I LIKE THE ISHIN SHISHI ...
BUT, I'VE GOTTA ADMIT, I'M A BIGGER FAN OF THE SHIN-SENGUMI.
HIJIKATA RULES!

和月伸宏

NOBUHIRO WATSUKI

WATSUKI IS A LIAR.

AS YOU MAY HAVE FIGURED FROM THE COMMENTS, I'VE REALLY GOT A THING FOR KENSHIN'S ENEMIES, THE SHINSENGUMI. GIVEN THAT I'M HISTORY-ILLITERATE AND DIDN'T EVEN TAKE JAPANESE HISTORY IN HIGH SCHOOL, I GUESS THAT MAKES ME AN IMPOSTER, HUH?

EVEN SO, THE BOOK YOU'RE NOW HOLDING IS NOT ONLY MY FIRST COLLECTED VOLUME, BUT MY DEBUT WORK. IDIOT CHILD OF MINE THOUGH IT MAY BE, PLEASE TRY AND LOVE IT, NONETHELESS.

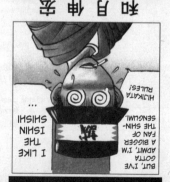

Rurouni Kenshin, which has found fans not only in Japan but around the world, first made its appearance in 1992 as an original short story in **Weekly Shonen Jump Special**. Later rewritten and published as a regular, continuing **Jump** series in 1994, **Rurouni Kenshin** ended serialization in 1999 but continued in popularity, as evidenced by the 2000 publication of **Yahiko no Sakabatô** (Yahiko's Reversed-Edge Sword) and the 2015 publication of **Rurouni Kenshin: Restoration** in **Weekly Shonen Jump.** The series has also inspired novels, anime and films. Watsuki is also the author of the popular series **Buso Renkin**, published by VIZ Media.

RUROUNI KENSHIN
3-in-1 Edition Volume 1
A compilation of the graphic novel volumes 1-2-3

STORY AND ART BY
NOBUHIRO WATSUKI

Translation/Kenichiro Yagi
English Adaptation/Gerard Jones
Touch-Up Art & Lettering/Steve Dutro
Design/Sean Lee (Manga Edition)
Design/Izumi Evers (Omnibus Edition)
Editor/Avery Gotoh (Manga Edition)
Editor/Shaenon Garrity (Omnibus Edition)

Printed in Canada

Published by VIZ Media, LLC
P.O. Box 77010
San Francisco, CA 94107

10 9 8 7 6 5 4 3 2
Omnibus edition first printing, January 2017
Second printing, October 2022

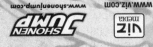

www.viz.com

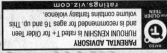

www.shonenjump.com

SHONEN JUMP MANGA

Rurouni Kenshin

Vol. 1
MEIJI SWORDSMAN ROMANTIC STORY

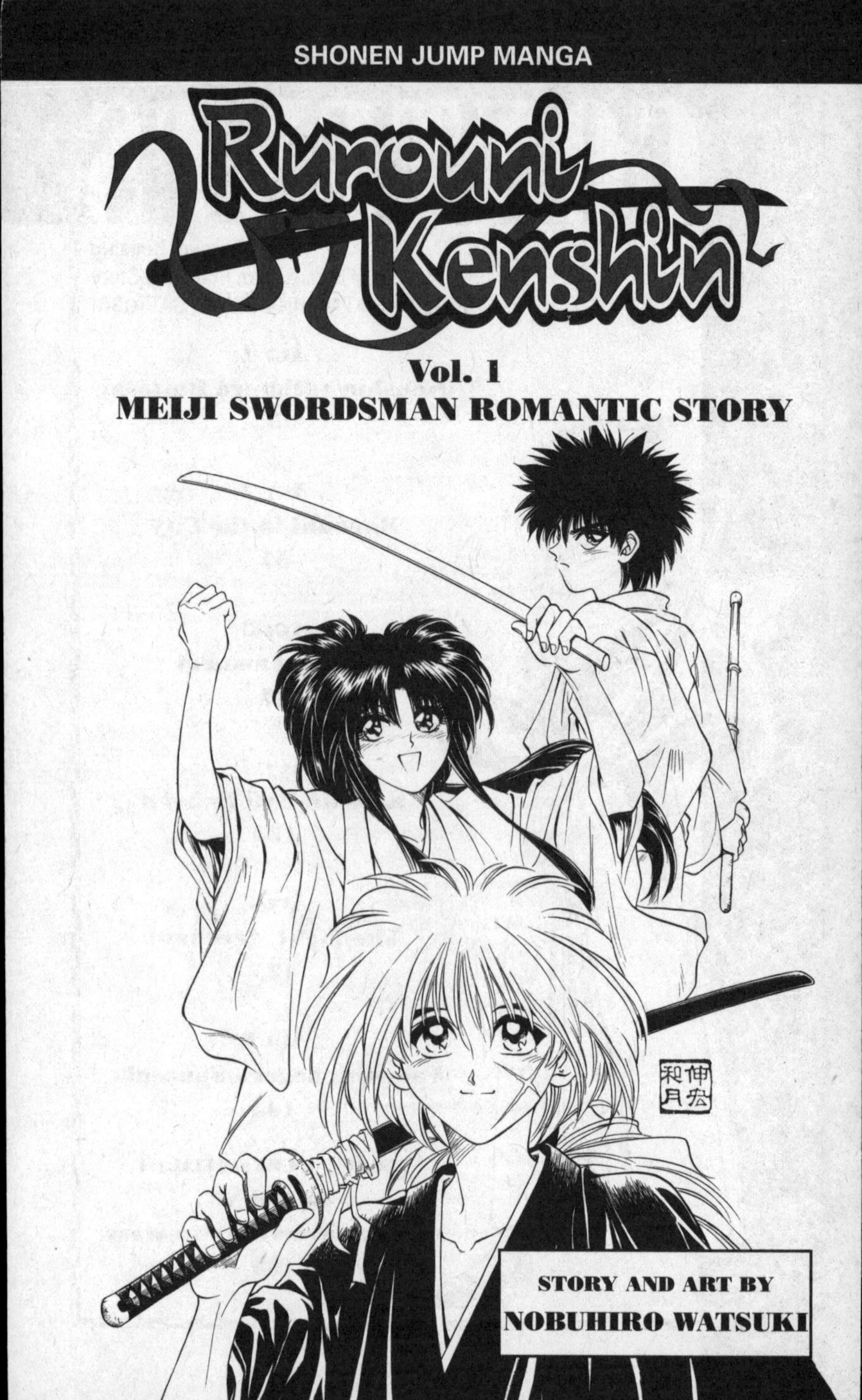
伸宏
和月

STORY AND ART BY
NOBUHIRO WATSUKI

CONTENTS

Rurouni Kenshin
Meiji Swordsman Romantic Story
BOOK ONE: KENSHIN HIMURA BATTŌSAI

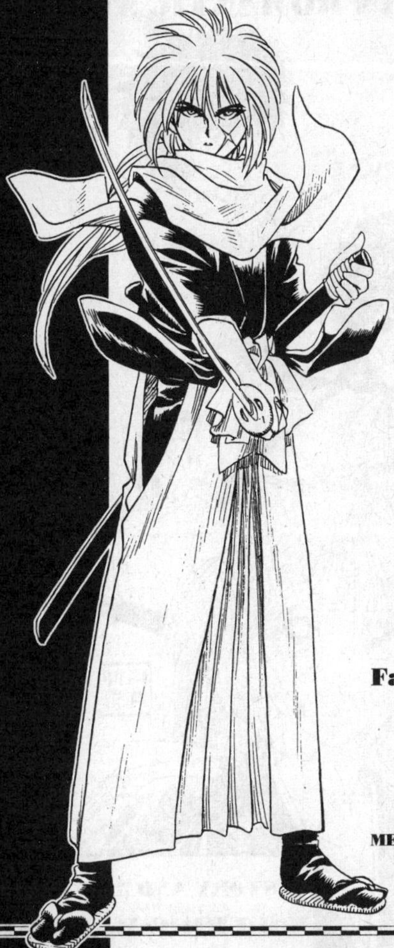

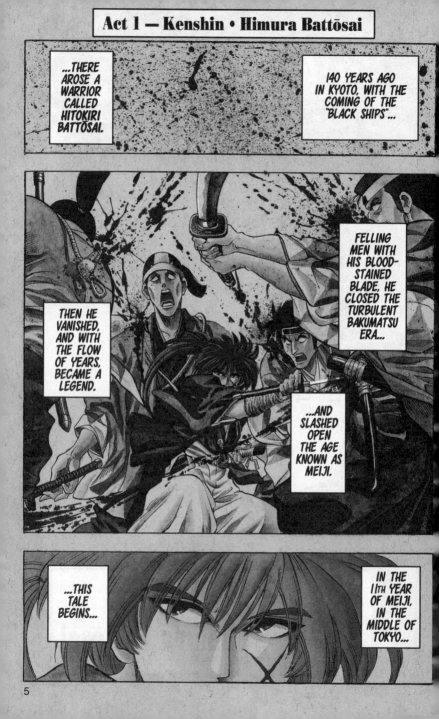

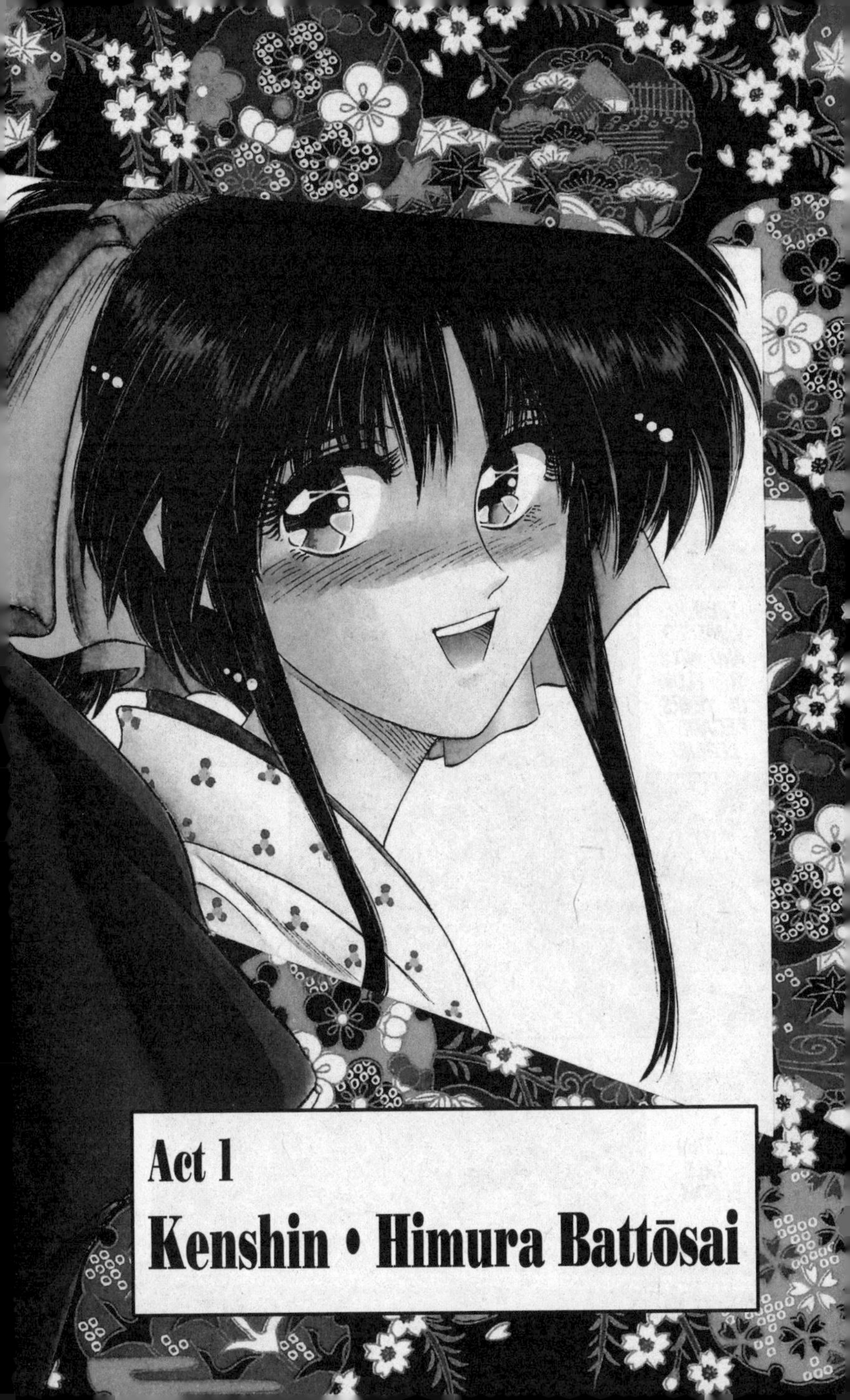
Act 1
Kenshin • Himura Battōsai

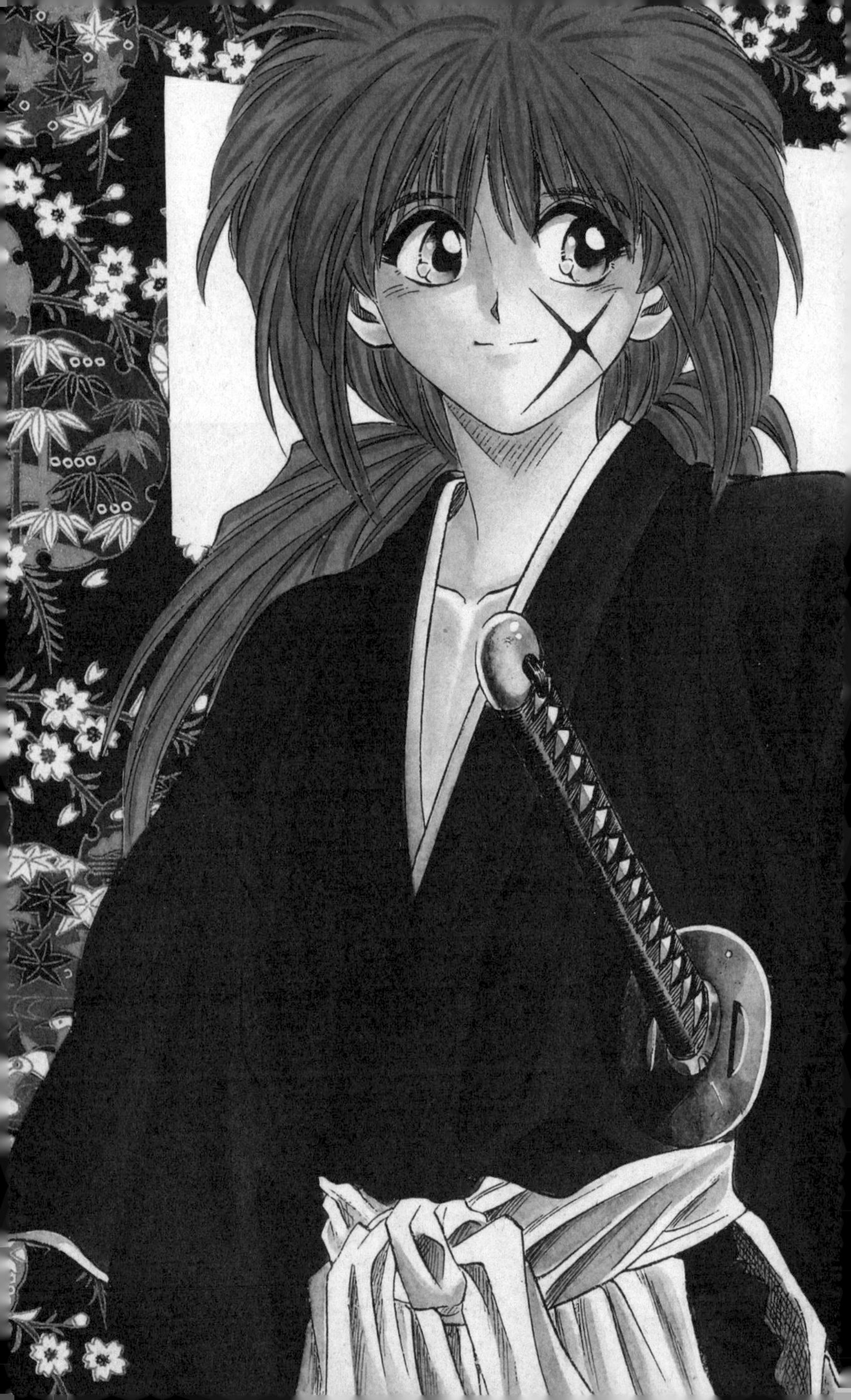

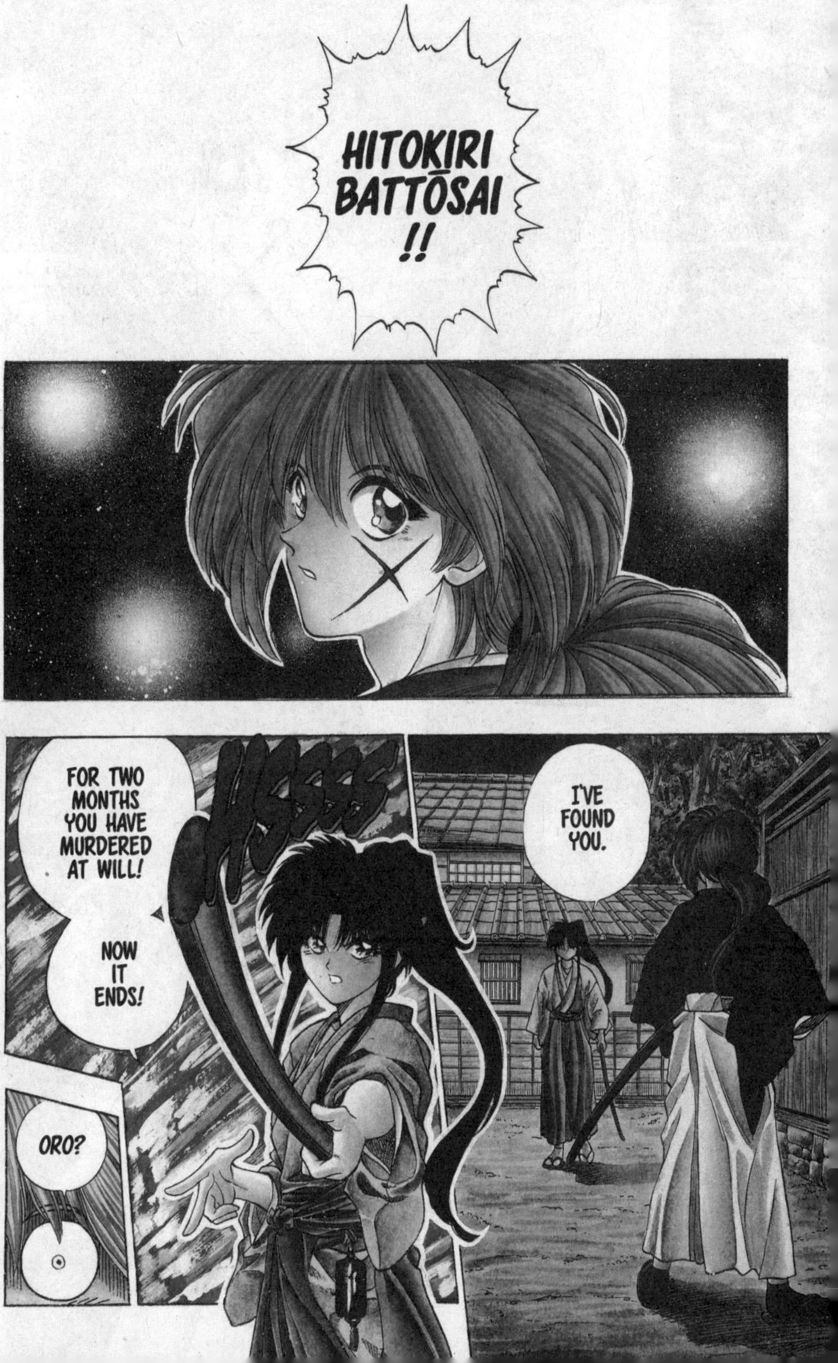
HITOKIRI BATTŌSAI !!
I'VE FOUND YOU.
HISSSS
FOR TWO MONTHS YOU HAVE MURDERED AT WILL!
NOW IT ENDS!
ORO?

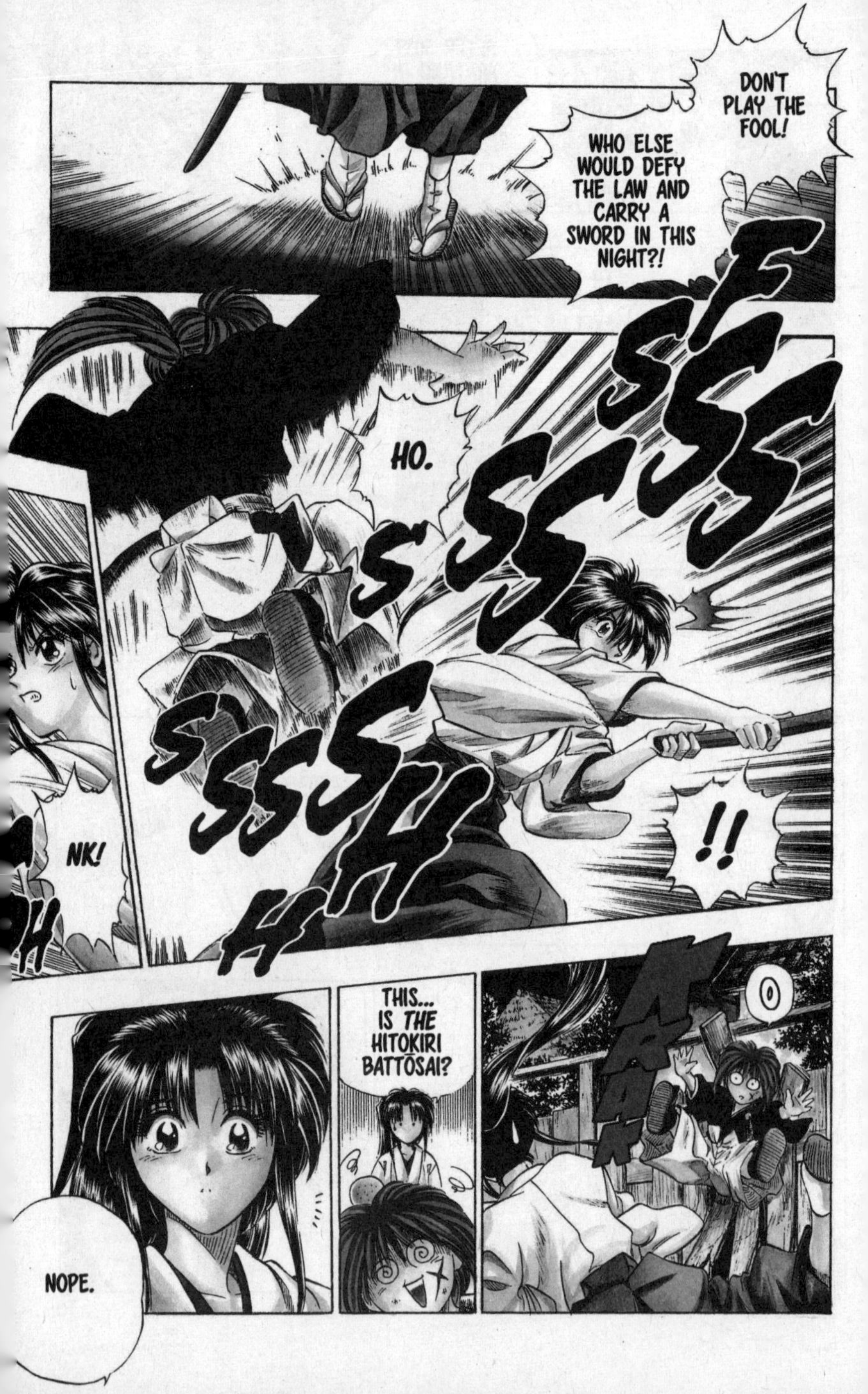
DON'T PLAY THE FOOL!
WHO ELSE WOULD DEFY THE LAW AND CARRY A SWORD IN THIS NIGHT?!
HO.
!!
NK!
O
THIS... IS THE HITOKIRI BATTŌSAI?
NOPE.

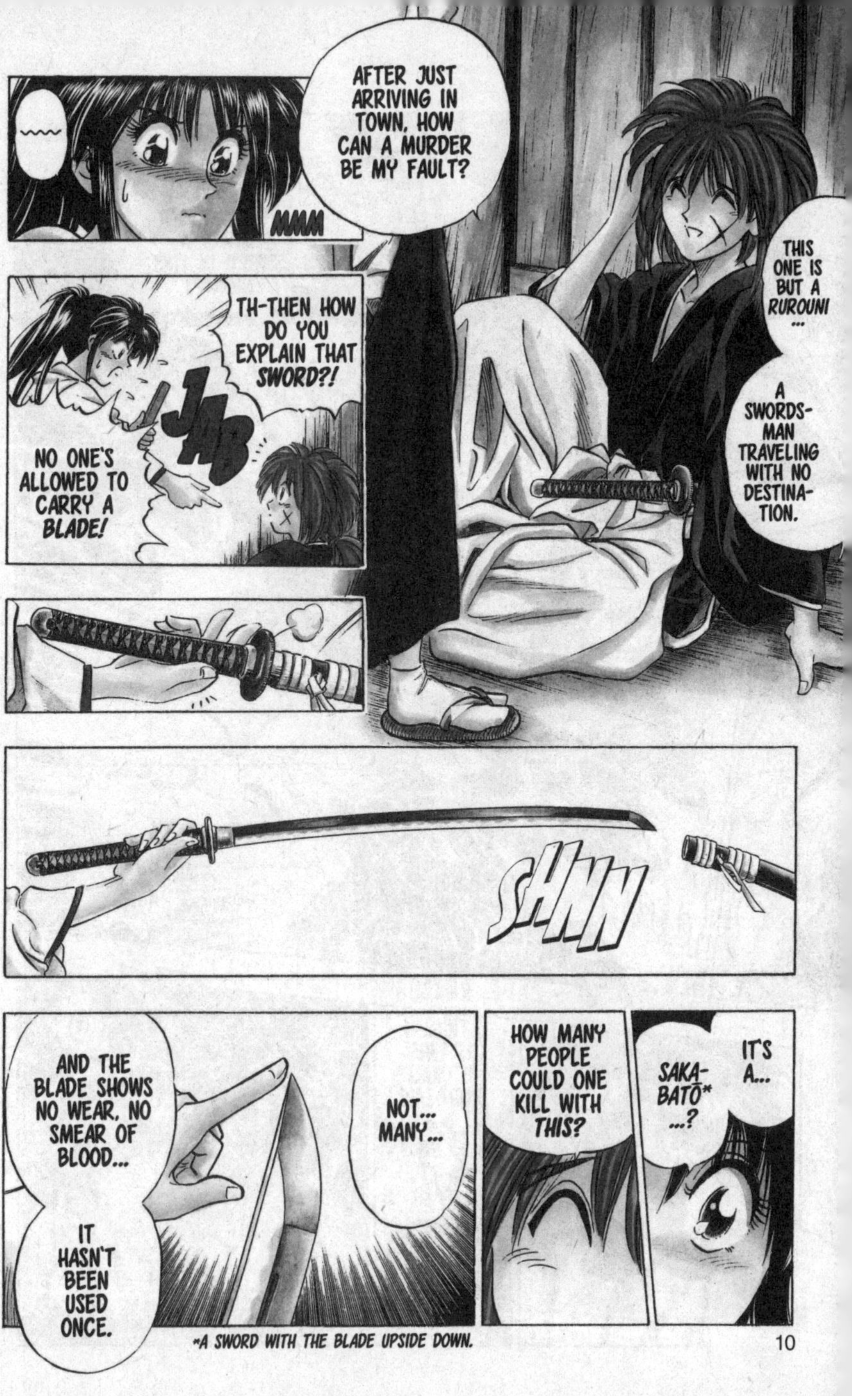
AFTER JUST ARRIVING IN TOWN, HOW CAN A MURDER BE MY FAULT?
THIS ONE IS BUT A RUROUNI...
A SWORDS-MAN TRAVELING WITH NO DESTINA-TION.
~~~
MMM
TH-THEN HOW DO YOU EXPLAIN THAT SWORD?!
JAB
NO ONE'S ALLOWED TO CARRY A BLADE!
SHNN
IT'S A...
SAKA-BATŌ* ...?
HOW MANY PEOPLE COULD ONE KILL WITH THIS?
NOT... MANY...
AND THE BLADE SHOWS NO WEAR, NO SMEAR OF BLOOD...
IT HASN'T BEEN USED ONCE.

*A SWORD WITH THE BLADE UPSIDE DOWN.
~~~

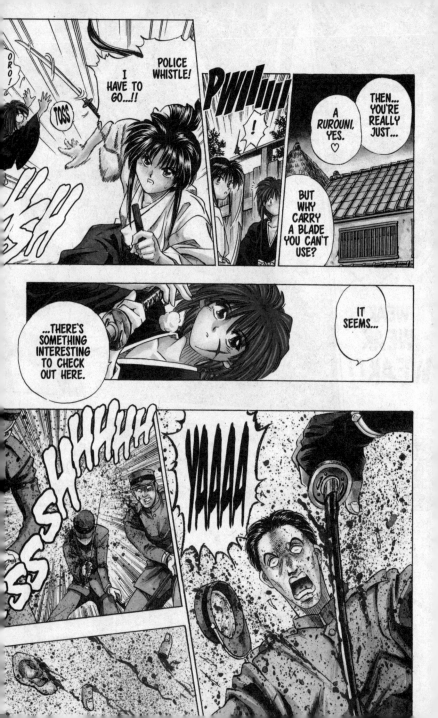

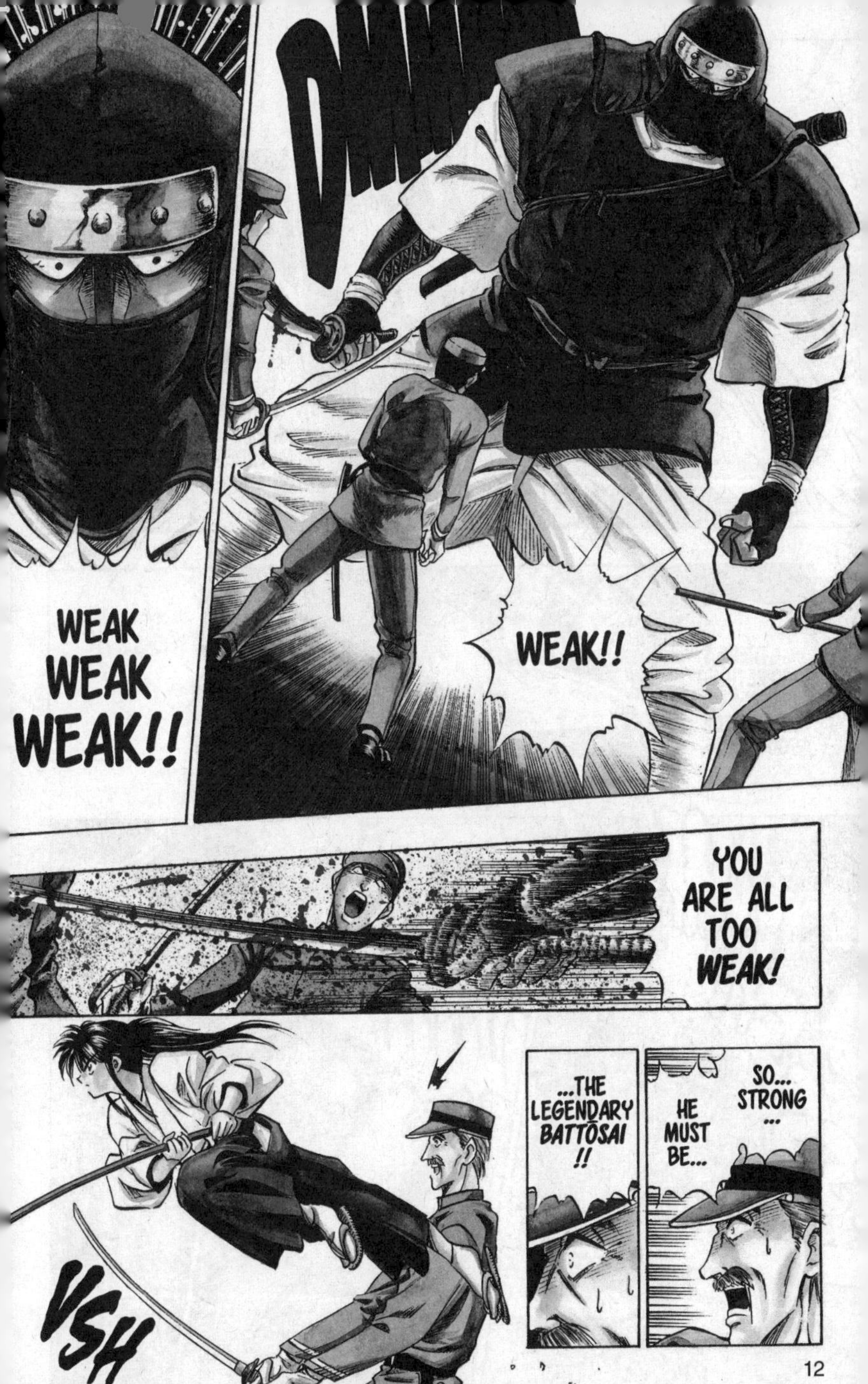
WEAK!!
WEAK WEAK WEAK!!
YOU ARE ALL TOO WEAK!
SO... STRONG ...
HE MUST BE...
...THE LEGENDARY BATTŌSAI !!
VSH

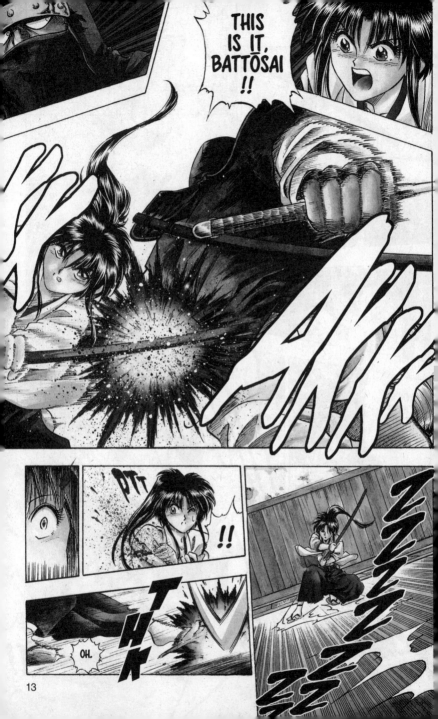

THIS IS IT, BATTŌSAI!!

BRAK

PTT

!!

THK

OH.

ZZZZZZZZ

13

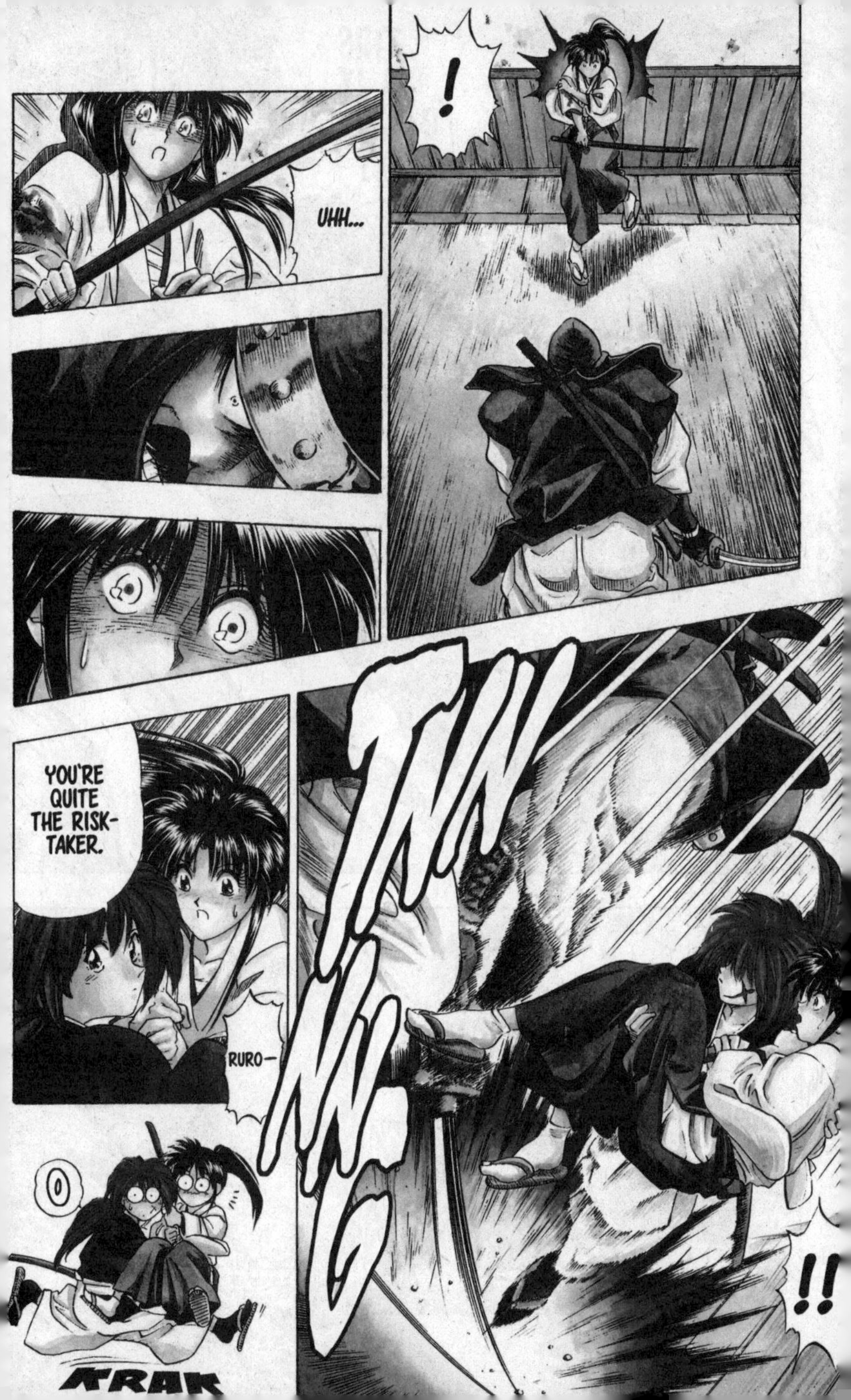
!
UHH...
!!
YOU'RE QUITE THE RISK-TAKER.
RURO-
KRAK

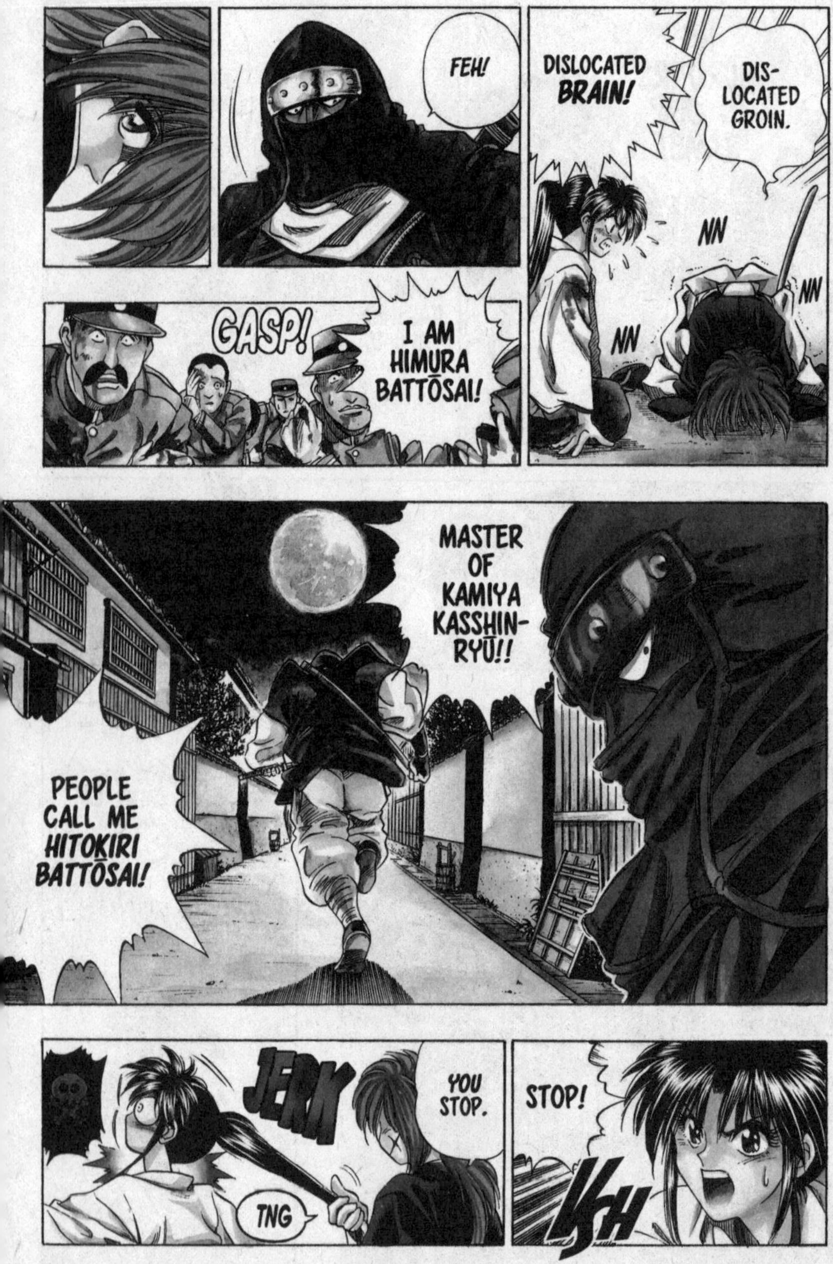

DIS-LOCATED GROIN.
DISLOCATED BRAIN!
NN
NN
NN
FEH!
I AM HIMURA BATTŌSAI!
GASP!
MASTER OF KAMIYA KASSHIN-RYŪ!!
PEOPLE CALL ME HITOKIRI BATTŌSAI!
STOP!
KSH
YOU STOP.
JERK
TNG

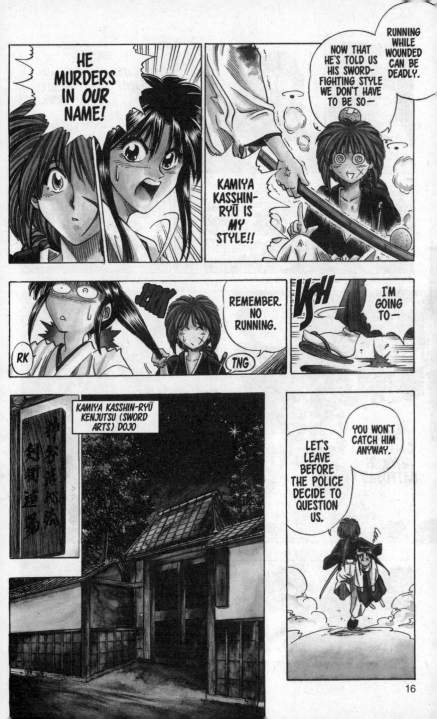

HE MURDERS IN OUR NAME!

NOW THAT HE'S TOLD US HIS SWORD-FIGHTING STYLE WE DON'T HAVE TO BE SO—

RUNNING WHILE WOUNDED CAN BE DEADLY.

KAMIYA KASSHIN-RYŪ IS MY STYLE!!

REMEMBER. NO RUNNING.

RK

JERK

TNG

USH

I'M GOING TO—

KAMIYA KASSHIN-RYŪ KENJUTSU (SWORD ARTS) DOJO

LET'S LEAVE BEFORE THE POLICE DECIDE TO QUESTION US.

YOU WON'T CATCH HIM ANYWAY.

16

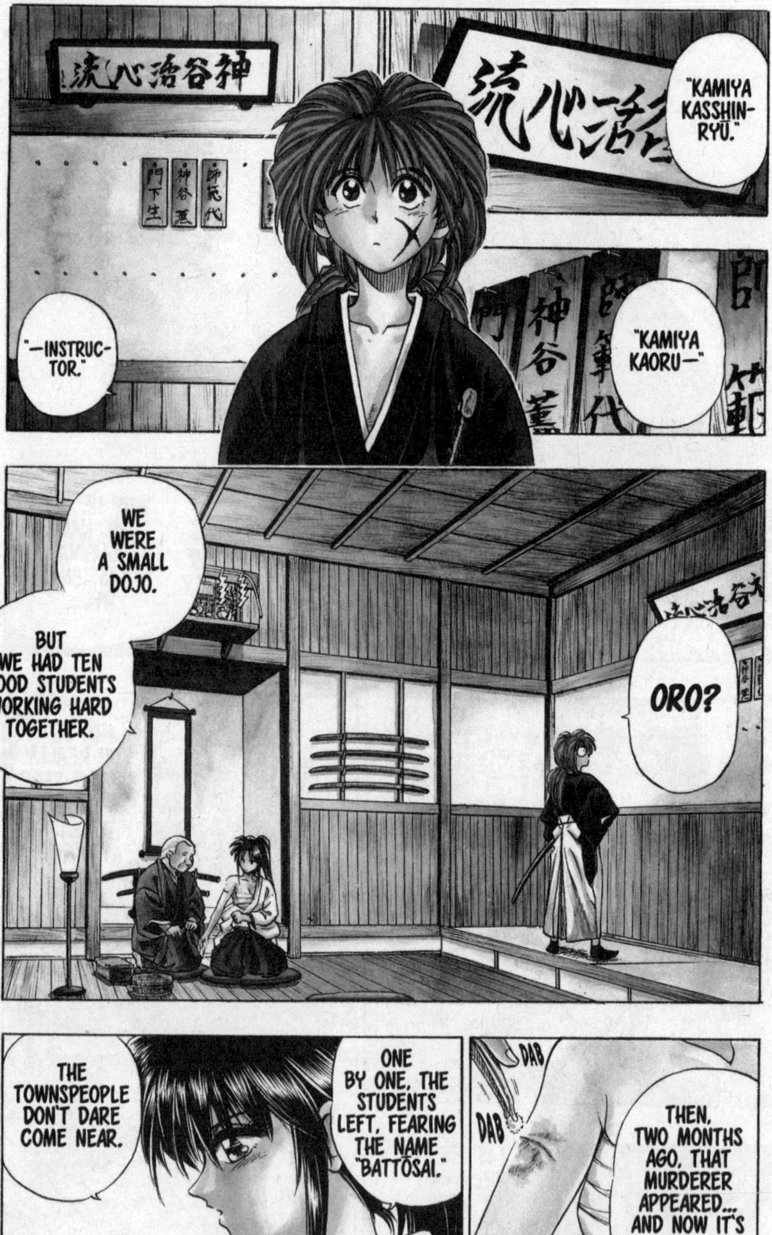
"KAMIYA KASSHIN-RYŪ."
"KAMIYA KAORU—"
"—INSTRUCTOR."
WE WERE A SMALL DOJO.
BUT WE HAD TEN GOOD STUDENTS WORKING HARD TOGETHER.
ORO?
DAB
DAB
THEN, TWO MONTHS AGO, THAT MURDERER APPEARED... AND NOW IT'S LIKE THIS.
ONE BY ONE, THE STUDENTS LEFT, FEARING THE NAME "BATTŌSAI."
THE TOWNSPEOPLE DON'T DARE COME NEAR.

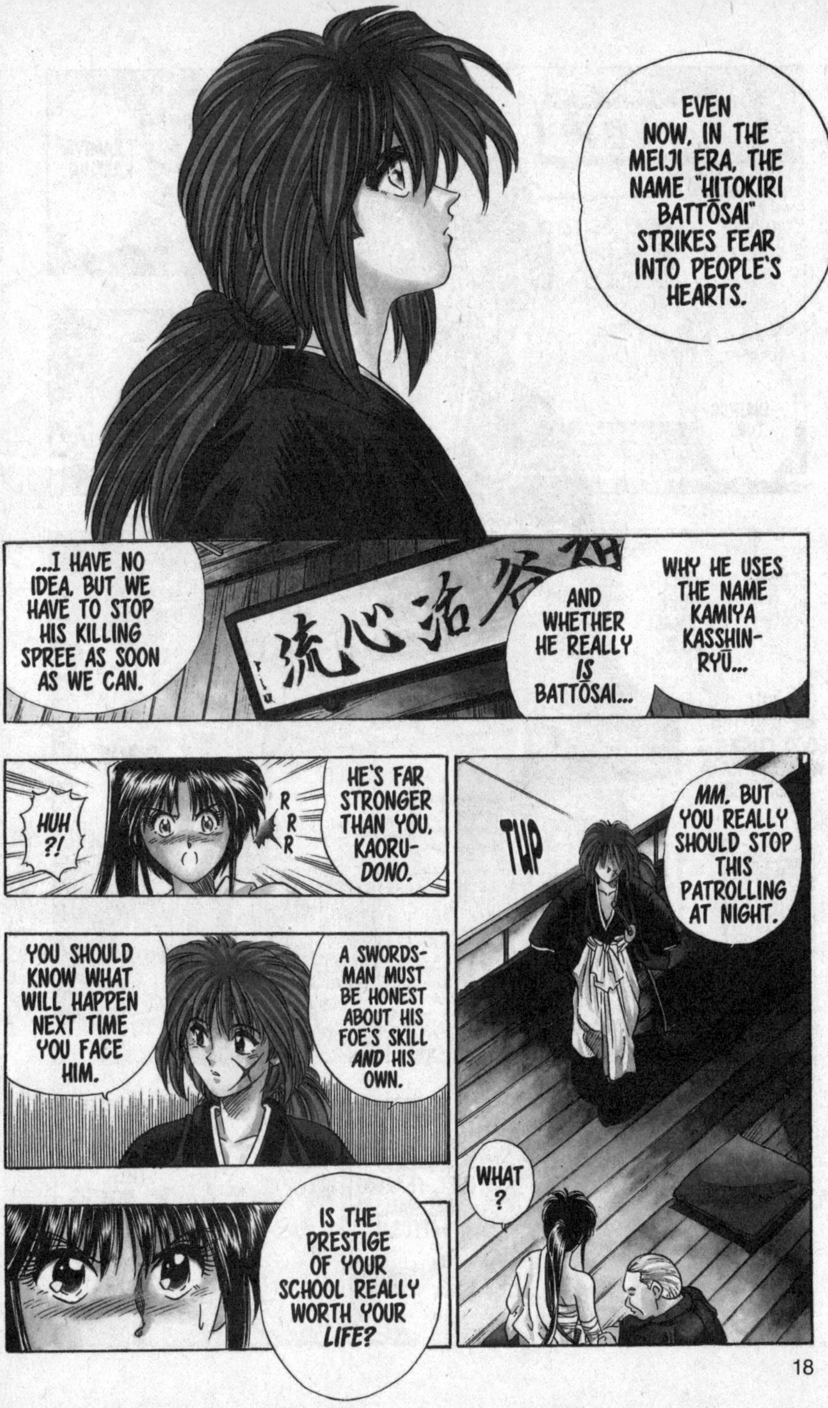
EVEN NOW, IN THE MEIJI ERA, THE NAME "HITOKIRI BATTŌSAI" STRIKES FEAR INTO PEOPLE'S HEARTS.
WHY HE USES THE NAME KAMIYA KASSHIN-RYŪ...
AND WHETHER HE REALLY *IS* BATTŌSAI...
...I HAVE NO IDEA, BUT WE HAVE TO STOP HIS KILLING SPREE AS SOON AS WE CAN.
TUP
MM. BUT YOU REALLY SHOULD STOP THIS PATROLLING AT NIGHT.
WHAT?
HE'S FAR STRONGER THAN YOU, KAORU-DONO.
RRR
HUH?!
A SWORDSMAN MUST BE HONEST ABOUT HIS FOE'S SKILL *AND* HIS OWN.
YOU SHOULD KNOW WHAT WILL HAPPEN NEXT TIME YOU FACE HIM.
IS THE PRESTIGE OF YOUR SCHOOL REALLY WORTH YOUR *LIFE*?

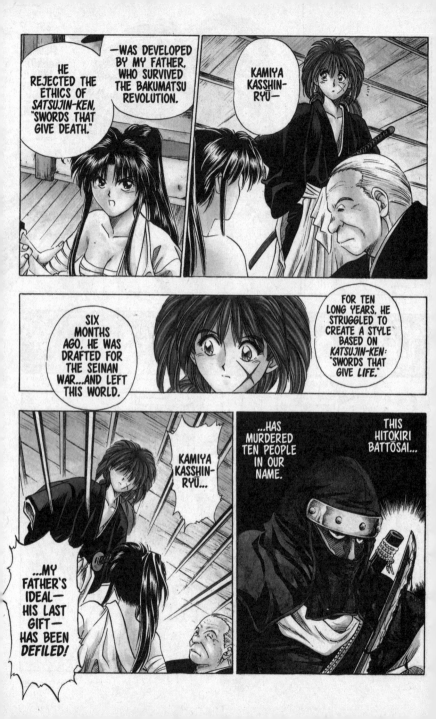

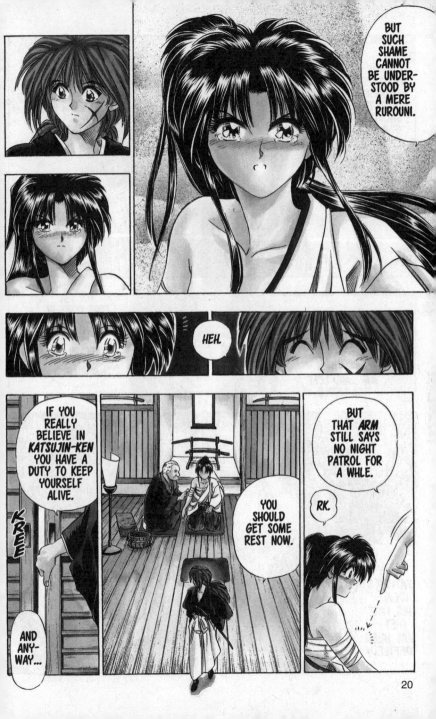

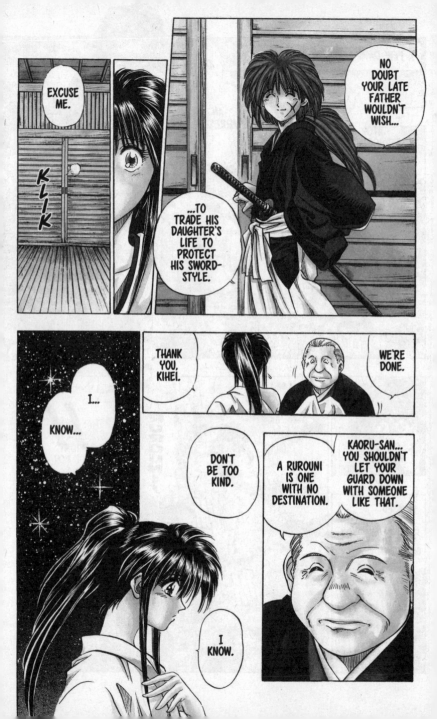

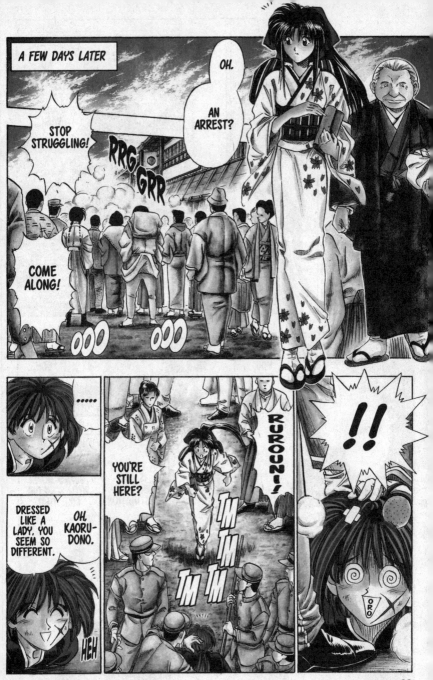

A FEW DAYS LATER

OH.

AN ARREST?

STOP STRUGGLING!

RRG GRR

COME ALONG!

.....

YOU'RE STILL HERE?

RUROUNI!

!!

DRESSED LIKE A LADY, YOU SEEM SO DIFFERENT.

OH, KAORU-DONO.

HEH

TM TM TM TM

ORO

22

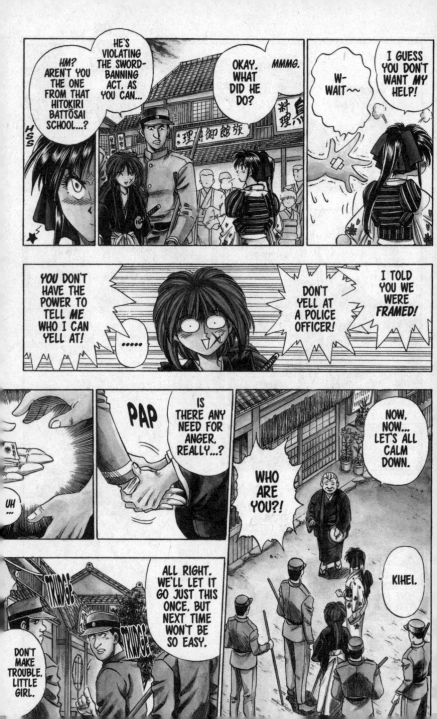

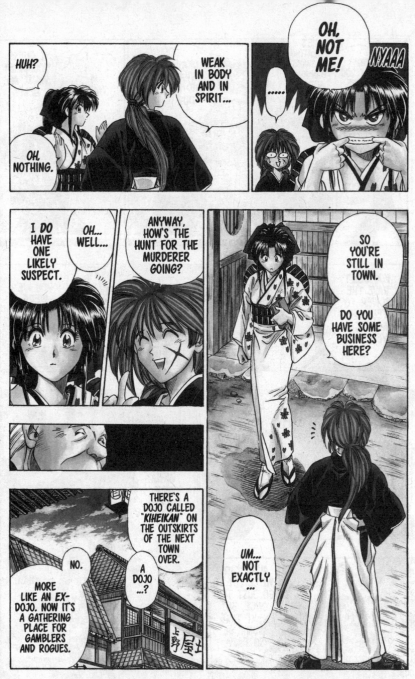

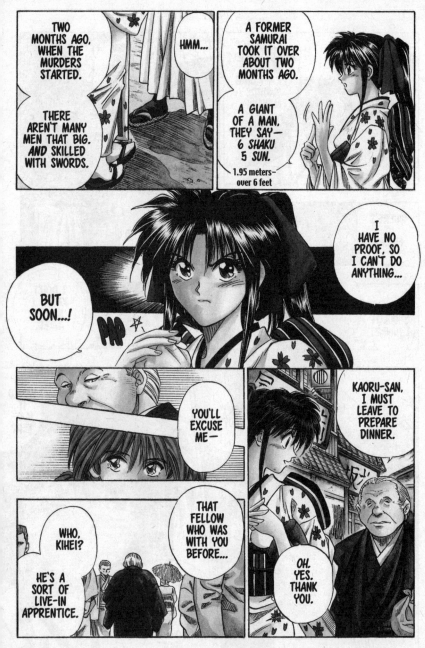

TWO MONTHS AGO, WHEN THE MURDERS STARTED.

THERE AREN'T MANY MEN THAT BIG. *AND* SKILLED WITH SWORDS.

HMM...

A FORMER SAMURAI TOOK IT OVER ABOUT TWO MONTHS AGO.

A GIANT OF A MAN, THEY SAY— 6 *SHAKU* 5 *SUN*.

1.95 meters— over 6 feet

I HAVE NO PROOF, SO I CAN'T DO ANYTHING...

BUT SOON...!

PAP

YOU'LL EXCUSE ME—

KAORU-SAN, I MUST LEAVE TO PREPARE DINNER.

WHO, KIHEI?

HE'S A SORT OF LIVE-IN APPRENTICE.

THAT FELLOW WHO WAS WITH YOU BEFORE...

OH. YES. THANK YOU.

25

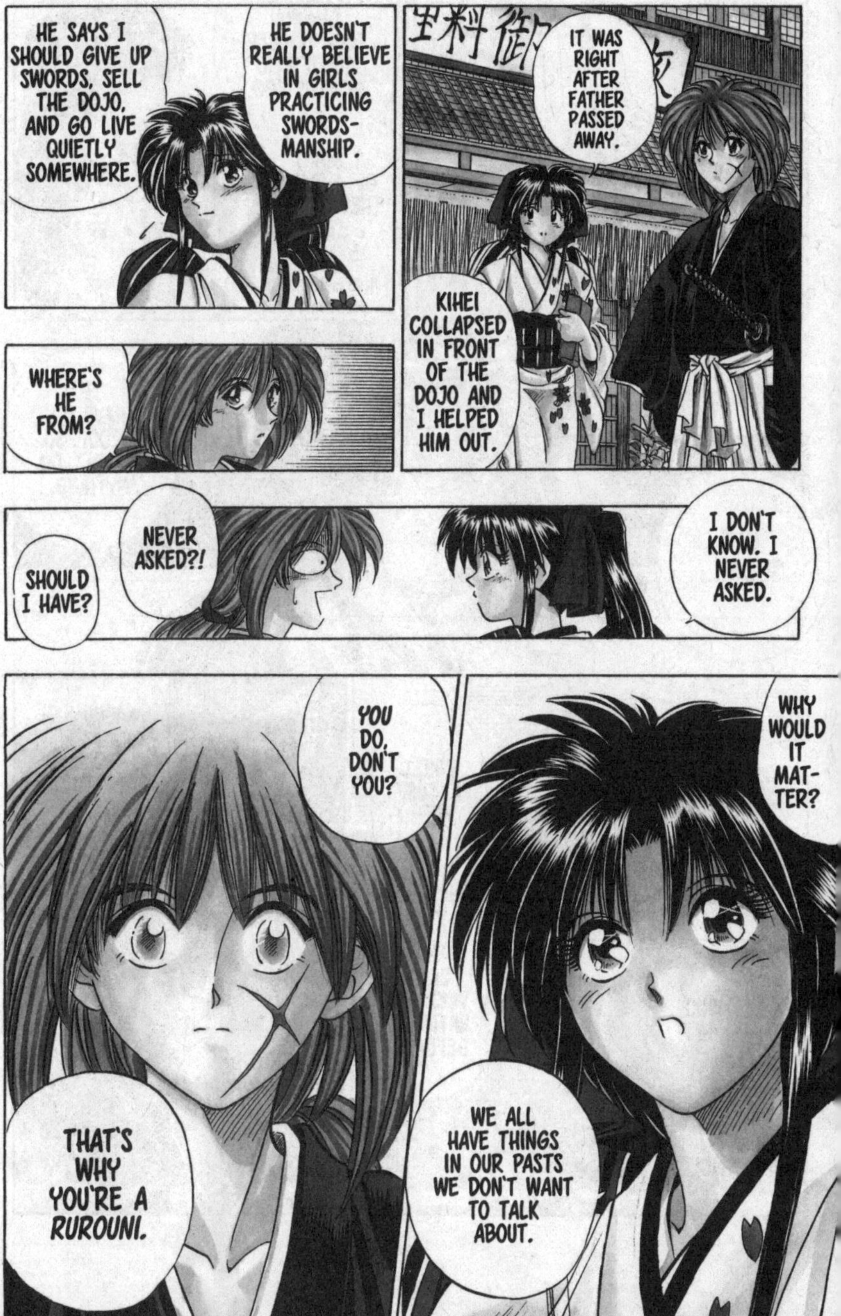
IT WAS RIGHT AFTER FATHER PASSED AWAY.
KIHEI COLLAPSED IN FRONT OF THE DOJO AND I HELPED HIM OUT.
HE DOESN'T REALLY BELIEVE IN GIRLS PRACTICING SWORDS-MANSHIP.
HE SAYS I SHOULD GIVE UP SWORDS, SELL THE DOJO, AND GO LIVE QUIETLY SOMEWHERE.
WHERE'S HE FROM?
I DON'T KNOW. I NEVER ASKED.
NEVER ASKED?!
SHOULD I HAVE?
WHY WOULD IT MAT-TER?
WE ALL HAVE THINGS IN OUR PASTS WE DON'T WANT TO TALK ABOUT.
YOU DO, DON'T YOU?
THAT'S WHY YOU'RE A RUROUNI.

READ THIS WAY

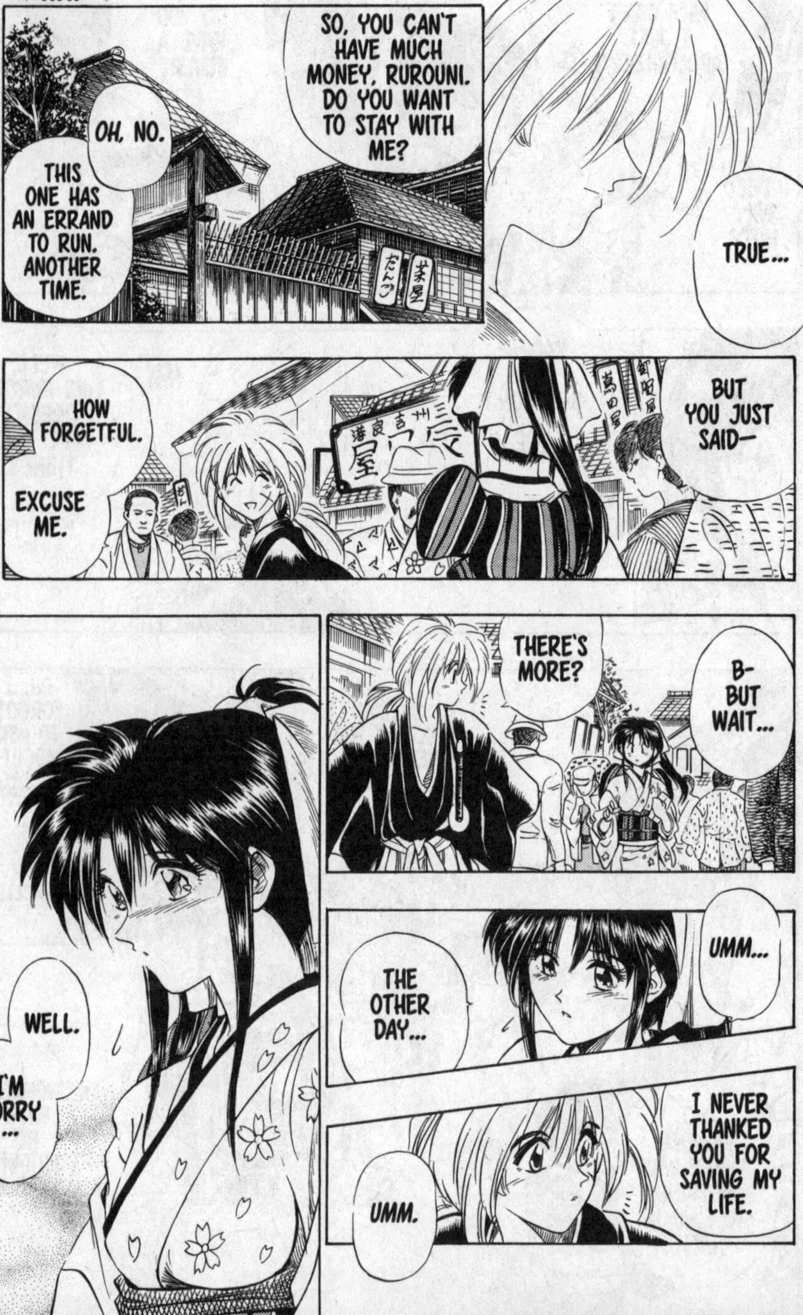
TRUE...
SO, YOU CAN'T HAVE MUCH MONEY, RUROUNI. DO YOU WANT TO STAY WITH ME?
OH, NO.
THIS ONE HAS AN ERRAND TO RUN. ANOTHER TIME.
BUT YOU JUST SAID—
HOW FORGETFUL.
EXCUSE ME.
B-BUT WAIT...
THERE'S MORE?
UMM...
THE OTHER DAY...
I NEVER THANKED YOU FOR SAVING MY LIFE.
UMM.
WELL.
I'M SORRY ...

READ THIS WAY

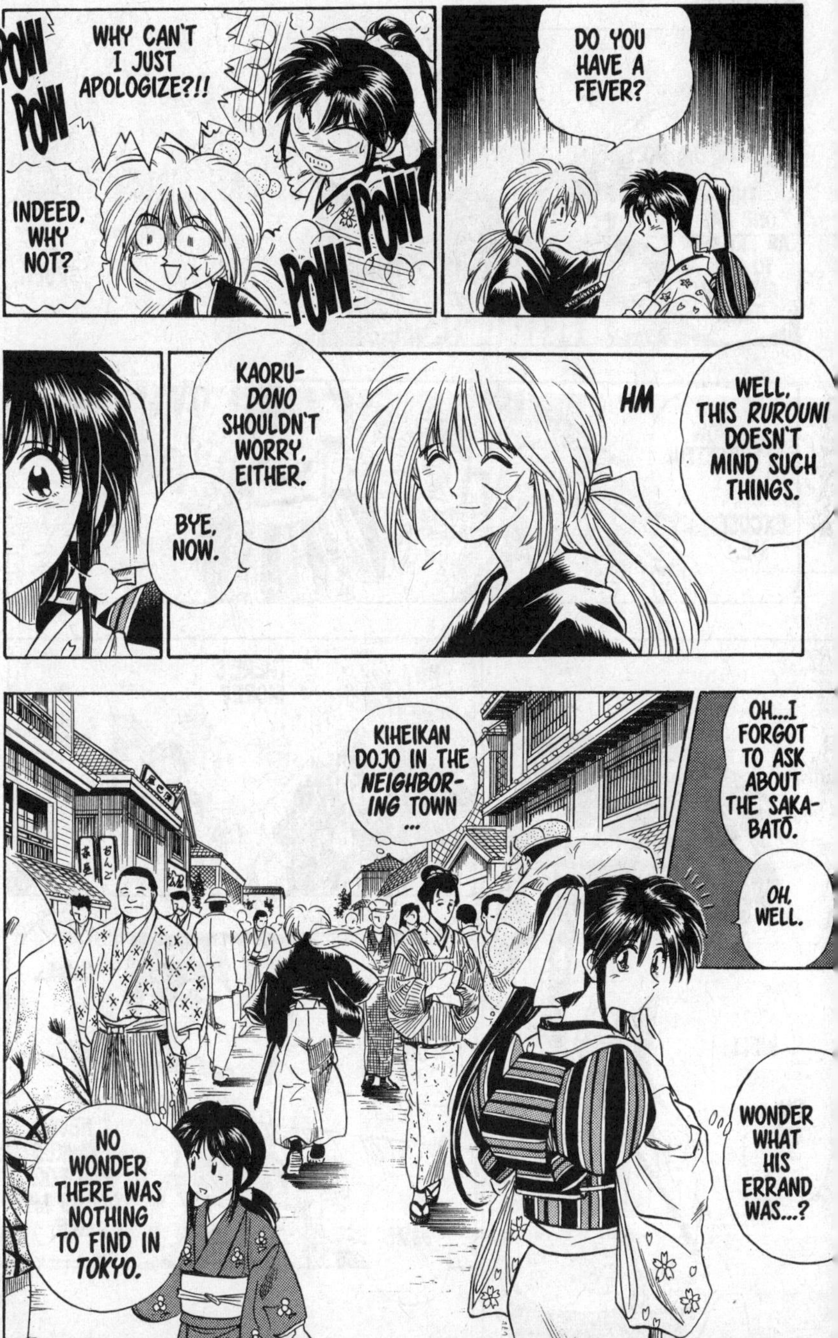
DO YOU HAVE A FEVER?
WHY CAN'T I JUST APOLOGIZE?!!
POW POW
POW POW
INDEED, WHY NOT?
WELL, THIS *RUROUNI* DOESN'T MIND SUCH THINGS.
HM
KAORU-*DONO* SHOULDN'T WORRY, EITHER.
BYE, NOW.
OH...I FORGOT TO ASK ABOUT THE SAKABATŌ.
OH, WELL.
KIHEIKAN DOJO IN THE *NEIGHBORING* TOWN ...
WONDER WHAT HIS ERRAND WAS...?
NO WONDER THERE WAS NOTHING TO FIND IN *TOKYO*.

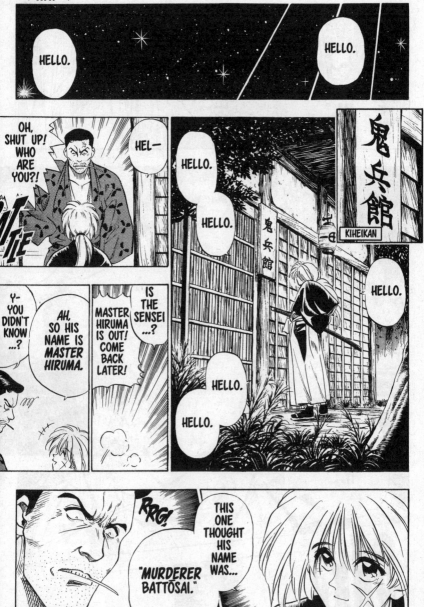

29

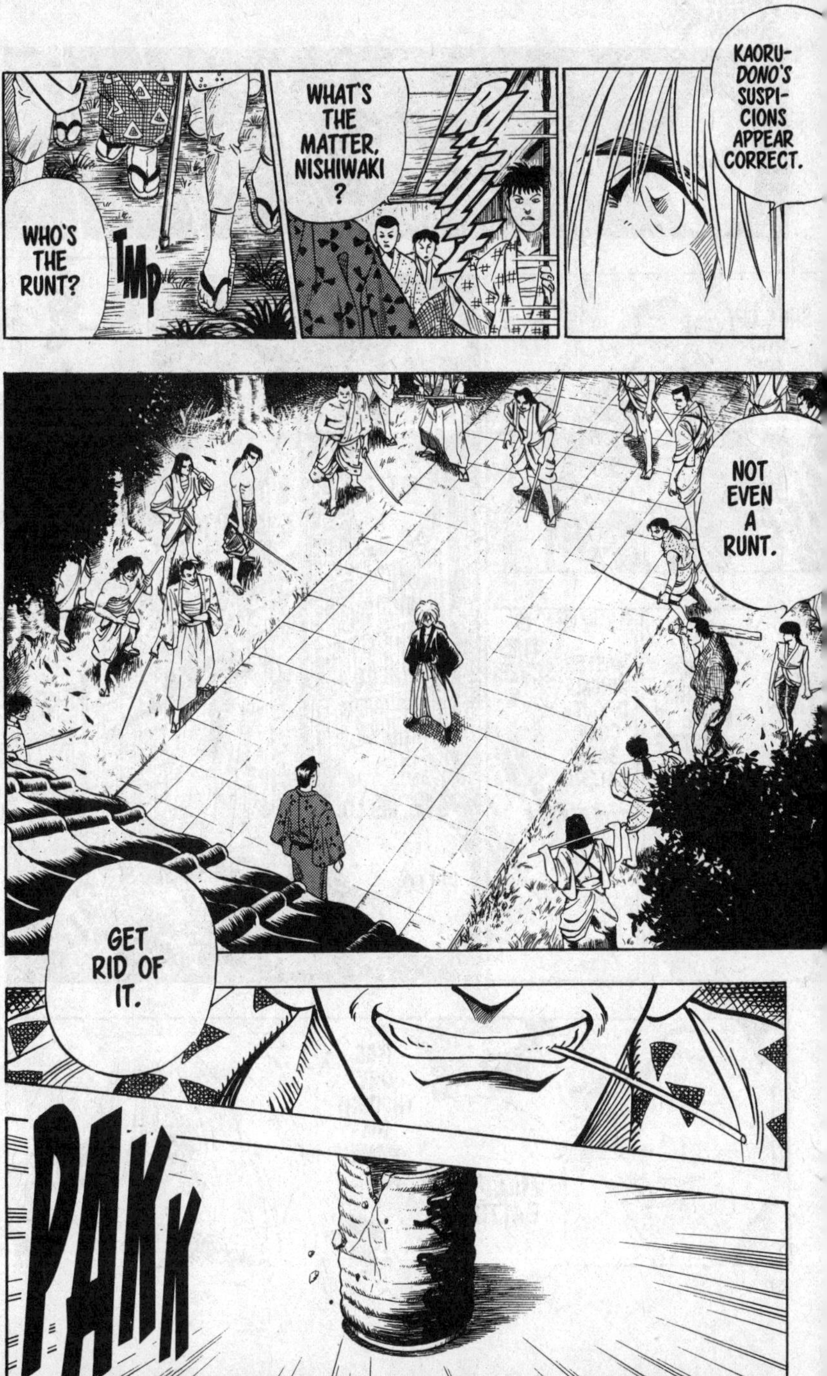
KAORU-DONO'S SUSPICIONS APPEAR CORRECT.
RATTLE
WHAT'S THE MATTER, NISHIWAKI?
WHO'S THE RUNT?
TMP
NOT EVEN A RUNT.
GET RID OF IT.
PAKK

READ THIS WAY

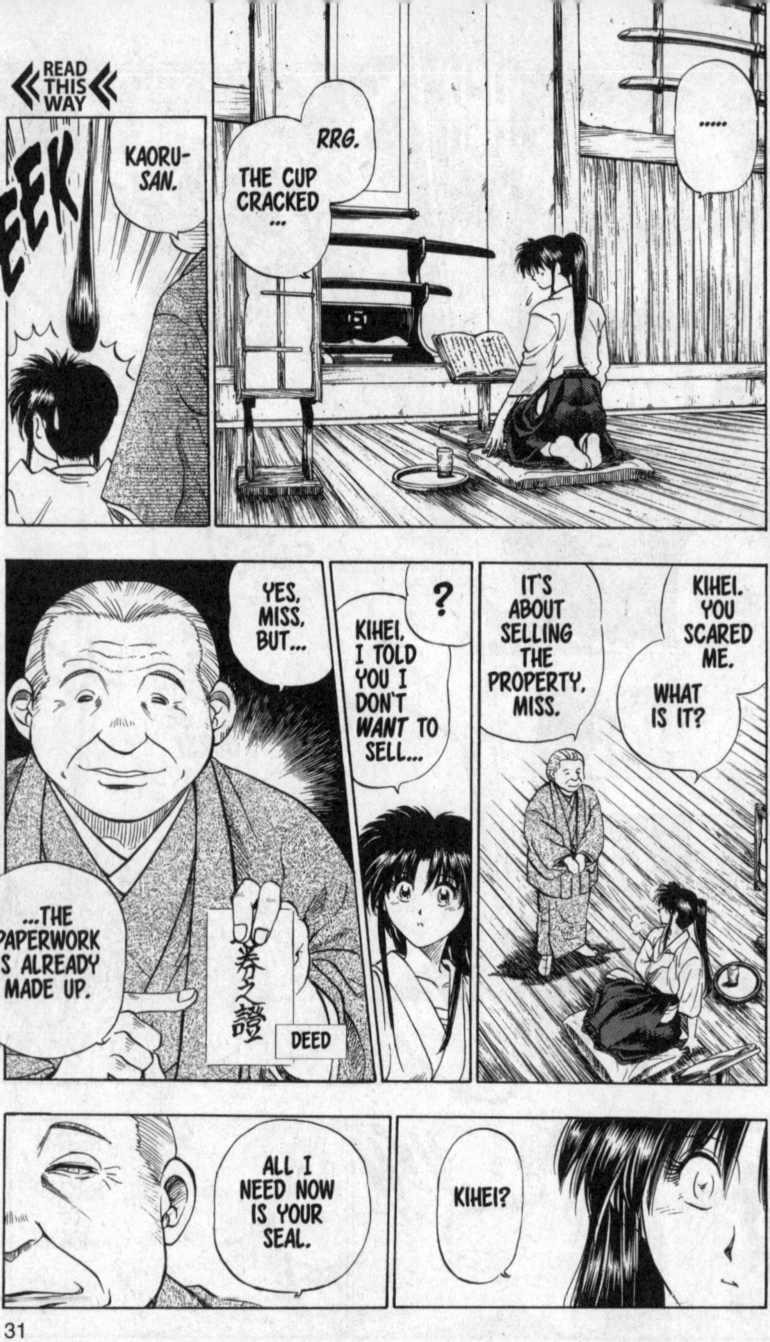
.....
RRG. THE CUP CRACKED ...
KAORU-SAN.
EEK
KIHEI. YOU SCARED ME.
WHAT IS IT?
IT'S ABOUT SELLING THE PROPERTY, MISS.
?
KIHEI, I TOLD YOU I DON'T *WANT* TO SELL...
YES, MISS, BUT...
...THE PAPERWORK IS ALREADY MADE UP.
DEED
KIHEI?
ALL I NEED NOW IS YOUR SEAL.

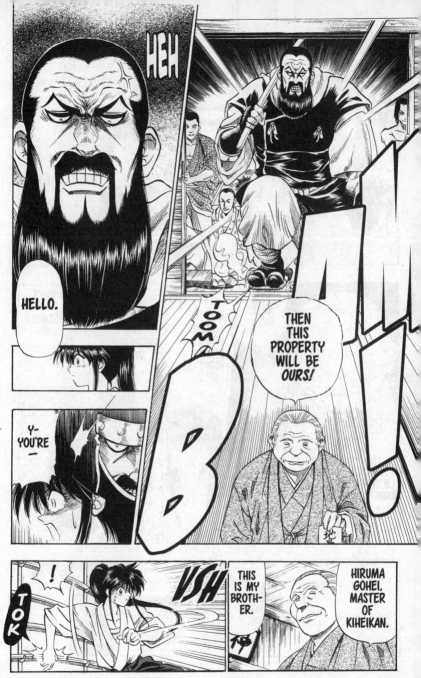

32

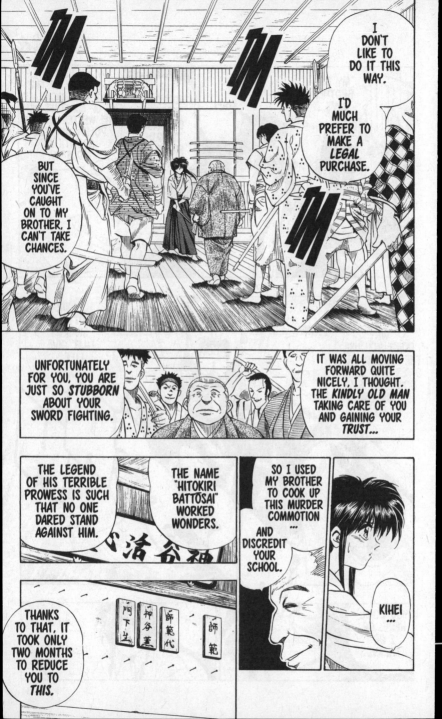

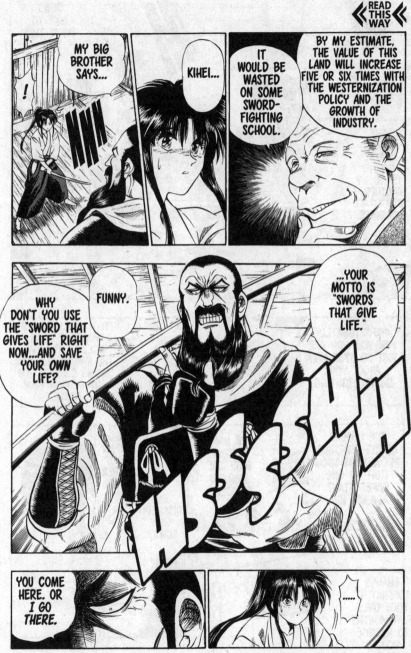

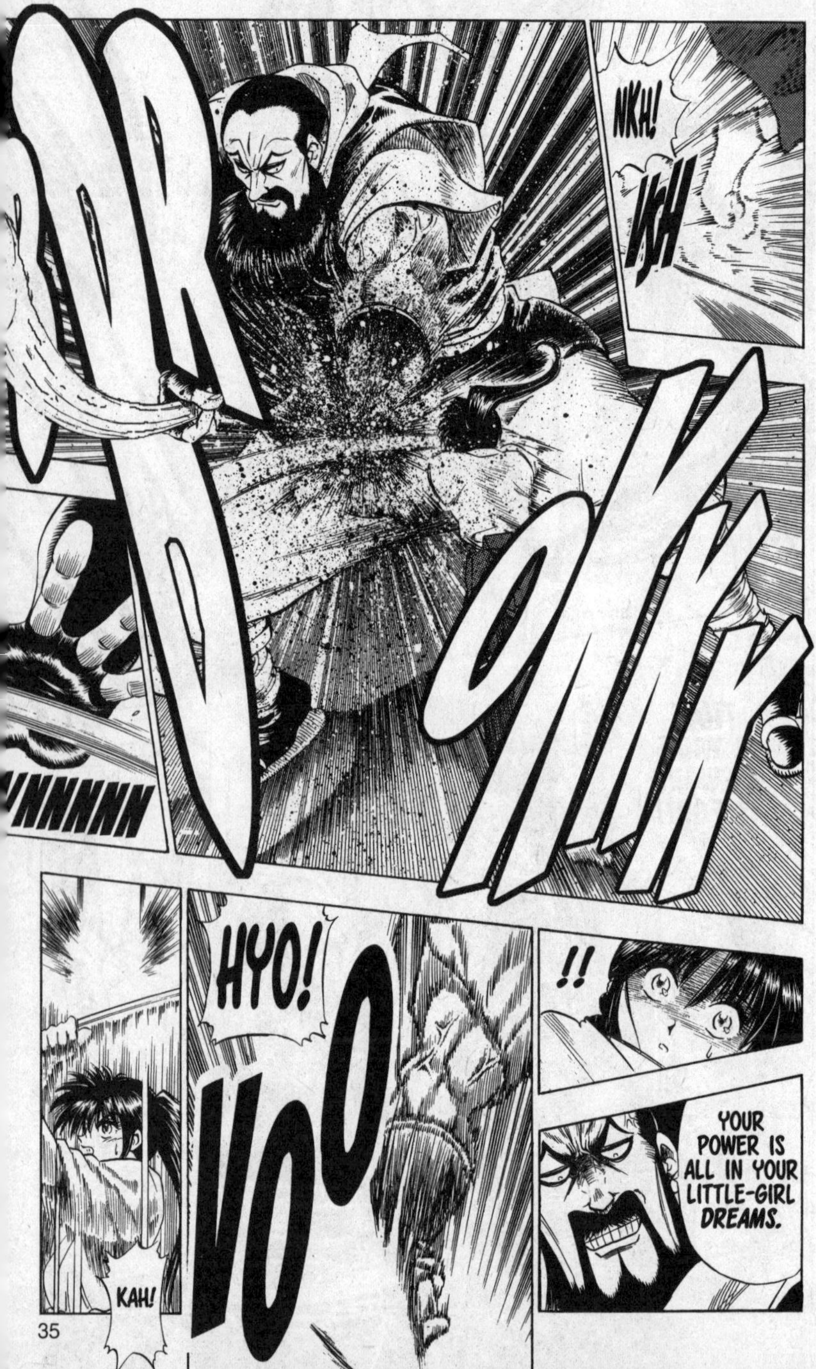
NKH!
!!
YOUR POWER IS ALL IN YOUR LITTLE-GIRL DREAMS.
HYO!
KAH!

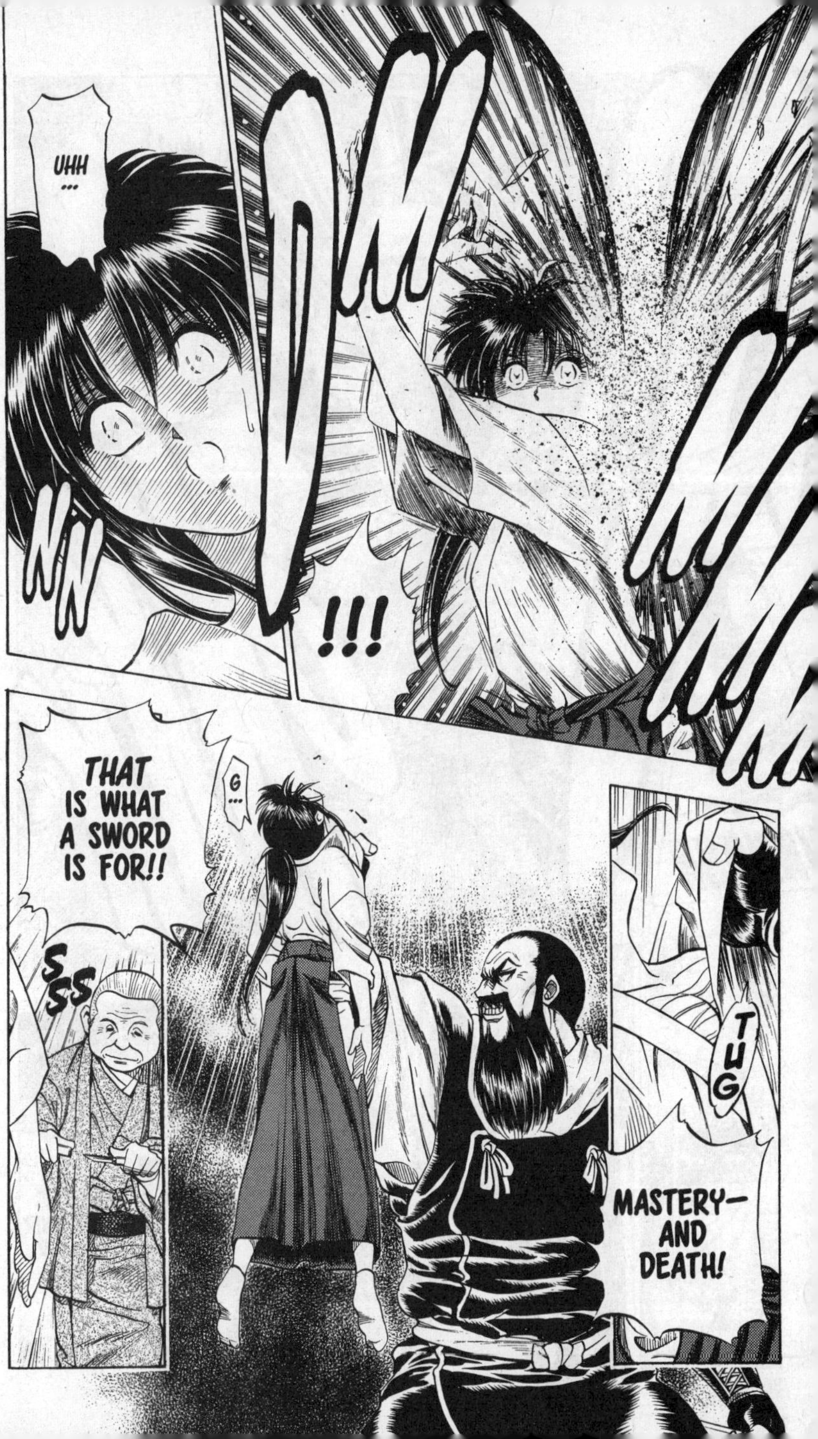
!!!
UHH ...
NN
TUG
MASTERY—AND DEATH!
G ...
THAT IS WHAT A SWORD IS FOR!!
SSS

READ THIS WAY

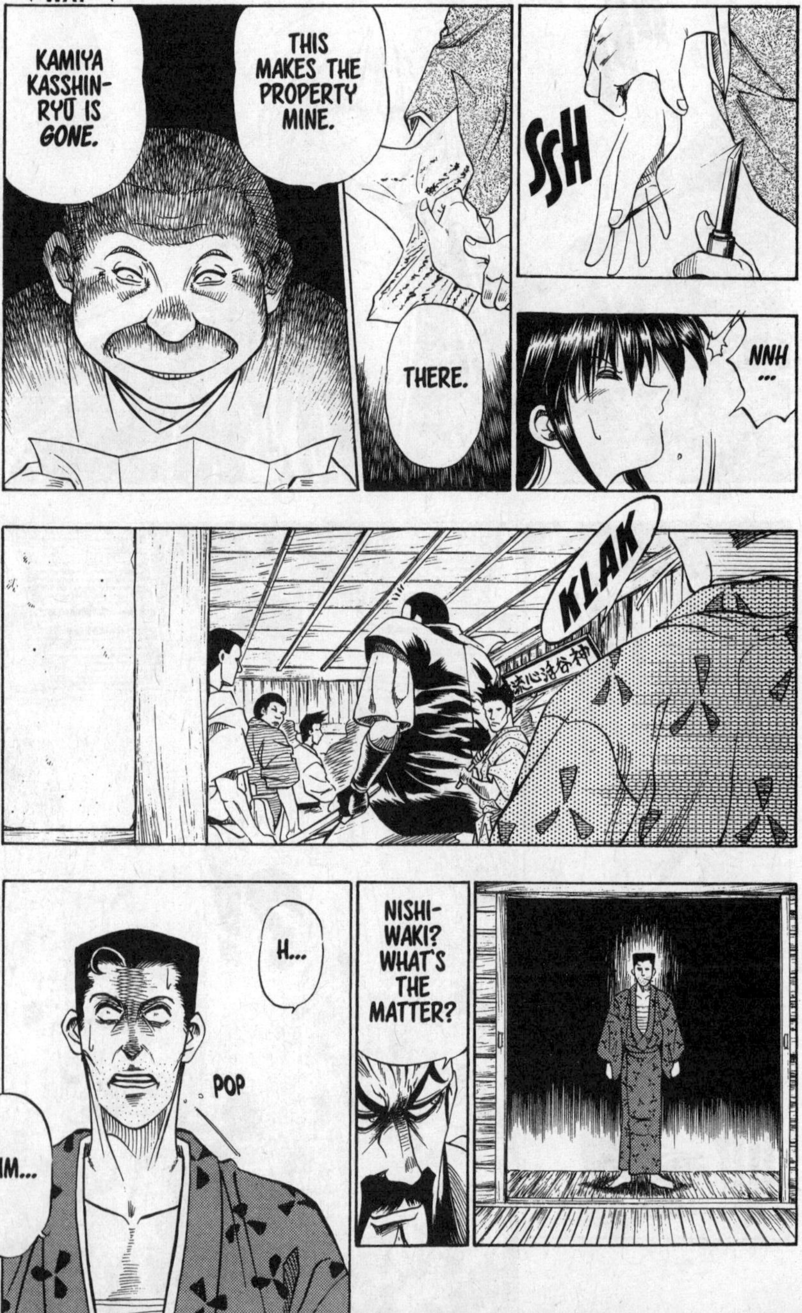
SSH
NNH...
THIS MAKES THE PROPERTY MINE.
THERE.
KAMIYA KASSHIN-RYŪ IS GONE.
KLAK
神谷活心流
NISHI-WAKI? WHAT'S THE MATTER?
H...
POP
HIM...

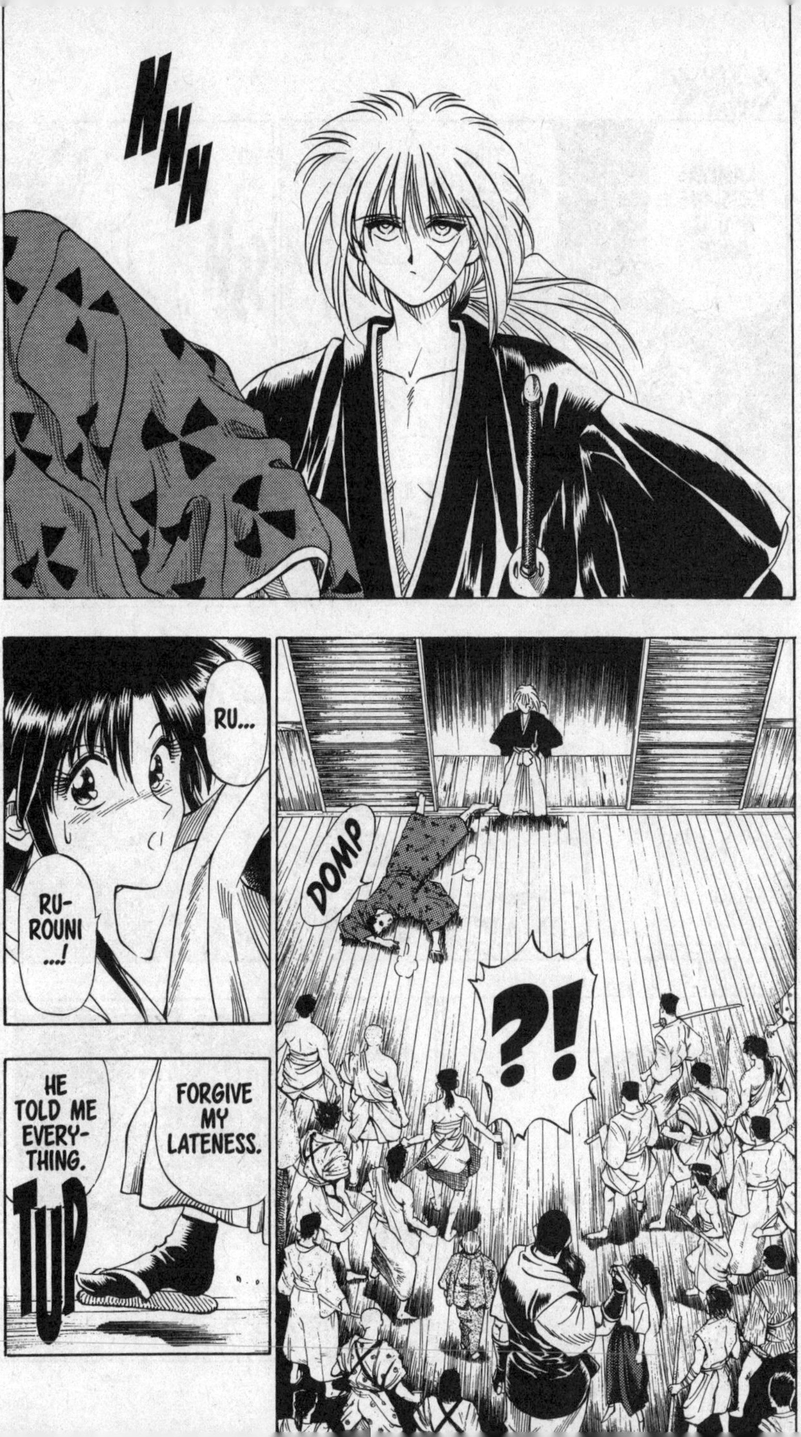
NNN
DOMP
?!
RU...
RU-ROUNI ...!
FORGIVE MY LATENESS.
HE TOLD ME EVERY-THING.
TUP

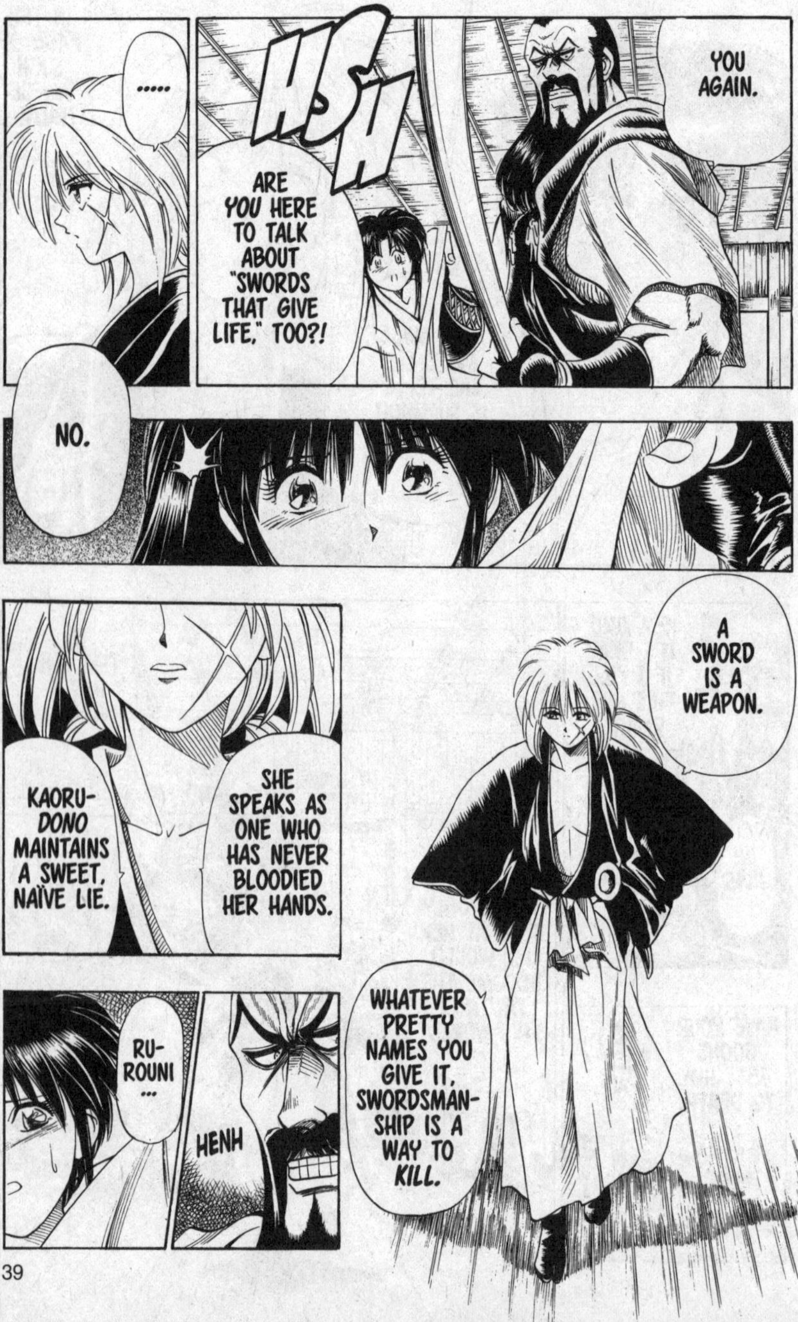
YOU AGAIN.
HSH
ARE YOU HERE TO TALK ABOUT "SWORDS THAT GIVE LIFE," TOO?!
......
NO.
A SWORD IS A WEAPON.
WHATEVER PRETTY NAMES YOU GIVE IT, SWORDSMAN-SHIP IS A WAY TO KILL.
SHE SPEAKS AS ONE WHO HAS NEVER BLOODIED HER HANDS.
KAORU-DONO MAINTAINS A SWEET, NAÏVE LIE.
HENH
RU-ROUNI...

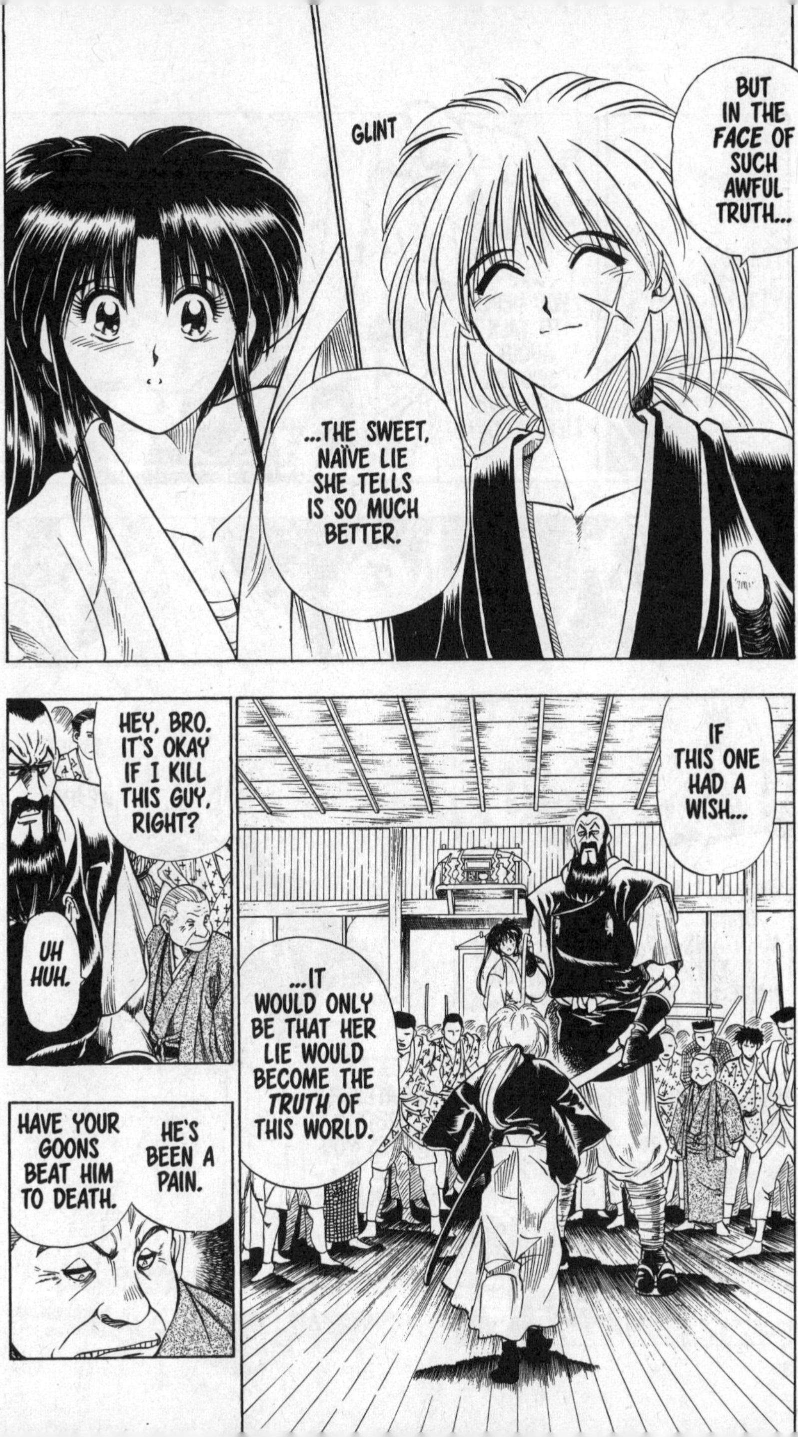
BUT IN THE FACE OF SUCH AWFUL TRUTH...
GLINT
...THE SWEET, NAÏVE LIE SHE TELLS IS SO MUCH BETTER.
IF THIS ONE HAD A WISH...
...IT WOULD ONLY BE THAT HER LIE WOULD BECOME THE TRUTH OF THIS WORLD.
HEY, BRO. IT'S OKAY IF I KILL THIS GUY, RIGHT?
UH HUH.
HE'S BEEN A PAIN.
HAVE YOUR GOONS BEAT HIM TO DEATH.

READ THIS WAY

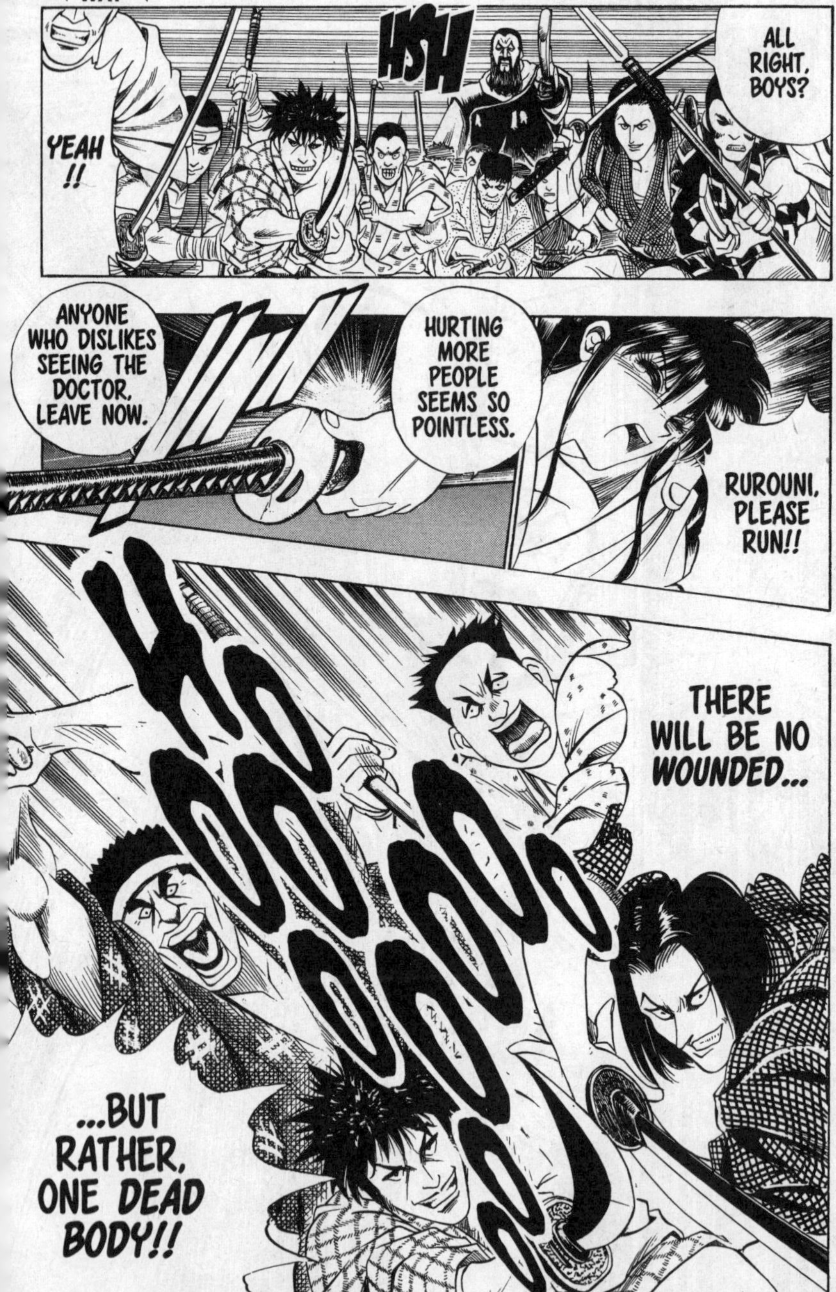

ALL RIGHT, BOYS?
HSH
YEAH!!
HURTING MORE PEOPLE SEEMS SO POINTLESS.
ANYONE WHO DISLIKES SEEING THE DOCTOR, LEAVE NOW.
RUROUNI, PLEASE RUN!!
THERE WILL BE NO WOUNDED...
...BUT RATHER, ONE DEAD BODY!!

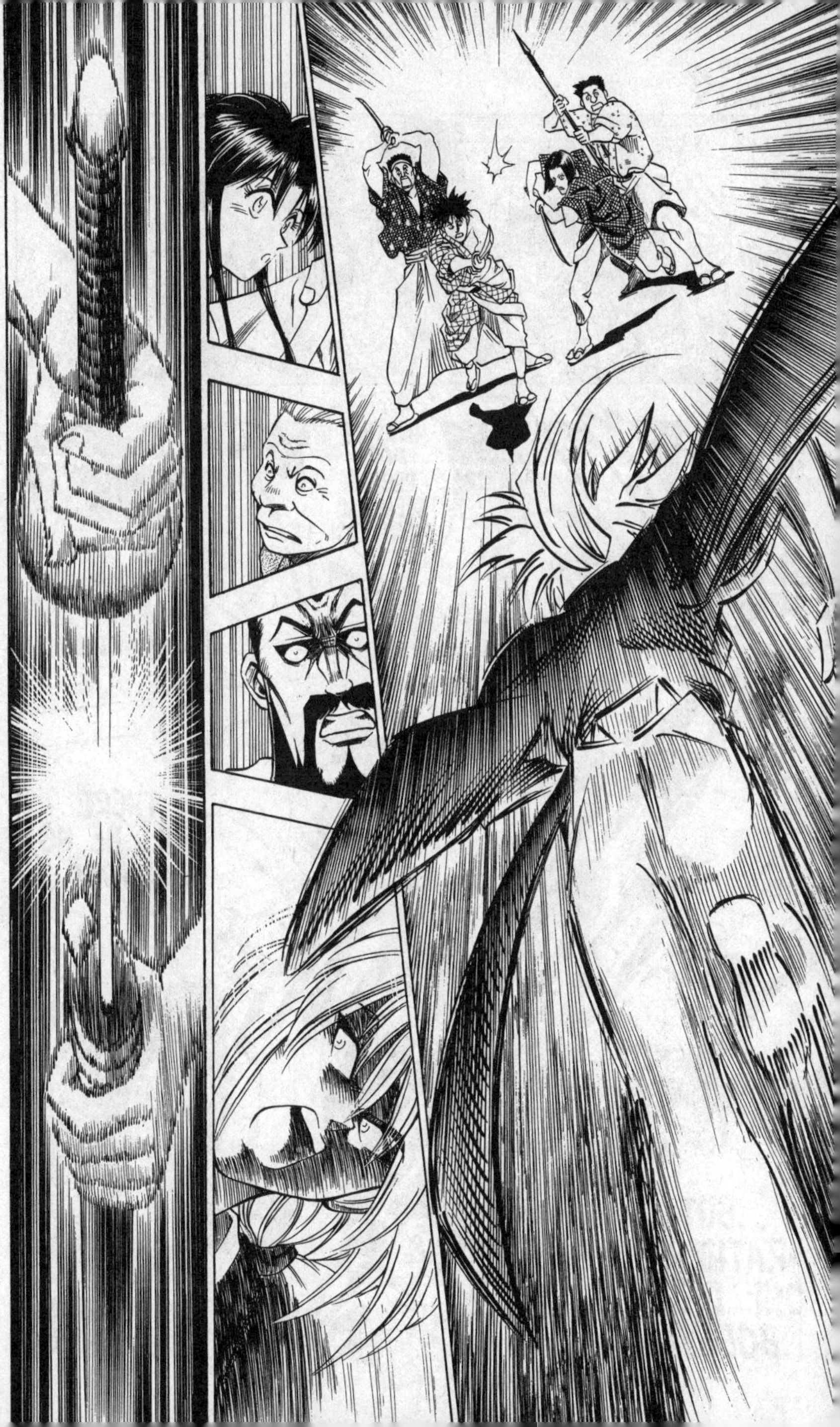

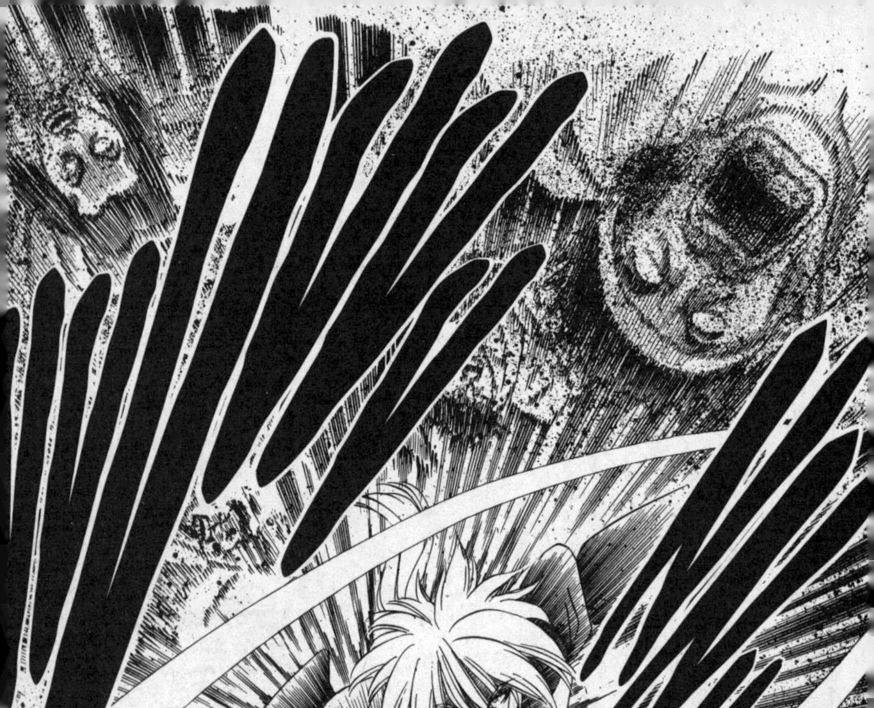

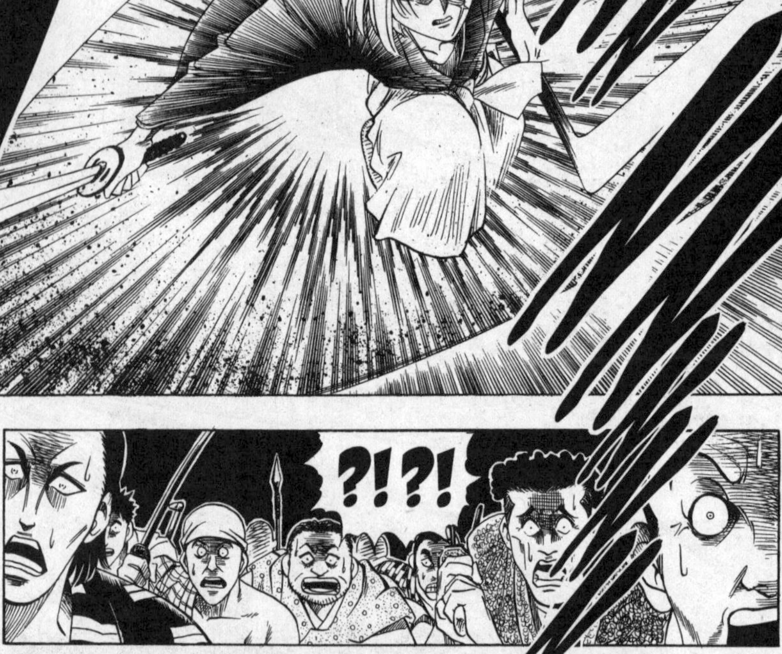
?!?!

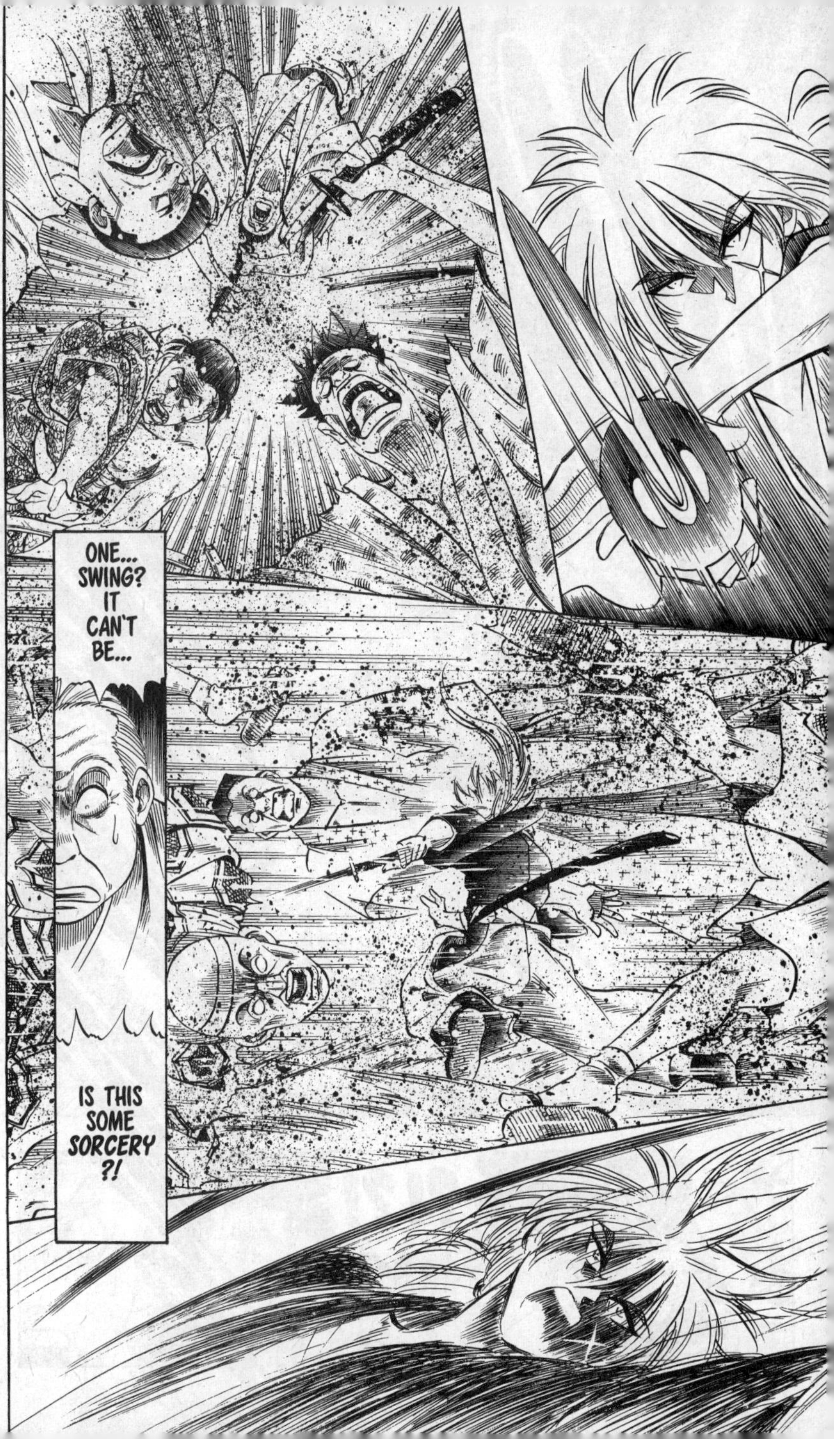
ONE... SWING? IT CAN'T BE...
IS THIS SOME SORCERY ?!

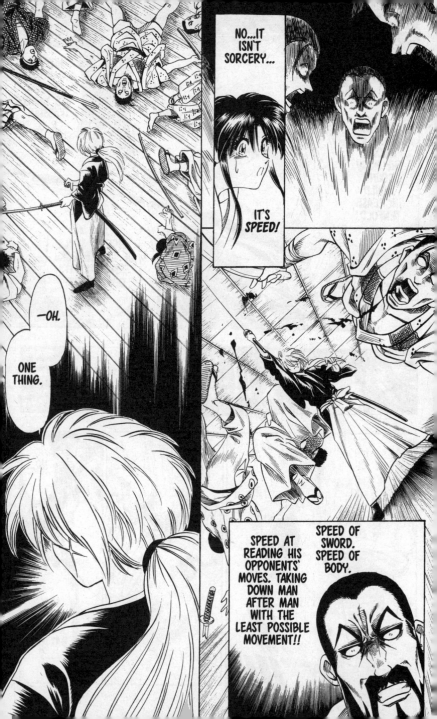

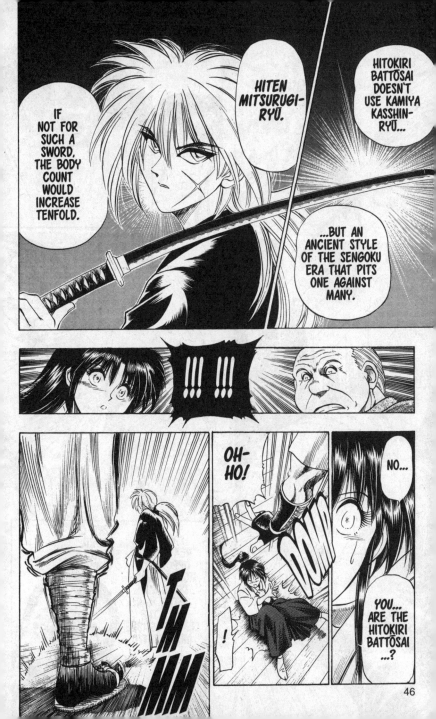

46

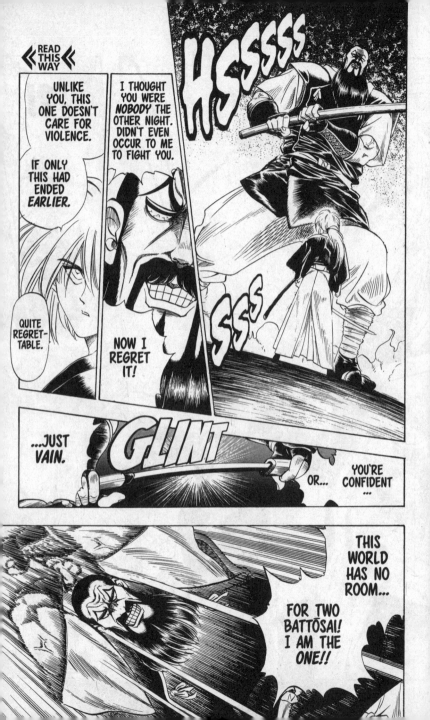

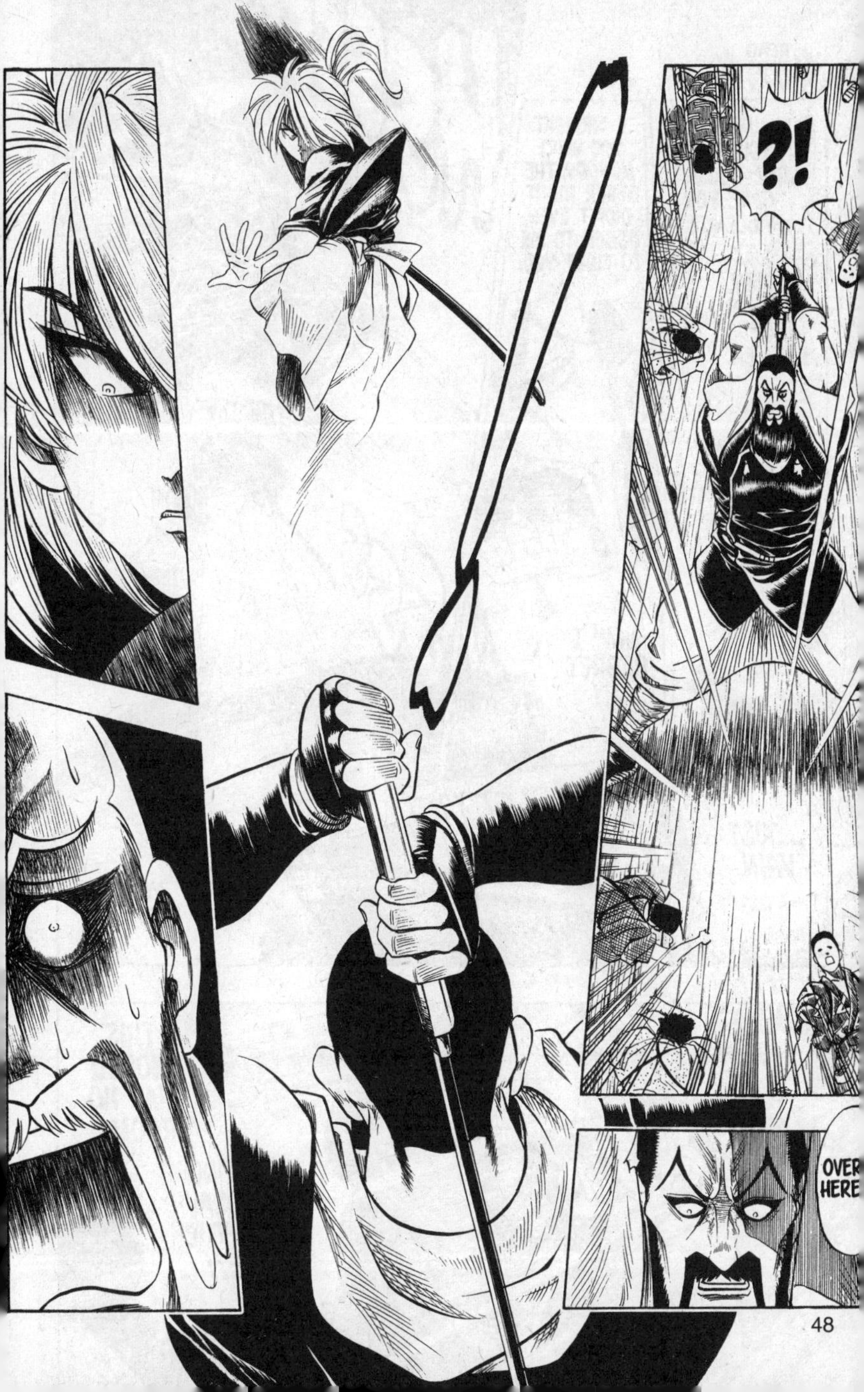
?!
OVER HERE

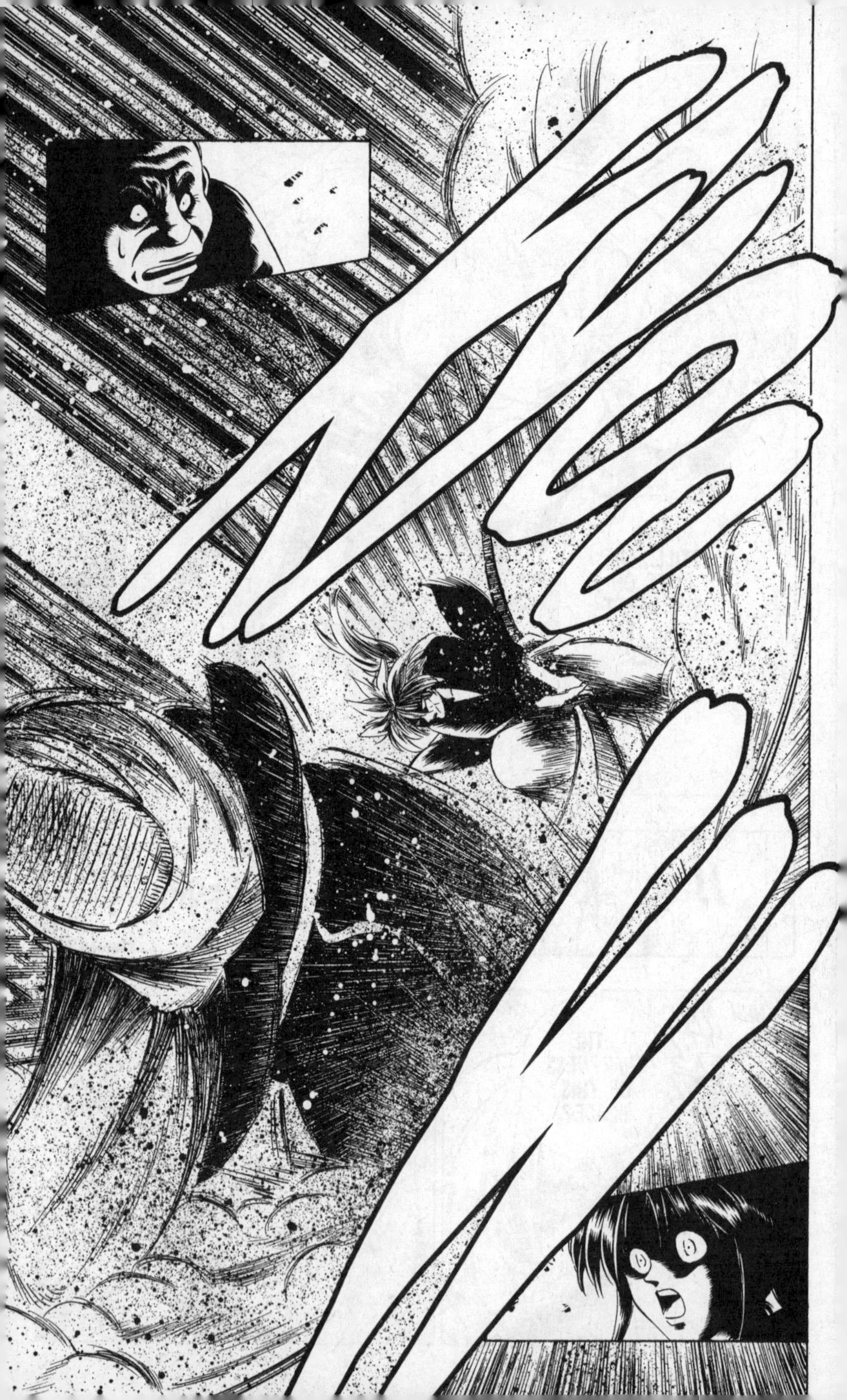

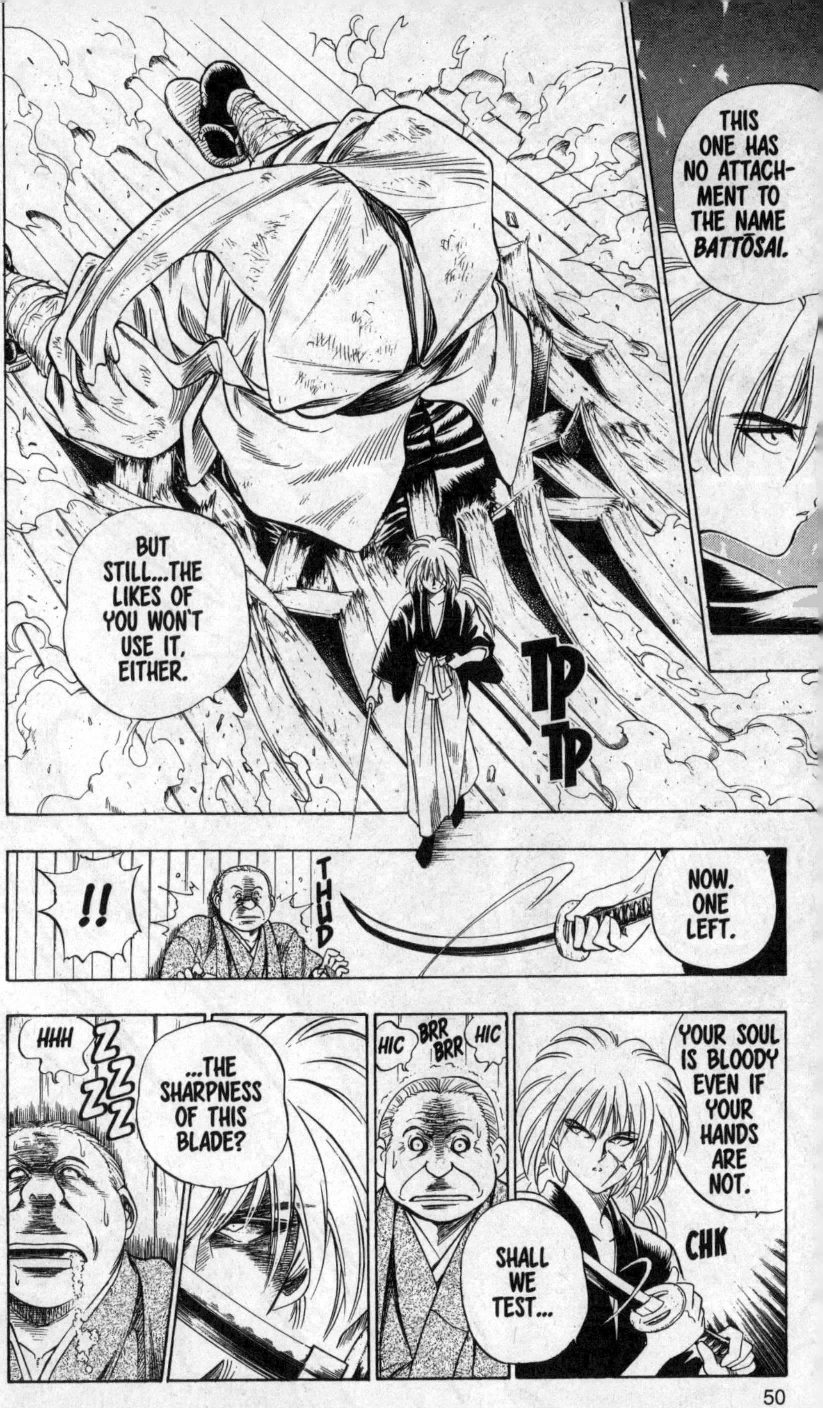
THIS ONE HAS NO ATTACHMENT TO THE NAME BATTŌSAI.
BUT STILL...THE LIKES OF YOU WON'T USE IT, EITHER.
TP TP
NOW. ONE LEFT.
THUD
!!
YOUR SOUL IS BLOODY EVEN IF YOUR HANDS ARE NOT.
CHK
HIC
BRR BRR
HIC
SHALL WE TEST...
...THE SHARPNESS OF THIS BLADE?
HHH
ZZZZ

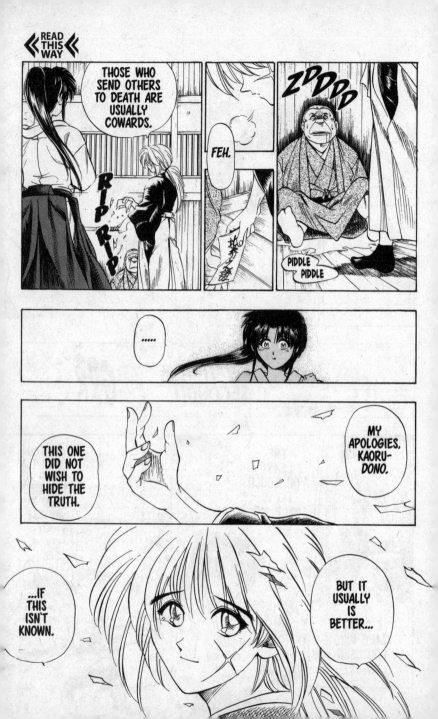

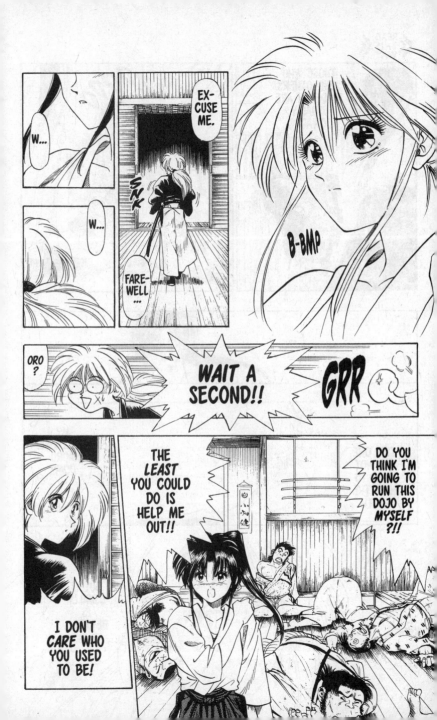

READ THIS WAY

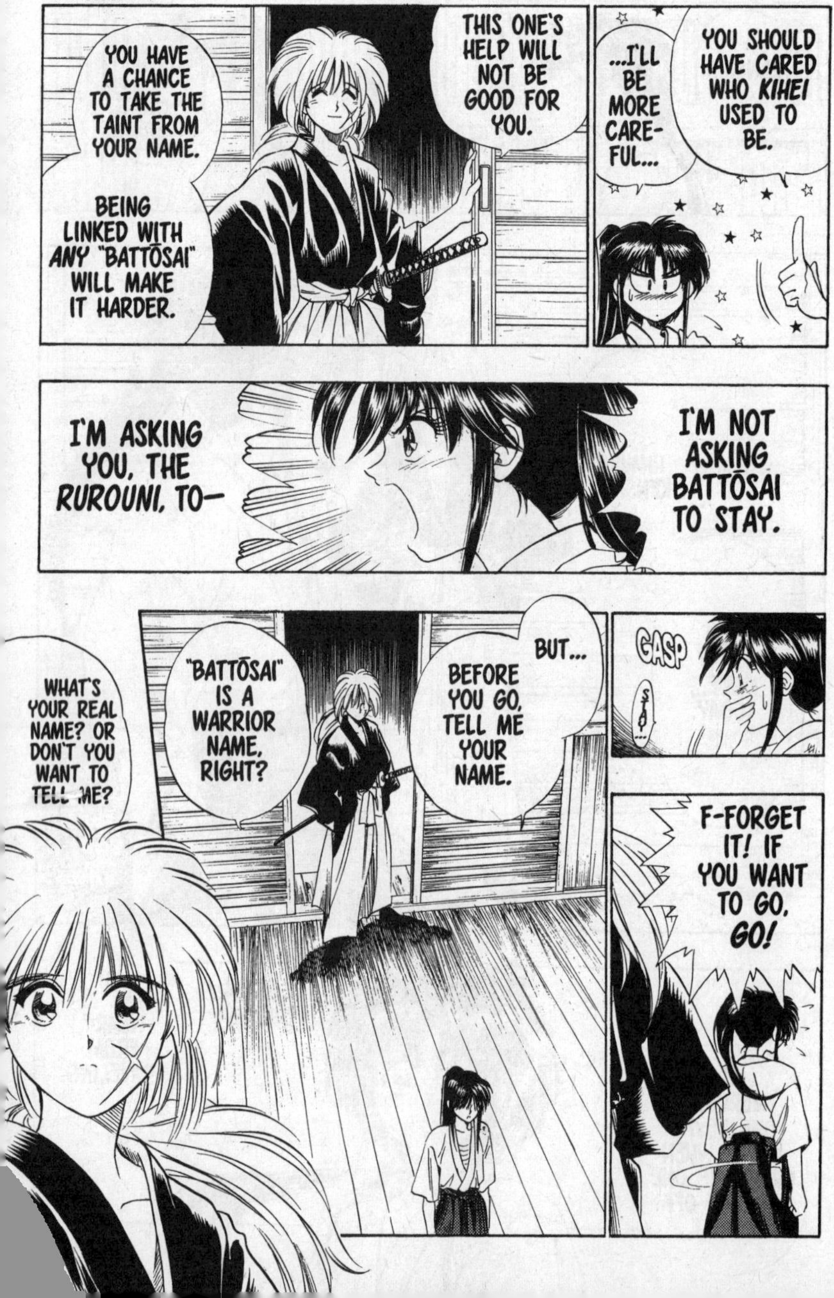
YOU SHOULD HAVE CARED WHO *KIHEI* USED TO BE.
...I'LL BE MORE CARE-FUL...
THIS ONE'S HELP WILL NOT BE GOOD FOR YOU.
YOU HAVE A CHANCE TO TAKE THE TAINT FROM YOUR NAME.
BEING LINKED WITH *ANY* "BATTŌSAI" WILL MAKE IT HARDER.
I'M NOT ASKING BATTŌSAI TO STAY.
I'M ASKING YOU, THE *RUROUNI*, TO—
GASP
STAY...
F-FORGET IT! IF YOU WANT TO GO, *GO!*
BUT...
BEFORE YOU GO, TELL ME YOUR NAME.
"BATTŌSAI" IS A WARRIOR NAME, RIGHT?
WHAT'S YOUR REAL NAME? OR DON'T YOU WANT TO TELL ME?

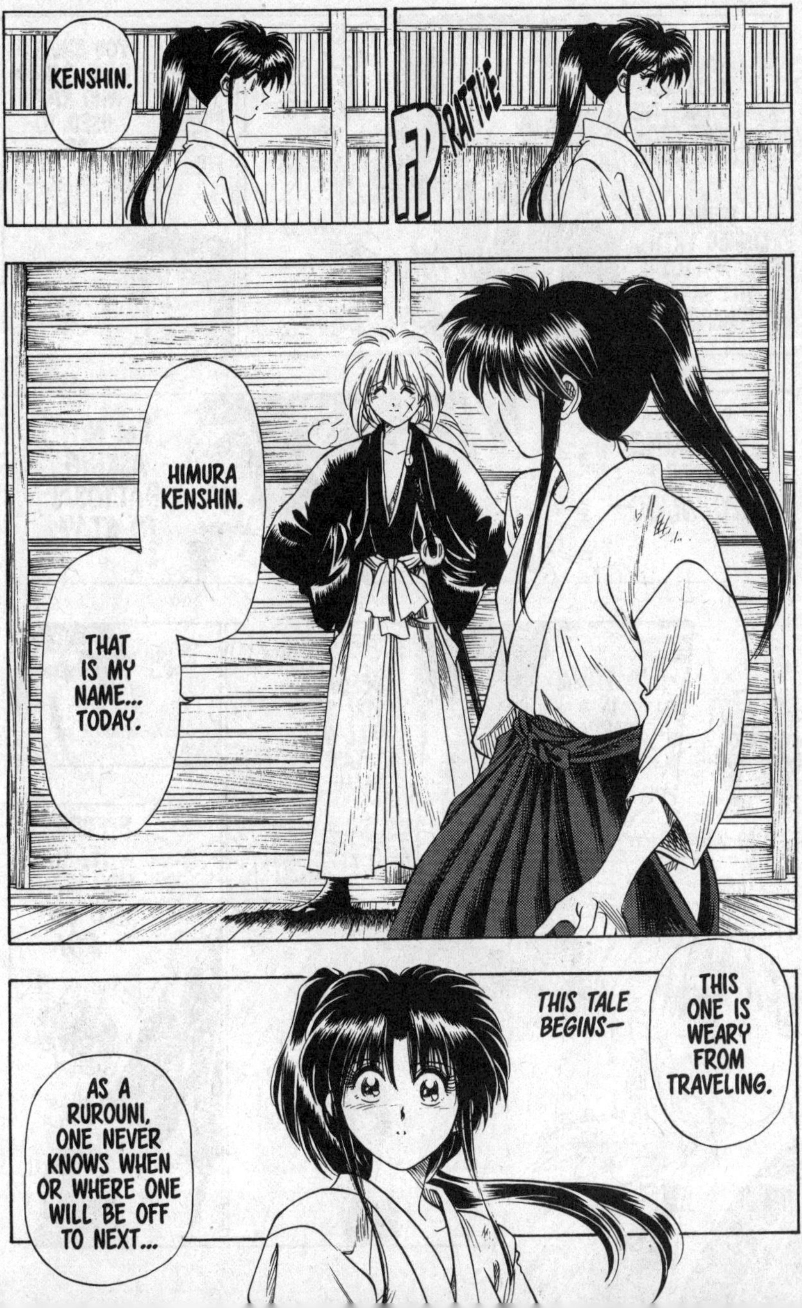
FP
RATTLE
KENSHIN.
HIMURA KENSHIN.
THAT IS MY NAME... TODAY.
THIS ONE IS WEARY FROM TRAVELING.
THIS TALE BEGINS—
AS A RUROUNI, ONE NEVER KNOWS WHEN OR WHERE ONE WILL BE OFF TO NEXT...

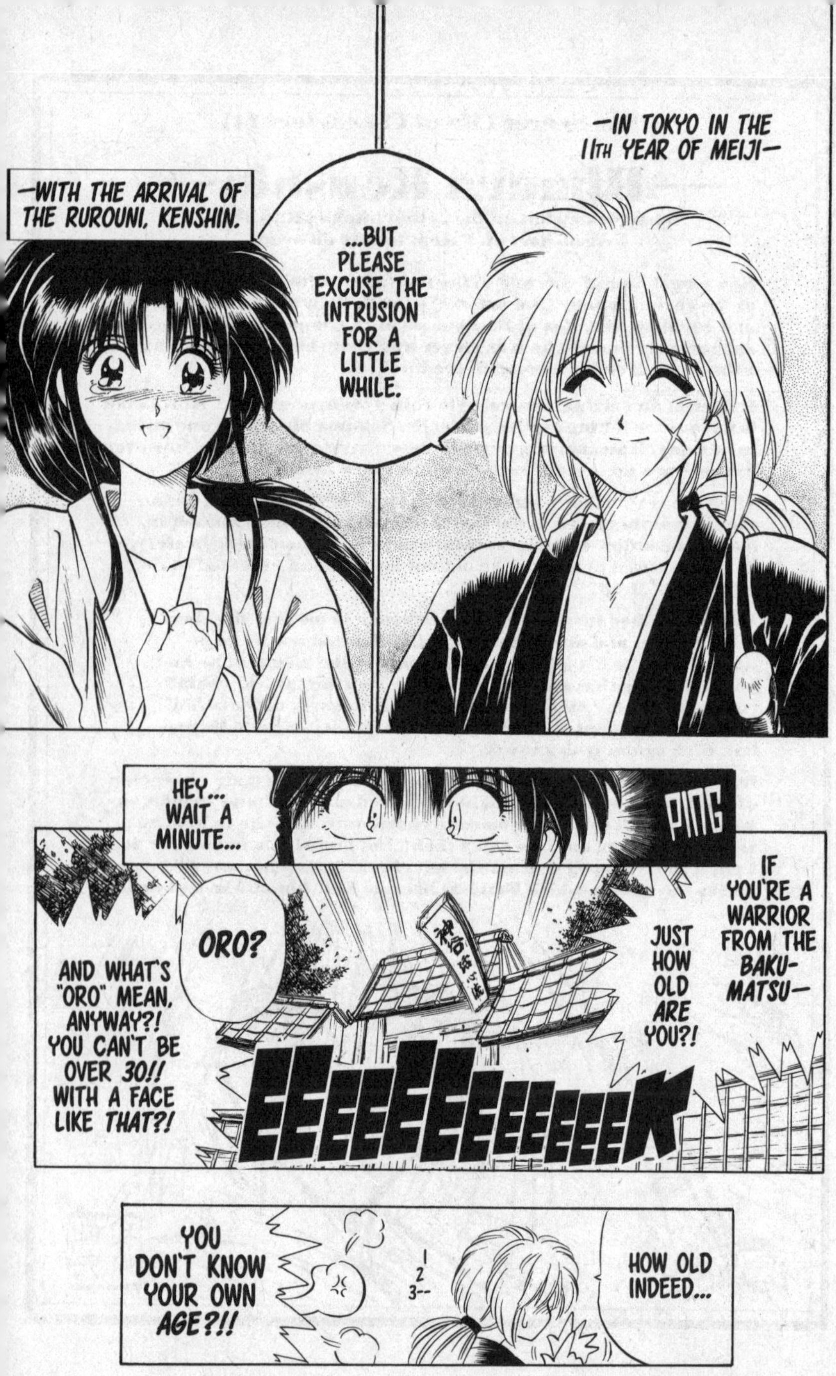

—IN TOKYO IN THE 11TH YEAR OF MEIJI—
...BUT PLEASE EXCUSE THE INTRUSION FOR A LITTLE WHILE.
—WITH THE ARRIVAL OF THE RUROUNI, KENSHIN.
PING
HEY... WAIT A MINUTE...
IF YOU'RE A WARRIOR FROM THE BAKU-MATSU—
JUST HOW OLD ARE YOU?!
ORO?
AND WHAT'S "ORO" MEAN, ANYWAY?! YOU CAN'T BE OVER 30!! WITH A FACE LIKE THAT?!
EEEEEEEEEEEEK
HOW OLD INDEED...
1
2
3--
YOU DON'T KNOW YOUR OWN AGE?!!

The Secret Life of Characters (1)

—Himura Kenshin—

Based somewhat on the actual hitokiri Kawakami Gensai. Sort of. Except totally different.

Kawakami Gensai was one of the four great hitokiri, or assassins, of the revolutionary (Bakumatsu) period. He was short and skinny, and could be mistaken at first glance for a woman. Contrary to his appearance, though, he was clever and clear-headed despite also being most dreaded among all the hitokiri.

Master of an original sword-style called "Shiranui-ryū," Kawakami is famous for felling the great idealist Sakuma Shōzan in one swing, in mid-day. Kawakami is nevertheless a mysterious figure, however, as there are no certain records of his other assassinations.

After the revolution—and unable to let go of the idea that Japan should remain closed to the world—Kawakami found himself in frequent conflict with the revolutionary government. Ultimately, he was accused of a crime he did not commit and executed in the 4th year of Meiji.

As I researched further, it began to occur to me that the story wasn't so cut and dry. What this hitokiri could not let go of was his duty to his fallen comrades and to the men that he had killed. It's this that gave me the initial idea for the "Kenshin" character. As for others, there is the selflessness of Okita Sōji of the Shinsengumi and the mysterious quality of Saitō Hajime... but, then again, who knows?

In terms of graphic design, I had no real motif. The main character of my debut work was a tall, black-haired man in showy armor, so when I set out to design someone completely opposite to him, he ended up coming out like a girl (heh). Not knowing what else to do, I put a cross-shaped scar on the left cheek. Now that same "X" marks the spot at which Battōsai became Kenshin...Or so I've heard!

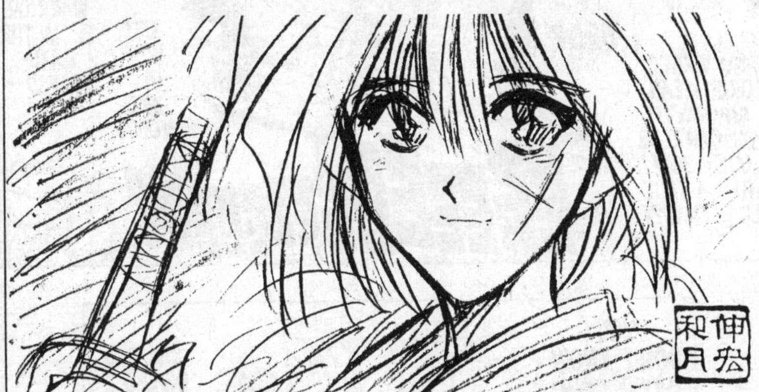

伸宏
和月

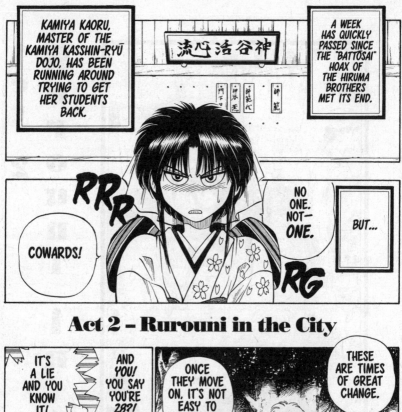

KAMIYA KAORU, MASTER OF THE KAMIYA KASSHIN-RYŪ DOJO, HAS BEEN RUNNING AROUND TRYING TO GET HER STUDENTS BACK.

A WEEK HAS QUICKLY PASSED SINCE THE "BATTŌSAI" HOAX OF THE HIRUMA BROTHERS MET ITS END.

流心活谷神

神谷活心流

師範 師範代 神谷活心 門下生

RRR

COWARDS!

NO ONE. NOT ONE.

BUT...

RG

Act 2 – Rurouni in the City

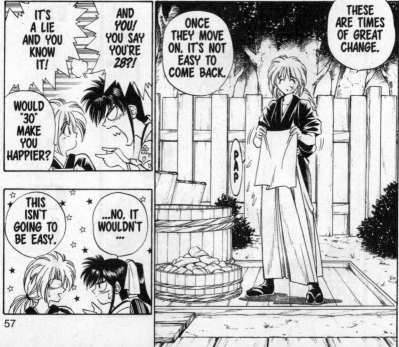

IT'S A LIE AND YOU KNOW IT!

AND YOU! YOU SAY YOU'RE 28?!

ONCE THEY MOVE ON, IT'S NOT EASY TO COME BACK.

THESE ARE TIMES OF GREAT CHANGE.

WOULD "30" MAKE YOU HAPPIER?

PAP

THIS ISN'T GOING TO BE EASY.

...NO, IT WOULDN'T...

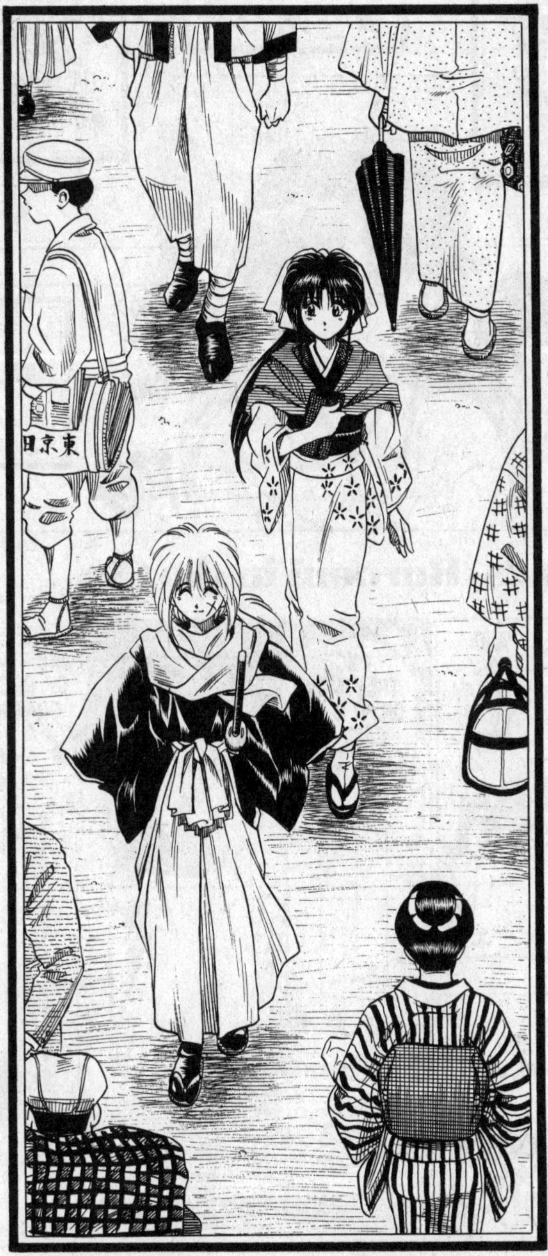
東京日

Act 2
Rurouni in the City

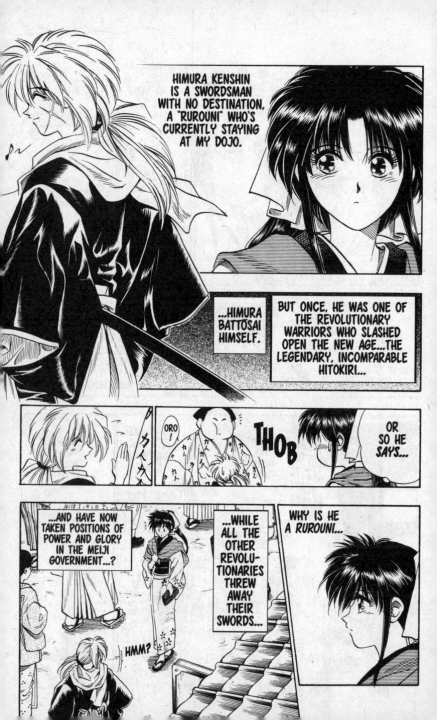

HIMURA KENSHIN IS A SWORDSMAN WITH NO DESTINATION, A "RUROUNI" WHO'S CURRENTLY STAYING AT MY DOJO.

...HIMURA BATTOSAI HIMSELF.

BUT ONCE, HE WAS ONE OF THE REVOLUTIONARY WARRIORS WHO SLASHED OPEN THE NEW AGE...THE LEGENDARY, INCOMPARABLE HITOKIRI...

ORO!

THOB

OR SO HE SAYS...

...AND HAVE NOW TAKEN POSITIONS OF POWER AND GLORY IN THE MEIJI GOVERNMENT...?

...WHILE ALL THE OTHER REVOLU-TIONARIES THREW AWAY THEIR SWORDS...

WHY IS HE A RUROUNI...

HMM?

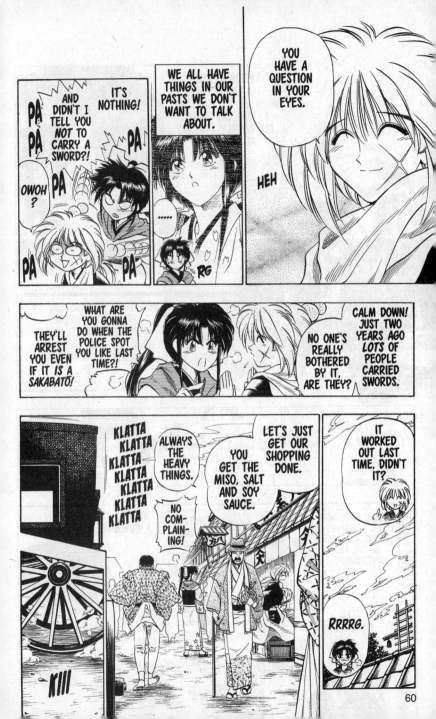

60

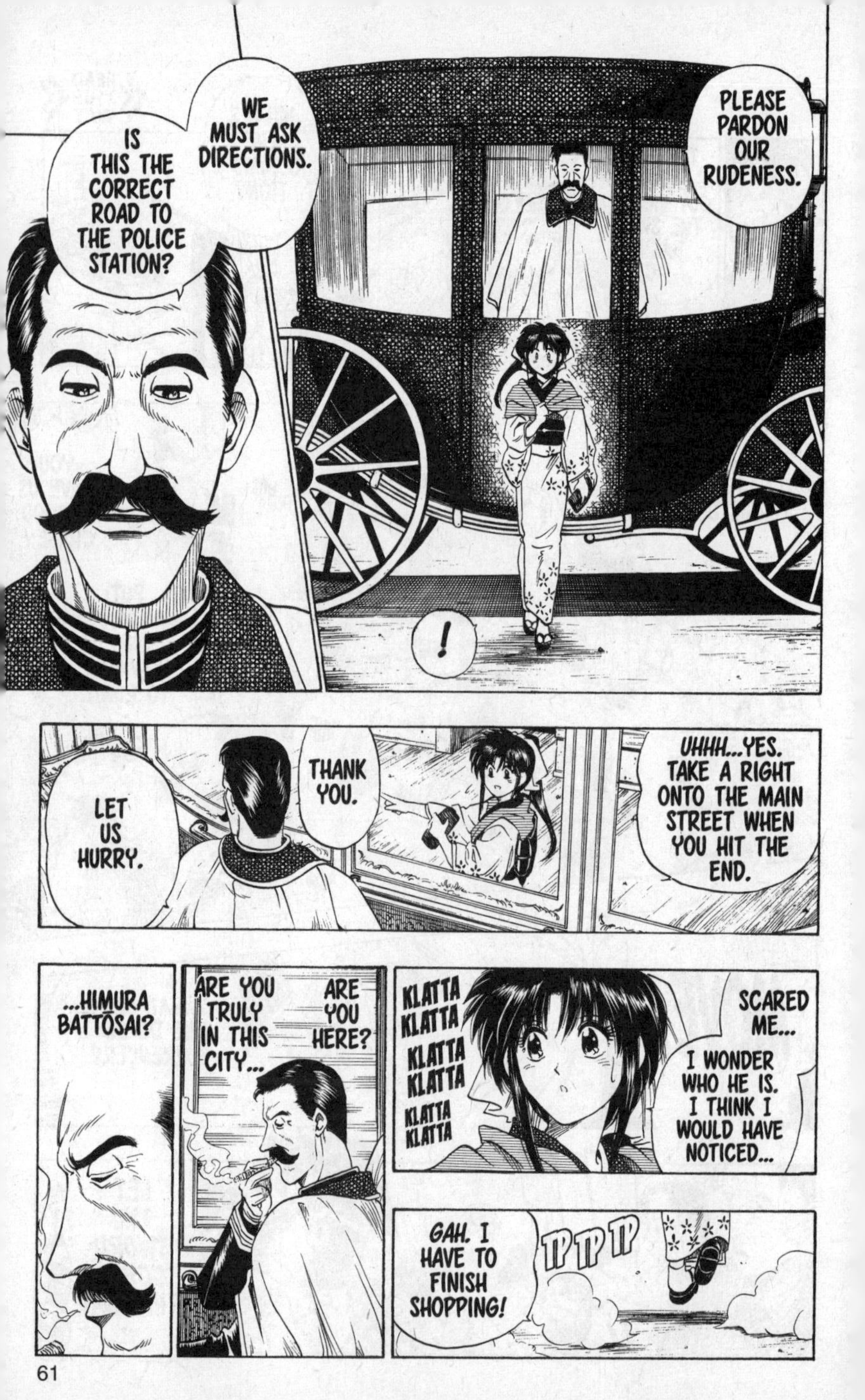
PLEASE PARDON OUR RUDENESS.
!
WE MUST ASK DIRECTIONS.
IS THIS THE CORRECT ROAD TO THE POLICE STATION?
UHHH...YES. TAKE A RIGHT ONTO THE MAIN STREET WHEN YOU HIT THE END.
THANK YOU.
LET US HURRY.
SCARED ME...
I WONDER WHO HE IS. I THINK I WOULD HAVE NOTICED...
KLATTA KLATTA
KLATTA KLATTA
KLATTA KLATTA
TP TP TP
GAH. I HAVE TO FINISH SHOPPING!
ARE YOU HERE?
ARE YOU TRULY IN THIS CITY...
...HIMURA BATTŌSAI?

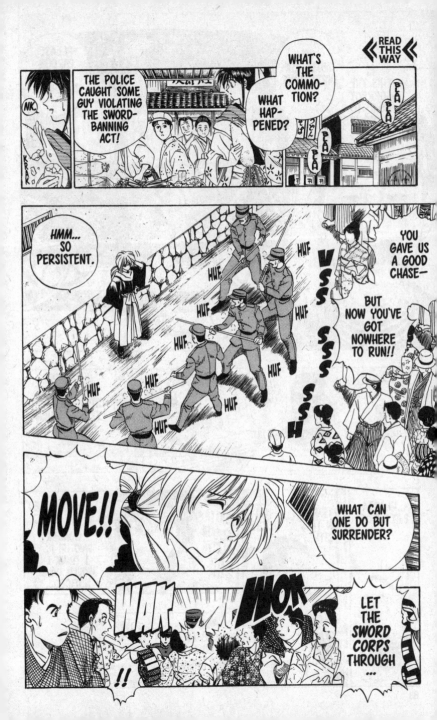

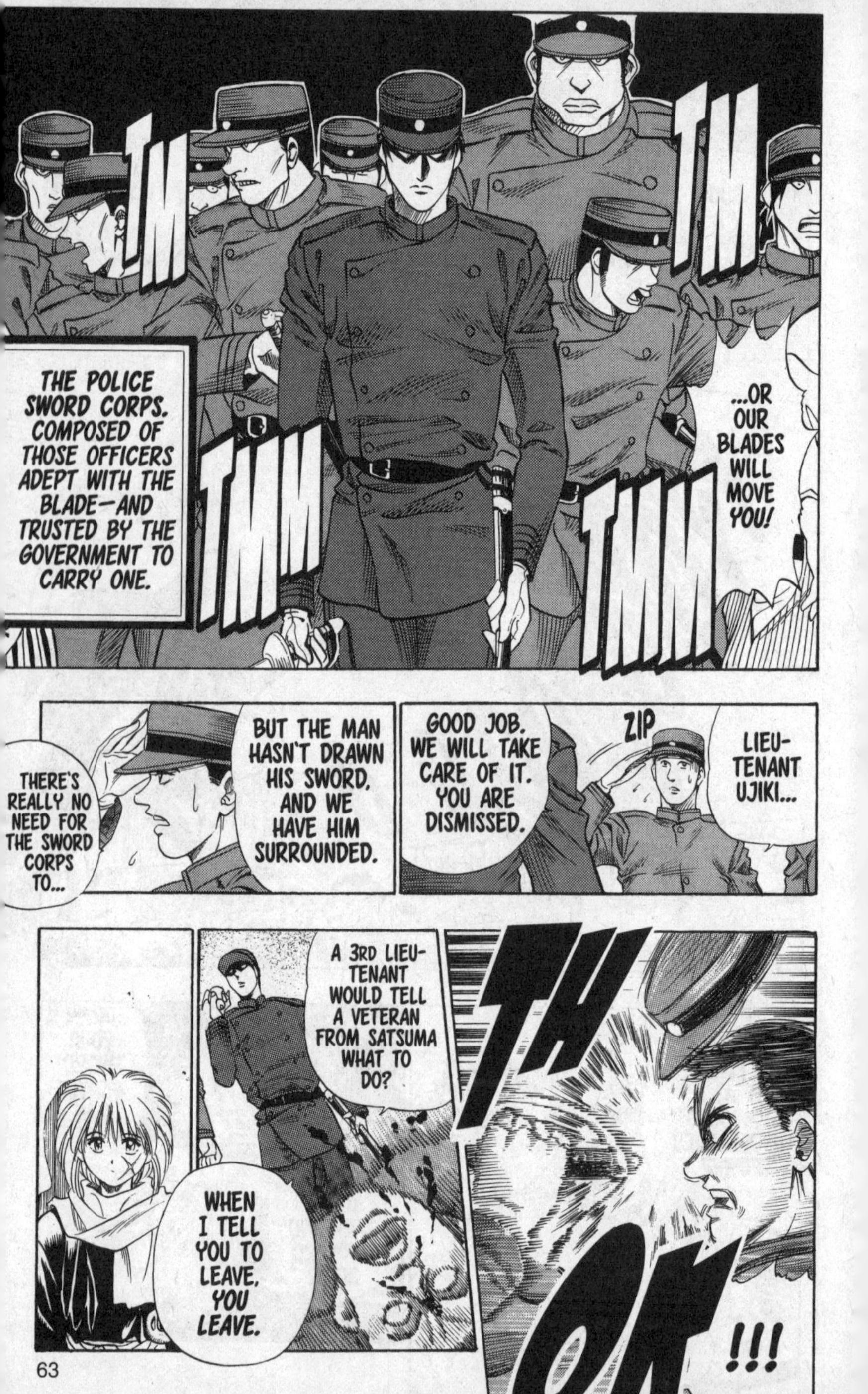
TM
...OR OUR BLADES WILL MOVE YOU!
TMM
TM
TMM
THE POLICE SWORD CORPS. COMPOSED OF THOSE OFFICERS ADEPT WITH THE BLADE—AND TRUSTED BY THE GOVERNMENT TO CARRY ONE.
LIEU-TENANT UJIKI...
ZIP
GOOD JOB. WE WILL TAKE CARE OF IT. YOU ARE DISMISSED.
BUT THE MAN HASN'T DRAWN HIS SWORD, AND WE HAVE HIM SURROUNDED.
THERE'S REALLY NO NEED FOR THE SWORD CORPS TO...
THOK!!!
A 3RD LIEU-TENANT WOULD TELL A VETERAN FROM SATSUMA WHAT TO DO?
WHEN I TELL YOU TO LEAVE, YOU LEAVE.

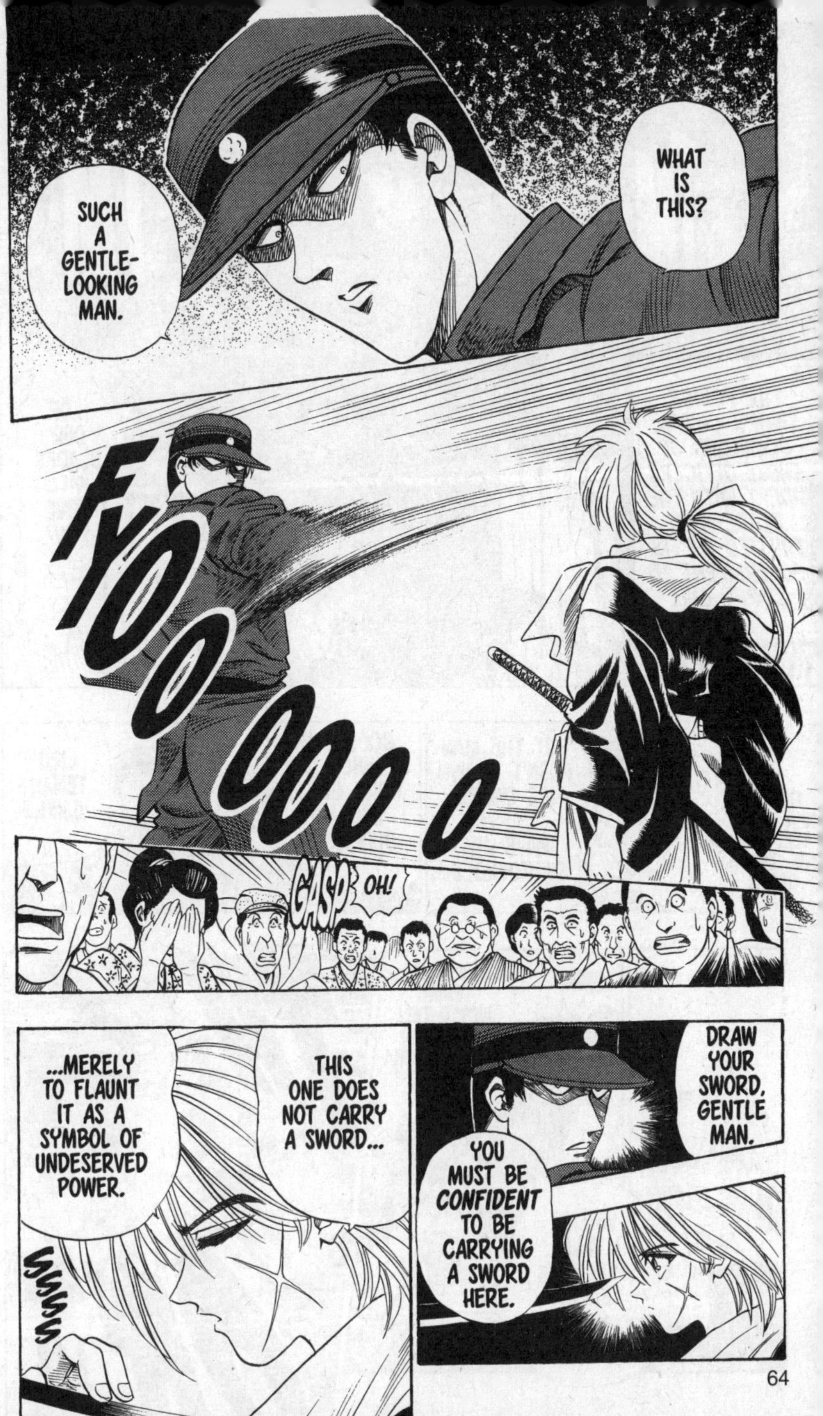
WHAT IS THIS?
SUCH A GENTLE-LOOKING MAN.
FYOOOOOOOO
OH!
GASP
DRAW YOUR SWORD, GENTLE MAN.
YOU MUST BE ***CONFIDENT*** TO BE CARRYING A SWORD HERE.
THIS ONE DOES NOT CARRY A SWORD...
...MERELY TO FLAUNT IT AS A SYMBOL OF UNDESERVED POWER.
SSSS

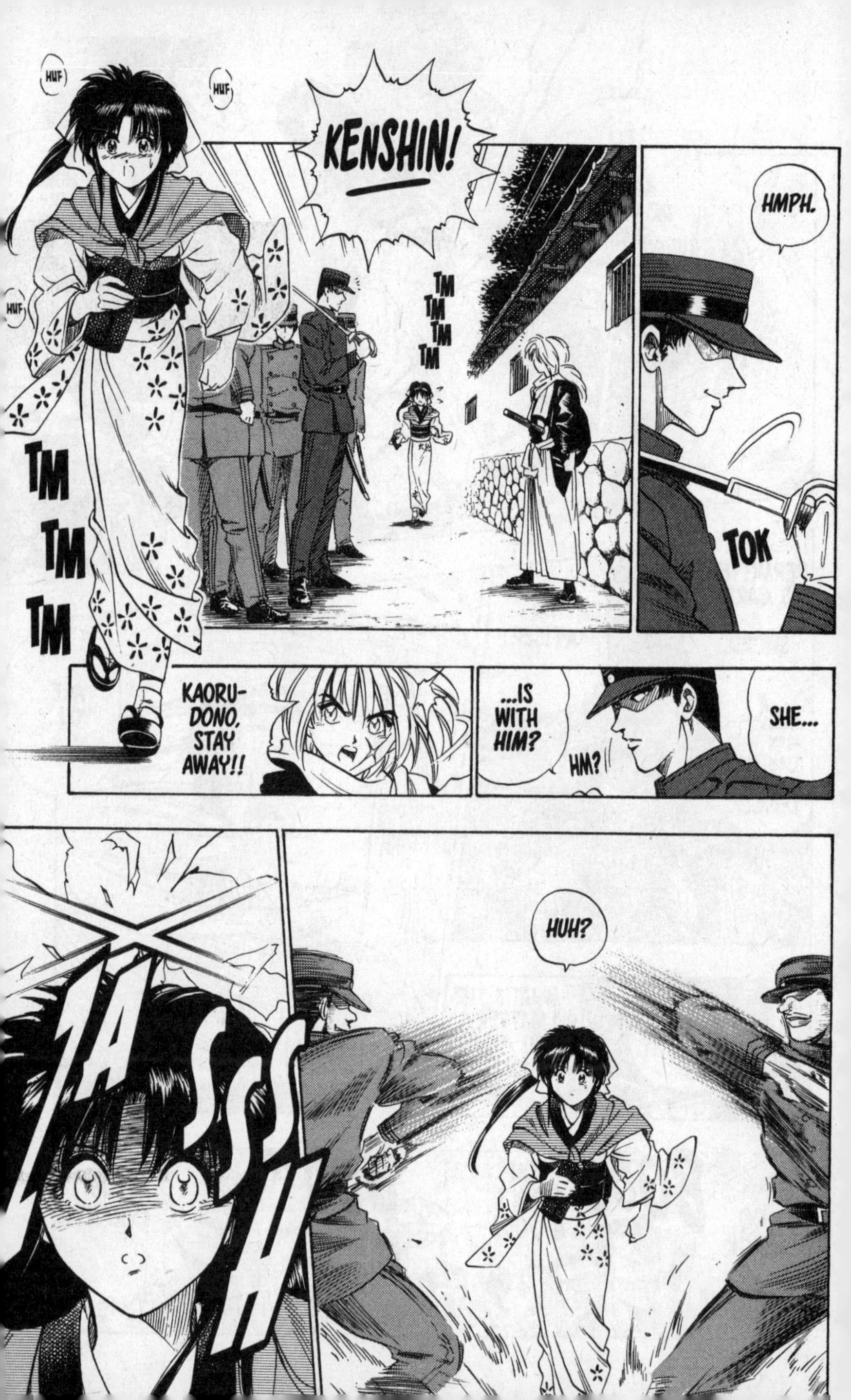
HMPH.
TOK
HUF
HUF
KENSHIN!
TM TM TM TM
HUF
TM TM TM
SHE...
HM?
...IS WITH HIM?
KAORU-DONO, STAY AWAY!!
HUH?
ZASSH

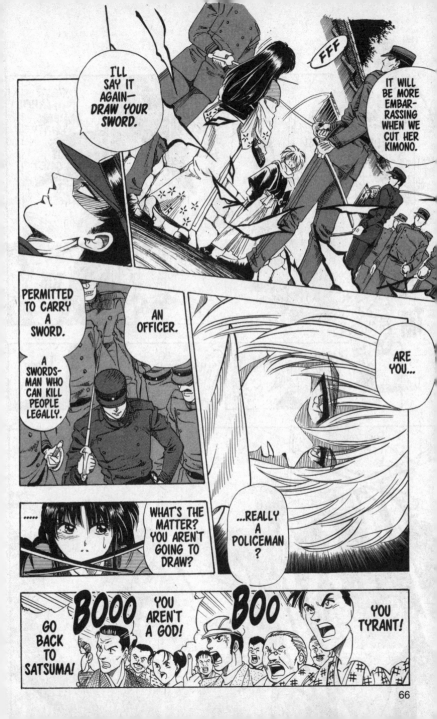

66

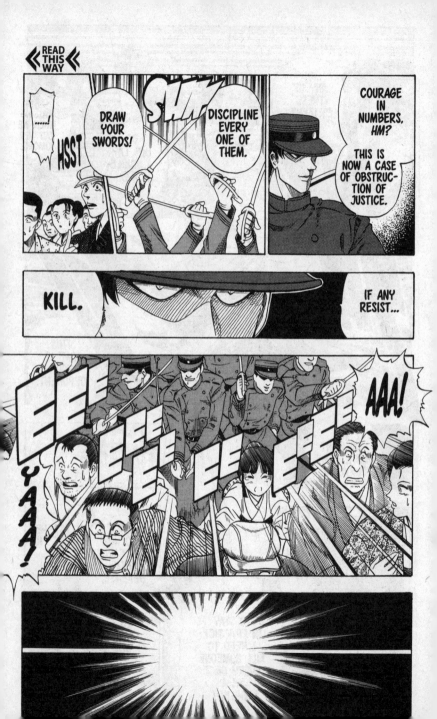

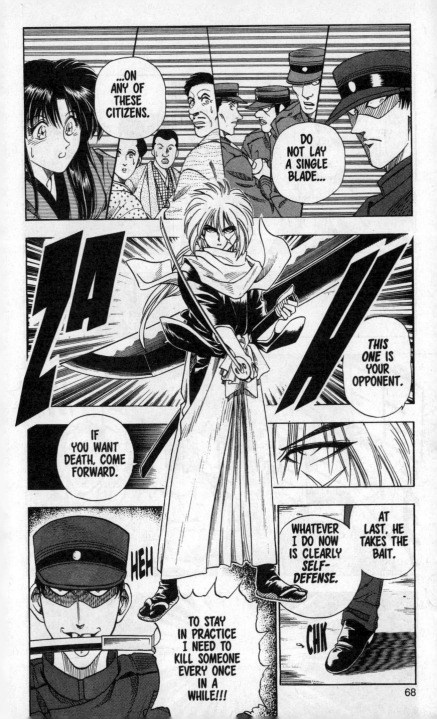

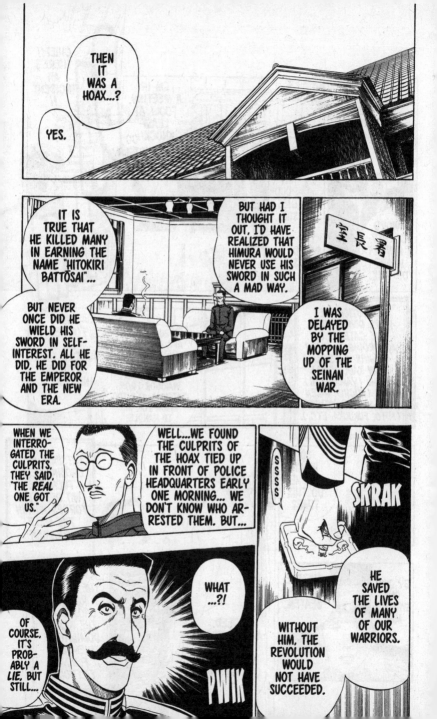

THEN IT WAS A HOAX...?

YES.

IT IS TRUE THAT HE KILLED MANY IN EARNING THE NAME "HITOKIRI BATTŌSAI"...

BUT NEVER ONCE DID HE WIELD HIS SWORD IN SELF-INTEREST. ALL HE DID, HE DID FOR THE EMPEROR AND THE NEW ERA.

BUT HAD I THOUGHT IT OUT, I'D HAVE REALIZED THAT HIMURA WOULD NEVER USE HIS SWORD IN SUCH A MAD WAY.

I WAS DELAYED BY THE MOPPING UP OF THE SEINAN WAR.

WHEN WE INTERROGATED THE CULPRITS, THEY SAID, "THE REAL ONE GOT US."

WELL...WE FOUND THE CULPRITS OF THE HOAX TIED UP IN FRONT OF POLICE HEADQUARTERS EARLY ONE MORNING... WE DON'T KNOW WHO ARRESTED THEM. BUT...

SSSSS

SKRAK

HE SAVED THE LIVES OF MANY OF OUR WARRIORS.

WHAT ...?!

OF COURSE, IT'S PROBABLY A LIE, BUT STILL...

PWIK

WITHOUT HIM, THE REVOLUTION WOULD NOT HAVE SUCCEEDED.

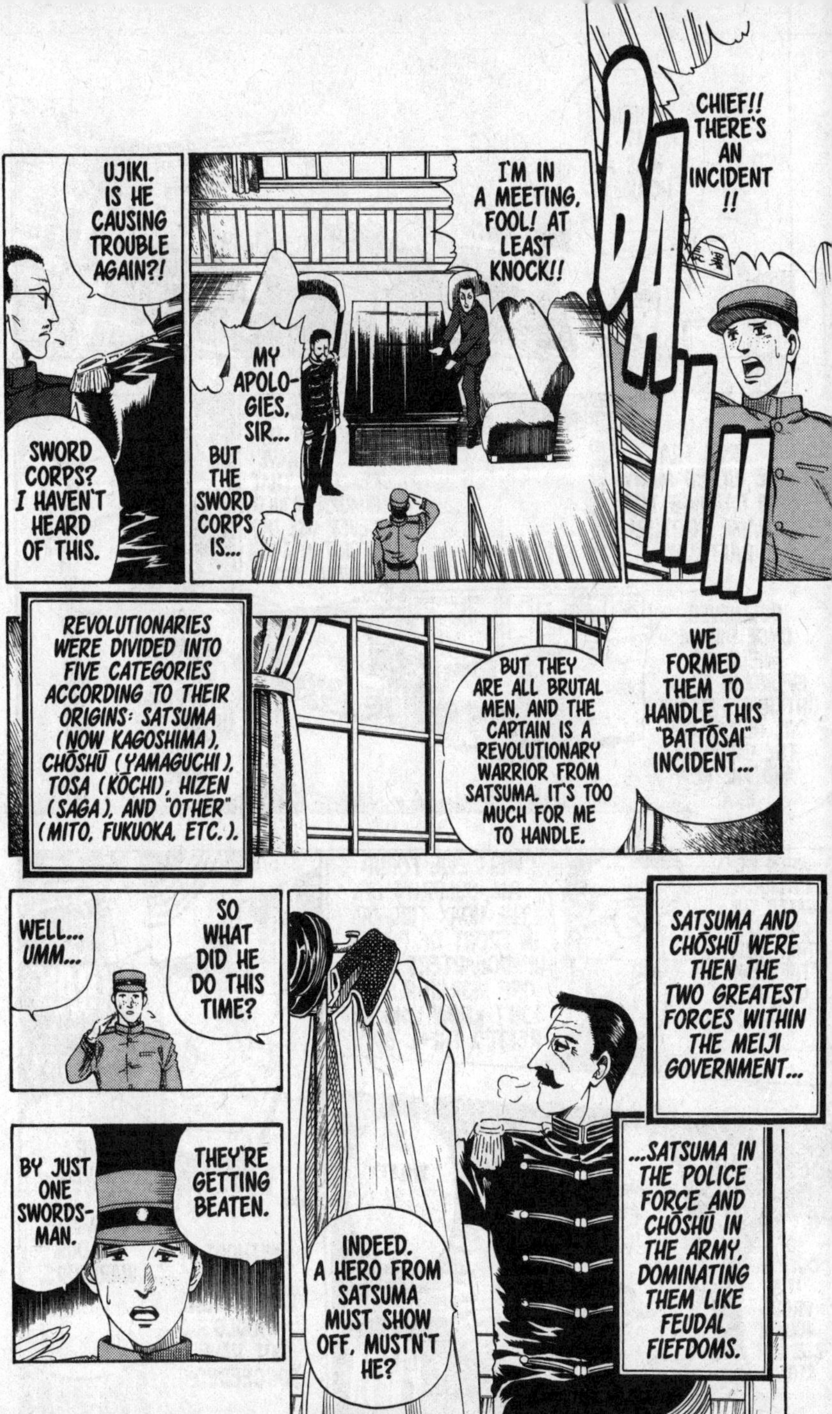
BAMM
CHIEF!! THERE'S AN INCIDENT!!
I'M IN A MEETING, FOOL! AT LEAST KNOCK!!
MY APOLOGIES, SIR...
BUT THE SWORD CORPS IS...
UJIKI. IS HE CAUSING TROUBLE AGAIN?!
SWORD CORPS? I HAVEN'T HEARD OF THIS.
WE FORMED THEM TO HANDLE THIS "BATTŌSAI" INCIDENT...
BUT THEY ARE ALL BRUTAL MEN, AND THE CAPTAIN IS A REVOLUTIONARY WARRIOR FROM SATSUMA. IT'S TOO MUCH FOR ME TO HANDLE.
REVOLUTIONARIES WERE DIVIDED INTO FIVE CATEGORIES ACCORDING TO THEIR ORIGINS: SATSUMA (NOW KAGOSHIMA), CHŌSHŪ (YAMAGUCHI), TOSA (KŌCHI), HIZEN (SAGA), AND "OTHER" (MITO, FUKUOKA, ETC.).
SATSUMA AND CHŌSHŪ WERE THEN THE TWO GREATEST FORCES WITHIN THE MEIJI GOVERNMENT...
...SATSUMA IN THE POLICE FORCE AND CHŌSHŪ IN THE ARMY, DOMINATING THEM LIKE FEUDAL FIEFDOMS.
INDEED. A HERO FROM SATSUMA MUST SHOW OFF, MUSTN'T HE?
SO WHAT DID HE DO THIS TIME?
WELL... UMM...
THEY'RE GETTING BEATEN.
BY JUST ONE SWORDSMAN.

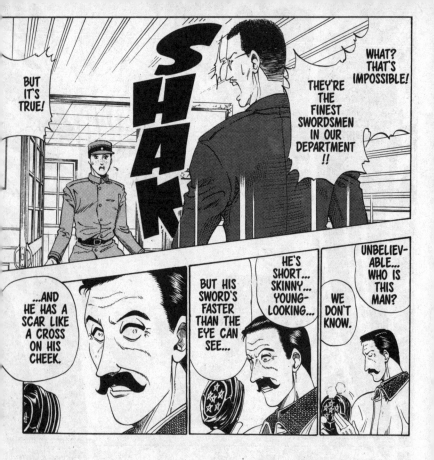

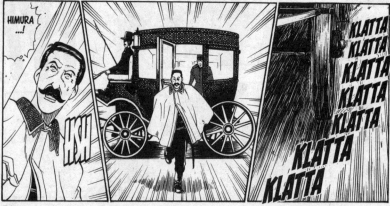

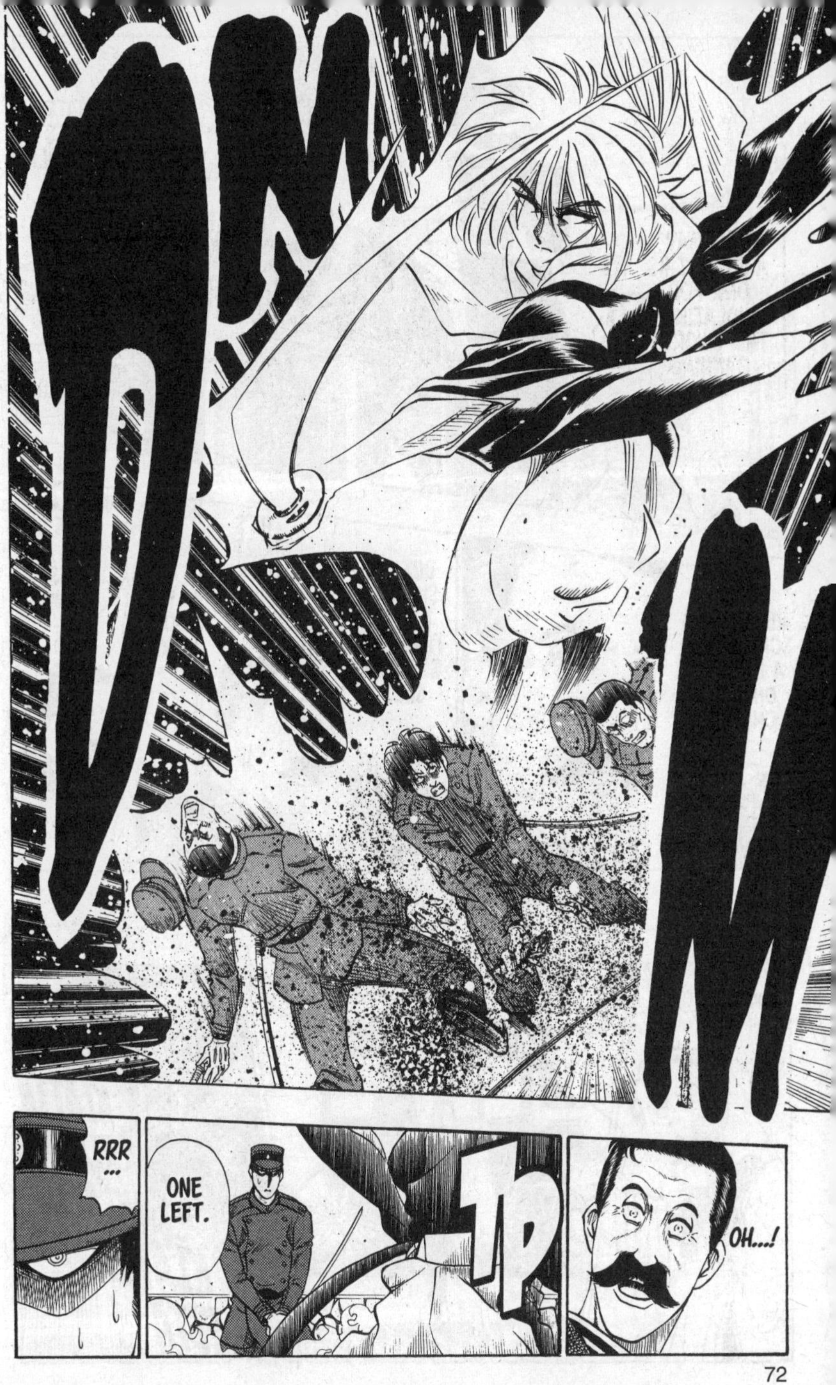
OH...!
TP
ONE LEFT.
RRR ...

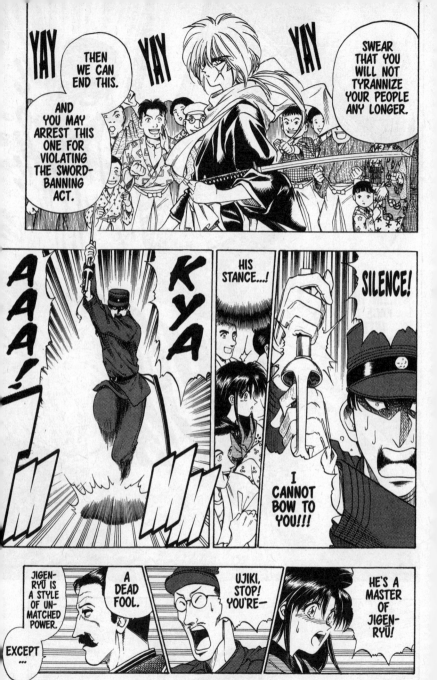

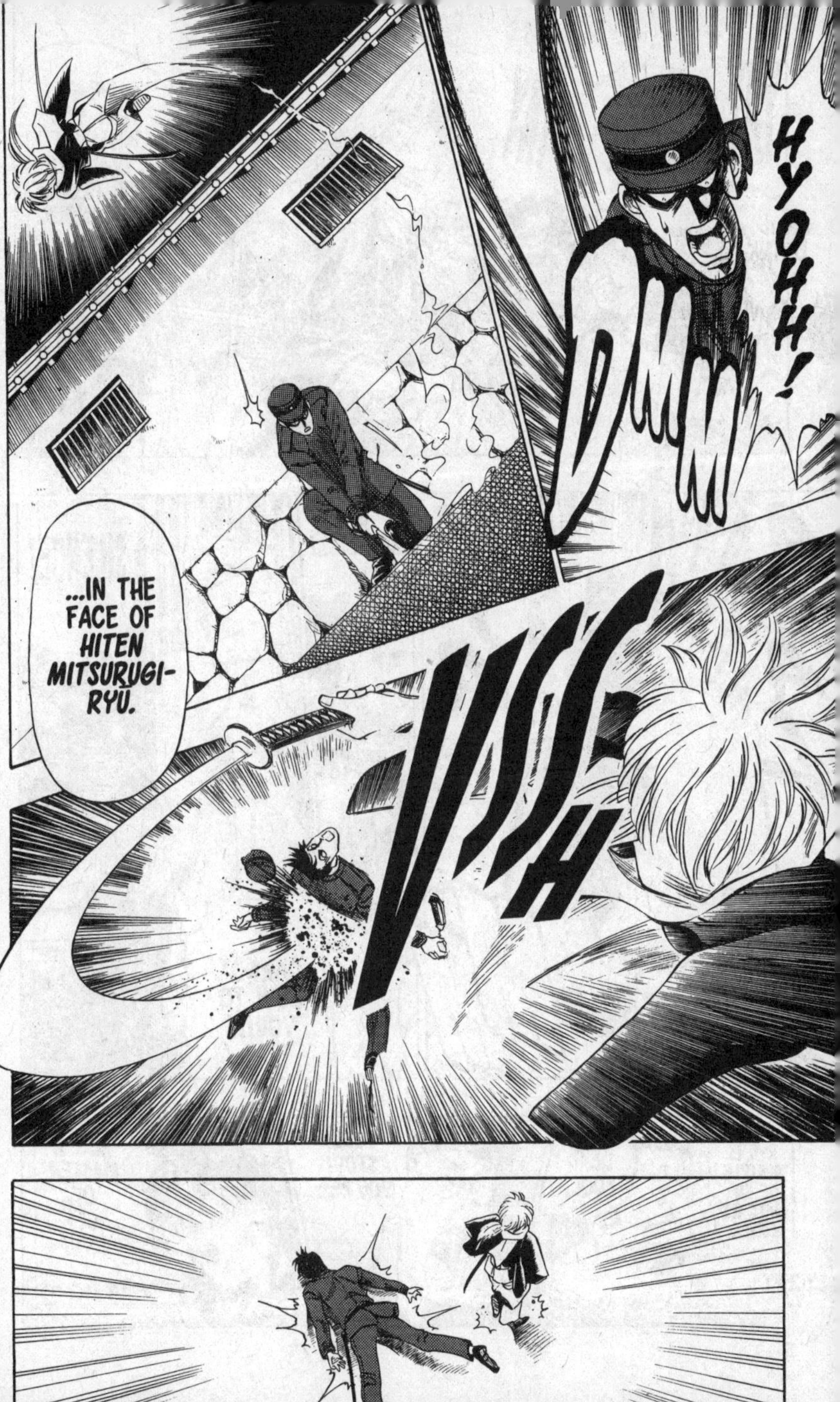
HYOHH!
DMM
...IN THE FACE OF HITEN MITSURUGI-RYŪ.
VASH

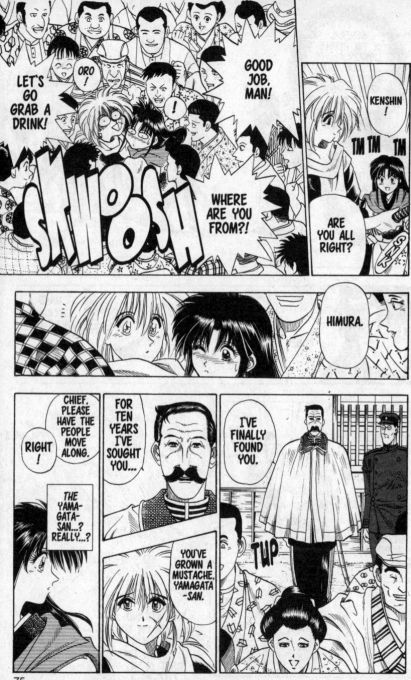

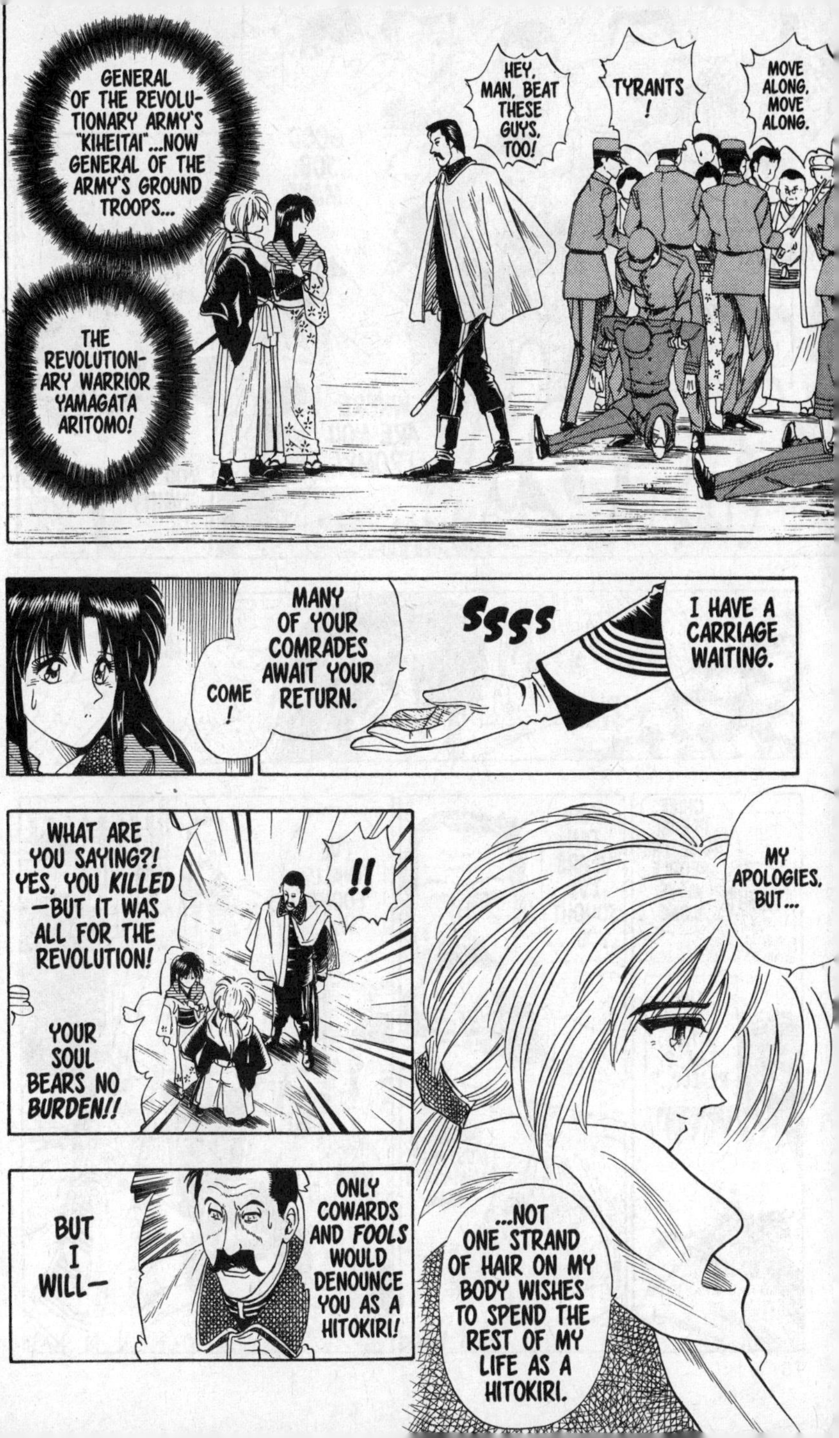
MOVE ALONG, MOVE ALONG.
TYRANTS!
HEY, MAN, BEAT THESE GUYS, TOO!
GENERAL OF THE REVOLUTIONARY ARMY'S "KIHEITAI"...NOW GENERAL OF THE ARMY'S GROUND TROOPS...
THE REVOLUTIONARY WARRIOR YAMAGATA ARITOMO!
I HAVE A CARRIAGE WAITING.
SSSS
MANY OF YOUR COMRADES AWAIT YOUR RETURN.
COME!
MY APOLOGIES, BUT...
...NOT ONE STRAND OF HAIR ON MY BODY WISHES TO SPEND THE REST OF MY LIFE AS A HITOKIRI.
!!
WHAT ARE YOU SAYING?! YES, YOU *KILLED* —BUT IT WAS ALL FOR THE REVOLUTION!
YOUR SOUL BEARS NO *BURDEN!!*
ONLY COWARDS AND *FOOLS* WOULD DENOUNCE YOU AS A HITOKIRI!
BUT I WILL—

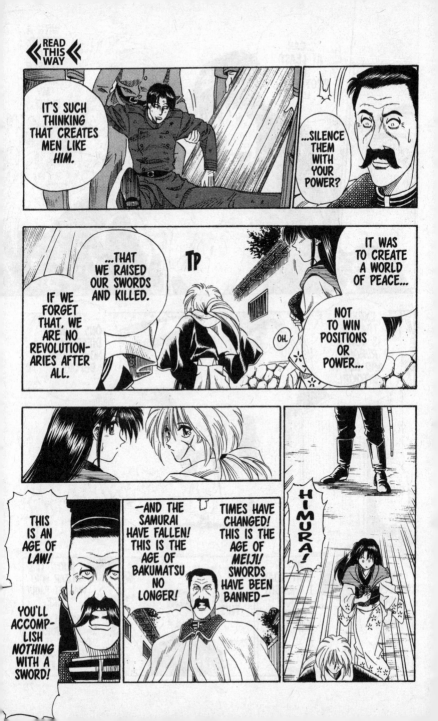

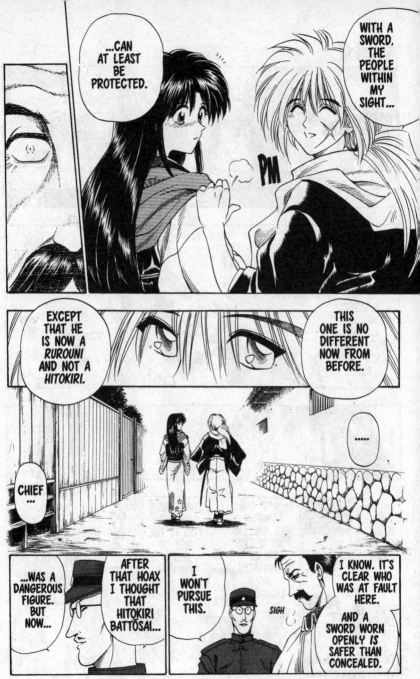

...CAN AT LEAST BE PROTECTED.

WITH A SWORD, THE PEOPLE WITHIN MY SIGHT...

PM

EXCEPT THAT HE IS NOW A *RUROUNI* AND NOT A *HITOKIRI*.

THIS ONE IS NO DIFFERENT NOW FROM BEFORE.

CHIEF...

.....

...WAS A DANGEROUS FIGURE. BUT NOW...

AFTER THAT HOAX I THOUGHT THAT HITOKIRI BATTŌSAI...

I WON'T PURSUE THIS.

SIGH

I KNOW. IT'S CLEAR WHO WAS AT FAULT HERE.

AND A SWORD WORN OPENLY *IS* SAFER THAN CONCEALED.

78

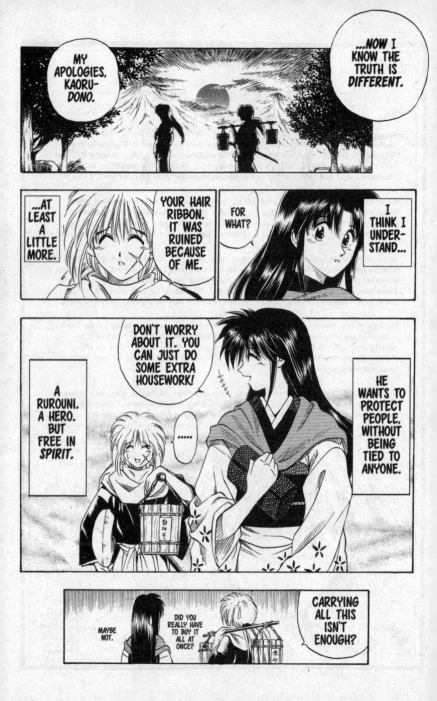

The Secret Life of Characters (2)

—Kamiya Kaoru—

No specific model here. If pressed, I'd probably have to say the character Chiba Sanako from the novel *Ryōma no Koibito*—the self-proclaimed "Ryōma's Girl." There's also that "commanding" quality which I tried to incorporate of Sasaki Mifuyu in *Kenkyaku Shōbai* by novelist Ikenami Shōtarō...but Kaoru wound up a plain, regular girl regardless. (Ah, well.)

As it turns out, though, "just plain Kaoru" seems to be working out for now, so I can't complain. Certainly many of my female readers seem to be relating to her. Some of them write that they can't tell if she's "strong" or "weak" as a fighter, but the truth is that she *is* strong.

Kaoru is quite independent for her age and can hold her own against the kendō masters of the many dojos in town. That makes her at very least a national-level champion. If Kaoru does appear weak, it's only because Kenshin and Sanosuke are so powerful. Whether or not she'll become Kenshin's love interest in the future, even I haven't quite yet decided.

Design-wise, there's no real motif here, either. You could say her look was inevitable. For a girl involved in kendō, after all, a ponytail is *de rigueur.* (Heh.) A blade, a kimono, a ponytail...what's not to like, right? Drawing her is enjoyable enough, although filling in her hair is sometimes a pain.

In that I am a "men, glorious and women, cute" kind of guy, it's true that ideally I'd like Kaoru to be drawn a bit more cutely. "Down-to-earth" and "poor" are also parts of her character though, and I can't overlook that. I do wish I could improve the pattern of her kimono and let her be at least a little more fashionable.

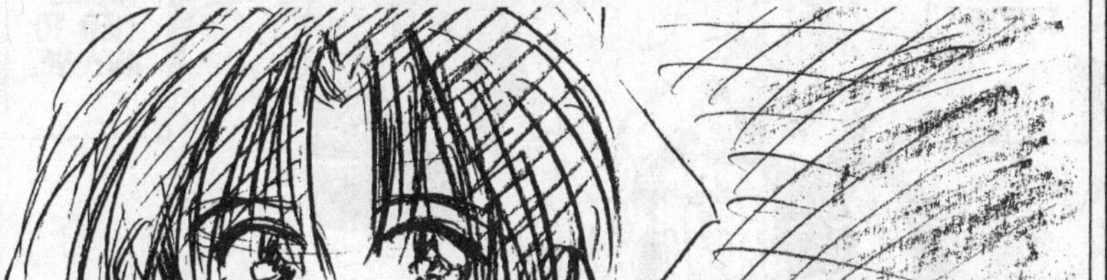

伸宏
和月

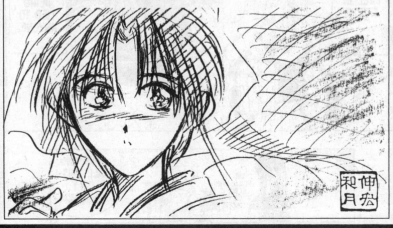

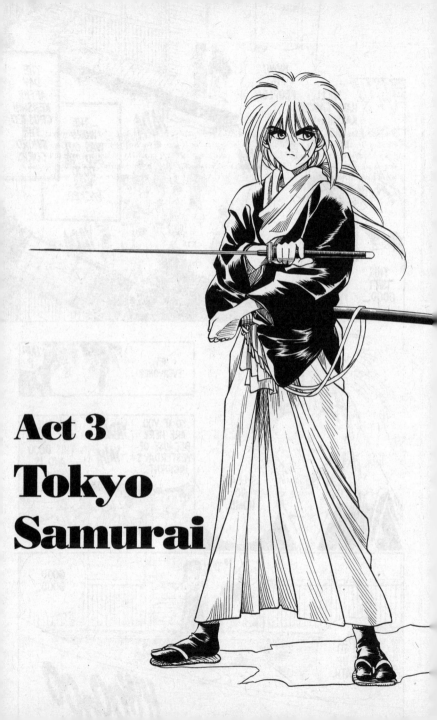

Act 3
Tokyo
Samurai

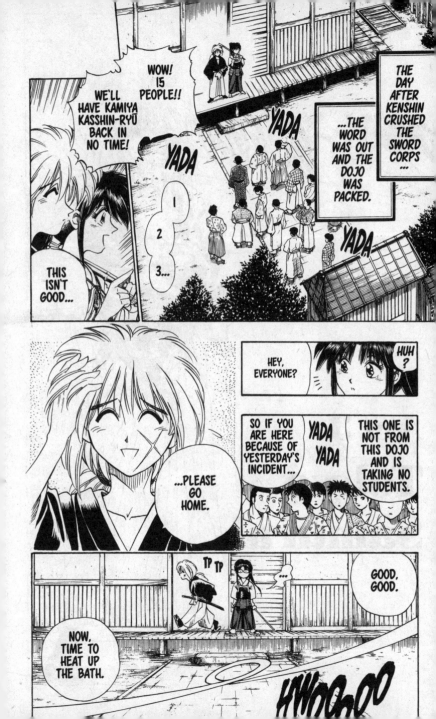

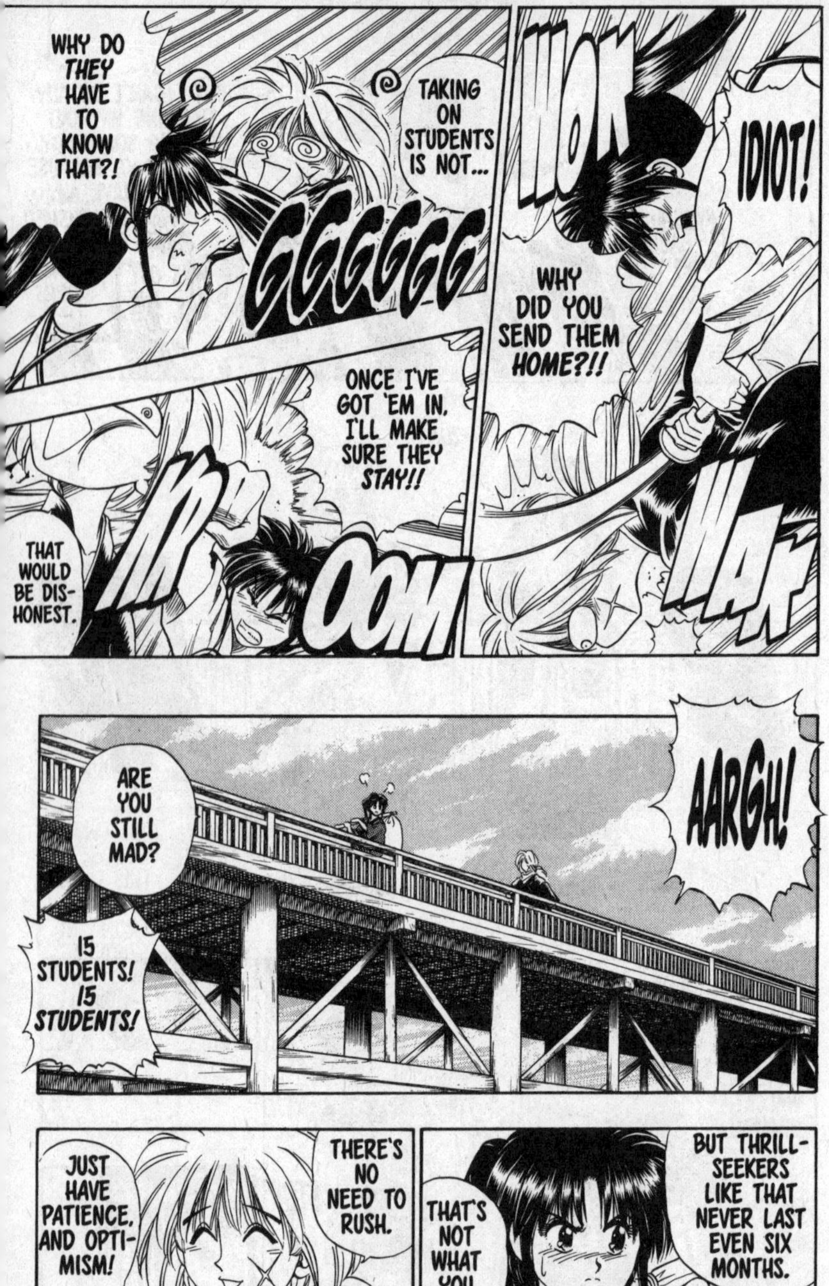
WHOK
IDIOT!
WHY DID YOU SEND THEM HOME?!!
WHAK
TAKING ON STUDENTS IS NOT...
WHY DO THEY HAVE TO KNOW THAT?!
GGGGGG
ONCE I'VE GOT 'EM IN, I'LL MAKE SURE THEY STAY!!
WHOOM
THAT WOULD BE DIS-HONEST.
AARGH!
ARE YOU STILL MAD?
15 STUDENTS! 15 STUDENTS!
BUT THRILL-SEEKERS LIKE THAT NEVER LAST EVEN SIX MONTHS.
...
RRR
THAT'S NOT WHAT YOU WANT.
THERE'S NO NEED TO RUSH.
JUST HAVE PATIENCE, AND OPTI-MISM!

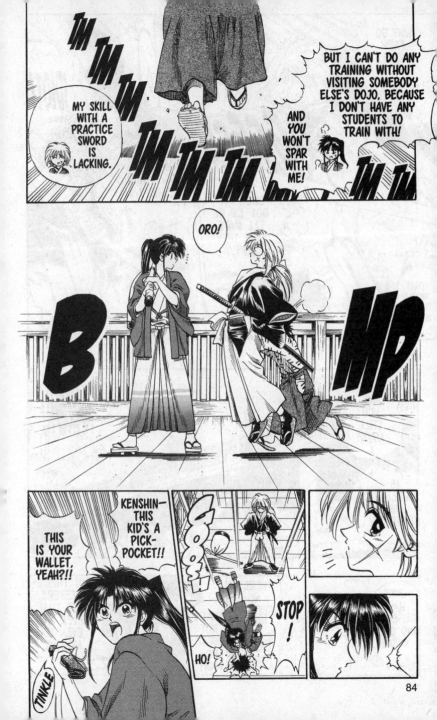

MY SKILL WITH A PRACTICE SWORD IS LACKING.

TM TM TM TM TM TM TM TM TM

AND YOU WON'T SPAR WITH ME!

BUT I CAN'T DO ANY TRAINING WITHOUT VISITING SOMEBODY ELSE'S DOJO, BECAUSE I DON'T HAVE ANY STUDENTS TO TRAIN WITH!

ORO!

B MP

THIS IS YOUR WALLET, YEAH?!!

KENSHIN— THIS KID'S A PICK- POCKET!!

OOO!

HO!

STOP !

TINKLE

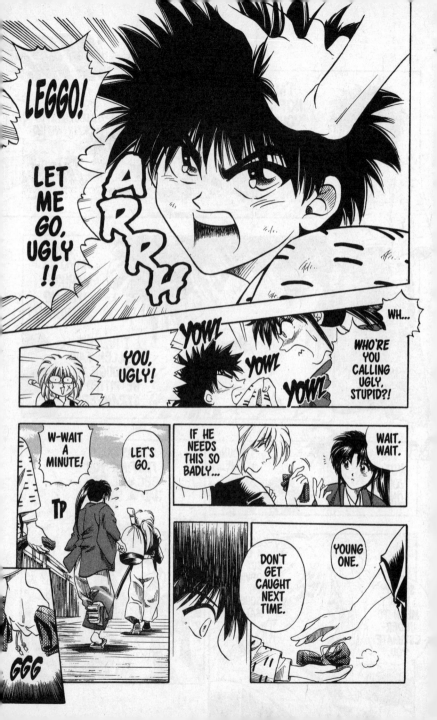

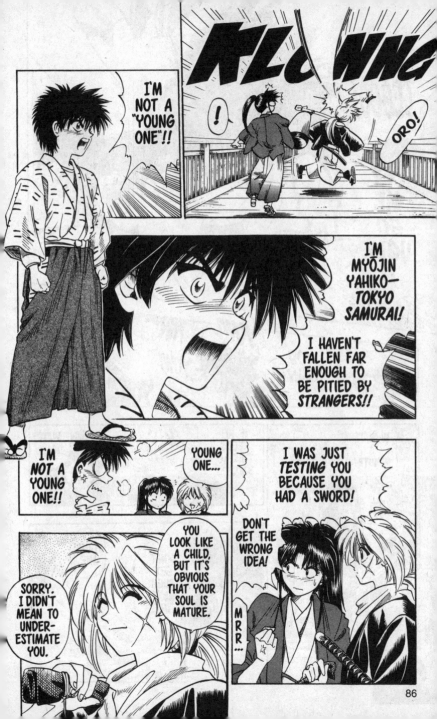

86

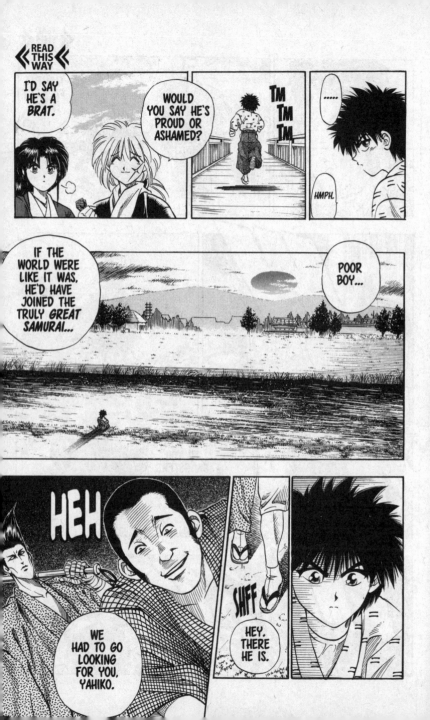

READ THIS WAY

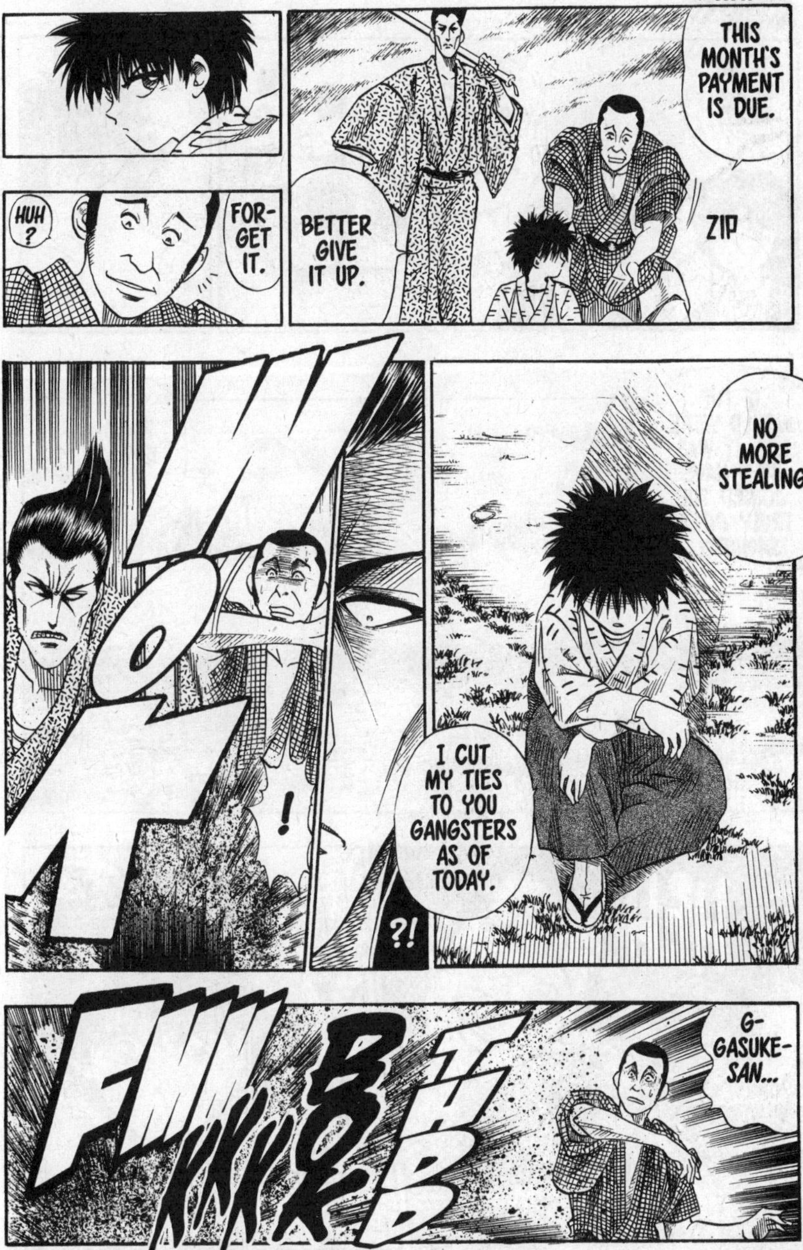

THIS MONTH'S PAYMENT IS DUE.
ZIP
BETTER GIVE IT UP.
FOR-GET IT.
HUH?
NO MORE STEALING.
I CUT MY TIES TO YOU GANGSTERS AS OF TODAY.
!
?!
G-GASUKE-SAN...

READ THIS WAY

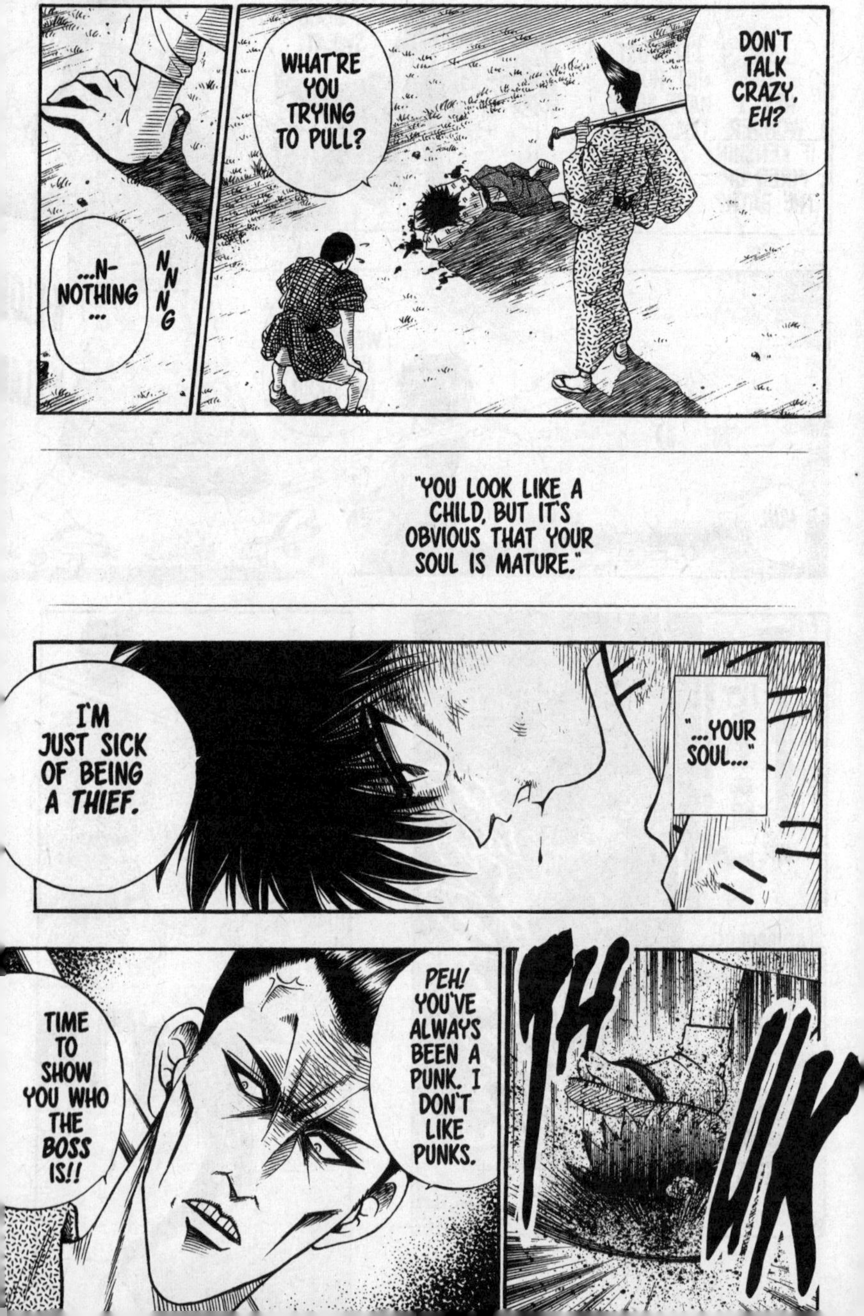
DON'T TALK CRAZY, EH?
WHAT'RE YOU TRYING TO PULL?
NNNG
...N-NOTHING...
"YOU LOOK LIKE A CHILD, BUT IT'S OBVIOUS THAT YOUR SOUL IS MATURE."
"...YOUR SOUL..."
I'M JUST SICK OF BEING A *THIEF*.
THUK
PEH! YOU'VE ALWAYS BEEN A PUNK. I DON'T LIKE PUNKS.
TIME TO SHOW YOU WHO THE BOSS IS!!

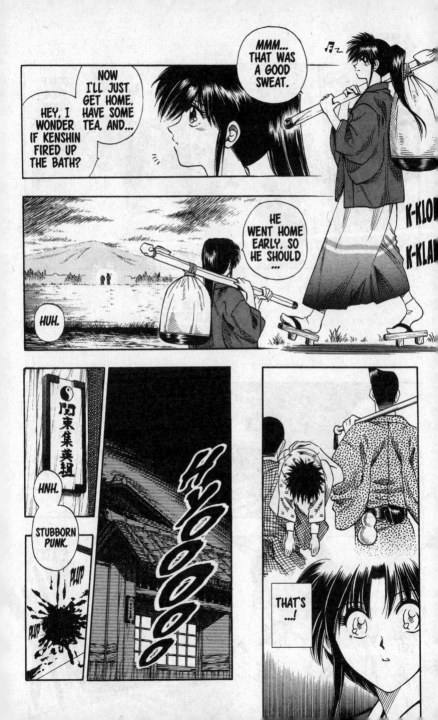

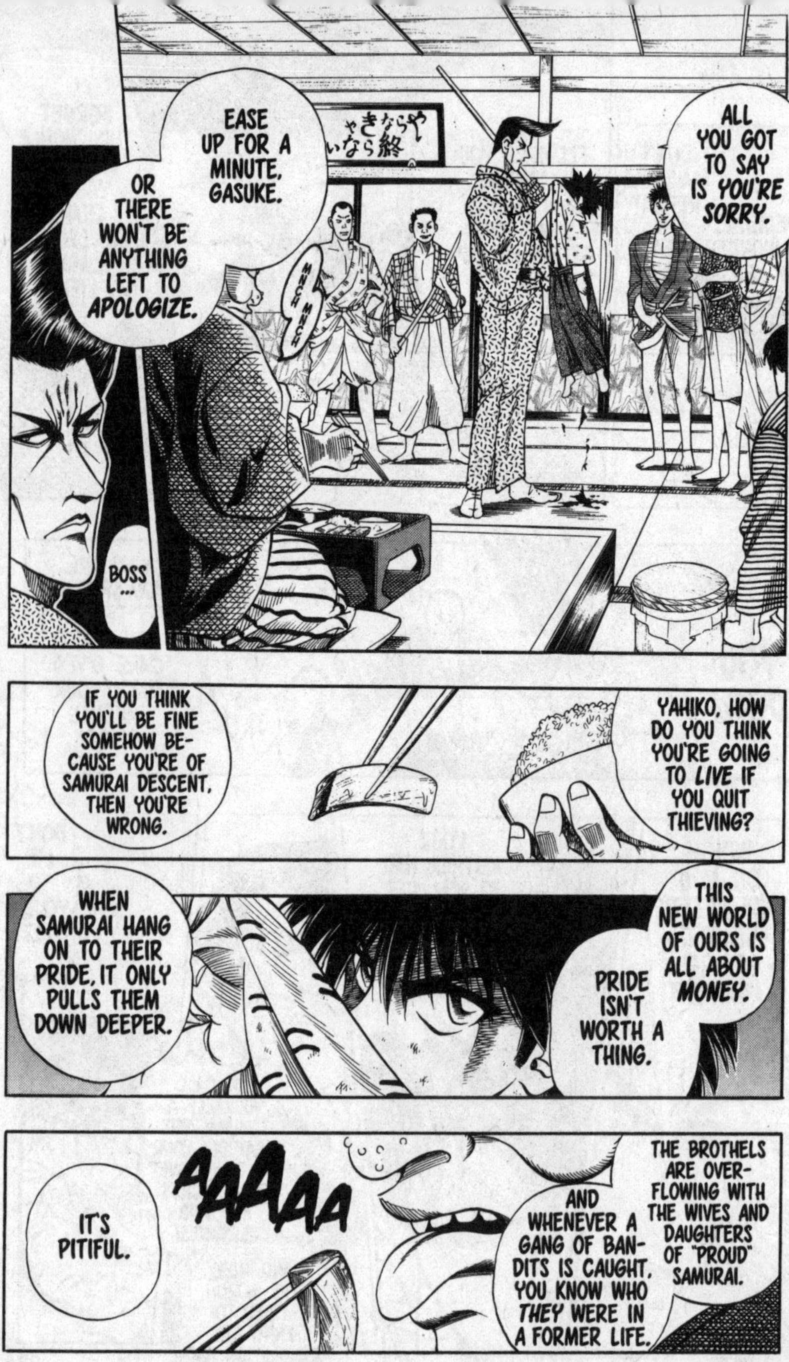
ALL YOU GOT TO SAY IS YOU'RE SORRY.
EASE UP FOR A MINUTE, GASUKE.
OR THERE WON'T BE ANYTHING LEFT TO APOLOGIZE.
MNCH MNCH
BOSS...
YAHIKO, HOW DO YOU THINK YOU'RE GOING TO LIVE IF YOU QUIT THIEVING?
IF YOU THINK YOU'LL BE FINE SOMEHOW BE-CAUSE YOU'RE OF SAMURAI DESCENT, THEN YOU'RE WRONG.
THIS NEW WORLD OF OURS IS ALL ABOUT MONEY.
PRIDE ISN'T WORTH A THING.
WHEN SAMURAI HANG ON TO THEIR PRIDE, IT ONLY PULLS THEM DOWN DEEPER.
THE BROTHELS ARE OVER-FLOWING WITH THE WIVES AND DAUGHTERS OF "PROUD" SAMURAI.
AND WHENEVER A GANG OF BAN-DITS IS CAUGHT, YOU KNOW WHO THEY WERE IN A FORMER LIFE.
AAAAA
IT'S PITIFUL.

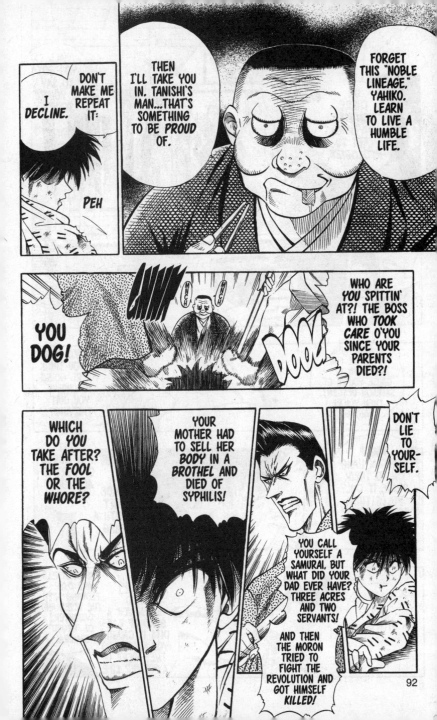

92

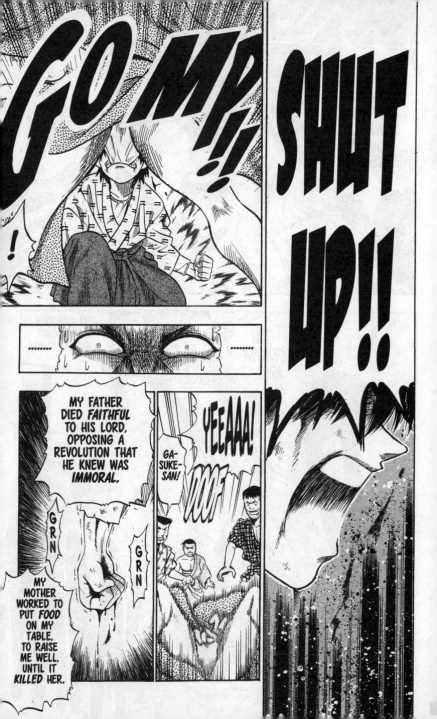

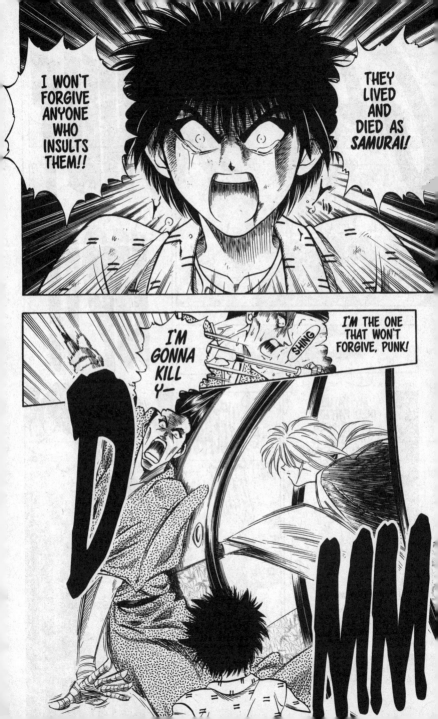

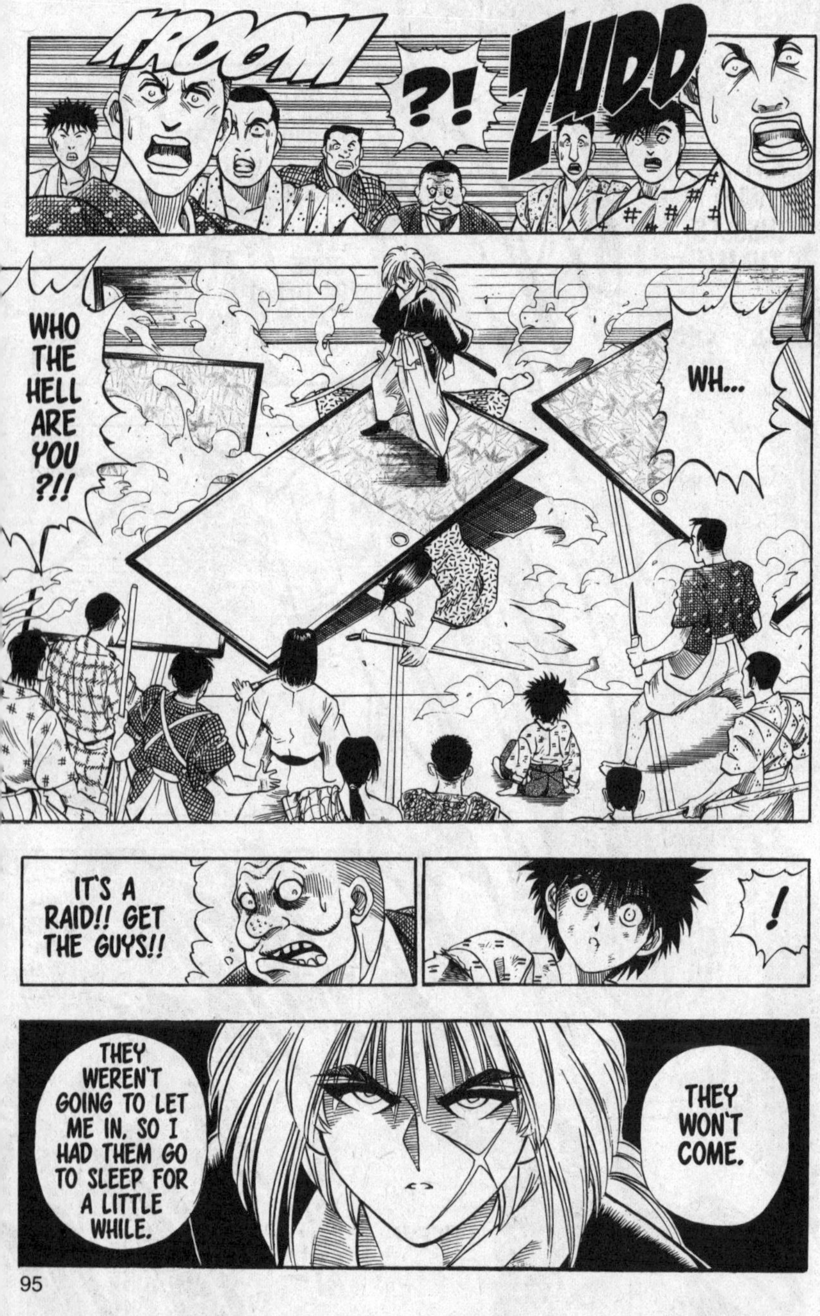

ZUDD
?!
KROOM
WH...
WHO THE HELL ARE YOU?!!
!
IT'S A RAID!! GET THE GUYS!!
THEY WON'T COME.
THEY WEREN'T GOING TO LET ME IN, SO I HAD THEM GO TO SLEEP FOR A LITTLE WHILE.

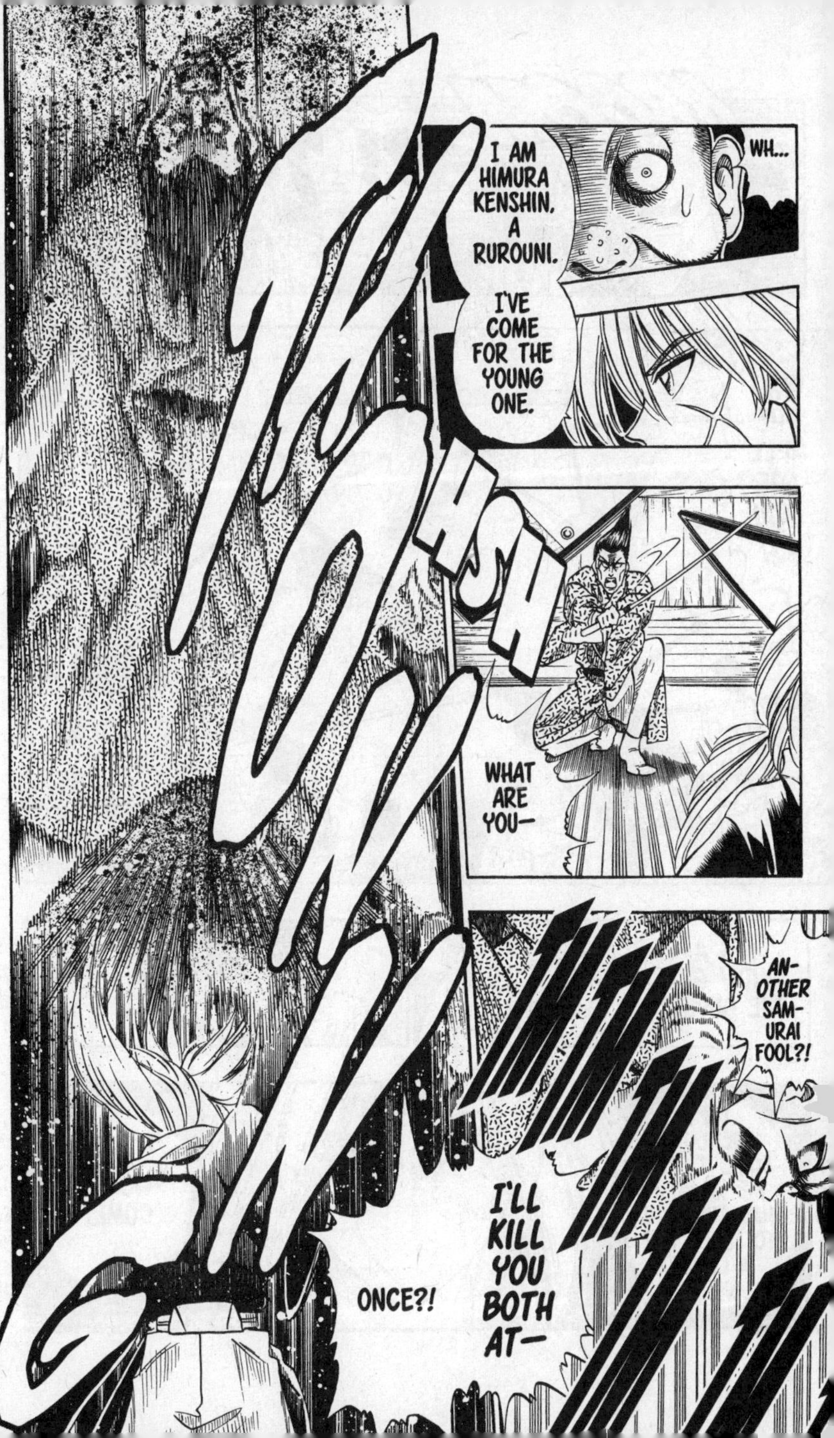
WH...
I AM HIMURA KENSHIN, A RUROUNI.
I'VE COME FOR THE YOUNG ONE.
WHAT ARE YOU—
ANOTHER SAMURAI FOOL?!
I'LL KILL YOU BOTH AT—
ONCE?!

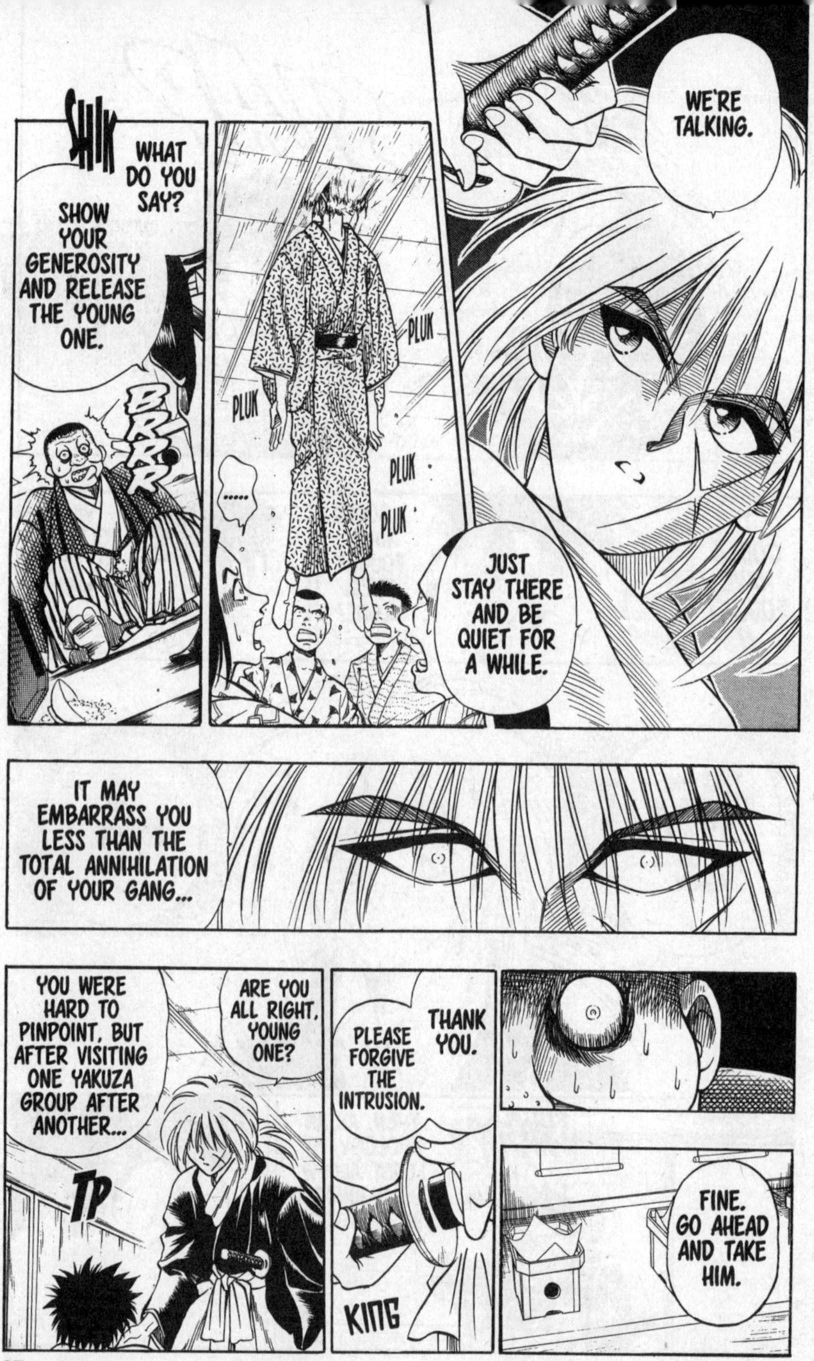
WE'RE TALKING.
JUST STAY THERE AND BE QUIET FOR A WHILE.
PLUK
PLUK
PLUK
PLUK
.....
SHIK
WHAT DO YOU SAY?
SHOW YOUR GENEROSITY AND RELEASE THE YOUNG ONE.
BRRR
IT MAY EMBARRASS YOU LESS THAN THE TOTAL ANNIHILATION OF YOUR GANG...
FINE. GO AHEAD AND TAKE HIM.
THANK YOU.
PLEASE FORGIVE THE INTRUSION.
KING
ARE YOU ALL RIGHT, YOUNG ONE?
YOU WERE HARD TO PINPOINT, BUT AFTER VISITING ONE YAKUZA GROUP AFTER ANOTHER...
TP

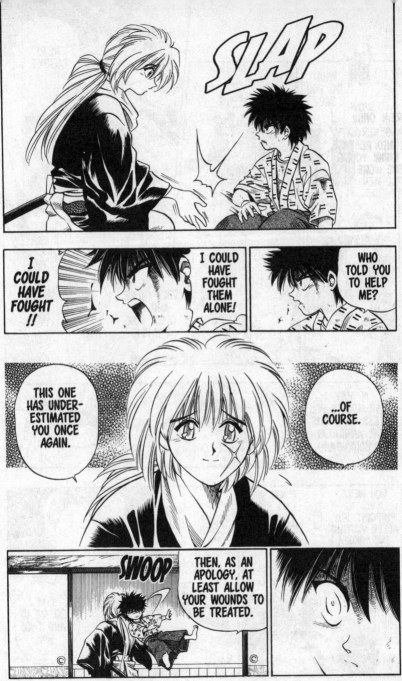

98

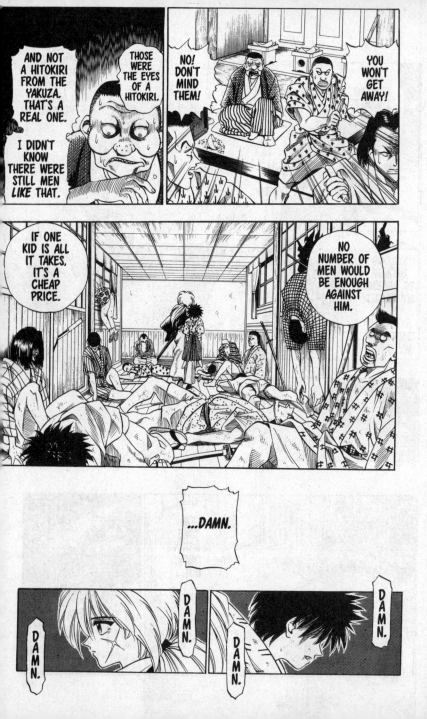

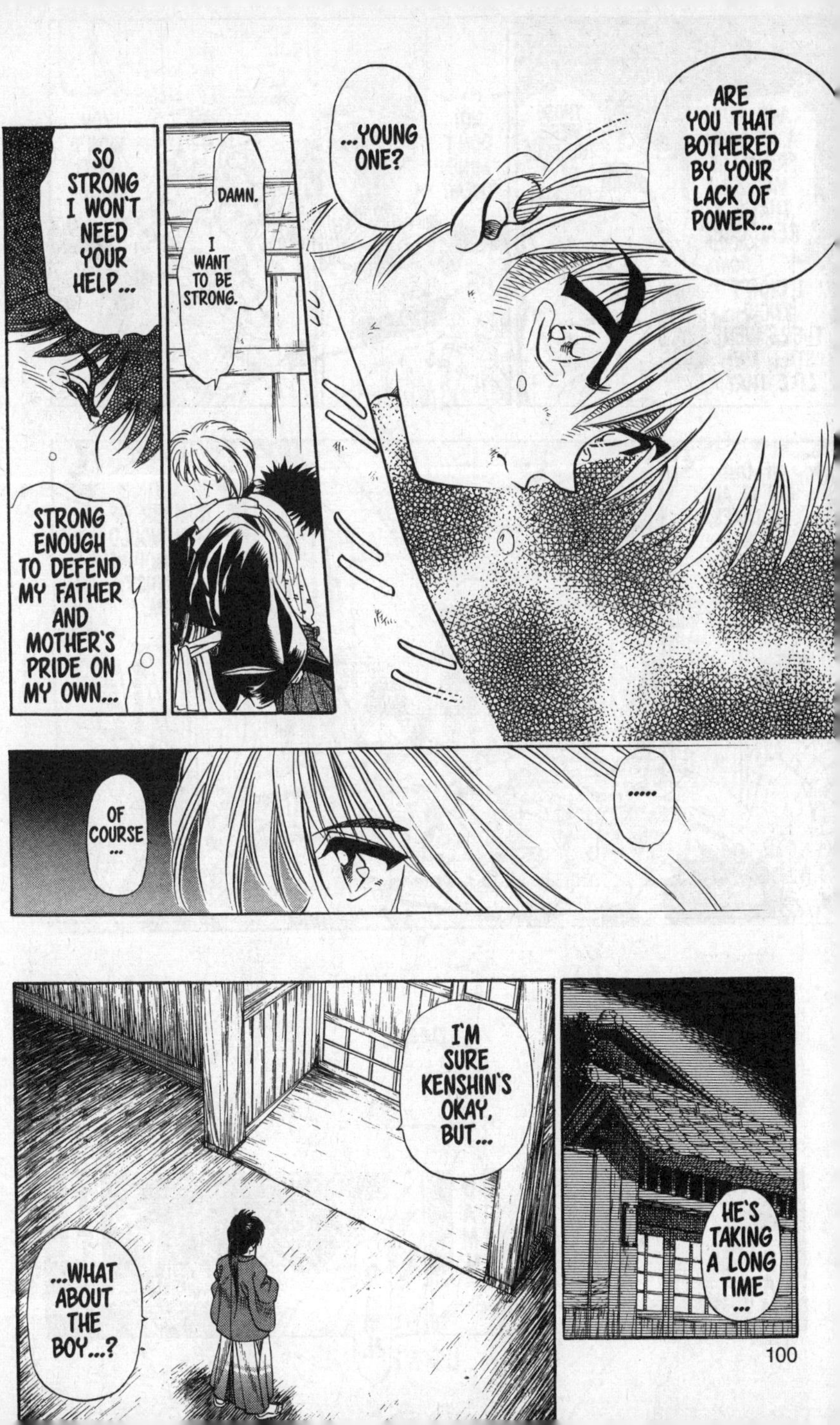
ARE YOU THAT BOTHERED BY YOUR LACK OF POWER...
...YOUNG ONE?
DAMN.
I WANT TO BE STRONG.
SO STRONG I WON'T NEED YOUR HELP...
STRONG ENOUGH TO DEFEND MY FATHER AND MOTHER'S PRIDE ON MY OWN...
......
OF COURSE ...
HE'S TAKING A LONG TIME ...
I'M SURE KENSHIN'S OKAY, BUT...
...WHAT ABOUT THE BOY...?

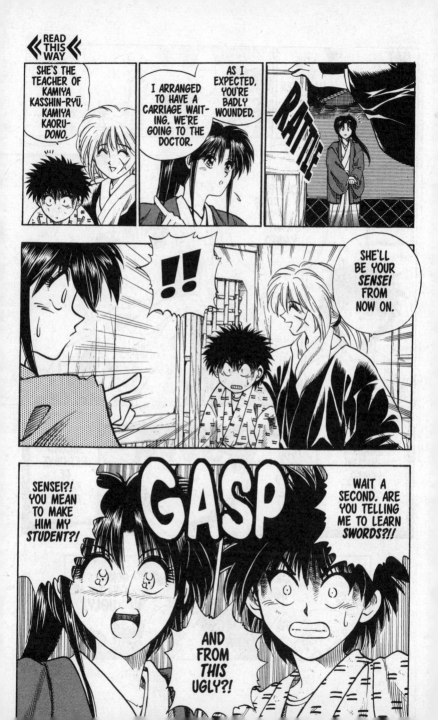

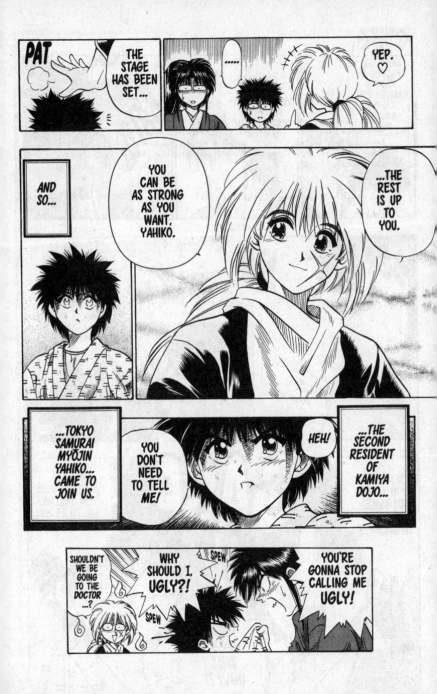

The Secret Life of Characters (3)

—Myōjin Yahiko—

More than any historical reality, the character of Yahiko grew out of feelings I had in middle school. I was in the kendo club—at first just because it was something to do—but then I got hooked on it as much as drawing manga, and soon I was swinging the *shinai* every day to the point of exhaustion.

The problem, though, was that I was weak. So weak, in fact, that I was an embarrassment to my 183 centimeters of height! In three years of middle school, I was a member of a starting squad only once, and then only because the kid who was *supposed* to be a starter got suspended for causing trouble, and I got bumped up by luck of the draw. Even then, still I was unable to score a win in a league tournament.

The disgrace I felt at kendo, the wanting to be stronger, the still being awful no matter how much I longed to be great, all of that has found an outlet in little Yahiko. Yahiko knows a pain that hero-types like Kenshin and Sanosuke can never know. Of late, he's turned more into a comedic character, but still my wish is to draw him in such a way that, five or ten years down the road, readers can envision him as a great swordsman.

As with Kaoru, there's no particular logic in Yahiko's design...that is, of course, unless you consider that having a defiant-eyed young man with mussed hair is itself a must in a comic for young men.

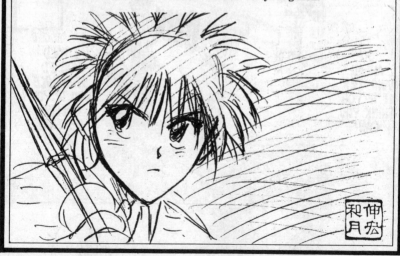

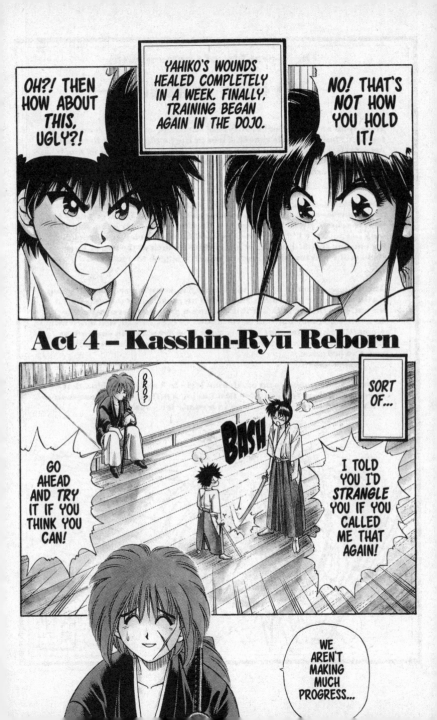

Act 4 – Kasshin-Ryū Reborn

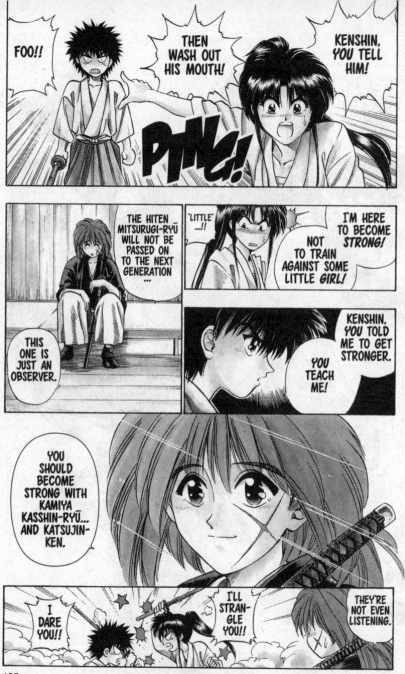

FOO!!

THEN WASH OUT HIS MOUTH!

KENSHIN, YOU TELL HIM!

PYNG!

THE HITEN MITSURUGI-RYŪ WILL NOT BE PASSED ON TO THE NEXT GENERATION...

THIS ONE IS JUST AN OBSERVER.

"LITTLE"...!!

I'M HERE TO BECOME STRONG! NOT TO TRAIN AGAINST SOME LITTLE GIRL!

KENSHIN, YOU TOLD ME TO GET STRONGER.

YOU TEACH ME!

YOU SHOULD BECOME STRONG WITH KAMIYA KASSHIN-RYŪ... AND KATSUJIN-KEN.

I DARE YOU!!

I'LL STRANGLE YOU!!

THEY'RE NOT EVEN LISTENING.

105

Act 4
Kasshin-Ryū Reborn

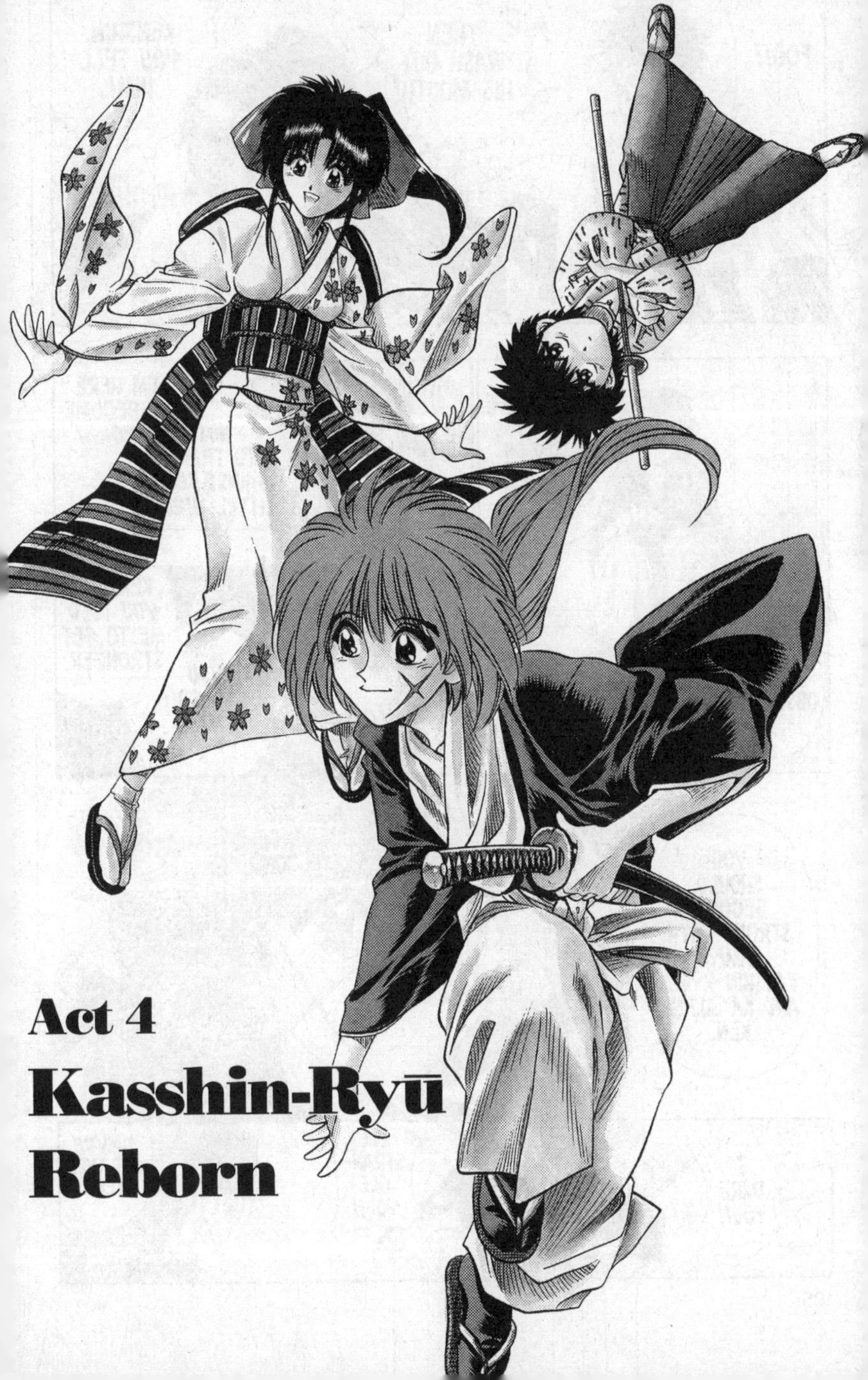

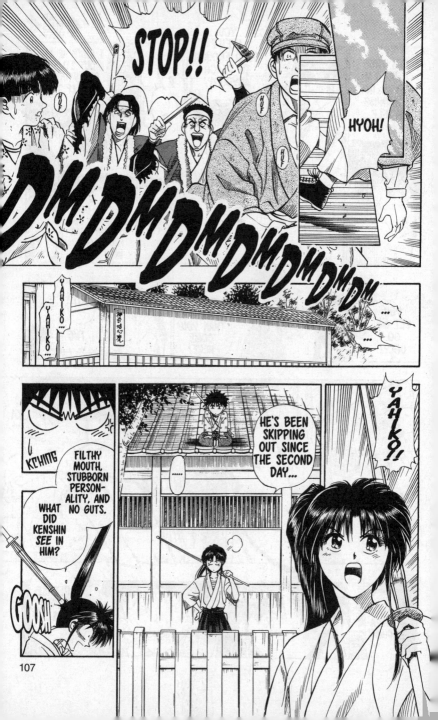

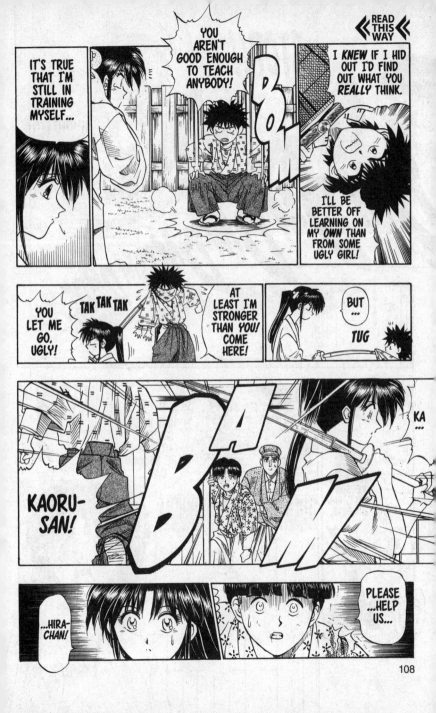

108

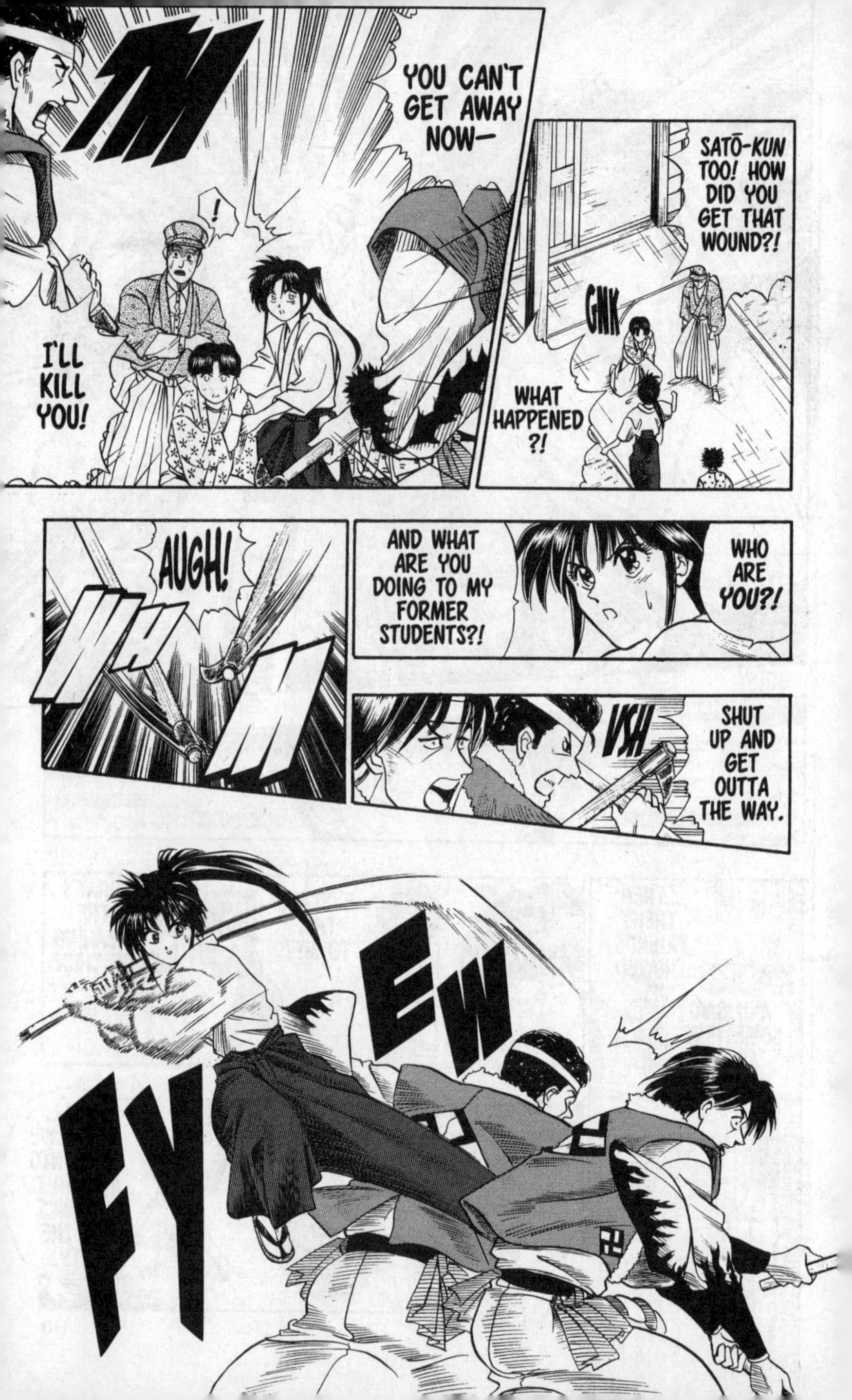
SATŌ-KUN TOO! HOW DID YOU GET THAT WOUND?!
GNK
WHAT HAPPENED ?!
YOU CAN'T GET AWAY NOW—
!
I'LL KILL YOU!
WHO ARE YOU?!
AND WHAT ARE YOU DOING TO MY FORMER STUDENTS?!
SHUT UP AND GET OUTTA THE WAY.
VSH
AUGH!

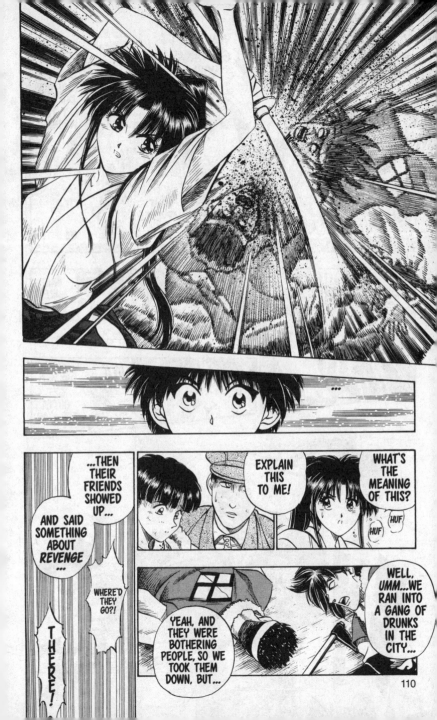

...THEN THEIR FRIENDS SHOWED UP...

AND SAID SOMETHING ABOUT REVENGE...

WHERE'D THEY GO?!

THERE!

EXPLAIN THIS TO ME!

WHAT'S THE MEANING OF THIS?

HUF

HUF

WELL, UMM...WE RAN INTO A GANG OF DRUNKS IN THE CITY...

YEAH, AND THEY WERE BOTHERING PEOPLE, SO WE TOOK THEM DOWN, BUT...

110

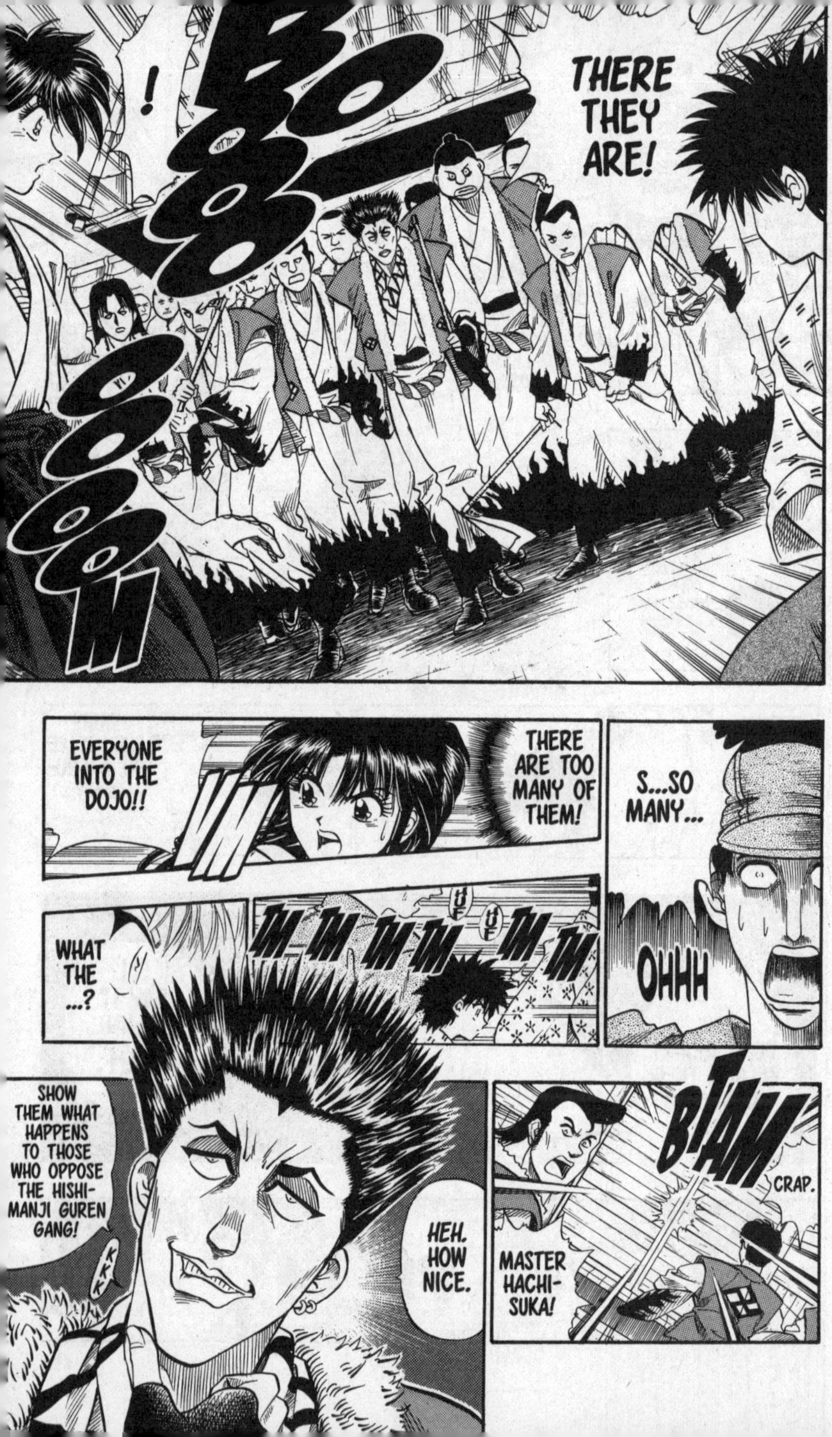
THERE THEY ARE!
BOOOOOOOOM
!
S...SO MANY...
OHHH
THERE ARE TOO MANY OF THEM!
EVERYONE INTO THE DOJO!!
HUF
HUF
WHAT THE ...?
BTAM
CRAP.
MASTER HACHI-SUKA!
HEH. HOW NICE.
SHOW THEM WHAT HAPPENS TO THOSE WHO OPPOSE THE HISHI-MANJI GUREN GANG!
KKK

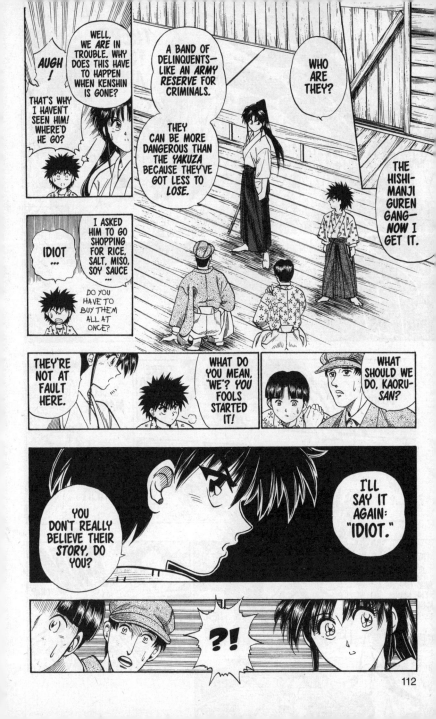

112

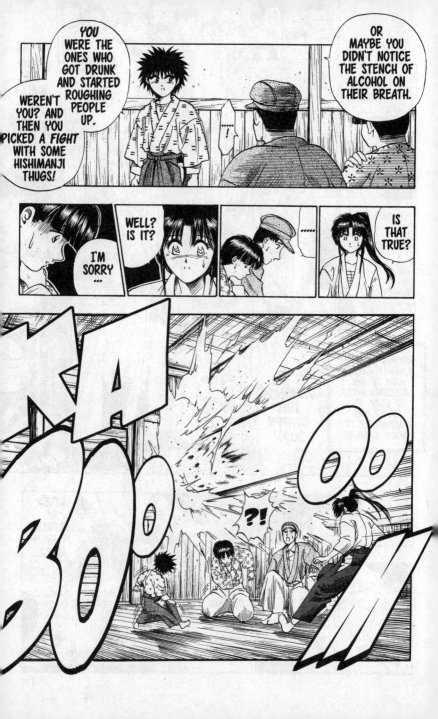

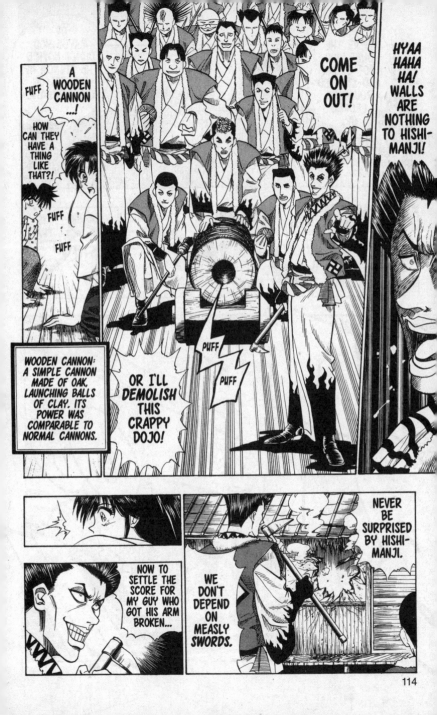

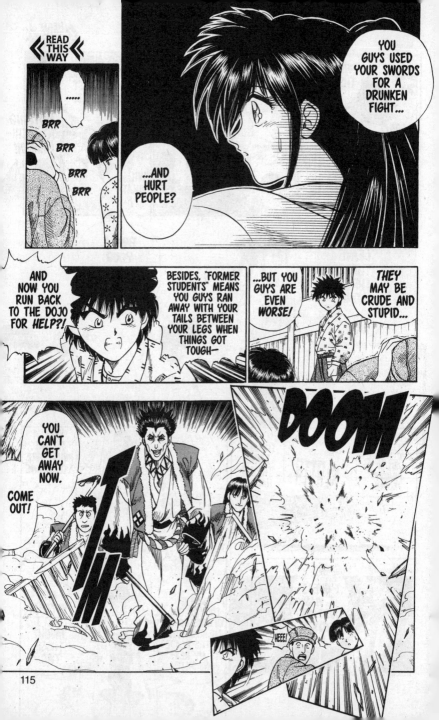

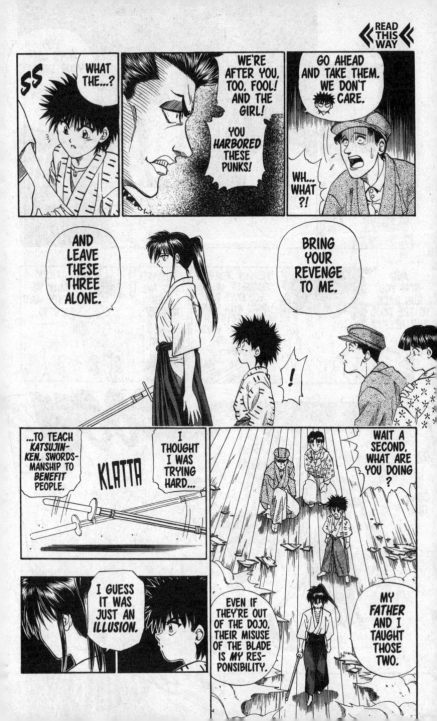

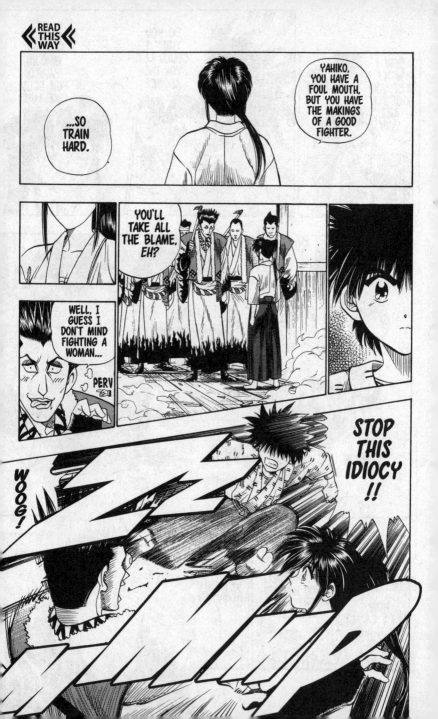

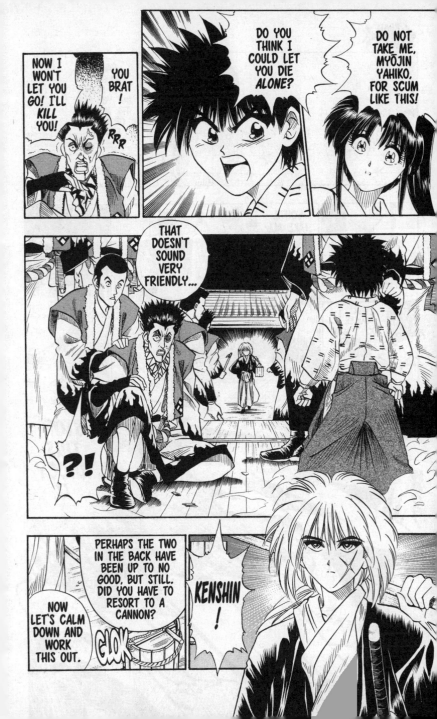

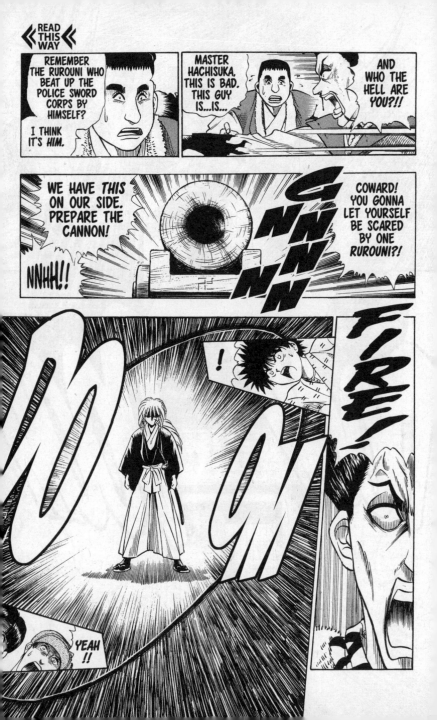

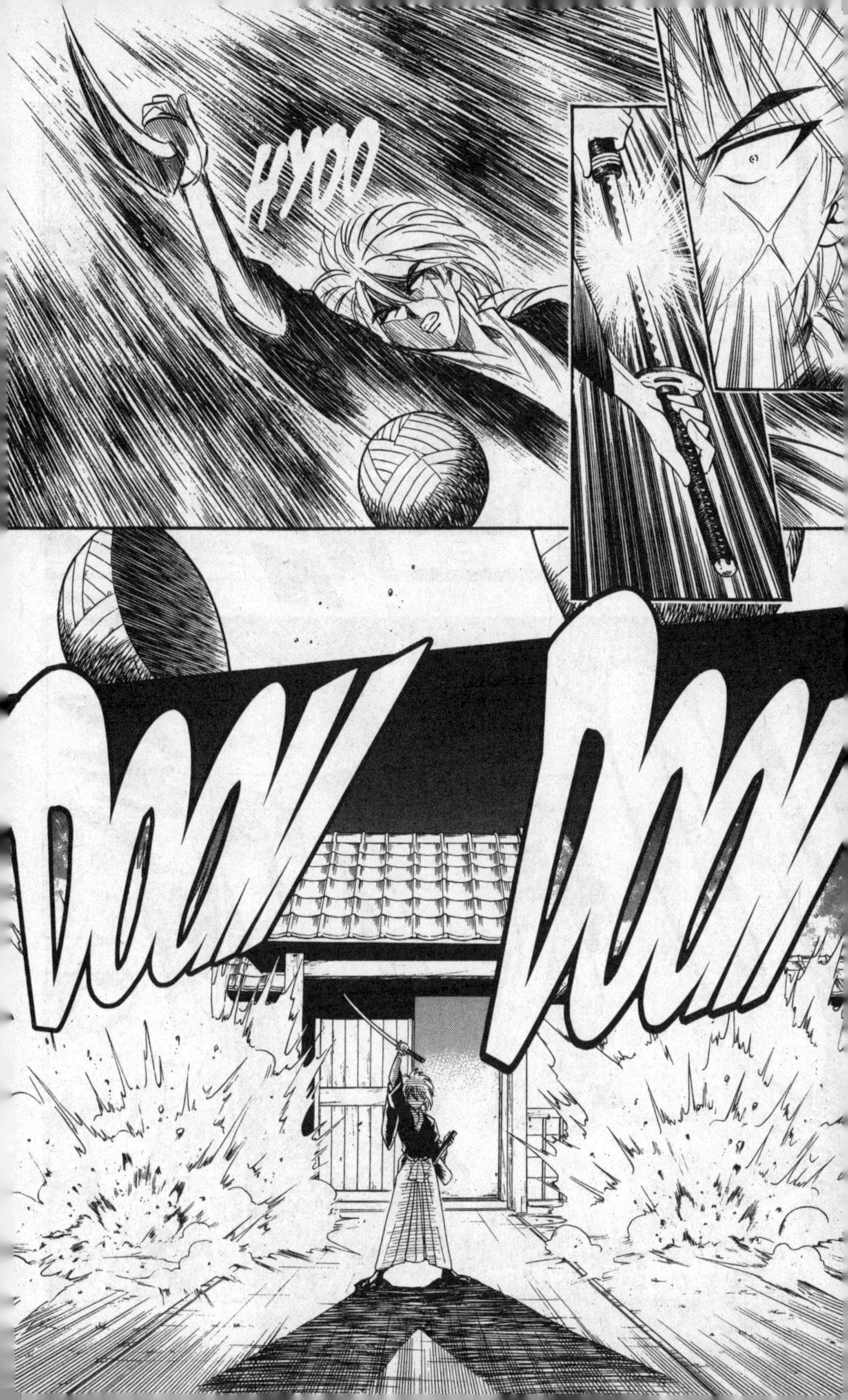
HYOO

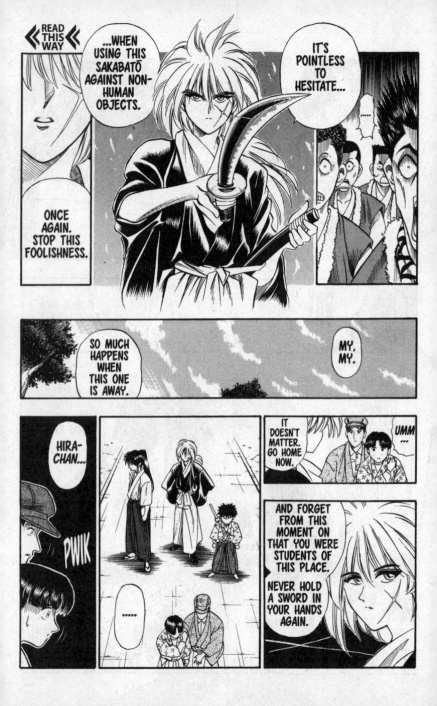

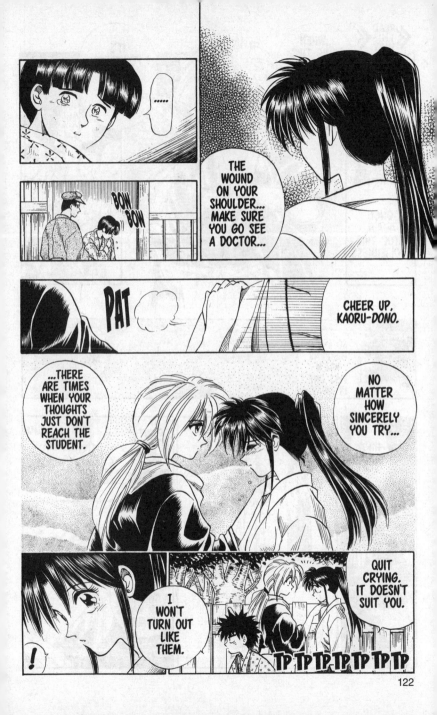

122

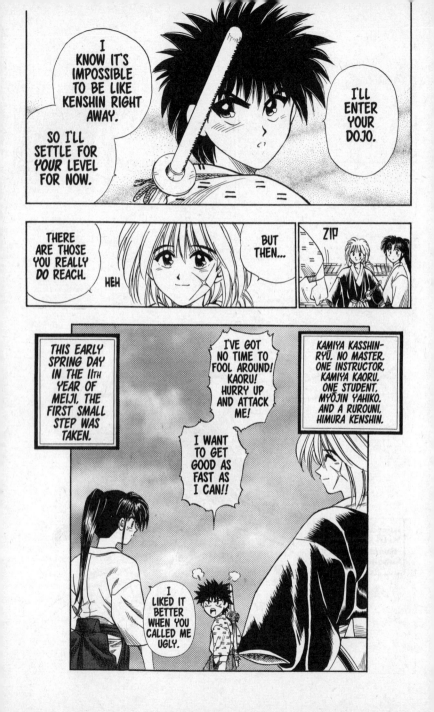

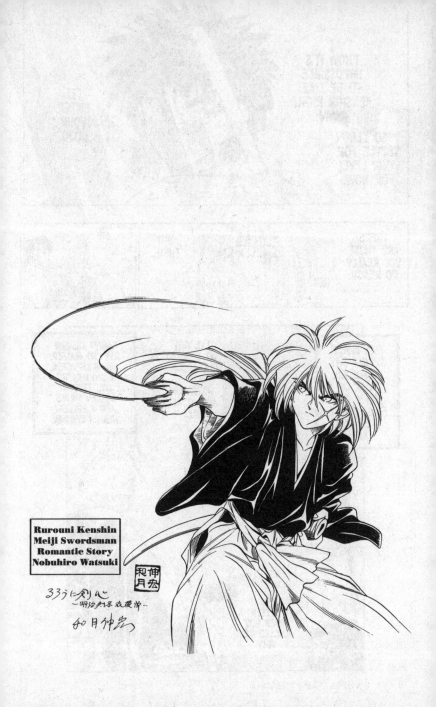

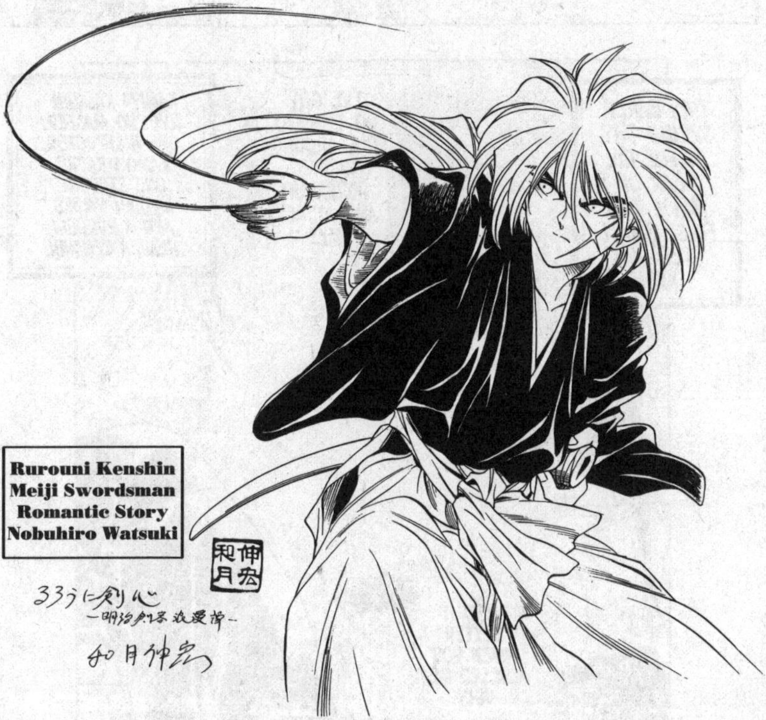
Rurouni Kenshin
Meiji Swordsman
Romantic Story
Nobuhiro Watsuki
伸宏 和月
るろうに剣心
ー明治剣客浪漫譚ー
和月伸宏

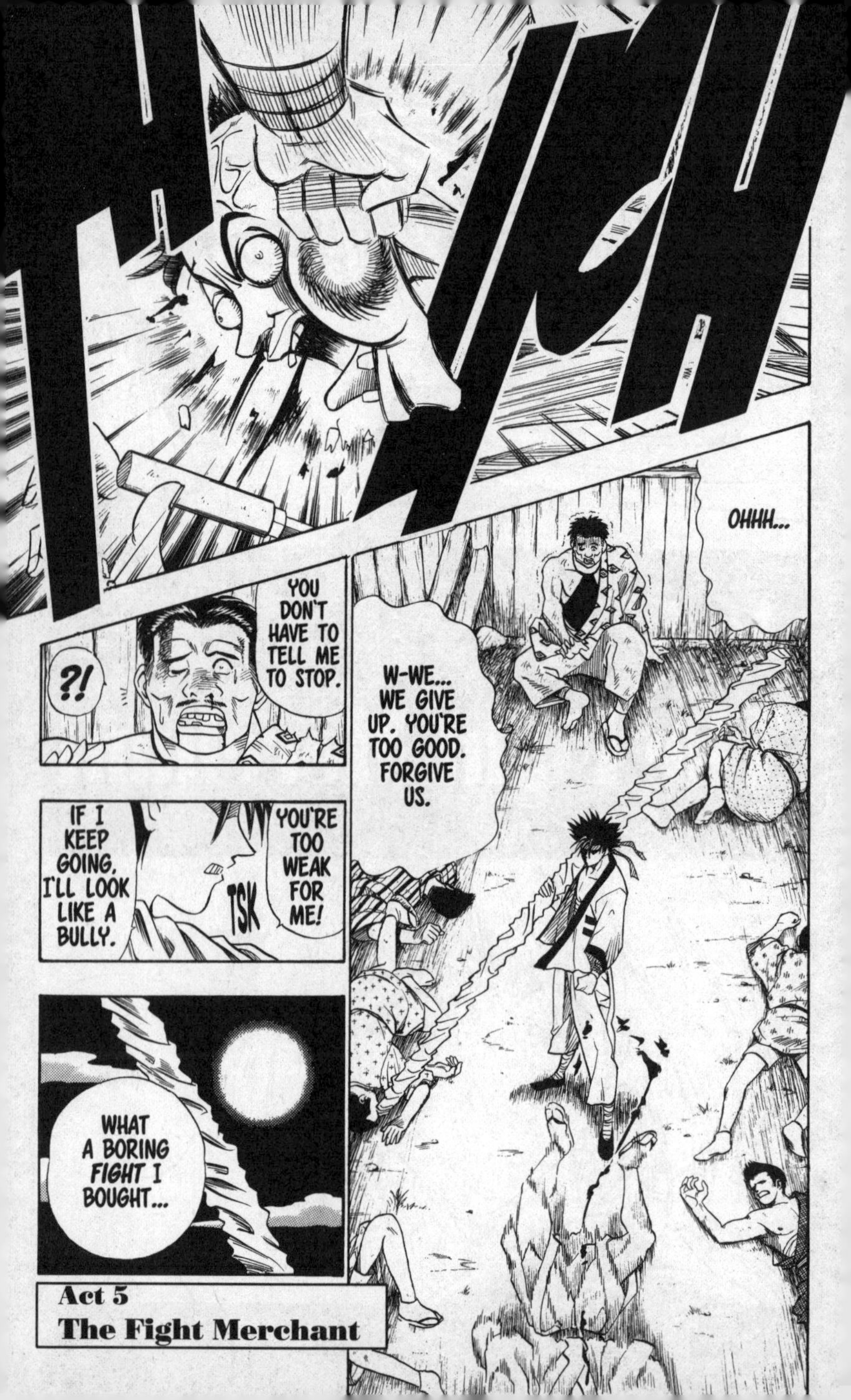
OHHH...
W-WE... WE GIVE UP. YOU'RE TOO GOOD. FORGIVE US.
YOU DON'T HAVE TO TELL ME TO STOP.
?!
YOU'RE TOO WEAK FOR ME!
TSK
IF I KEEP GOING, I'LL LOOK LIKE A BULLY.
WHAT A BORING FIGHT I BOUGHT...

Act 5
The Fight Merchant

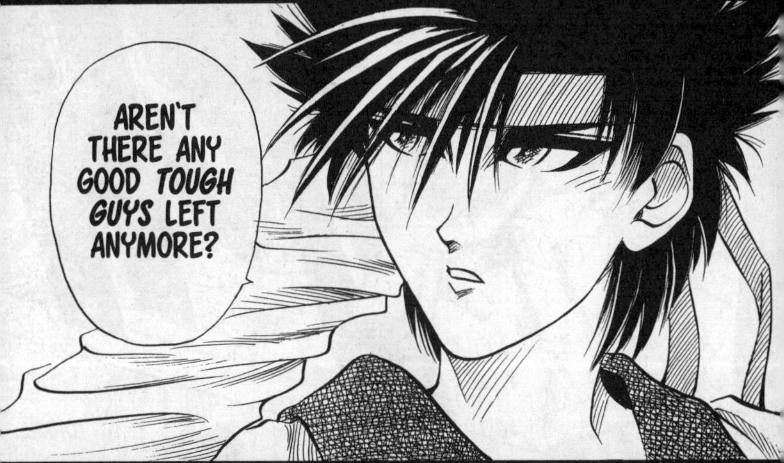
AREN'T THERE ANY GOOD TOUGH GUYS LEFT ANYMORE?

Act 5
The Fight Merchant

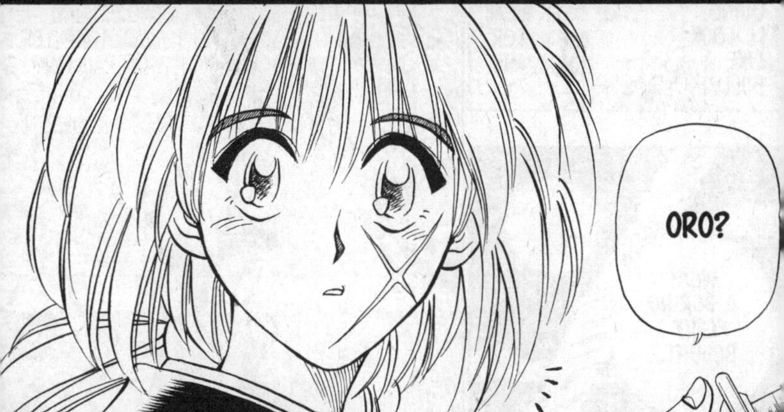
ORO?

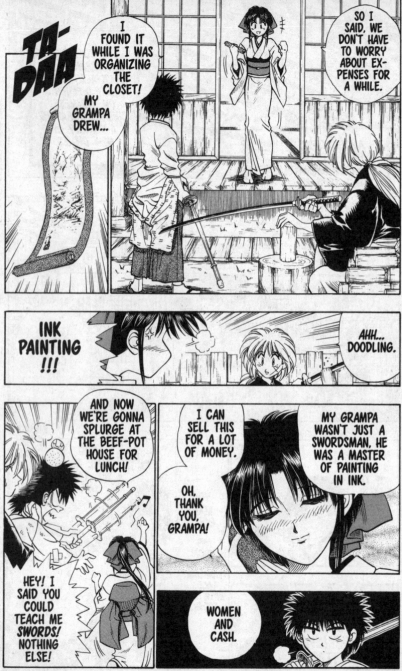

127

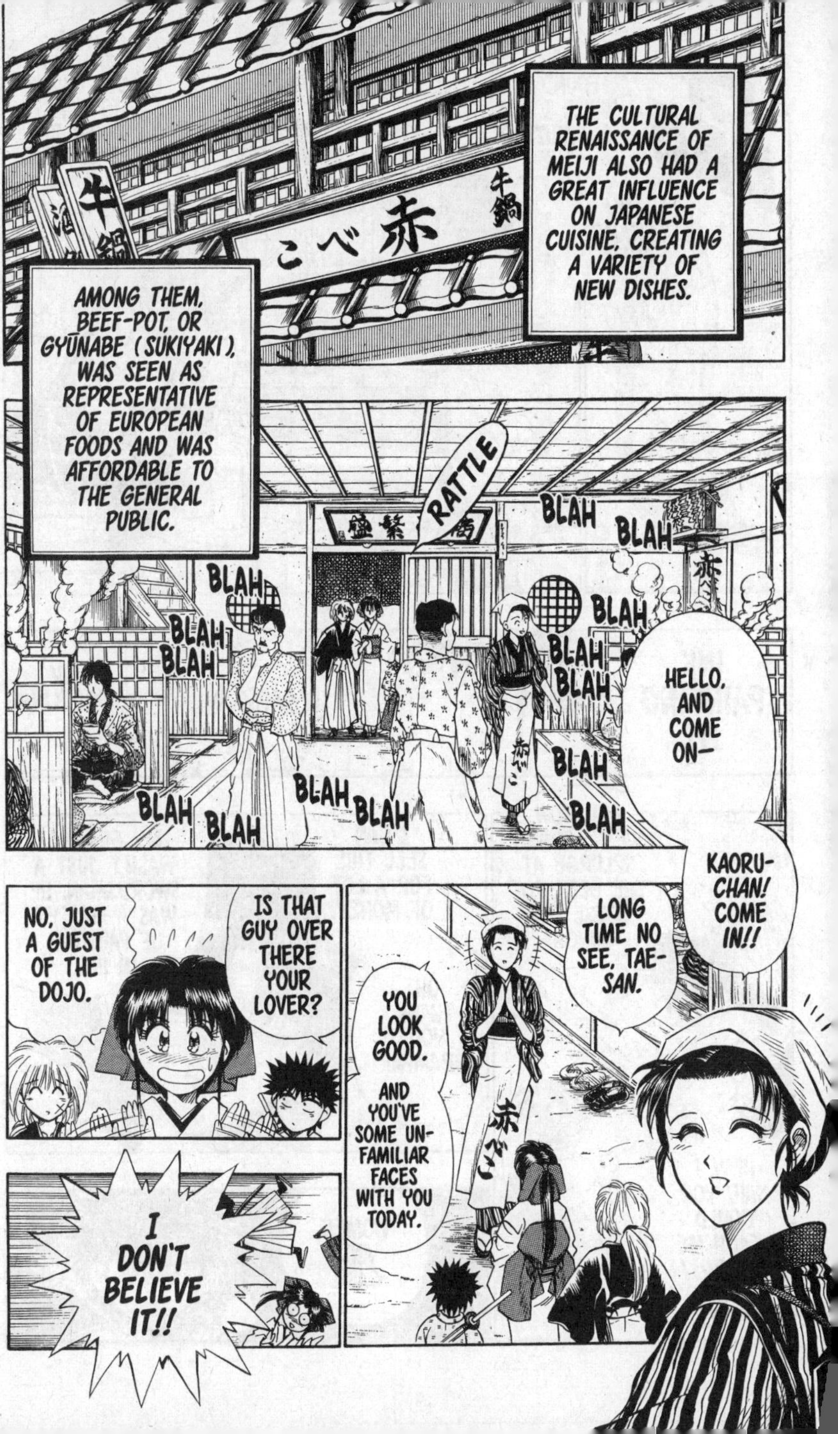

THE CULTURAL RENAISSANCE OF MEIJI ALSO HAD A GREAT INFLUENCE ON JAPANESE CUISINE, CREATING A VARIETY OF NEW DISHES.
牛鍋
赤べこ
AMONG THEM, BEEF-POT, OR GYŪNABE (SUKIYAKI), WAS SEEN AS REPRESENTATIVE OF EUROPEAN FOODS AND WAS AFFORDABLE TO THE GENERAL PUBLIC.
RATTLE
BLAH BLAH
BLAH BLAH BLAH
BLAH BLAH BLAH
BLAH BLAH BLAH BLAH
BLAH BLAH
HELLO, AND COME ON—
KAORU-CHAN! COME IN!!
LONG TIME NO SEE, TAE-SAN.
YOU LOOK GOOD.
AND YOU'VE SOME UNFAMILIAR FACES WITH YOU TODAY.
IS THAT GUY OVER THERE YOUR LOVER?
NO, JUST A GUEST OF THE DOJO.
I DON'T BELIEVE IT!!

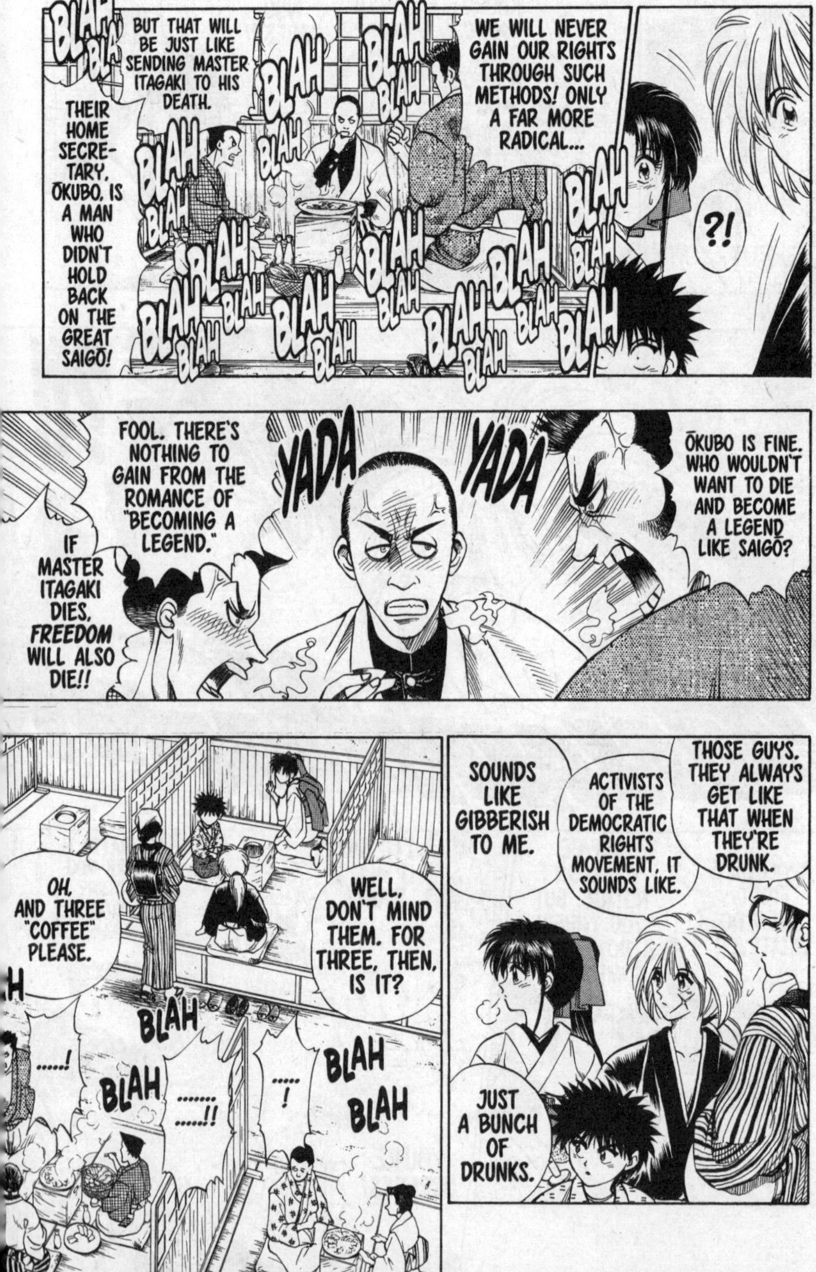
?!
WE WILL NEVER GAIN OUR RIGHTS THROUGH SUCH METHODS! ONLY A FAR MORE RADICAL...
BLAH BLAH
BLAH BLAH
BUT THAT WILL BE JUST LIKE SENDING MASTER ITAGAKI TO HIS DEATH.
BLAH BLAH
THEIR HOME SECRETARY, ŌKUBO, IS A MAN WHO DIDN'T HOLD BACK ON THE GREAT SAIGŌ!
BLAH BLAH
BLAH BLAH
BLAH BLAH
BLAH BLAH
BLAH BLAH
BLAH BLAH
BLAH BLAH
ŌKUBO IS FINE. WHO WOULDN'T WANT TO DIE AND BECOME A LEGEND LIKE SAIGŌ?
YADA
YADA
FOOL. THERE'S NOTHING TO GAIN FROM THE ROMANCE OF "BECOMING A LEGEND."
IF MASTER ITAGAKI DIES, FREEDOM WILL ALSO DIE!!
THOSE GUYS. THEY ALWAYS GET LIKE THAT WHEN THEY'RE DRUNK.
ACTIVISTS OF THE DEMOCRATIC RIGHTS MOVEMENT, IT SOUNDS LIKE.
SOUNDS LIKE GIBBERISH TO ME.
JUST A BUNCH OF DRUNKS.
WELL, DON'T MIND THEM. FOR THREE, THEN, IS IT?
OH, AND THREE "COFFEE" PLEASE.
BLAH
BLAH BLAH
......!
BLAH
....!!
...... !

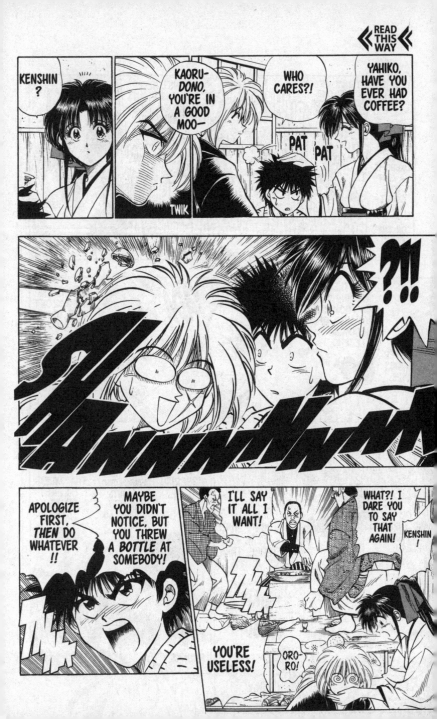

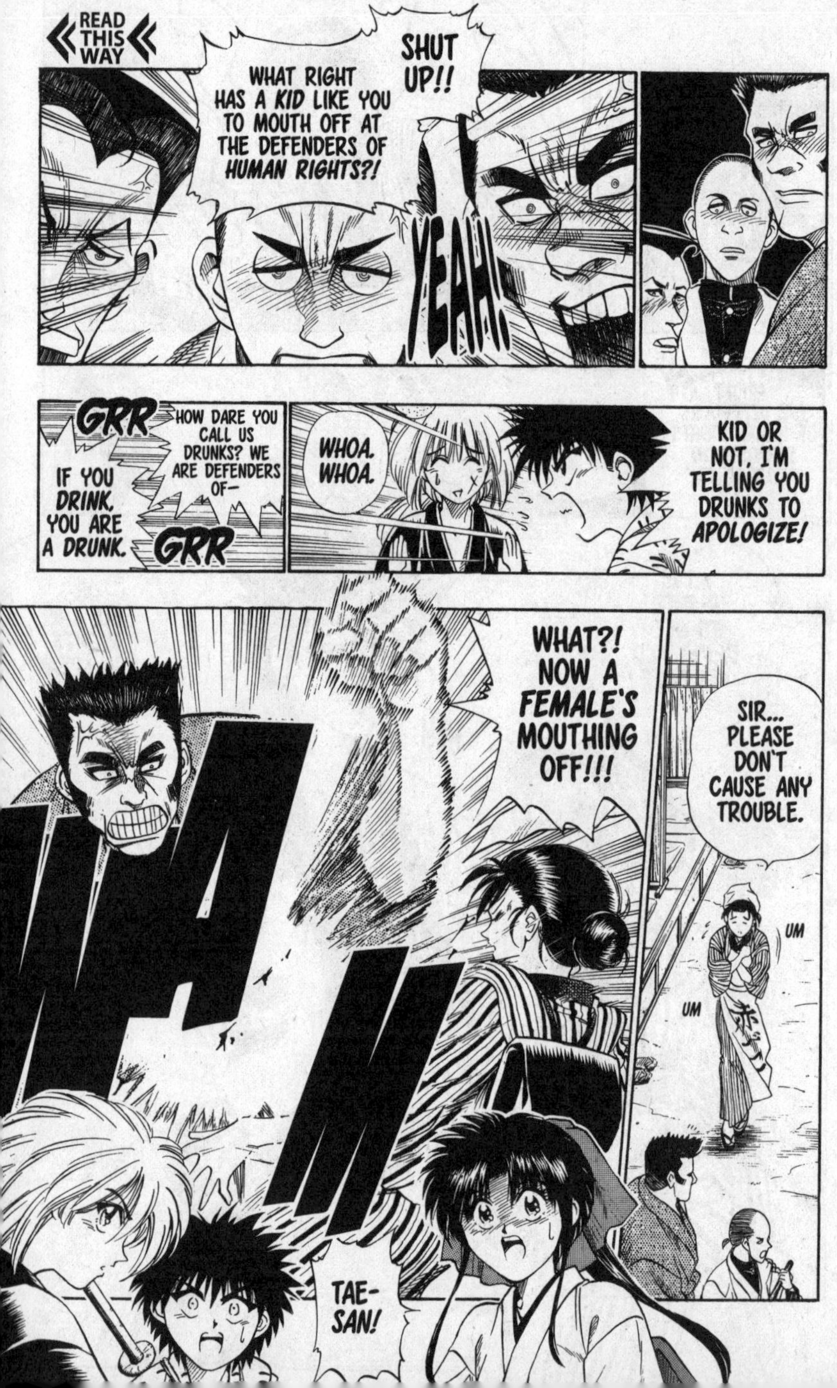
READ THIS WAY
SHUT UP!!
WHAT RIGHT HAS A KID LIKE YOU TO MOUTH OFF AT THE DEFENDERS OF HUMAN RIGHTS?!
YEAH!!
KID OR NOT, I'M TELLING YOU DRUNKS TO APOLOGIZE!
WHOA. WHOA.
GRR
HOW DARE YOU CALL US DRUNKS? WE ARE DEFENDERS OF—
IF YOU DRINK, YOU ARE A DRUNK.
GRR
SIR... PLEASE DON'T CAUSE ANY TROUBLE.
UM
UM
WHAT?! NOW A FEMALE'S MOUTHING OFF!!!
TAE-SAN!

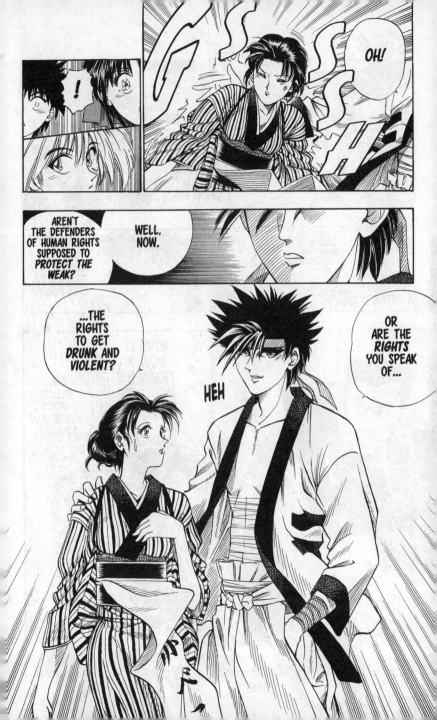

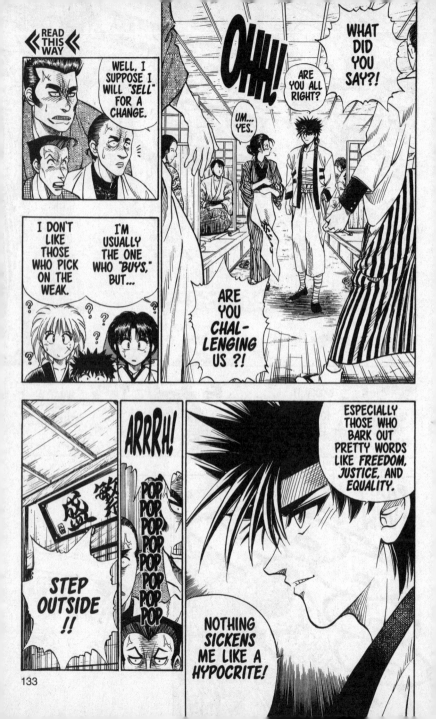

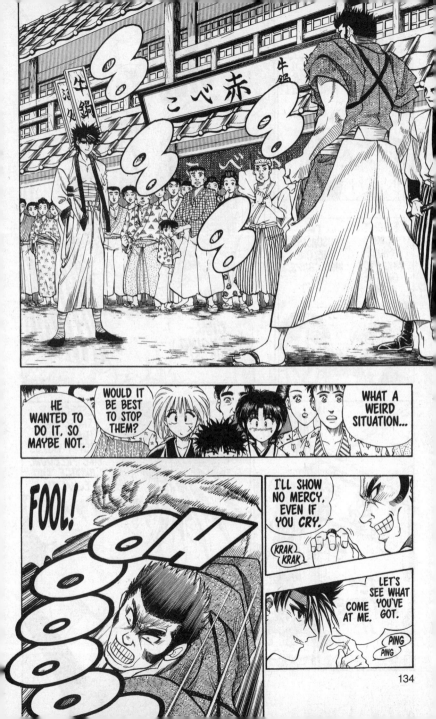

134

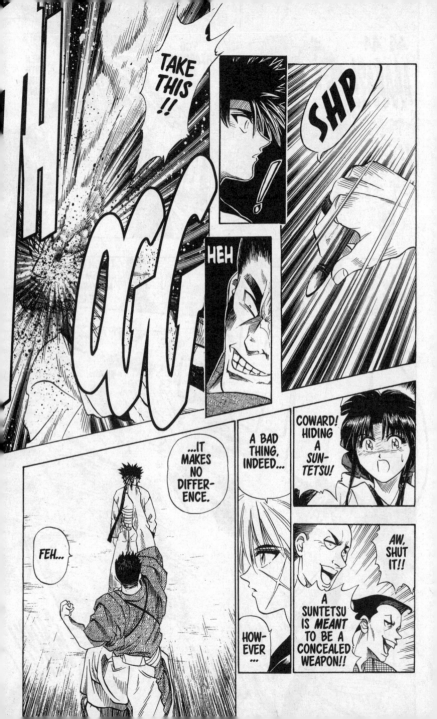

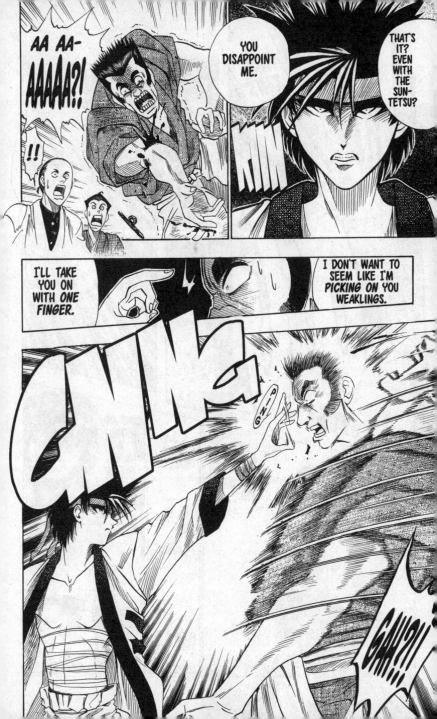

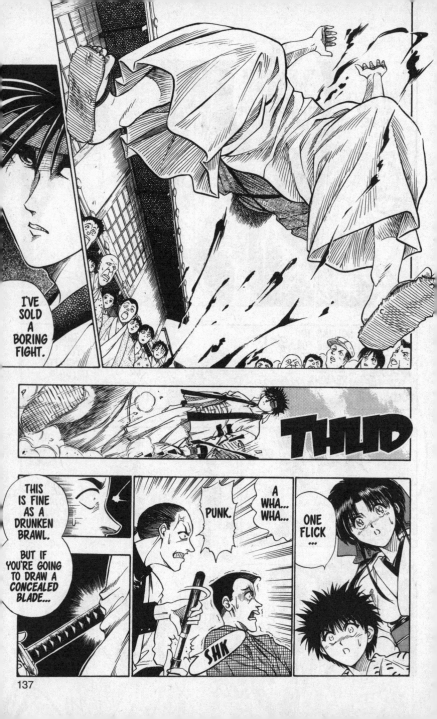

I'VE SOLD A BORING FIGHT.

THUD

THIS IS FINE AS A DRUNKEN BRAWL.

BUT IF YOU'RE GOING TO DRAW A CONCEALED BLADE...

PUNK.

A WHA... WHA...

ONE FLICK...

SHK

137

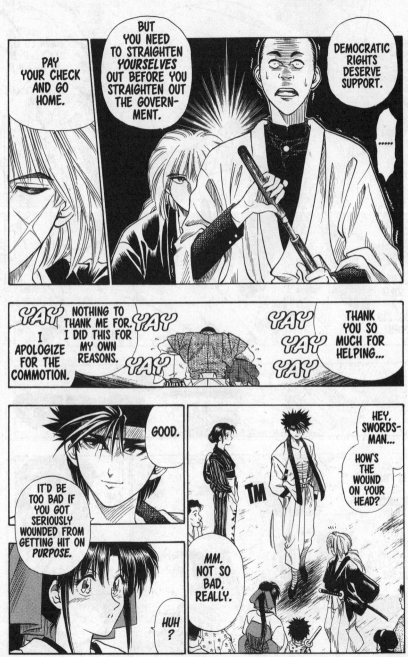

138

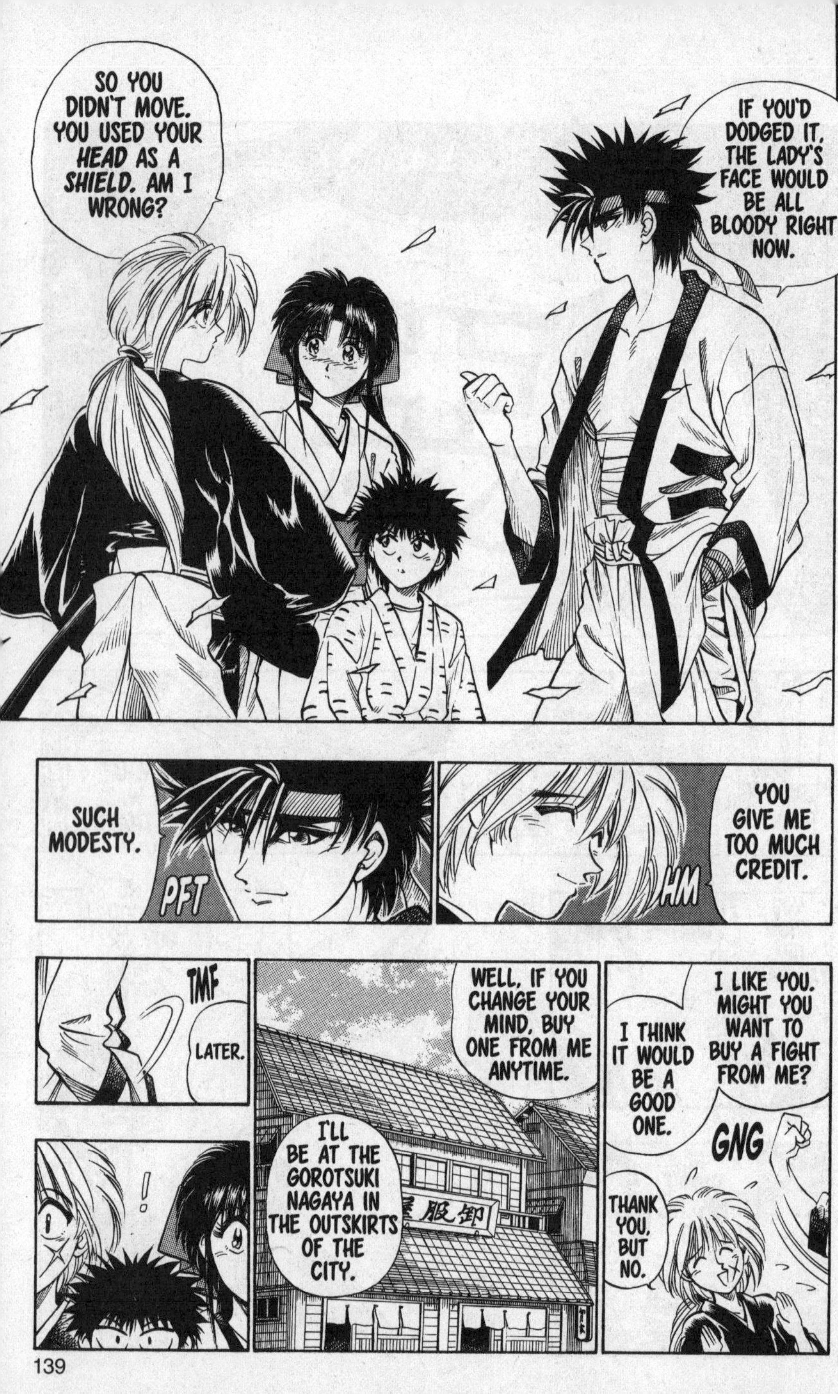
IF YOU'D DODGED IT, THE LADY'S FACE WOULD BE ALL BLOODY RIGHT NOW.
SO YOU DIDN'T MOVE. YOU USED YOUR *HEAD* AS A *SHIELD*. AM I WRONG?
YOU GIVE ME TOO MUCH CREDIT.
HM
PFT
SUCH MODESTY.
I LIKE YOU. MIGHT YOU WANT TO BUY A FIGHT FROM ME?
I THINK IT WOULD BE A GOOD ONE.
GNG
THANK YOU, BUT NO.
WELL, IF YOU CHANGE YOUR MIND, BUY ONE FROM ME ANYTIME.
I'LL BE AT THE GOROTSUKI NAGAYA IN THE OUTSKIRTS OF THE CITY.
御服屋
TMF
LATER.
!

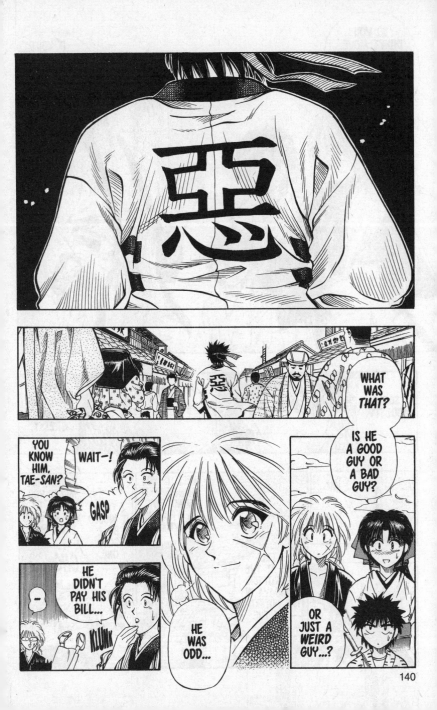

140

READ THIS WAY

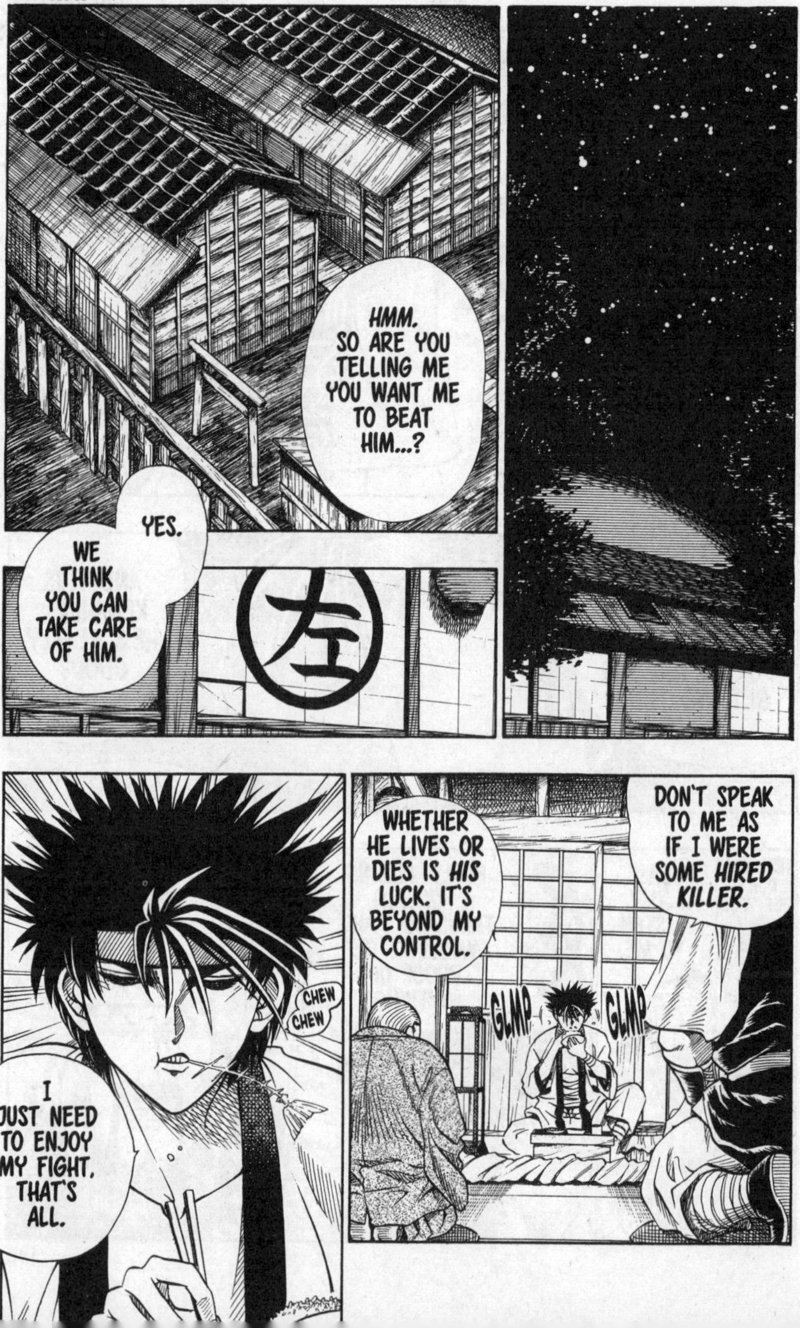
HMM. SO ARE YOU TELLING ME YOU WANT ME TO BEAT HIM...?
YES.
WE THINK YOU CAN TAKE CARE OF HIM.
DON'T SPEAK TO ME AS IF I WERE SOME *HIRED KILLER.*
WHETHER HE LIVES OR DIES IS *HIS* LUCK. IT'S BEYOND MY CONTROL.
GLMP
GLMP
CHEW
CHEW
I JUST NEED TO ENJOY MY FIGHT, THAT'S ALL.

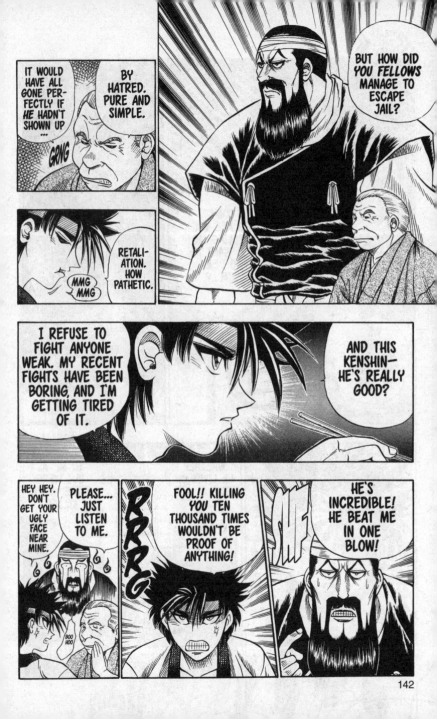

IT WOULD HAVE ALL GONE PERFECTLY IF HE HADN'T SHOWN UP...

GRNG

BY HATRED. PURE AND SIMPLE.

MMG MMG

RETALIATION. HOW PATHETIC.

BUT HOW DID *YOU FELLOWS* MANAGE TO ESCAPE JAIL?

I REFUSE TO FIGHT ANYONE WEAK. MY RECENT FIGHTS HAVE BEEN BORING, AND I'M GETTING TIRED OF IT.

AND THIS KENSHIN—HE'S REALLY GOOD?

HEY HEY. DON'T GET YOUR UGLY FACE NEAR MINE.

PLEASE... JUST LISTEN TO ME.

BOO HOO

RRRG

FOOL!! KILLING YOU TEN THOUSAND TIMES WOULDN'T BE PROOF OF ANYTHING!

HE'S INCREDIBLE! HE BEAT ME IN ONE BLOW!

142

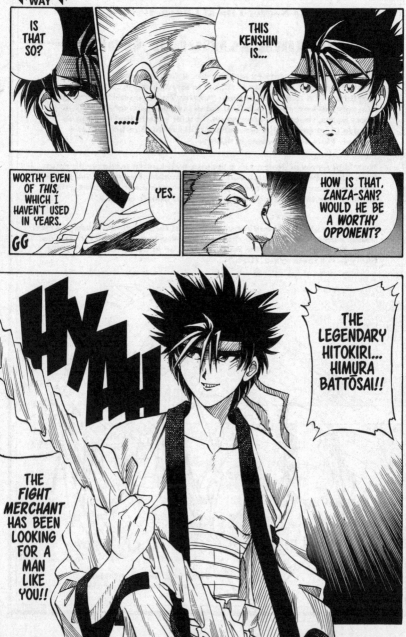

The Secret Life of Characters (4)

—Hiruma Kihei & Gohei—

The way these two turned out is a direct function of the story. I wanted a pair of interesting villains to start things off with a bang, and figured I'd make one of them "brainy" and one of them "wild." The story of how these two first came together was taking up too many pages, though, so after some thought I made the decision to change them from being circumstantially related to being blood-related. Thus, they became brothers.

Models in terms of design are a certain well-known manager/director from Obata Takeshi's sumō manga "*Chikarabito Densetsu*" for Kihei... and some character spotted in a magazine who made me think, "Ooh, *impact!*" for Gohei. (Much more than that, I don't recall.)

Unlike Kenshin and the others, the faces of these two are made of basic, simple shapes, making them that much easier to draw. The closer I got to my deadlines, in fact, the fonder I became of them. Alas, we're not likely to see them again. (Heh.)

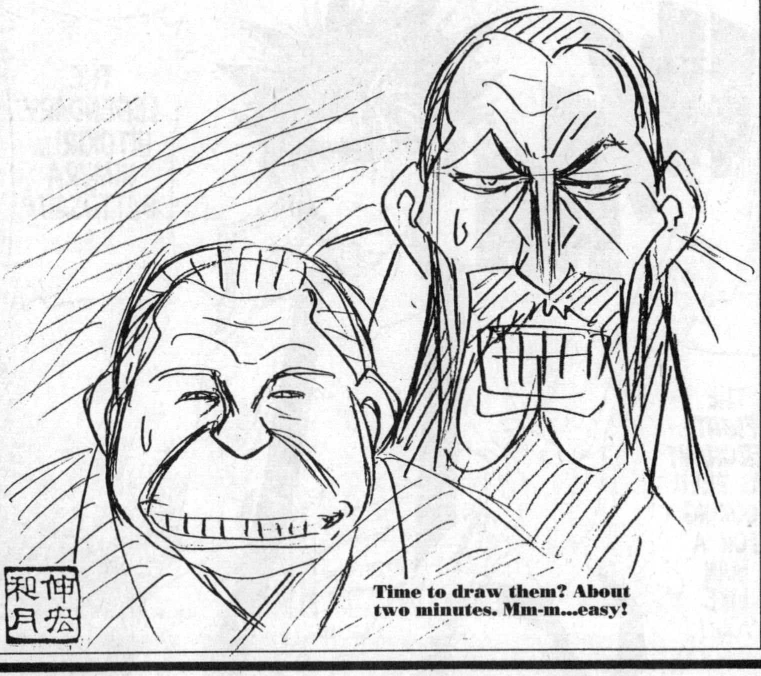
伸宏
和月

Time to draw them? About two minutes. Mm-m...easy!

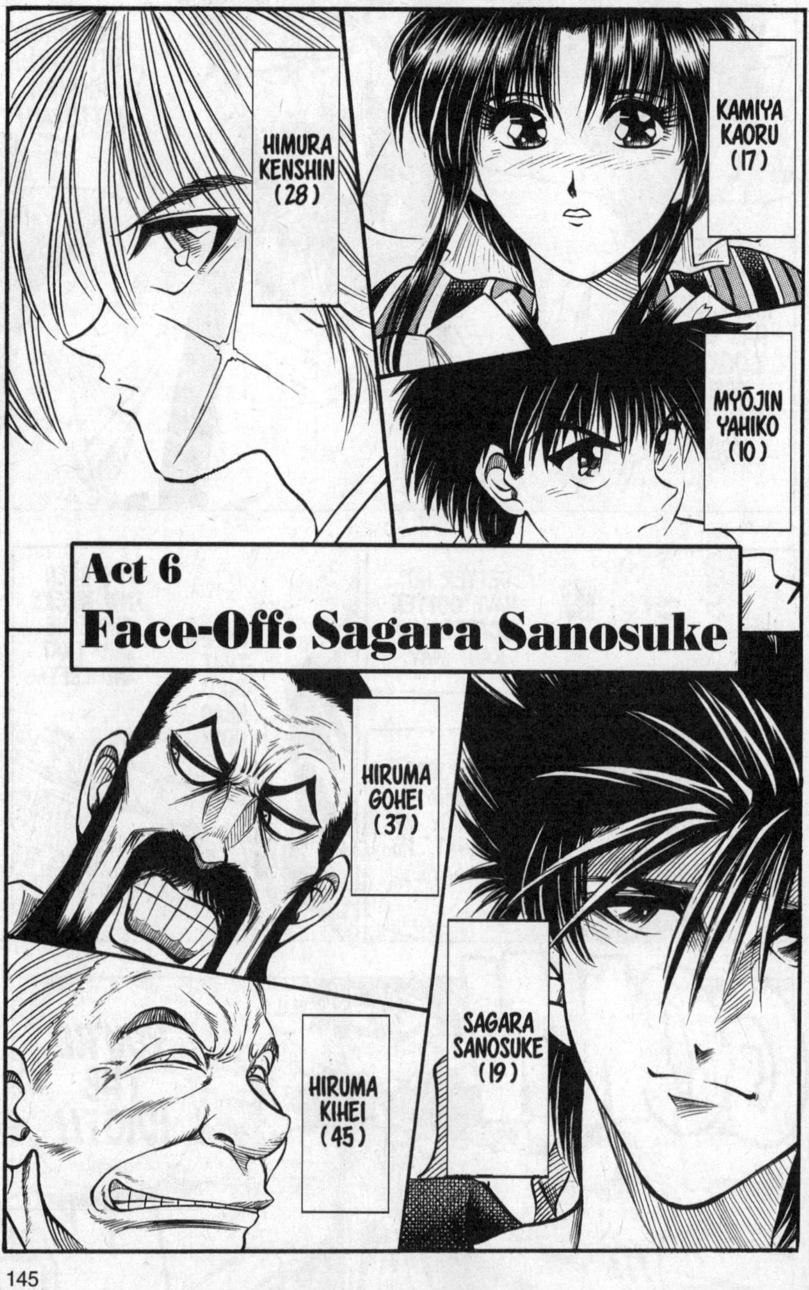
KAMIYA KAORU (17)
MYŌJIN YAHIKO (10)
HIMURA KENSHIN (28)
Act 6
Face-Off: Sagara Sanosuke
SAGARA SANOSUKE (19)
HIRUMA GOHEI (37)
HIRUMA KIHEI (45)

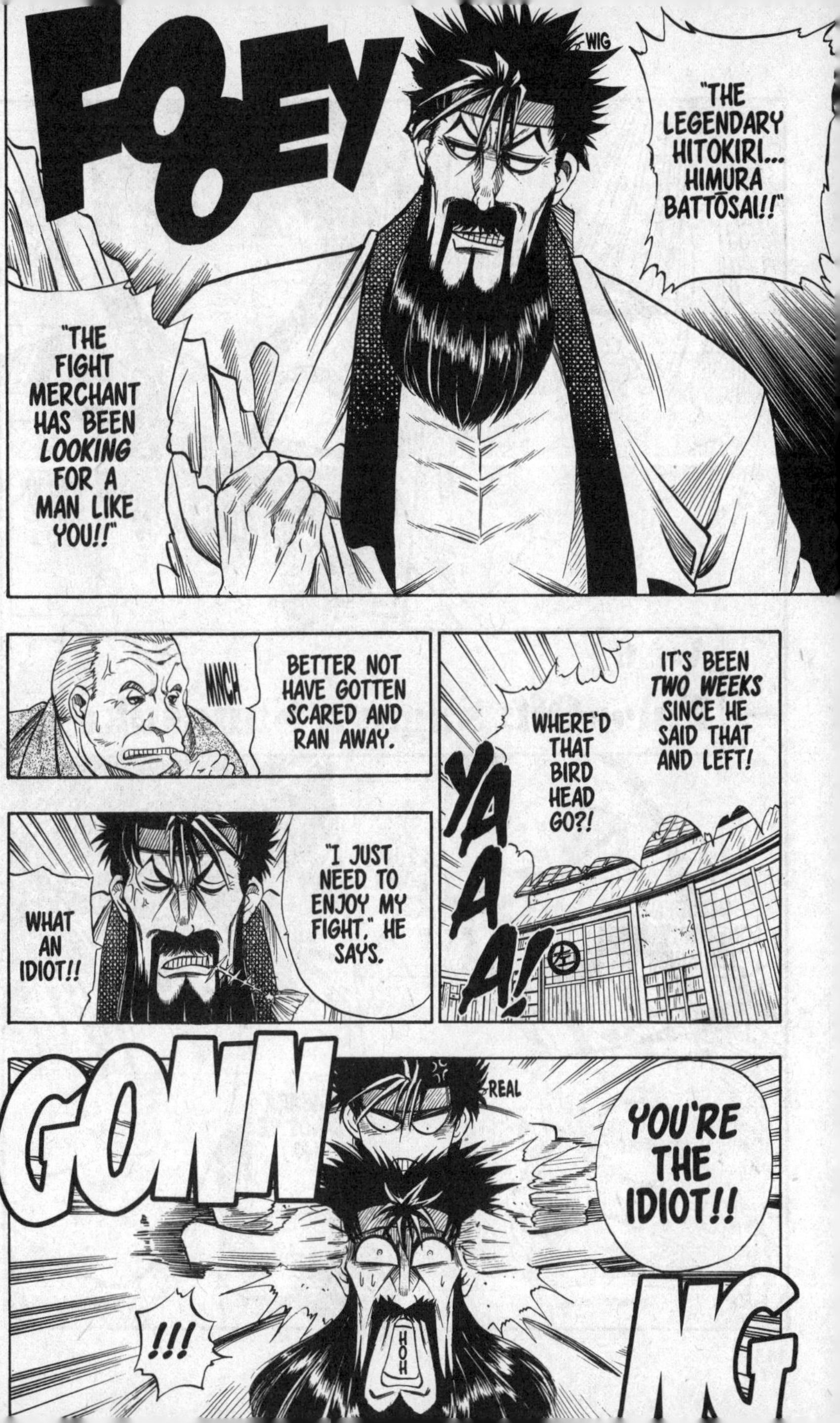
"THE LEGENDARY HITOKIRI... HIMURA BATTŌSAI!!"
WIG
FOOEY
"THE FIGHT MERCHANT HAS BEEN *LOOKING* FOR A MAN LIKE YOU!!"
IT'S BEEN *TWO WEEKS* SINCE HE SAID THAT AND LEFT!
WHERE'D THAT BIRD HEAD GO?!
YAAAA!
BETTER NOT HAVE GOTTEN SCARED AND RAN AWAY.
MNCH
"I JUST NEED TO ENJOY MY FIGHT," HE SAYS.
WHAT AN IDIOT!!
REAL
YOU'RE THE IDIOT!!
GONN
NG
!!!
HOH

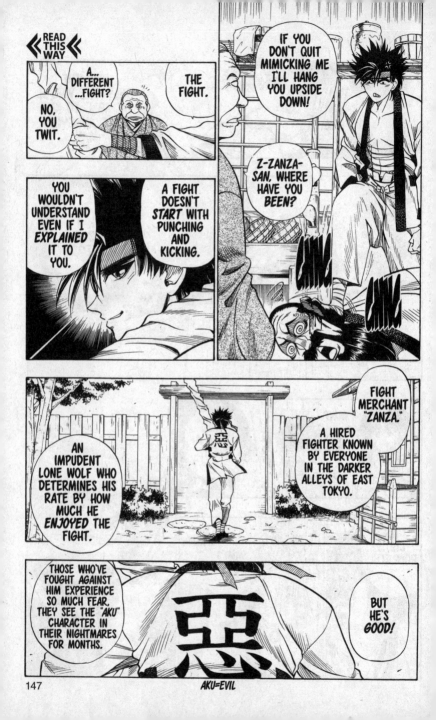

AKU=EVIL

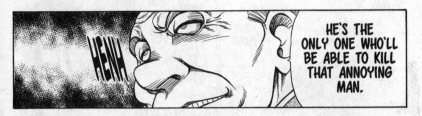

HE'S THE ONLY ONE WHO'LL BE ABLE TO KILL THAT ANNOYING MAN.

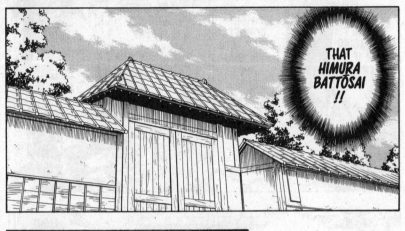

THAT HIMURA BATTŌSAI!!

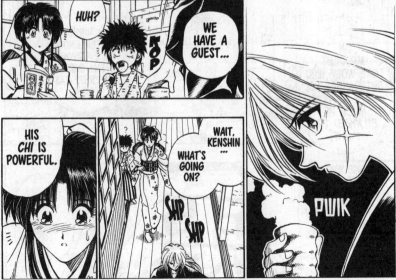

HUH?

TOP

WE HAVE A GUEST...

HIS CHI IS POWERFUL.

WAIT, KENSHIN...

WHAT'S GOING ON?

SLP SLP

PWIK

148

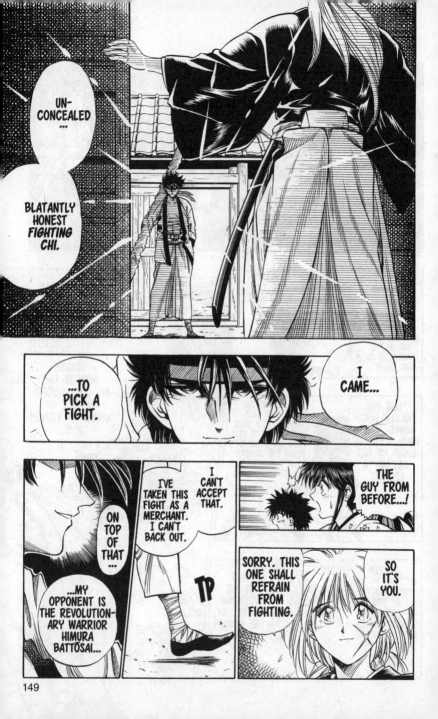

UN-CONCEALED...

BLATANTLY HONEST FIGHTING CHI.

...TO PICK A FIGHT.

I CAME...

ON TOP OF THAT...

...MY OPPONENT IS THE REVOLUTIONARY WARRIOR HIMURA BATTOSAI...

I'VE TAKEN THIS FIGHT AS A MERCHANT. I CAN'T BACK OUT.

I CAN'T ACCEPT THAT.

THE GUY FROM BEFORE...!

SORRY. THIS ONE SHALL REFRAIN FROM FIGHTING.

SO IT'S YOU.

TP

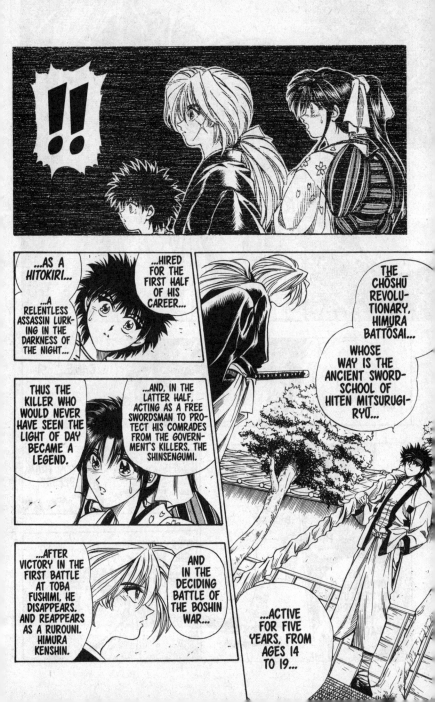

!!

...AS A HITOKIRI... A RELENTLESS ASSASSIN LURKING IN THE DARKNESS OF THE NIGHT...

...HIRED FOR THE FIRST HALF OF HIS CAREER...

THE CHŌSHŪ REVOLUTIONARY, HIMURA BATTŌSAI...

WHOSE WAY IS THE ANCIENT SWORD-SCHOOL OF HITEN MITSURUGI-RYŪ...

THUS THE KILLER WHO WOULD NEVER HAVE SEEN THE LIGHT OF DAY BECAME A LEGEND.

...AND, IN THE LATTER HALF, ACTING AS A FREE SWORDSMAN TO PROTECT HIS COMRADES FROM THE GOVERNMENT'S KILLERS, THE SHINSENGUMI.

...AFTER VICTORY IN THE FIRST BATTLE AT TOBA FUSHIMI, HE DISAPPEARS. AND REAPPEARS AS A RUROUNI. HIMURA KENSHIN.

AND IN THE DECIDING BATTLE OF THE BOSHIN WAR...

...ACTIVE FOR FIVE YEARS, FROM AGES 14 TO 19...

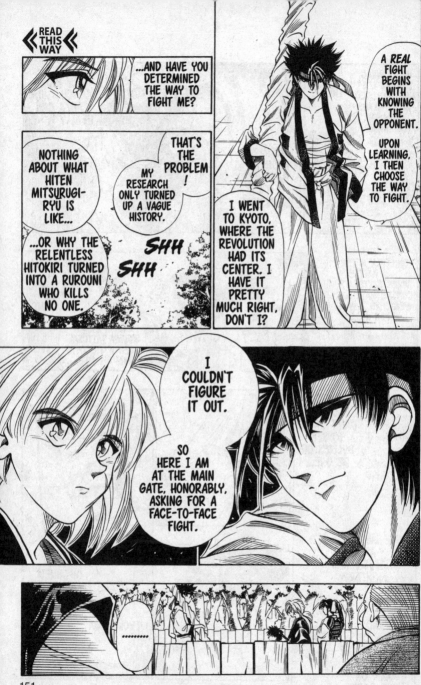

...AND HAVE YOU DETERMINED THE WAY TO FIGHT ME?

A REAL FIGHT BEGINS WITH KNOWING THE OPPONENT.

UPON LEARNING, I THEN CHOOSE THE WAY TO FIGHT.

NOTHING ABOUT WHAT HITEN MITSURUGI-RYU IS LIKE...

THAT'S THE PROBLEM!

MY RESEARCH ONLY TURNED UP A VAGUE HISTORY.

...OR WHY THE RELENTLESS HITOKIRI TURNED INTO A RUROUNI WHO KILLS NO ONE.

SHH SHH

I WENT TO KYOTO, WHERE THE REVOLUTION HAD ITS CENTER. I HAVE IT PRETTY MUCH RIGHT, DON'T I?

I COULDN'T FIGURE IT OUT.

SO HERE I AM AT THE MAIN GATE, HONORABLY, ASKING FOR A FACE-TO-FACE FIGHT.

....

151

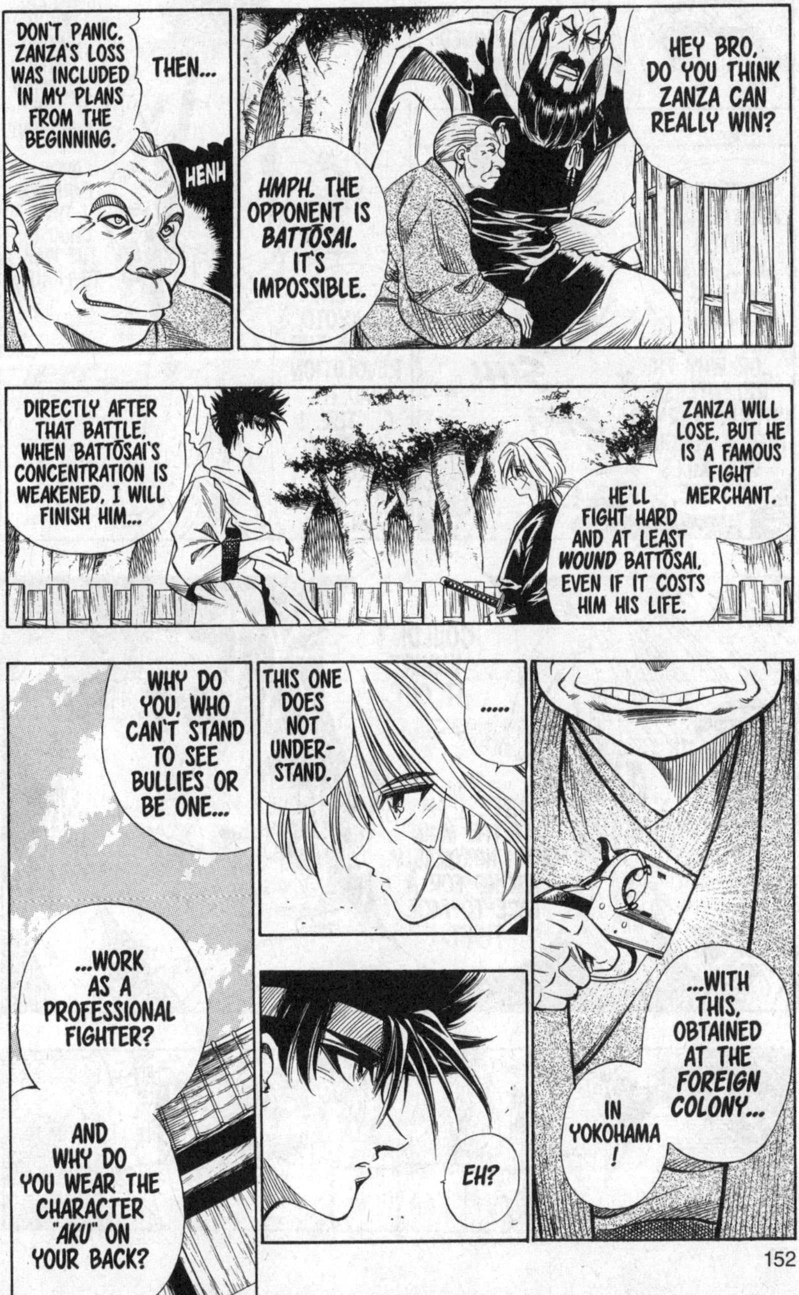
HEY BRO, DO YOU THINK ZANZA CAN REALLY WIN?
HMPH. THE OPPONENT IS BATTŌSAI. IT'S IMPOSSIBLE.
THEN...
DON'T PANIC. ZANZA'S LOSS WAS INCLUDED IN MY PLANS FROM THE BEGINNING.
HENH
ZANZA WILL LOSE, BUT HE IS A FAMOUS FIGHT MERCHANT.
HE'LL FIGHT HARD AND AT LEAST *WOUND* BATTŌSAI, EVEN IF IT COSTS HIM HIS LIFE.
DIRECTLY AFTER THAT BATTLE, WHEN BATTŌSAI'S CONCENTRATION IS WEAKENED, I WILL FINISH HIM...
...WITH THIS, OBTAINED AT THE *FOREIGN COLONY*...
IN YOKOHAMA!
.....
THIS ONE DOES NOT UNDERSTAND.
EH?
WHY DO YOU, WHO CAN'T STAND TO SEE BULLIES OR BE ONE...
...WORK AS A PROFESSIONAL FIGHTER?
AND WHY DO YOU WEAR THE CHARACTER "*AKU*" ON YOUR BACK?

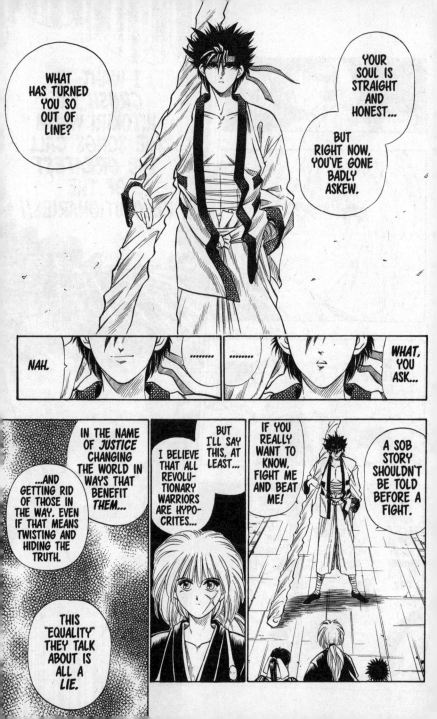

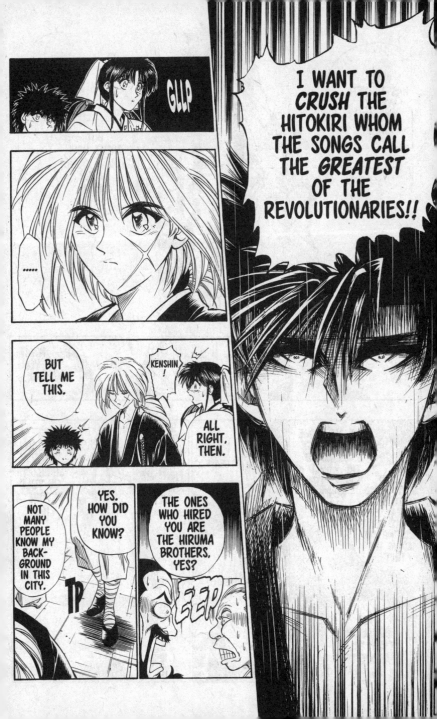

READ THIS WAY

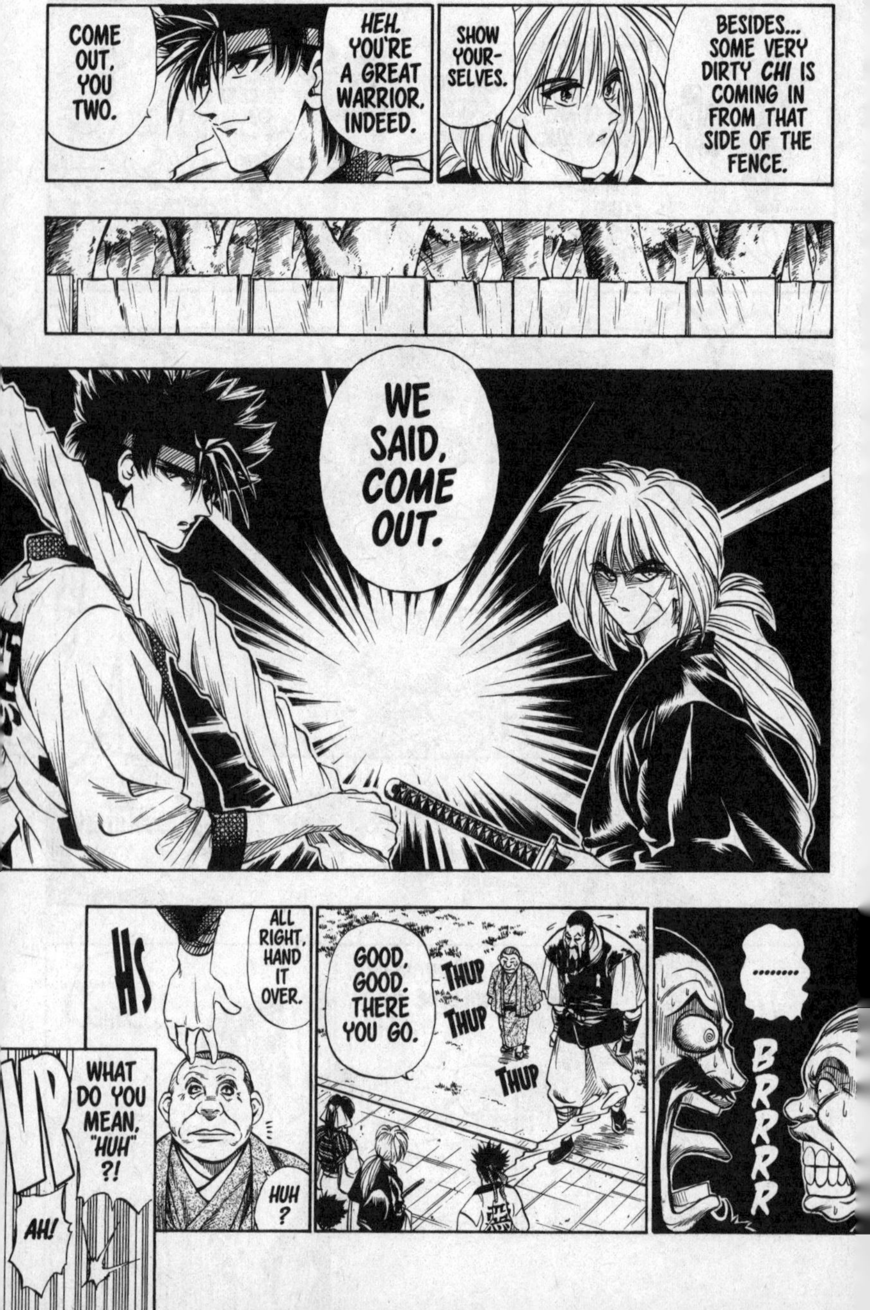
BESIDES... SOME VERY DIRTY CHI IS COMING IN FROM THAT SIDE OF THE FENCE.
SHOW YOUR-SELVES.
HEH. YOU'RE A GREAT WARRIOR, INDEED.
COME OUT, YOU TWO.
WE SAID, COME OUT.
....
BRRRR
THUP
THUP
THUP
GOOD, GOOD. THERE YOU GO.
ALL RIGHT, HAND IT OVER.
HS
HUH ?
WHAT DO YOU MEAN, "HUH" ?!
AH!

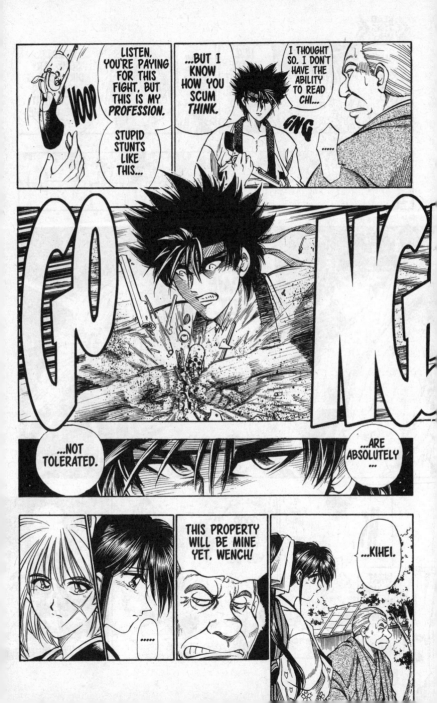

« READ THIS WAY «

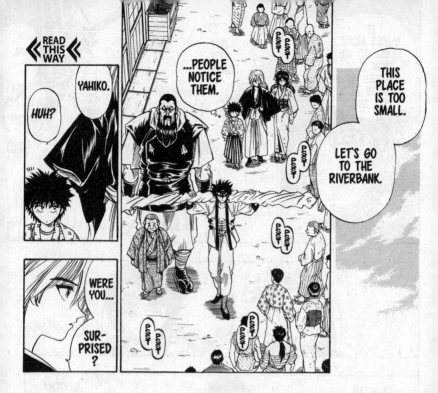

Thanks for all the fan letters. For a new author, it's sure a lot of encouragement! A couple of you are mailing me every week, and 90% of you seem to be female—has *Shonen Jump* gone suddenly *shōjo*, I wonder? Anyway, these are the kinds of things I think of as I continue working on the series. I can't quite say I'll ever be able to reply to you, but I will always be sure to read each letter that comes my way. Thanks again for your support!

—Watsuki

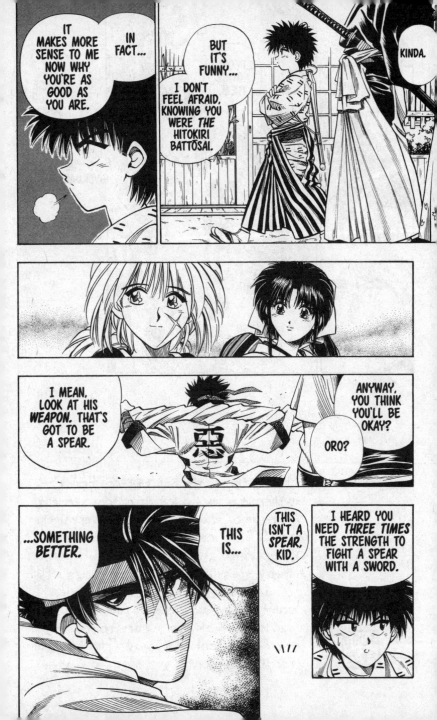

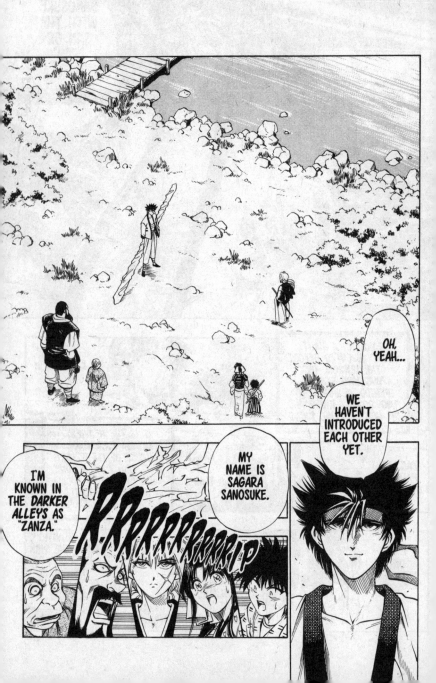

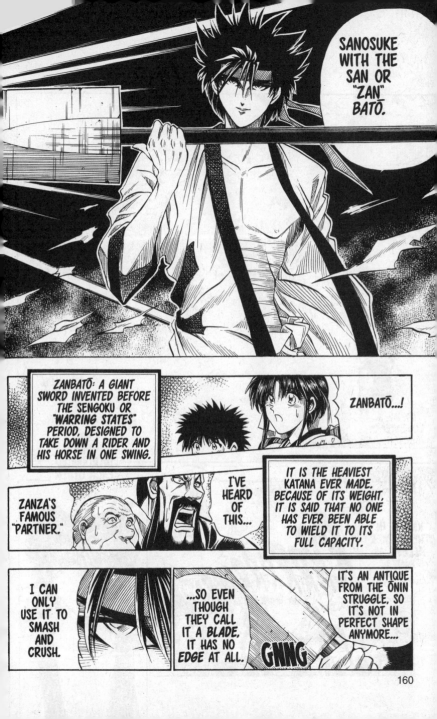

SANOSUKE WITH THE SAN OR "ZAN" BATŌ.

ZANBATŌ: A GIANT SWORD INVENTED BEFORE THE SENGOKU OR "WARRING STATES" PERIOD, DESIGNED TO TAKE DOWN A RIDER AND HIS HORSE IN ONE SWING.

ZANBATŌ...!

ZANZA'S FAMOUS "PARTNER."

I'VE HEARD OF THIS...

IT IS THE HEAVIEST KATANA EVER MADE. BECAUSE OF ITS WEIGHT, IT IS SAID THAT NO ONE HAS EVER BEEN ABLE TO WIELD IT TO ITS FULL CAPACITY.

I CAN ONLY USE IT TO SMASH AND CRUSH.

...SO EVEN THOUGH THEY CALL IT A BLADE, IT HAS NO EDGE AT ALL.

GNNG

IT'S AN ANTIQUE FROM THE ŌNIN STRUGGLE, SO IT'S NOT IN PERFECT SHAPE ANYMORE...

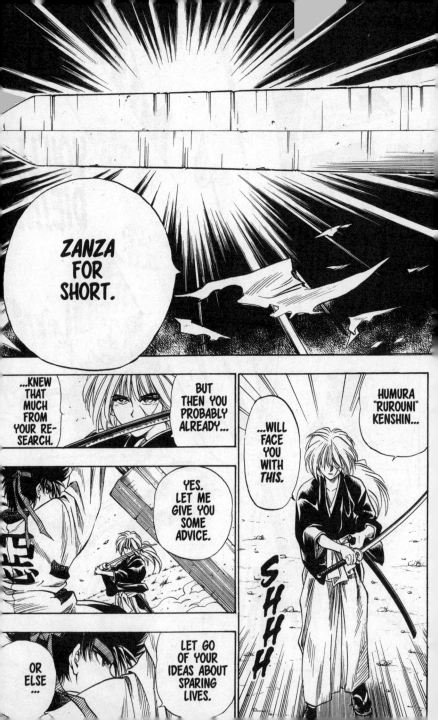

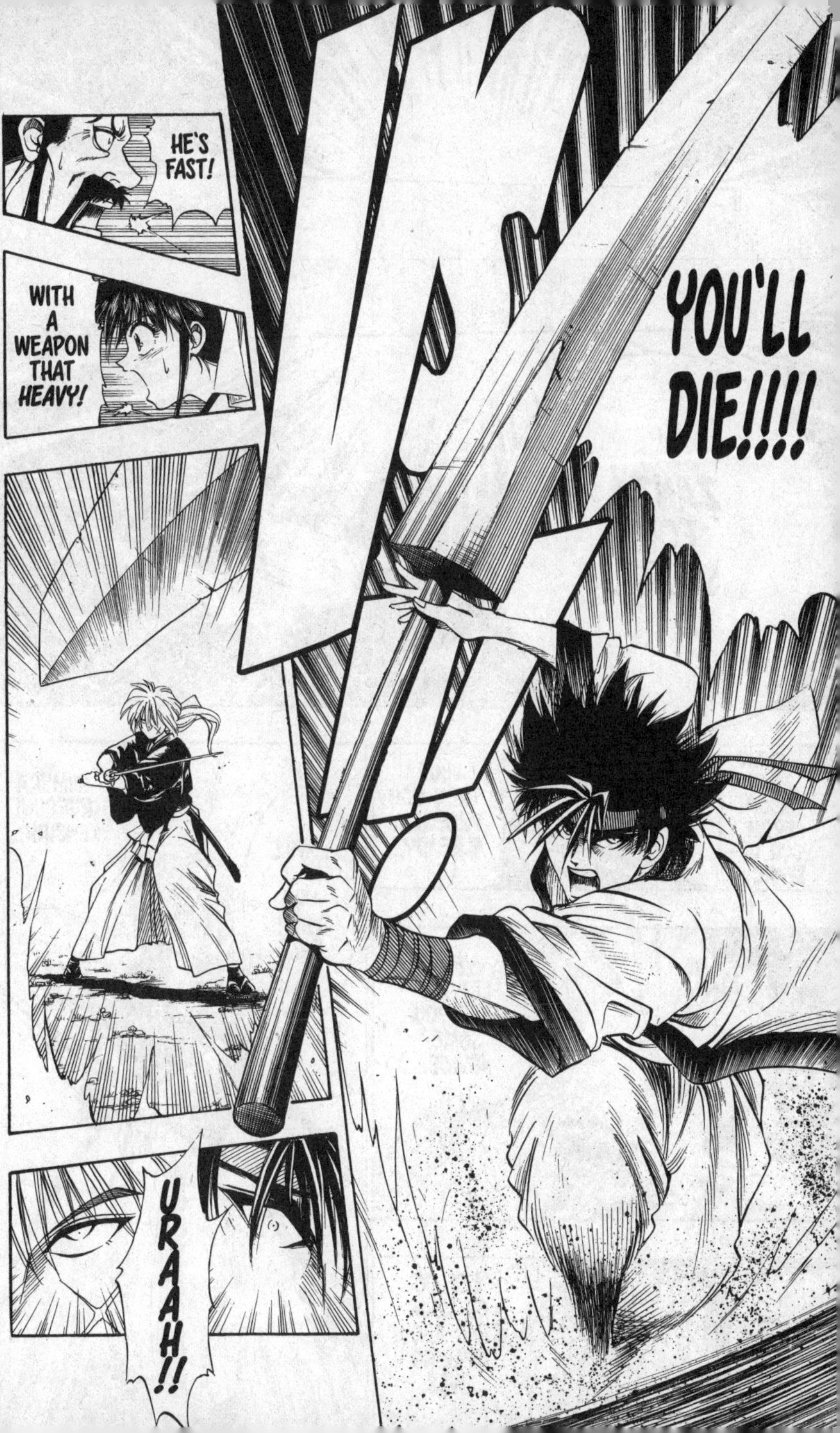
YOU'LL DIE!!!!
HE'S FAST!
WITH A WEAPON THAT HEAVY!
URAAAH!!

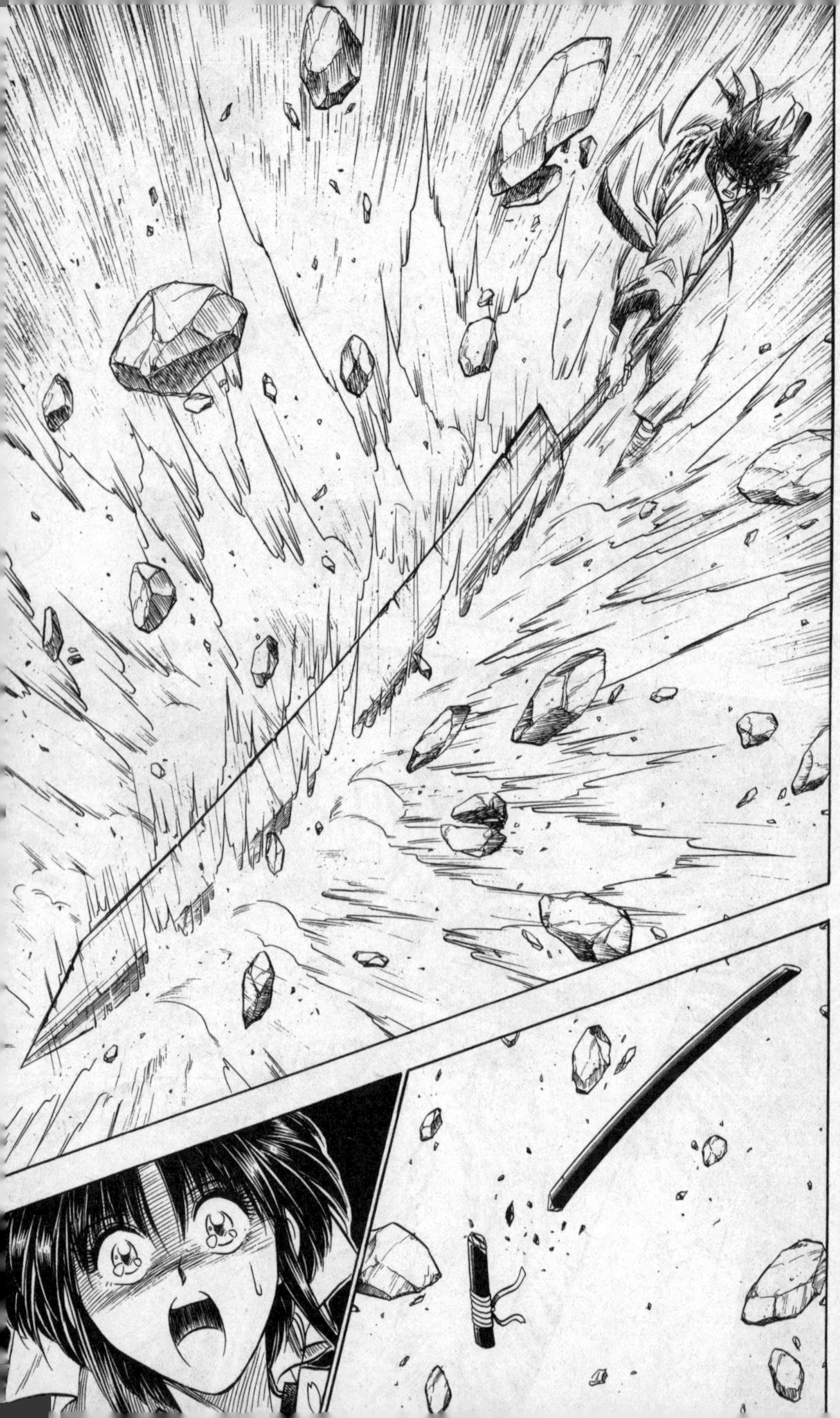

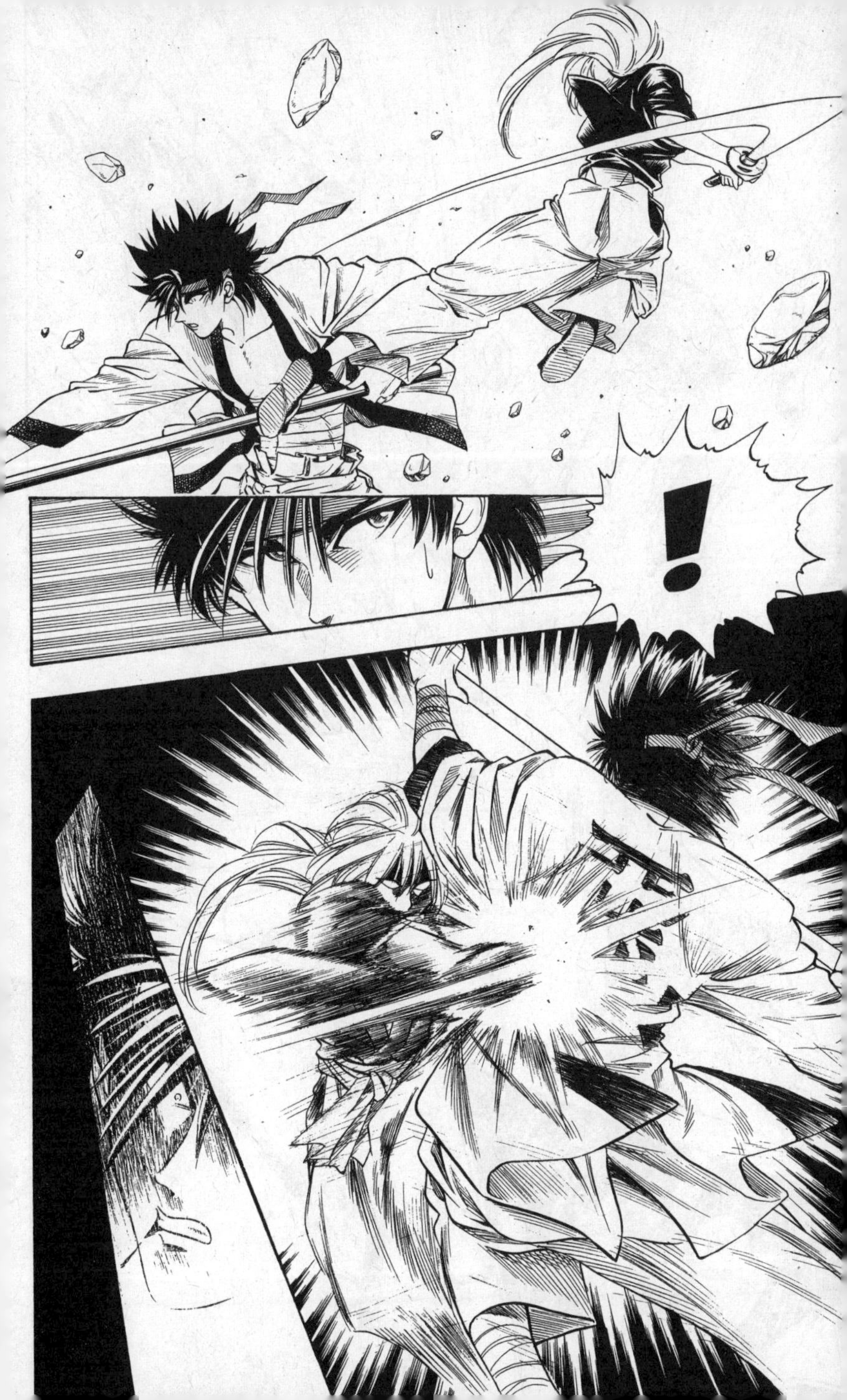
!

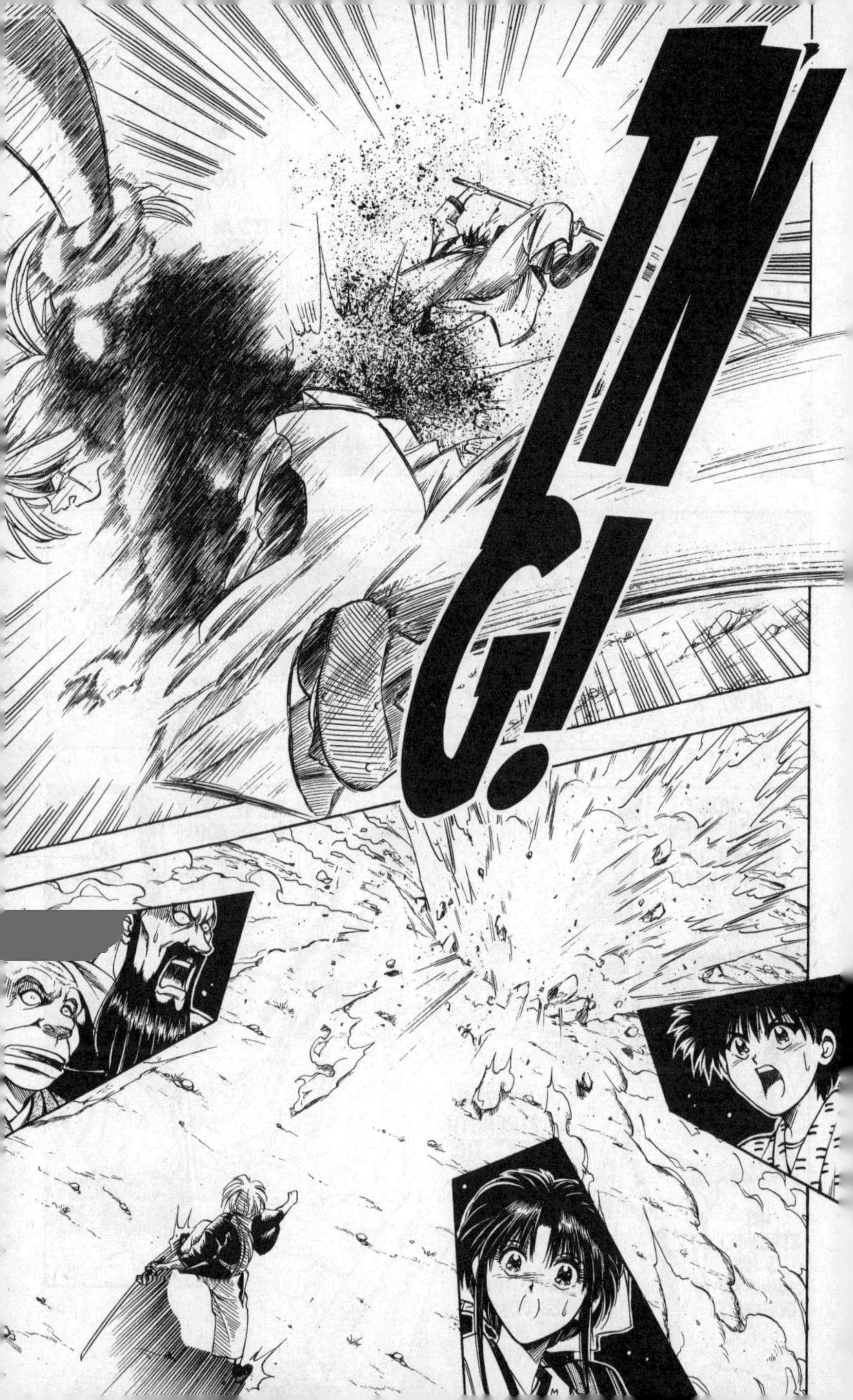

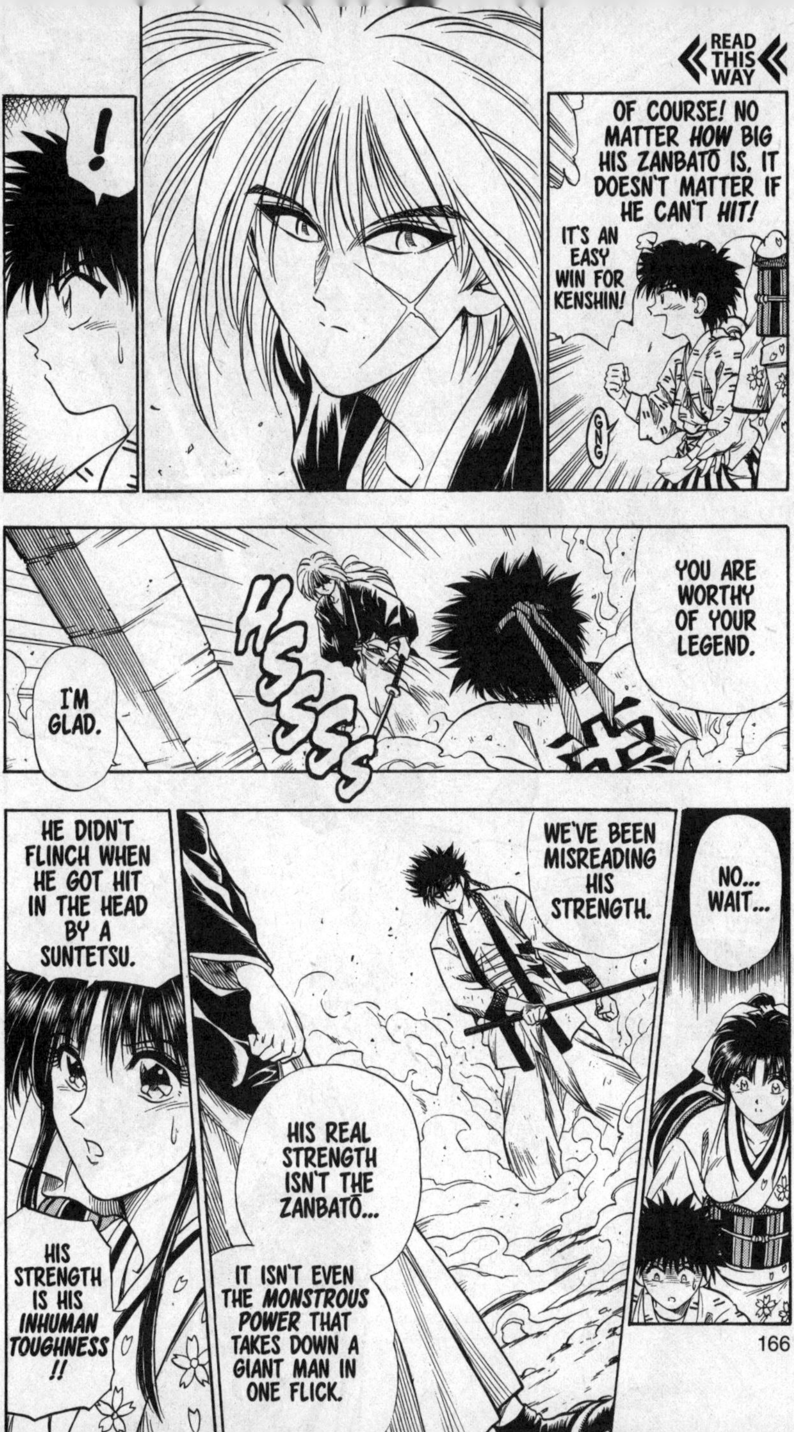
READ THIS WAY
OF COURSE! NO MATTER HOW BIG HIS ZANBATŌ IS, IT DOESN'T MATTER IF HE CAN'T HIT!
IT'S AN EASY WIN FOR KENSHIN!
GNG
!
YOU ARE WORTHY OF YOUR LEGEND.
HSSSSS
I'M GLAD.
NO... WAIT...
WE'VE BEEN MISREADING HIS STRENGTH.
HIS REAL STRENGTH ISN'T THE ZANBATŌ...
IT ISN'T EVEN THE MONSTROUS POWER THAT TAKES DOWN A GIANT MAN IN ONE FLICK.
HE DIDN'T FLINCH WHEN HE GOT HIT IN THE HEAD BY A SUNTETSU.
HIS STRENGTH IS HIS INHUMAN TOUGHNESS!!

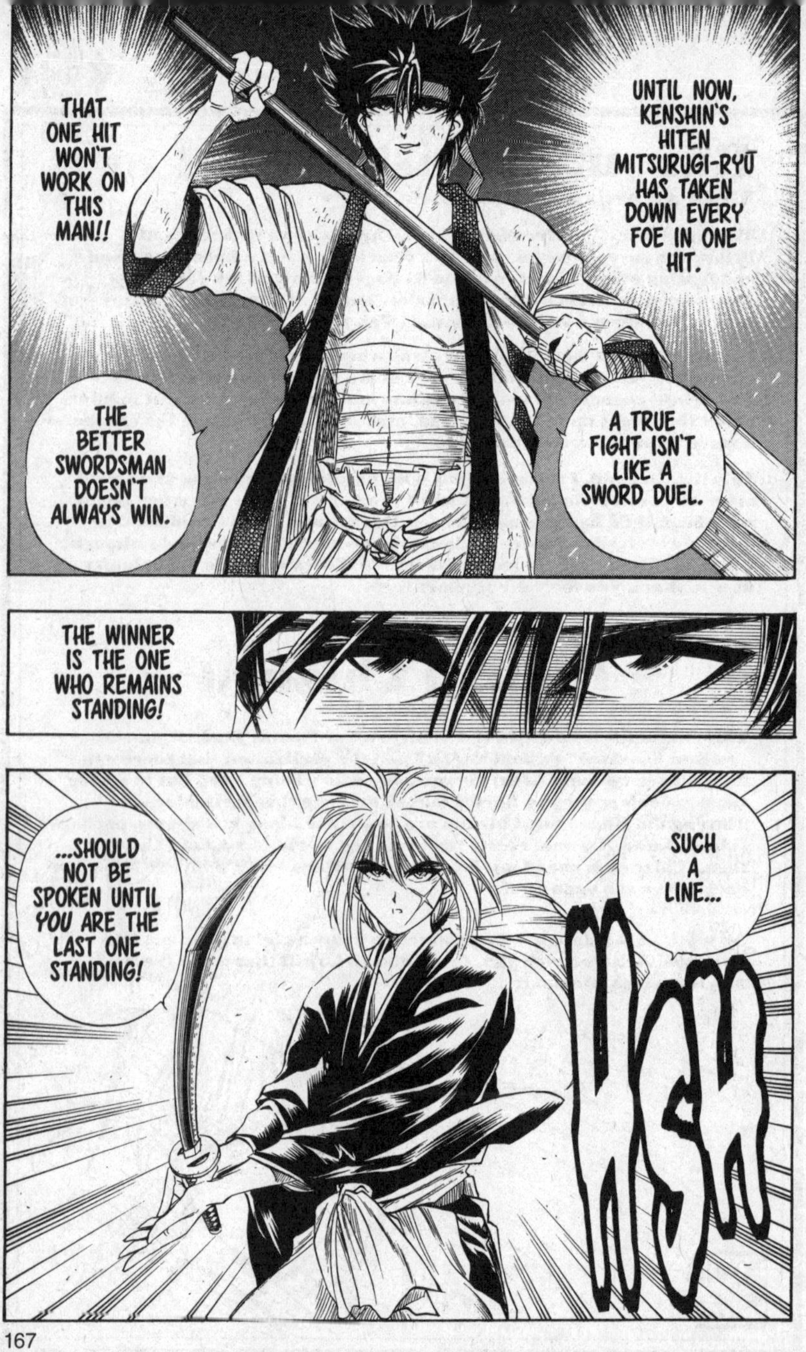
UNTIL NOW, KENSHIN'S HITEN MITSURUGI-RYU HAS TAKEN DOWN EVERY FOE IN ONE HIT.
THAT ONE HIT WON'T WORK ON THIS MAN!!
A TRUE FIGHT ISN'T LIKE A SWORD DUEL.
THE BETTER SWORDSMAN DOESN'T ALWAYS WIN.
THE WINNER IS THE ONE WHO REMAINS STANDING!
SUCH A LINE...
...SHOULD NOT BE SPOKEN UNTIL *YOU* ARE THE LAST ONE STANDING!
WSH

READ THIS WAY

Rurouni Kenshin

Meiji Swordsman Romantic Story

The "side-story" you're about to read next was published about a year before the current series started. I remember what a hard time I had condensing everything down into 31 pages. This was my very first appearance in *Shonen Jump* magazine, and so of course I put all my soul into it, but when I look back now.... (Sigh.)

For me, the most memorable part was when Kenshin—his name wasn't mentioned yet, but Battōsai's "real" name was set a year before this saw print—changes his tone. My editor and I had very different opinions about this, right up to the very end, and ultimately we gave the character a more "slangy" speech pattern.

This time around, I tinkered a bit with his dialogue, making him sound more as I prefer him now, and still I think about what this story might have been if I'd had two more pages. Once it was finally published in *Jump*, I received mediocre reviews and about 200 letters, and although I was unable to reply to most of them, I'd like to take this opportunity now to thank you for your support then.

—Raikōji Chizuru—

This character is based on the "Chizuru" of Tomita Tsuneo's novel "*Sugata Sanshirō*" (whom else?). Upon the realization that there can be romance not only in saving someone who's being hurt, but in saving someone *before* they're hurt, I longed to write this particular story. Then again, Kaoru and Chizuru are so similar...long-lost sisters, perhaps? (Uh-oh. Guess it would *really* turn into the world of Sugata Sanshirō, then.) Chizuru is one of my favorite characters, and I'd love to bring her back, given the opportunity.

No motif in her design; I just wanted to draw a girl in *hakama*. I've done the sheltered rich girl, the kendō girl...will that make the next a priestess, eh, Watsuki?

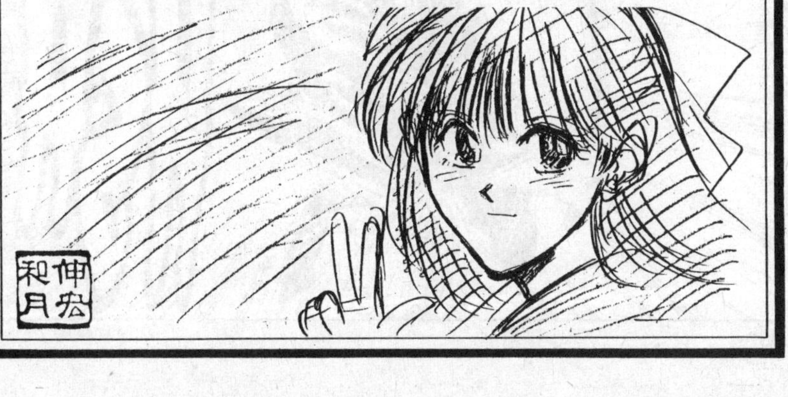

伸宏
和月

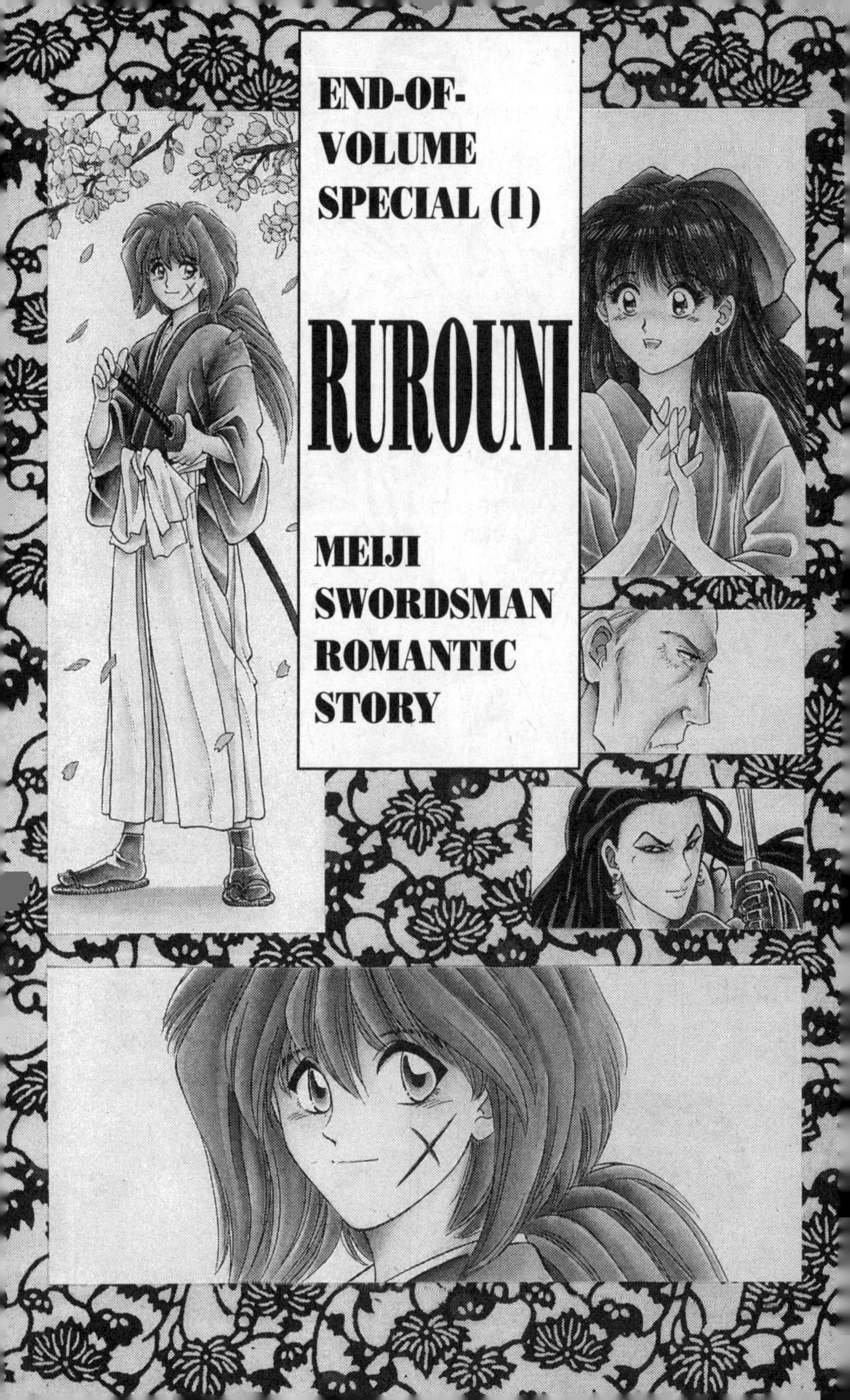
END-OF-
VOLUME
SPECIAL (1)
RUROUNI
MEIJI
SWORDSMAN
ROMANTIC
STORY

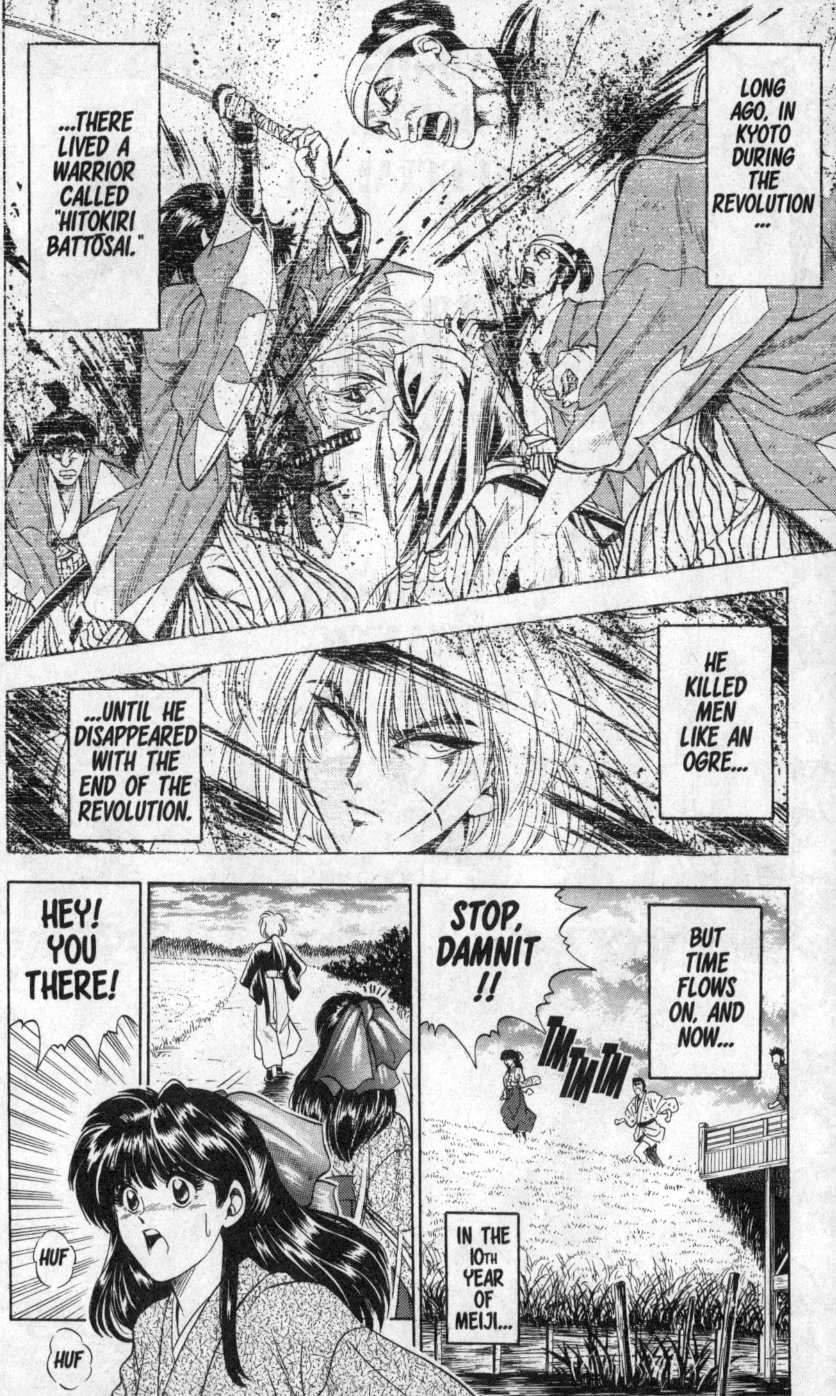
LONG AGO, IN KYOTO DURING THE REVOLUTION...
...THERE LIVED A WARRIOR CALLED "HITOKIRI BATTŌSAI."
HE KILLED MEN LIKE AN OGRE...
...UNTIL HE DISAPPEARED WITH THE END OF THE REVOLUTION.
BUT TIME FLOWS ON, AND NOW...
STOP, DAMNIT !!
TMTMTM
IN THE 10TH YEAR OF MEIJI...
HEY! YOU THERE!
HUF
HUF

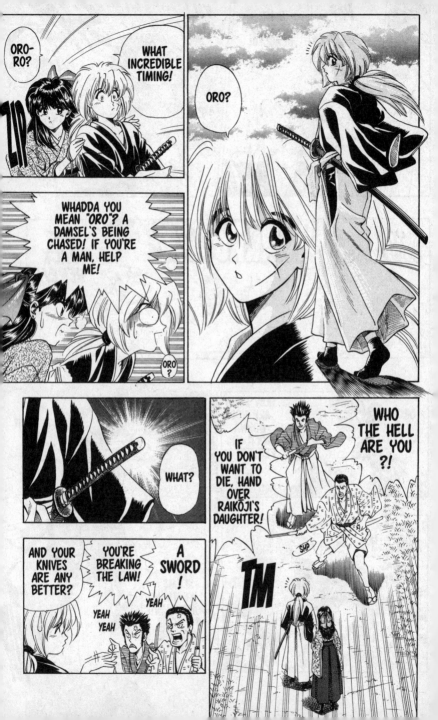

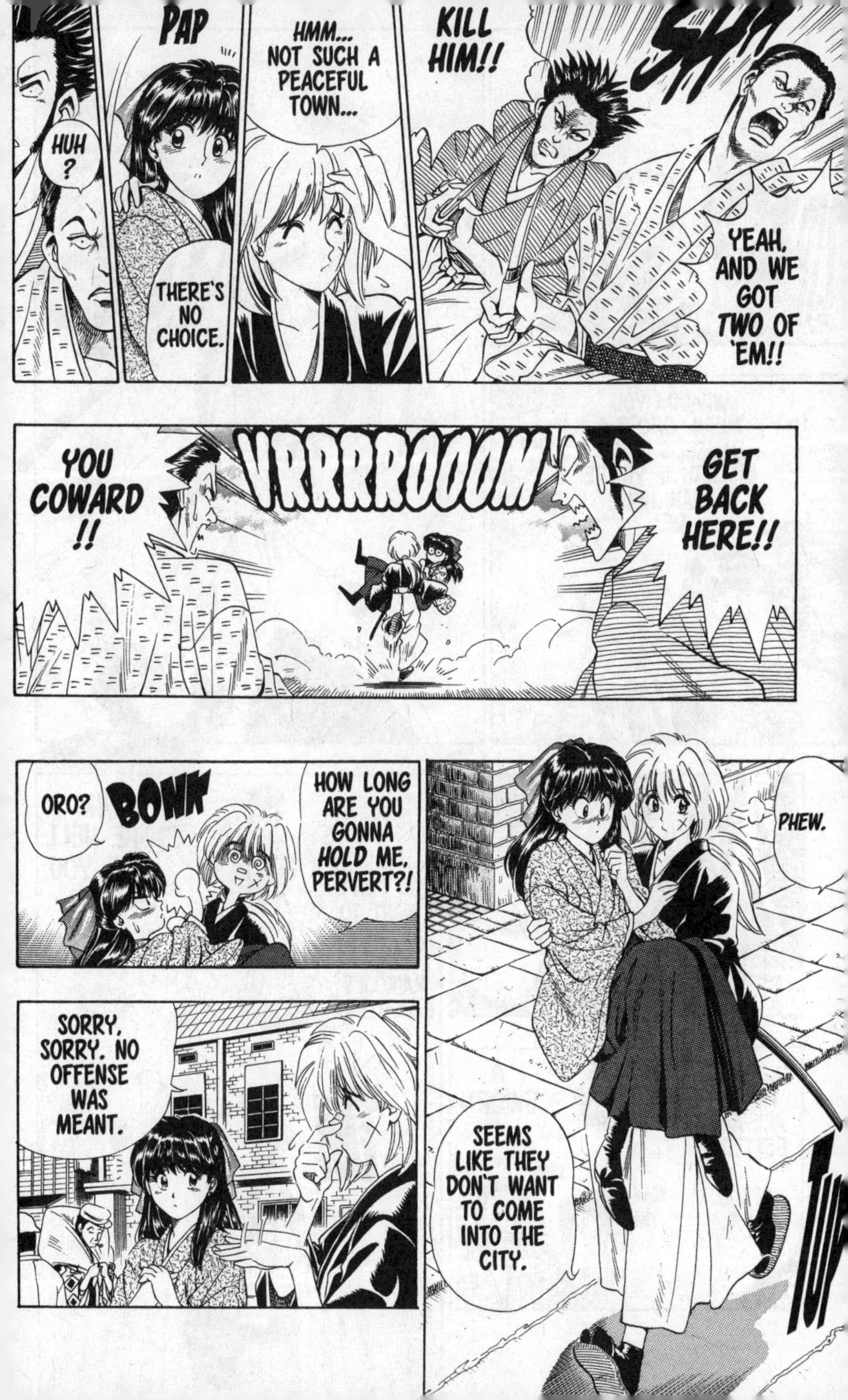

SHA
KILL HIM!!
YEAH, AND WE GOT TWO OF 'EM!!
HMM... NOT SUCH A PEACEFUL TOWN...
PAP
THERE'S NO CHOICE.
HUH?
GET BACK HERE!!
VRRRROOOM
YOU COWARD!!
PHEW.
SEEMS LIKE THEY DON'T WANT TO COME INTO THE CITY.
TUP
HOW LONG ARE YOU GONNA HOLD ME, PERVERT?!
BONK
ORO?
SORRY, SORRY. NO OFFENSE WAS MEANT.

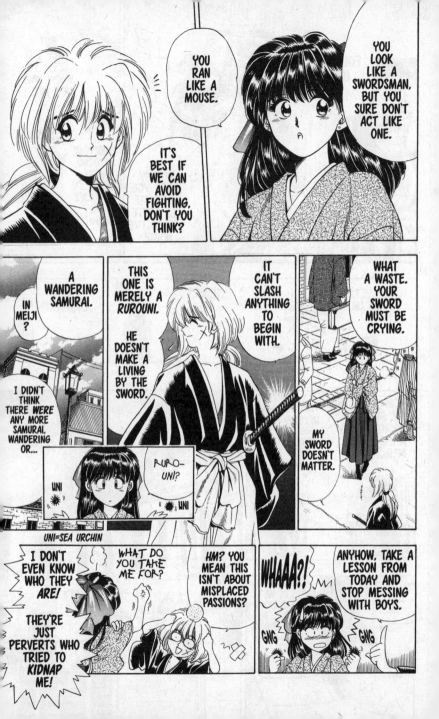

YOU RAN LIKE A MOUSE.

YOU LOOK LIKE A SWORDSMAN, BUT YOU SURE DON'T ACT LIKE ONE.

IT'S BEST IF WE CAN AVOID FIGHTING, DON'T YOU THINK?

IN MEIJI?

A WANDERING SAMURAI.

THIS ONE IS MERELY A RUROUNI.

HE DOESN'T MAKE A LIVING BY THE SWORD.

IT CAN'T SLASH ANYTHING TO BEGIN WITH.

WHAT A WASTE. YOUR SWORD MUST BE CRYING.

I DIDN'T THINK THERE WERE ANY MORE SAMURAI, WANDERING OR...

RURO-UNI?

UNI

UNI

MY SWORD DOESN'T MATTER.

UNI=SEA URCHIN

I DON'T EVEN KNOW WHO THEY ARE!

THEY'RE JUST PERVERTS WHO TRIED TO KIDNAP ME!

WHAT DO YOU TAKE ME FOR?

HM? YOU MEAN THIS ISN'T ABOUT MISPLACED PASSIONS?

WHAAA?!

ANYHOW, TAKE A LESSON FROM TODAY AND STOP MESSING WITH BOYS.

GNG

GNG

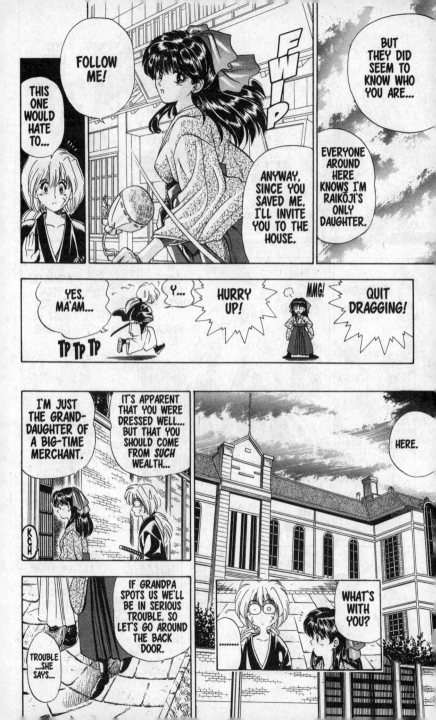

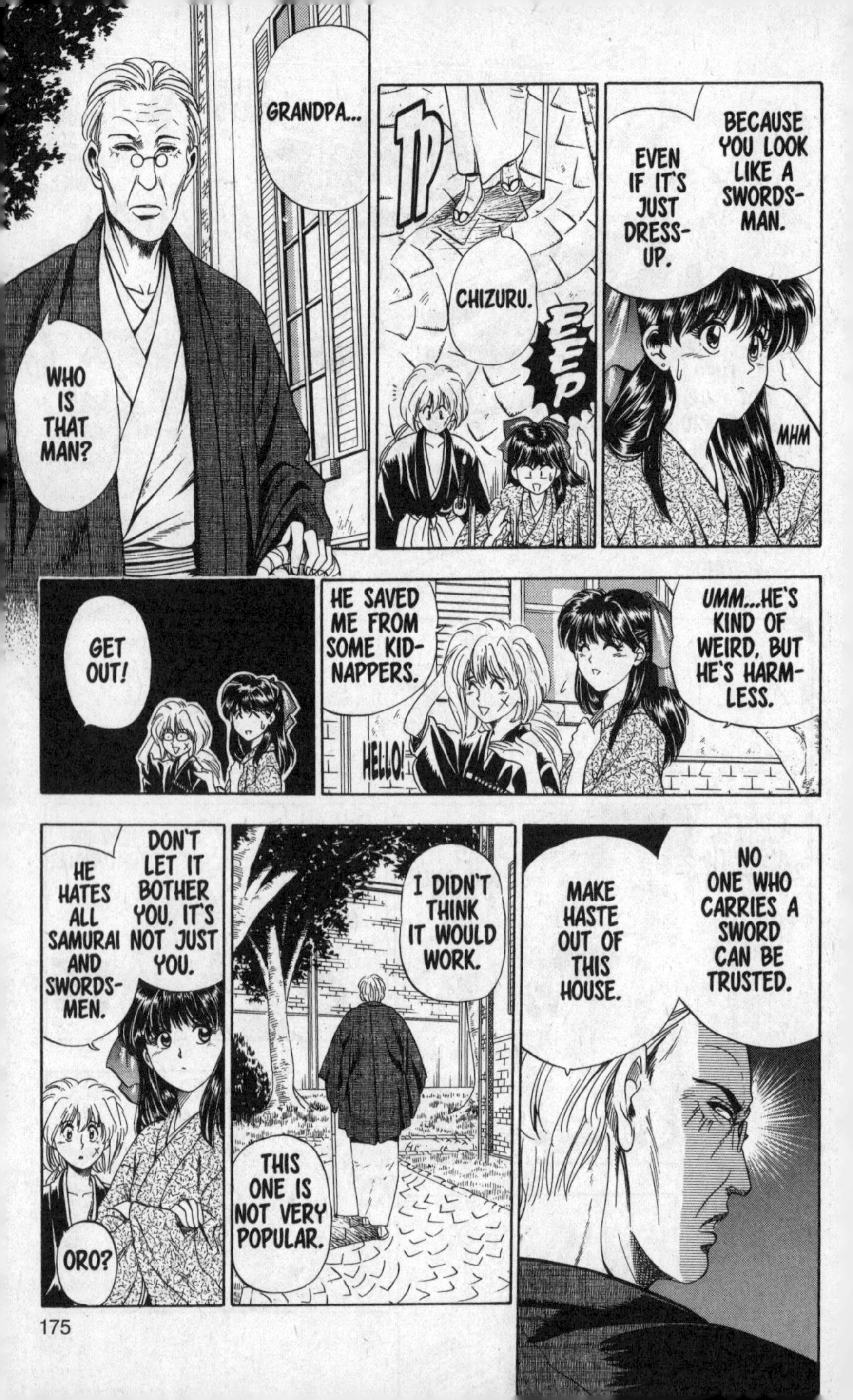
BECAUSE YOU LOOK LIKE A SWORDSMAN.
EVEN IF IT'S JUST DRESS-UP.
MHM
Tp
CHIZURU.
EEP
GRANDPA...
WHO IS THAT MAN?
UMM...HE'S KIND OF WEIRD, BUT HE'S HARMLESS.
HE SAVED ME FROM SOME KIDNAPPERS.
HELLO!
GET OUT!
NO ONE WHO CARRIES A SWORD CAN BE TRUSTED.
MAKE HASTE OUT OF THIS HOUSE.
I DIDN'T THINK IT WOULD WORK.
THIS ONE IS NOT VERY POPULAR.
DON'T LET IT BOTHER YOU, IT'S NOT JUST YOU.
HE HATES ALL SAMURAI AND SWORDSMEN.
ORO?

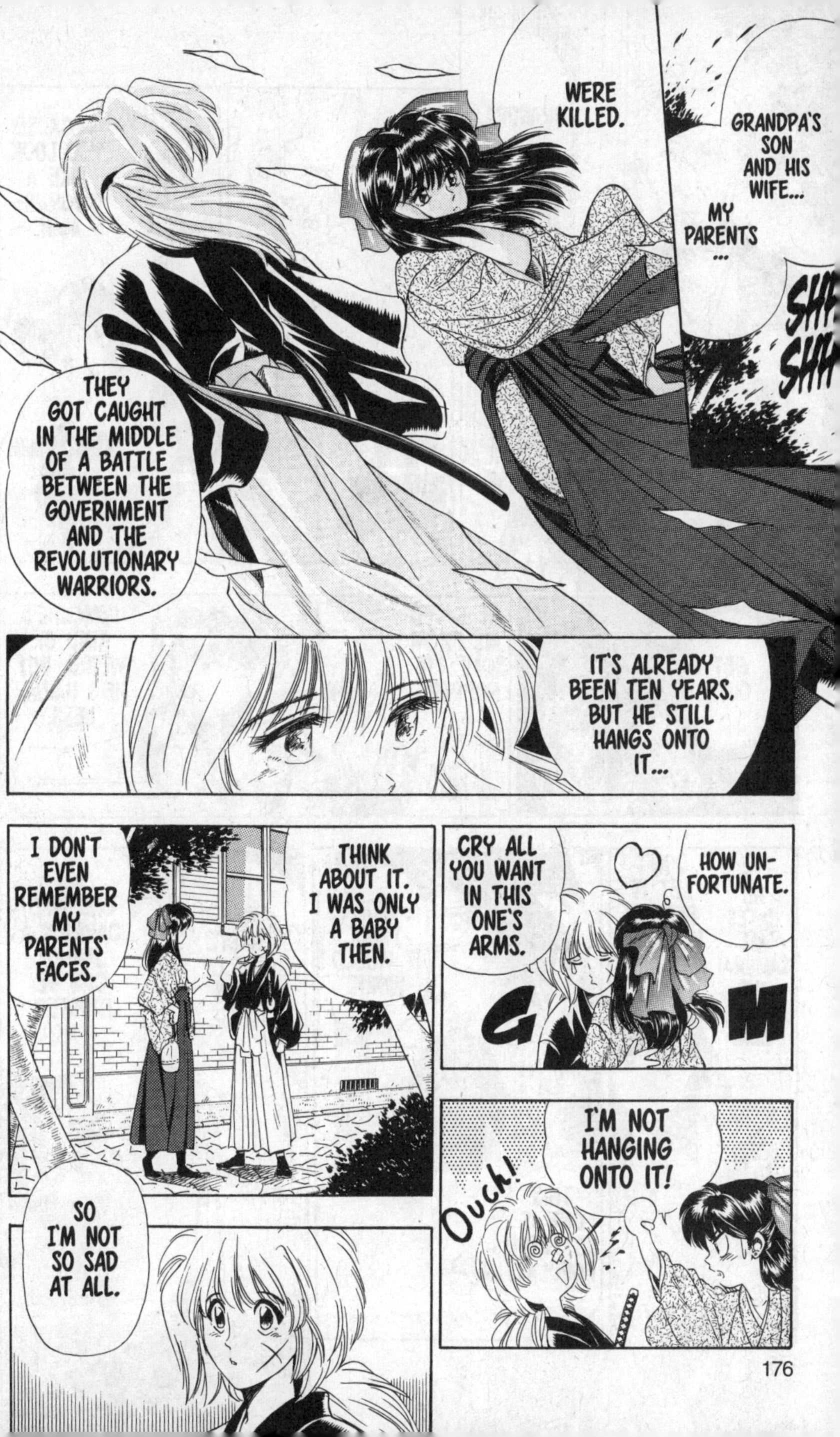
GRANDPA'S SON AND HIS WIFE...
MY PARENTS ...
SHH SHH
WERE KILLED.
THEY GOT CAUGHT IN THE MIDDLE OF A BATTLE BETWEEN THE GOVERNMENT AND THE REVOLUTIONARY WARRIORS.
IT'S ALREADY BEEN TEN YEARS, BUT HE STILL HANGS ONTO IT...
HOW UN-FORTUNATE.
CRY ALL YOU WANT IN THIS ONE'S ARMS.
G M
I'M NOT HANGING ONTO IT!
Ouch!
THINK ABOUT IT. I WAS ONLY A BABY THEN.
I DON'T EVEN REMEMBER MY PARENTS' FACES.
SO I'M NOT SO SAD AT ALL.

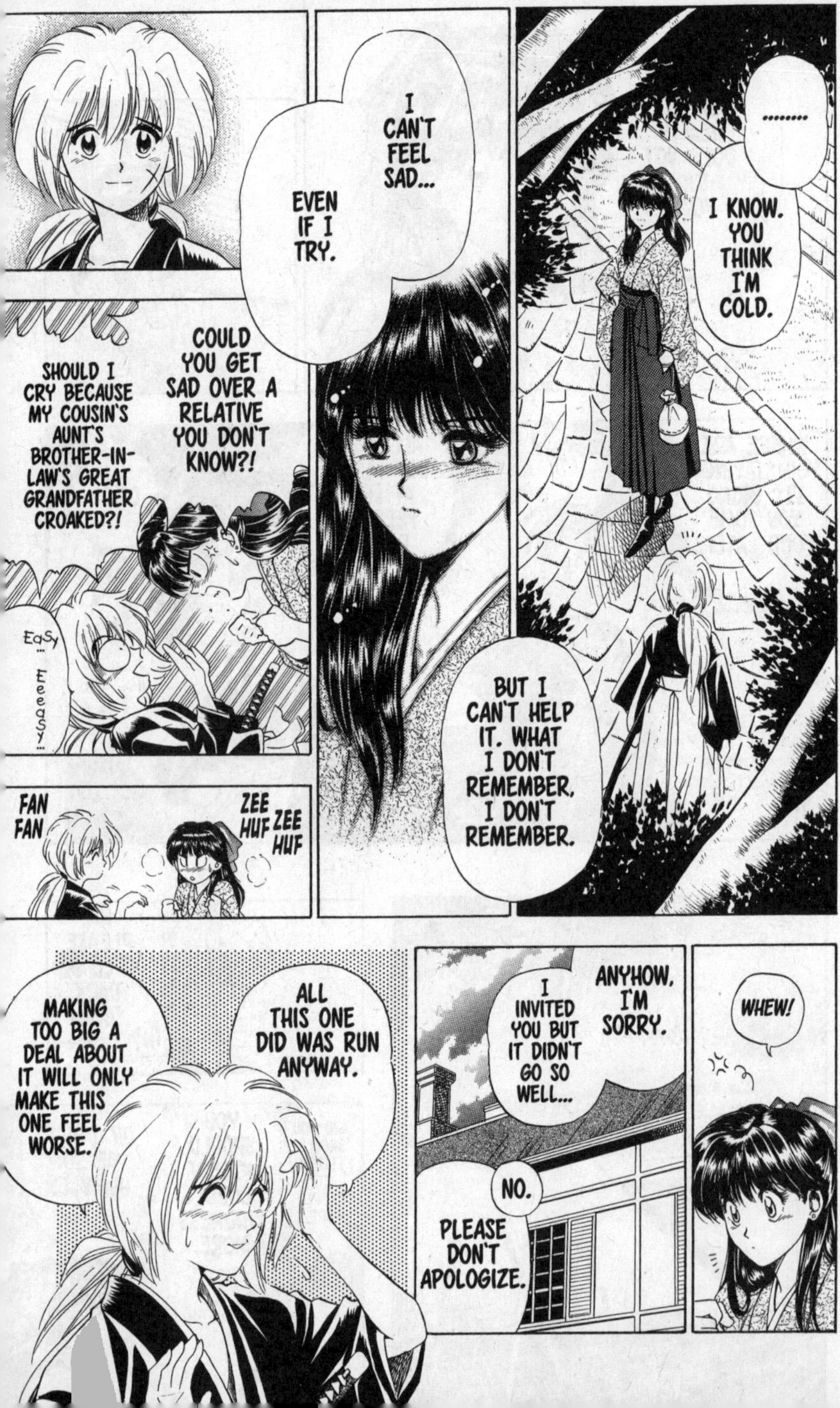
....
I KNOW. YOU THINK I'M COLD.
BUT I CAN'T HELP IT. WHAT I DON'T REMEMBER, I DON'T REMEMBER.
I CAN'T FEEL SAD...
EVEN IF I TRY.
COULD YOU GET SAD OVER A RELATIVE YOU DON'T KNOW?!
SHOULD I CRY BECAUSE MY COUSIN'S AUNT'S BROTHER-IN-LAW'S GREAT GRANDFATHER CROAKED?!
Easy...
Eeeasy...
ZEE HUF ZEE HUF
FAN FAN
WHEW!
ANYHOW, I'M SORRY.
I INVITED YOU BUT IT DIDN'T GO SO WELL...
NO.
PLEASE DON'T APOLOGIZE.
ALL THIS ONE DID WAS RUN ANYWAY.
MAKING TOO BIG A DEAL ABOUT IT WILL ONLY MAKE THIS ONE FEEL WORSE.

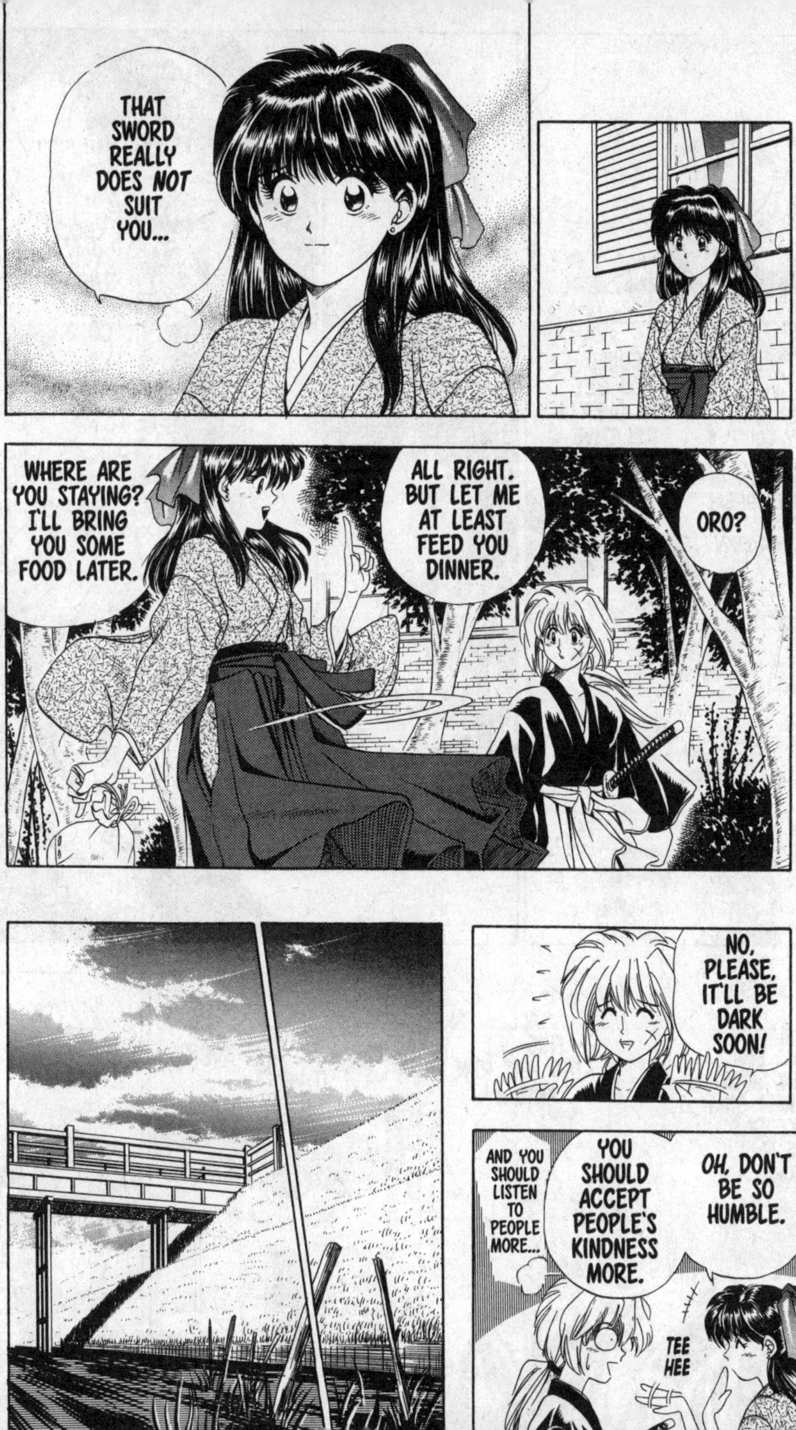
THAT SWORD REALLY DOES NOT SUIT YOU...
ORO?
ALL RIGHT. BUT LET ME AT LEAST FEED YOU DINNER.
WHERE ARE YOU STAYING? I'LL BRING YOU SOME FOOD LATER.
NO, PLEASE, IT'LL BE DARK SOON!
OH, DON'T BE SO HUMBLE.
YOU SHOULD ACCEPT PEOPLE'S KINDNESS MORE.
AND YOU SHOULD LISTEN TO PEOPLE MORE...
TEE HEE

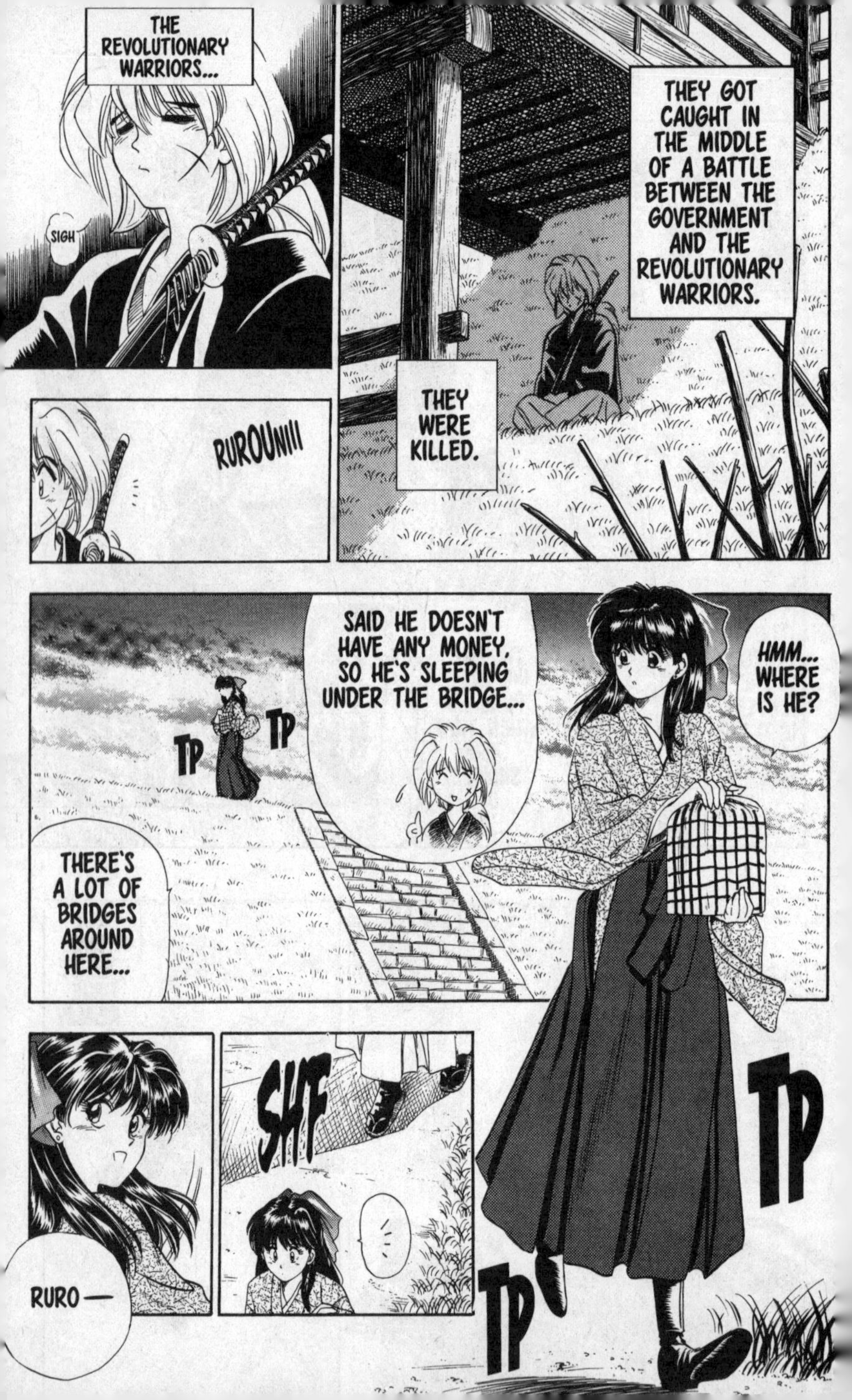
THEY GOT CAUGHT IN THE MIDDLE OF A BATTLE BETWEEN THE GOVERNMENT AND THE REVOLUTIONARY WARRIORS.
THEY WERE KILLED.
THE REVOLUTIONARY WARRIORS...
SIGH
RUROUNIII
HMM... WHERE IS HE?
SAID HE DOESN'T HAVE ANY MONEY, SO HE'S SLEEPING UNDER THE BRIDGE...
TP
TP
THERE'S A LOT OF BRIDGES AROUND HERE...
TP
TP
SHF
RURO—

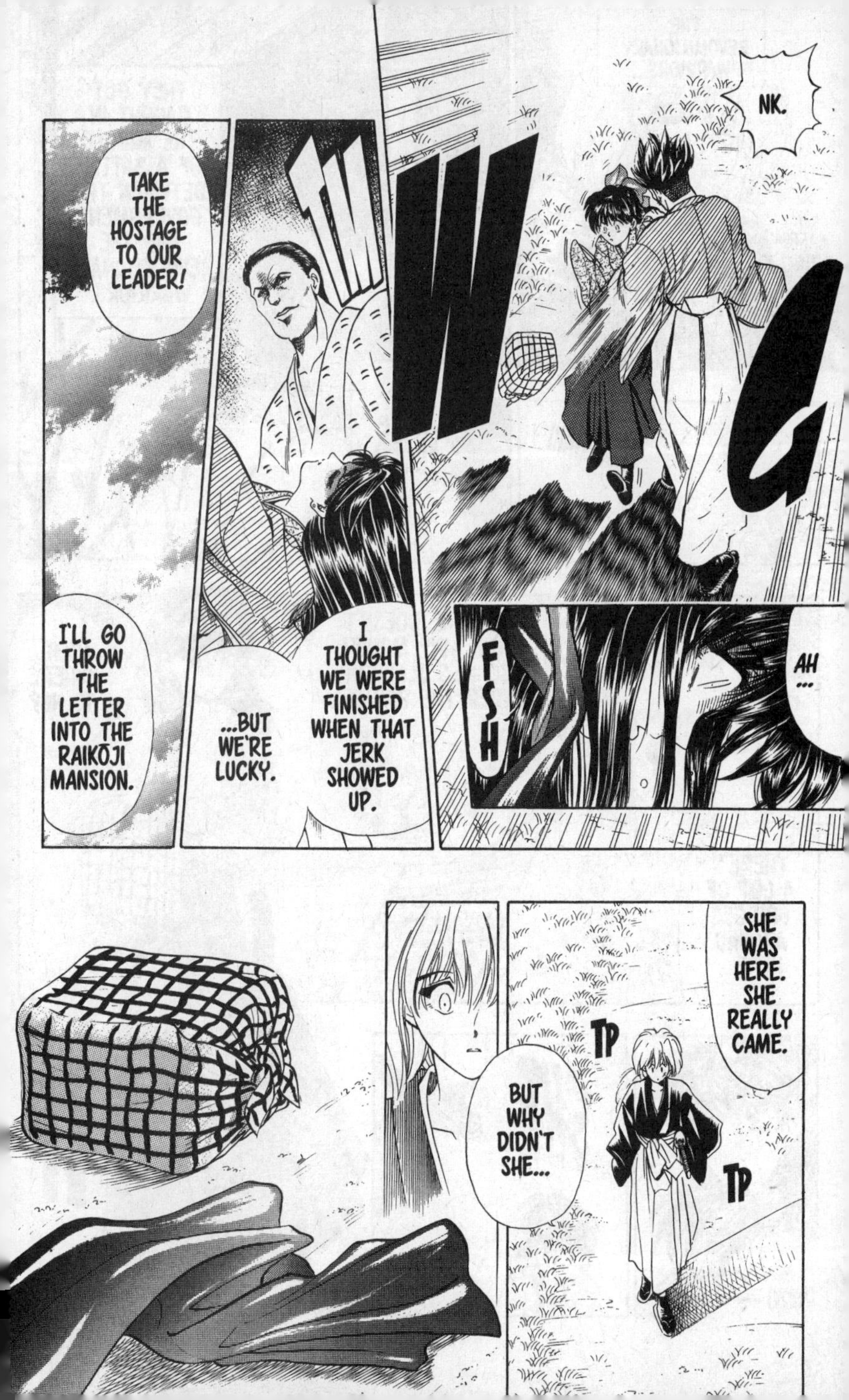
NK.
AH...
FSH
I THOUGHT WE WERE FINISHED WHEN THAT JERK SHOWED UP.
...BUT WE'RE LUCKY.
TAKE THE HOSTAGE TO OUR LEADER!
I'LL GO THROW THE LETTER INTO THE RAIKŌJI MANSION.
SHE WAS HERE. SHE REALLY CAME.
TP
TP
BUT WHY DIDN'T SHE...

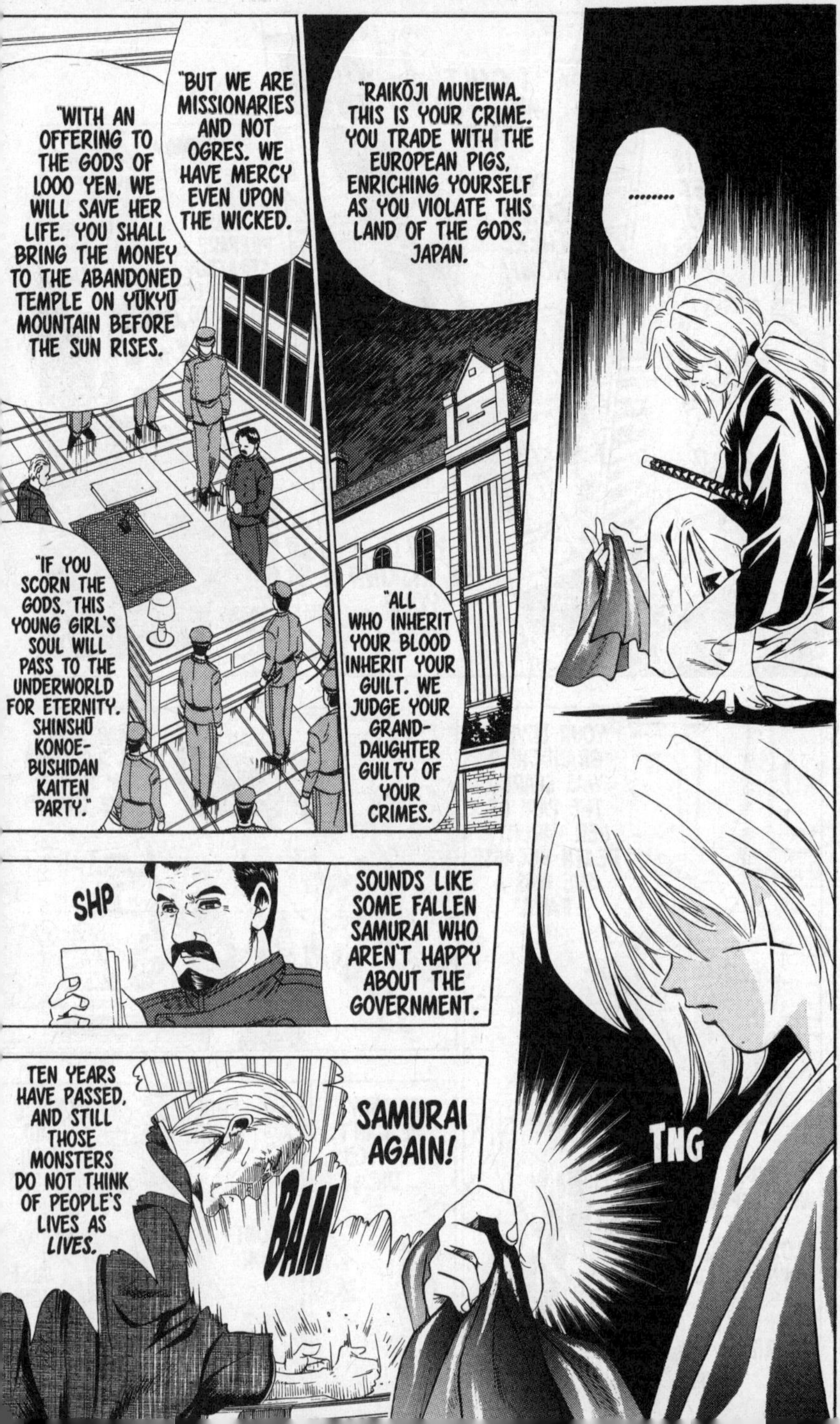
....
TNG
"RAIKŌJI MUNEIWA. THIS IS YOUR CRIME. YOU TRADE WITH THE EUROPEAN PIGS, ENRICHING YOURSELF AS YOU VIOLATE THIS LAND OF THE GODS, JAPAN.
"ALL WHO INHERIT YOUR BLOOD INHERIT YOUR GUILT. WE JUDGE YOUR GRAND-DAUGHTER GUILTY OF YOUR CRIMES.
"BUT WE ARE MISSIONARIES AND NOT OGRES. WE HAVE MERCY EVEN UPON THE WICKED.
"WITH AN OFFERING TO THE GODS OF 1,000 YEN, WE WILL SAVE HER LIFE. YOU SHALL BRING THE MONEY TO THE ABANDONED TEMPLE ON YŪKYŪ MOUNTAIN BEFORE THE SUN RISES.
"IF YOU SCORN THE GODS, THIS YOUNG GIRL'S SOUL WILL PASS TO THE UNDERWORLD FOR ETERNITY. SHINSHŪ KONOE-BUSHIDAN KAITEN PARTY."
SOUNDS LIKE SOME FALLEN SAMURAI WHO AREN'T HAPPY ABOUT THE GOVERNMENT.
SHP
SAMURAI AGAIN!
TEN YEARS HAVE PASSED, AND STILL THOSE MONSTERS DO NOT THINK OF PEOPLE'S LIVES AS *LIVES*.
BAM

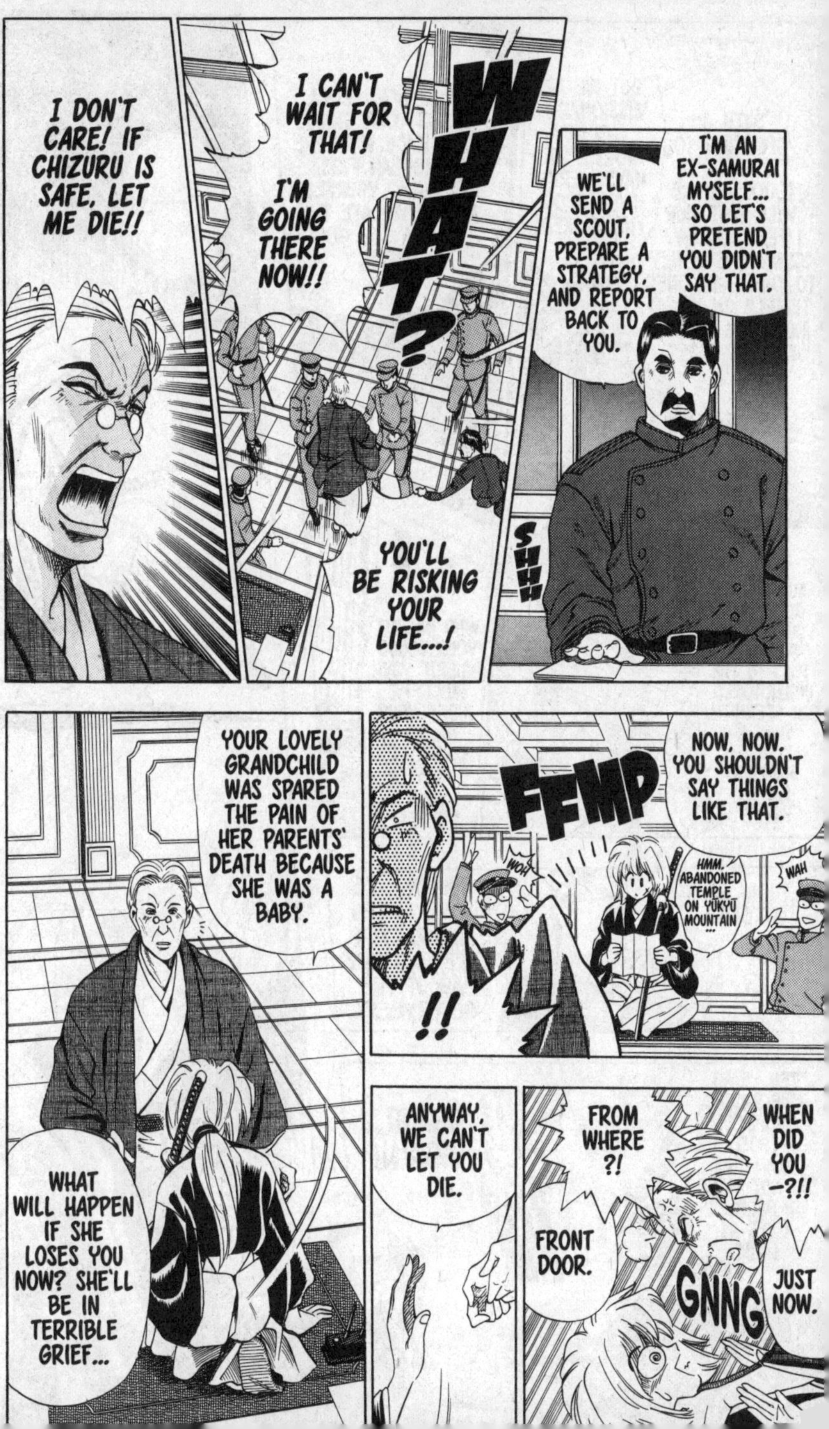
I'M AN EX-SAMURAI MYSELF... SO LET'S PRETEND YOU DIDN'T SAY THAT.
WE'LL SEND A SCOUT, PREPARE A STRATEGY, AND REPORT BACK TO YOU.
SHHH
WHAT?
YOU'LL BE RISKING YOUR LIFE...!
I CAN'T WAIT FOR THAT!
I'M GOING THERE NOW!!
I DON'T CARE! IF CHIZURU IS SAFE, LET ME DIE!!
NOW, NOW. YOU SHOULDN'T SAY THINGS LIKE THAT.
WAH
HMM. ABANDONED TEMPLE ON YUKYU MOUNTAIN...
FFMP
WOH
!!
WHEN DID YOU-?!!
JUST NOW.
GNNG
FROM WHERE?!
FRONT DOOR.
ANYWAY, WE CAN'T LET YOU DIE.
YOUR LOVELY GRANDCHILD WAS SPARED THE PAIN OF HER PARENTS' DEATH BECAUSE SHE WAS A BABY.
WHAT WILL HAPPEN IF SHE LOSES YOU NOW? SHE'LL BE IN TERRIBLE GRIEF...

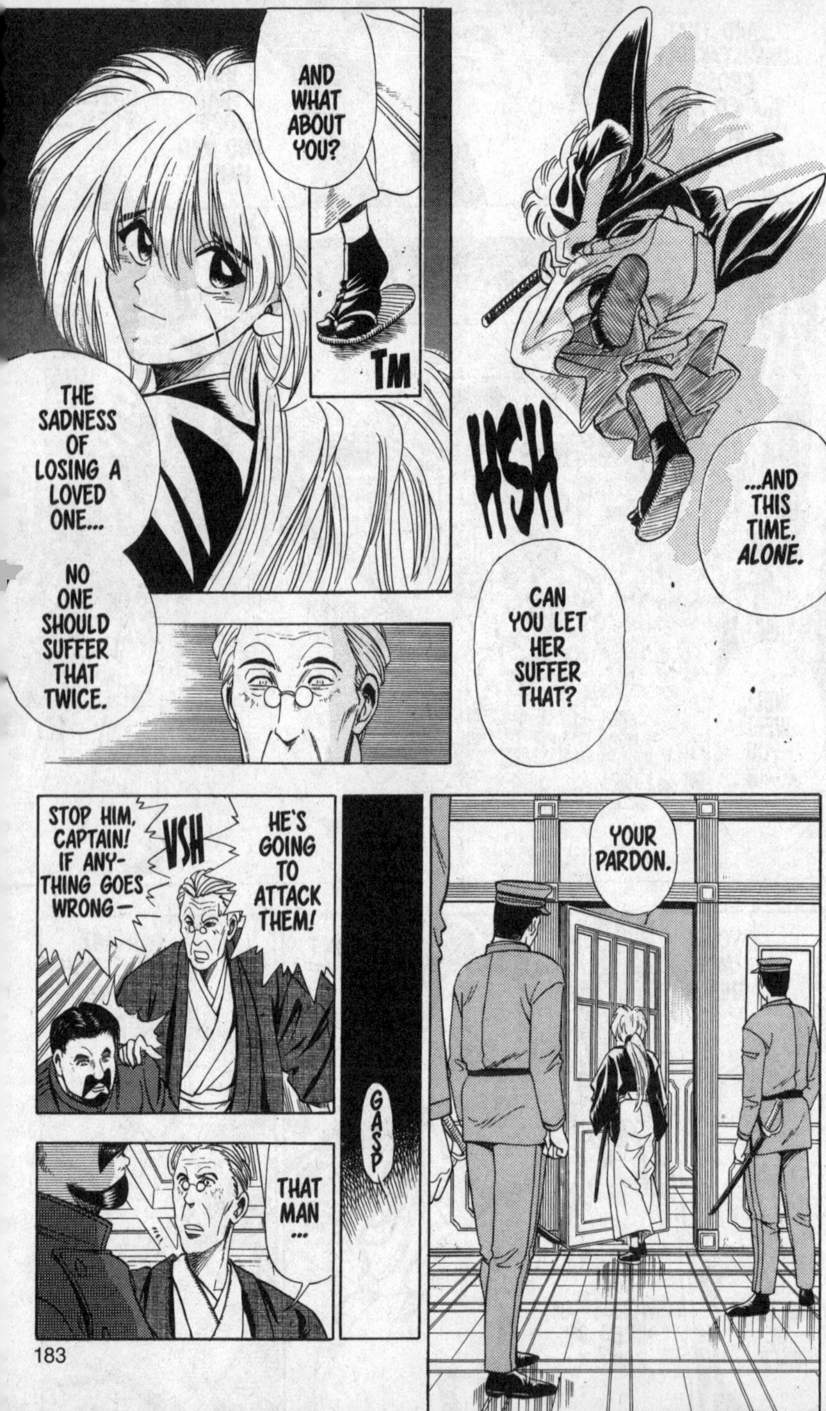
AND WHAT ABOUT YOU?
TM
THE SADNESS OF LOSING A LOVED ONE...
NO ONE SHOULD SUFFER THAT TWICE.
VSH
...AND THIS TIME, ALONE.
CAN YOU LET HER SUFFER THAT?
YOUR PARDON.
GASP
HE'S GOING TO ATTACK THEM!
VSH
STOP HIM, CAPTAIN! IF ANY-THING GOES WRONG—
THAT MAN ...

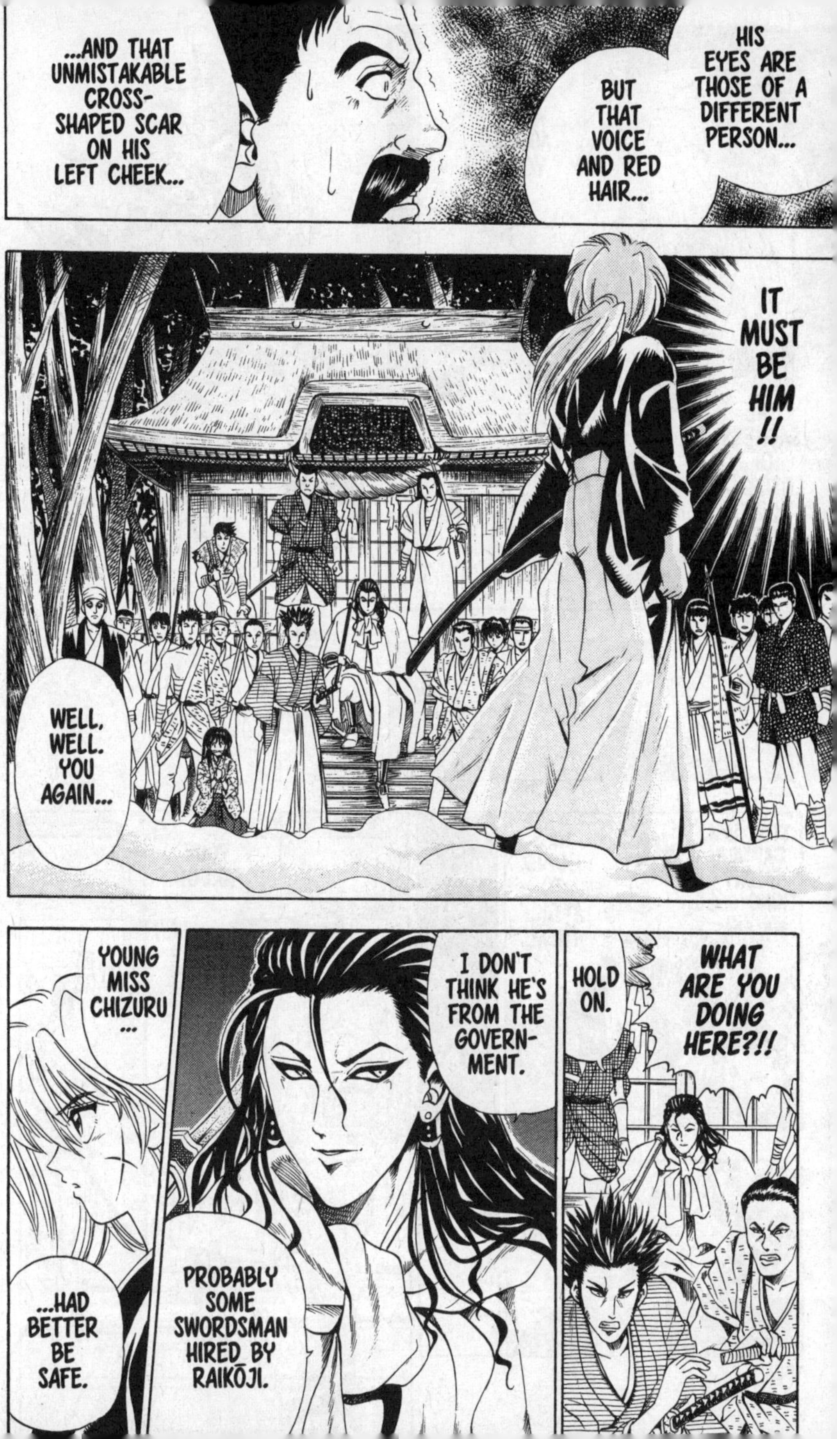
HIS EYES ARE THOSE OF A DIFFERENT PERSON...
BUT THAT VOICE AND RED HAIR...
...AND THAT UNMISTAKABLE CROSS-SHAPED SCAR ON HIS LEFT CHEEK...
IT MUST BE HIM!!
WELL, WELL. YOU AGAIN...
WHAT ARE YOU DOING HERE?!!
HOLD ON.
I DON'T THINK HE'S FROM THE GOVERNMENT.
PROBABLY SOME SWORDSMAN HIRED BY RAIKŌJI.
YOUNG MISS CHIZURU...
...HAD BETTER BE SAFE.

READ THIS WAY

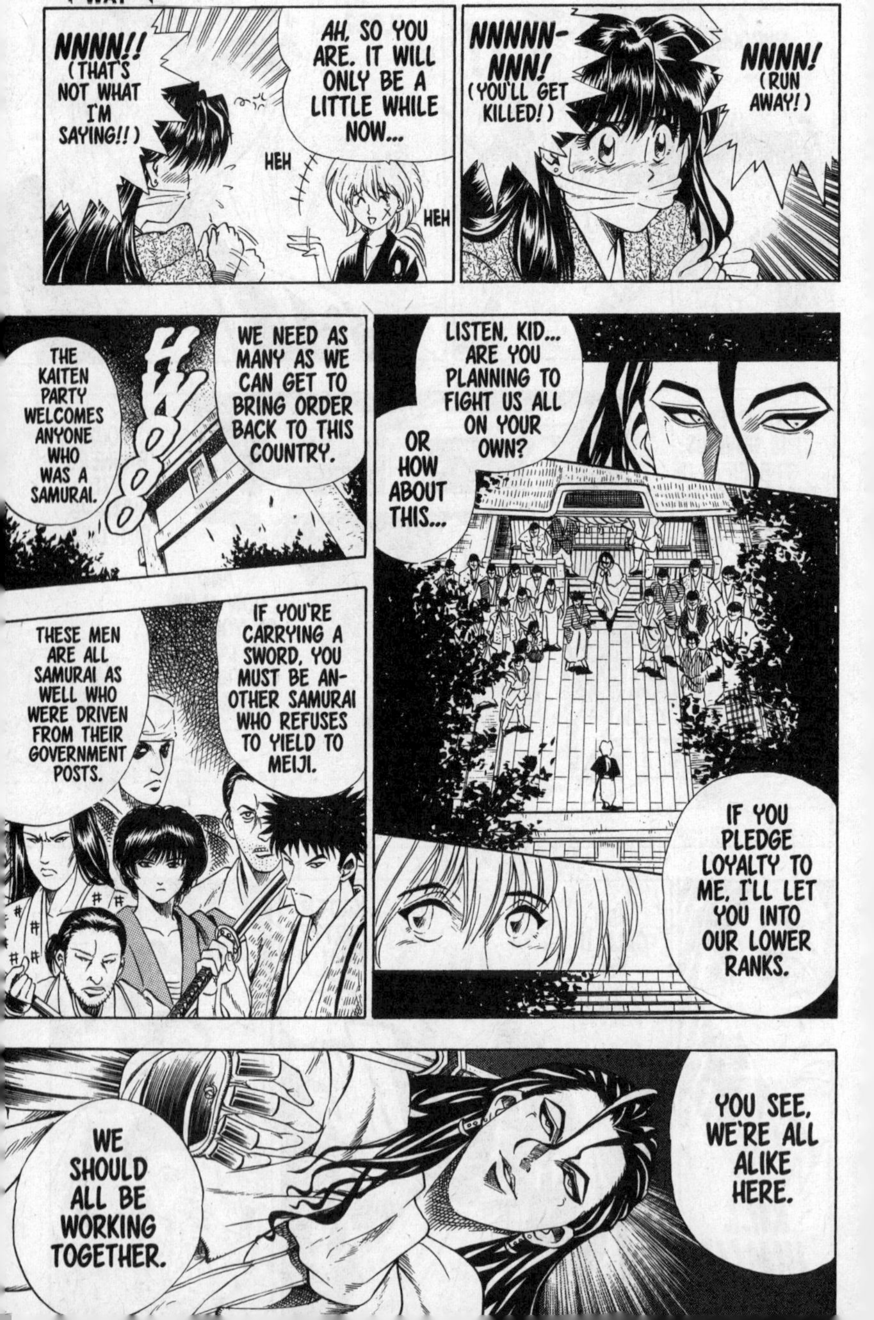
NNNN! (RUN AWAY!)
NNNNN-NNN! (YOU'LL GET KILLED!)
AH, SO YOU ARE. IT WILL ONLY BE A LITTLE WHILE NOW...
NNNN!! (THAT'S NOT WHAT I'M SAYING!!)
HEH
HEH
LISTEN, KID... ARE YOU PLANNING TO FIGHT US ALL ON YOUR OWN?
OR HOW ABOUT THIS...
IF YOU PLEDGE LOYALTY TO ME, I'LL LET YOU INTO OUR LOWER RANKS.
WE NEED AS MANY AS WE CAN GET TO BRING ORDER BACK TO THIS COUNTRY.
THE KAITEN PARTY WELCOMES ANYONE WHO WAS A SAMURAI.
IF YOU'RE CARRYING A SWORD, YOU MUST BE AN-OTHER SAMURAI WHO REFUSES TO YIELD TO MEIJI.
THESE MEN ARE ALL SAMURAI AS WELL WHO WERE DRIVEN FROM THEIR GOVERNMENT POSTS.
YOU SEE, WE'RE ALL ALIKE HERE.
WE SHOULD ALL BE WORKING TOGETHER.

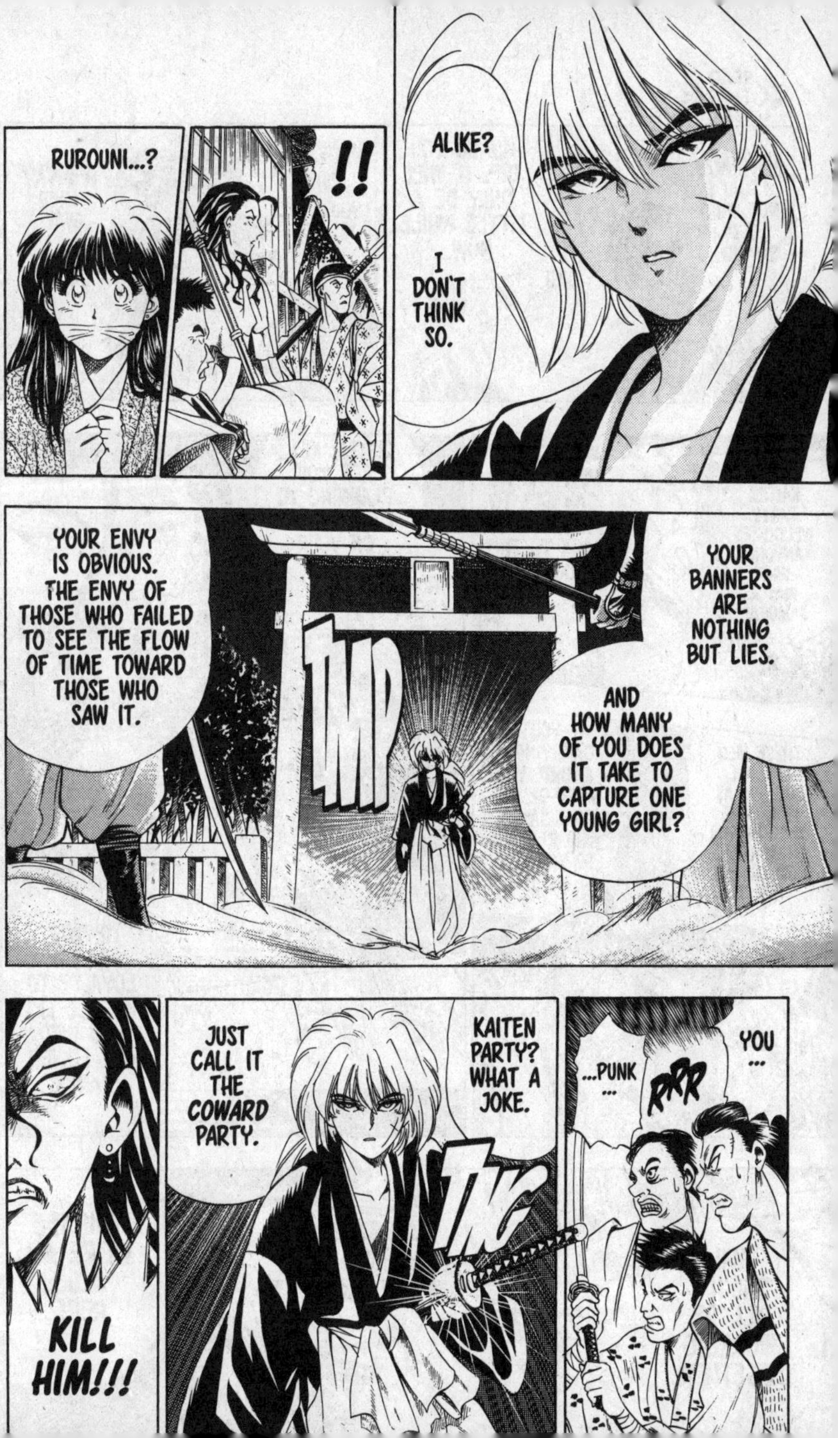
ALIKE?
I DON'T THINK SO.
!!
RUROUNI...?
YOUR ENVY IS OBVIOUS. THE ENVY OF THOSE WHO FAILED TO SEE THE FLOW OF TIME TOWARD THOSE WHO SAW IT.
YOUR BANNERS ARE NOTHING BUT LIES.
AND HOW MANY OF YOU DOES IT TAKE TO CAPTURE ONE YOUNG GIRL?
TMP
YOU ...
RRR
...PUNK ...
KAITEN PARTY? WHAT A JOKE.
JUST CALL IT THE COWARD PARTY.
TNG
KILL HIM!!!

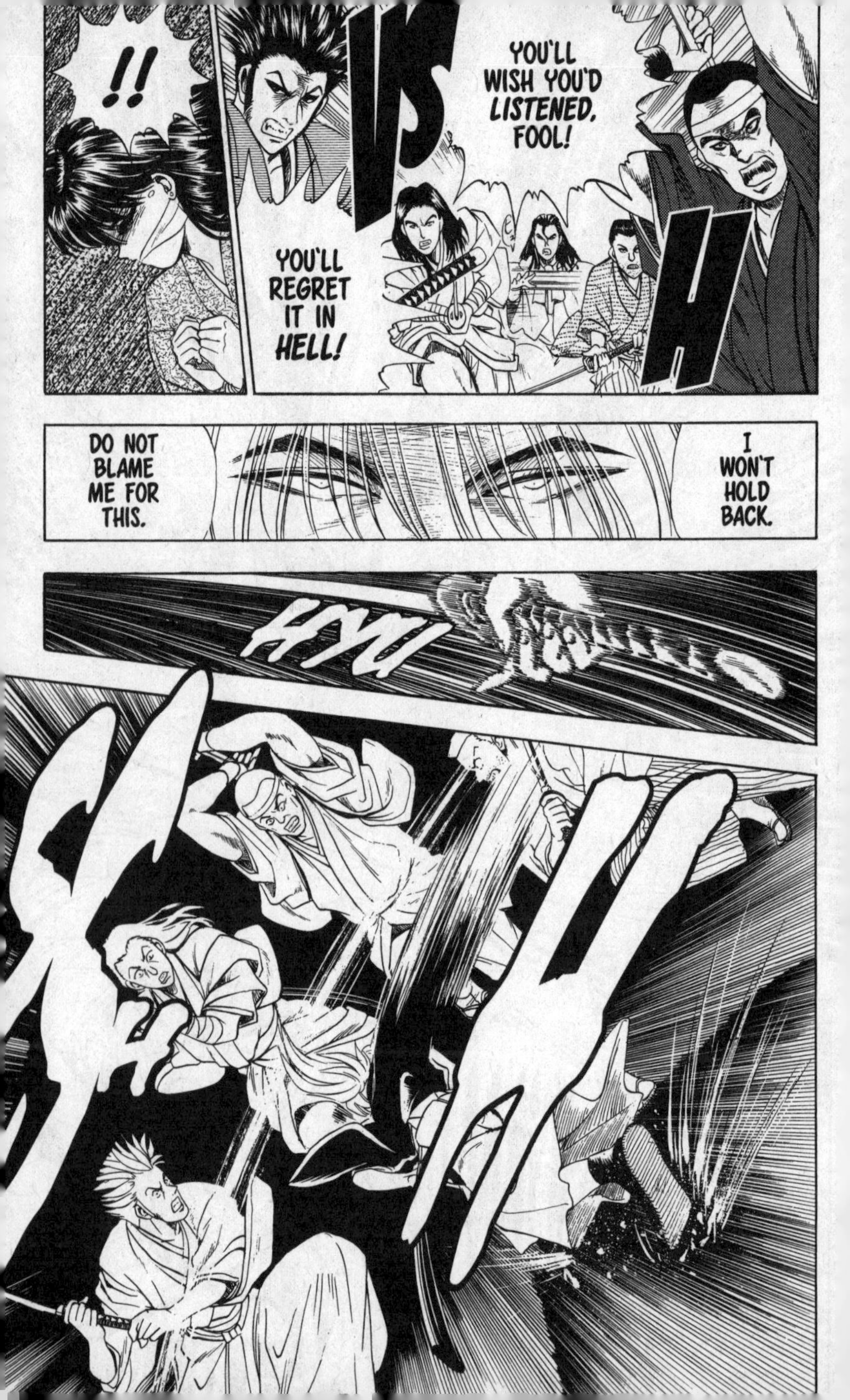

YOU'LL WISH YOU'D LISTENED, FOOL!
YOU'LL REGRET IT IN HELL!
!!
I WON'T HOLD BACK.
DO NOT BLAME ME FOR THIS.
HYU

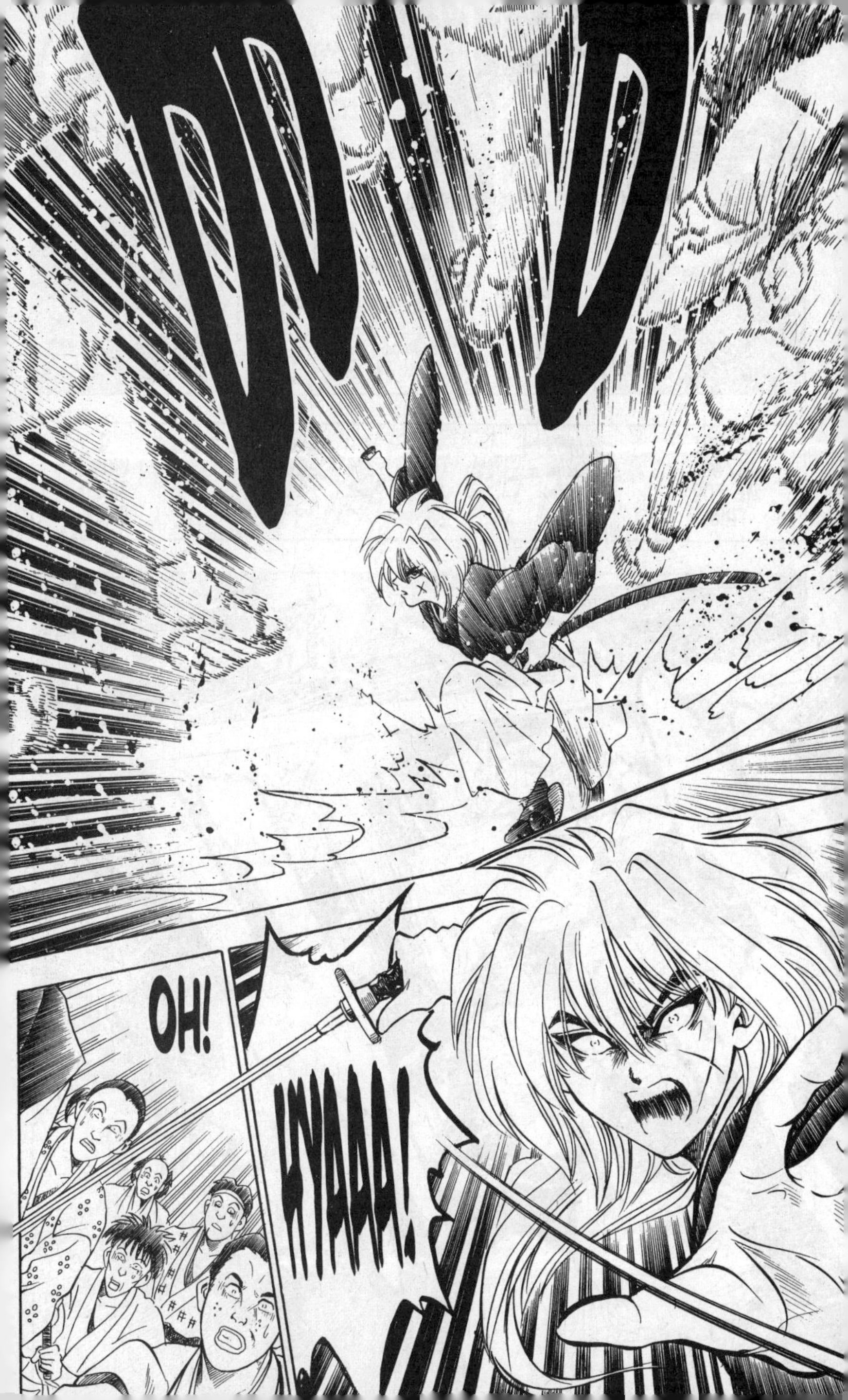
HYAAA!
OH!

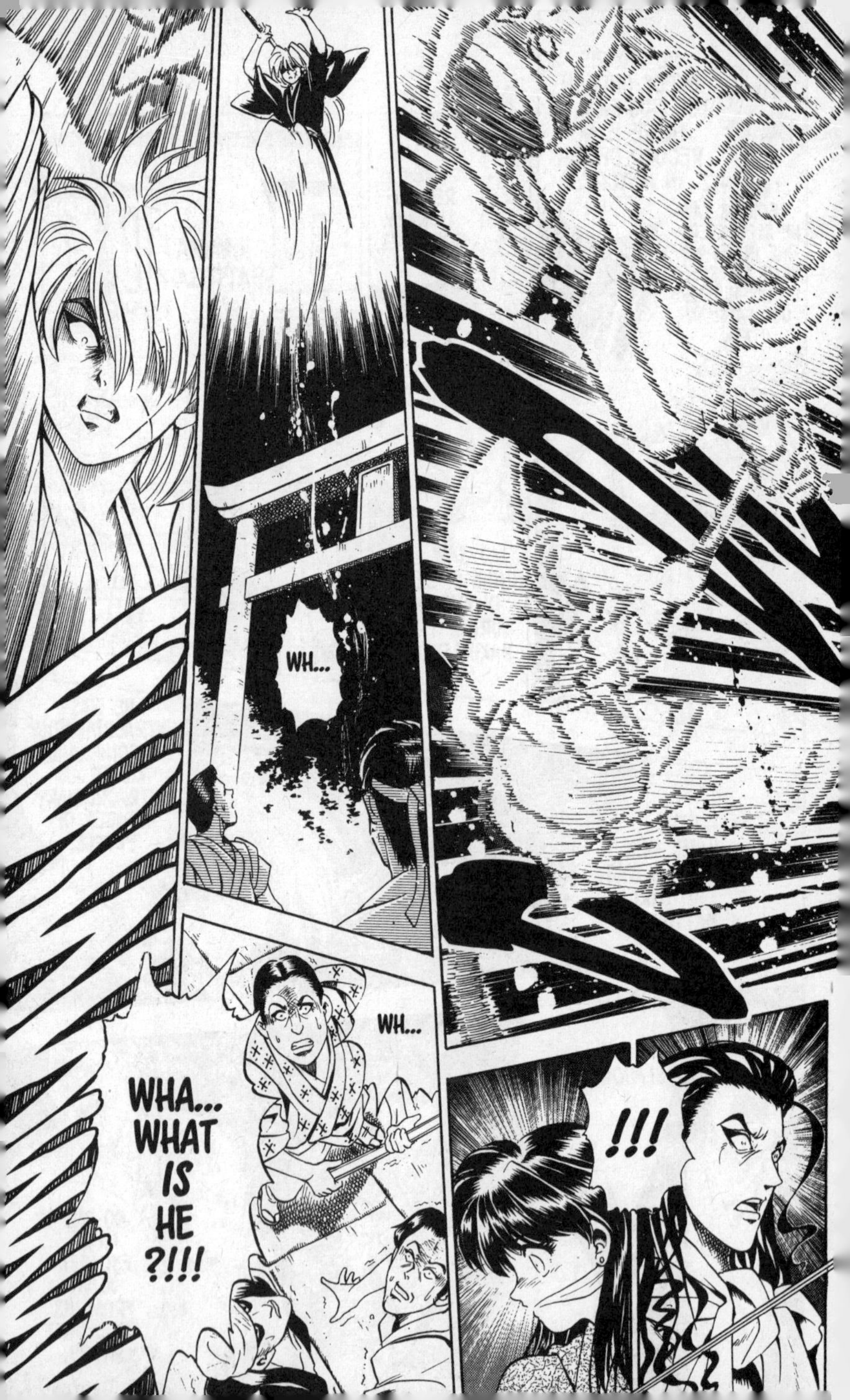
WH...
!!!
WH...
WHA... WHAT IS HE?!!!

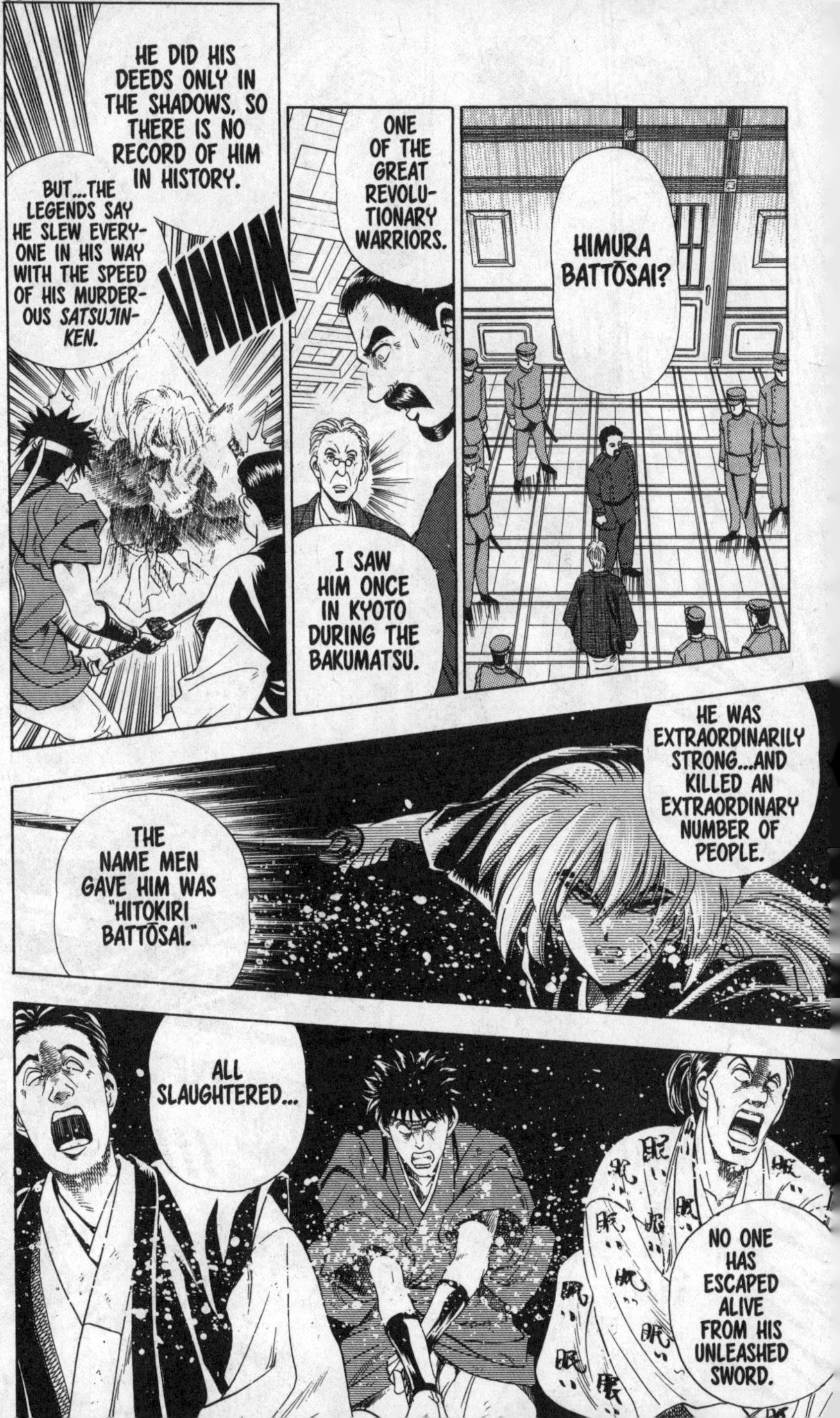
HIMURA BATTŌSAI?
ONE OF THE GREAT REVOLUTIONARY WARRIORS.
I SAW HIM ONCE IN KYOTO DURING THE BAKUMATSU.
HE DID HIS DEEDS ONLY IN THE SHADOWS, SO THERE IS NO RECORD OF HIM IN HISTORY.
BUT...THE LEGENDS SAY HE SLEW EVERYONE IN HIS WAY WITH THE SPEED OF HIS MURDEROUS *SATSUJINKEN.*
VNNNN
HE WAS EXTRAORDINARILY STRONG...AND KILLED AN EXTRAORDINARY NUMBER OF PEOPLE.
THE NAME MEN GAVE HIM WAS "HITOKIRI BATTŌSAI."
NO ONE HAS ESCAPED ALIVE FROM HIS UNLEASHED SWORD.
ALL SLAUGHTERED...

READ THIS WAY

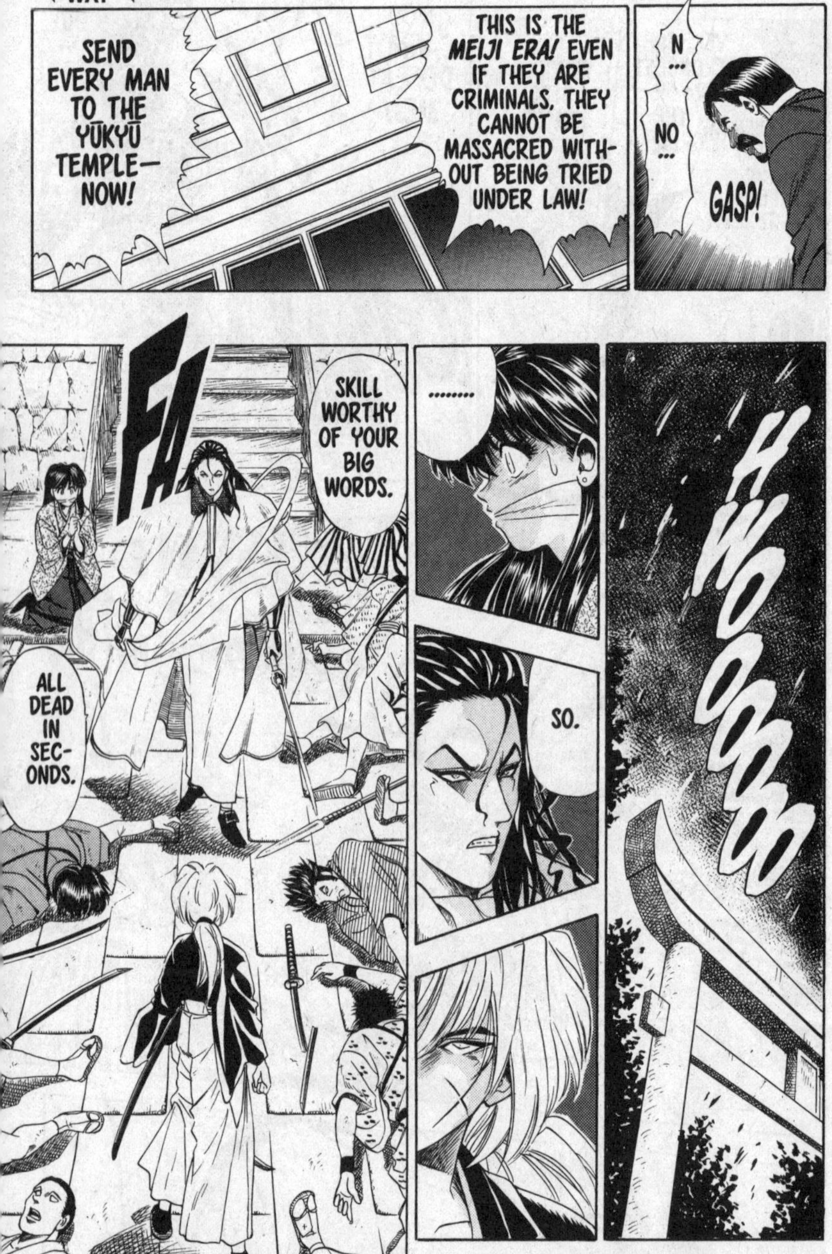

N...
NO...
GASP!
THIS IS THE MEIJI ERA! EVEN IF THEY ARE CRIMINALS, THEY CANNOT BE MASSACRED WITHOUT BEING TRIED UNDER LAW!
SEND EVERY MAN TO THE YŪKYŪ TEMPLE—NOW!
HWOOOOOO
....
SO.
SKILL WORTHY OF YOUR BIG WORDS.
FA
ALL DEAD IN SECONDS.

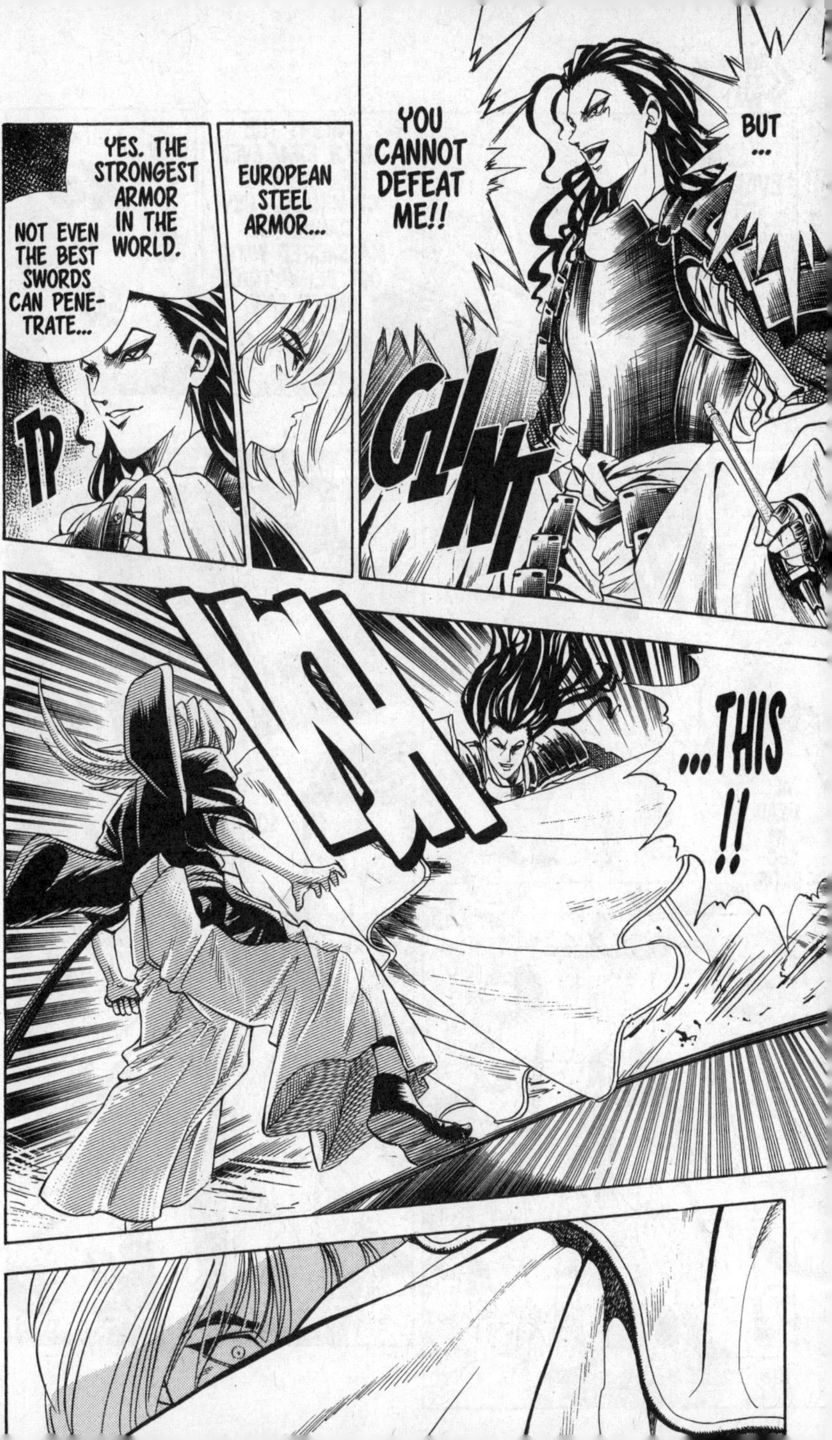
BUT ...
YOU CANNOT DEFEAT ME!!
GLINT
EUROPEAN STEEL ARMOR...
YES. THE STRONGEST ARMOR IN THE WORLD.
NOT EVEN THE BEST SWORDS CAN PENE-TRATE...
TP
...THIS !!

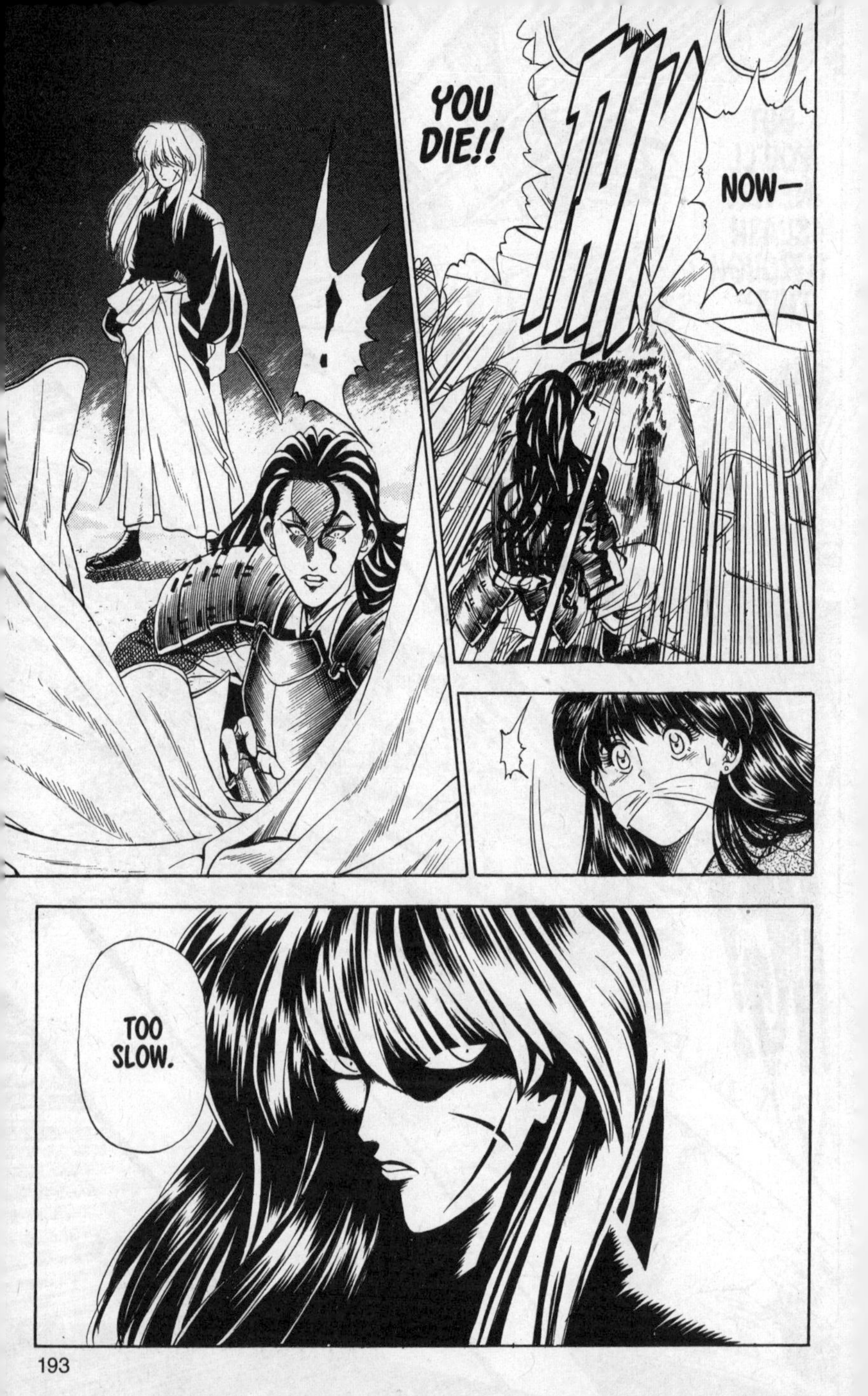
NOW—
YOU DIE!!
!
TOO SLOW.

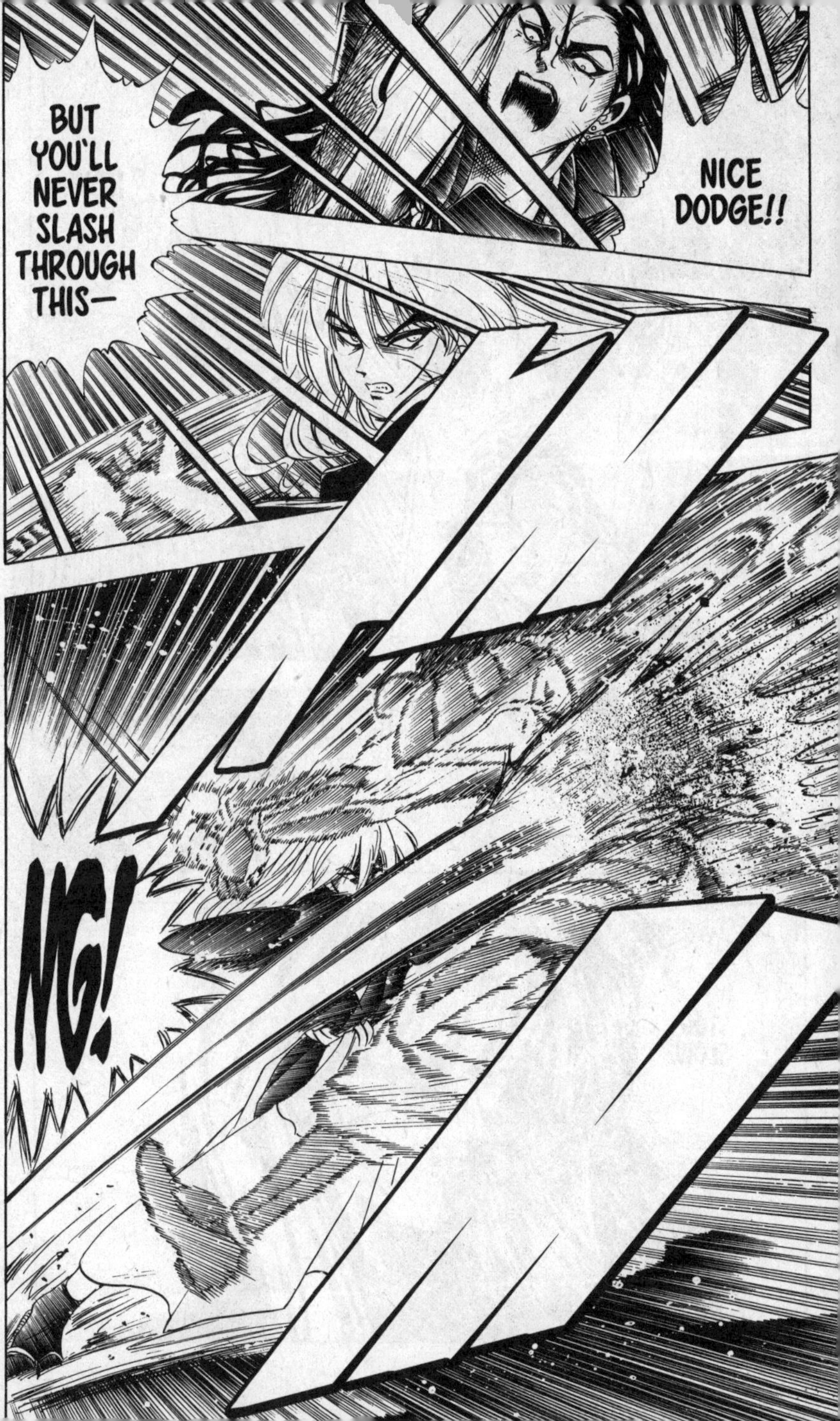
NICE DODGE!!
BUT YOU'LL NEVER SLASH THROUGH THIS—
NG!

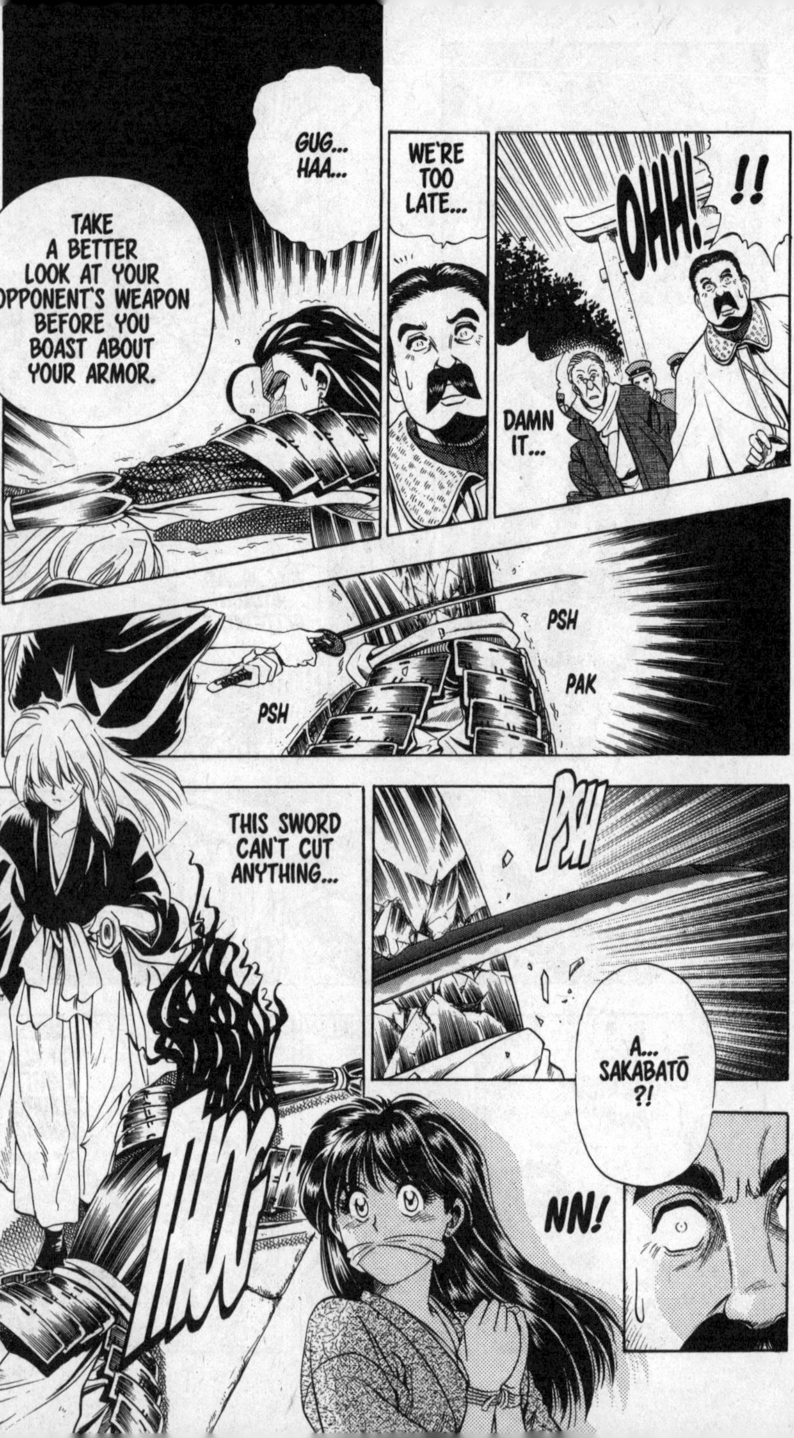
OHH!
!!
DAMN IT...
WE'RE TOO LATE...
GUG... HAA...
TAKE A BETTER LOOK AT YOUR OPPONENT'S WEAPON BEFORE YOU BOAST ABOUT YOUR ARMOR.
PSH
PAK
PSH
PSH
A... SAKABATŌ ?!
NN!
THIS SWORD CAN'T CUT ANYTHING...
SHP

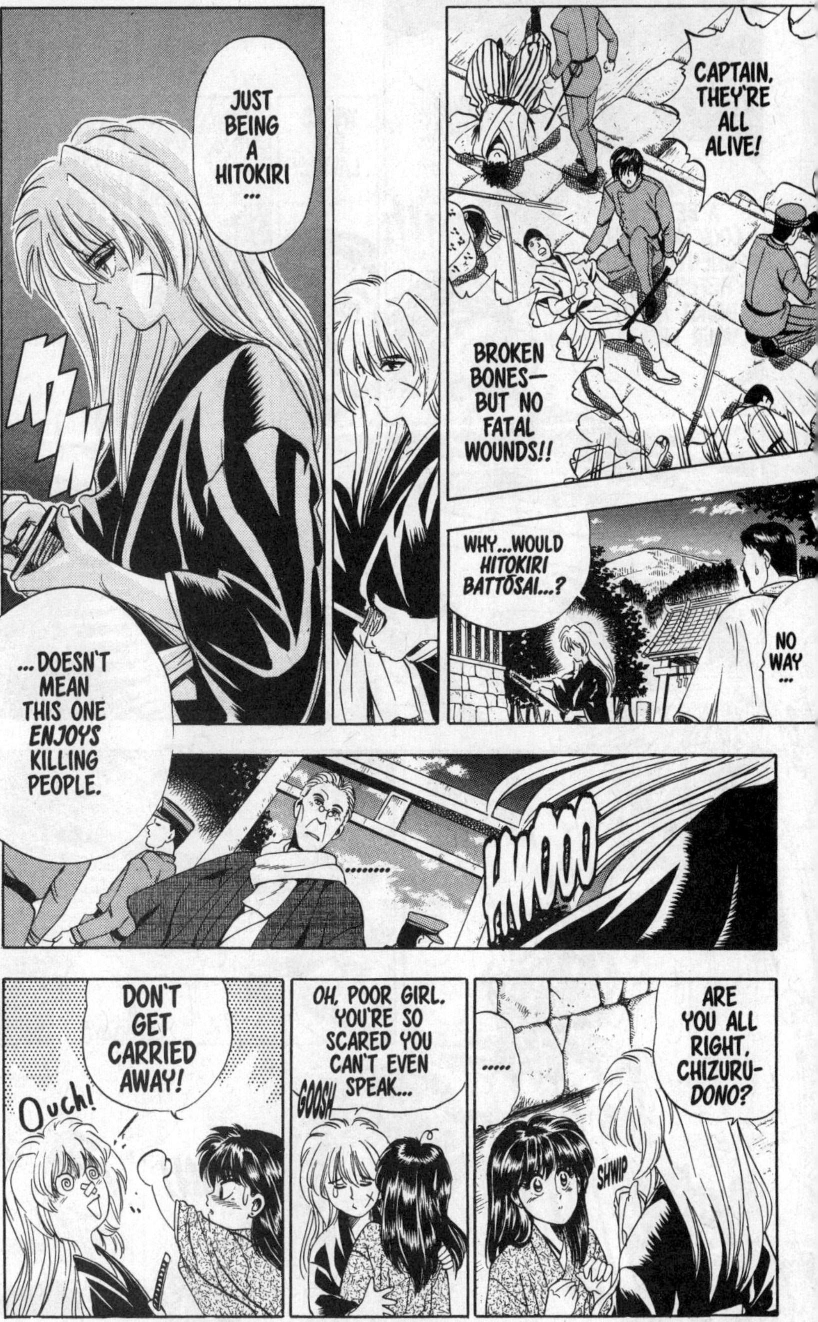
CAPTAIN, THEY'RE ALL ALIVE!
BROKEN BONES— BUT NO FATAL WOUNDS!!
WHY...WOULD HITOKIRI BATTŌSAI...?
NO WAY...
KIN
JUST BEING A HITOKIRI...
...DOESN'T MEAN THIS ONE ENJOYS KILLING PEOPLE.
WHOOO
....
ARE YOU ALL RIGHT, CHIZURU-DONO?
SHWIP
.....
OH, POOR GIRL. YOU'RE SO SCARED YOU CAN'T EVEN SPEAK...
GOOSH
DON'T GET CARRIED AWAY!
Ouch!

READ THIS WAY

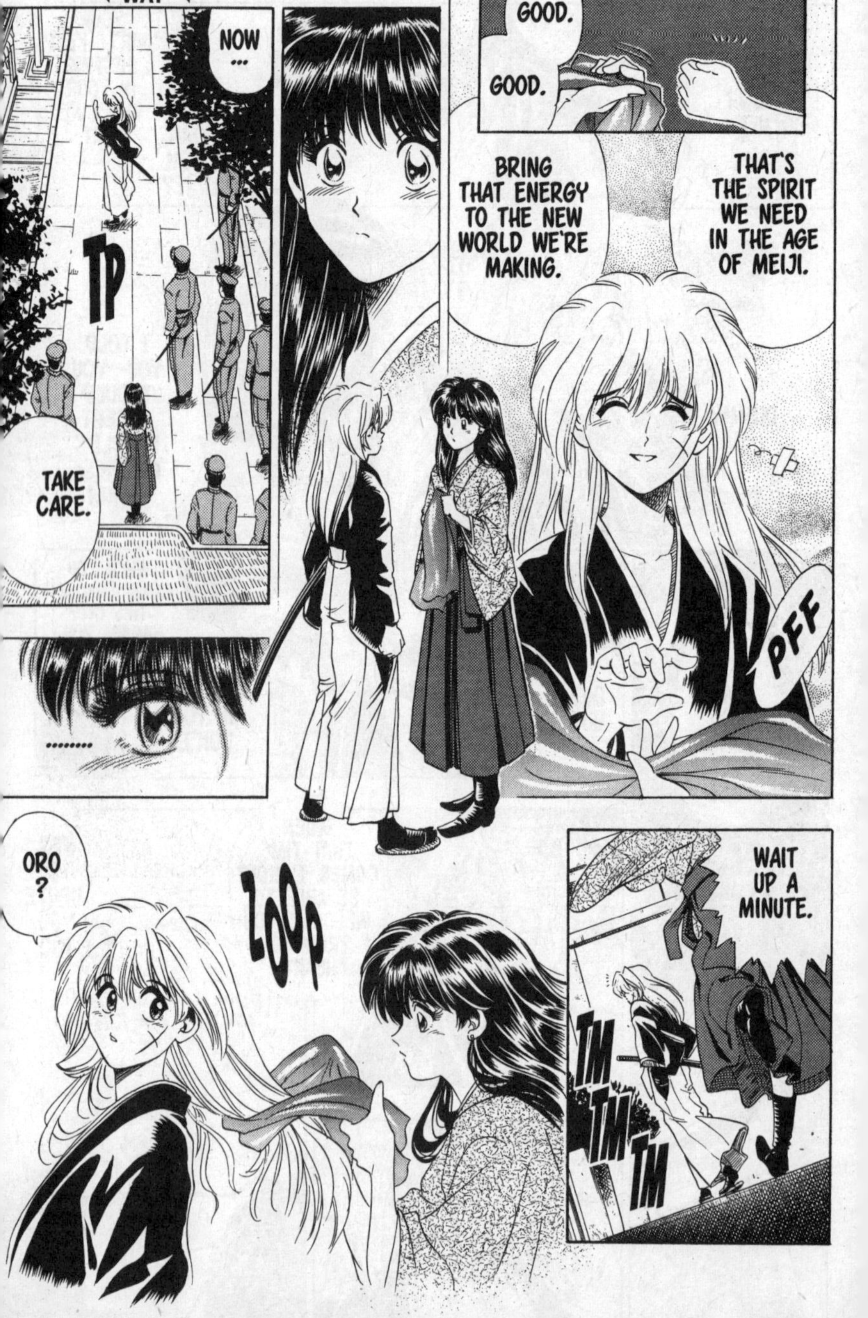
GOOD.
GOOD.
THAT'S THE SPIRIT WE NEED IN THE AGE OF MEIJI.
BRING THAT ENERGY TO THE NEW WORLD WE'RE MAKING.
PFF
NOW...
TP
TAKE CARE.
....
WAIT UP A MINUTE.
TM TM TM TM
ZOOP
ORO?

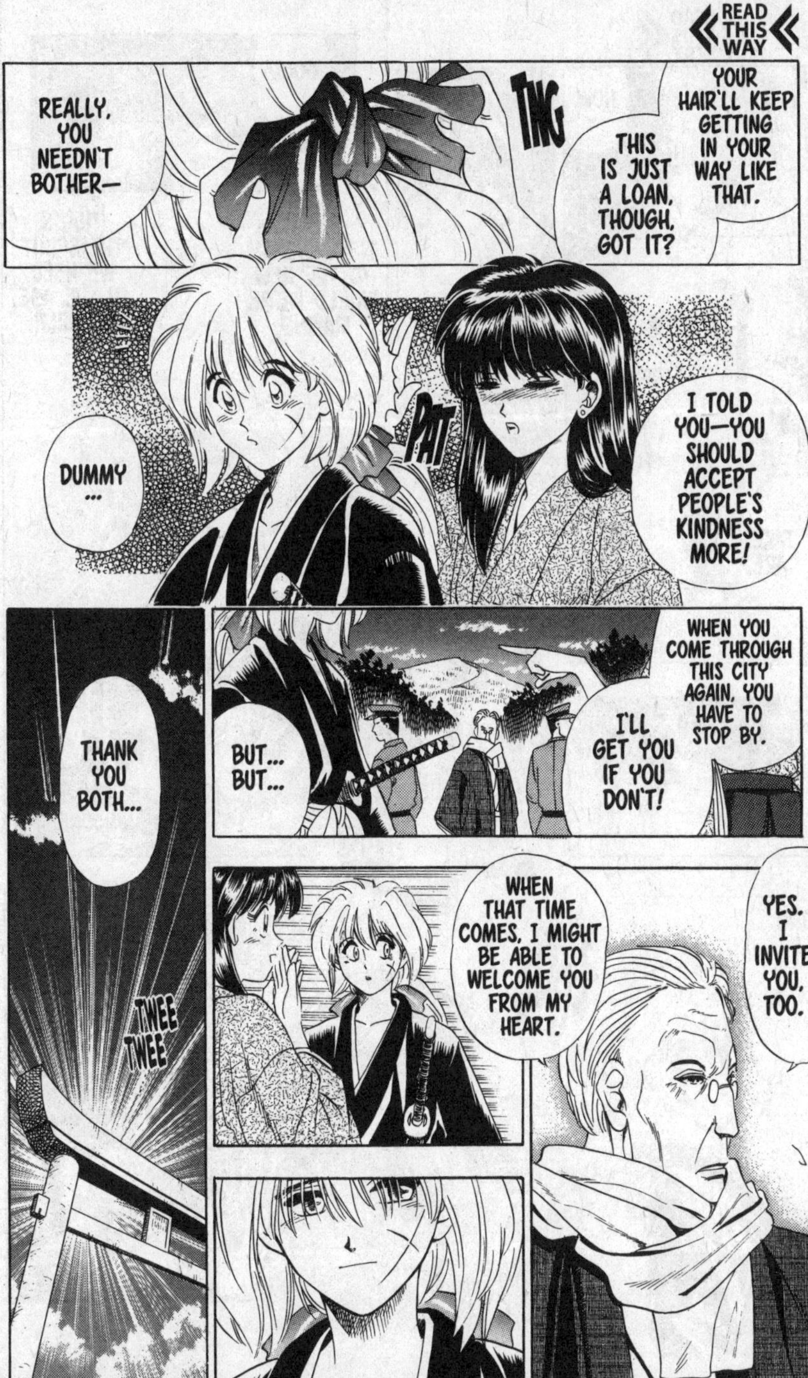
READ THIS WAY
YOUR HAIR'LL KEEP GETTING IN YOUR WAY LIKE THAT.
THIS IS JUST A LOAN, THOUGH, GOT IT?
TNG
REALLY, YOU NEEDN'T BOTHER—
I TOLD YOU—YOU SHOULD ACCEPT PEOPLE'S KINDNESS MORE!
PAT
DUMMY ...
WHEN YOU COME THROUGH THIS CITY AGAIN, YOU HAVE TO STOP BY.
I'LL GET YOU IF YOU DON'T!
BUT... BUT...
YES. I INVITE YOU, TOO.
WHEN THAT TIME COMES, I MIGHT BE ABLE TO WELCOME YOU FROM MY HEART.
THANK YOU BOTH...
TWEE TWEE

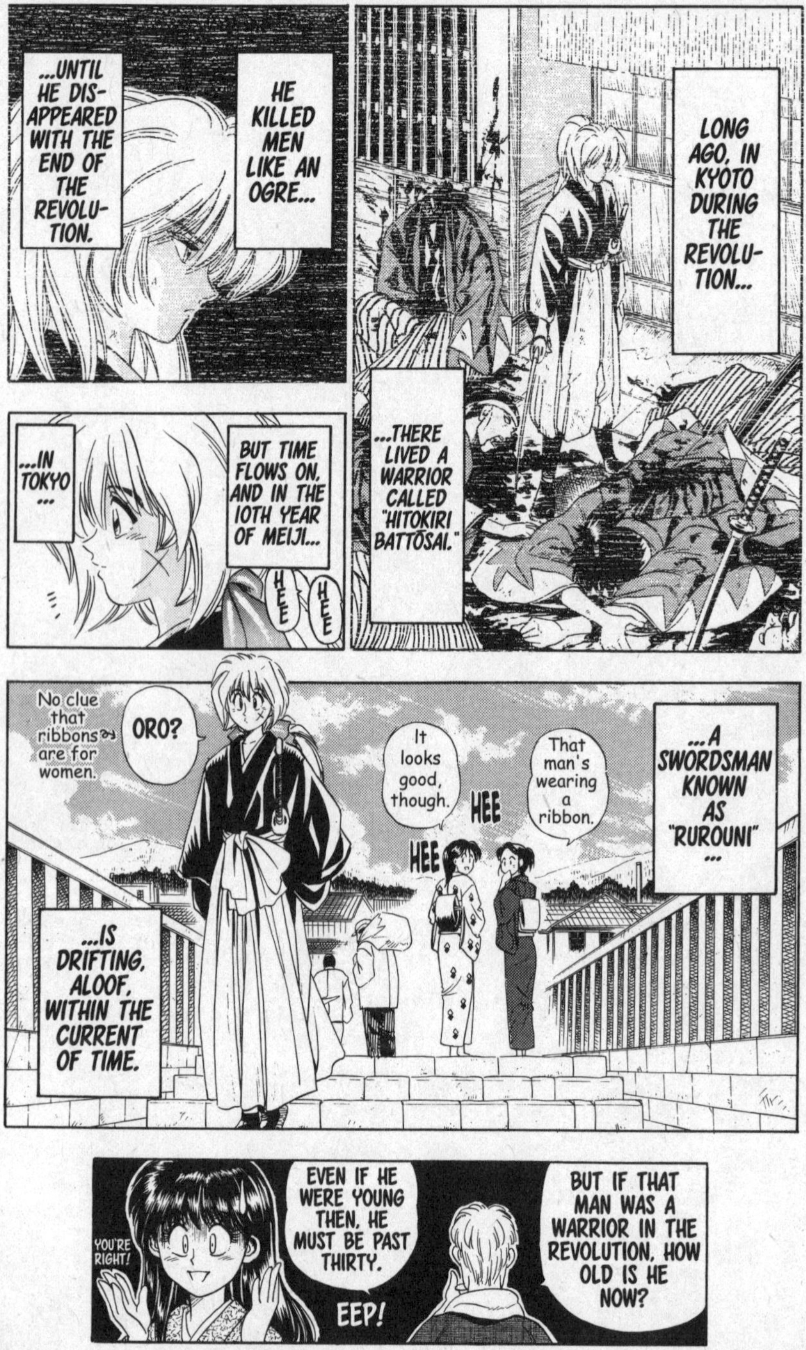
LONG AGO, IN KYOTO DURING THE REVOLUTION...
...THERE LIVED A WARRIOR CALLED "HITOKIRI BATTŌSAI."
HE KILLED MEN LIKE AN OGRE...
...UNTIL HE DISAPPEARED WITH THE END OF THE REVOLUTION.
BUT TIME FLOWS ON, AND IN THE 10TH YEAR OF MEIJI...
HEE
HEE
...IN TOKYO...
...A SWORDSMAN KNOWN AS "RUROUNI"...
That man's wearing a ribbon.
HEE
It looks good, though.
HEE
ORO?
No clue that ribbons are for women.
...IS DRIFTING, ALOOF, WITHIN THE CURRENT OF TIME.
BUT IF THAT MAN WAS A WARRIOR IN THE REVOLUTION, HOW OLD IS HE NOW?
EVEN IF HE WERE YOUNG THEN, HE MUST BE PAST THIRTY.
EEP!
YOU'RE RIGHT!

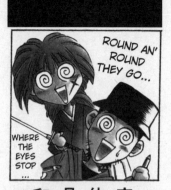

ROUND AN' ROUND THEY GO...

WHERE THE EYES STOP...

和月伸宏

NOBUHIRO WATSUKI

WATSUKI IS STILL A LIAR.

IN THE INTERESTS OF FULL DISCLOSURE, THE KANJI FOR "RUROUNI" ISN'T READ "RUROUNI" AT ALL—YOU SURE WON'T FIND IT IN ANY DICTIONARY! ONCE AGAIN, WATSUKI HAS BEEN PULLING YOUR LEG. (IF YOU'RE ONE OF THOSE PEOPLE TAKEN IN BY THE LITTLE RUSE, SORRY!)

THAT ASIDE, IT'S BEEN SO CRAZY-BUSY LATELY THAT I FEEL EXACTLY LIKE THE LITTLE SKETCH UP THERE. I HAVEN'T EVEN HAD TIME TO DO A NEW, ORIGINAL ILLUSTRATION FOR THIS GRAPHIC NOVEL. IT DOESN'T LOOK LIKE I'LL HAVE TIME TO DO IT FOR VOLUME 3, EITHER, BUT I WILL FOR VOLUME 4 PROMISE! CROSS MY HEART!!

SHONEN JUMP MANGA

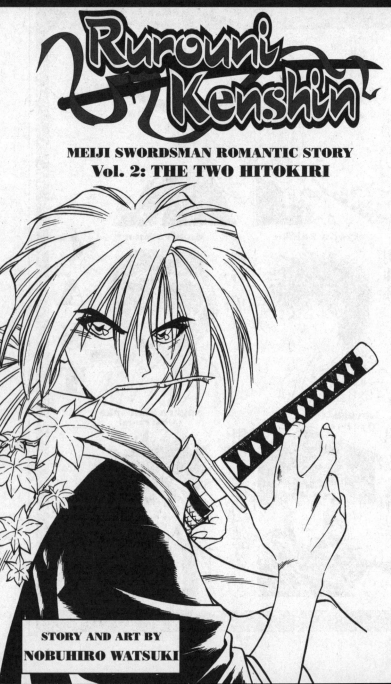

Rurouni Kenshin

MEIJI SWORDSMAN ROMANTIC STORY

Vol. 2: THE TWO HITOKIRI

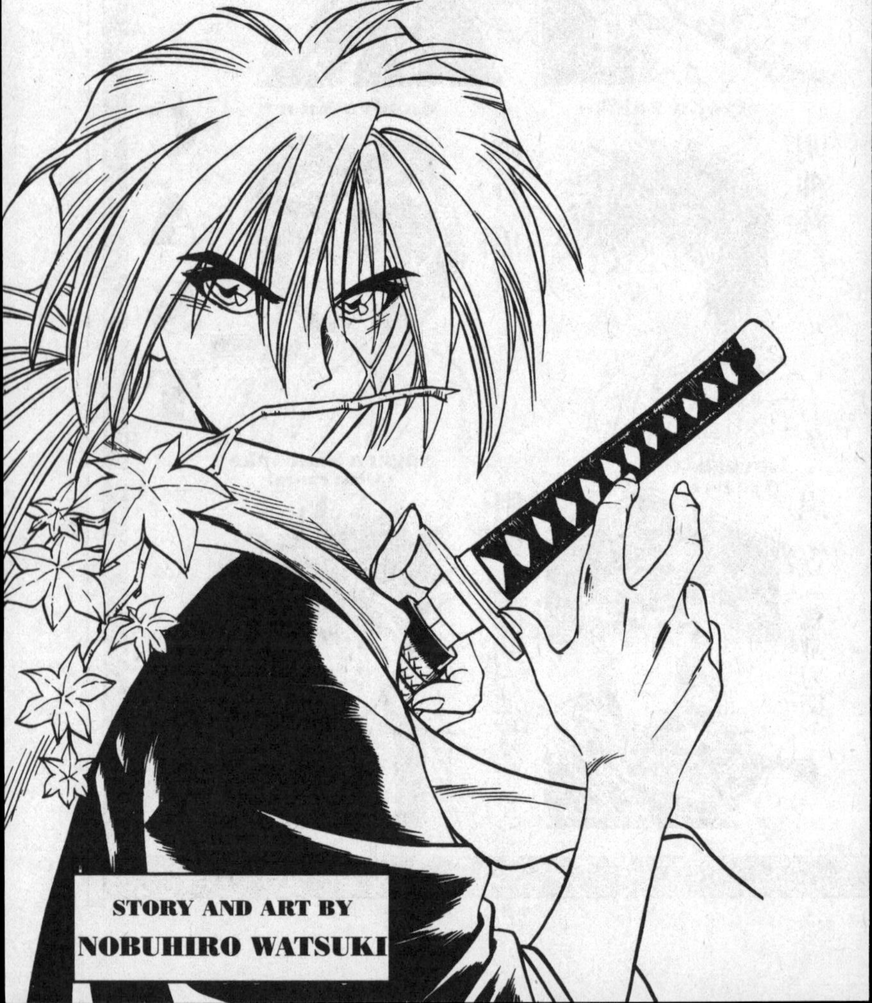

STORY AND ART BY

NOBUHIRO WATSUKI

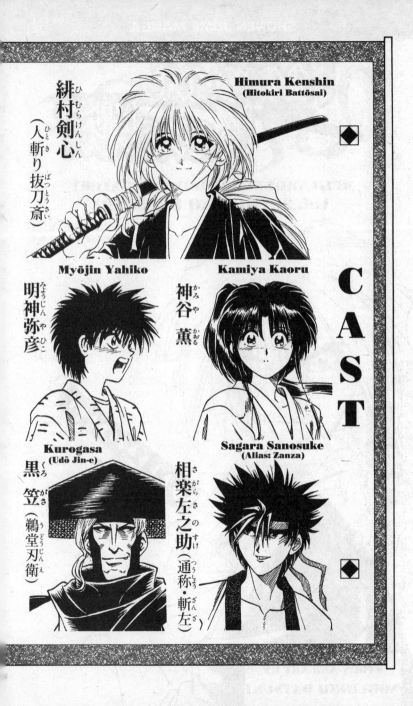

緋村剣心
（ひむらけんしん）
（人斬り抜刀斎）
（ひときりばっとうさい）

Himura Kenshin
(Hitokiri Battōsai)

明神弥彦
（みょうじんやひこ）

Myōjin Yahiko

神谷薫
（かみやかおる）

Kamiya Kaoru

黒笠
（くろがさ）
（鵜堂刃衛）
（うどうじんえ）

Kurogasa
(Udō Jin-e)

相楽左之助
（さがらさのすけ）
（通称・斬左）
（つうしょう・ざんざ）

Sagara Sanosuke
(Alias: Zanza)

C A S T

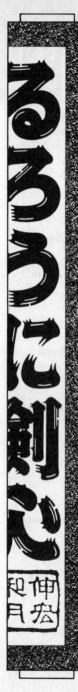

るろうに剣心

和月伸宏

Once he was a *hitokiri*, an assassin, called *Battōsai.*

His name was legend among the *Ishin Shishi* or "patriot" warriors who launched the Meiji Era.

Now Himura Kenshin is a *rurouni*, a wanderer, who carries a reversed-edge *sakabatō* blade to prohibit himself from killing.

Having exposed the scheme of the Hiruma Brothers to steal the Kamiya school's property with a "fake Battōsai," Kenshin's decided to stay on at the dojo for a while.

Hiruma Kihei

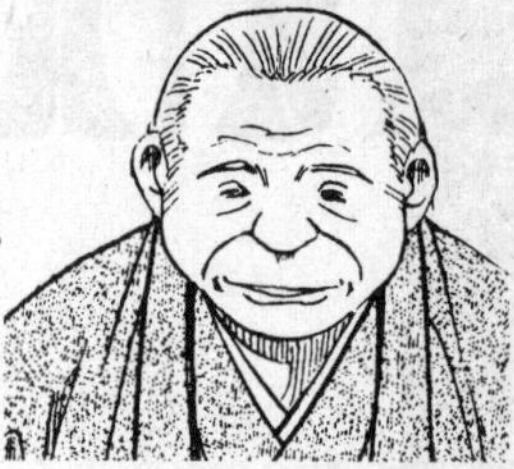

Hiruma Gohei

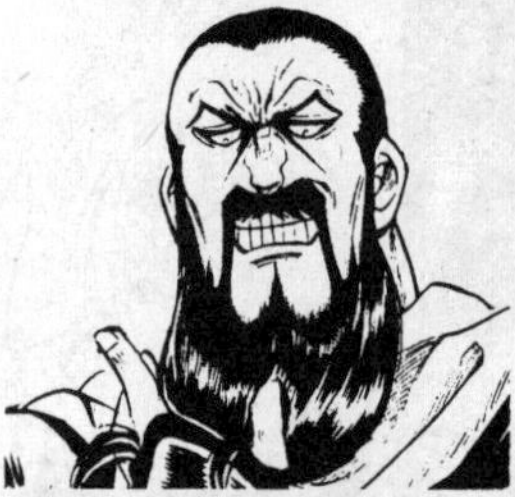

比留間喜兵衛・伍兵衛

THUS FAR

After losing all its students because of the hoax, the Kamiya dojo and its "*Kasshin-ryū*" sword style is taking its first steps toward revival.

Kenshin brings in Myōjin Yahiko, the son of an ex-samurai whom he rescued from the yakuza, to become its first new student.

But, still greedy for the property, the Hiruma Brothers escape from jail and hire Sagara Sanosuke, who fights the fights of others for a living, to get rid of the annoying Kenshin.

At first unwilling, Sanosuke takes the job when he learns who Kenshin *really* is—Sanosuke hates the so-called patriots and the chance to humble the greatest of them all is too tempting to pass by.

Ultimately Kenshin accepts Sanosuke's challenge, and while Kaoru, Yahiko, and the Hiruma Brothers watch, the deadly serious battle begins.

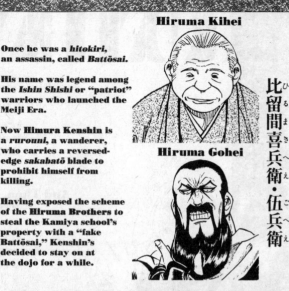

CONTENTS

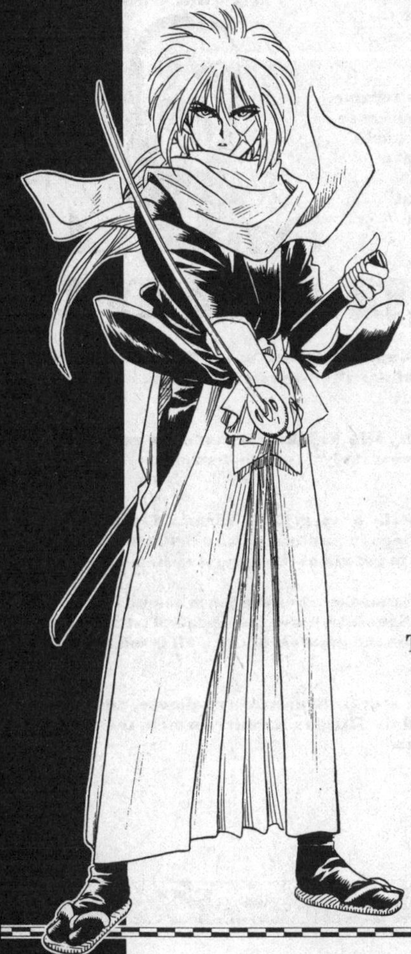

Act 7 - Mark of Evil

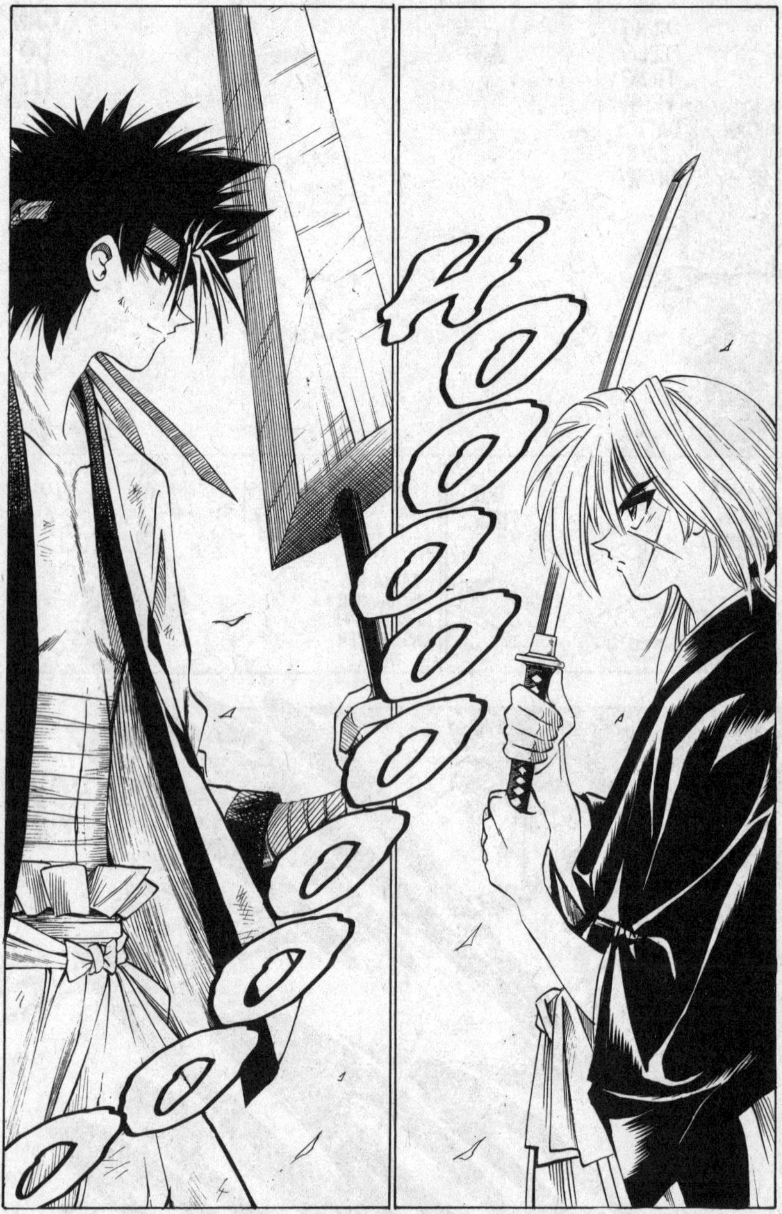
HOOOOOOOOOOO

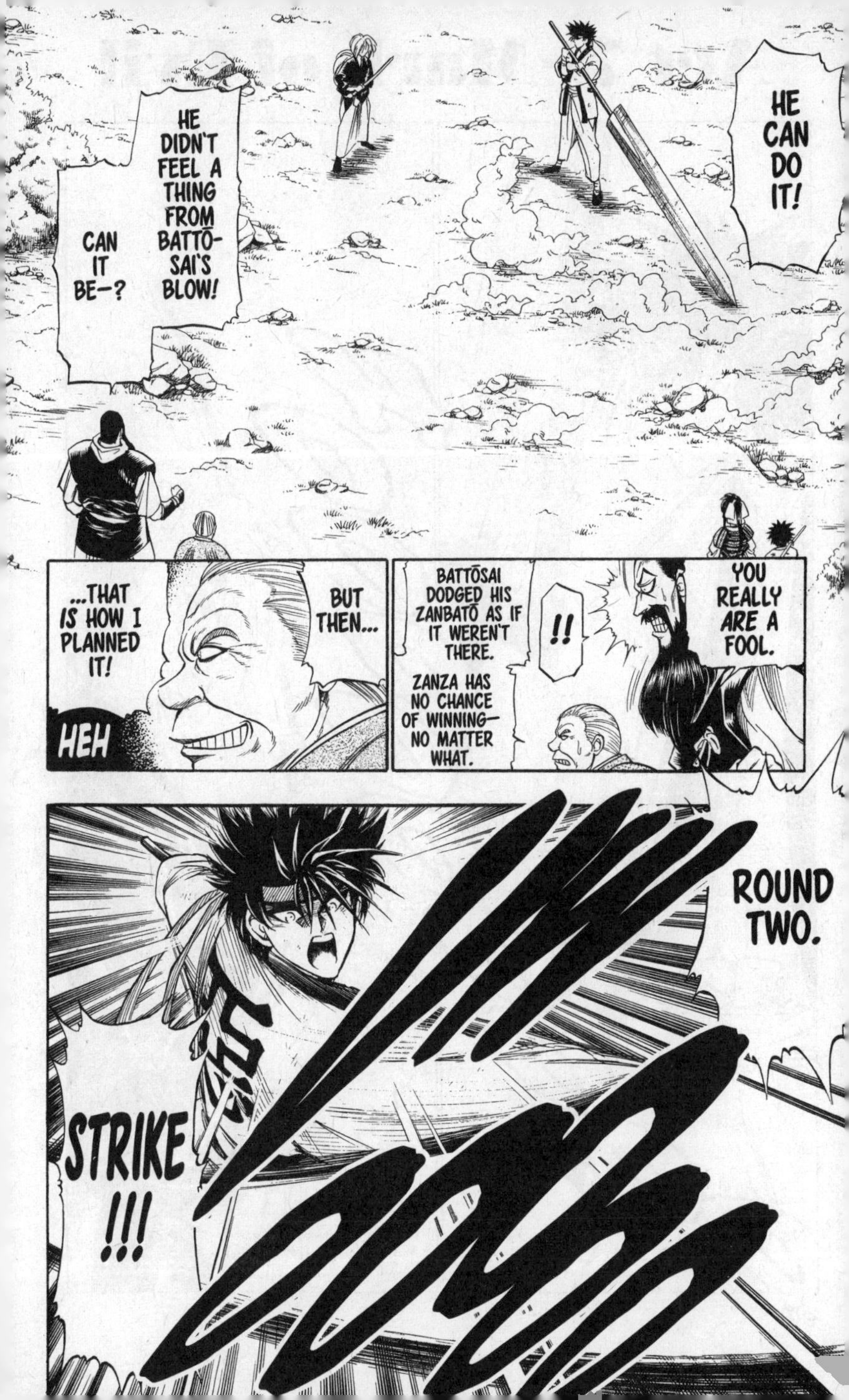
HE CAN DO IT!
HE DIDN'T FEEL A THING FROM BATTŌSAI'S BLOW!
CAN IT BE—?
YOU REALLY ARE A FOOL.
!!
BATTŌSAI DODGED HIS ZANBATŌ AS IF IT WEREN'T THERE.
ZANZA HAS NO CHANCE OF WINNING—NO MATTER WHAT.
BUT THEN...
...THAT IS HOW I PLANNED IT!
HEH
ROUND TWO.
STRIKE !!!

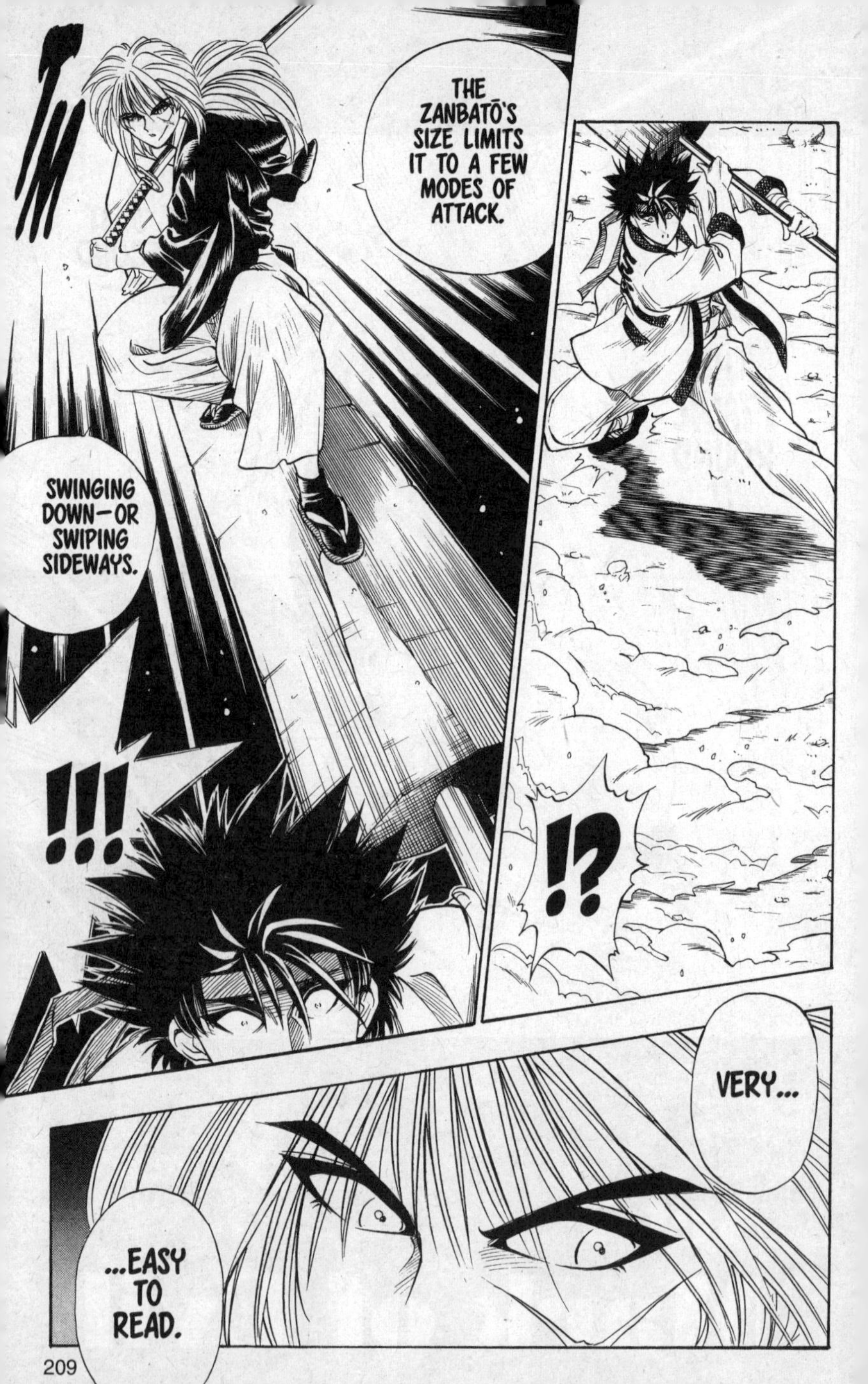
!?
THE ZANBATŌ'S SIZE LIMITS IT TO A FEW MODES OF ATTACK.
SWINGING DOWN—OR SWIPING SIDEWAYS.
!!!
VERY...
...EASY TO READ.

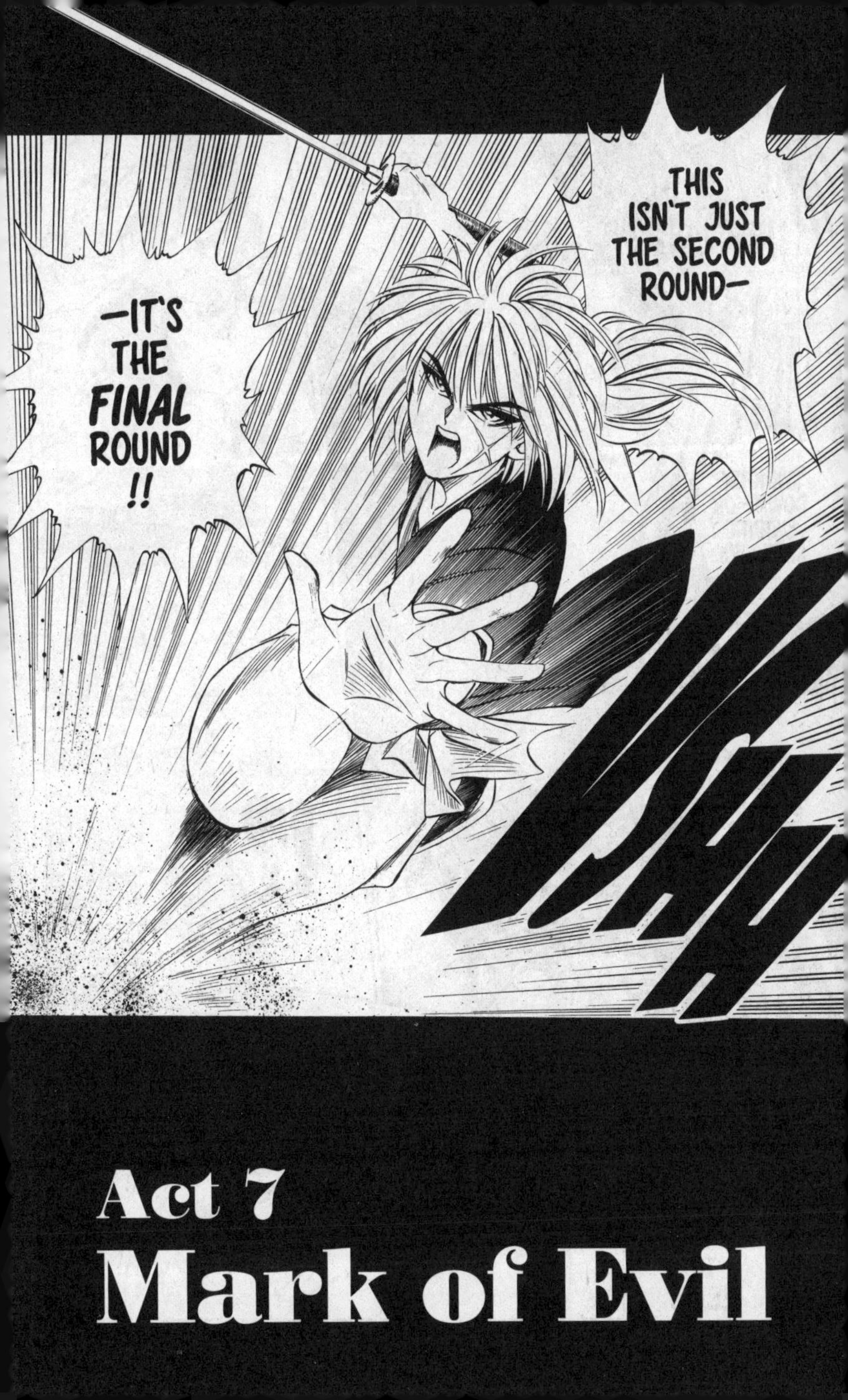
THIS ISN'T JUST THE SECOND ROUND—
—IT'S THE FINAL ROUND!!

Act 7
Mark of Evil

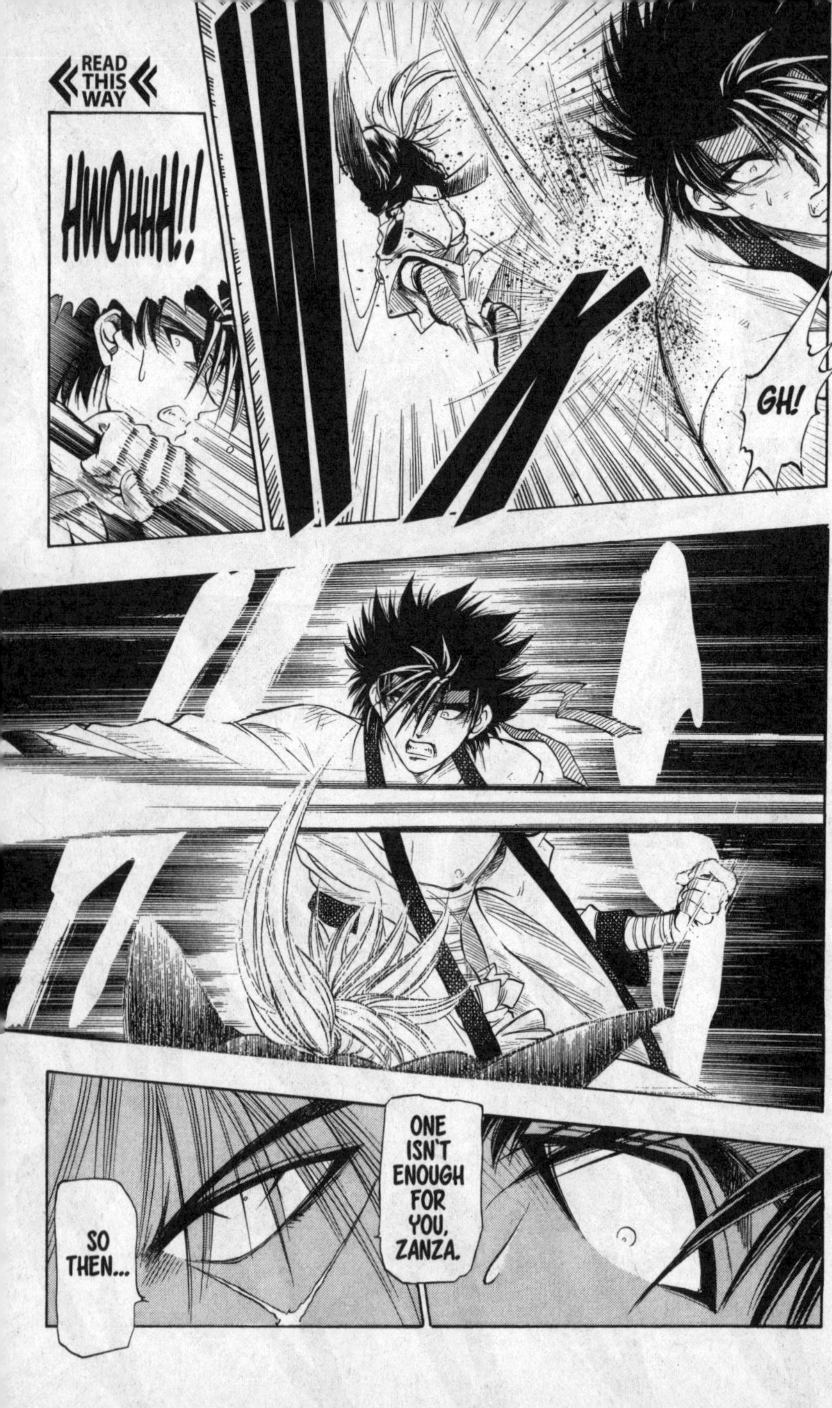

READ THIS WAY
GH!
HWOHHH!!
ONE ISN'T ENOUGH FOR YOU, ZANZA.
SO THEN...

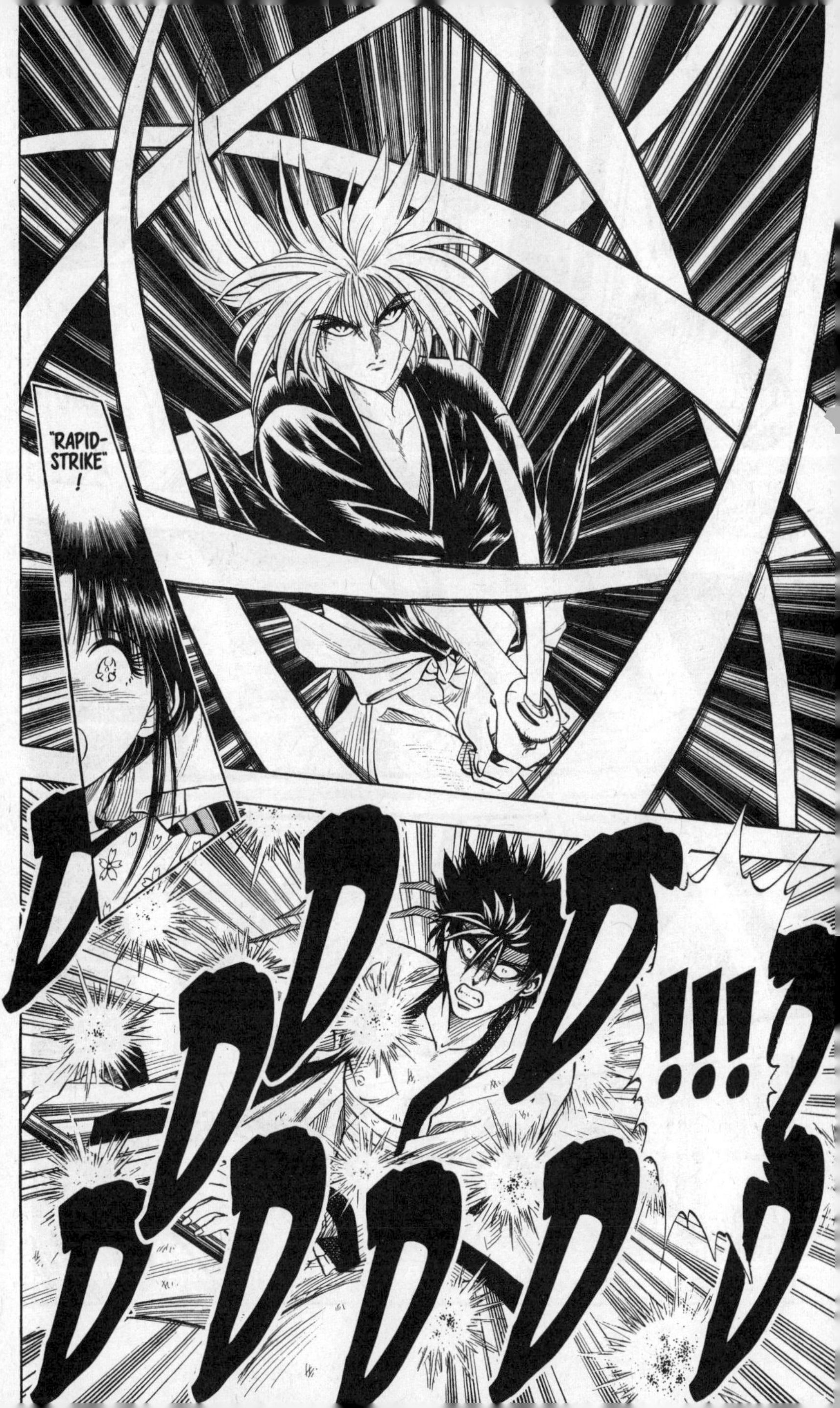
"RAPID-STRIKE" !

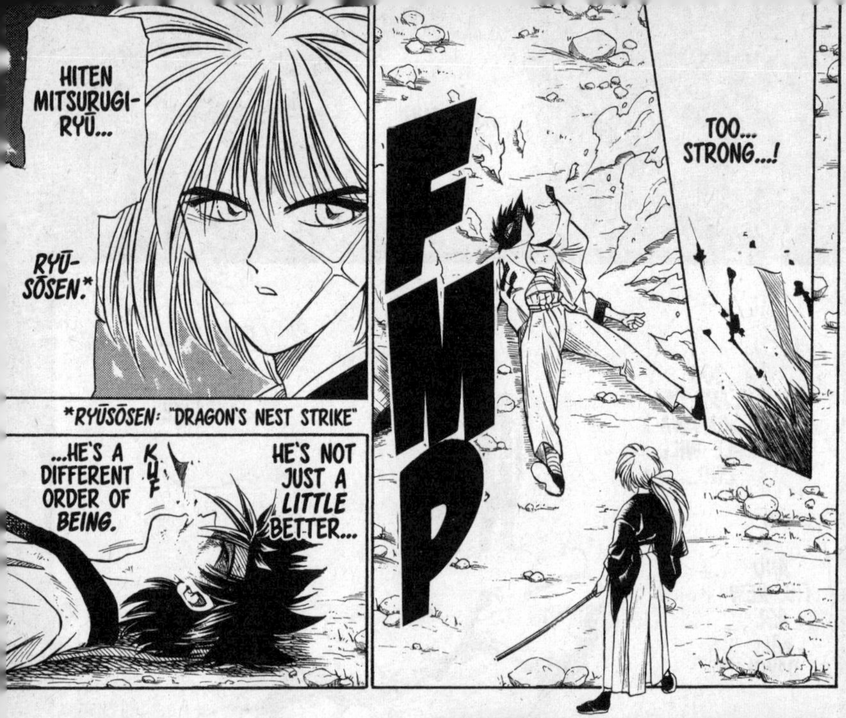
FMP
TOO... STRONG...!
HITEN MITSURUGI-RYŪ...
RYŪ-SŌSEN.*
*RYŪSŌSEN: "DRAGON'S NEST STRIKE"
HE'S NOT JUST A LITTLE BETTER...
KUF
...HE'S A DIFFERENT ORDER OF BEING.

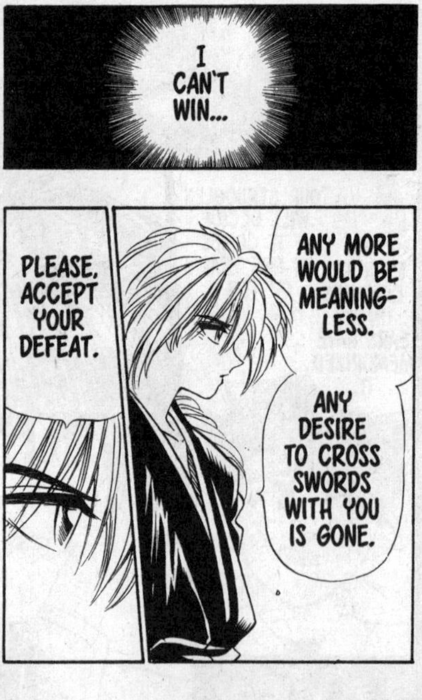
I CAN'T WIN...
ANY MORE WOULD BE MEANING-LESS.
ANY DESIRE TO CROSS SWORDS WITH YOU IS GONE.
PLEASE, ACCEPT YOUR DEFEAT.

So-o-o, *Rurouni Kenshin* is to become a CD book! I bet you're all surprised...but none more so than me. It's only been half a year, and already Kenshin is crossing over to other media...thanks to your support. Thank you—really!—so much.

和月伸宏

Watsuki

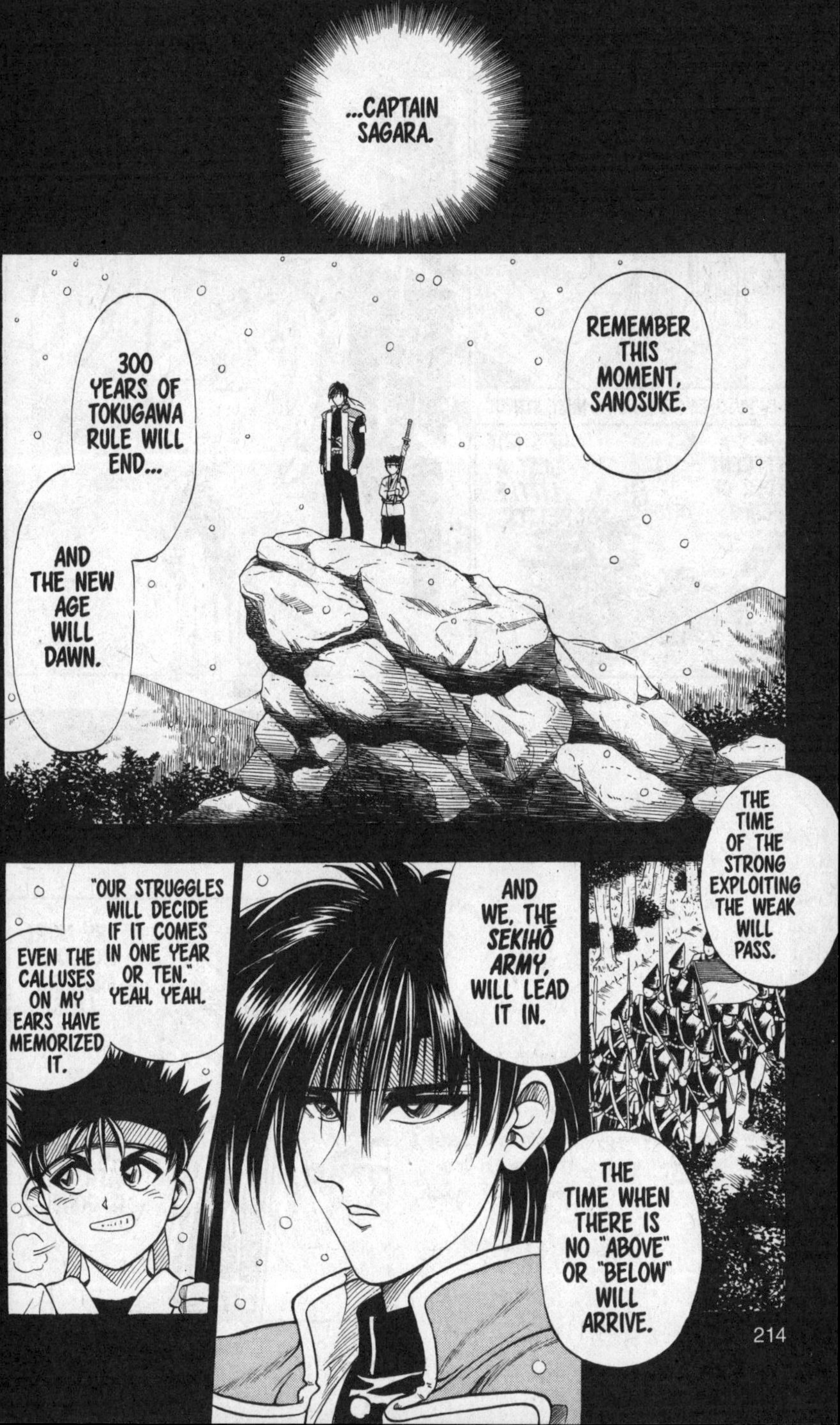
...CAPTAIN SAGARA.
REMEMBER THIS MOMENT, SANOSUKE.
300 YEARS OF TOKUGAWA RULE WILL END...
AND THE NEW AGE WILL DAWN.
THE TIME OF THE STRONG EXPLOITING THE WEAK WILL PASS.
AND WE, THE *SEKIHŌ ARMY*, WILL LEAD IT IN.
THE TIME WHEN THERE IS NO "ABOVE" OR "BELOW" WILL ARRIVE.
"OUR STRUGGLES WILL DECIDE IF IT COMES IN ONE YEAR OR TEN." YEAH, YEAH.
EVEN THE CALLUSES ON MY EARS HAVE MEMORIZED IT.

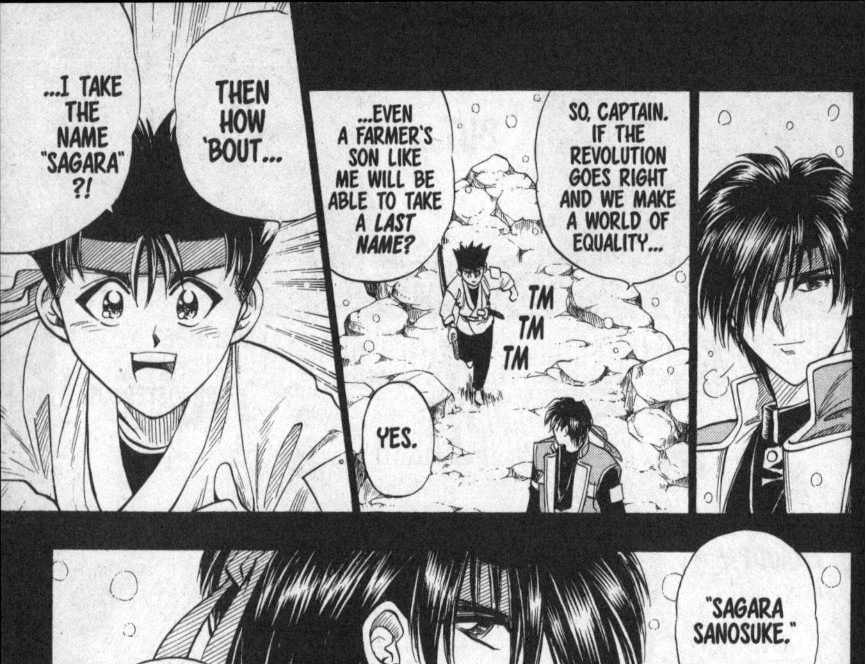
SO, CAPTAIN. IF THE REVOLUTION GOES RIGHT AND WE MAKE A WORLD OF EQUALITY...
...EVEN A FARMER'S SON LIKE ME WILL BE ABLE TO TAKE A LAST NAME?
TM TM TM
YES.
THEN HOW 'BOUT...
...I TAKE THE NAME "SAGARA"?!
"SAGARA SANOSUKE."
SOUNDS GOOFY. DON'T DO IT.
HEH

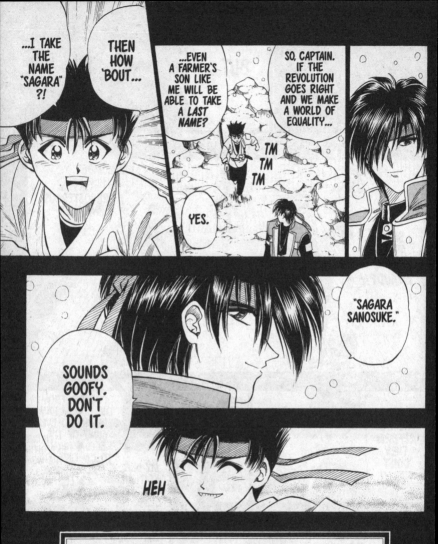

Sekihō Army

A unit formed of civilians in 1868, immediately after the battle of Toba Fushimi. Advancing before the revolutionary army, it collected intelligence about future targets and gathered recruits.

The 1st unit of the Army, led by Sagara Sōzō, was at this time marching north through the eastern mountain roads to spread the "halving of taxes" proclaimed by the revolution.

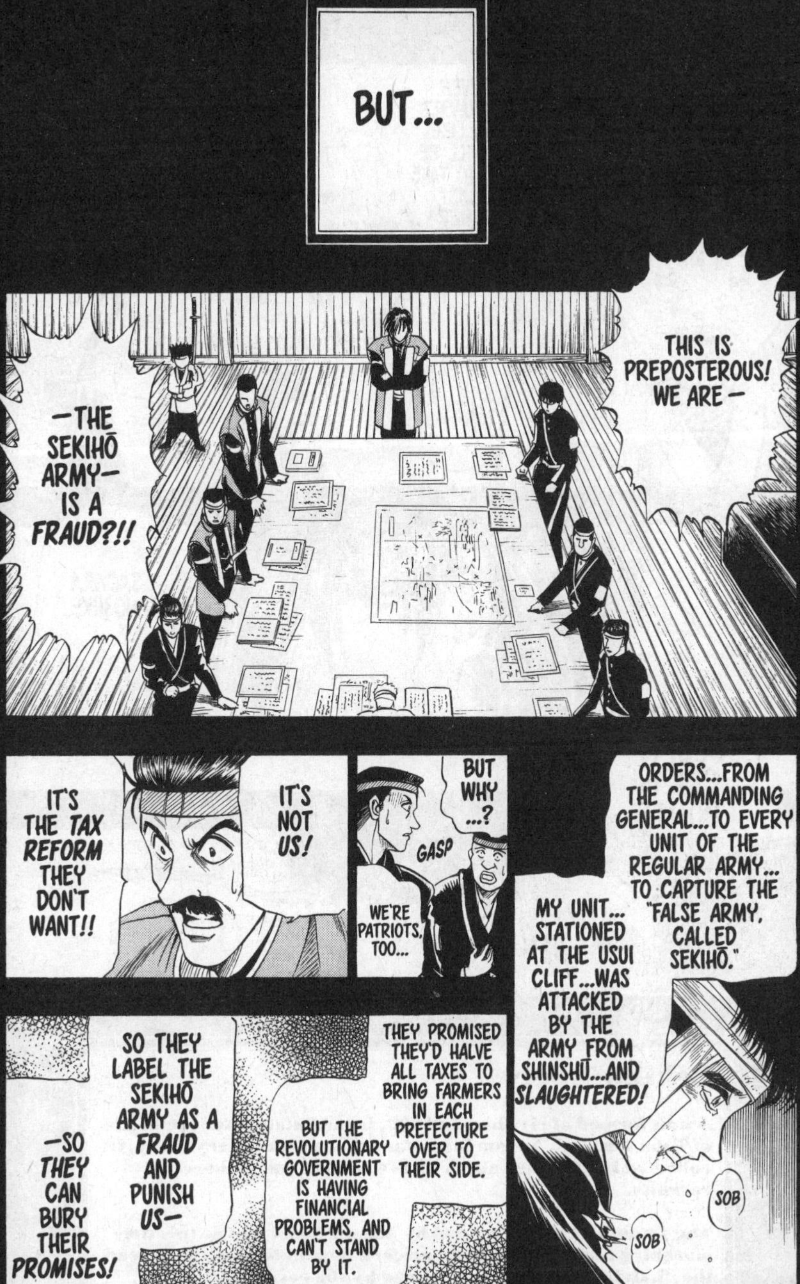
BUT...
THIS IS PREPOSTEROUS! WE ARE—
—THE SEKIHŌ ARMY— IS A FRAUD?!!
ORDERS...FROM THE COMMANDING GENERAL...TO EVERY UNIT OF THE REGULAR ARMY... TO CAPTURE THE "FALSE ARMY, CALLED SEKIHŌ."
MY UNIT... STATIONED AT THE USUI CLIFF...WAS ATTACKED BY THE ARMY FROM SHINSHŪ...AND SLAUGHTERED!
SOB
SOB
BUT WHY ...?
GASP
WE'RE PATRIOTS, TOO...
IT'S NOT US!
IT'S THE TAX REFORM THEY DON'T WANT!!
THEY PROMISED THEY'D HALVE ALL TAXES TO BRING FARMERS IN EACH PREFECTURE OVER TO THEIR SIDE.
BUT THE REVOLUTIONARY GOVERNMENT IS HAVING FINANCIAL PROBLEMS, AND CAN'T STAND BY IT.
SO THEY LABEL THE SEKIHŌ ARMY AS A FRAUD AND PUNISH US—
—SO THEY CAN BURY THEIR PROMISES!

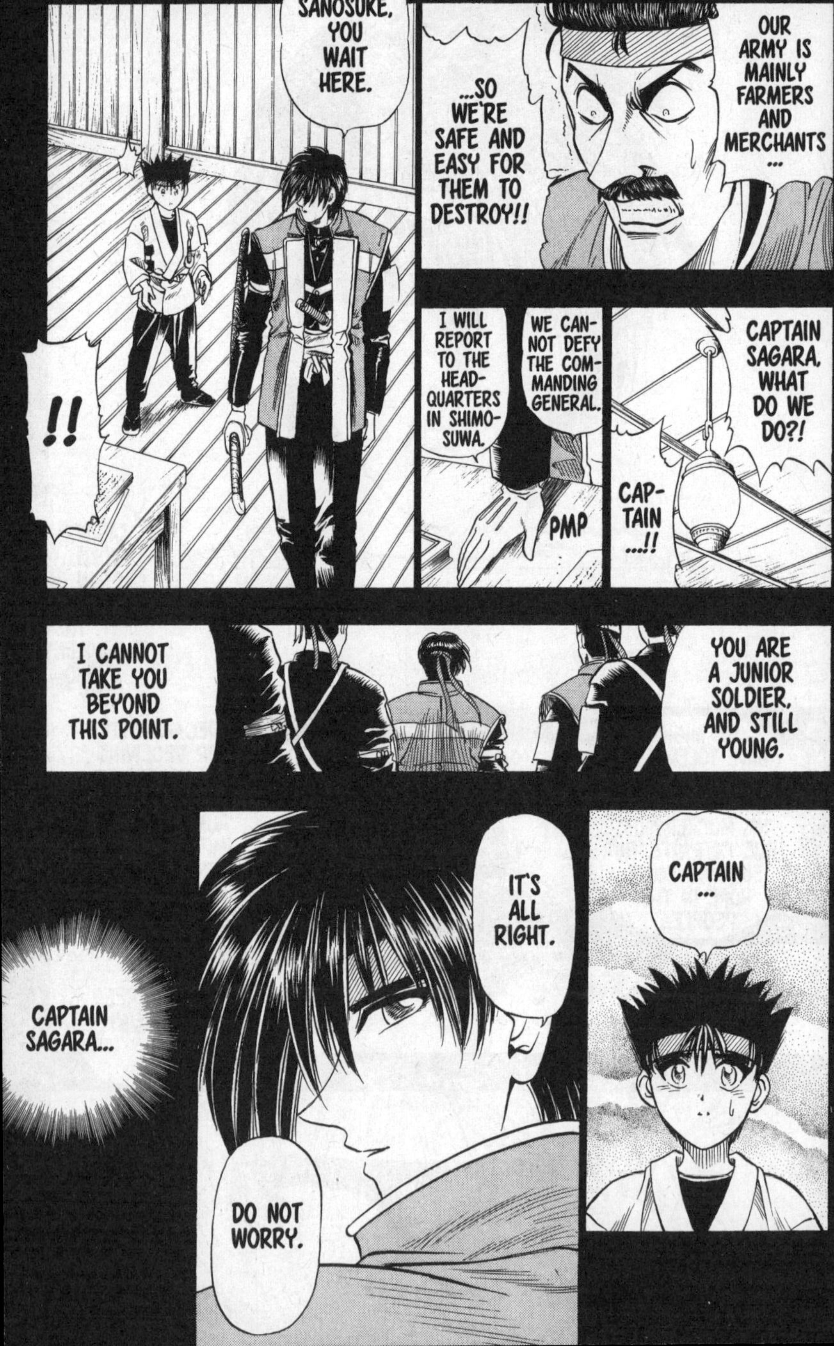
OUR ARMY IS MAINLY FARMERS AND MERCHANTS...
...SO WE'RE SAFE AND EASY FOR THEM TO DESTROY!!
CAPTAIN SAGARA, WHAT DO WE DO?!
CAP-TAIN...!!
WE CAN-NOT DEFY THE COM-MANDING GENERAL.
I WILL REPORT TO THE HEAD-QUARTERS IN SHIMO-SUWA.
PMP
SANOSUKE, YOU WAIT HERE.
!!
YOU ARE A JUNIOR SOLDIER, AND STILL YOUNG.
I CANNOT TAKE YOU BEYOND THIS POINT.
CAPTAIN...
IT'S ALL RIGHT.
DO NOT WORRY.
CAPTAIN SAGARA...

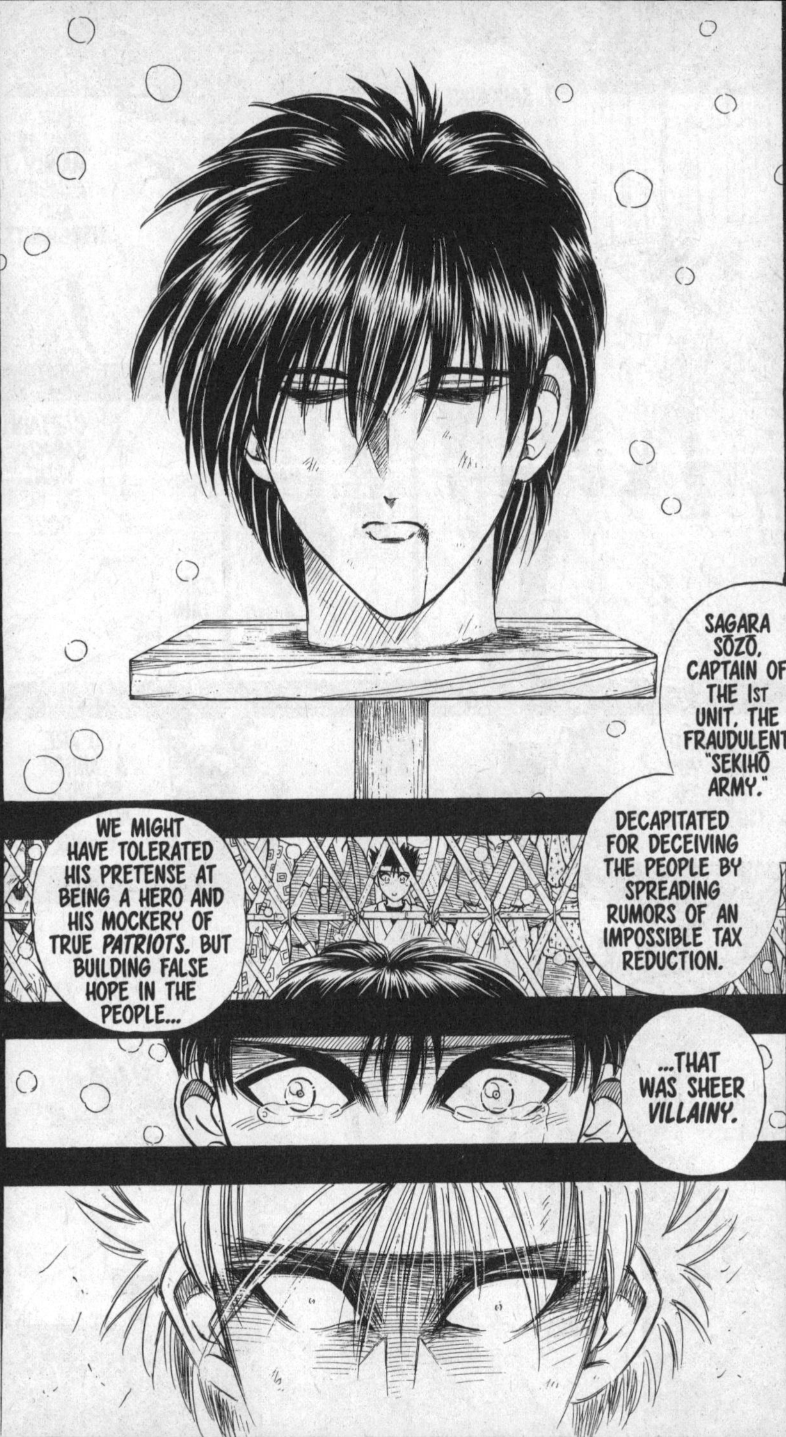
SAGARA SŌZŌ, CAPTAIN OF THE 1ST UNIT, THE FRAUDULENT "SEKIHŌ ARMY."
DECAPITATED FOR DECEIVING THE PEOPLE BY SPREADING RUMORS OF AN IMPOSSIBLE TAX REDUCTION.
WE MIGHT HAVE TOLERATED HIS PRETENSE AT BEING A HERO AND HIS MOCKERY OF TRUE *PATRIOTS.* BUT BUILDING FALSE HOPE IN THE PEOPLE...
...THAT WAS SHEER *VILLAINY.*

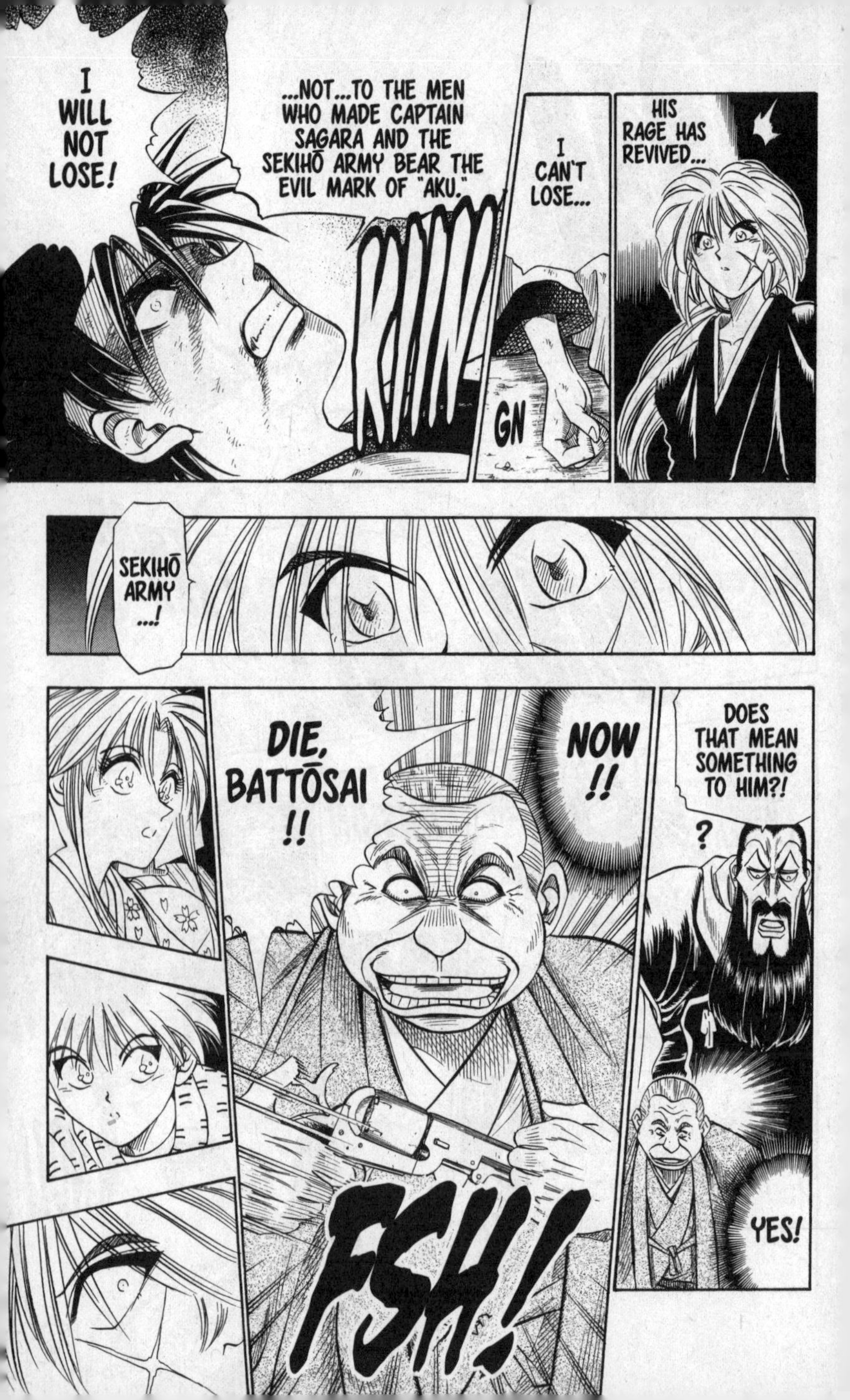
HIS RAGE HAS REVIVED...
I CAN'T LOSE...
GN
...NOT...TO THE MEN WHO MADE CAPTAIN SAGARA AND THE SEKIHŌ ARMY BEAR THE EVIL MARK OF "AKU."
I WILL NOT LOSE!
SEKIHŌ ARMY ...!
DOES THAT MEAN SOMETHING TO HIM?!
?
YES!
NOW!!
DIE, BATTŌSAI!!
FSH!

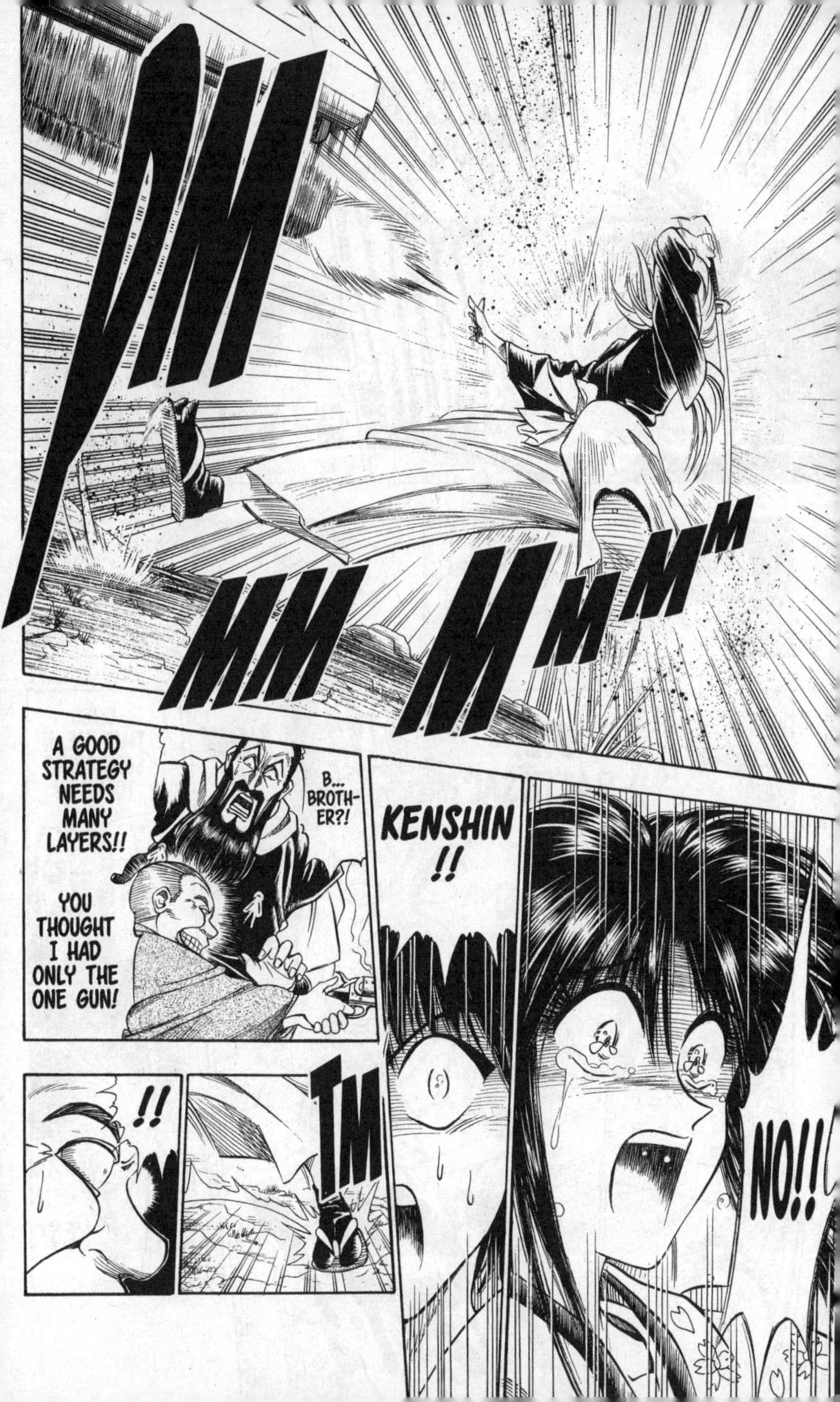
DM
MM M MMM
KENSHIN!!
NO!!
B... BROTHER?!
A GOOD STRATEGY NEEDS MANY LAYERS!!
YOU THOUGHT I HAD ONLY THE ONE GUN!
TM
!!

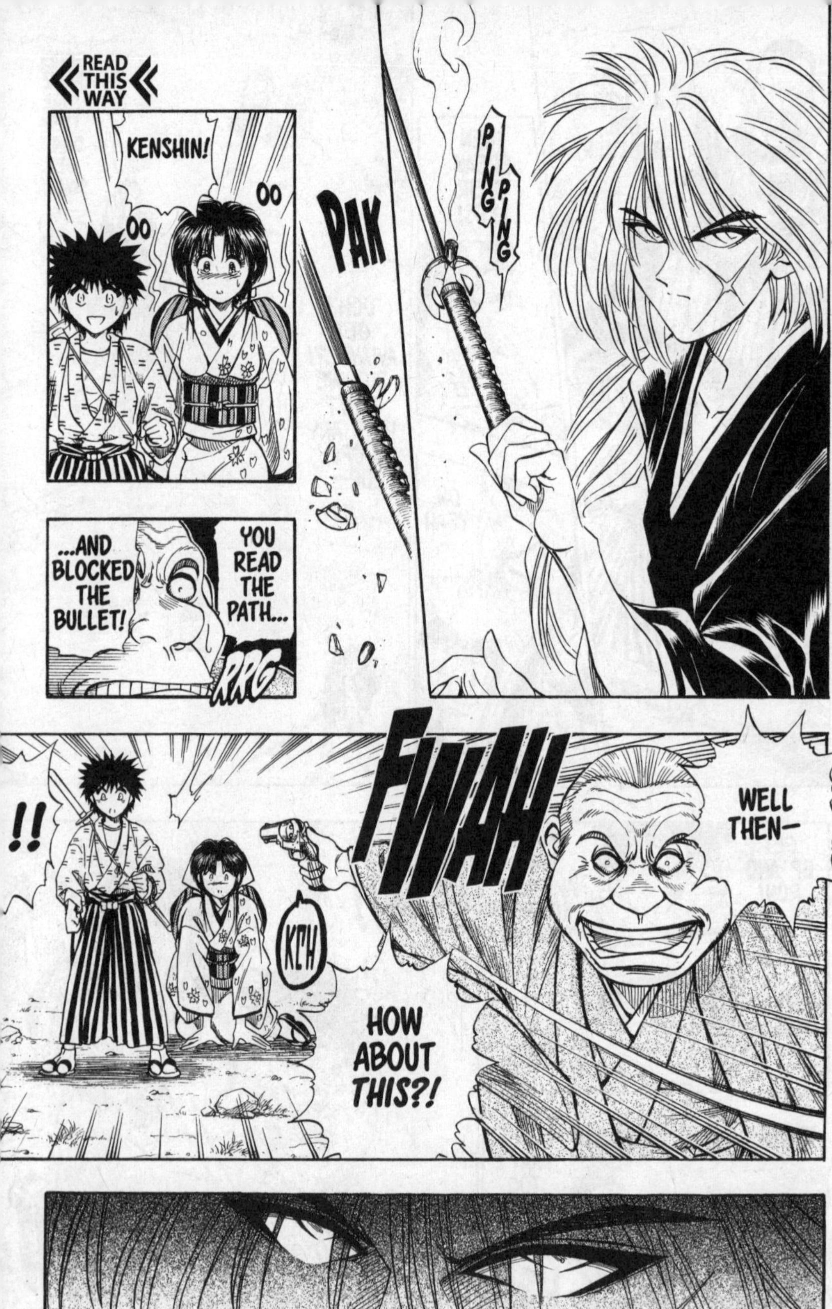
READ THIS WAY
PING PING
PAK
KENSHIN!
OO
OO
YOU READ THE PATH...
...AND BLOCKED THE BULLET!
RRG
WELL THEN—
FWAH
HOW ABOUT THIS?!
KCH
!!

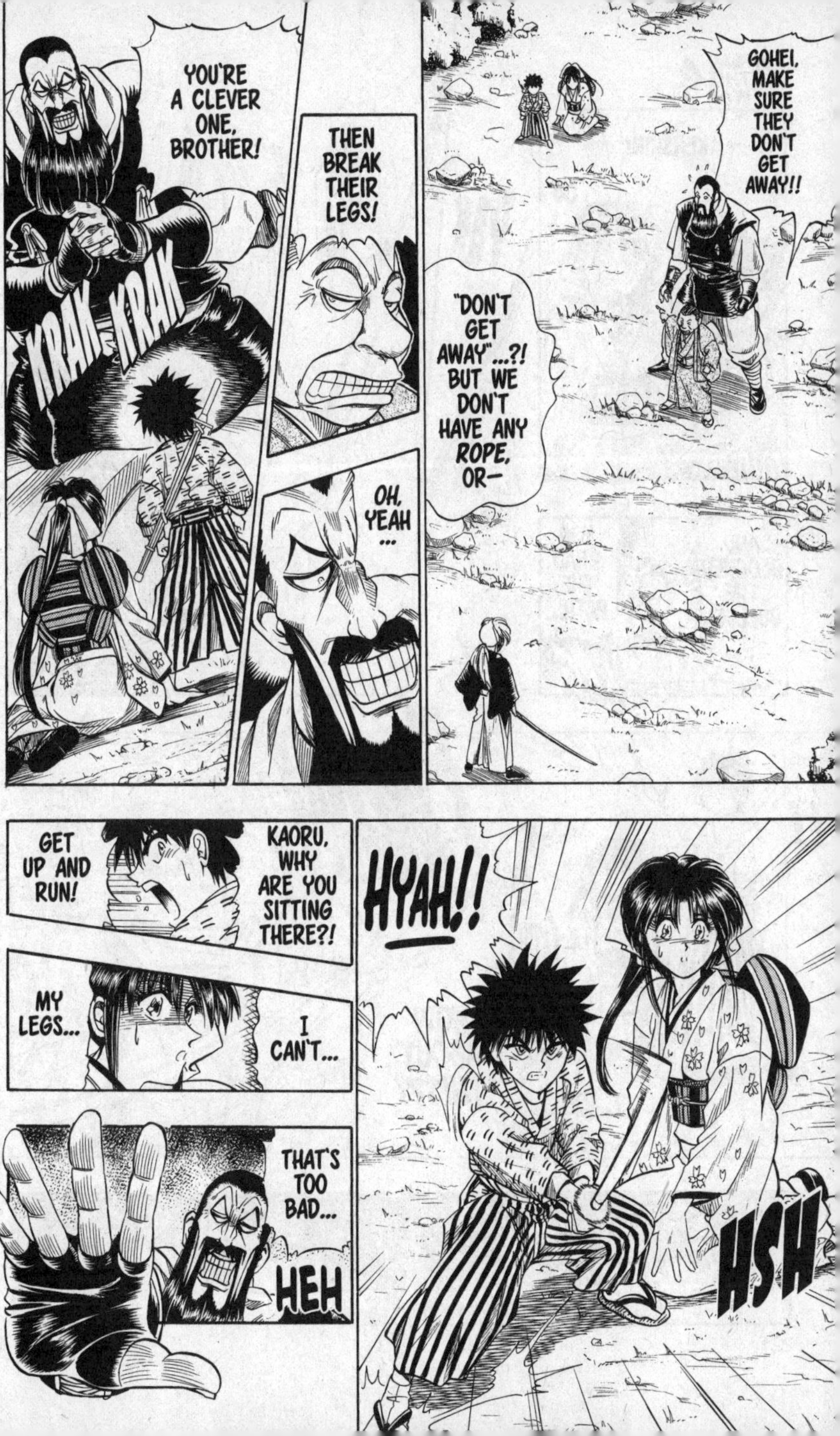
GOHEI, MAKE SURE THEY DON'T GET AWAY!!
"DON'T GET AWAY"...?! BUT WE DON'T HAVE ANY ROPE, OR—
THEN BREAK THEIR LEGS!
OH, YEAH ...
YOU'RE A CLEVER ONE, BROTHER!
KRAK KRAK
HYAH!!
HSH
KAORU, WHY ARE YOU SITTING THERE?!
GET UP AND RUN!
MY LEGS...
I CAN'T...
THAT'S TOO BAD...
HEH

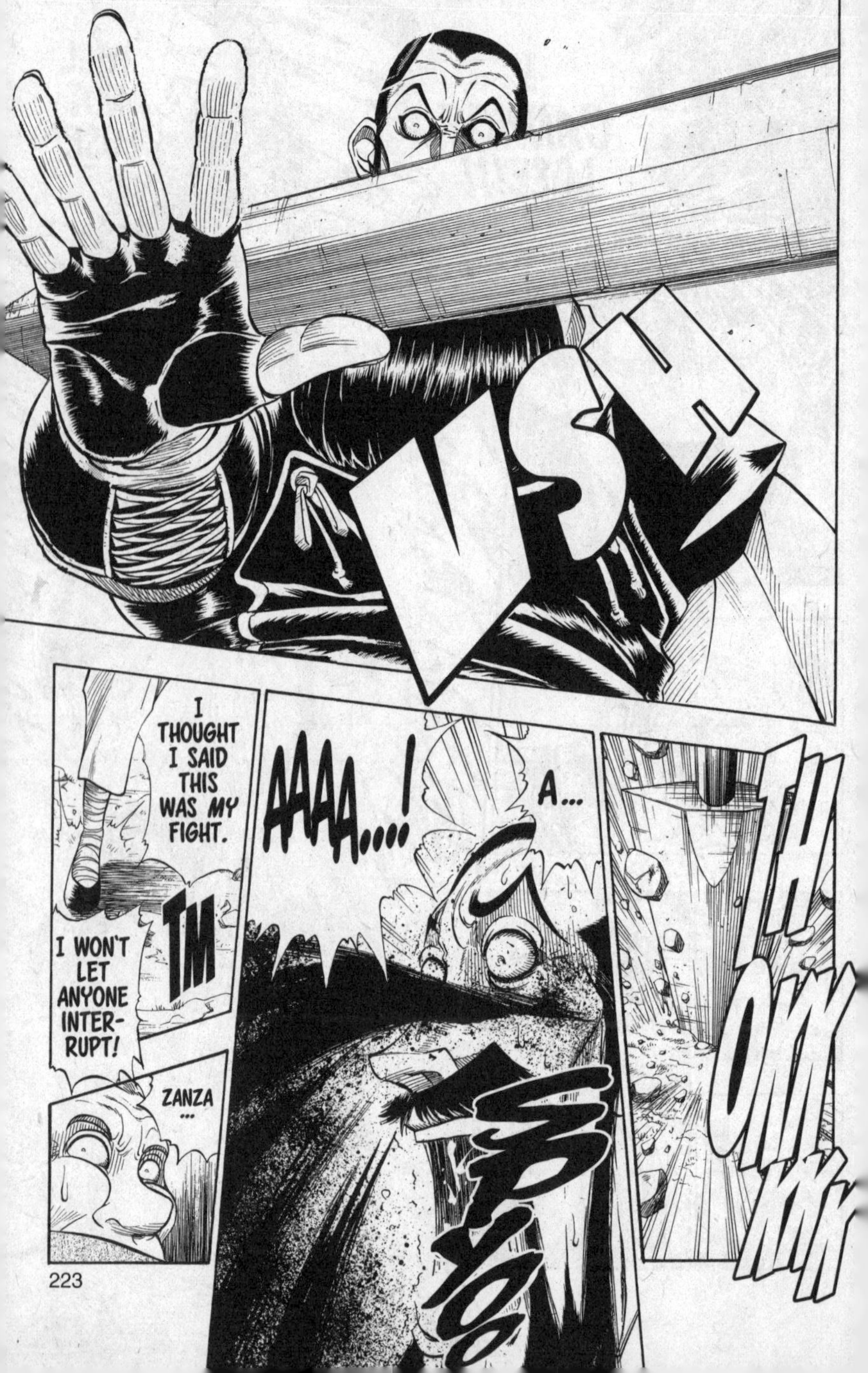
VSH
AAAA...!
A...
I THOUGHT I SAID THIS WAS MY FIGHT.
TM
I WON'T LET ANYONE INTER-RUPT!
ZANZA...

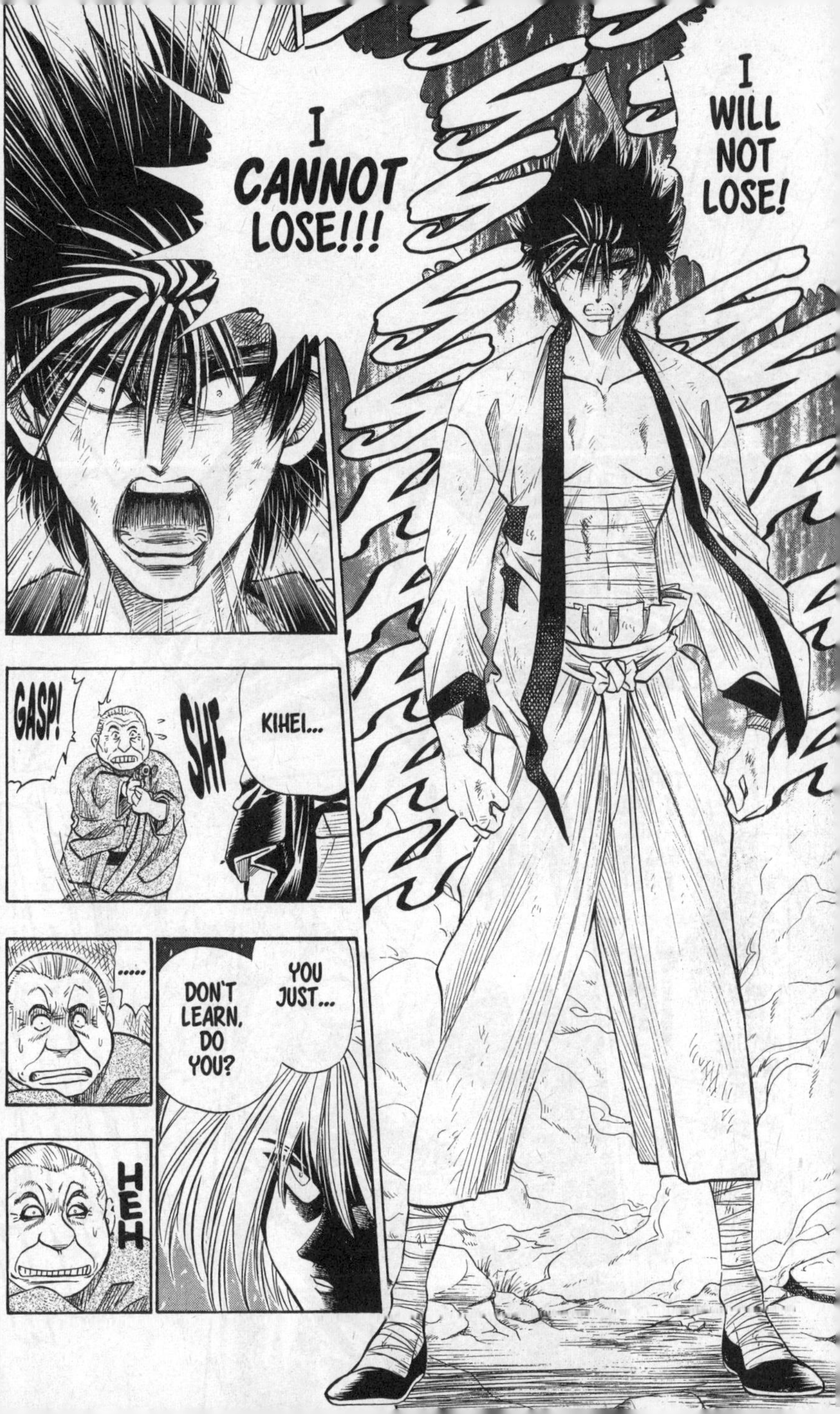
I WILL NOT LOSE!
I CANNOT LOSE!!!
KIHEI...
SHF
GASP!
YOU JUST... DON'T LEARN, DO YOU?
......
HEH

READ THIS WAY

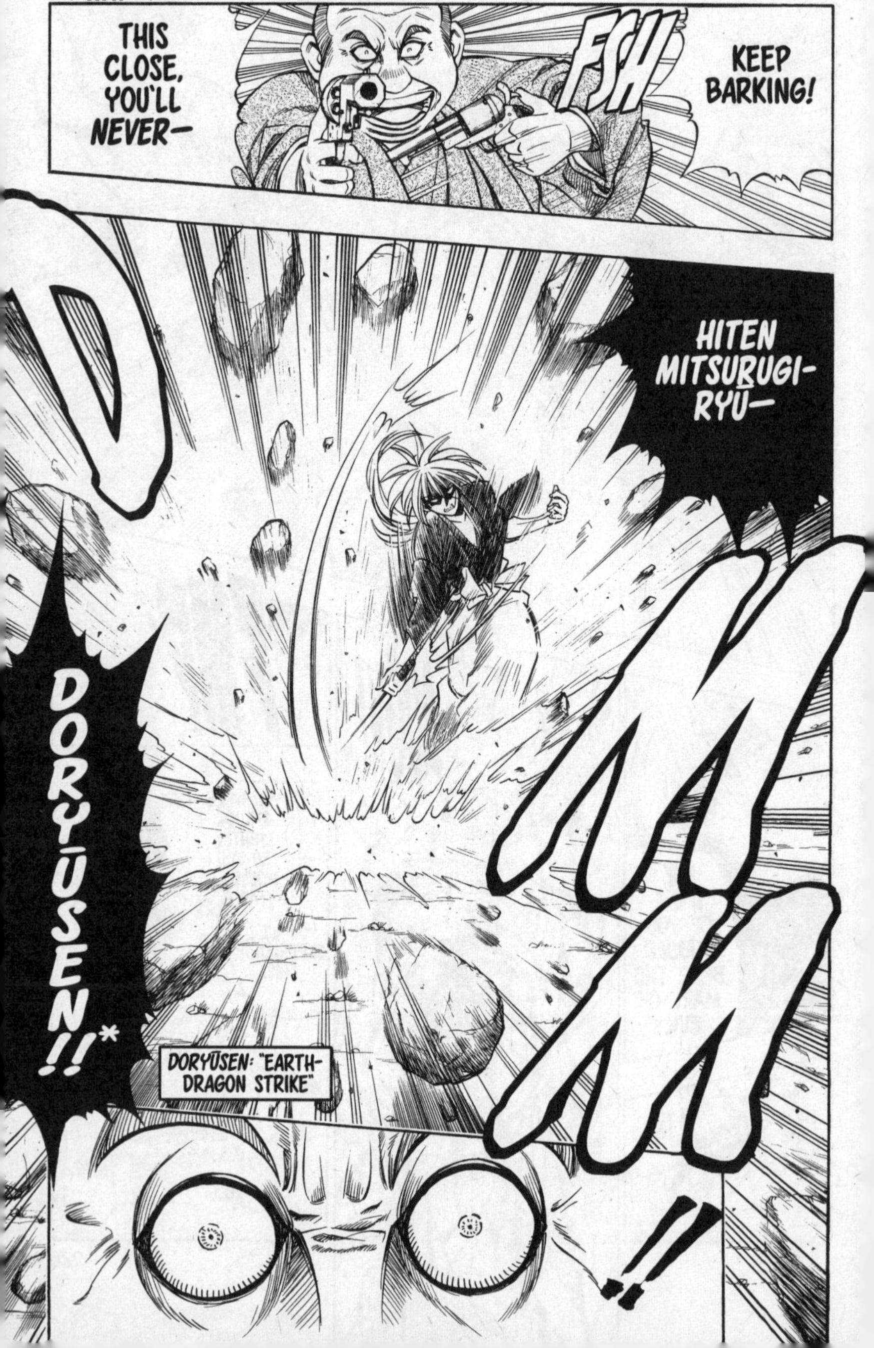
KEEP BARKING!
FSH
THIS CLOSE, YOU'LL NEVER—
HITEN MITSURUGI-RYŪ—
DORYŪSEN!!*
DORYŪSEN: "EARTH-DRAGON STRIKE"

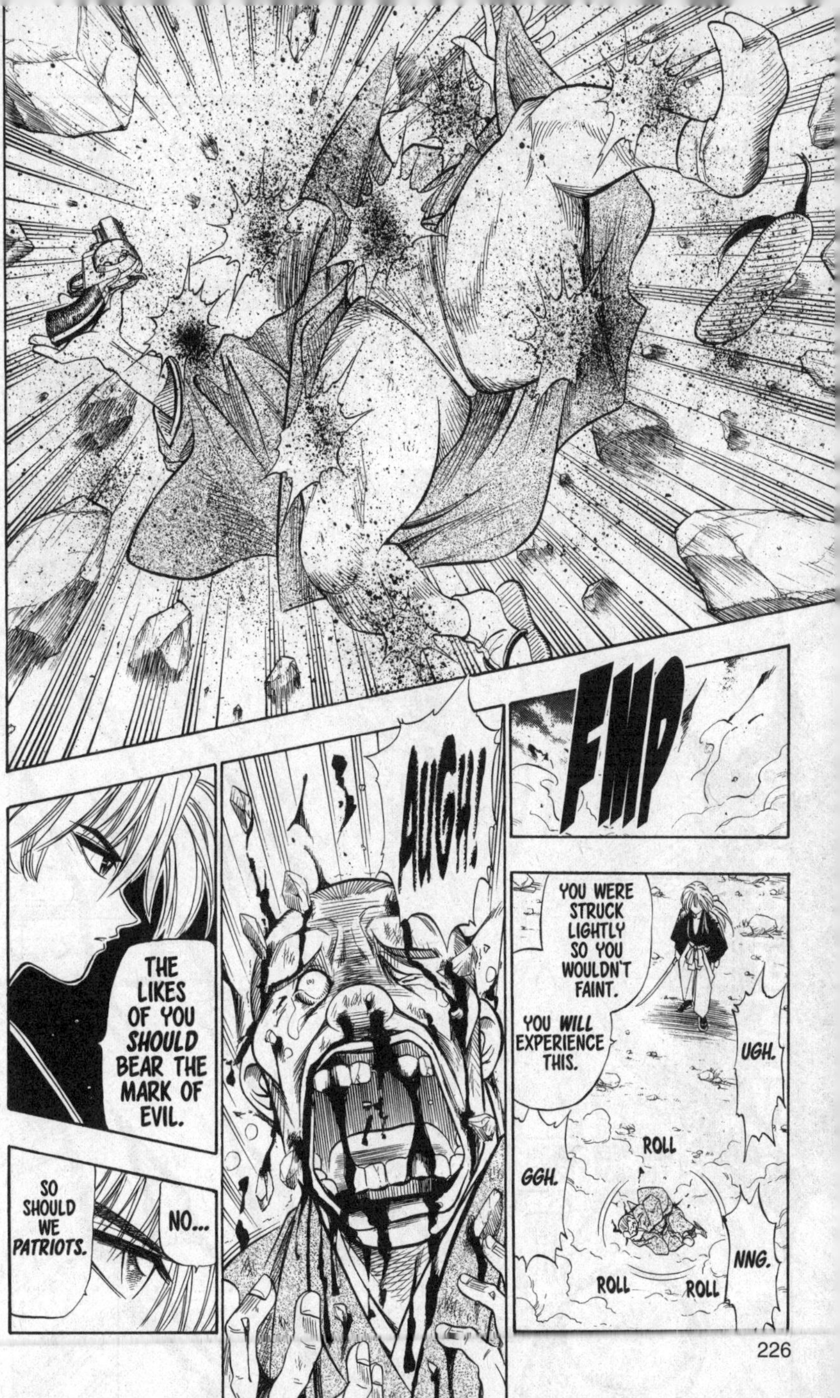
FMP
YOU WERE STRUCK LIGHTLY SO YOU WOULDN'T FAINT.
YOU *WILL* EXPERIENCE THIS.
UGH.
ROLL
GGH.
NNG.
ROLL
ROLL
AUGH!
THE LIKES OF YOU *SHOULD* BEAR THE MARK OF EVIL.
NO...
SO SHOULD WE PATRIOTS.

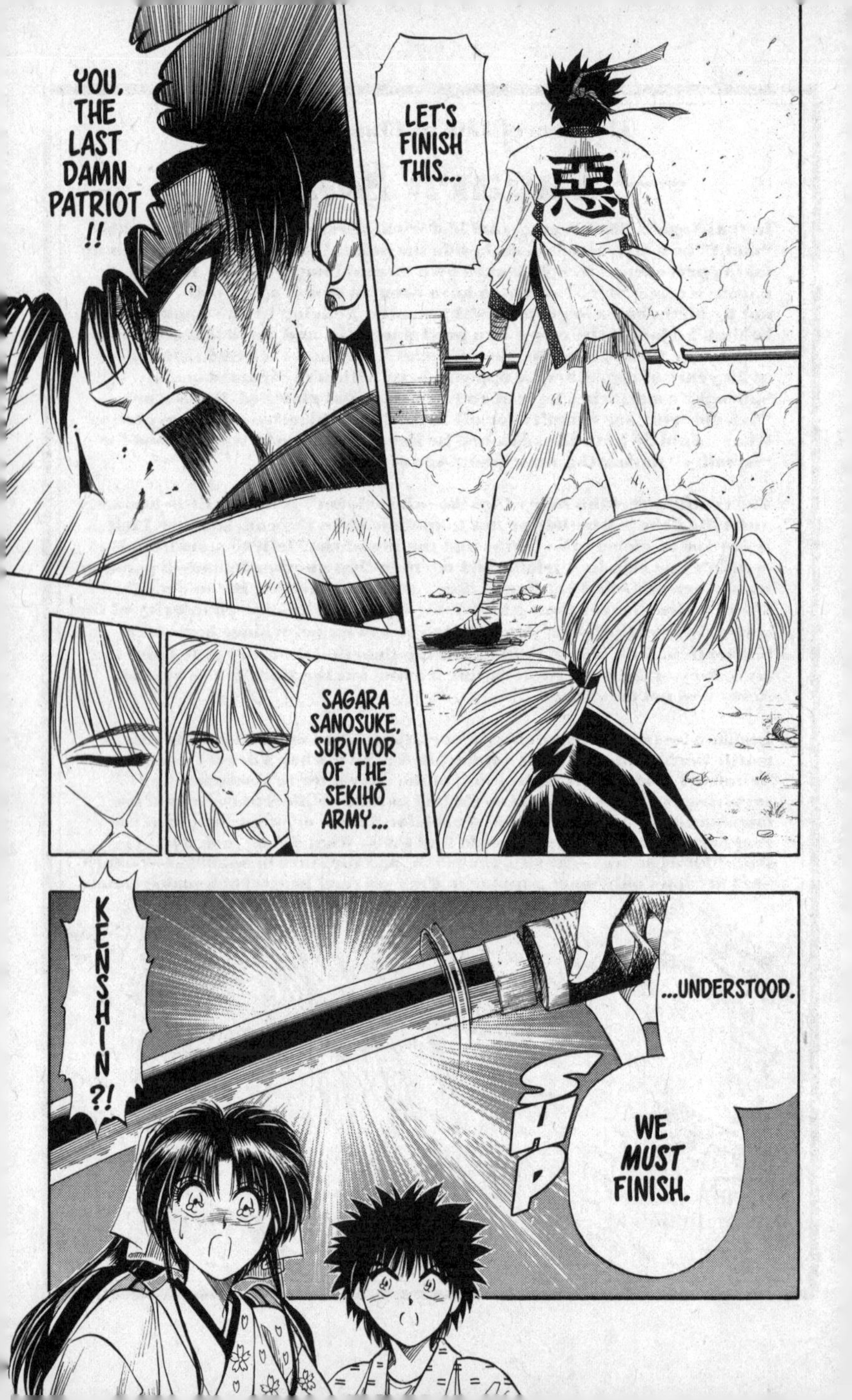
LET'S FINISH THIS...
YOU, THE LAST DAMN PATRIOT!!
SAGARA SANOSUKE, SURVIVOR OF THE SEKIHŌ ARMY...
...UNDERSTOOD.
WE MUST FINISH.
SHP
KENSHIN?!

The Secret Life of Characters (5)

—Sagara Sōzō—

In that Sagara Sōzō is an actual historical personage, talking about his "motif" as a character seems beside the point. Ultimately, what ended up taking precedence was Watsuki's own mental image. Sagara Sōzō (real name: Kojima Shirō) seems to have been an extravagant man, samurai not by birth, but scion of a wealthy family. Leaving his wife and children behind, he joined the cause as a pro-Imperialist and, as in this story, was eventually turned upon by the Imperial Army and executed (beheaded) at 29 years of age. Since he appears here within the framework of Sanosuke's memories, he is of course somewhat glorified. But Sagara Sōzō did truly see equality for all as the final objective of the revolution. What would he have thought, had he lived, had he seen what passed for "equality" during the subsequent Age of Meiji...?

The real-life "Sekihō Army (*Sekihō-tai*) Incident" is in fact little-known, and I did debate whether or not to include it. In the end, because I felt it showed so clearly the truths and the lies of the Meiji Restoration, I couldn't just skip it. A friend told me then that another friend—a popular manga creator—had cautioned that I might be "getting in too deep." There's also the fact that, while doing this storyline, the popularity of the series (in *Weekly Shonen Jump*) fell to its lowest point since beginning publication. Still, Watsuki did feel at the time that, in order to explore the true story of the Meiji Restoration, leaving out the story of the Sekihō Army was not an option.

Design-wise (and as mentioned above), there's not much reason to discuss motif. Back in the previous volume, in Act Two when I drew Yamagata Aritomo, I couldn't get my version of the character to resemble the surviving photos of him, and so I'd had to take a different route and use imagination as my guide. (I did search for photos or other images of the real Sagara Sōzō, but never could find them. What did he look like...?) Beautiful as he was—the sun, the moon, and the stars to Sanosuke—Sagara Sōzō becomes only more popular in the eyes (and hearts) of female readers.

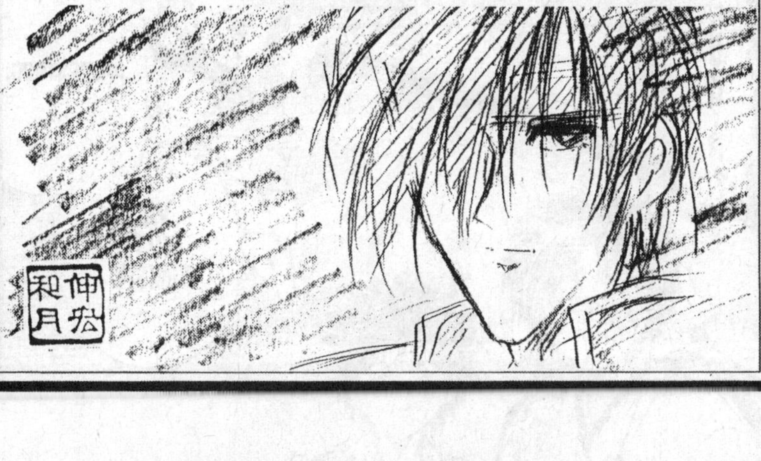
伸宏
和月

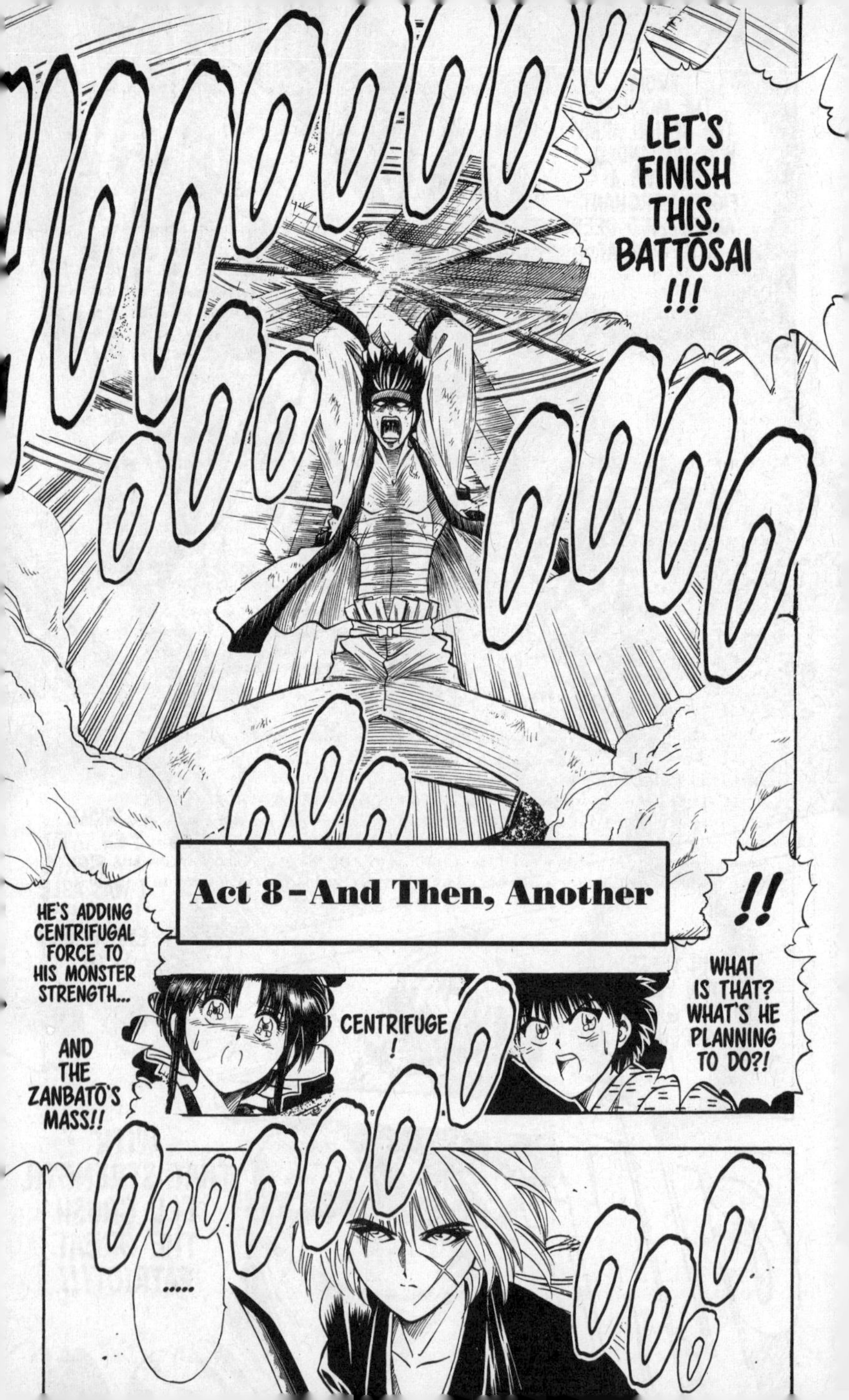
LET'S FINISH THIS, BATTŌSAI!!!
Act 8 – And Then, Another
!!
WHAT IS THAT? WHAT'S HE PLANNING TO DO?!
CENTRIFUGE!
HE'S ADDING CENTRIFUGAL FORCE TO HIS MONSTER STRENGTH...
AND THE ZANBATŌ'S MASS!!
......

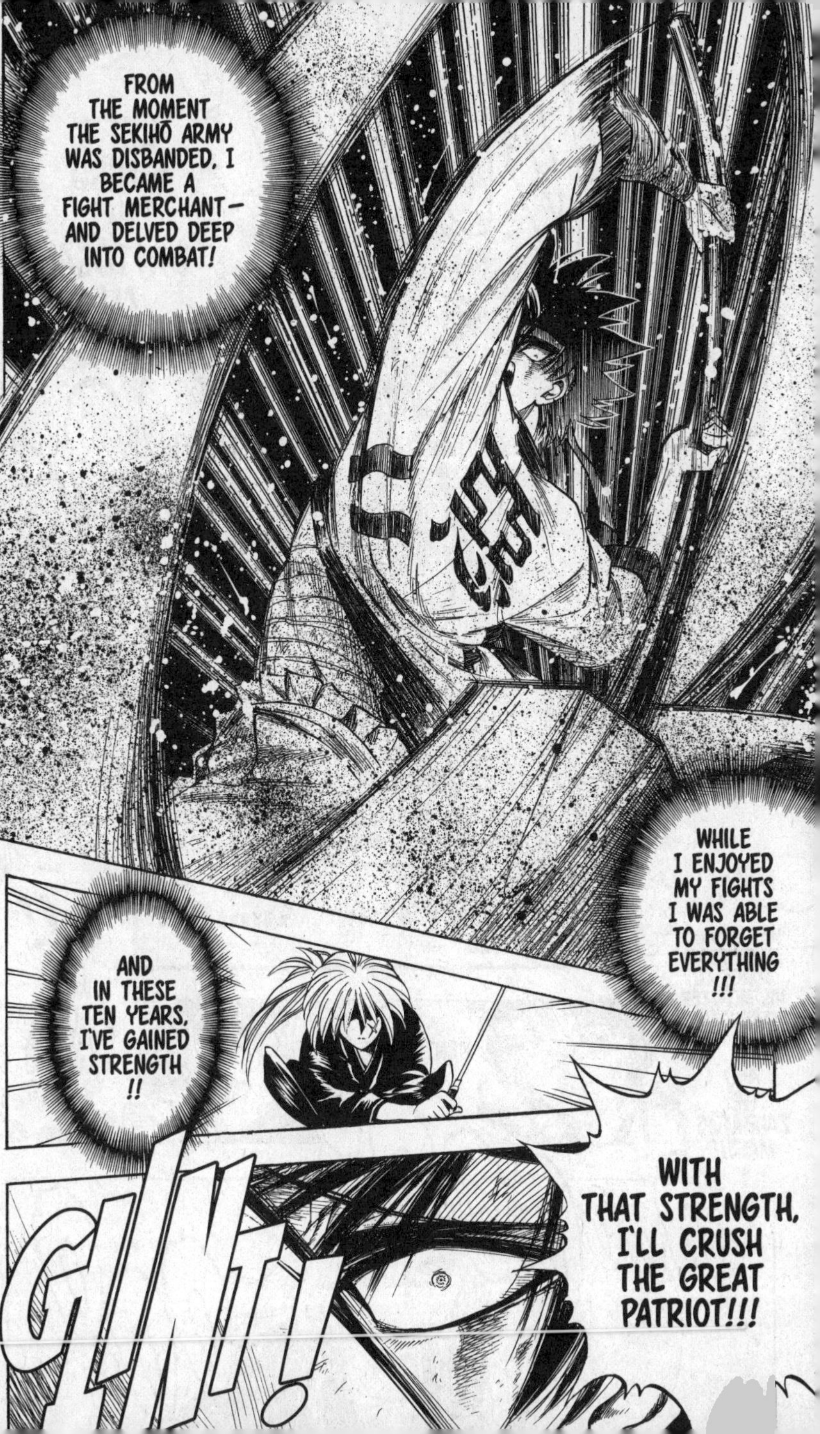
FROM THE MOMENT THE SEKIHŌ ARMY WAS DISBANDED, I BECAME A FIGHT MERCHANT—AND DELVED DEEP INTO COMBAT!
WHILE I ENJOYED MY FIGHTS I WAS ABLE TO FORGET EVERYTHING!!!
AND IN THESE TEN YEARS, I'VE GAINED STRENGTH!!
WITH THAT STRENGTH, I'LL CRUSH THE GREAT PATRIOT!!!

READ THIS WAY

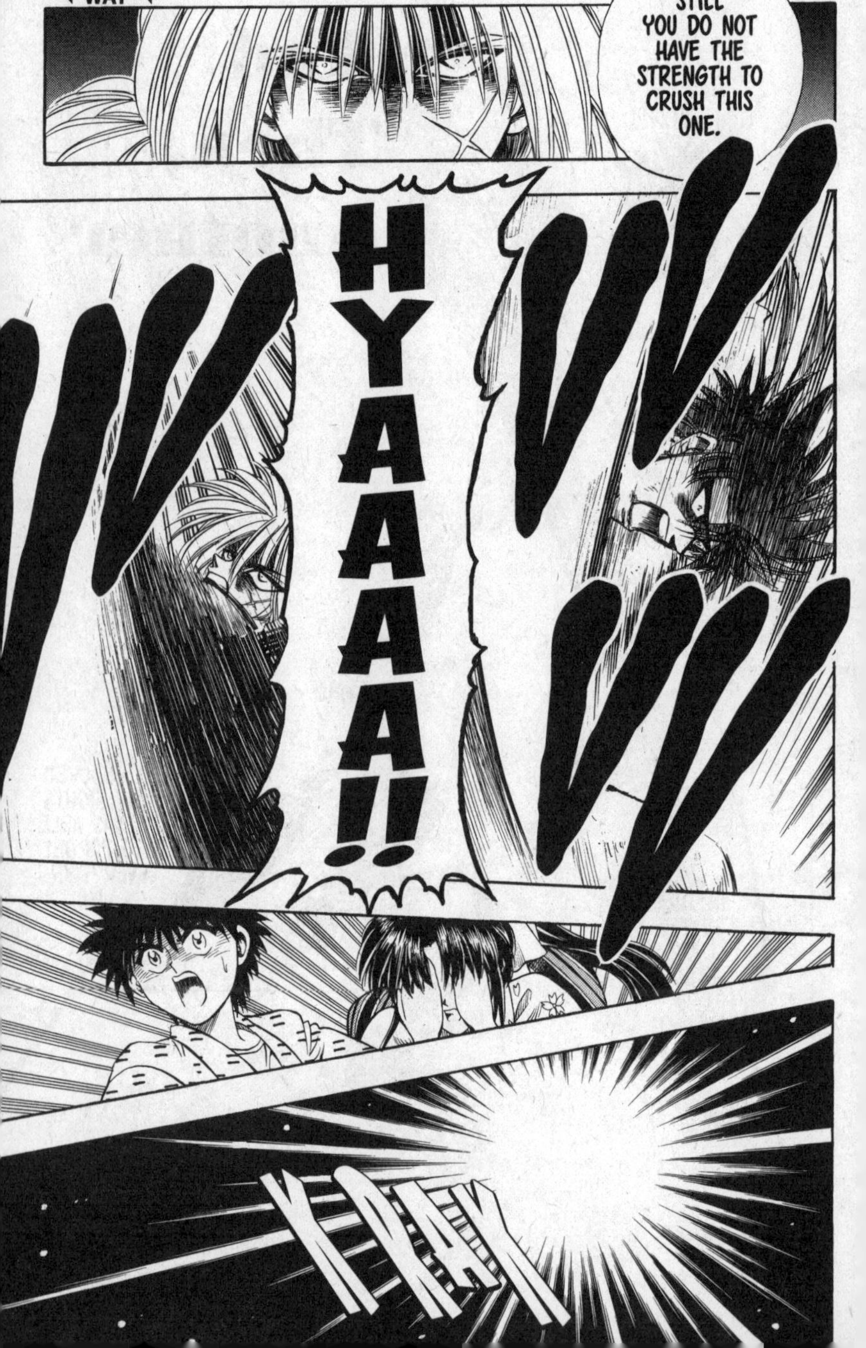

STILL YOU DO NOT HAVE THE STRENGTH TO CRUSH THIS ONE.
HYAAAA!!

Act 8
And Then, Another

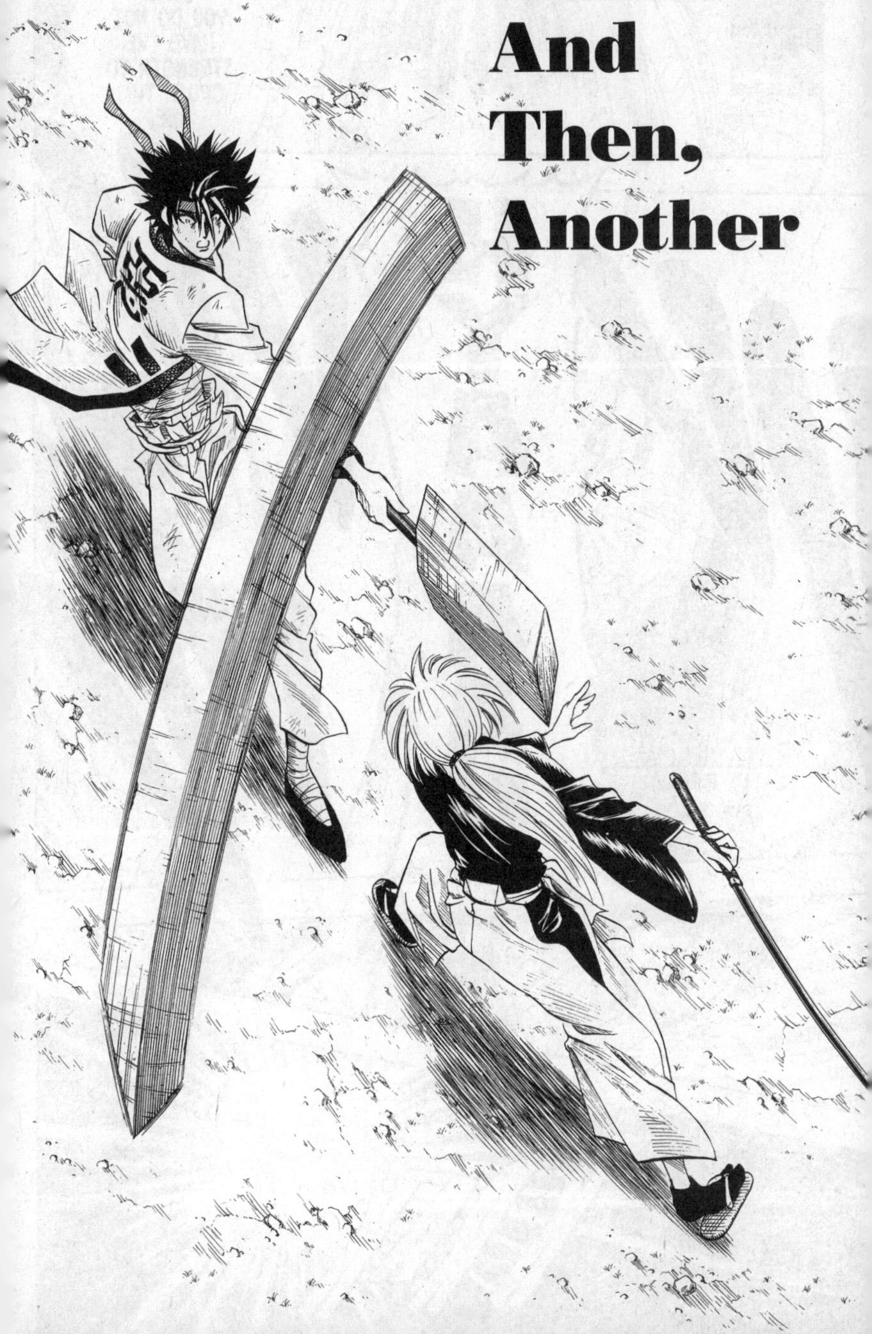

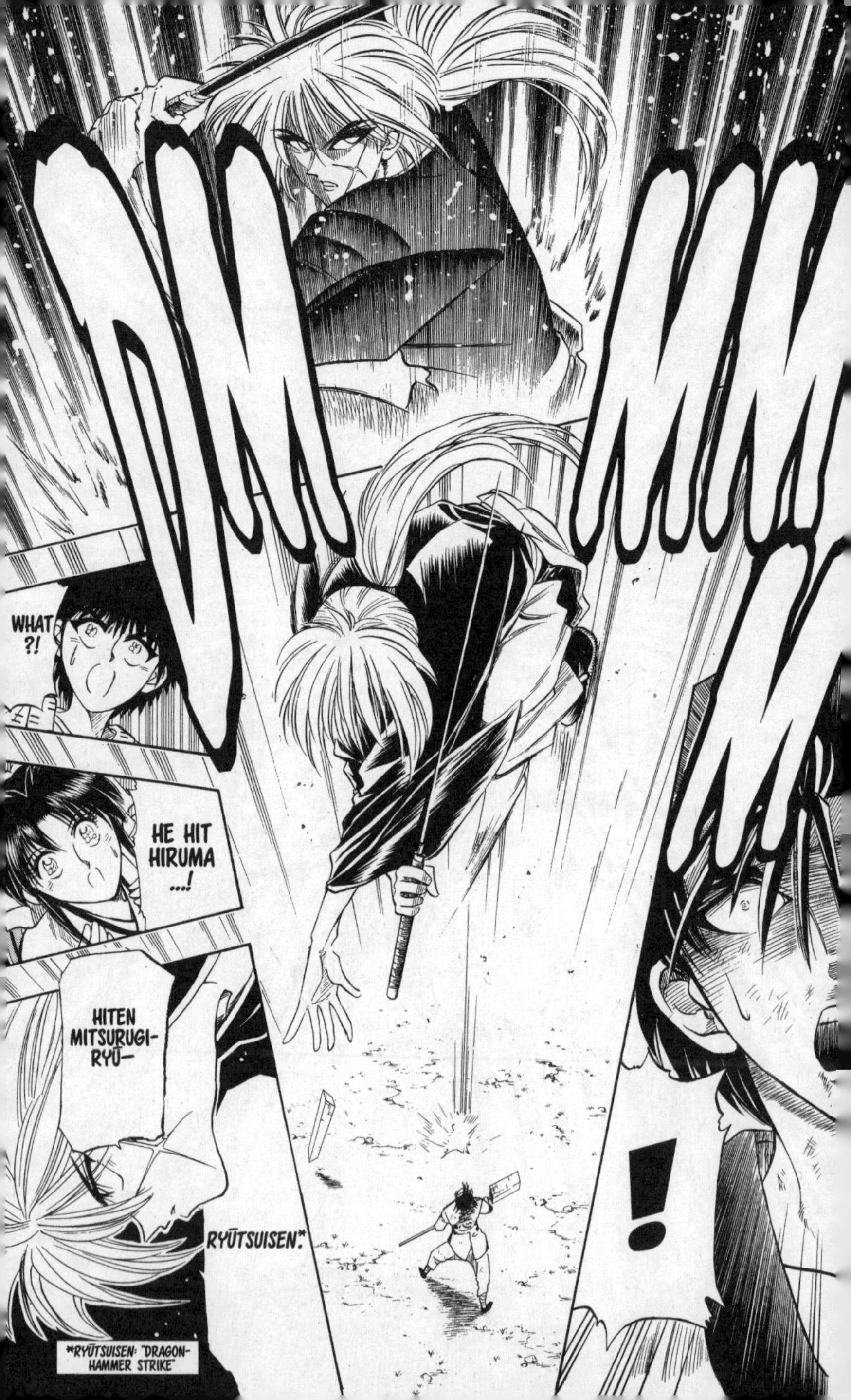
!
WHAT ?!
HE HIT HIRUMA ...!
HITEN MITSURUGI-RYŪ—
RYŪTSUISEN!*
*RYŪTSUISEN: "DRAGON-HAMMER STRIKE"

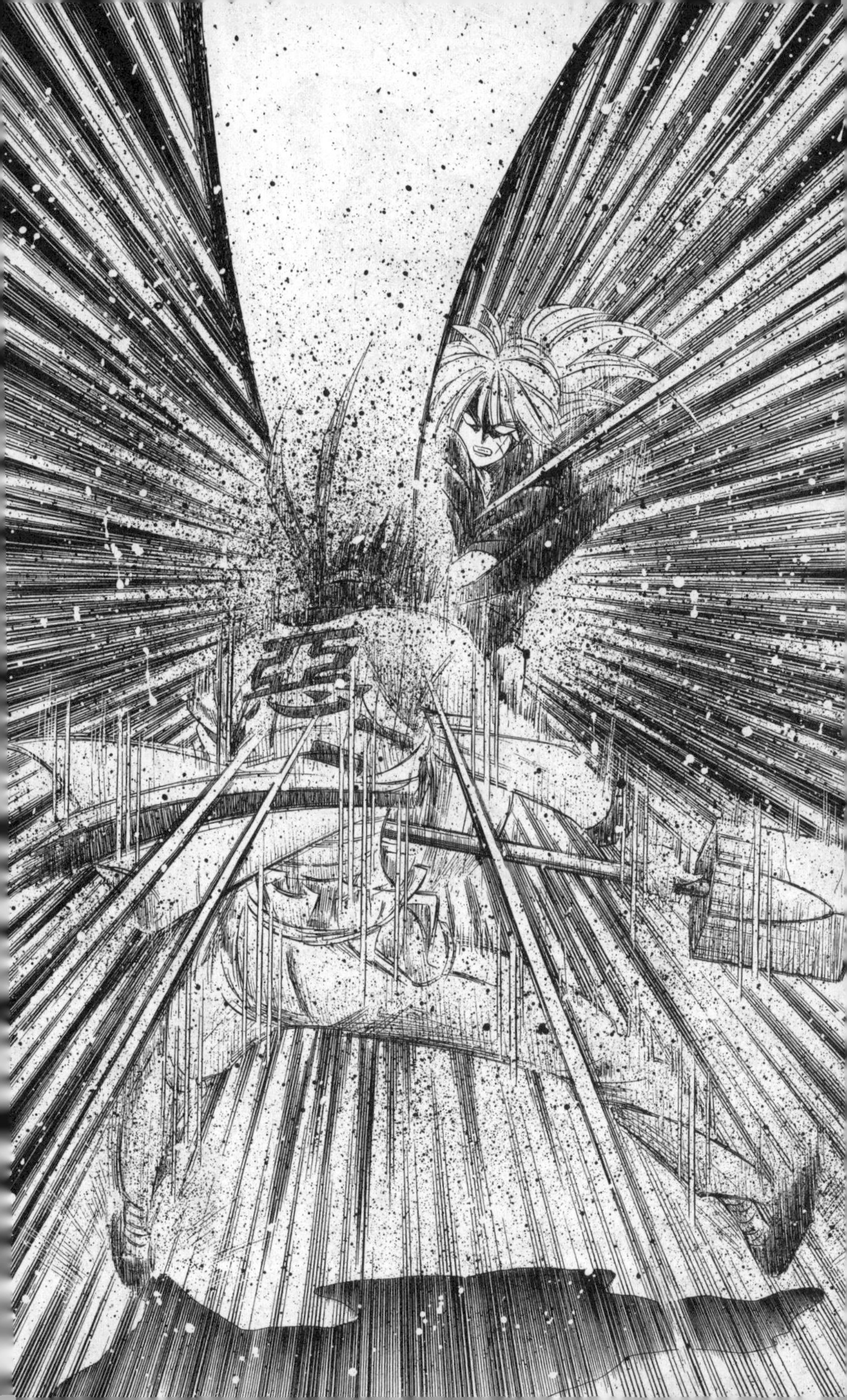

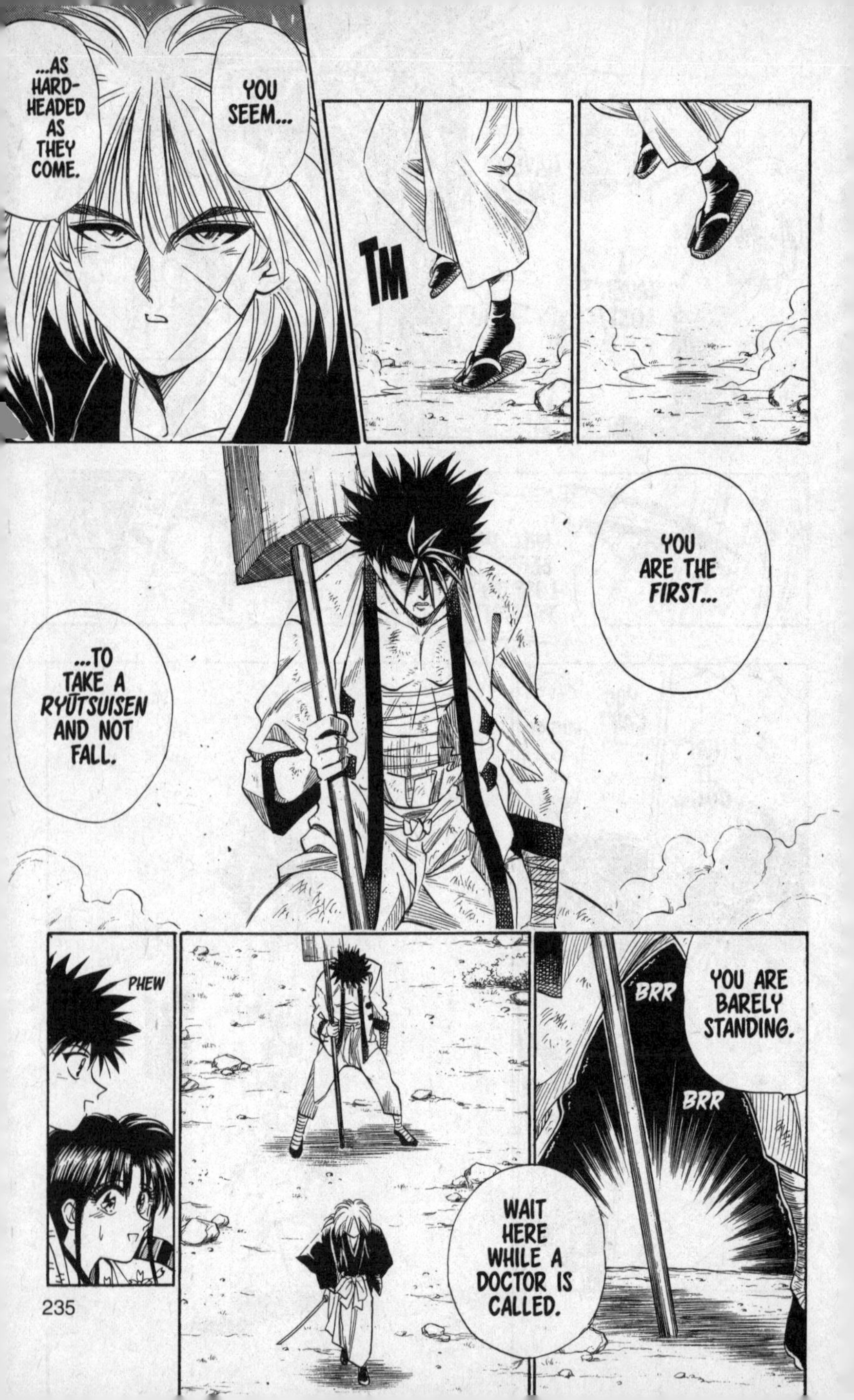
TM
YOU SEEM...
...AS HARD-HEADED AS THEY COME.
YOU ARE THE FIRST...
...TO TAKE A RYŪTSUISEN AND NOT FALL.
BRR
YOU ARE BARELY STANDING.
BRR
WAIT HERE WHILE A DOCTOR IS CALLED.
PHEW

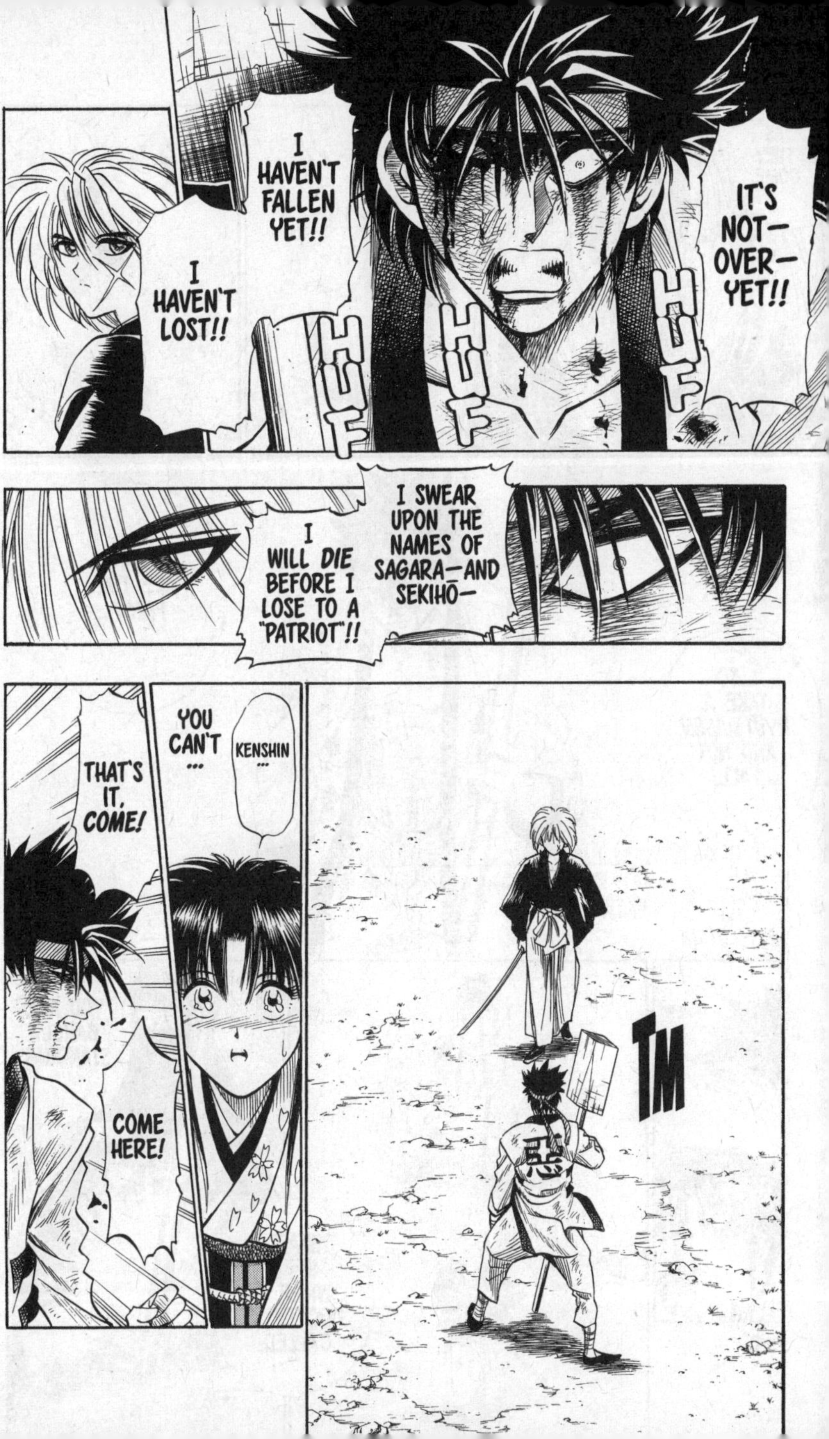
IT'S NOT—OVER—YET!!
HUF
HUF
HUF
I HAVEN'T FALLEN YET!!
I HAVEN'T LOST!!
I SWEAR UPON THE NAMES OF SAGARA—AND SEKIHŌ—
I WILL DIE BEFORE I LOSE TO A "PATRIOT"!!
TM
KENSHIN...
YOU CAN'T...
THAT'S IT, COME!
COME HERE!

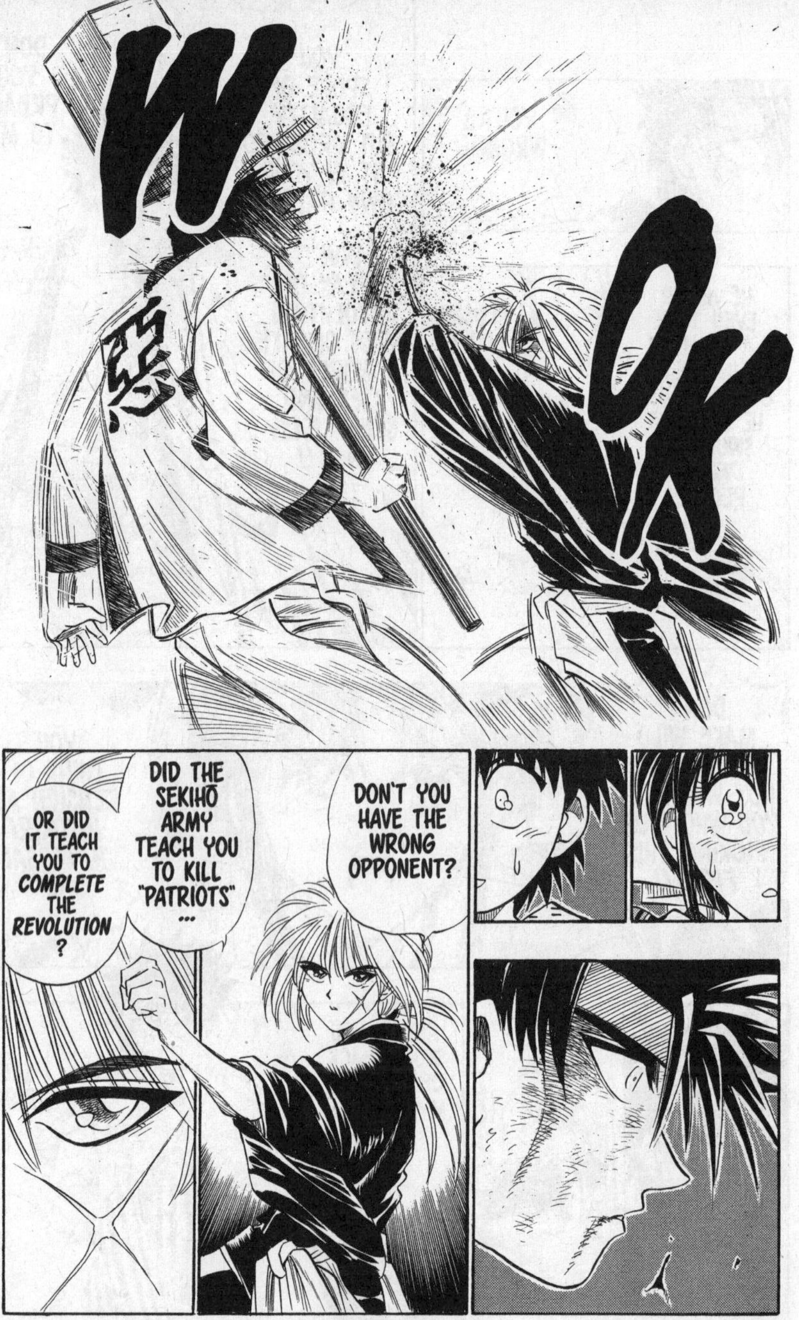
WOK
DON'T YOU HAVE THE WRONG OPPONENT?
DID THE SEKIHŌ ARMY TEACH YOU TO KILL "PATRIOTS" ...
OR DID IT TEACH YOU TO COMPLETE THE REVOLUTION ?

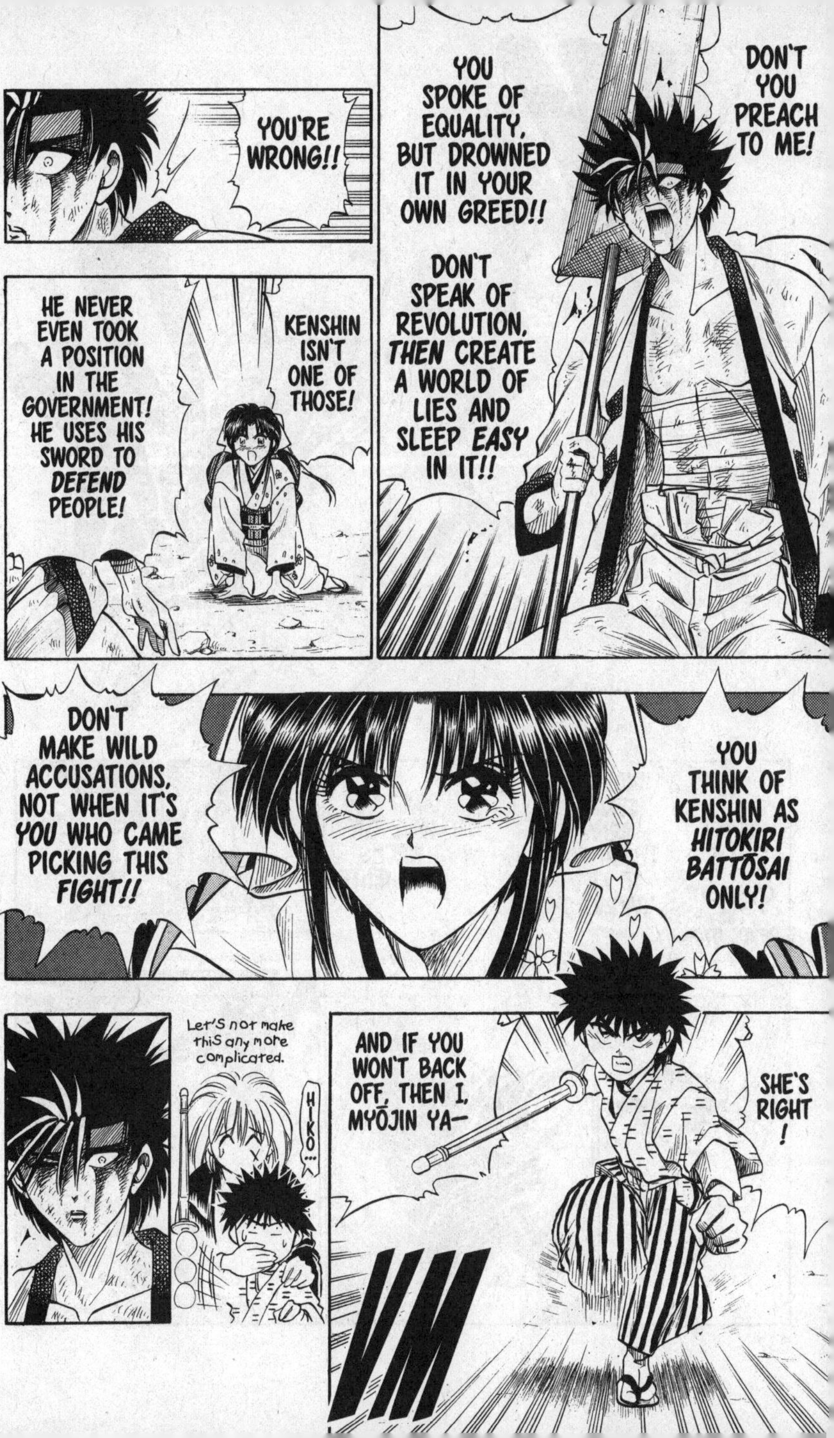
DON'T YOU PREACH TO ME!
YOU SPOKE OF EQUALITY, BUT DROWNED IT IN YOUR OWN GREED!!
DON'T SPEAK OF REVOLUTION, THEN CREATE A WORLD OF LIES AND SLEEP EASY IN IT!!
YOU'RE WRONG!!
KENSHIN ISN'T ONE OF THOSE!
HE NEVER EVEN TOOK A POSITION IN THE GOVERNMENT! HE USES HIS SWORD TO DEFEND PEOPLE!
YOU THINK OF KENSHIN AS HITOKIRI BATTŌSAI ONLY!
DON'T MAKE WILD ACCUSATIONS, NOT WHEN IT'S YOU WHO CAME PICKING THIS FIGHT!!
SHE'S RIGHT!
AND IF YOU WON'T BACK OFF, THEN I, MYŌJIN YA—
HIKO...
Let's not make this any more complicated.

READ THIS WAY

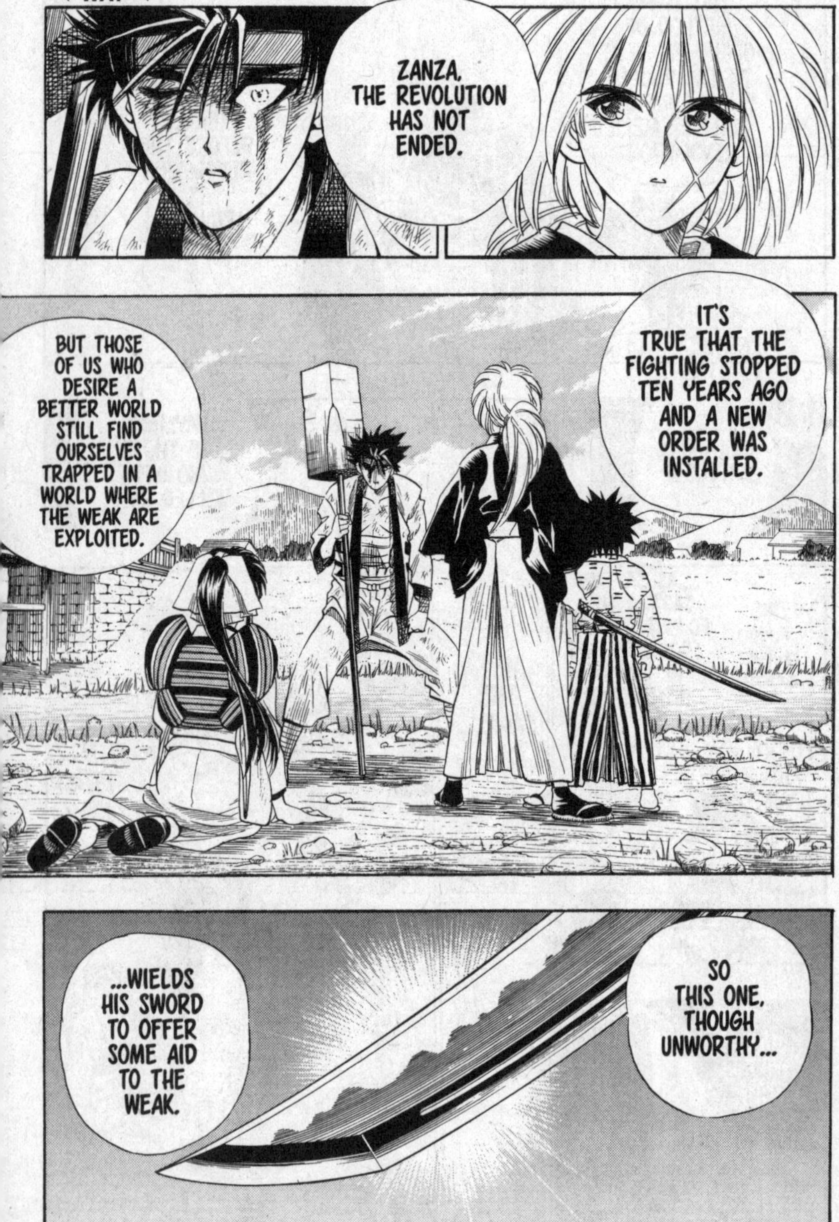
ZANZA, THE REVOLUTION HAS NOT ENDED.
IT'S TRUE THAT THE FIGHTING STOPPED TEN YEARS AGO AND A NEW ORDER WAS INSTALLED.
BUT THOSE OF US WHO DESIRE A BETTER WORLD STILL FIND OURSELVES TRAPPED IN A WORLD WHERE THE WEAK ARE EXPLOITED.
SO THIS ONE, THOUGH UNWORTHY...
...WIELDS HIS SWORD TO OFFER SOME AID TO THE WEAK.

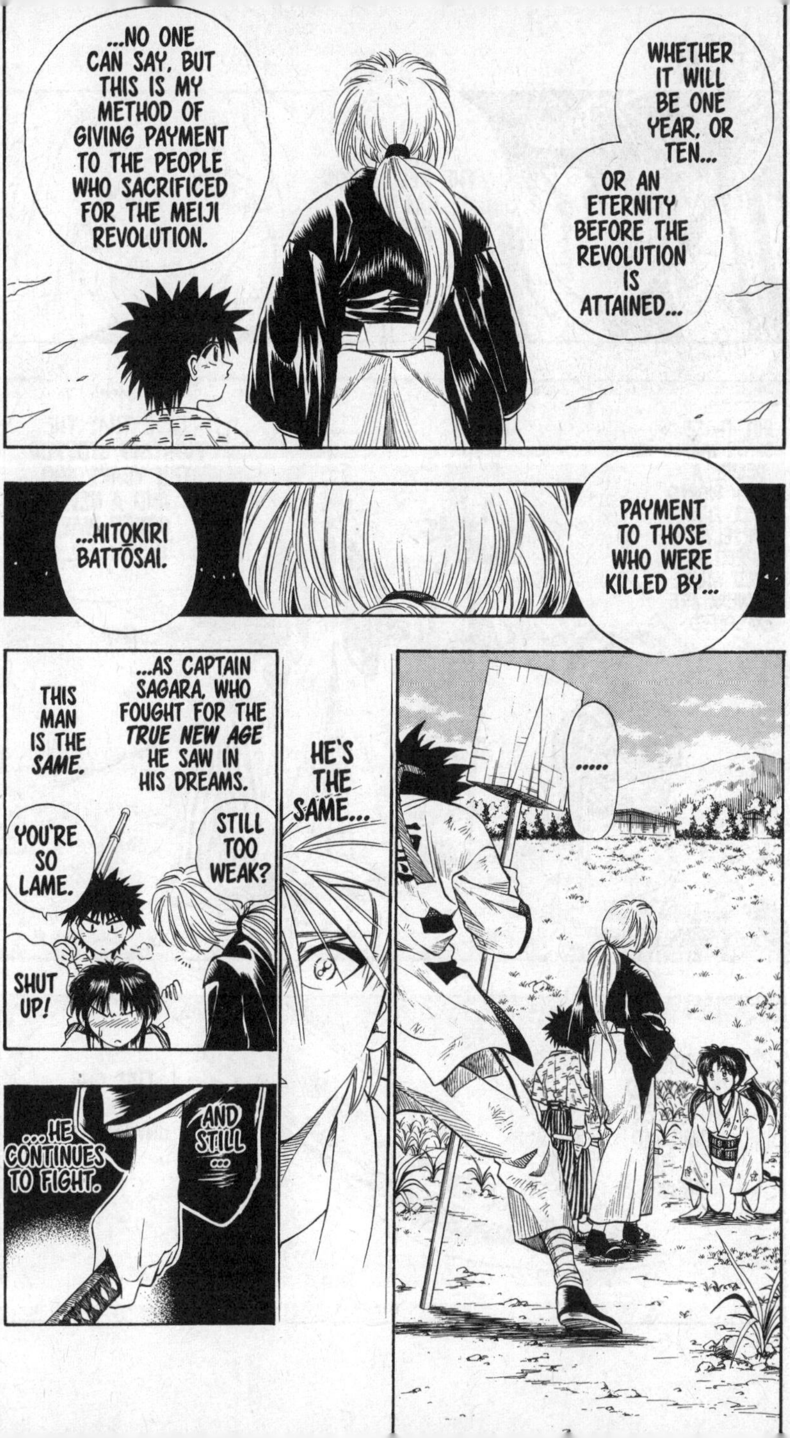
WHETHER IT WILL BE ONE YEAR, OR TEN...
OR AN ETERNITY BEFORE THE REVOLUTION IS ATTAINED...
...NO ONE CAN SAY, BUT THIS IS MY METHOD OF GIVING PAYMENT TO THE PEOPLE WHO SACRIFICED FOR THE MEIJI REVOLUTION.
PAYMENT TO THOSE WHO WERE KILLED BY...
...HITOKIRI BATTŌSAI.
.....
HE'S THE SAME...
...AS CAPTAIN SAGARA, WHO FOUGHT FOR THE *TRUE NEW AGE* HE SAW IN HIS DREAMS.
THIS MAN IS THE *SAME.*
STILL TOO WEAK?
YOU'RE SO LAME.
SHUT UP!
AND STILL...
...HE CONTINUES TO FIGHT.

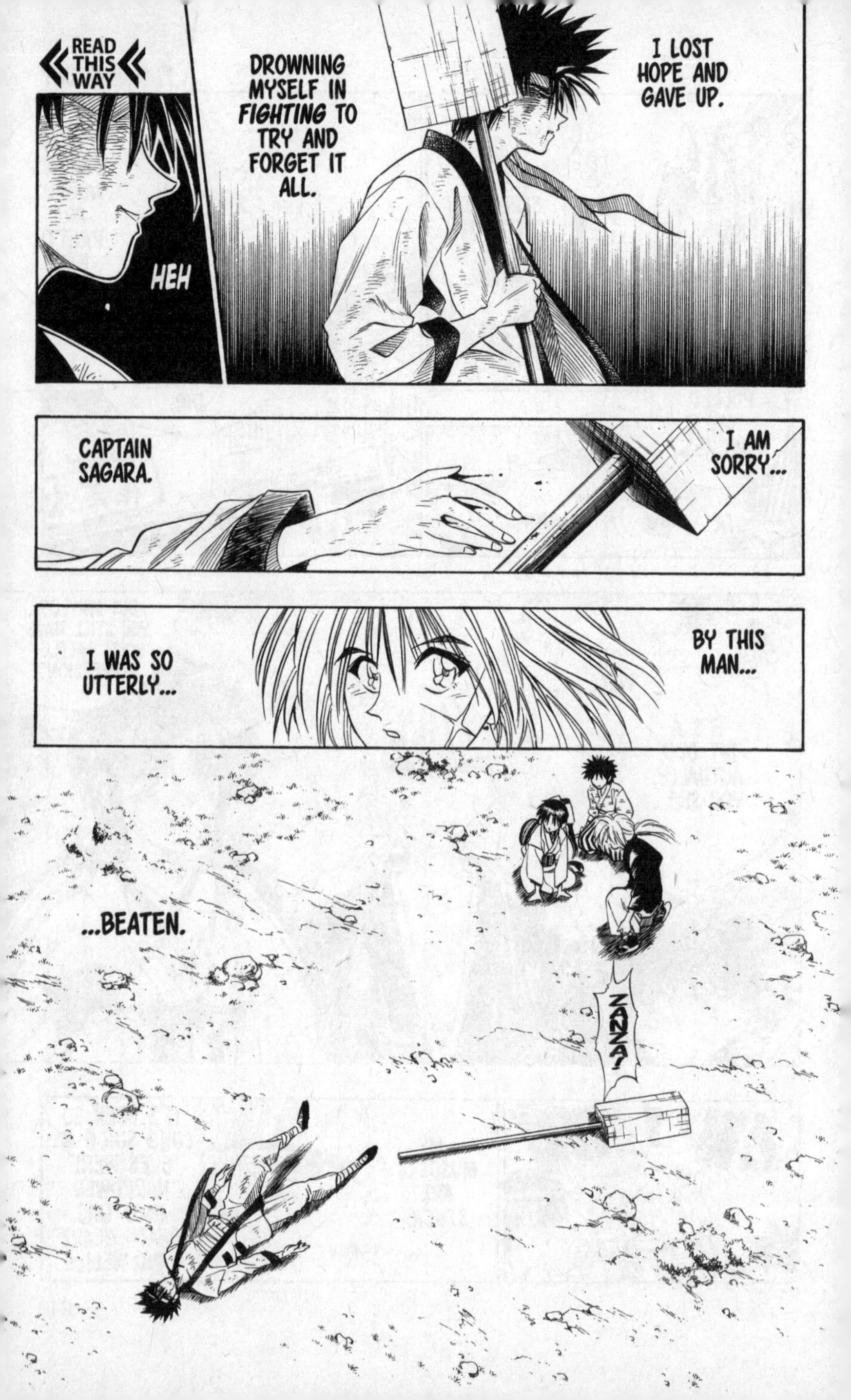

READ THIS WAY
I LOST HOPE AND GAVE UP.
DROWNING MYSELF IN FIGHTING TO TRY AND FORGET IT ALL.
HEH
I AM SORRY...
CAPTAIN SAGARA.
BY THIS MAN...
I WAS SO UTTERLY...
ZANZA!
...BEATEN.

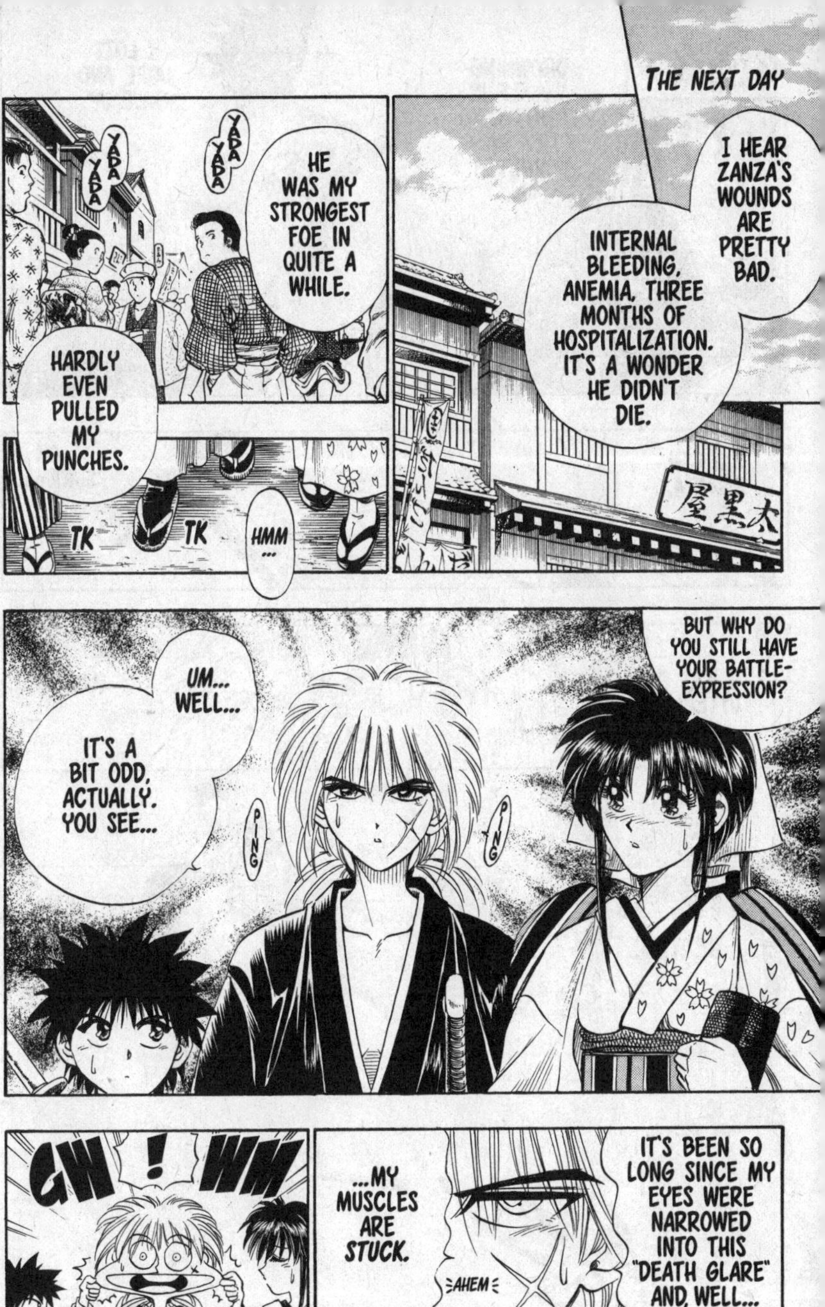
THE NEXT DAY
I HEAR ZANZA'S WOUNDS ARE PRETTY BAD.
INTERNAL BLEEDING, ANEMIA, THREE MONTHS OF HOSPITALIZATION. IT'S A WONDER HE DIDN'T DIE.
大黒屋
YADA YADA
YADA YADA
HE WAS MY STRONGEST FOE IN QUITE A WHILE.
HARDLY EVEN PULLED MY PUNCHES.
TK
TK
HMM...
BUT WHY DO YOU STILL HAVE YOUR BATTLE-EXPRESSION?
PING
PING
UM... WELL...
IT'S A BIT ODD, ACTUALLY. YOU SEE...
IT'S BEEN SO LONG SINCE MY EYES WERE NARROWED INTO THIS "DEATH GLARE" AND, WELL...
AHEM
...MY MUSCLES ARE STUCK.
GN ! WM

READ THIS WAY

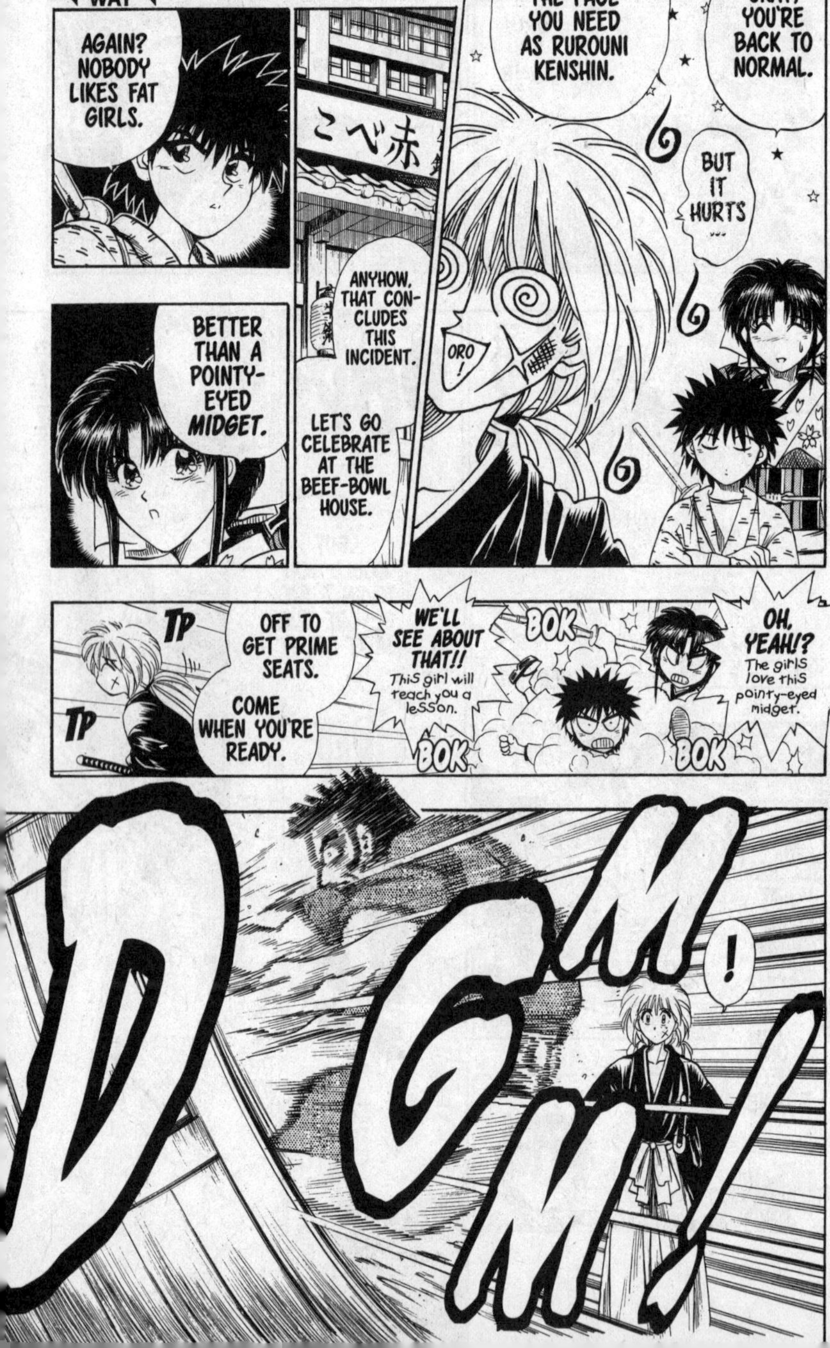

OKAY, YOU'RE BACK TO NORMAL.
THIS IS THE FACE YOU NEED AS RUROUNI KENSHIN.
BUT IT HURTS...
ORO!
ANYHOW, THAT CONCLUDES THIS INCIDENT.
LET'S GO CELEBRATE AT THE BEEF-BOWL HOUSE.
AGAIN? NOBODY LIKES FAT GIRLS.
BETTER THAN A POINTY-EYED MIDGET.
OH, YEAH!? The girls love this pointy-eyed midget.
BOK
WE'LL SEE ABOUT THAT!! This girl will teach you a lesson.
BOK
BOK
OFF TO GET PRIME SEATS.
COME WHEN YOU'RE READY.
TP
TP
DOM
DOM
!

READ THIS WAY

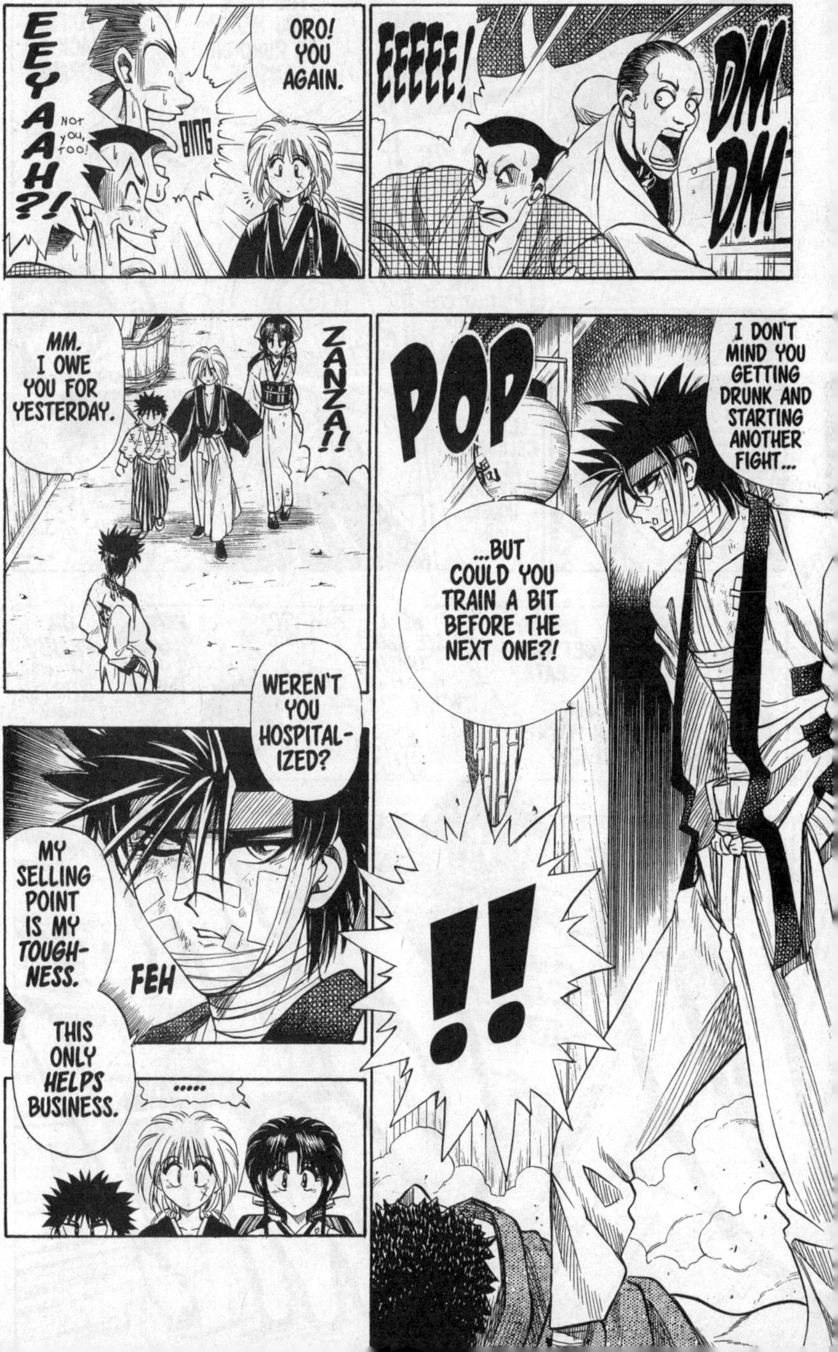

DM DM
EEEEE!
ORO! YOU AGAIN.
BING
Not you, too!
EEYAAAH?!
I DON'T MIND YOU GETTING DRUNK AND STARTING ANOTHER FIGHT...
POP
...BUT COULD YOU TRAIN A BIT BEFORE THE NEXT ONE?!
!!
ZANZA!!
MM. I OWE YOU FOR YESTERDAY.
WEREN'T YOU HOSPITAL-IZED?
MY SELLING POINT IS MY TOUGH-NESS.
FEH
THIS ONLY HELPS BUSINESS.
.....

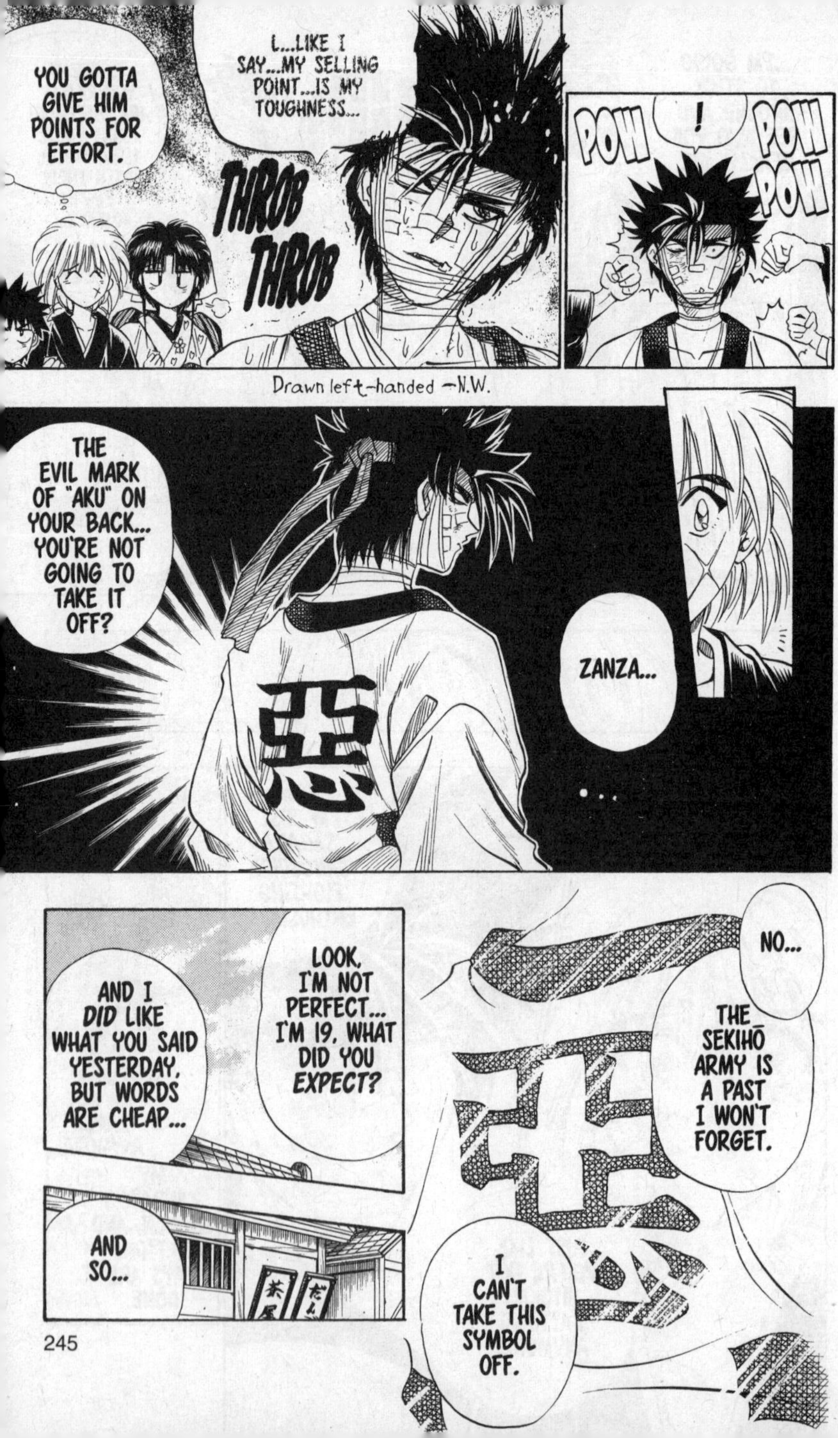
!
POW POW POW
L...LIKE I SAY...MY SELLING POINT...IS MY TOUGHNESS...
YOU GOTTA GIVE HIM POINTS FOR EFFORT.
THROB THROB
Drawn left-handed —N.W.
ZANZA...
THE EVIL MARK OF "AKU" ON YOUR BACK... YOU'RE NOT GOING TO TAKE IT OFF?
...
NO...
THE SEKIHŌ ARMY IS A PAST I WON'T FORGET.
I CAN'T TAKE THIS SYMBOL OFF.
LOOK, I'M NOT PERFECT... I'M 19. WHAT DID YOU *EXPECT?*
AND I *DID* LIKE WHAT YOU SAID YESTERDAY, BUT WORDS ARE CHEAP...
AND SO...

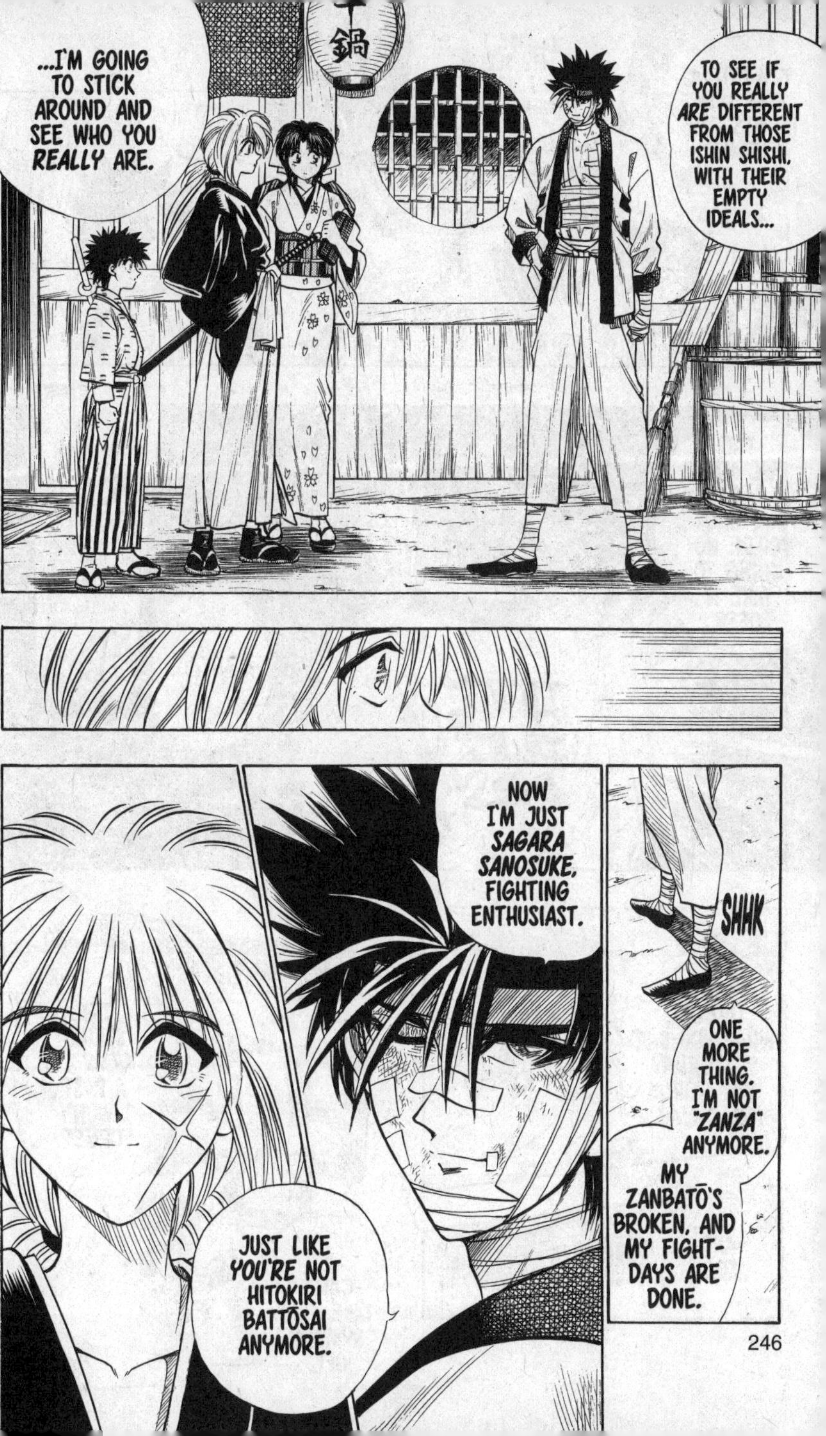

TO SEE IF YOU REALLY ARE DIFFERENT FROM THOSE ISHIN SHISHI, WITH THEIR EMPTY IDEALS...
鍋
...I'M GOING TO STICK AROUND AND SEE WHO YOU REALLY ARE.
SHHK
ONE MORE THING. I'M NOT "ZANZA" ANYMORE.
MY ZANBATŌ'S BROKEN, AND MY FIGHT-DAYS ARE DONE.
NOW I'M JUST SAGARA SANOSUKE, FIGHTING ENTHUSIAST.
JUST LIKE YOU'RE NOT HITOKIRI BATTŌSAI ANYMORE.

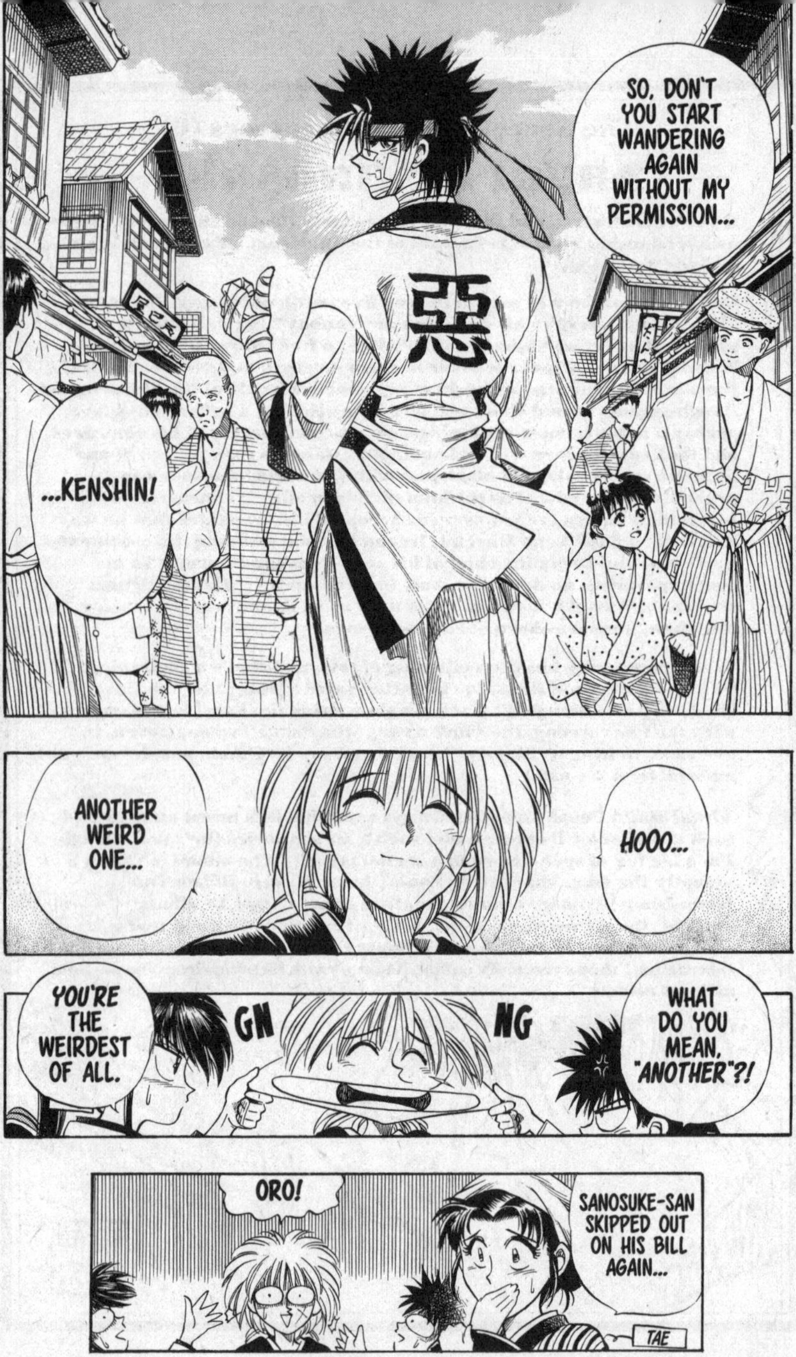
SO, DON'T YOU START WANDERING AGAIN WITHOUT MY PERMISSION...
...KENSHIN!
HOOO...
ANOTHER WEIRD ONE...
WHAT DO YOU MEAN, "ANOTHER"?!
GN NG
YOU'RE THE WEIRDEST OF ALL.
SANOSUKE-SAN SKIPPED OUT ON HIS BILL AGAIN...
TAE
ORO!

The Secret Life of Characters (6)

—Sagara Sanosuke—

If you're a Shinsengumi fan, you've probably figured this one out right away: Sanosuke's motif is Captain of the Shinsengumi's 10th division, Harada Sanosuke.

Harada Sanosuke was among the top five best-looking guys in the Shinsengumi...despite his depiction as "chubby" in (well-known historical novelist) Shiba Ryōtarō's *Moeyo Ken* [*Burn, O Sword*]—Watsuki's bible! A spear-wielder of great strength and forever fighting, Harada Sanosuke was active in every decisive battle of the Shinsengumi. Rough-mannered and short-tempered, he also had a softer side—due, perhaps, to his humble beginnings. He was considerate of his comrades and took special care with subordinates. Quick to pass judgment and prone to seeing things in black and white, Harada Sanosuke can probably be thought of as the kind of "big brother" character so common in manga for young men. Accepted history states that he was K.I.A. during the Ueno War, but legend has him crossing the continent (to China) and becoming chief of his very own bandit army. To his contemporaries, no doubt, he must have cut quite a dashing figure; obviously, Watsuki liked him quite a bit as well, and wanted him for *RuroKen.* Thus was born Sagara Sanosuke.

Sano's popularity has been climbing of late, and that's a good thing. But as the *Rurouni Kenshin* character voted "Most Likely to Have His First Name Mangled" (I see people writing the *kanji* for "Sanosuke" with the "*Sa*" wrong, the "*no*" wrong, the "*suke*" wrong...even, in one case, writing it "*Sasuke*"!!), all I can say is: C'mon, people—he's not a *ninja!* (Sad...so sad.)

***Visual Motif:* People are also always assuming he's based on such-and-such a character from such-and-such a manga series (he's not, though I'm a big fan of such-and-such a series, myself). The model for Sano is actually the main character "Lamp" from *Mashin Bōken Tan Lamp-Lamp* [*Arabian Genie Adventure Lamp-Lamp*] by Obata Takeshi, the *Hikaru No Go* artist. As for where *that* all started, that was with me, doodling in sketchbooks during my days as an assistant, adding and subtracting, then eventually calling it Sano—with blessings from the original artist, of course.**

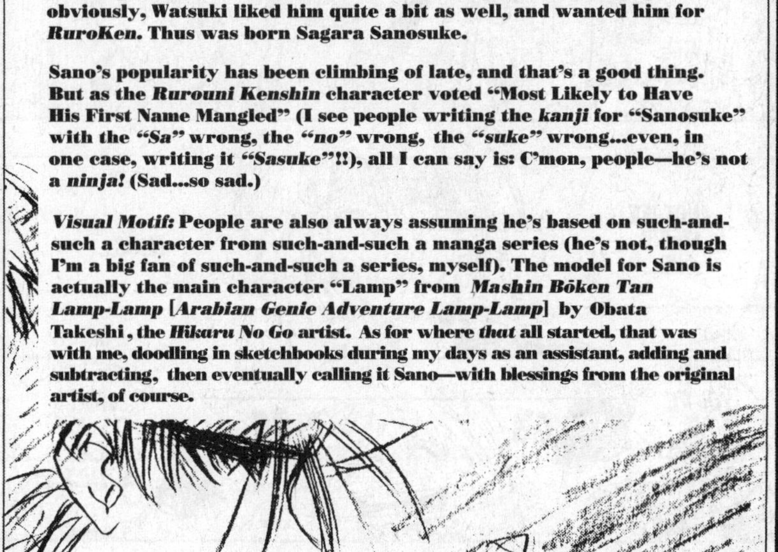
伸宏
和月

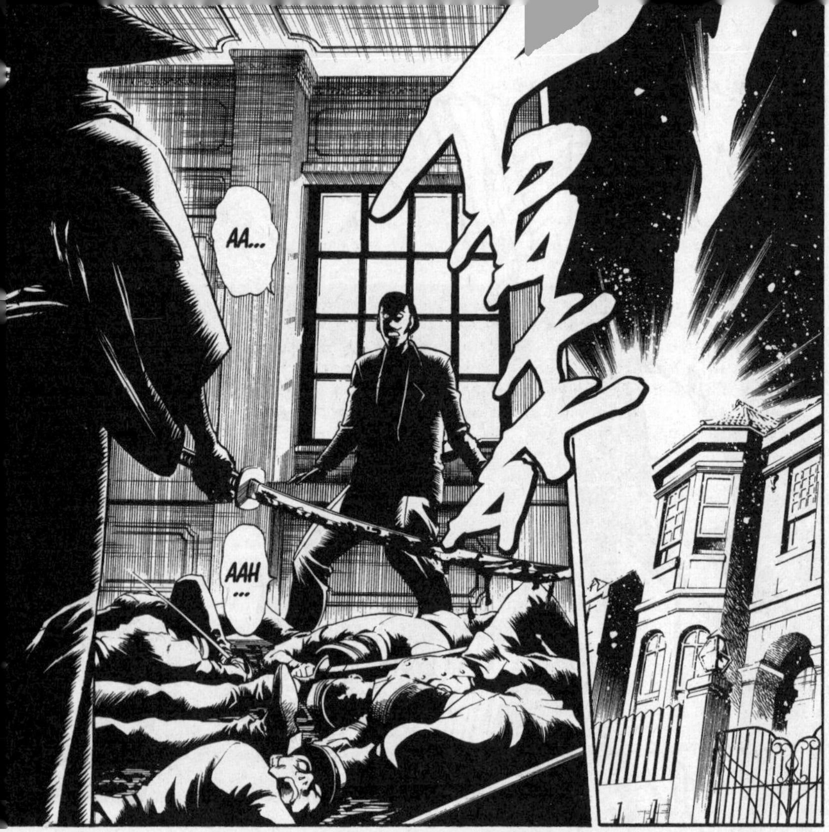
AA...
AAH ...

Act 9 – Kurogasa

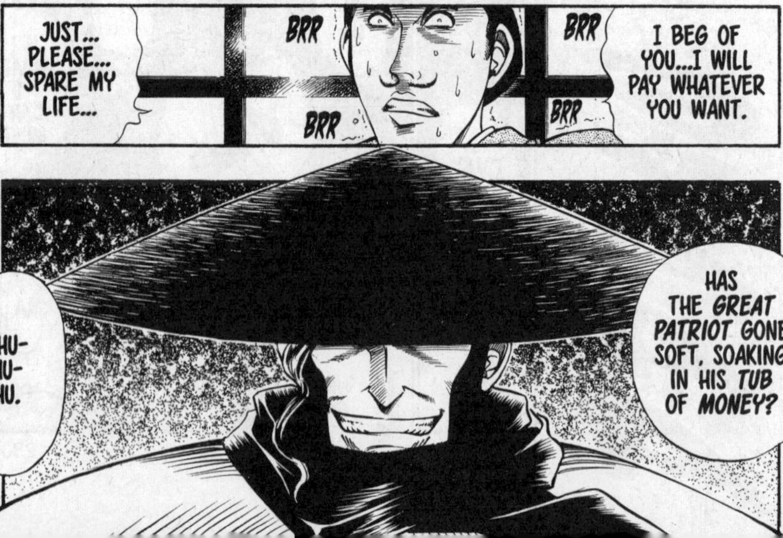
BRR
BRR
I BEG OF YOU...I WILL PAY WHATEVER YOU WANT.
BRR
BRR
JUST... PLEASE... SPARE MY LIFE...
HAS THE *GREAT PATRIOT* GONE SOFT, SOAKING IN HIS *TUB* OF *MONEY?*
UHU-HU-HU.

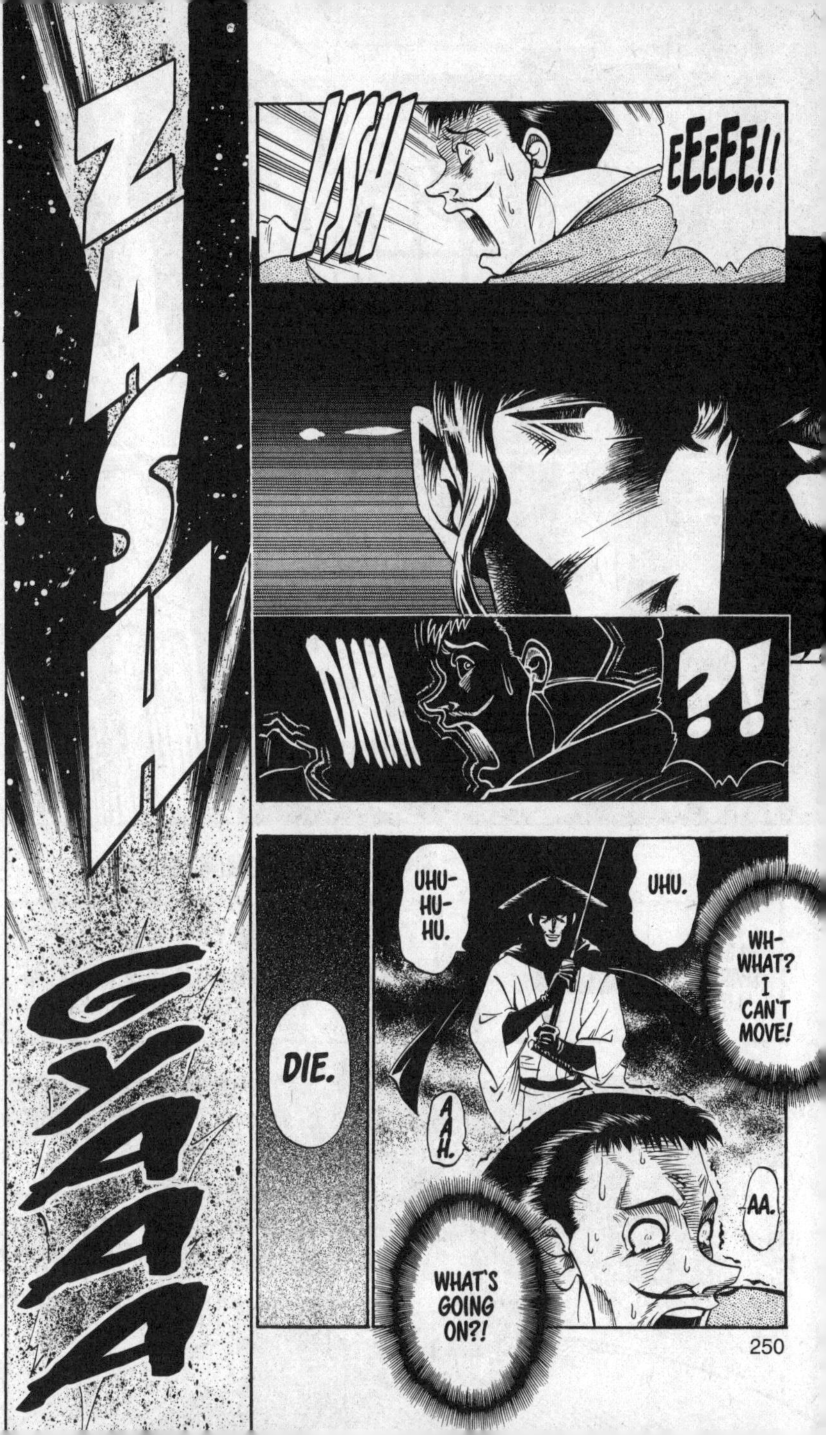
EEEEE!!
VSH
?!
DMM
WH-WHAT? I CAN'T MOVE!
UHU.
UHU-HU-HU.
AA.
AAH.
WHAT'S GOING ON?!
DIE.
ZASH
GYAAAA

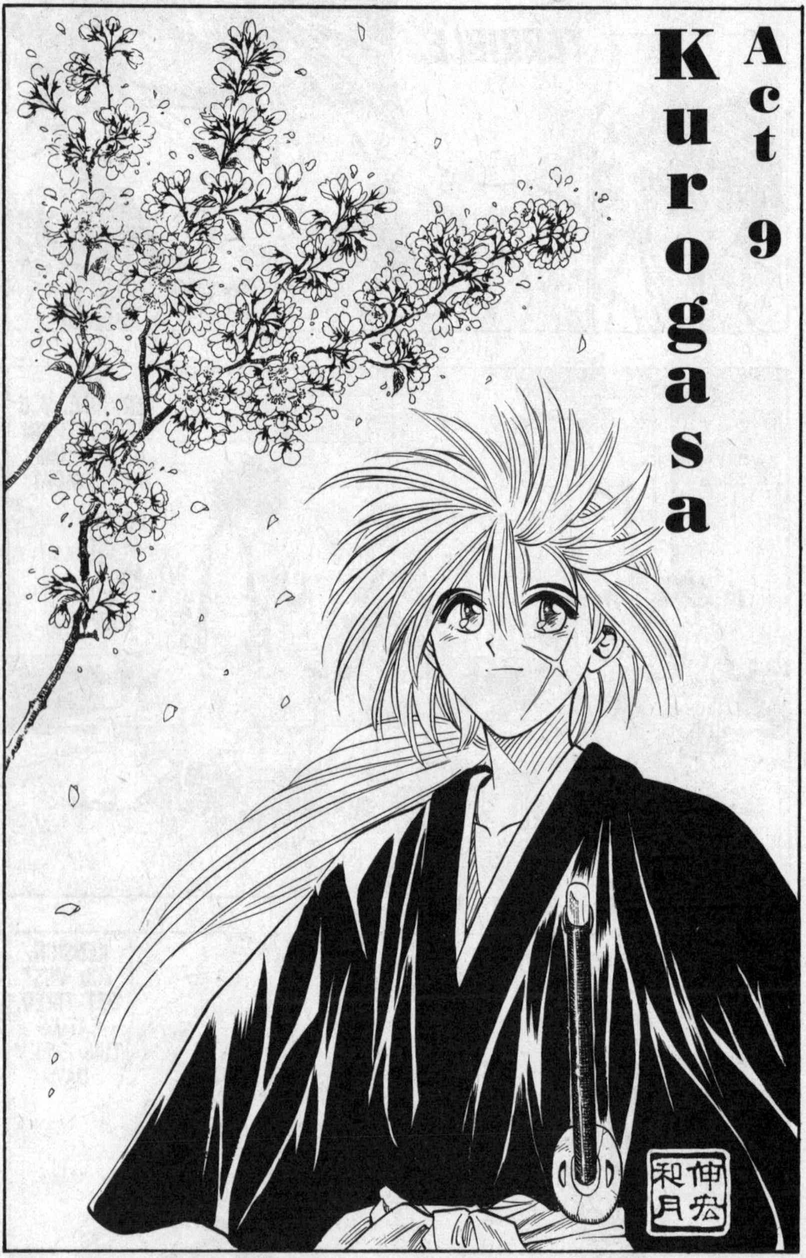
Act 9
Kurogasa

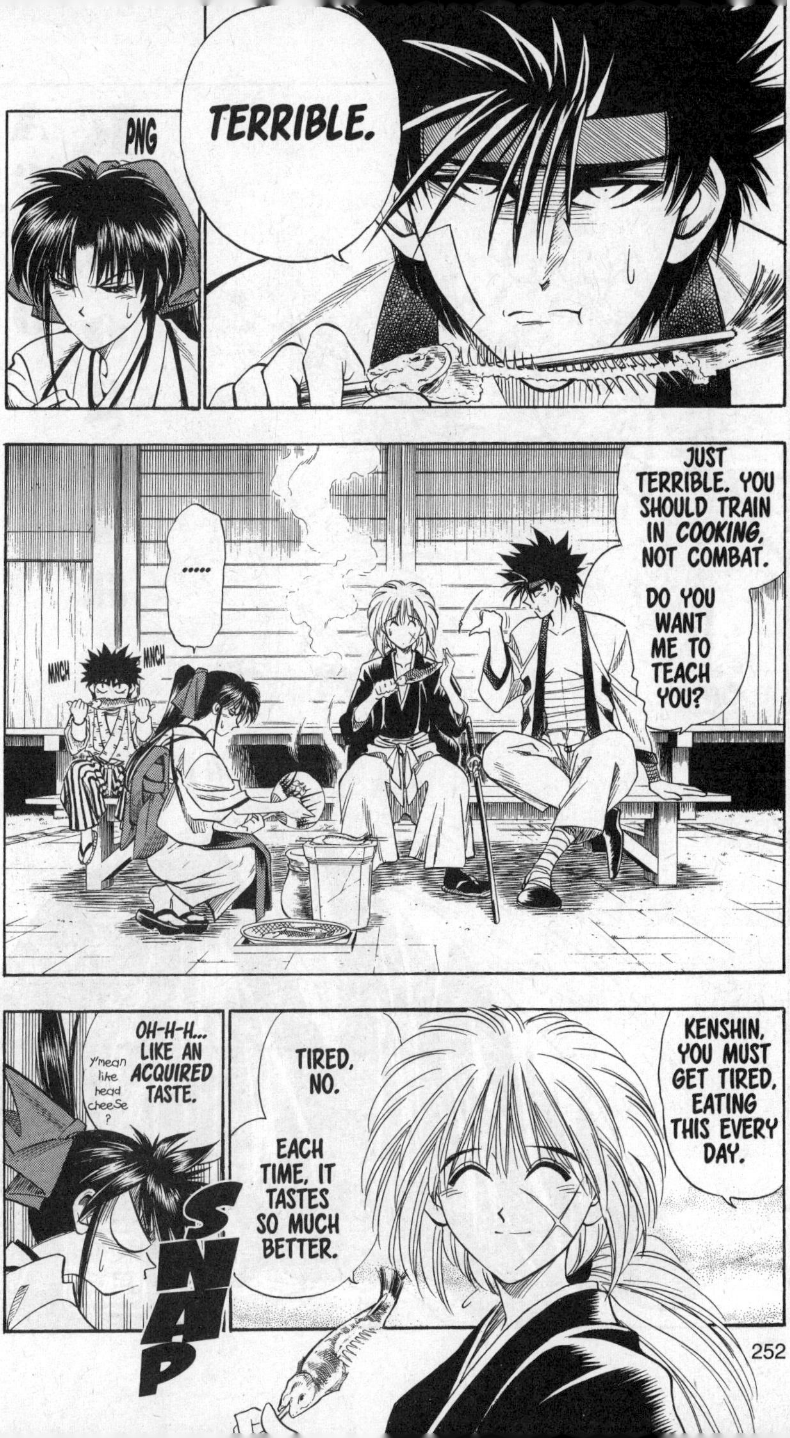
TERRIBLE.
PNG
JUST TERRIBLE. YOU SHOULD TRAIN IN *COOKING*, NOT COMBAT.
DO YOU WANT ME TO TEACH YOU?
.....
MNCH
MNCH
KENSHIN, YOU MUST GET TIRED, EATING THIS EVERY DAY.
TIRED, NO.
EACH TIME, IT TASTES SO MUCH BETTER.
OH-H-H... LIKE AN ACQUIRED TASTE.
Y'mean like head cheese?
SNAP

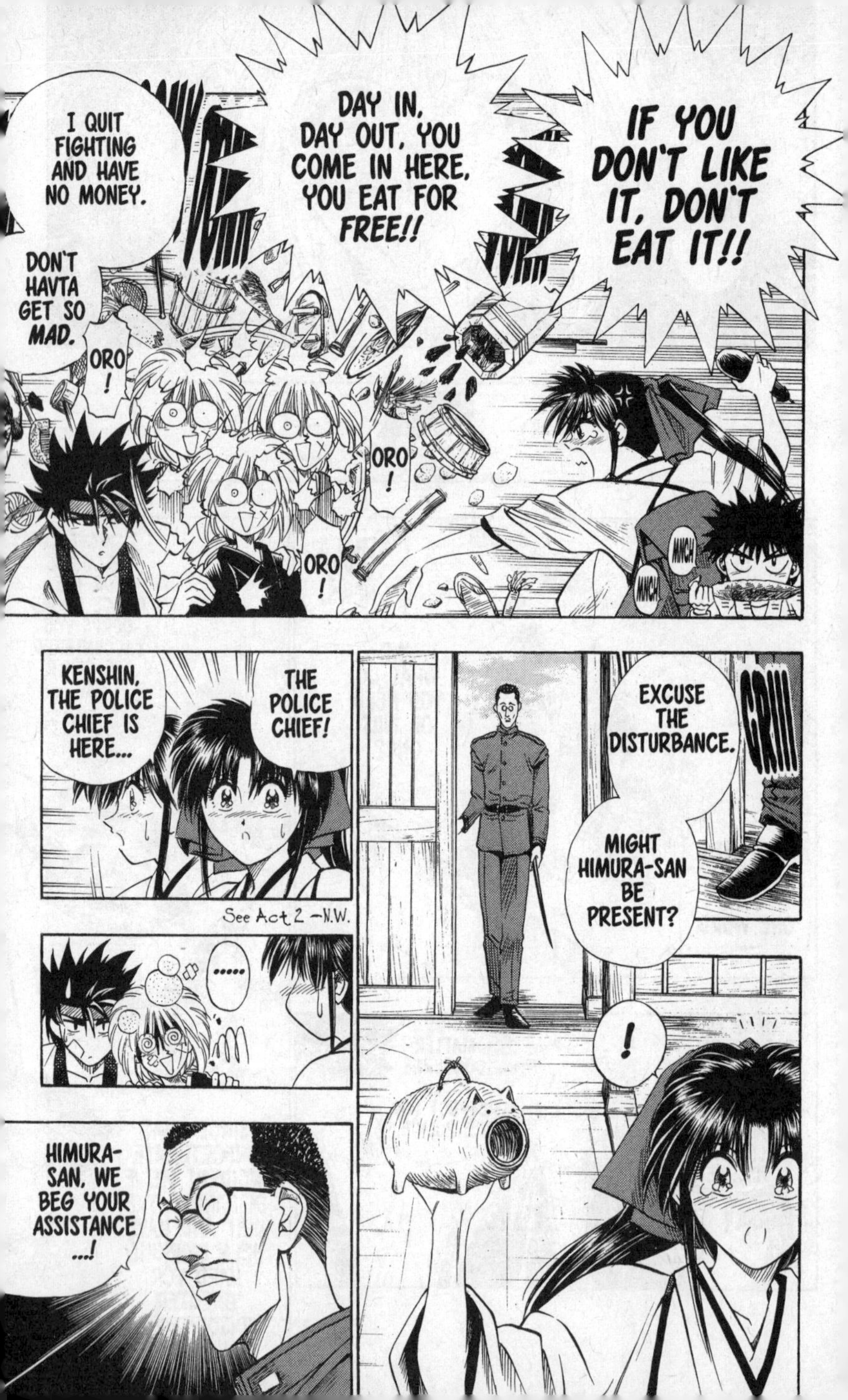

IF YOU DON'T LIKE IT, DON'T EAT IT!!
DAY IN, DAY OUT, YOU COME IN HERE, YOU EAT FOR FREE!!
MNCH
MNCH
I QUIT FIGHTING AND HAVE NO MONEY.
DON'T HAVTA GET SO MAD.
ORO!
ORO!
ORO!
GRIII
EXCUSE THE DISTURBANCE.
MIGHT HIMURA-SAN BE PRESENT?
!
KENSHIN, THE POLICE CHIEF IS HERE...
THE POLICE CHIEF!
See Act 2 —N.W.
......
HIMURA-SAN, WE BEG YOUR ASSISTANCE ...!

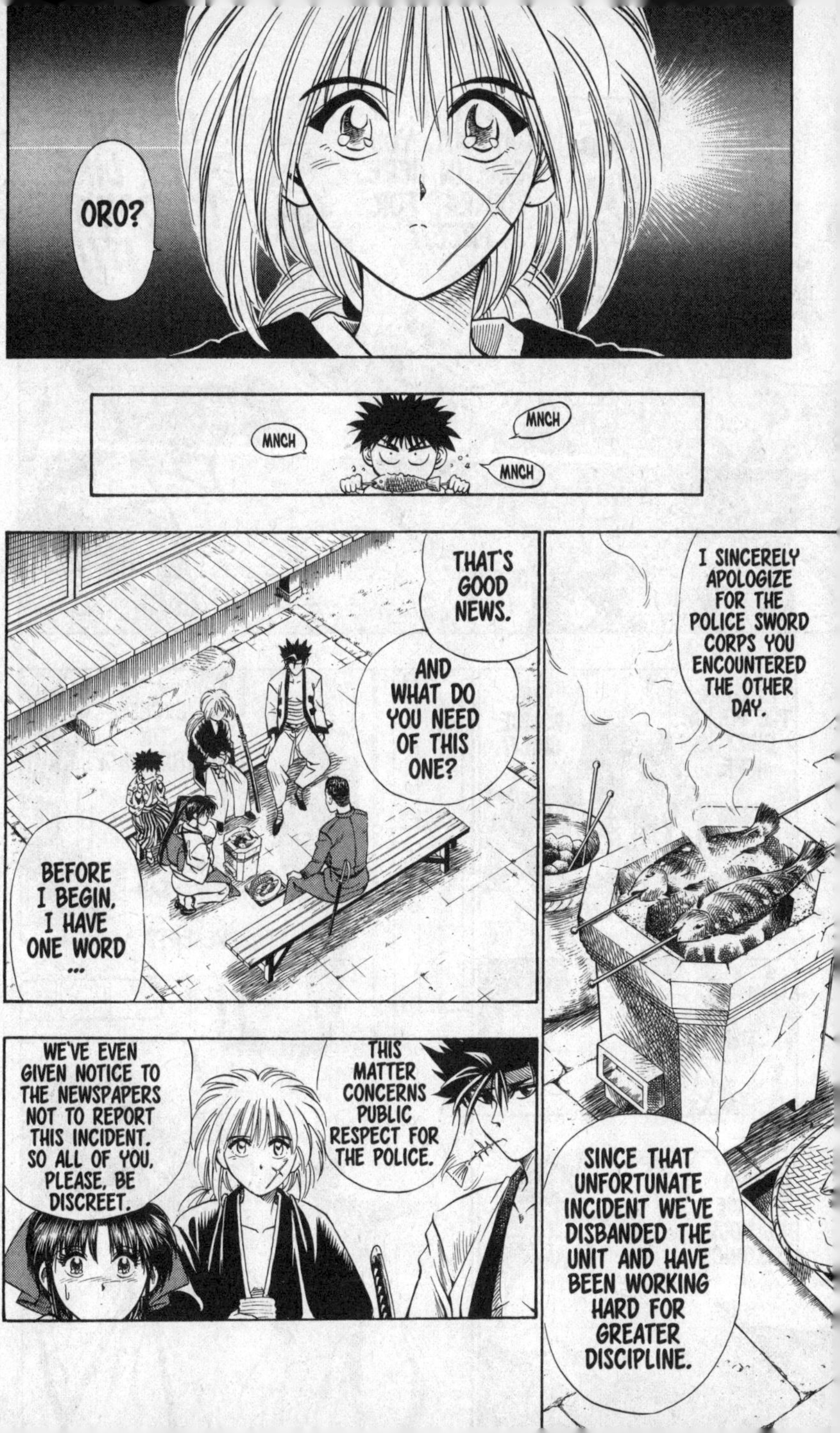
ORO?
MNCH
MNCH
MNCH
I SINCERELY APOLOGIZE FOR THE POLICE SWORD CORPS YOU ENCOUNTERED THE OTHER DAY.
SINCE THAT UNFORTUNATE INCIDENT WE'VE DISBANDED THE UNIT AND HAVE BEEN WORKING HARD FOR GREATER DISCIPLINE.
THAT'S GOOD NEWS.
AND WHAT DO YOU NEED OF THIS ONE?
BEFORE I BEGIN, I HAVE ONE WORD ...
THIS MATTER CONCERNS PUBLIC RESPECT FOR THE POLICE.
WE'VE EVEN GIVEN NOTICE TO THE NEWSPAPERS NOT TO REPORT THIS INCIDENT. SO ALL OF YOU, PLEASE, BE DISCREET.

READ THIS WAY

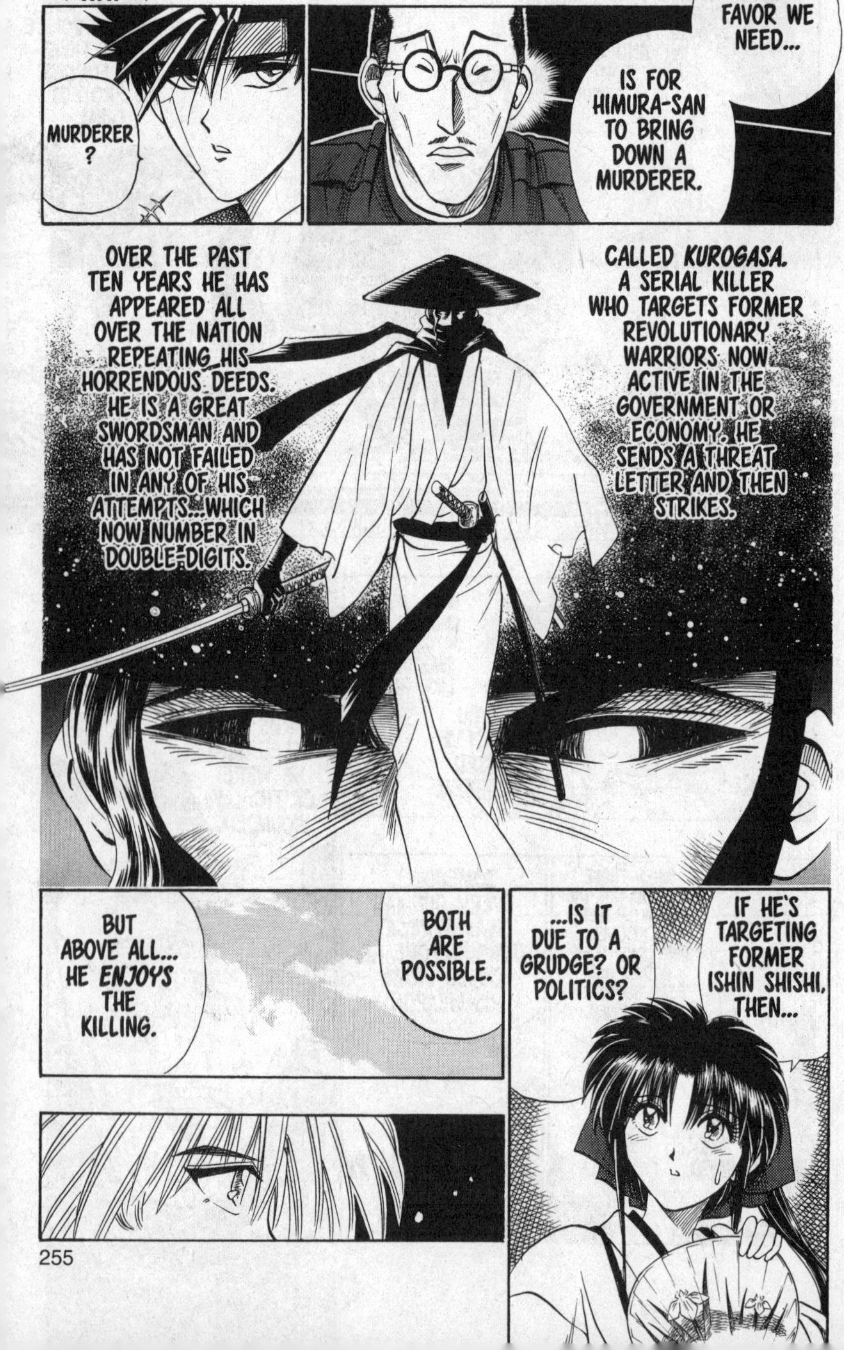
THE FAVOR WE NEED...
IS FOR HIMURA-SAN TO BRING DOWN A MURDERER.
MURDERER?
CALLED *KUROGASA.* A SERIAL KILLER WHO TARGETS FORMER REVOLUTIONARY WARRIORS NOW ACTIVE IN THE GOVERNMENT OR ECONOMY. HE SENDS A THREAT LETTER AND THEN STRIKES.
OVER THE PAST TEN YEARS HE HAS APPEARED ALL OVER THE NATION REPEATING HIS HORRENDOUS DEEDS. HE IS A GREAT SWORDSMAN AND HAS NOT FAILED IN ANY OF HIS ATTEMPTS...WHICH NOW NUMBER IN DOUBLE-DIGITS.
IF HE'S TARGETING FORMER ISHIN SHISHI, THEN...
...IS IT DUE TO A GRUDGE? OR POLITICS?
BOTH ARE POSSIBLE.
BUT ABOVE ALL... HE *ENJOYS* THE KILLING.

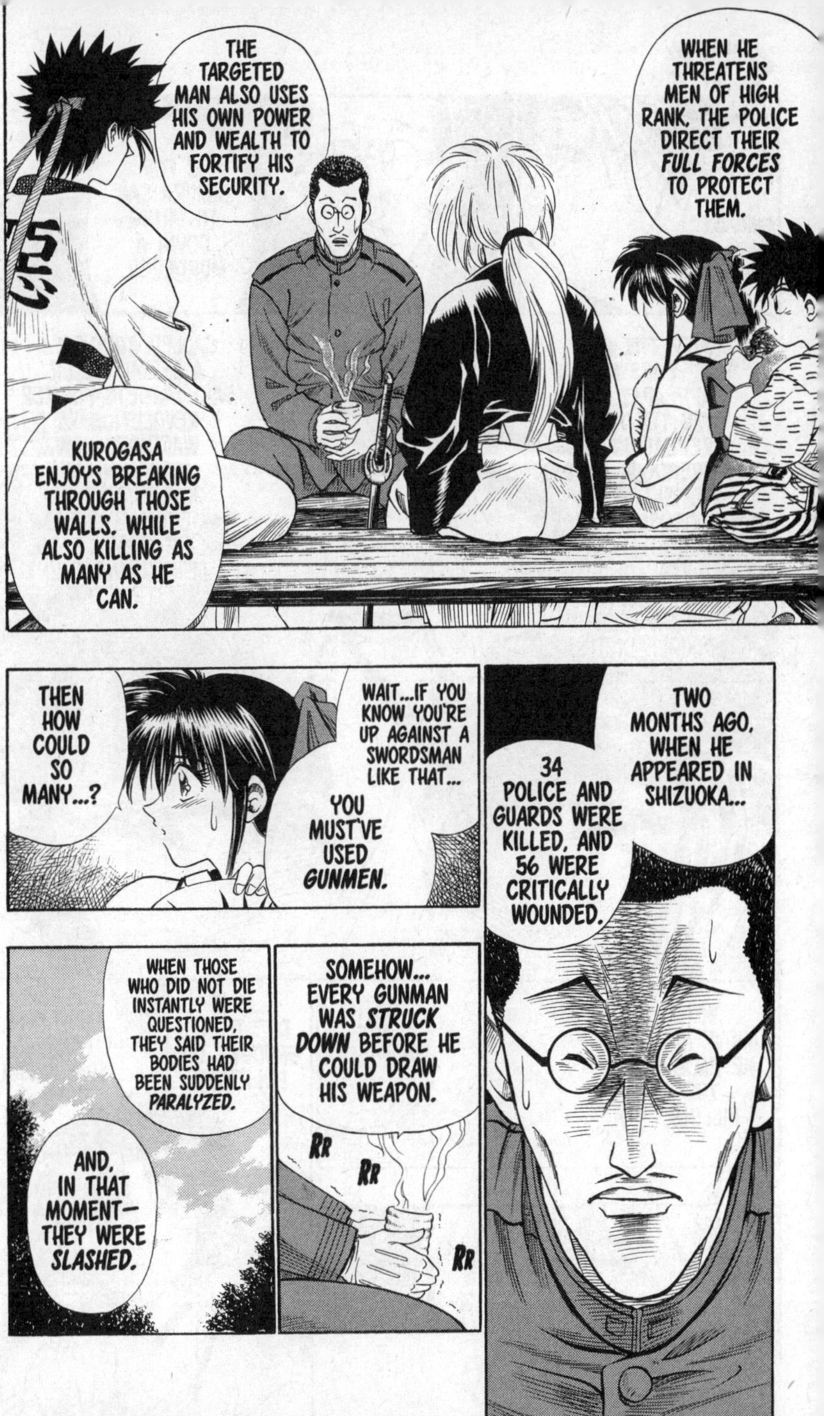
WHEN HE THREATENS MEN OF HIGH RANK, THE POLICE DIRECT THEIR *FULL FORCES* TO PROTECT THEM.
THE TARGETED MAN ALSO USES HIS OWN POWER AND WEALTH TO FORTIFY HIS SECURITY.
KUROGASA ENJOYS BREAKING THROUGH THOSE WALLS. WHILE ALSO KILLING AS MANY AS HE CAN.
TWO MONTHS AGO, WHEN HE APPEARED IN SHIZUOKA...
34 POLICE AND GUARDS WERE KILLED, AND 56 WERE CRITICALLY WOUNDED.
WAIT...IF YOU KNOW YOU'RE UP AGAINST A SWORDSMAN LIKE THAT...
YOU MUST'VE USED *GUNMEN.*
THEN HOW COULD SO MANY...?
SOMEHOW... EVERY GUNMAN WAS *STRUCK DOWN* BEFORE HE COULD DRAW HIS WEAPON.
RR
RR
RR
WHEN THOSE WHO DID NOT DIE INSTANTLY WERE QUESTIONED, THEY SAID THEIR BODIES HAD BEEN SUDDENLY *PARALYZED.*
AND, IN THAT MOMENT— THEY WERE *SLASHED.*

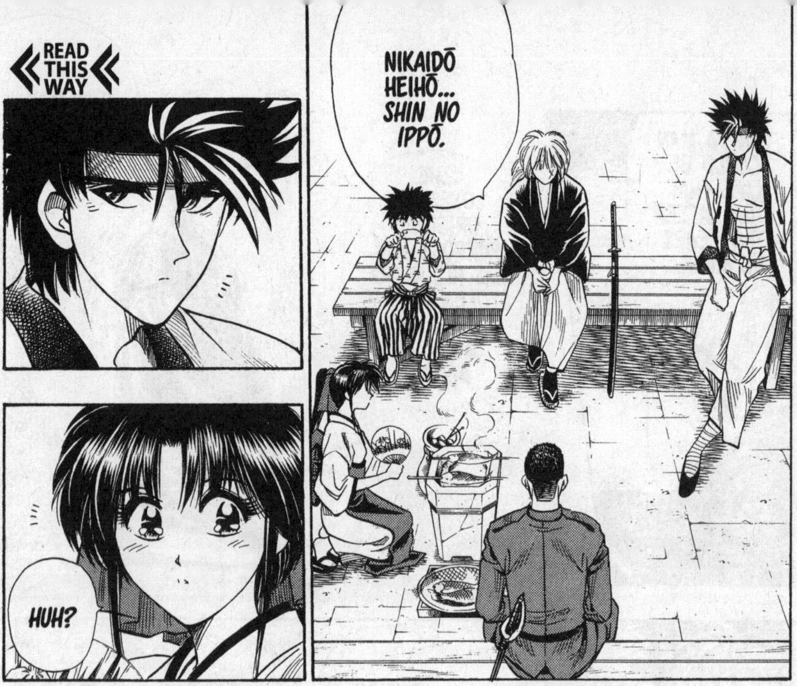
READ THIS WAY
NIKAIDŌ HEIHŌ... SHIN NO IPPŌ.
HUH?

The voice-actors of (the CD book) *Rurouni Kenshin*:

Himura Kenshin	Ogata Megumi
Kamiya Kaoru	Sakurai Tomo
Myōjin Yahiko	Takayama Minami

Sanosuke's not in the group because the CD book is based on the first four manga chapters only. Sorry, Sanosuke fans! Even so, you should check it out. Really! Besides, with the start of the anime, you can check him out there. (You believe me, don't you?) Despite all my worries, then—and even though the casting was Watsuki-hands free! —I'm thinking it works.

和月伸宏

...to be continued

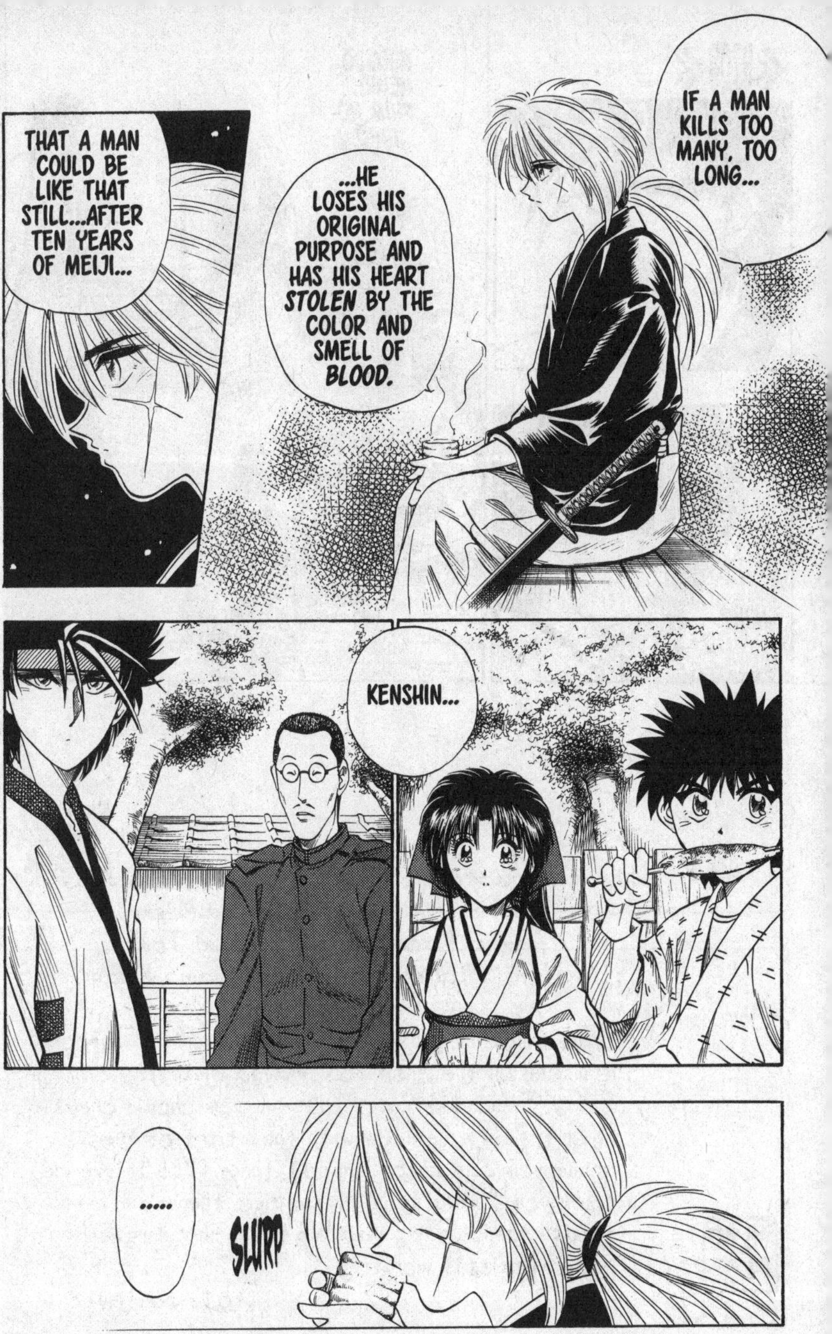
IF A MAN KILLS TOO MANY, TOO LONG...
...HE LOSES HIS ORIGINAL PURPOSE AND HAS HIS HEART STOLEN BY THE COLOR AND SMELL OF BLOOD.
THAT A MAN COULD BE LIKE THAT STILL...AFTER TEN YEARS OF MEIJI...
KENSHIN...
......
SLURP

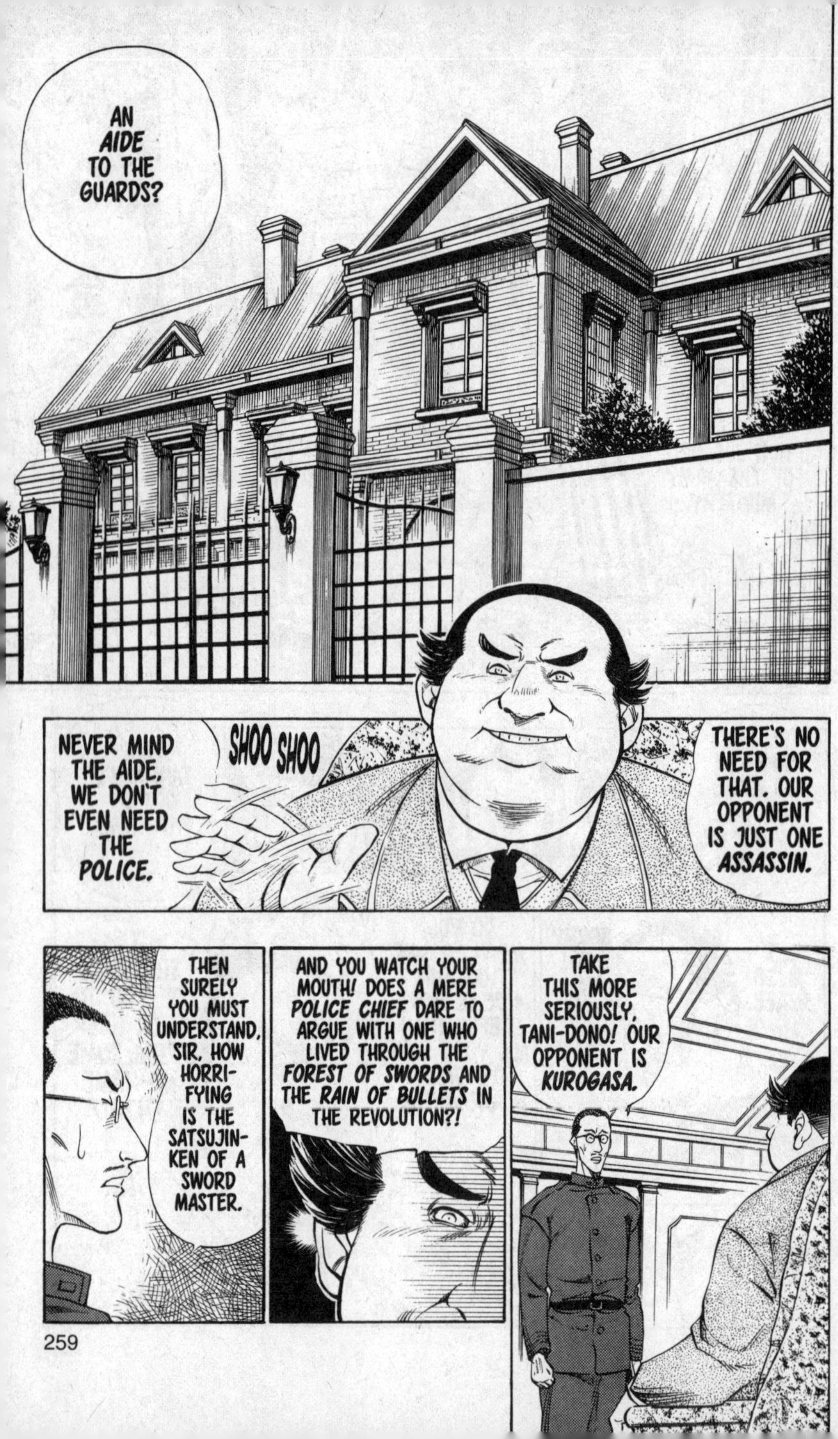
AN AIDE TO THE GUARDS?
THERE'S NO NEED FOR THAT. OUR OPPONENT IS JUST ONE ASSASSIN.
SHOO SHOO
NEVER MIND THE AIDE, WE DON'T EVEN NEED THE POLICE.
TAKE THIS MORE SERIOUSLY, TANI-DONO! OUR OPPONENT IS KUROGASA.
AND YOU WATCH YOUR MOUTH! DOES A MERE POLICE CHIEF DARE TO ARGUE WITH ONE WHO LIVED THROUGH THE FOREST OF SWORDS AND THE RAIN OF BULLETS IN THE REVOLUTION?!
THEN SURELY YOU MUST UNDERSTAND, SIR, HOW HORRI-FYING IS THE SATSUJIN-KEN OF A SWORD MASTER.

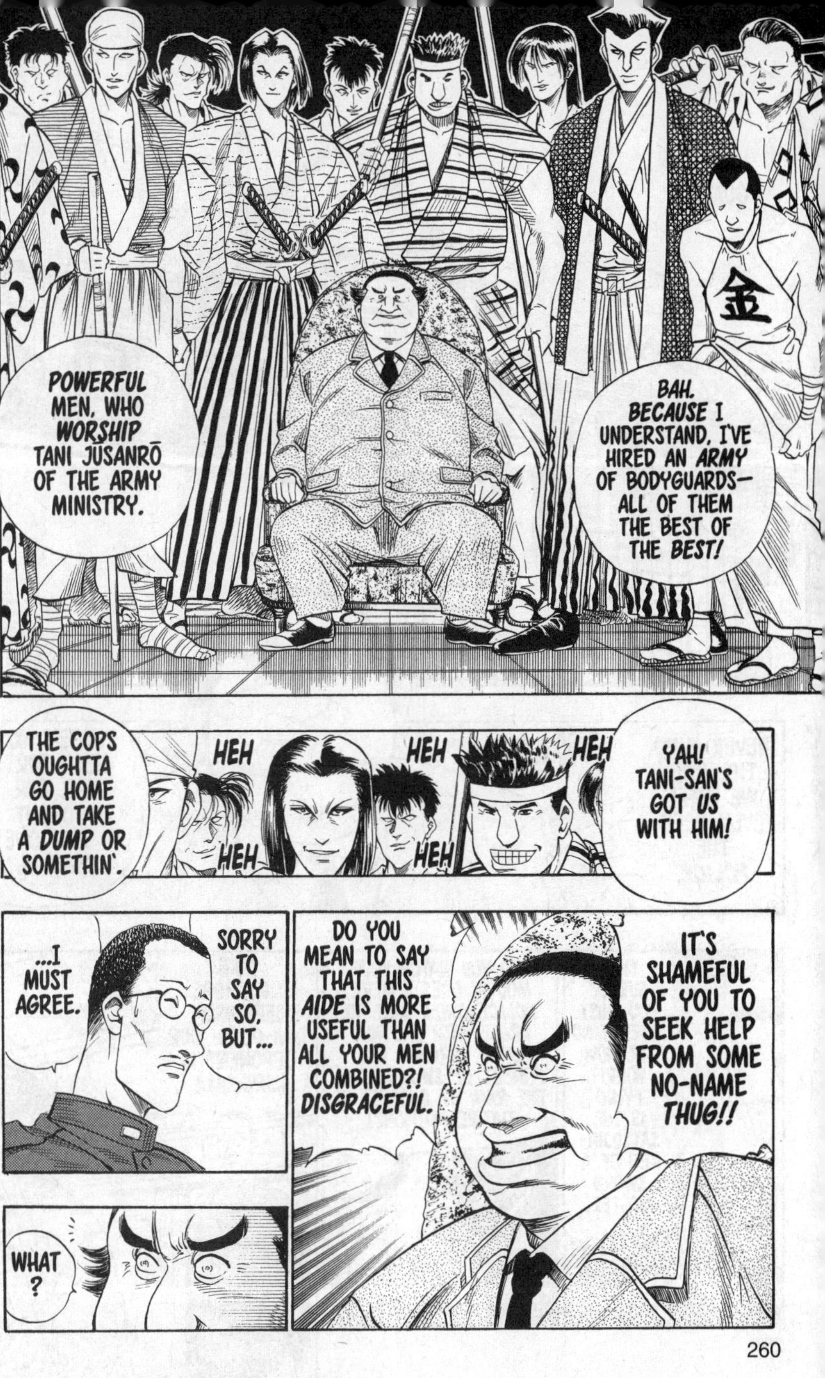
BAH. BECAUSE I UNDERSTAND, I'VE HIRED AN ARMY OF BODYGUARDS— ALL OF THEM THE BEST OF THE BEST!
POWERFUL MEN, WHO WORSHIP TANI JŪSANRŌ OF THE ARMY MINISTRY.
YAH! TANI-SAN'S GOT US WITH HIM!
HEH
HEH
HEH
HEH
HEH
THE COPS OUGHTTA GO HOME AND TAKE A DUMP OR SOMETHIN'.
IT'S SHAMEFUL OF YOU TO SEEK HELP FROM SOME NO-NAME THUG!!
DO YOU MEAN TO SAY THAT THIS AIDE IS MORE USEFUL THAN ALL YOUR MEN COMBINED?! DISGRACEFUL.
SORRY TO SAY SO, BUT...
...I MUST AGREE.
WHAT?

READ THIS WAY

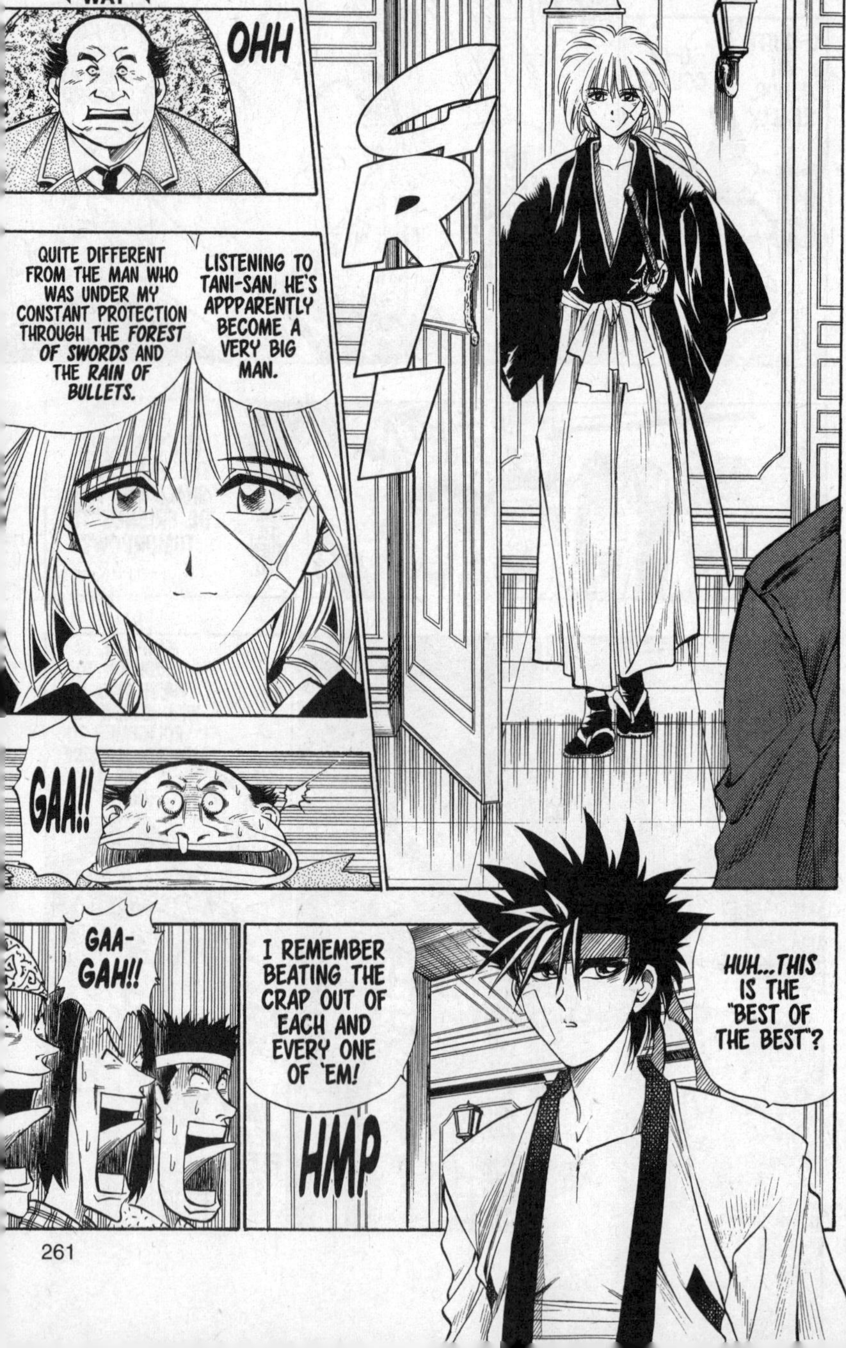
OHH
LISTENING TO TANI-SAN, HE'S APPPARENTLY BECOME A VERY BIG MAN.
QUITE DIFFERENT FROM THE MAN WHO WAS UNDER MY CONSTANT PROTECTION THROUGH THE FOREST OF SWORDS AND THE RAIN OF BULLETS.
GAA!!
HUH...THIS IS THE "BEST OF THE BEST"?
I REMEMBER BEATING THE CRAP OUT OF EACH AND EVERY ONE OF 'EM!
HMP
GAA-GAH!!

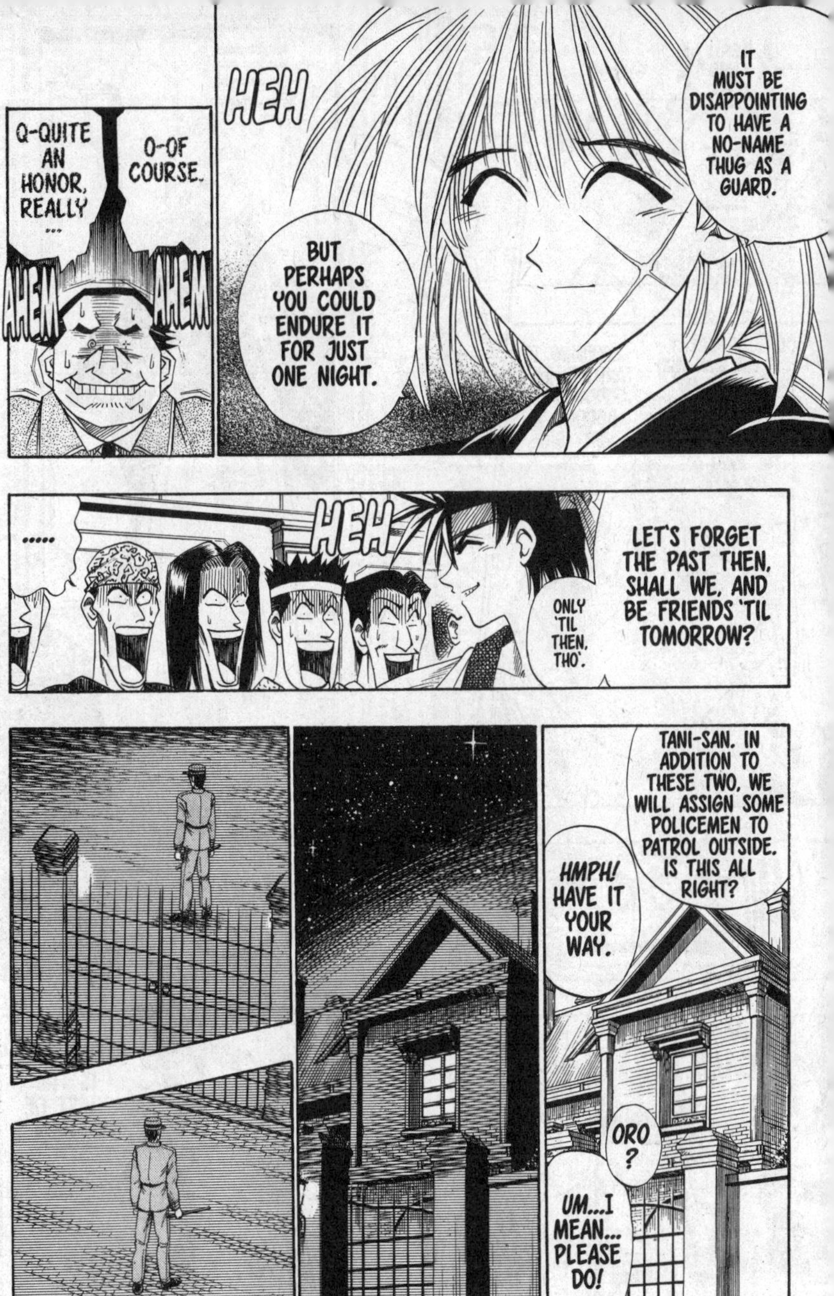

HEH
IT MUST BE DISAPPOINTING TO HAVE A NO-NAME THUG AS A GUARD.
BUT PERHAPS YOU COULD ENDURE IT FOR JUST ONE NIGHT.
O-OF COURSE...
Q-QUITE AN HONOR, REALLY...
AHEM
AHEM
LET'S FORGET THE PAST THEN, SHALL WE, AND BE FRIENDS 'TIL TOMORROW?
ONLY 'TIL THEN, THO'.
HEH
.....
TANI-SAN. IN ADDITION TO THESE TWO, WE WILL ASSIGN SOME POLICEMEN TO PATROL OUTSIDE. IS THIS ALL RIGHT?
HMPH! HAVE IT YOUR WAY.
ORO?
UM...I MEAN... PLEASE DO!

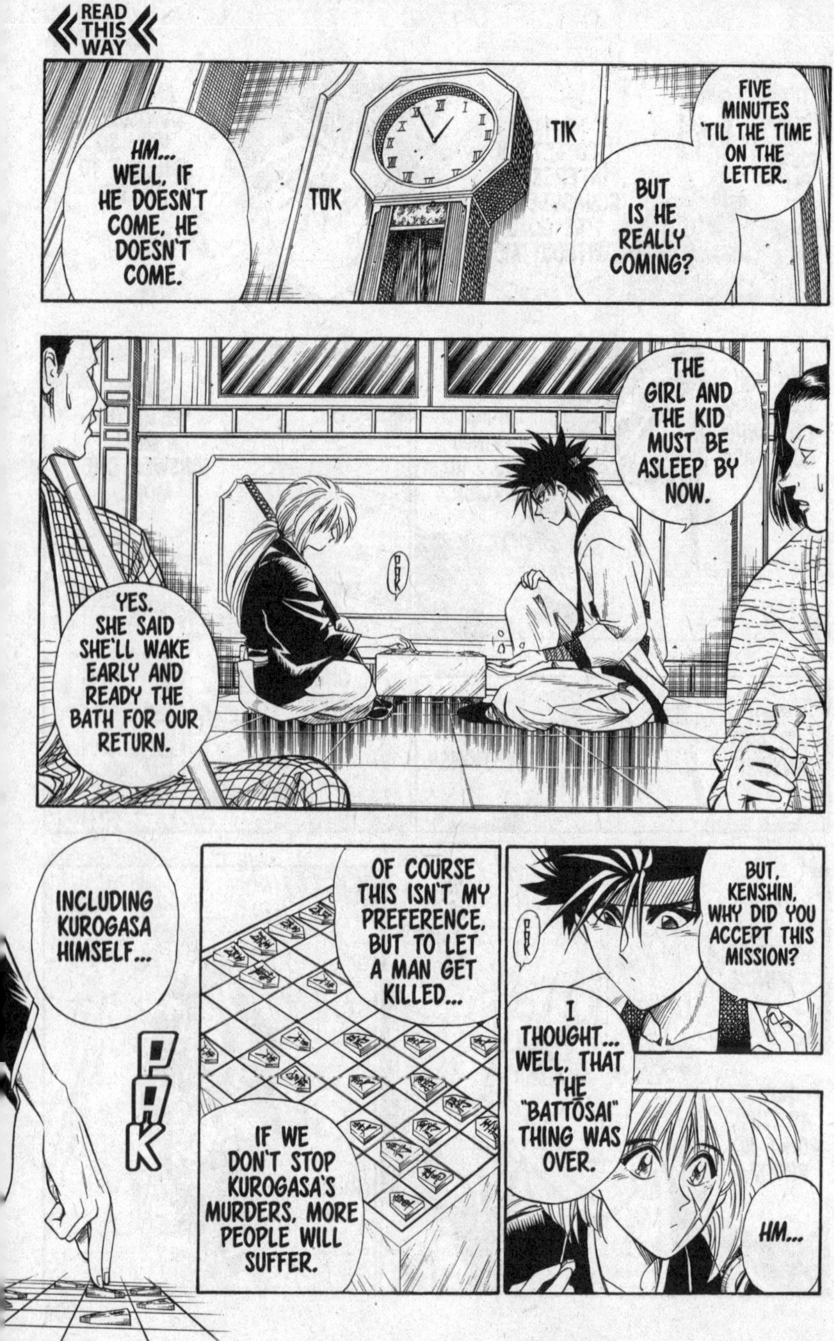
READ THIS WAY
FIVE MINUTES 'TIL THE TIME ON THE LETTER.
TIK
BUT IS HE REALLY COMING?
TOK
HM... WELL, IF HE DOESN'T COME, HE DOESN'T COME.
THE GIRL AND THE KID MUST BE ASLEEP BY NOW.
YES. SHE SAID SHE'LL WAKE EARLY AND READY THE BATH FOR OUR RETURN.
BUT, KENSHIN, WHY DID YOU ACCEPT THIS MISSION?
I THOUGHT... WELL, THAT THE "BATTŌSAI" THING WAS OVER.
HM...
OF COURSE THIS ISN'T MY PREFERENCE, BUT TO LET A MAN GET KILLED...
IF WE DON'T STOP KUROGASA'S MURDERS, MORE PEOPLE WILL SUFFER.
INCLUDING KUROGASA HIMSELF...
PAK

READ THIS WAY

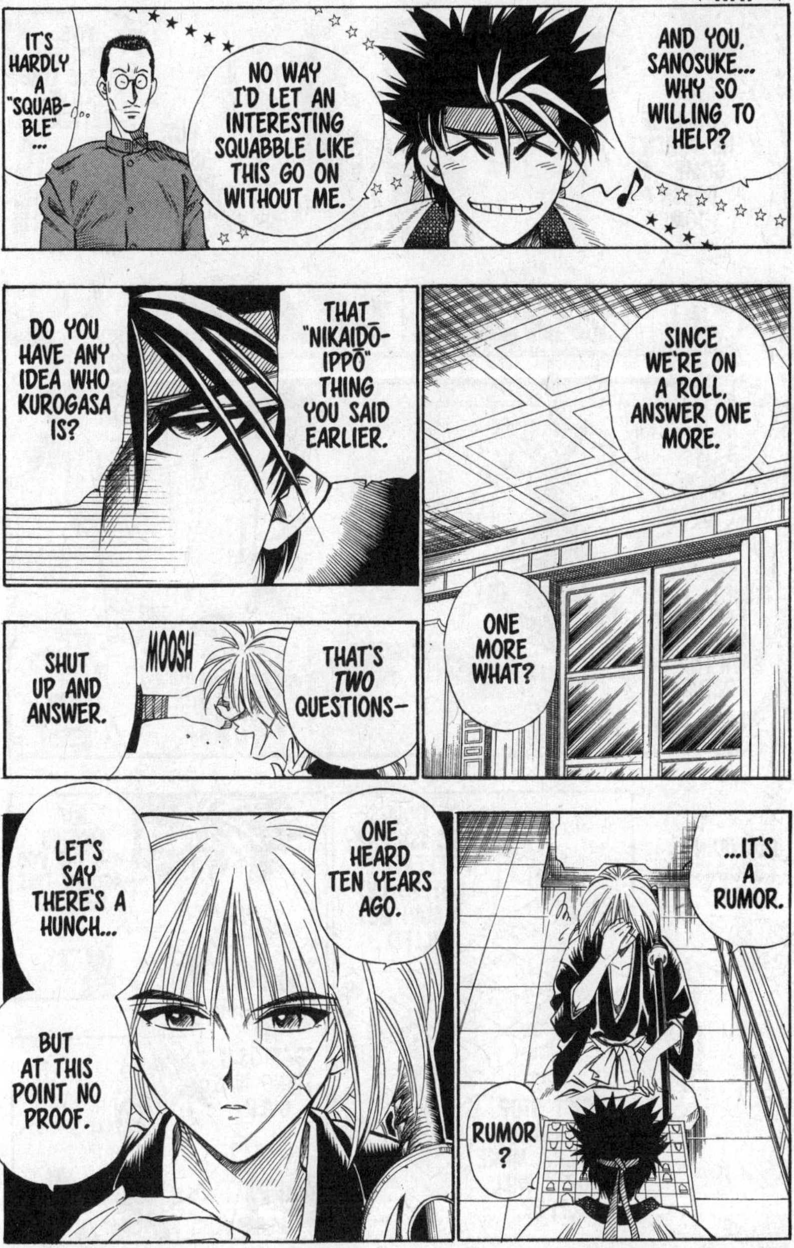
AND YOU, SANOSUKE... WHY SO WILLING TO HELP?
NO WAY I'D LET AN INTERESTING SQUABBLE LIKE THIS GO ON WITHOUT ME.
IT'S HARDLY A "SQUABBLE"...
SINCE WE'RE ON A ROLL, ANSWER ONE MORE.
ONE MORE WHAT?
THAT "NIKAIDŌ-IPPŌ" THING YOU SAID EARLIER.
DO YOU HAVE ANY IDEA WHO KUROGASA IS?
THAT'S *TWO* QUESTIONS—
MOOSH
SHUT UP AND ANSWER.
...IT'S A RUMOR.
RUMOR?
ONE HEARD TEN YEARS AGO.
LET'S SAY THERE'S A HUNCH...
BUT AT THIS POINT NO PROOF.

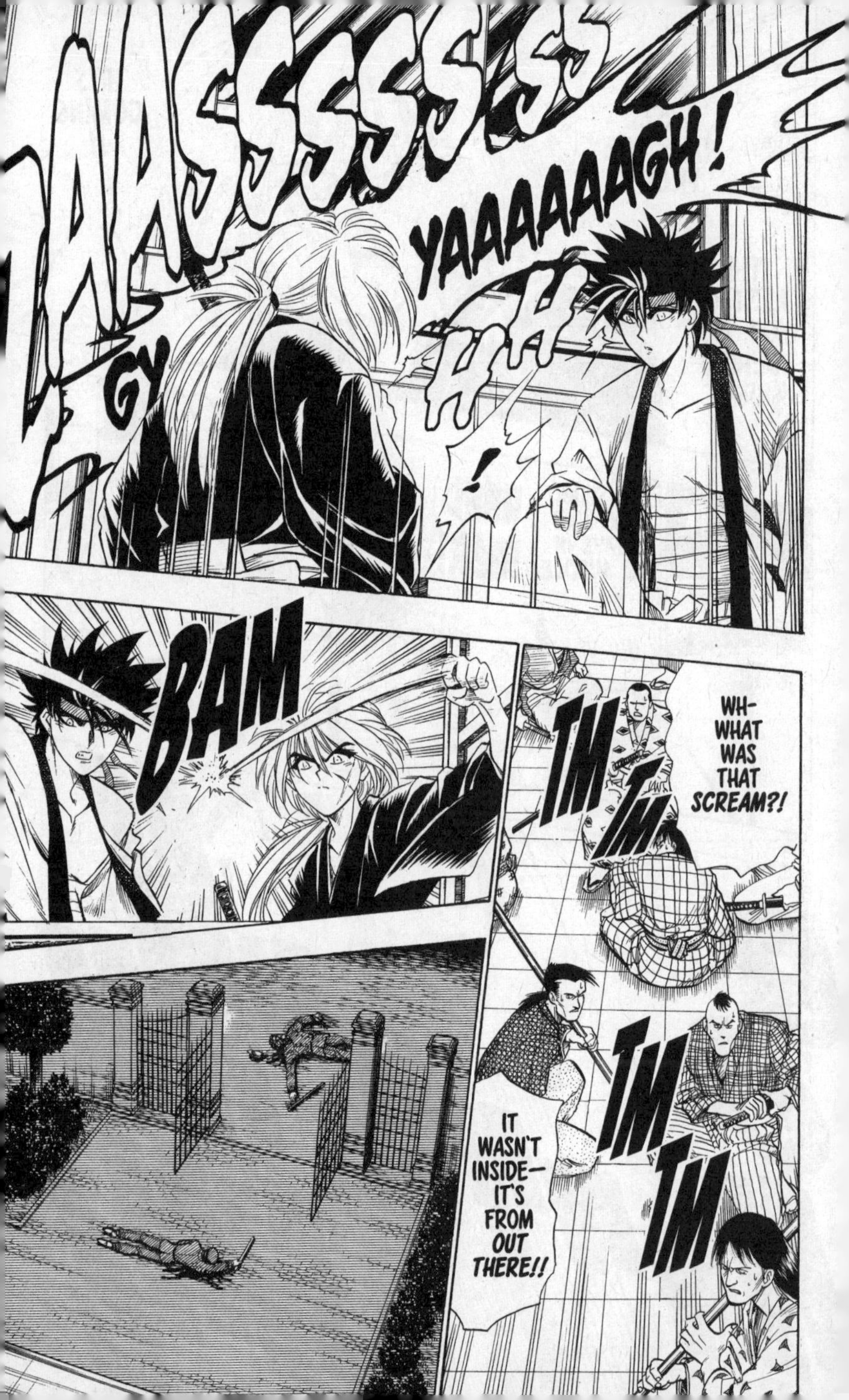
ZASSSSSS
GY
AH
YAAAAAAGH!
!
WH- WHAT WAS THAT SCREAM?!
TM TM
TM TM TM
IT WASN'T INSIDE— IT'S FROM OUT THERE!!
BAM

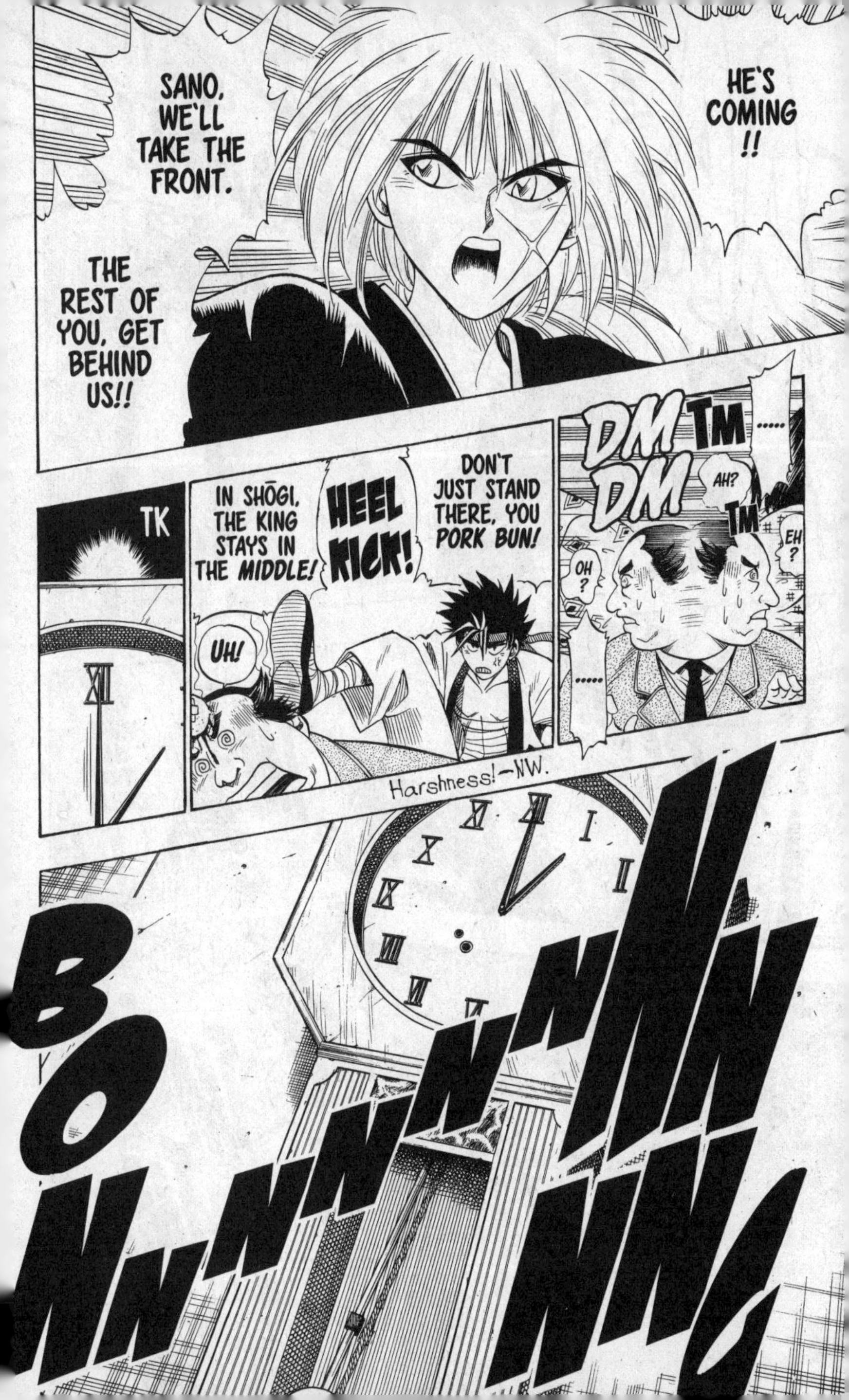
HE'S COMING !!
SANO, WE'LL TAKE THE FRONT.
THE REST OF YOU, GET BEHIND US!!
DM DM
TM TM .....
AH?
EH?
OH?
.....
DON'T JUST STAND THERE, YOU PORK BUN!
HEEL KICK!
IN SHŌGI, THE KING STAYS IN THE MIDDLE!
UH!
Harshness!—NW.
TK
BONNNNNNNNNNNN!

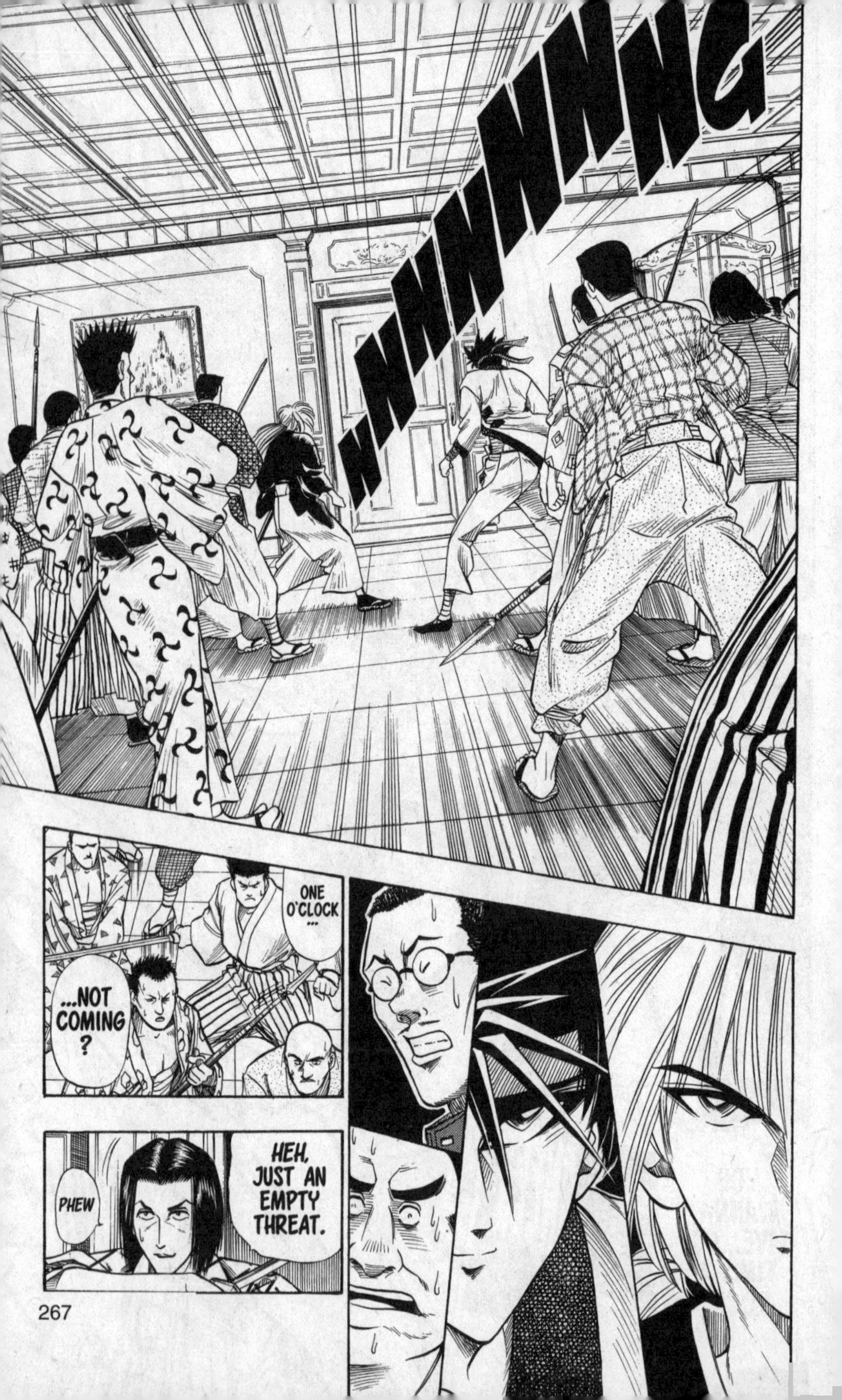
N-NNNNNNNNG
ONE O'CLOCK...
...NOT COMING?
HEH, JUST AN EMPTY THREAT.
PHEW

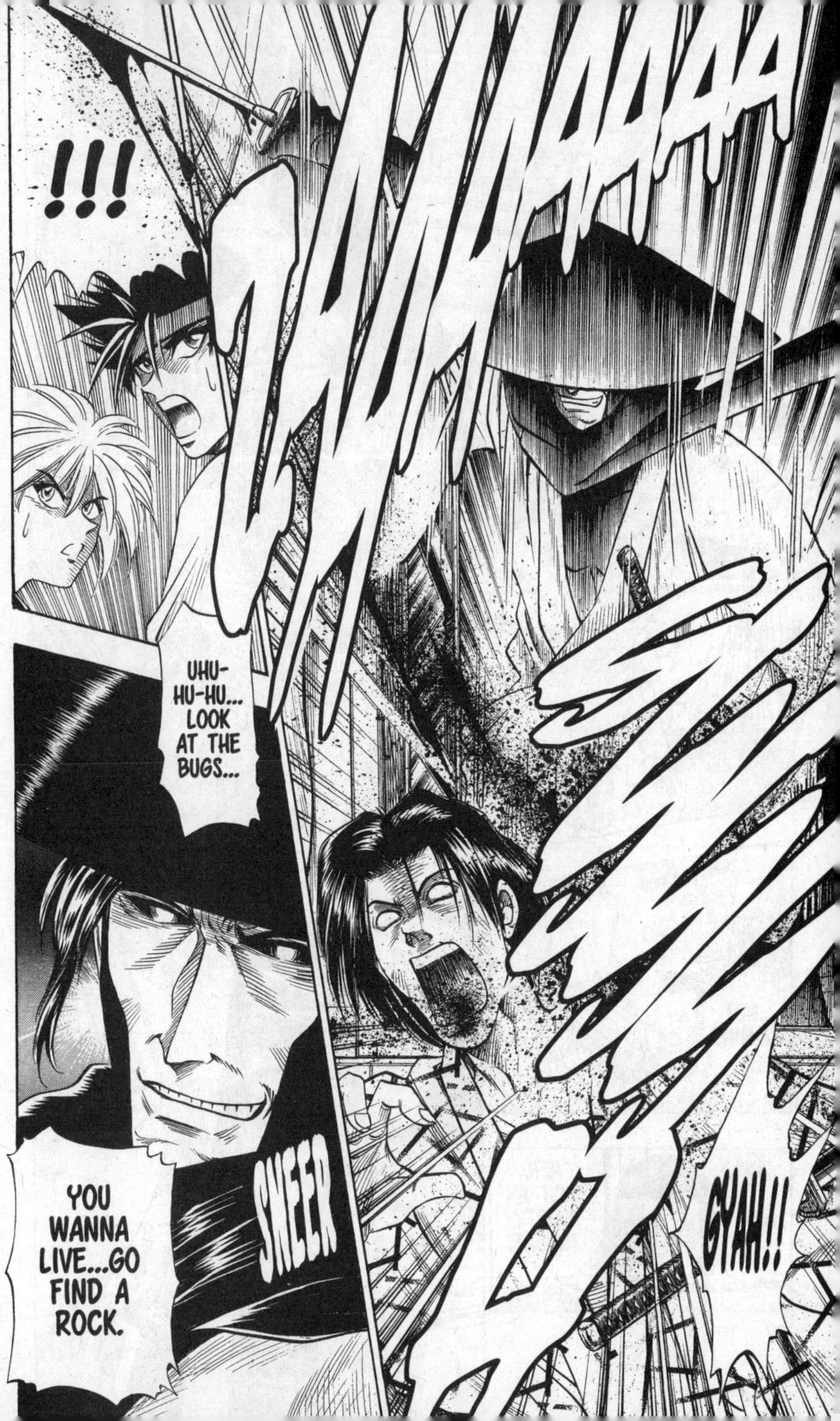
!!!
GYAH!!
UHU-HU-HU... LOOK AT THE BUGS...
SNEER
YOU WANNA LIVE...GO FIND A ROCK.

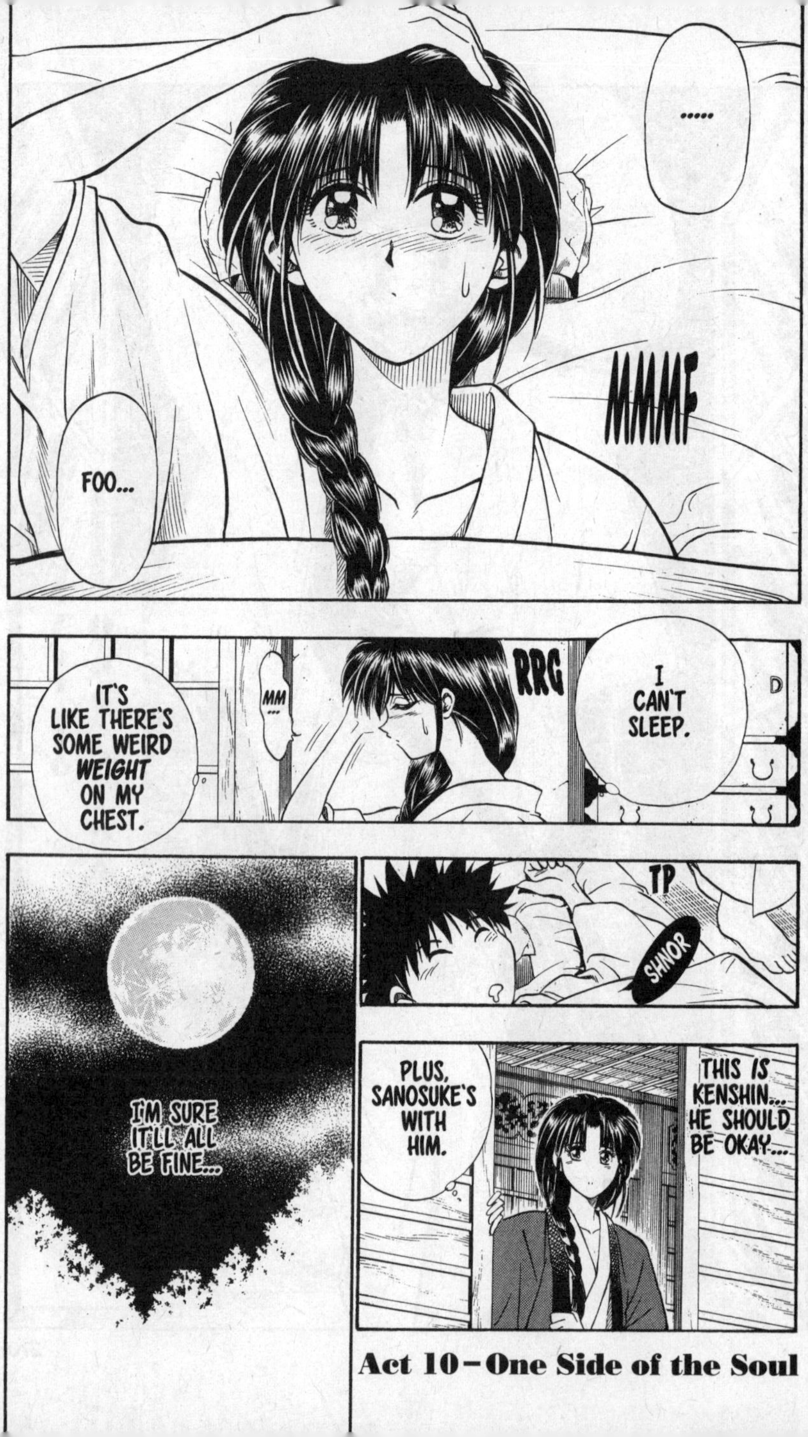
.....
MMMF
FOO...
I CAN'T SLEEP.
RRG
MM...
IT'S LIKE THERE'S SOME WEIRD WEIGHT ON MY CHEST.
TP
SHNOR
THIS IS KENSHIN... HE SHOULD BE OKAY...
PLUS, SANOSUKE'S WITH HIM.
I'M SURE IT'LL ALL BE FINE...

Act 10 – One Side of the Soul

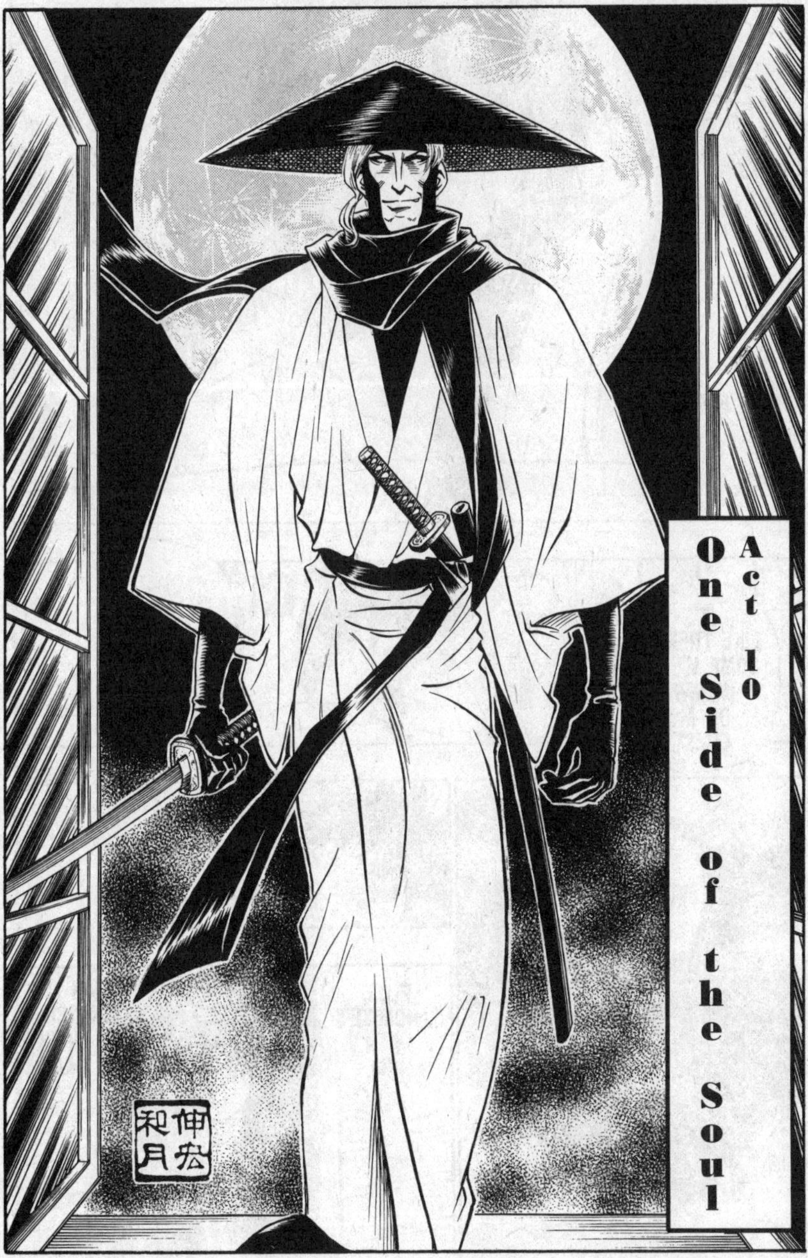
Act 10
One Side of the Soul

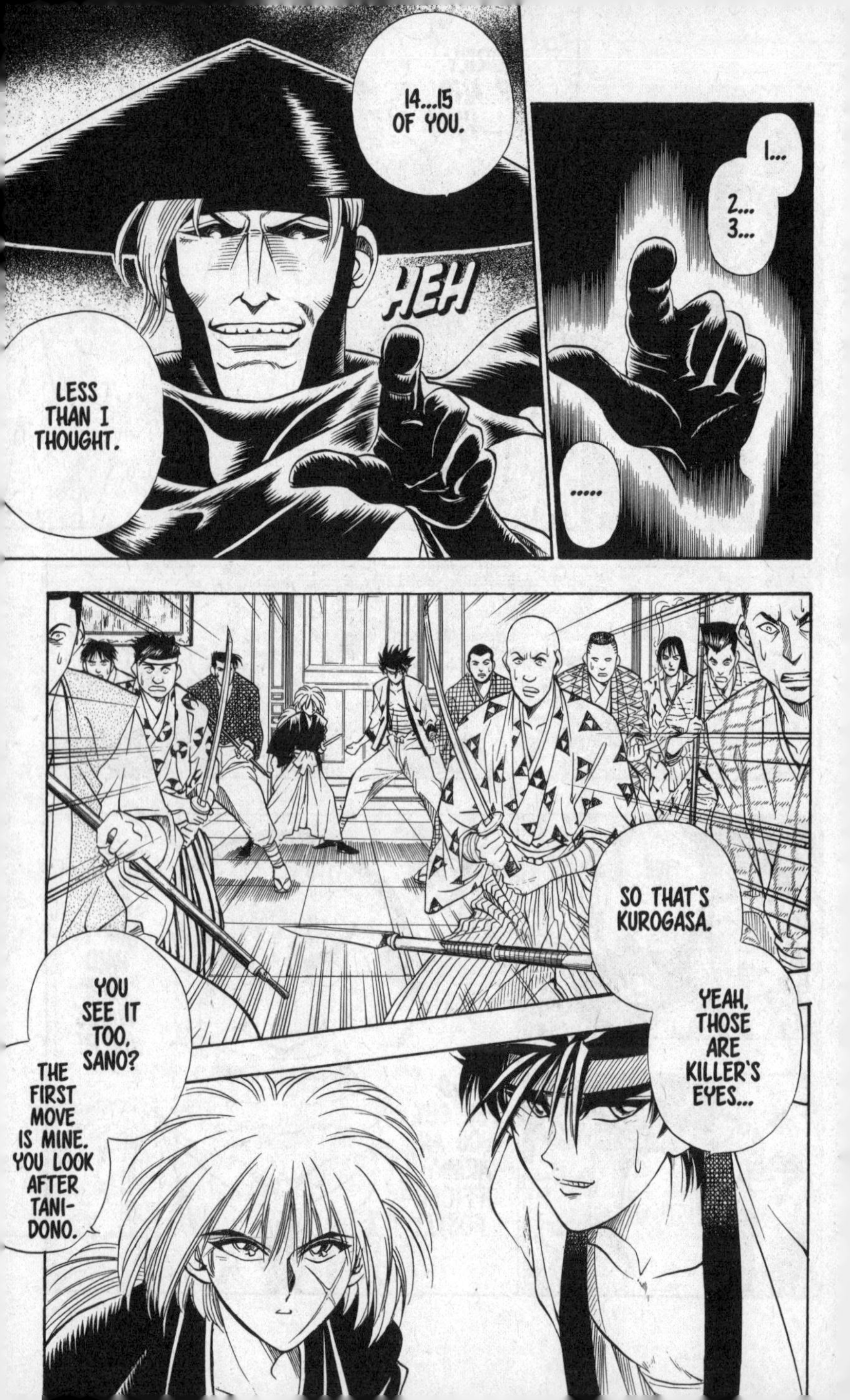
1...
2...
3...
......
14...15
OF YOU.
HEH
LESS THAN I THOUGHT.
SO THAT'S KUROGASA.
YOU SEE IT TOO, SANO?
YEAH, THOSE ARE KILLER'S EYES...
THE FIRST MOVE IS MINE. YOU LOOK AFTER TANI-DONO.

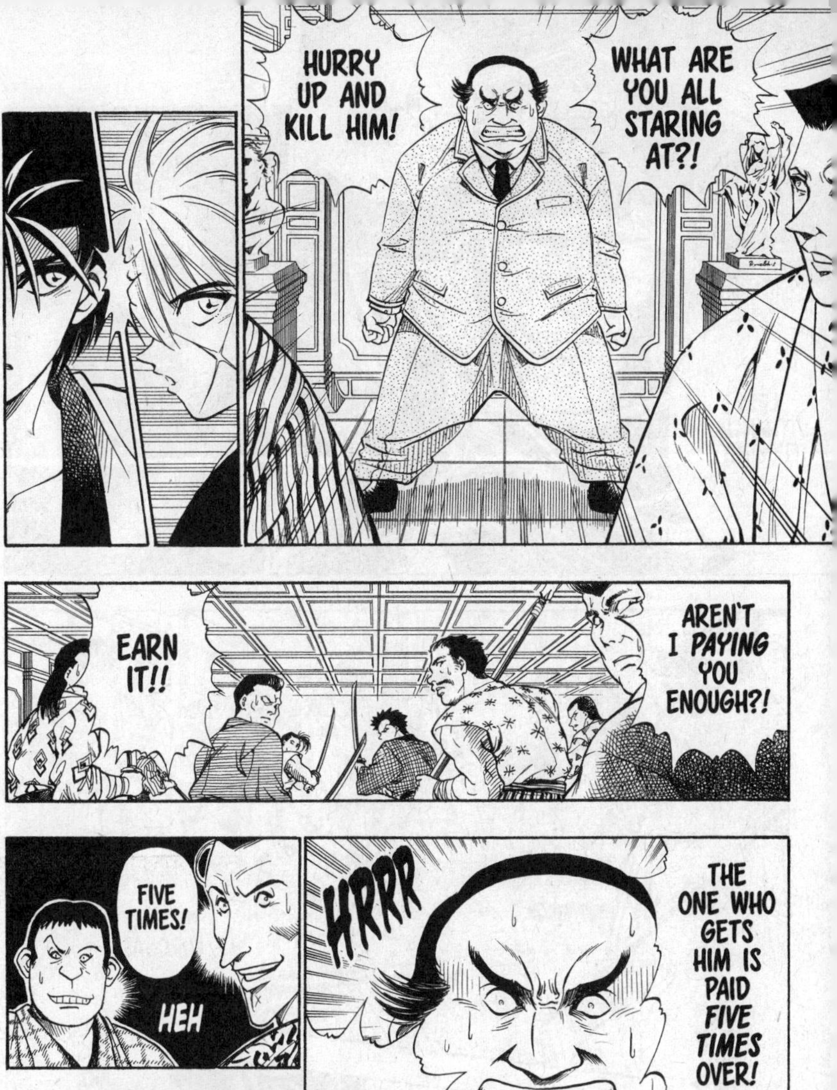
WHAT ARE YOU ALL STARING AT?!
HURRY UP AND KILL HIM!
AREN'T I *PAYING* YOU ENOUGH?!
EARN IT!!
THE ONE WHO GETS HIM IS PAID *FIVE TIMES* OVER!
HRRR
AND, I'LL GET YOU AN ARMY-OFFICER POST!
FIVE TIMES!
HEH
HEH
OFFICER!

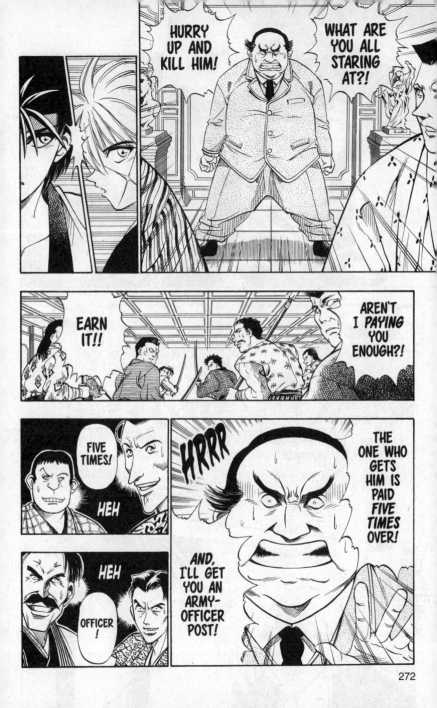

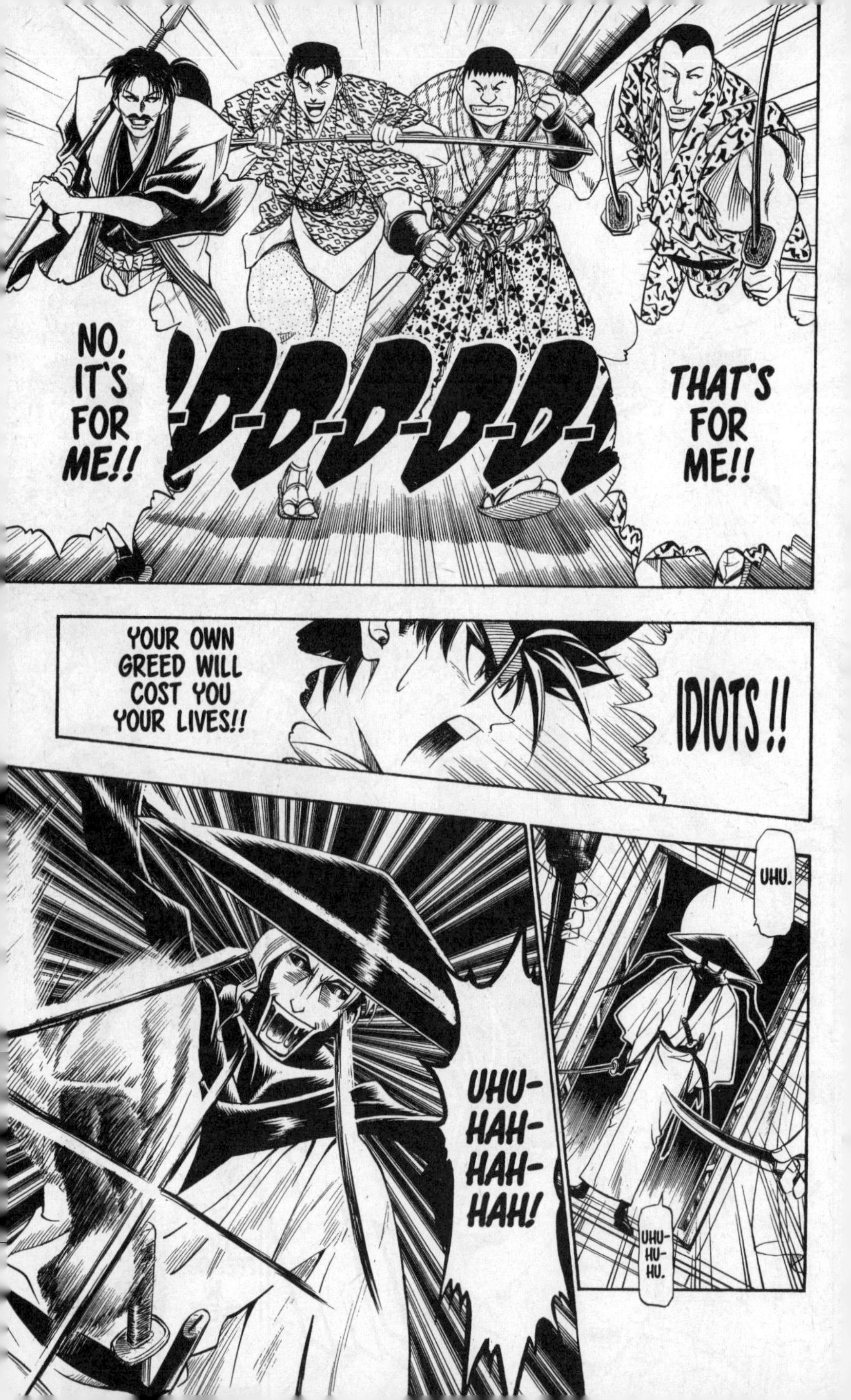
THAT'S FOR ME!!
D-D-D-D-D-D-D
NO, IT'S FOR ME!!
IDIOTS!!
YOUR OWN GREED WILL COST YOU YOUR LIVES!!
UHU.
UHU-HU-HU.
UHU-HAH-HAH-HAH!

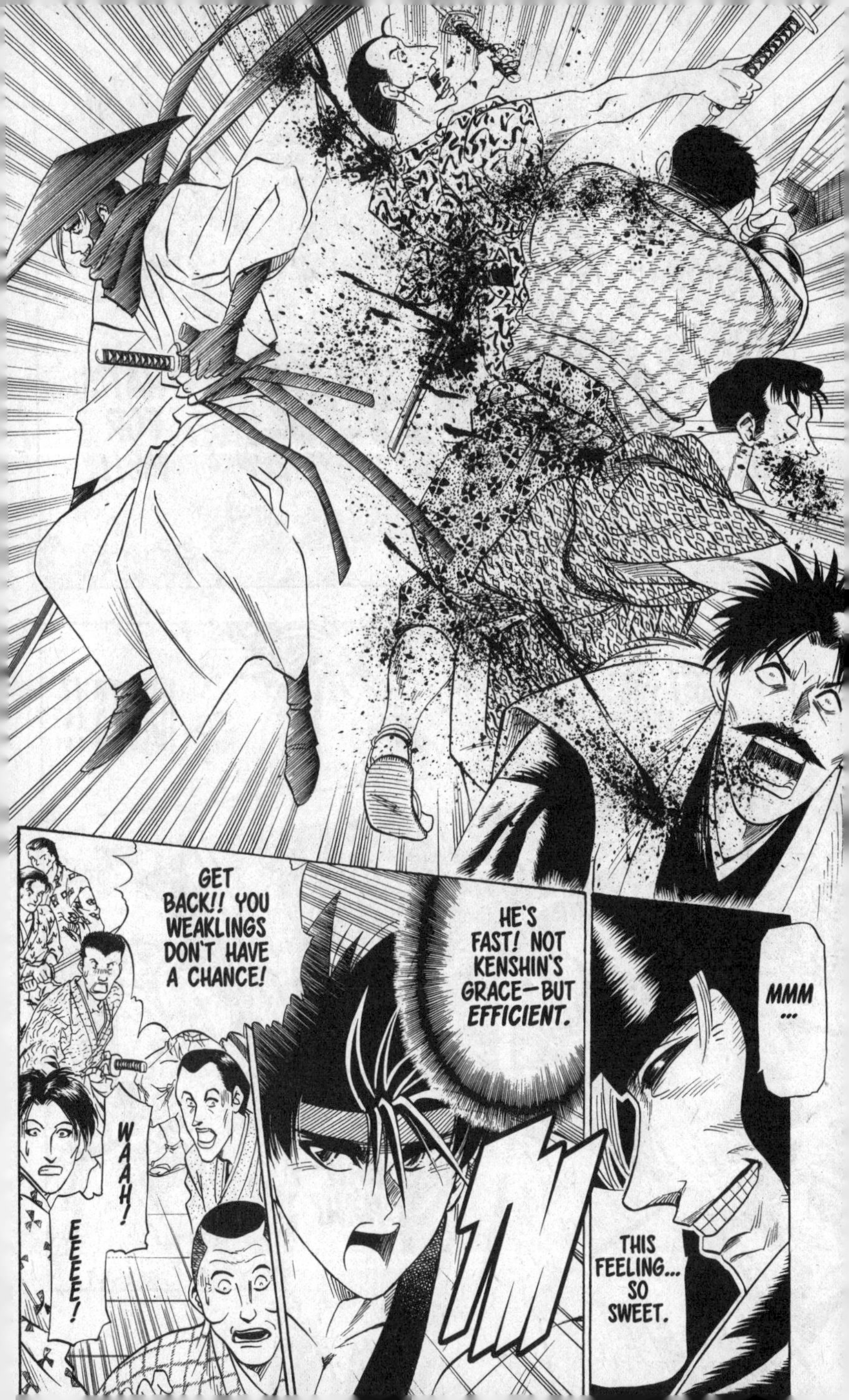
MMM...
THIS FEELING... SO SWEET.
HE'S FAST! NOT KENSHIN'S GRACE—BUT EFFICIENT.
GET BACK!! YOU WEAKLINGS DON'T HAVE A CHANCE!
WAAAH!
EEEEE!

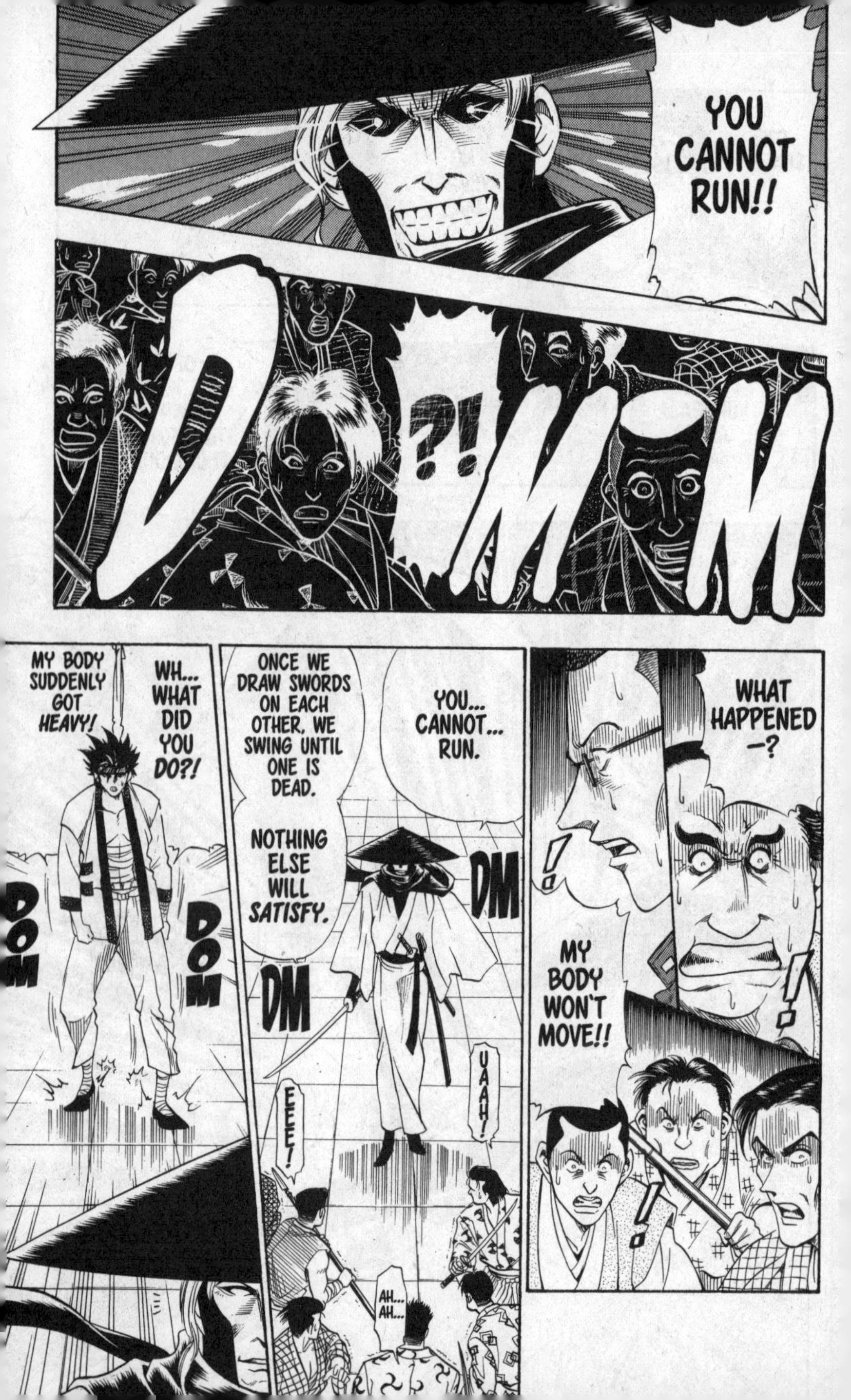
YOU CANNOT RUN!!
DMMM
?!
WHAT HAPPENED—?
!
!
MY BODY WON'T MOVE!!
!
YOU... CANNOT... RUN.
ONCE WE DRAW SWORDS ON EACH OTHER, WE SWING UNTIL ONE IS DEAD.
NOTHING ELSE WILL SATISFY.
DM
DM
UAAH!
EEE!
AH... AH...
WH... WHAT DID YOU DO?!
MY BODY SUDDENLY GOT HEAVY!
DOM
DOM

READ THIS WAY

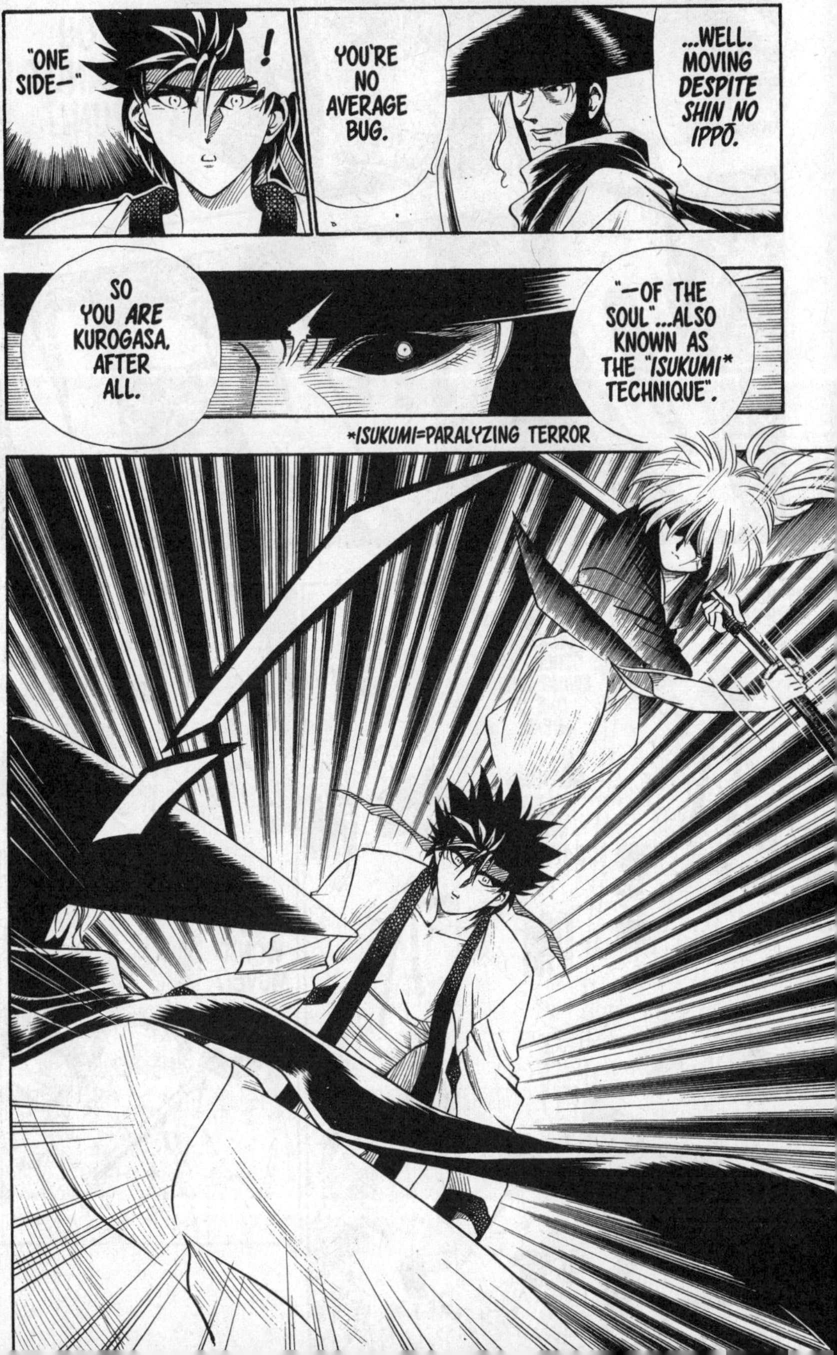
...WELL. MOVING DESPITE SHIN NO IPPŌ.
YOU'RE NO AVERAGE BUG.
!
"ONE SIDE—"
"—OF THE SOUL"...ALSO KNOWN AS THE "ISUKUMI*" TECHNIQUE".
SO YOU ARE KUROGASA, AFTER ALL.
*ISUKUMI=PARALYZING TERROR

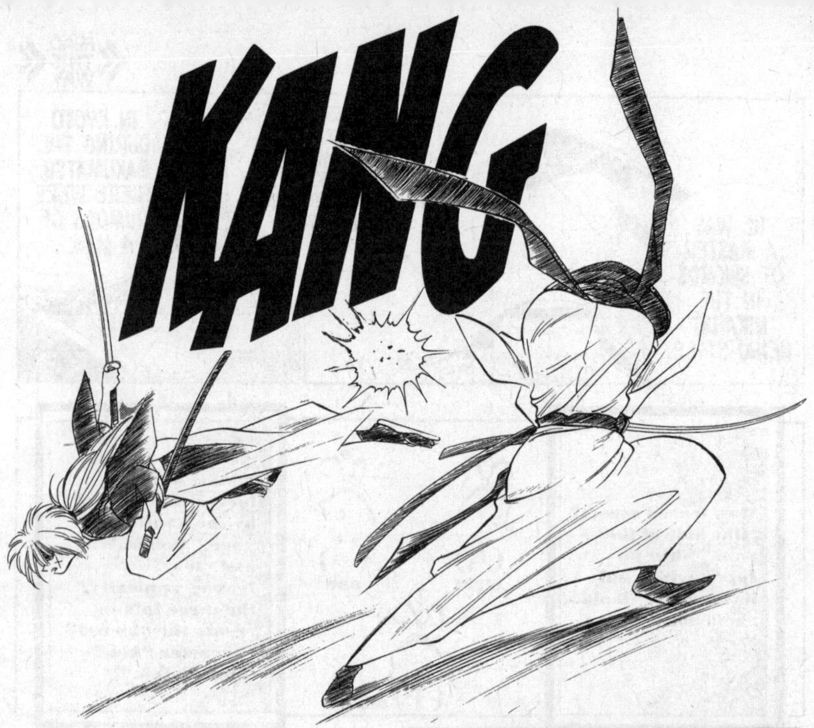
KANG

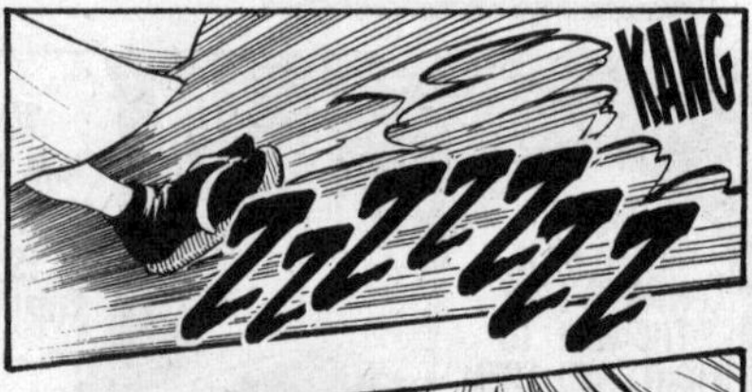
KANG
ZZZZZZZ

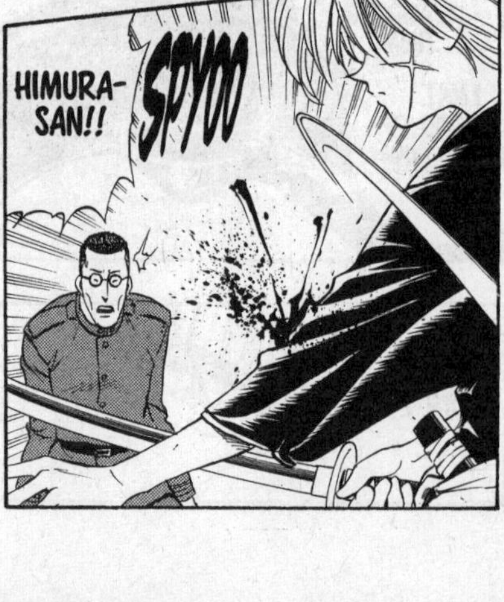
SPYOO
HIMURA-SAN!!

Even Watsuki, who watches anime yet knows little of anime voice-actors, knows (Kenshin "CD book" voice-actor) Ogata. That is how good and popular she is. To be fair, quite a few fan letters mention how well her voice fits (indicating, to me, how many *Kenshin* readers were also reading a certain, other, super-popular manga...and how sad and complicated a realization is that!). Given that Watsuki had imagined Kenshin's voice more "neutral," it's a good thing, having Ogata bring his voice to life.

伸宏和月

...to be continued

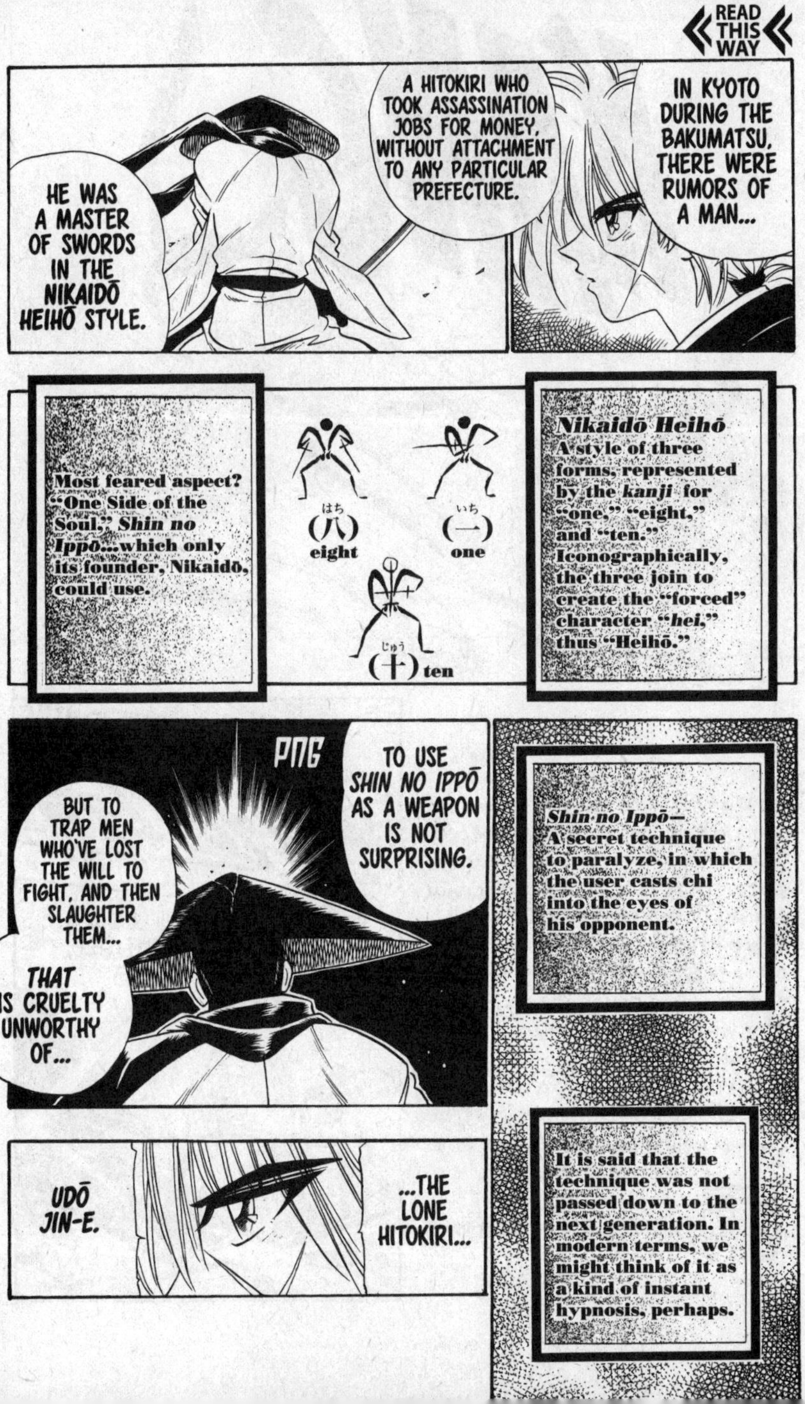
READ THIS WAY
IN KYOTO DURING THE BAKUMATSU, THERE WERE RUMORS OF A MAN...
A HITOKIRI WHO TOOK ASSASSINATION JOBS FOR MONEY, WITHOUT ATTACHMENT TO ANY PARTICULAR PREFECTURE.
HE WAS A MASTER OF SWORDS IN THE NIKAIDŌ HEIHŌ STYLE.
Nikaidō Heihō
A style of three forms, represented by the kanji for "one," "eight," and "ten." Iconographically, the three join to create the "forced" character "hei," thus "Heihō."
いち
(一) one
はち
(八) eight
じゅう
(十) ten
Most feared aspect? "One Side of the Soul," Shin no Ippō...which only its founder, Nikaidō, could use.
Shin no Ippō—
A secret technique to paralyze, in which the user casts chi into the eyes of his opponent.
It is said that the technique was not passed down to the next generation. In modern terms, we might think of it as a kind of instant hypnosis, perhaps.
PNG
TO USE SHIN NO IPPŌ AS A WEAPON IS NOT SURPRISING.
BUT TO TRAP MEN WHO'VE LOST THE WILL TO FIGHT, AND THEN SLAUGHTER THEM...
THAT IS CRUELTY UNWORTHY OF...
...THE LONE HITOKIRI...
UDŌ JIN-E.

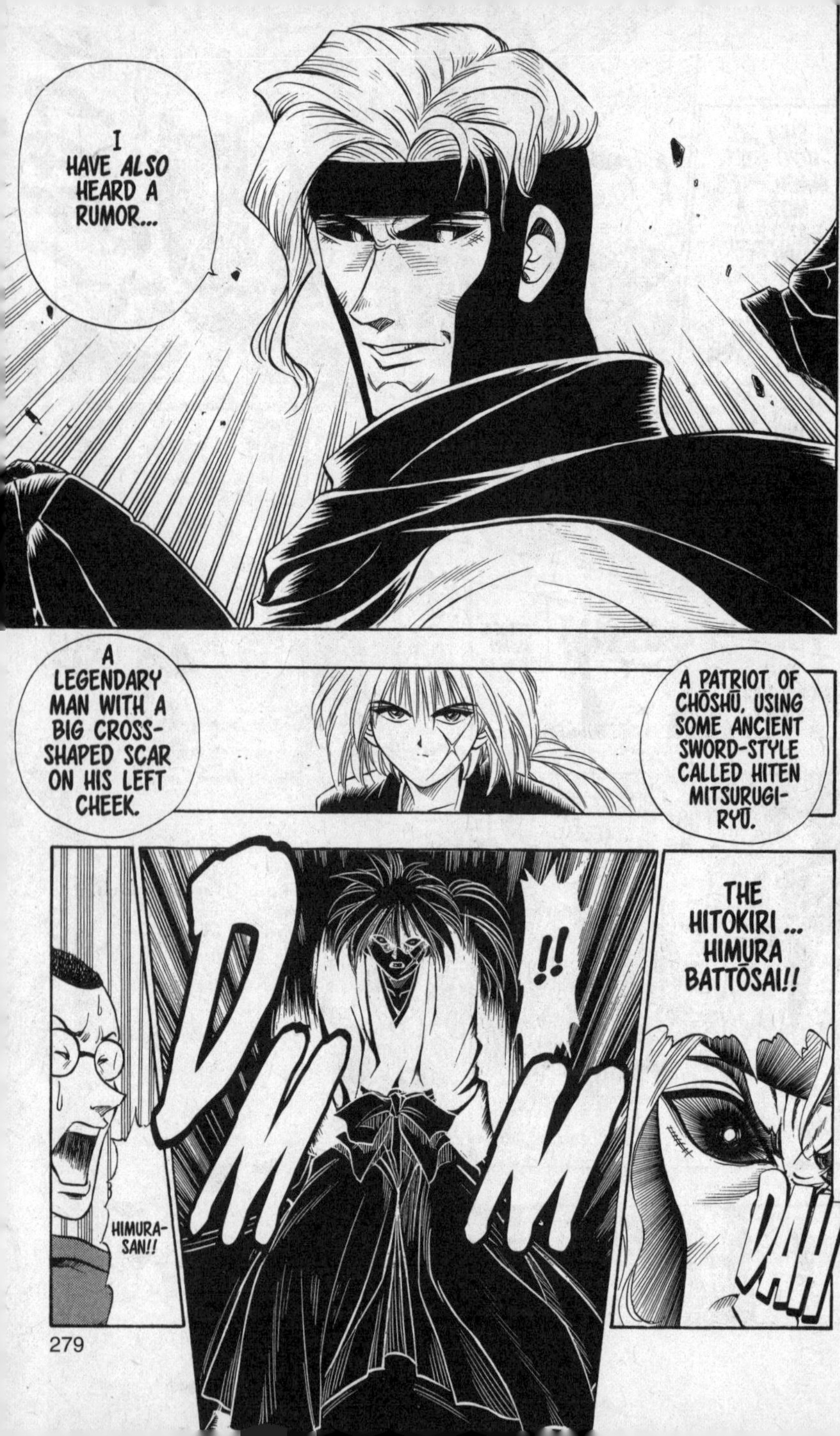
I HAVE ALSO HEARD A RUMOR...
A PATRIOT OF CHŌSHŪ, USING SOME ANCIENT SWORD-STYLE CALLED HITEN MITSURUGI-RYŪ.
A LEGENDARY MAN WITH A BIG CROSS-SHAPED SCAR ON HIS LEFT CHEEK.
THE HITOKIRI ... HIMURA BATTŌSAI!!
DAH
DMM
!!
HIMURA-SAN!!

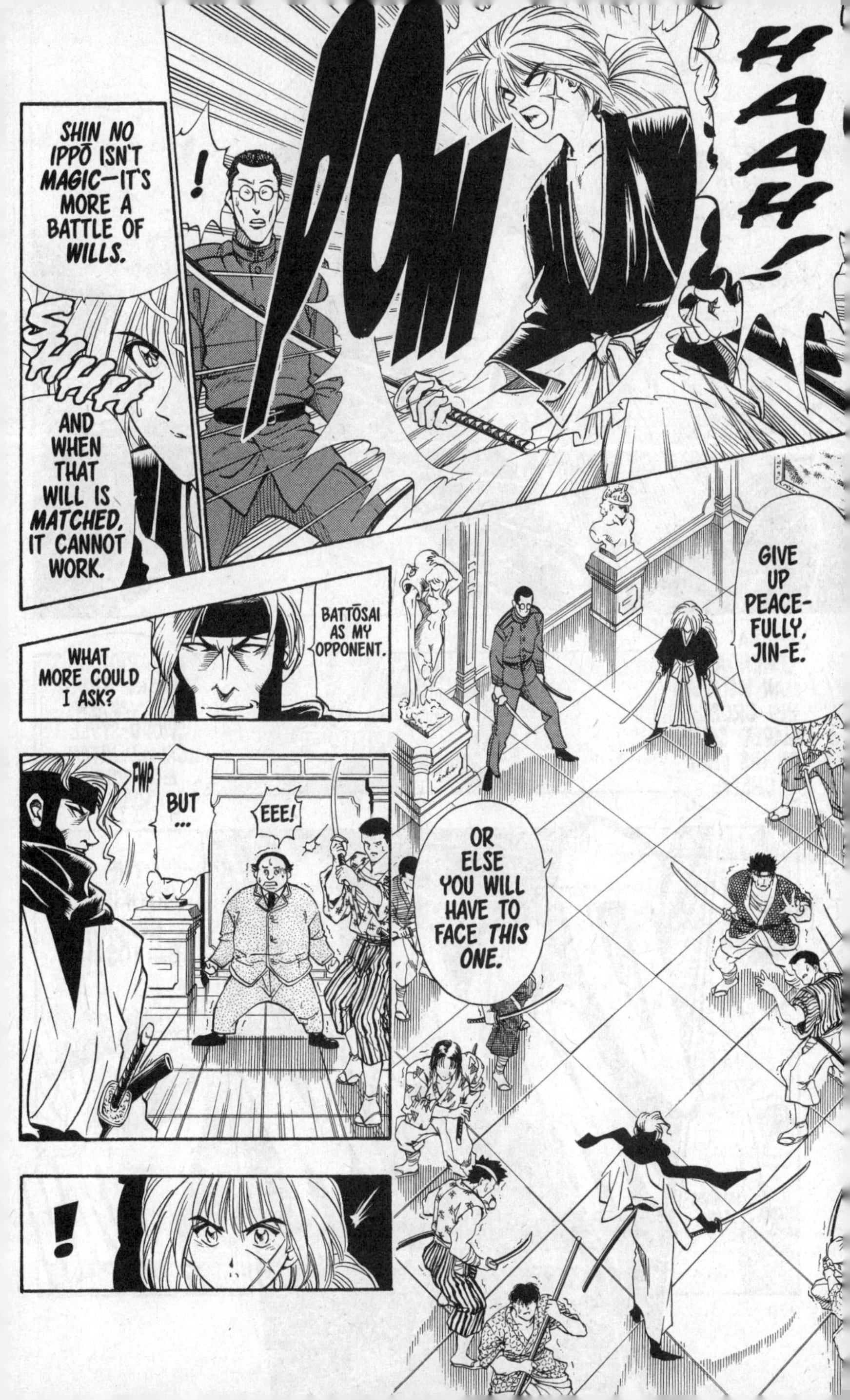
HAAH!
POW
!
SHIN NO IPPŌ ISN'T *MAGIC*—IT'S MORE A BATTLE OF *WILLS.*
SHHH
AND WHEN THAT WILL IS *MATCHED,* IT CANNOT WORK.
GIVE UP PEACE-FULLY, JIN-E.
OR ELSE YOU WILL HAVE TO FACE *THIS ONE.*
BATTŌSAI AS MY OPPONENT.
WHAT MORE COULD I ASK?
FWP
BUT ...
EEE!
!

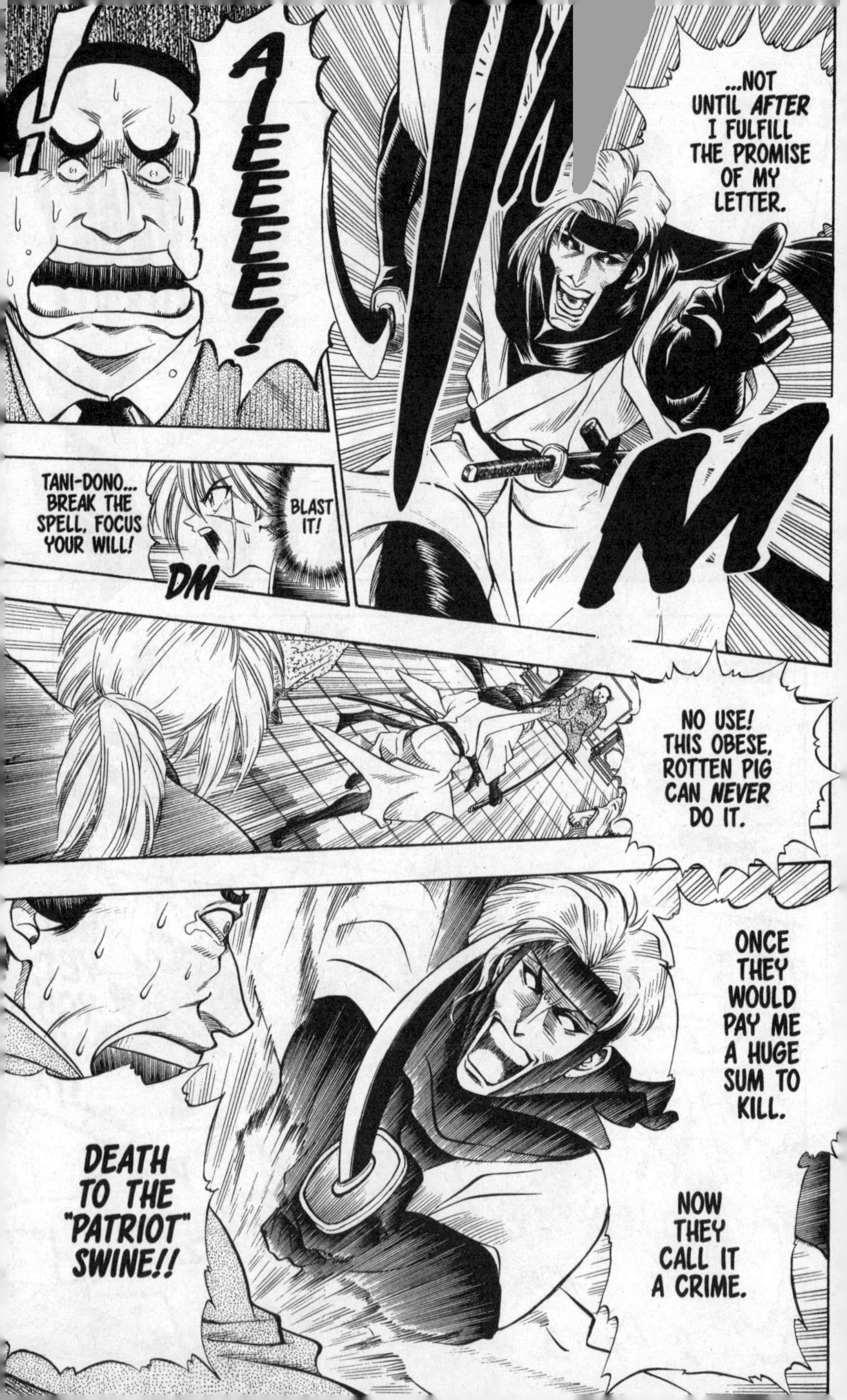
...NOT UNTIL AFTER I FULFILL THE PROMISE OF MY LETTER.
AIEEEEE!
BLAST IT!
TANI-DONO... BREAK THE SPELL, FOCUS YOUR WILL!
DM
NO USE! THIS OBESE, ROTTEN PIG CAN NEVER DO IT.
ONCE THEY WOULD PAY ME A HUGE SUM TO KILL.
NOW THEY CALL IT A CRIME.
DEATH TO THE "PATRIOT" SWINE!!

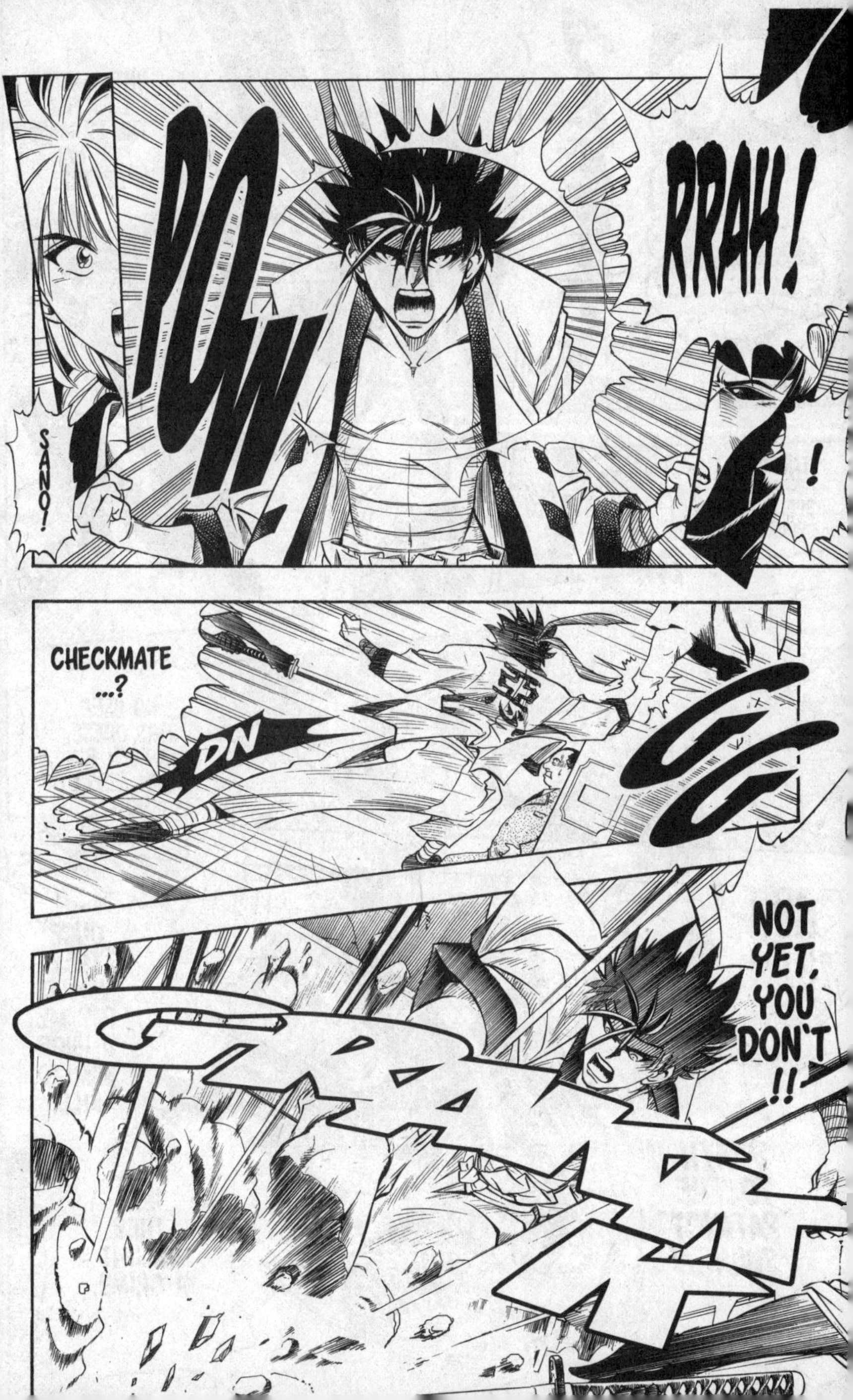
RRAH!
!
POW
SANO!
GG
DN
CHECKMATE ...?
NOT YET, YOU DON'T!!

READ THIS WAY

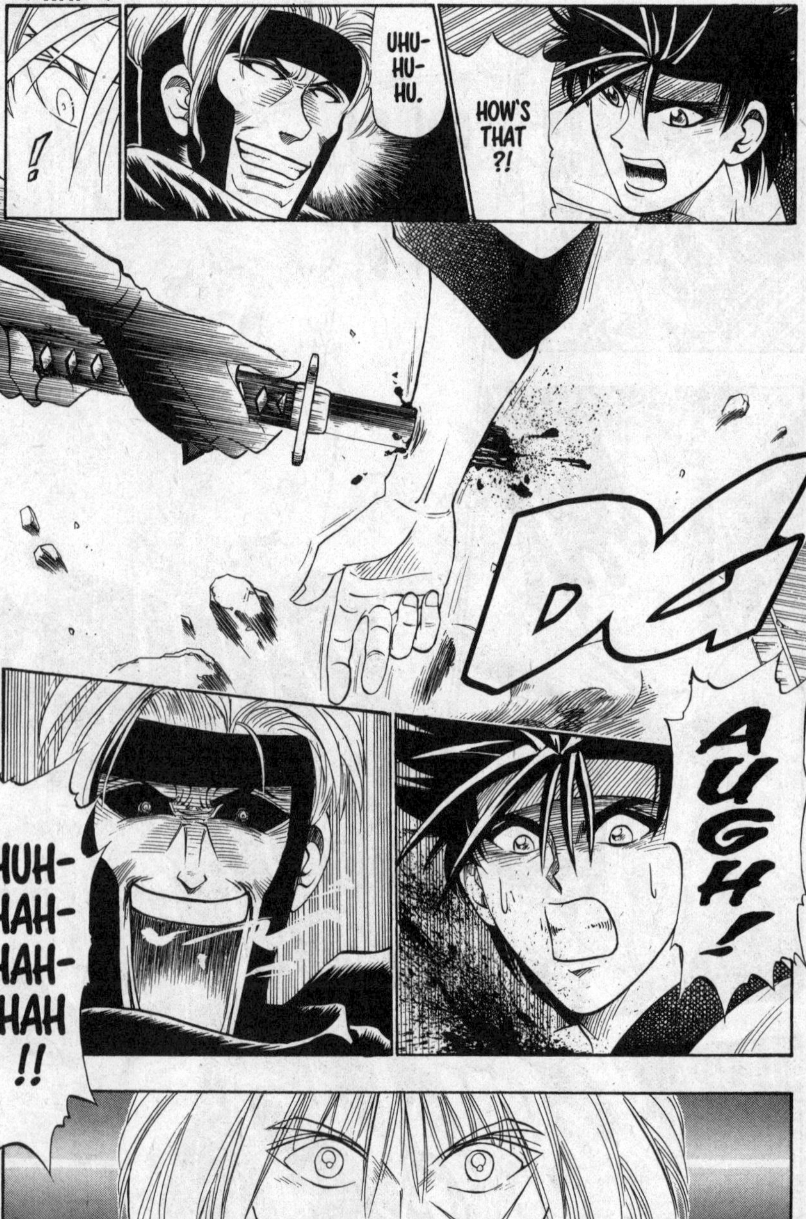
HOW'S THAT ?!
UHU-HU-HU.
!
AUGH!
HUH-HAH-HAH-HAH !!

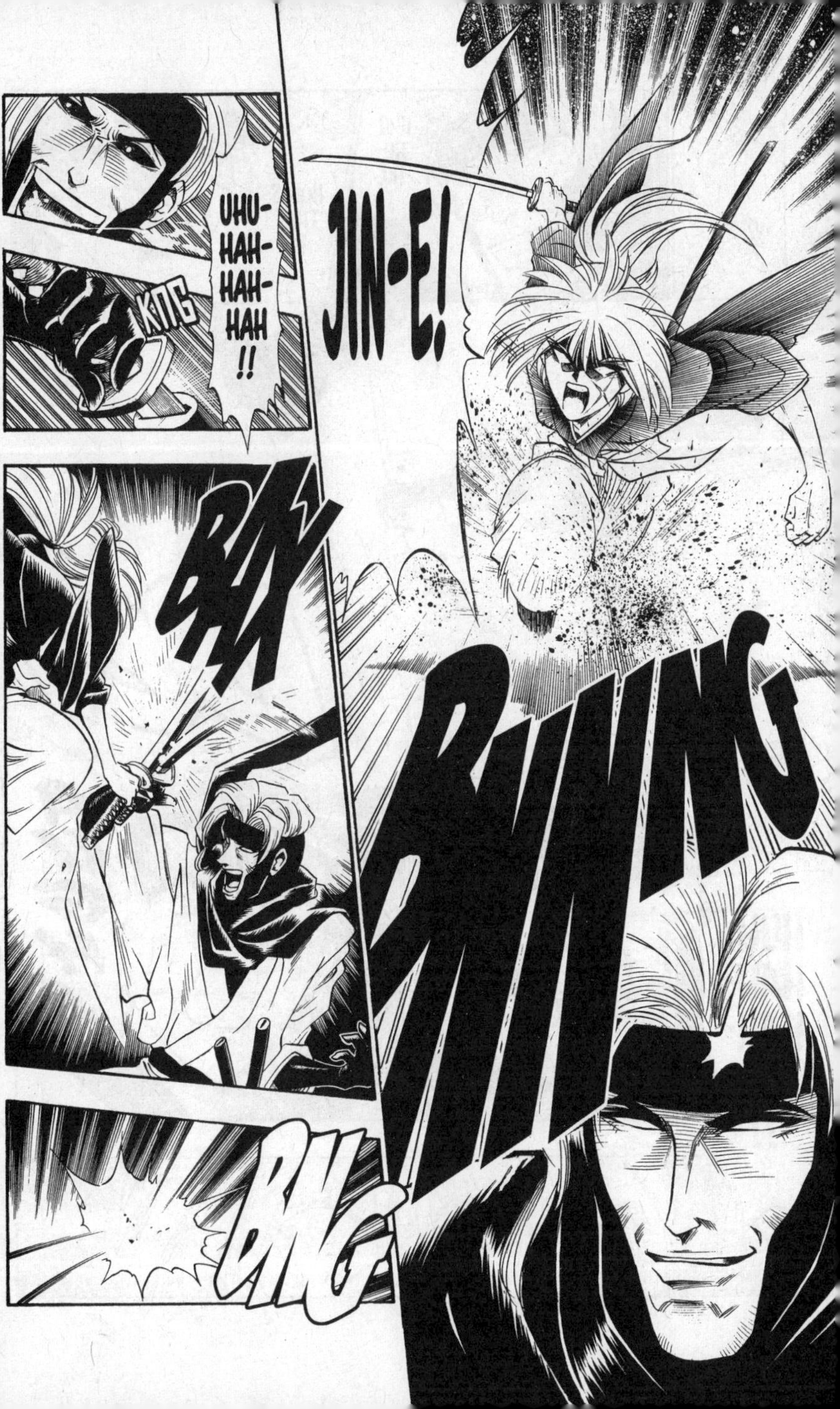
JIN-E!
UHU-HAH-HAH-HAH!!
KNG
BAM BAM
BANG

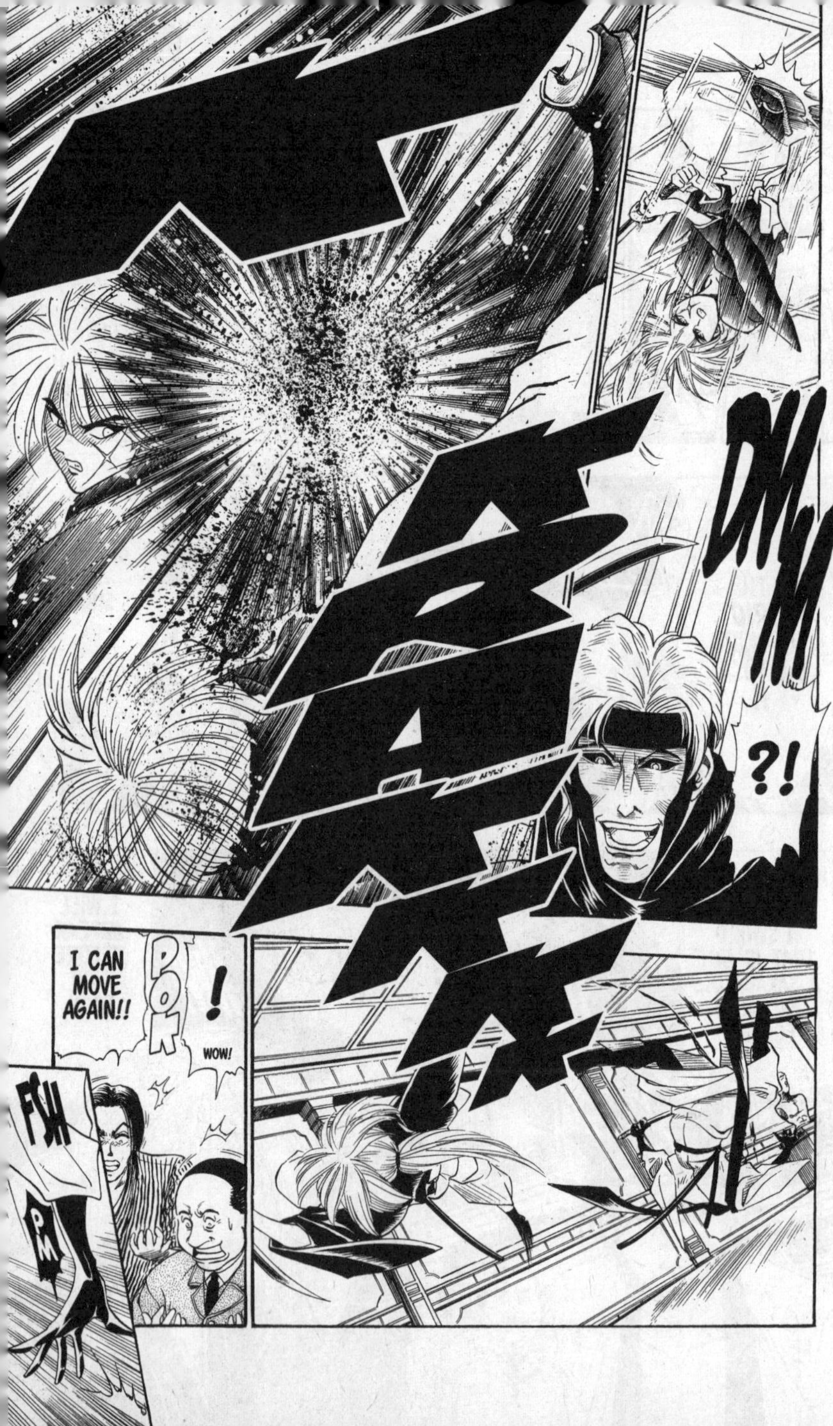
DMMM
?!
!
POK
I CAN MOVE AGAIN!!
WOW!
FSH
PM

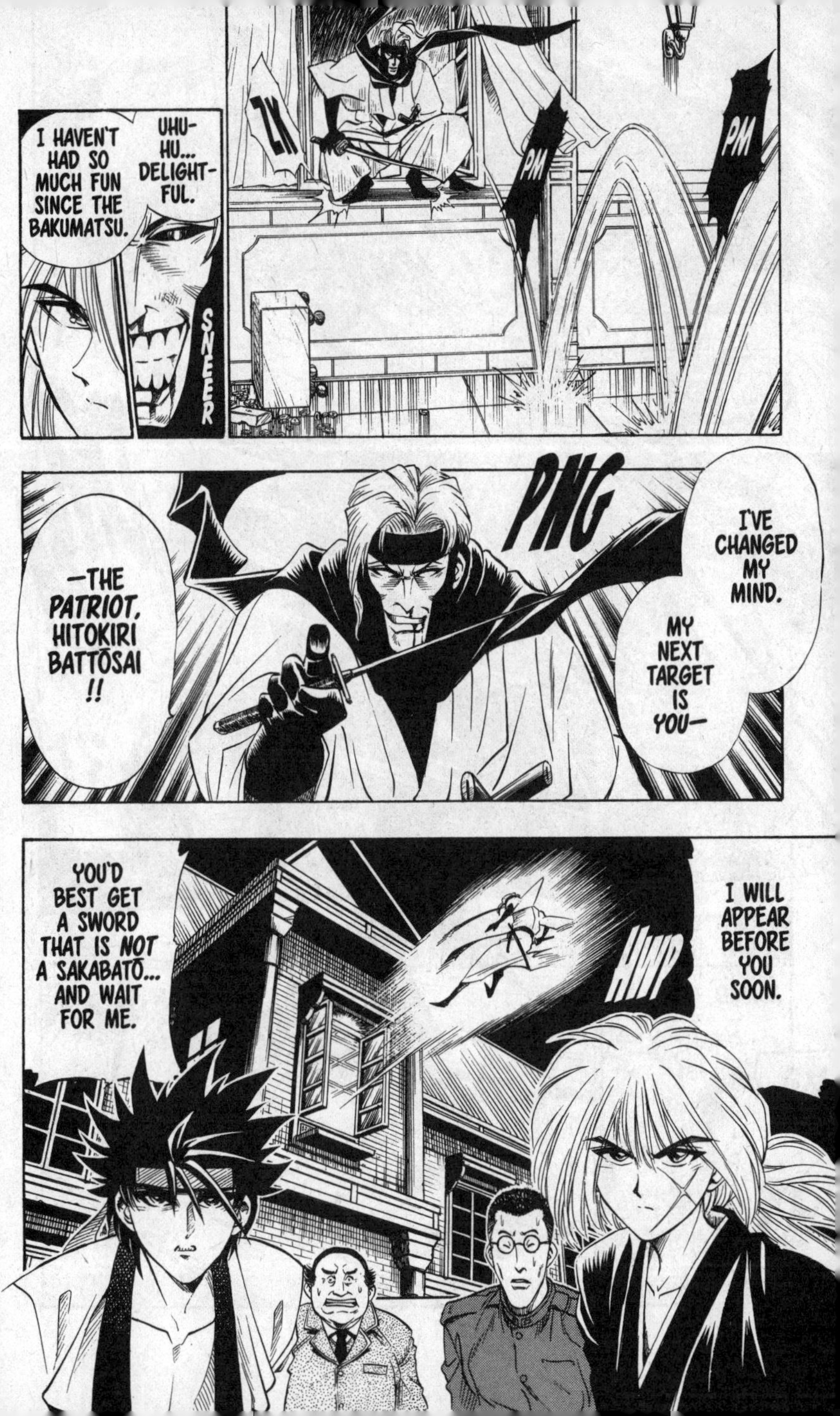
ZK
PM
PM
UHU-HU... DELIGHT-FUL.
I HAVEN'T HAD SO MUCH FUN SINCE THE BAKUMATSU.
SNEER
I'VE CHANGED MY MIND.
MY NEXT TARGET IS YOU—
PNG
—THE PATRIOT, HITOKIRI BATTŌSAI !!
I WILL APPEAR BEFORE YOU SOON.
HWP
YOU'D BEST GET A SWORD THAT IS NOT A SAKABATŌ... AND WAIT FOR ME.

READ THIS WAY

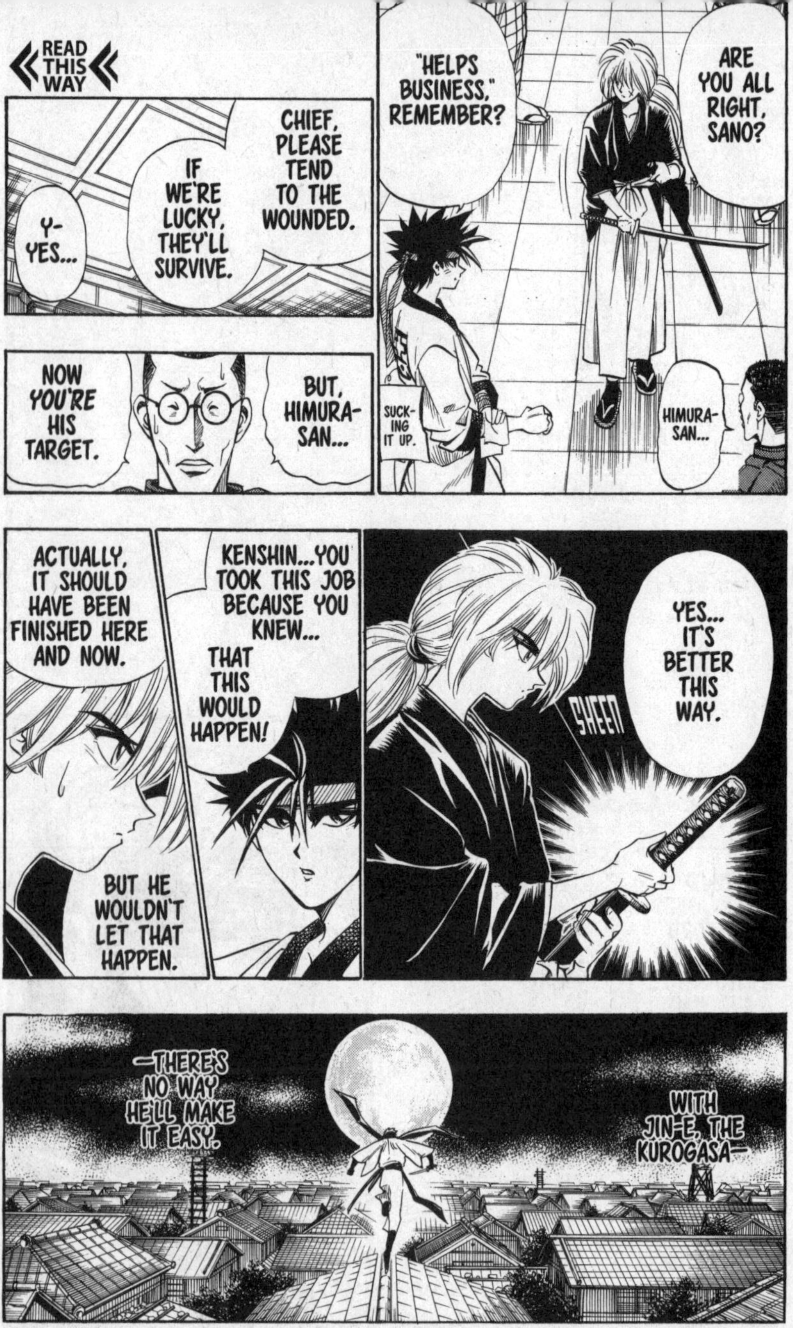
ARE YOU ALL RIGHT, SANO?
"HELPS BUSINESS," REMEMBER?
HIMURA-SAN...
SUCKING IT UP.
CHIEF, PLEASE TEND TO THE WOUNDED.
IF WE'RE LUCKY, THEY'LL SURVIVE.
Y-YES...
BUT, HIMURA-SAN...
NOW YOU'RE HIS TARGET.
YES... IT'S BETTER THIS WAY.
SHEEN
KENSHIN...YOU TOOK THIS JOB BECAUSE YOU KNEW...
THAT THIS WOULD HAPPEN!
ACTUALLY, IT SHOULD HAVE BEEN FINISHED HERE AND NOW.
BUT HE WOULDN'T LET THAT HAPPEN.
WITH JIN-E, THE KUROGASA—
—THERE'S NO WAY HE'LL MAKE IT EASY.

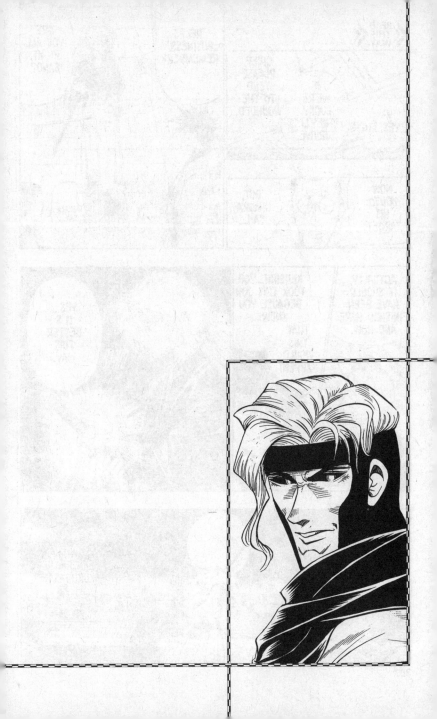

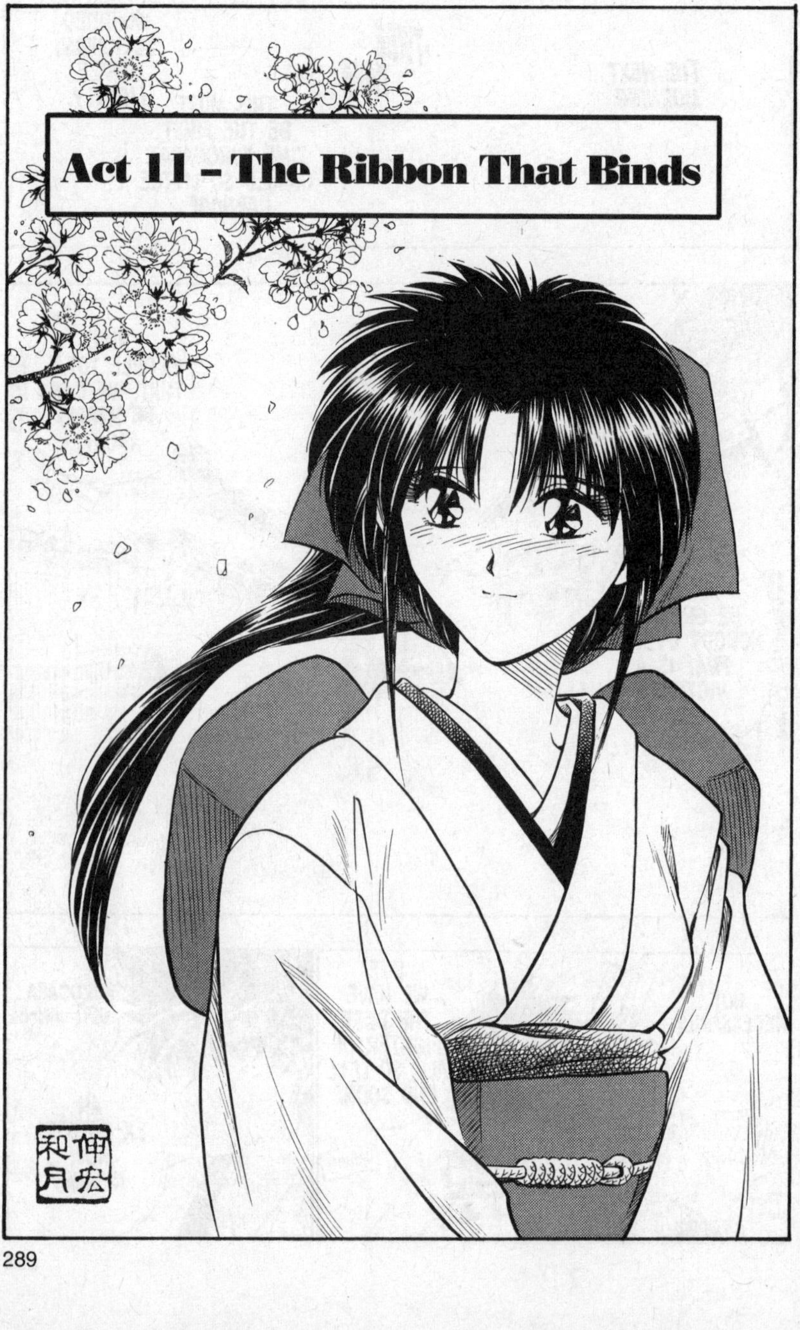

Act 11 – The Ribbon That Binds
伸宏
和月

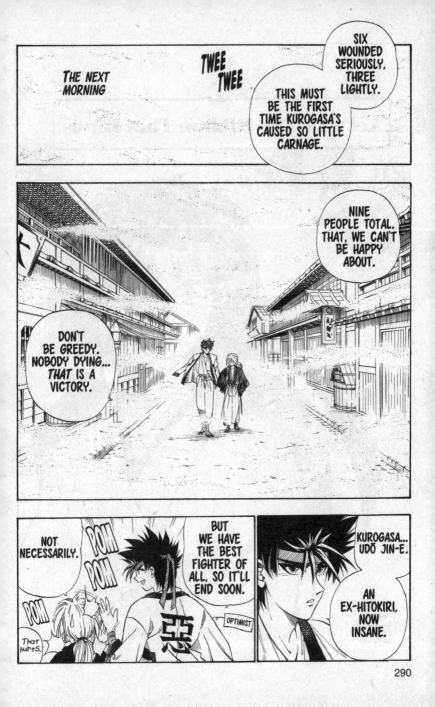

SIX WOUNDED SERIOUSLY, THREE LIGHTLY.
TWEE TWEE
THIS MUST BE THE FIRST TIME KUROGASA'S CAUSED SO LITTLE CARNAGE.
THE NEXT MORNING
NINE PEOPLE TOTAL. THAT, WE CAN'T BE HAPPY ABOUT.
DON'T BE GREEDY. NOBODY DYING... *THAT* IS A VICTORY.
KUROGASA... UDŌ JIN-E.
AN EX-HITOKIRI, NOW INSANE.
BUT WE HAVE THE BEST FIGHTER OF ALL, SO IT'LL END SOON.
POM POM
NOT NECESSARILY.
OPTIMIST
POM
That hurts.

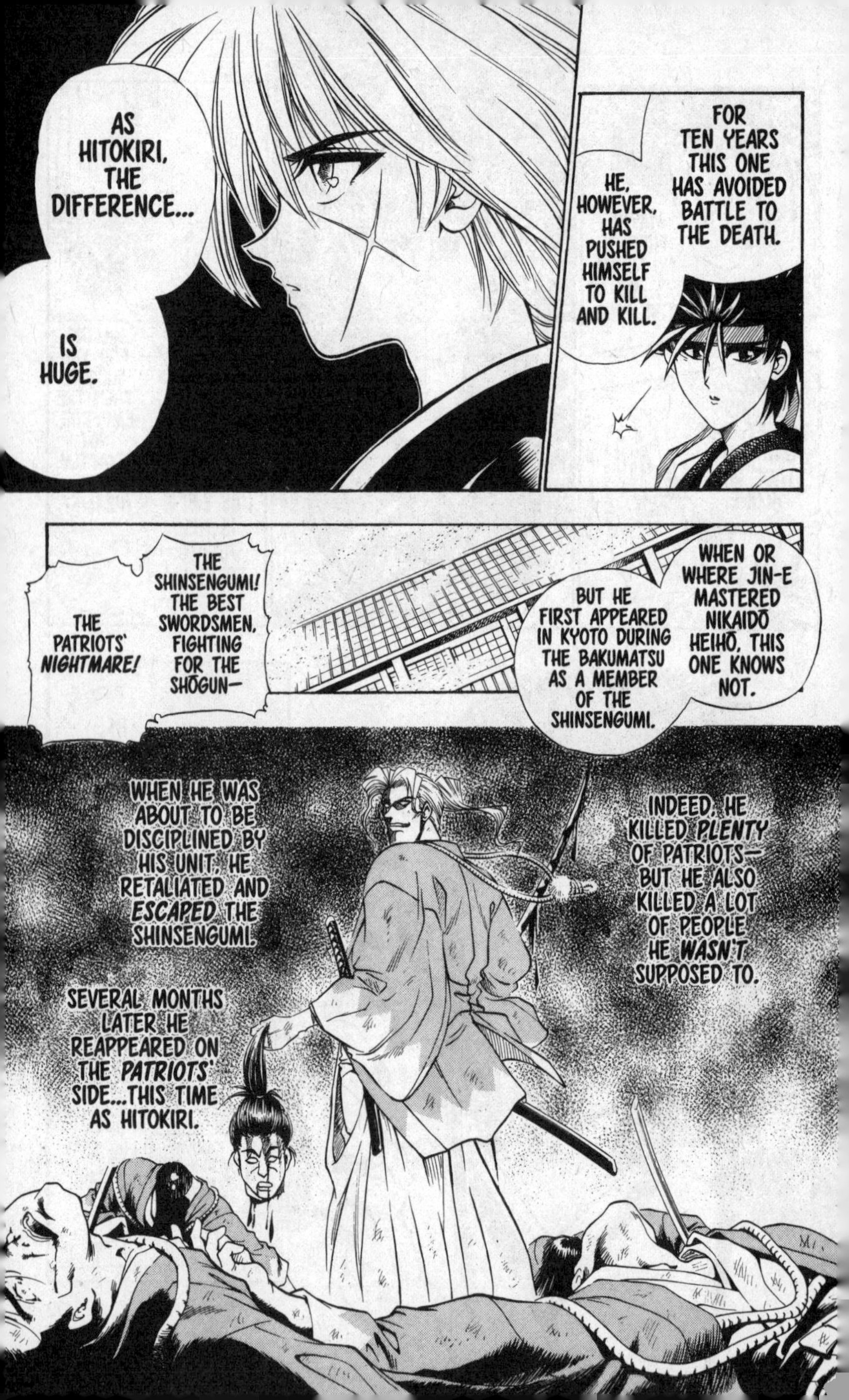

FOR TEN YEARS THIS ONE HAS AVOIDED BATTLE TO THE DEATH.
HE, HOWEVER, HAS PUSHED HIMSELF TO KILL AND KILL.
AS HITOKIRI, THE DIFFERENCE...
IS HUGE.
WHEN OR WHERE JIN-E MASTERED NIKAIDŌ HEIHŌ, THIS ONE KNOWS NOT.
BUT HE FIRST APPEARED IN KYOTO DURING THE BAKUMATSU AS A MEMBER OF THE SHINSENGUMI.
THE SHINSENGUMI! THE BEST SWORDSMEN, FIGHTING FOR THE SHŌGUN—
THE PATRIOTS' *NIGHTMARE!*
INDEED, HE KILLED *PLENTY* OF PATRIOTS—BUT HE ALSO KILLED A LOT OF PEOPLE HE *WASN'T* SUPPOSED TO.
WHEN HE WAS ABOUT TO BE DISCIPLINED BY HIS UNIT, HE RETALIATED AND *ESCAPED* THE SHINSENGUMI.
SEVERAL MONTHS LATER HE REAPPEARED ON THE *PATRIOTS'* SIDE...THIS TIME AS HITOKIRI.

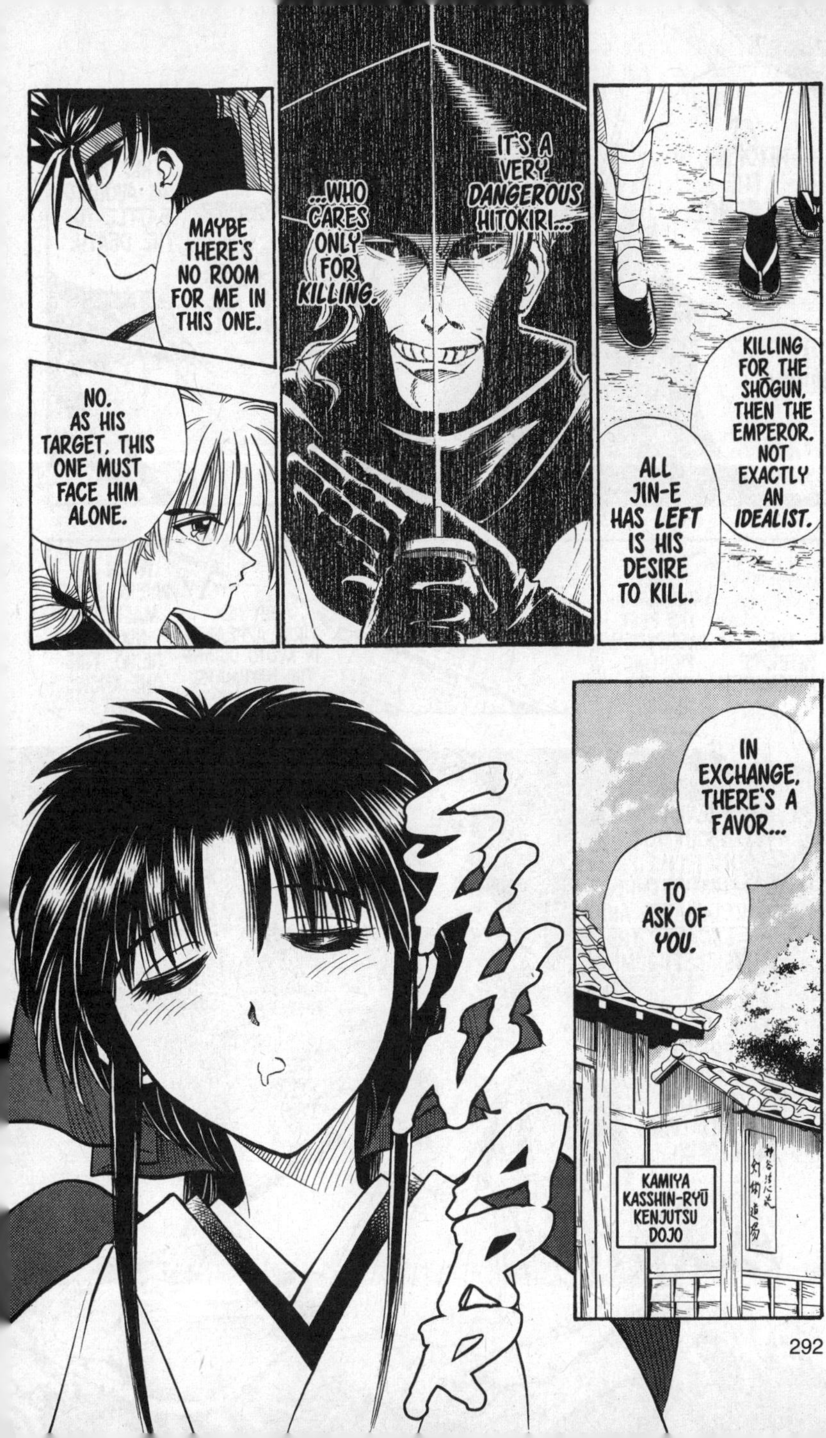
KILLING FOR THE SHŌGUN, THEN THE EMPEROR. NOT EXACTLY AN IDEALIST.
ALL JIN-E HAS LEFT IS HIS DESIRE TO KILL.
IT'S A VERY DANGEROUS HITOKIRI...
...WHO CARES ONLY FOR KILLING.
MAYBE THERE'S NO ROOM FOR ME IN THIS ONE.
NO. AS HIS TARGET, THIS ONE MUST FACE HIM ALONE.
IN EXCHANGE, THERE'S A FAVOR...
TO ASK OF YOU.
KAMIYA KASSHIN-RYŪ KENJUTSU DOJO

READ THIS WAY

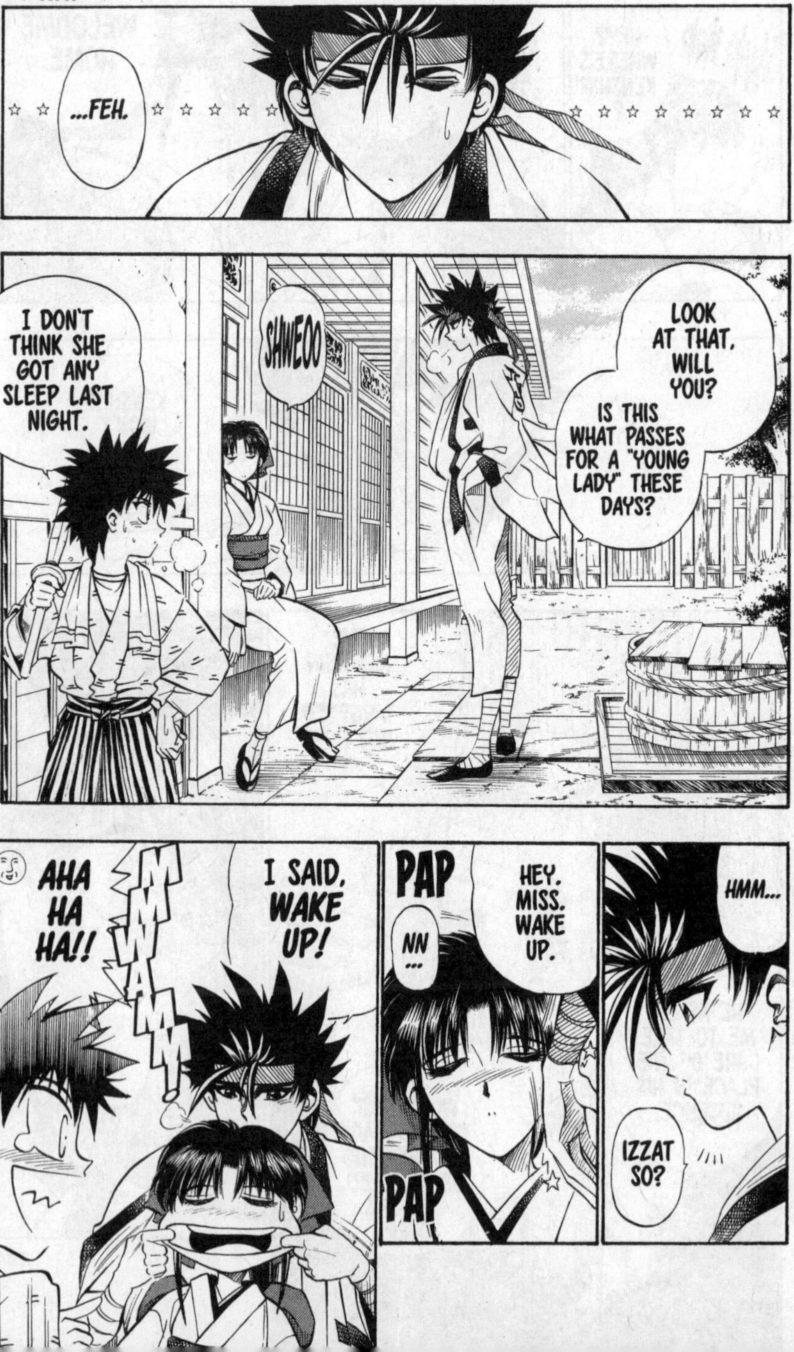
...FEH.
LOOK AT THAT, WILL YOU?
IS THIS WHAT PASSES FOR A "YOUNG LADY" THESE DAYS?
SHWEOO
I DON'T THINK SHE GOT ANY SLEEP LAST NIGHT.
HMM...
IZZAT SO?
PAP
HEY. MISS. WAKE UP.
NN...
PAP
I SAID, WAKE UP!
MMWAMM!
AHA HA HA!!

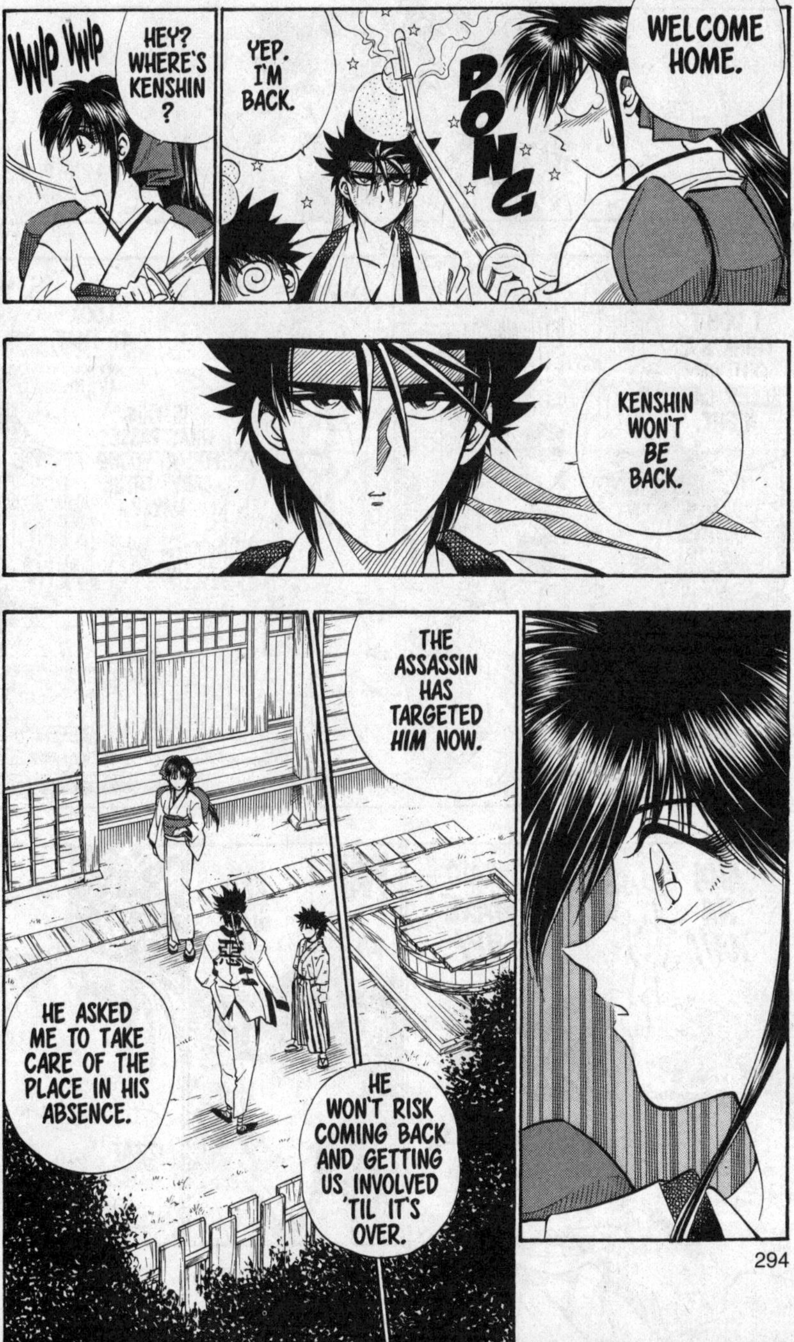
WELCOME HOME.
PONG
YEP. I'M BACK.
VWIP VWIP
HEY? WHERE'S KENSHIN?
KENSHIN WON'T BE BACK.
THE ASSASSIN HAS TARGETED HIM NOW.
HE WON'T RISK COMING BACK AND GETTING US INVOLVED 'TIL IT'S OVER.
HE ASKED ME TO TAKE CARE OF THE PLACE IN HIS ABSENCE.

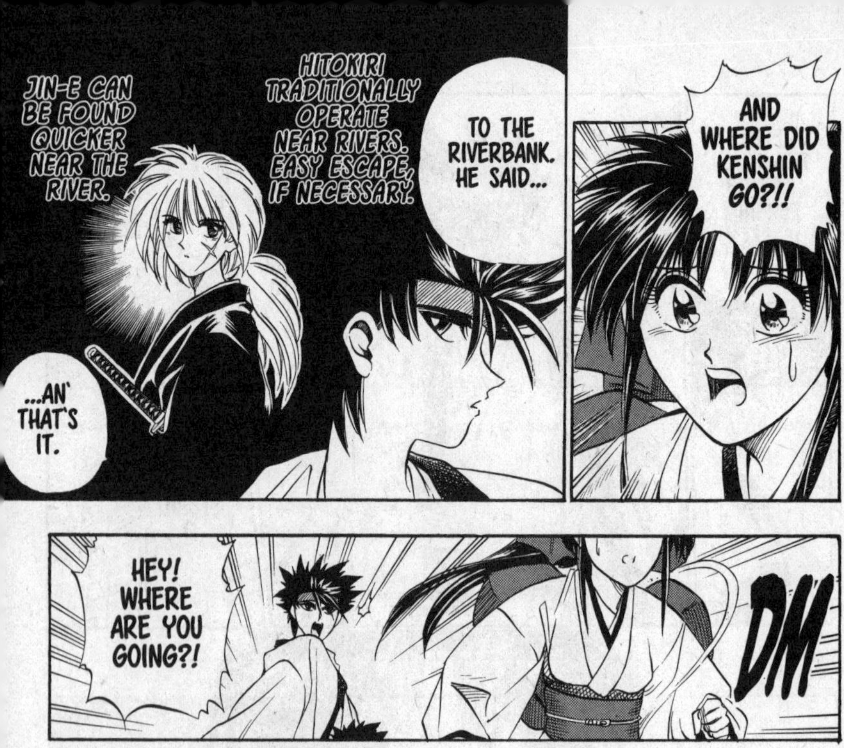
AND WHERE DID KENSHIN GO?!!
TO THE RIVERBANK. HE SAID...
HITOKIRI TRADITIONALLY OPERATE NEAR RIVERS. EASY ESCAPE, IF NECESSARY.
JIN-E CAN BE FOUND QUICKER NEAR THE RIVER.
...AN' THAT'S IT.
DM
HEY! WHERE ARE YOU GOING?!

I didn't know who Sakurai was—sorry, my bad!—so, when I asked a friend, I found out she was also voicing the heroine of a new anime series to start that fall. Eventually, I watched it and thought she was good—not too high, not too low. That "not too airhead-y" tone was close to what Watsuki had imagined for Kaoru's voice..."bang on," I thought. Takayama, they tell me, is "Kiki" in "Kiki's Delivery Service" (I'm sorry, I really do not know voice-actors). She's got a lot of energy, and is a great fit for "the kid," Yahiko.

伸宏和月

...to be continued

READ THIS WAY

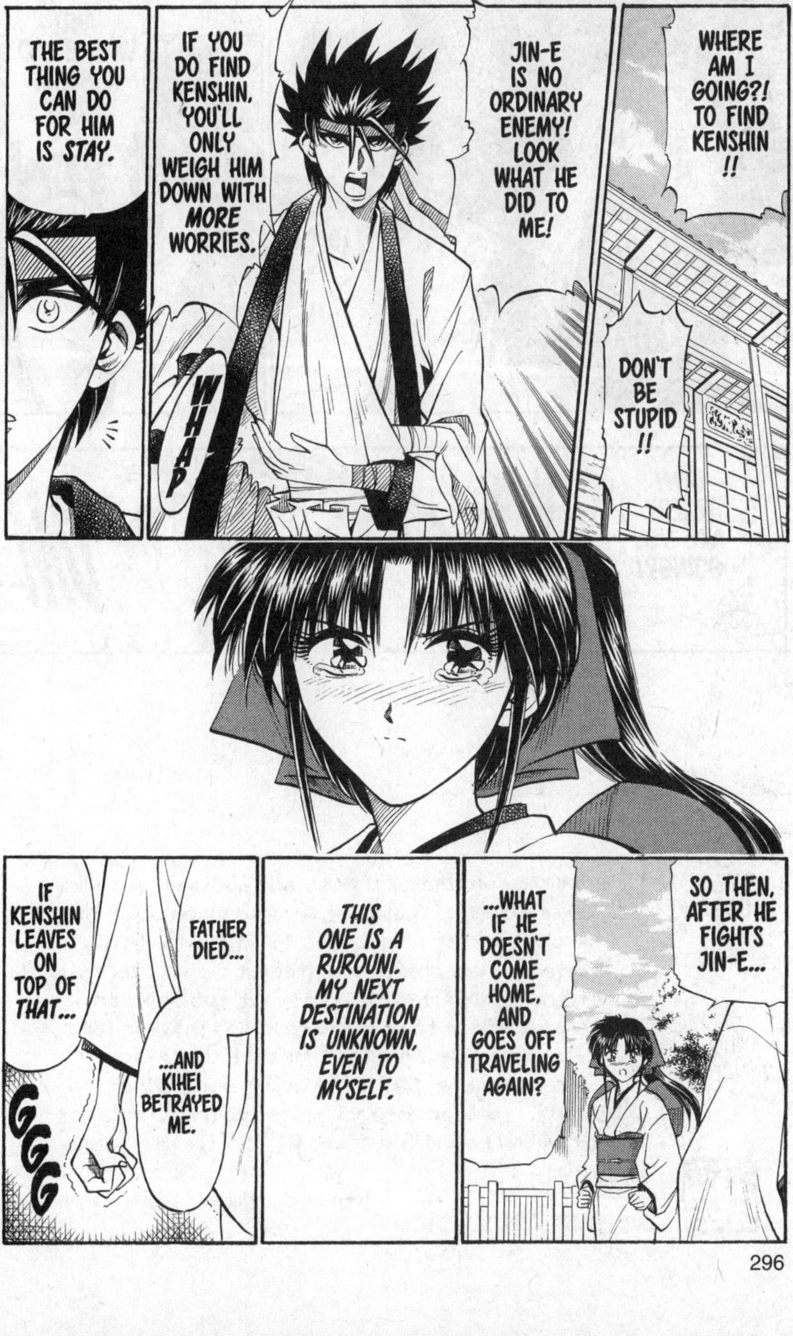

WHERE AM I GOING?! TO FIND KENSHIN!!
DON'T BE STUPID!!
JIN-E IS NO ORDINARY ENEMY! LOOK WHAT HE DID TO ME!
IF YOU DO FIND KENSHIN, YOU'LL ONLY WEIGH HIM DOWN WITH MORE WORRIES.
WHAP
THE BEST THING YOU CAN DO FOR HIM IS STAY.
SO THEN, AFTER HE FIGHTS JIN-E...
...WHAT IF HE DOESN'T COME HOME, AND GOES OFF TRAVELING AGAIN?
THIS ONE IS A RUROUNI. MY NEXT DESTINATION IS UNKNOWN, EVEN TO MYSELF.
FATHER DIED...
...AND KIHEI BETRAYED ME.
IF KENSHIN LEAVES ON TOP OF THAT...
GGG

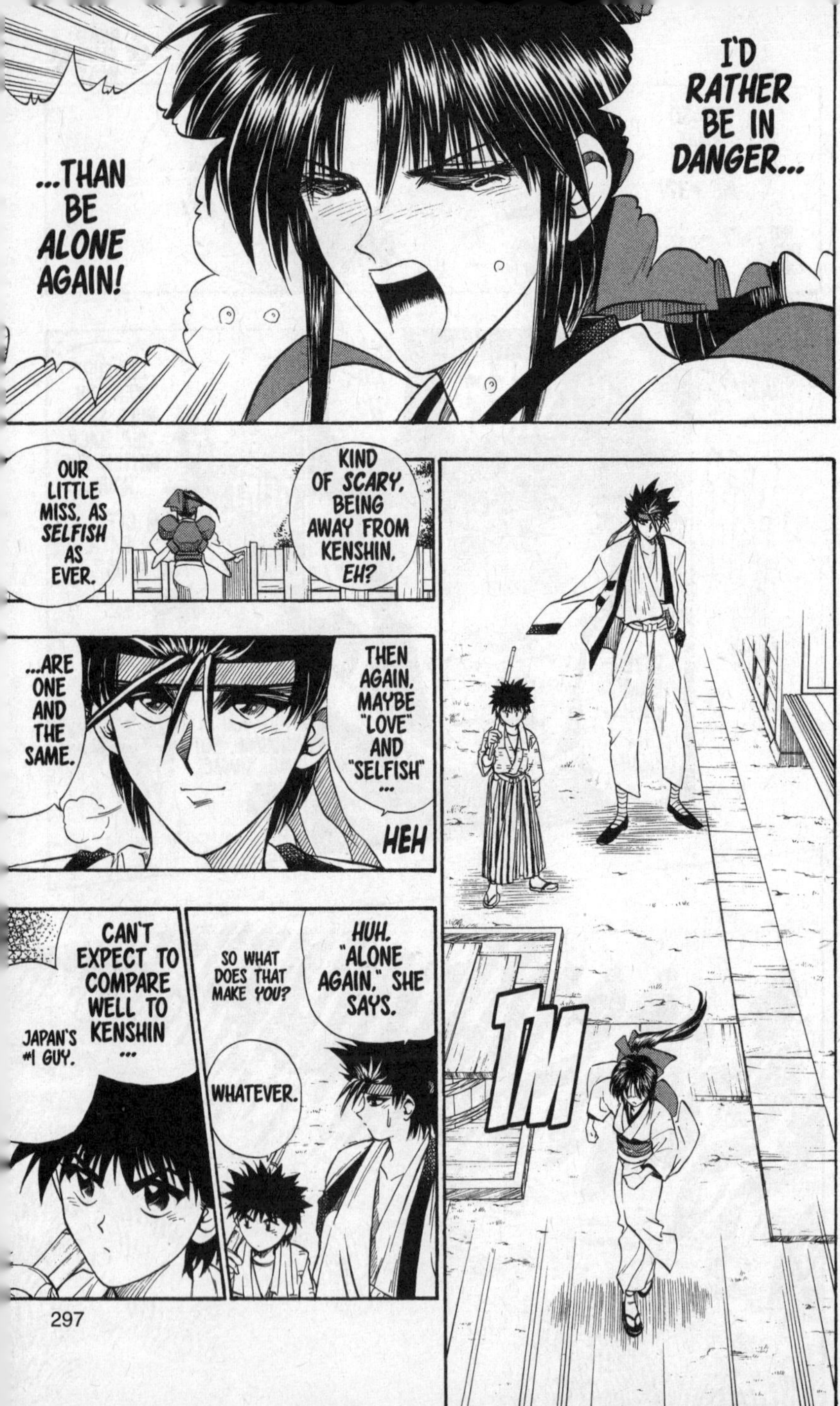
I'D RATHER BE IN DANGER...
...THAN BE ALONE AGAIN!
TM
KIND OF SCARY, BEING AWAY FROM KENSHIN, EH?
OUR LITTLE MISS, AS SELFISH AS EVER.
THEN AGAIN, MAYBE "LOVE" AND "SELFISH"...
HEH
...ARE ONE AND THE SAME.
HUH. "ALONE AGAIN," SHE SAYS.
SO WHAT DOES THAT MAKE YOU?
WHATEVER.
CAN'T EXPECT TO COMPARE WELL TO KENSHIN...
JAPAN'S #1 GUY.

READ THIS WAY

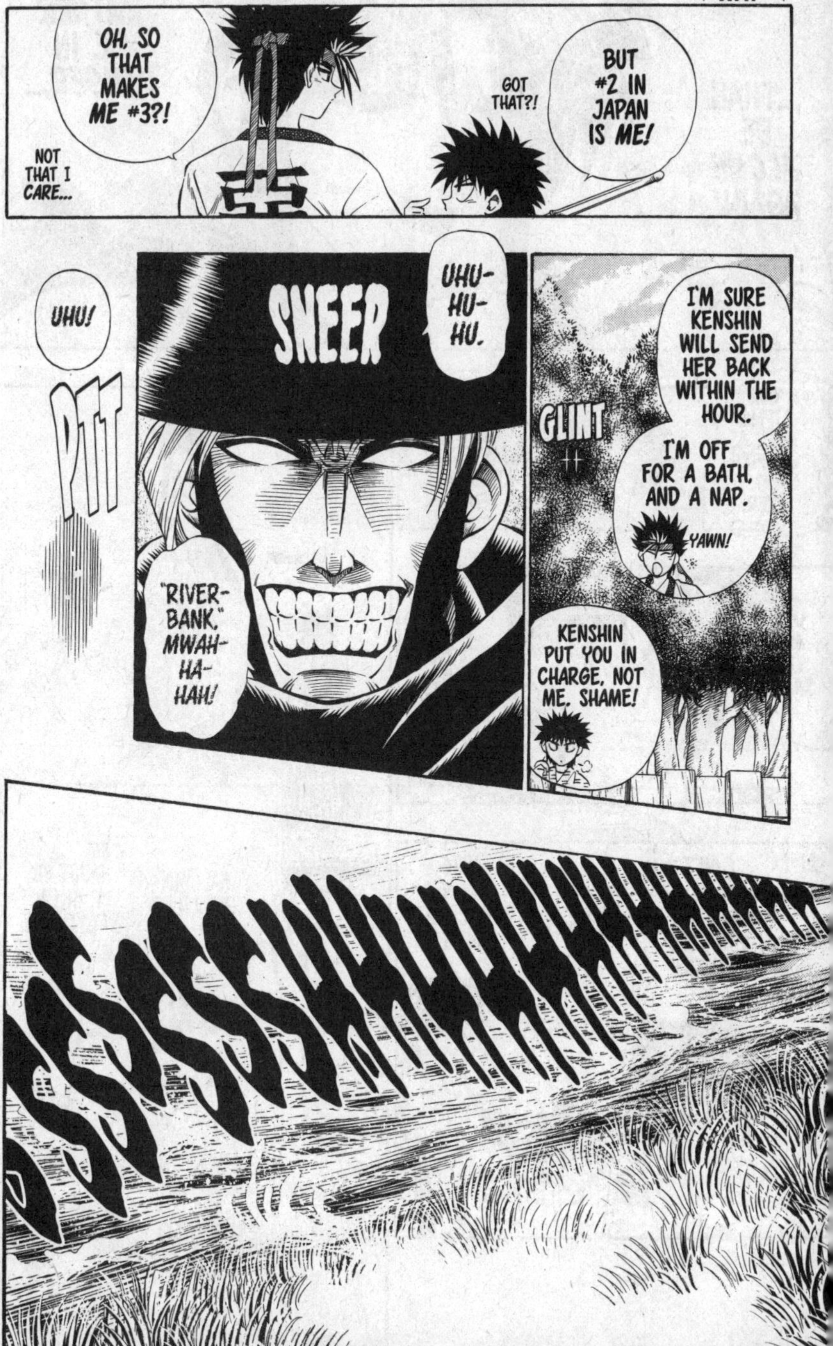

BUT #2 IN JAPAN IS ME!
GOT THAT?!
OH, SO THAT MAKES ME #3?!
NOT THAT I CARE...
I'M SURE KENSHIN WILL SEND HER BACK WITHIN THE HOUR.
GLINT
I'M OFF FOR A BATH, AND A NAP.
YAWN!
KENSHIN PUT YOU IN CHARGE, NOT ME, SHAME!
UHU-HU-HU.
SNEER
"RIVER-BANK," MWAH-HA-HAH!
UHU!
PTT
SSSSSHHHHHHHHHHHH

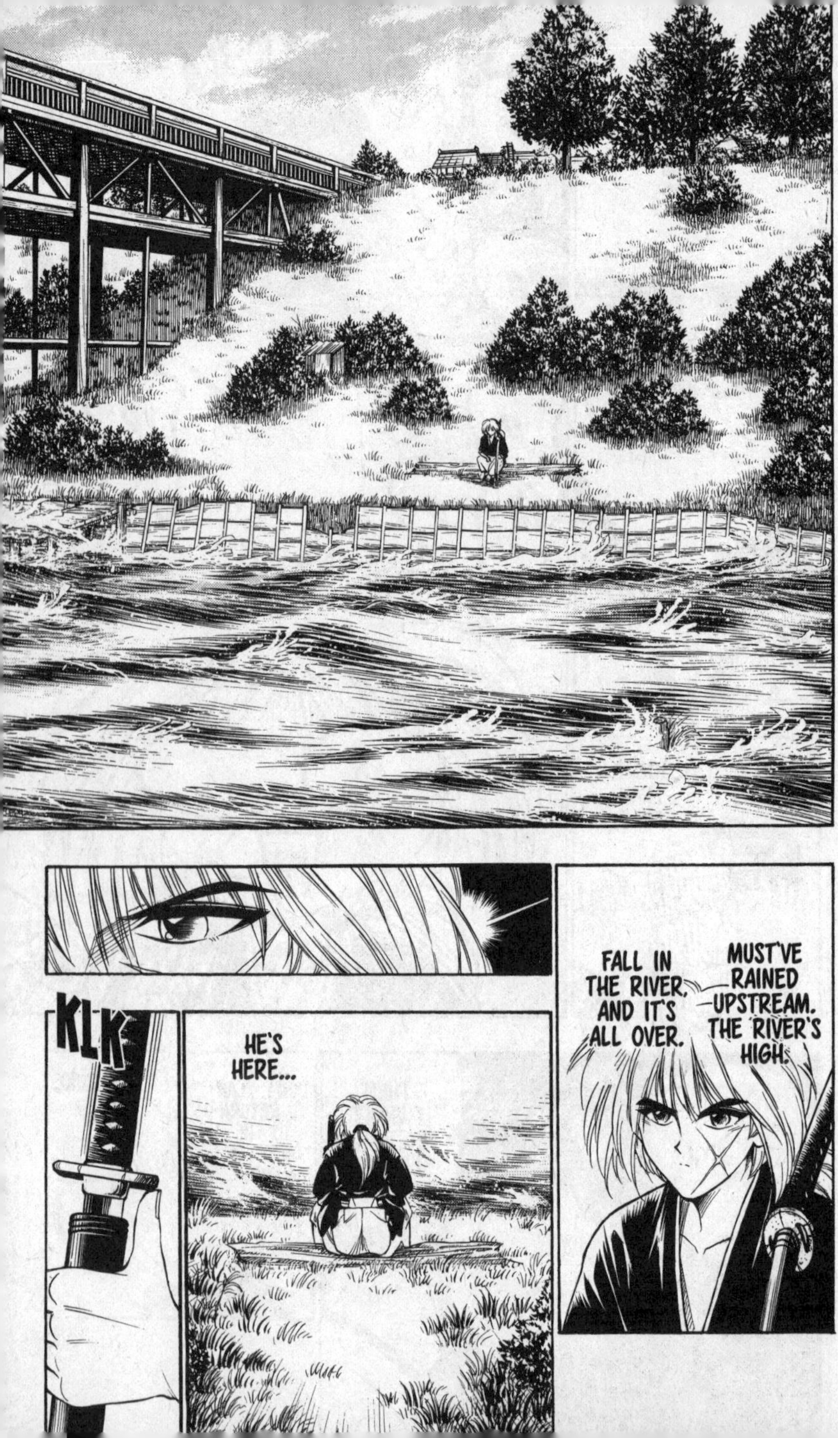
MUST'VE RAINED UPSTREAM. THE RIVER'S HIGH.
FALL IN THE RIVER, AND IT'S ALL OVER.
HE'S HERE...
KLK

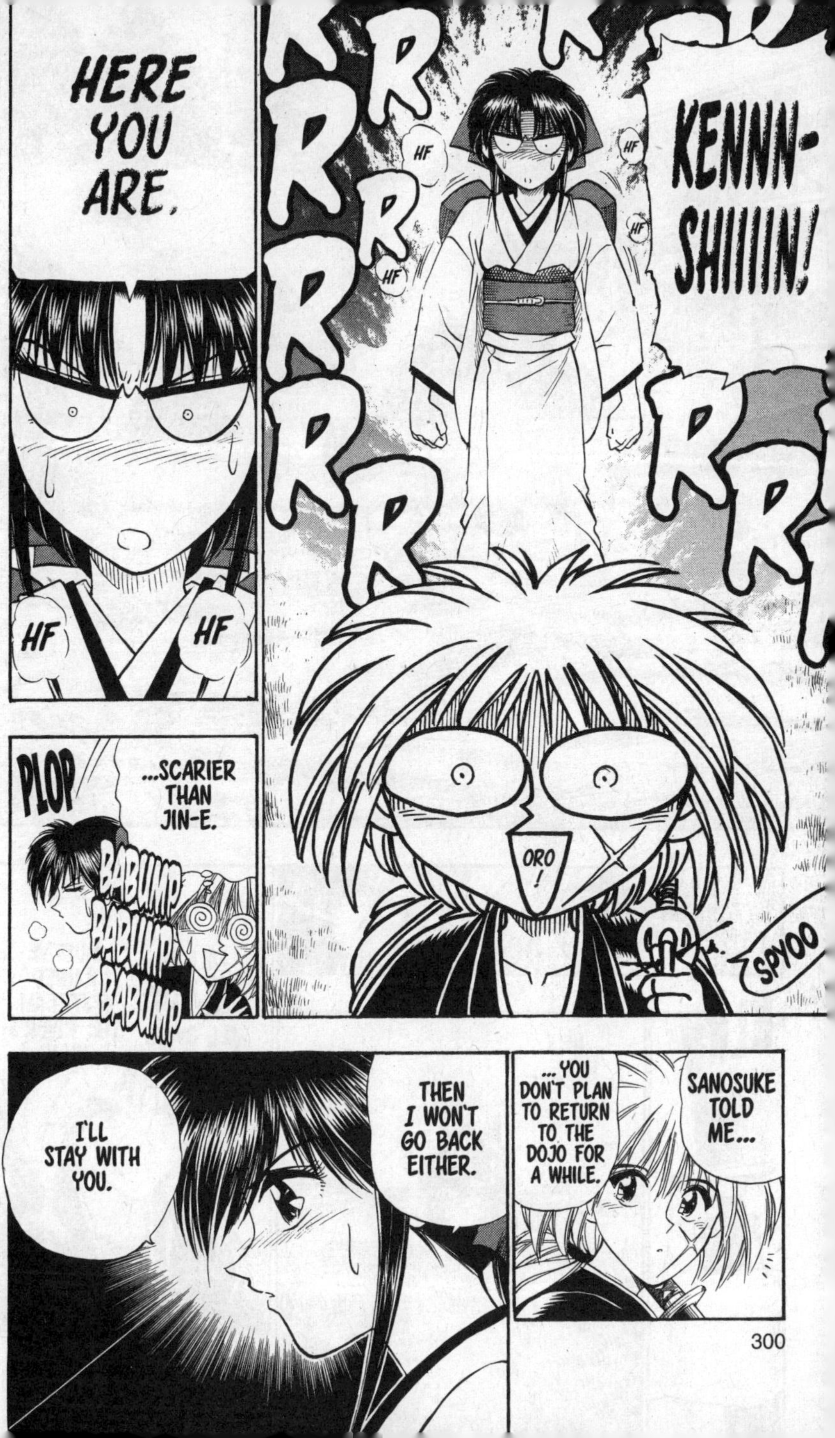
RRRRRR
KENNN-SHIIIN!
HF
HF
HF
HF
RRR
ORO!
SPYOO
HERE YOU ARE.
HF
HF
PLOP
...SCARIER THAN JIN-E.
BABUMP
BABUMP
BABUMP
BABUMP
SANOSUKE TOLD ME...
...YOU DON'T PLAN TO RETURN TO THE DOJO FOR A WHILE.
THEN I WON'T GO BACK EITHER.
I'LL STAY WITH YOU.

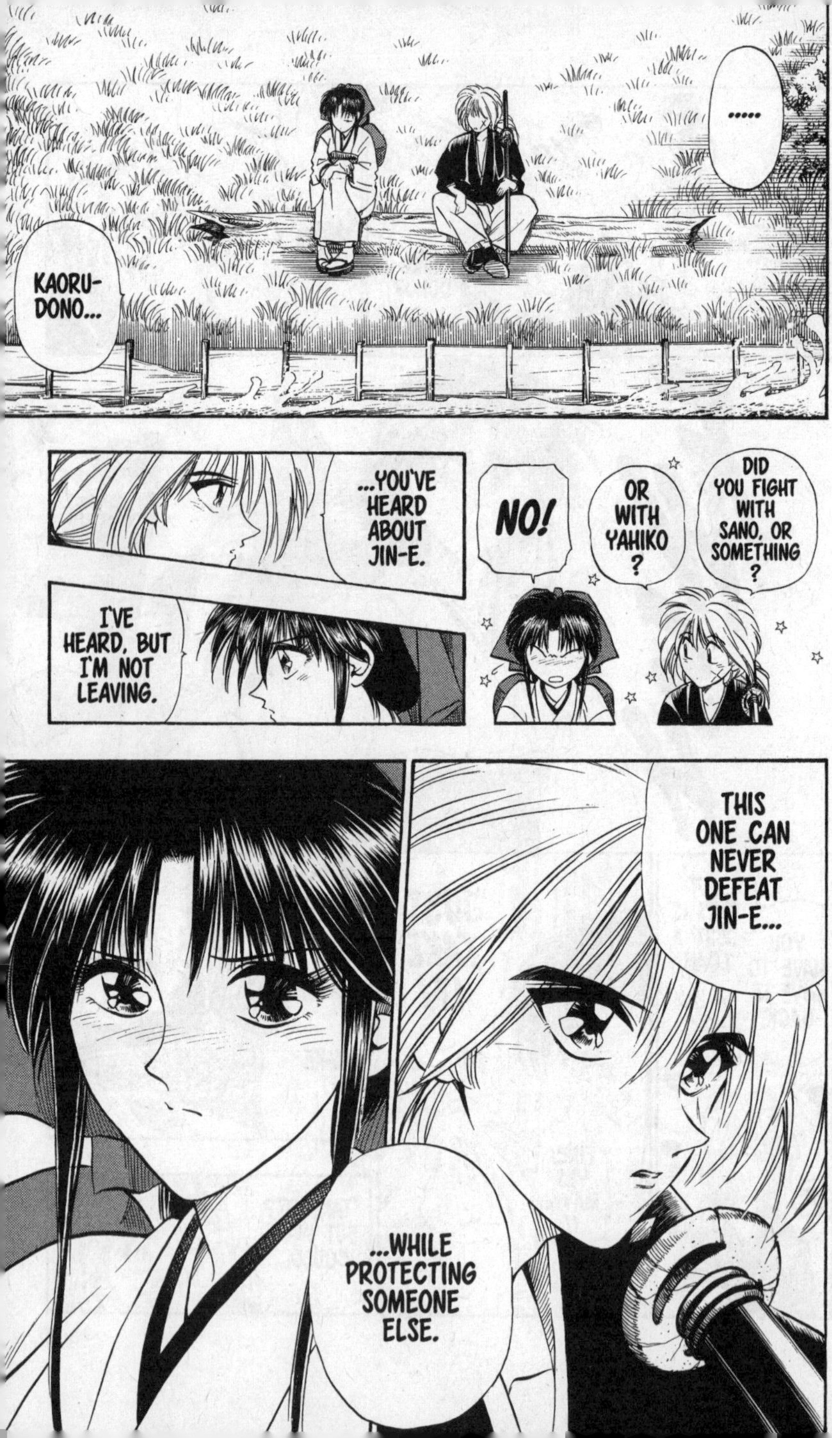
......
KAORU-DONO...
DID YOU FIGHT WITH SANO, OR SOMETHING?
OR WITH YAHIKO?
NO!
...YOU'VE HEARD ABOUT JIN-E.
I'VE HEARD, BUT I'M NOT LEAVING.
THIS ONE CAN NEVER DEFEAT JIN-E...
...WHILE PROTECTING SOMEONE ELSE.

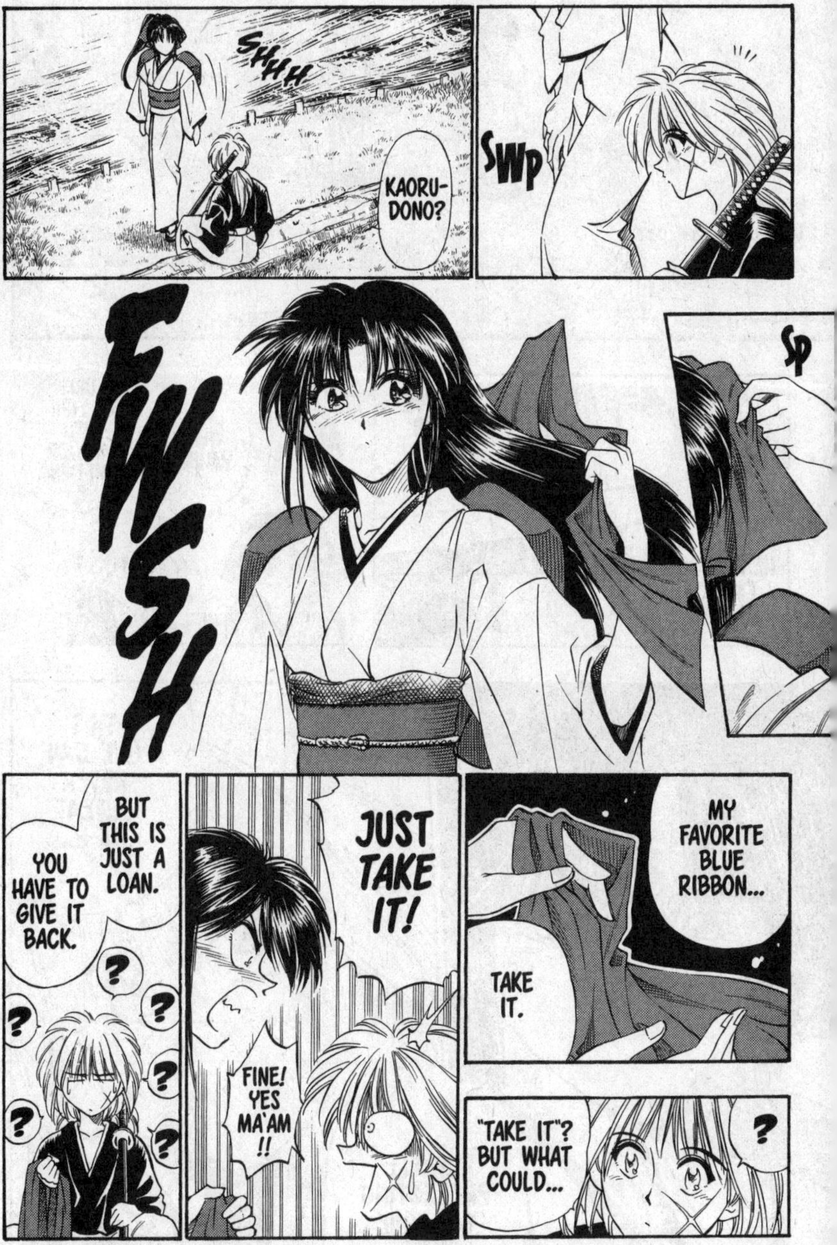
SWP
SHHH
KAORU-DONO?
SP
FWSH
MY FAVORITE BLUE RIBBON...
TAKE IT.
"TAKE IT"? BUT WHAT COULD...
JUST TAKE IT!
FINE! YES MA'AM!!
BUT THIS IS JUST A LOAN.
YOU HAVE TO GIVE IT BACK.

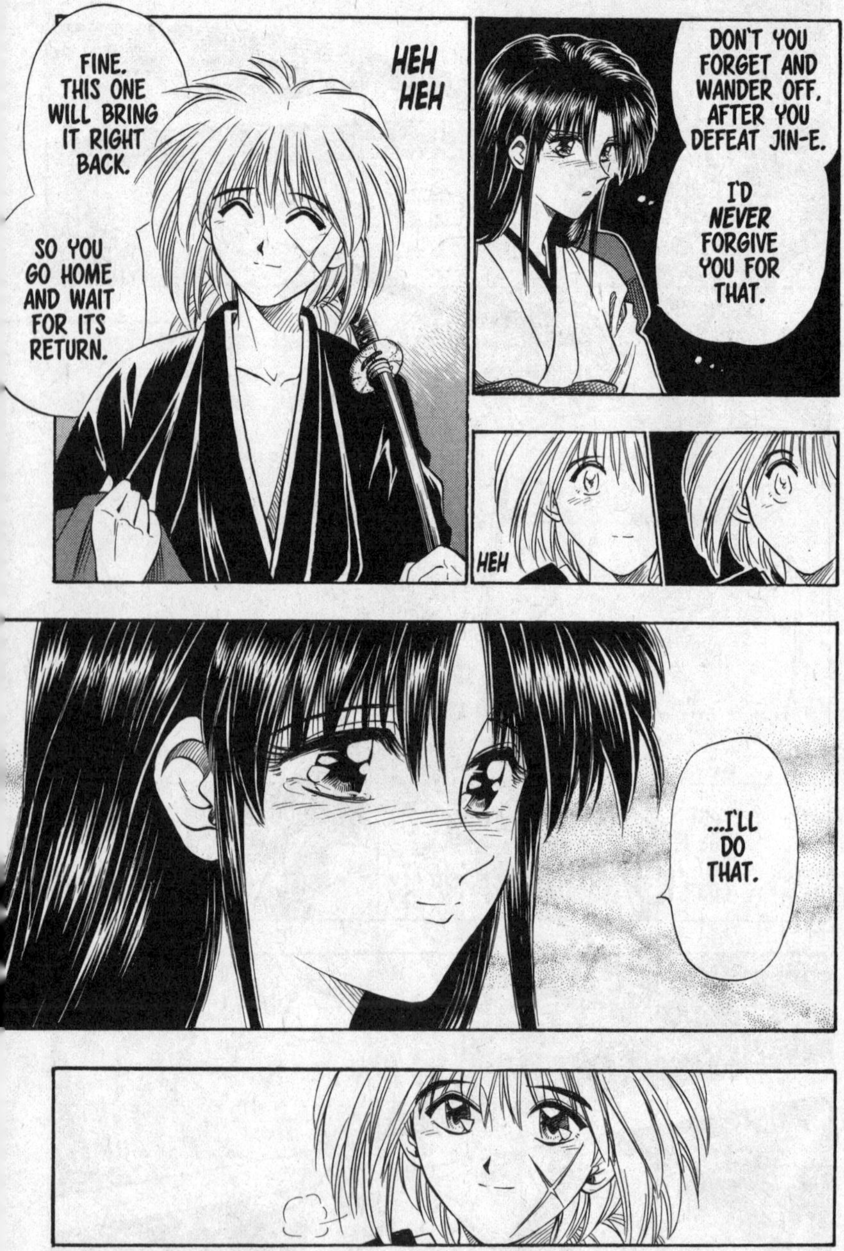
DON'T YOU FORGET AND WANDER OFF, AFTER YOU DEFEAT JIN-E.
I'D NEVER FORGIVE YOU FOR THAT.
HEH
HEH HEH
FINE. THIS ONE WILL BRING IT RIGHT BACK.
SO YOU GO HOME AND WAIT FOR ITS RETURN.
...I'LL DO THAT.

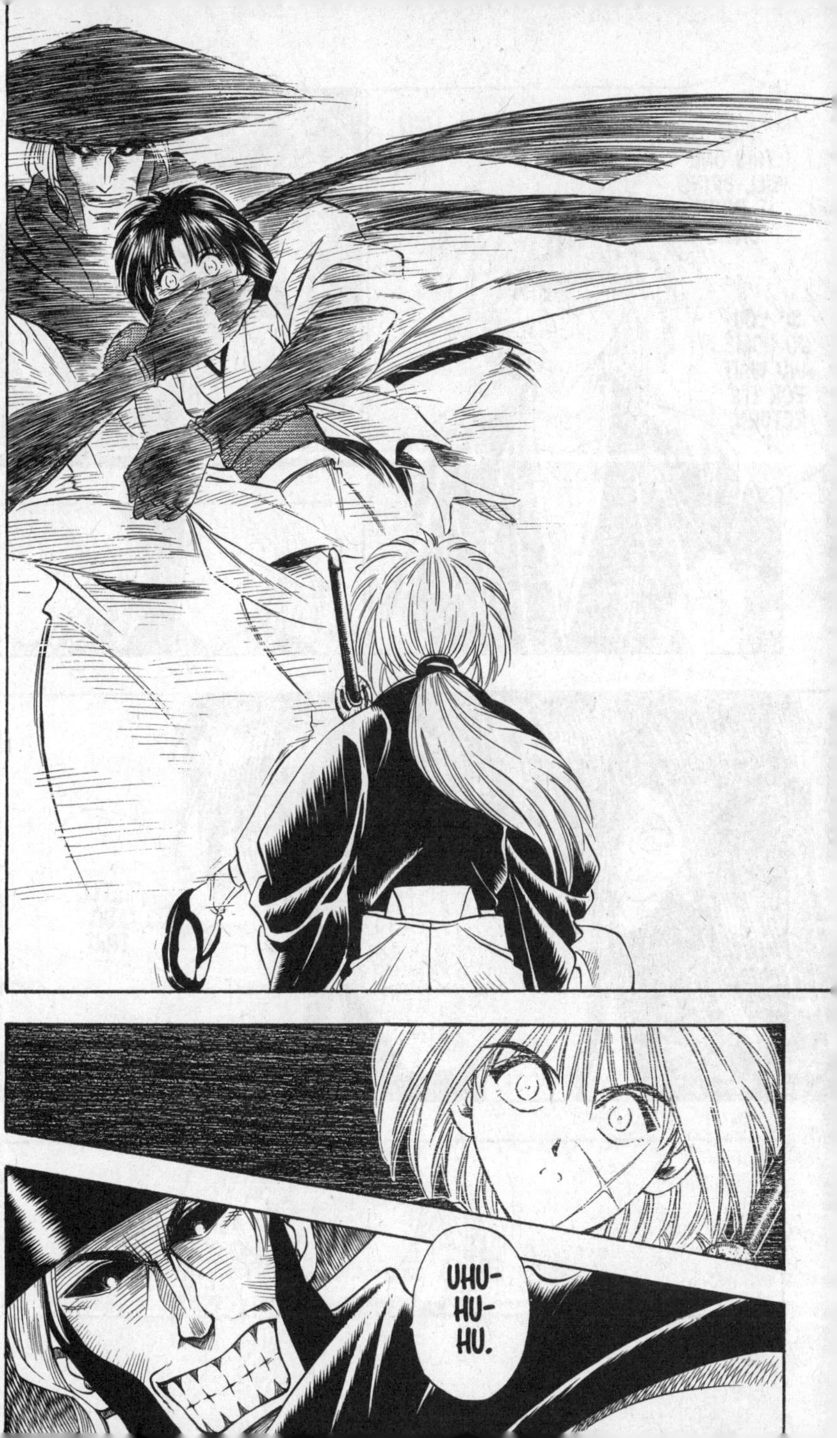
UHU-
HU-
HU.

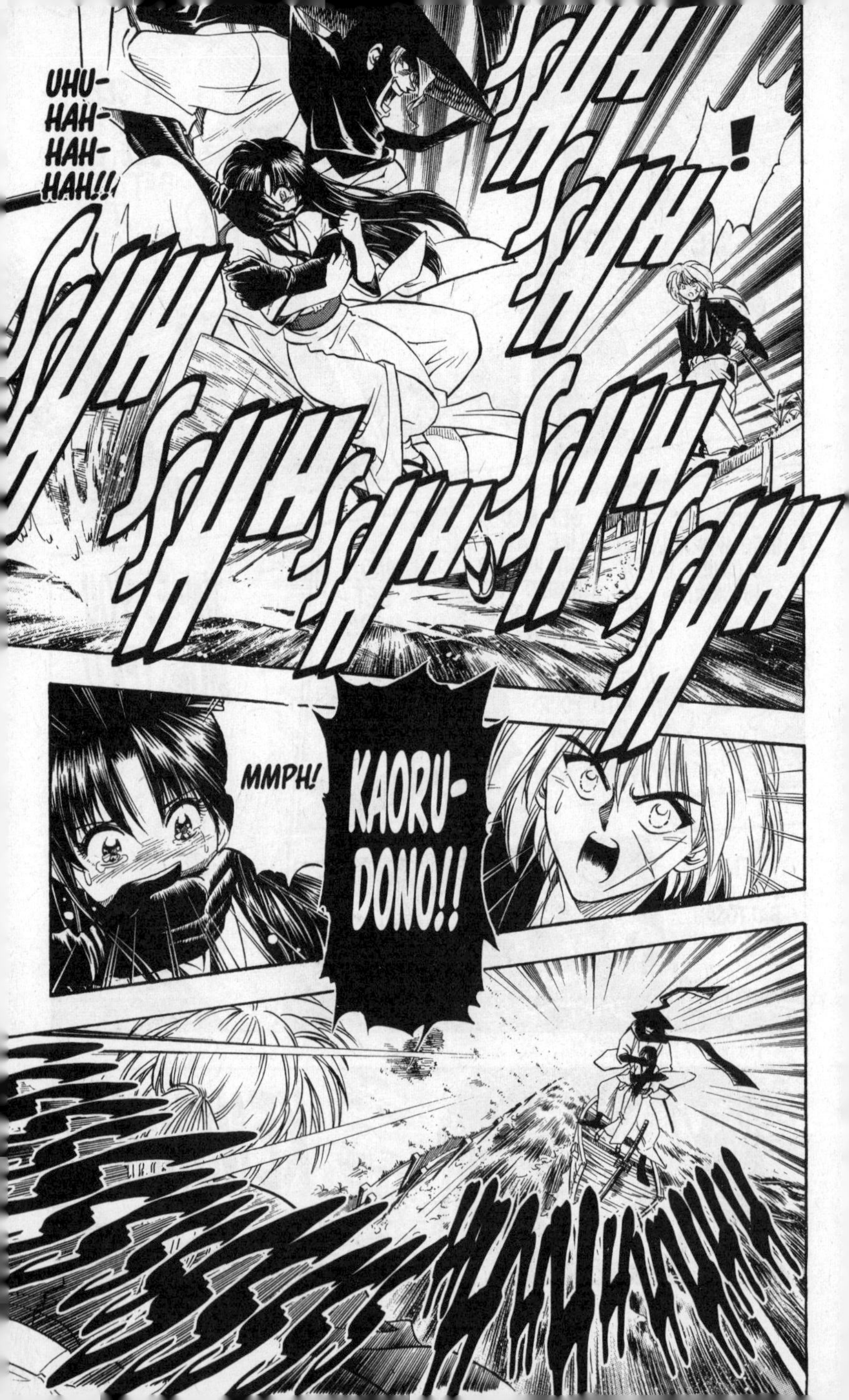
!
UHU-HAH-HAH-HAH!!
KAORU-DONO!!
MMPH!

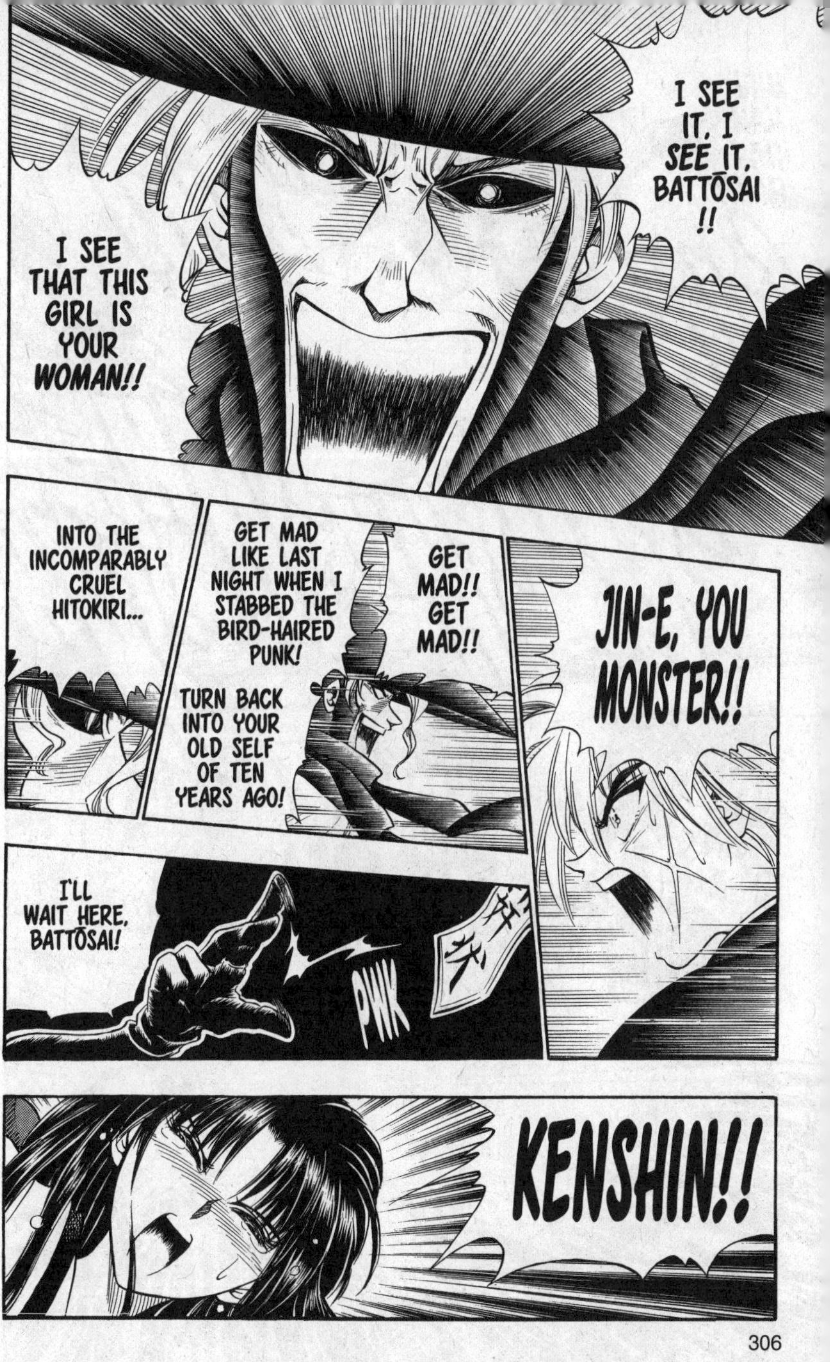
I SEE IT, I SEE IT, BATTŌSAI!!
I SEE THAT THIS GIRL IS YOUR WOMAN!!
JIN-E, YOU MONSTER!!
GET MAD!! GET MAD!!
GET MAD LIKE LAST NIGHT WHEN I STABBED THE BIRD-HAIRED PUNK!
TURN BACK INTO YOUR OLD SELF OF TEN YEARS AGO!
INTO THE INCOMPARABLY CRUEL HITOKIRI...
I'LL WAIT HERE, BATTŌSAI!
PWK
KENSHIN!!

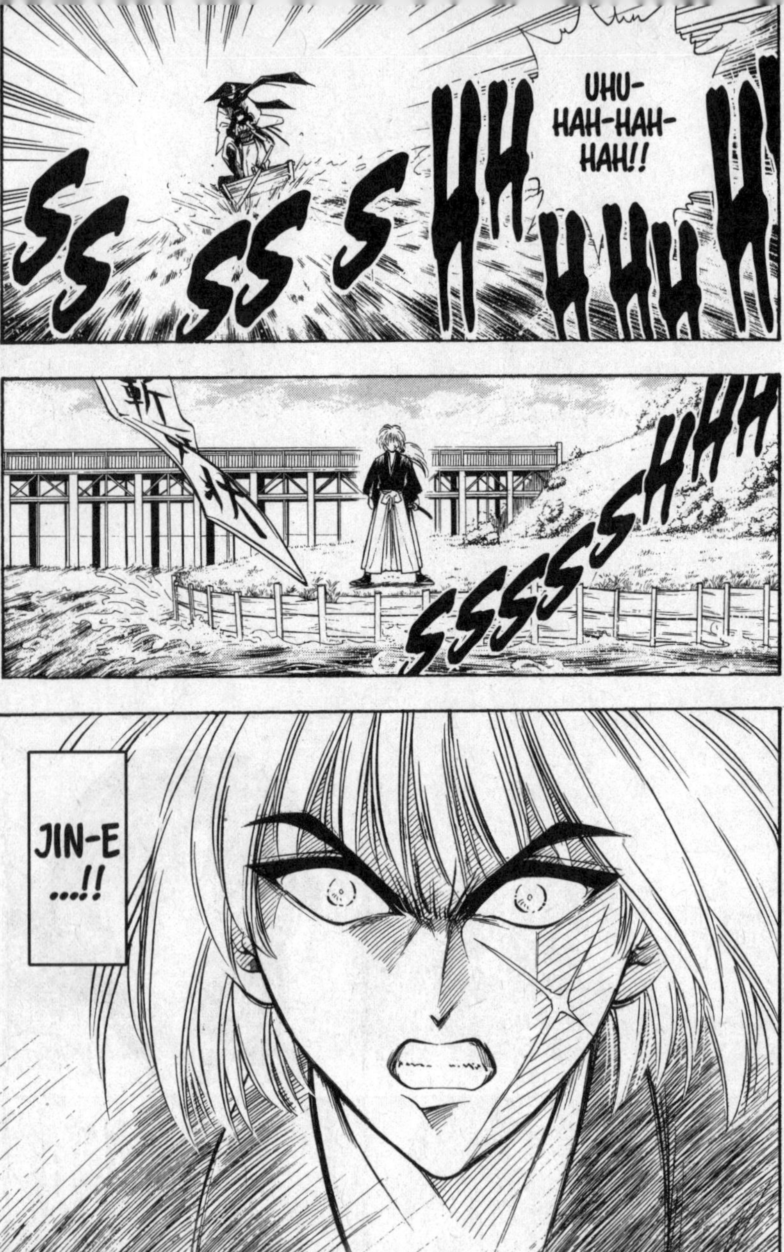
UHU-HAH-HAH-HAH!!
SSSSSHHHHHHH
SSSSSHHHH
JIN-E ...!!

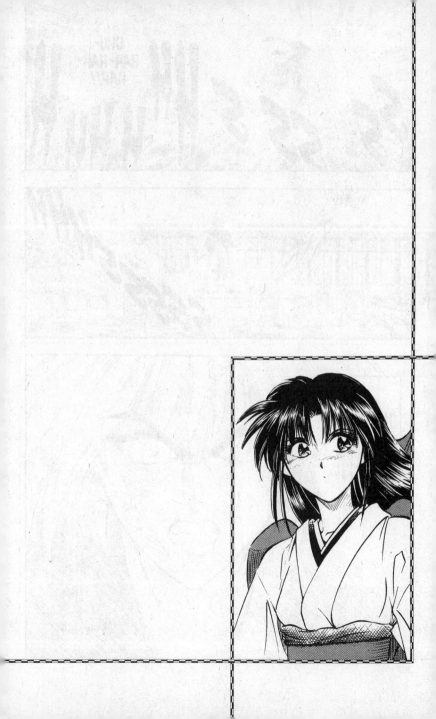

Act 12 – The Two Hitokiri

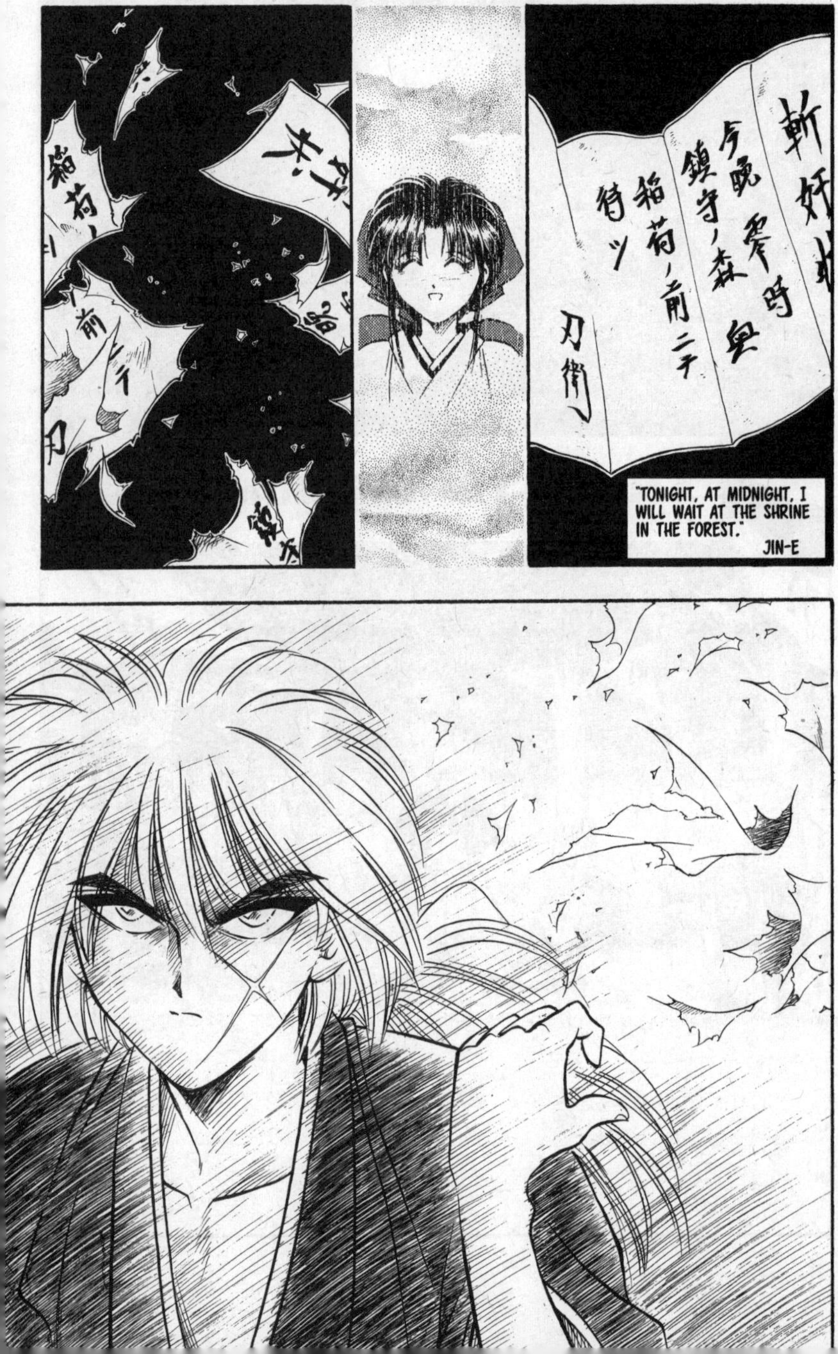
斬奸
今晩 零時
鎮守ノ森奥
稲荷ノ前ニテ
待ツ
刃衛
"TONIGHT, AT MIDNIGHT, I WILL WAIT AT THE SHRINE IN THE FOREST."
JIN-E

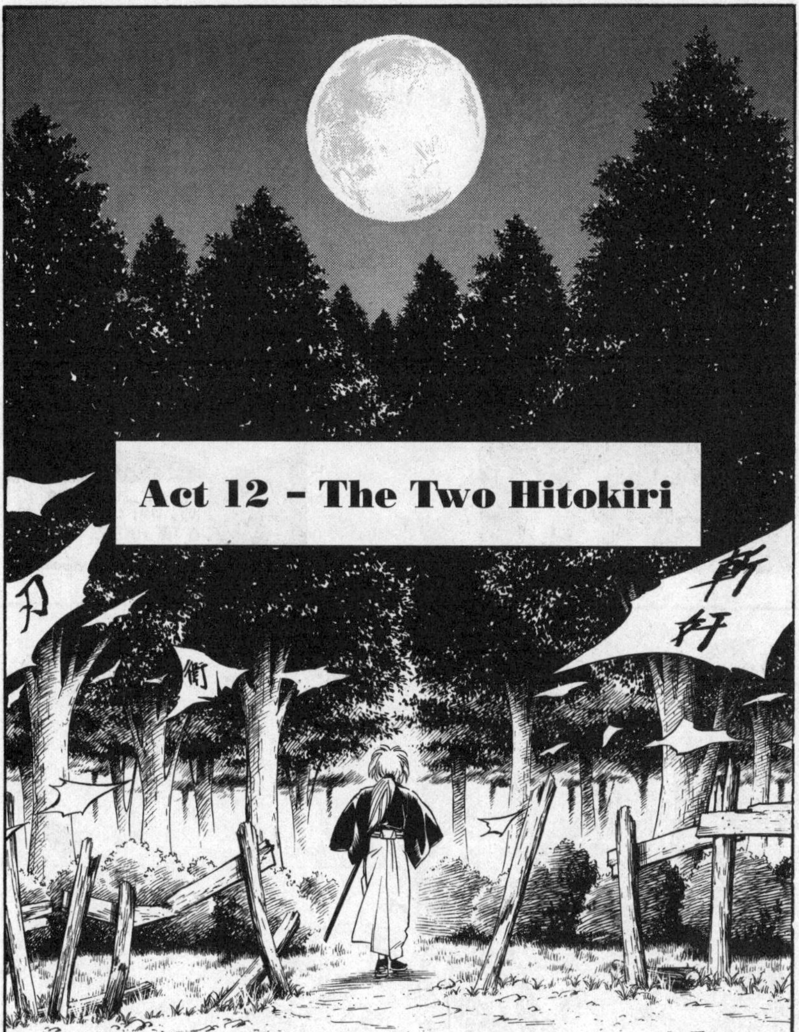
Act 12 - The Two Hitokiri
和月伸宏

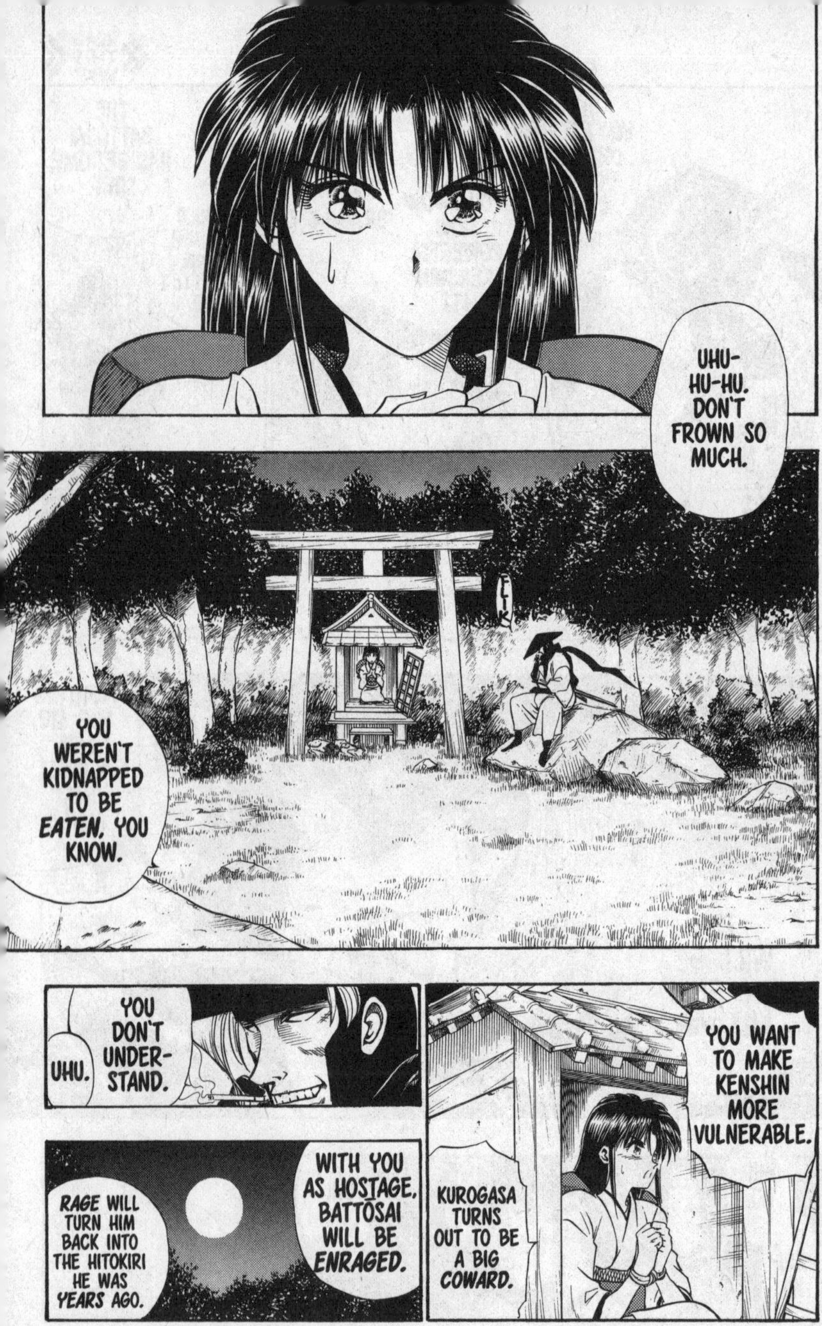
UHU-HU-HU. DON'T FROWN SO MUCH.
FLIK
YOU WEREN'T KIDNAPPED TO BE *EATEN*, YOU KNOW.
YOU WANT TO MAKE KENSHIN MORE VULNERABLE.
KUROGASA TURNS OUT TO BE A BIG *COWARD.*
YOU DON'T UNDER-STAND.
UHU.
WITH YOU AS HOSTAGE, BATTŌSAI WILL BE *ENRAGED.*
RAGE WILL TURN HIM BACK INTO THE HITOKIRI HE WAS *YEARS* AGO.

READ THIS WAY

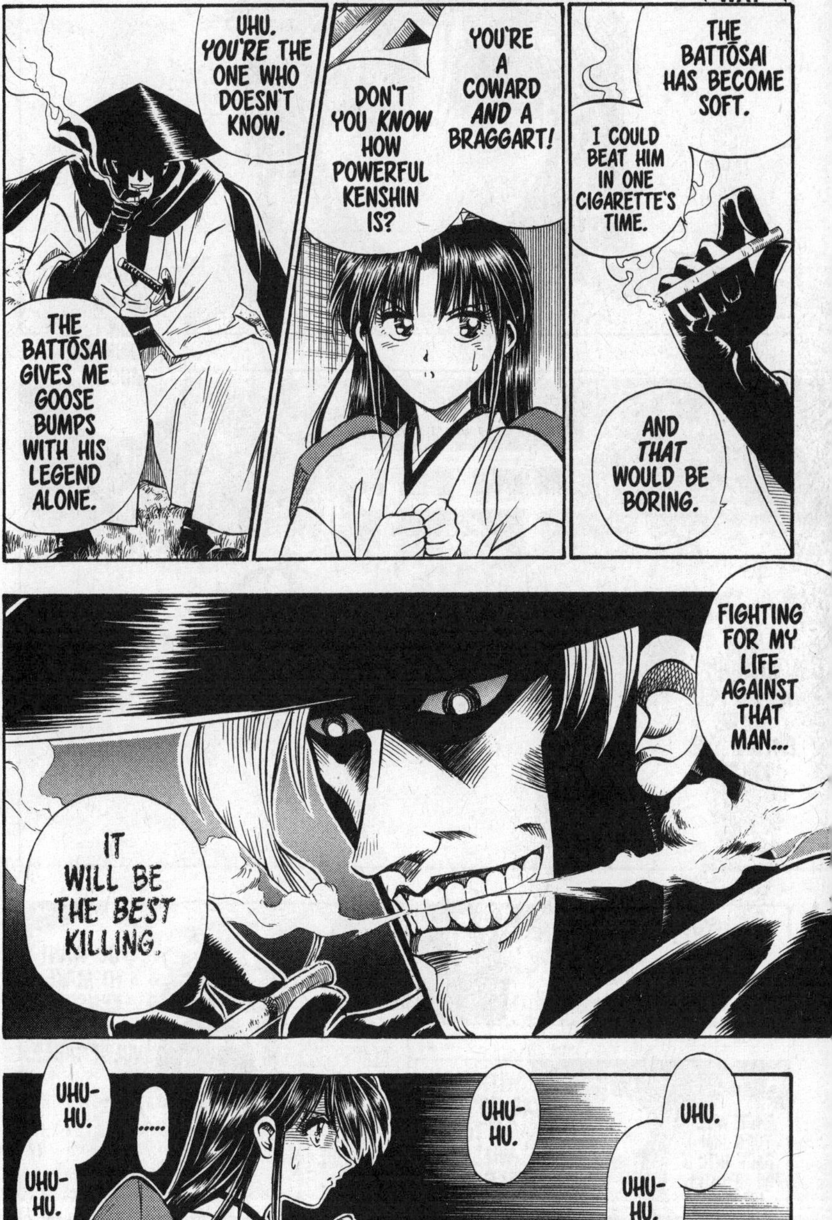
THE BATTŌSAI HAS BECOME SOFT.
I COULD BEAT HIM IN ONE CIGARETTE'S TIME.
AND *THAT* WOULD BE BORING.
YOU'RE A COWARD *AND* A BRAGGART!
DON'T YOU *KNOW* HOW POWERFUL KENSHIN IS?
UHU. *YOU'RE* THE ONE WHO DOESN'T KNOW.
THE BATTŌSAI GIVES ME GOOSE BUMPS WITH HIS LEGEND ALONE.
FIGHTING FOR MY LIFE AGAINST THAT MAN...
IT WILL BE THE *BEST* KILLING.
UHU.
UHU-HU.
UHU-HU.
.....
UHU-HU.
UHU-HU.

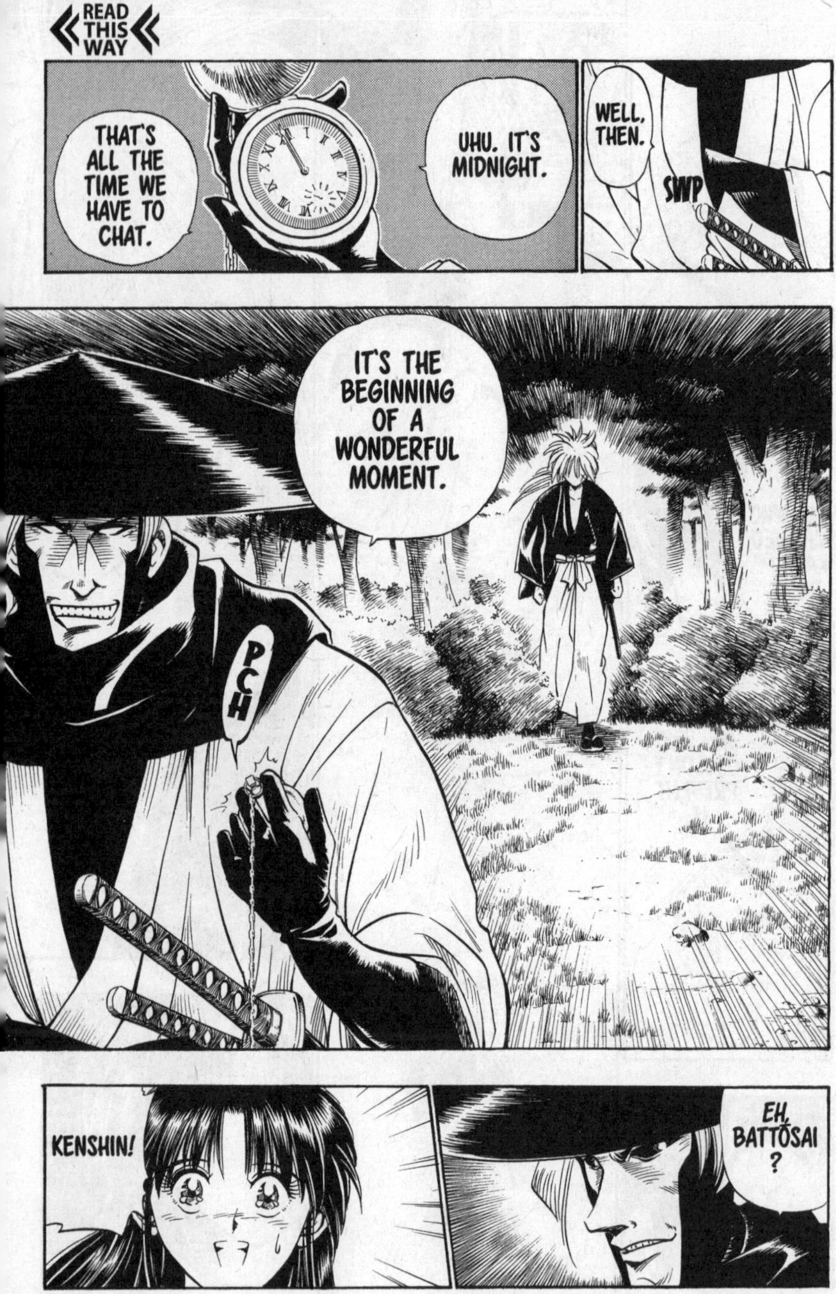
READ THIS WAY
WELL, THEN.
SWP
UHU. IT'S MIDNIGHT.
THAT'S ALL THE TIME WE HAVE TO CHAT.
IT'S THE BEGINNING OF A WONDERFUL MOMENT.
PCH
EH, BATTŌSAI?
KENSHIN!

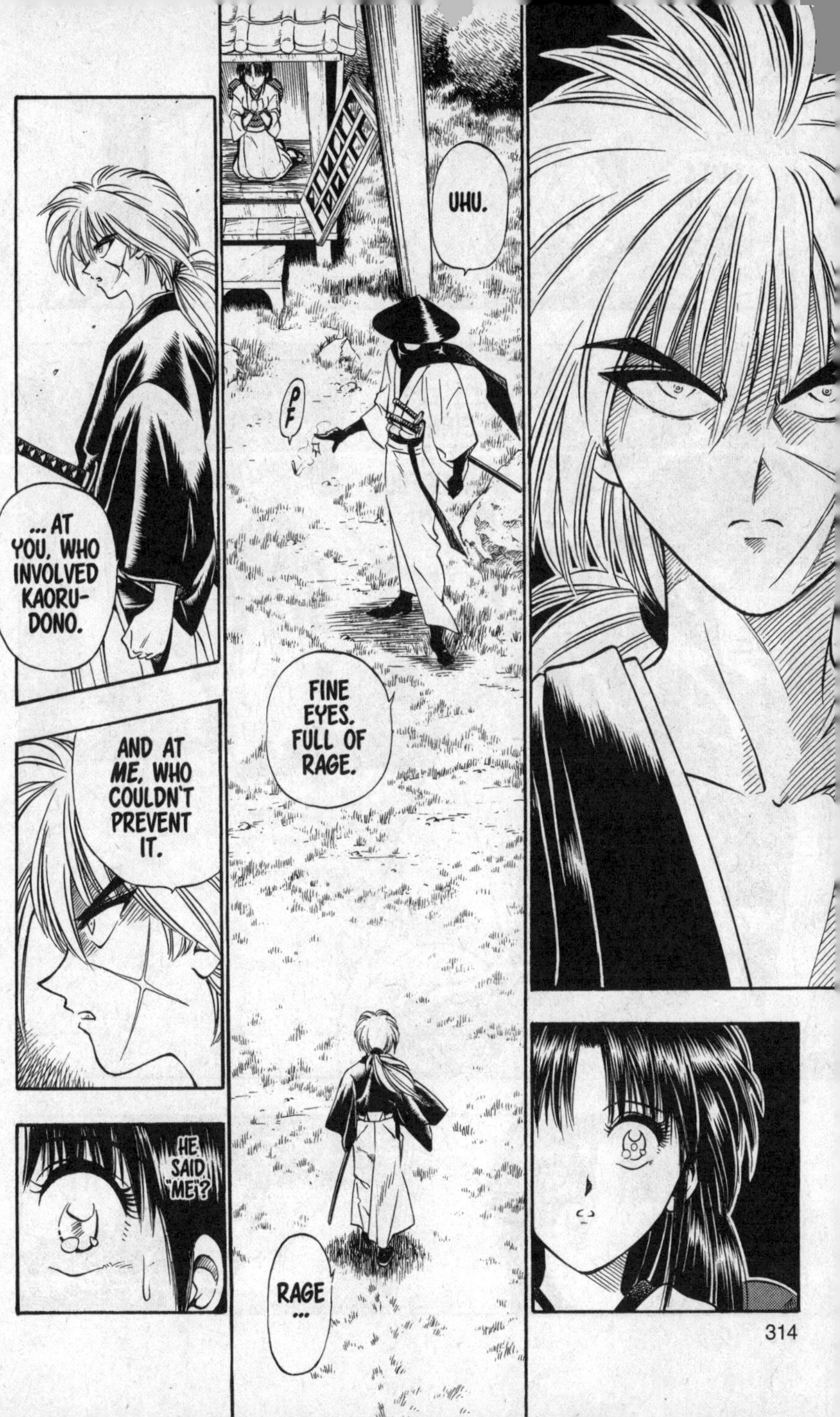
UHU.
PF
FINE EYES. FULL OF RAGE.
RAGE...
...AT YOU, WHO INVOLVED KAORU-DONO.
AND AT ME, WHO COULDN'T PREVENT IT.
HE SAID "ME"?

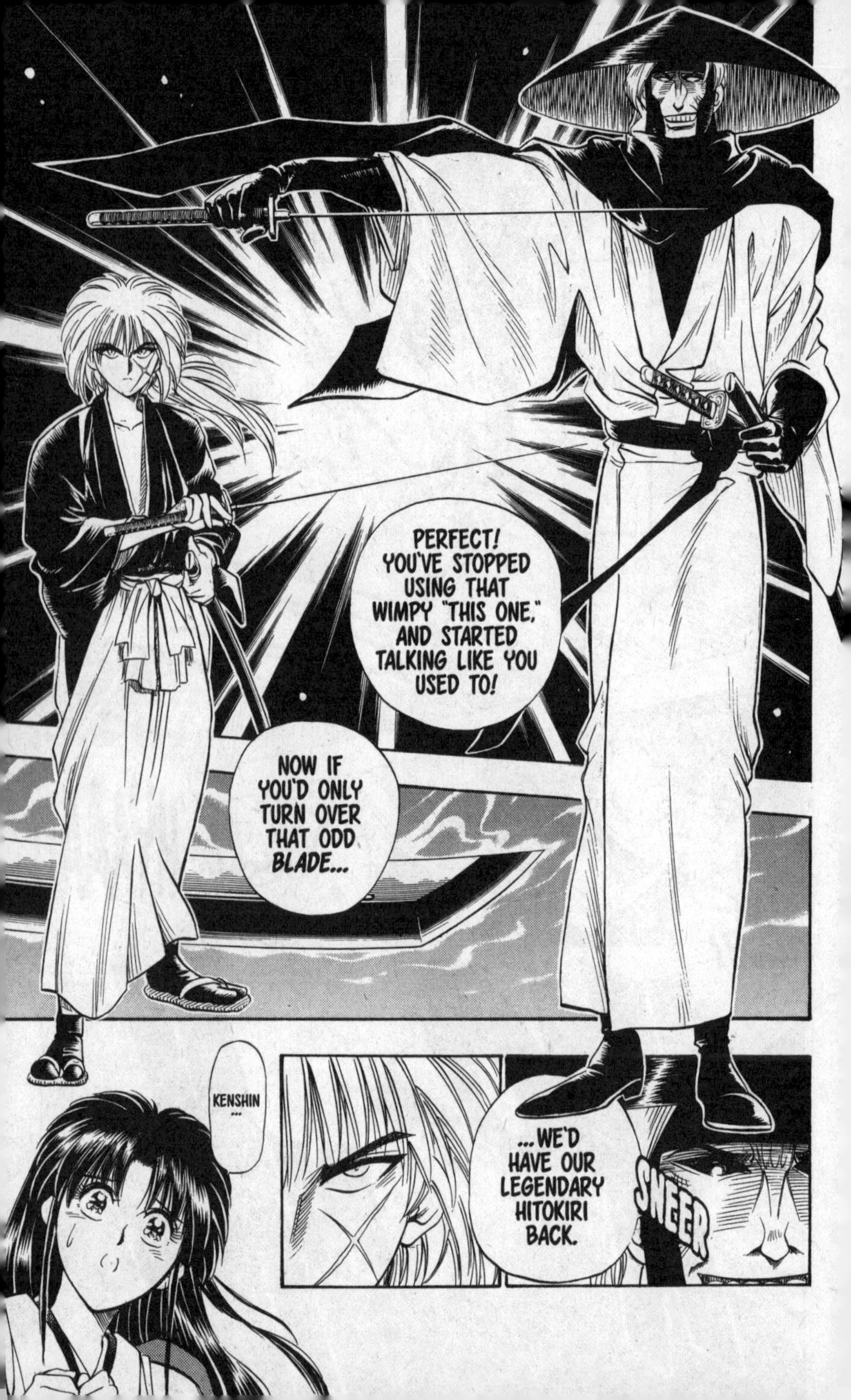
PERFECT! YOU'VE STOPPED USING THAT WIMPY "THIS ONE," AND STARTED TALKING LIKE YOU USED TO!
NOW IF YOU'D ONLY TURN OVER THAT ODD BLADE...
...WE'D HAVE OUR LEGENDARY HITOKIRI BACK.
SNEER
KENSHIN...

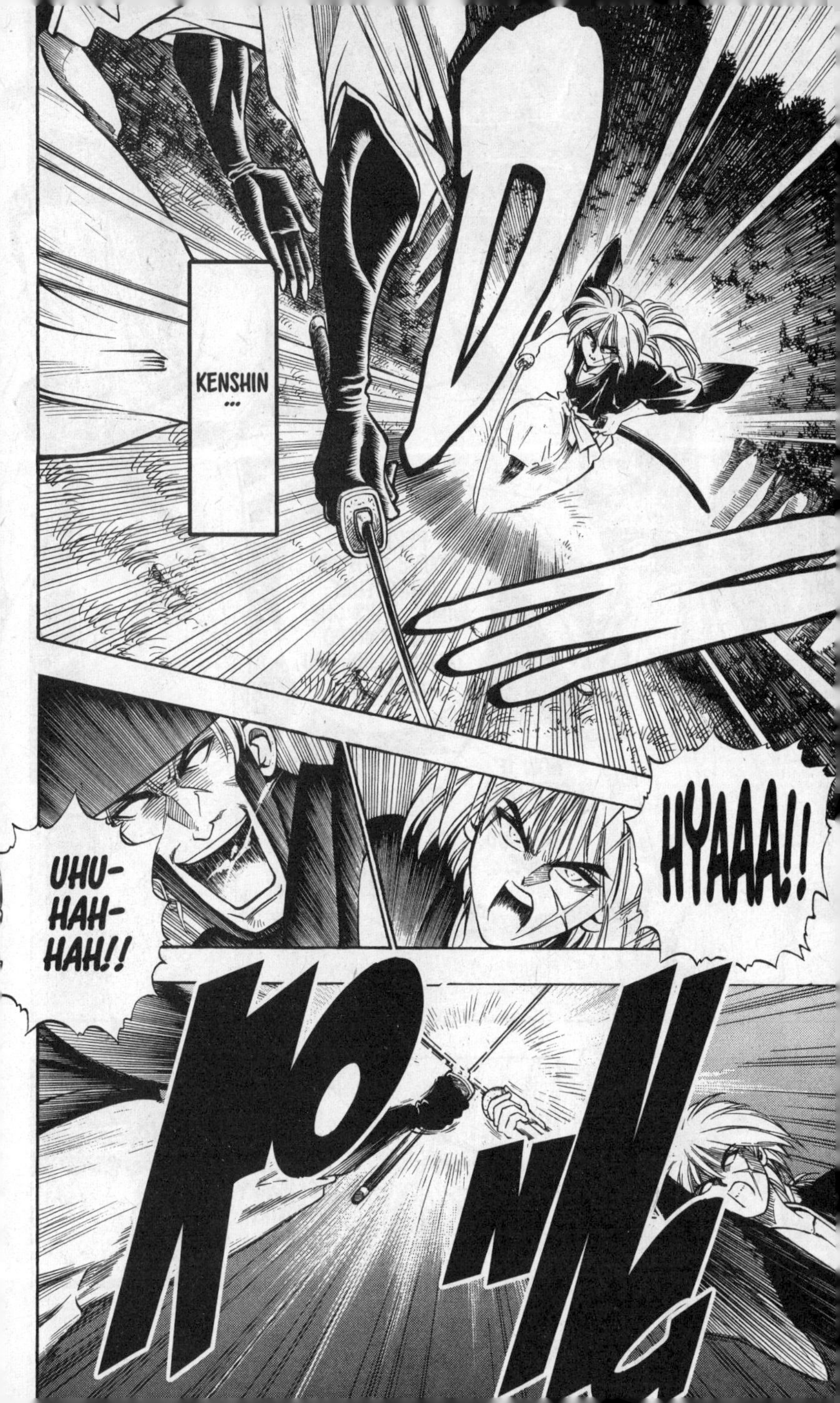
KENSHIN ...
HYAAA!!
UHU-HAH-HAH!!

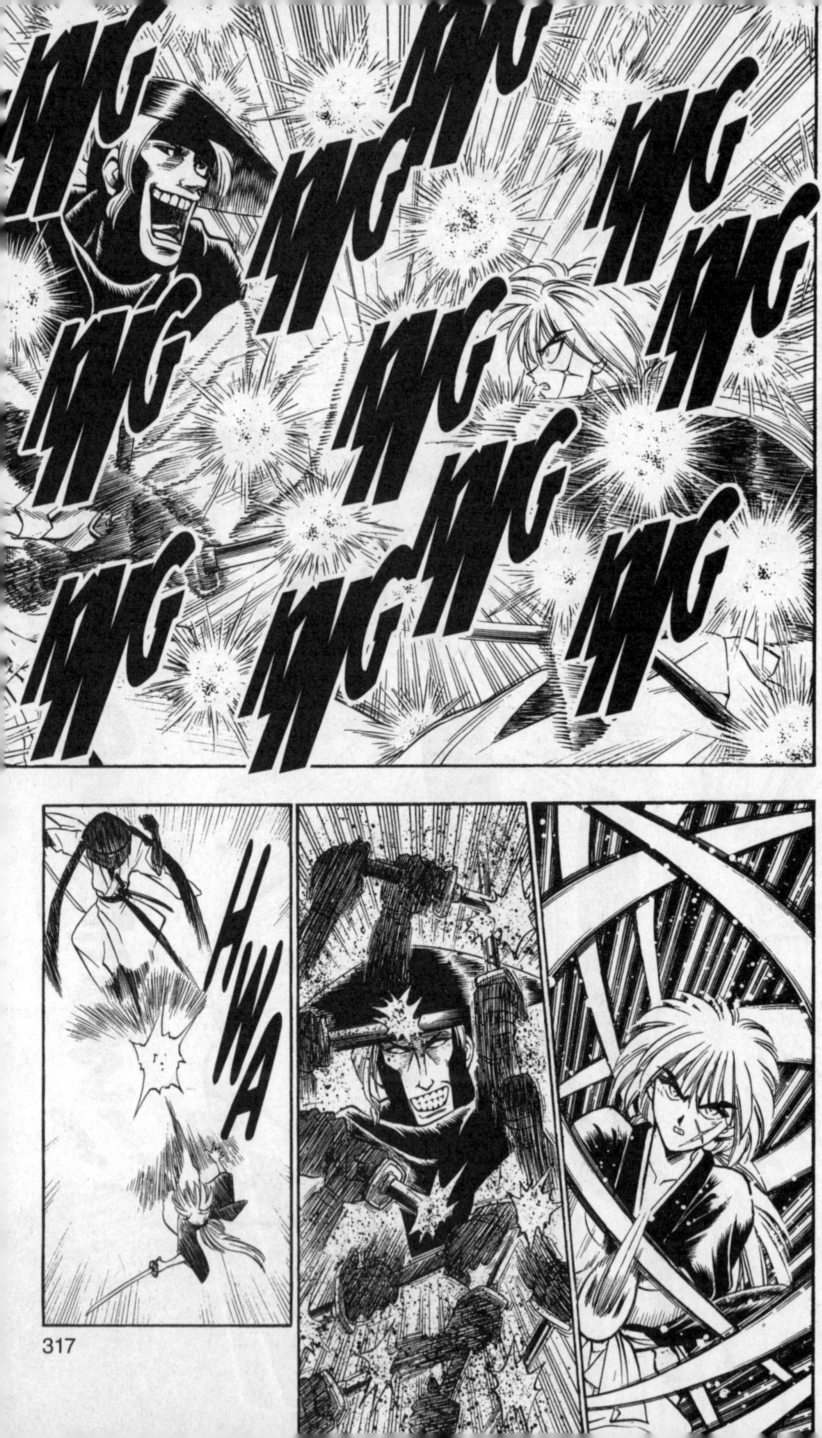
NG
NG
NG
NG
NG
NG
NG
NG
NG
NG
NG
NG
HWA

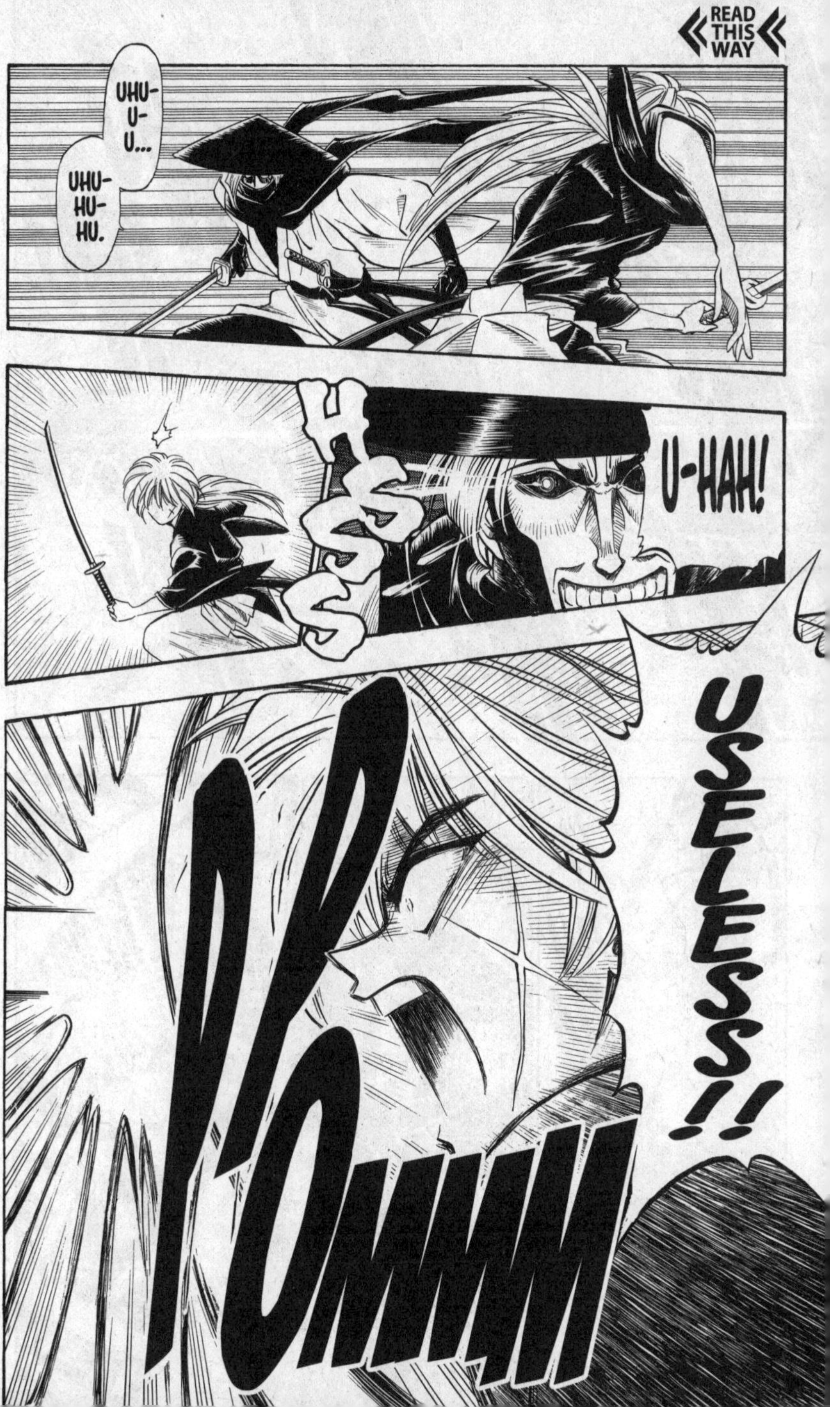
READ THIS WAY
UHU-U-U...
UHU-HU-HU.
U-HAH!
HSSS
USELESS!!

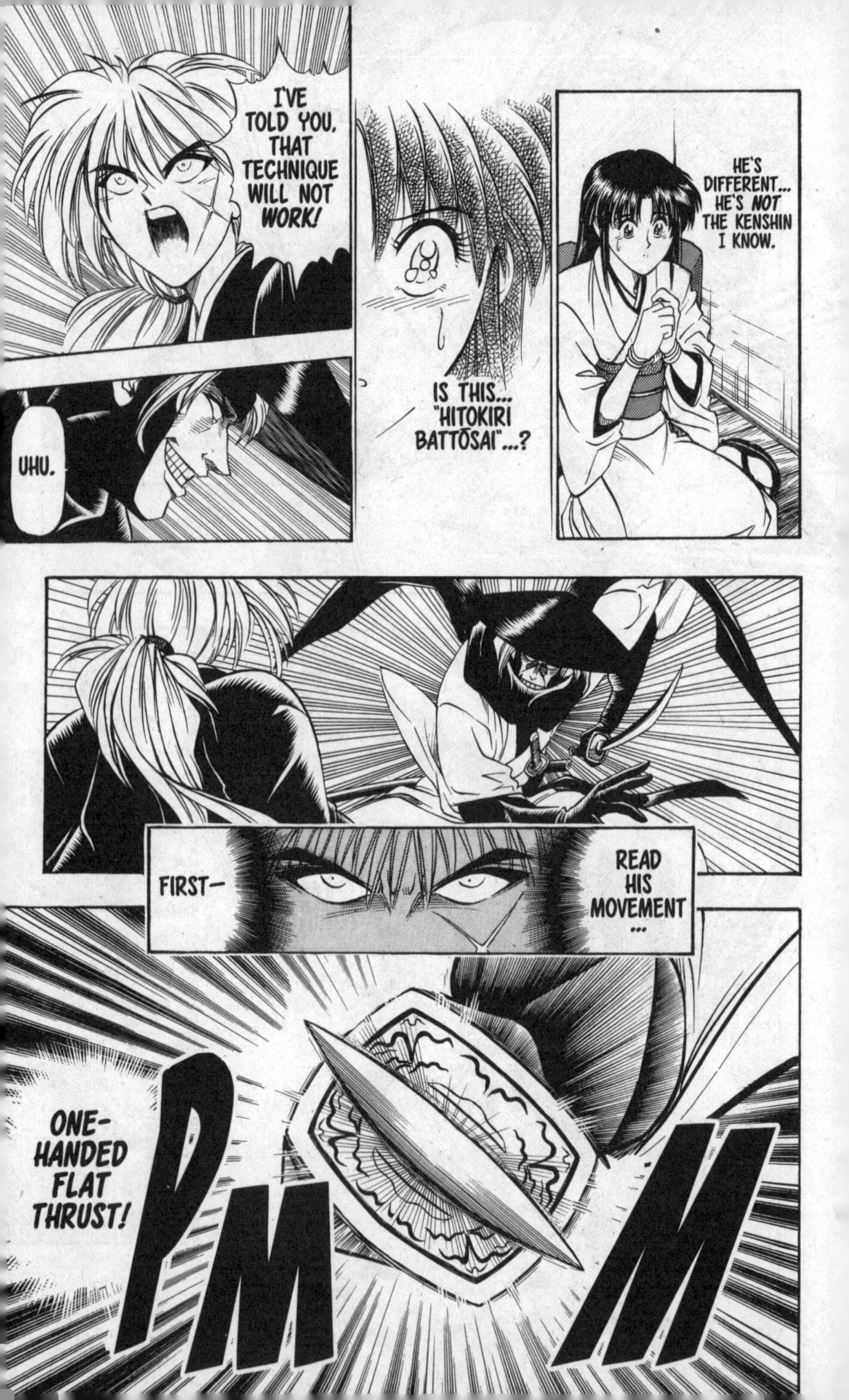
HE'S DIFFERENT... HE'S NOT THE KENSHIN I KNOW.
IS THIS... "HITOKIRI BATTŌSAI"...?
I'VE TOLD YOU, THAT TECHNIQUE WILL NOT WORK!
UHU.
READ HIS MOVEMENT...
FIRST–
ONE-HANDED FLAT THRUST!
PMM

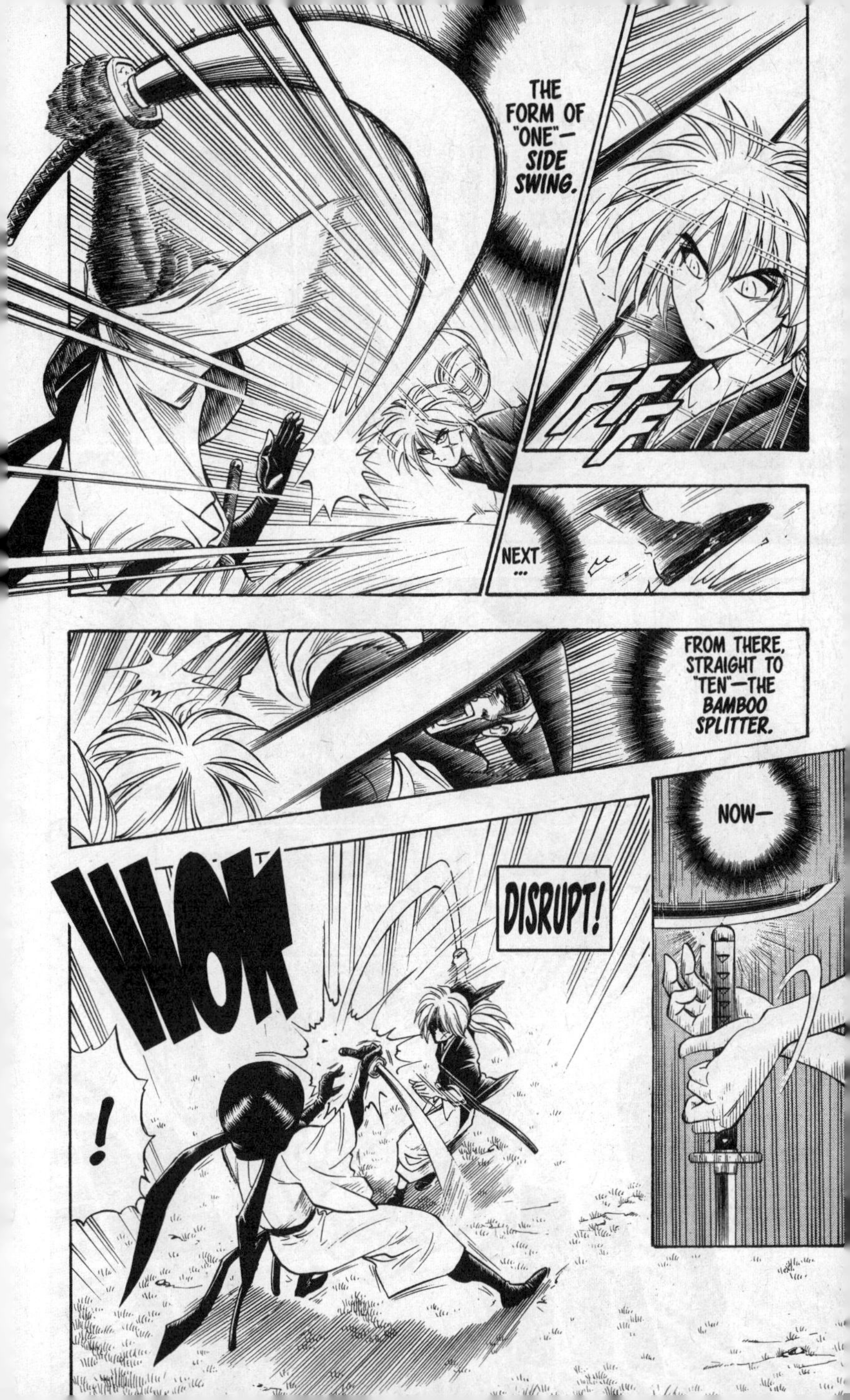
THE FORM OF "ONE"— SIDE SWING.
FFF
NEXT ...
FROM THERE, STRAIGHT TO "TEN"—THE BAMBOO SPLITTER.
NOW—
DISRUPT!
WOK
!

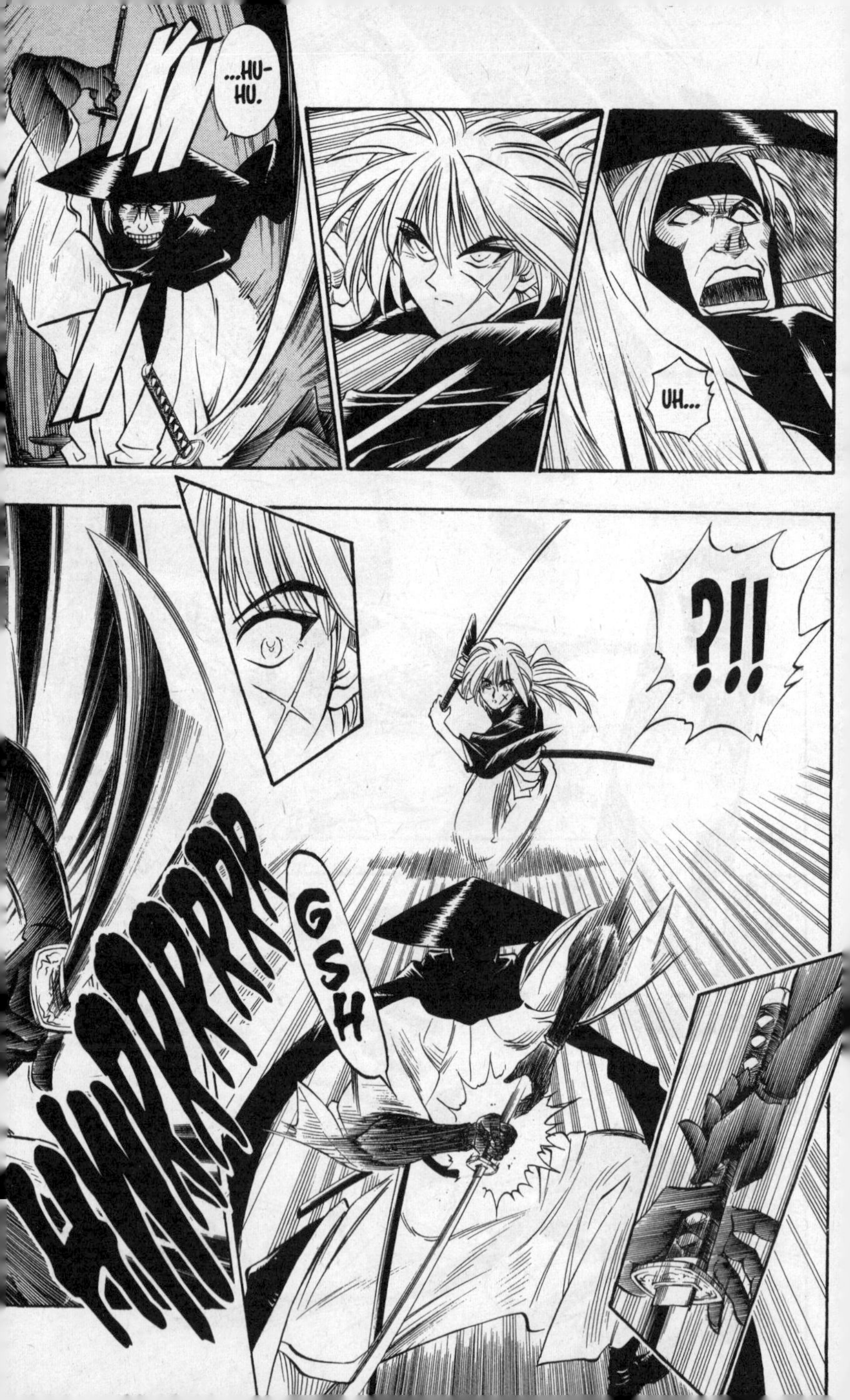
UH...
...HU-HU.
?!!
GSH

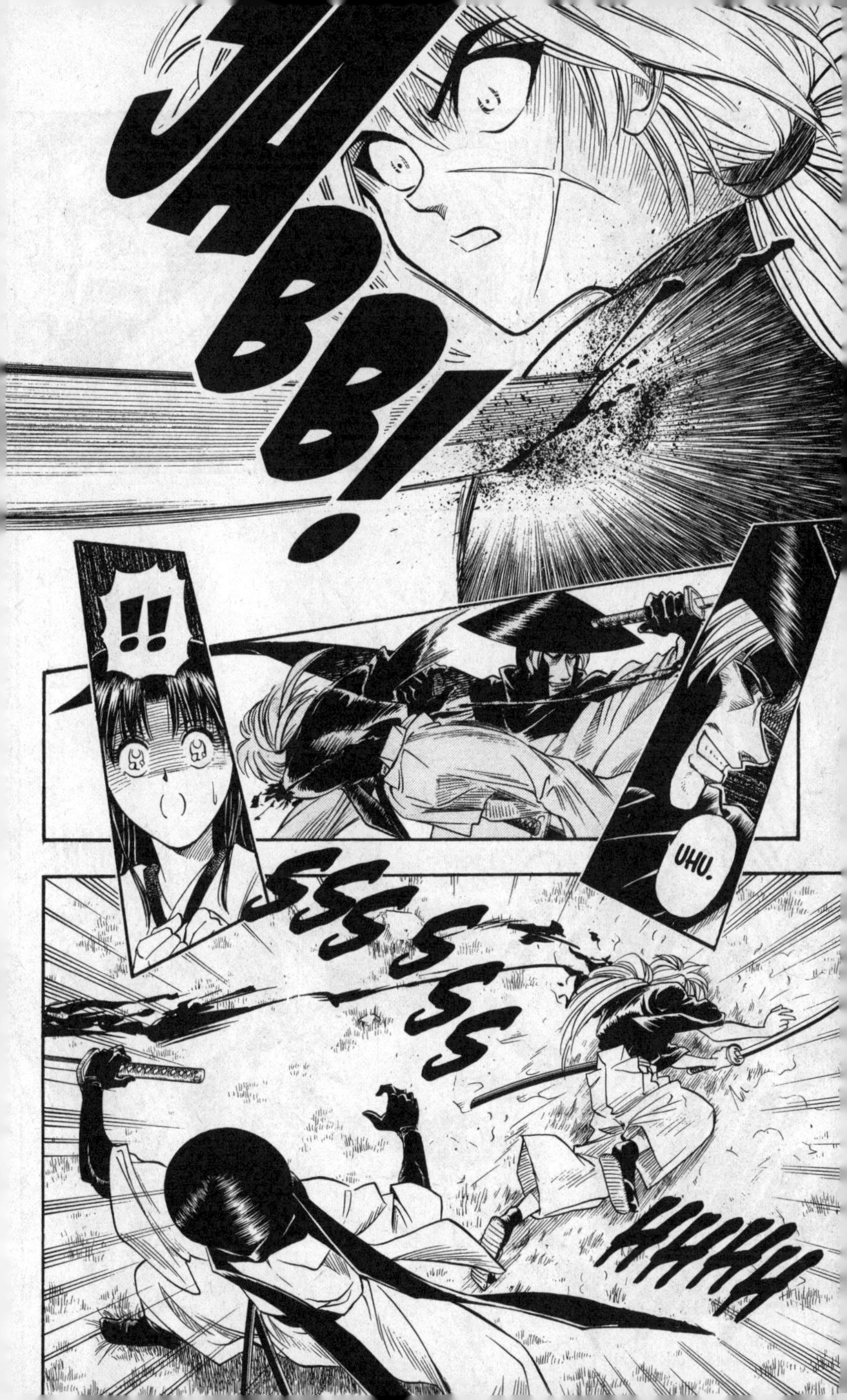
JABBB!
UHU.
!!
SSSSSSSS
HHHHH

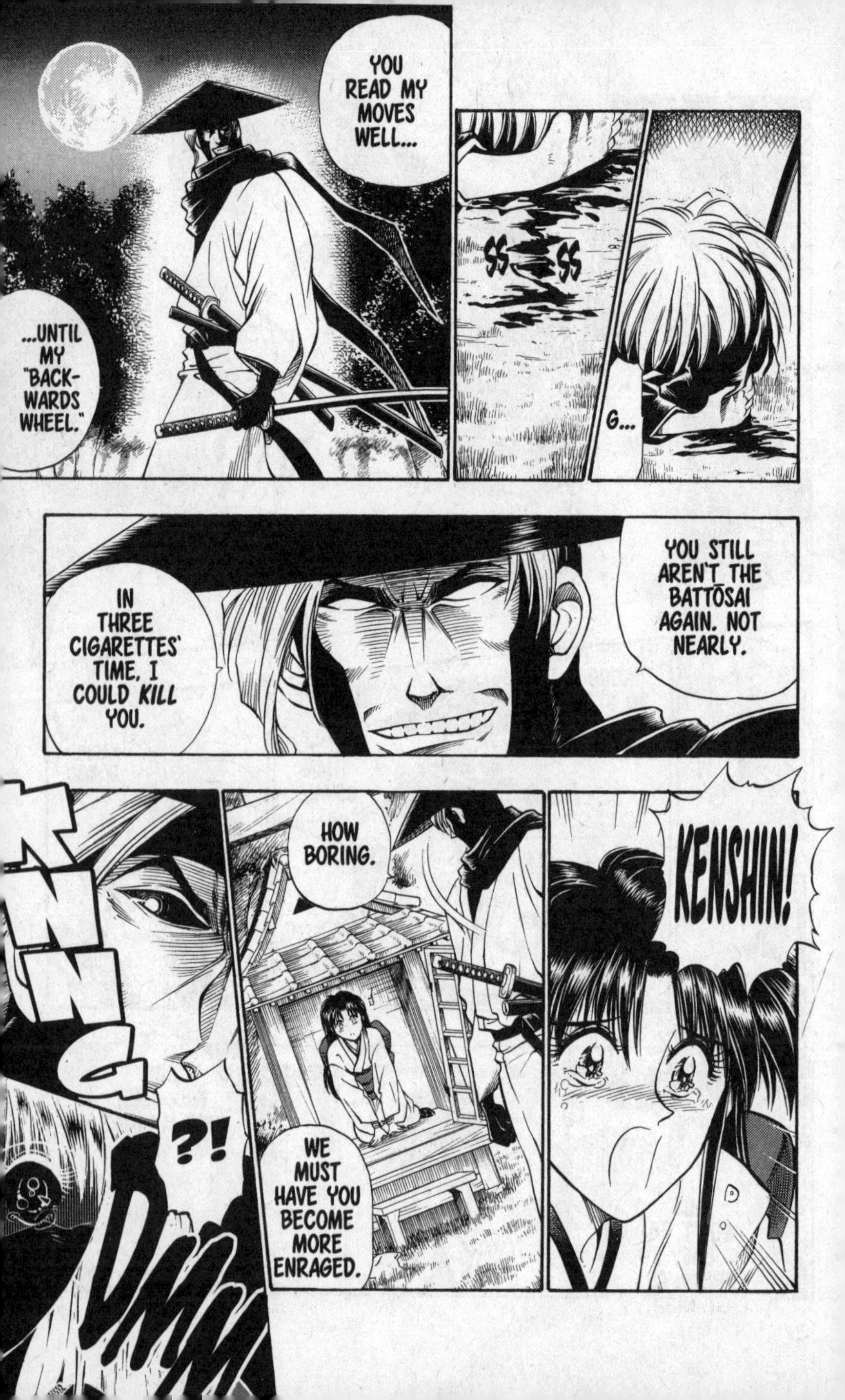
G...
SS SS
YOU READ MY MOVES WELL...
...UNTIL MY "BACKWARDS WHEEL."
YOU STILL AREN'T THE BATTŌSAI AGAIN. NOT NEARLY.
IN THREE CIGARETTES' TIME, I COULD KILL YOU.
KENSHIN!
HOW BORING.
WE MUST HAVE YOU BECOME MORE ENRAGED.
?!

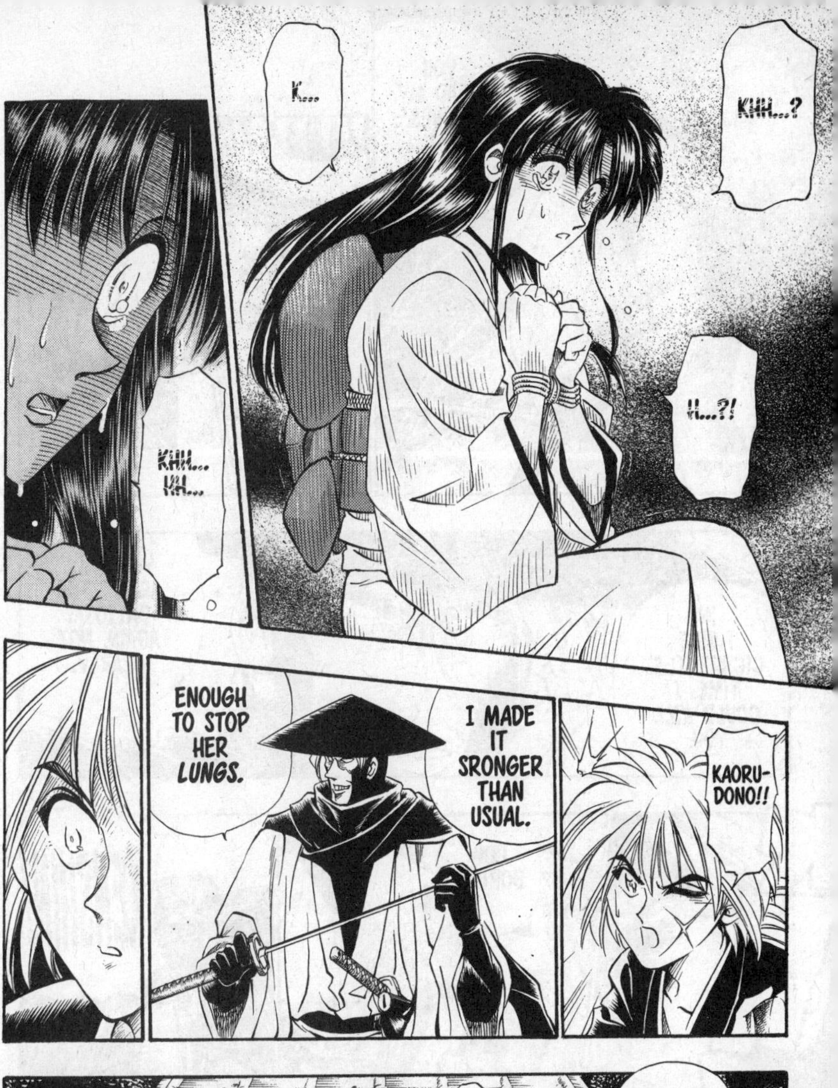
KHH...?
K...
H...?!
KHH... KH...
KAORU-DONO!!
I MADE IT SRONGER THAN USUAL.
ENOUGH TO STOP HER LUNGS.
SHE WILL LAST TWO MINUTES, AT MOST.
.....
.....
THIS WON'T BE AS EASY TO BREAK AS LAST NIGHT.

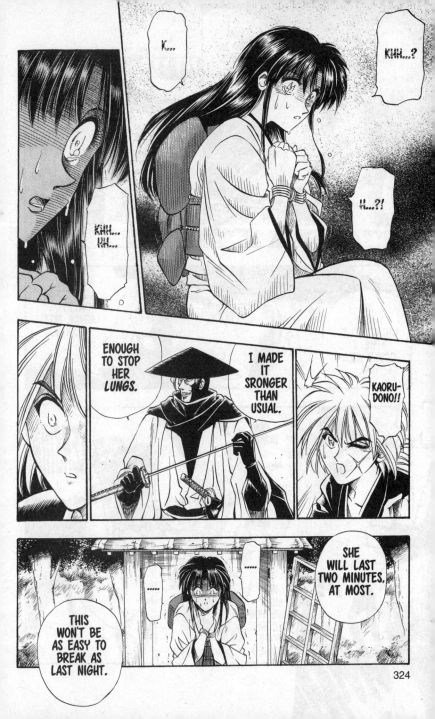

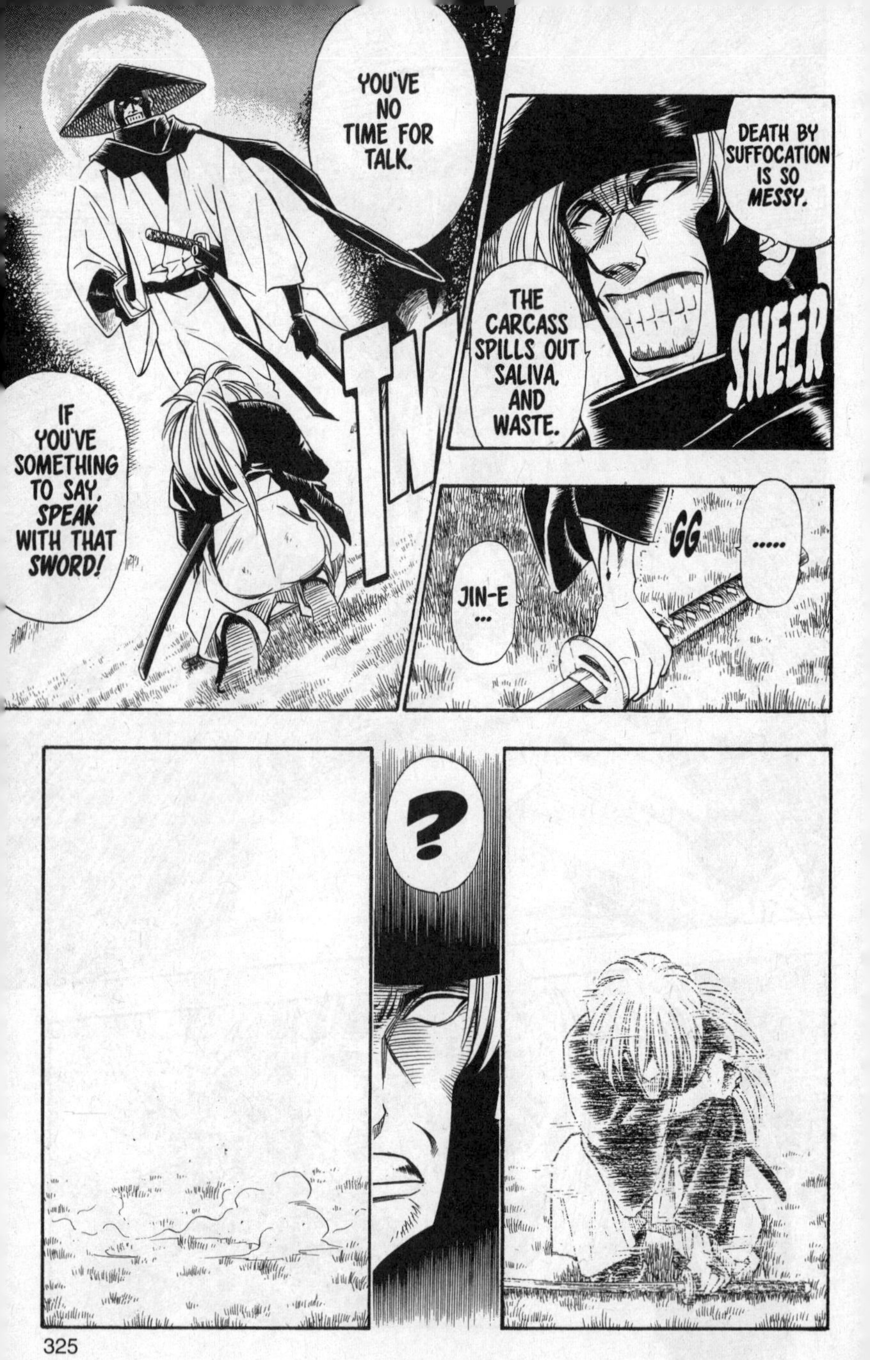
DEATH BY SUFFOCATION IS SO *MESSY.*
THE CARCASS SPILLS OUT SALIVA, AND WASTE.
SNEER
.....
GG
JIN-E ...
YOU'VE NO TIME FOR TALK.
TM
IF YOU'VE SOMETHING TO SAY, *SPEAK* WITH THAT *SWORD!*
?

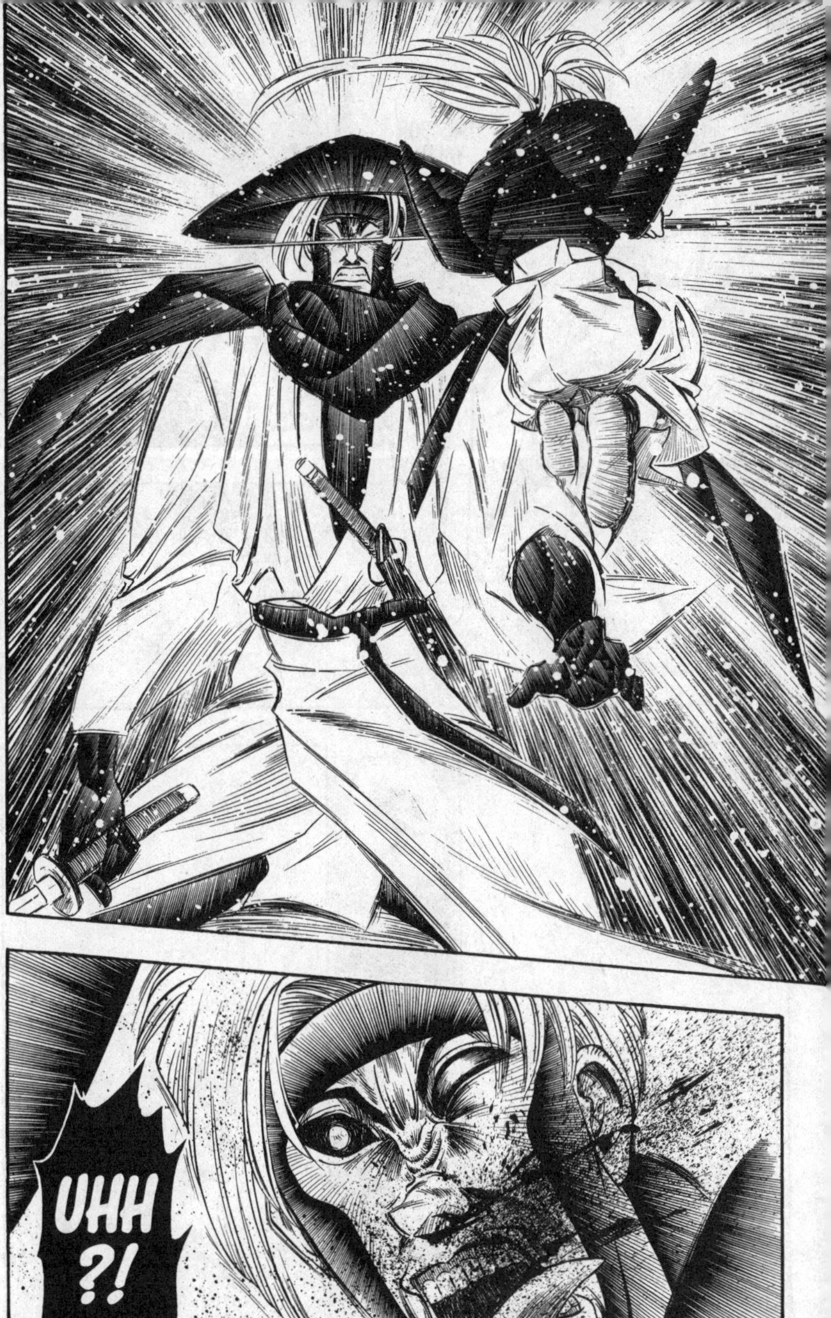
UHH
?!

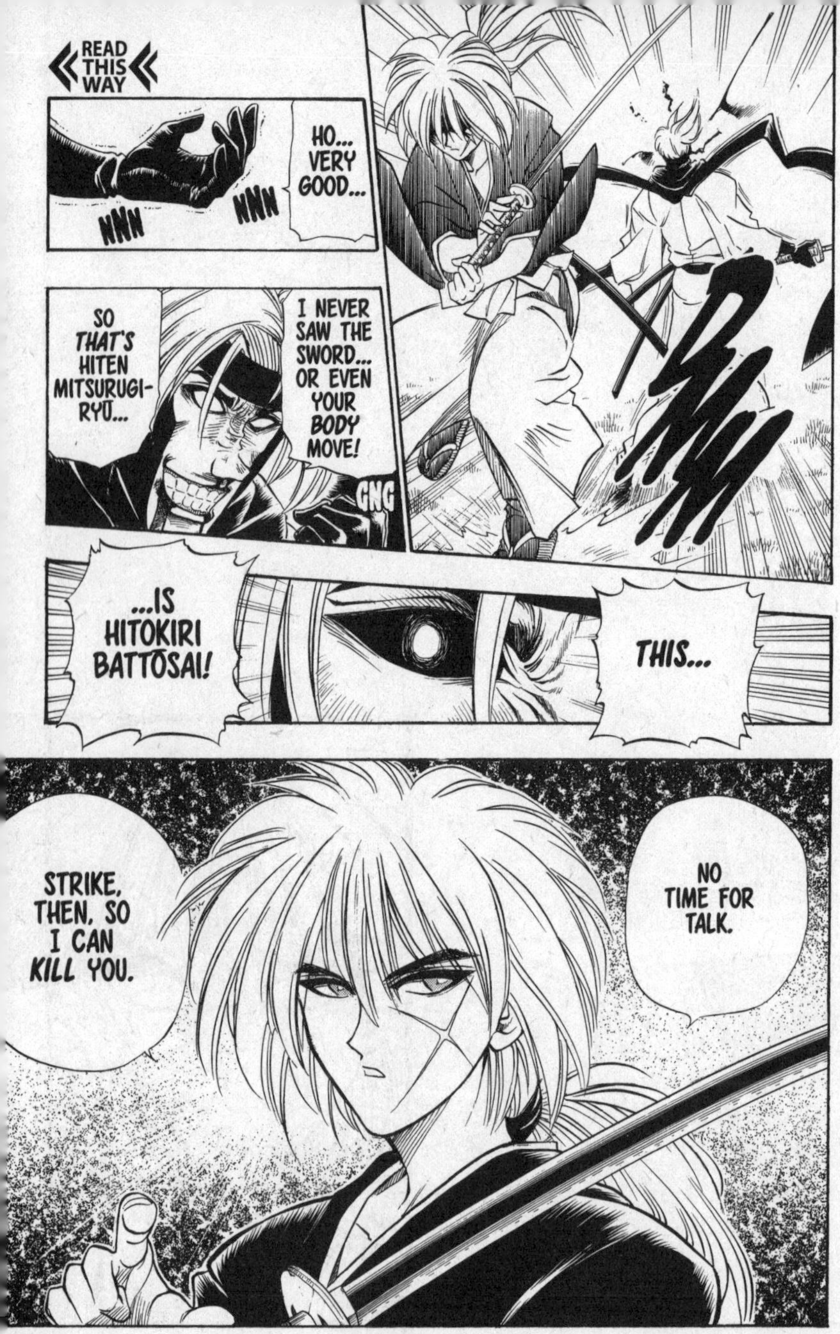
READ THIS WAY
HO... VERY GOOD...
NNN
NNN
I NEVER SAW THE SWORD... OR EVEN YOUR *BODY* MOVE!
SO *THAT'S* HITEN MITSURUGI-RYŪ...
GNG
THIS...
...IS HITOKIRI BATTŌSAI!
NO TIME FOR TALK.
STRIKE, THEN, SO I CAN *KILL* YOU.

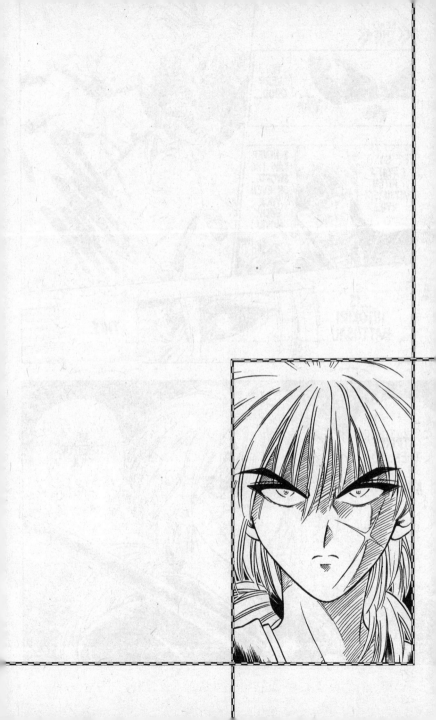

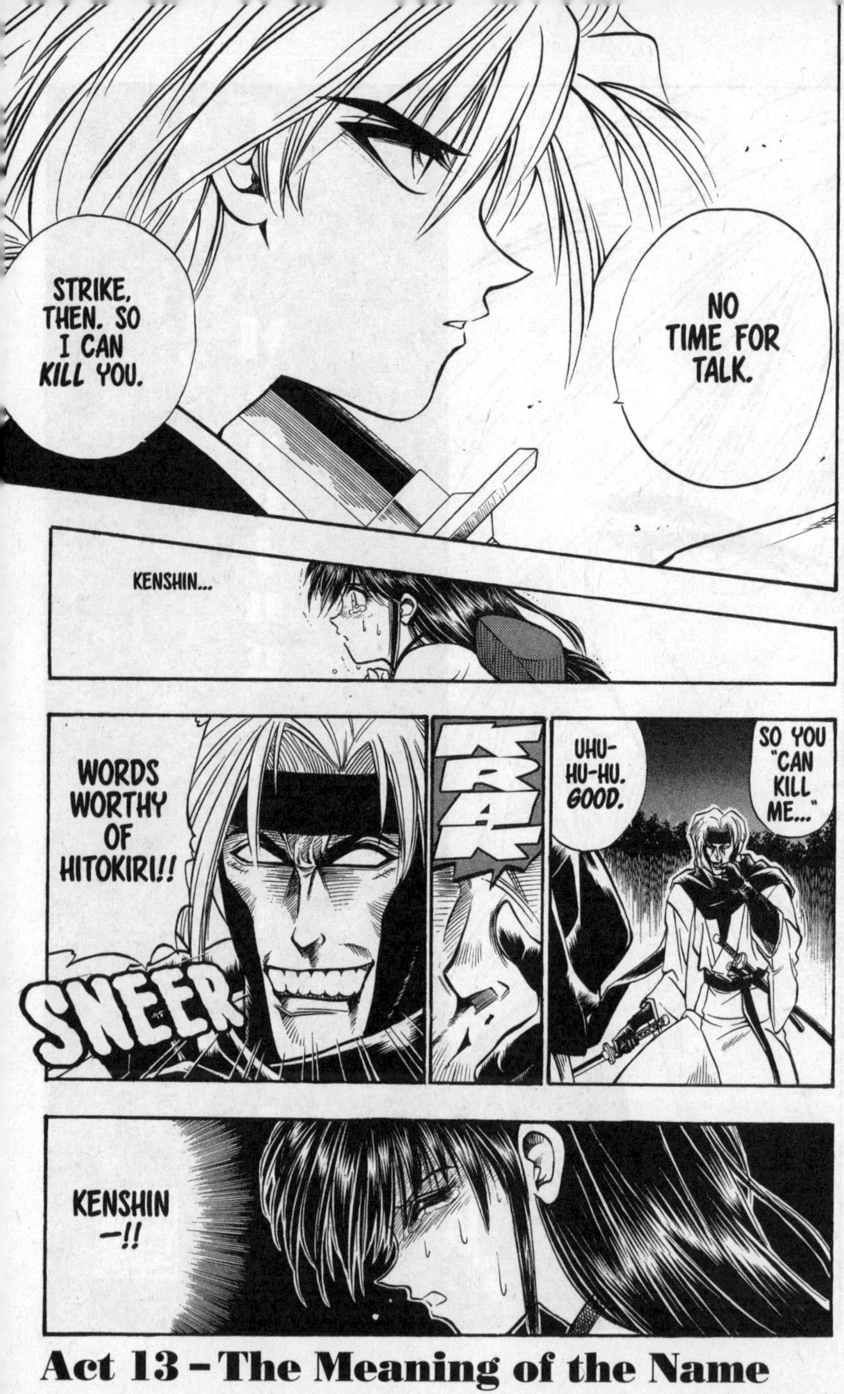
NO TIME FOR TALK.
STRIKE, THEN. SO I CAN KILL YOU.
KENSHIN...
SO YOU "CAN KILL ME..."
UHU-HU-HU. GOOD.
KRAK
WORDS WORTHY OF HITOKIRI!!
SNEER
KENSHIN—!!

Act 13 - The Meaning of the Name

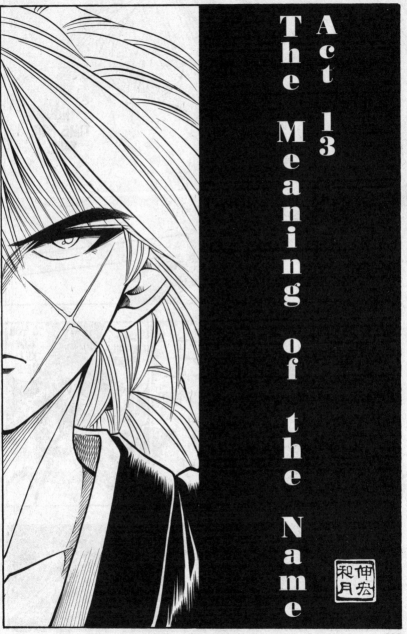

Act 13
The Meaning of the Name

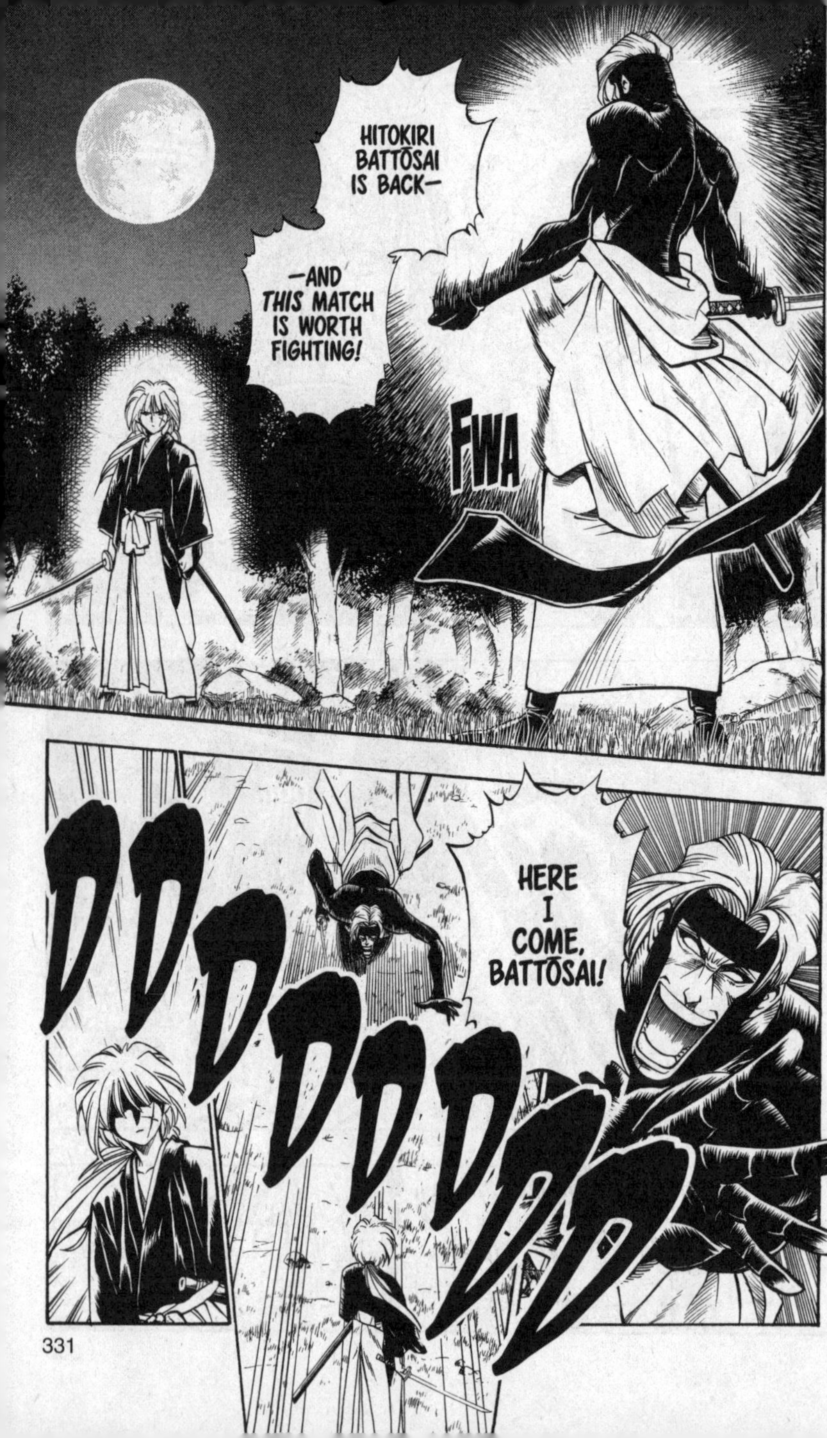
HITOKIRI BATTŌSAI IS BACK—
—AND *THIS* MATCH IS WORTH FIGHTING!
FWA
HERE I COME, BATTŌSAI!
DDDDDDD

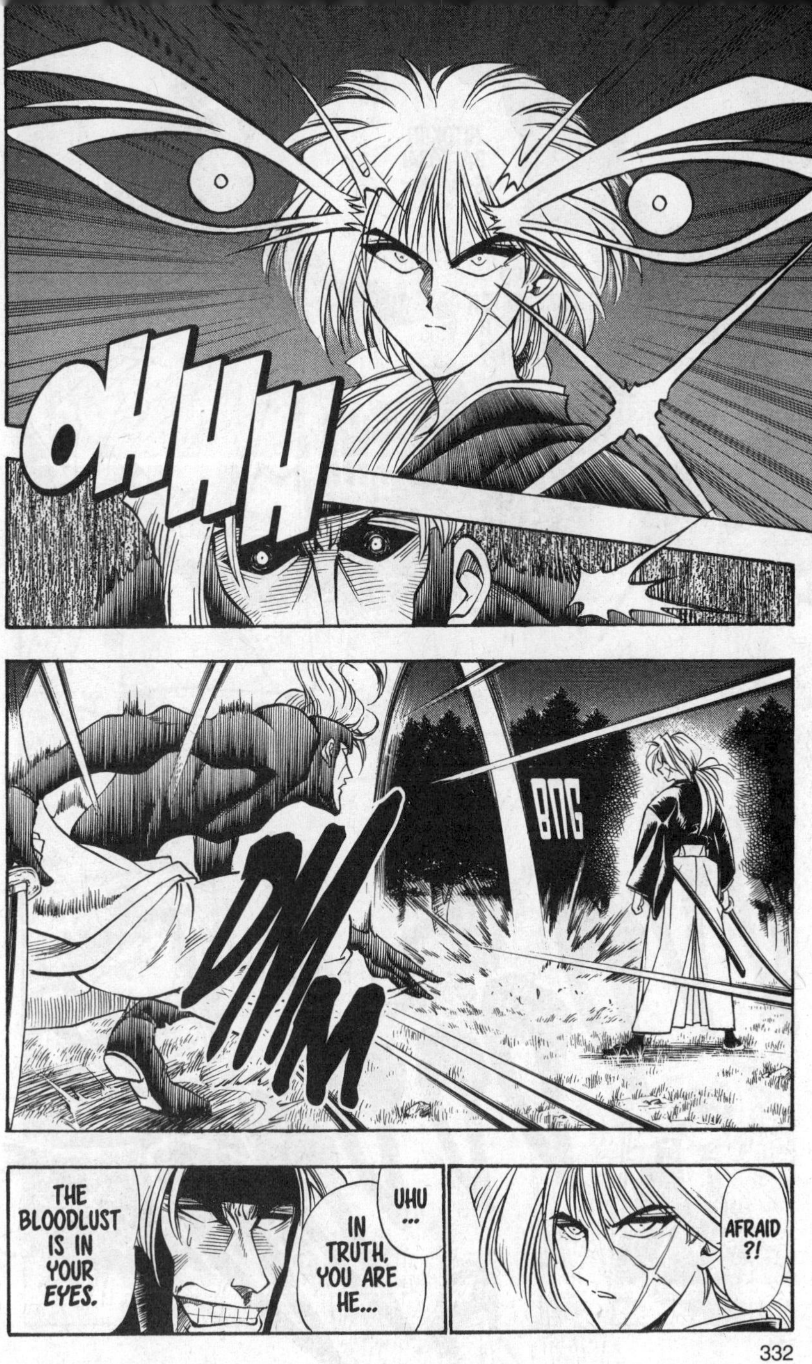
OHHH
BNG
VMM
AFRAID ?!
UHU ...
IN TRUTH, YOU ARE HE...
THE BLOODLUST IS IN YOUR EYES.

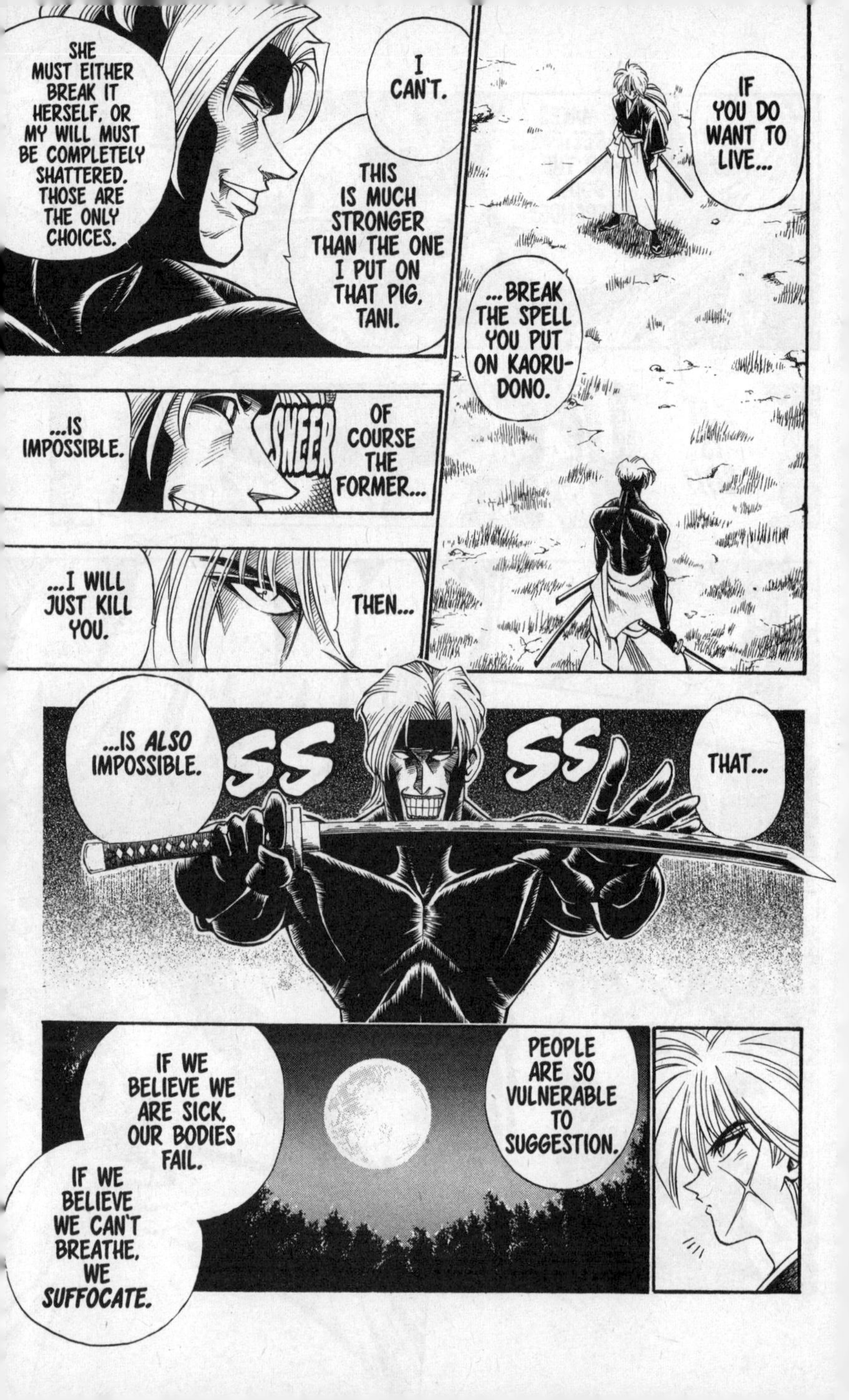
IF YOU DO WANT TO LIVE...
...BREAK THE SPELL YOU PUT ON KAORU-DONO.
I CAN'T.
THIS IS MUCH STRONGER THAN THE ONE I PUT ON THAT PIG, TANI.
SHE MUST EITHER BREAK IT HERSELF, OR MY WILL MUST BE COMPLETELY SHATTERED. THOSE ARE THE ONLY CHOICES.
OF COURSE THE FORMER...
SNEER
...IS IMPOSSIBLE.
THEN...
...I WILL JUST KILL YOU.
THAT...
SS
SS
...IS *ALSO* IMPOSSIBLE.
PEOPLE ARE SO VULNERABLE TO SUGGESTION.
IF WE BELIEVE WE ARE SICK, OUR BODIES FAIL.
IF WE BELIEVE WE CAN'T BREATHE, WE *SUFFOCATE.*

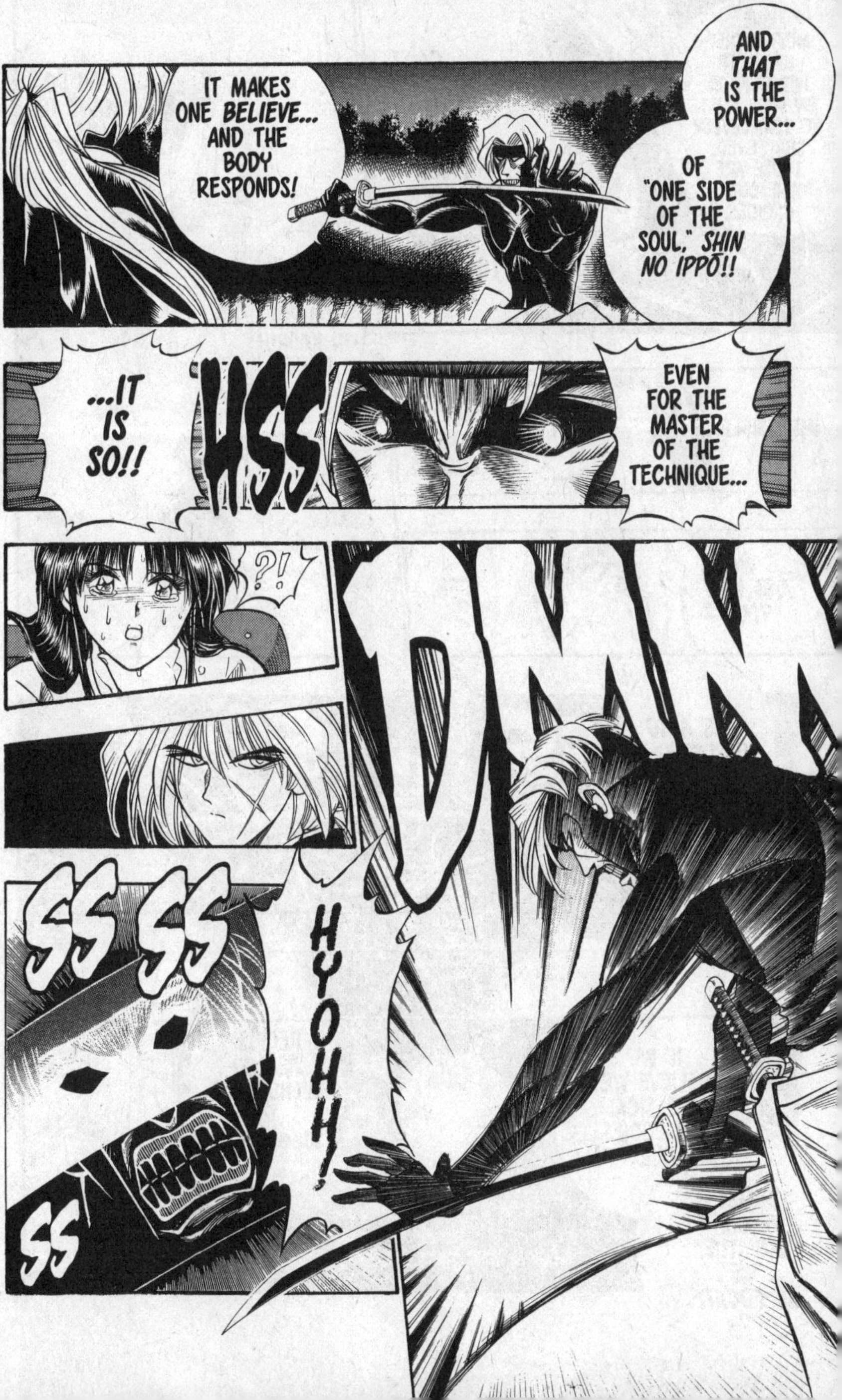
IT MAKES ONE BELIEVE... AND THE BODY RESPONDS!
AND THAT IS THE POWER...
OF "ONE SIDE OF THE SOUL," SHIN NO IPPŌ!!
EVEN FOR THE MASTER OF THE TECHNIQUE...
HSS
...IT IS SO!!
DMN
HYOHH!
?!
SS SS
SS

READ THIS WAY

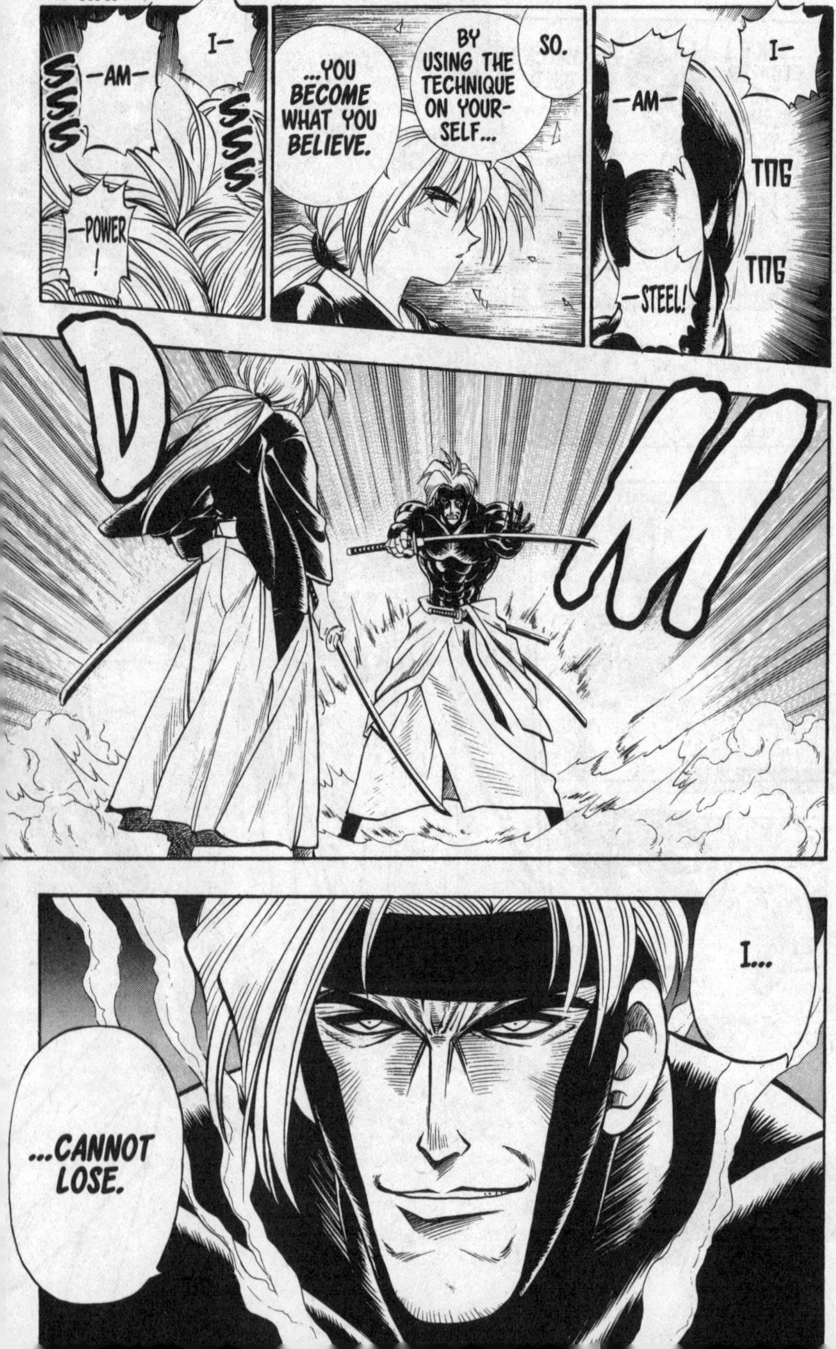
I—
—AM—
TNG
TNG
—STEEL!
SO.
BY USING THE TECHNIQUE ON YOUR-SELF...
...YOU BECOME WHAT YOU BELIEVE.
I—
—AM—
SSS
SSS
—POWER!
D
M
I...
...CANNOT LOSE.

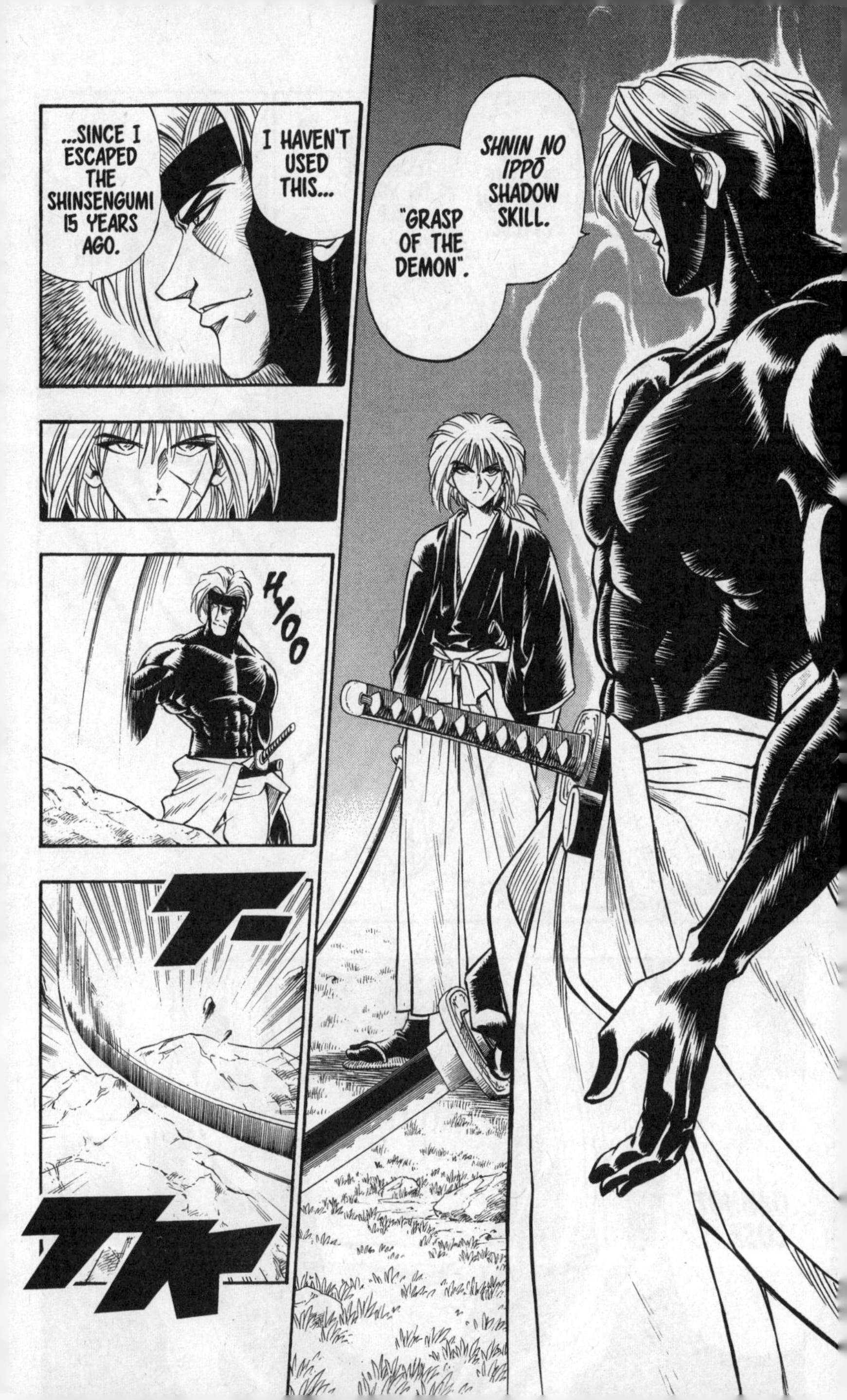
SHNIN NO IPPŌ SHADOW SKILL.
"GRASP OF THE DEMON".
I HAVEN'T USED THIS...
...SINCE I ESCAPED THE SHINSENGUMI 15 YEARS AGO.
HYOO

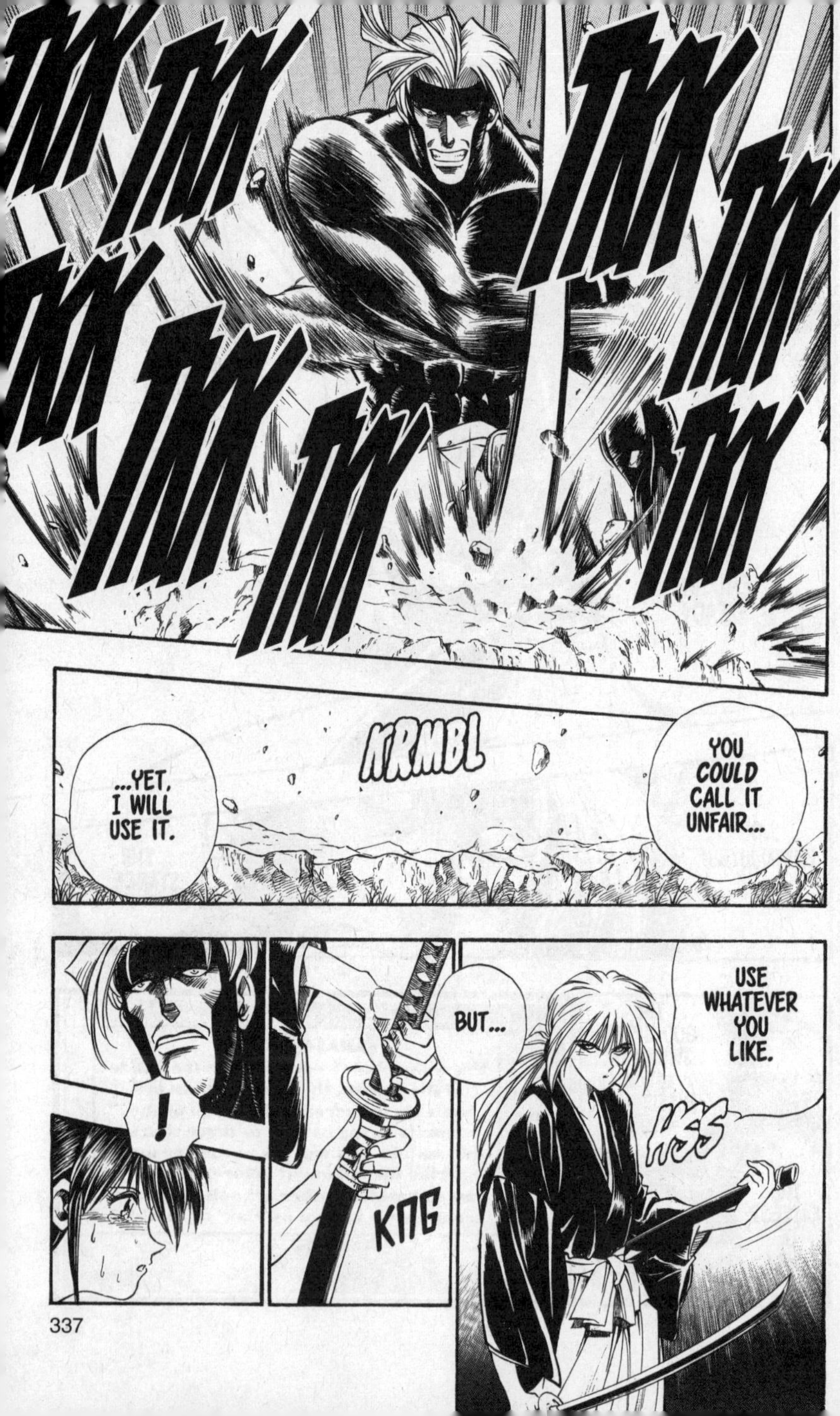
YOU COULD CALL IT UNFAIR...
KRMBL
...YET, I WILL USE IT.
USE WHATEVER YOU LIKE.
HSS
BUT...
KNG
!

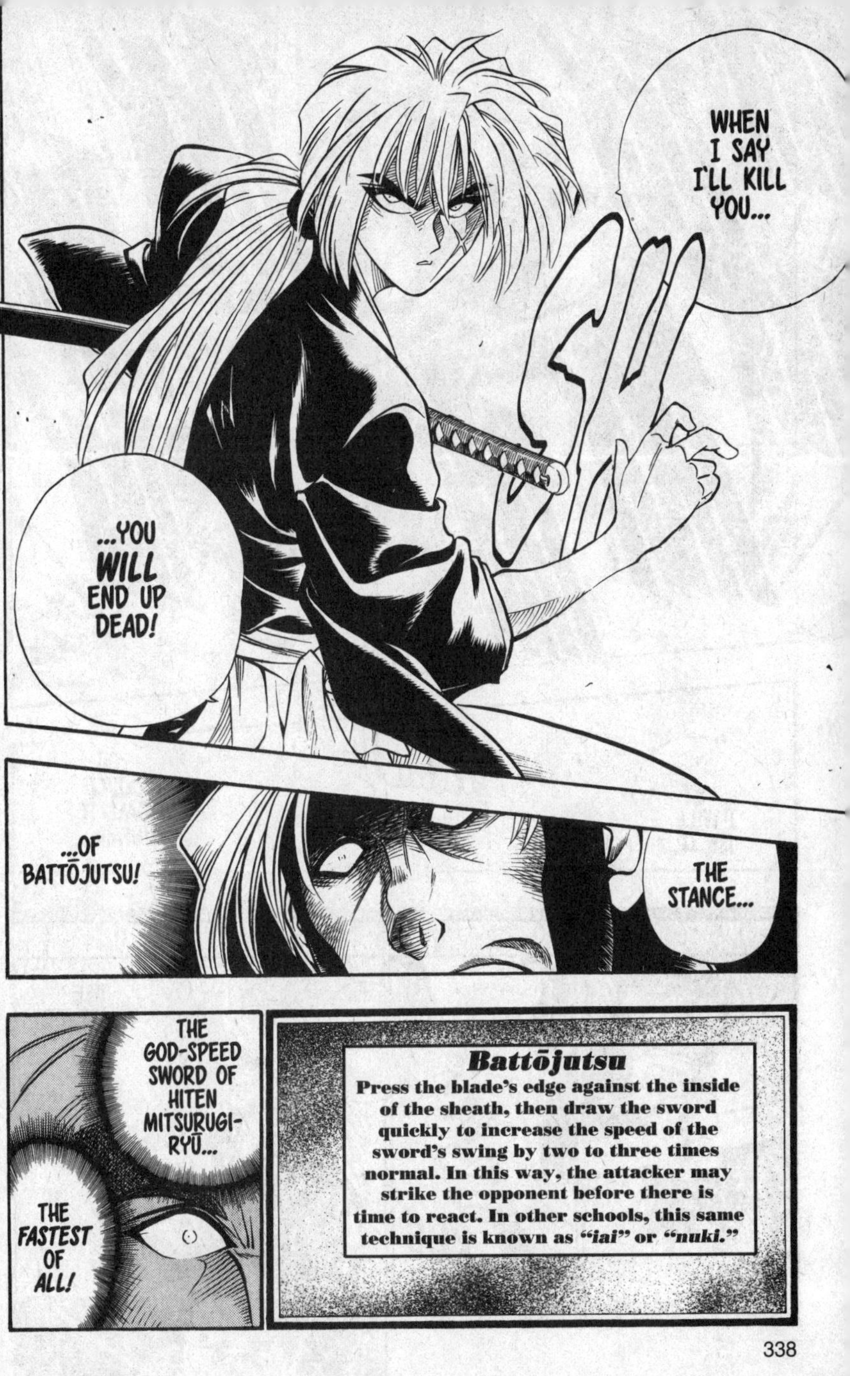
WHEN I SAY I'LL KILL YOU...
...YOU WILL END UP DEAD!
THE STANCE...
...OF BATTŌJUTSU!
Battōjutsu
Press the blade's edge against the inside of the sheath, then draw the sword quickly to increase the speed of the sword's swing by two to three times normal. In this way, the attacker may strike the opponent before there is time to react. In other schools, this same technique is known as "iai" or "nuki."
THE GOD-SPEED SWORD OF HITEN MITSURUGI-RYŪ...
THE FASTEST OF ALL!

READ THIS WAY

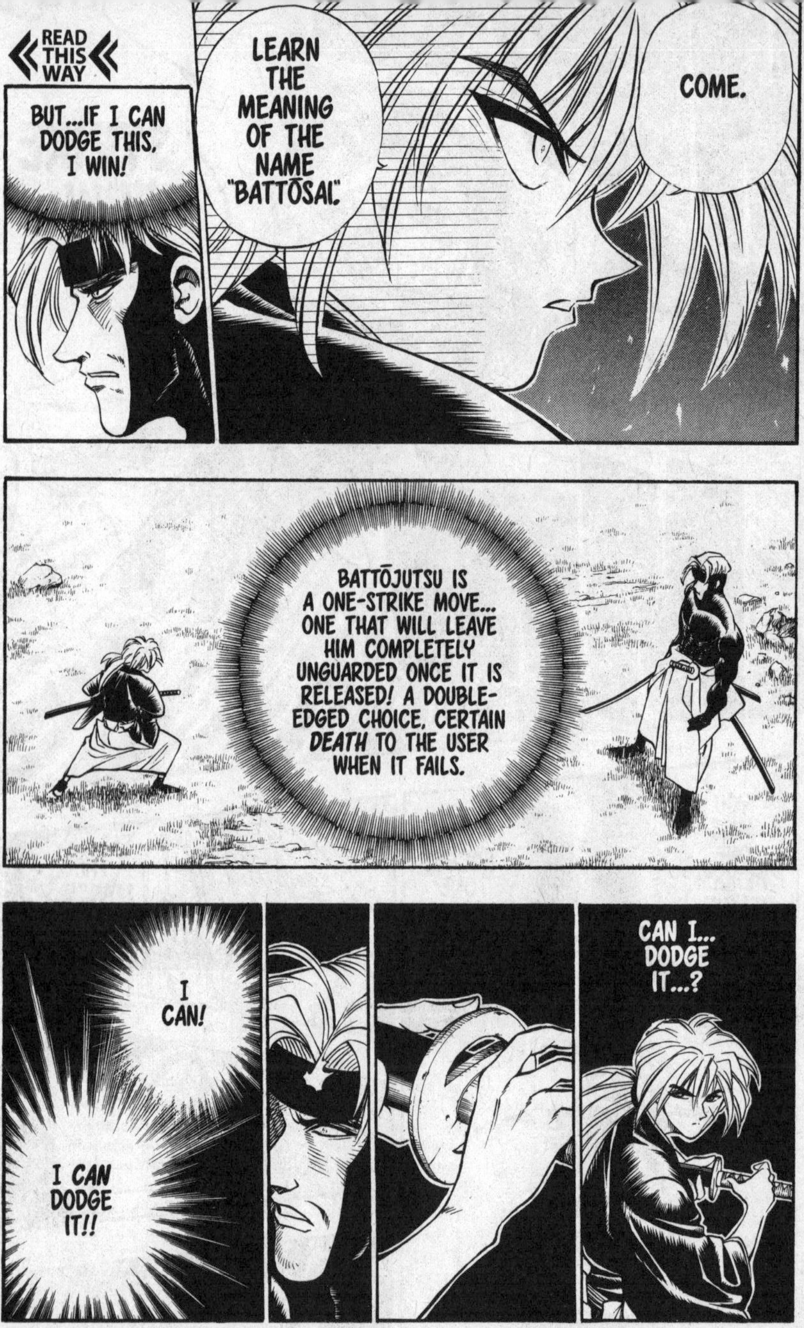
COME.
LEARN THE MEANING OF THE NAME "BATTŌSAI."
BUT...IF I CAN DODGE THIS, I WIN!
BATTŌJUTSU IS A ONE-STRIKE MOVE... ONE THAT WILL LEAVE HIM COMPLETELY UNGUARDED ONCE IT IS RELEASED! A DOUBLE-EDGED CHOICE, CERTAIN *DEATH* TO THE USER WHEN IT FAILS.
CAN I... DODGE IT...?
I CAN!
I *CAN* DODGE IT!!

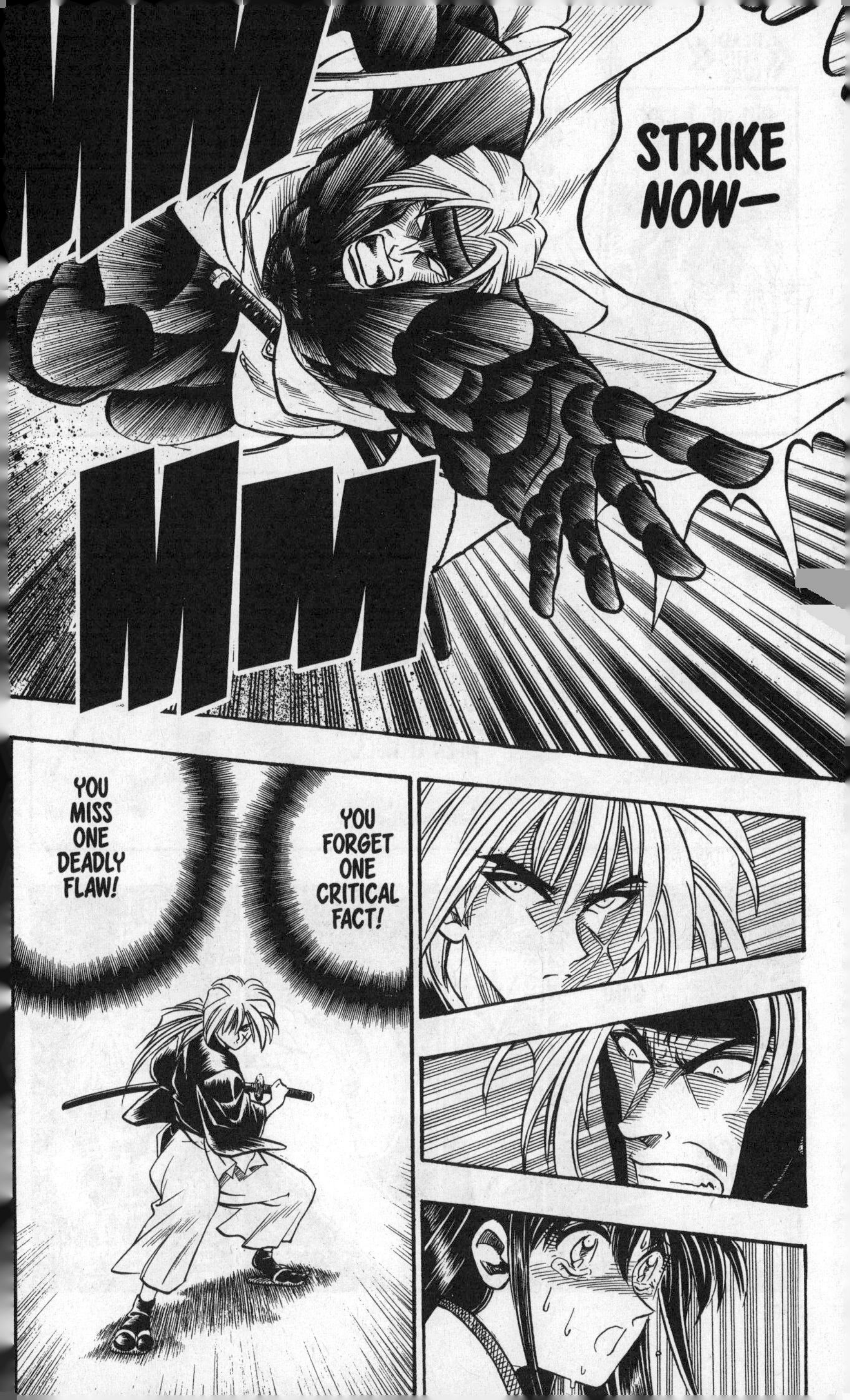
STRIKE NOW—
YOU FORGET ONE CRITICAL FACT!
YOU MISS ONE DEADLY FLAW!

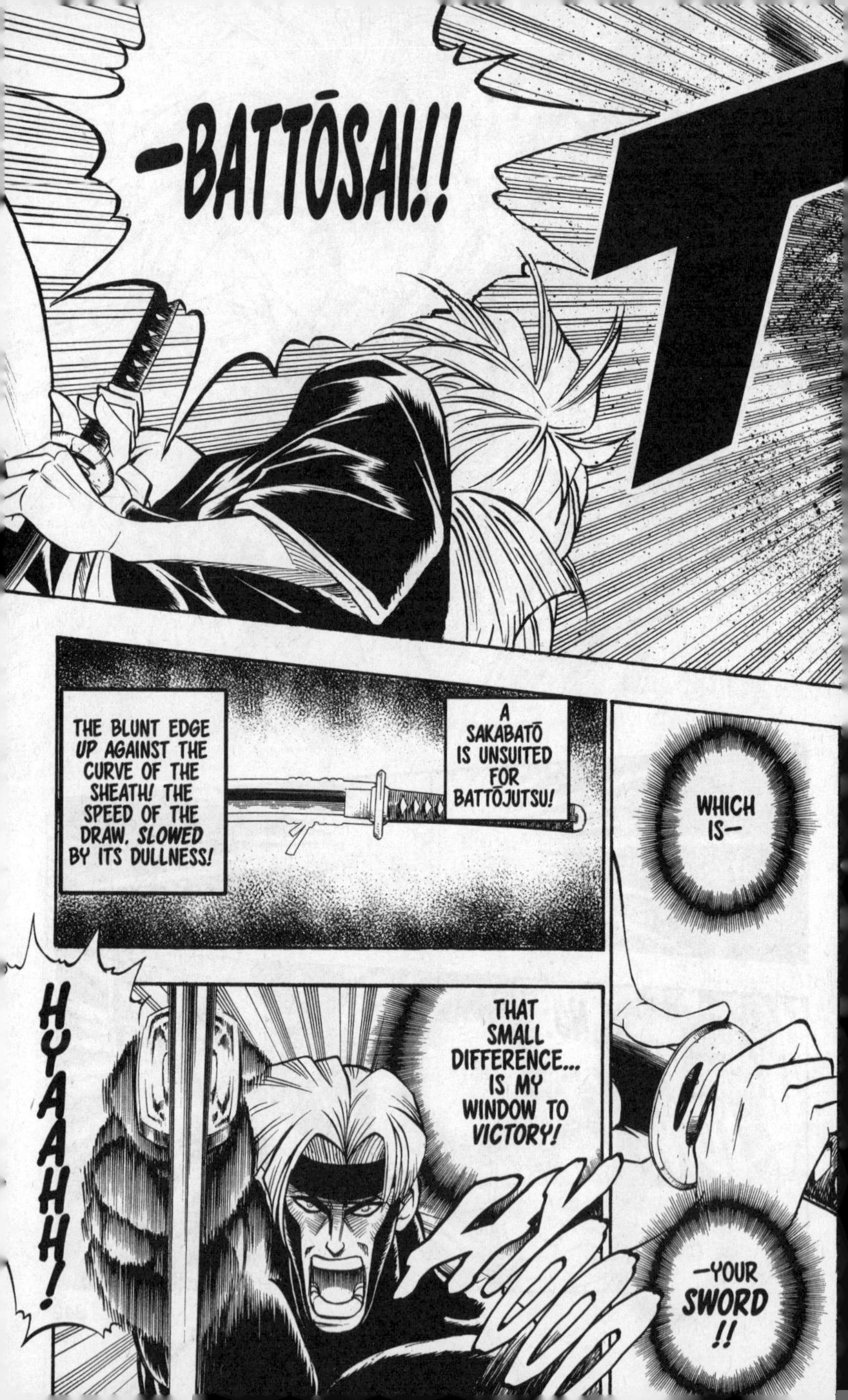
—BATTŌSAI!!
WHICH IS—
—YOUR SWORD!!
A SAKABATŌ IS UNSUITED FOR BATTŌJUTSU!
THE BLUNT EDGE UP AGAINST THE CURVE OF THE SHEATH! THE SPEED OF THE DRAW, SLOWED BY ITS DULLNESS!
THAT SMALL DIFFERENCE... IS MY WINDOW TO VICTORY!
HYAAAHH!

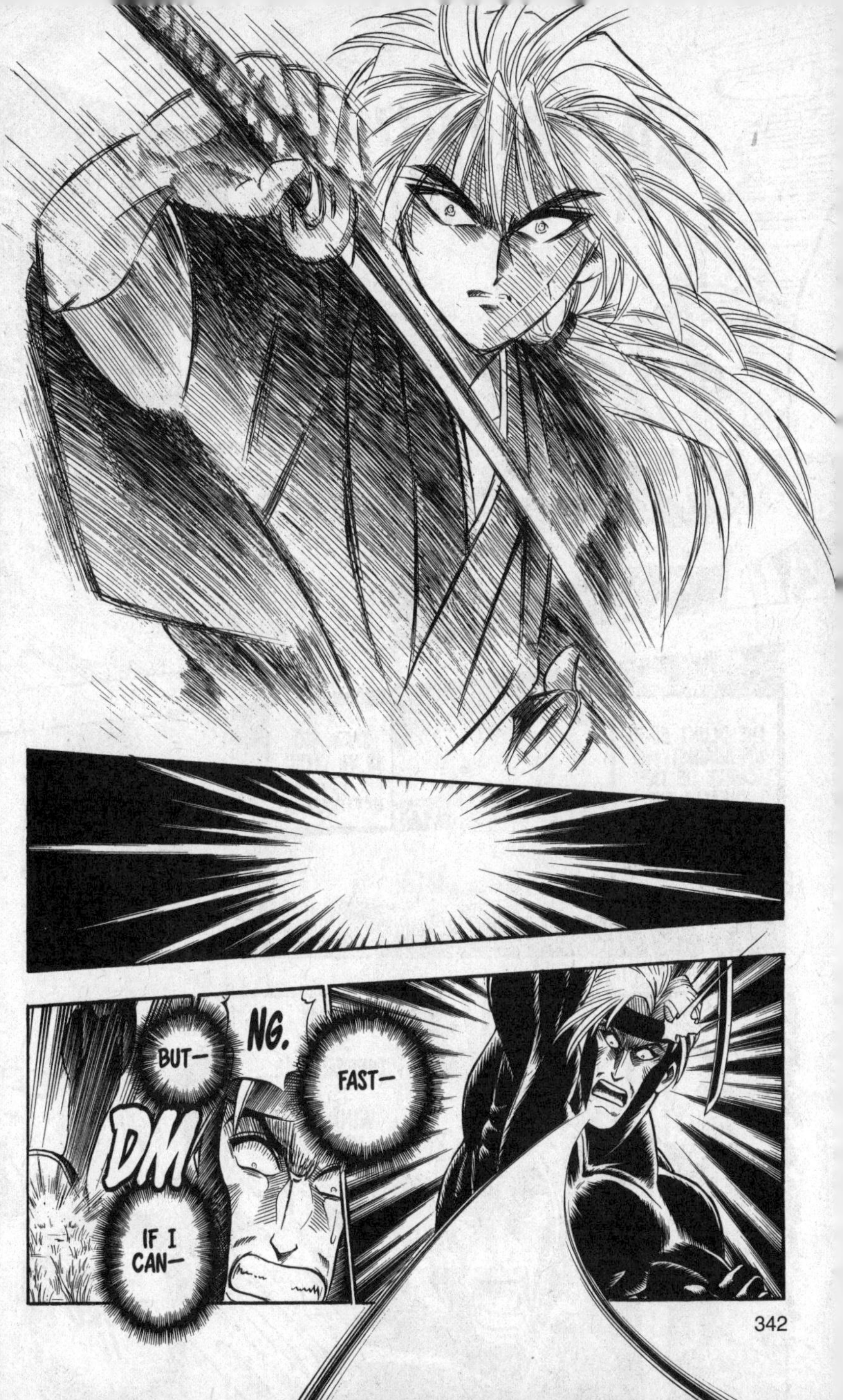
FAST—
NG.
BUT—
DM
IF I CAN—

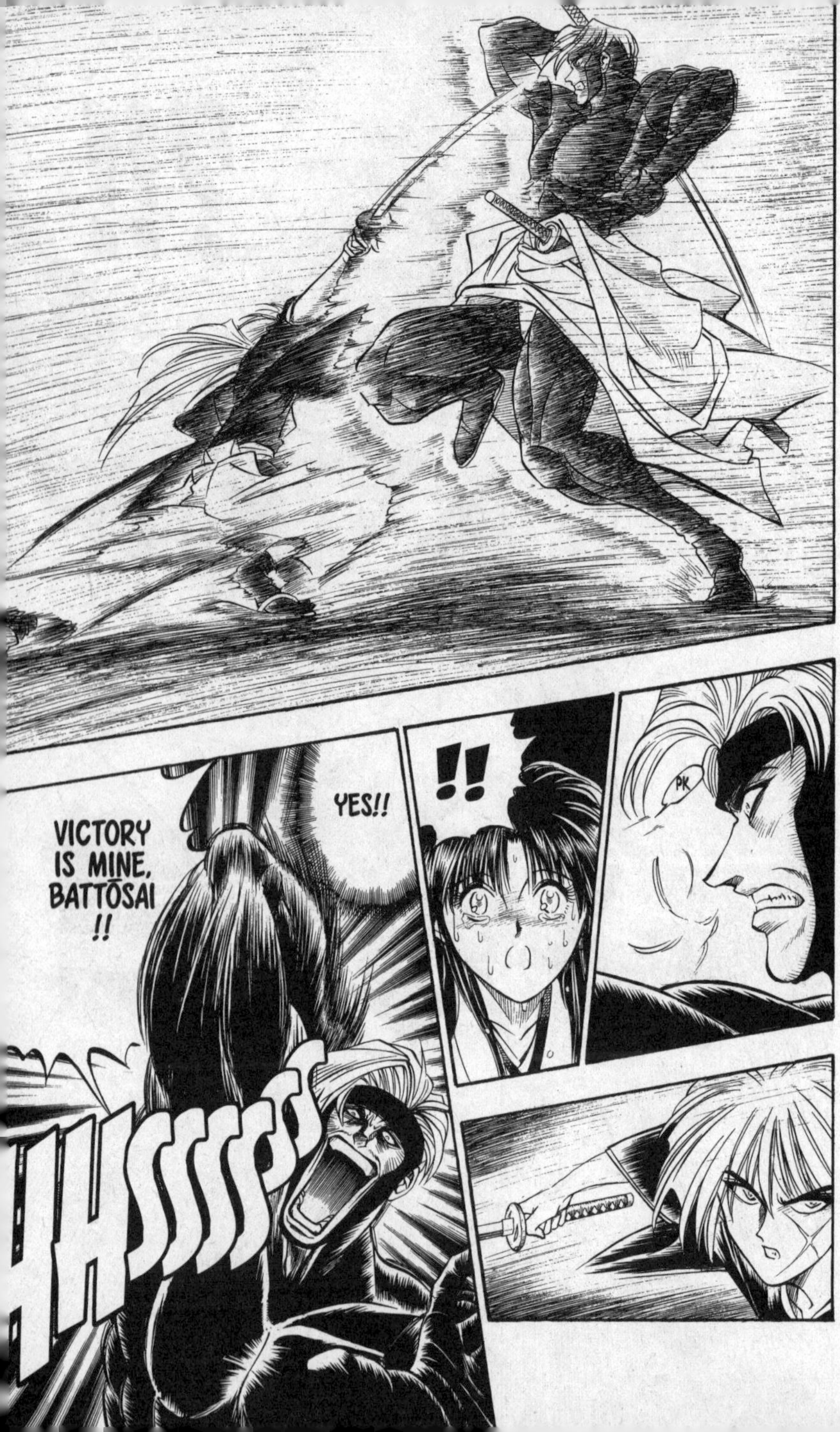
PK
!!
YES!!
VICTORY IS MINE, BATTŌSAI !!
HSSSSSS

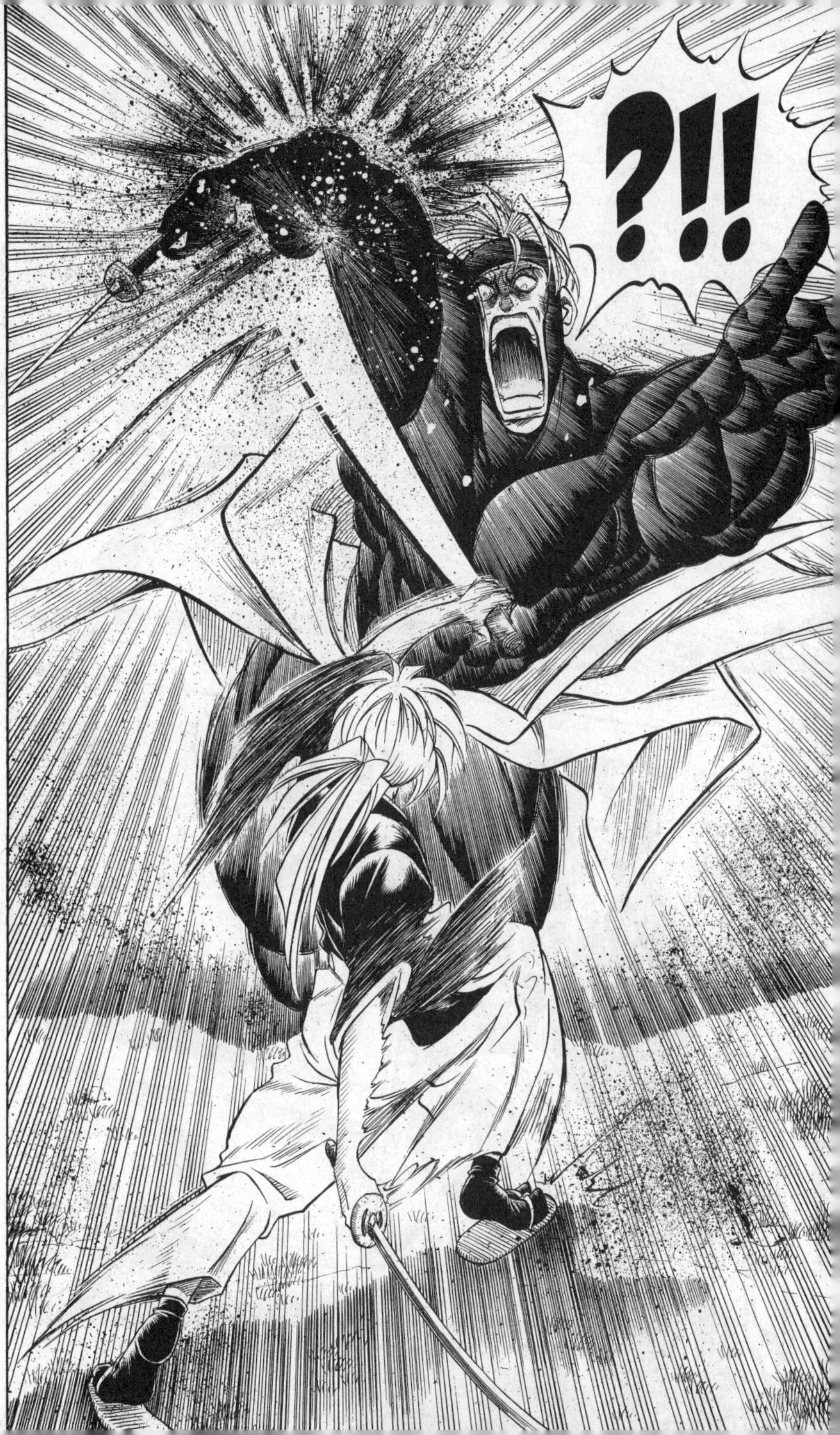
?!!

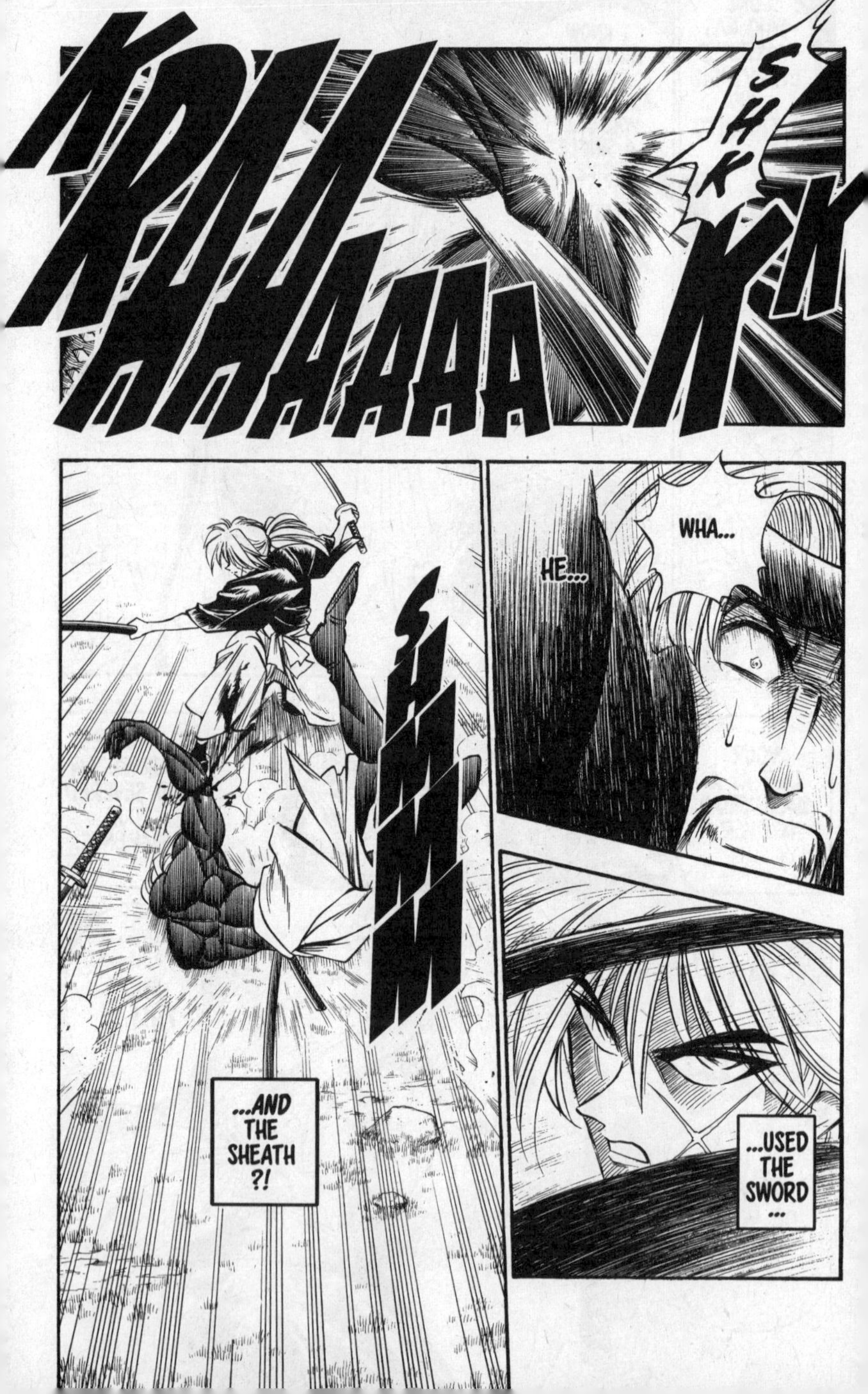
SHK
WHA...
HE...
...USED THE SWORD ...
...AND THE SHEATH ?!

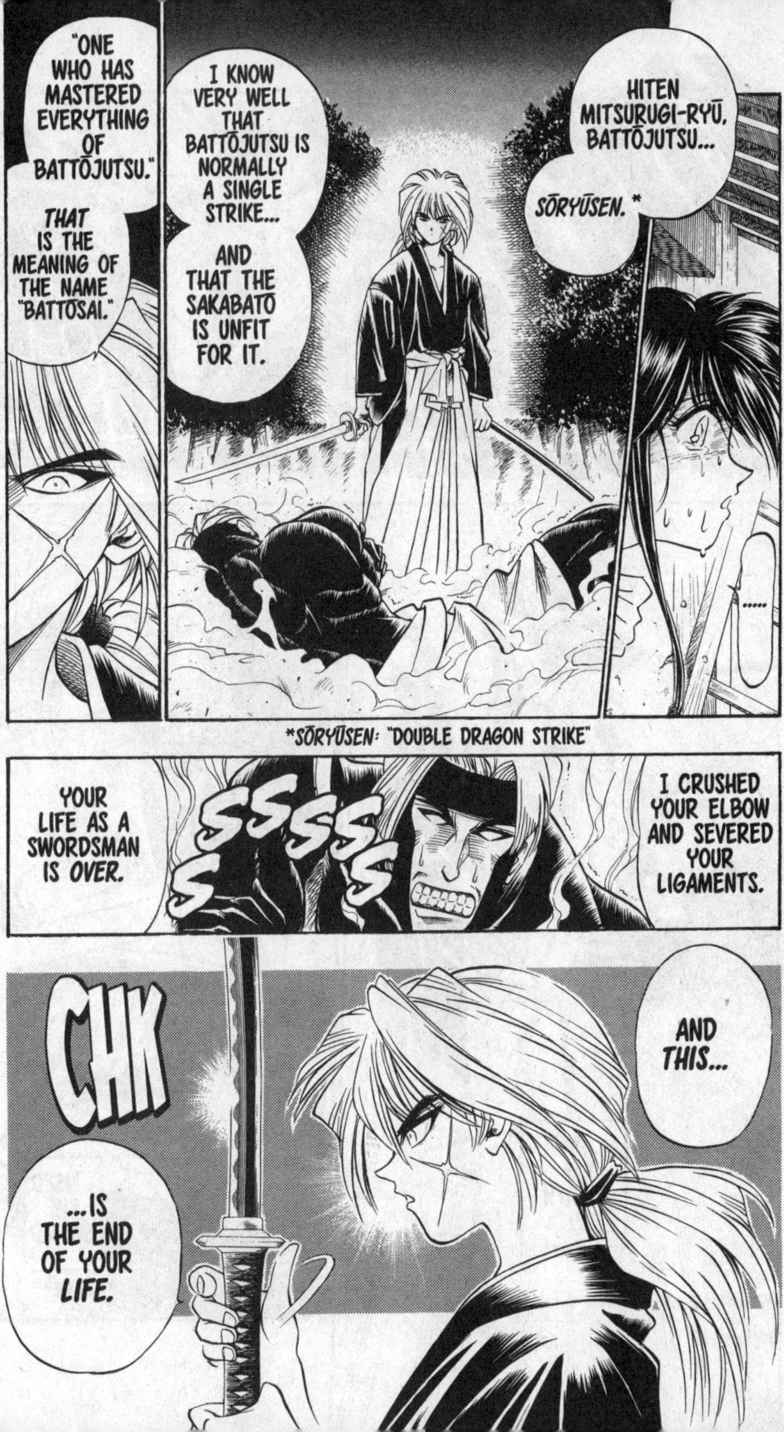
HITEN MITSURUGI-RYŪ, BATTŌJUTSU...
SŌRYŪSEN. *
.....
I KNOW VERY WELL THAT BATTŌJUTSU IS NORMALLY A SINGLE STRIKE...
AND THAT THE SAKABATŌ IS UNFIT FOR IT.
"ONE WHO HAS MASTERED EVERYTHING OF BATTŌJUTSU."
THAT IS THE MEANING OF THE NAME "BATTŌSAI."
I CRUSHED YOUR ELBOW AND SEVERED YOUR LIGAMENTS.
SSSSSS
YOUR LIFE AS A SWORDSMAN IS *OVER*.
AND *THIS*...
CHK
...IS THE END OF YOUR *LIFE*.

*SŌRYŪSEN: "DOUBLE DRAGON STRIKE"

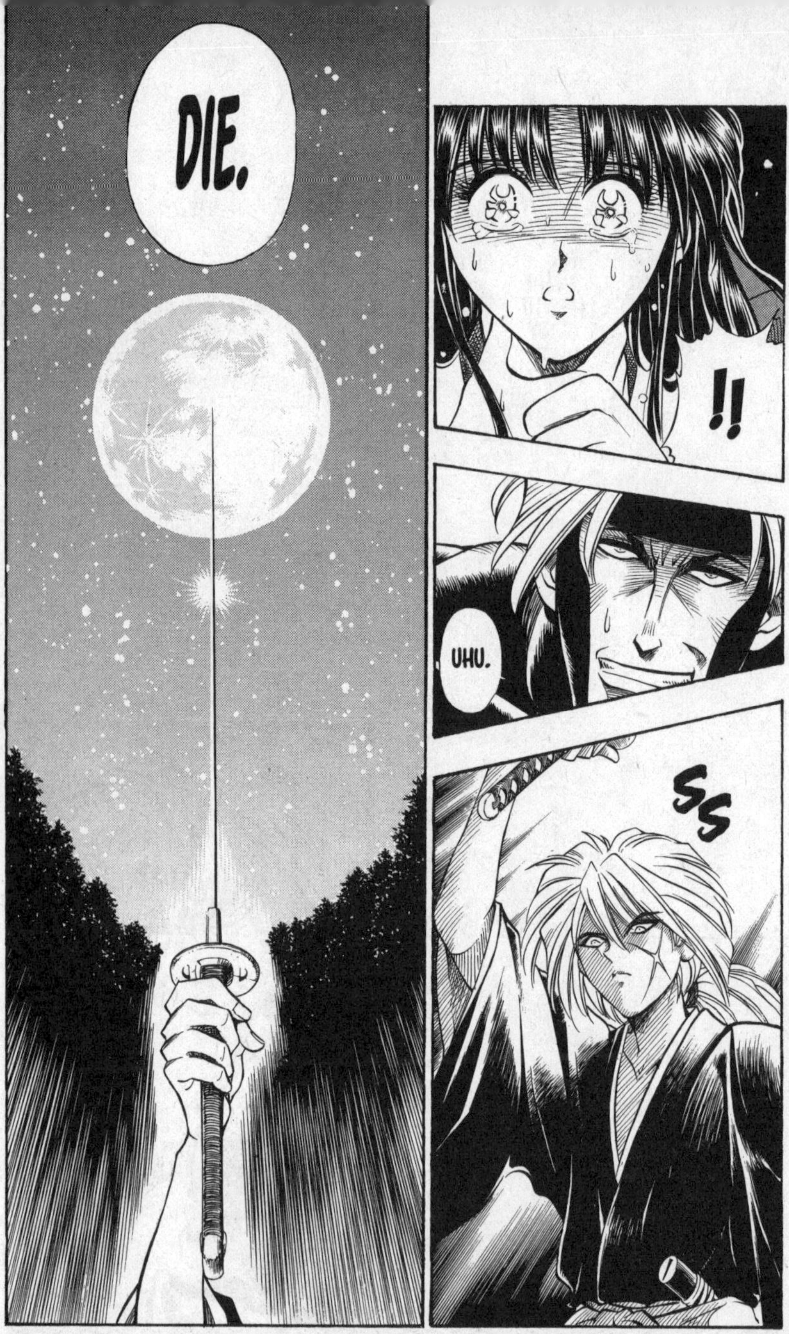
!!
UHU.
SS
DIE.

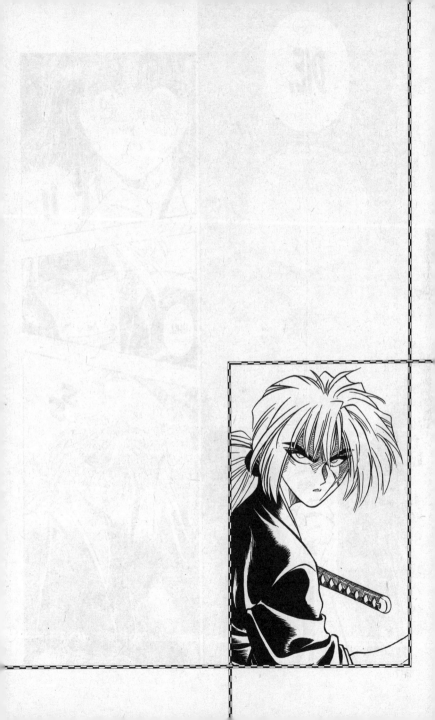

Act 14 – End Beneath the Moon

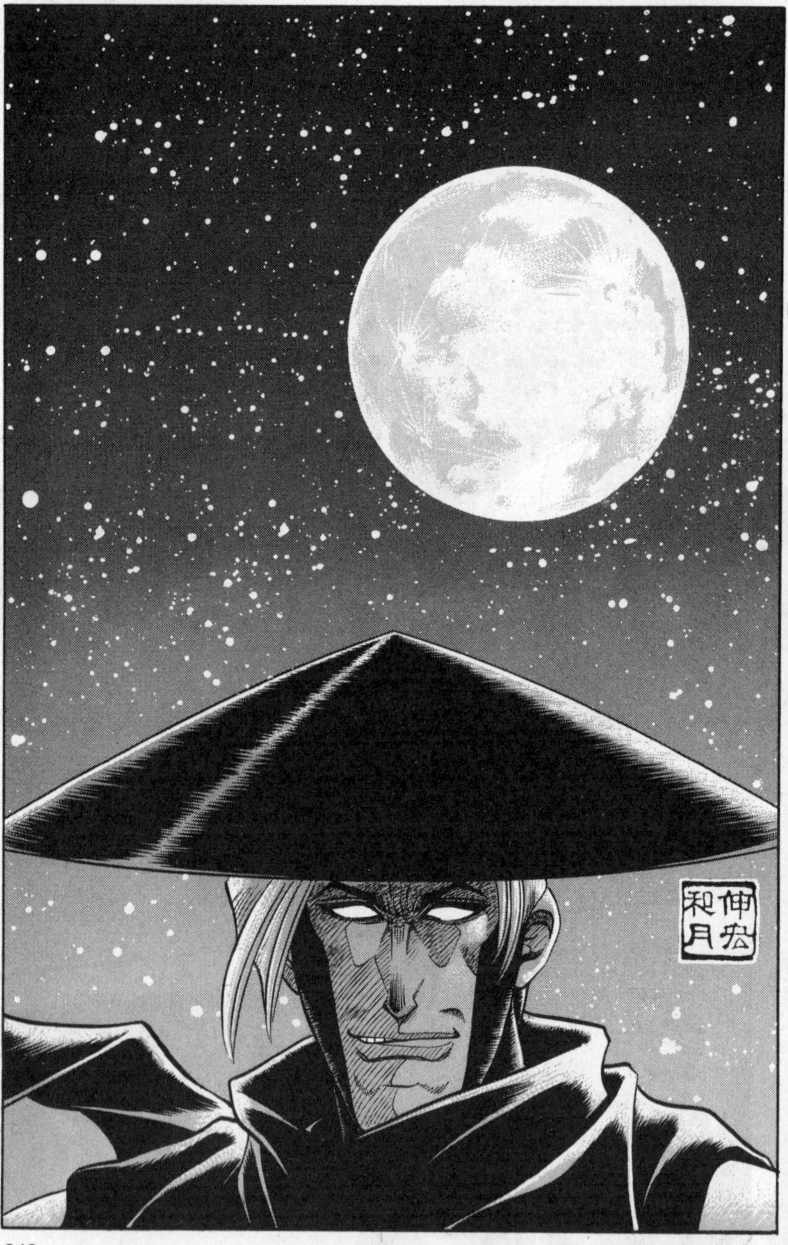

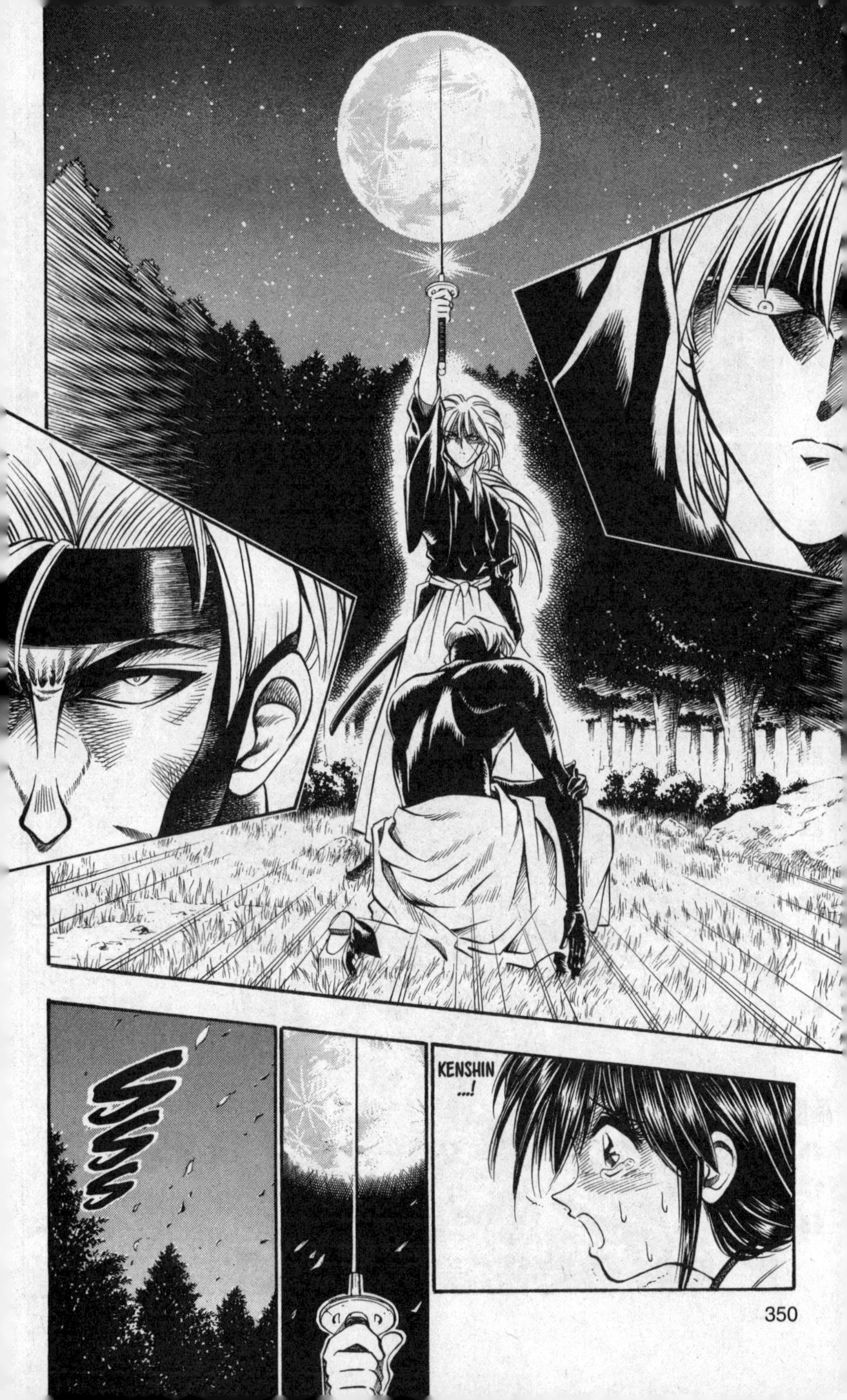
KENSHIN
...!
SJJJJ

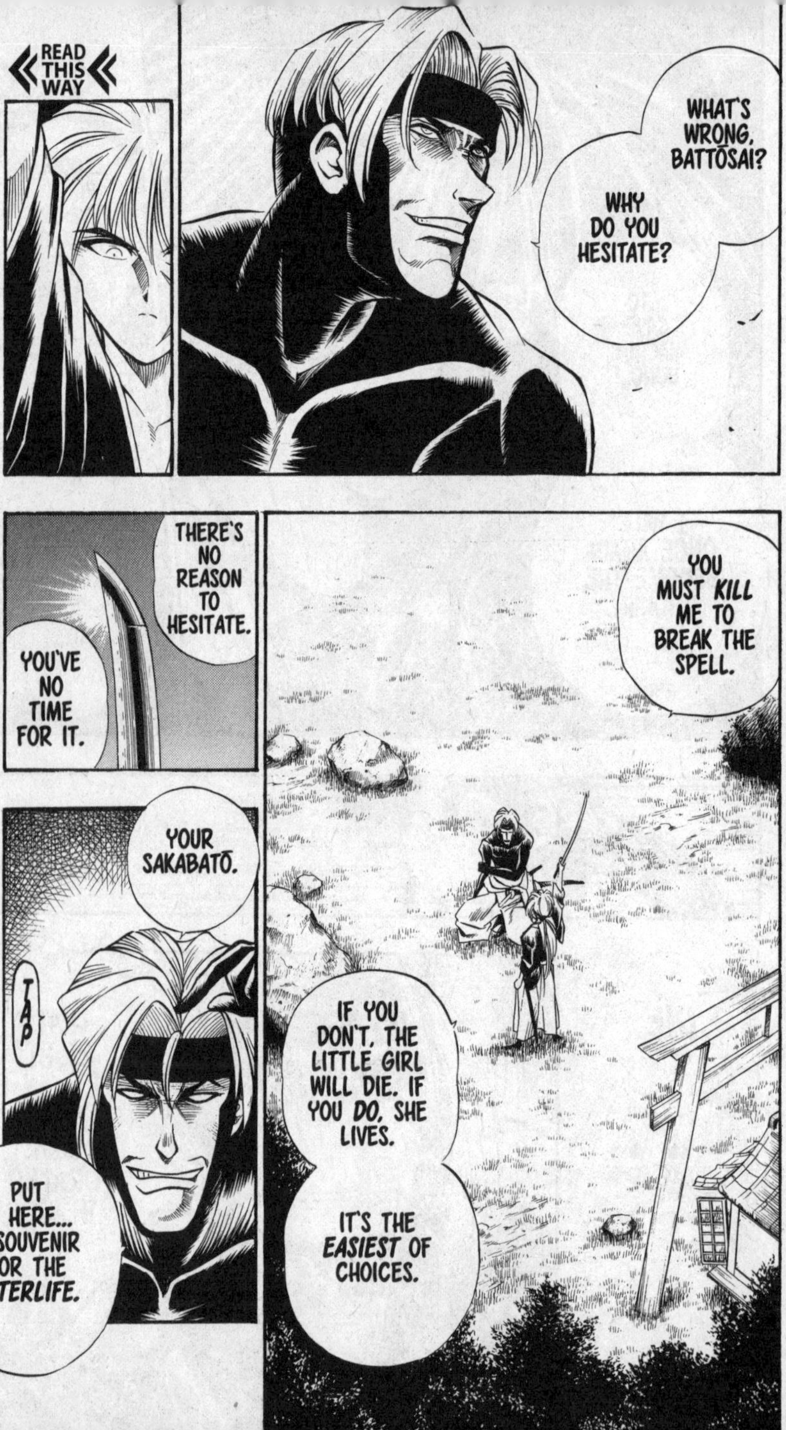
READ THIS WAY
WHAT'S WRONG, BATTŌSAI?
WHY DO YOU HESITATE?
YOU MUST *KILL* ME TO BREAK THE SPELL.
IF YOU DON'T, THE LITTLE GIRL WILL DIE. IF YOU *DO*, SHE LIVES.
IT'S THE *EASIEST* OF CHOICES.
THERE'S NO REASON TO HESITATE.
YOU'VE NO TIME FOR IT.
YOUR SAKABATŌ.
TAP
PUT IT HERE... A SOUVENIR FOR THE *AFTERLIFE.*

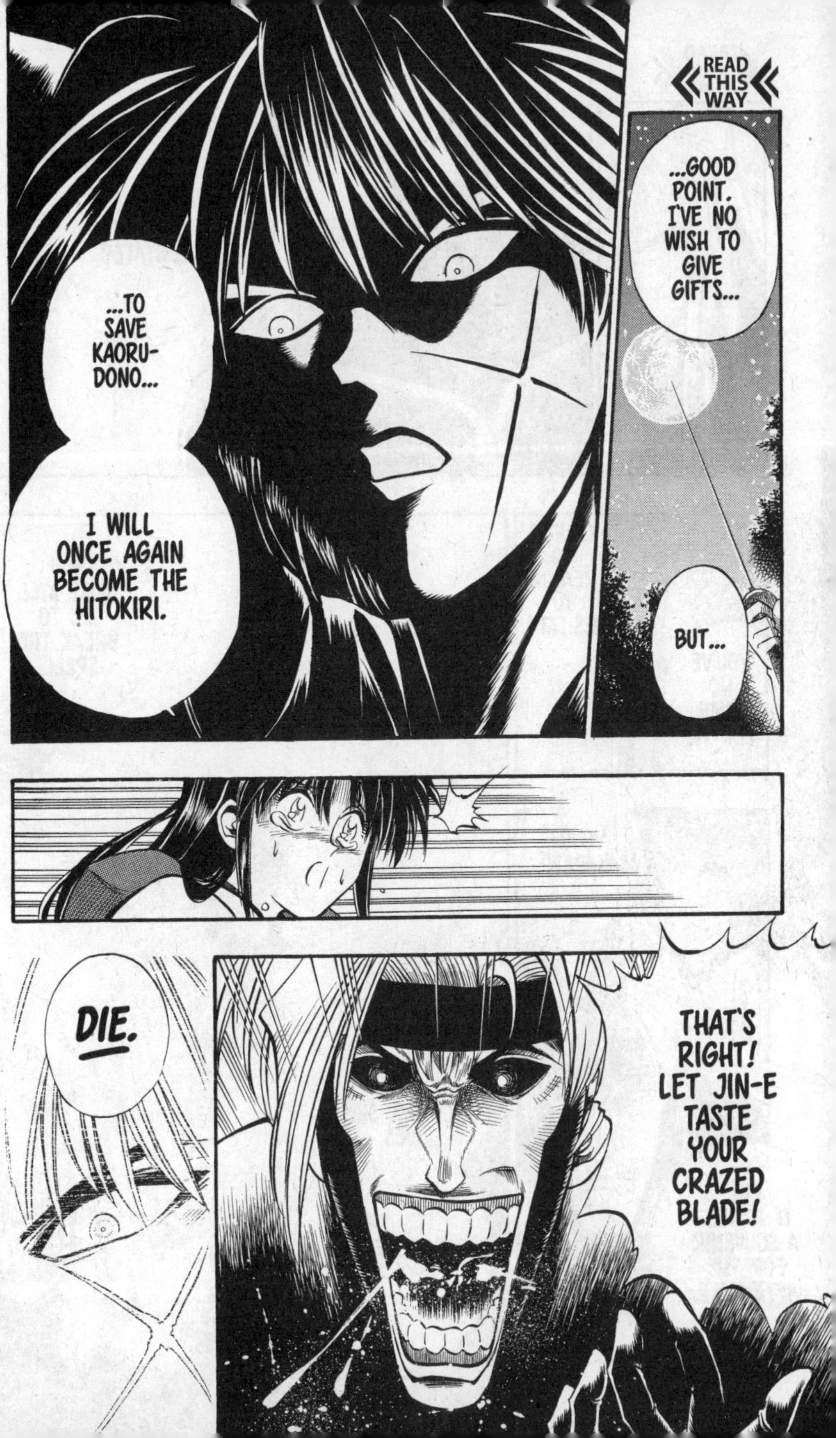
READ THIS WAY
...GOOD POINT. I'VE NO WISH TO GIVE GIFTS...
BUT...
...TO SAVE KAORU-DONO...
I WILL ONCE AGAIN BECOME THE HITOKIRI.
THAT'S RIGHT! LET JIN-E TASTE YOUR CRAZED BLADE!
DIE.

READ THIS WAY

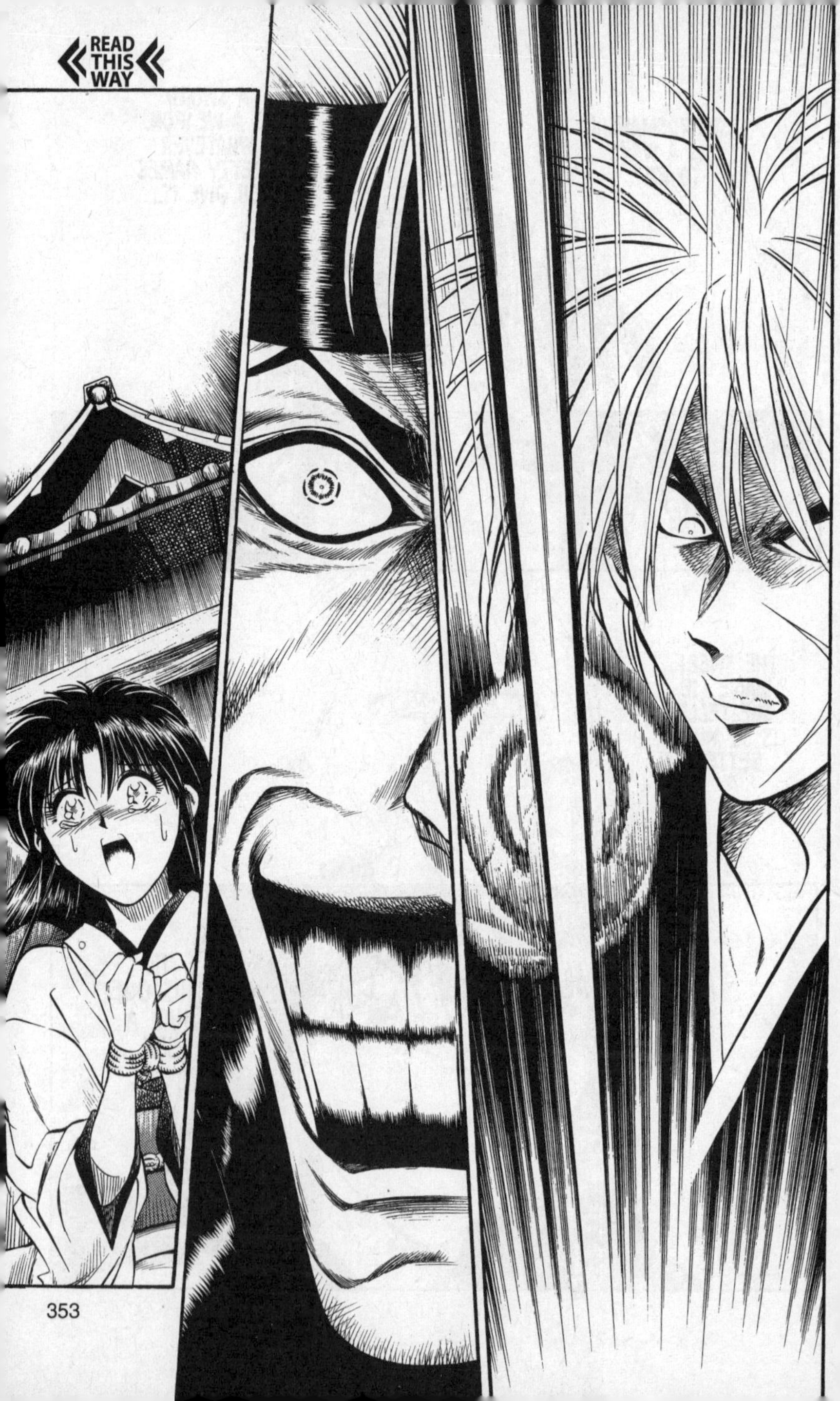

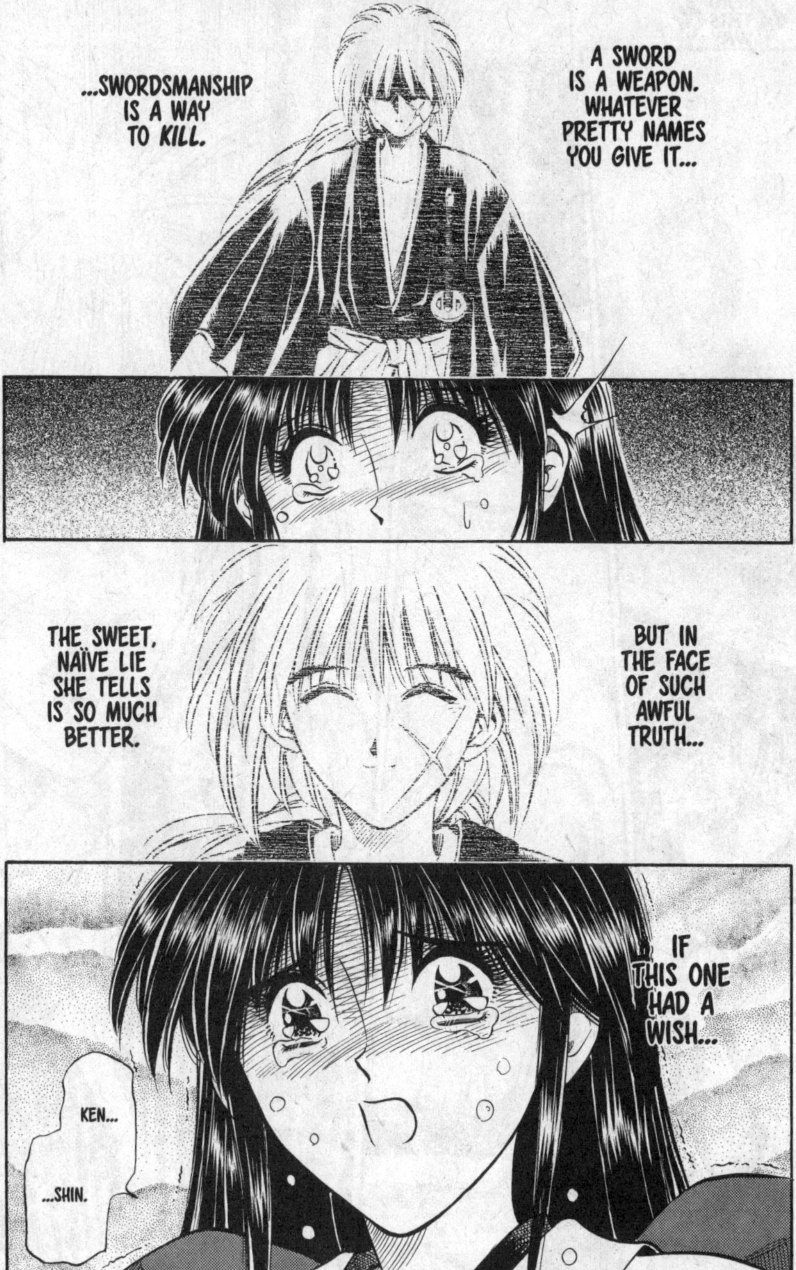
A SWORD IS A WEAPON. WHATEVER PRETTY NAMES YOU GIVE IT...
...SWORDSMANSHIP IS A WAY TO *KILL.*
BUT IN THE FACE OF SUCH AWFUL TRUTH...
THE SWEET, NAÏVE LIE SHE TELLS IS SO MUCH BETTER.
IF THIS ONE HAD A WISH...
KEN...
...SHIN.

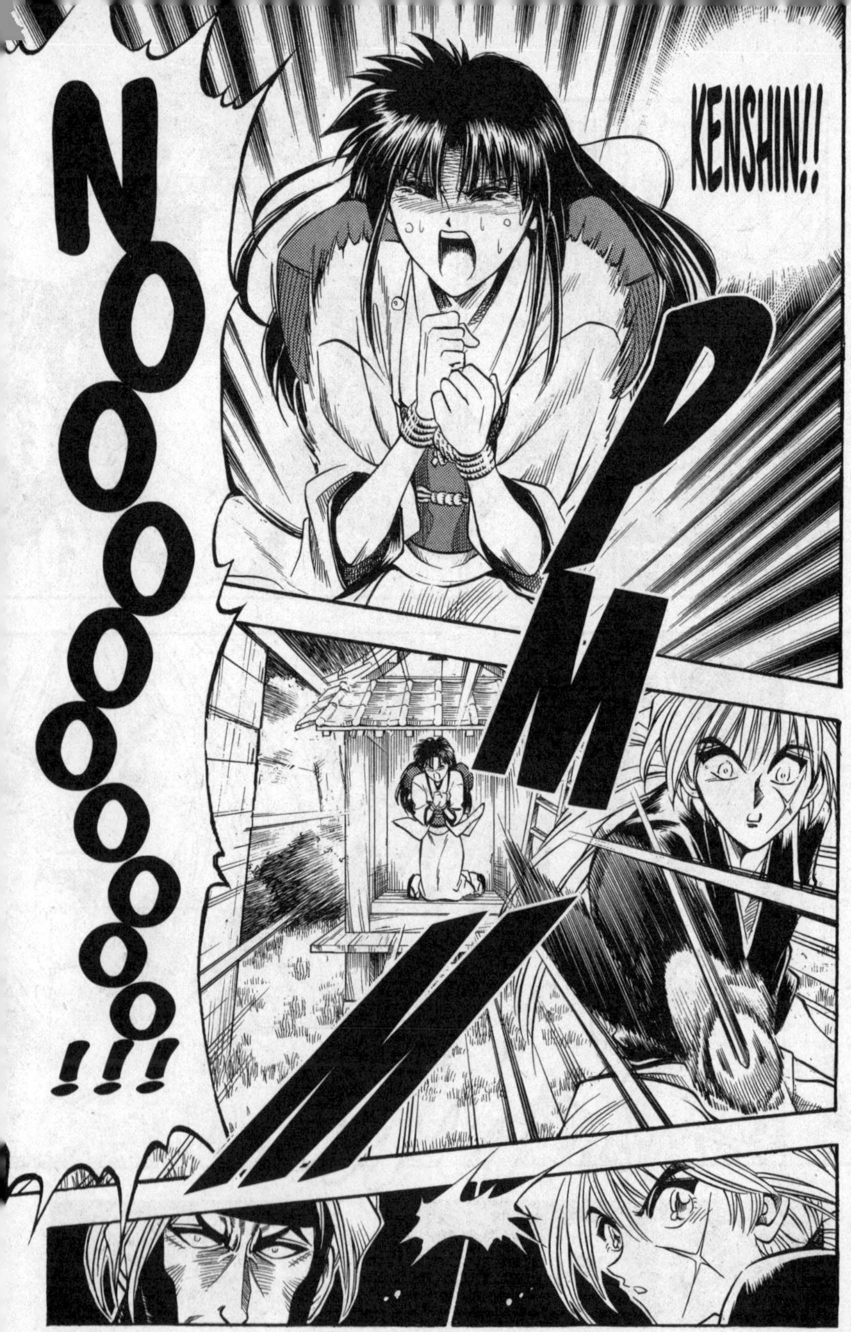
KENSHIN!!
NOOOOOOOOOO!!!
DOM

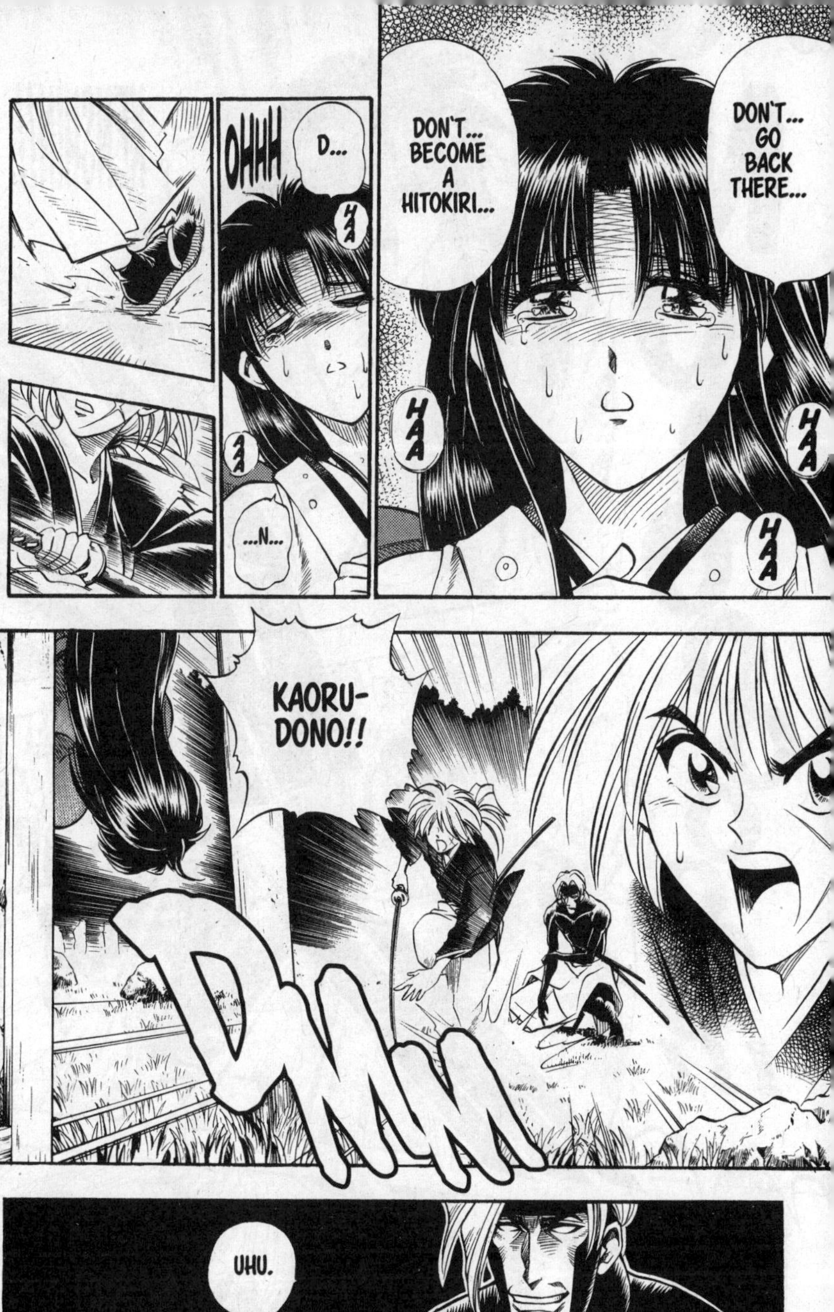
DON'T... GO BACK THERE...
DON'T... BECOME A HITOKIRI...
HAA
HAA
HAA
HAA
OHHH
D...
HAA
...N...
KAORU-DONO!!
DMM
UHU.

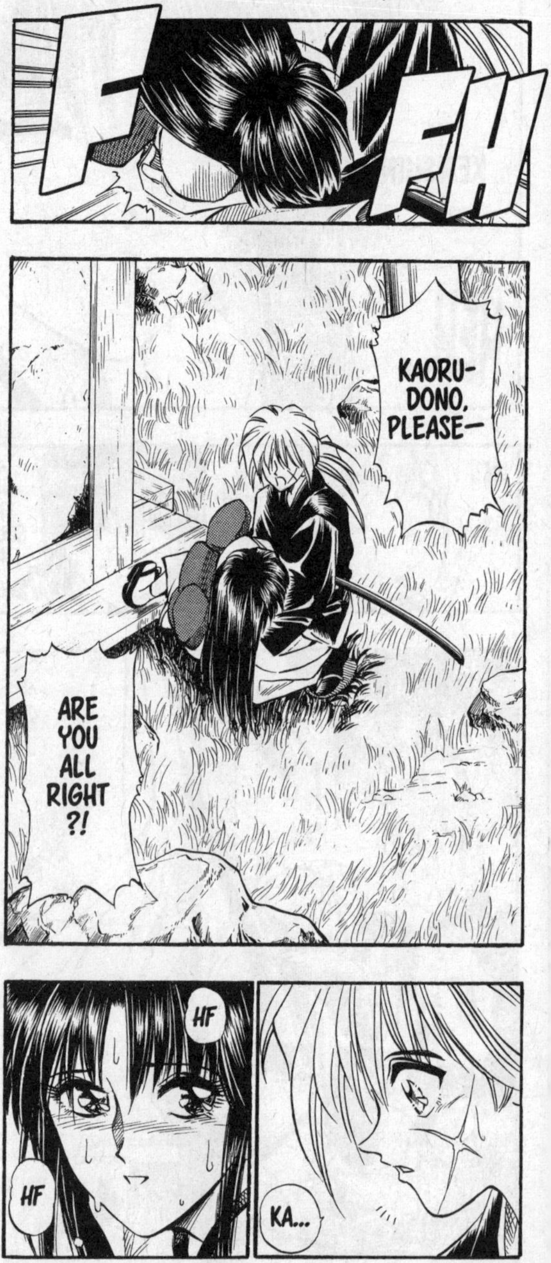
F-
EH
KAORU-DONO, PLEASE—
ARE YOU ALL RIGHT?!
KA...
HF
HF

Okay! So! The "CD book" version of *Rurouni Kenshin*...! The recording script looks great and I'm really excited. I just wish I weren't so busy with work so I could sit in on the recording...But... is this real? Is *Rurouni Kenshin* REALLY real?

I think I may be dreaming....We'll find out, I guess. Hoping you're enjoying this as much as I am (I'm a little scared, myself...).

Watsuki

和月伸宏

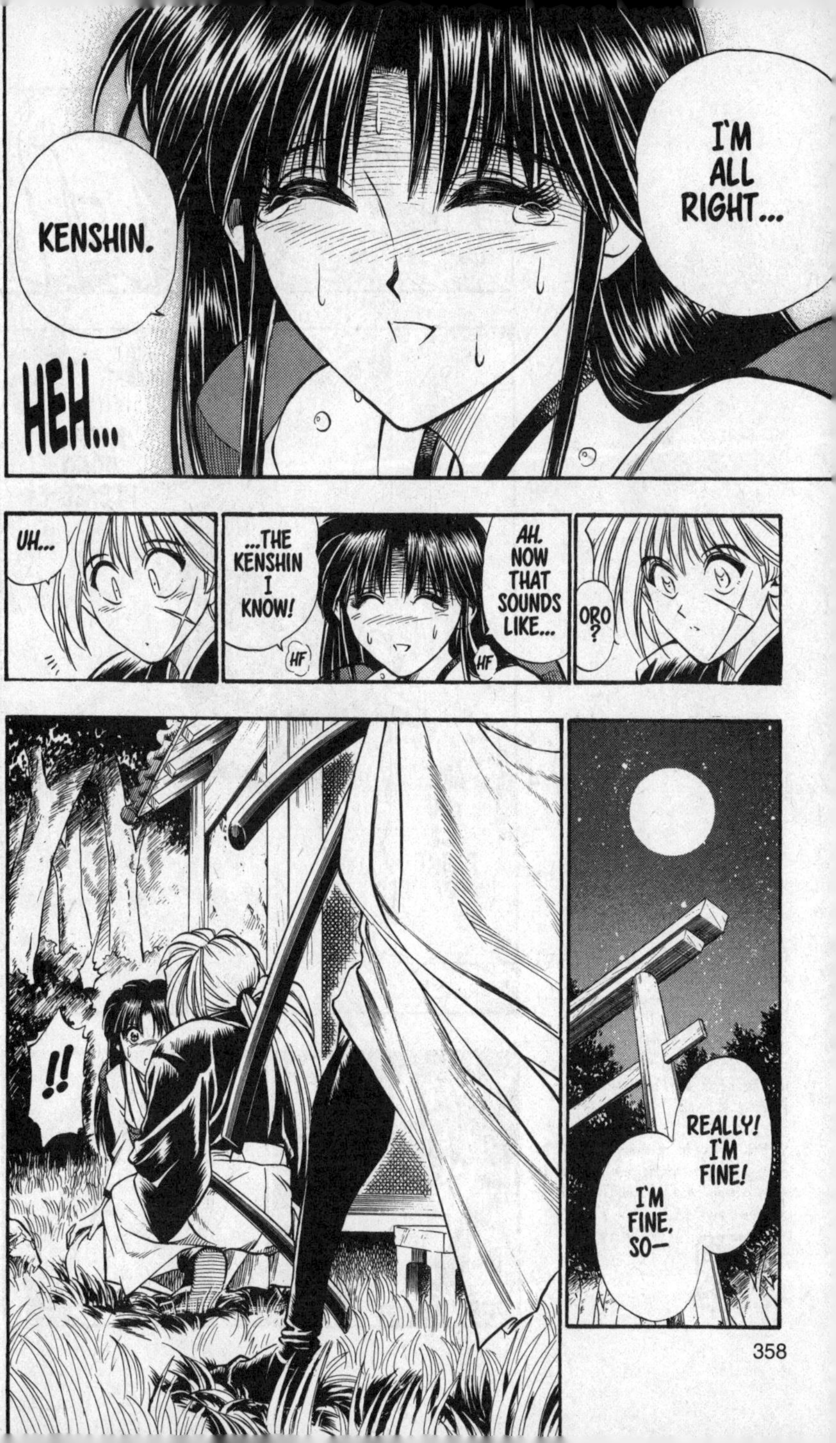
I'M ALL RIGHT...
KENSHIN.
HEH...
ORO?
AH. NOW THAT SOUNDS LIKE...
HF
...THE KENSHIN I KNOW!
HF
UH...
REALLY! I'M FINE!
I'M FINE, SO—
!!

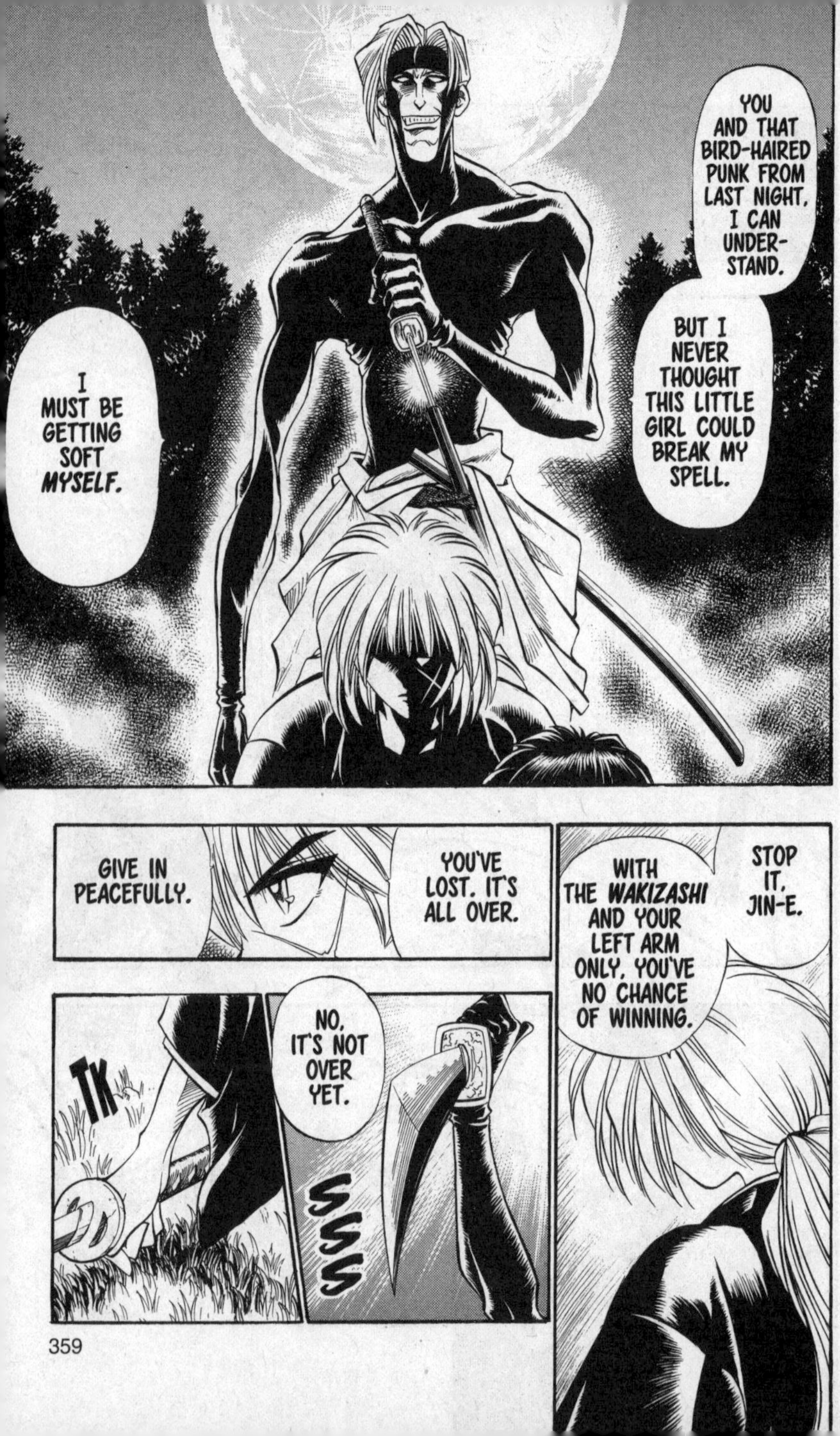
YOU AND THAT BIRD-HAIRED PUNK FROM LAST NIGHT, I CAN UNDER-STAND.
BUT I NEVER THOUGHT THIS LITTLE GIRL COULD BREAK MY SPELL.
I MUST BE GETTING SOFT *MYSELF.*
STOP IT, JIN-E.
WITH THE *WAKIZASHI* AND YOUR LEFT ARM ONLY, YOU'VE NO CHANCE OF WINNING.
YOU'VE LOST. IT'S ALL OVER.
GIVE IN PEACEFULLY.
NO, IT'S NOT OVER YET.
SSS
TK

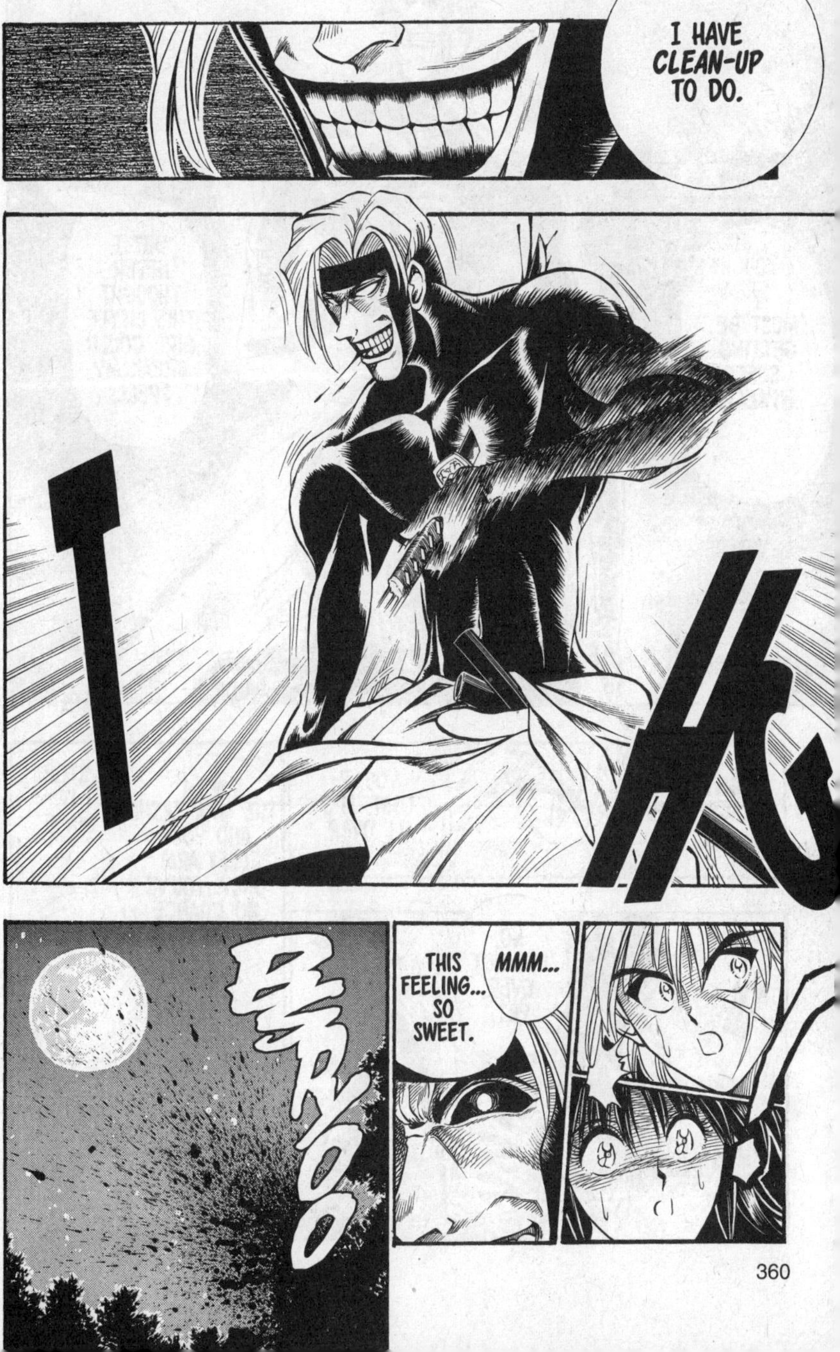

I HAVE CLEAN-UP TO DO.
THG
MMM...
THIS FEELING... SO SWEET.

READ THIS WAY

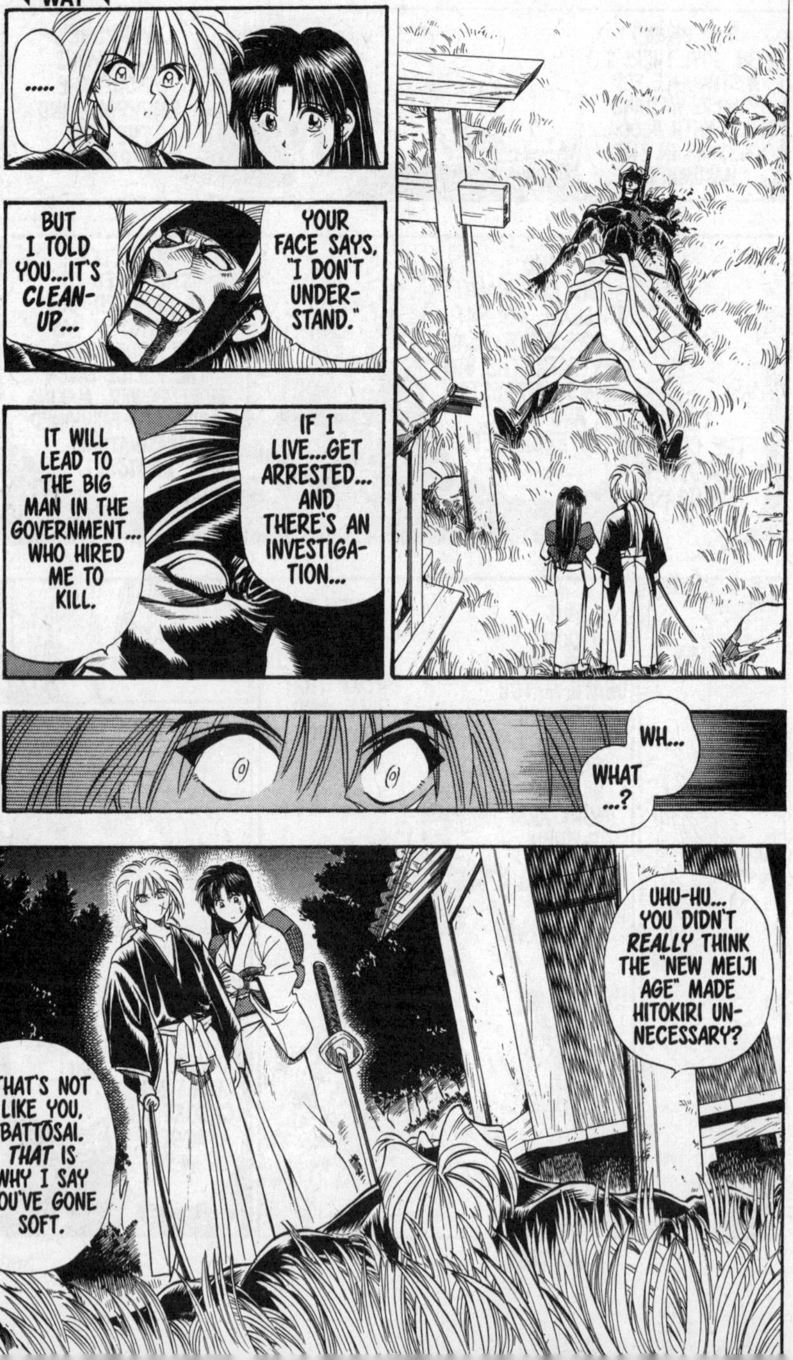
.....
YOUR FACE SAYS, "I DON'T UNDER-STAND."
BUT I TOLD YOU...IT'S *CLEAN-UP*...
IF I LIVE...GET ARRESTED... AND THERE'S AN INVESTIGA-TION...
IT WILL LEAD TO THE BIG MAN IN THE GOVERNMENT... WHO HIRED ME TO KILL.
WH...
WHAT ...?
UHU-HU... YOU DIDN'T *REALLY* THINK THE "NEW MEIJI AGE" MADE HITOKIRI UN-NECESSARY?
THAT'S NOT LIKE YOU, BATTOSAI. *THAT* IS WHY I SAY YOU'VE GONE SOFT.

READ THIS WAY

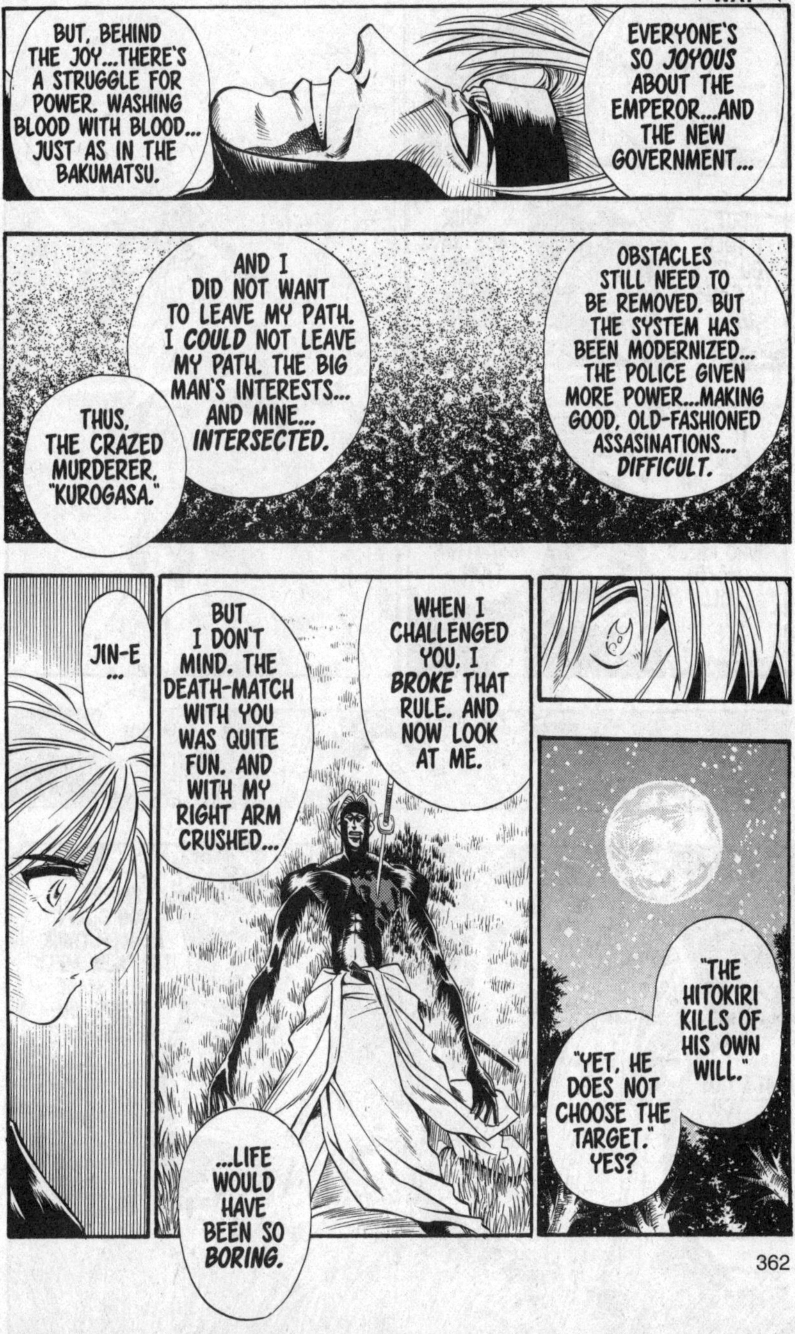
EVERYONE'S SO JOYOUS ABOUT THE EMPEROR...AND THE NEW GOVERNMENT...
BUT, BEHIND THE JOY...THERE'S A STRUGGLE FOR POWER. WASHING BLOOD WITH BLOOD... JUST AS IN THE BAKUMATSU.
OBSTACLES STILL NEED TO BE REMOVED. BUT THE SYSTEM HAS BEEN MODERNIZED... THE POLICE GIVEN MORE POWER...MAKING GOOD, OLD-FASHIONED ASSASINATIONS... DIFFICULT.
AND I DID NOT WANT TO LEAVE MY PATH. I COULD NOT LEAVE MY PATH. THE BIG MAN'S INTERESTS... AND MINE... INTERSECTED.
THUS, THE CRAZED MURDERER, "KUROGASA."
"THE HITOKIRI KILLS OF HIS OWN WILL."
"YET, HE DOES NOT CHOOSE THE TARGET." YES?
WHEN I CHALLENGED YOU, I BROKE THAT RULE. AND NOW LOOK AT ME.
BUT I DON'T MIND. THE DEATH-MATCH WITH YOU WAS QUITE FUN. AND WITH MY RIGHT ARM CRUSHED...
...LIFE WOULD HAVE BEEN SO BORING.
JIN-E ...

READ THIS WAY

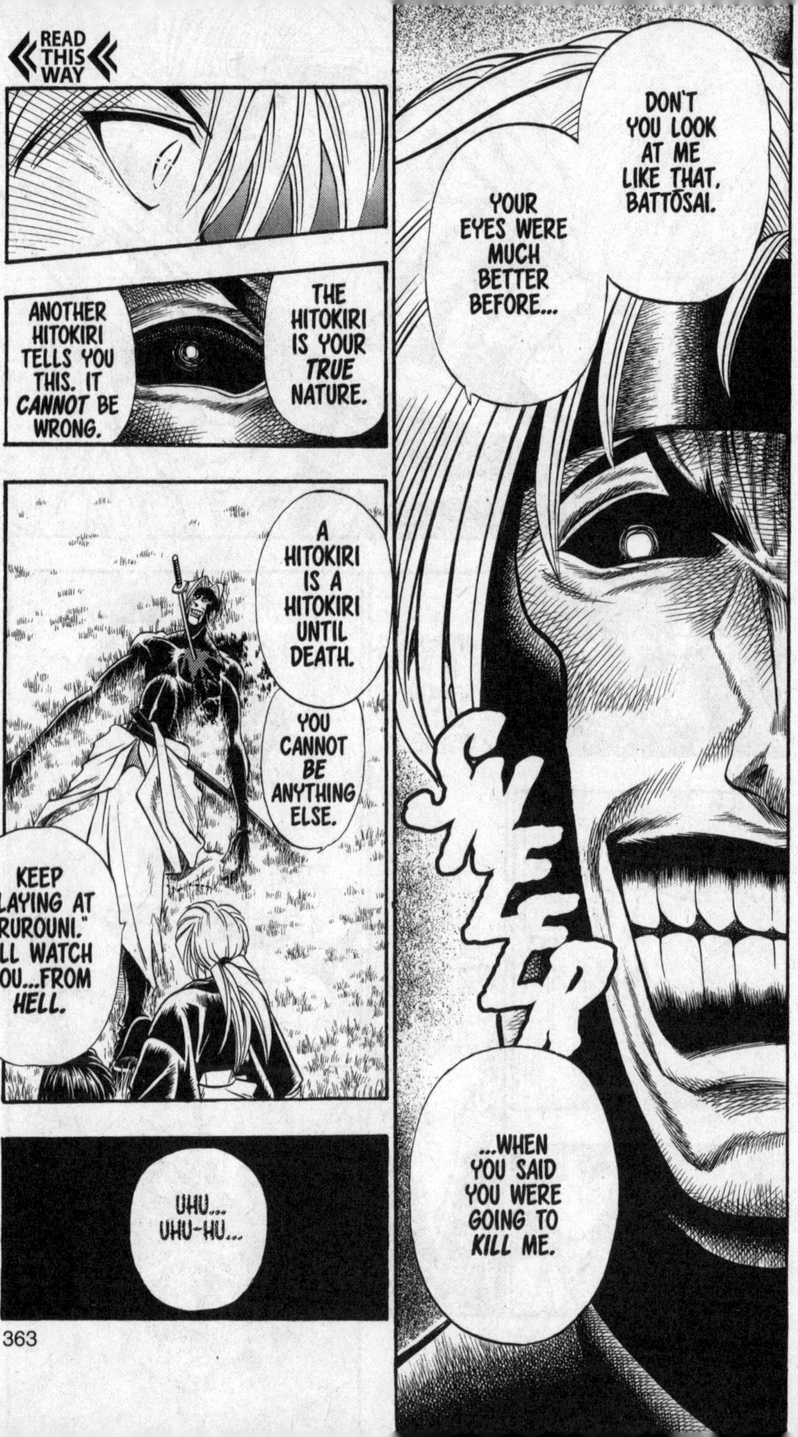

DON'T YOU LOOK AT ME LIKE THAT, BATTŌSAI.
YOUR EYES WERE MUCH BETTER BEFORE...
SNEER
...WHEN YOU SAID YOU WERE GOING TO KILL ME.
THE HITOKIRI IS YOUR TRUE NATURE.
ANOTHER HITOKIRI TELLS YOU THIS. IT CANNOT BE WRONG.
A HITOKIRI IS A HITOKIRI UNTIL DEATH.
YOU CANNOT BE ANYTHING ELSE.
KEEP PLAYING AT "RUROUNI." I'LL WATCH YOU...FROM HELL.
UHU... UHU-HU...

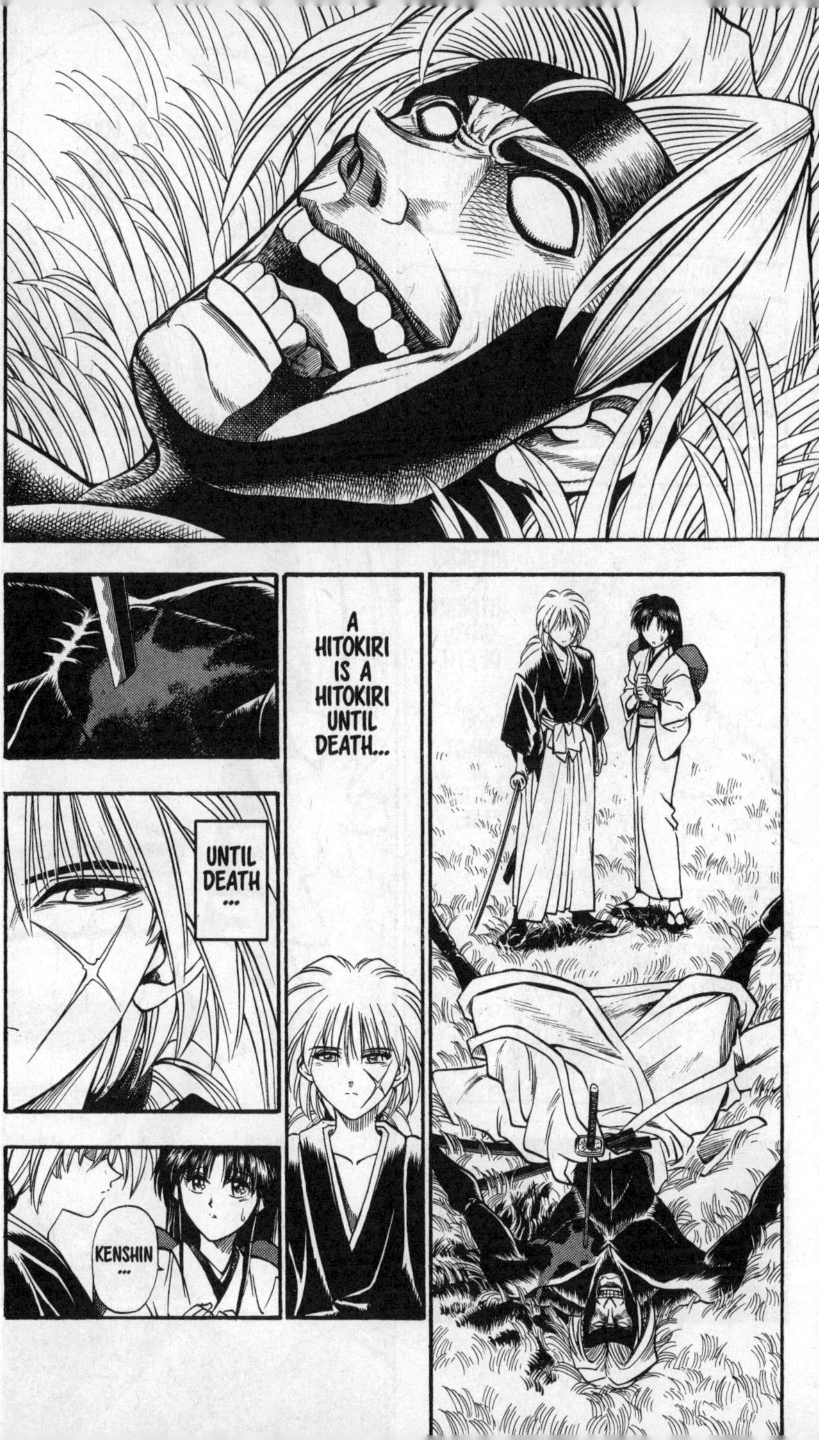
A HITOKIRI IS A HITOKIRI UNTIL DEATH...
UNTIL DEATH...
KENSHIN...

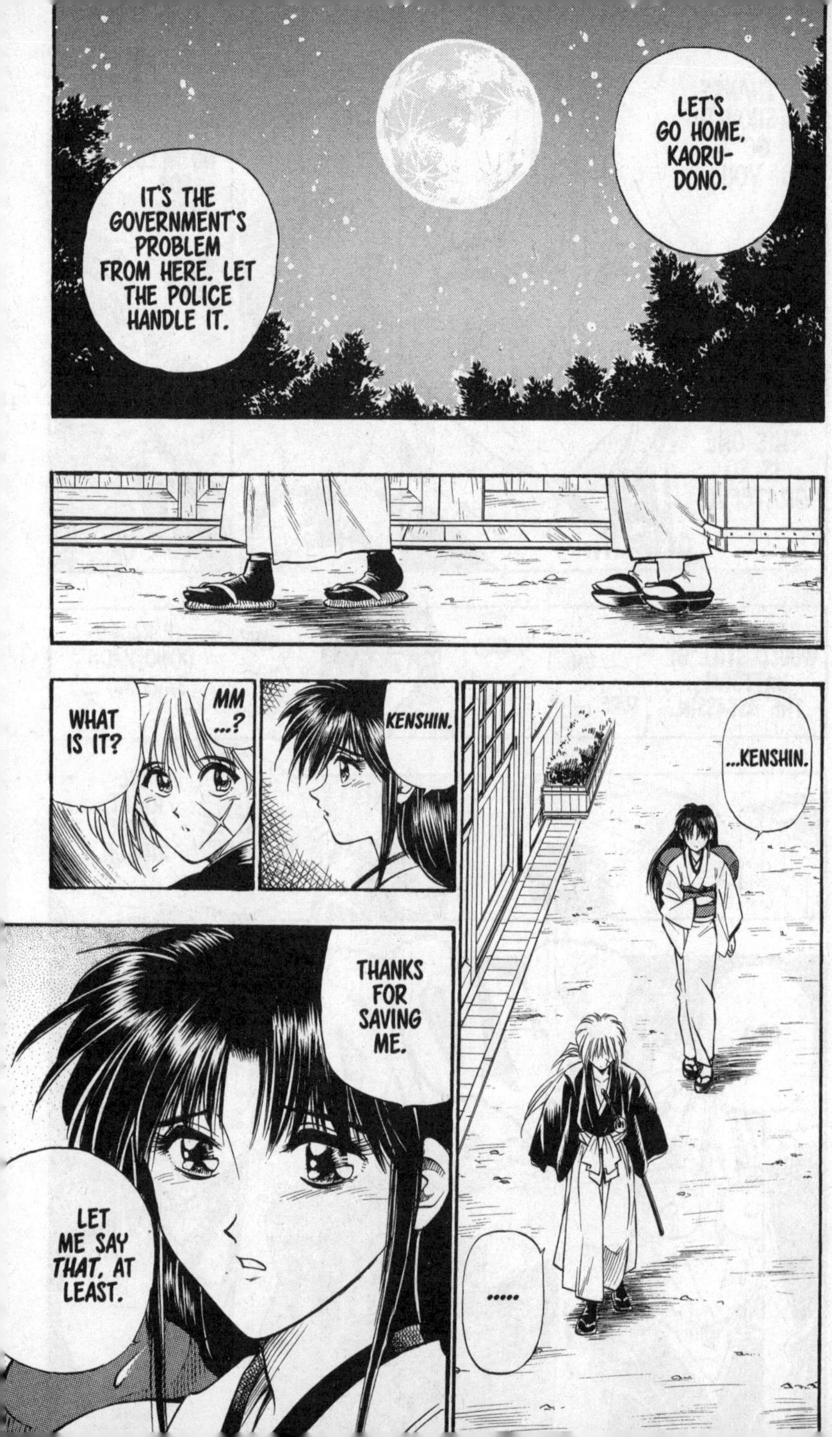
LET'S GO HOME, KAORU-DONO.
IT'S THE GOVERNMENT'S PROBLEM FROM HERE. LET THE POLICE HANDLE IT.
...KENSHIN.
.....
KENSHIN.
MM ...?
WHAT IS IT?
THANKS FOR SAVING ME.
LET ME SAY THAT, AT LEAST.

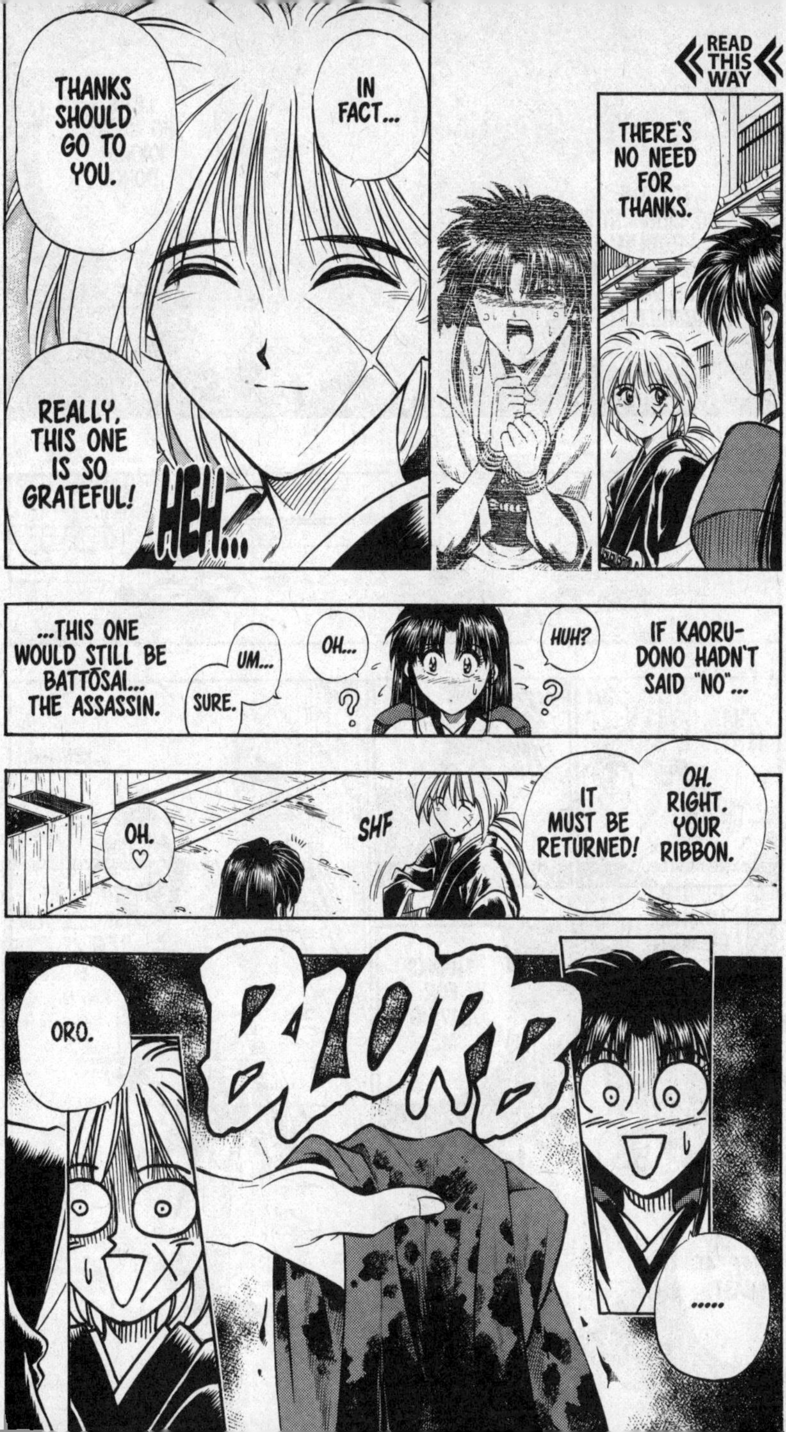
READ THIS WAY
THERE'S NO NEED FOR THANKS.
IN FACT...
THANKS SHOULD GO TO YOU.
REALLY, THIS ONE IS SO GRATEFUL!
HEH...
IF KAORU-DONO HADN'T SAID "NO"...
HUH?
OH...
UM... SURE.
...THIS ONE WOULD STILL BE BATTŌSAI... THE ASSASSIN.
OH. RIGHT. YOUR RIBBON.
IT MUST BE RETURNED!
SHF
OH. ♥
......
BLORB
ORO.

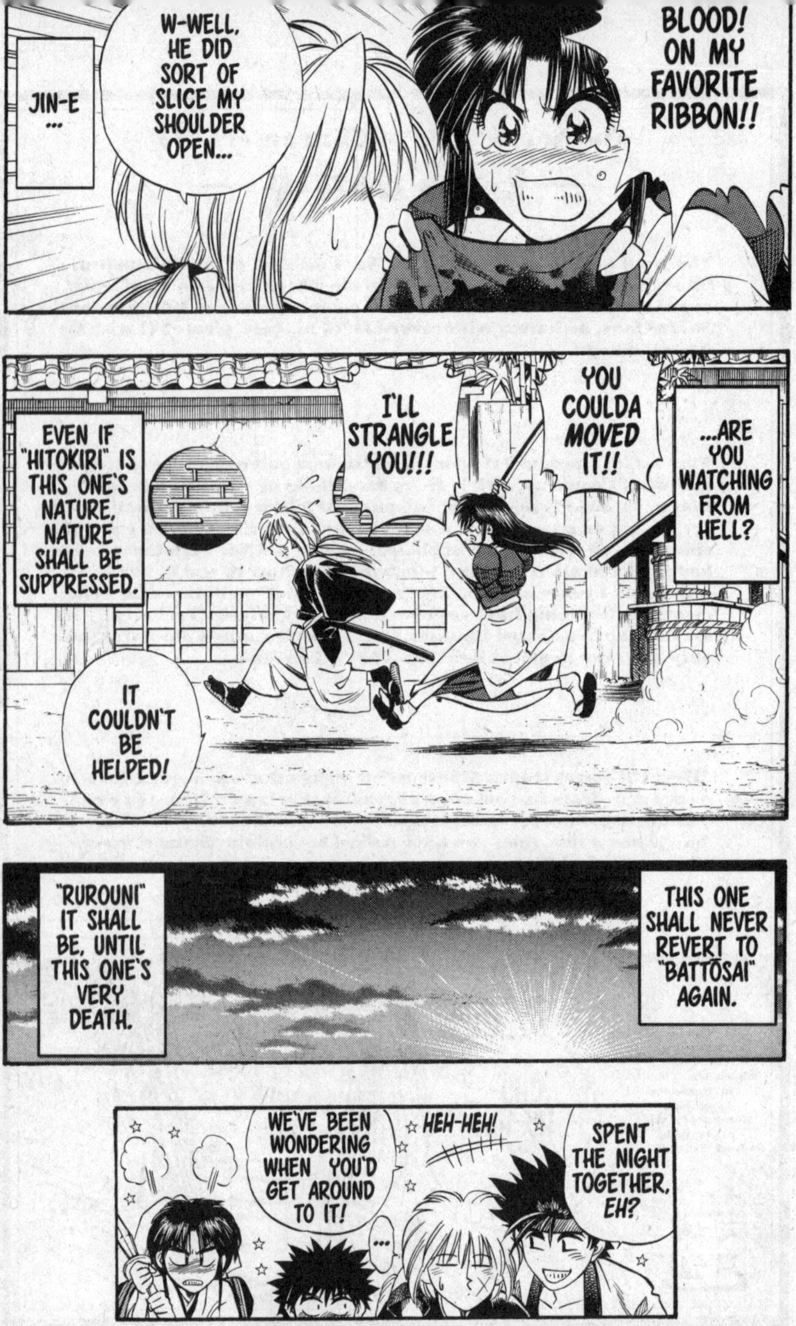
BLOOD! ON MY FAVORITE RIBBON!!
W-WELL, HE DID SORT OF SLICE MY SHOULDER OPEN...
JIN-E ...
...ARE YOU WATCHING FROM HELL?
YOU COULDA MOVED IT!!
I'LL STRANGLE YOU!!!
EVEN IF "HITOKIRI" IS THIS ONE'S NATURE, NATURE SHALL BE SUPPRESSED.
IT COULDN'T BE HELPED!
THIS ONE SHALL NEVER REVERT TO "BATTŌSAI" AGAIN.
"RUROUNI" IT SHALL BE, UNTIL THIS ONE'S VERY DEATH.
SPENT THE NIGHT TOGETHER, EH?
HEH-HEH!
WE'VE BEEN WONDERING WHEN YOU'D GET AROUND TO IT!
...

The Secret Life of Characters (7)

—Udō Jin-e—

The motif for this character is the No. 1 hitokiri of the Bakumatsu, Okada Izō...or so it was *supposed* to have been, but Udō Jin-e looks even less like his real-life, historical counterpart than Kenshin does. So, Izō fans, no letters with razor-blades in them, please? (I wish I were kidding.)

That aside, I designed the character to be a polar opposite of Kenshin, and what I came up with is Jin-e. *Satsujin-ki* or "murderous ogre" that he is, Jin-e is the sort of complicated fellow who's not only crazy-acting, but *crazy*-crazy. It was tough, but both the character and the story proved worth the trouble. Jin-e being the No. 1 fan favorite for bad guys and all, it was also tough deciding how to end it, but ultimately I reasoned that, his "art of hitokiri" not otherwise being complete, he would have to commit a tearful suicide. Technically he may not have defeated Battōsai, but in another sense, Jin-e was the only one ever to defeat Kenshin. *That* is Udō Jin-e.

His outfit comes from a Shinsengumi manga that came out 14, 15 years ago—from its cool main character, Serizawa Kamo (we're talking Hijikata-cool here, kids). If you by chance happen to already have *known* this, then you have passed beyond the realm of mere Shinsengumi otakudom. You, my friend, are a Shinsengumi *master*.

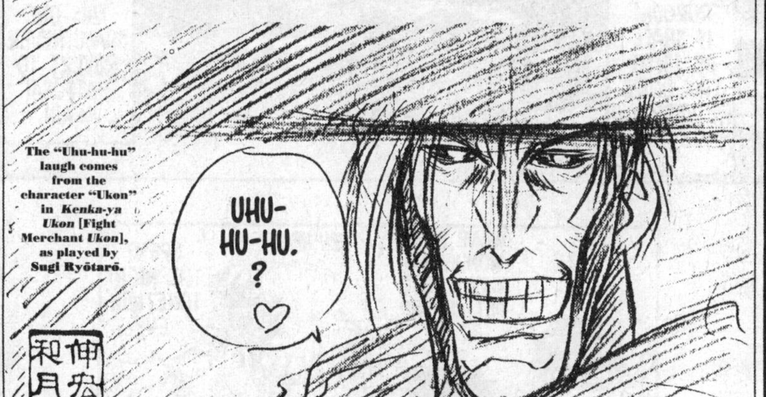
UHU-HU-HU.
?
♡
伸宏
和月

The "Uhu-hu-hu" laugh comes from the character "Ukon" in *Kenka-ya Ukon* [Fight Merchant *Ukon*], as played by Sugi Ryōtarō.

Act 15
Beauty on the Run

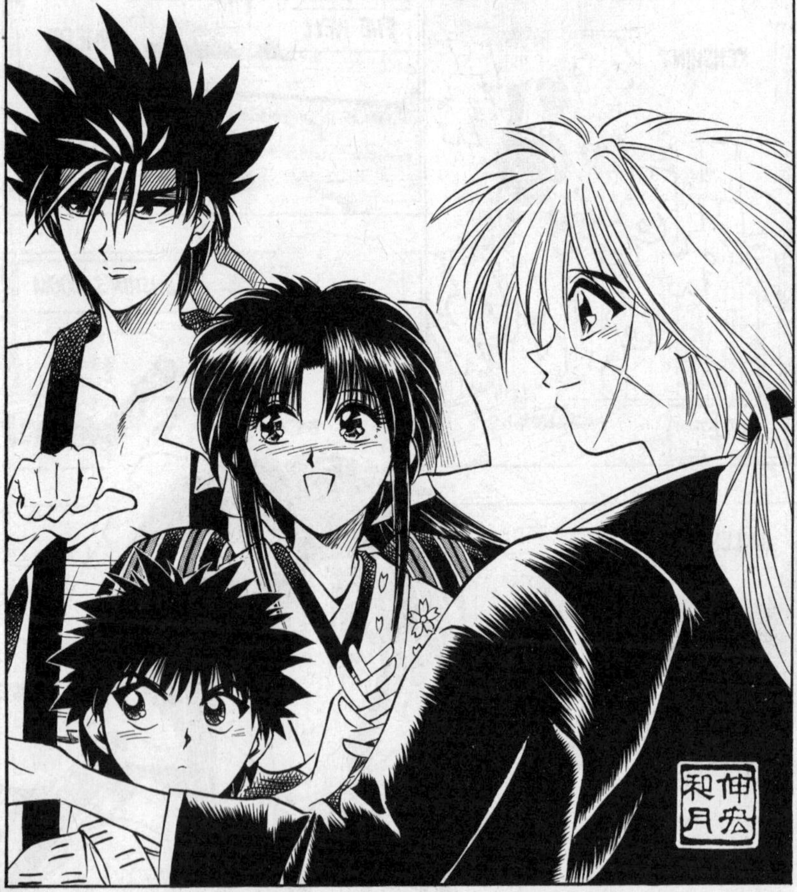
伸宏
和月

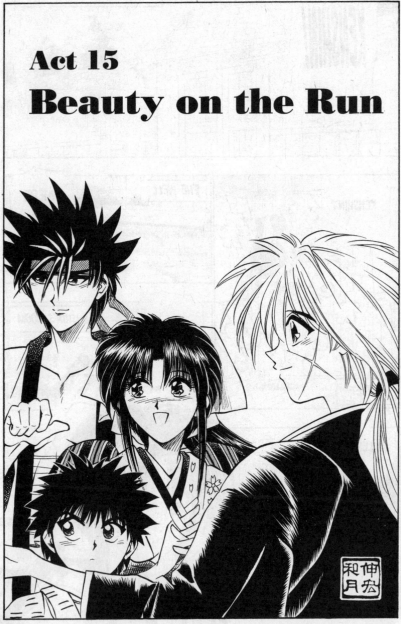

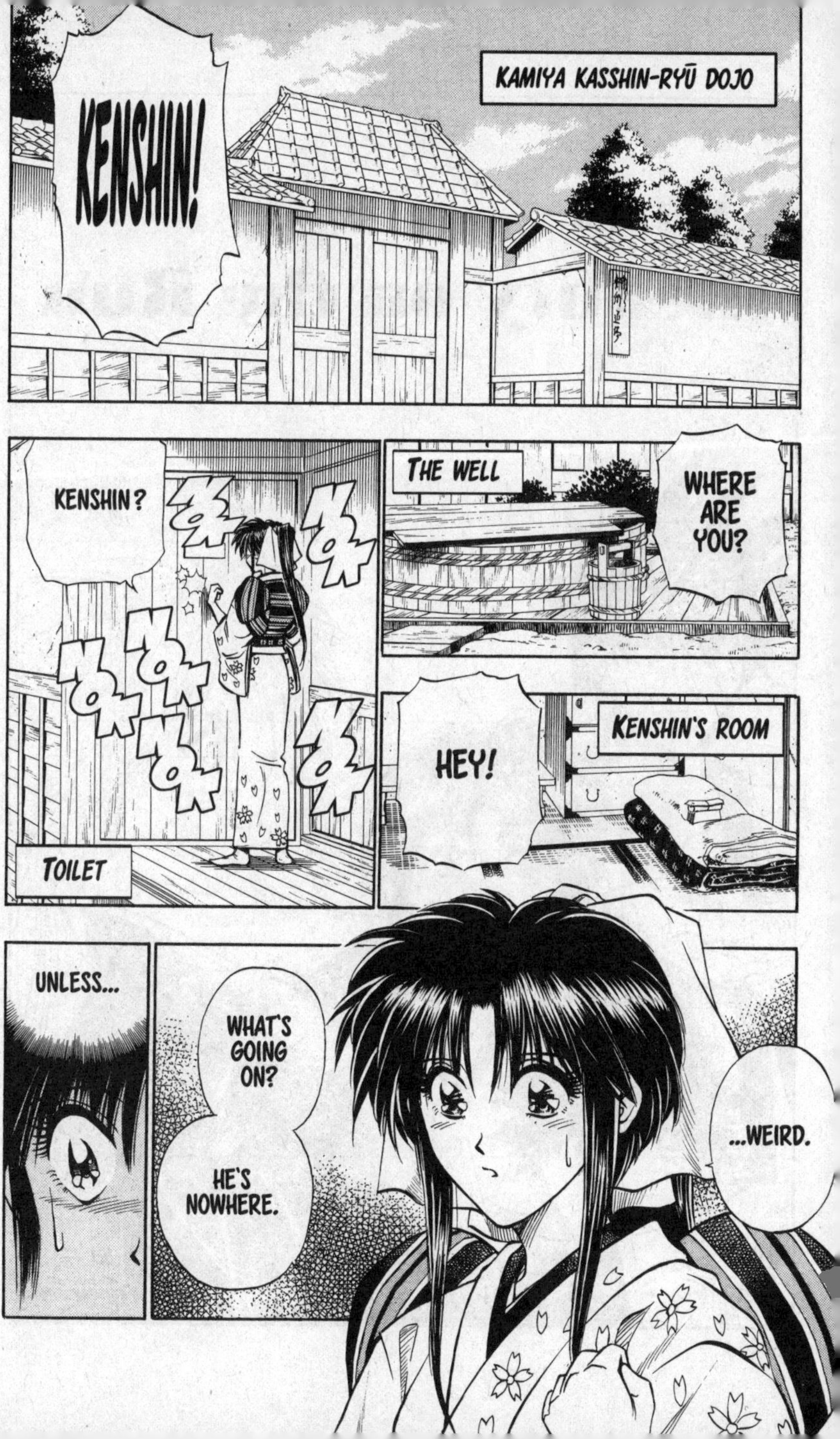
KAMIYA KASSHIN-RYŪ DOJO
KENSHIN!
WHERE ARE YOU?
THE WELL
KENSHIN'S ROOM
HEY!
KENSHIN?
TOILET
...WEIRD.
WHAT'S GOING ON?
HE'S NOWHERE.
UNLESS...

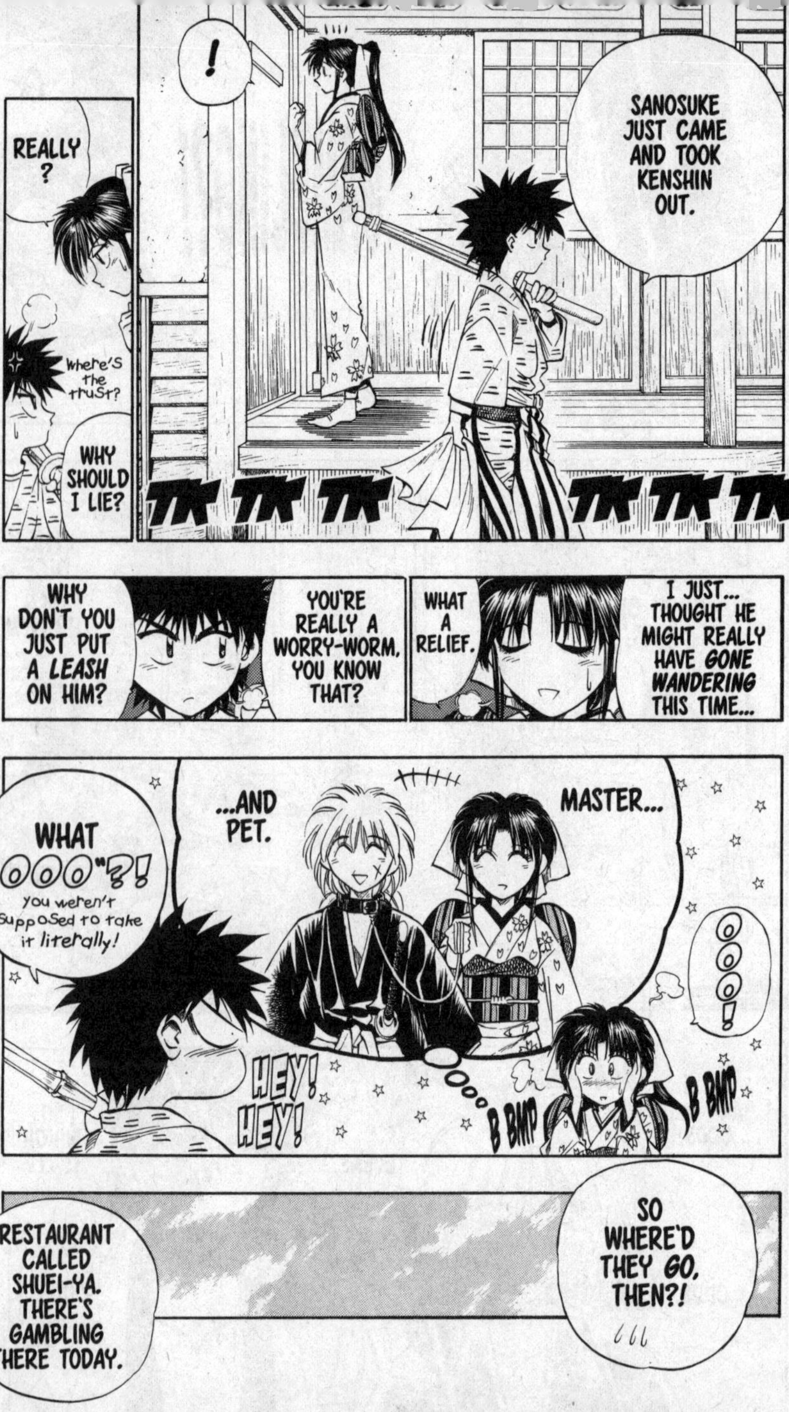
!
SANOSUKE JUST CAME AND TOOK KENSHIN OUT.
TK TK TK TK TK TK
REALLY?
Where's the trust?
WHY SHOULD I LIE?
I JUST... THOUGHT HE MIGHT REALLY HAVE GONE WANDERING THIS TIME...
WHAT A RELIEF.
YOU'RE REALLY A WORRY-WORM, YOU KNOW THAT?
WHY DON'T YOU JUST PUT A LEASH ON HIM?
MASTER...
...AND PET.
ooo!
WHAT "ooo"?! you weren't supposed to take it literally!
HEY! HEY!
B BMP
B BMP
SO WHERE'D THEY GO, THEN?!
RESTAURANT CALLED SHUEI-YA. THERE'S GAMBLING THERE TODAY.

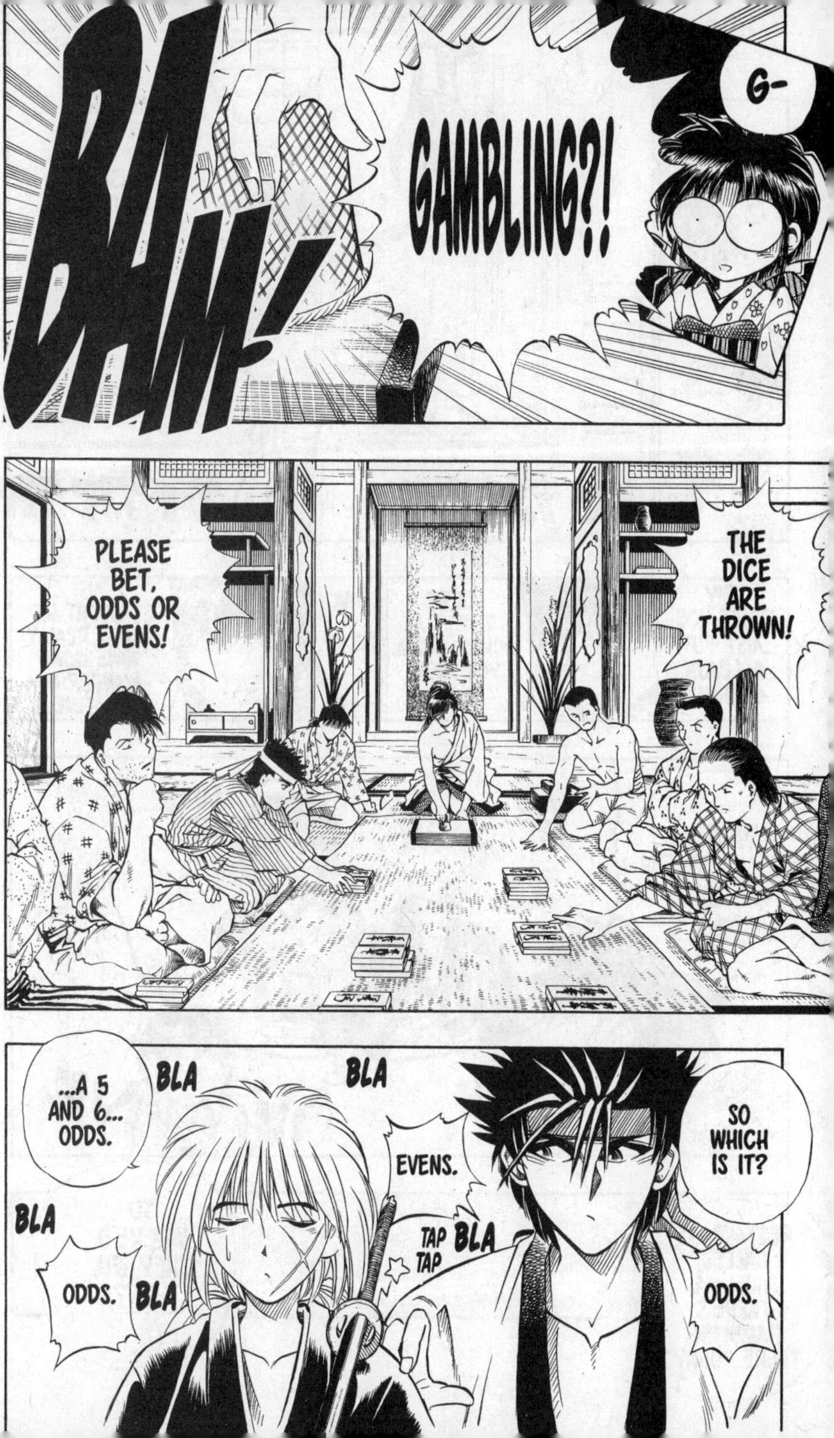
G-
GAMBLING?!
BAM!
THE DICE ARE THROWN!
PLEASE BET, ODDS OR EVENS!
SO WHICH IS IT?
BLA
ODDS.
EVENS.
TAP TAP
BLA
BLA
...A 5 AND 6... ODDS.
BLA
BLA
ODDS.

READ THIS WAY

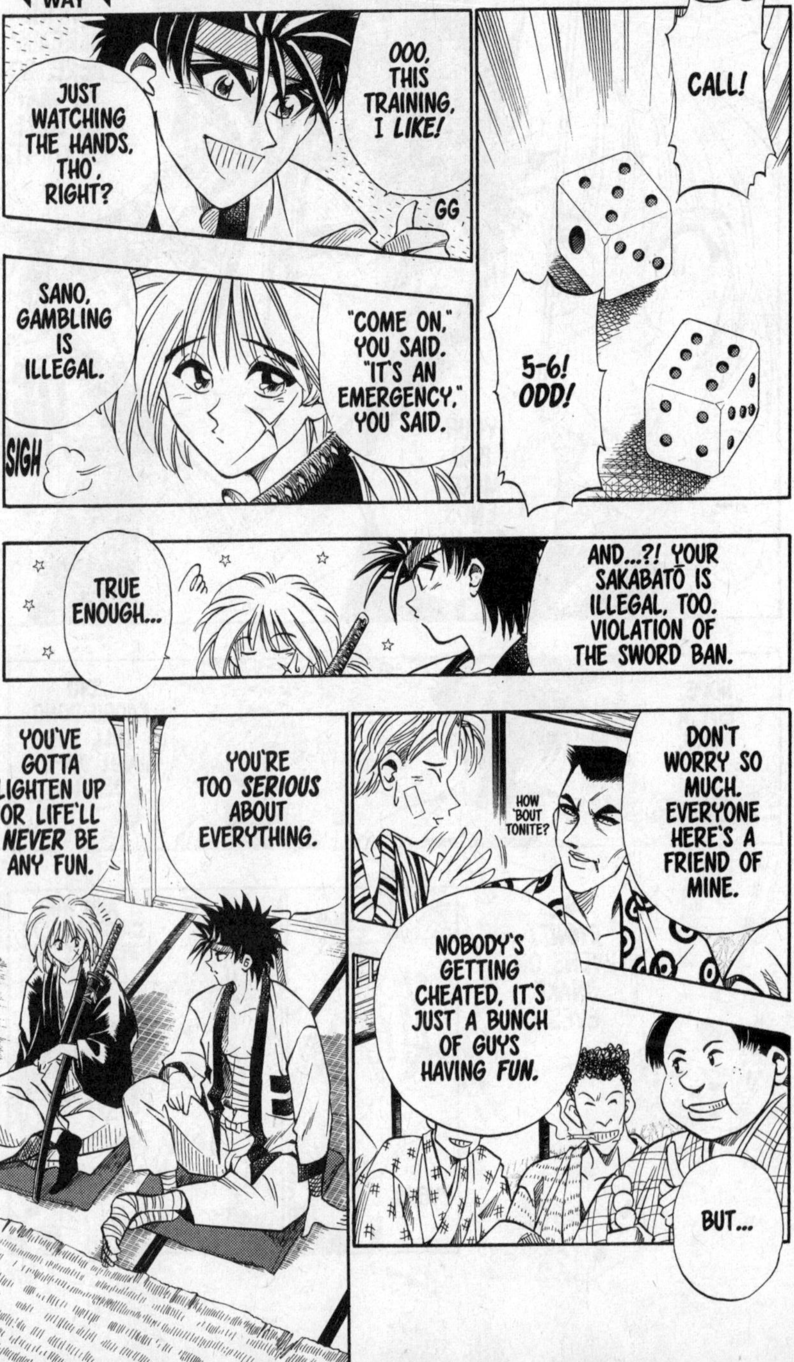

CALL!
5-6! ODD!
OOO, THIS TRAINING, I LIKE!
GG
JUST WATCHING THE HANDS, THO', RIGHT?
"COME ON," YOU SAID. "IT'S AN EMERGENCY," YOU SAID.
SANO, GAMBLING IS ILLEGAL.
SIGH
AND...?! YOUR SAKABATŌ IS ILLEGAL, TOO. VIOLATION OF THE SWORD BAN.
TRUE ENOUGH...
DON'T WORRY SO MUCH. EVERYONE HERE'S A FRIEND OF MINE.
HOW 'BOUT TONITE?
NOBODY'S GETTING CHEATED, IT'S JUST A BUNCH OF GUYS HAVING FUN.
BUT...
YOU'RE TOO SERIOUS ABOUT EVERYTHING.
YOU'VE GOTTA LIGHTEN UP OR LIFE'LL NEVER BE ANY FUN.

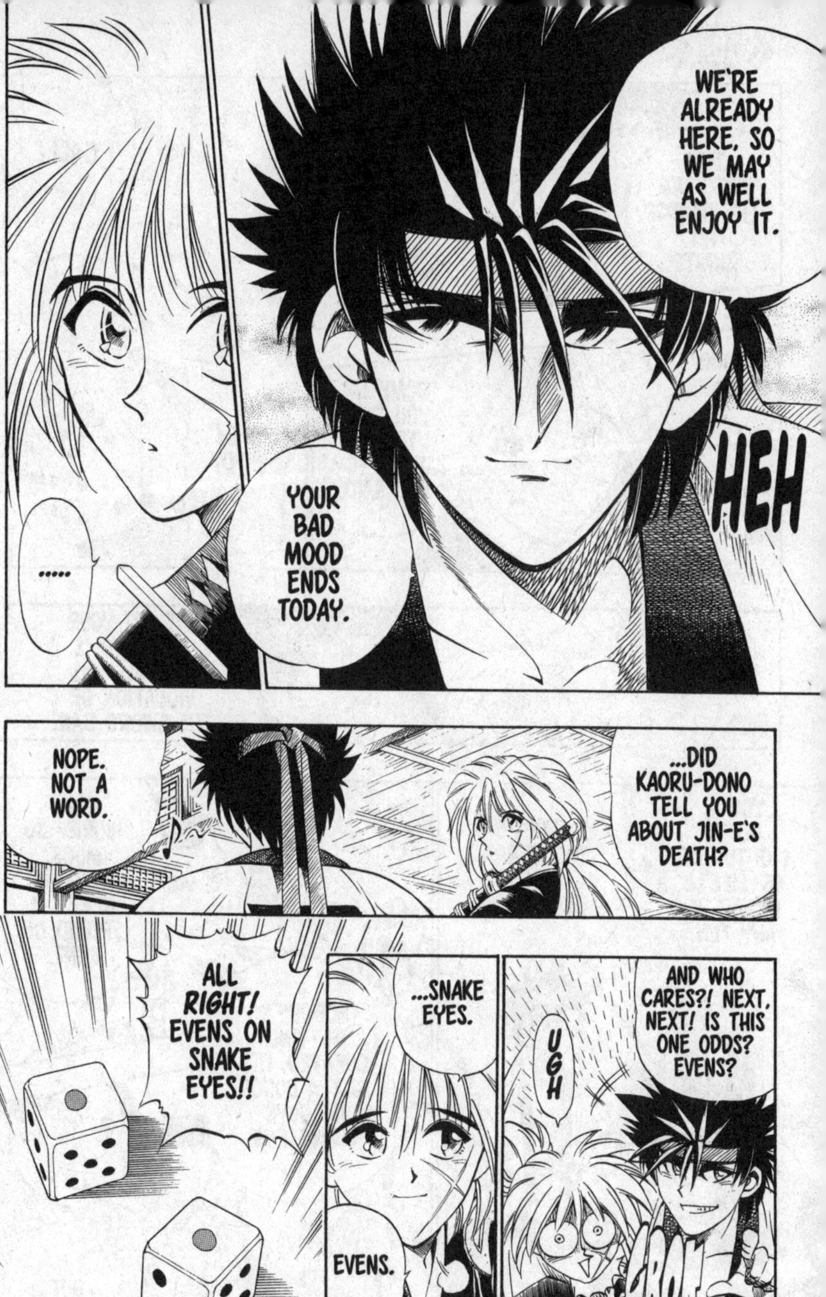
WE'RE ALREADY HERE, SO WE MAY AS WELL ENJOY IT.
HEH
YOUR BAD MOOD ENDS TODAY.
......
...DID KAORU-DONO TELL YOU ABOUT JIN-E'S DEATH?
NOPE. NOT A WORD.
AND WHO CARES?! NEXT, NEXT! IS THIS ONE ODDS? EVENS?
UGH
GROM
...SNAKE EYES.
EVENS.
ALL RIGHT! EVENS ON SNAKE EYES!!

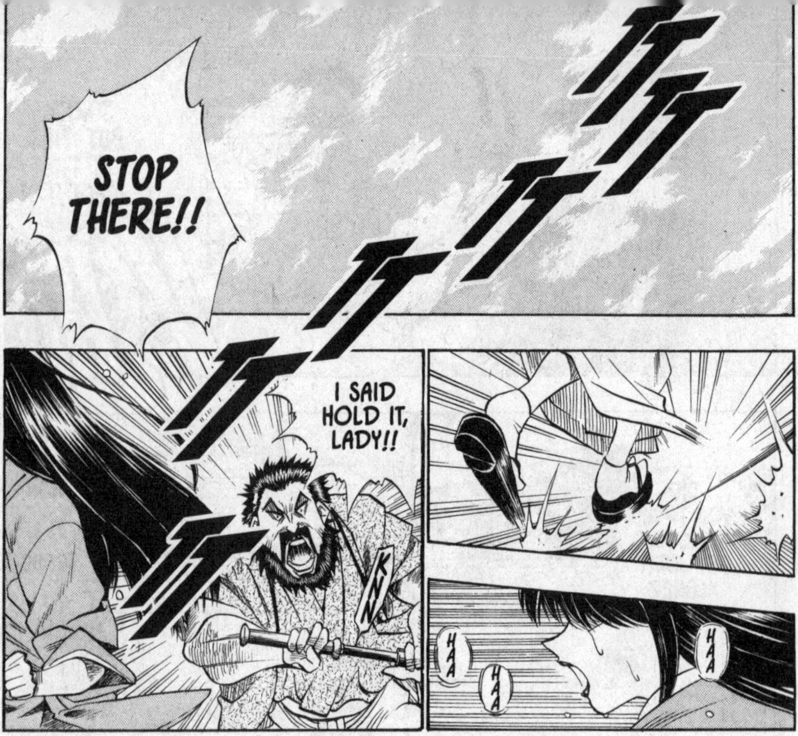
STOP THERE!!
HAA
HAA
HAA
I SAID HOLD IT, LADY!!
KNN

Finally, a note about something OTHER than the CD book. First, thank you for the fan letters which keep coming in. Recently, even though the male-female readership ratio has changed a bit, it's still running around 2:8, with females in the lead. I'm always wanting to pen replies to your letters, but the amount you guys keep SENDING isn't even funny. Worse, work's been piling up and there's no "days off" in sight...not for another couple weeks, anyway. Forgive me!! Sometimes you write, saying you've made dōjinshi "fanzines" and ask if it's okay to send them. Bring 'em on! I've got like 20 of them here already. As it happens, I'm "pro-dōjinshi" myself, so send them on in without fear. For now, then, see you in Volume 3!

Watsuki

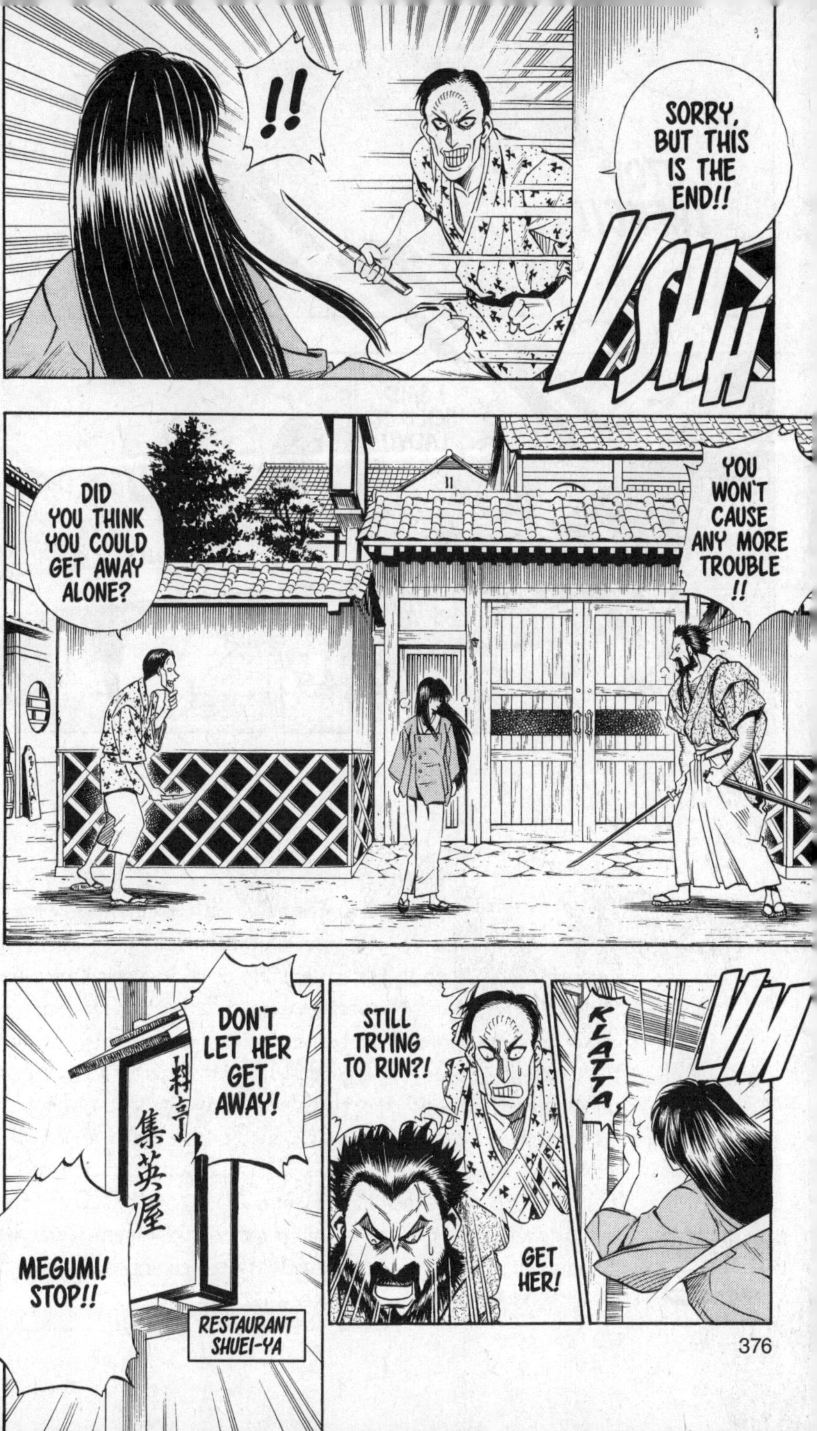
SORRY, BUT THIS IS THE END!!
VSHH
!!
YOU WON'T CAUSE ANY MORE TROUBLE!!
DID YOU THINK YOU COULD GET AWAY ALONE?
VM
KLATTA
STILL TRYING TO RUN?!
GET HER!
DON'T LET HER GET AWAY!
料亭
集英屋
RESTAURANT SHUEI-YA
MEGUMI! STOP!!

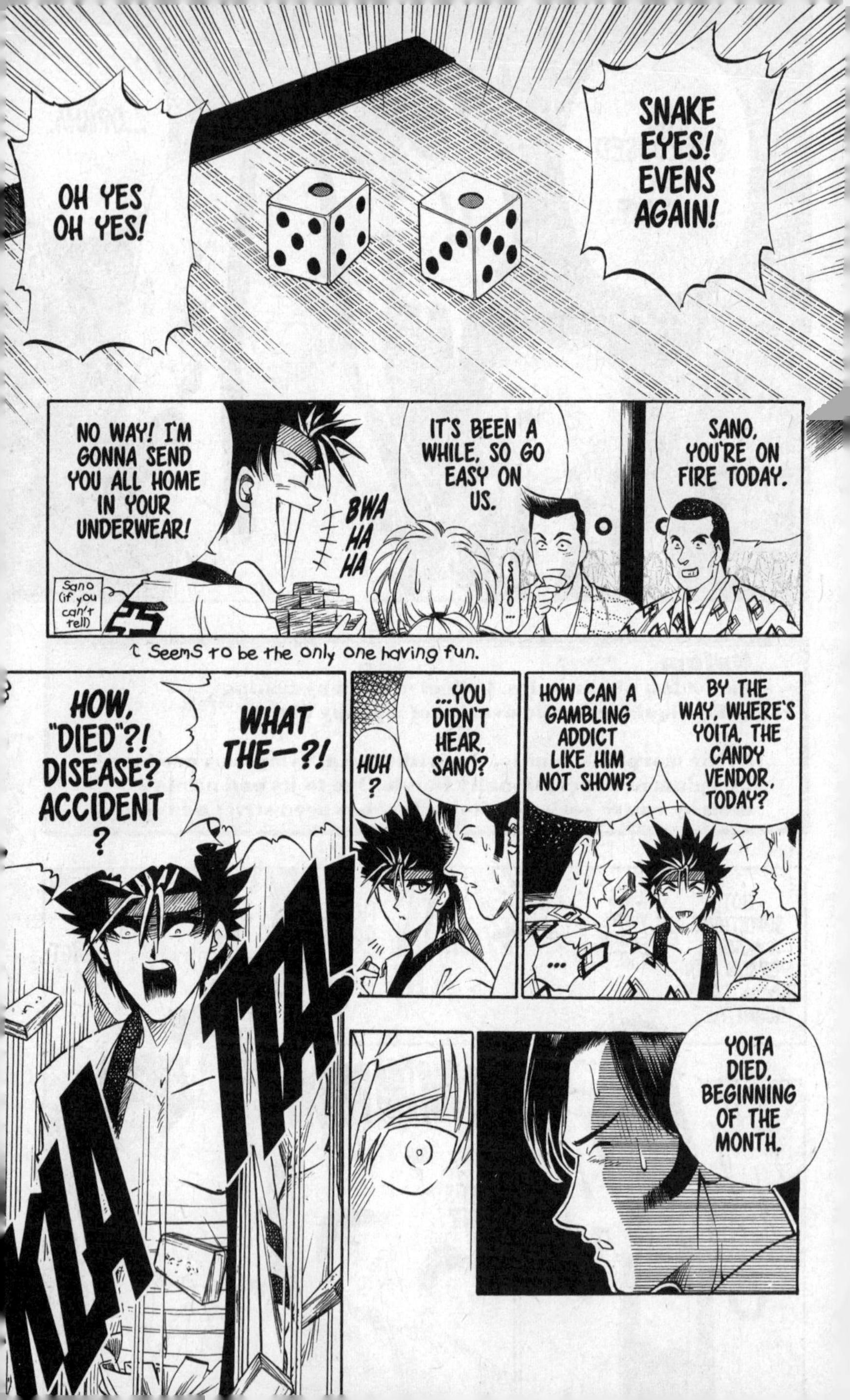
SNAKE EYES! EVENS AGAIN!
OH YES OH YES!
SANO, YOU'RE ON FIRE TODAY.
IT'S BEEN A WHILE, SO GO EASY ON US.
SANO...
BWA HA HA
NO WAY! I'M GONNA SEND YOU ALL HOME IN YOUR UNDERWEAR!
Sano (if you can't tell)
↑ Seems to be the only one having fun.
BY THE WAY, WHERE'S YOITA, THE CANDY VENDOR, TODAY?
HOW CAN A GAMBLING ADDICT LIKE HIM NOT SHOW?
...
...YOU DIDN'T HEAR, SANO?
HUH?
YOITA DIED, BEGINNING OF THE MONTH.
WHAT THE—?!
HOW, "DIED"?! DISEASE? ACCIDENT?
KLA TTA!

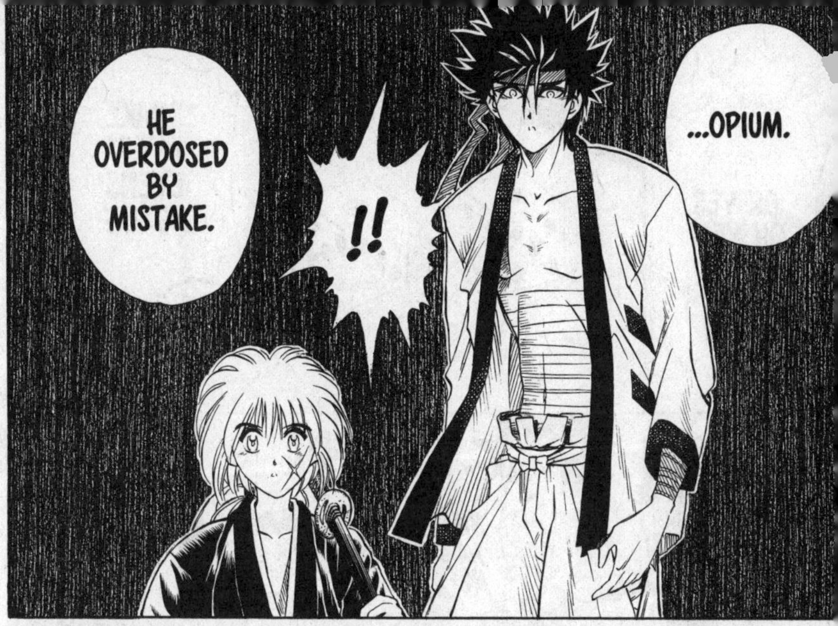
...OPIUM.
!!
HE OVERDOSED BY MISTAKE.

Opium
The oldest of narcotics. Collected by dehydrating milky liquid from the ovaries of a poppy plant.

Of the morphine family, the withdrawal symptoms produced by opium are exceptionally harsh. Due to its potential to destroy entire societies, its outlaw has been strict and total.

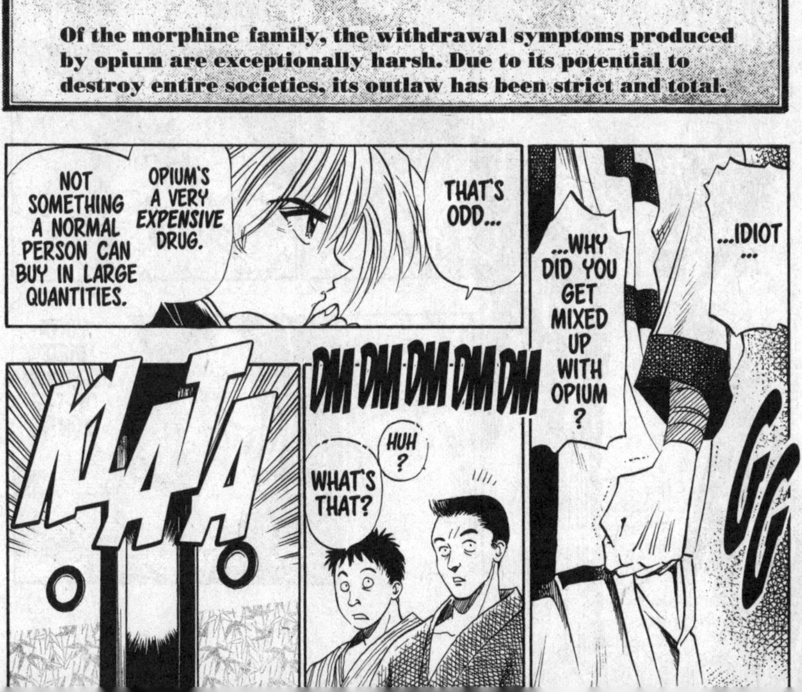
...IDIOT ...
...WHY DID YOU GET MIXED UP WITH OPIUM?
THAT'S ODD...
OPIUM'S A VERY EXPENSIVE DRUG.
NOT SOMETHING A NORMAL PERSON CAN BUY IN LARGE QUANTITIES.
DM DM DM DM DM
HUH ?
WHAT'S THAT?
KATA

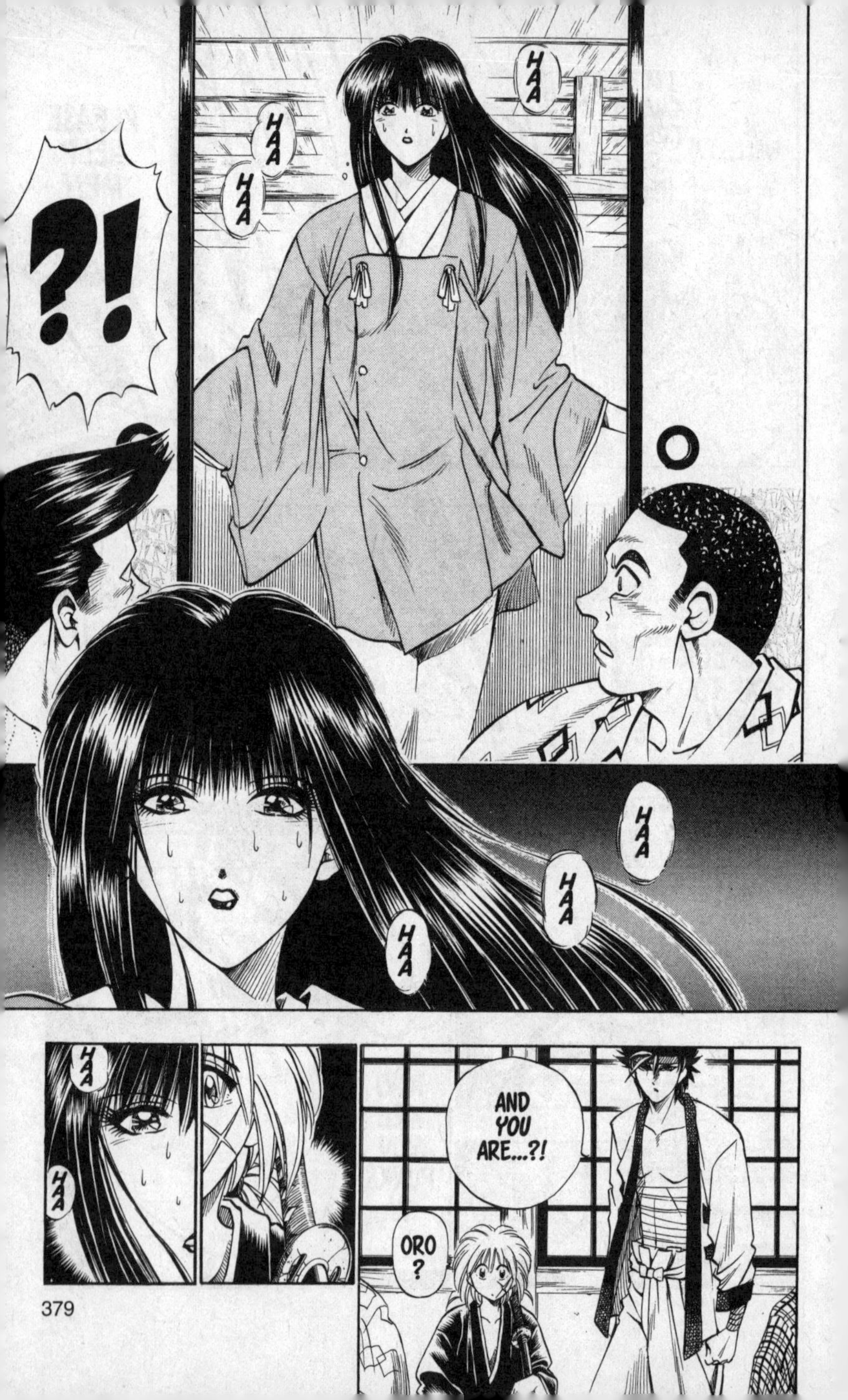
HAA
HAA
HAA
?!
HAA
HAA
HAA
AND YOU ARE...?!
ORO?
HAA
HAA

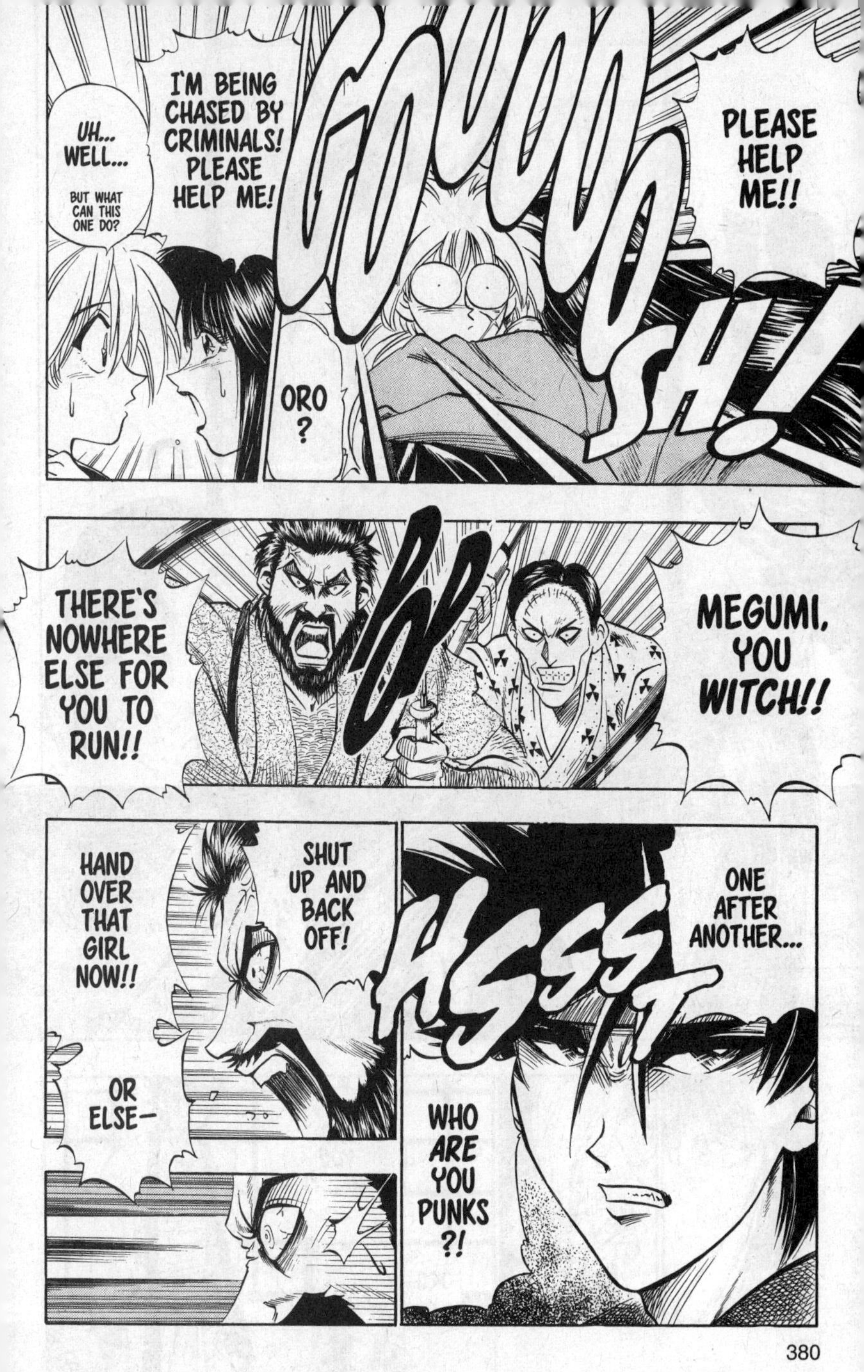
PLEASE HELP ME!!
ORO?
I'M BEING CHASED BY CRIMINALS! PLEASE HELP ME!
UH... WELL...
BUT WHAT CAN THIS ONE DO?
MEGUMI, YOU WITCH!!
THERE'S NOWHERE ELSE FOR YOU TO RUN!!
ONE AFTER ANOTHER...
HSSS
WHO ARE YOU PUNKS?!
SHUT UP AND BACK OFF!
HAND OVER THAT GIRL NOW!!
OR ELSE—

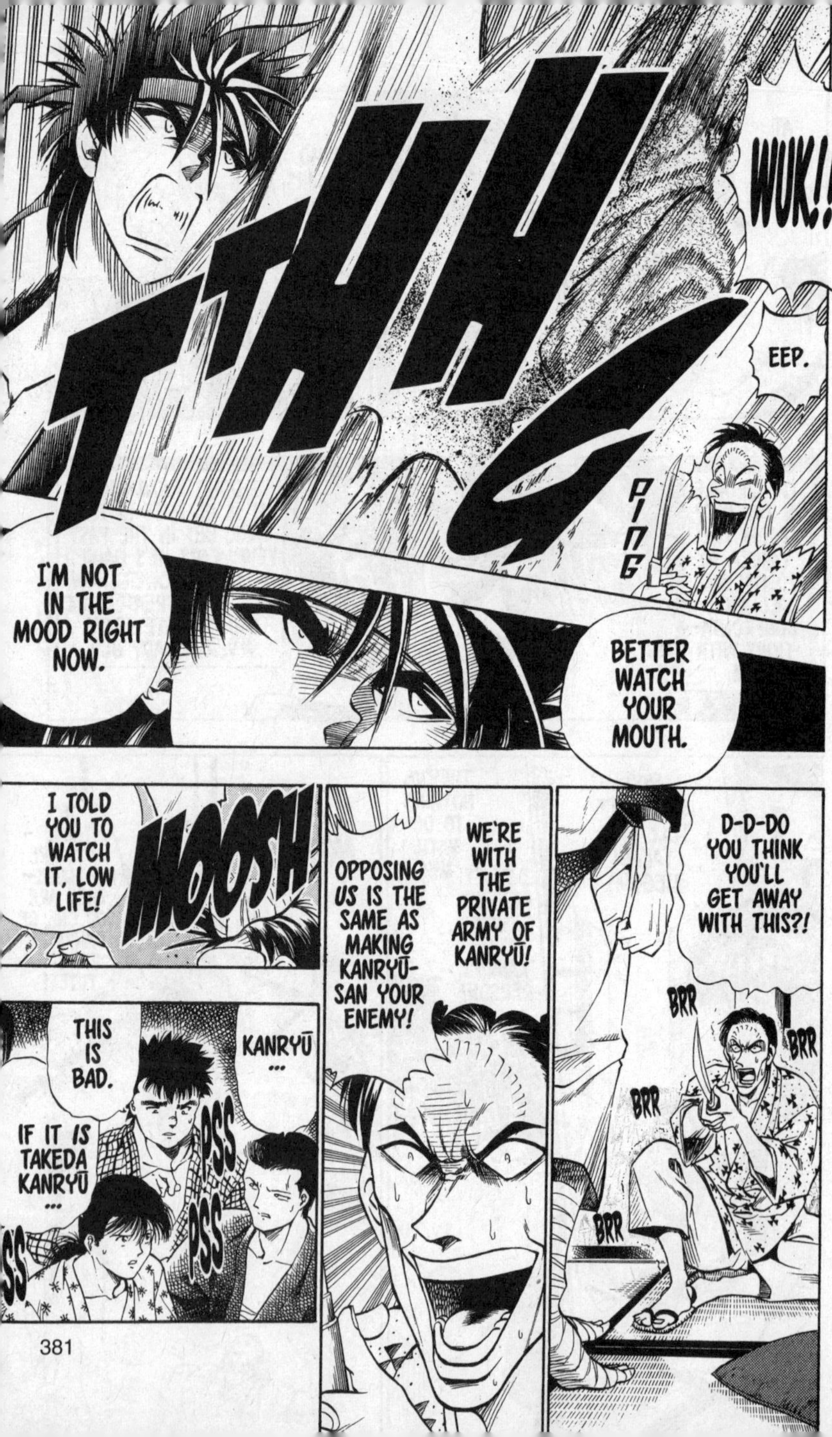
WUK!!
EEP.
PING
BETTER WATCH YOUR MOUTH.
I'M NOT IN THE MOOD RIGHT NOW.
D-D-DO YOU THINK YOU'LL GET AWAY WITH THIS?!
BRR
BRR
BRR
BRR
WE'RE WITH THE PRIVATE ARMY OF KANRYŪ!
OPPOSING US IS THE SAME AS MAKING KANRYŪ-SAN YOUR ENEMY!
I TOLD YOU TO WATCH IT, LOW LIFE!
WHOOSH
KANRYŪ...
THIS IS BAD.
PSS
PSS
IF IT *IS* TAKEDA KANRYŪ...
SS

READ THIS WAY

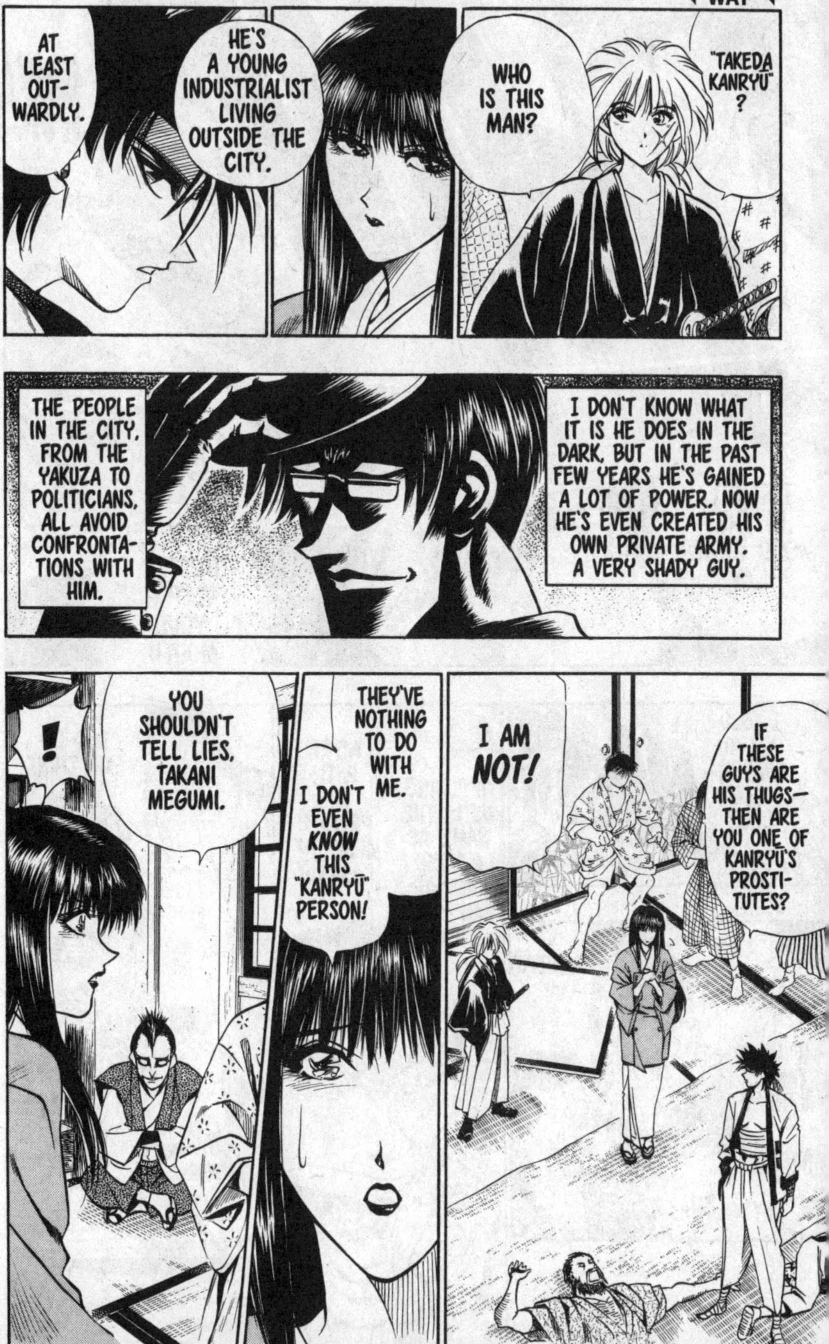
"TAKEDA KANRYŪ"?
WHO IS THIS MAN?
HE'S A YOUNG INDUSTRIALIST LIVING OUTSIDE THE CITY.
AT LEAST OUTWARDLY.
I DON'T KNOW WHAT IT IS HE DOES IN THE DARK, BUT IN THE PAST FEW YEARS HE'S GAINED A LOT OF POWER. NOW HE'S EVEN CREATED HIS OWN PRIVATE ARMY. A VERY SHADY GUY.
THE PEOPLE IN THE CITY, FROM THE YAKUZA TO POLITICIANS, ALL AVOID CONFRONTATIONS WITH HIM.
IF THESE GUYS ARE HIS THUGS—THEN ARE YOU ONE OF KANRYŪ'S PROSTITUTES?
I AM *NOT!*
THEY'VE NOTHING TO DO WITH ME.
I DON'T EVEN *KNOW* THIS "KANRYŪ" PERSON!
YOU SHOULDN'T TELL LIES, TAKANI MEGUMI.
!

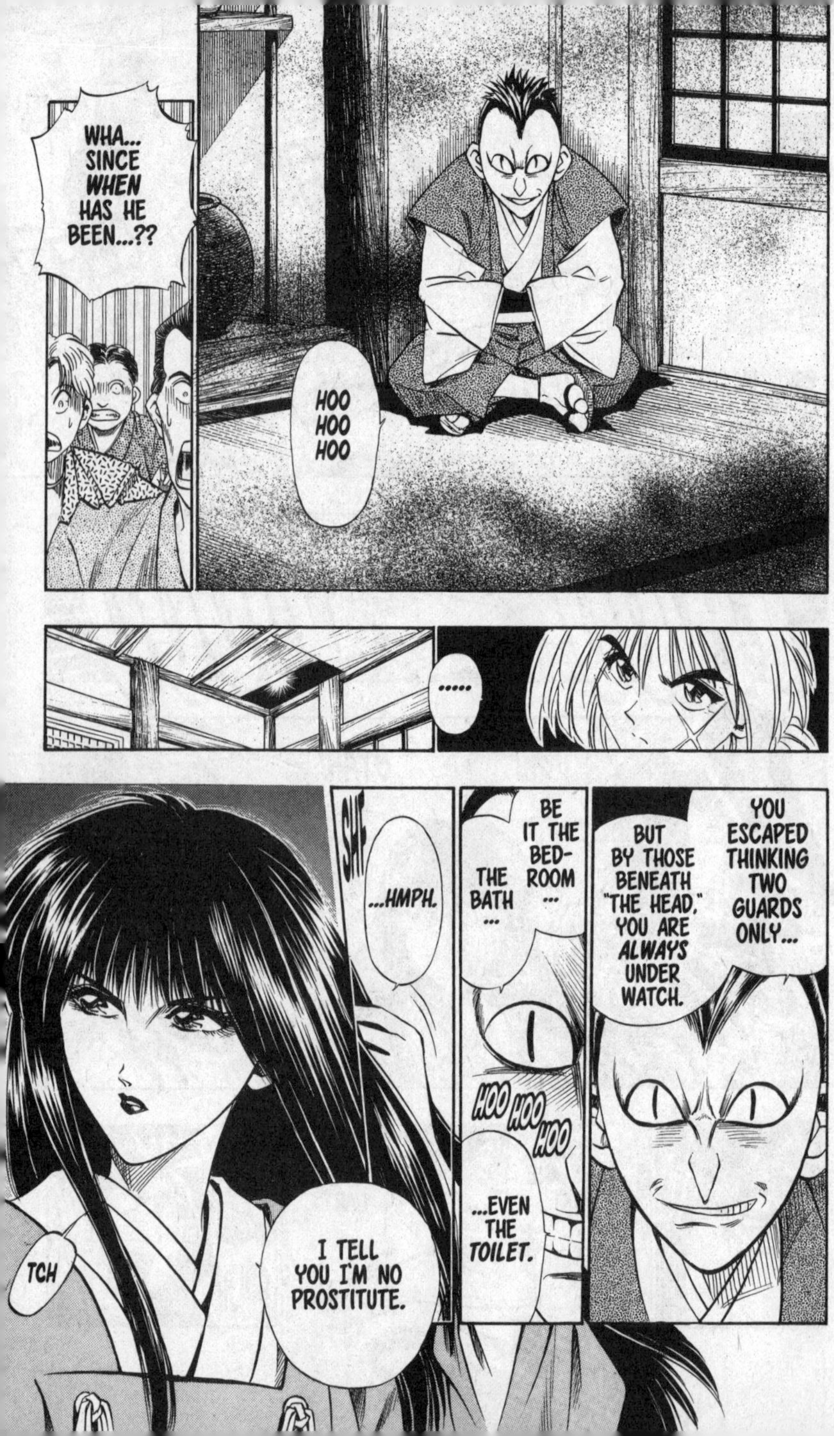
HOO HOO HOO
WHA... SINCE WHEN HAS HE BEEN...??
......
YOU ESCAPED THINKING TWO GUARDS ONLY...
BUT BY THOSE BENEATH "THE HEAD," YOU ARE ALWAYS UNDER WATCH.
BE IT THE BEDROOM...
THE BATH...
HOO HOO HOO
...EVEN THE TOILET.
SHF
...HMPH.
I TELL YOU I'M NO PROSTITUTE.
TCH

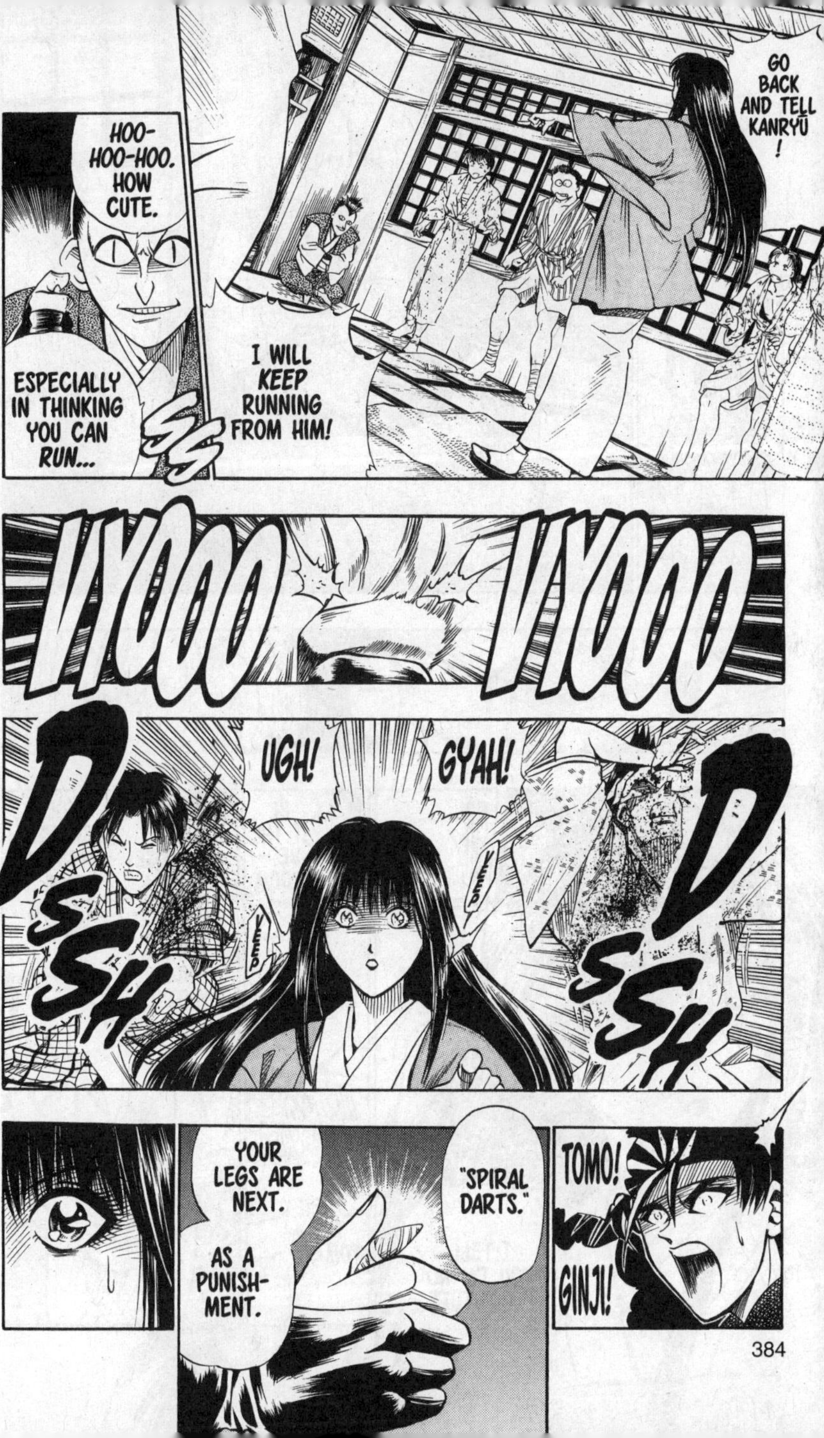
GO BACK AND TELL KANRYŪ!
I WILL KEEP RUNNING FROM HIM!
HOO-HOO-HOO. HOW CUTE.
ESPECIALLY IN THINKING YOU CAN RUN...
SS
VYOOO
VYOOO
DSSH
GYAH!
UGH!
DSSH
TOMO!
GINJI!
"SPIRAL DARTS."
YOUR LEGS ARE NEXT.
AS A PUNISHMENT.

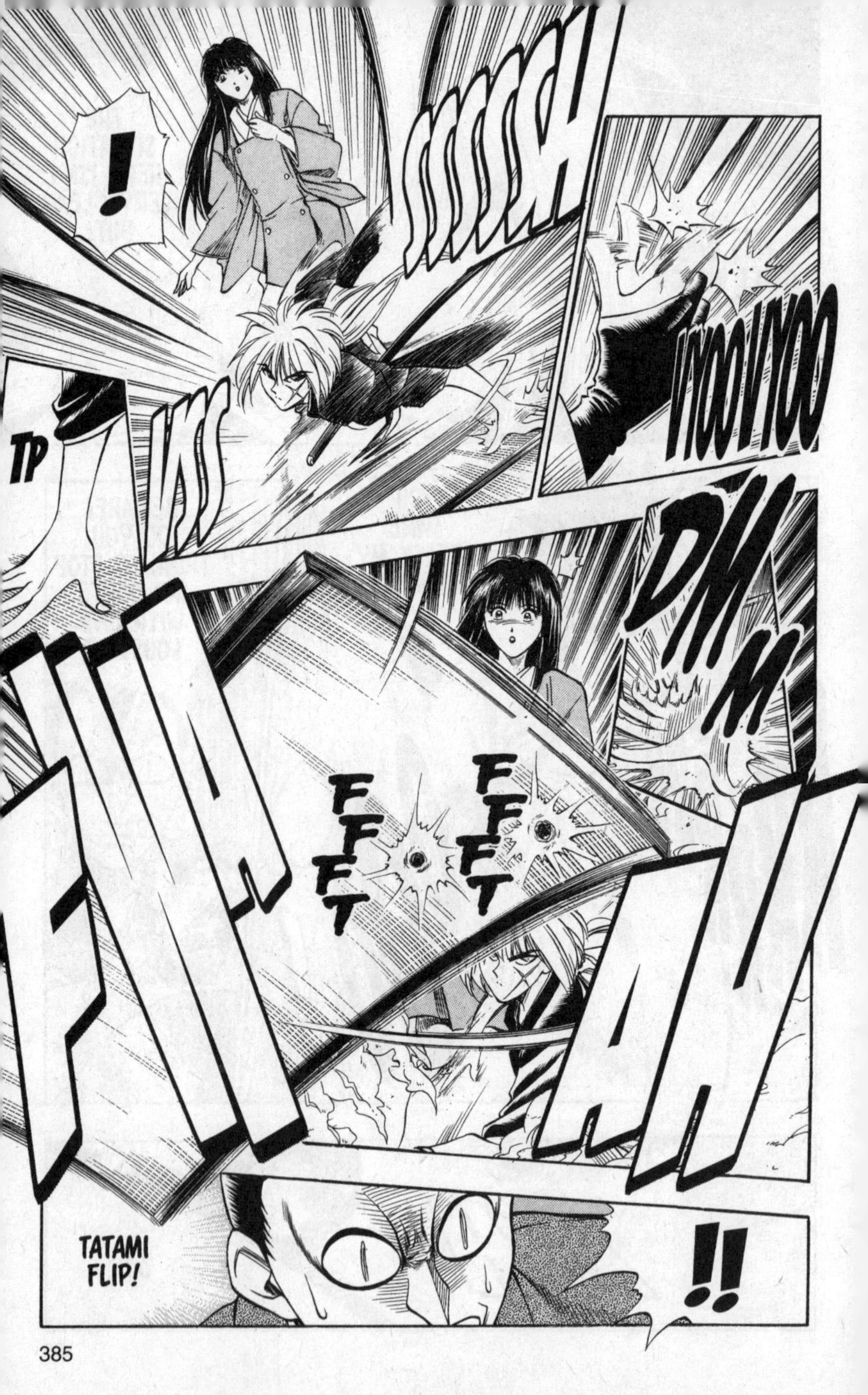
VYOO VYOO
!
SCCCCH
VSS
TP
FFFT
FFFT
!!
TATAMI FLIP!

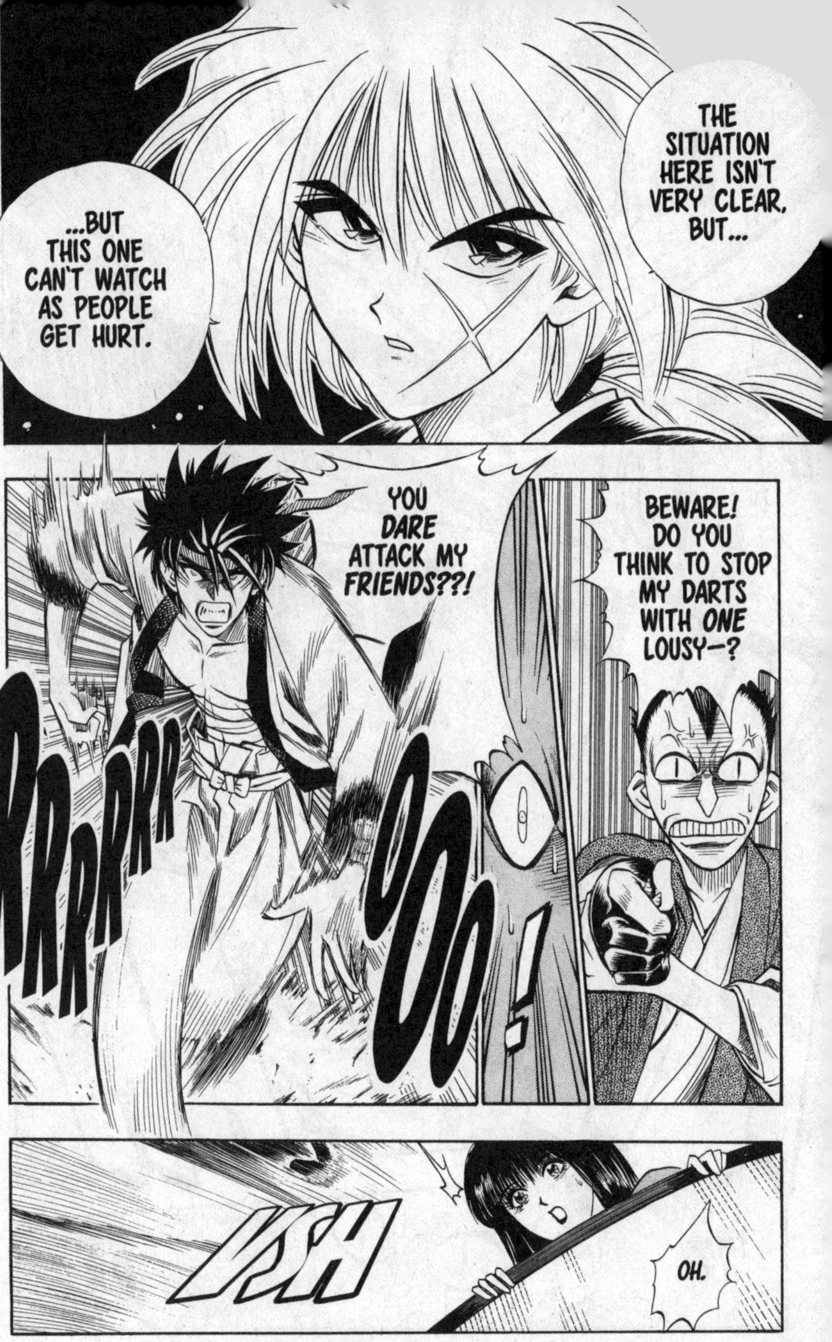
THE SITUATION HERE ISN'T VERY CLEAR, BUT...
...BUT THIS ONE CAN'T WATCH AS PEOPLE GET HURT.
BEWARE! DO YOU THINK TO STOP MY DARTS WITH ONE LOUSY—?
YOU DARE ATTACK MY FRIENDS??!
RRRRRR
OOOO!
OH.
VSH

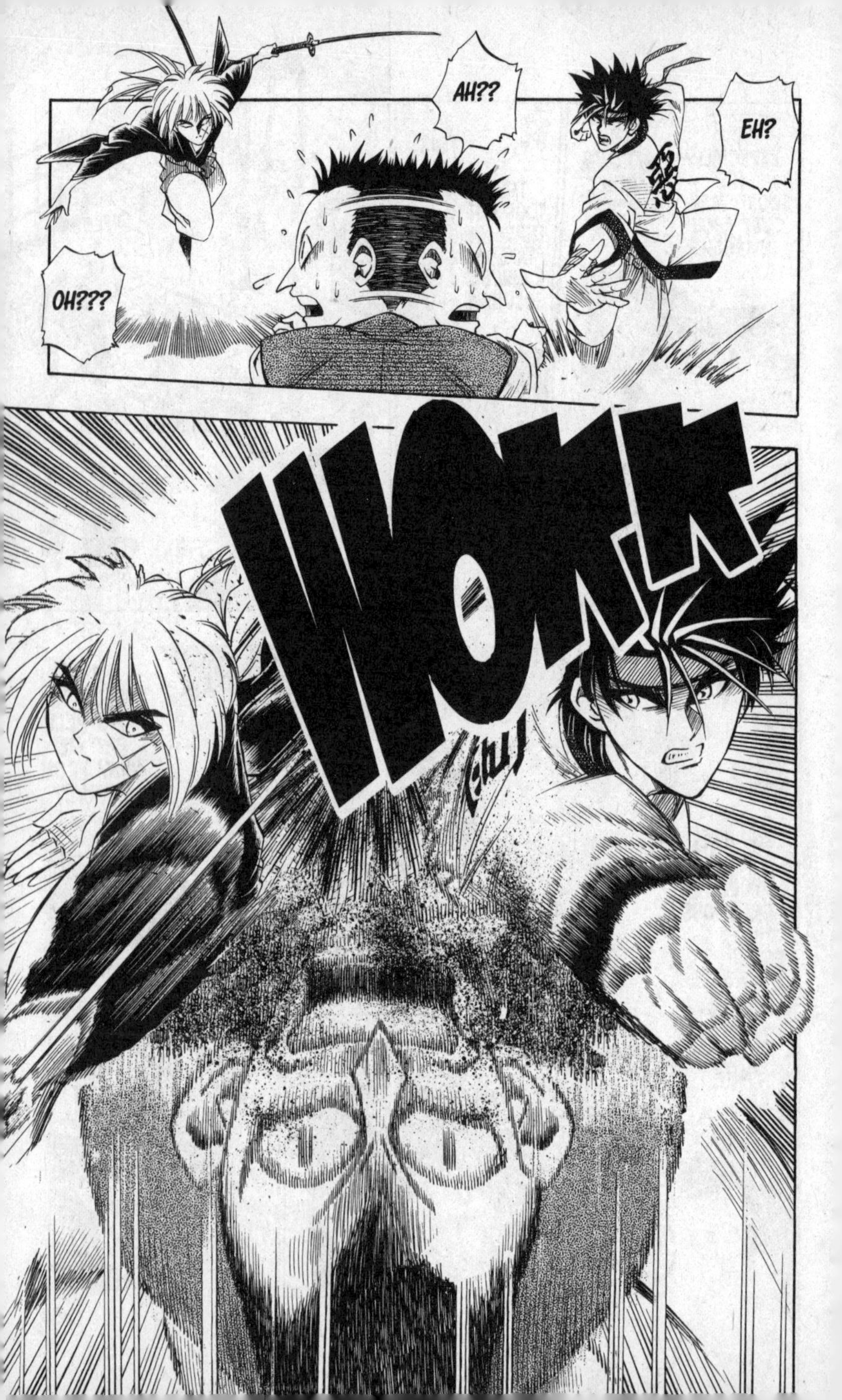
EH?
AH??
OH???
WONK

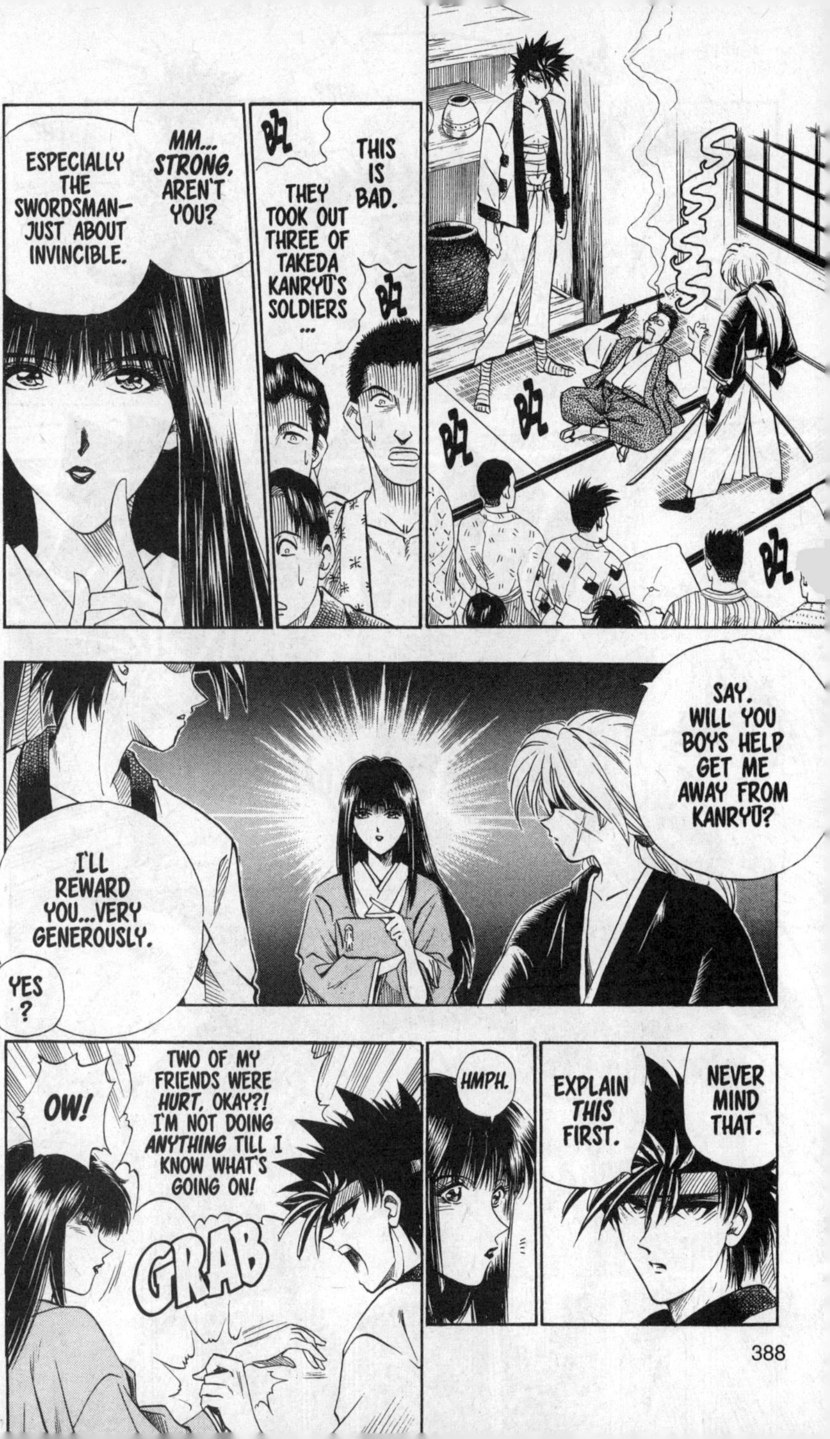
SSSS
THIS IS BAD.
THEY TOOK OUT THREE OF TAKEDA KANRYŪ'S SOLDIERS...
MM... STRONG, AREN'T YOU?
ESPECIALLY THE SWORDSMAN—JUST ABOUT INVINCIBLE.
SAY. WILL YOU BOYS HELP GET ME AWAY FROM KANRYŪ?
I'LL REWARD YOU...VERY GENEROUSLY.
YES ?
NEVER MIND THAT.
EXPLAIN THIS FIRST.
HMPH.
TWO OF MY FRIENDS WERE HURT, OKAY?! I'M NOT DOING ANYTHING TILL I KNOW WHAT'S GOING ON!
GRAB
OW!

READ THIS WAY

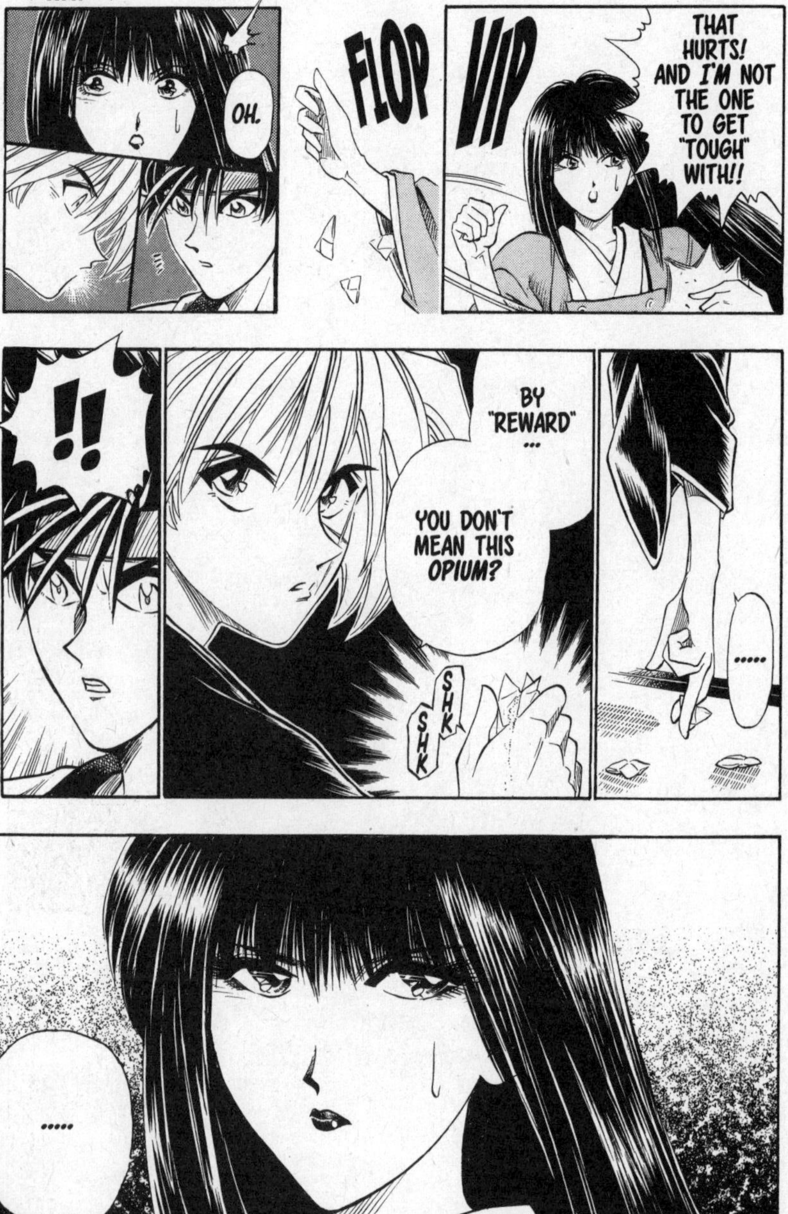

THAT HURTS! AND I'M NOT THE ONE TO GET "TOUGH" WITH!!
VIP
FLOP
OH.
……
BY "REWARD"…
YOU DON'T MEAN THIS OPIUM?
SHK
SHK
!!
……

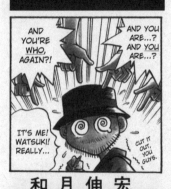

AND YOU ARE...? AND YOU ARE...?
AND YOU'RE WHO, AGAIN?!
CUT IT OUT, YOU GUYS.
IT'S ME! WATSUKI! REALLY...

和月伸宏

NOBUHIRO WATSUKI

PACKING IT ON.

HAVING HAD NO TIME FOR EXERCISE, IT'S TO BE EXPECTED ...REALLY, CAN'T BE HELPED, BUT.... WHAT'S WORSE IS, BECAUSE I'VE BEEN SO BUSY AND THERE'S BEEN NO TIME EVEN TO SHAVE, EVERYONE I KNOW IS TREATING ME LIKE YOU SEE HERE.

THE GOAL FOR THIS YEAR, THEN, IS TO DIET, AND TO REMEMBER TO SHAVE. THAT, AND GIVING *RUROUNI KENSHIN* MY ALL, OF COURSE! I SO-O-O WANNA PLAY *SHIN (NEW) SAMURAI SPIRITS*, BUT... (SHAPE-UP! PUNISHMENT!! *KRACK!!*)

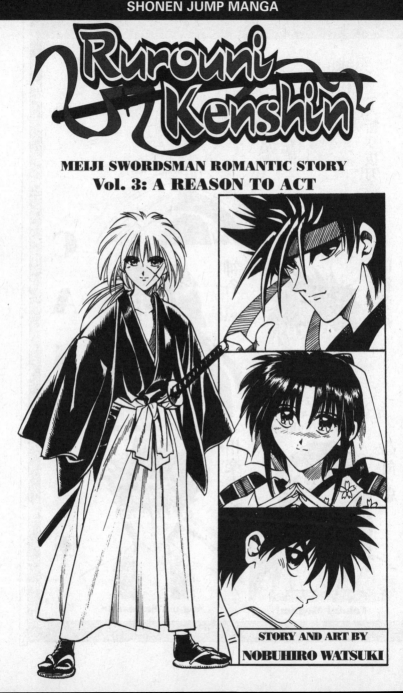

READ THIS WAY

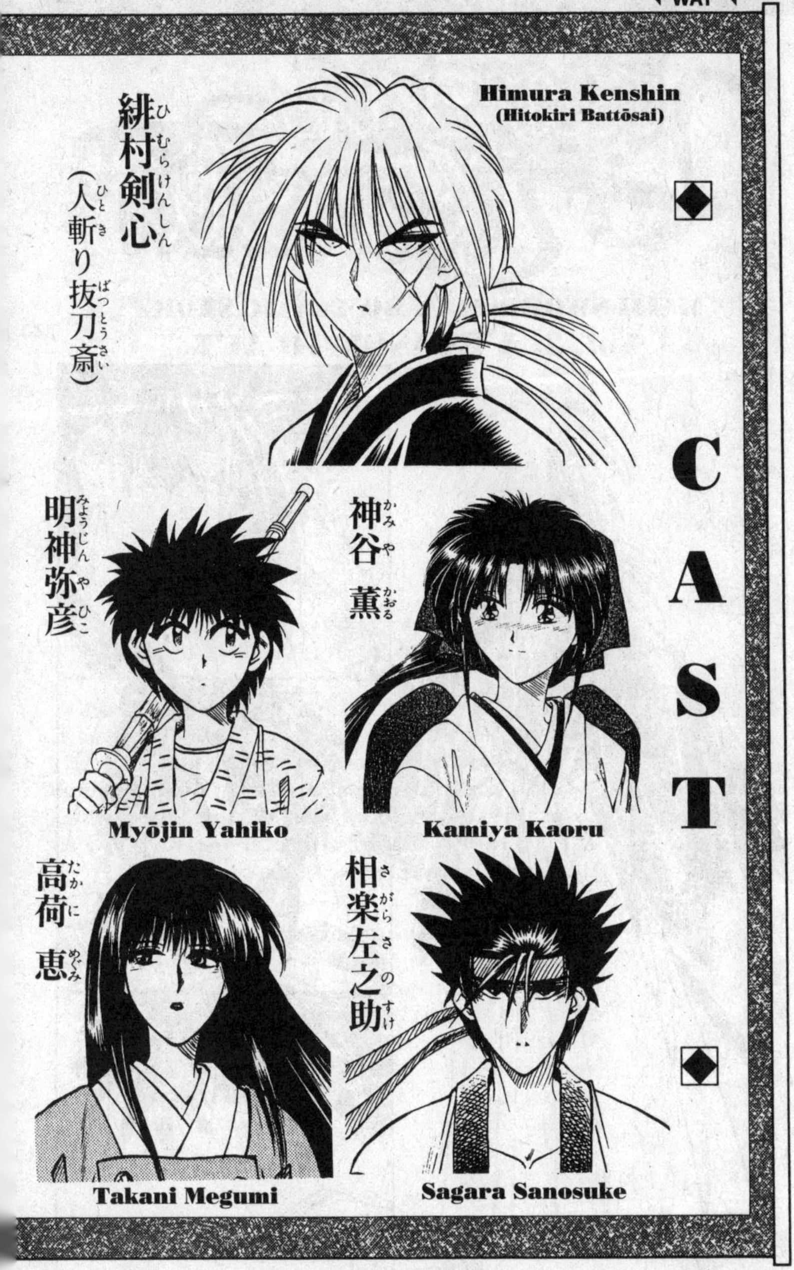

CAST
Himura Kenshin
(Hitokiri Battōsai)
緋村剣心
（人斬り抜刀斎）
神谷薫
Kamiya Kaoru
明神弥彦
Myōjin Yahiko
相楽左之助
Sagara Sanosuke
高荷恵
Takani Megumi

るろうに剣心

和月伸宏

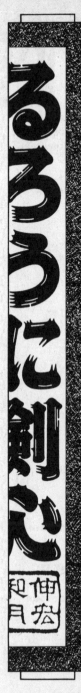

Takeda Kanryū

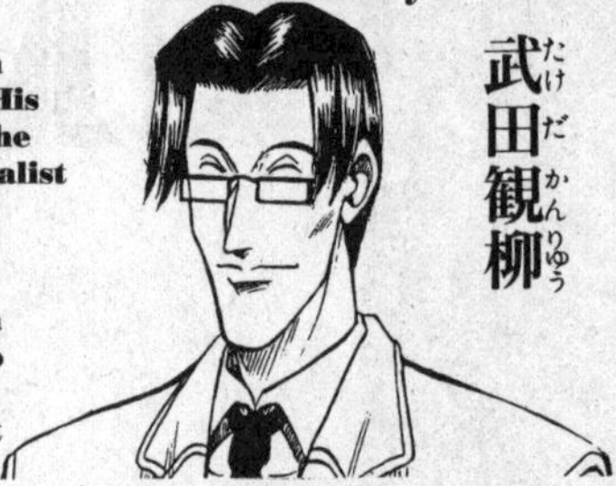

武田観柳

Once he was a *hitokiri*, an assassin, called *Battōsai.* His name was legend among the *Ishin Shishi* or pro-imperialist "patriot" warriors who launched the Meiji era.

Now Himura Kenshin is a *rurouni,* a wanderer, who carries a reversed-edge *sakabatō* blade to prohibit himself from killing.

Having rescued the Kamiya dojo from the hoax of a "fake Battōsai," Kenshin's decided to stay on at the dojo for a while.

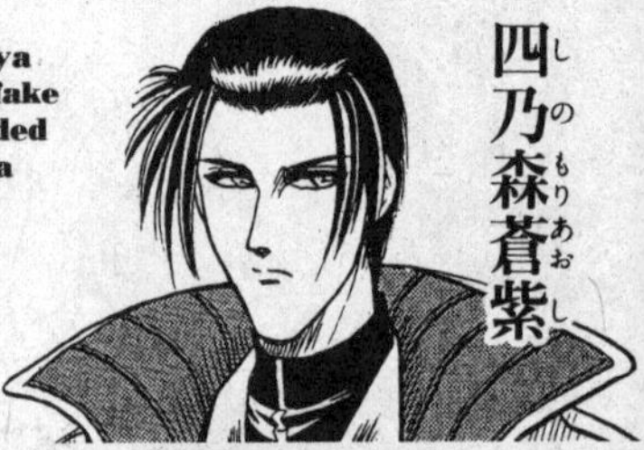

四乃森蒼紫

Shinomori Aoshi

THUS FAR

After losing all its students, the Kamiya dojo and its "*Kasshin-ryū*" sword style is taking its first steps toward revival. Kenshin brings in Myōjin Yahiko, son of an ex-samurai rescued from the yakuza, and also Sagara Sanosuke, who gave up a life as a fighter-for-hire due to Kenshin's example.

One evening, Kenshin is dragged to a gambling den by Sanosuke. There they learn that one of Sanosuke's gambling buddies is dead because of opium use. Suddenly, Takani Megumi bursts in, asking for Kenshin's protection from the private army of Takeda Kanryū...for reasons apparently having something to do with the drug....

CONTENTS

Rurouni Kenshin
Meiji Swordsman Romantic Story
BOOK THREE: A REASON TO ACT

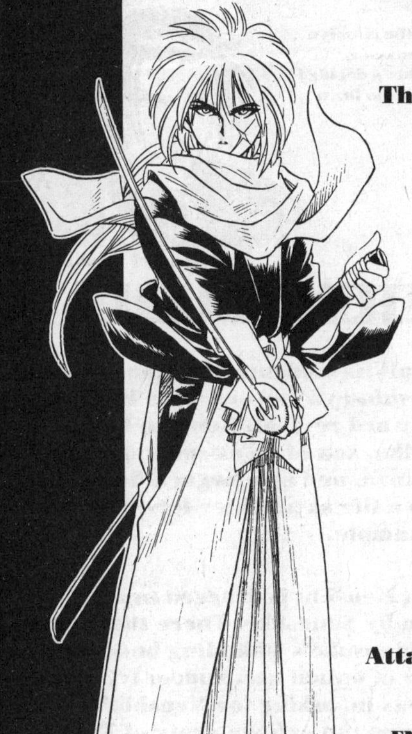

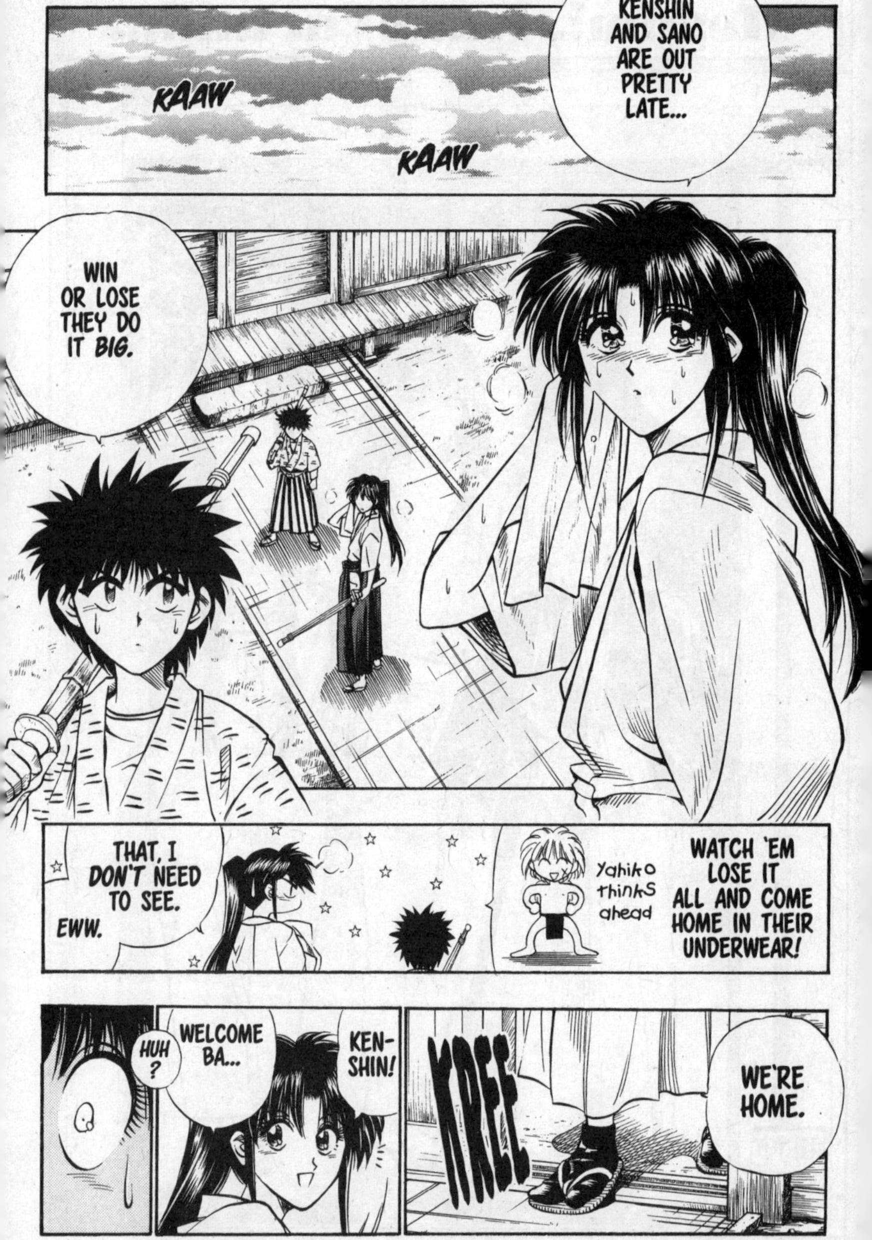
KENSHIN AND SANO ARE OUT PRETTY LATE...
KAAW
KAAW
WIN OR LOSE THEY DO IT BIG.
WATCH 'EM LOSE IT ALL AND COME HOME IN THEIR UNDERWEAR!
Yahiko thinks ahead
THAT, I DON'T NEED TO SEE.
EWW.
WE'RE HOME.
KREE
KEN-SHIN!
WELCOME BA...
HUH?

Act 16—Megumi, Kanryū, and...

Act 16
Megumi, Kanryū, and...

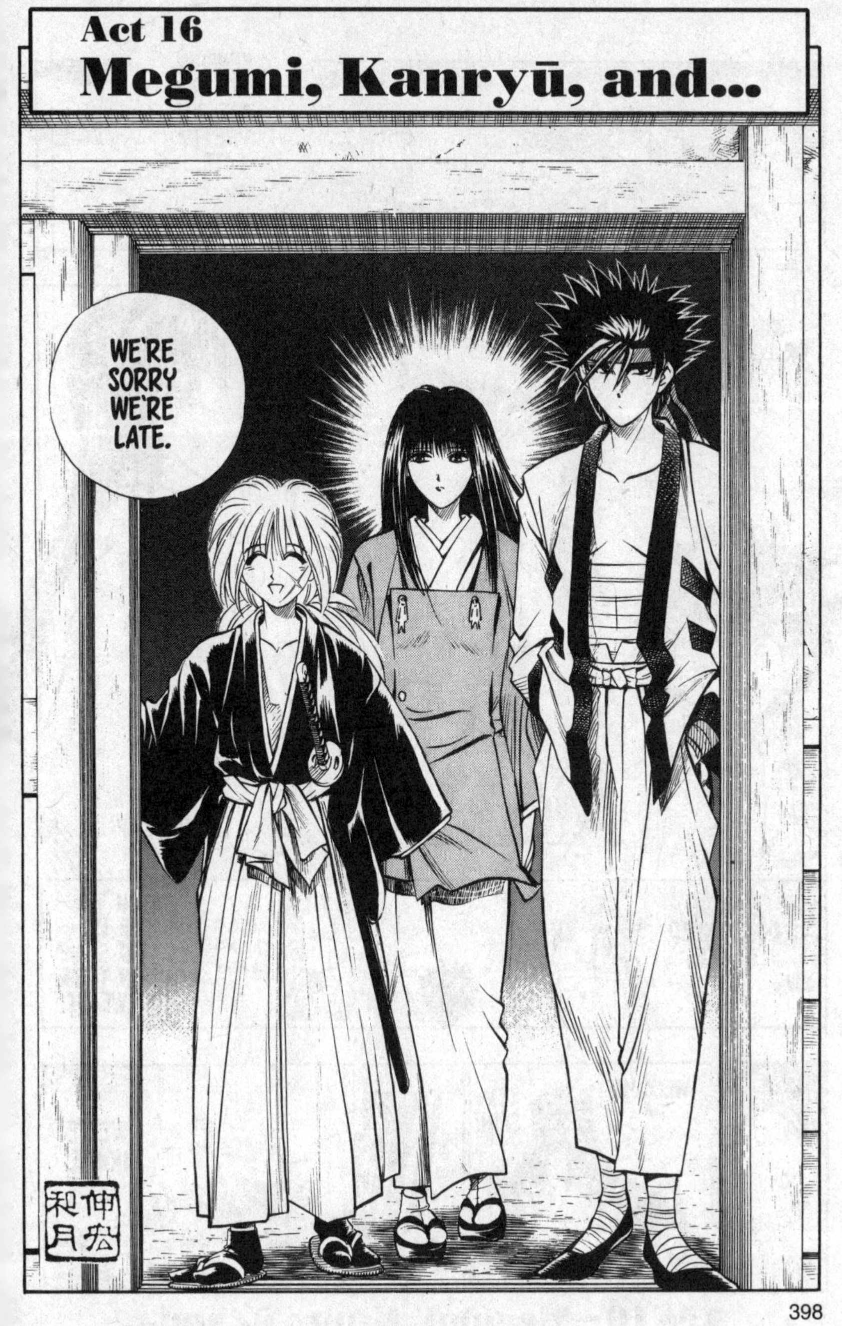
WE'RE SORRY WE'RE LATE.
伸宏和月

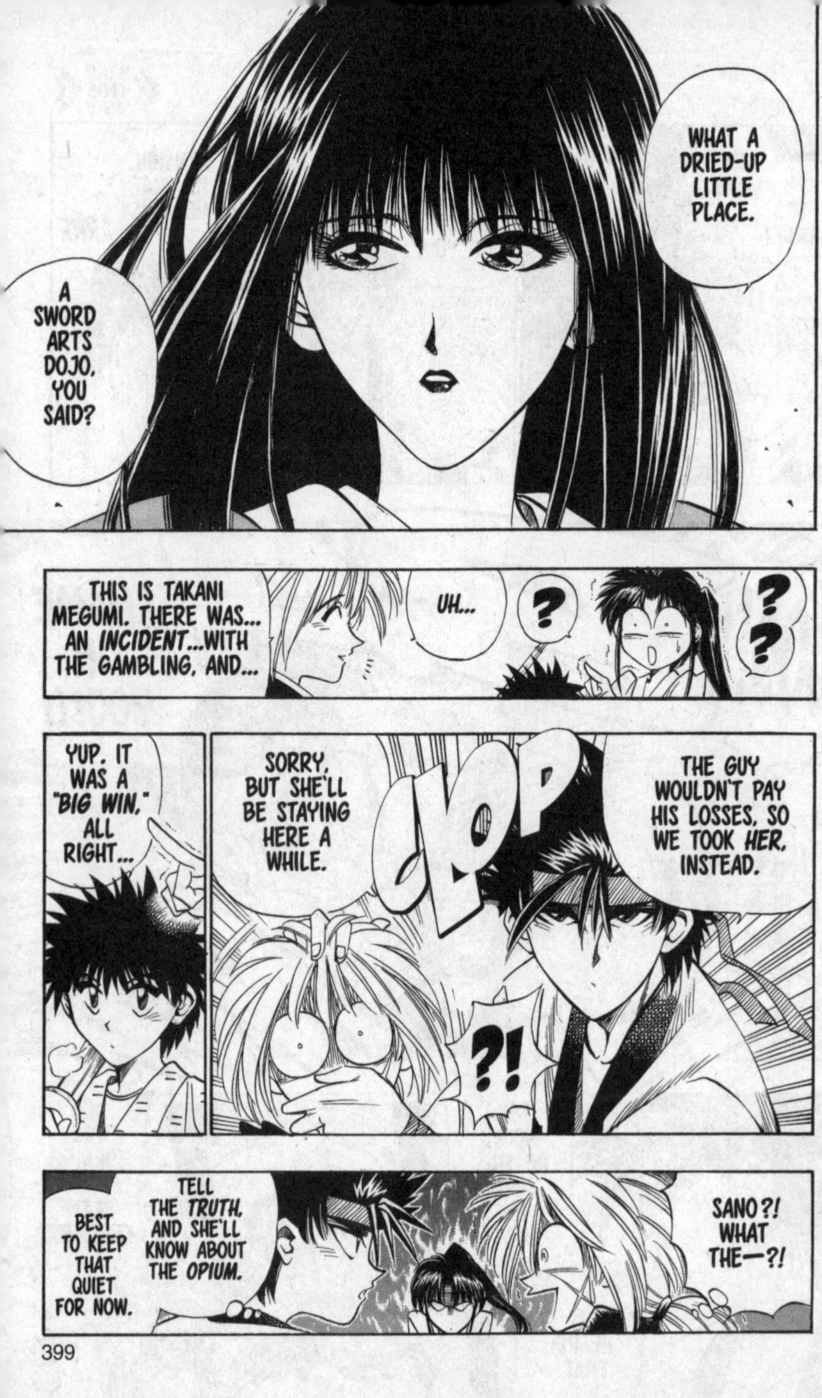
WHAT A DRIED-UP LITTLE PLACE.
A SWORD ARTS DOJO, YOU SAID?
??
?
UH...
THIS IS TAKANI MEGUMI. THERE WAS... AN *INCIDENT*...WITH THE GAMBLING, AND...
THE GUY WOULDN'T PAY HIS LOSSES, SO WE TOOK *HER*, INSTEAD.
CHOP
?!
SORRY, BUT SHE'LL BE STAYING HERE A WHILE.
YUP. IT WAS A "*BIG WIN*," ALL RIGHT...
SANO?! WHAT THE—?!
TELL THE *TRUTH*, AND SHE'LL KNOW ABOUT THE *OPIUM*.
BEST TO KEEP THAT QUIET FOR NOW.

READ THIS WAY

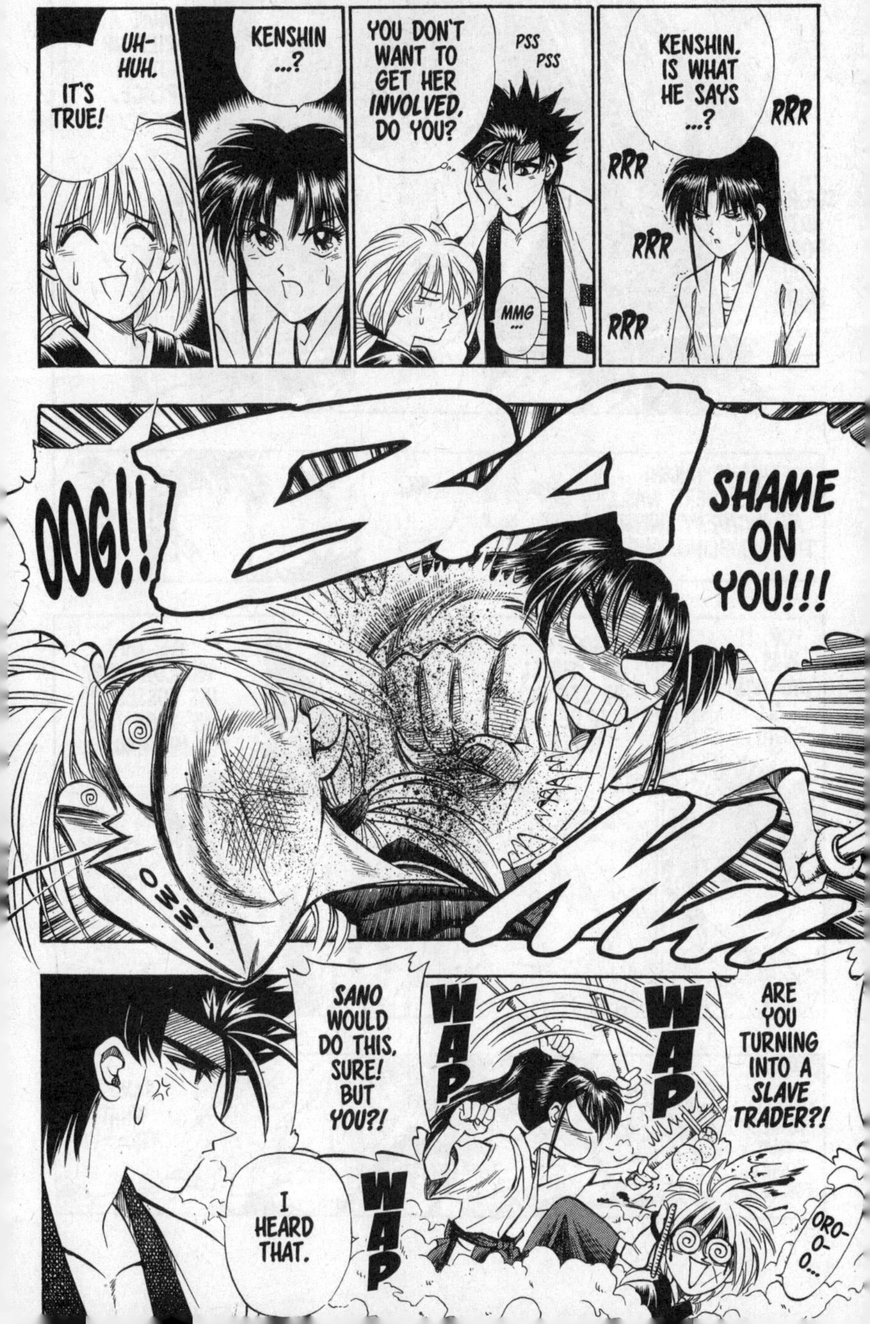
KENSHIN. IS WHAT HE SAYS ...?
RRR
RRR
RRR
RRR
PSS PSS
YOU DON'T WANT TO GET HER INVOLVED, DO YOU?
MMG ...
KENSHIN ...?
UH-HUH.
IT'S TRUE!
SHAME ON YOU!!!
OOG!!
OWW!
ARE YOU TURNING INTO A SLAVE TRADER?!
WAP
WAP
SANO WOULD DO THIS, SURE! BUT YOU?!
ORO-O-O-O...
WAP
I HEARD THAT.

READ THIS WAY

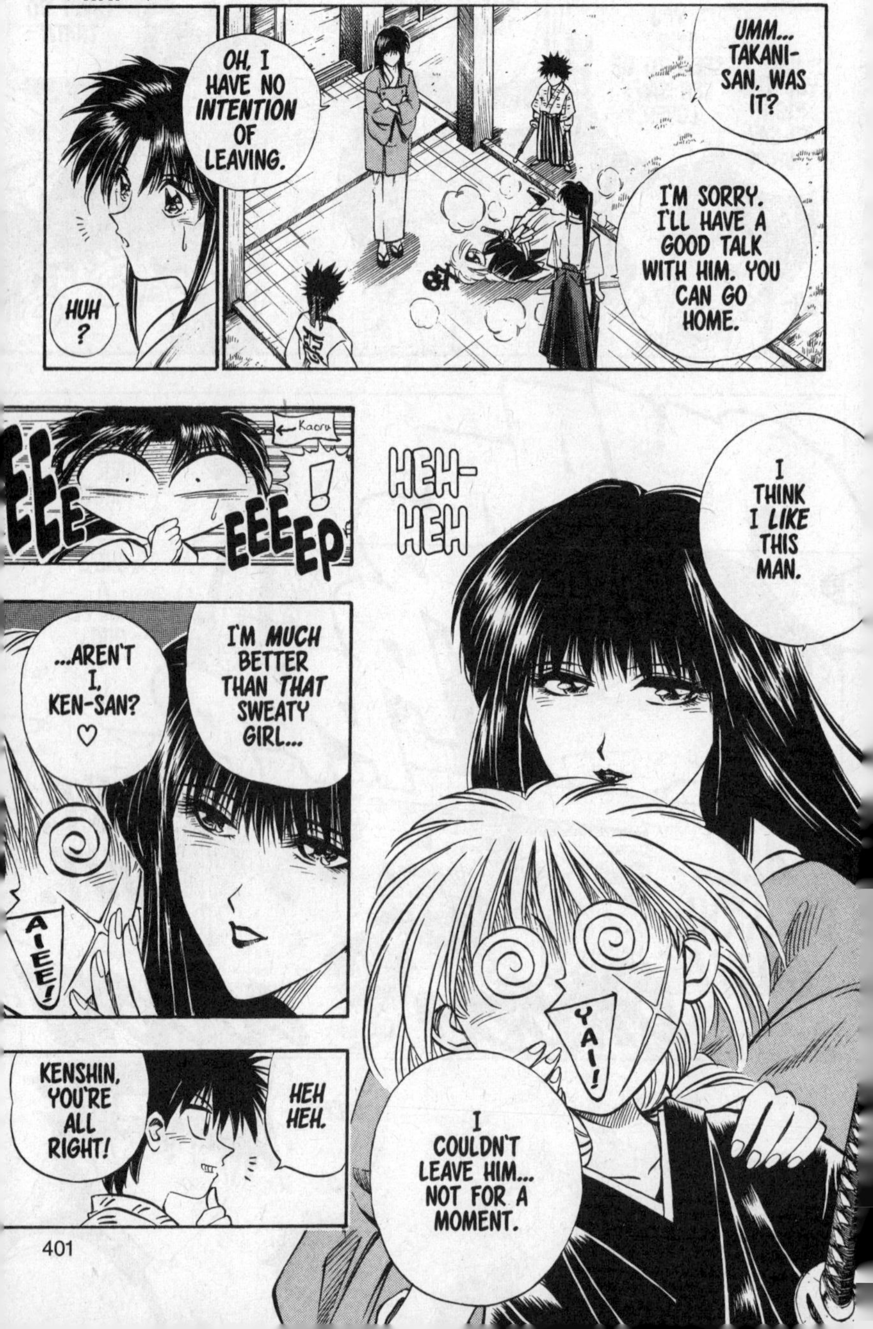

UMM... TAKANI-SAN, WAS IT?
I'M SORRY. I'LL HAVE A GOOD TALK WITH HIM. YOU CAN GO HOME.
OH, I HAVE NO INTENTION OF LEAVING.
HUH?
HEH-HEH
I THINK I LIKE THIS MAN.
YAI!
I COULDN'T LEAVE HIM... NOT FOR A MOMENT.
← Kaoru
!
EEEEEEEP
I'M MUCH BETTER THAN THAT SWEATY GIRL...
...AREN'T I, KEN-SAN? ♡
AIEE!
HEH HEH.
KENSHIN, YOU'RE ALL RIGHT!

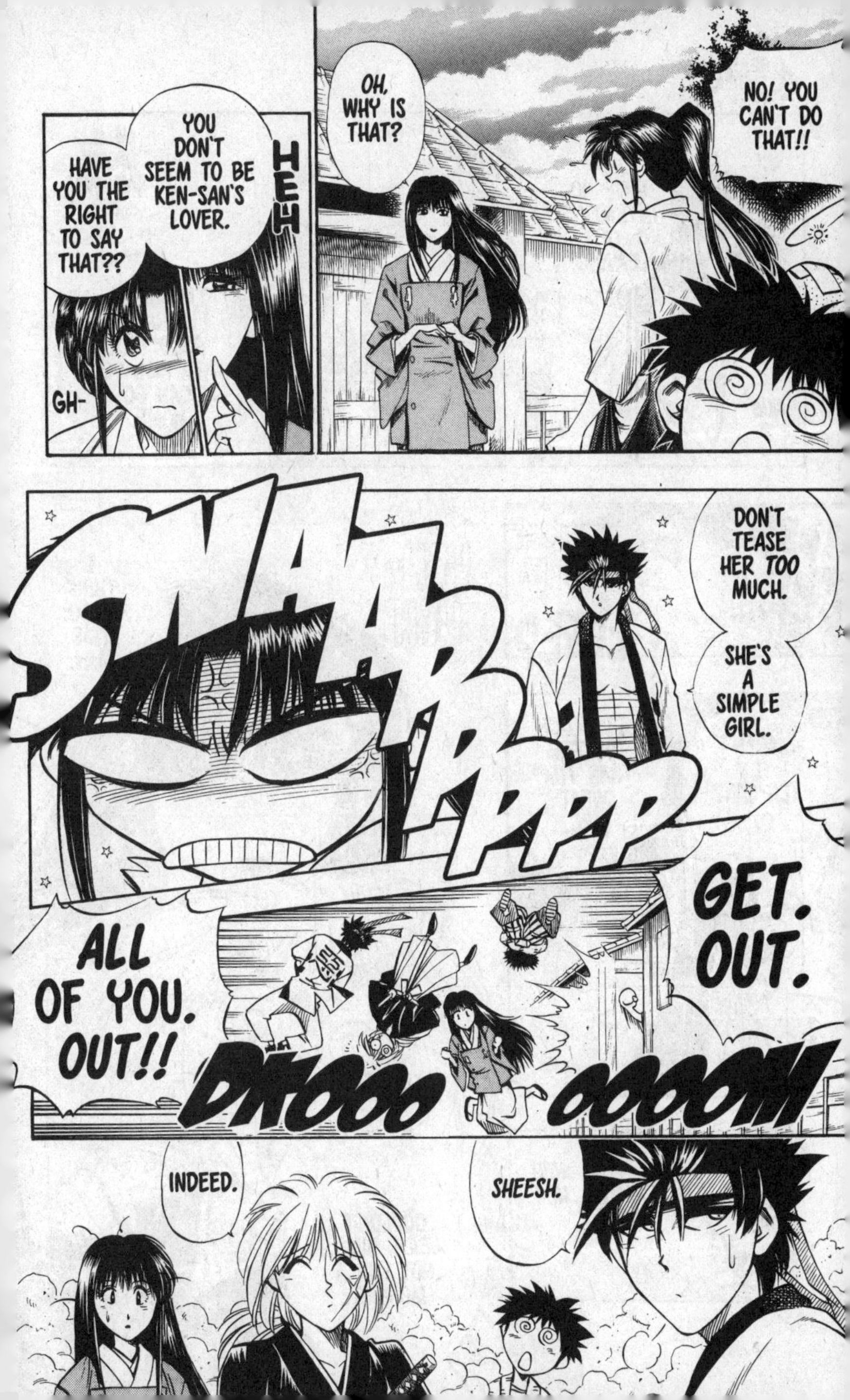
NO! YOU CAN'T DO THAT!!
OH, WHY IS THAT?
HEH
YOU DON'T SEEM TO BE KEN-SAN'S LOVER.
HAVE YOU THE RIGHT TO SAY THAT??
GH-
DON'T TEASE HER TOO MUCH.
SHE'S A SIMPLE GIRL.
GET. OUT.
ALL OF YOU. OUT!!
SHEESH.
INDEED.

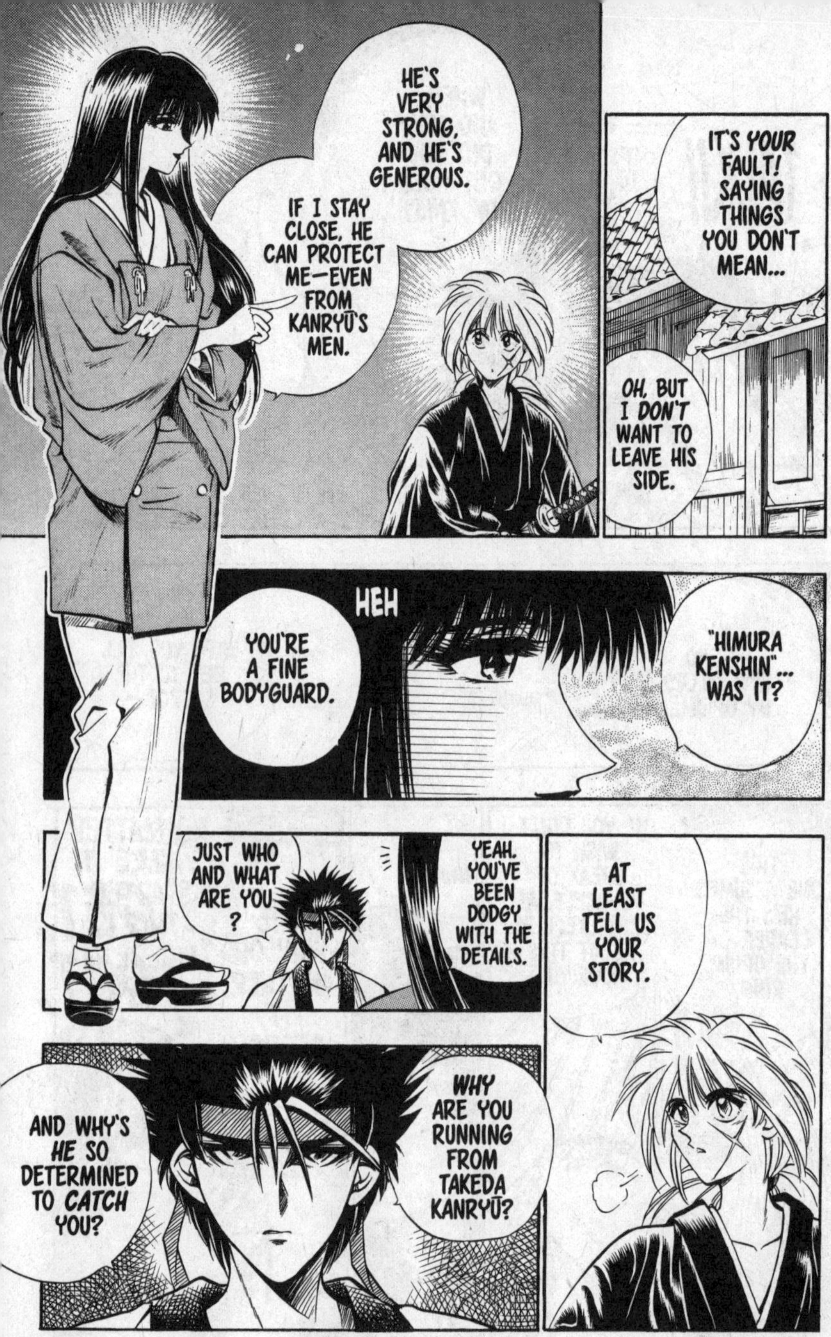
IT'S *YOUR* FAULT! SAYING THINGS YOU DON'T MEAN...
OH, BUT I *DON'T* WANT TO LEAVE HIS SIDE.
HE'S VERY STRONG, AND HE'S GENEROUS.
IF I STAY CLOSE, HE CAN PROTECT ME—EVEN FROM KANRYŪ'S MEN.
"HIMURA KENSHIN"... WAS IT?
HEH
YOU'RE A FINE BODYGUARD.
AT LEAST TELL US YOUR STORY.
YEAH. YOU'VE BEEN DODGY WITH THE DETAILS.
JUST WHO AND WHAT ARE YOU ?
WHY ARE YOU RUNNING FROM TAKEDA KANRYŪ?
AND WHY'S *HE* SO DETERMINED TO *CATCH* YOU?

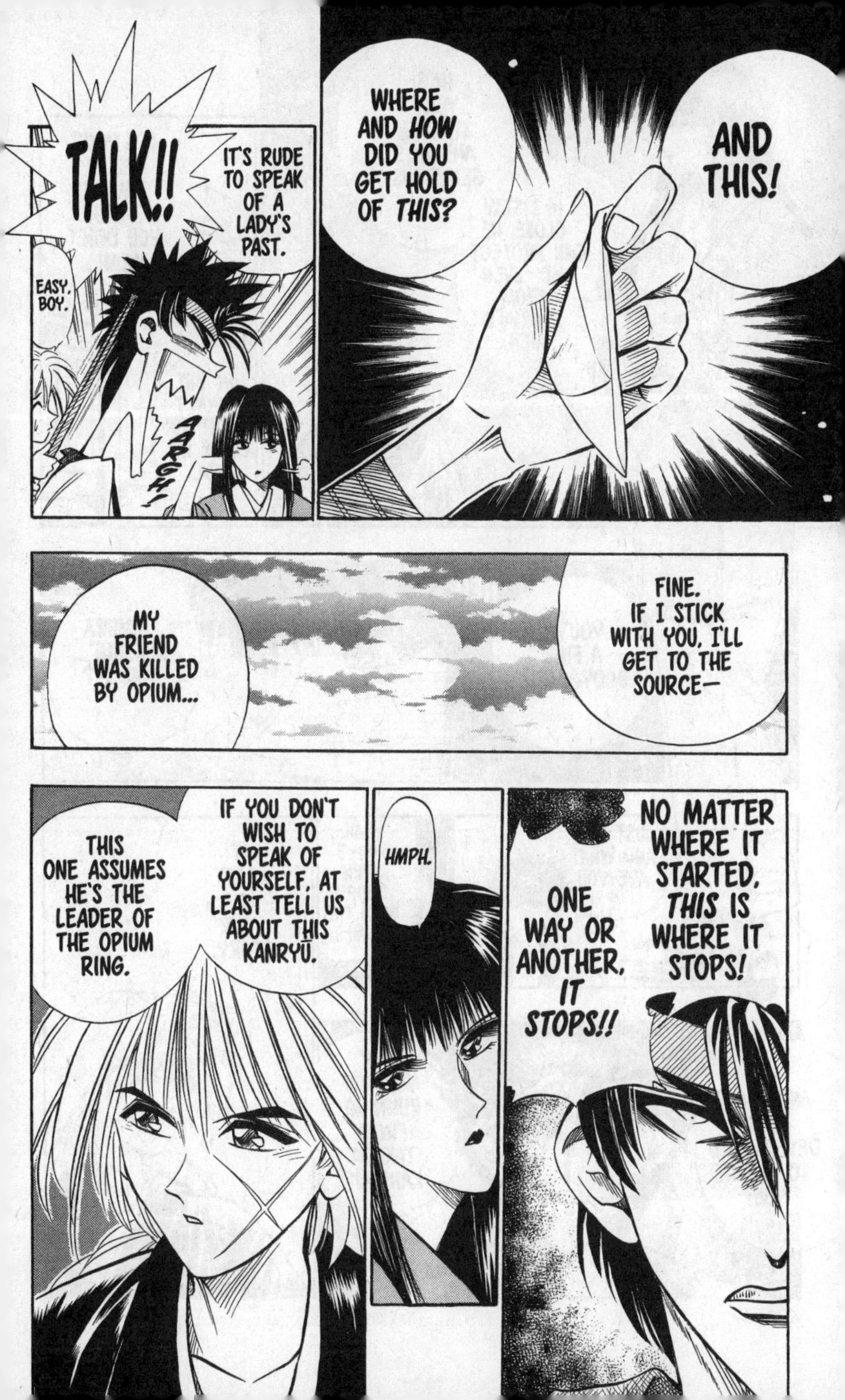
WHERE AND HOW DID YOU GET HOLD OF THIS?
AND THIS!
TALK!!
IT'S RUDE TO SPEAK OF A LADY'S PAST.
EASY, BOY.
AARGH!
FINE. IF I STICK WITH YOU, I'LL GET TO THE SOURCE—
MY FRIEND WAS KILLED BY OPIUM...
NO MATTER WHERE IT STARTED, THIS IS WHERE IT STOPS!
ONE WAY OR ANOTHER, IT STOPS!!
HMPH.
IF YOU DON'T WISH TO SPEAK OF YOURSELF, AT LEAST TELL US ABOUT THIS KANRYŪ.
THIS ONE ASSUMES HE'S THE LEADER OF THE OPIUM RING.

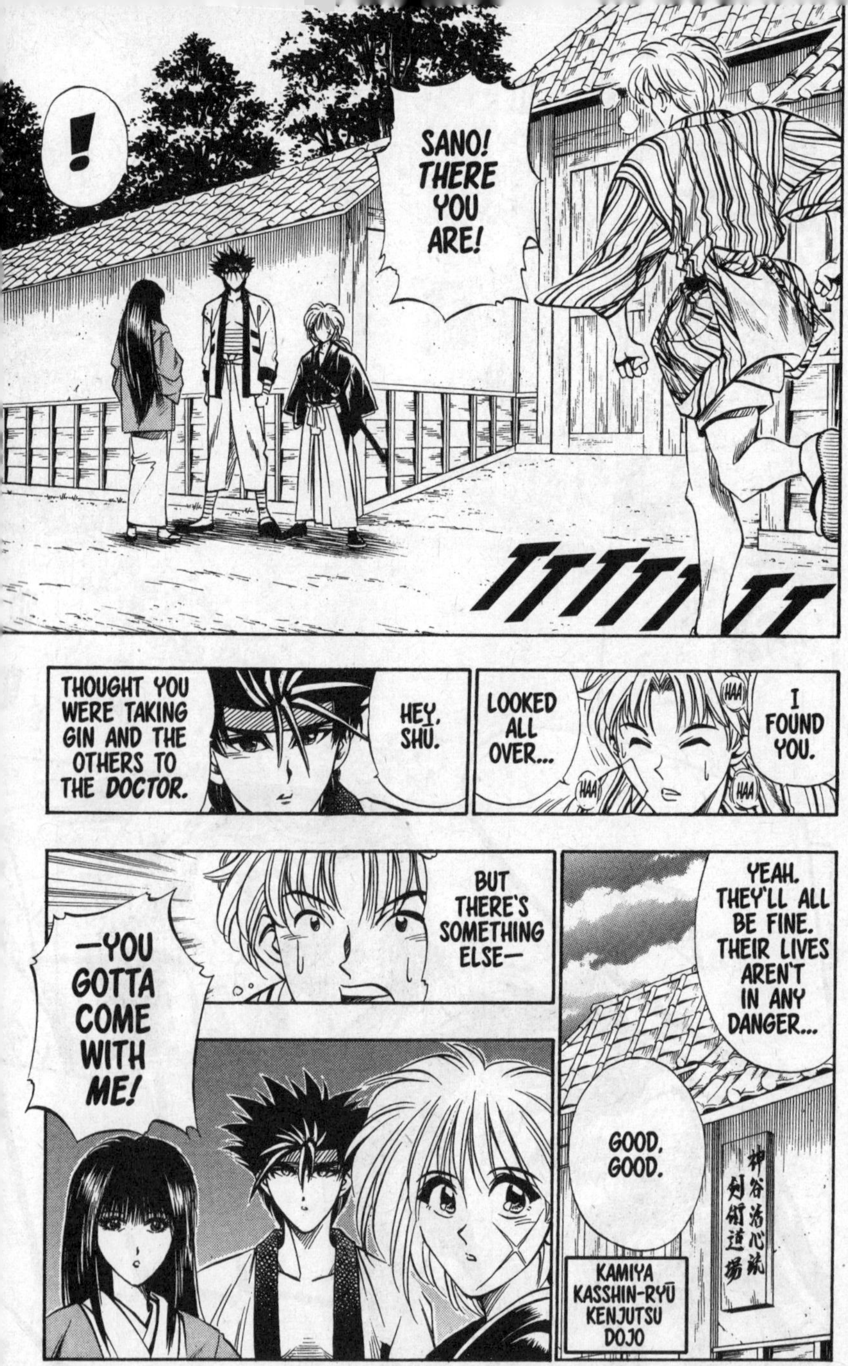
SANO! THERE YOU ARE!
!
TTTTTTT
I FOUND YOU.
HAA
HAA
HAA
LOOKED ALL OVER...
HEY, SHU.
THOUGHT YOU WERE TAKING GIN AND THE OTHERS TO THE DOCTOR.
YEAH. THEY'LL ALL BE FINE. THEIR LIVES AREN'T IN ANY DANGER...
GOOD. GOOD.
神谷活心流剣術道場
KAMIYA KASSHIN-RYŪ KENJUTSU DOJO
BUT THERE'S SOMETHING ELSE—
—YOU GOTTA COME WITH ME!

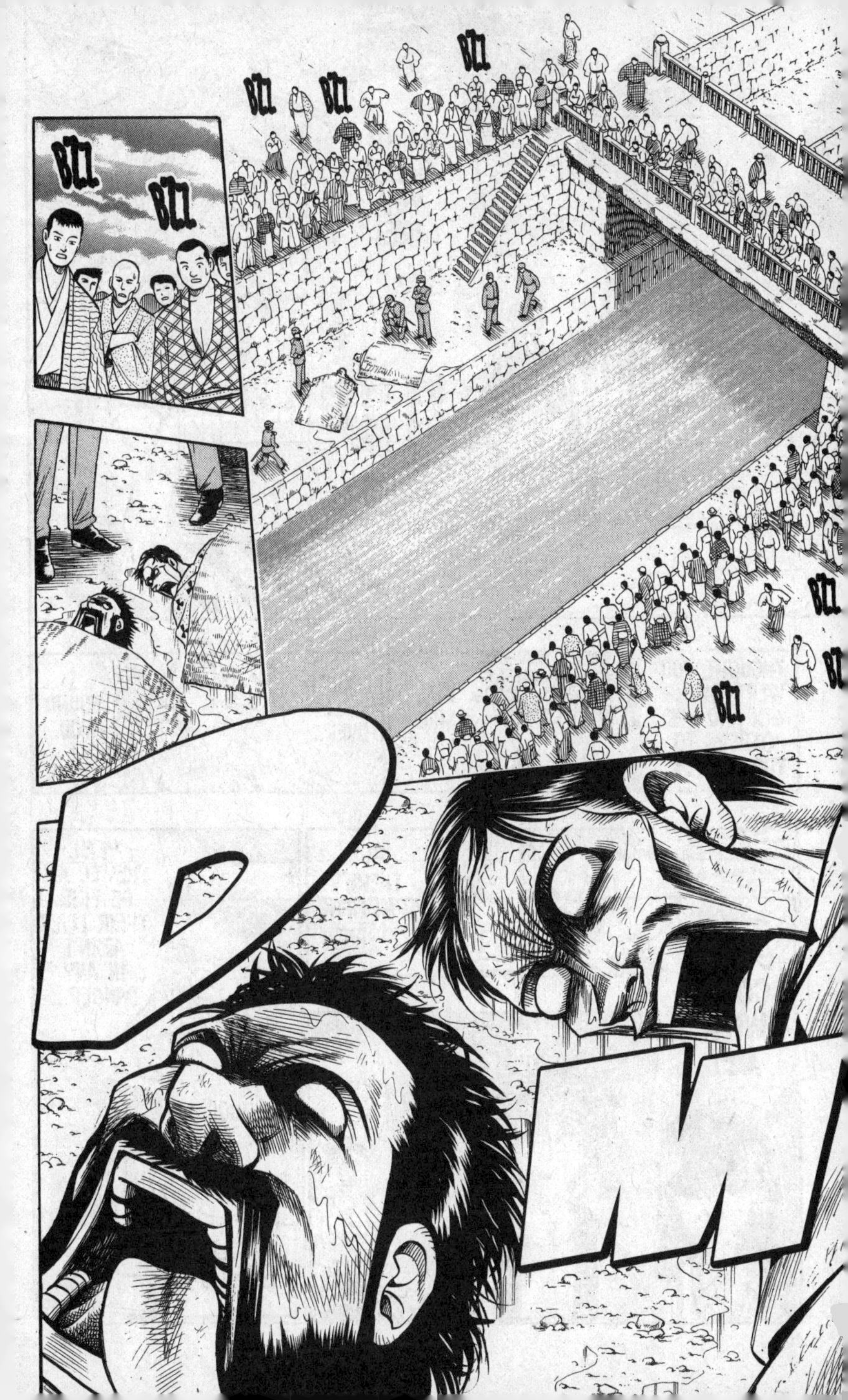
BZZ
BZZ
BZZ
BZZ
BZZ
BZZ
BZZ
BZZ

READ THIS WAY

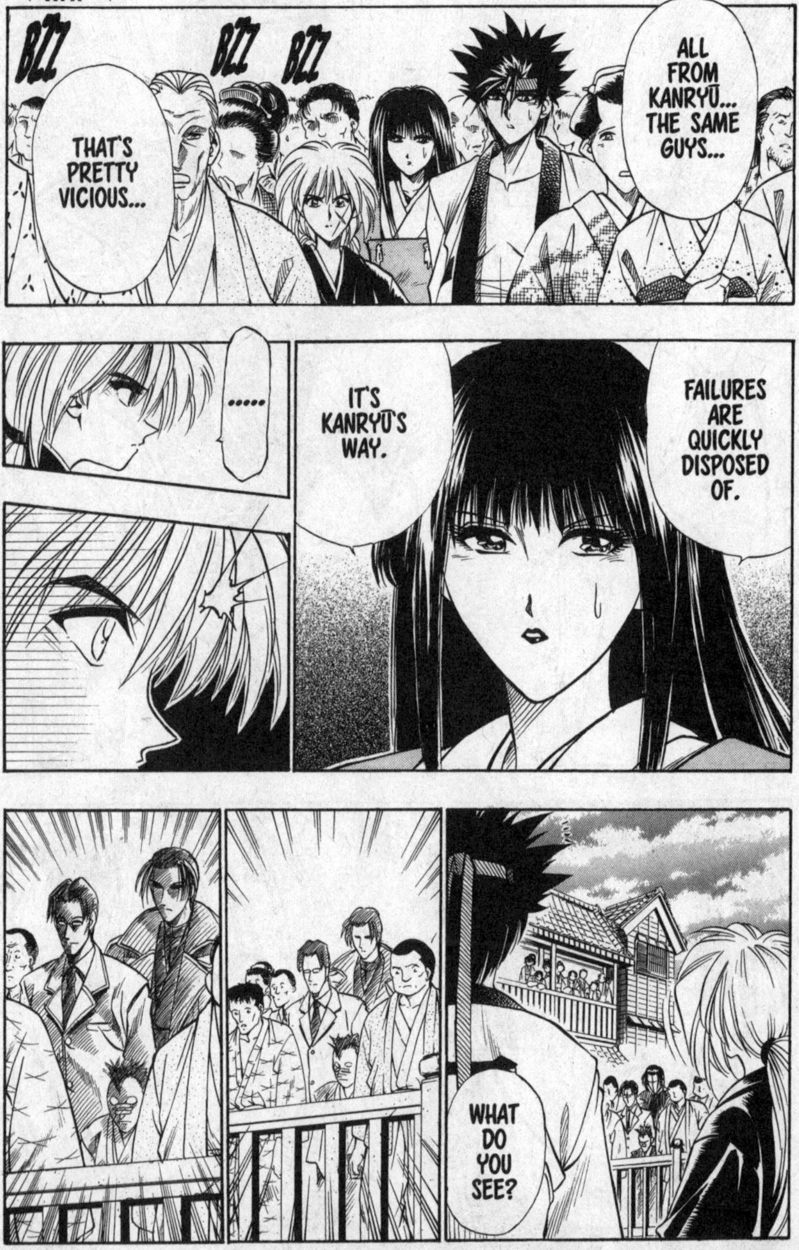
ALL FROM KANRYŪ... THE SAME GUYS...
BZZ
BZZ
BZZ
THAT'S PRETTY VICIOUS...
FAILURES ARE QUICKLY DISPOSED OF.
IT'S KANRYŪ'S WAY.
......
WHAT DO YOU SEE?

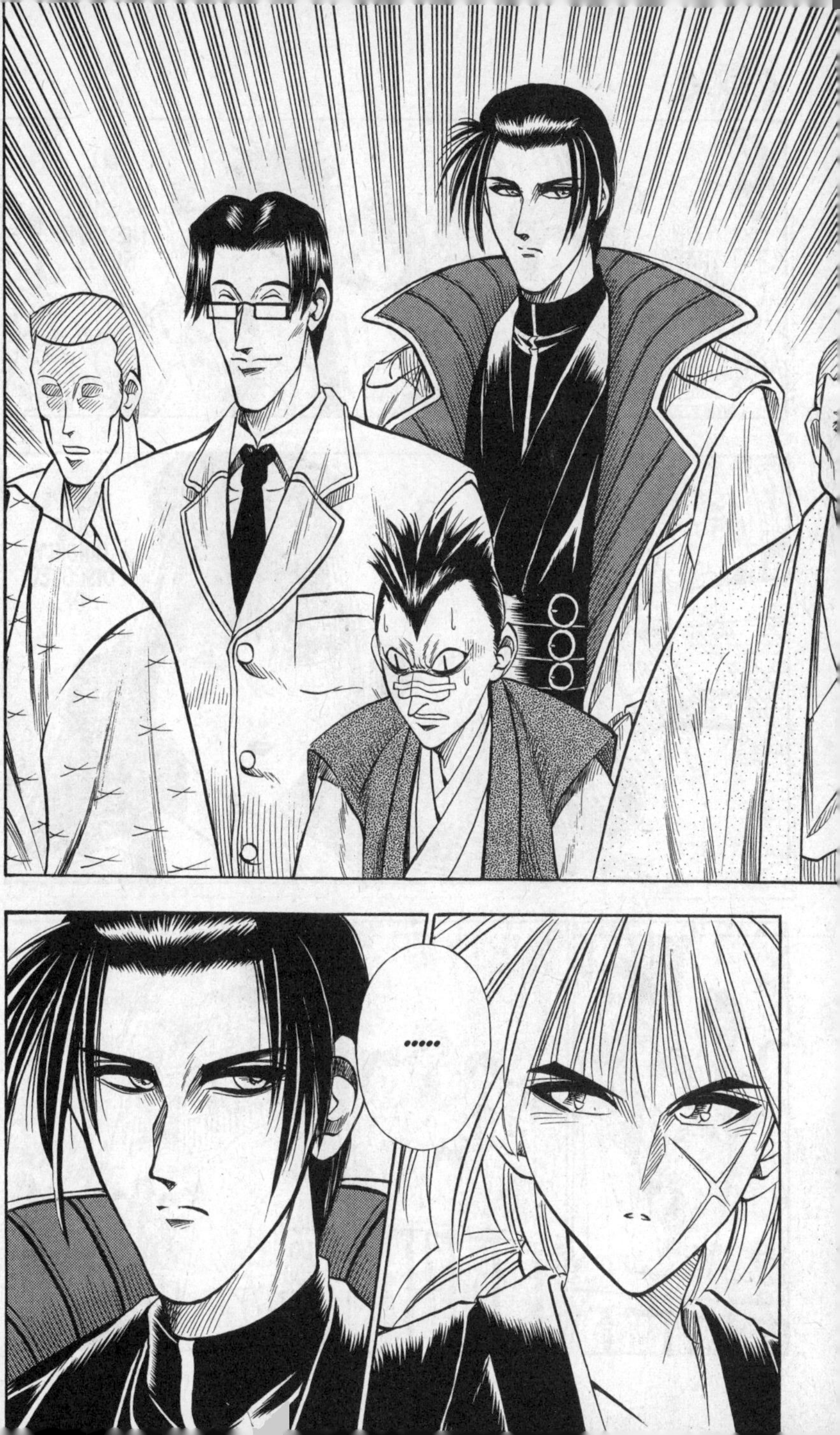
.....

READ THIS WAY

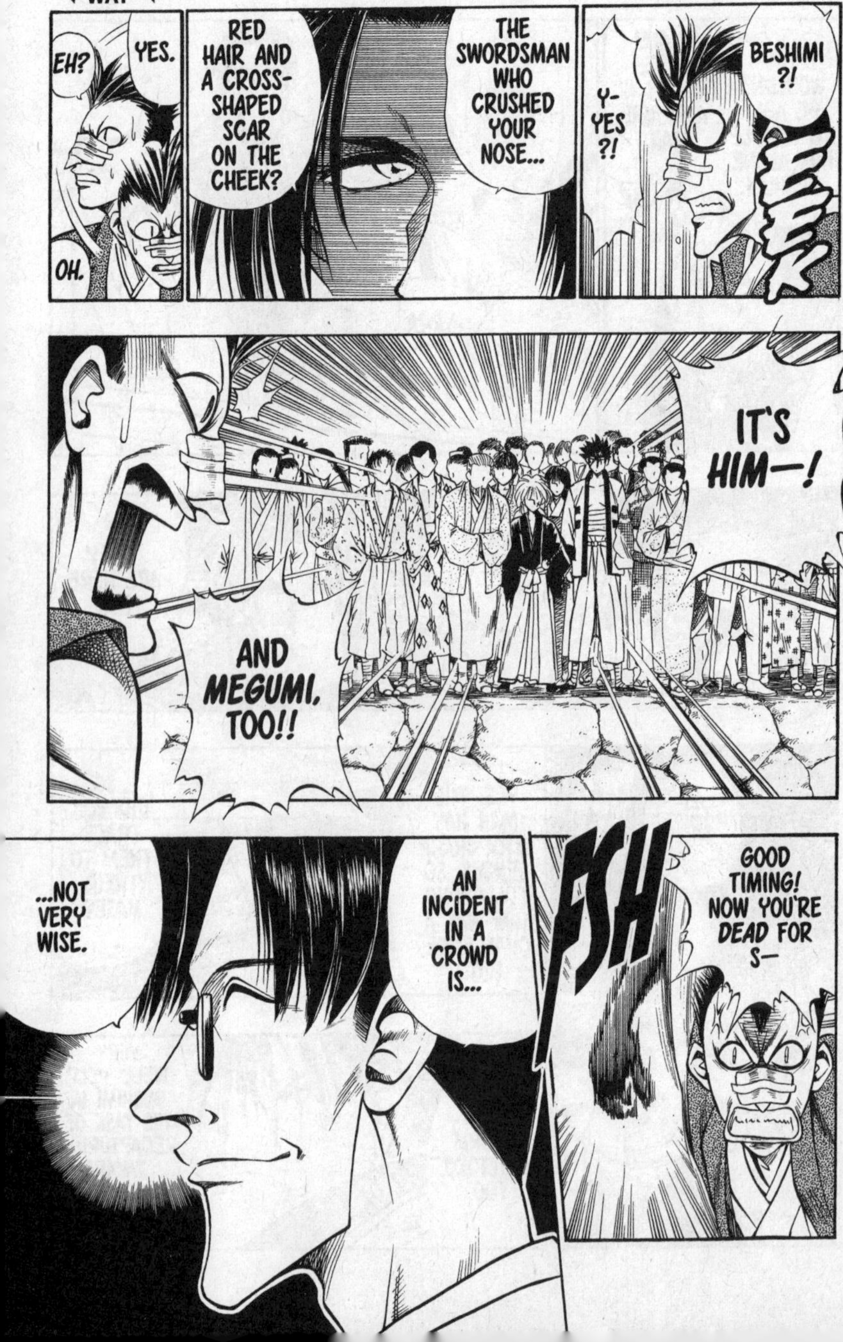
BESHIMI?!
Y-YES?!
THE SWORDSMAN WHO CRUSHED YOUR NOSE...
RED HAIR AND A CROSS-SHAPED SCAR ON THE CHEEK?
YES.
EH?
OH.
IT'S HIM—!
AND MEGUMI, TOO!!
GOOD TIMING! NOW YOU'RE DEAD FOR S—
FSH
AN INCIDENT IN A CROWD IS...
...NOT VERY WISE.

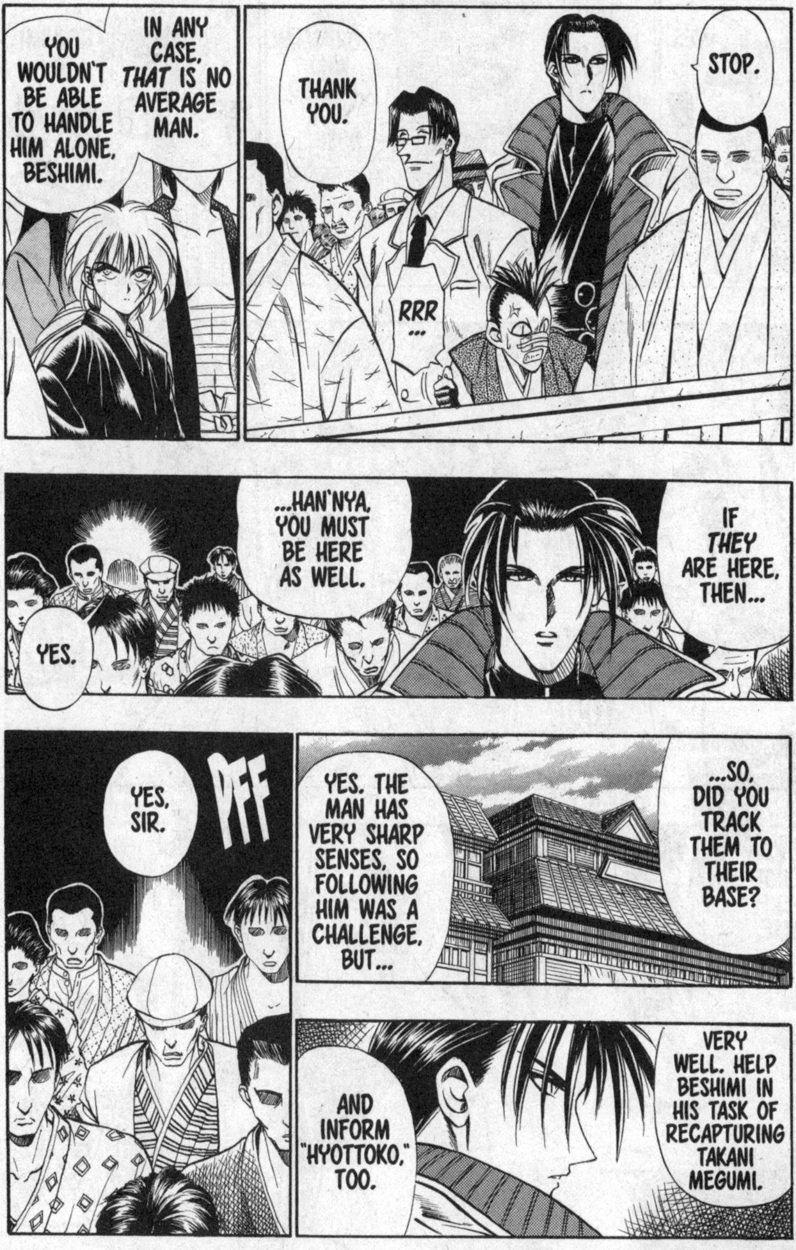
STOP.
THANK YOU.
RRR...
IN ANY CASE, THAT IS NO AVERAGE MAN.
YOU WOULDN'T BE ABLE TO HANDLE HIM ALONE, BESHIMI.
IF THEY ARE HERE, THEN...
...HAN'NYA, YOU MUST BE HERE AS WELL.
YES.
...SO, DID YOU TRACK THEM TO THEIR BASE?
YES. THE MAN HAS VERY SHARP SENSES, SO FOLLOWING HIM WAS A CHALLENGE, BUT...
VERY WELL. HELP BESHIMI IN HIS TASK OF RECAPTURING TAKANI MEGUMI.
AND INFORM "HYOTTOKO," TOO.
YES, SIR.
PFF

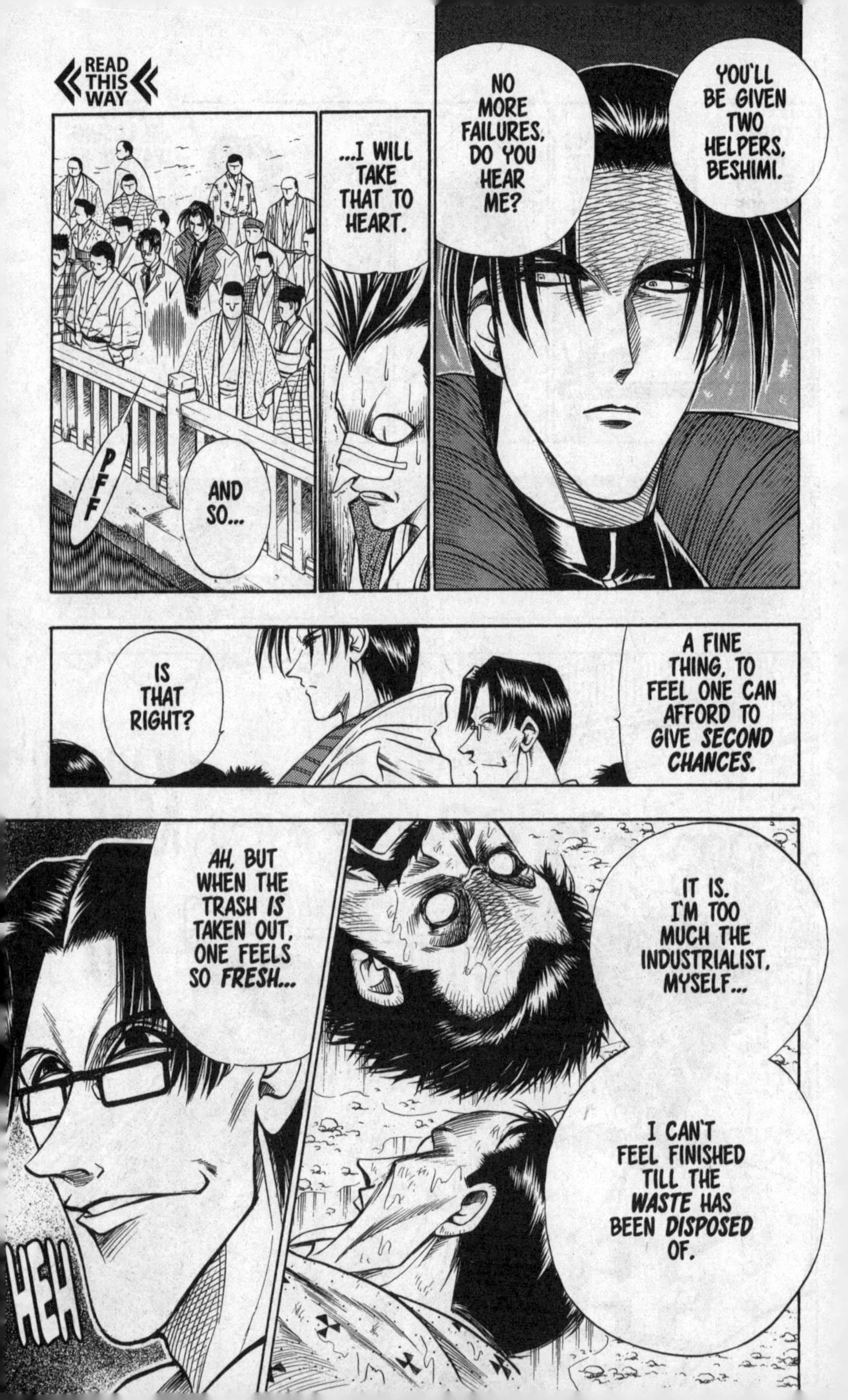
READ THIS WAY
YOU'LL BE GIVEN TWO HELPERS, BESHIMI.
NO MORE FAILURES, DO YOU HEAR ME?
...I WILL TAKE THAT TO HEART.
AND SO...
PFF
A FINE THING, TO FEEL ONE CAN AFFORD TO GIVE *SECOND CHANCES.*
IS THAT RIGHT?
IT IS. I'M TOO MUCH THE INDUSTRIALIST, MYSELF...
I CAN'T FEEL FINISHED TILL THE *WASTE* HAS BEEN *DISPOSED* OF.
AH, BUT WHEN THE TRASH *IS* TAKEN OUT, ONE FEELS SO *FRESH...*
HEH

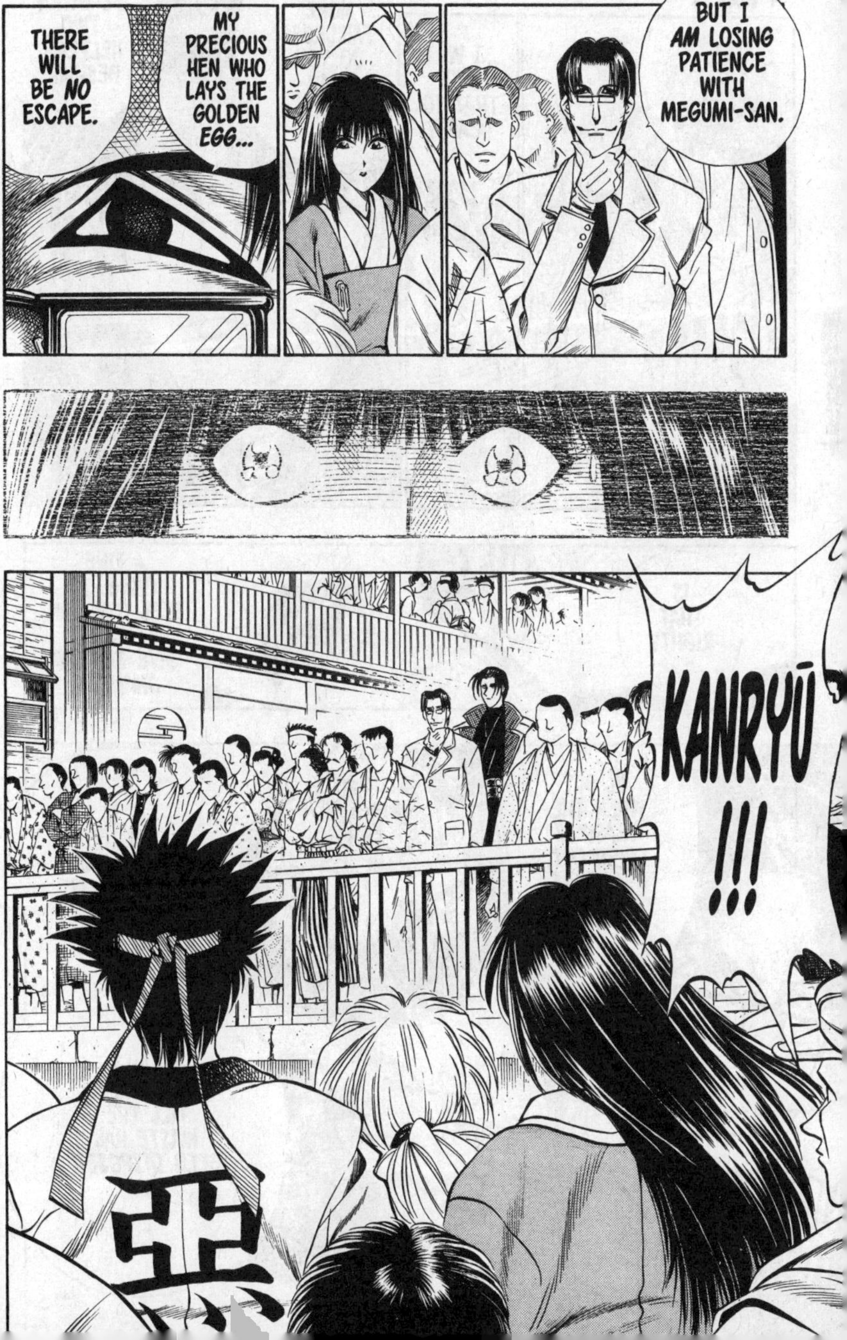
BUT I AM LOSING PATIENCE WITH MEGUMI-SAN.
MY PRECIOUS HEN WHO LAYS THE GOLDEN EGG...
THERE WILL BE NO ESCAPE.
KANRYŪ!!!

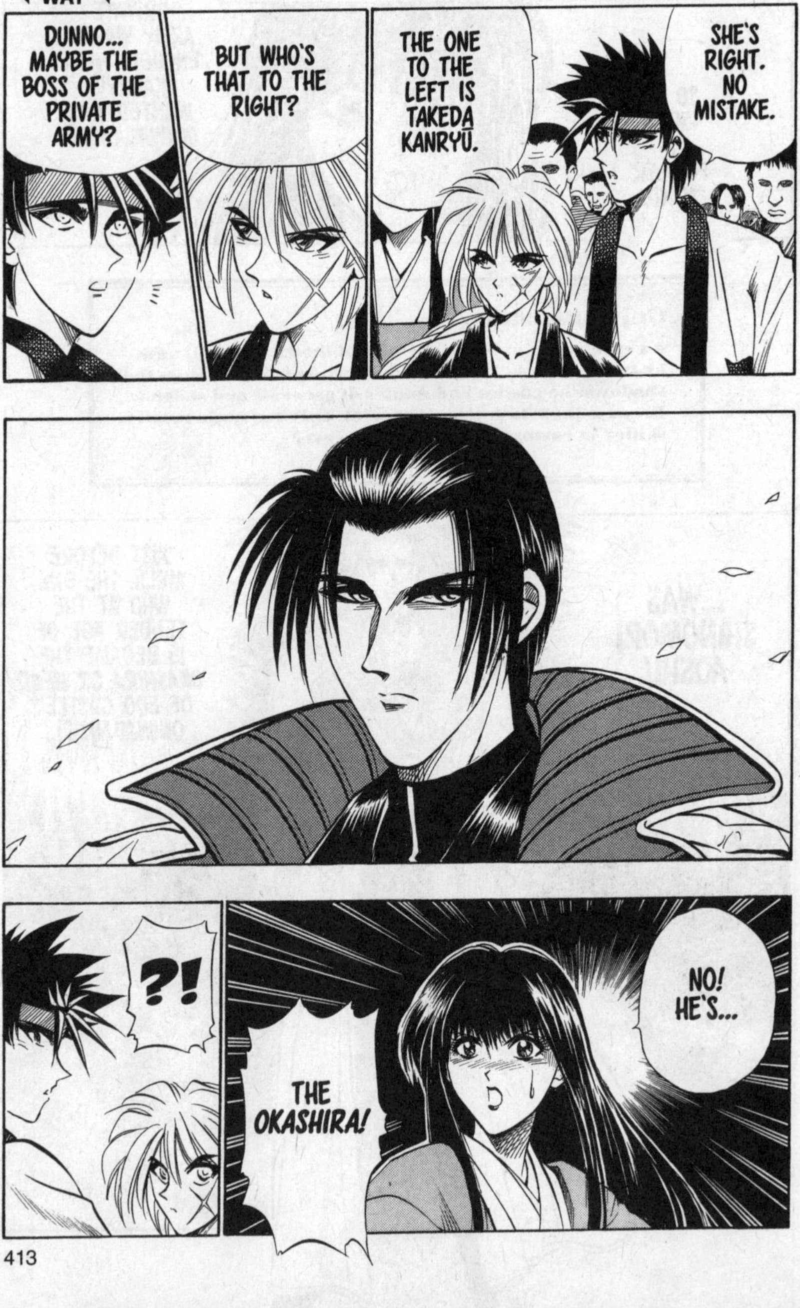
SHE'S RIGHT. NO MISTAKE.
THE ONE TO THE LEFT IS TAKEDA KANRYŪ.
BUT WHO'S THAT TO THE RIGHT?
DUNNO... MAYBE THE BOSS OF THE PRIVATE ARMY?
NO! HE'S...
THE OKASHIRA!
?!

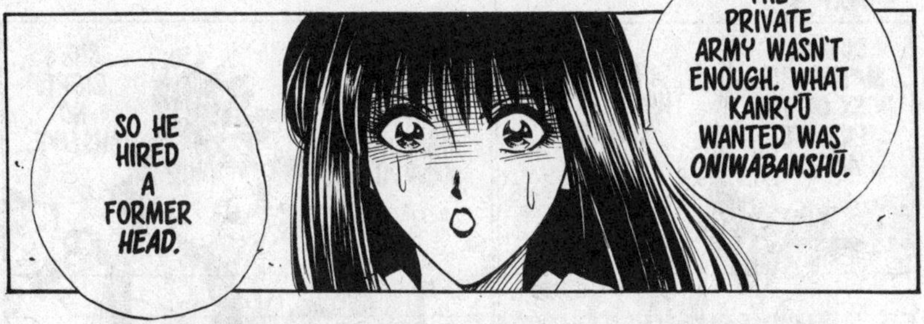
THE PRIVATE ARMY WASN'T ENOUGH. WHAT KANRYŪ WANTED WAS ONIWABANSHŪ.
SO HE HIRED A FORMER HEAD.

Oniwabanshū

An elite group of *onmitsu* (spies of the Edo period, now known as "ninja" or "shinobi") who protected from the shadows the castles and estates of generals and shōgun. Because their task was so crucial, only the ninja most skilled in combat were called to serve.

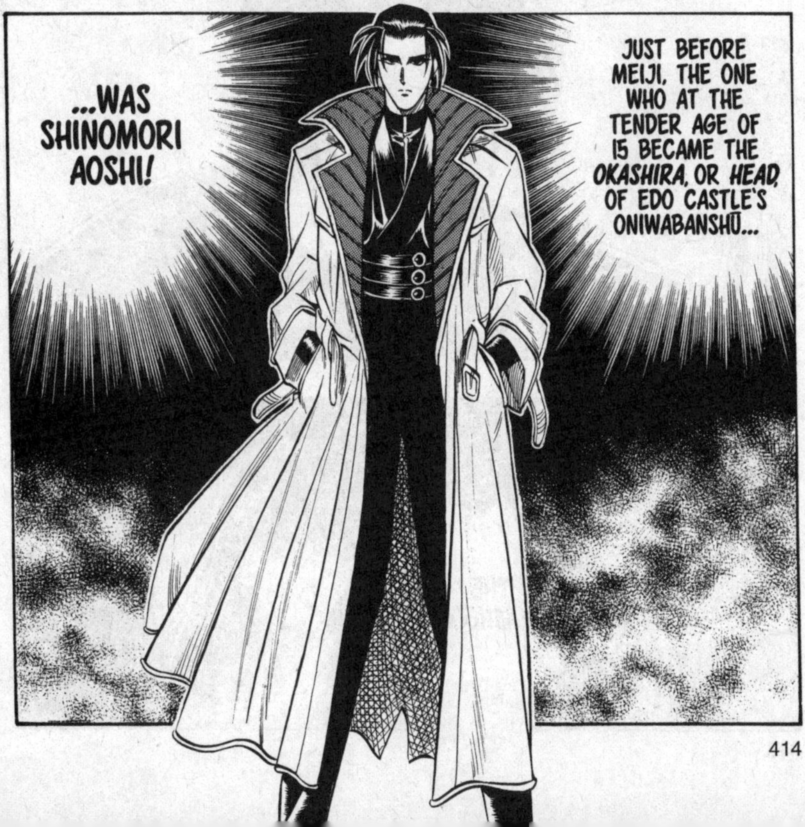
JUST BEFORE MEIJI, THE ONE WHO AT THE TENDER AGE OF 15 BECAME THE OKASHIRA, OR HEAD, OF EDO CASTLE'S ONIWABANSHŪ...
...WAS SHINOMORI AOSHI!

READ THIS WAY

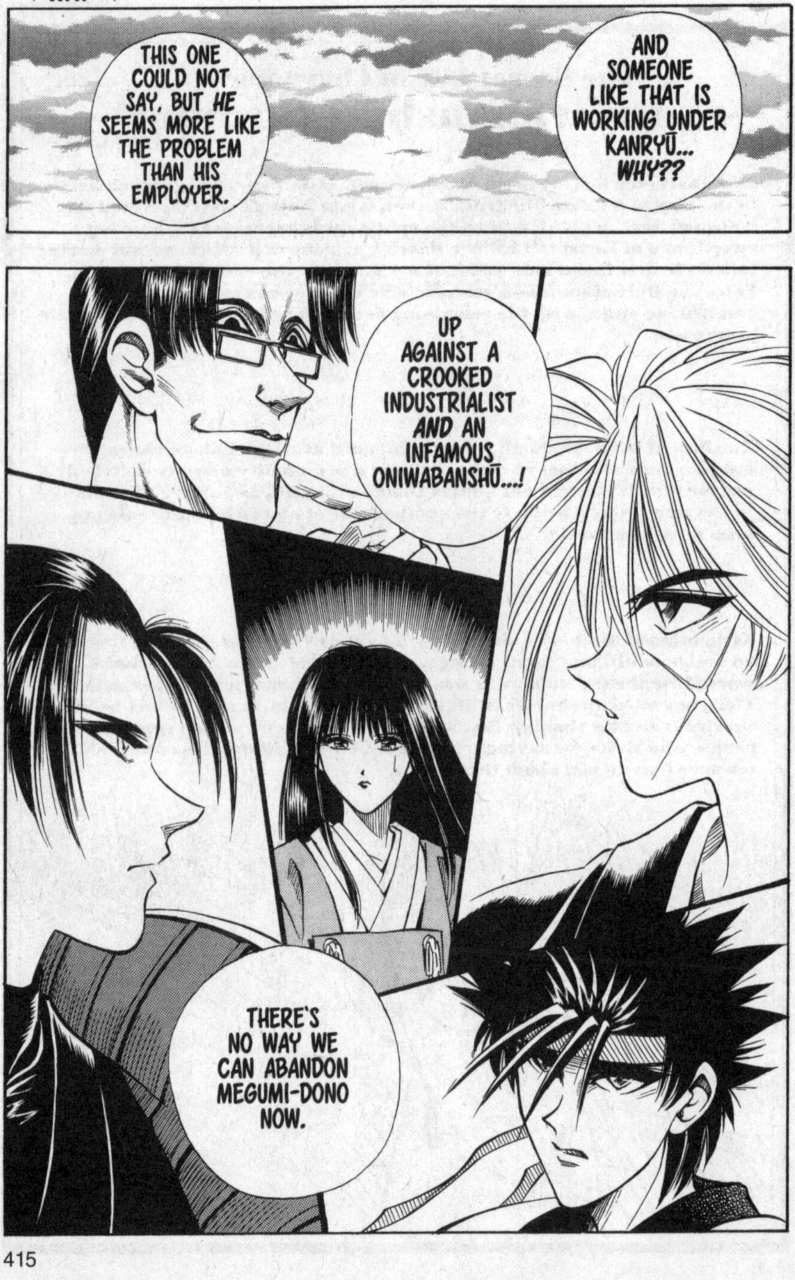
AND SOMEONE LIKE THAT IS WORKING UNDER KANRYŪ... WHY??
THIS ONE COULD NOT SAY, BUT HE SEEMS MORE LIKE THE PROBLEM THAN HIS EMPLOYER.
UP AGAINST A CROOKED INDUSTRIALIST AND AN INFAMOUS ONIWABANSHŪ...!
THERE'S NO WAY WE CAN ABANDON MEGUMI-DONO NOW.

The Secret Life of Characters (8)
—Oniwabanshū • Beshimi—

As a character largely created on-the-spot, I can't say there's much here in the way of a motif. The truth is that, when Watsuki first discussed the "Megumi Arc" with his editor, the opinion was expressed that having a swordsman of Kenshin's caliber fighting a group of punk-thugs still coming into their first facial hair mi-i-ight not make for the most epic of manga. Enter the Oniwabanshū—a real, historic entity—soon made over into onmitsu, or ninja, with the remaining details to be fleshed out as the story progressed.

The first of them, Beshimi, was not intended as a stand-alone character, but as a taste of things to come. Without a personality already sketched out for him, he turned out kind of timid...although, as you read further in the story, you'll begin to see another side of him (which I'm going to keep secret, for now).

As mentioned, Beshimi's kind of an "as-you-go" character and so there's no design motif. One thing, though, was that aside from Aoshi, what I wanted for the Oniwabanshū was a variety of shapes and temperaments. Thus, he ended up shorter in stature than Kenshin. It may in fact be his shortness and his timidity that's garnered him his own little group of fans, people who write me saying, "Beshimi KAWAI'I [Beshimi is cute]!!" Not too sure how to feel about that one....

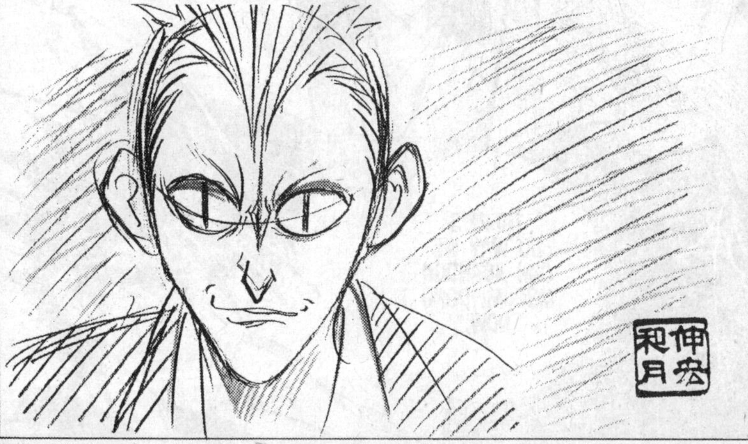
伸宏
和月

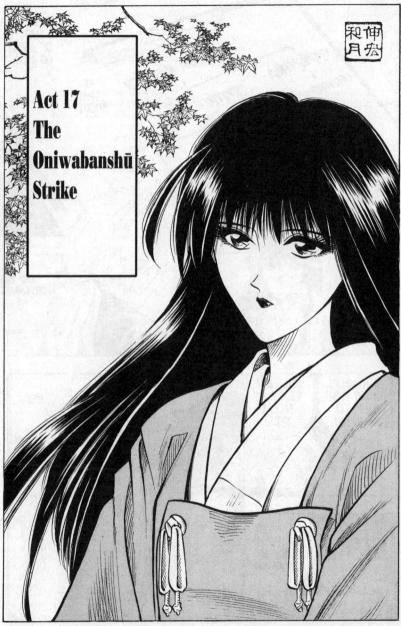

Act 17
The Oniwabanshū Strike

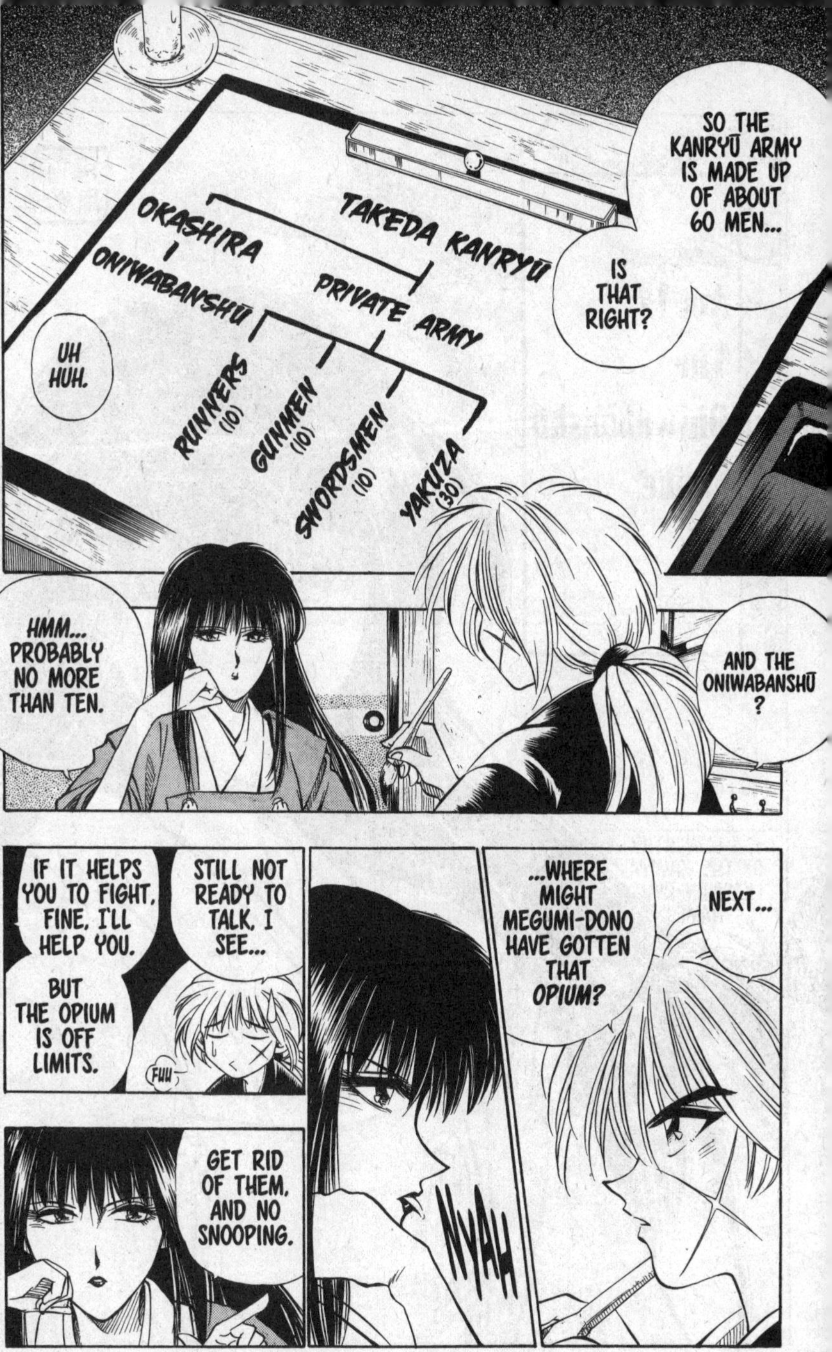
SO THE KANRYŪ ARMY IS MADE UP OF ABOUT 60 MEN...
IS THAT RIGHT?
TAKEDA KANRYŪ
OKASHIRA
ONIWABANSHŪ
PRIVATE ARMY
RUNNERS (10)
GUNMEN (10)
SWORDSMEN (10)
YAKUZA (30)
UH HUH.
AND THE ONIWABANSHŪ?
HMM... PROBABLY NO MORE THAN TEN.
NEXT...
...WHERE MIGHT MEGUMI-DONO HAVE GOTTEN THAT OPIUM?
NYAH
STILL NOT READY TO TALK, I SEE...
IF IT HELPS YOU TO FIGHT, FINE, I'LL HELP YOU.
BUT THE OPIUM IS OFF LIMITS.
FUU
GET RID OF THEM, AND NO SNOOPING.

READ THIS WAY

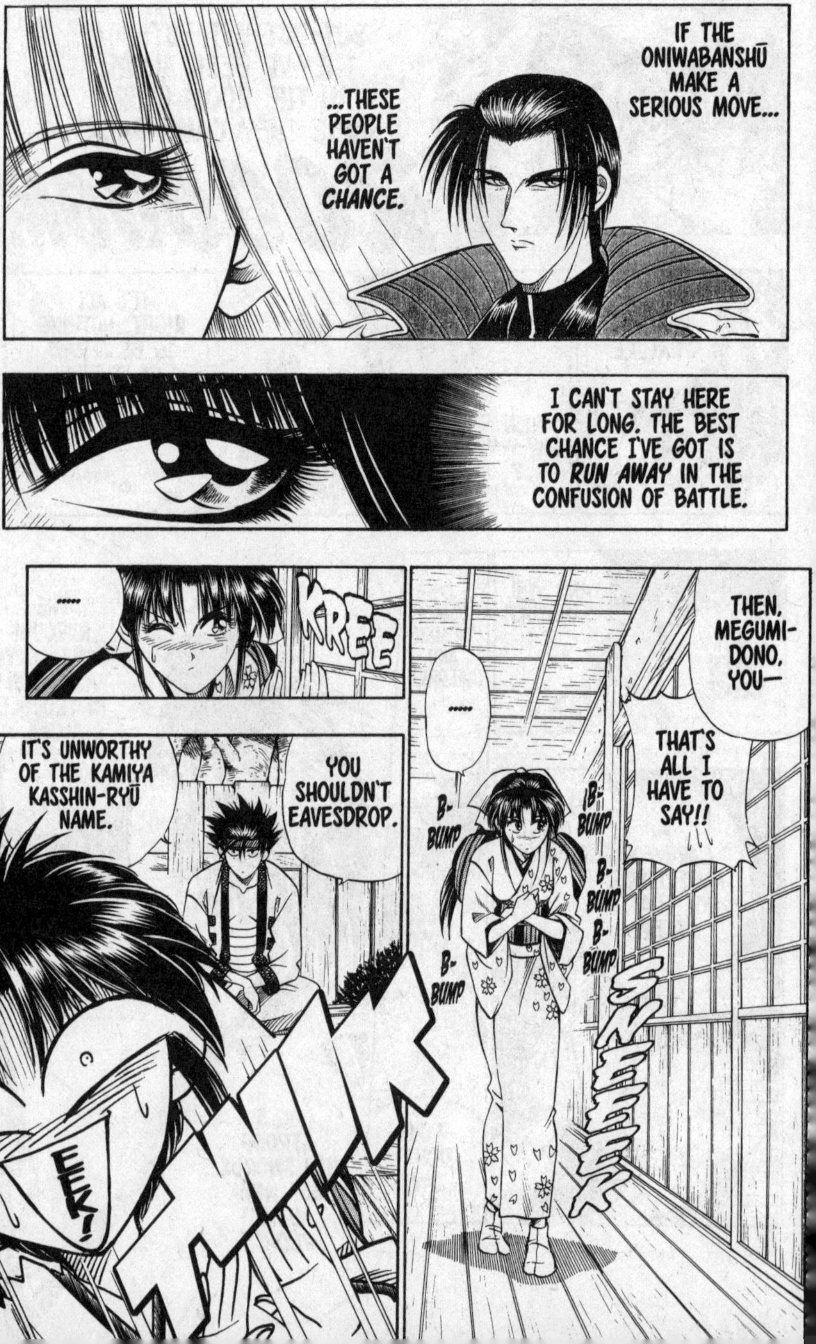
IF THE ONIWABANSHŪ MAKE A SERIOUS MOVE...
...THESE PEOPLE HAVEN'T GOT A *CHANCE.*
I CAN'T STAY HERE FOR LONG. THE BEST CHANCE I'VE GOT IS TO *RUN AWAY* IN THE CONFUSION OF BATTLE.
THEN, MEGUMI-DONO, YOU—
THAT'S ALL I HAVE TO SAY!!
......
B-BUMP
B-BUMP
B-BUMP
B-BUMP
B-BUMP
SNEEEEK
......
KREE
YOU SHOULDN'T EAVESDROP.
IT'S UNWORTHY OF THE KAMIYA KASSHIN-RYŪ NAME.
EEK!

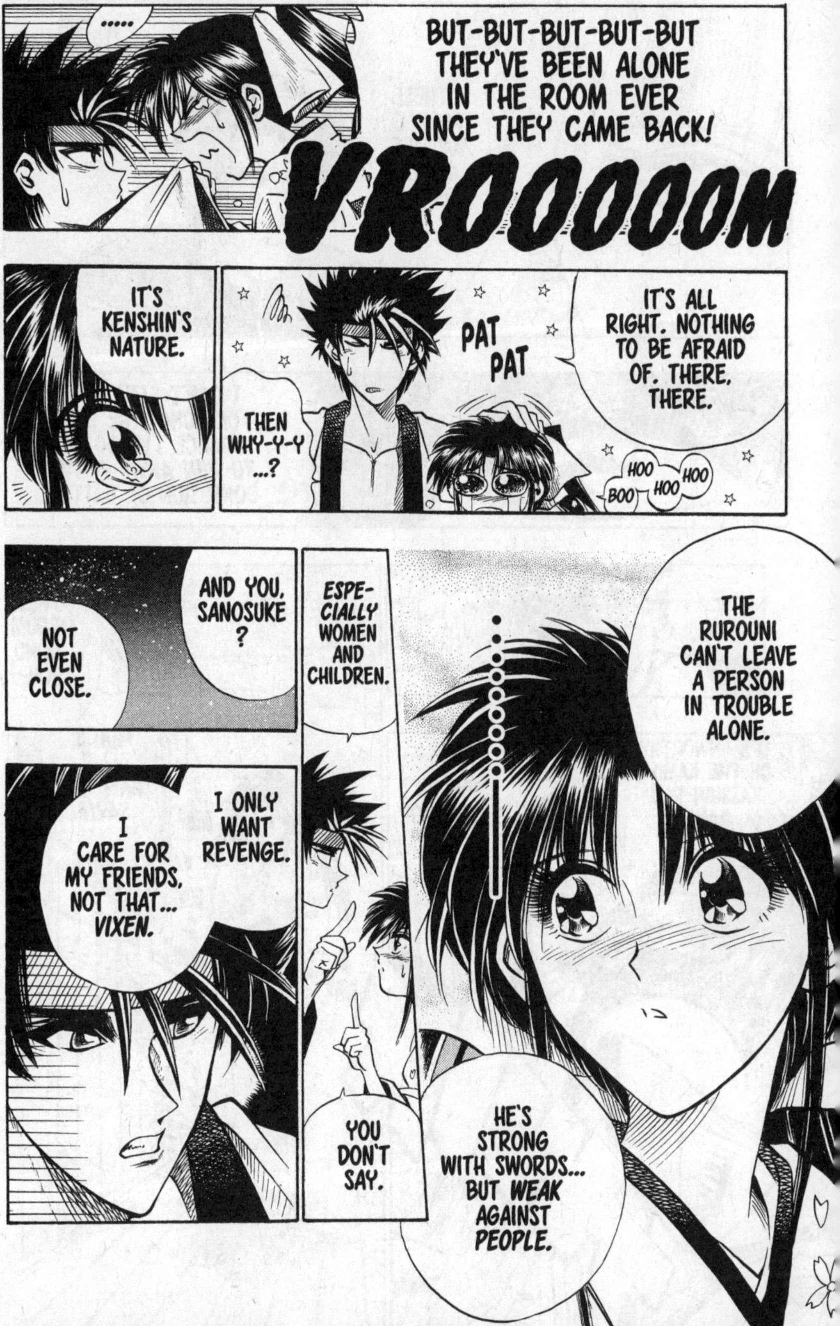
BUT-BUT-BUT-BUT-BUT THEY'VE BEEN ALONE IN THE ROOM EVER SINCE THEY CAME BACK!
VROOOOOM
......
IT'S ALL RIGHT. NOTHING TO BE AFRAID OF. THERE, THERE.
PAT PAT
HOO HOO BOO HOO
THEN WHY-Y-Y ...?
IT'S KENSHIN'S NATURE.
THE RUROUNI CAN'T LEAVE A PERSON IN TROUBLE ALONE.
HE'S STRONG WITH SWORDS... BUT WEAK AGAINST PEOPLE.
ESPE-CIALLY WOMEN AND CHILDREN.
YOU DON'T SAY.
AND YOU, SANOSUKE?
NOT EVEN CLOSE.
I ONLY WANT REVENGE.
I CARE FOR MY FRIENDS, NOT THAT... VIXEN.

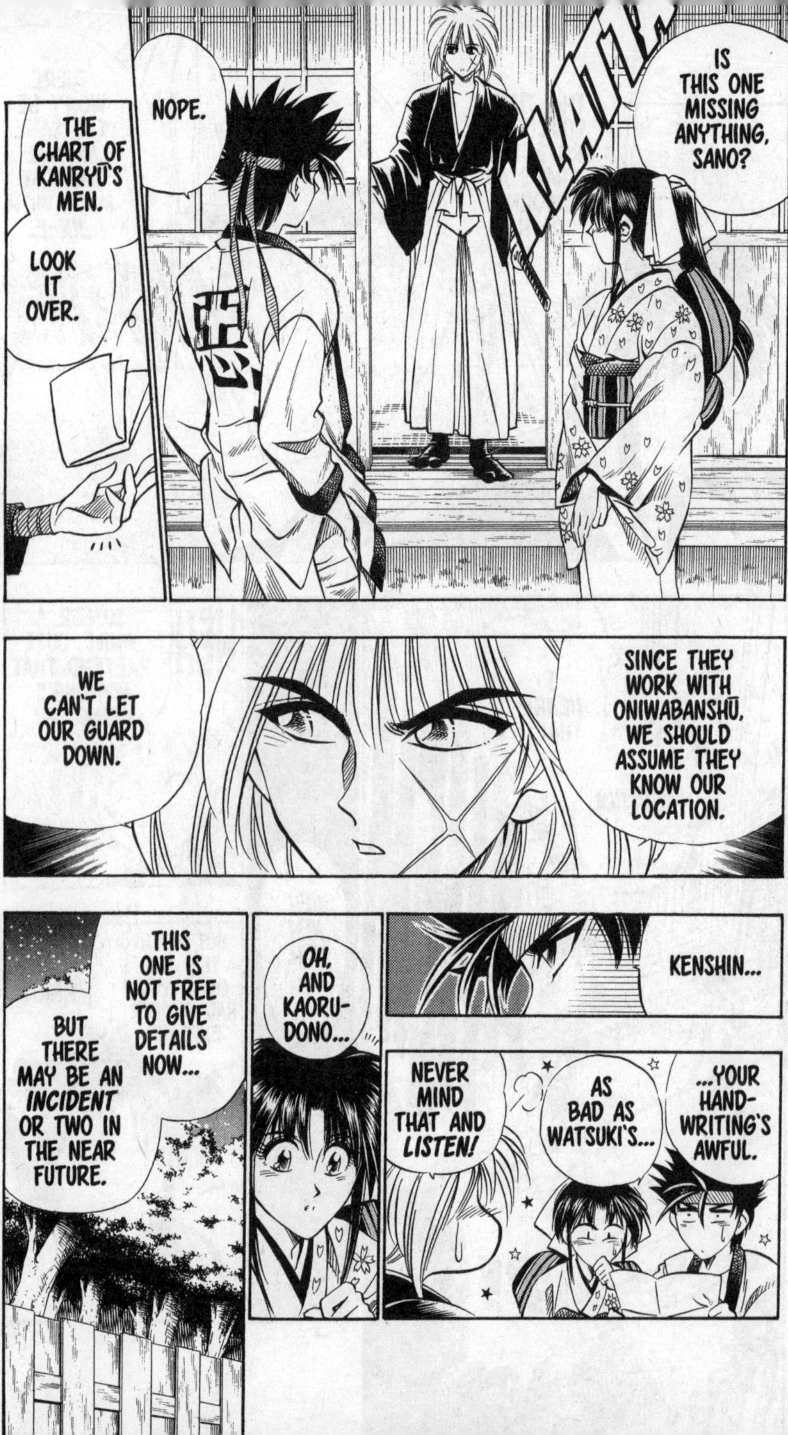
IS THIS ONE MISSING ANYTHING, SANO?
NOPE.
THE CHART OF KANRYŪ'S MEN.
LOOK IT OVER.
SINCE THEY WORK WITH ONIWABANSHŪ, WE SHOULD ASSUME THEY KNOW OUR LOCATION.
WE CAN'T LET OUR GUARD DOWN.
KENSHIN...
...YOUR HAND-WRITING'S AWFUL.
AS BAD AS WATSUKI'S...
NEVER MIND THAT AND *LISTEN!*
OH, AND KAORU-DONO...
THIS ONE IS NOT FREE TO GIVE DETAILS NOW...
BUT THERE MAY BE AN *INCIDENT* OR TWO IN THE NEAR FUTURE.

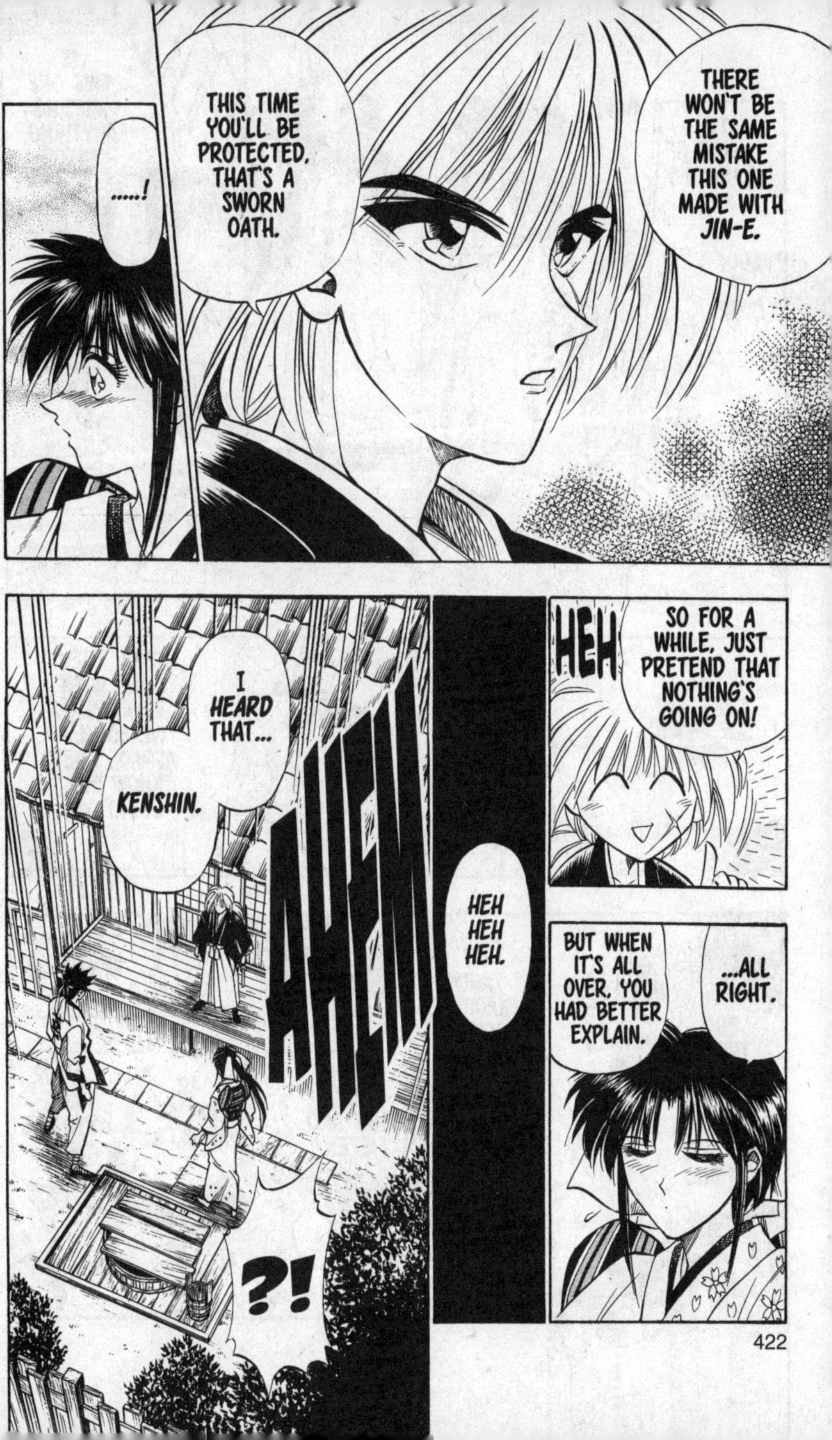
THERE WON'T BE THE SAME MISTAKE THIS ONE MADE WITH JIN-E.
THIS TIME YOU'LL BE PROTECTED. THAT'S A SWORN OATH.
......!
SO FOR A WHILE, JUST PRETEND THAT NOTHING'S GOING ON!
HEH
...ALL RIGHT.
BUT WHEN IT'S ALL OVER, YOU HAD BETTER EXPLAIN.
HEH HEH HEH.
AHEM
I HEARD THAT...
KENSHIN.
?!

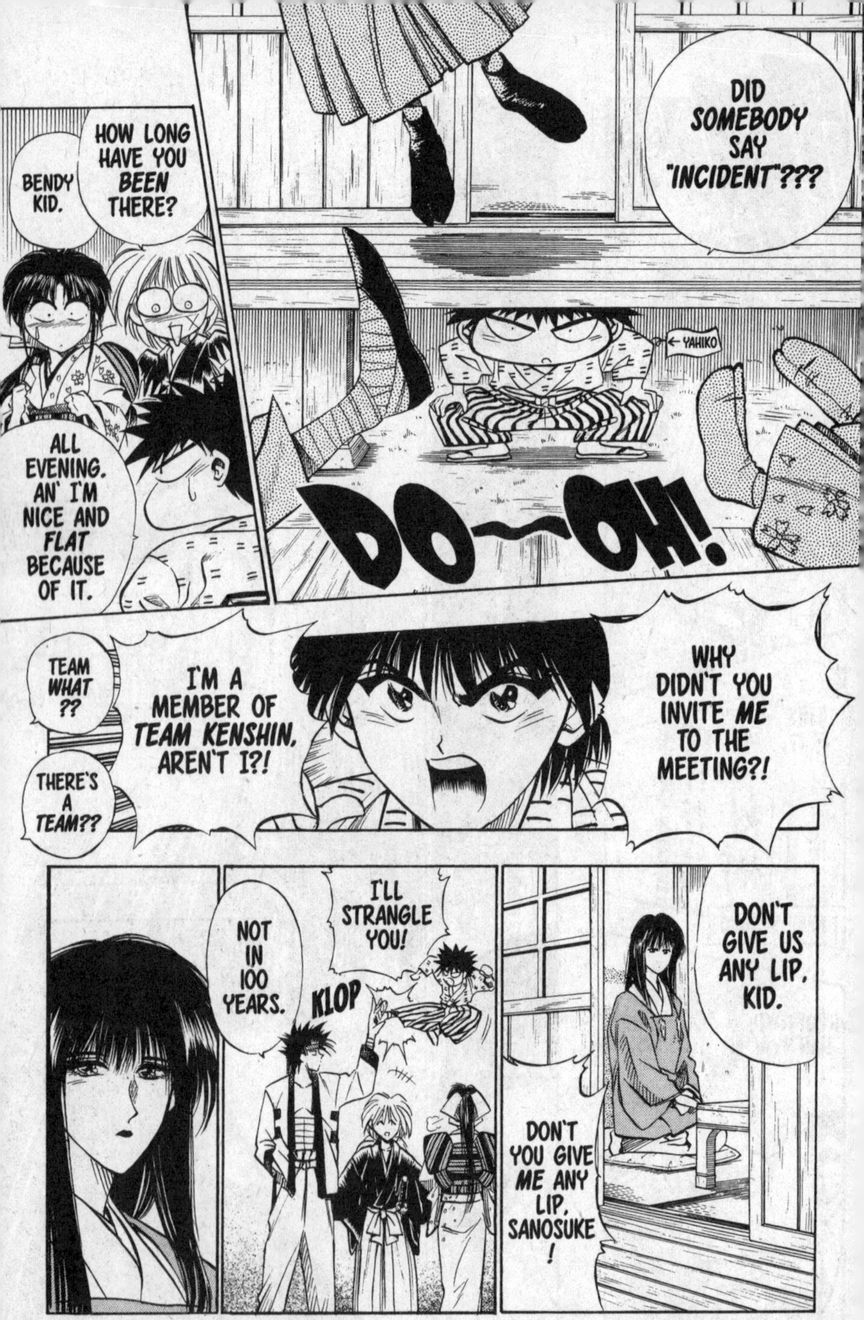
DID SOMEBODY SAY "INCIDENT"???
YAHIKO
DO--OH!
HOW LONG HAVE YOU BEEN THERE?
BENDY KID.
ALL EVENING. AN' I'M NICE AND FLAT BECAUSE OF IT.
WHY DIDN'T YOU INVITE ME TO THE MEETING?!
I'M A MEMBER OF TEAM KENSHIN, AREN'T I?!
TEAM WHAT??
THERE'S A TEAM??
DON'T GIVE US ANY LIP, KID.
DON'T YOU GIVE ME ANY LIP, SANOSUKE!
I'LL STRANGLE YOU!
NOT IN 100 YEARS.
KLOP

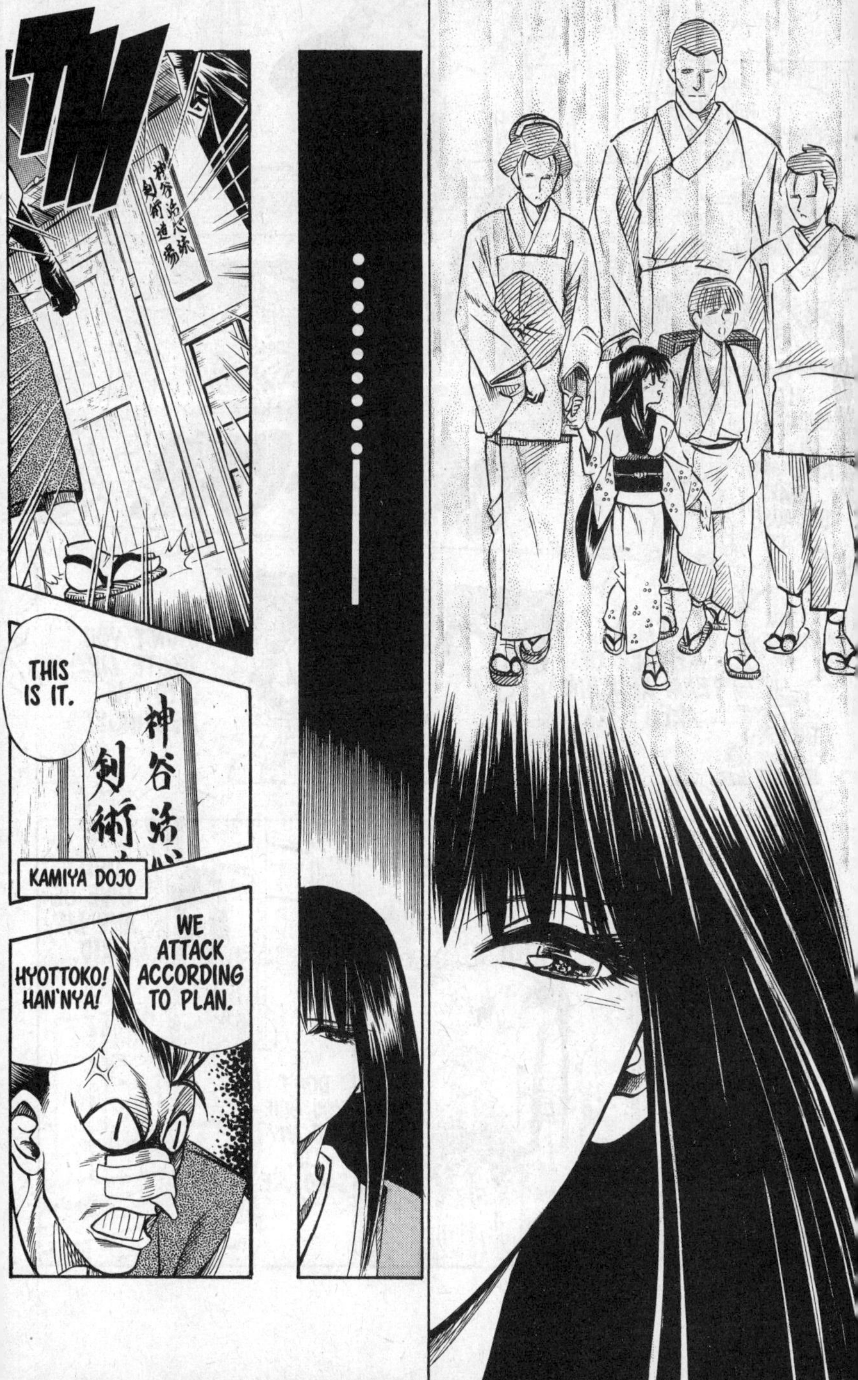

神谷活心流
剣術道場
THIS IS IT.
KAMIYA DOJO
WE ATTACK ACCORDING TO PLAN.
HYOTTOKO! HAN'NYA!

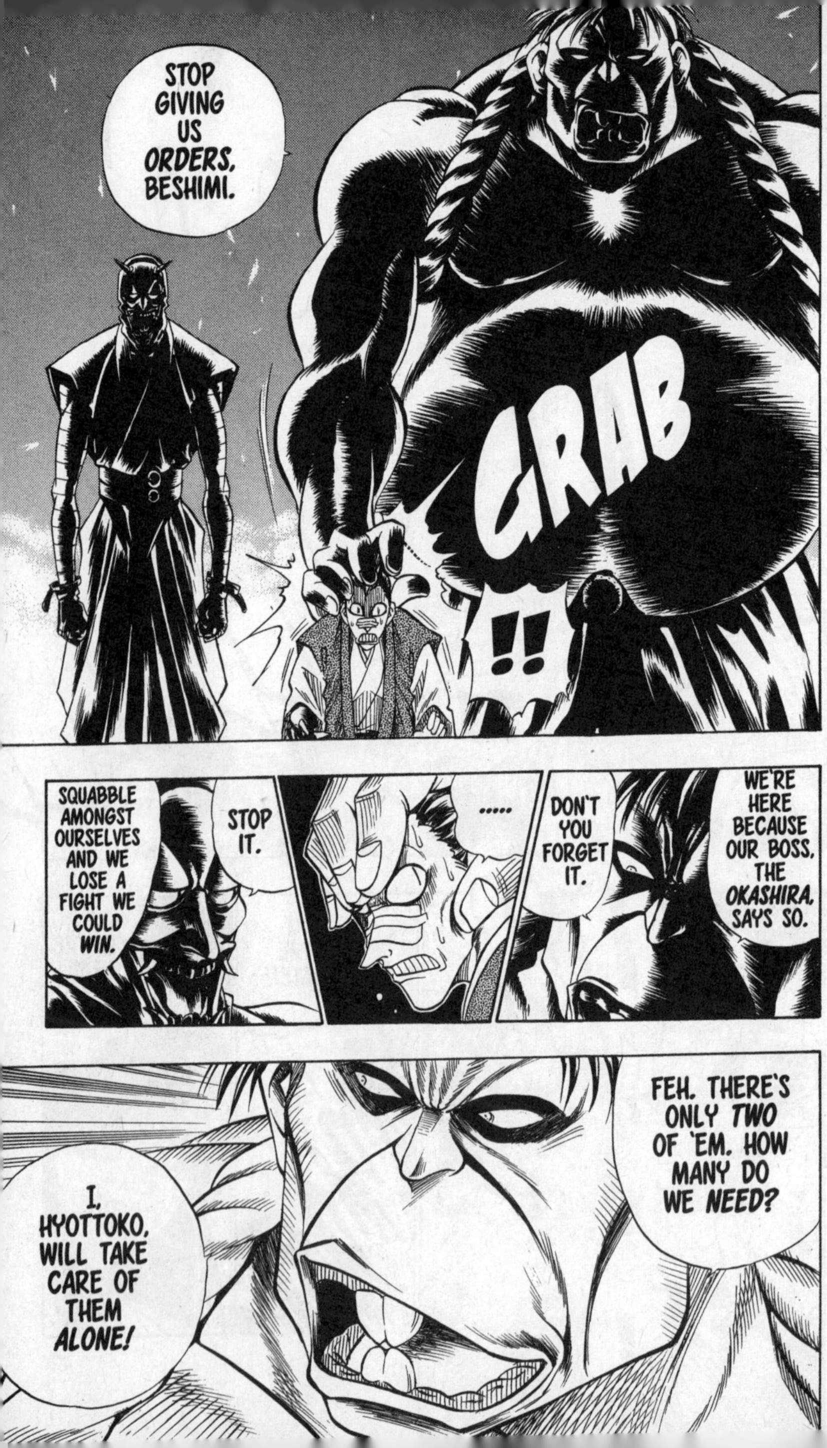
STOP GIVING US ORDERS, BESHIMI.
GRAB
!!
WE'RE HERE BECAUSE OUR BOSS, THE OKASHIRA, SAYS SO.
DON'T YOU FORGET IT.
.....
STOP IT.
SQUABBLE AMONGST OURSELVES AND WE LOSE A FIGHT WE COULD WIN.
FEH. THERE'S ONLY TWO OF 'EM. HOW MANY DO WE NEED?
I, HYOTTOKO, WILL TAKE CARE OF THEM ALONE!

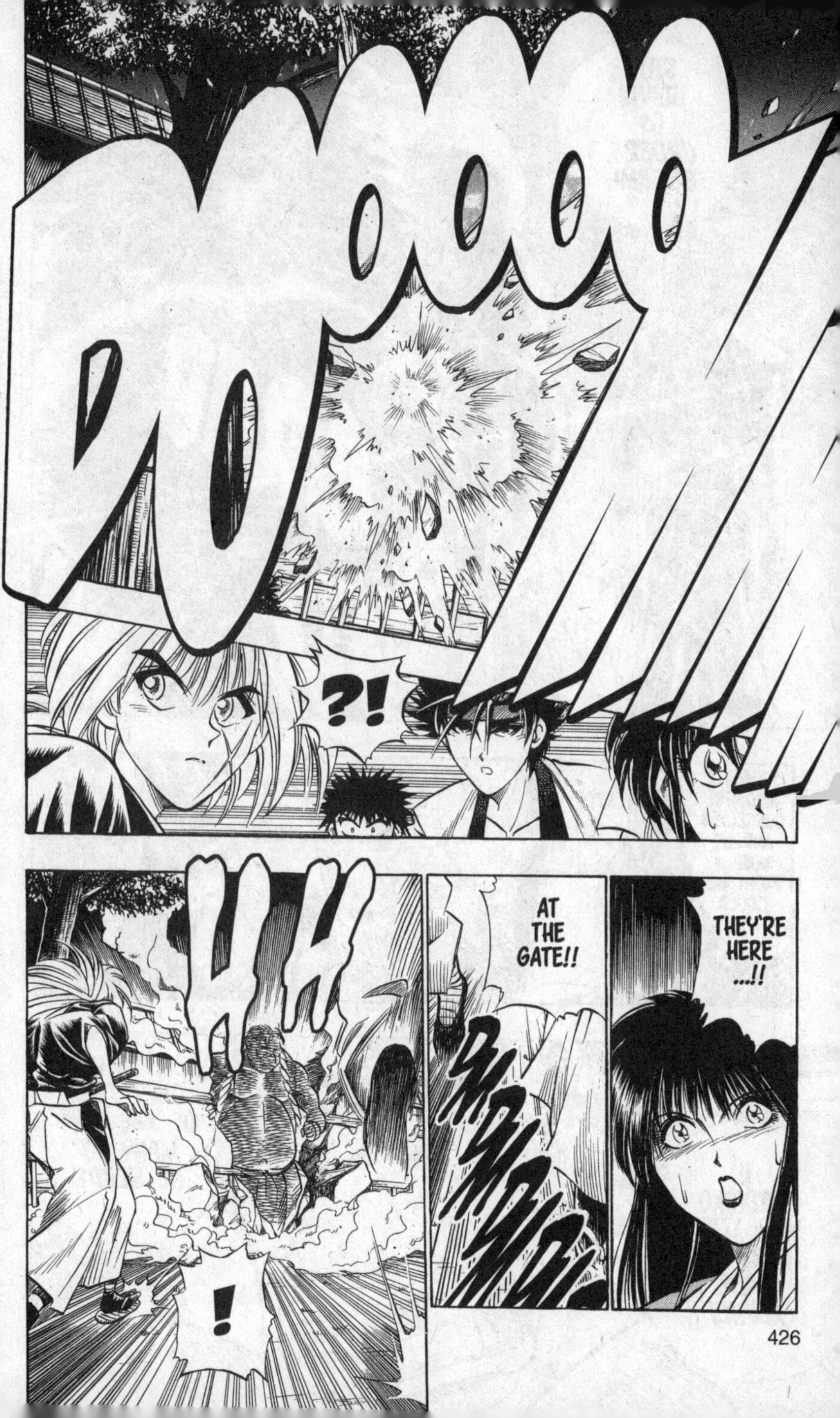
DOOOOM
?!
THEY'RE HERE ...!!
AT THE GATE!!
!

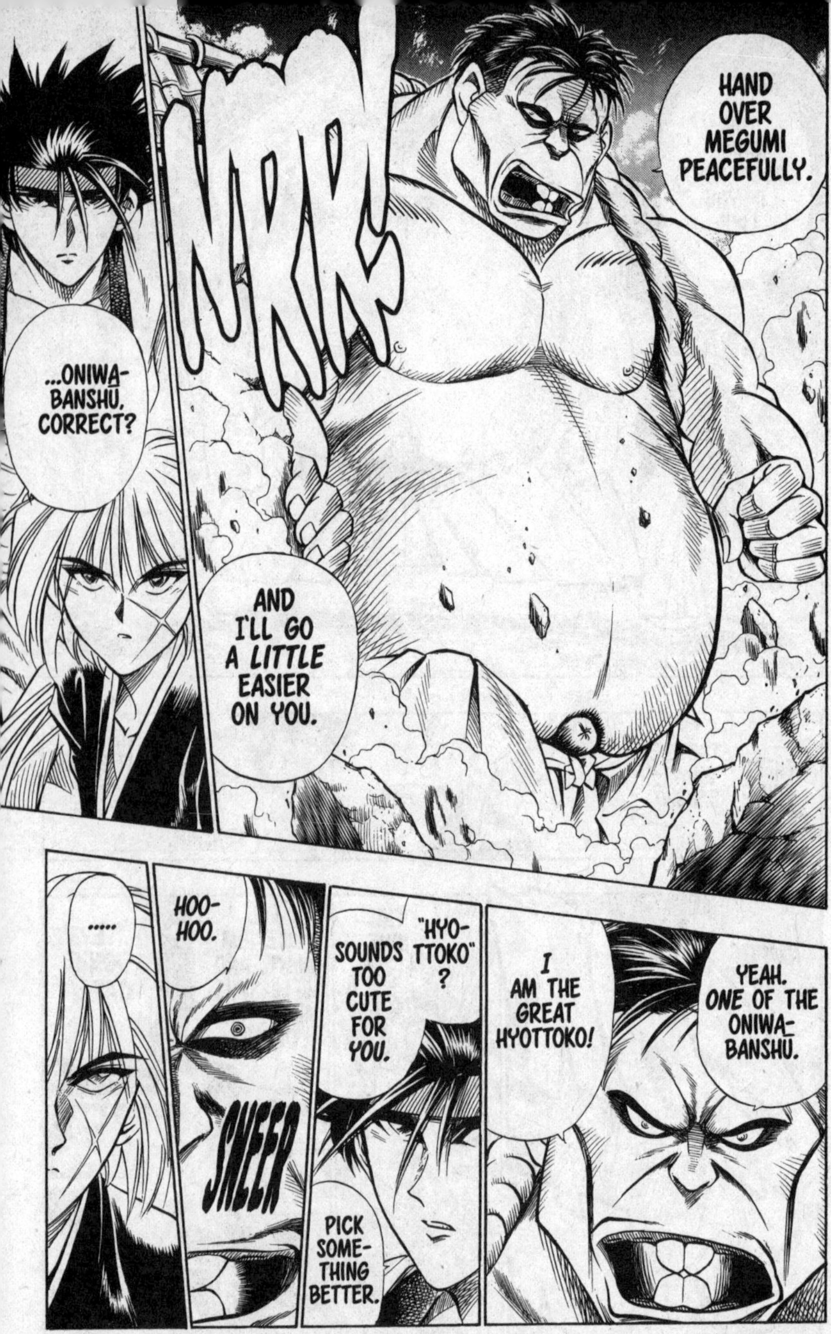
HAND OVER MEGUMI PEACEFULLY.
AND I'LL GO A *LITTLE* EASIER ON YOU.
...ONIWA-BANSHU, CORRECT?
YEAH. *ONE* OF THE ONIWA-BANSHU.
I AM THE GREAT HYOTTOKO!
"HYOTTOKO"?
SOUNDS TOO CUTE FOR YOU.
PICK SOMETHING BETTER.
HOO-HOO.
SNEER
......

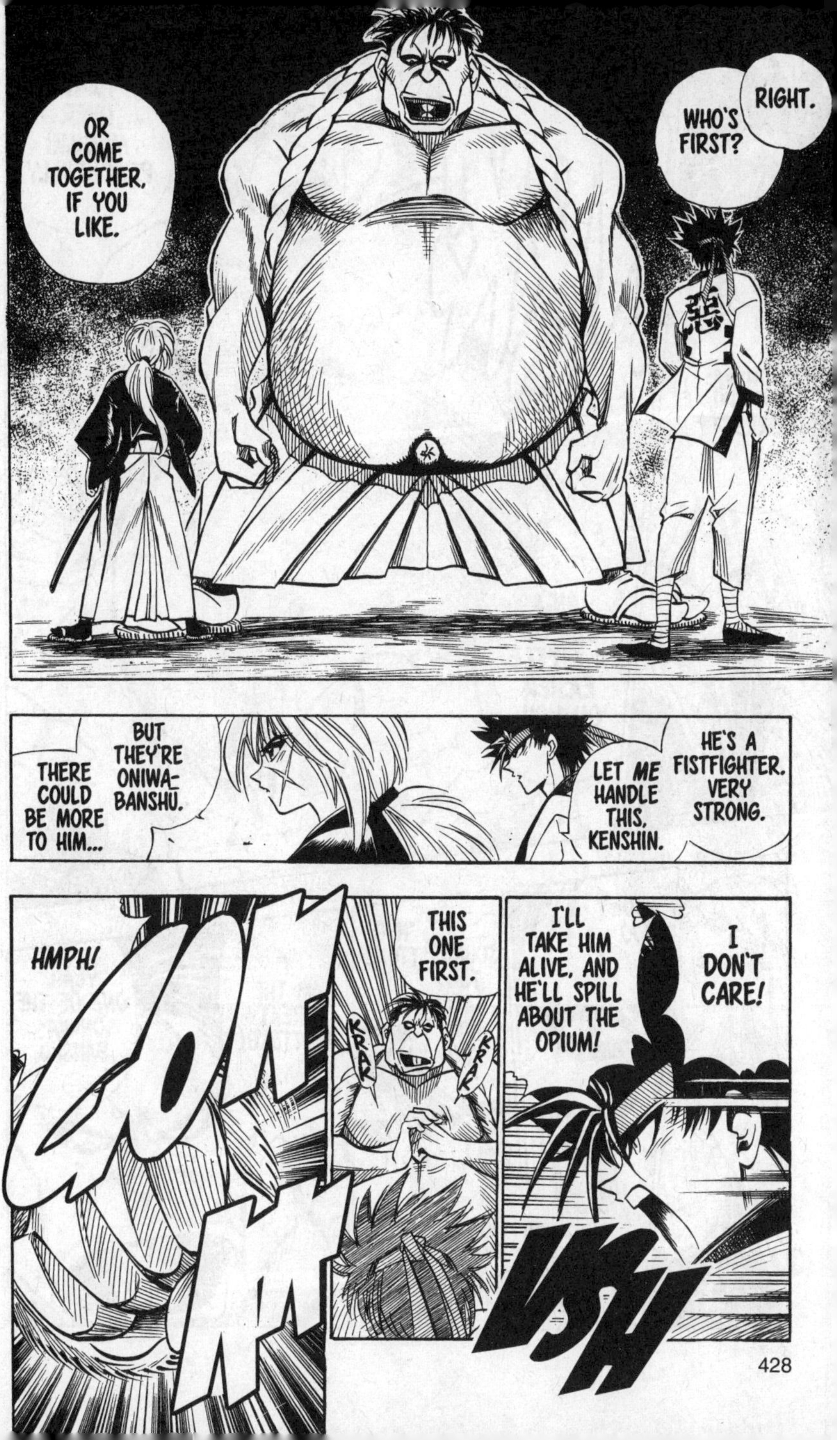
RIGHT.
WHO'S FIRST?
OR COME TOGETHER, IF YOU LIKE.
HE'S A FISTFIGHTER. VERY STRONG.
LET *ME* HANDLE THIS, KENSHIN.
BUT THEY'RE ONIWA-BANSHU.
THERE COULD BE MORE TO HIM...
I DON'T CARE!
I'LL TAKE HIM ALIVE, AND HE'LL SPILL ABOUT THE OPIUM!
THIS ONE FIRST.
KRAK
KRAK
HMPH!

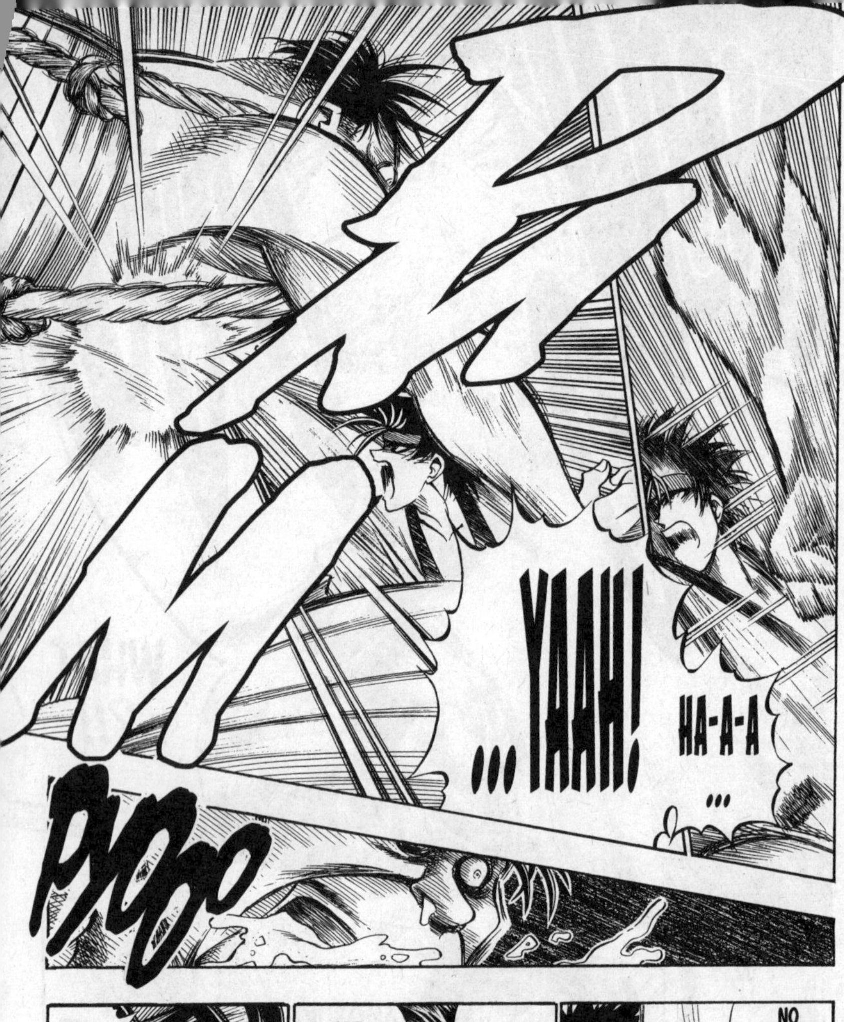
HA-A-A ...
...YAAH!
NO MATTER HOW STRONG YOU ARE...
...STILL YOU GOTTA LAND THE HIT.
MMG... THANKS.
FOR COMING WITHIN RANGE...
?

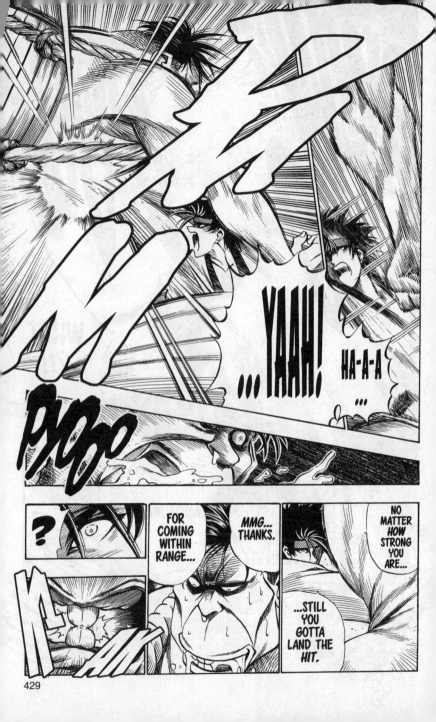

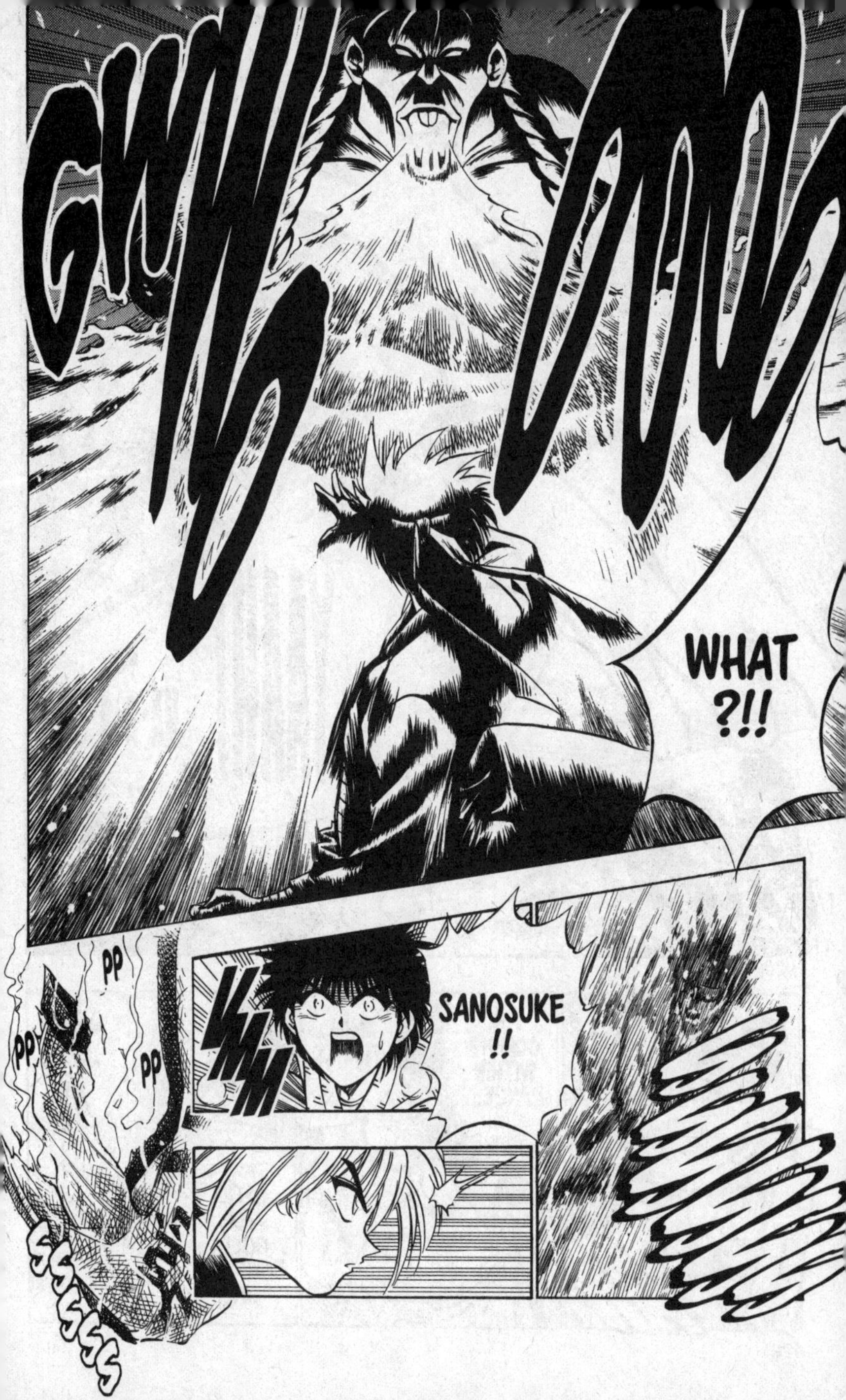
GHUUOOO
WHAT ?!!
SANOSUKE !!
PP
PP
PP
SSSSSS

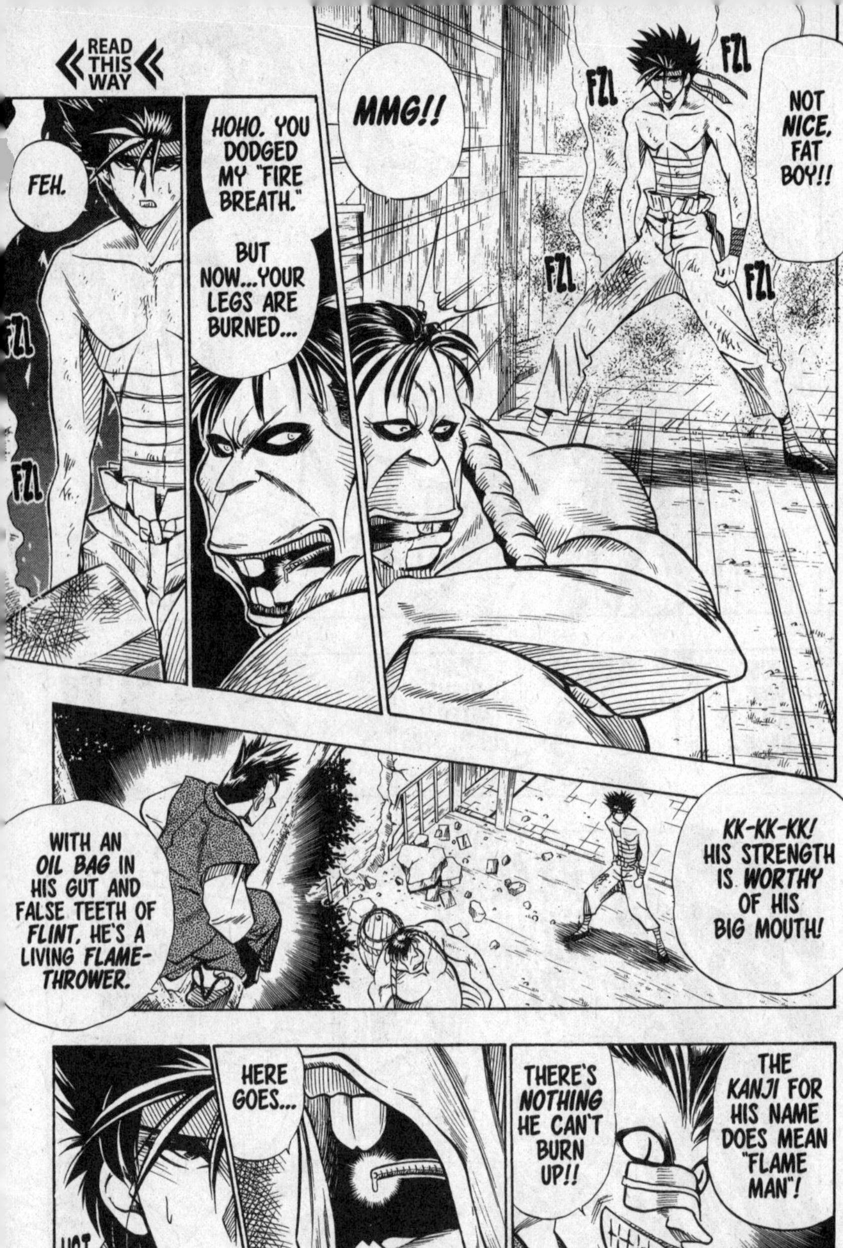
READ THIS WAY
FZL
FZL
NOT NICE, FAT BOY!!
FZL
FZL
MMG!!
HOHO. YOU DODGED MY "FIRE BREATH."
BUT NOW...YOUR LEGS ARE BURNED...
FEH.
FZL
FZL
KK-KK-KK! HIS STRENGTH IS WORTHY OF HIS BIG MOUTH!
WITH AN OIL BAG IN HIS GUT AND FALSE TEETH OF FLINT, HE'S A LIVING FLAME-THROWER.
THE KANJI FOR HIS NAME DOES MEAN "FLAME MAN"!
THERE'S NOTHING HE CAN'T BURN UP!!
HERE GOES...
HST

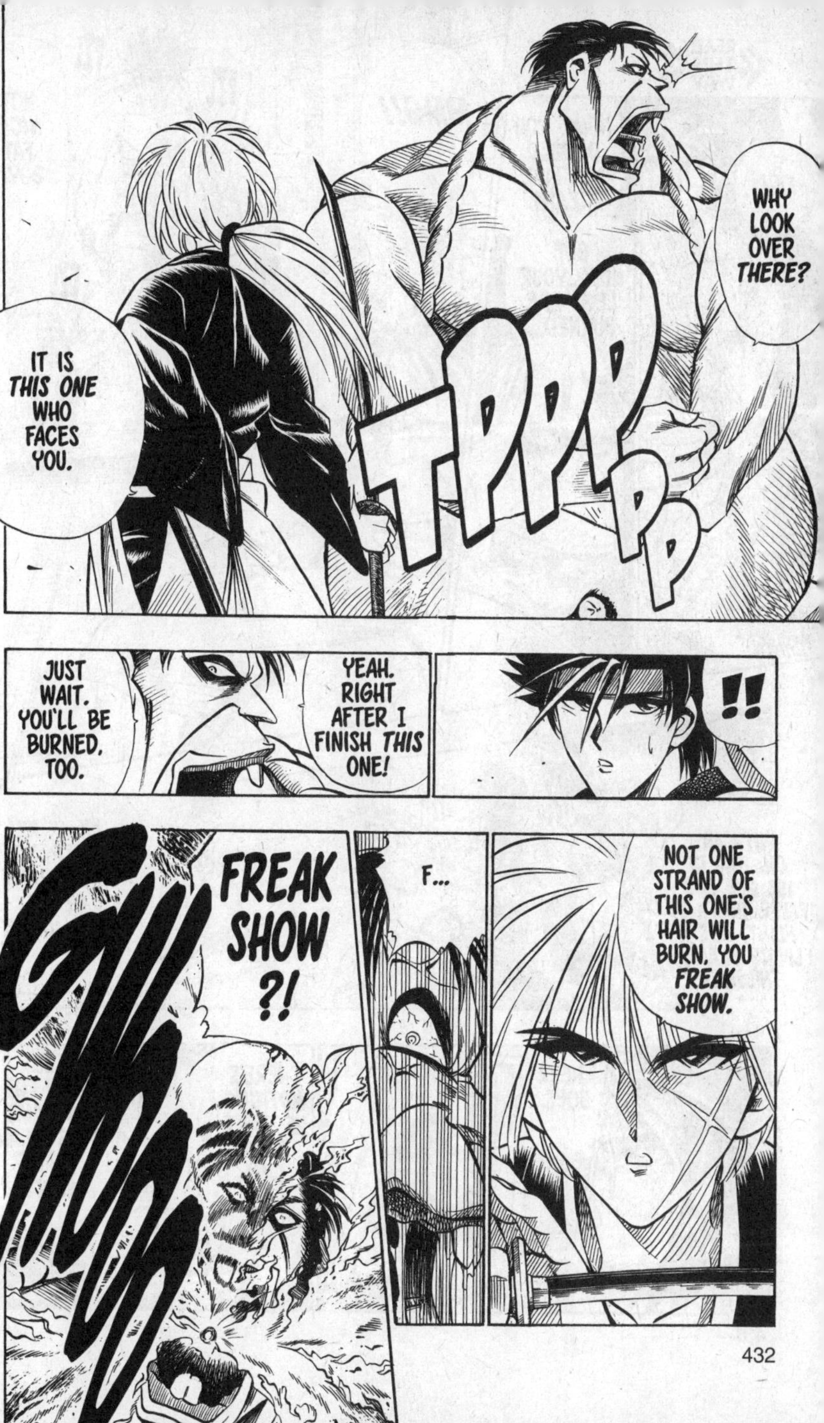
WHY LOOK OVER THERE?
T-PPP PP
IT IS THIS ONE WHO FACES YOU.
!!
YEAH. RIGHT AFTER I FINISH THIS ONE!
JUST WAIT. YOU'LL BE BURNED, TOO.
NOT ONE STRAND OF THIS ONE'S HAIR WILL BURN, YOU FREAK SHOW.
F...
FREAK SHOW?!

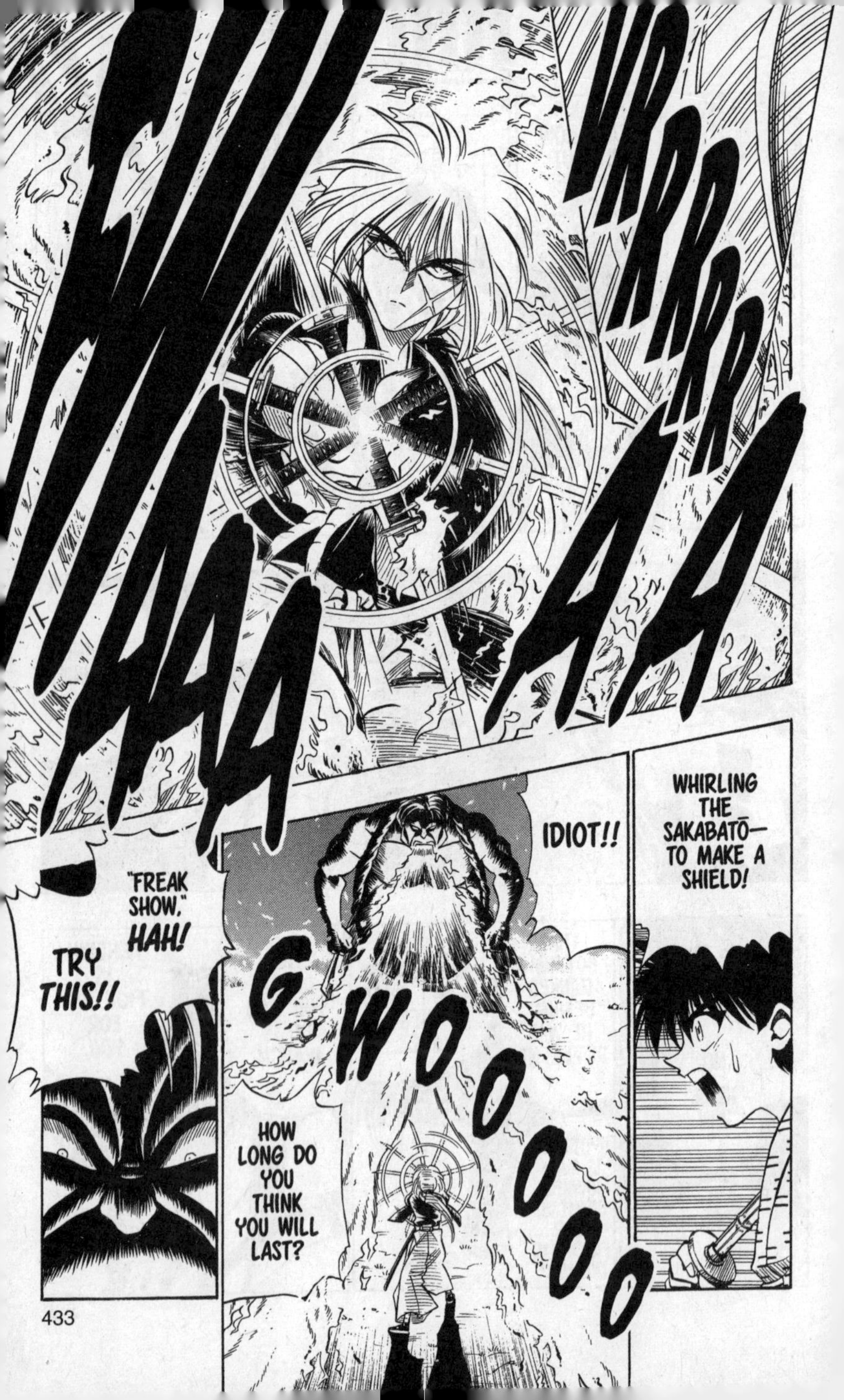
WHIRLING THE SAKABATŌ—TO MAKE A SHIELD!
IDIOT!!
GWOOOOOOO
HOW LONG DO YOU THINK YOU WILL LAST?
"FREAK SHOW." HAH!
TRY THIS!!

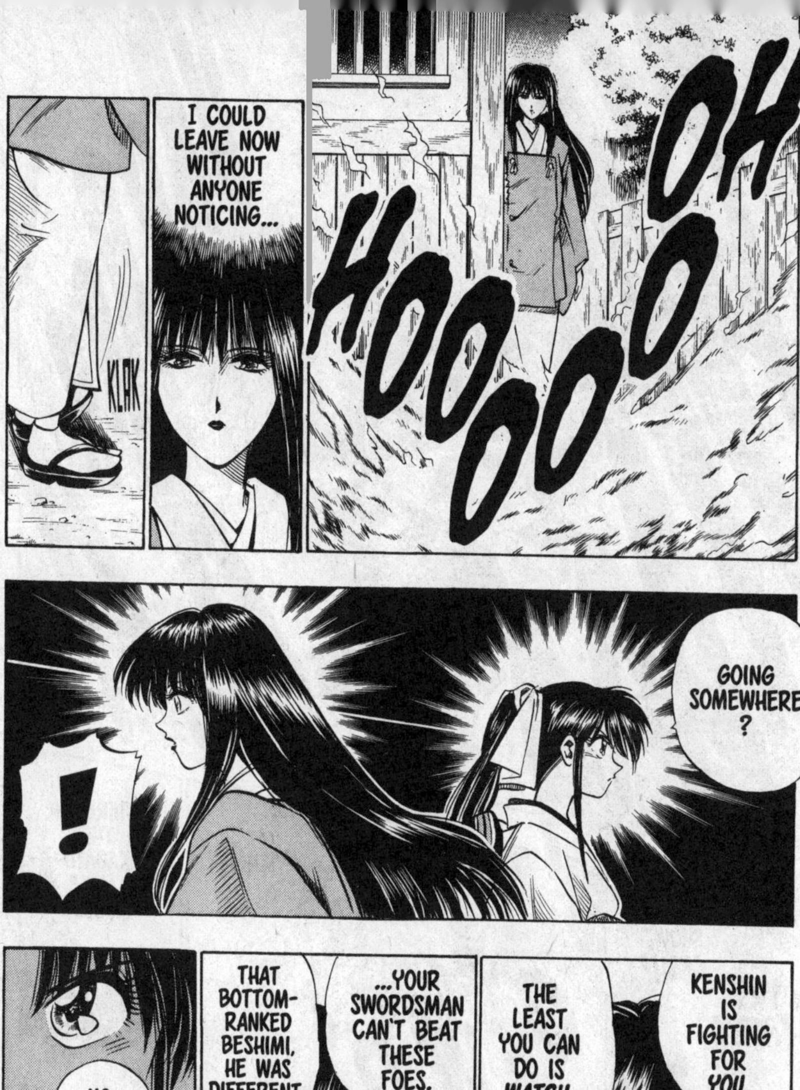
HOOOOOOOOH
I COULD LEAVE NOW WITHOUT ANYONE NOTICING...
KLAK
GOING SOMEWHERE?
!
KENSHIN IS FIGHTING FOR YOU.
THE LEAST YOU CAN DO IS WATCH.
...YOUR SWORDSMAN CAN'T BEAT THESE FOES.
THAT BOTTOM-RANKED BESHIMI, HE WAS DIFFERENT.
HYOTTOKO IS MID-RANKED ONMITSU. YOUR FRIEND IS DOOMED.
NO. HE'LL WIN.

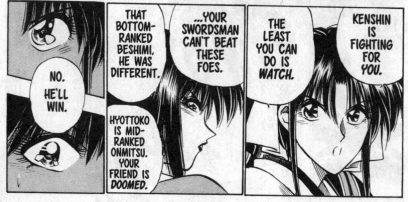

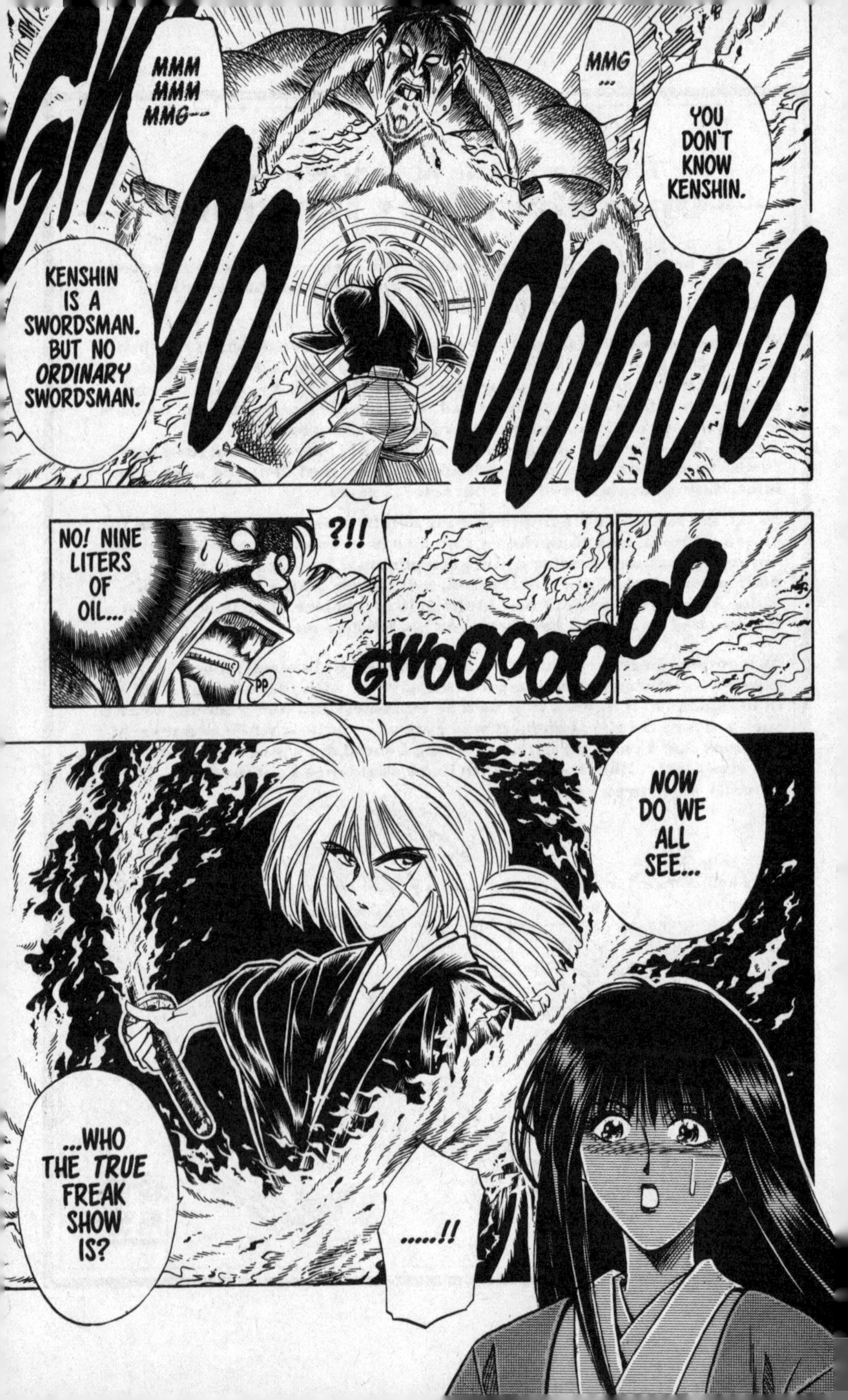
MMG...
YOU DON'T KNOW KENSHIN.
MMM MMM MMG--
KENSHIN IS A SWORDSMAN. BUT NO *ORDINARY* SWORDSMAN.
GWOOOOOOOO
?!!
NO! NINE LITERS OF OIL...
PP
GWOOOOOOOO
NOW DO WE ALL SEE...
...WHO THE *TRUE* FREAK SHOW IS?
.....!!

The Secret Life of Characters (9)

—Oniwabanshū • Hyottoko—

No motif here, either. Drawing upon my rudimentary kanji knowledge for the name (Hyottoko=fire+man), I eventually got a character who was, what do you know! A fire-breather.

Since he's an onmitsu (a ninja, in other words, although when you just write it like that, "ninja," it seems so cheesy, which is why it's onmitsu), I figured it was only natural for him to be a little flashy. In that sense, the fire-breathing didn't seem so bad. Looking back now, though, he does seem a bit out of place, not really organic to the world he's in. Personality-wise, he's the guy who makes a big entrance and then gets just as spectacularly beaten—ridiculously overconfident and a bit of an idiot. Natural evolution of the character, I guess.

As for the matter of the fire-breathing and its defeat by Kenshin with the sword-spinning technique, know that I've been roundly criticized by fans, dōjinshi "fanzine" creators, and even personal friends for it. "They're both circus-freaks!" they exclaimed, leaving me with a bit of puzzled sadness. (In my defense, I was in the grip of summer doldrums at the time—not much of an excuse, but there you go. Forgive me.)

As mentioned earlier, what I'd wanted for the Oniwabanshū was an assortment of shapes and temperaments. What with there being an oil bag in his stomach, it figured that he'd be extremely fat. Never having drawn such a figure before, though, it was only after quite a while and several versions that I came up with something I could draw not only comfortably, but repeatedly. How cool was it to know that, once I got used to it, it actually came pretty easily.

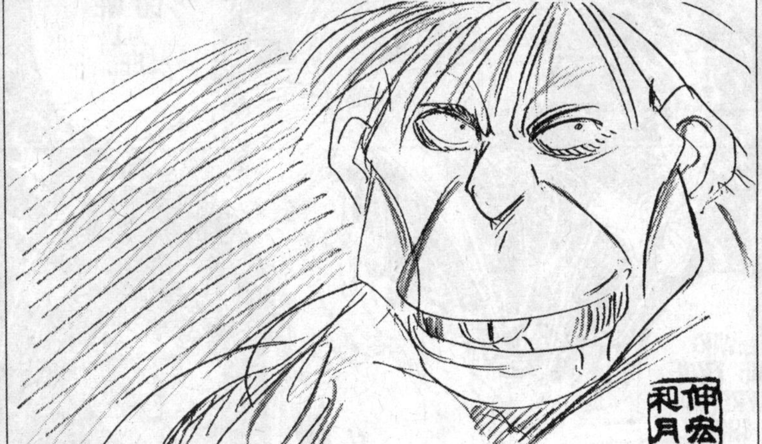
伸宏
和月

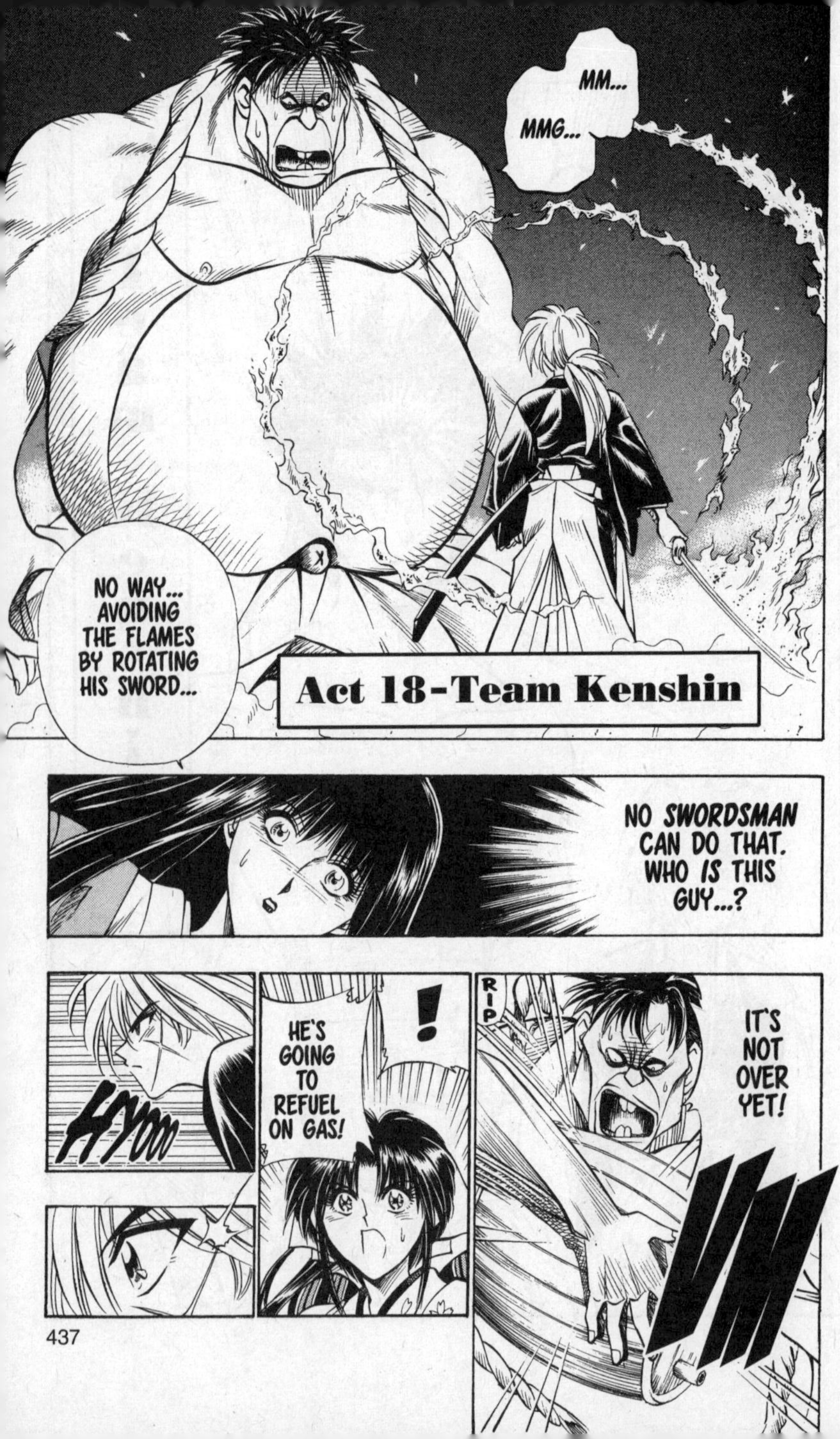
MM... MMG...
NO WAY... AVOIDING THE FLAMES BY ROTATING HIS SWORD...
Act 18-Team Kenshin
NO SWORDSMAN CAN DO THAT. WHO IS THIS GUY...?
RIP
IT'S NOT OVER YET!
!
HE'S GOING TO REFUEL ON GAS!
HYOOO

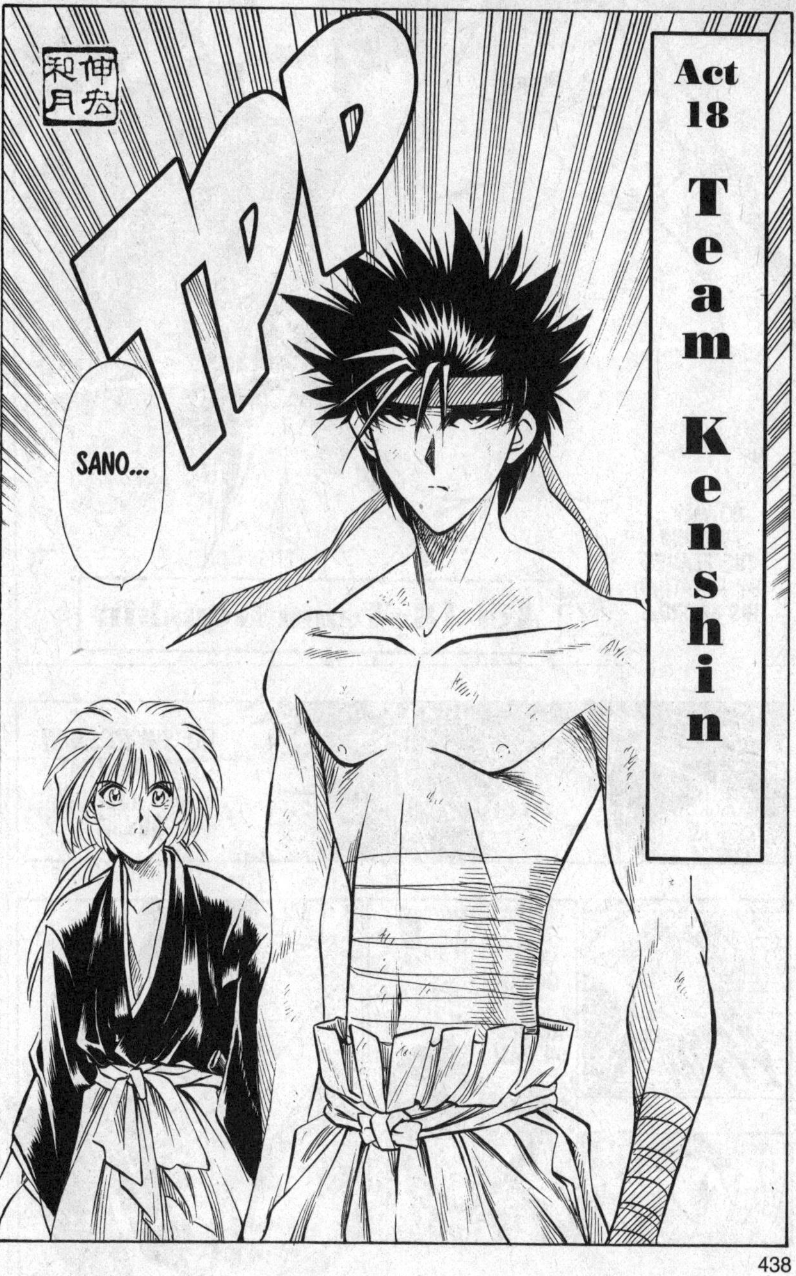
Act 18
Team Kenshin
TAP
伸宏和月
SANO...

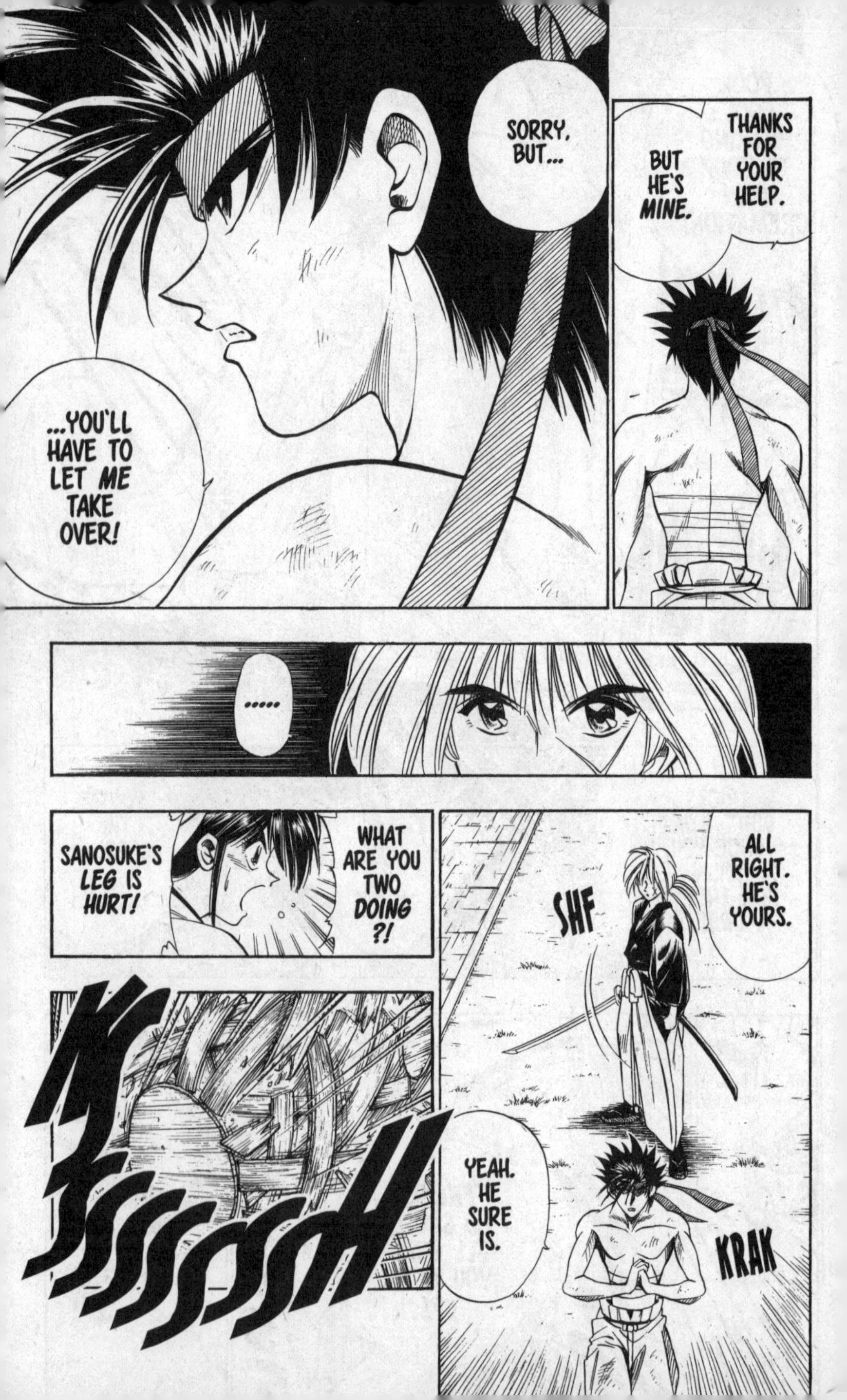
THANKS FOR YOUR HELP.
BUT HE'S *MINE.*
SORRY, BUT...
...YOU'LL HAVE TO LET *ME* TAKE OVER!
......
ALL RIGHT. HE'S YOURS.
SHF
YEAH. HE SURE IS.
KRAK
WHAT ARE YOU TWO *DOING* ?!
SANOSUKE'S *LEG* IS *HURT!*
KSSSSSSSH!!

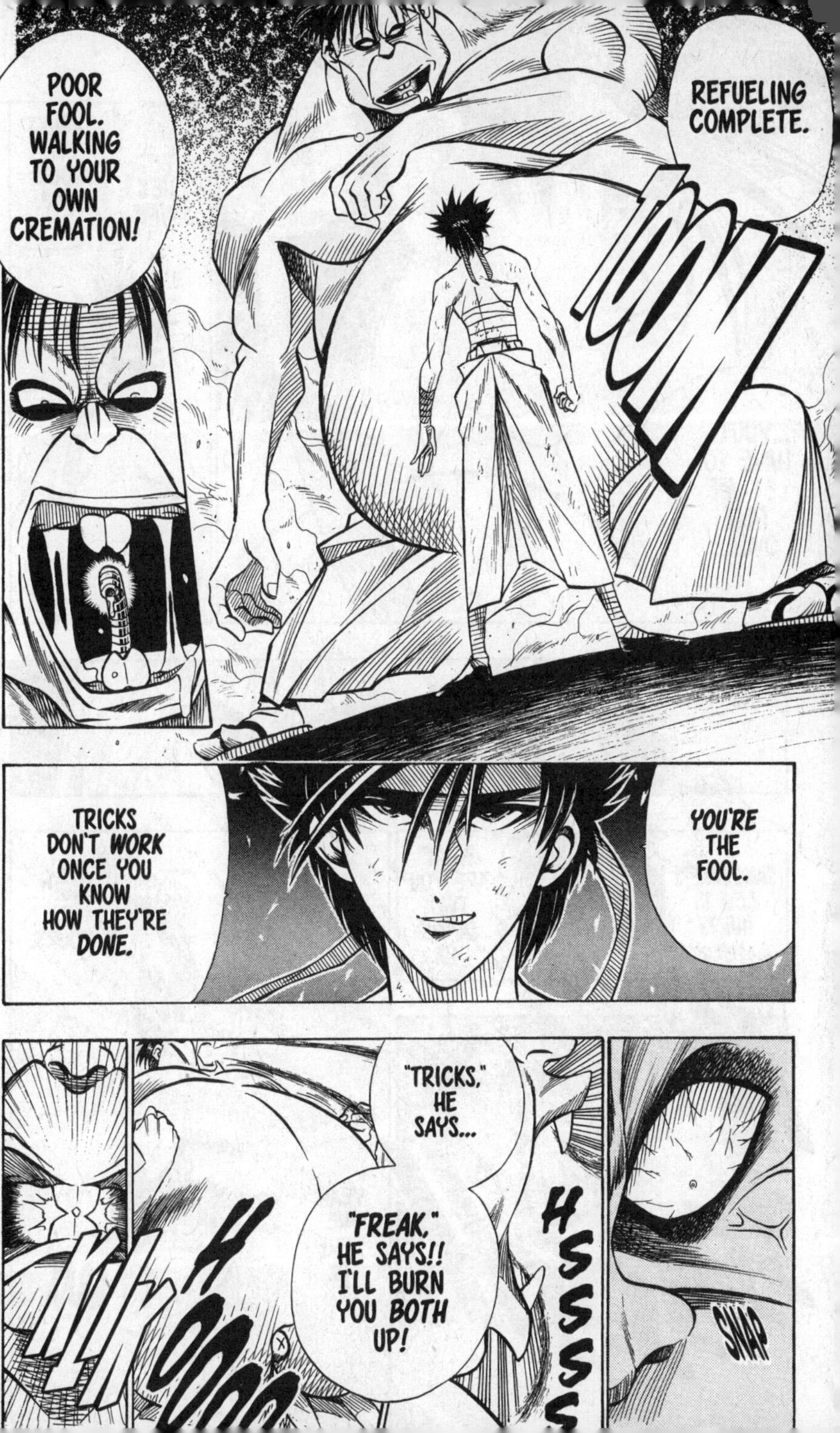
REFUELING COMPLETE.
TOOM
POOR FOOL. WALKING TO YOUR OWN CREMATION!
YOU'RE THE FOOL.
TRICKS DON'T *WORK* ONCE YOU KNOW HOW THEY'RE *DONE.*
SNAP
HSSS
"TRICKS," HE SAYS...
"FREAK," HE SAYS!! I'LL BURN YOU *BOTH* UP!

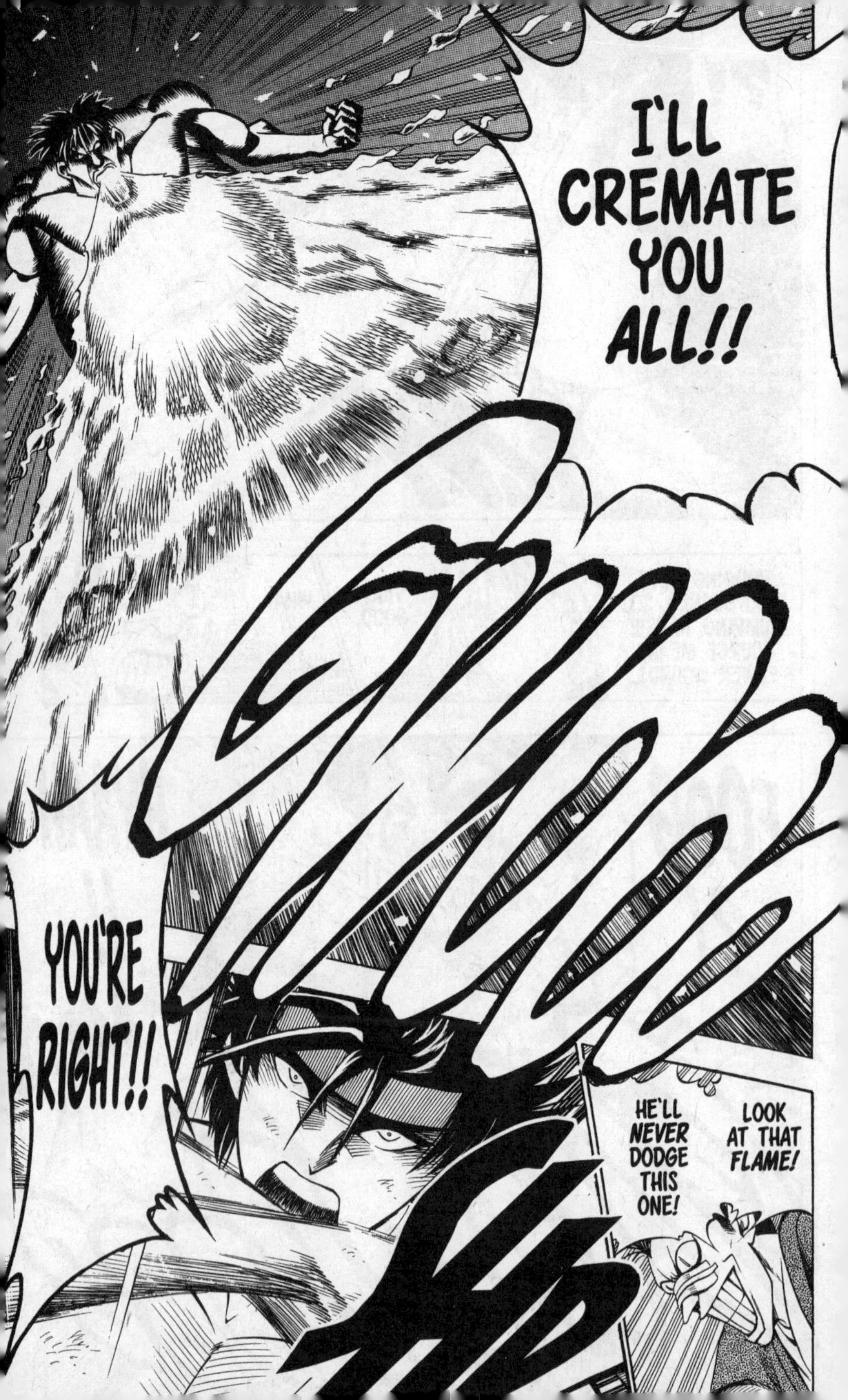
I'LL CREMATE YOU ALL!!
LOOK AT THAT FLAME!
HE'LL NEVER DODGE THIS ONE!
YOU'RE RIGHT!!

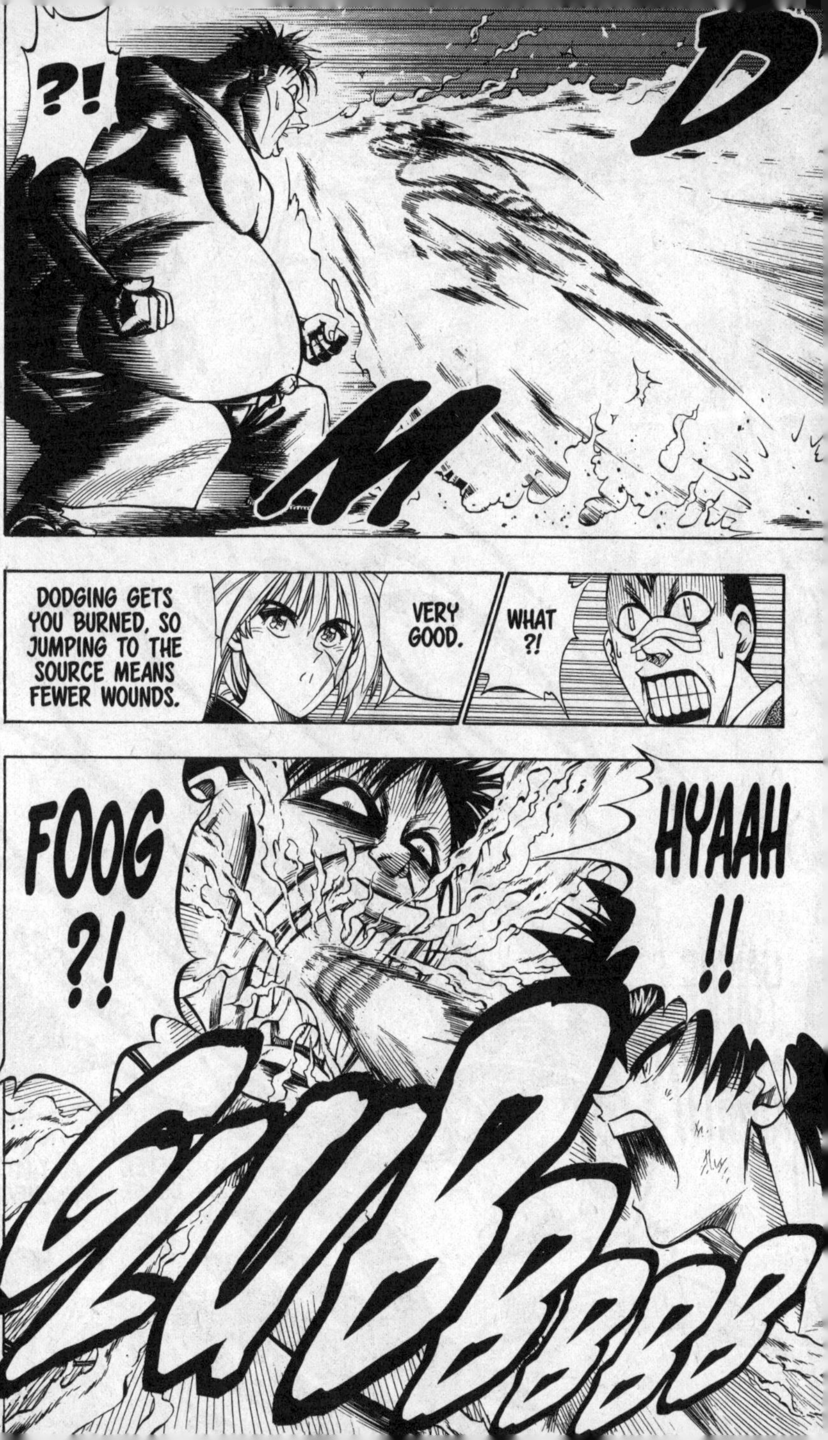
D
?!
M
WHAT ?!
VERY GOOD.
DODGING GETS YOU BURNED, SO JUMPING TO THE SOURCE MEANS FEWER WOUNDS.
HYAAH !!
FOOG ?!

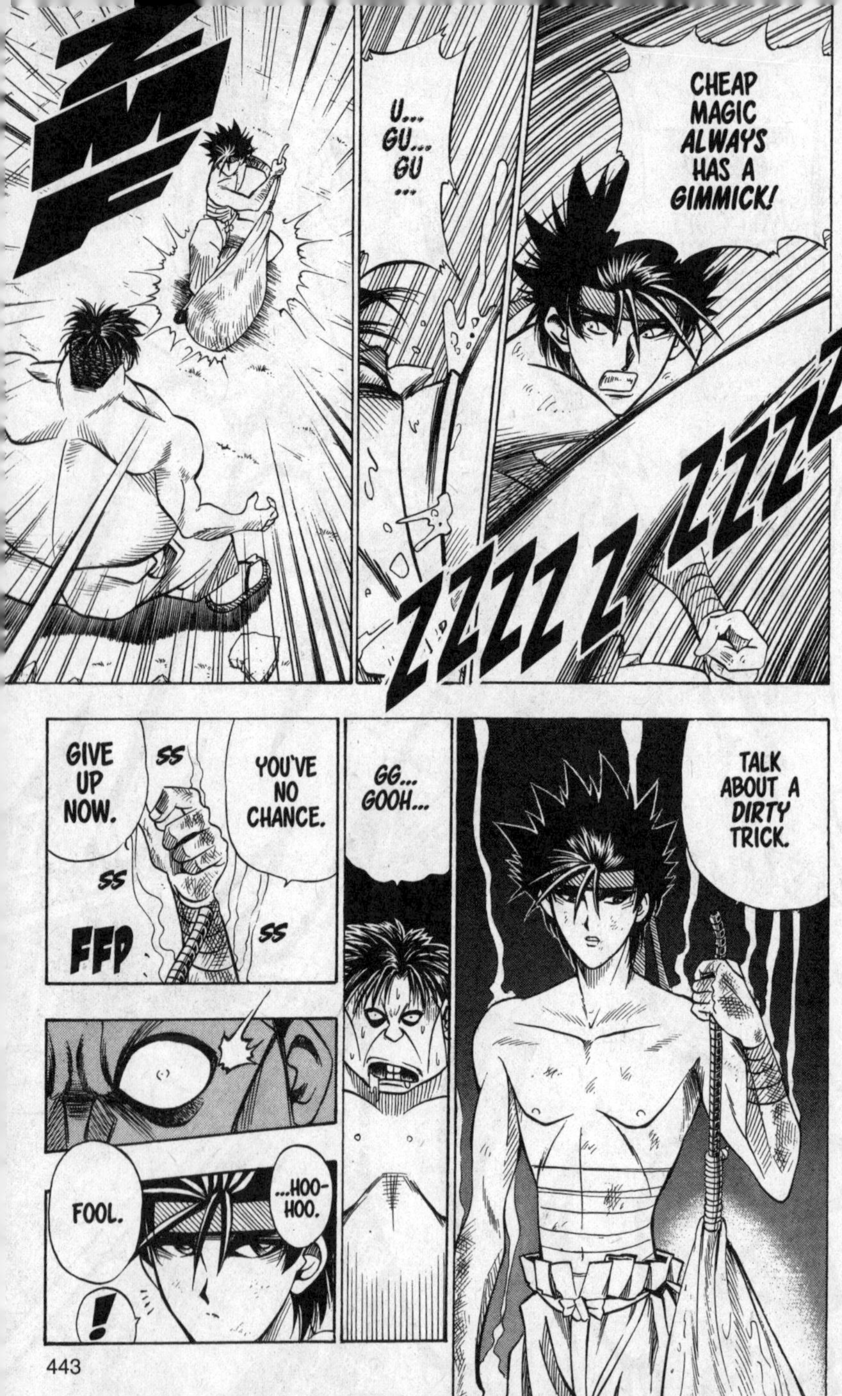
CHEAP MAGIC ALWAYS HAS A GIMMICK!
ZZZZ Z
ZZZZ
U... GU... GU ...
TALK ABOUT A DIRTY TRICK.
GG... GOOH...
YOU'VE NO CHANCE.
GIVE UP NOW.
SS
SS
SS
FFP
...HOO-HOO.
FOOL.
!

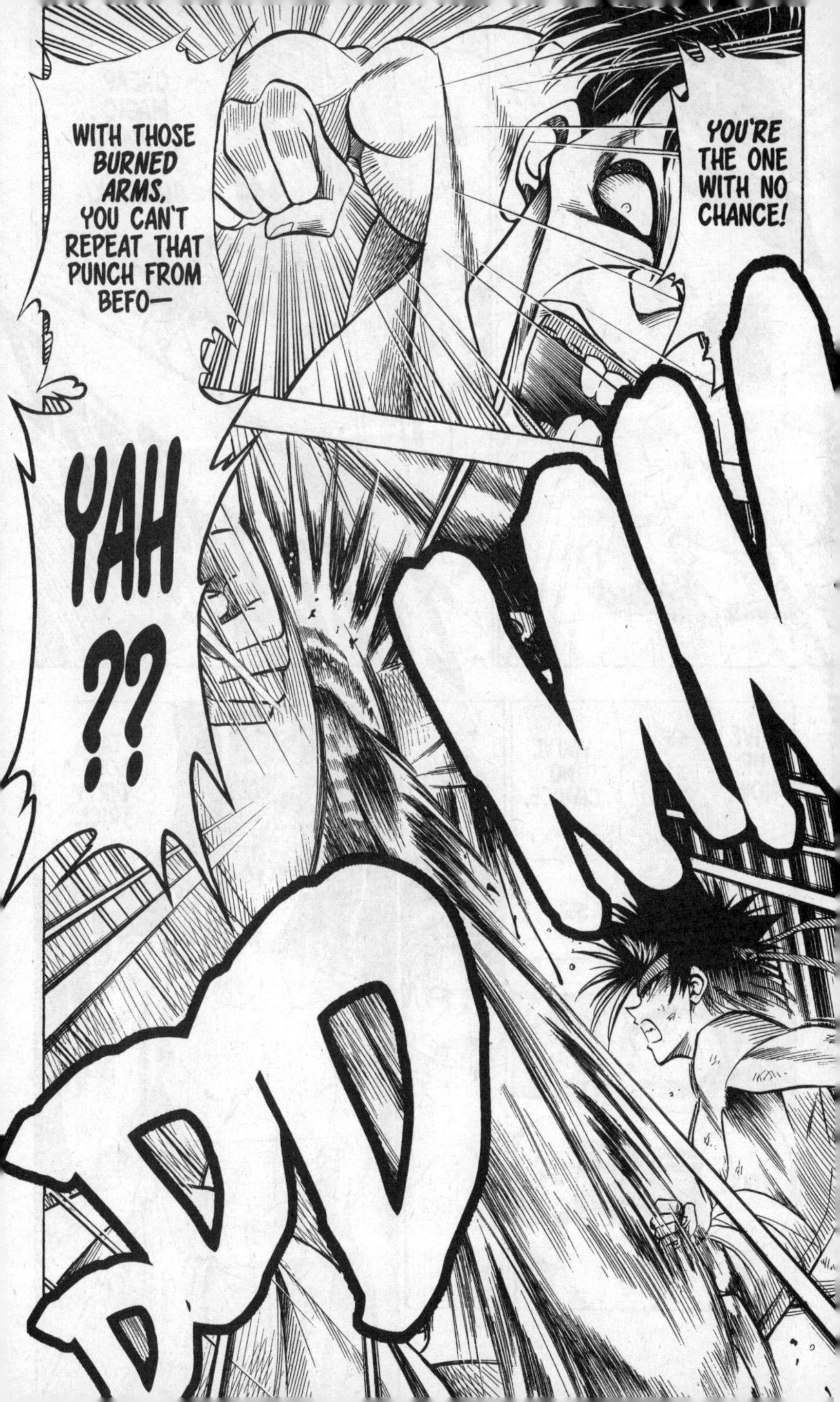
YOU'RE THE ONE WITH NO CHANCE!
WITH THOSE BURNED ARMS, YOU CAN'T REPEAT THAT PUNCH FROM BEFO—
YAH??
BAM

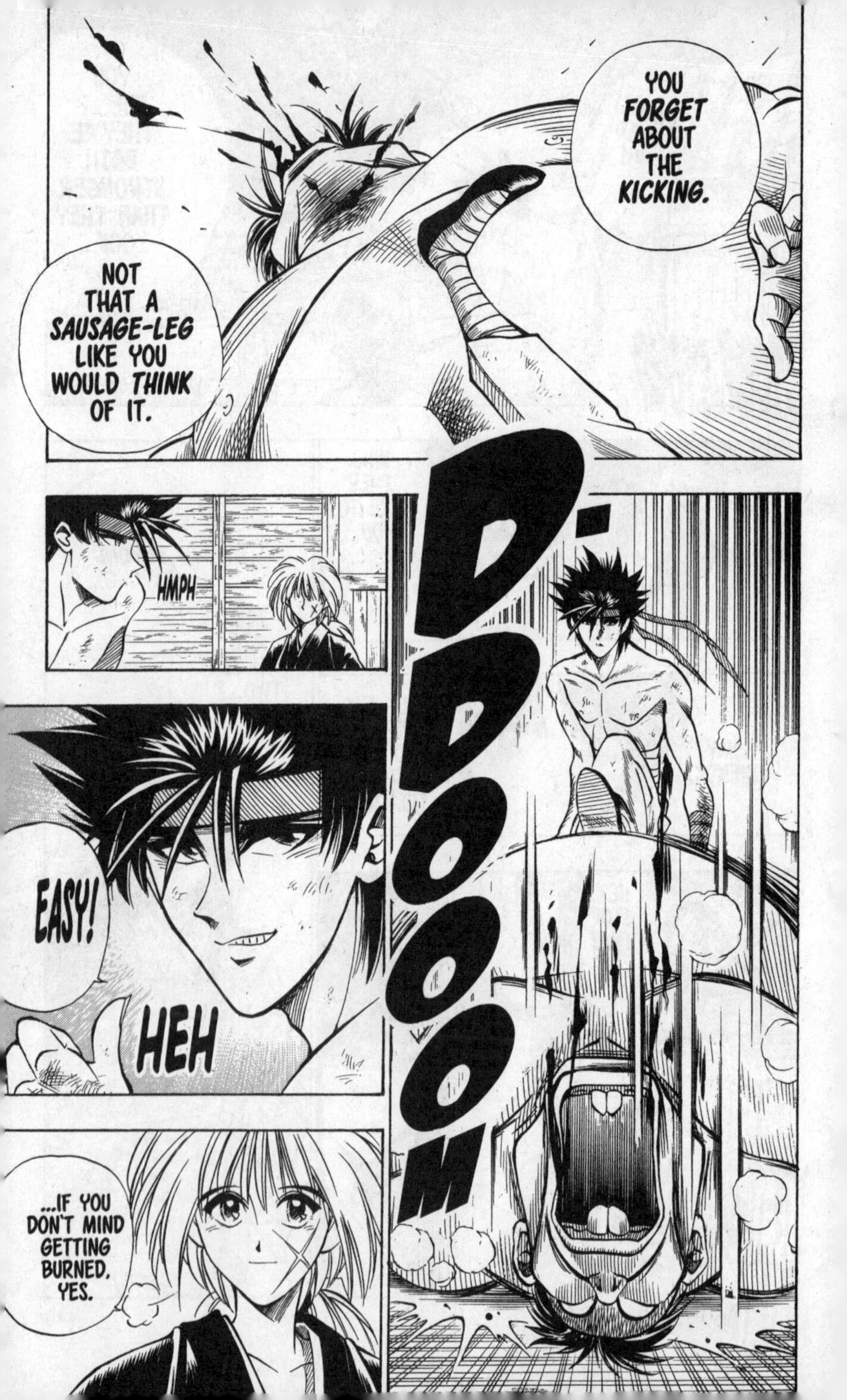
YOU FORGET ABOUT THE KICKING.
NOT THAT A SAUSAGE-LEG LIKE YOU WOULD THINK OF IT.
D-DOOOOM
HMPH
EASY!
HEH
...IF YOU DON'T MIND GETTING BURNED, YES.

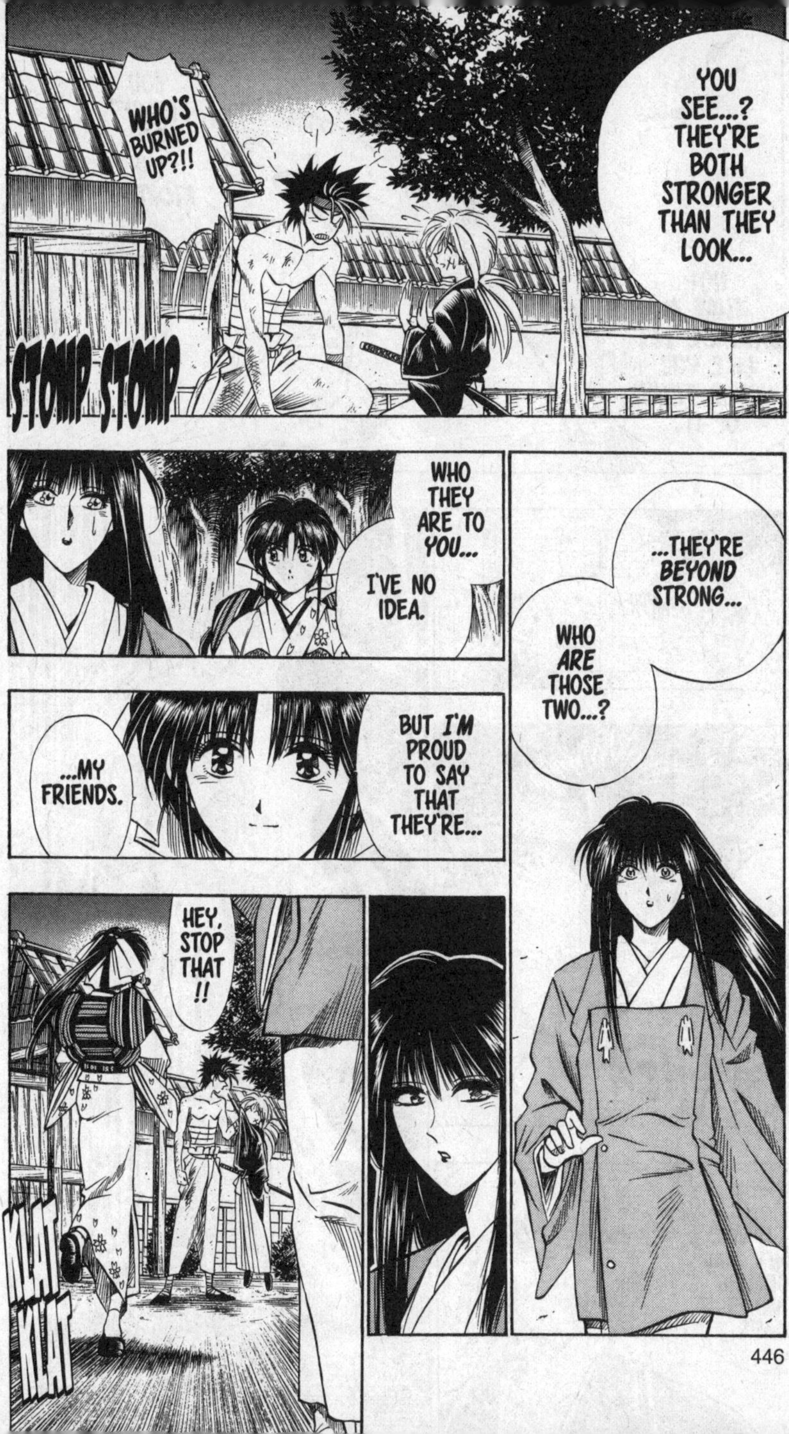
YOU SEE...? THEY'RE BOTH STRONGER THAN THEY LOOK...
WHO'S BURNED UP?!!
STOMP STOMP
...THEY'RE BEYOND STRONG...
WHO ARE THOSE TWO...?
WHO THEY ARE TO YOU...
I'VE NO IDEA.
BUT I'M PROUD TO SAY THAT THEY'RE...
...MY FRIENDS.
HEY, STOP THAT!!
KLAT KLAT

READ THIS WAY

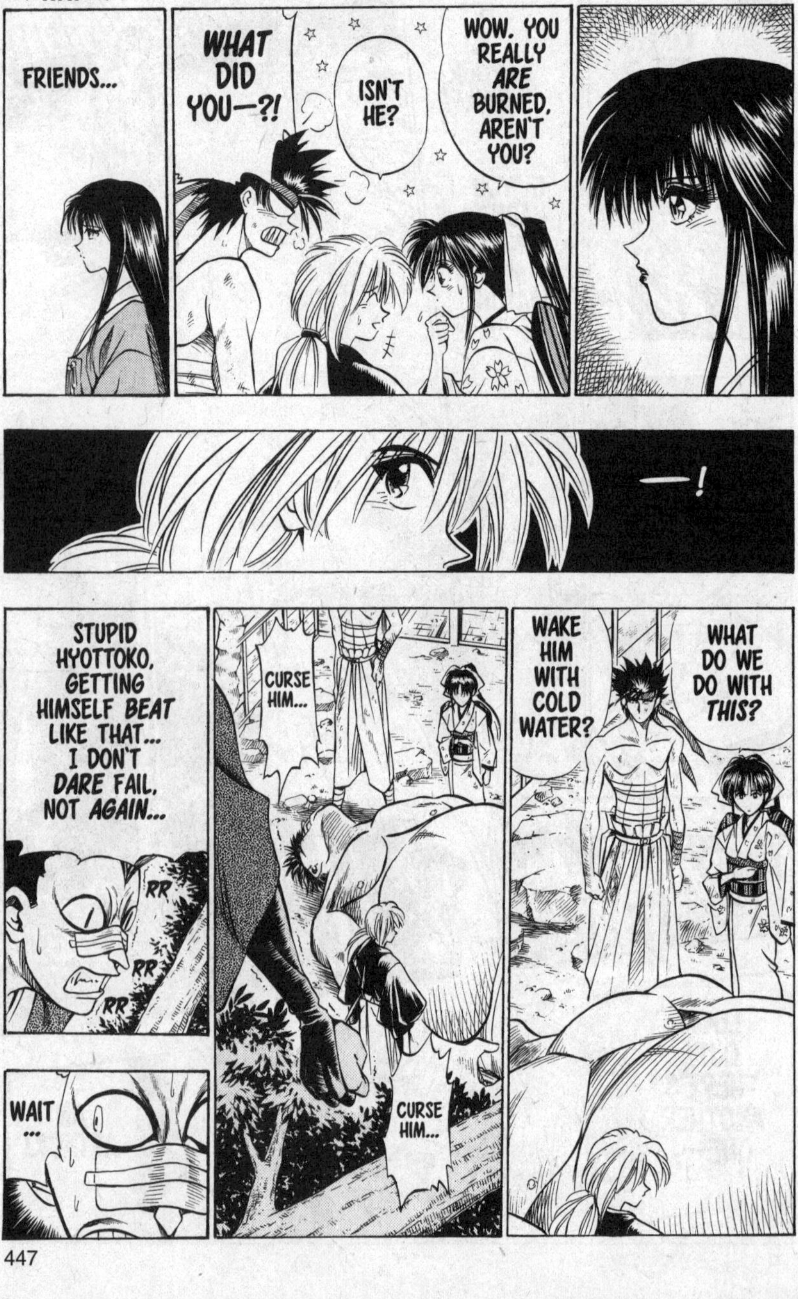

WOW. YOU REALLY ARE BURNED, AREN'T YOU?
ISN'T HE?
WHAT DID YOU—?!
FRIENDS...
—!
WHAT DO WE DO WITH THIS?
WAKE HIM WITH COLD WATER?
CURSE HIM...
CURSE HIM...
STUPID HYOTTOKO, GETTING HIMSELF BEAT LIKE THAT... I DON'T DARE FAIL, NOT AGAIN...
RR
RR
RR
WAIT ...

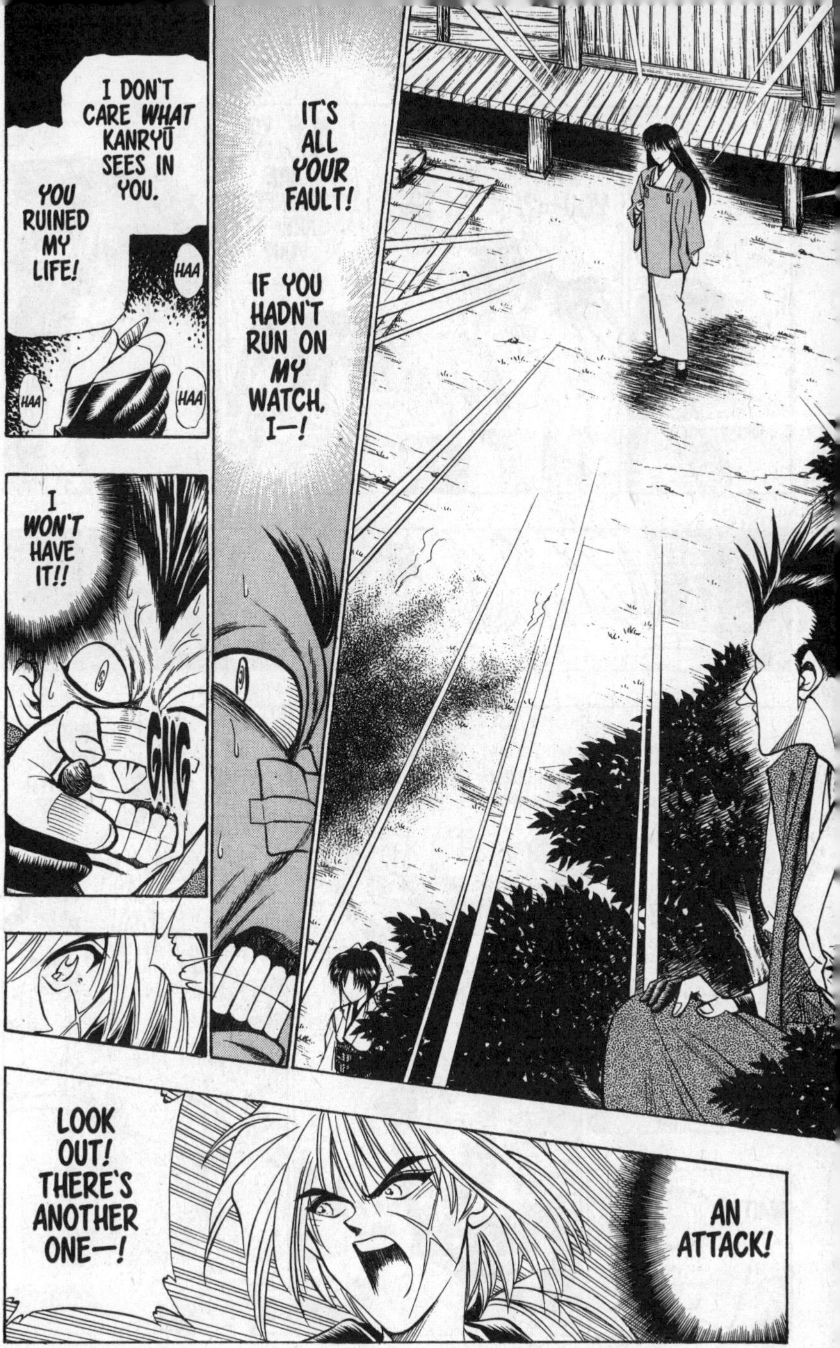
IT'S ALL YOUR FAULT!
IF YOU HADN'T RUN ON MY WATCH, I—!
I DON'T CARE WHAT KANRYŪ SEES IN YOU.
YOU RUINED MY LIFE!
HAA
HAA
HAA
I WON'T HAVE IT!!
GNG
AN ATTACK!
LOOK OUT! THERE'S ANOTHER ONE—!

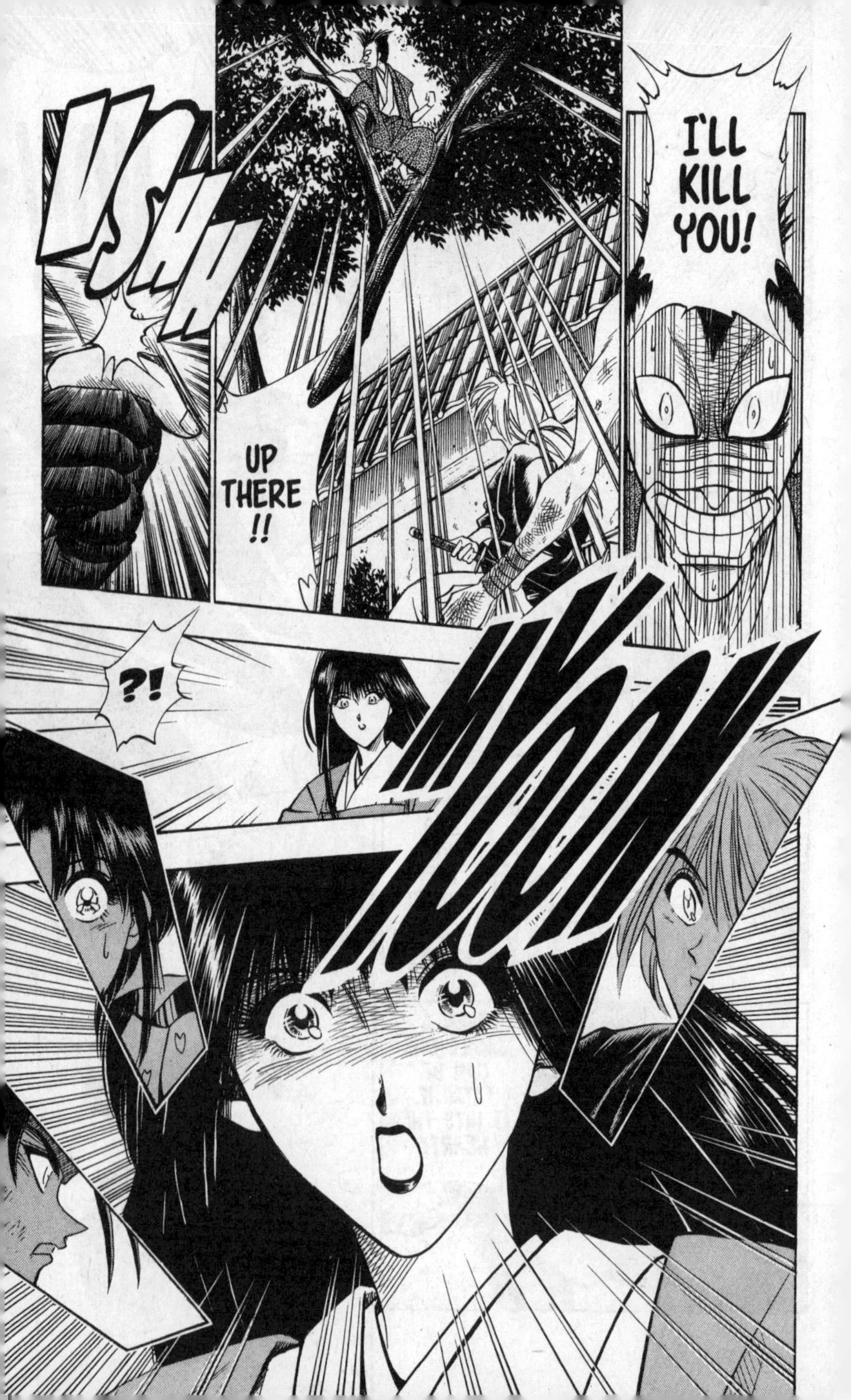
I'LL KILL YOU!
UP THERE!!
?!

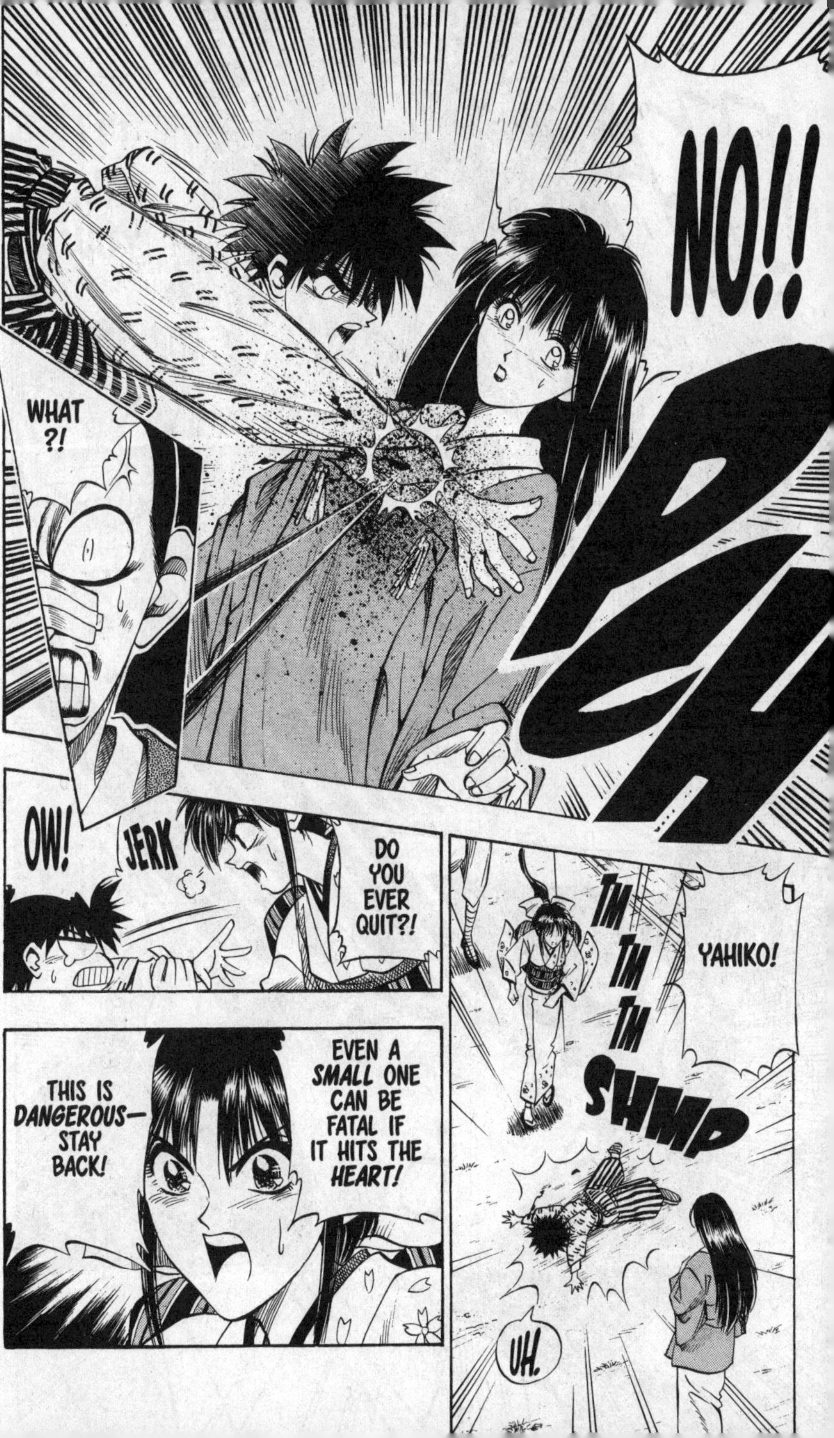
NO!!
WHAT ?!
YAHIKO!
TM TM TM
SHMP
UH.
DO YOU EVER QUIT?!
JERK
OW!
EVEN A SMALL ONE CAN BE FATAL IF IT HITS THE HEART!
THIS IS DANGEROUS— STAY BACK!

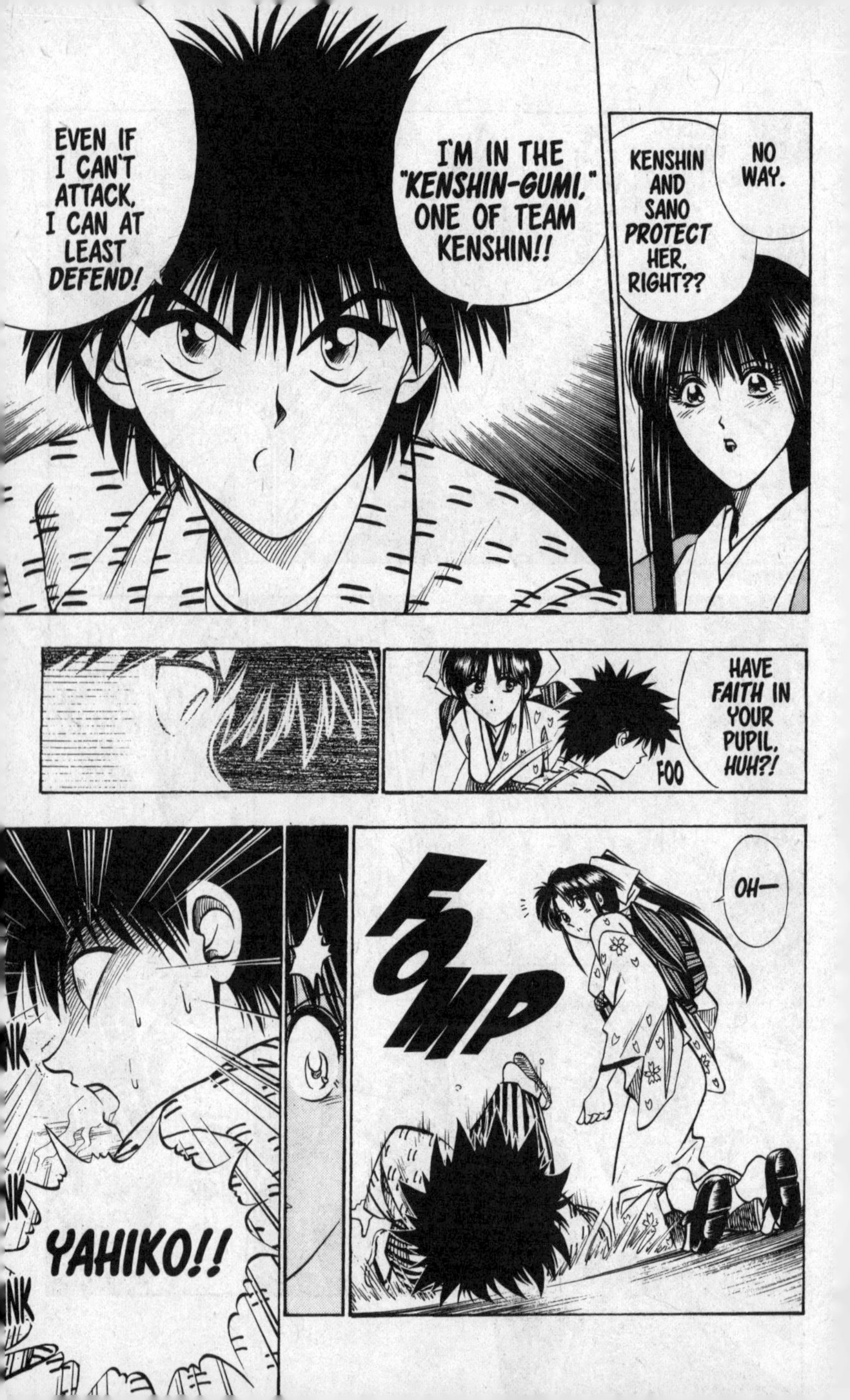
NO WAY.
KENSHIN AND SANO PROTECT HER, RIGHT??
I'M IN THE "KENSHIN-GUMI," ONE OF TEAM KENSHIN!!
EVEN IF I CAN'T ATTACK, I CAN AT LEAST DEFEND!
HAVE FAITH IN YOUR PUPIL, HUH?!
FOO
OH—
FOMP
YAHIKO!!

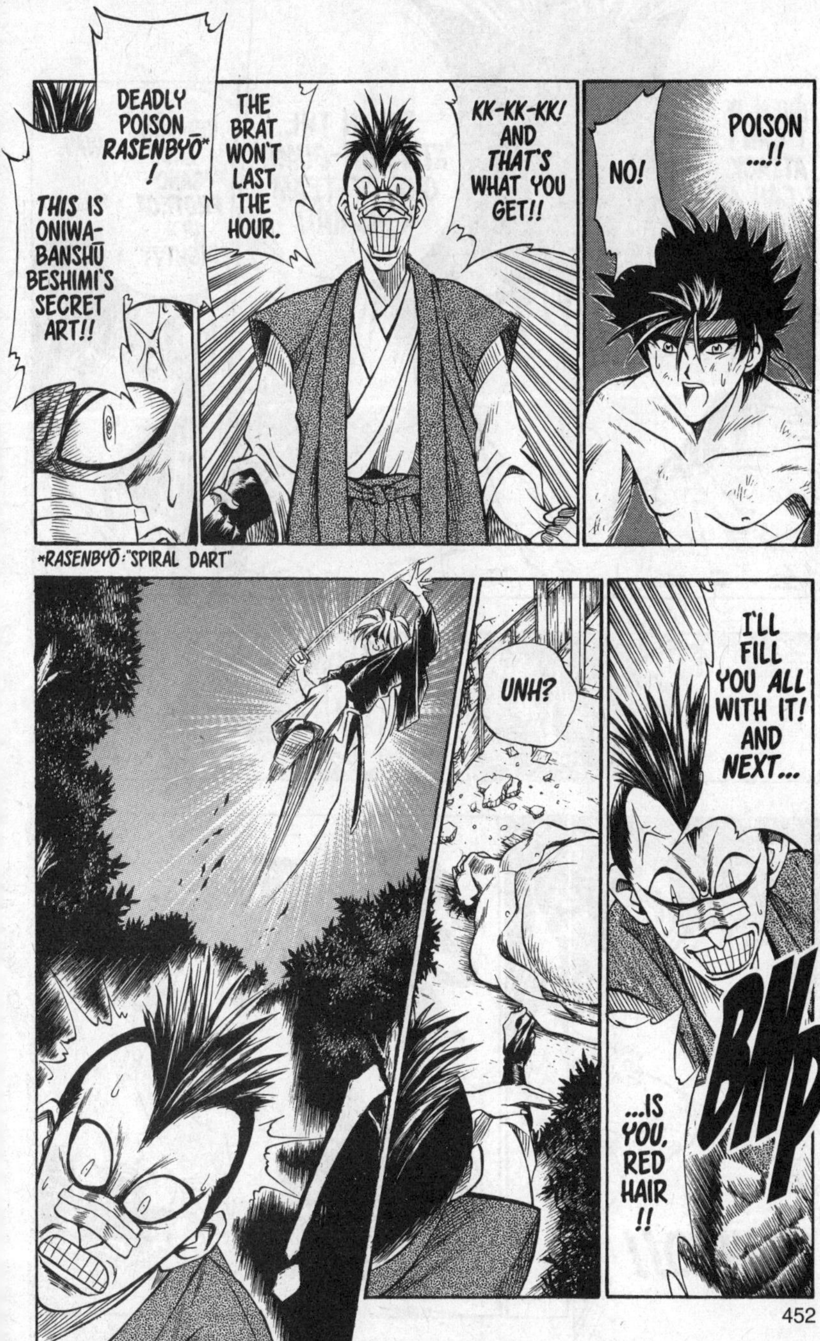
POISON ...!!
NO!
KK-KK-KK! AND THAT'S WHAT YOU GET!!
THE BRAT WON'T LAST THE HOUR.
DEADLY POISON RASENBYŌ* !
THIS IS ONIWA-BANSHŪ BESHIMI'S SECRET ART!!
I'LL FILL YOU ALL WITH IT! AND NEXT...
...IS YOU, RED HAIR !!
UNH?

*RASENBYŌ: "SPIRAL DART"

READ THIS WAY

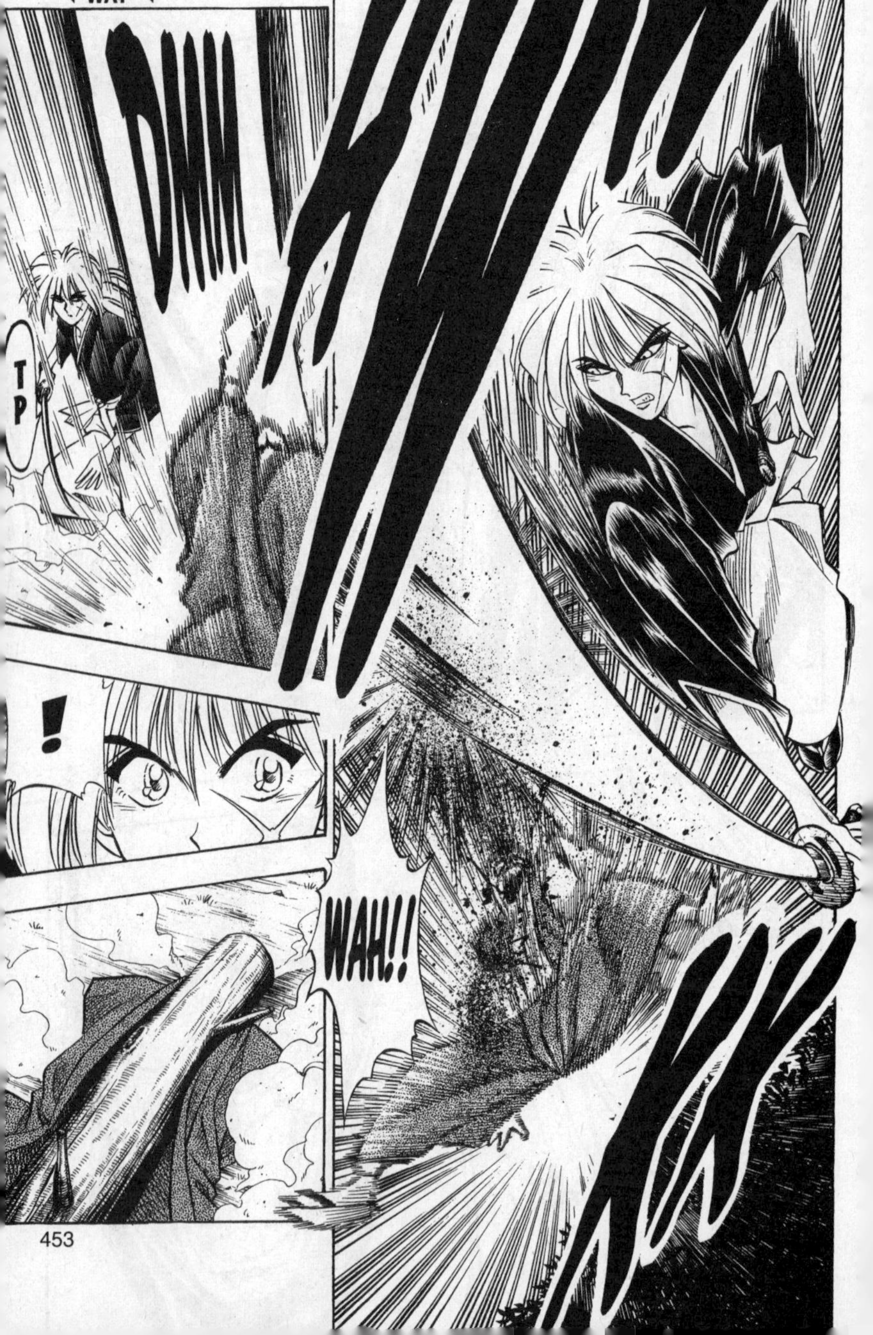
WAH!!
DMM
TP
!

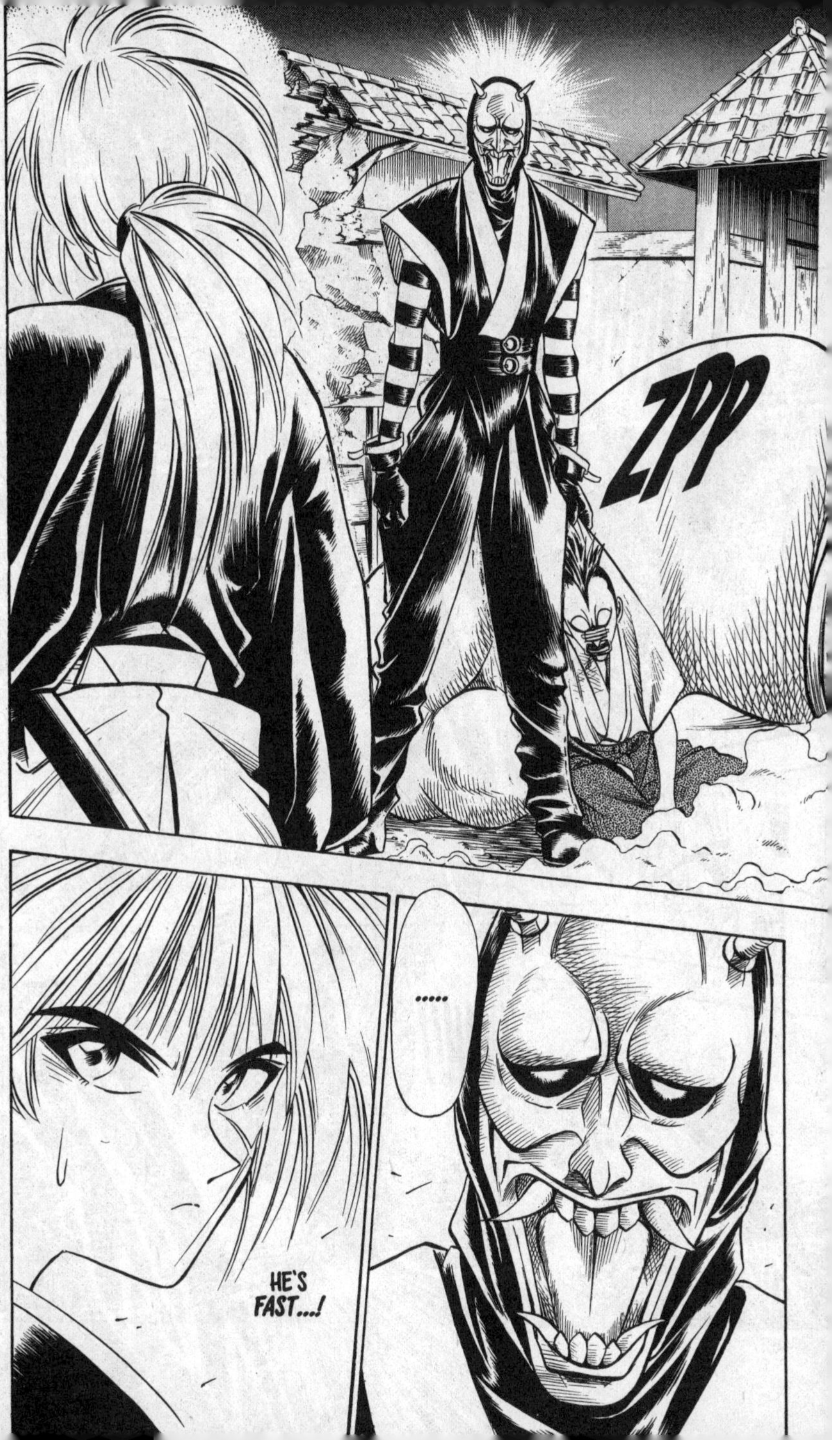
ZPP
......
HE'S FAST...!

READ THIS WAY

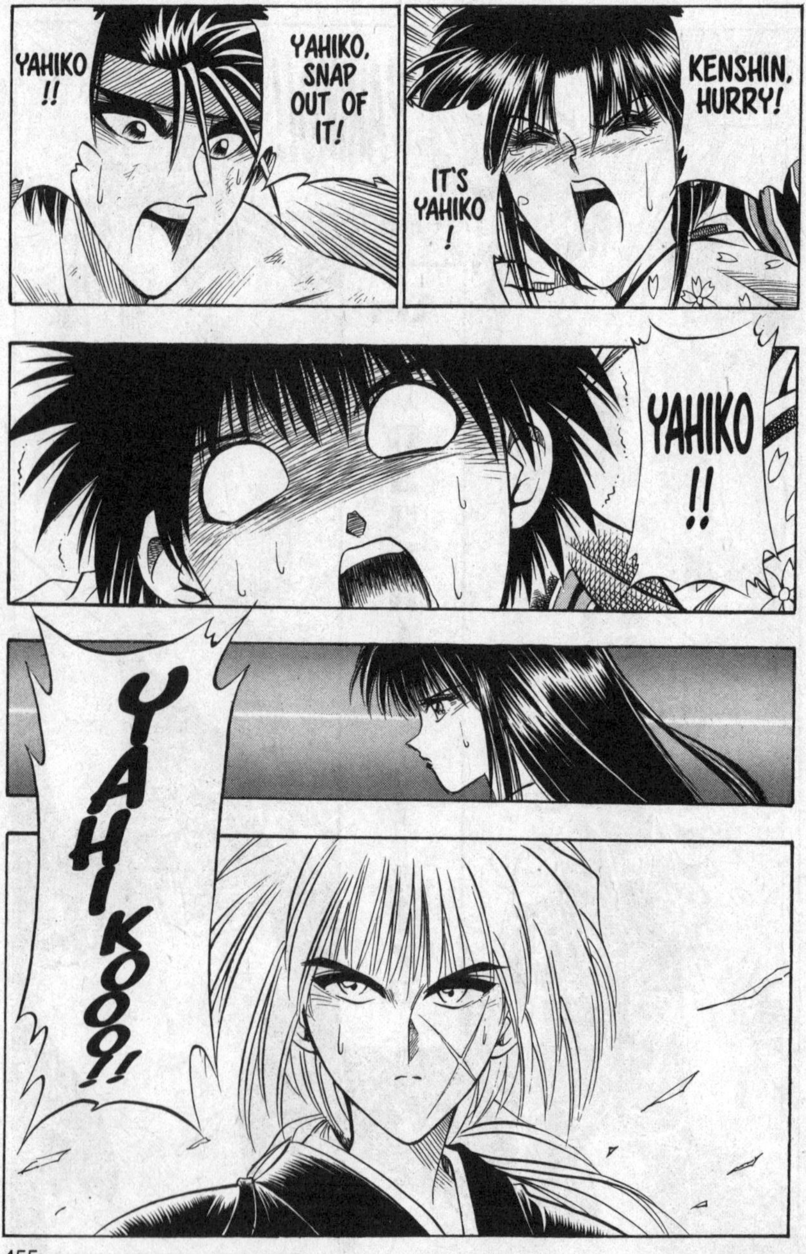
KENSHIN, HURRY!
IT'S YAHIKO!
YAHIKO, SNAP OUT OF IT!
YAHIKO!!
YAHIKO!!
YAHIKOOO!!

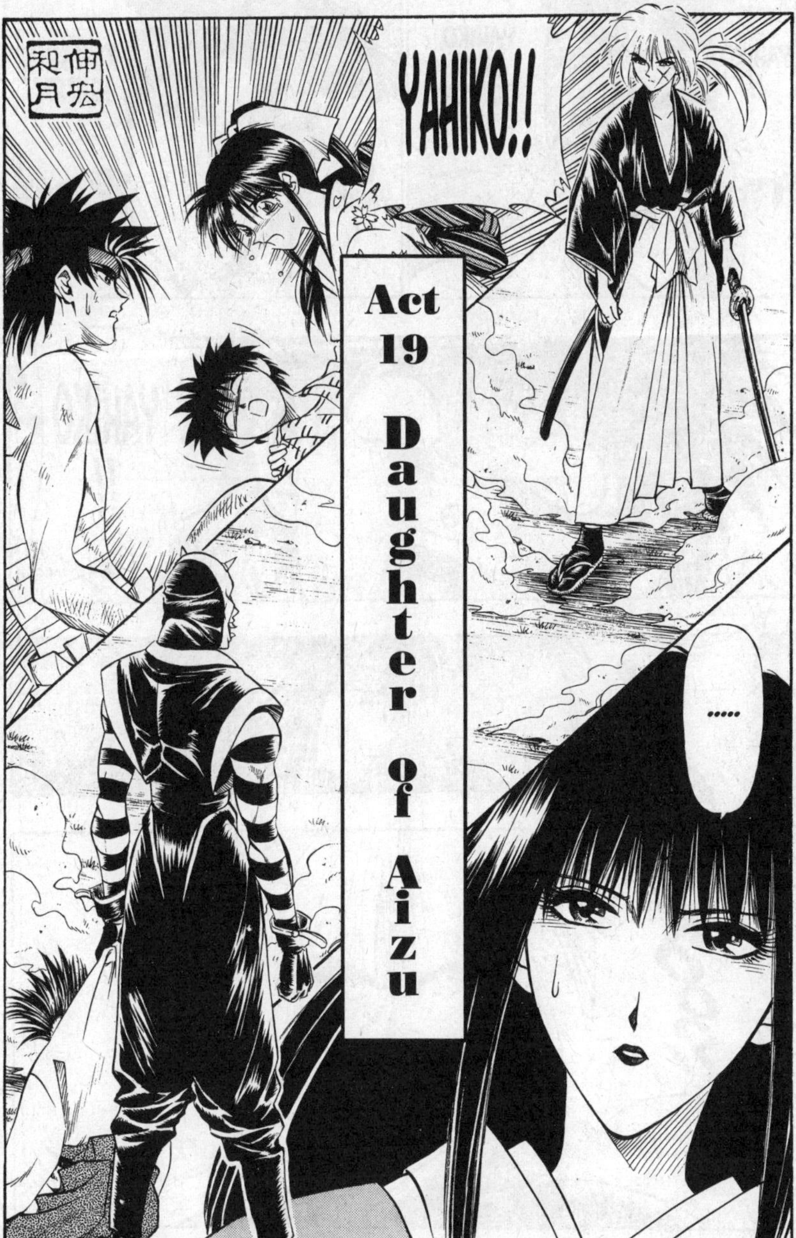
YAHIKO!!
Act 19 Daughter of Aizu
......

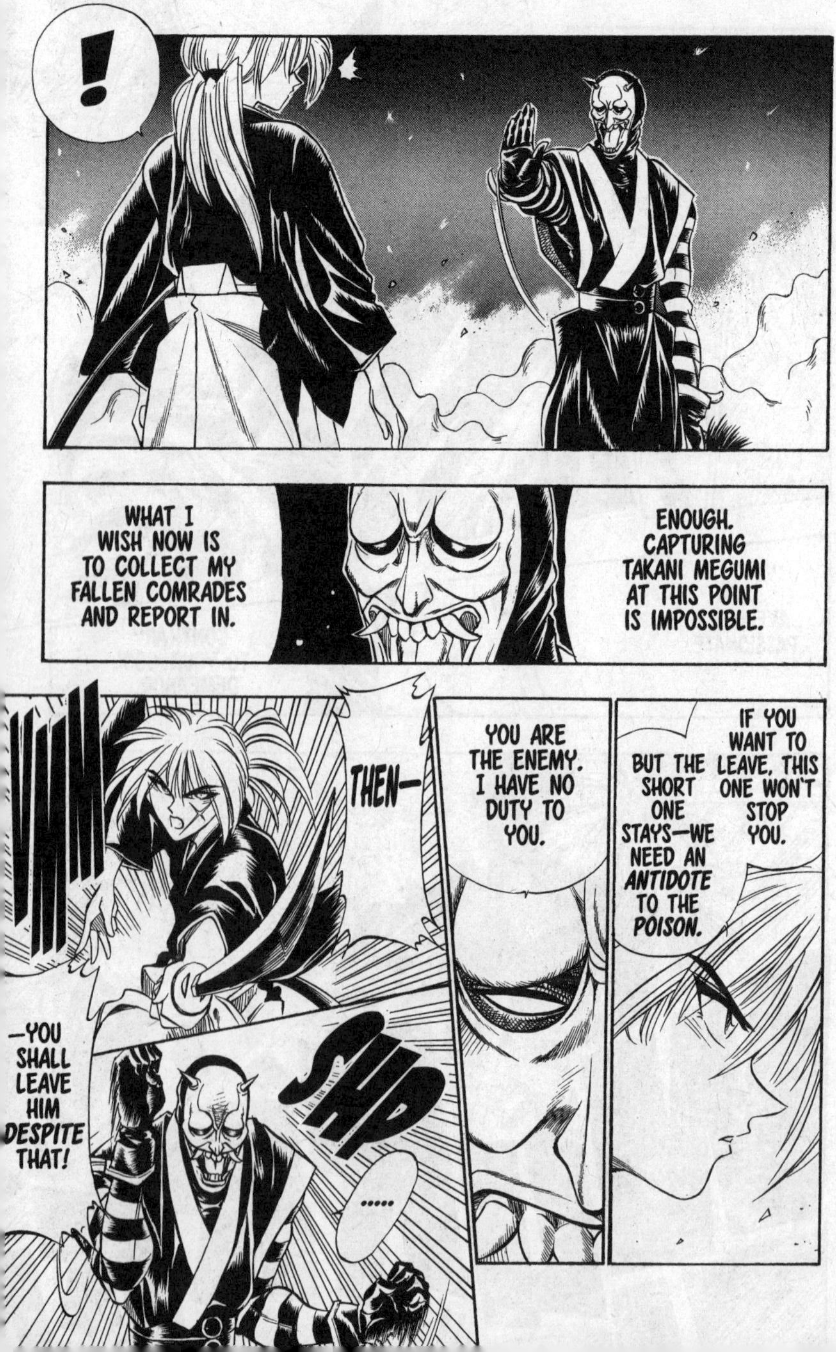
!
ENOUGH. CAPTURING TAKANI MEGUMI AT THIS POINT IS IMPOSSIBLE.
WHAT I WISH NOW IS TO COLLECT MY FALLEN COMRADES AND REPORT IN.
IF YOU WANT TO LEAVE, THIS ONE WON'T STOP YOU.
BUT THE SHORT ONE STAYS—WE NEED AN *ANTIDOTE* TO THE *POISON*.
YOU ARE THE ENEMY. I HAVE NO DUTY TO YOU.
THEN—
SHP
......
—YOU SHALL LEAVE HIM DESPITE THAT!

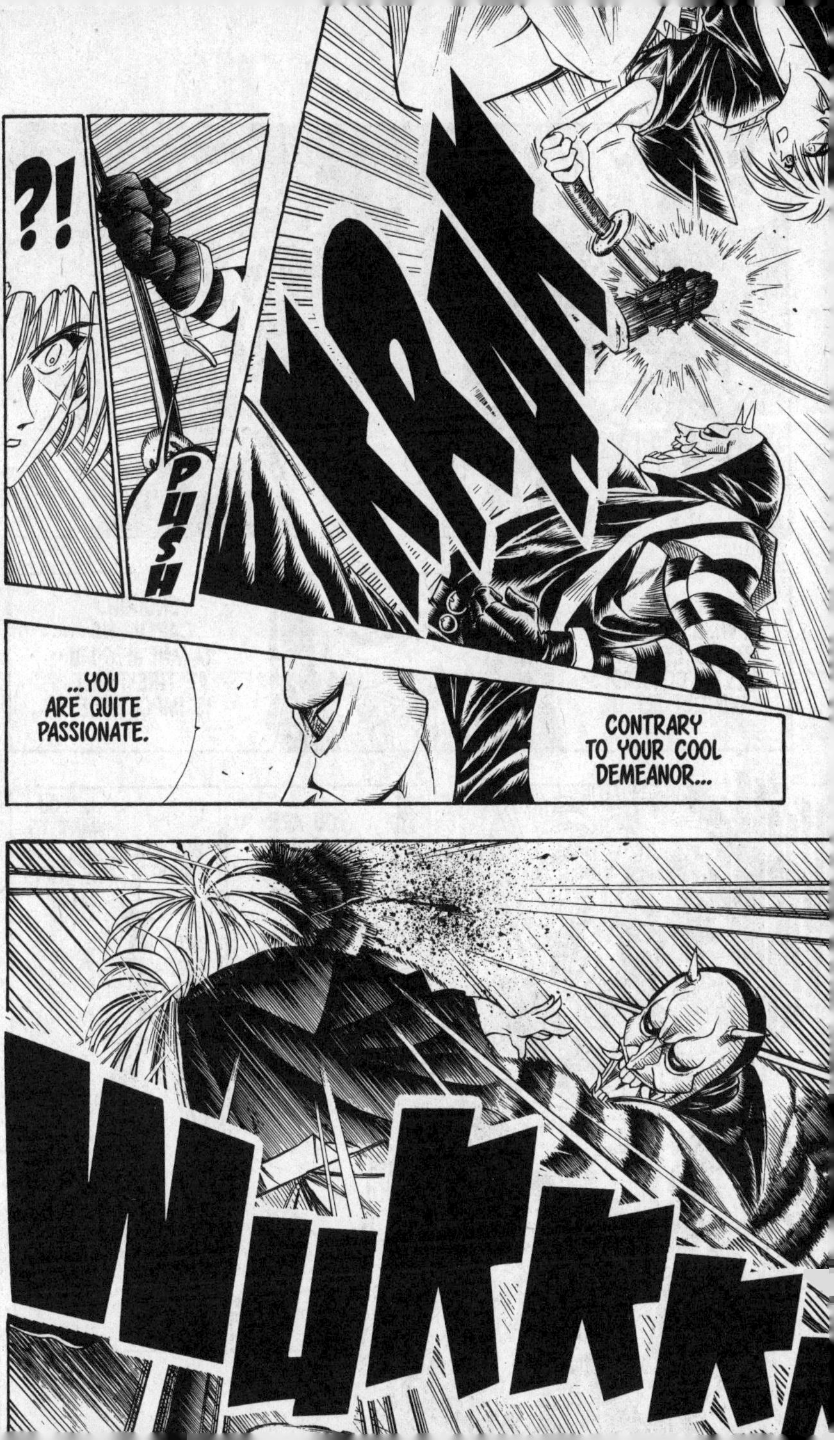
PUSH
?!
CONTRARY TO YOUR COOL DEMEANOR...
...YOU ARE QUITE PASSIONATE.

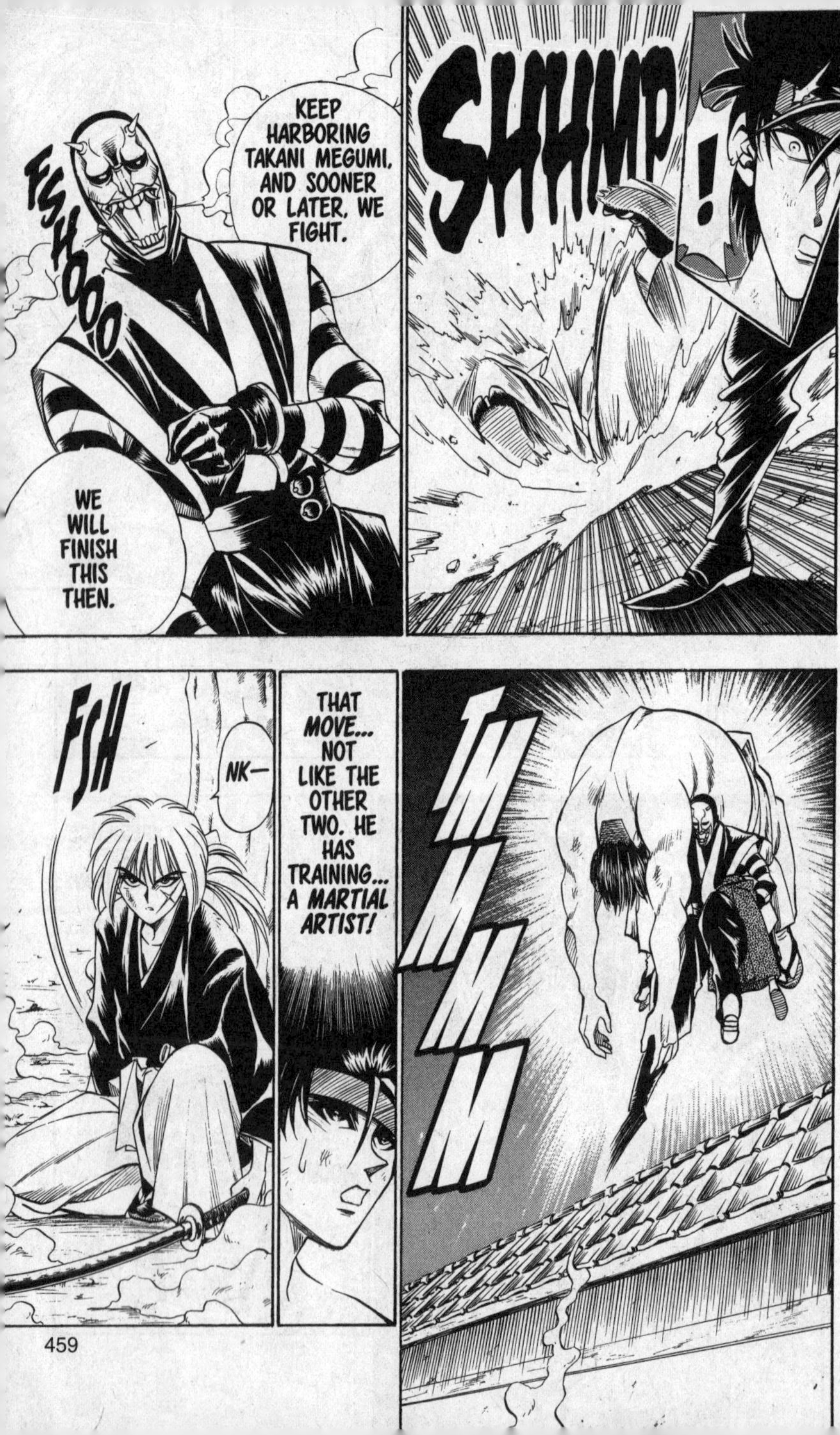

SHHMP
!
FSHOOO
KEEP HARBORING TAKANI MEGUMI, AND SOONER OR LATER, WE FIGHT.
WE WILL FINISH THIS THEN.
THMMM
THAT *MOVE*... NOT LIKE THE OTHER TWO. HE HAS TRAINING... A *MARTIAL ARTIST!*
FSH
NK—

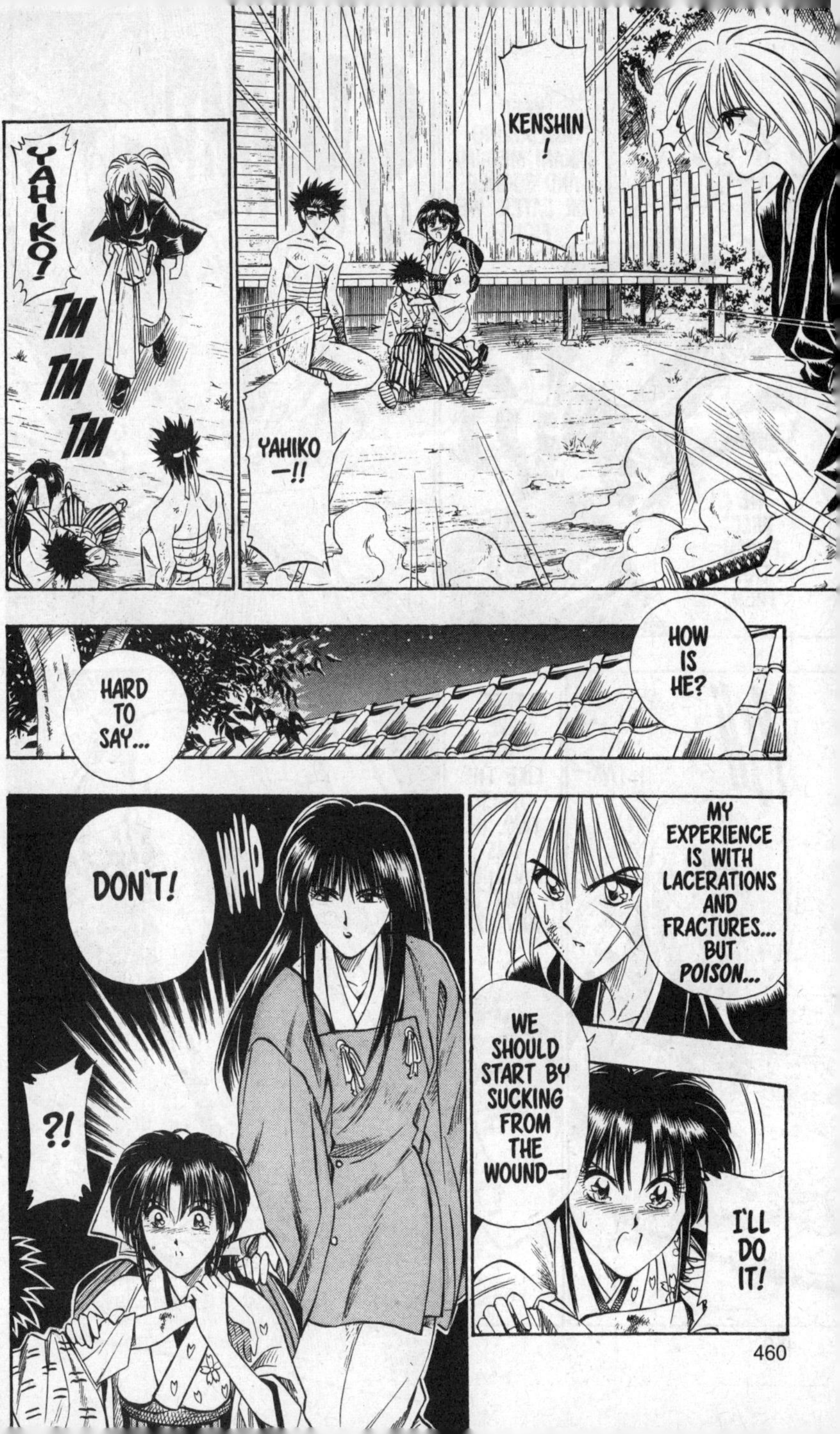
KENSHIN!
YAHIKO—!!
YAHIKO!
TM TM TM
HOW IS HE?
HARD TO SAY...
MY EXPERIENCE IS WITH LACERATIONS AND FRACTURES... BUT POISON...
WE SHOULD START BY SUCKING FROM THE WOUND—
I'LL DO IT!
DON'T!
WHP
?!

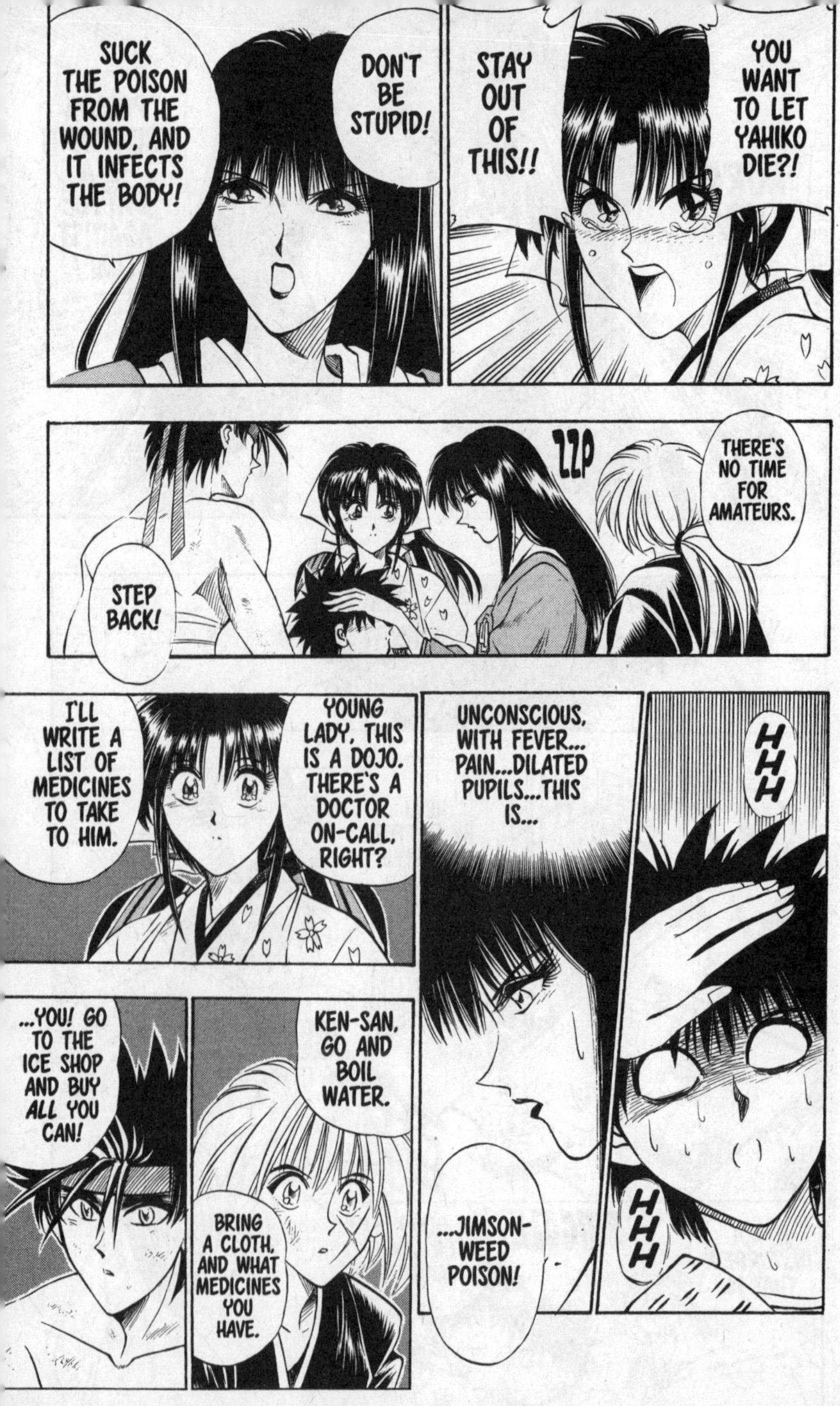
YOU WANT TO LET YAHIKO DIE?!
STAY OUT OF THIS!!
DON'T BE STUPID!
SUCK THE POISON FROM THE WOUND, AND IT INFECTS THE BODY!
THERE'S NO TIME FOR AMATEURS.
ZZP
STEP BACK!
HHH
HHH
UNCONSCIOUS, WITH FEVER... PAIN...DILATED PUPILS...THIS IS...
...JIMSON-WEED POISON!
YOUNG LADY, THIS IS A DOJO. THERE'S A DOCTOR ON-CALL, RIGHT?
I'LL WRITE A LIST OF MEDICINES TO TAKE TO HIM.
KEN-SAN, GO AND BOIL WATER.
BRING A CLOTH, AND WHAT MEDICINES YOU HAVE.
...YOU! GO TO THE ICE SHOP AND BUY ALL YOU CAN!

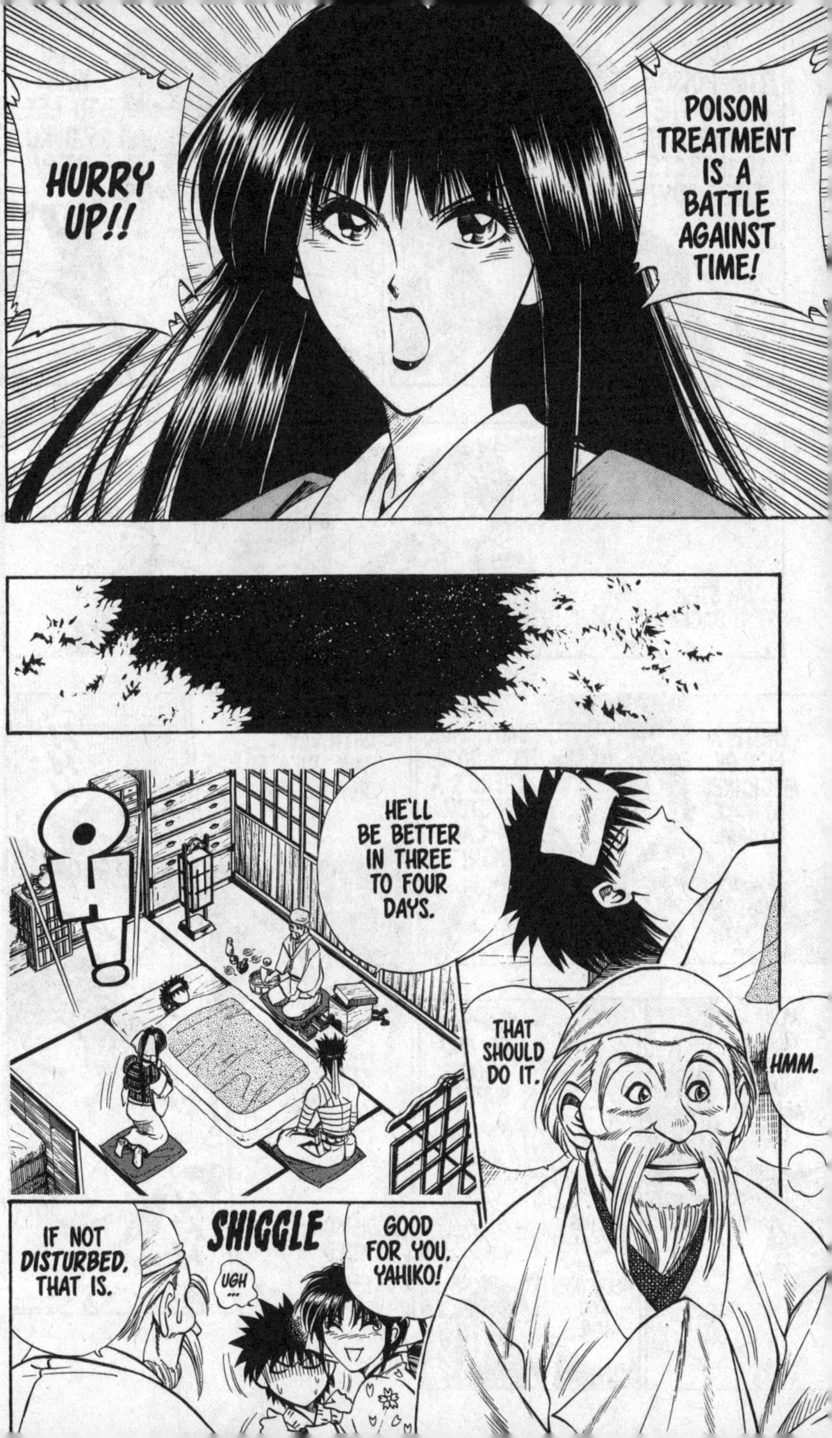
POISON TREATMENT IS A BATTLE AGAINST TIME!
HURRY UP!!
HMM.
THAT SHOULD DO IT.
OH!
HE'LL BE BETTER IN THREE TO FOUR DAYS.
GOOD FOR YOU, YAHIKO!
SHIGGLE
UGH...
IF NOT DISTURBED, THAT IS.

READ THIS WAY

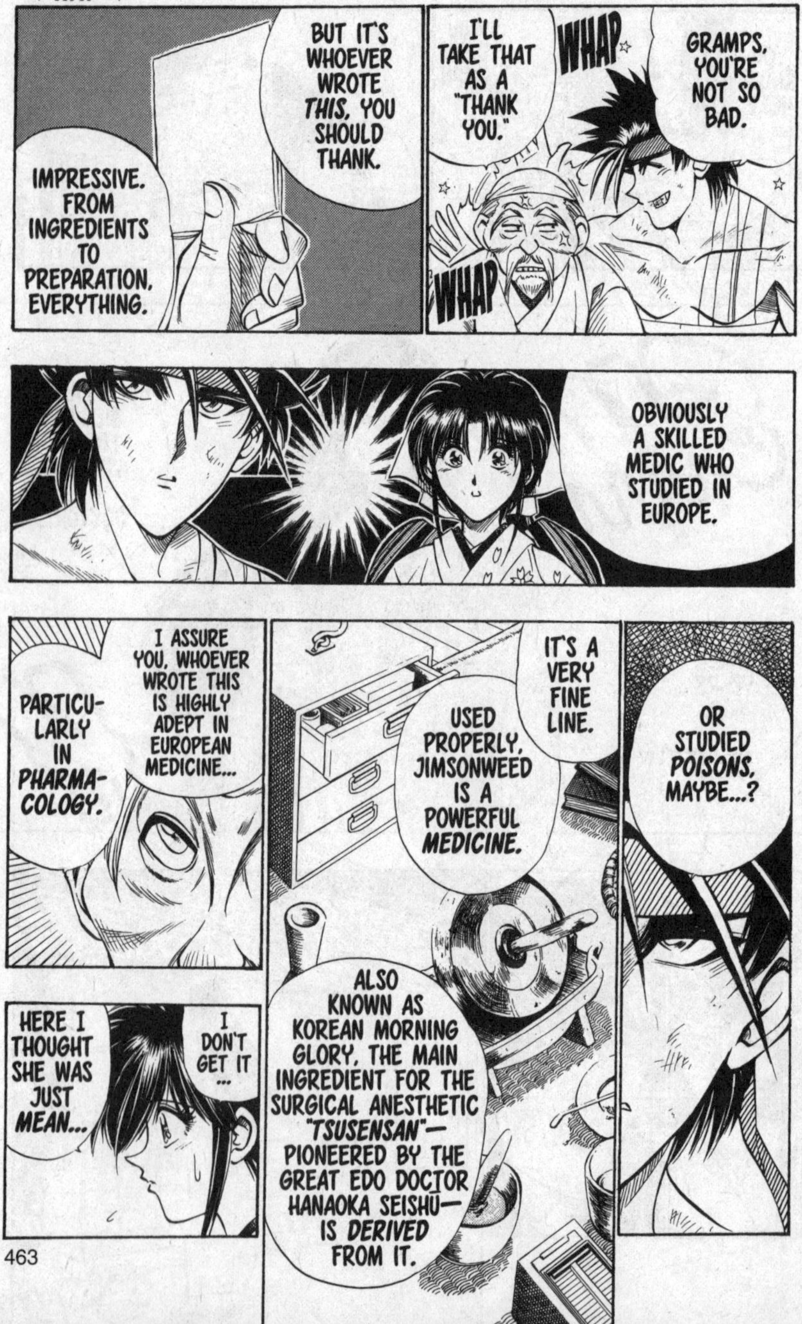
GRAMPS, YOU'RE NOT SO BAD.
WHAP
WHAP
I'LL TAKE THAT AS A "THANK YOU."
IMPRESSIVE. FROM INGREDIENTS TO PREPARATION, EVERYTHING.
BUT IT'S WHOEVER WROTE *THIS*, YOU SHOULD THANK.
OBVIOUSLY A SKILLED MEDIC WHO STUDIED IN EUROPE.
OR STUDIED *POISONS*, MAYBE...?
IT'S A VERY FINE LINE.
USED PROPERLY, JIMSONWEED IS A POWERFUL *MEDICINE*.
ALSO KNOWN AS KOREAN MORNING GLORY, THE MAIN INGREDIENT FOR THE SURGICAL ANESTHETIC *"TSUSENSAN"*—PIONEERED BY THE GREAT EDO DOCTOR HANAOKA SEISHŪ—IS *DERIVED* FROM IT.
I ASSURE YOU, WHOEVER WROTE THIS IS HIGHLY ADEPT IN EUROPEAN MEDICINE...
PARTICULARLY IN *PHARMACOLOGY*.
I DON'T GET IT ...
HERE I THOUGHT SHE WAS JUST *MEAN*...

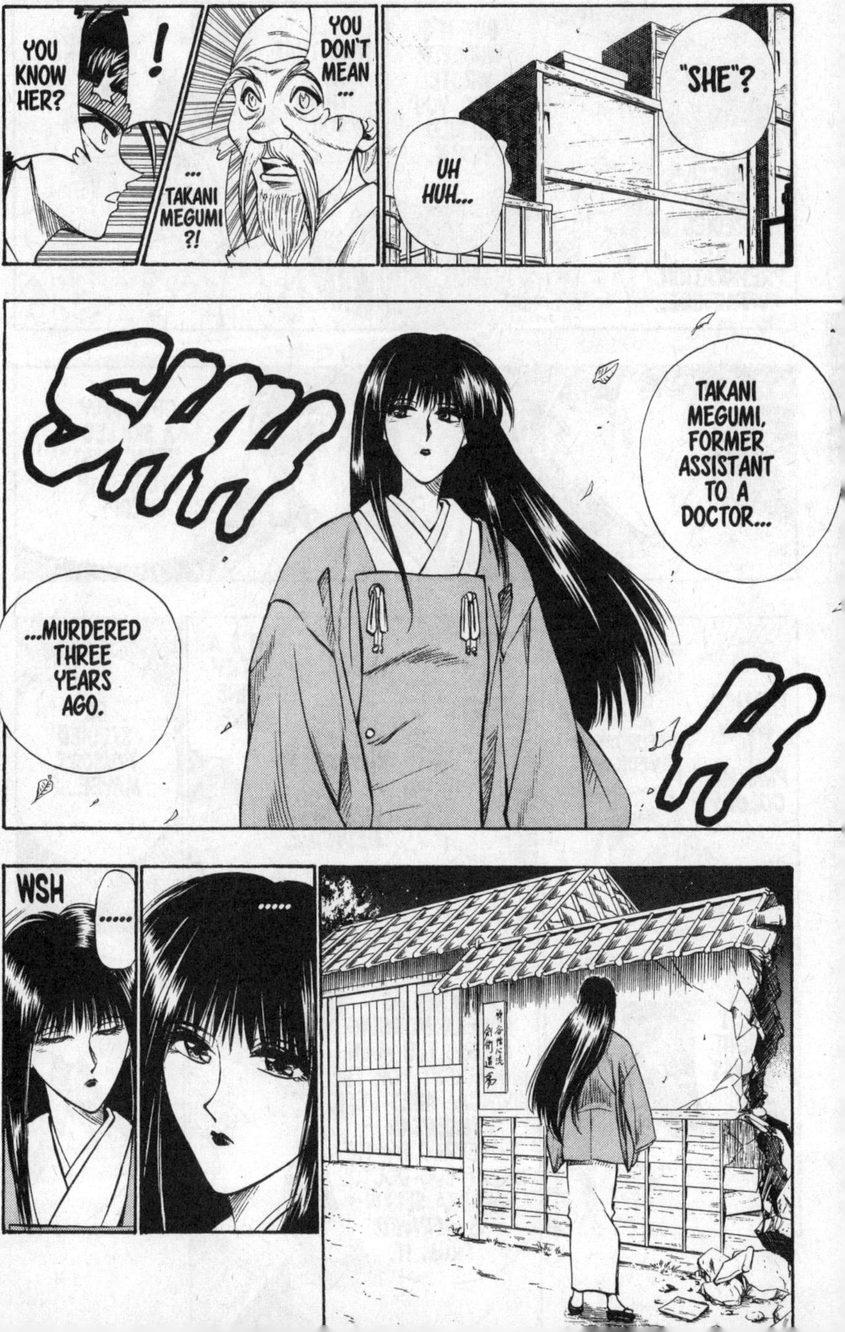
"SHE"?
UH HUH...
YOU DON'T MEAN ...
... TAKANI MEGUMI ?!
!
YOU KNOW HER?
TAKANI MEGUMI, FORMER ASSISTANT TO A DOCTOR...
...MURDERED THREE YEARS AGO.
......
WSH
......

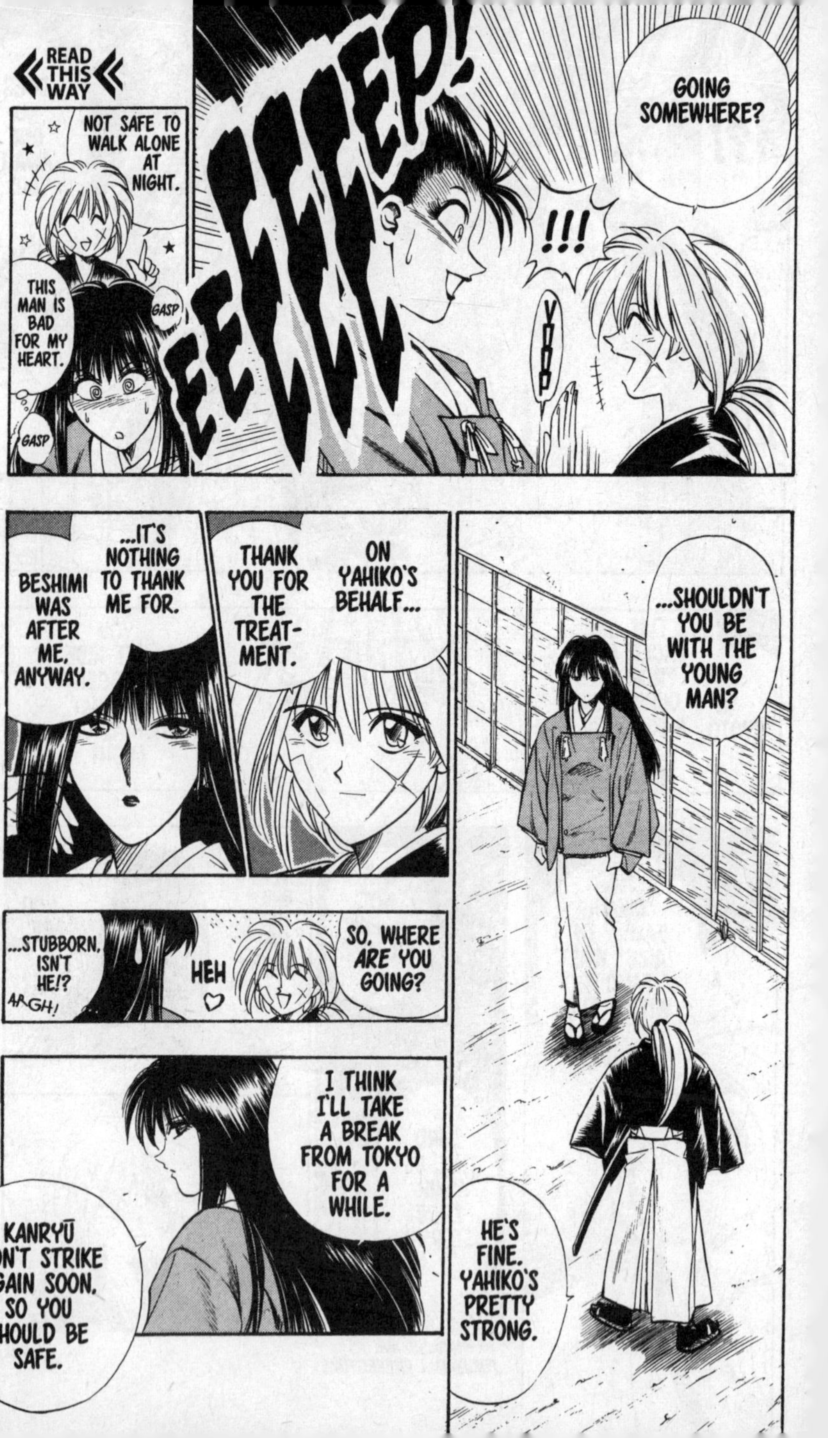
READ THIS WAY
GOING SOMEWHERE?
EEEEEEP!
!!!
VOOP
NOT SAFE TO WALK ALONE AT NIGHT.
THIS MAN IS BAD FOR MY HEART.
GASP
GASP
...SHOULDN'T YOU BE WITH THE YOUNG MAN?
HE'S FINE. YAHIKO'S PRETTY STRONG.
ON YAHIKO'S BEHALF...
THANK YOU FOR THE TREATMENT.
...IT'S NOTHING TO THANK ME FOR.
BESHIMI WAS AFTER ME, ANYWAY.
SO, WHERE ARE YOU GOING?
HEH ♡
...STUBBORN, ISN'T HE!?
ARGH!
I THINK I'LL TAKE A BREAK FROM TOKYO FOR A WHILE.
KANRYŪ WON'T STRIKE AGAIN SOON, SO YOU SHOULD BE SAFE.

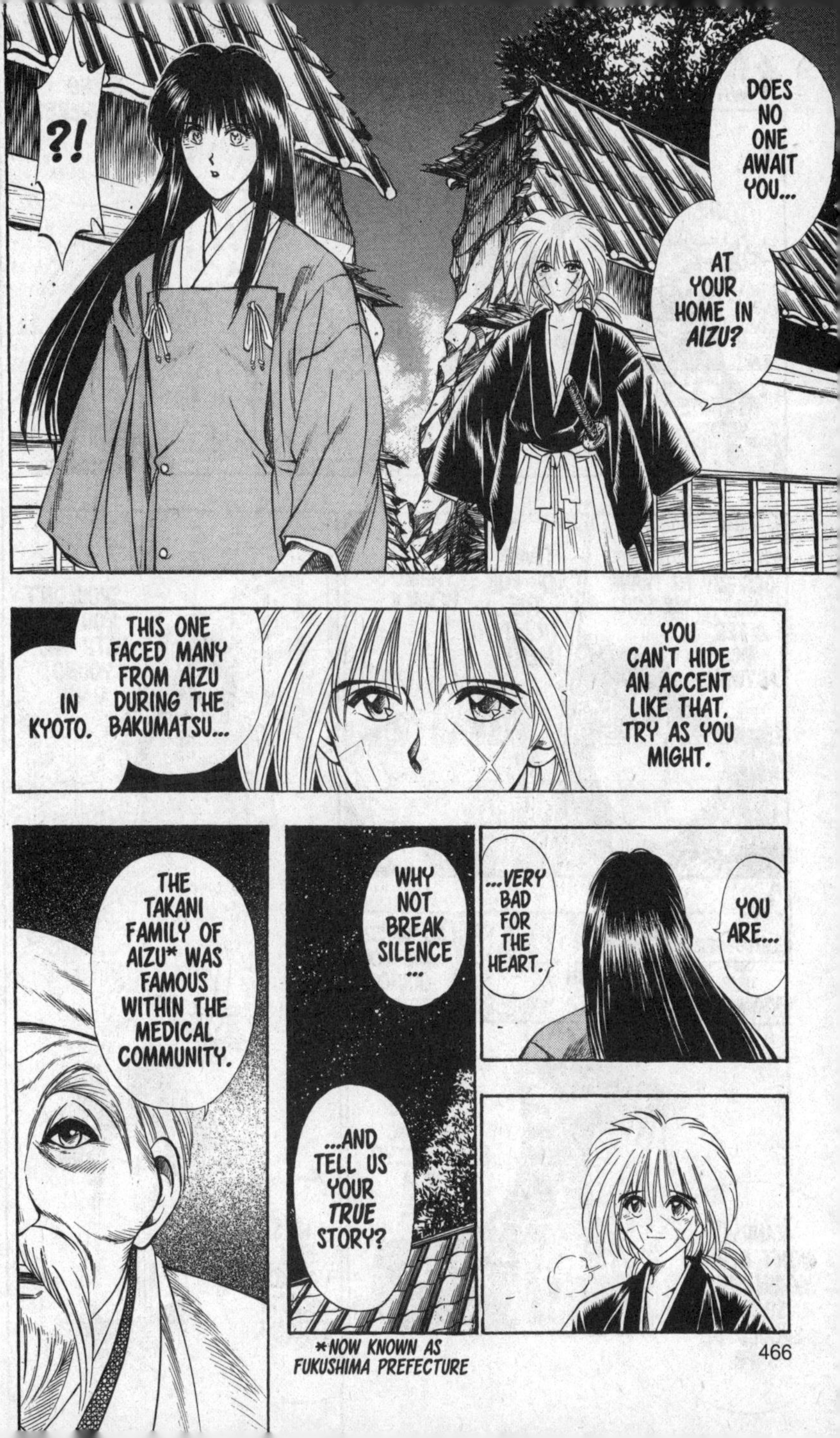
DOES NO ONE AWAIT YOU...
AT YOUR HOME IN *AIZU?*
?!
YOU CAN'T HIDE AN ACCENT LIKE THAT, TRY AS YOU MIGHT.
THIS ONE FACED MANY FROM AIZU DURING THE BAKUMATSU...
IN KYOTO.
YOU ARE...
...*VERY* BAD FOR THE HEART.
WHY NOT BREAK SILENCE...
...AND TELL US YOUR *TRUE* STORY?
THE TAKANI FAMILY OF AIZU* WAS FAMOUS WITHIN THE MEDICAL COMMUNITY.

*NOW KNOWN AS FUKUSHIMA PREFECTURE

READ THIS WAY

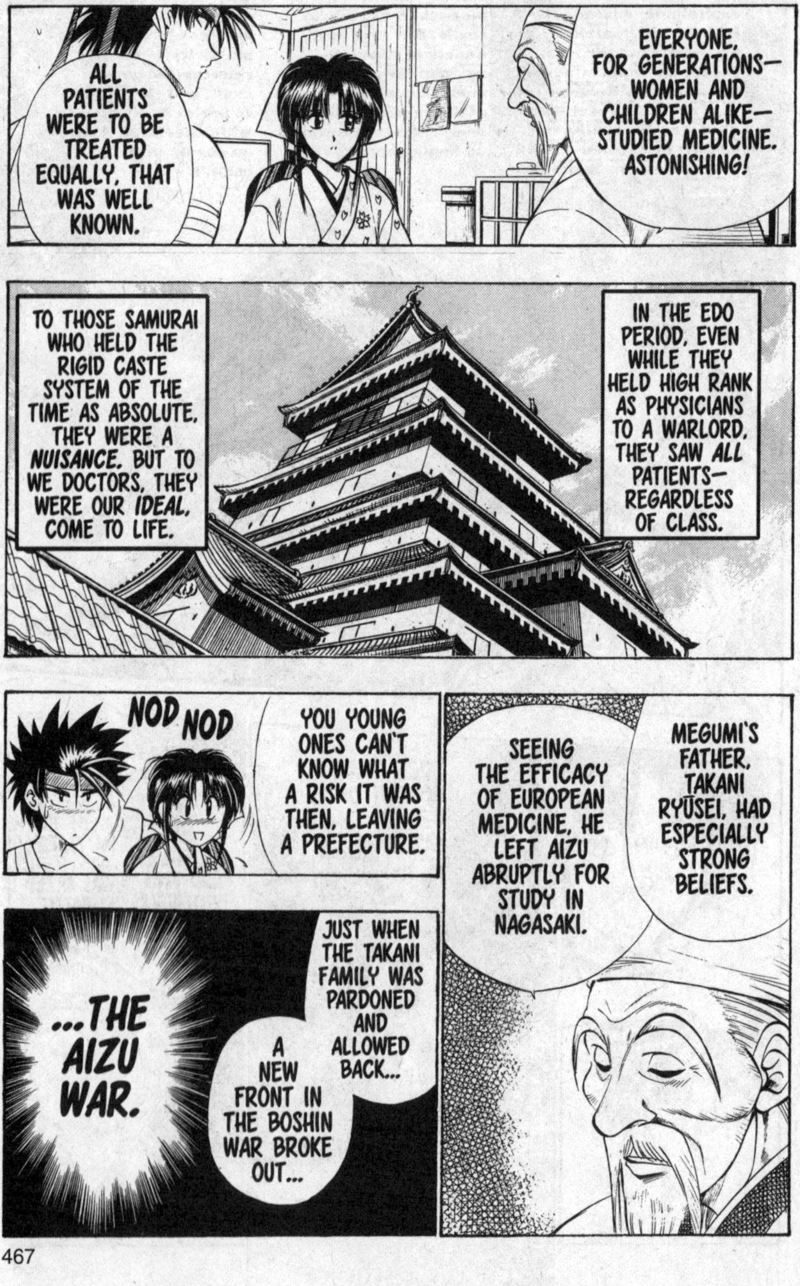
EVERYONE, FOR GENERATIONS—WOMEN AND CHILDREN ALIKE—STUDIED MEDICINE. ASTONISHING!
ALL PATIENTS WERE TO BE TREATED EQUALLY, THAT WAS WELL KNOWN.
IN THE EDO PERIOD, EVEN WHILE THEY HELD HIGH RANK AS PHYSICIANS TO A WARLORD, THEY SAW *ALL* PATIENTS—REGARDLESS OF CLASS.
TO THOSE SAMURAI WHO HELD THE RIGID CASTE SYSTEM OF THE TIME AS ABSOLUTE, THEY WERE A *NUISANCE*. BUT TO WE DOCTORS, THEY WERE OUR *IDEAL*, COME TO LIFE.
MEGUMI'S FATHER, TAKANI RYŪSEI, HAD ESPECIALLY STRONG BELIEFS.
SEEING THE EFFICACY OF EUROPEAN MEDICINE, HE LEFT AIZU ABRUPTLY FOR STUDY IN NAGASAKI.
YOU YOUNG ONES CAN'T KNOW WHAT A RISK IT WAS THEN, LEAVING A PREFECTURE.
NOD NOD
JUST WHEN THE TAKANI FAMILY WAS PARDONED AND ALLOWED BACK...
A NEW FRONT IN THE BOSHIN WAR BROKE OUT...
...THE AIZU WAR.

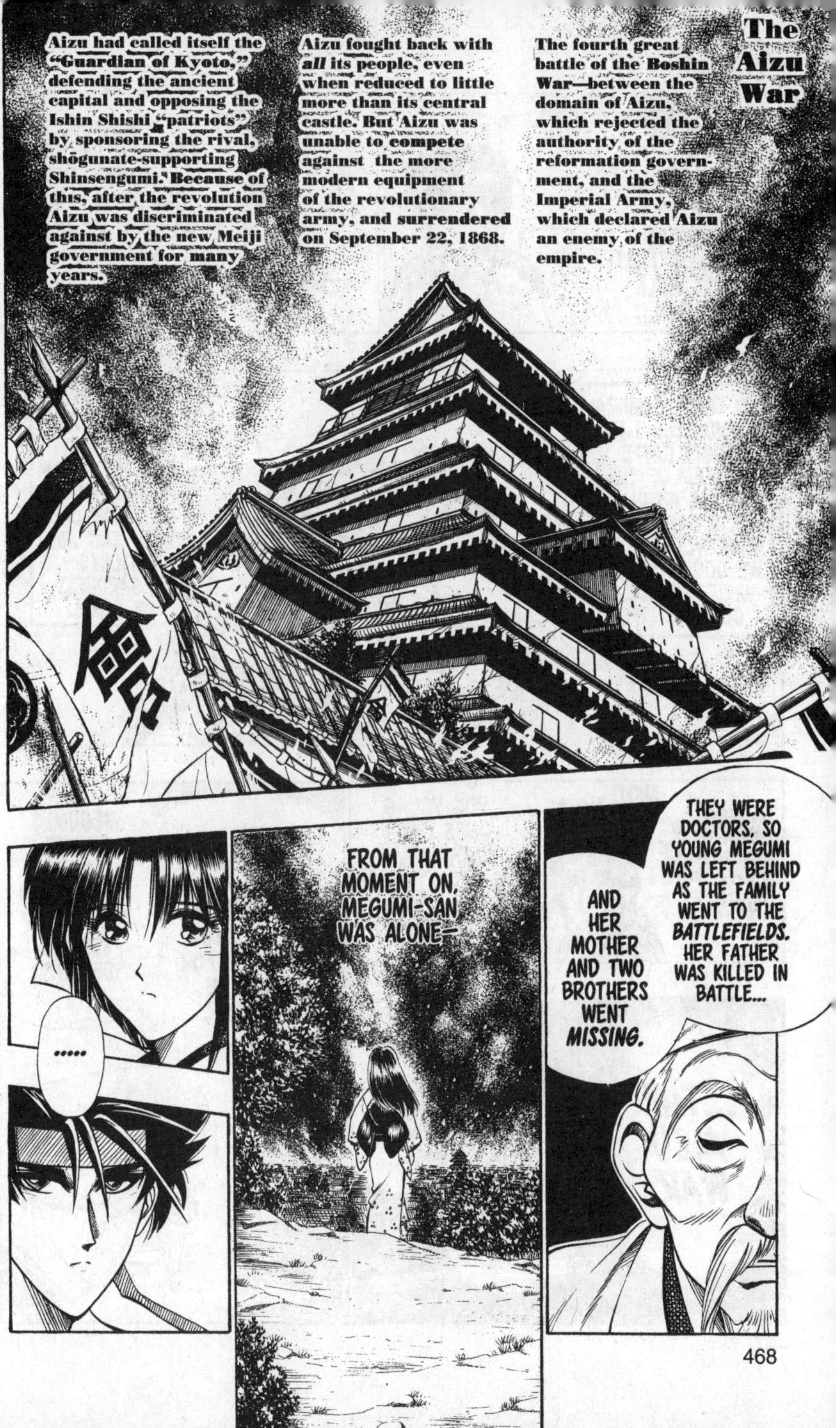
The Aizu War
The fourth great battle of the Boshin War—between the domain of Aizu, which rejected the authority of the reformation government, and the Imperial Army, which declared Aizu an enemy of the empire.
Aizu fought back with *all* its people, even when reduced to little more than its central castle. But Aizu was unable to compete against the more modern equipment of the revolutionary army, and surrendered on September 22, 1868.
Aizu had called itself the "Guardian of Kyoto," defending the ancient capital and opposing the Ishin Shishi "patriots" by sponsoring the rival, shōgunate-supporting Shinsengumi. Because of this, after the revolution Aizu was discriminated against by the new Meiji government for many years.
THEY WERE DOCTORS, SO YOUNG MEGUMI WAS LEFT BEHIND AS THE FAMILY WENT TO THE *BATTLEFIELDS.* HER FATHER WAS KILLED IN BATTLE...
AND HER MOTHER AND TWO BROTHERS WENT *MISSING.*
FROM THAT MOMENT ON, MEGUMI-SAN WAS ALONE—
......

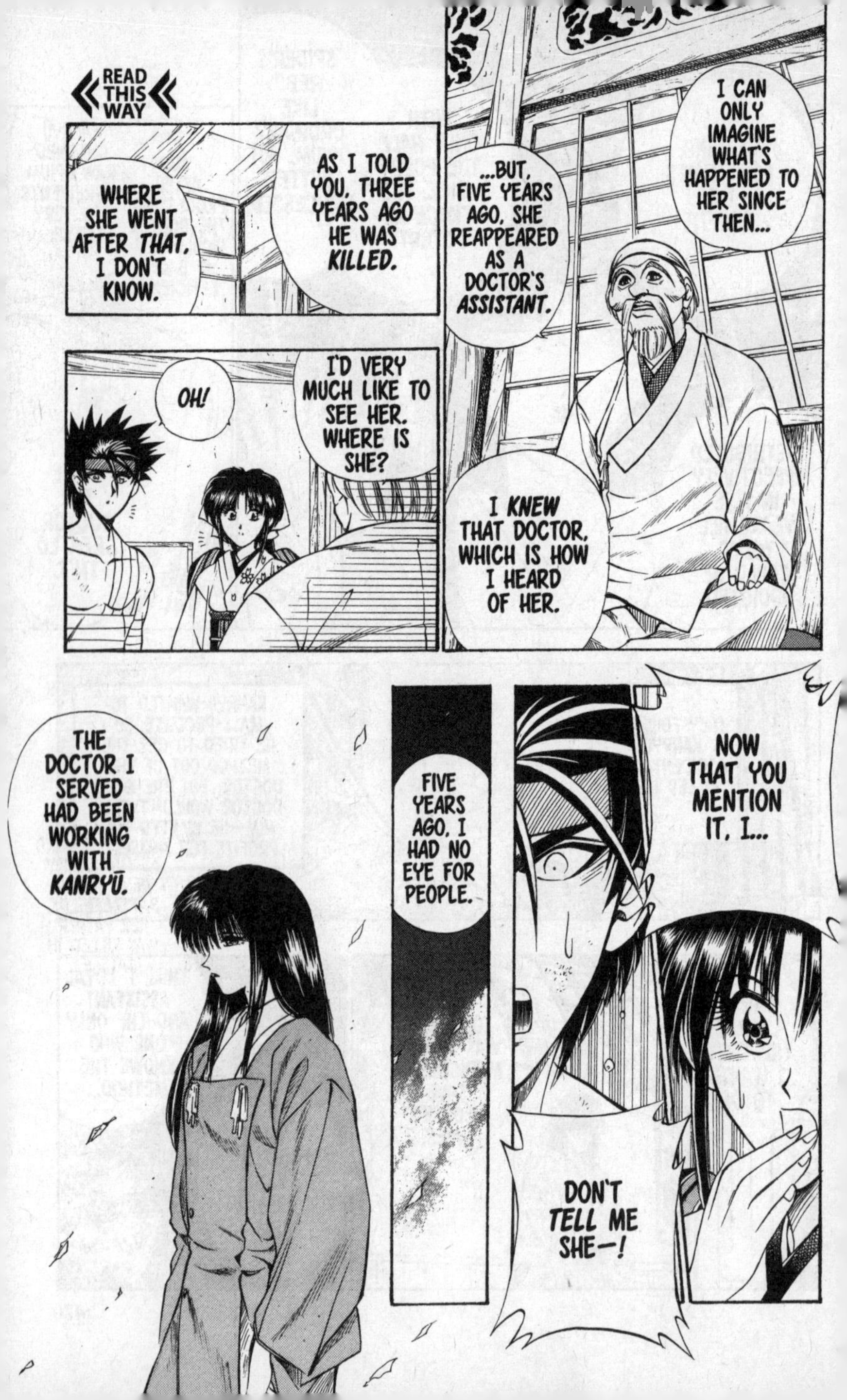
READ THIS WAY
I CAN ONLY IMAGINE WHAT'S HAPPENED TO HER SINCE THEN...
...BUT, FIVE YEARS AGO, SHE REAPPEARED AS A DOCTOR'S *ASSISTANT*.
I *KNEW* THAT DOCTOR, WHICH IS HOW I HEARD OF HER.
AS I TOLD YOU, THREE YEARS AGO HE WAS *KILLED*.
WHERE SHE WENT AFTER *THAT*, I DON'T KNOW.
I'D VERY MUCH LIKE TO SEE HER. WHERE IS SHE?
OH!
NOW THAT YOU MENTION IT, I...
DON'T *TELL* ME SHE—!
FIVE YEARS AGO, I HAD NO EYE FOR PEOPLE.
THE DOCTOR I SERVED HAD BEEN WORKING WITH *KANRYŪ*.

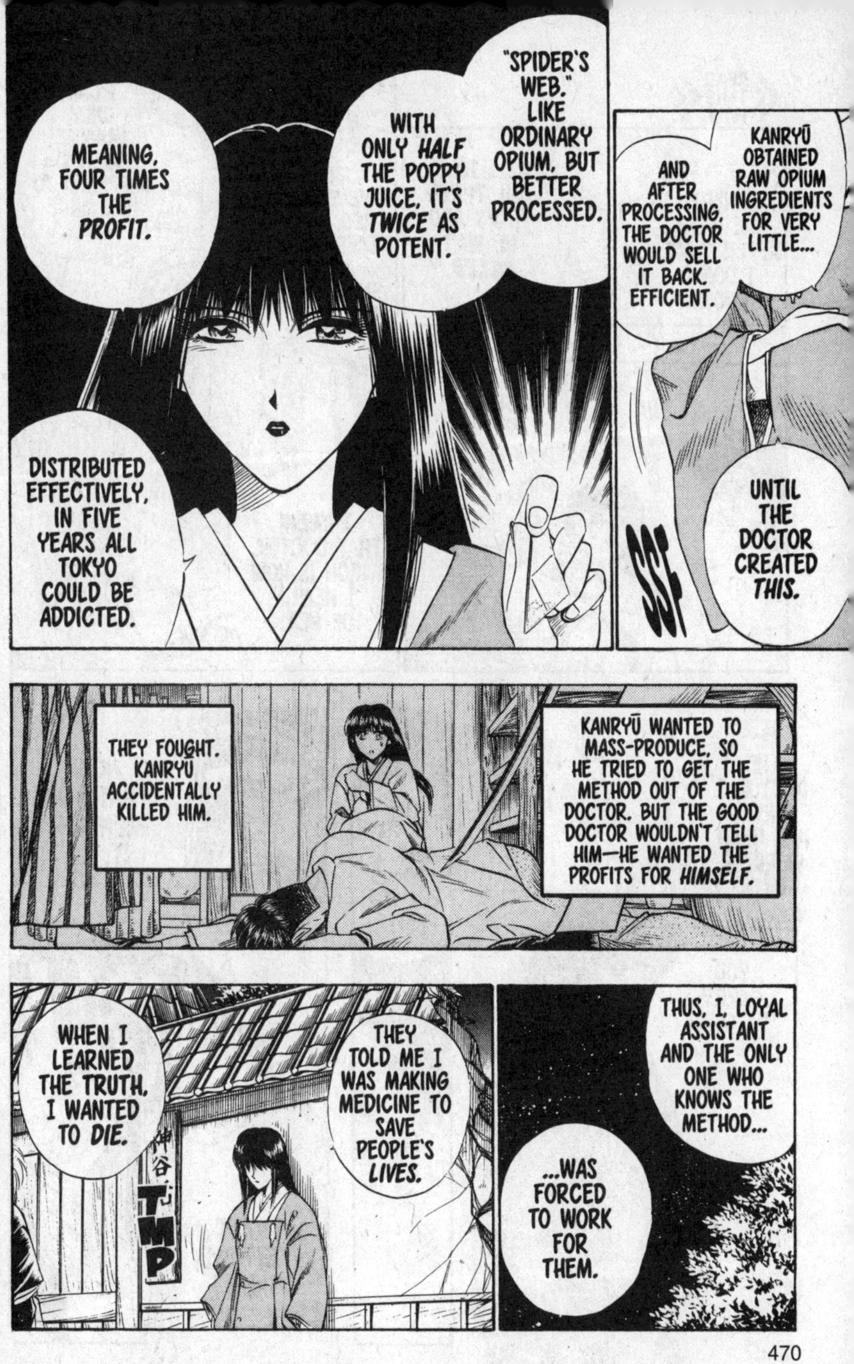
KANRYŪ OBTAINED RAW OPIUM INGREDIENTS FOR VERY LITTLE...
AND AFTER PROCESSING, THE DOCTOR WOULD SELL IT BACK. EFFICIENT.
UNTIL THE DOCTOR CREATED *THIS.*
"SPIDER'S WEB." LIKE ORDINARY OPIUM, BUT BETTER PROCESSED.
WITH ONLY *HALF* THE POPPY JUICE, IT'S *TWICE* AS POTENT.
MEANING, FOUR TIMES THE *PROFIT.*
DISTRIBUTED EFFECTIVELY, IN FIVE YEARS ALL TOKYO COULD BE ADDICTED.
KANRYŪ WANTED TO MASS-PRODUCE, SO HE TRIED TO GET THE METHOD OUT OF THE DOCTOR. BUT THE GOOD DOCTOR WOULDN'T TELL HIM—HE WANTED THE PROFITS FOR *HIMSELF.*
THEY FOUGHT. KANRYŪ ACCIDENTALLY KILLED HIM.
THUS, I, LOYAL ASSISTANT AND THE ONLY ONE WHO KNOWS THE METHOD...
...WAS FORCED TO WORK FOR THEM.
THEY TOLD ME I WAS MAKING MEDICINE TO SAVE PEOPLE'S *LIVES.*
WHEN I LEARNED THE TRUTH, I WANTED TO *DIE.*

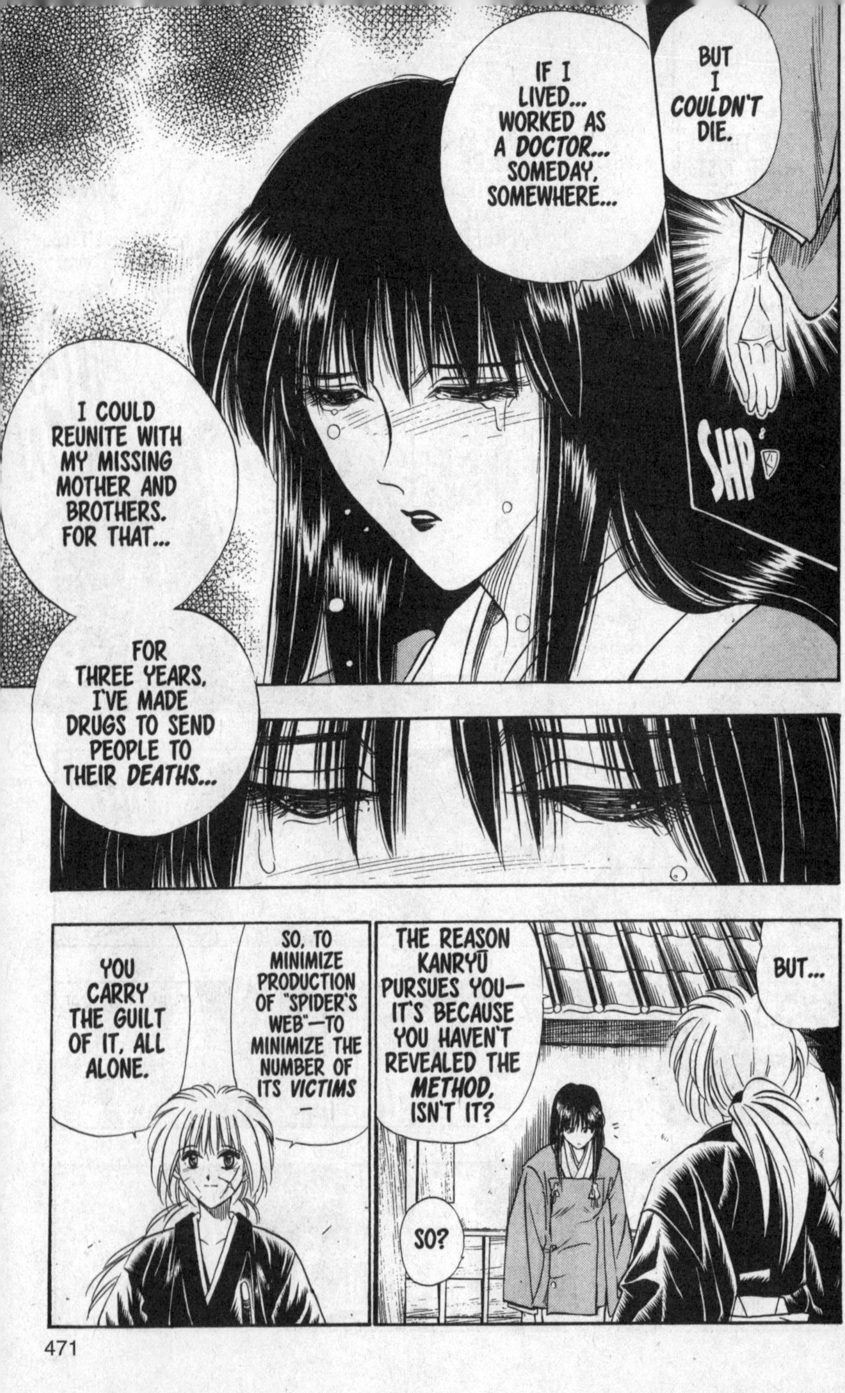
BUT I COULDN'T DIE.
IF I LIVED... WORKED AS A DOCTOR... SOMEDAY, SOMEWHERE...
SHP
I COULD REUNITE WITH MY MISSING MOTHER AND BROTHERS. FOR THAT...
FOR THREE YEARS, I'VE MADE DRUGS TO SEND PEOPLE TO THEIR DEATHS...
BUT...
THE REASON KANRYŪ PURSUES YOU—IT'S BECAUSE YOU HAVEN'T REVEALED THE METHOD, ISN'T IT?
SO?
SO, TO MINIMIZE PRODUCTION OF "SPIDER'S WEB"—TO MINIMIZE THE NUMBER OF ITS VICTIMS—
YOU CARRY THE GUILT OF IT, ALL ALONE.

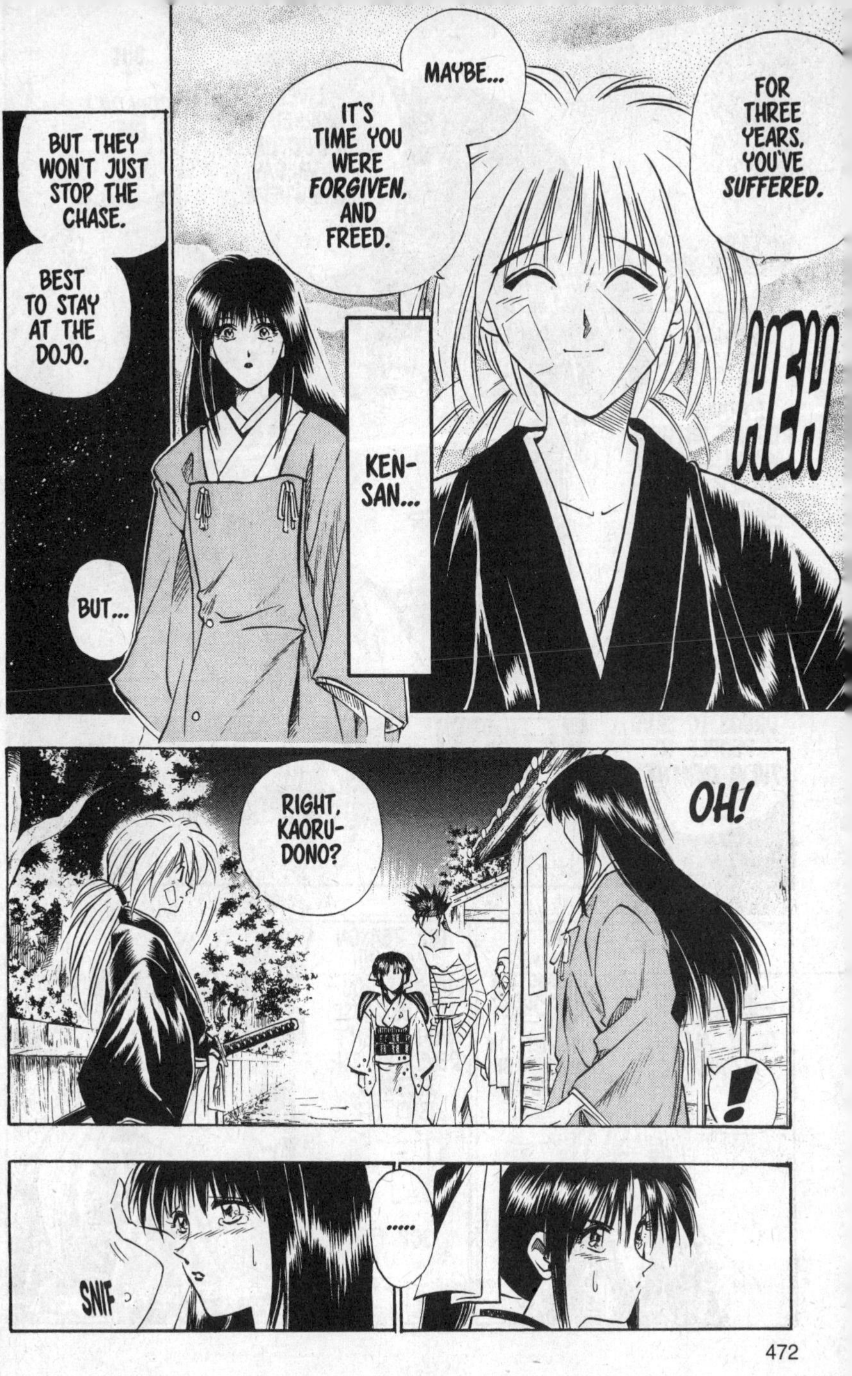
FOR THREE YEARS, YOU'VE SUFFERED.
HEH
MAYBE...
IT'S TIME YOU WERE FORGIVEN, AND FREED.
KEN-SAN...
BUT THEY WON'T JUST STOP THE CHASE.
BEST TO STAY AT THE DOJO.
BUT...
OH!
!
RIGHT, KAORU-DONO?
.....
SNIF

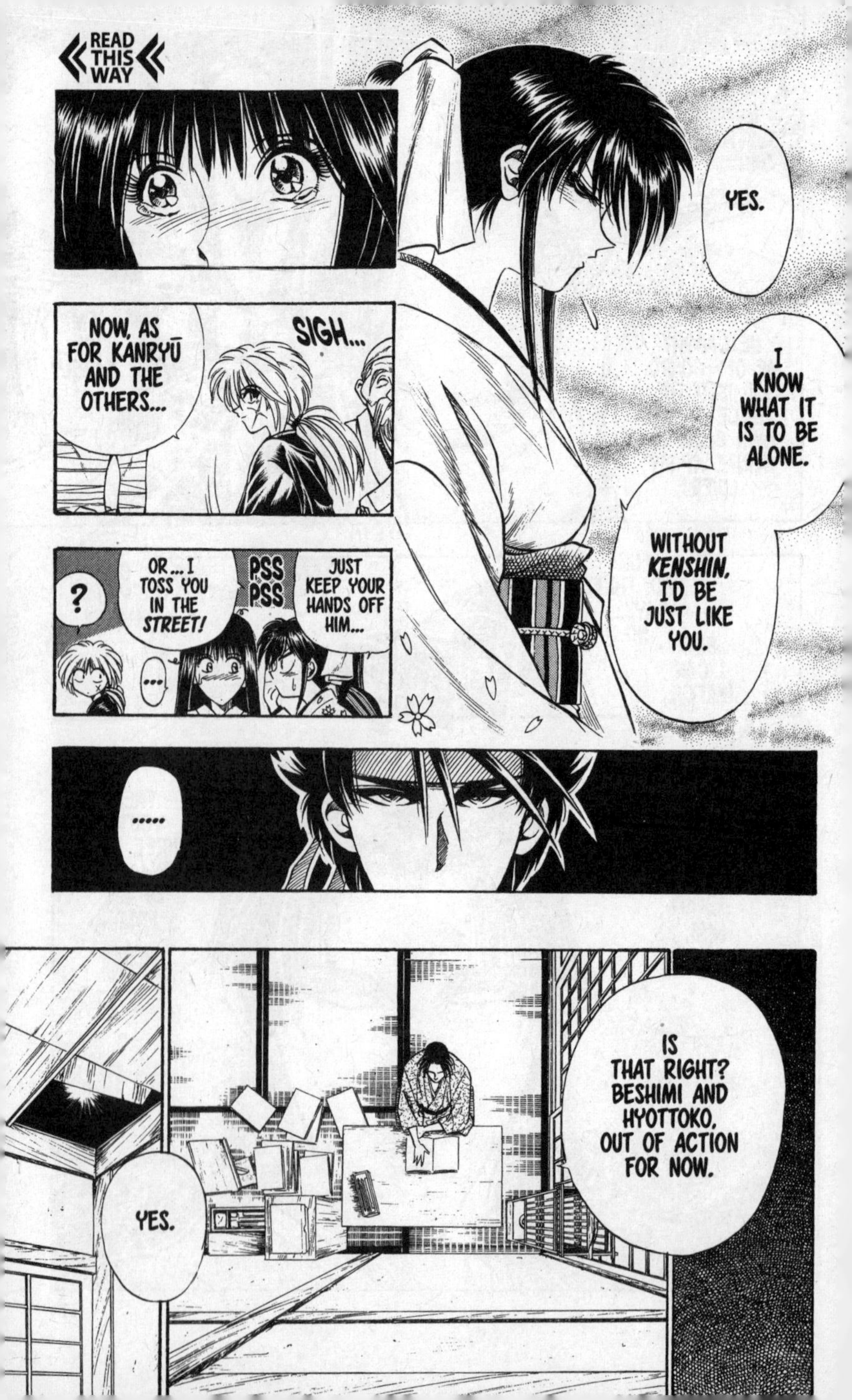
READ THIS WAY
YES.
I KNOW WHAT IT IS TO BE ALONE.
WITHOUT KENSHIN, I'D BE JUST LIKE YOU.
SIGH...
NOW, AS FOR KANRYŪ AND THE OTHERS...
JUST KEEP YOUR HANDS OFF HIM...
PSS PSS
OR... I TOSS YOU IN THE STREET!
?
...
......
IS THAT RIGHT? BESHIMI AND HYOTTOKO, OUT OF ACTION FOR NOW.
YES.

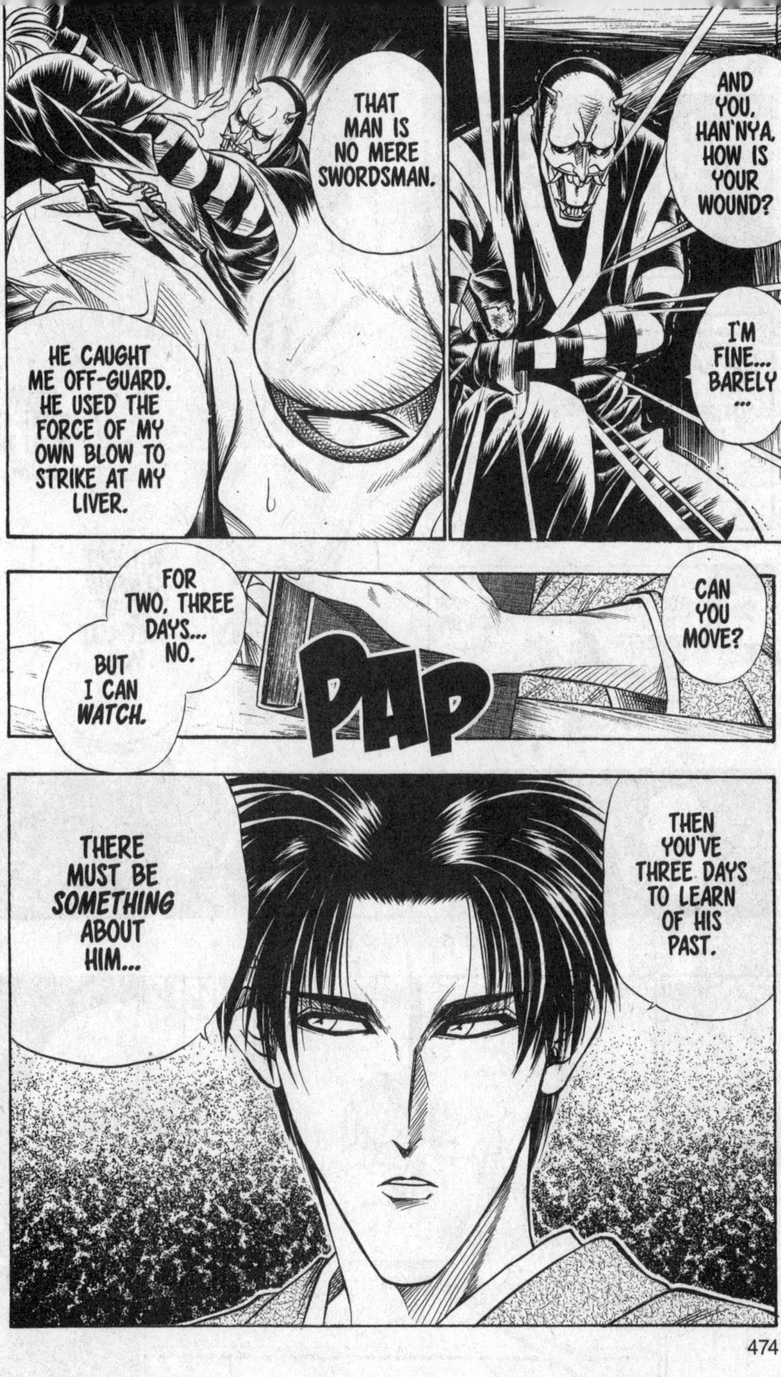

AND YOU, HAN'NYA, HOW IS YOUR WOUND?
I'M FINE... BARELY...
THAT MAN IS NO MERE SWORDSMAN.
HE CAUGHT ME OFF-GUARD. HE USED THE FORCE OF MY OWN BLOW TO STRIKE AT MY LIVER.
CAN YOU MOVE?
PAP
FOR TWO, THREE DAYS... NO.
BUT I CAN *WATCH.*
THEN YOU'VE THREE DAYS TO LEARN OF HIS PAST.
THERE MUST BE *SOMETHING* ABOUT HIM...

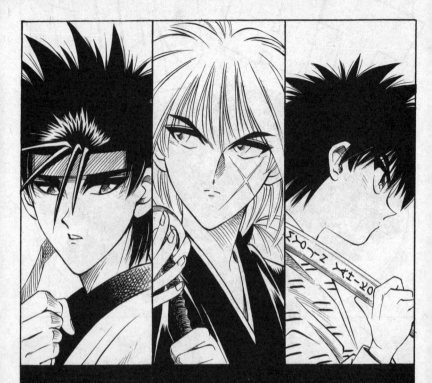

Act 20
A Reason to Act

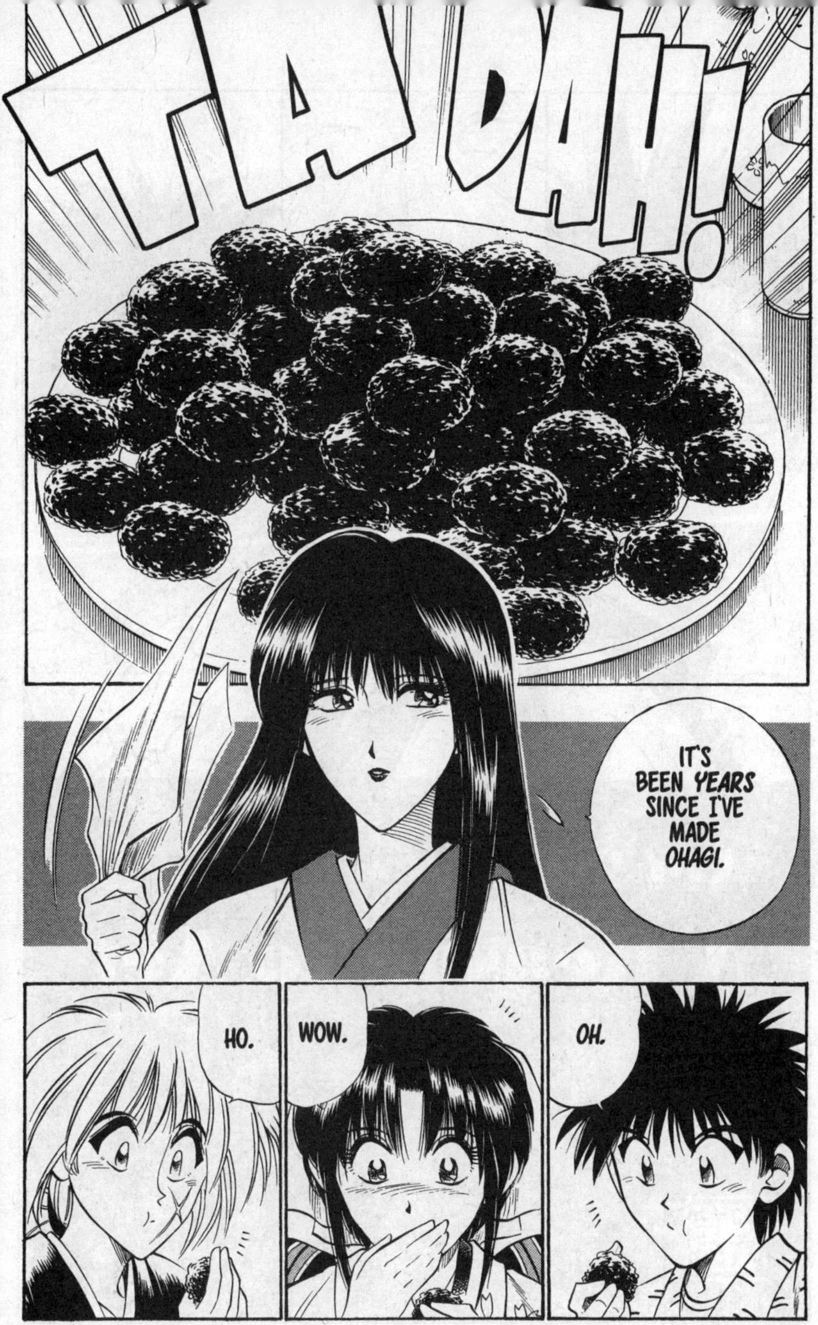
TA DAH!
IT'S BEEN YEARS SINCE I'VE MADE OHAGI.
OH.
WOW.
HO.

« READ THIS WAY «

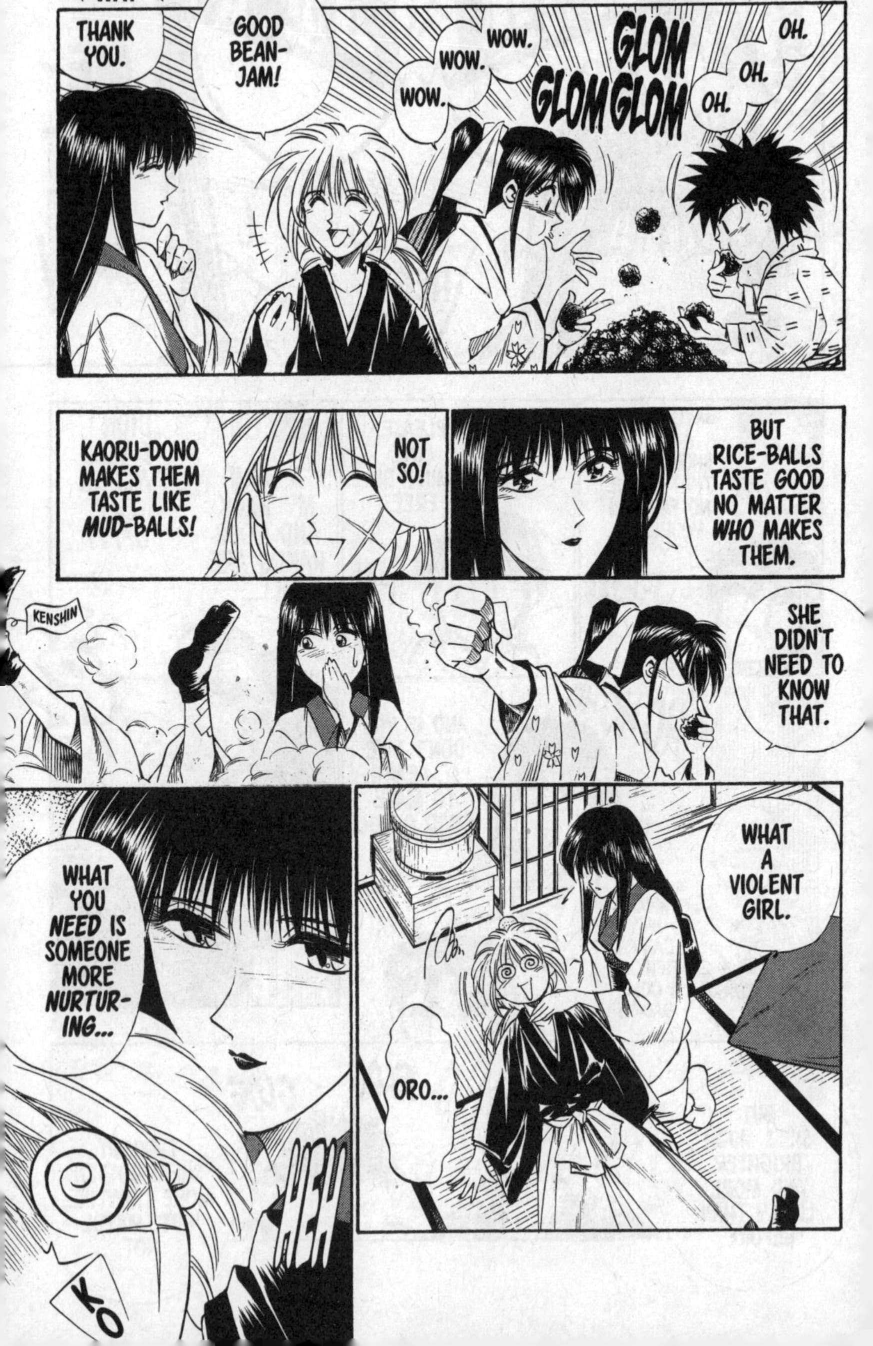
OH. OH. OH.
GLOM GLOM GLOM
WOW. WOW. WOW.
GOOD BEAN-JAM!
THANK YOU.
BUT RICE-BALLS TASTE GOOD NO MATTER WHO MAKES THEM.
NOT SO!
KAORU-DONO MAKES THEM TASTE LIKE MUD-BALLS!
SHE DIDN'T NEED TO KNOW THAT.
KENSHIN
WHAT A VIOLENT GIRL.
ORO...
WHAT YOU NEED IS SOMEONE MORE NURTURING...
HEH
KO

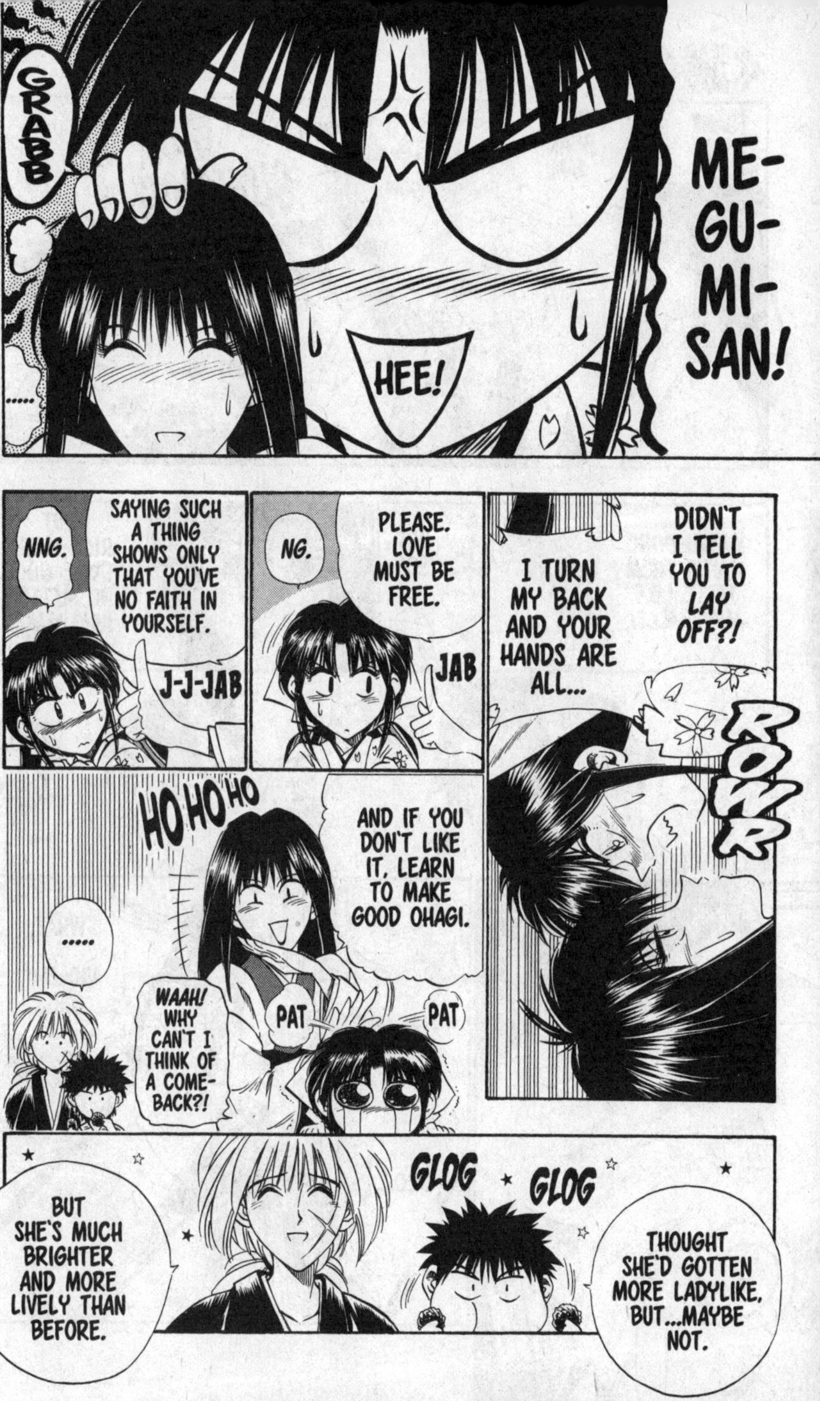
ME-GU-MI-SAN!
GRABB
HEE!
.....
DIDN'T I TELL YOU TO LAY OFF?!
I TURN MY BACK AND YOUR HANDS ARE ALL...
ROWR
PLEASE. LOVE MUST BE FREE.
NG.
JAB
SAYING SUCH A THING SHOWS ONLY THAT YOU'VE NO FAITH IN YOURSELF.
NNG.
J-J-JAB
AND IF YOU DON'T LIKE IT, LEARN TO MAKE GOOD OHAGI.
HO HO HO
PAT
PAT
WAAH! WHY CAN'T I THINK OF A COME-BACK?!
.....
THOUGHT SHE'D GOTTEN MORE LADYLIKE, BUT...MAYBE NOT.
GLOG
GLOG
BUT SHE'S MUCH BRIGHTER AND MORE LIVELY THAN BEFORE.

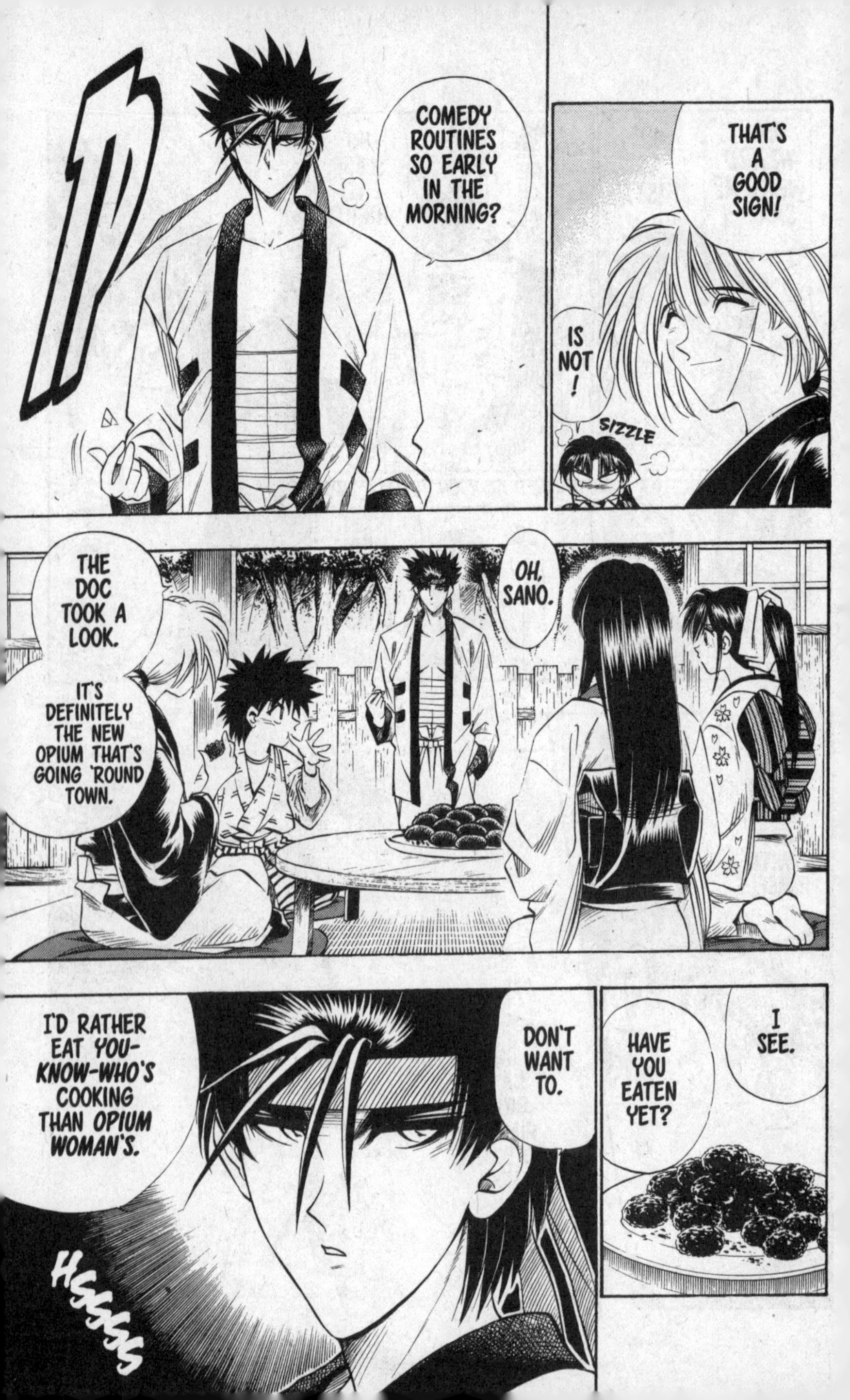
THAT'S A GOOD SIGN!
IS NOT!
SIZZLE
COMEDY ROUTINES SO EARLY IN THE MORNING?
OH, SANO.
THE DOC TOOK A LOOK.
IT'S DEFINITELY THE NEW OPIUM THAT'S GOING 'ROUND TOWN.
I SEE.
HAVE YOU EATEN YET?
DON'T WANT TO.
I'D RATHER EAT YOU-KNOW-WHO'S COOKING THAN OPIUM WOMAN'S.
HSSSSS

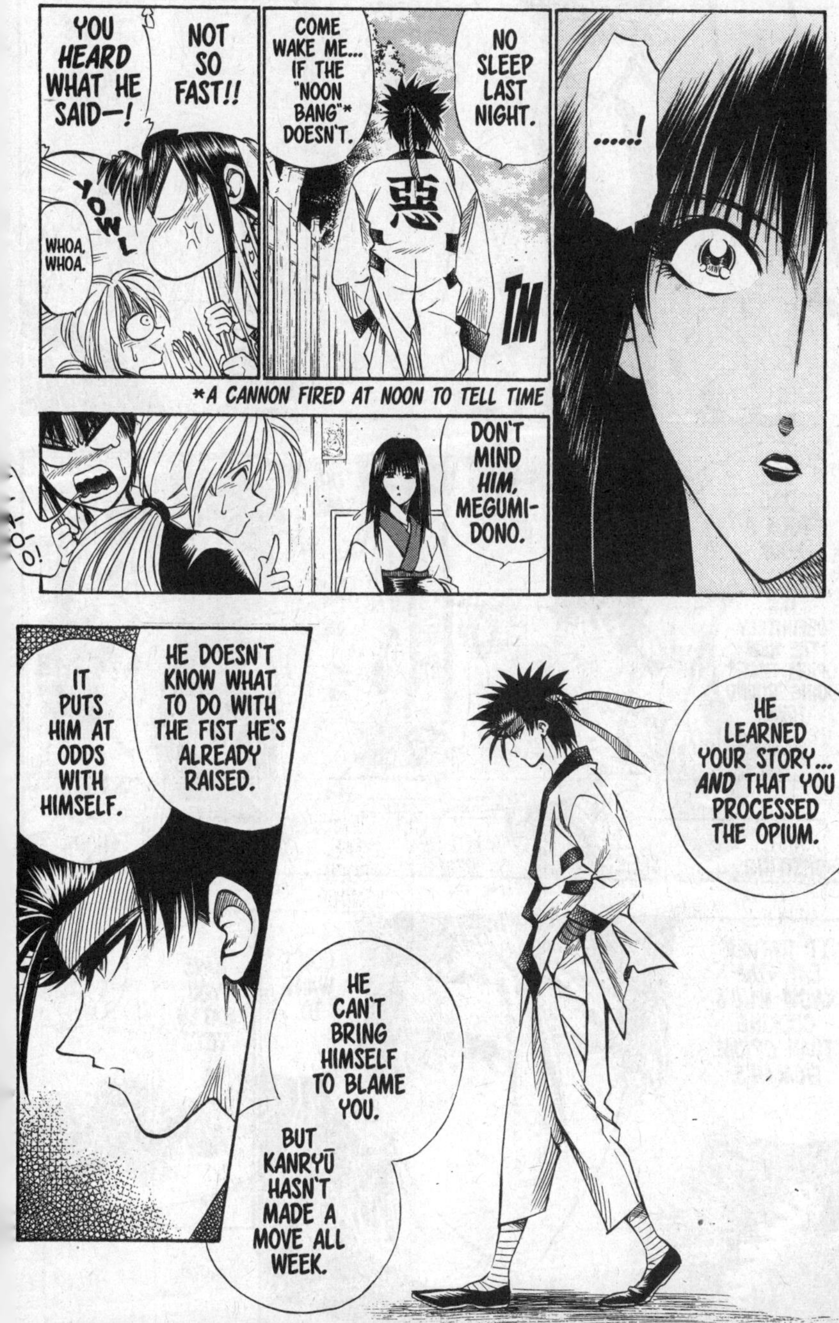
.....!
NO SLEEP LAST NIGHT.
COME WAKE ME... IF THE "NOON BANG"* DOESN'T.
TM
NOT SO FAST!!
YOU HEARD WHAT HE SAID—!
YOWL
WHOA, WHOA.
*A CANNON FIRED AT NOON TO TELL TIME
DON'T MIND HIM, MEGUMI-DONO.
O-O!
HE LEARNED YOUR STORY... AND THAT YOU PROCESSED THE OPIUM.
HE DOESN'T KNOW WHAT TO DO WITH THE FIST HE'S ALREADY RAISED.
IT PUTS HIM AT ODDS WITH HIMSELF.
HE CAN'T BRING HIMSELF TO BLAME YOU.
BUT KANRYŪ HASN'T MADE A MOVE ALL WEEK.

READ THIS WAY

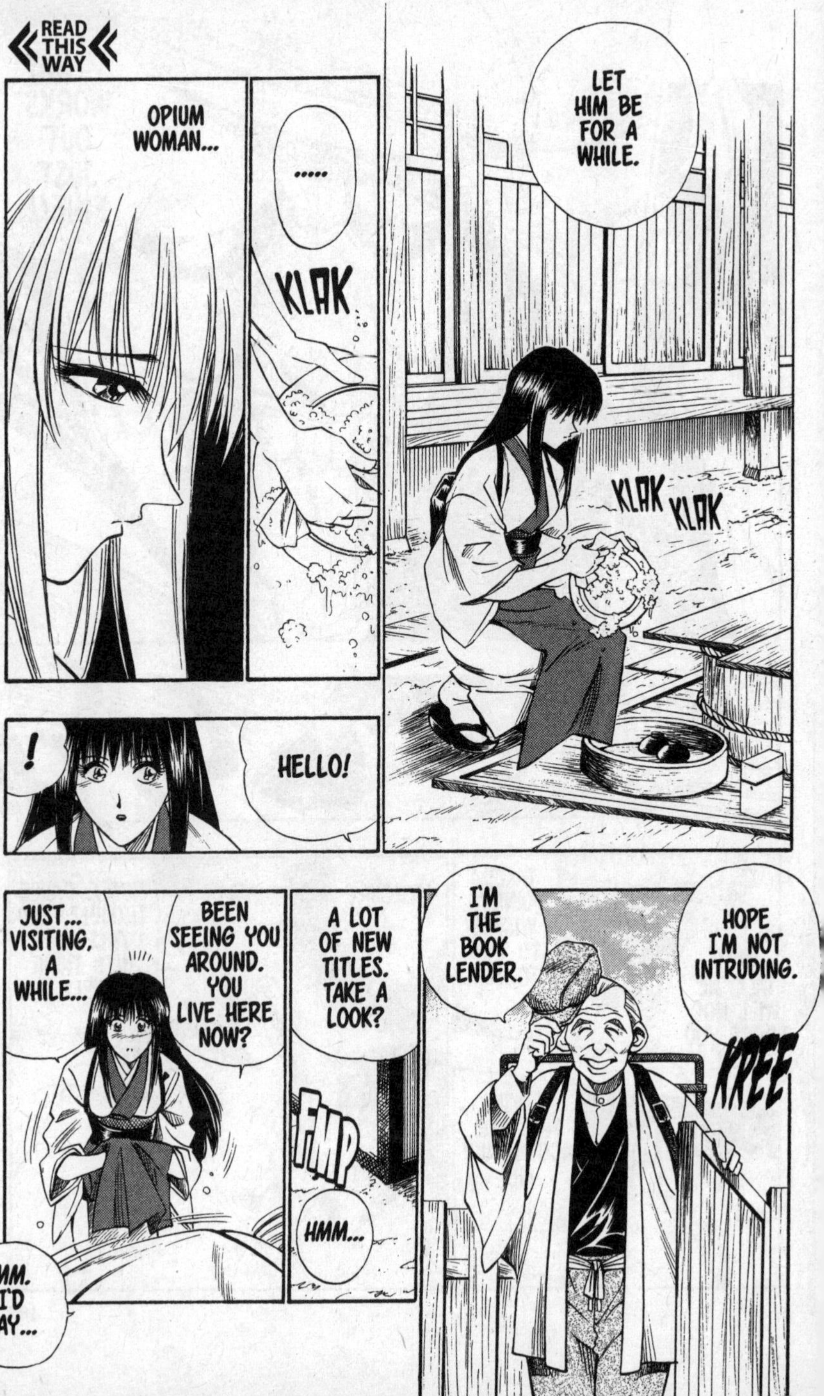
LET HIM BE FOR A WHILE.
KLAK KLAK
.....
KLAK
OPIUM WOMAN...
HELLO!
!
HOPE I'M NOT INTRUDING.
KREE
I'M THE BOOK LENDER.
A LOT OF NEW TITLES. TAKE A LOOK?
FMP
HMM...
BEEN SEEING YOU AROUND. YOU LIVE HERE NOW?
JUST... VISITING, A WHILE...
MM. I'D SAY...

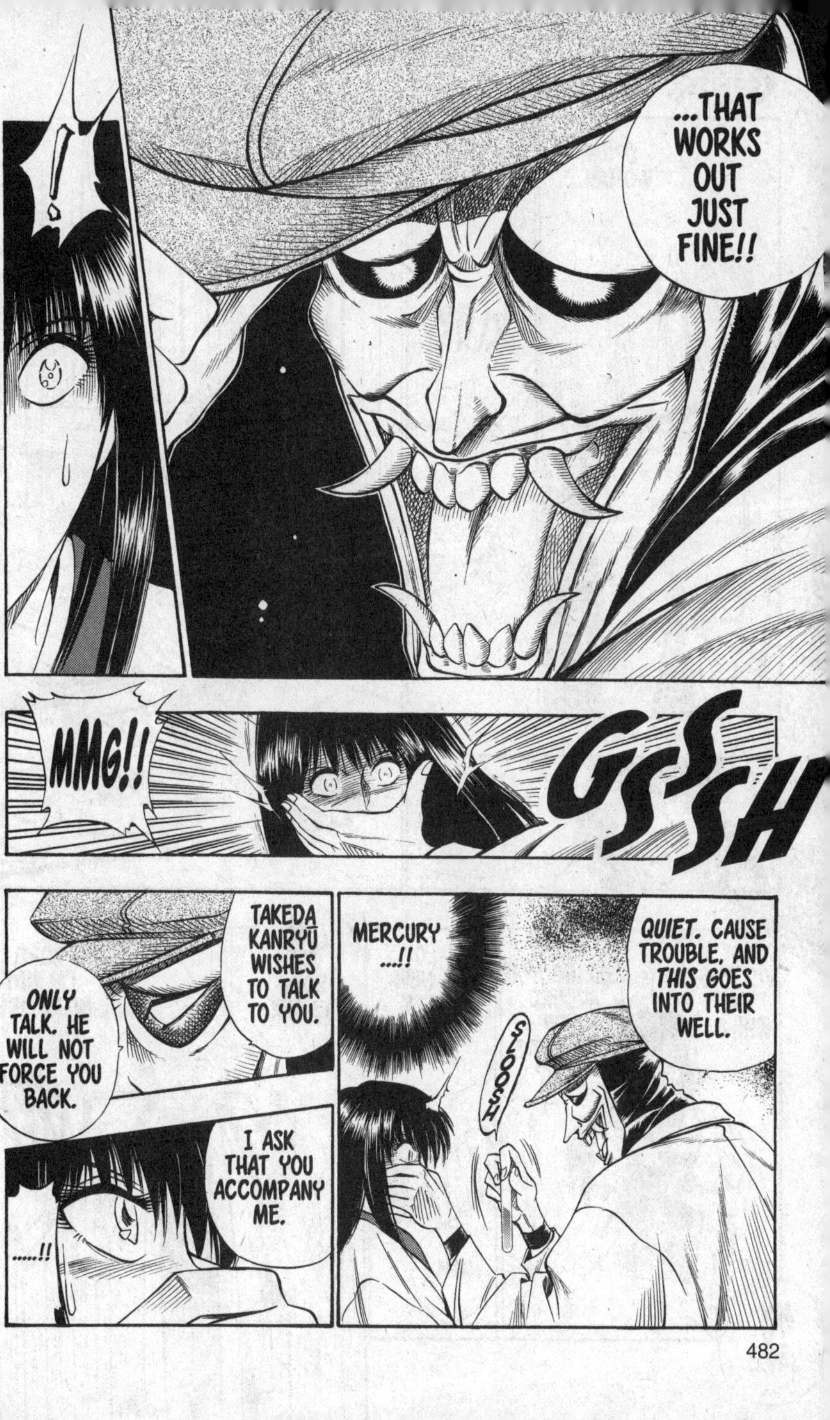
...THAT WORKS OUT JUST FINE!!
!
GSSSH
MMG!!
QUIET. CAUSE TROUBLE, AND THIS GOES INTO THEIR WELL.
MERCURY ...!!
SLOOSH
TAKEDA KANRYŪ WISHES TO TALK TO YOU.
ONLY TALK. HE WILL NOT FORCE YOU BACK.
I ASK THAT YOU ACCOMPANY ME.
......!!

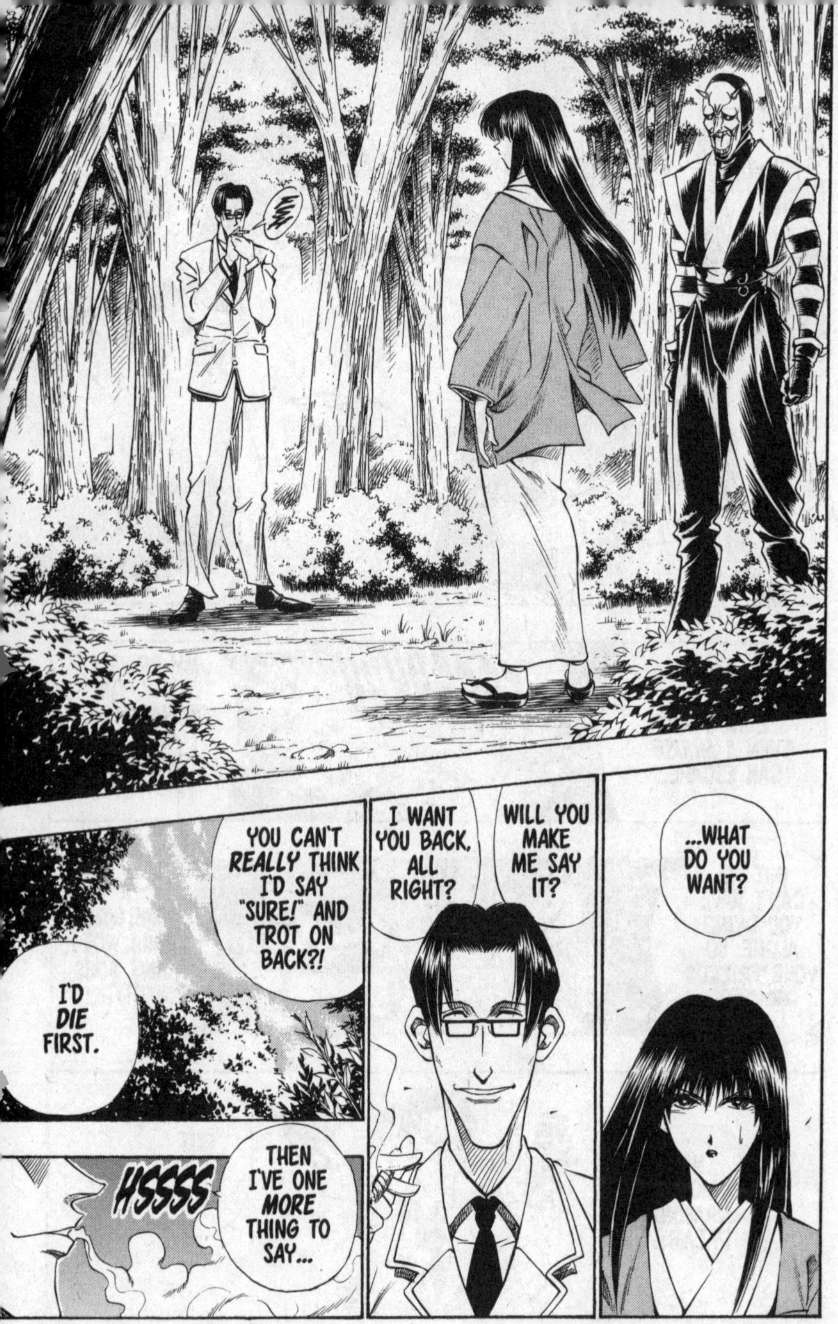
...WHAT DO YOU WANT?
WILL YOU MAKE ME SAY IT?
I WANT YOU BACK, ALL RIGHT?
YOU CAN'T *REALLY* THINK I'D SAY "SURE!" AND TROT ON BACK?!
I'D *DIE* FIRST.
THEN I'VE ONE *MORE* THING TO SAY...
HSSSS

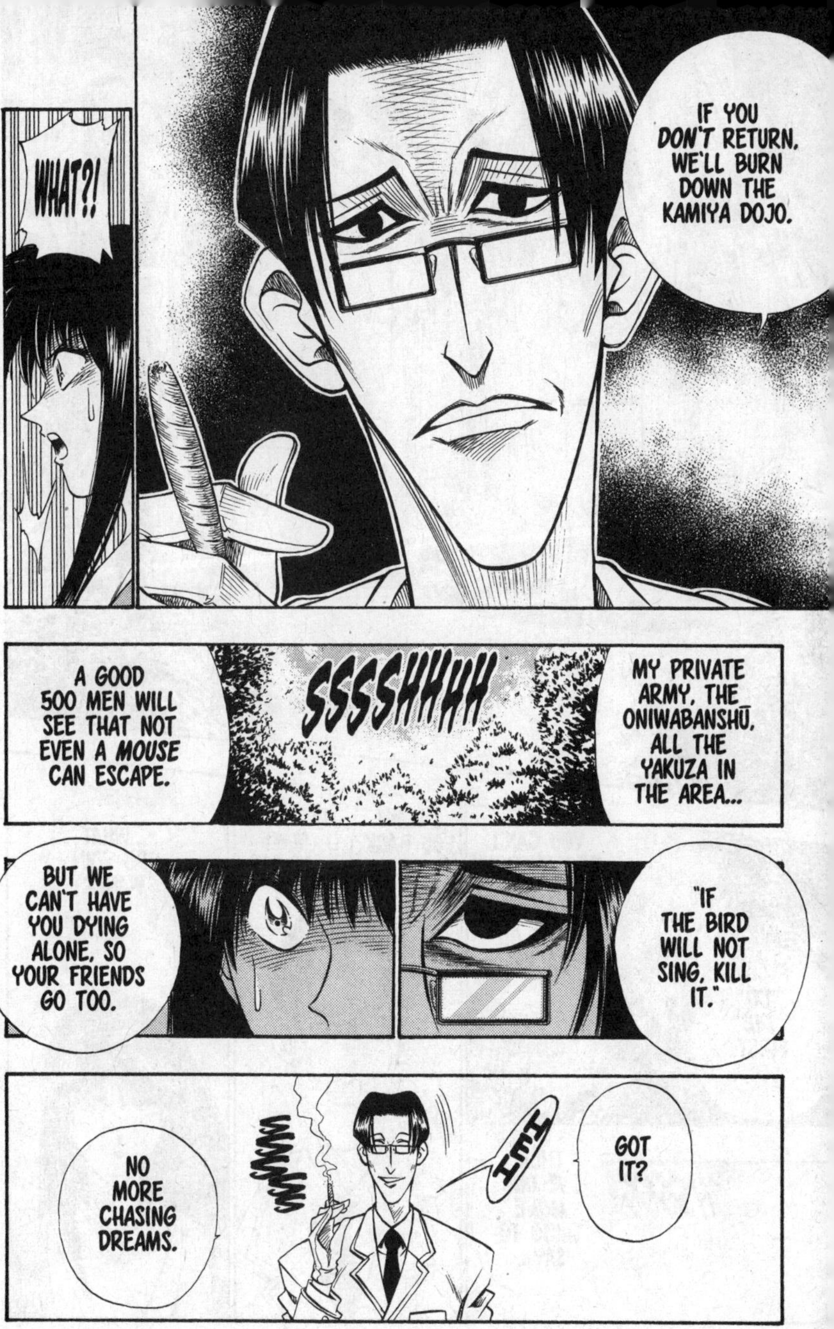
IF YOU DON'T RETURN, WE'LL BURN DOWN THE KAMIYA DOJO.
WHAT?!
MY PRIVATE ARMY, THE ONIWABANSHŪ, ALL THE YAKUZA IN THE AREA...
SSSSHHHH
A GOOD 500 MEN WILL SEE THAT NOT EVEN A MOUSE CAN ESCAPE.
"IF THE BIRD WILL NOT SING, KILL IT."
BUT WE CAN'T HAVE YOU DYING ALONE, SO YOUR FRIENDS GO TOO.
GOT IT?
NO MORE CHASING DREAMS.

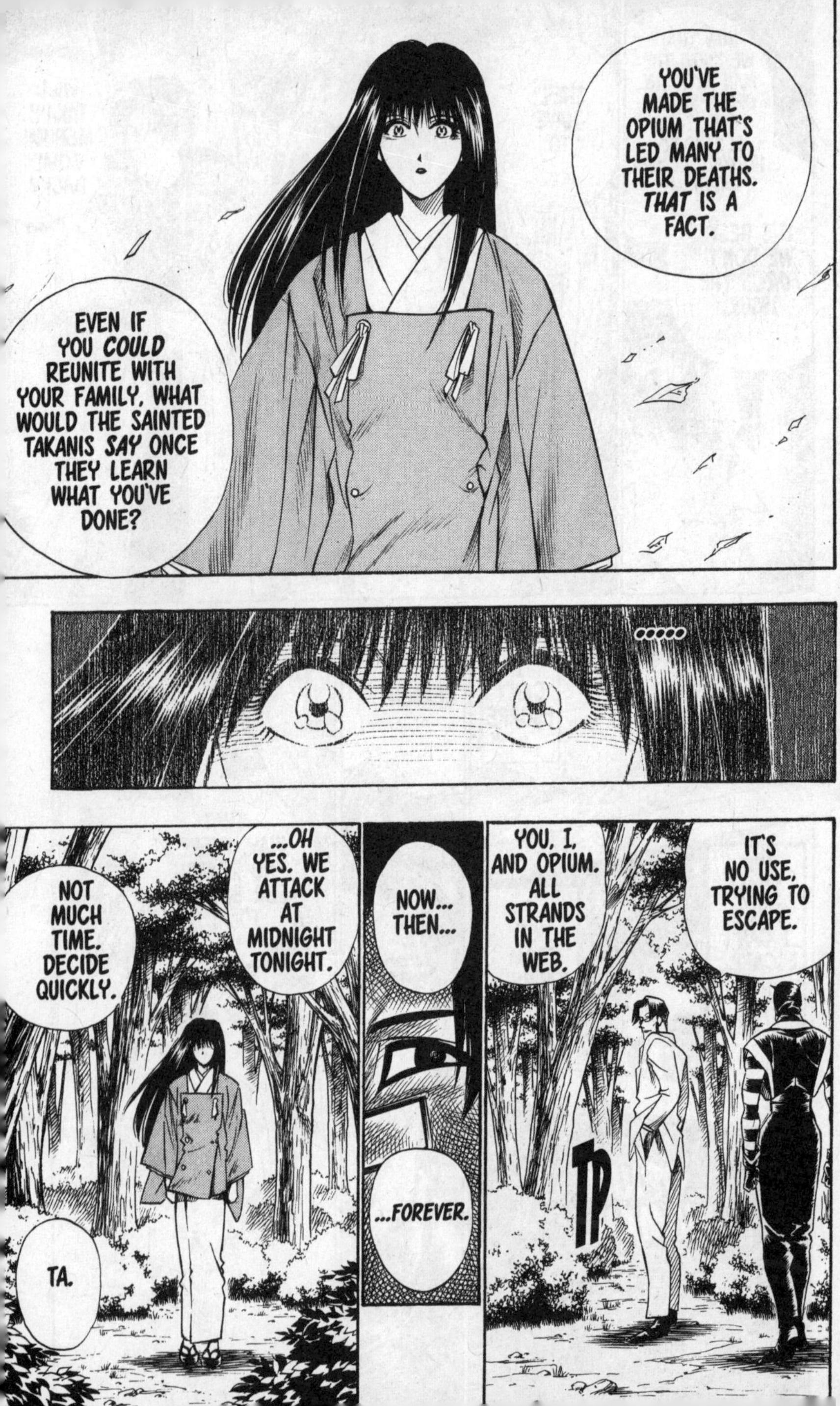
YOU'VE MADE THE OPIUM THAT'S LED MANY TO THEIR DEATHS. THAT IS A FACT.
EVEN IF YOU COULD REUNITE WITH YOUR FAMILY, WHAT WOULD THE SAINTED TAKANIS SAY ONCE THEY LEARN WHAT YOU'VE DONE?
.....
IT'S NO USE, TRYING TO ESCAPE.
YOU, I, AND OPIUM. ALL STRANDS IN THE WEB.
TP
NOW... THEN...
...FOREVER.
...OH YES. WE ATTACK AT MIDNIGHT TONIGHT.
NOT MUCH TIME. DECIDE QUICKLY.
TA.

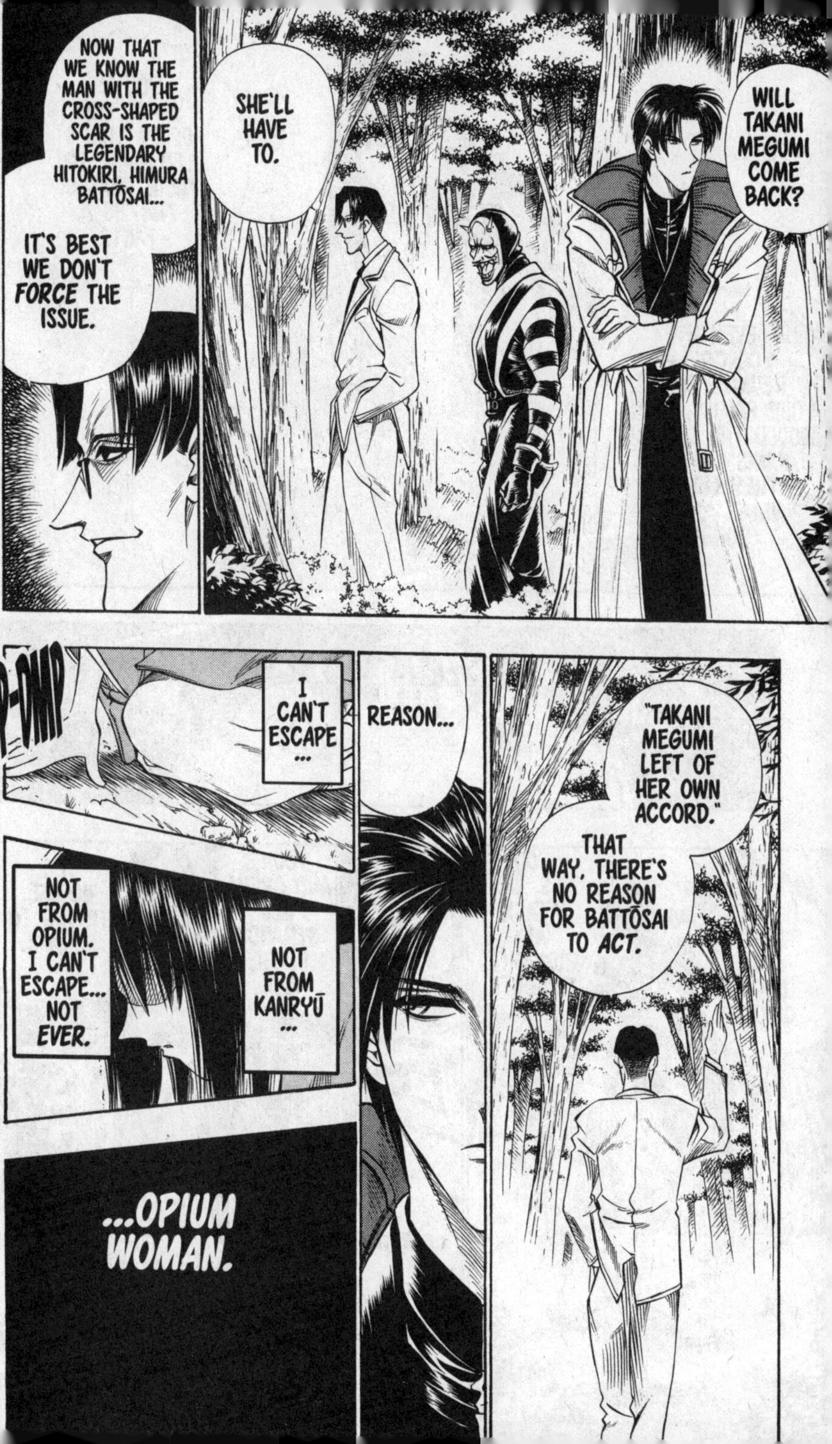
WILL TAKANI MEGUMI COME BACK?
SHE'LL HAVE TO.
NOW THAT WE KNOW THE MAN WITH THE CROSS-SHAPED SCAR IS THE LEGENDARY HITOKIRI, HIMURA BATTŌSAI...
IT'S BEST WE DON'T *FORCE* THE ISSUE.
"TAKANI MEGUMI LEFT OF HER OWN ACCORD."
THAT WAY, THERE'S NO REASON FOR BATTŌSAI TO *ACT.*
REASON...
P-DMP
I CAN'T ESCAPE...
NOT FROM KANRYŪ...
NOT FROM OPIUM. I CAN'T ESCAPE... NOT *EVER.*
...OPIUM WOMAN.

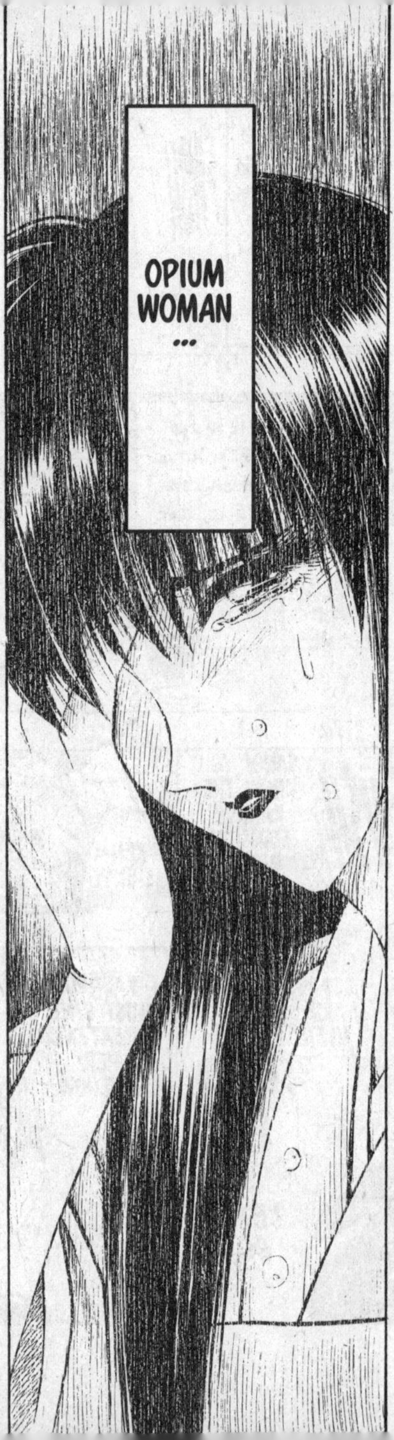
OPIUM WOMAN
...

READ THIS WAY

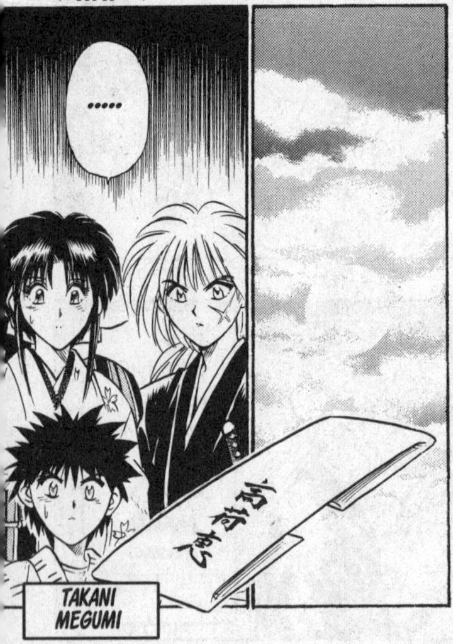
高荷恵
TAKANI MEGUMI
......

Long time no see! Watsuki here. About those fan letters, again— I've been getting more and more from you guys. We're becoming more like a "young men's" magazine, but even so, the ratio is still running 7:3, females over males. I do still plan to reply to you, so please be patient, just a bit longer—especially those of you who've sent multiple letters already. (I'm so sorry!)

Watsuki

READ THIS WAY

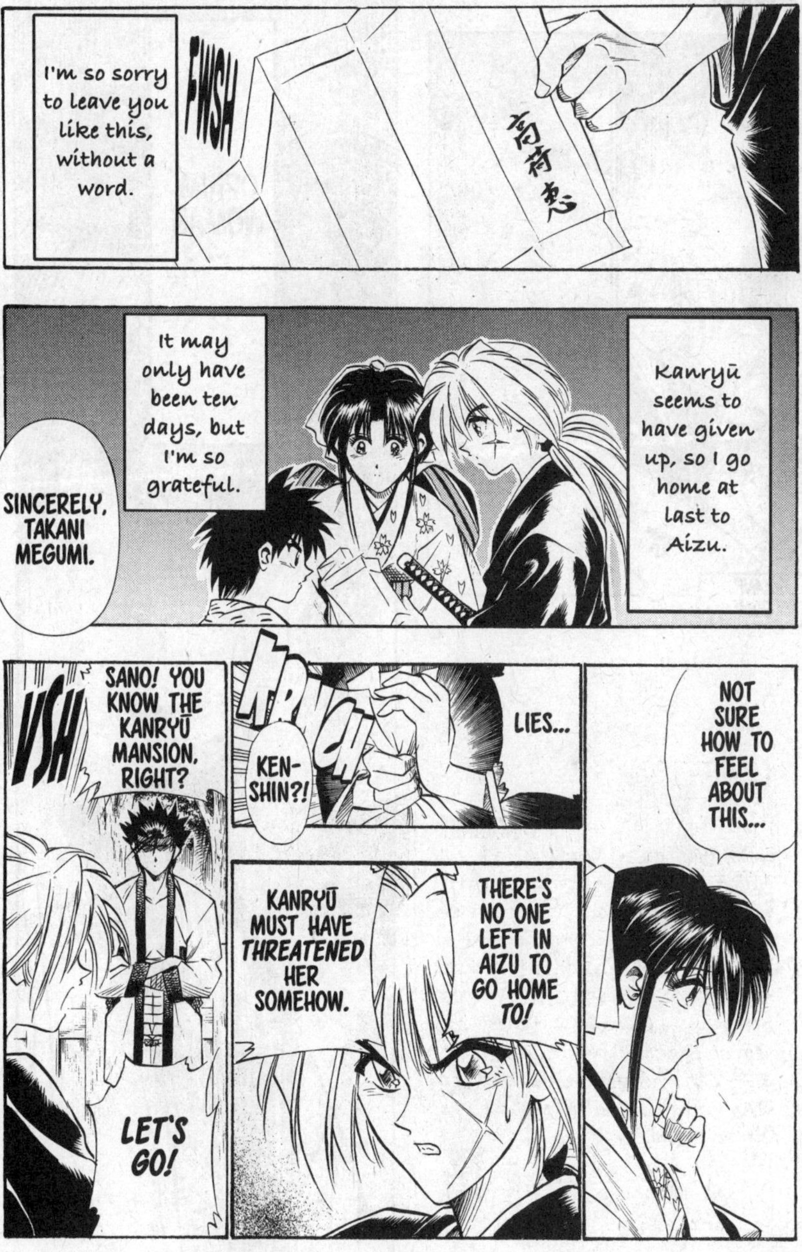

I'm so sorry to leave you like this, without a word.
FWSH
高荷恵
Kanryū seems to have given up, so I go home at last to Aizu.
It may only have been ten days, but I'm so grateful.
SINCERELY, TAKANI MEGUMI.
NOT SURE HOW TO FEEL ABOUT THIS...
LIES...
KRNCH
KEN-SHIN?!
THERE'S NO ONE LEFT IN AIZU TO GO HOME TO!
KANRYŪ MUST HAVE THREATENED HER SOMEHOW.
VSH
SANO! YOU KNOW THE KANRYŪ MANSION, RIGHT?
LET'S GO!

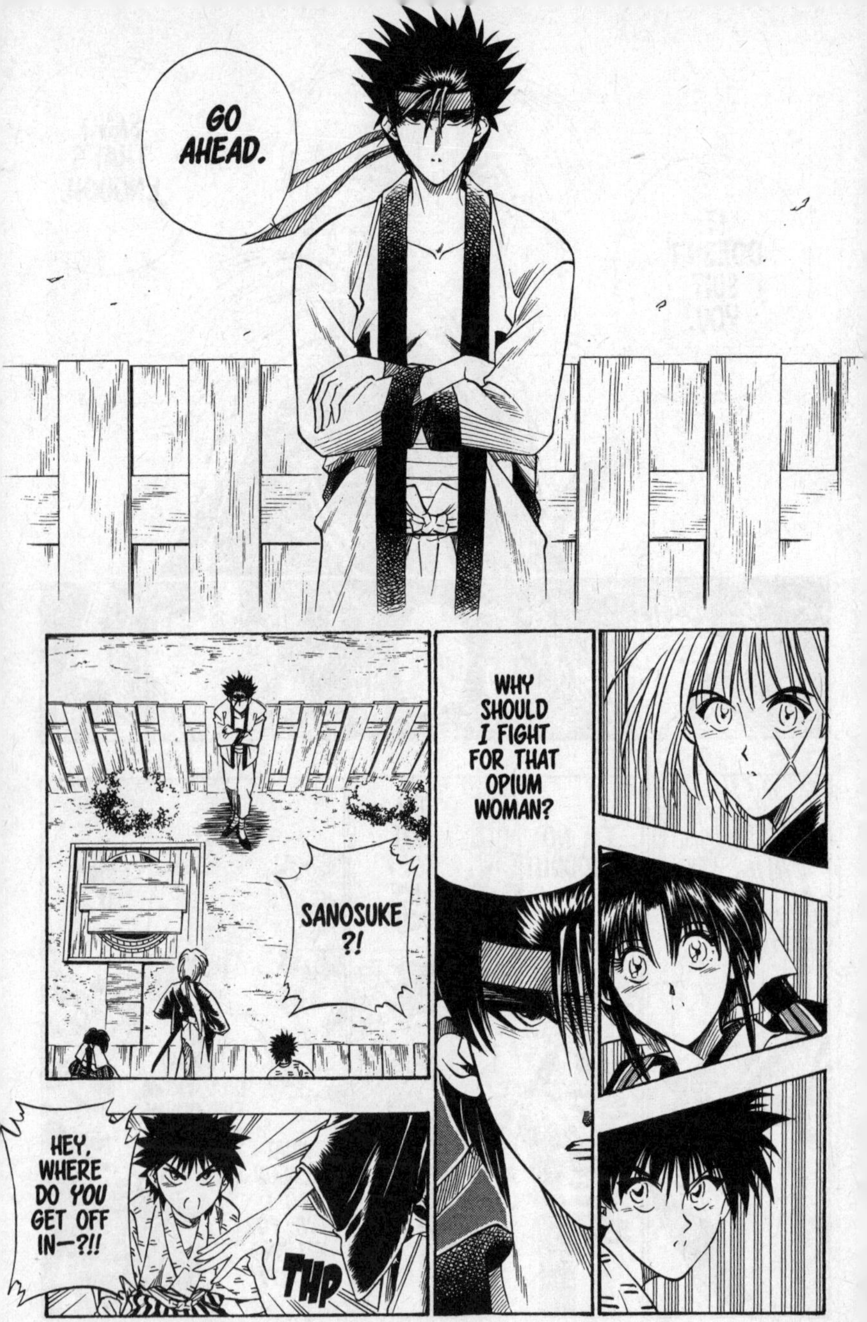
GO AHEAD.
WHY SHOULD I FIGHT FOR THAT OPIUM WOMAN?
SANOSUKE ?!
HEY, WHERE DO YOU GET OFF IN—?!!
THP

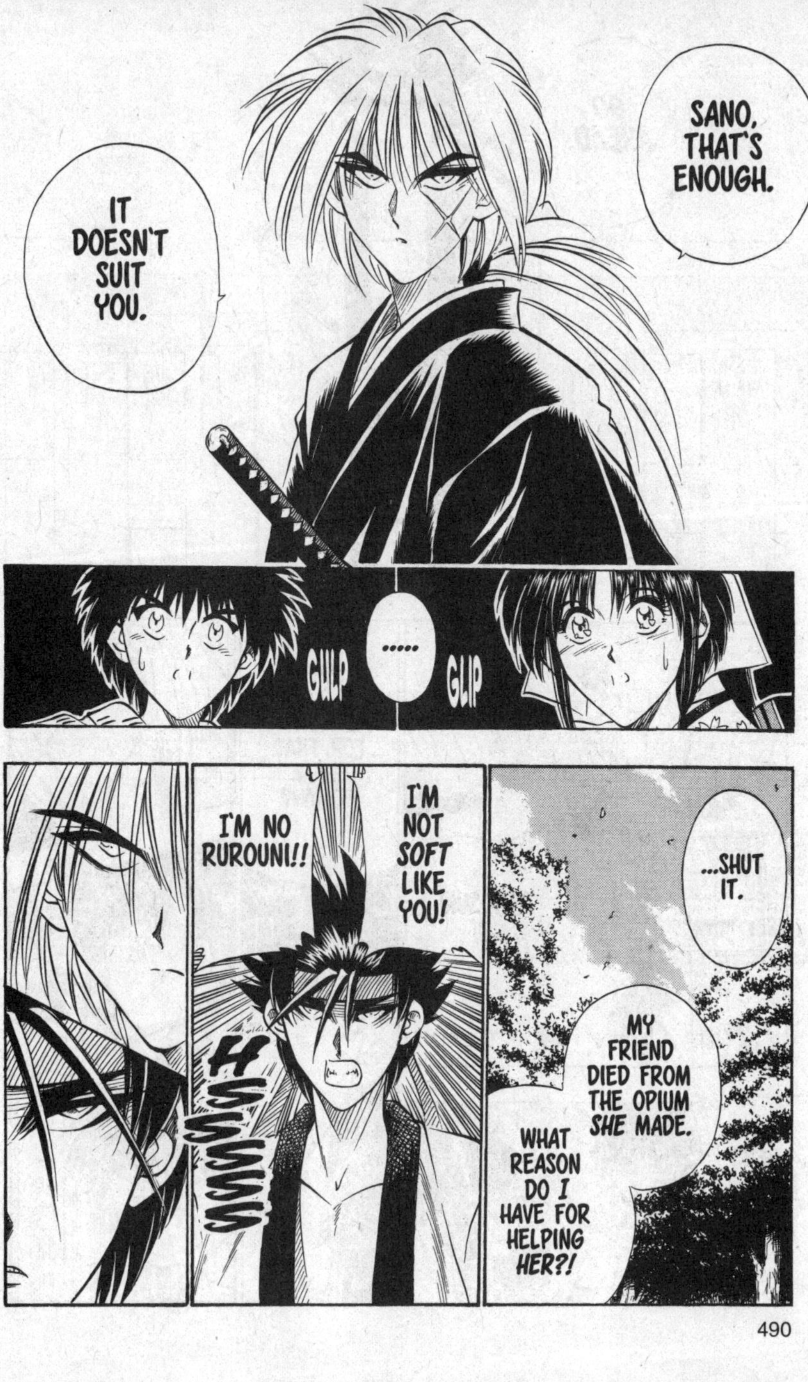
SANO, THAT'S ENOUGH.
IT DOESN'T SUIT YOU.
GLIP
......
GULP
...SHUT IT.
MY FRIEND DIED FROM THE OPIUM *SHE* MADE.
WHAT REASON DO I HAVE FOR HELPING *HER*?!
I'M NOT *SOFT* LIKE YOU!
I'M NO RUROUNI!!
HSSSSSS

READ THIS WAY

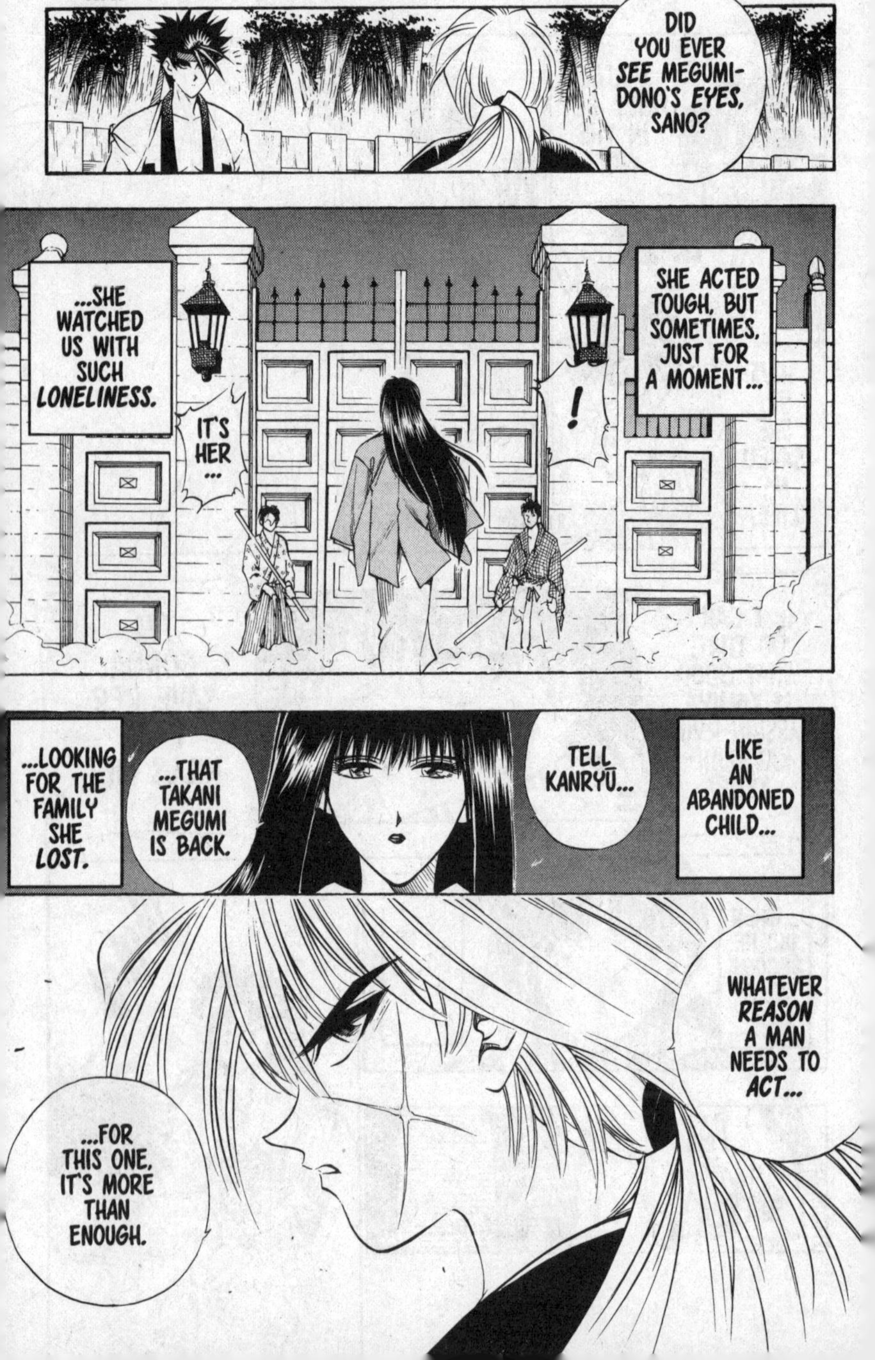
DID YOU EVER SEE MEGUMI-DONO'S EYES, SANO?
SHE ACTED TOUGH, BUT SOMETIMES, JUST FOR A MOMENT...
!
IT'S HER...
...SHE WATCHED US WITH SUCH LONELINESS.
LIKE AN ABANDONED CHILD...
TELL KANRYŪ...
...THAT TAKANI MEGUMI IS BACK.
...LOOKING FOR THE FAMILY SHE LOST.
WHATEVER REASON A MAN NEEDS TO ACT...
...FOR THIS ONE, IT'S MORE THAN ENOUGH.

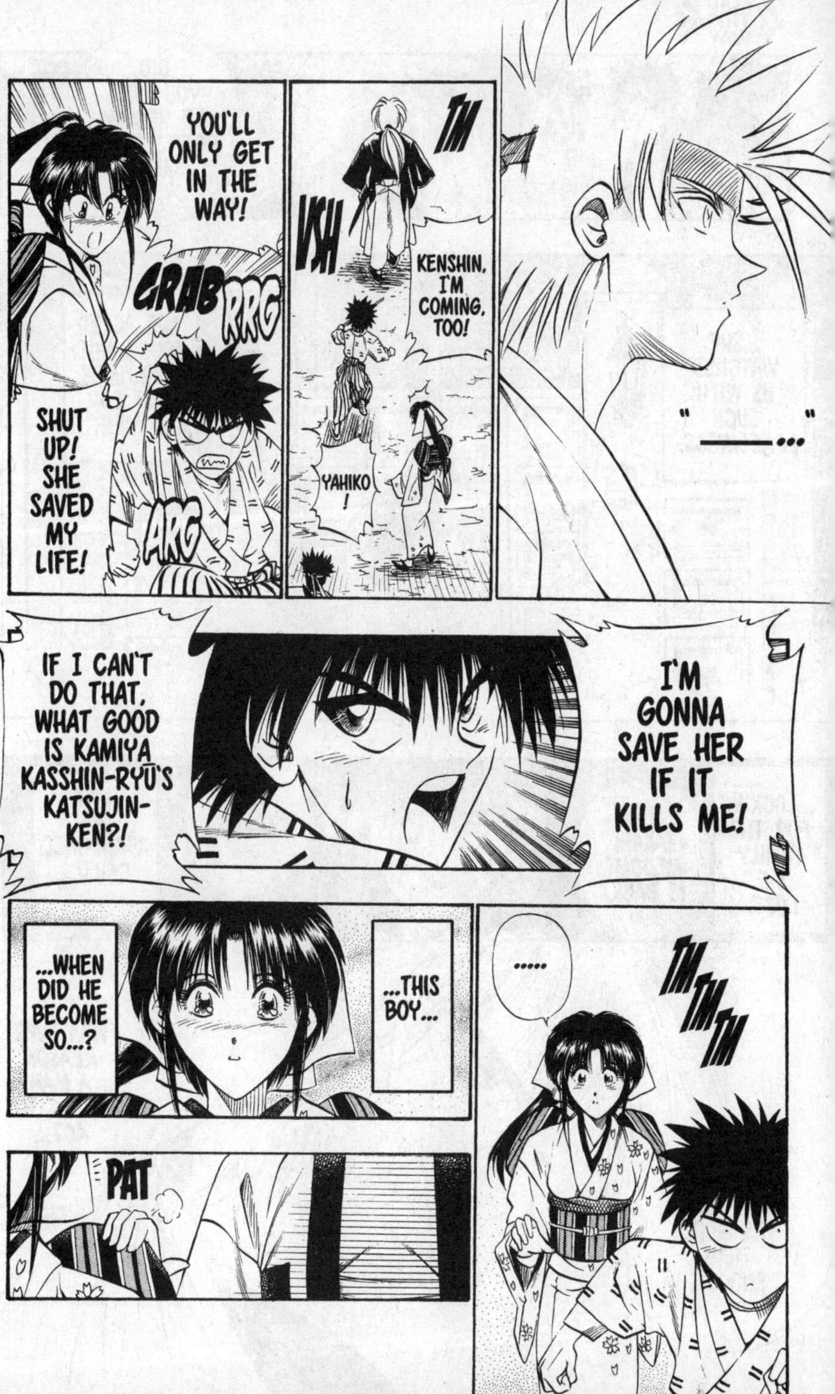

"——..."
TH
KENSHIN, I'M COMING, TOO!
VSH
YAHIKO!
YOU'LL ONLY GET IN THE WAY!
GRAB
RRG
SHUT UP! SHE SAVED MY LIFE!
ARG
I'M GONNA SAVE HER IF IT KILLS ME!
IF I CAN'T DO THAT, WHAT GOOD IS KAMIYA KASSHIN-RYŪ'S KATSUJIN-KEN?!
.....
TH TH TH
...THIS BOY...
...WHEN DID HE BECOME SO...?
PAT

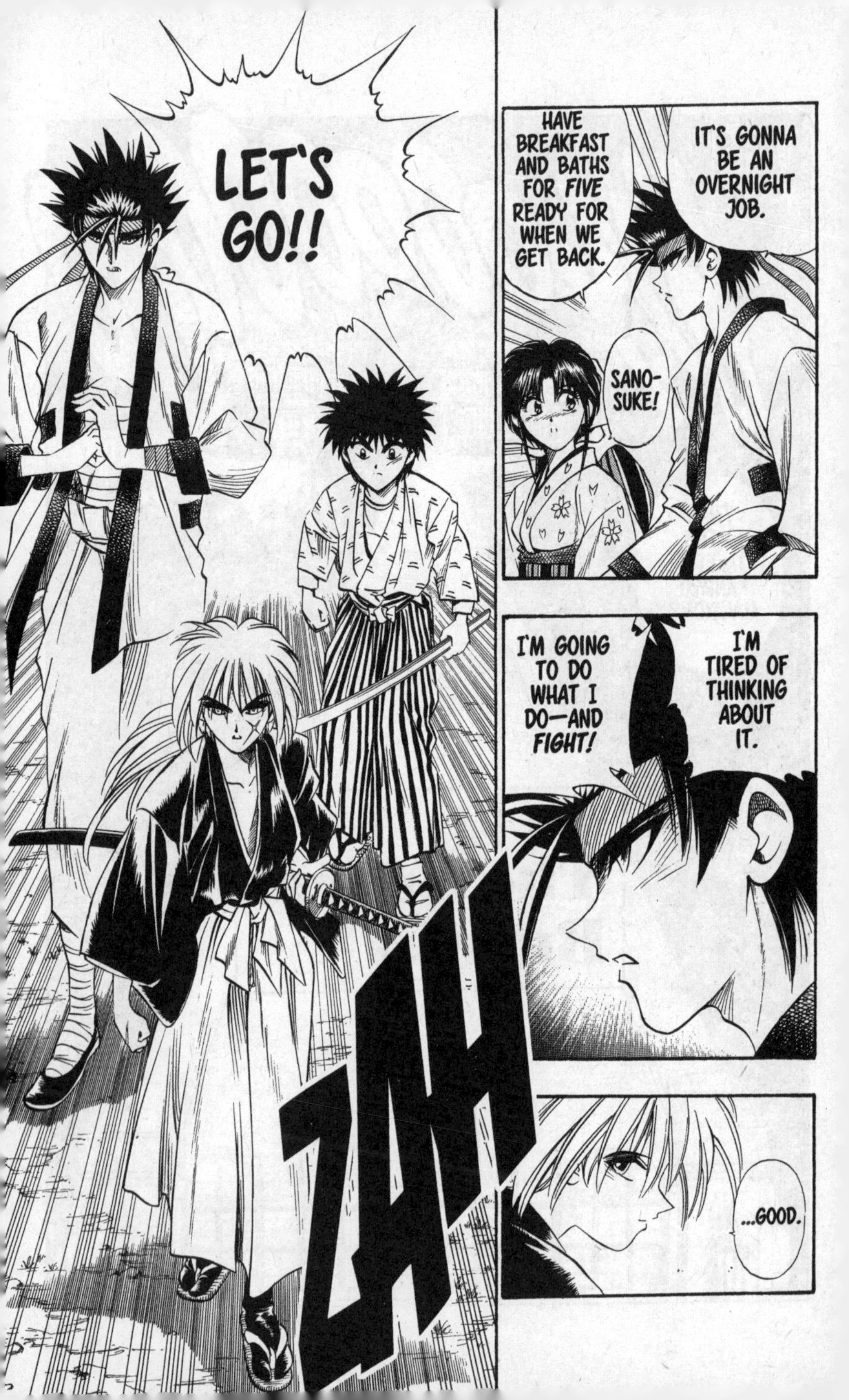
IT'S GONNA BE AN OVERNIGHT JOB.
HAVE BREAKFAST AND BATHS FOR *FIVE* READY FOR WHEN WE GET BACK.
SANO-SUKE!
I'M TIRED OF THINKING ABOUT IT.
I'M GOING TO DO WHAT I DO—AND FIGHT!
...GOOD.
LET'S GO!!
ZAH

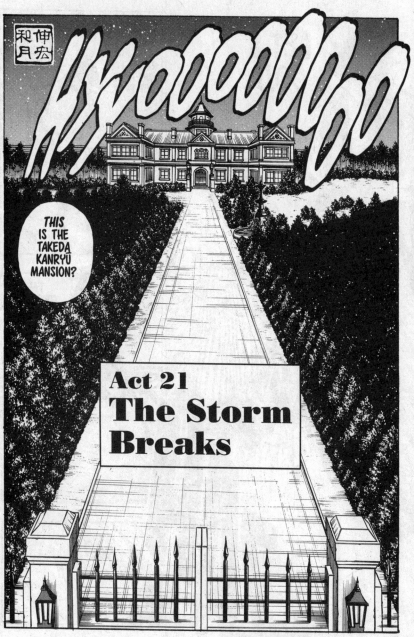

HYOOOOOOOO

THIS IS THE TAKEDA KANRYŪ MANSION?

Act 21
The Storm Breaks

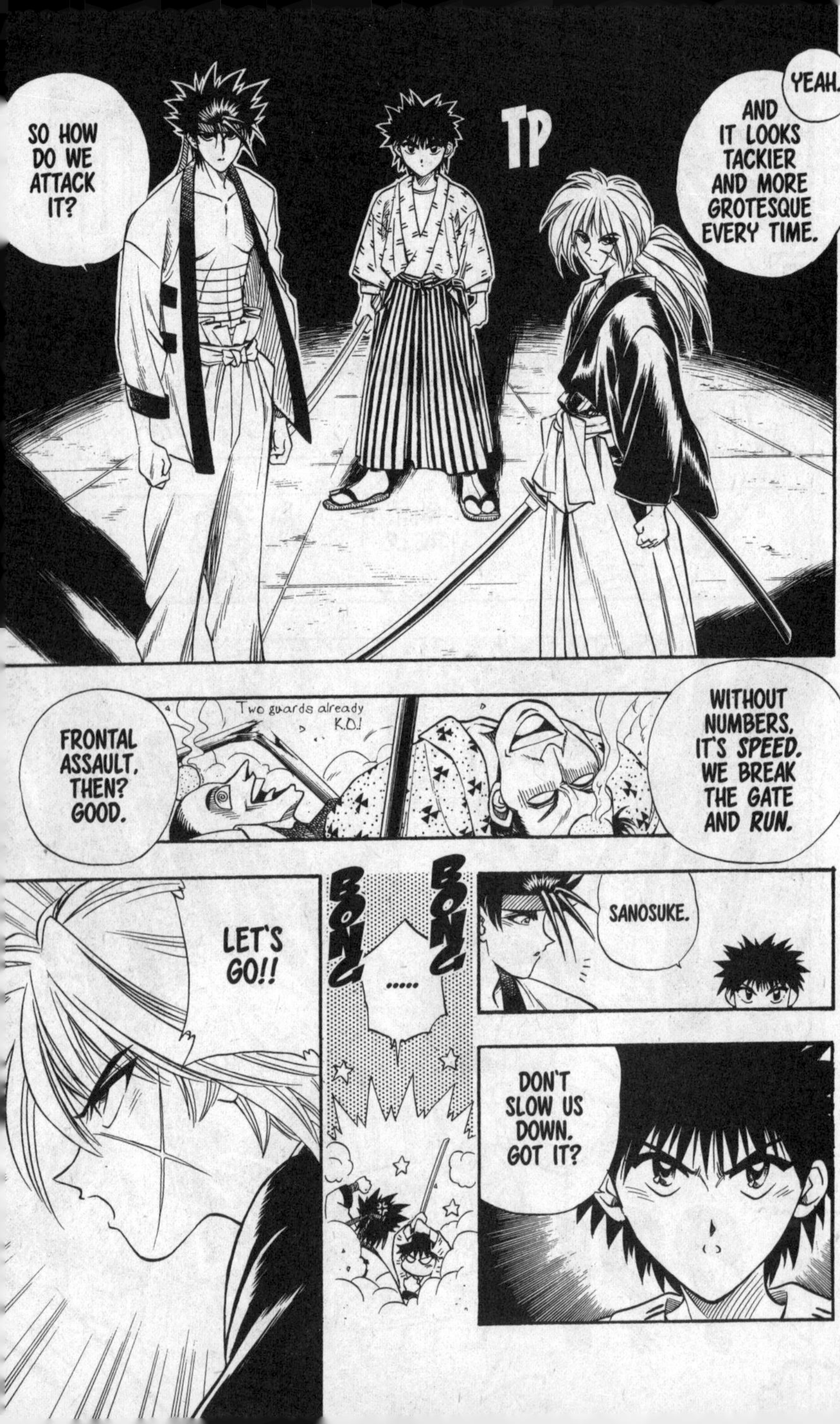
YEAH.
AND IT LOOKS TACKIER AND MORE GROTESQUE EVERY TIME.
TP
SO HOW DO WE ATTACK IT?
WITHOUT NUMBERS, IT'S *SPEED*. WE BREAK THE GATE AND *RUN*.
Two guards already K.O.!
FRONTAL ASSAULT, THEN? GOOD.
SANOSUKE.
DON'T SLOW US DOWN. GOT IT?
BONG
BONG
......
LET'S GO!!

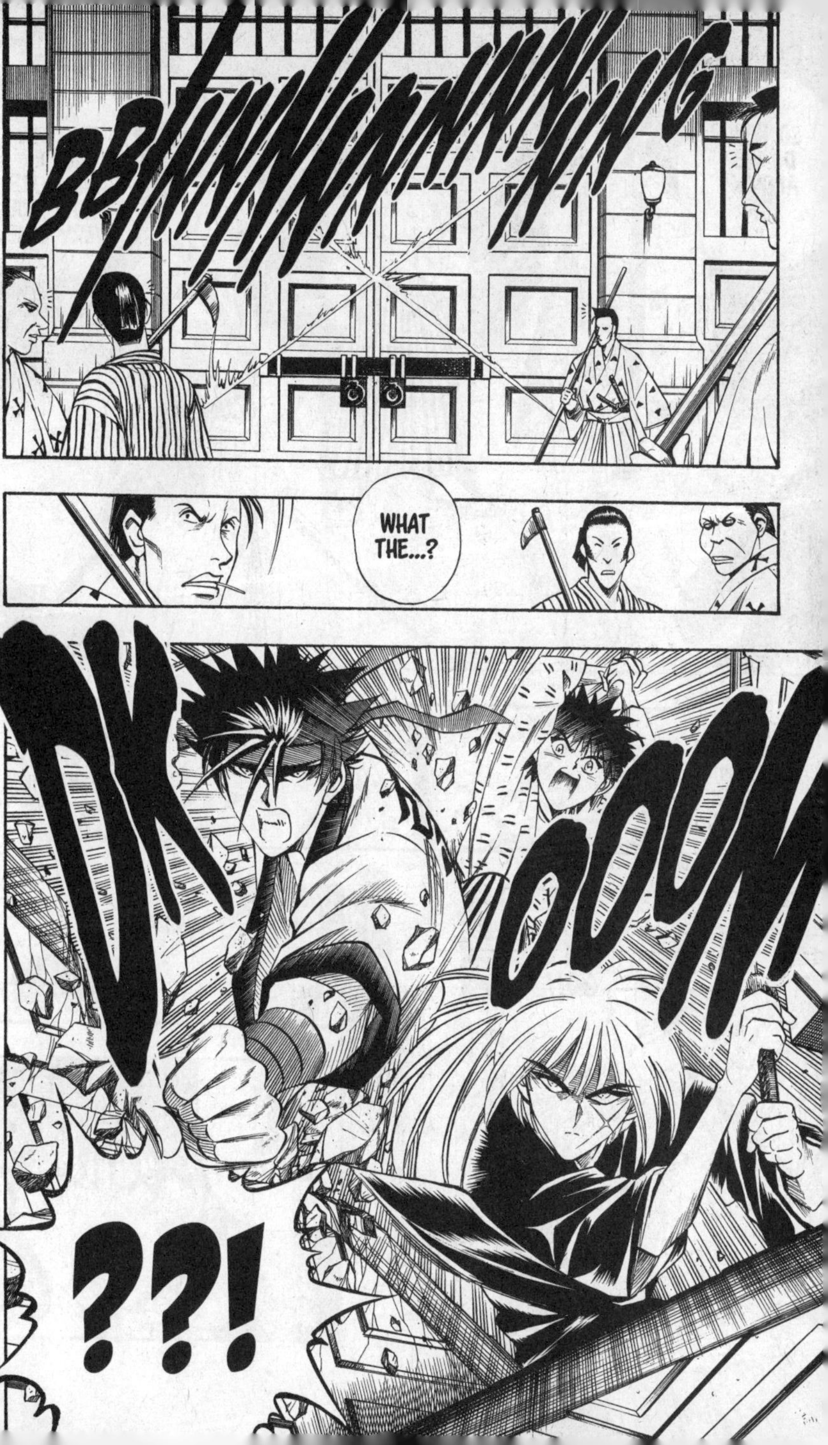
BBTWWANNNNNNNNNG
WHAT THE...?
DKOOOOM
??!

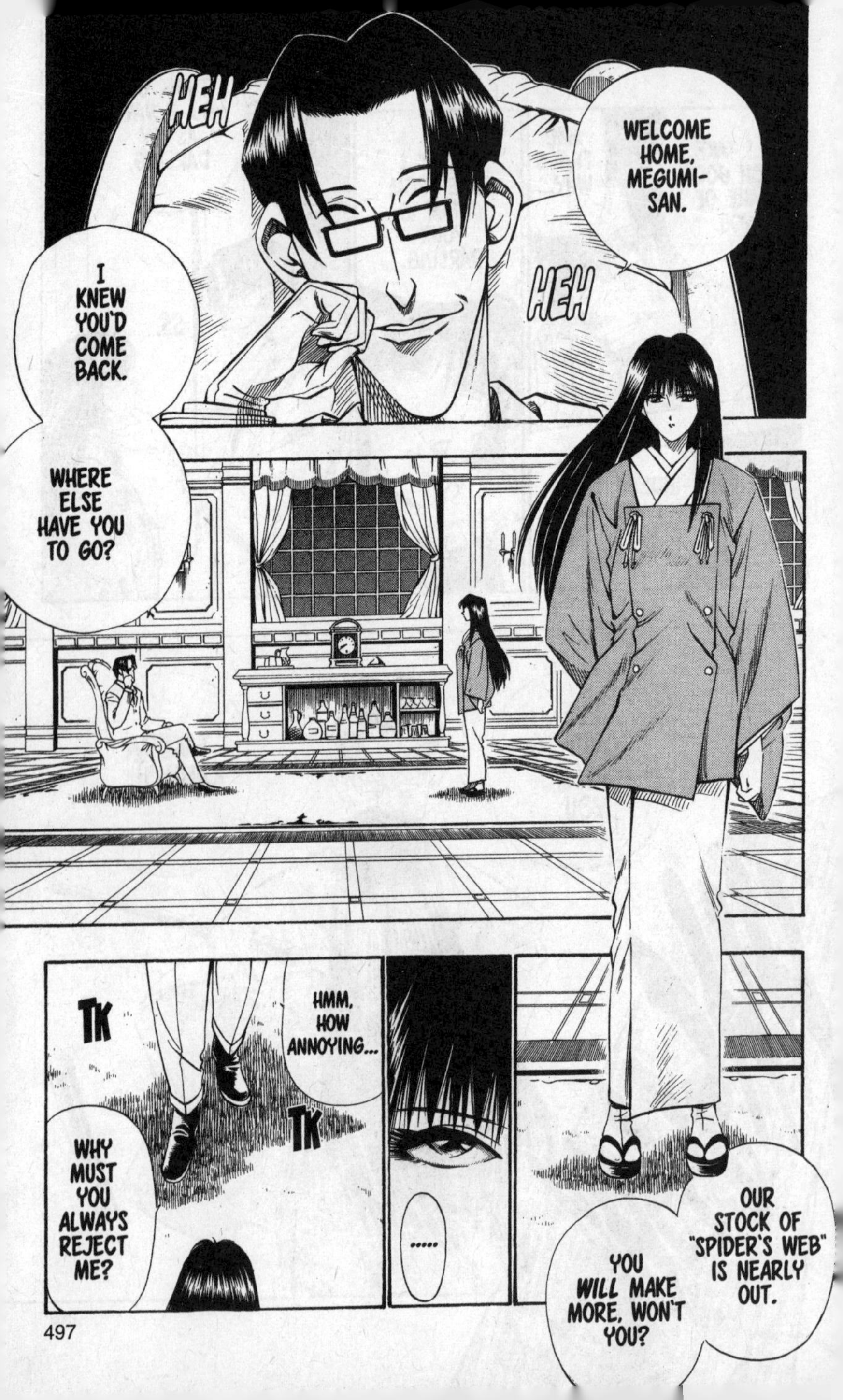
WELCOME HOME, MEGUMI-SAN.
HEH
HEH
I KNEW YOU'D COME BACK.
WHERE ELSE HAVE YOU TO GO?
OUR STOCK OF "SPIDER'S WEB" IS NEARLY OUT.
YOU *WILL* MAKE MORE, WON'T YOU?
......
TK
HMM, HOW ANNOYING...
TK
WHY MUST YOU ALWAYS REJECT ME?

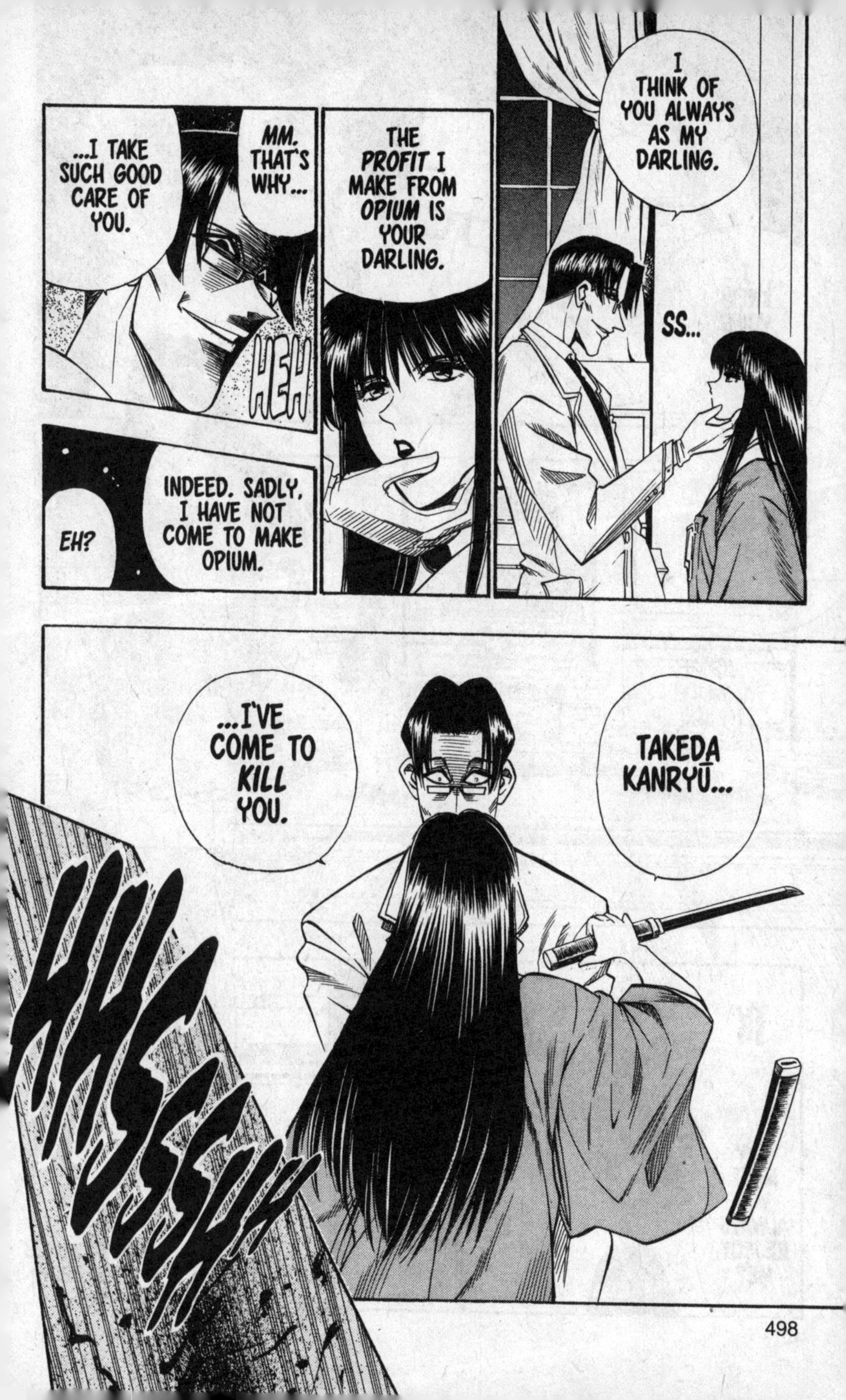
I THINK OF YOU ALWAYS AS MY DARLING.
SS...
THE PROFIT I MAKE FROM OPIUM IS YOUR DARLING.
MM. THAT'S WHY...
...I TAKE SUCH GOOD CARE OF YOU.
HEH
INDEED. SADLY, I HAVE NOT COME TO MAKE OPIUM.
EH?
TAKEDA KANRYŪ...
...I'VE COME TO KILL YOU.

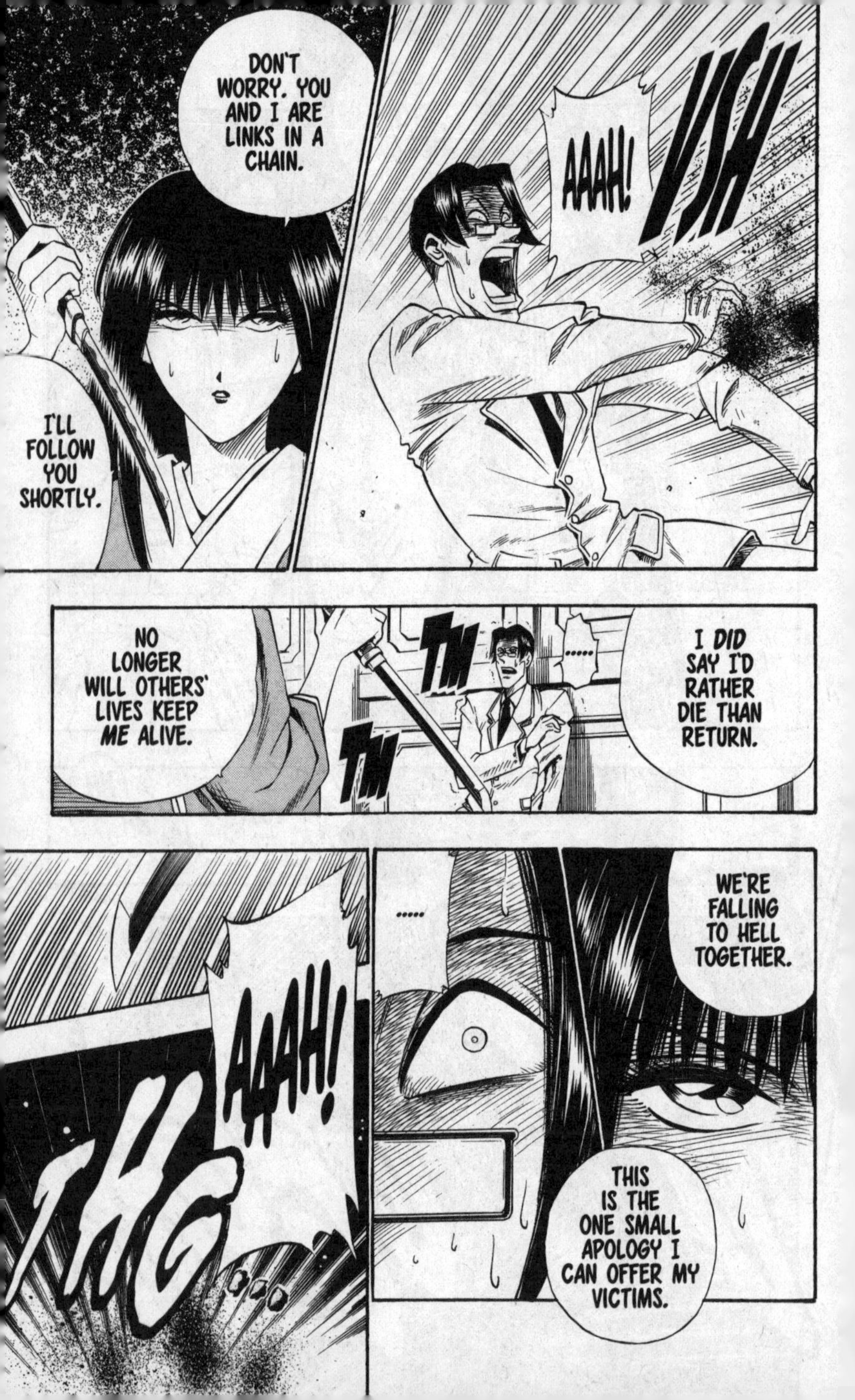

VISH
AAAH!
DON'T WORRY. YOU AND I ARE LINKS IN A CHAIN.
I'LL FOLLOW YOU SHORTLY.
I *DID* SAY I'D RATHER DIE THAN RETURN.
......
TM
TM
NO LONGER WILL OTHERS' LIVES KEEP *ME* ALIVE.
WE'RE FALLING TO HELL TOGETHER.
......
THIS IS THE ONE SMALL APOLOGY I CAN OFFER MY VICTIMS.
AAAH!
THG

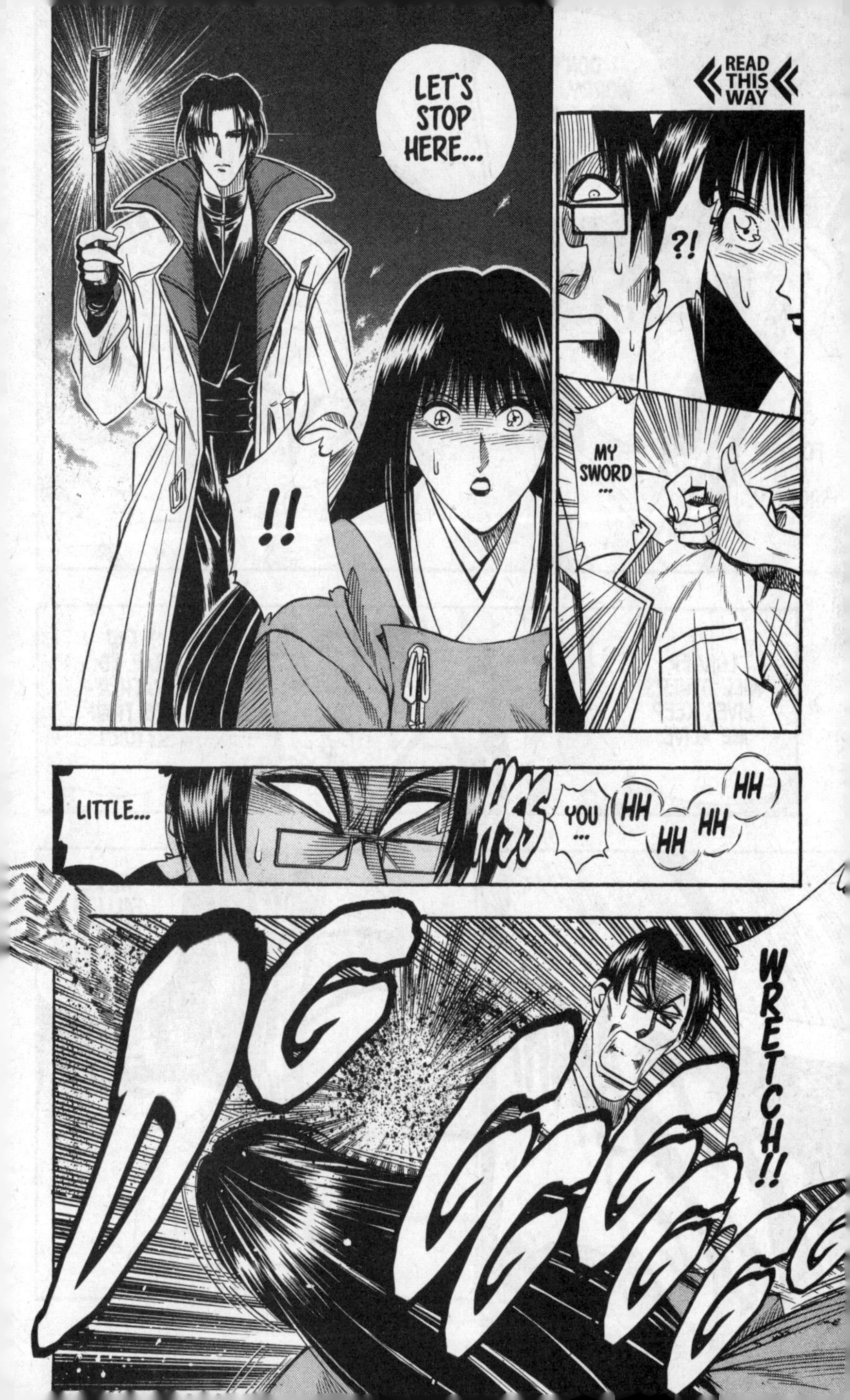
READ THIS WAY
?!
MY SWORD ...
LET'S STOP HERE...
!!
HH HH HH HH HH
YOU ...
HSS
LITTLE...
WRETCH!!

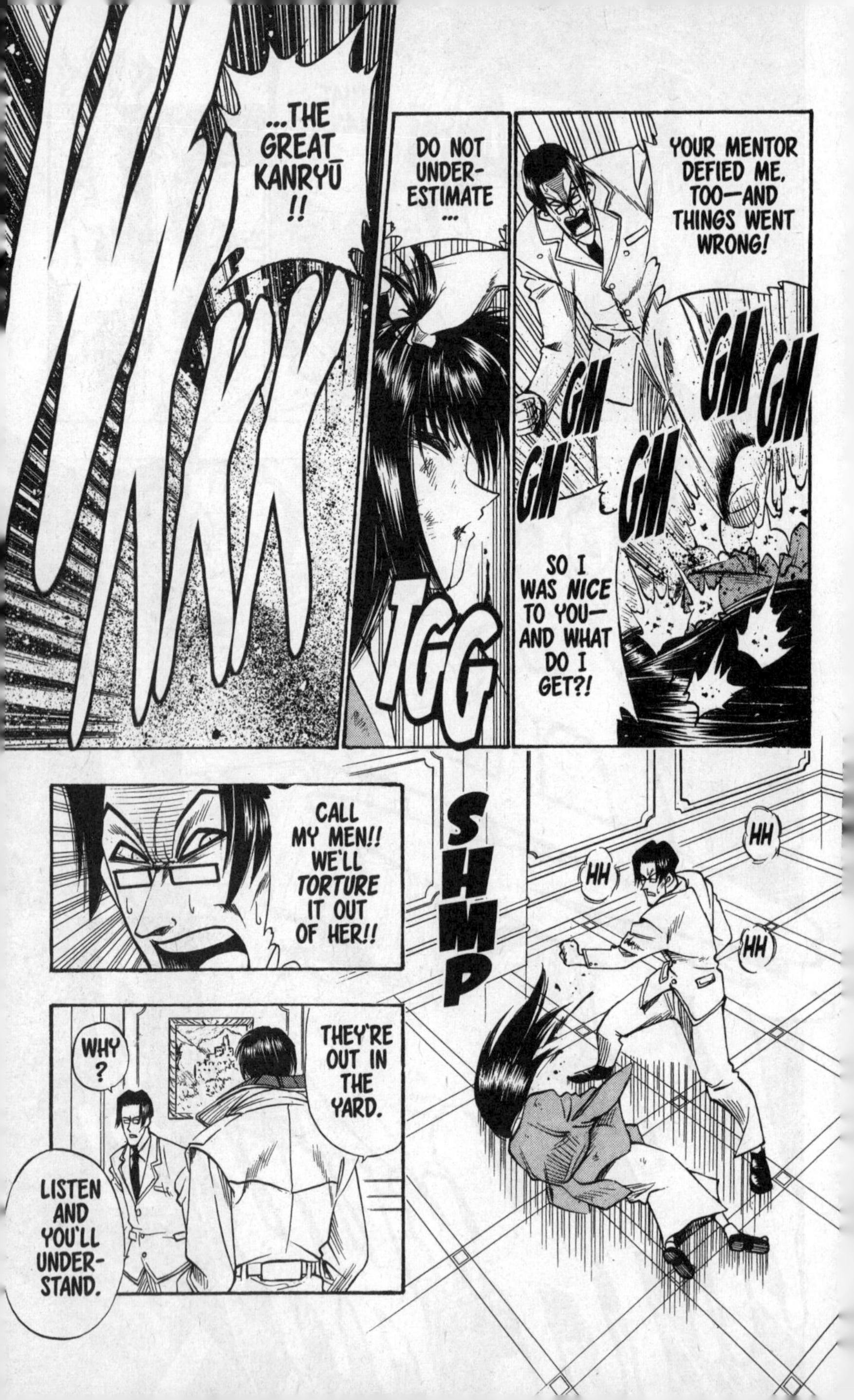
YOUR MENTOR DEFIED ME, TOO—AND THINGS WENT WRONG!
GM GM GM GM GM GM
SO I WAS *NICE* TO YOU—AND WHAT DO I GET?!
DO NOT UNDER-ESTIMATE...
TGG
...THE GREAT KANRYŪ!!
SHMP
HH
HH
HH
CALL MY MEN!! WE'LL *TORTURE* IT OUT OF HER!!
THEY'RE OUT IN THE YARD.
WHY?
LISTEN AND YOU'LL UNDER-STAND.

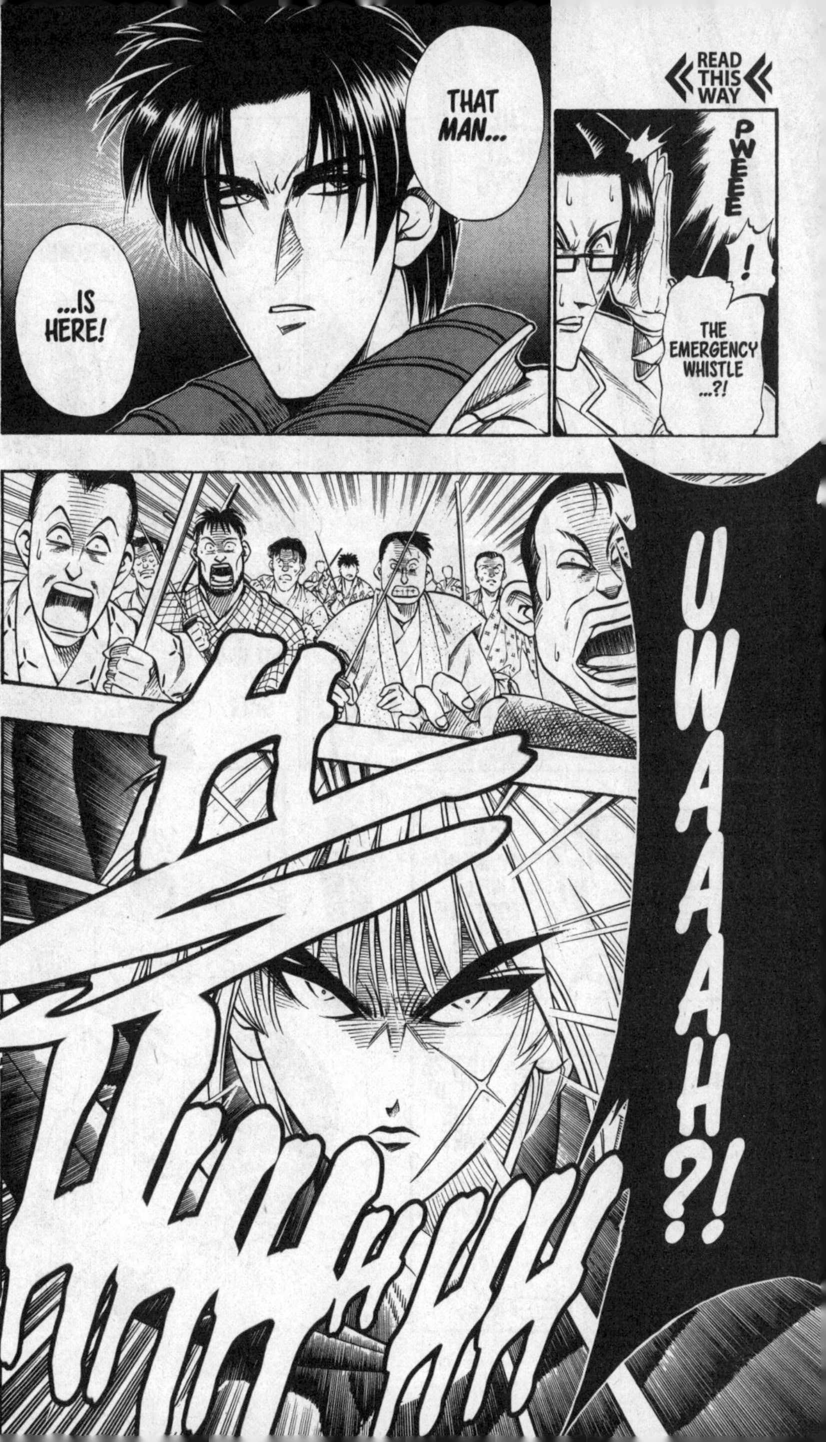
READ THIS WAY
PWEEE!
THE EMERGENCY WHISTLE ...?!
THAT MAN...
...IS HERE!
UWAAAH?!

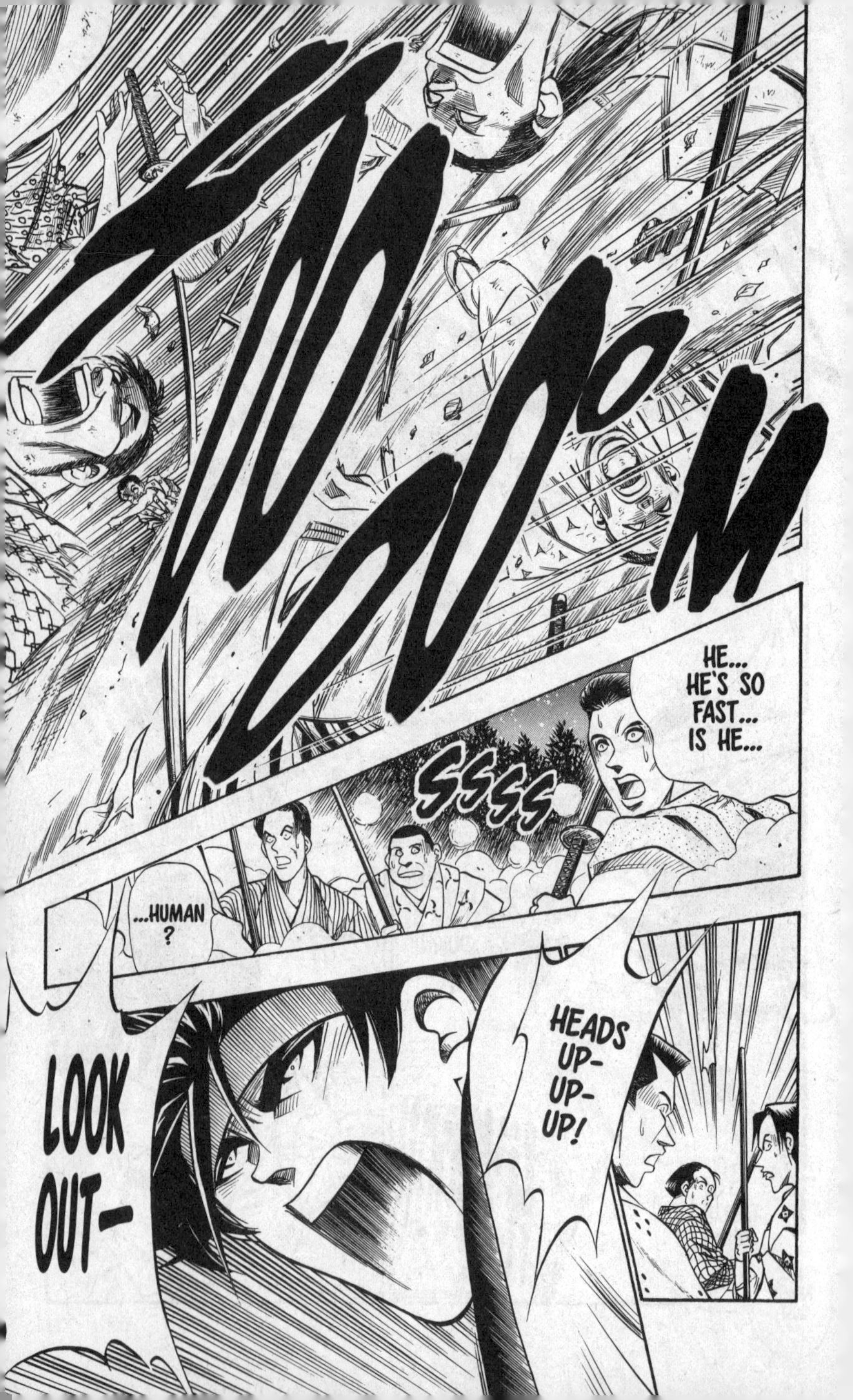

HE... HE'S SO FAST... IS HE...
SSSS
...HUMAN ?
HEADS UP-UP-UP!
LOOK OUT-

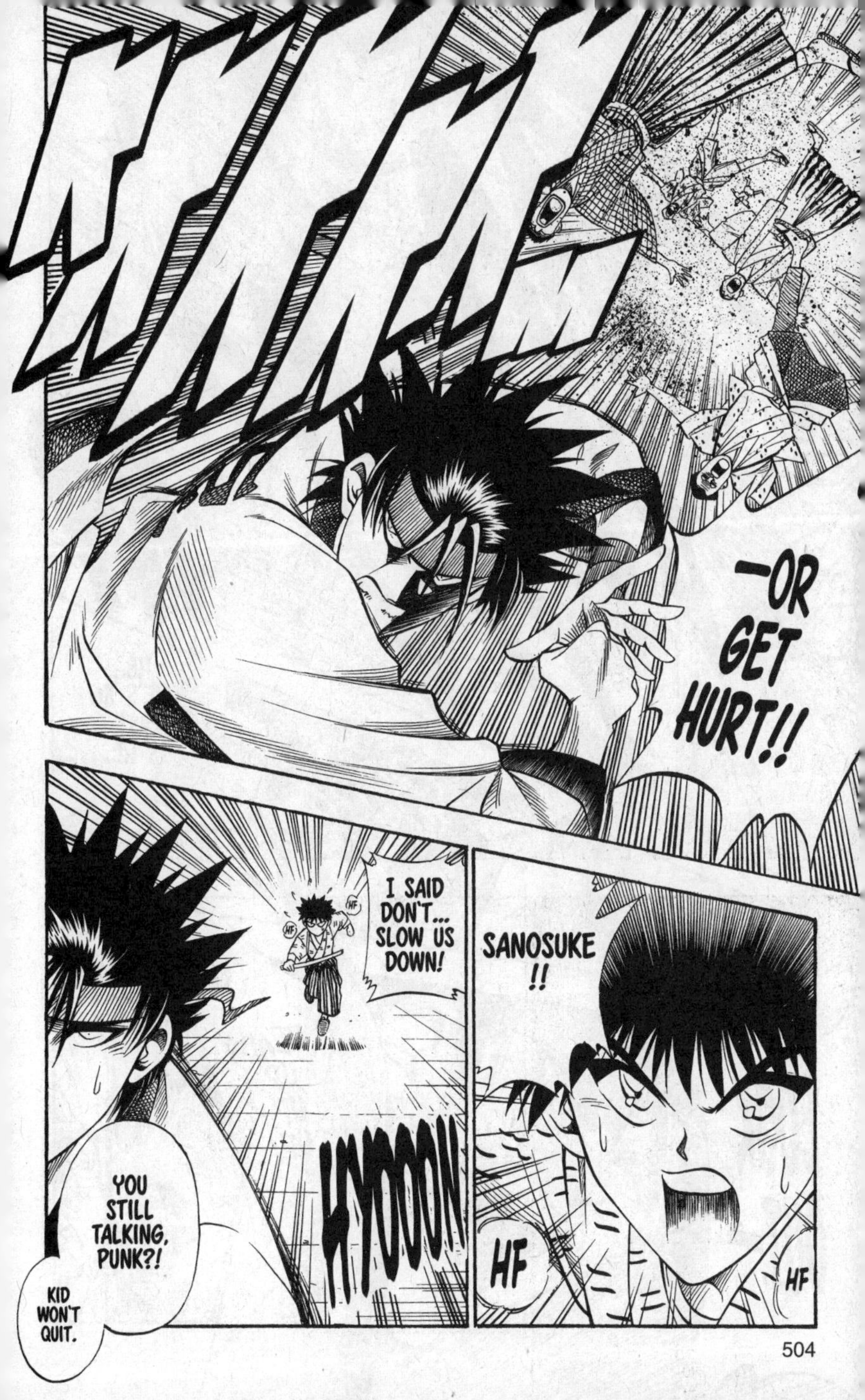

—OR GET HURT!!
SANOSUKE !!
HF
HF
I SAID DON'T... SLOW US DOWN!
HF
HF
HYOOON
YOU STILL TALKING, PUNK?!
KID WON'T QUIT.

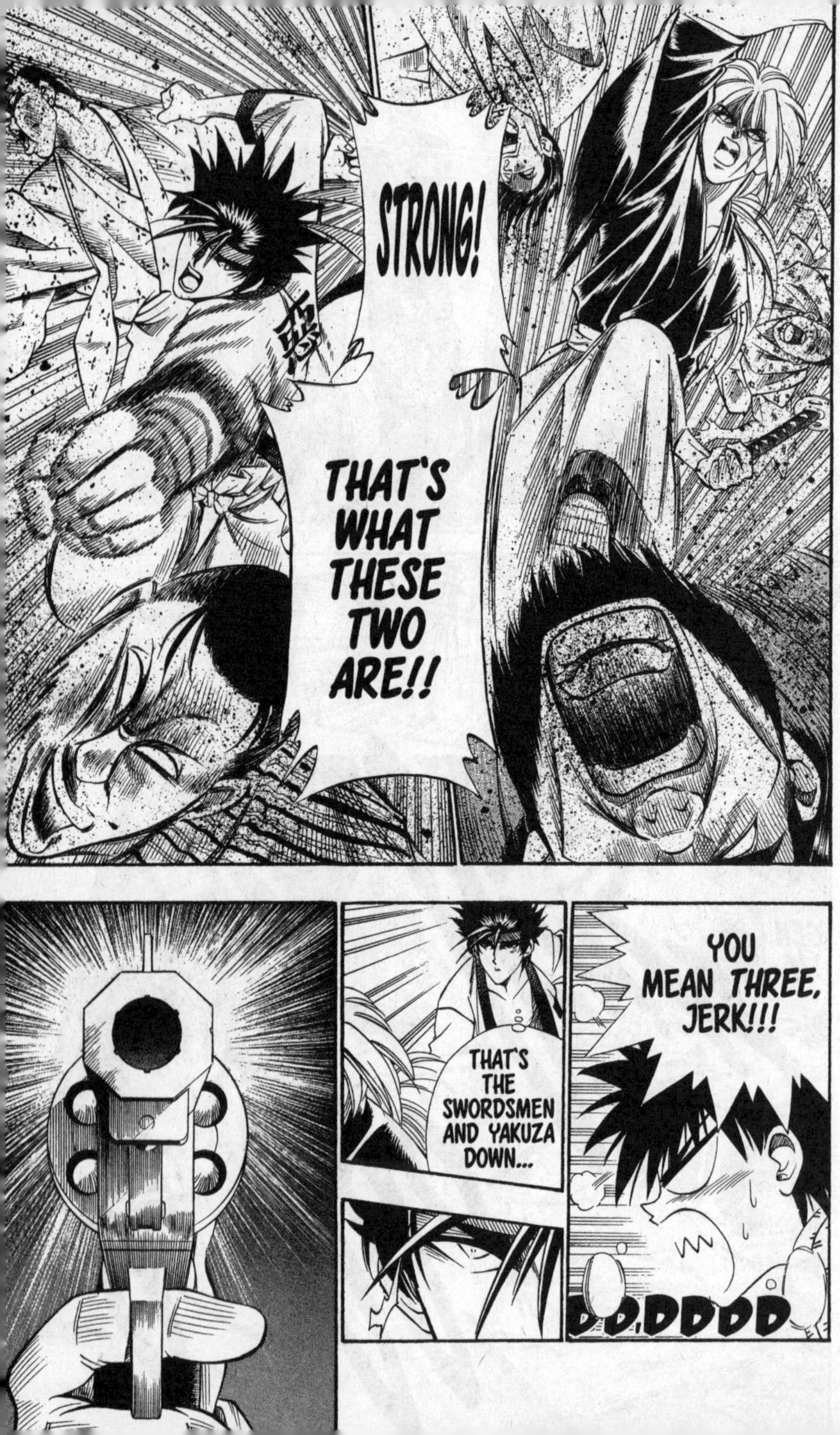
STRONG!
THAT'S WHAT THESE TWO ARE!!
YOU MEAN THREE, JERK!!!
DDDDDD
THAT'S THE SWORDSMEN AND YAKUZA DOWN...

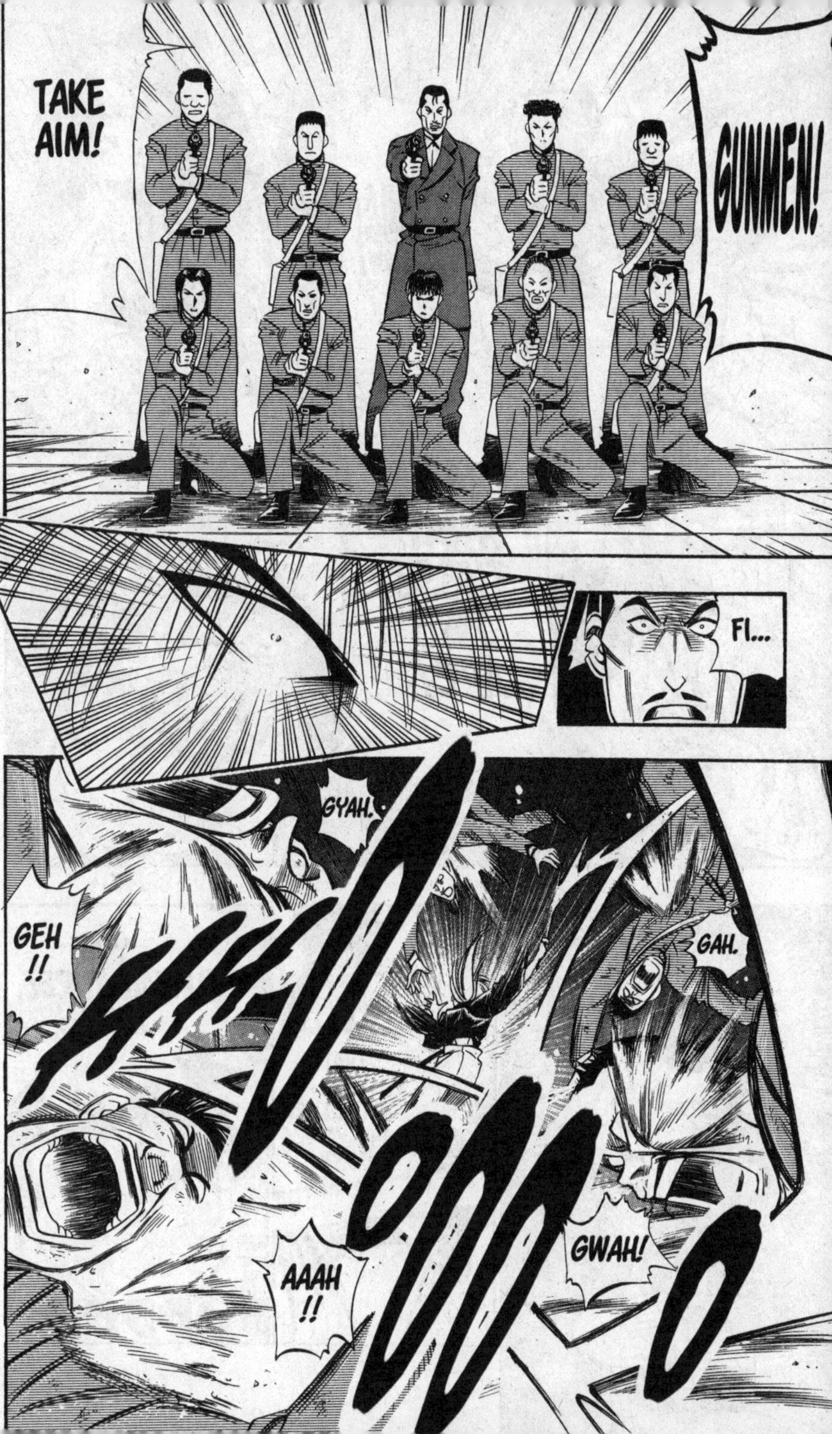
GUNMEN!
TAKE AIM!
FI...
GYAH.
GAH.
GEH !!
GWAH!
AAAH !!

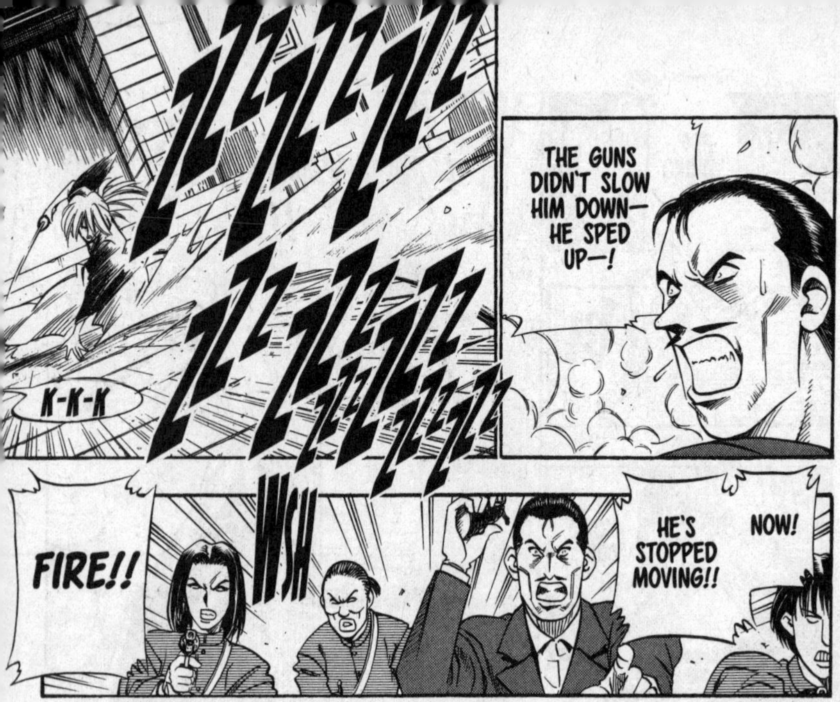
THE GUNS DIDN'T SLOW HIM DOWN— HE SPED UP—!
K-K-K
HE'S STOPPED MOVING!! NOW!
WSH
FIRE!!

Sure, you may THINK I'm behind the times, but lately I'm hooked on *Samurai Damashi'i* (*Samurai Spirits*, also known in the U.S. as *Samurai Shodown*). I even bought a NEO*GEO CD to play it!

So now you're thinking I'm a gamer, maybe, but that wouldn't be true. Watsuki has been to an arcade, like, five times in his life, and THAT's only because of his assistants, so I seriously suck. Even on "Easy Mode," I lose all the time, and Haohmaru is always dying. Worse, because I can play no more than one or two hours a week, I never get any better at it.

As I write this, I have yet to get my hands on *Shin (New) Samurai Damashi'i* (*Samurai Shodown II*), but as you read this, most likely Kibagami Genjuro has already begun dying his endless deaths by my hand. (Apologies to those of you who have no interest in video games, and have no idea what this is all about.)

和月伸宏

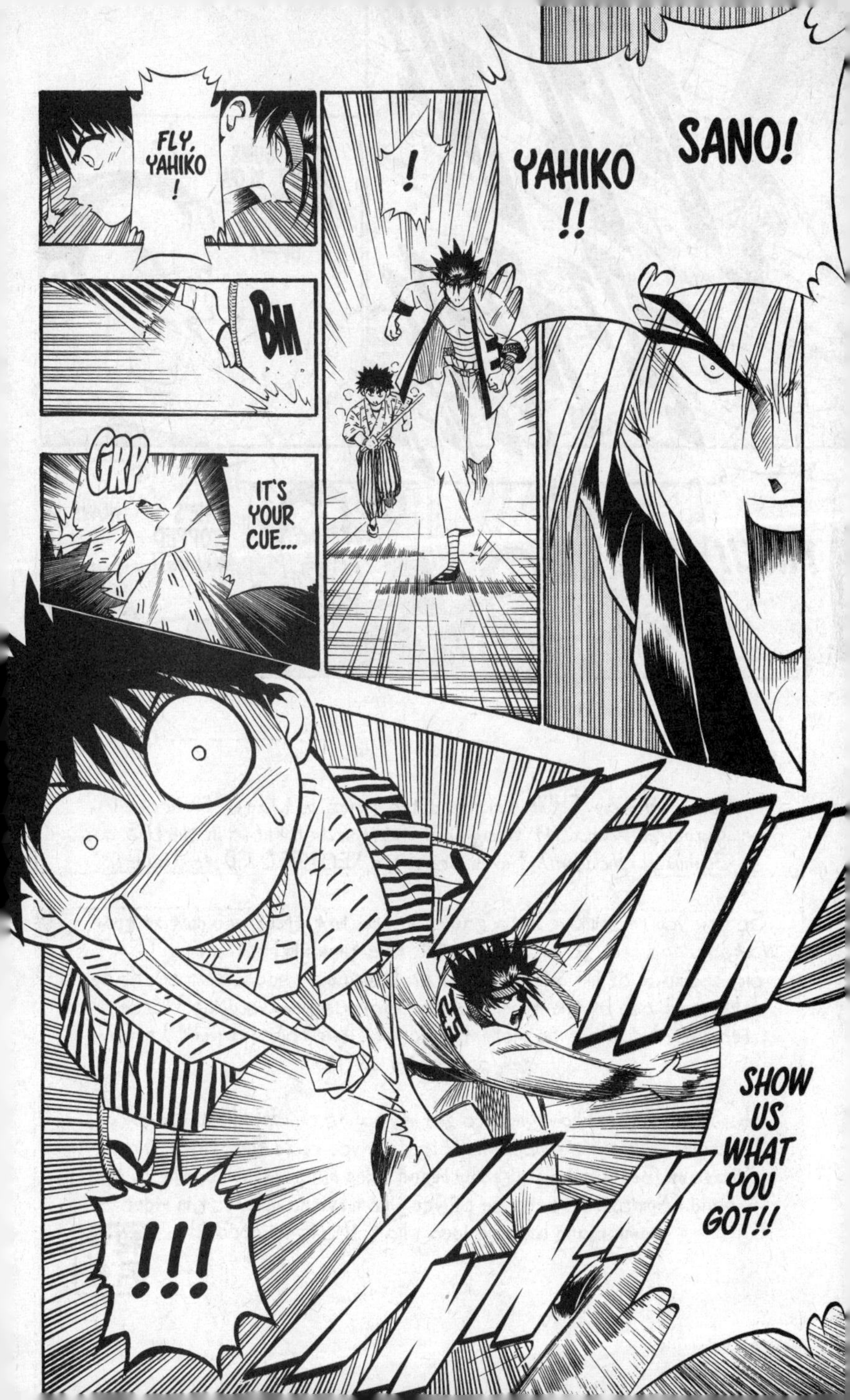
SANO!
YAHIKO !!
!
FLY, YAHIKO !
BM
GRP
IT'S YOUR CUE...
SHOW US WHAT YOU GOT!!
!!!

READ THIS WAY

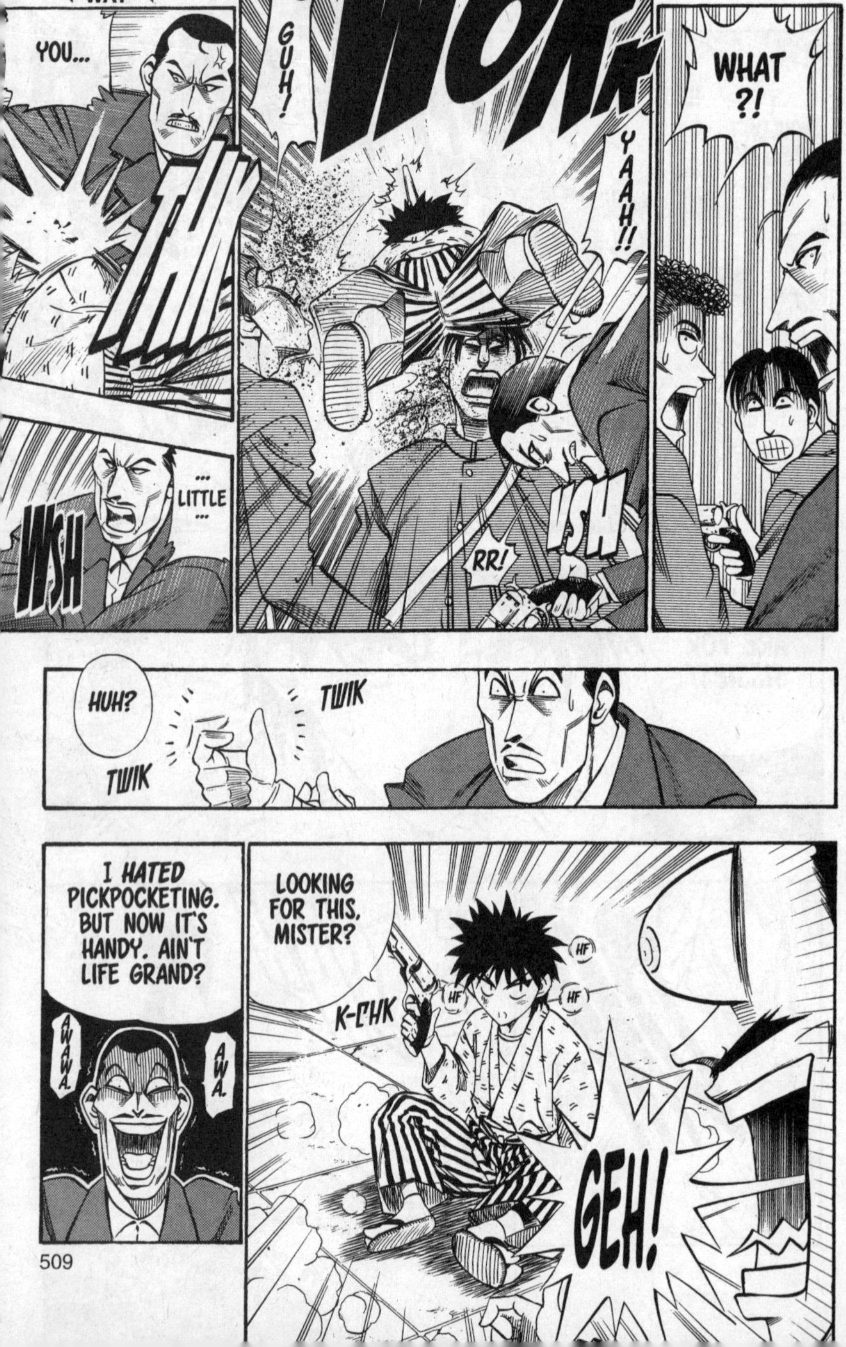

WHAT ?!
WOK!
GUH!
YAAAH!!
RR!
VSH
YOU...
THK
... LITTLE ...
VSH
HUH?
TWIK
TWIK
LOOKING FOR THIS, MISTER?
HF
HF
HF
K-CHK
GEH!
I HATED PICKPOCKETING. BUT NOW IT'S HANDY. AIN'T LIFE GRAND?
AWA.
AWAWA.

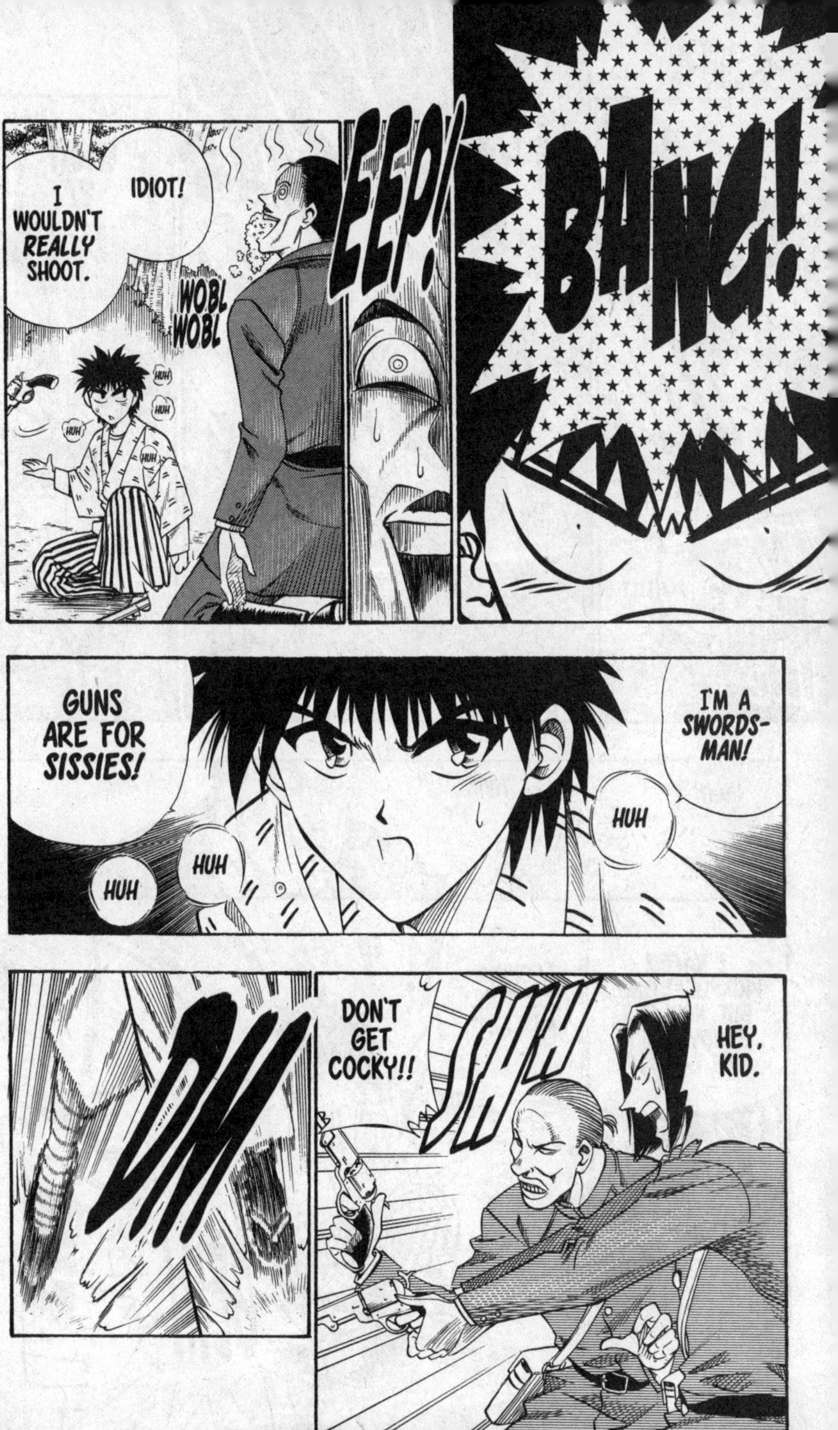
BANG!
EEP!
IDIOT!
I WOULDN'T REALLY SHOOT.
WOBL WOBL
HUH
HUH
HUH
HUH
I'M A SWORDS-MAN!
HUH
GUNS ARE FOR SISSIES!
HUH
HUH
HEY, KID.
SCHH
DON'T GET COCKY!!

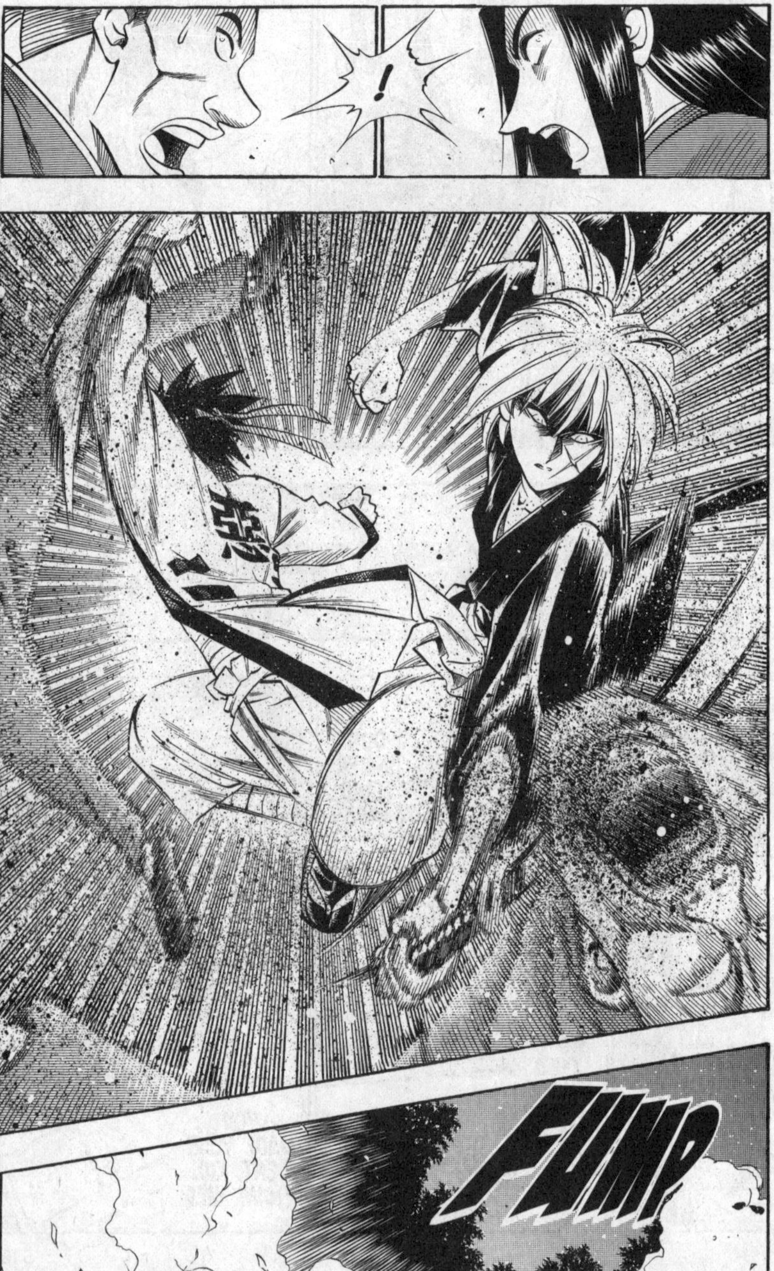
!
悪
FUMP

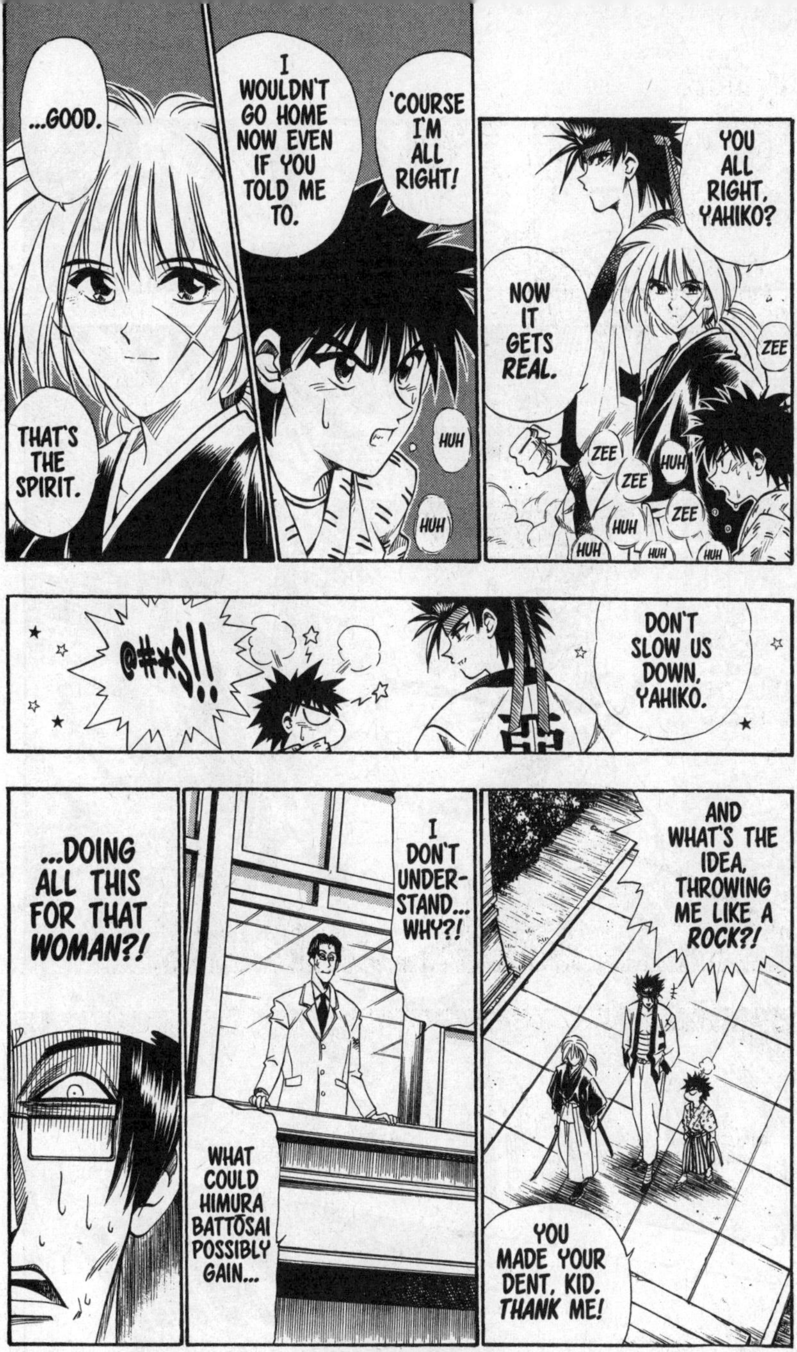
YOU ALL RIGHT, YAHIKO?
NOW IT GETS REAL.
ZEE
ZEE
HUH
ZEE
ZEE
HUH
HUH
HUH
HUH
'COURSE I'M ALL RIGHT!
I WOULDN'T GO HOME NOW EVEN IF YOU TOLD ME TO.
HUH
HUH
...GOOD.
THAT'S THE SPIRIT.
DON'T SLOW US DOWN, YAHIKO.
@#*$!!
AND WHAT'S THE IDEA, THROWING ME LIKE A ROCK?!
YOU MADE YOUR DENT, KID. THANK ME!
I DON'T UNDER-STAND... WHY?!
WHAT COULD HIMURA BATTOSAI POSSIBLY GAIN...
...DOING ALL THIS FOR THAT WOMAN?!

READ THIS WAY

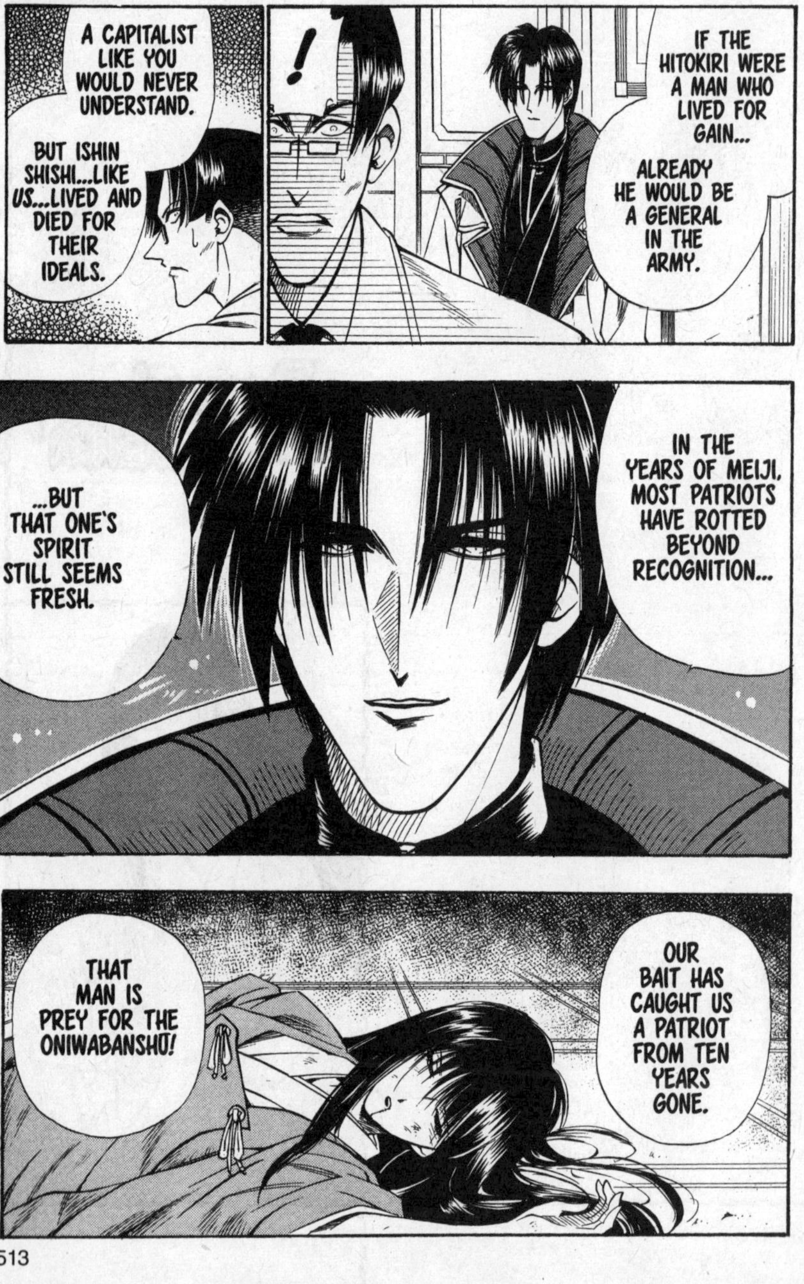

IF THE HITOKIRI WERE A MAN WHO LIVED FOR GAIN...
ALREADY HE WOULD BE A GENERAL IN THE ARMY.
!
A CAPITALIST LIKE YOU WOULD NEVER UNDERSTAND.
BUT ISHIN SHISHI...LIKE US...LIVED AND DIED FOR THEIR IDEALS.
IN THE YEARS OF MEIJI, MOST PATRIOTS HAVE ROTTED BEYOND RECOGNITION...
...BUT THAT ONE'S SPIRIT STILL SEEMS FRESH.
OUR BAIT HAS CAUGHT US A PATRIOT FROM TEN YEARS GONE.
THAT MAN IS PREY FOR THE ONIWABANSHŪ!

Rurouni Kenshin

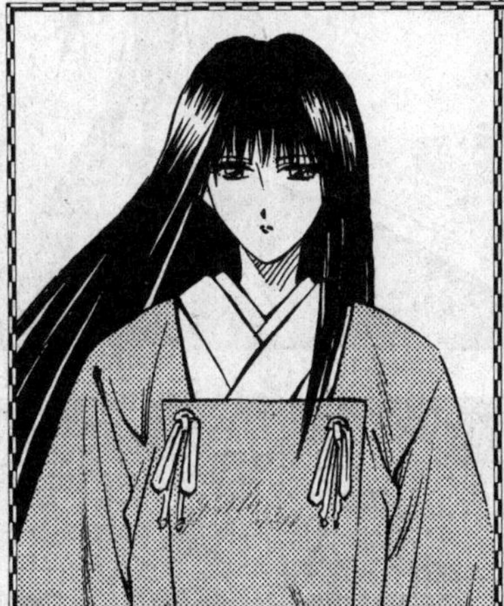

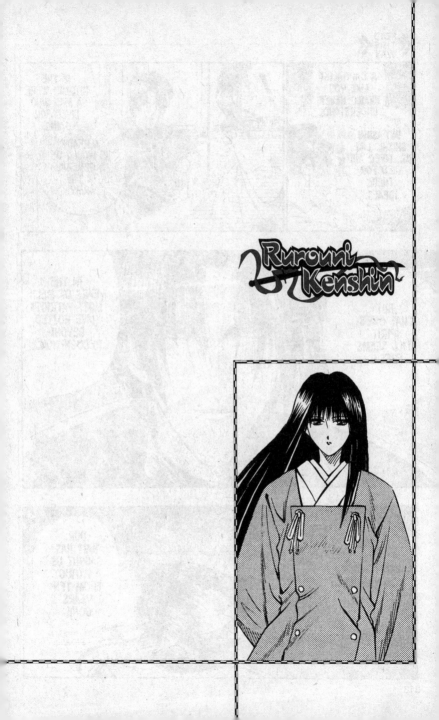

Act 22
Attack on Kanryū Mansion

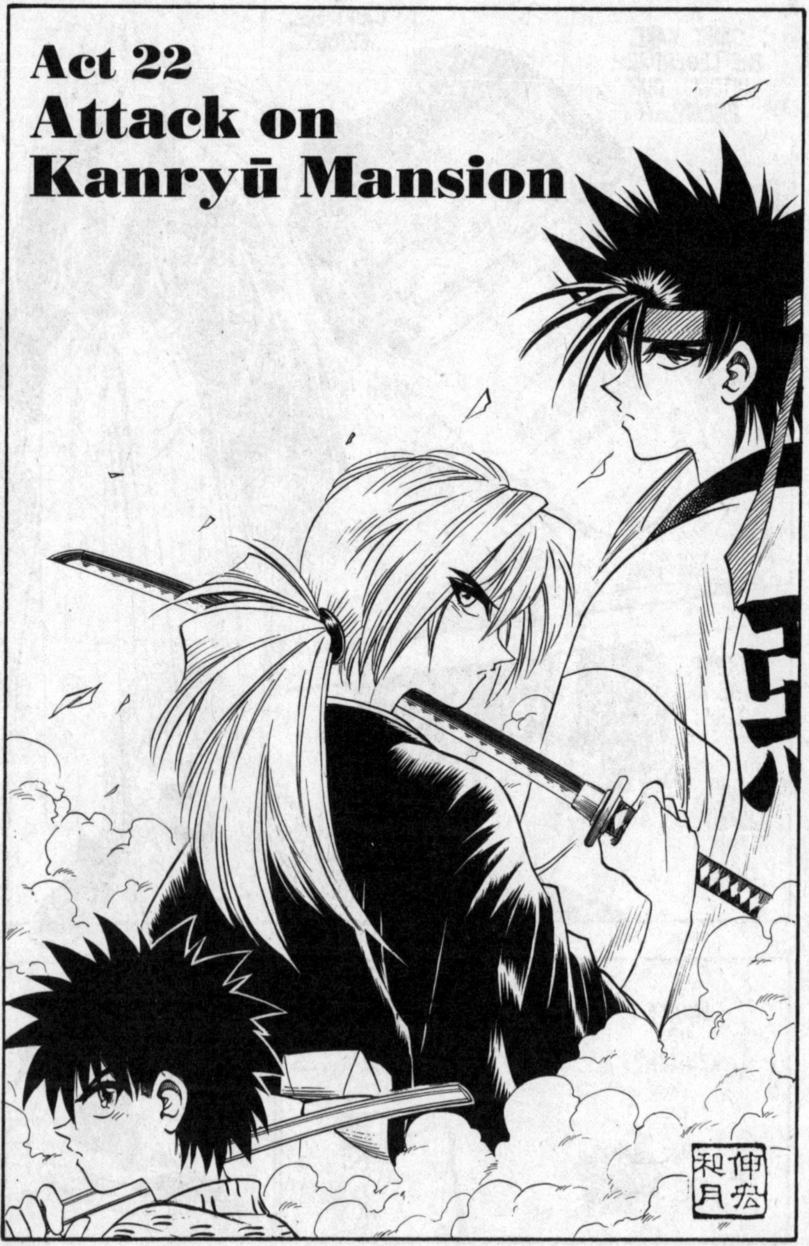
伸宏
和月

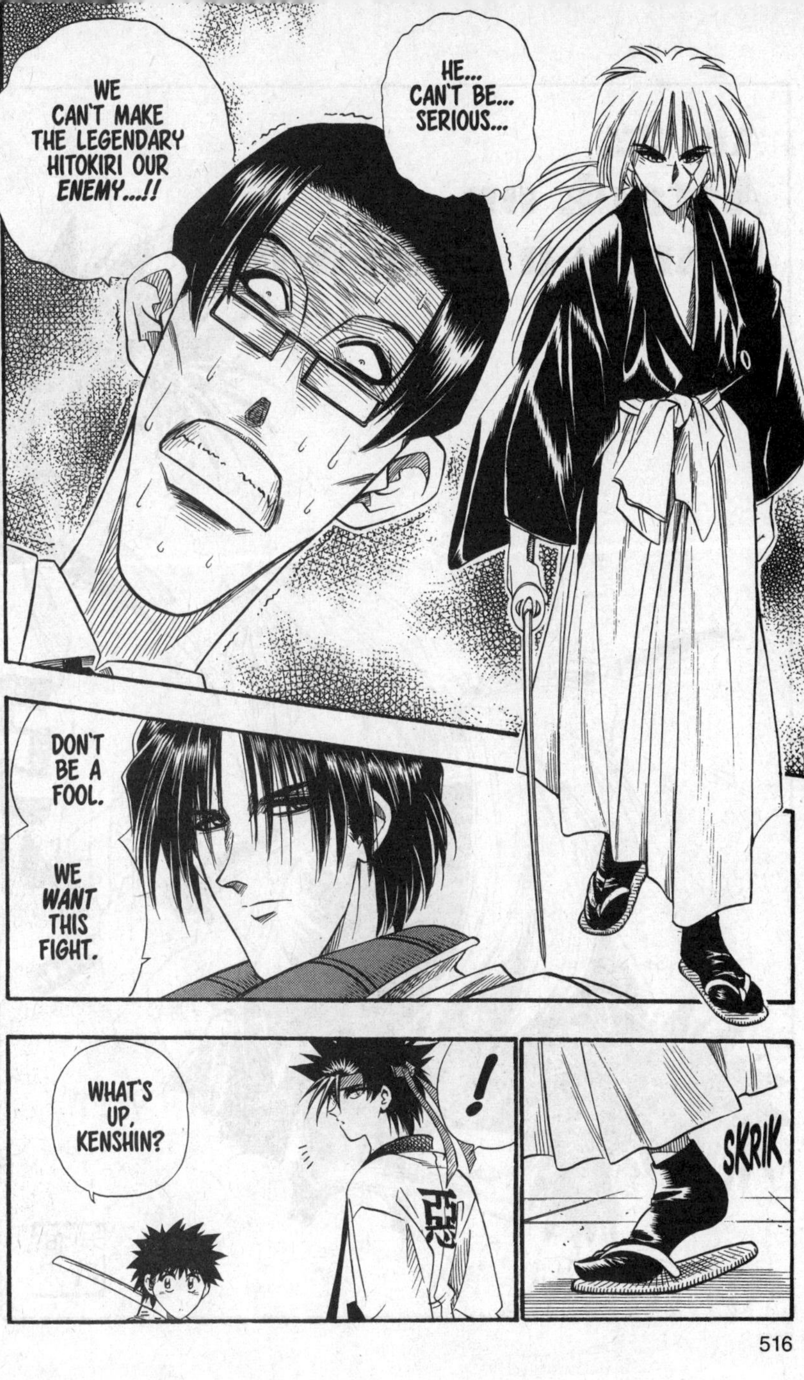
HE... CAN'T BE... SERIOUS...
WE CAN'T MAKE THE LEGENDARY HITOKIRI OUR *ENEMY*...!!
DON'T BE A FOOL.
WE *WANT* THIS FIGHT.
SKRIK
!
WHAT'S UP, KENSHIN?

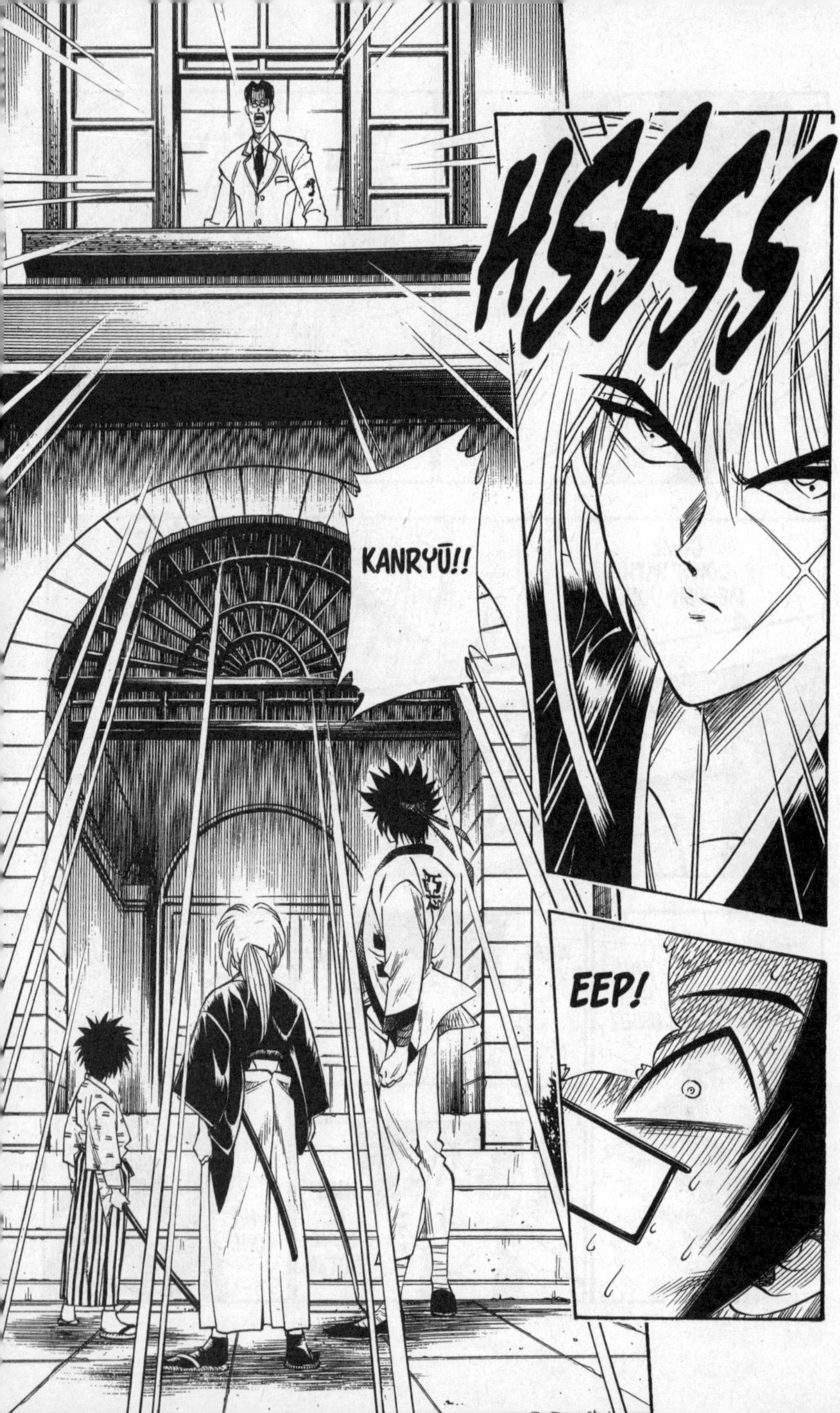
HSSSS
KANRYŪ!!
EEP!

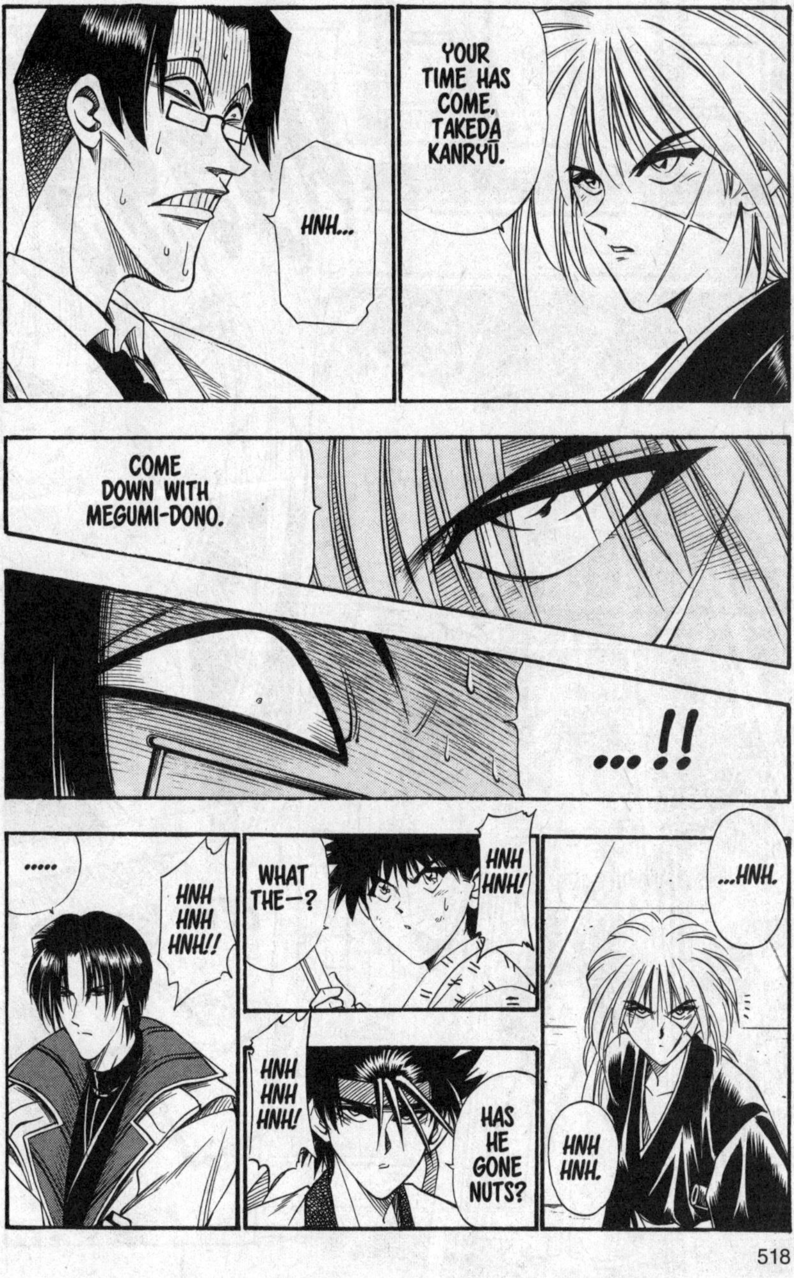
YOUR TIME HAS COME, TAKEDA KANRYŪ.
HNH...
COME DOWN WITH MEGUMI-DONO.
...!!
...HNH.
HNH HNH.
HNH HNH!
WHAT THE—?
HNH HNH HNH!
HAS HE GONE NUTS?
HNH HNH HNH!!
......

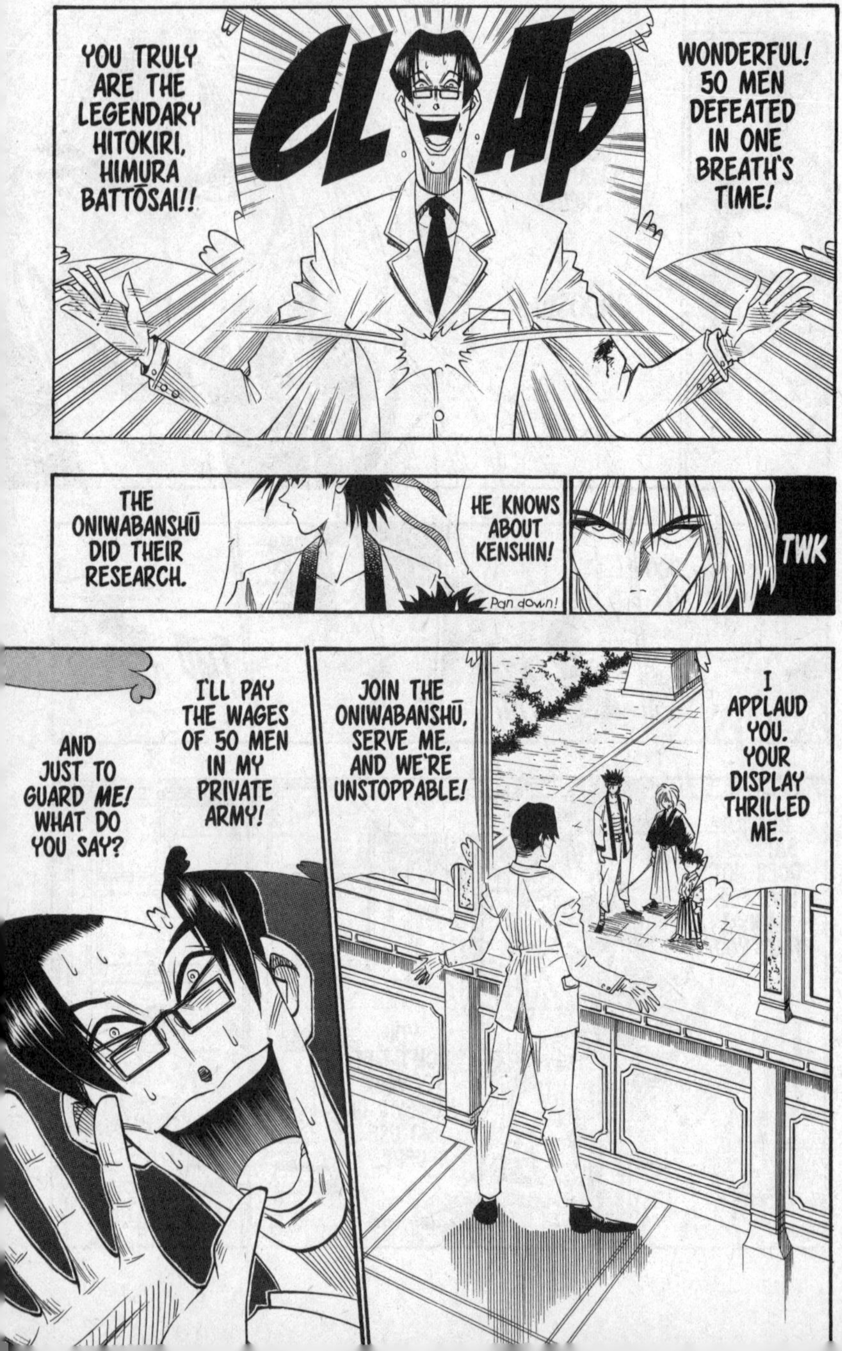
WONDERFUL! 50 MEN DEFEATED IN ONE BREATH'S TIME!
CLAP
YOU TRULY ARE THE LEGENDARY HITOKIRI, HIMURA BATTŌSAI!!
TWK
HE KNOWS ABOUT KENSHIN!
Pan down!
THE ONIWABANSHŪ DID THEIR RESEARCH.
I APPLAUD YOU. YOUR DISPLAY THRILLED ME.
JOIN THE ONIWABANSHŪ, SERVE ME, AND WE'RE UNSTOPPABLE!
I'LL PAY THE WAGES OF 50 MEN IN MY PRIVATE ARMY!
AND JUST TO GUARD *ME*! WHAT DO YOU SAY?

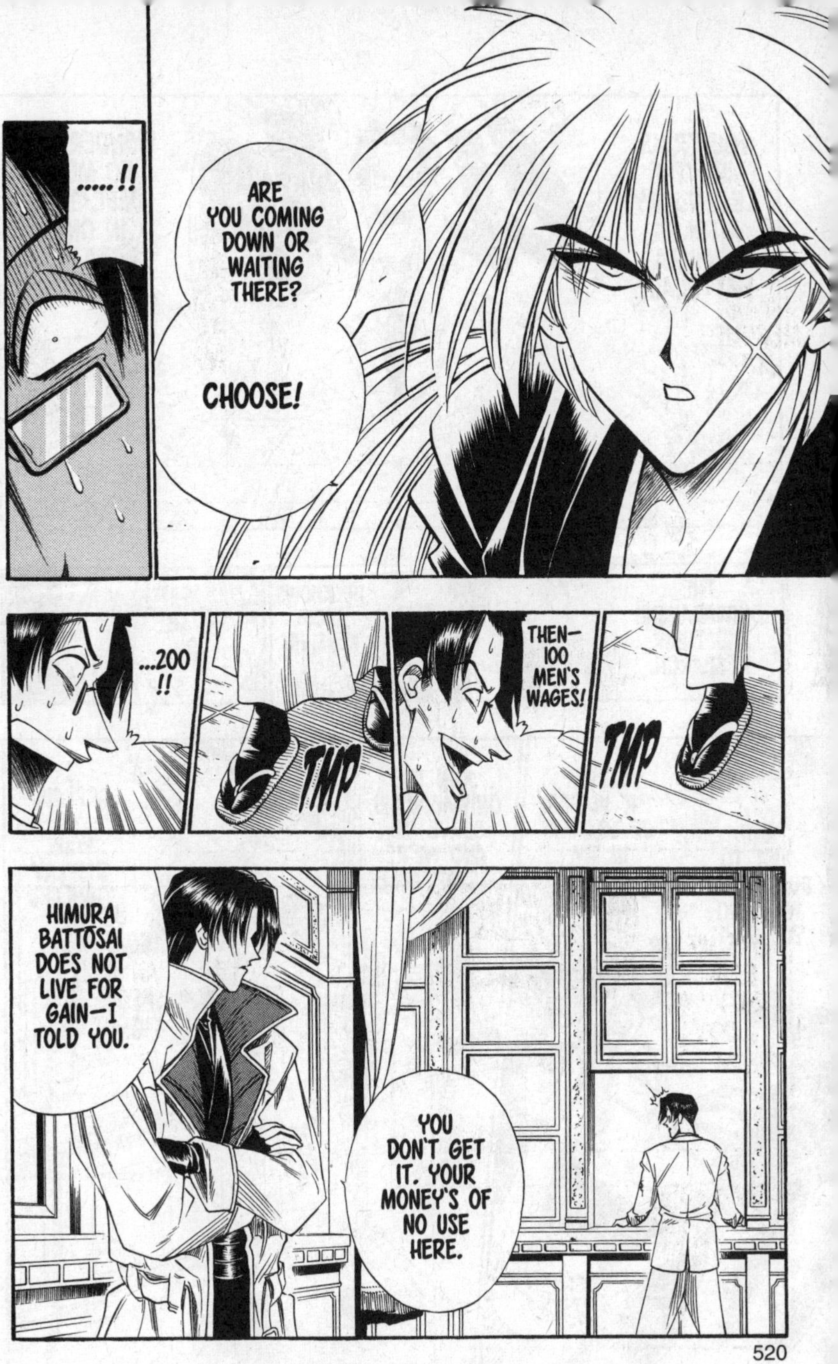
ARE YOU COMING DOWN OR WAITING THERE?
CHOOSE!
.....!!
TMP
THEN—100 MEN'S WAGES!
TMP
...200 !!
YOU DON'T GET IT. YOUR MONEY'S OF NO USE HERE.
HIMURA BATTŌSAI DOES NOT LIVE FOR GAIN—I TOLD YOU.

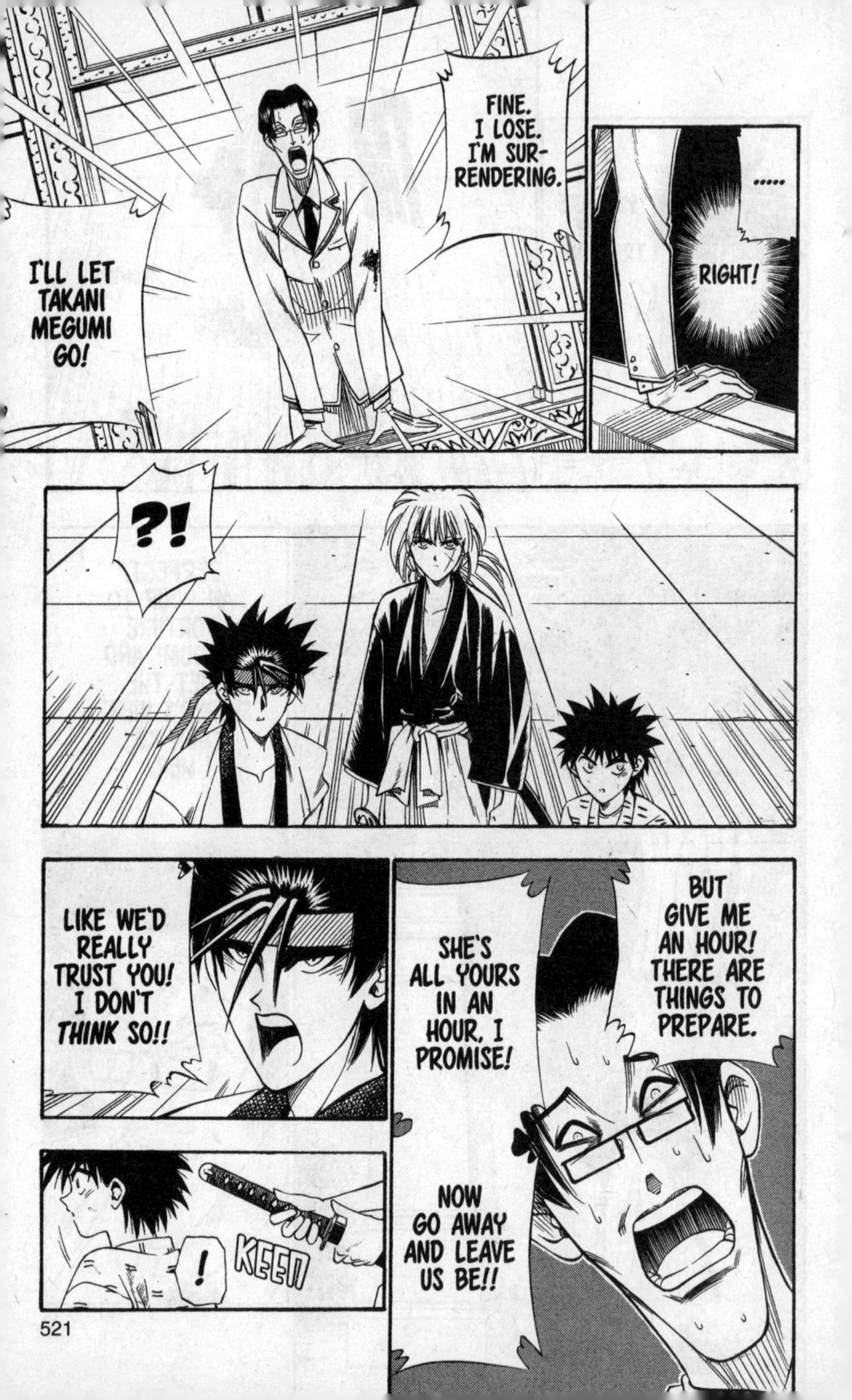

.....
RIGHT!
FINE. I LOSE. I'M SUR-RENDERING.
I'LL LET TAKANI MEGUMI GO!
?!
BUT GIVE ME AN HOUR! THERE ARE THINGS TO PREPARE.
SHE'S ALL YOURS IN AN HOUR, I PROMISE!
NOW GO AWAY AND LEAVE US BE!!
LIKE WE'D REALLY TRUST YOU! I DON'T *THINK* SO!!
KEEN
!

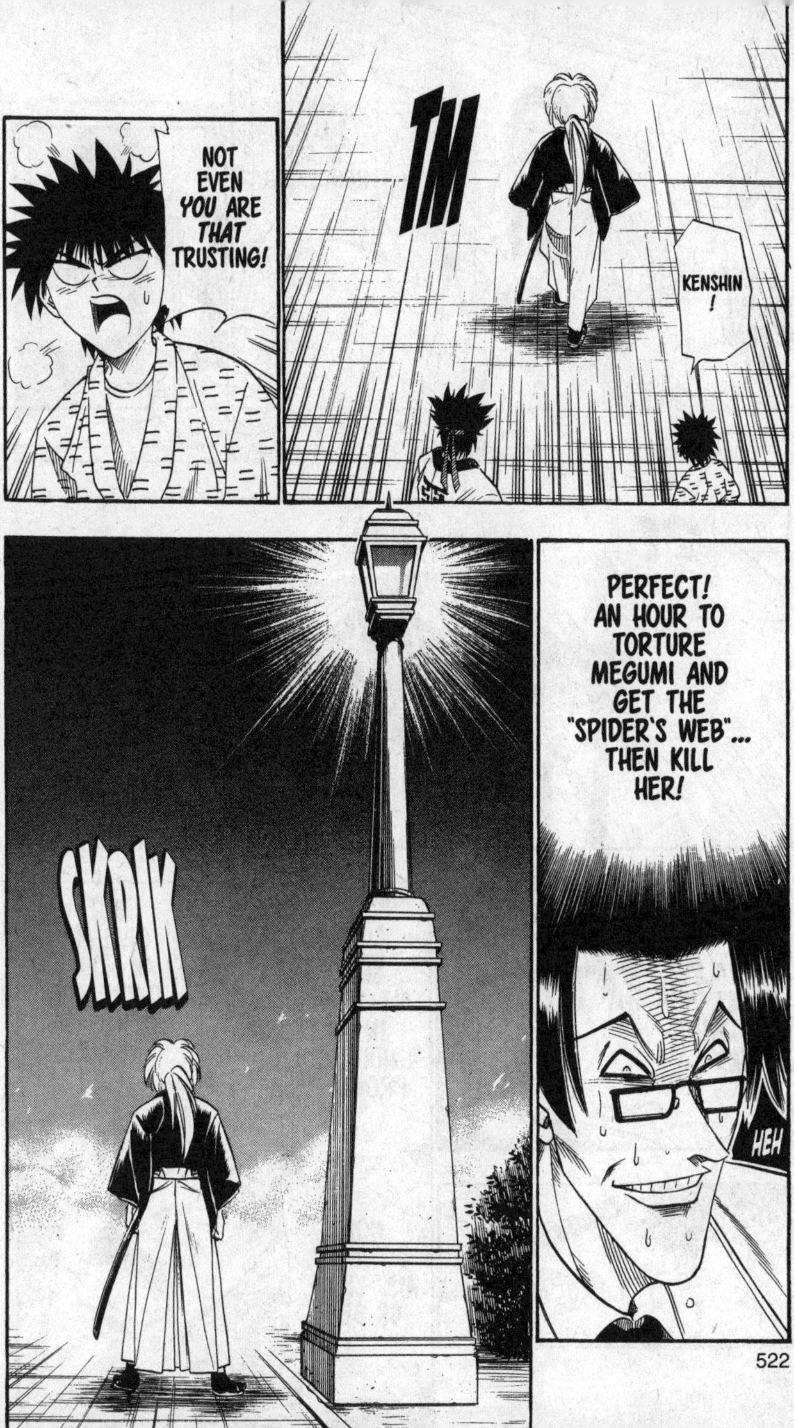
TM
KENSHIN!
NOT EVEN YOU ARE THAT TRUSTING!
PERFECT! AN HOUR TO TORTURE MEGUMI AND GET THE "SPIDER'S WEB"... THEN KILL HER!
HEH
SKRIK

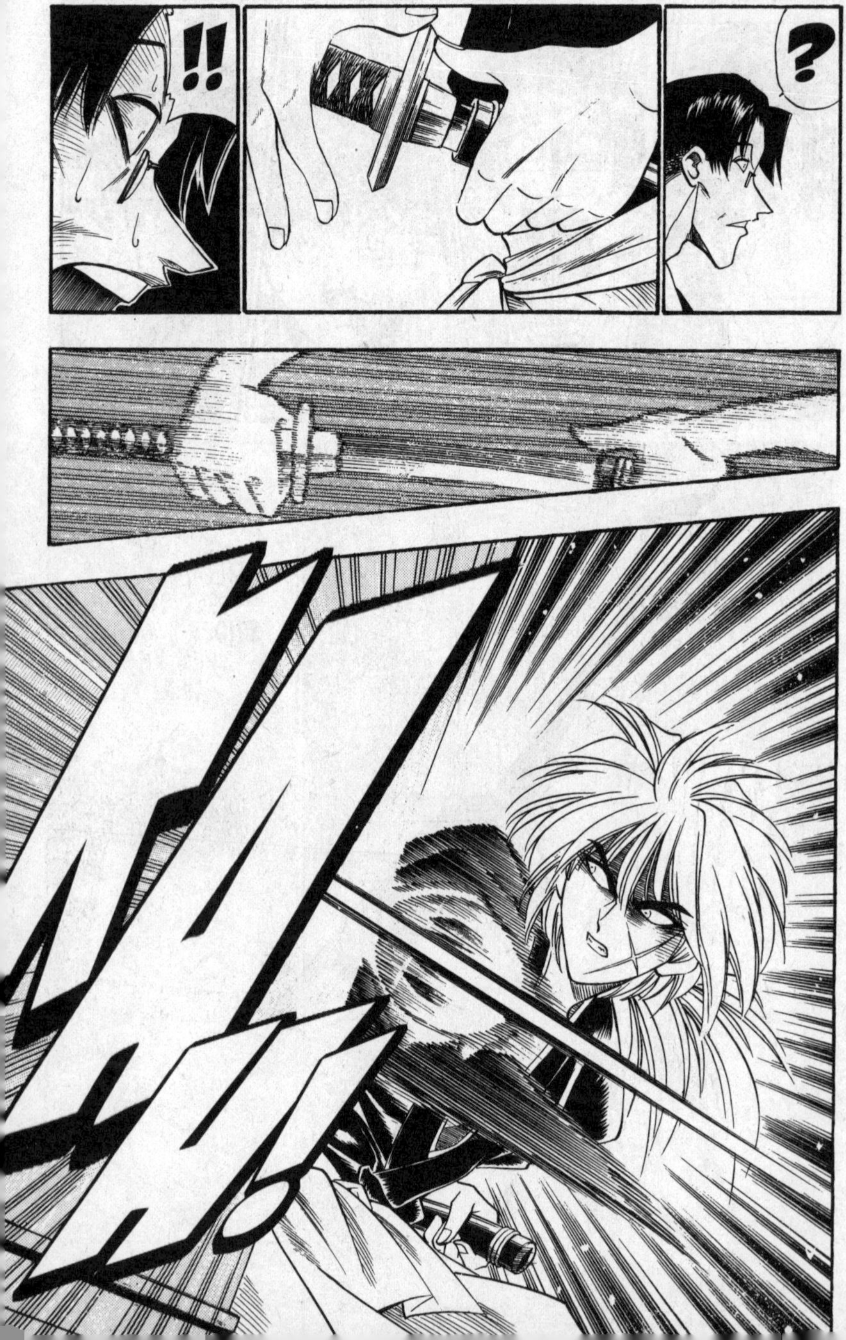
?
!!

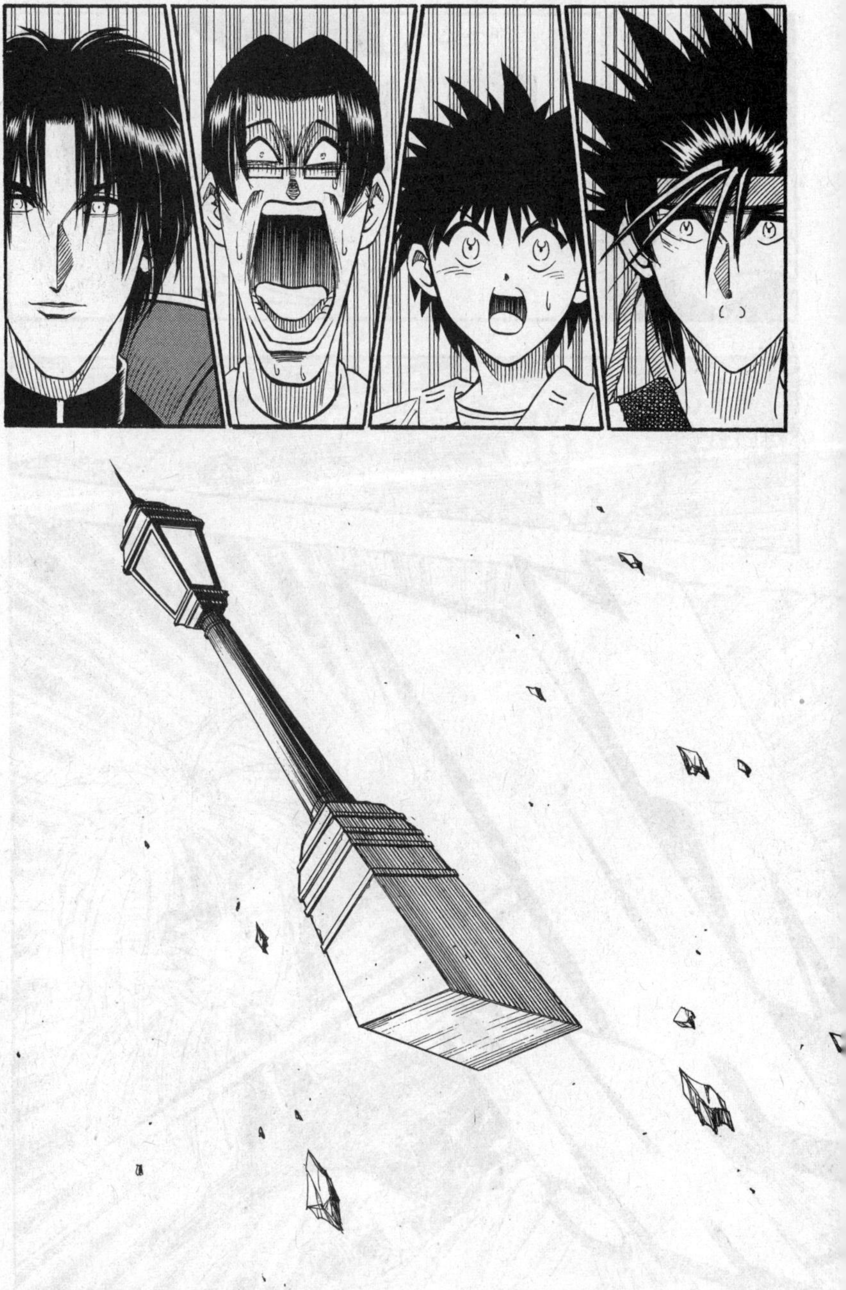

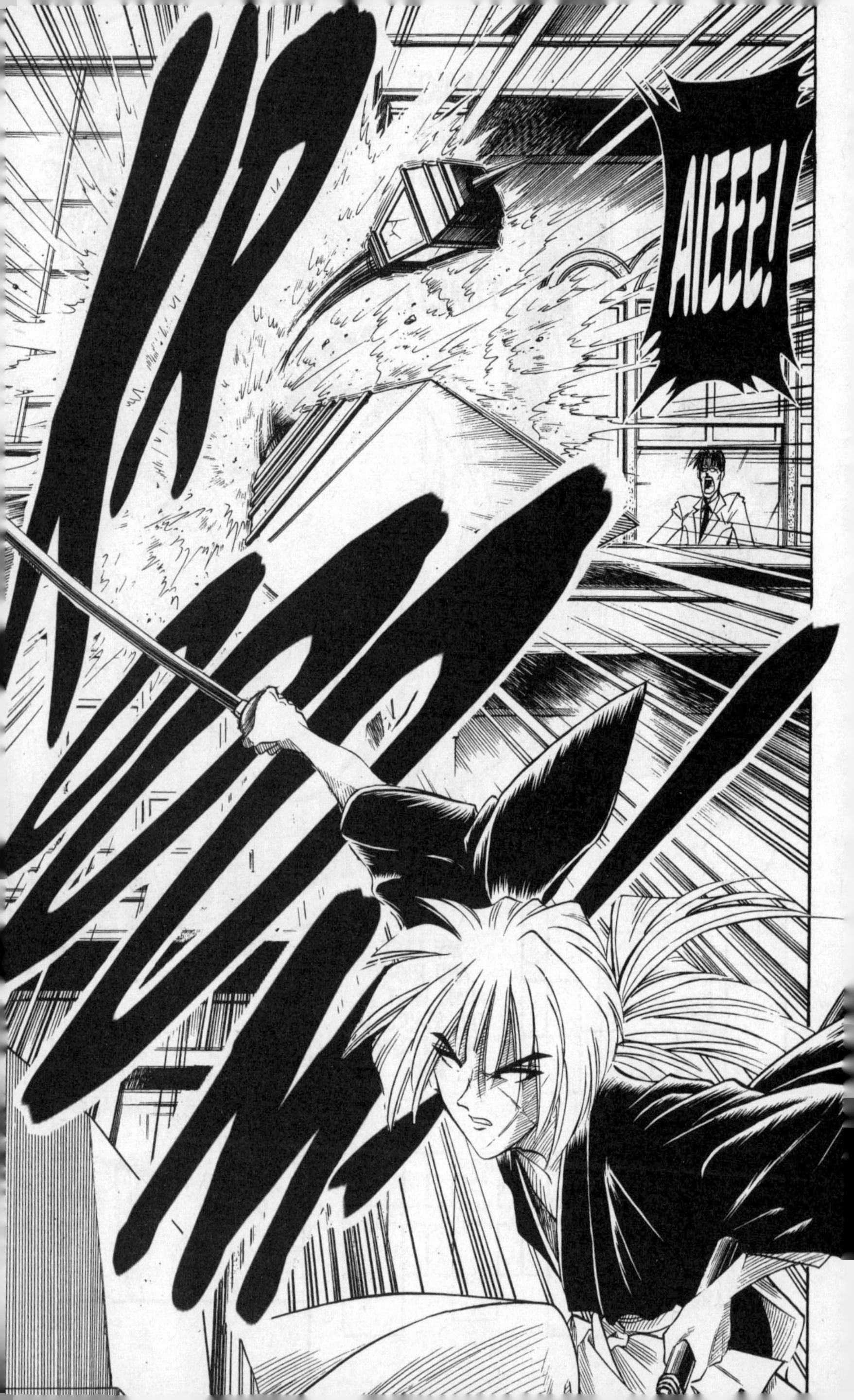
AIEEE!

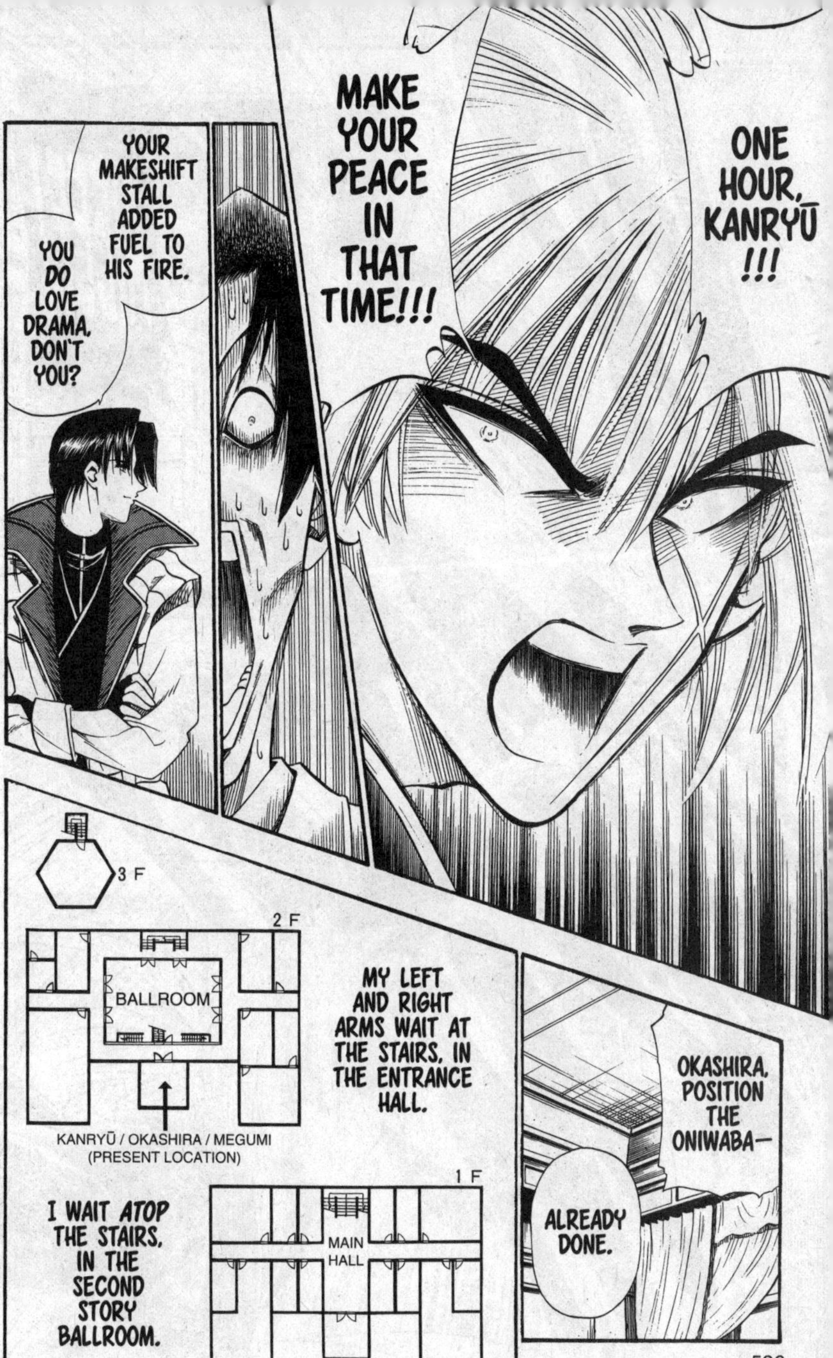
ONE HOUR, KANRYŪ!!!
MAKE YOUR PEACE IN THAT TIME!!!
YOUR MAKESHIFT STALL ADDED FUEL TO HIS FIRE.
YOU DO LOVE DRAMA, DON'T YOU?
OKASHIRA, POSITION THE ONIWABA—
ALREADY DONE.
MY LEFT AND RIGHT ARMS WAIT AT THE STAIRS, IN THE ENTRANCE HALL.
3 F
2 F
BALLROOM
KANRYŪ / OKASHIRA / MEGUMI (PRESENT LOCATION)
1 F
MAIN HALL
I WAIT ATOP THE STAIRS, IN THE SECOND STORY BALLROOM.

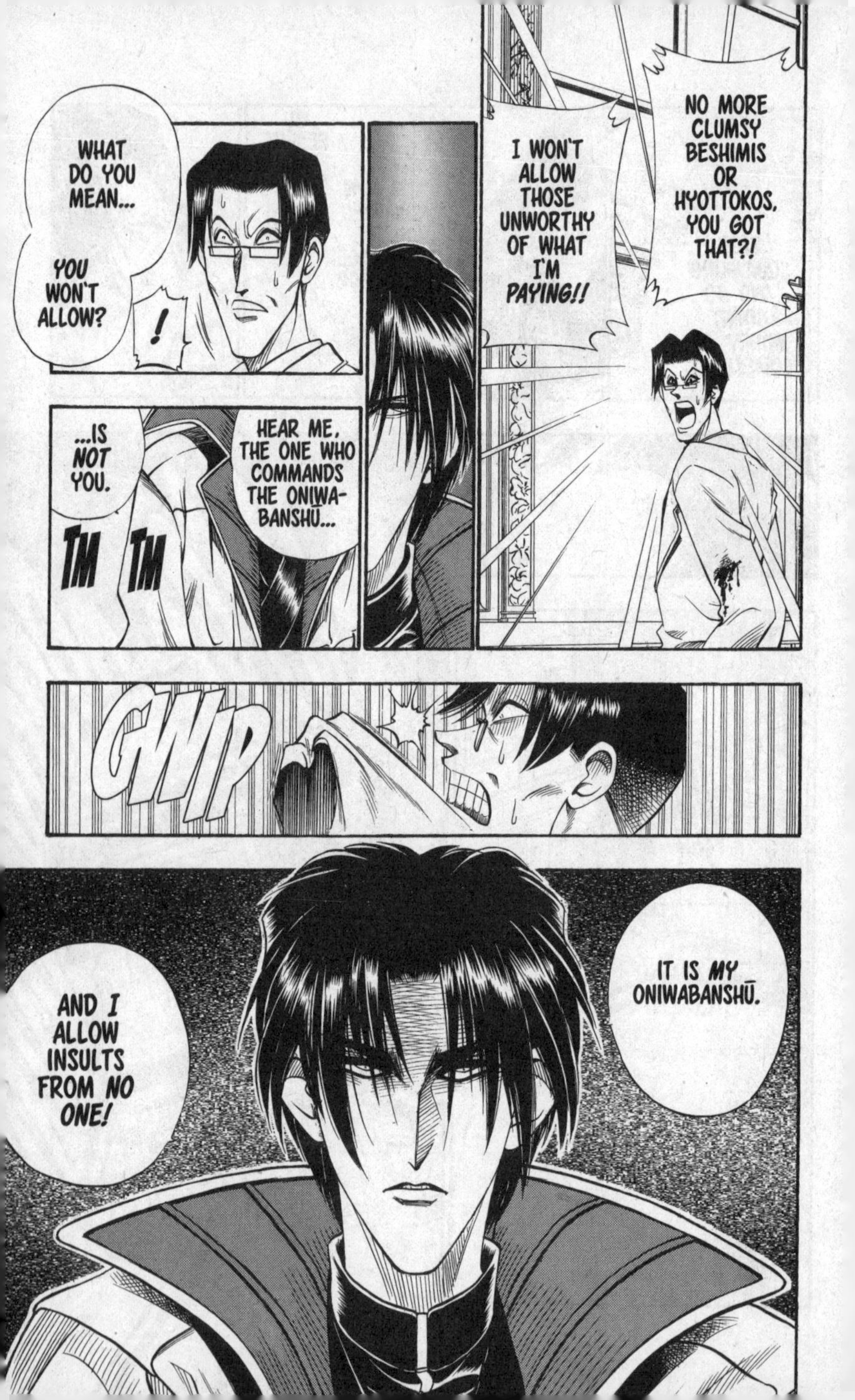
NO MORE CLUMSY BESHIMIS OR HYOTTOKOS, YOU GOT THAT?!
I WON'T ALLOW THOSE UNWORTHY OF WHAT I'M *PAYING!!*
WHAT DO YOU MEAN...
YOU WON'T ALLOW?
!
HEAR ME, THE ONE WHO COMMANDS THE ONIWABANSHŪ...
...IS *NOT* YOU.
TM TM
GNIP
IT IS *MY* ONIWABANSHŪ.
AND I ALLOW INSULTS FROM *NO ONE!*

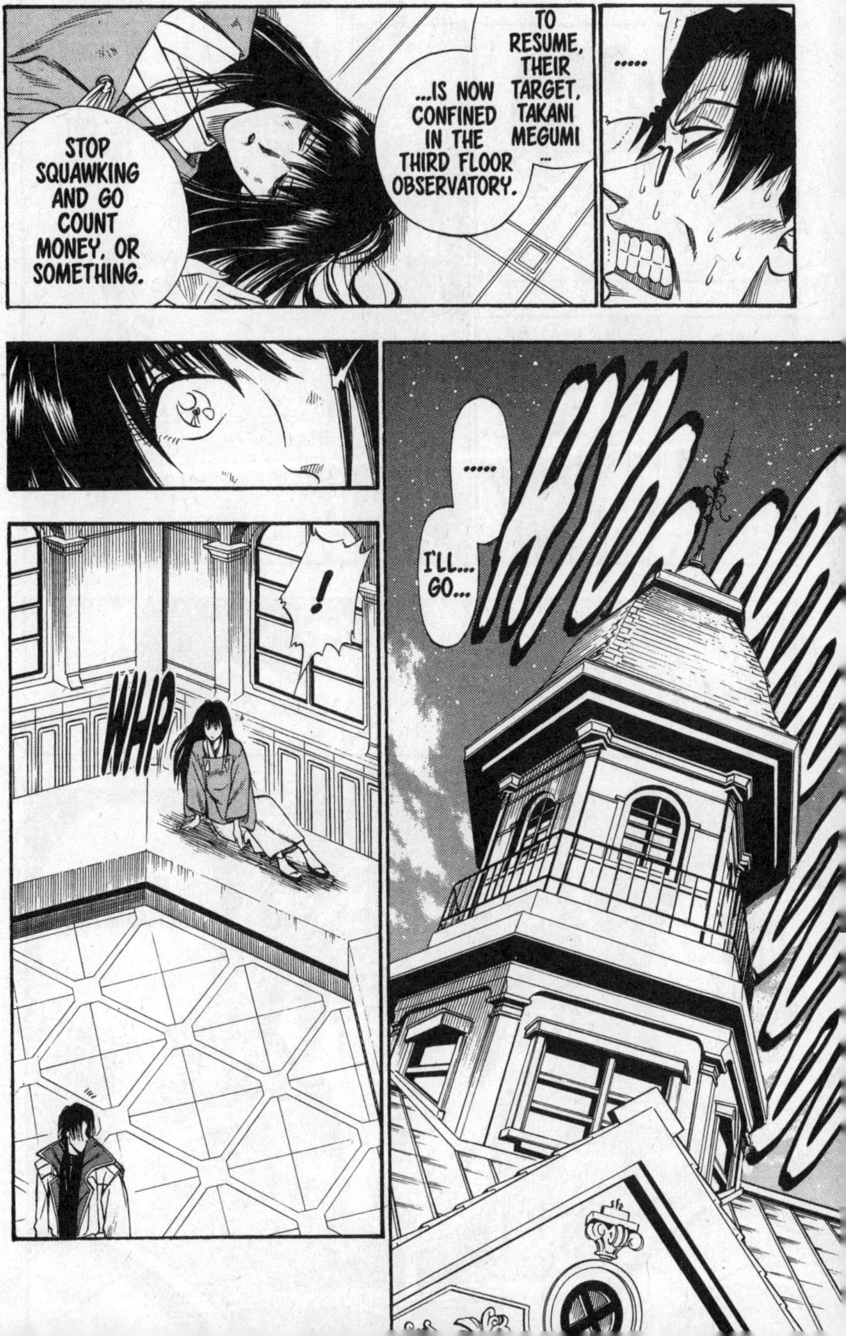
.....
TO RESUME, THEIR TARGET, TAKANI MEGUMI...
...IS NOW CONFINED IN THE THIRD FLOOR OBSERVATORY.
STOP SQUAWKING AND GO COUNT MONEY, OR SOMETHING.
HOOOOO
.....
I'LL... GO...
!
WHP

READ THIS WAY

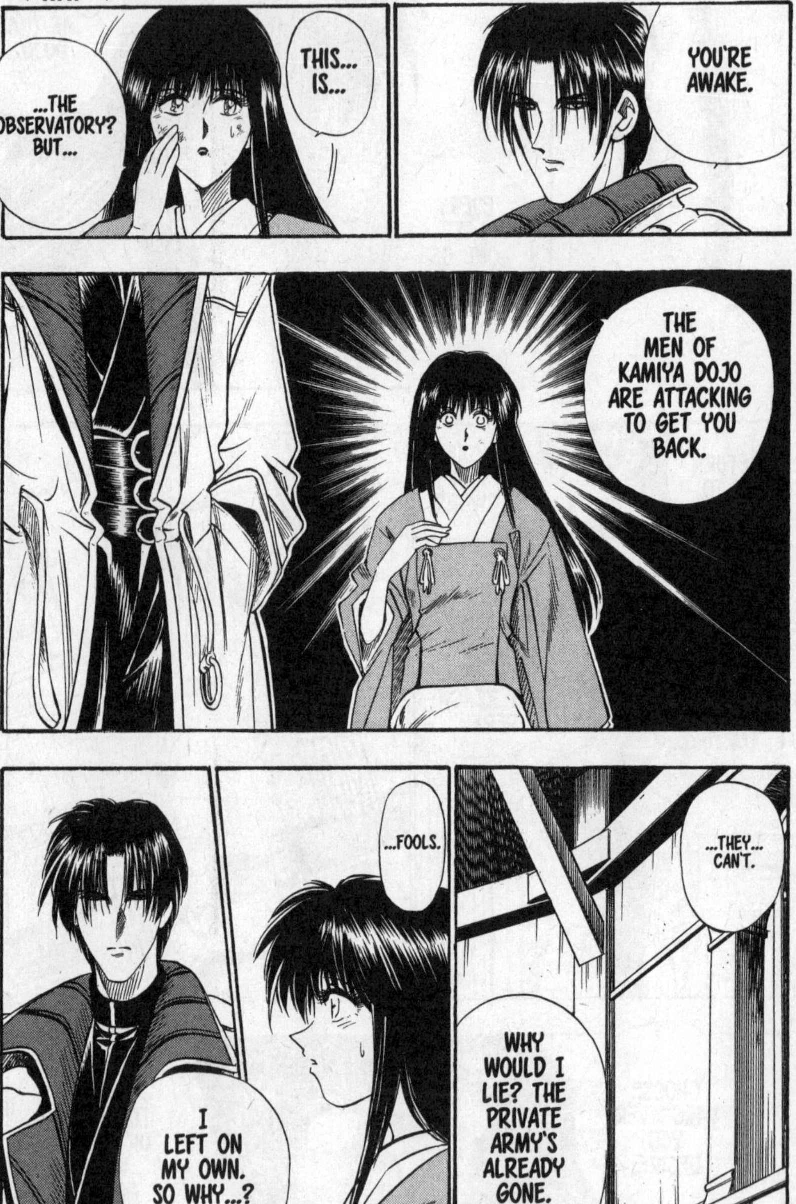
YOU'RE AWAKE.
THIS... IS...
...THE OBSERVATORY? BUT...
THE MEN OF KAMIYA DOJO ARE ATTACKING TO GET YOU BACK.
...THEY... CAN'T.
WHY WOULD I LIE? THE PRIVATE ARMY'S ALREADY GONE.
...FOOLS.
I LEFT ON MY OWN. SO WHY...?

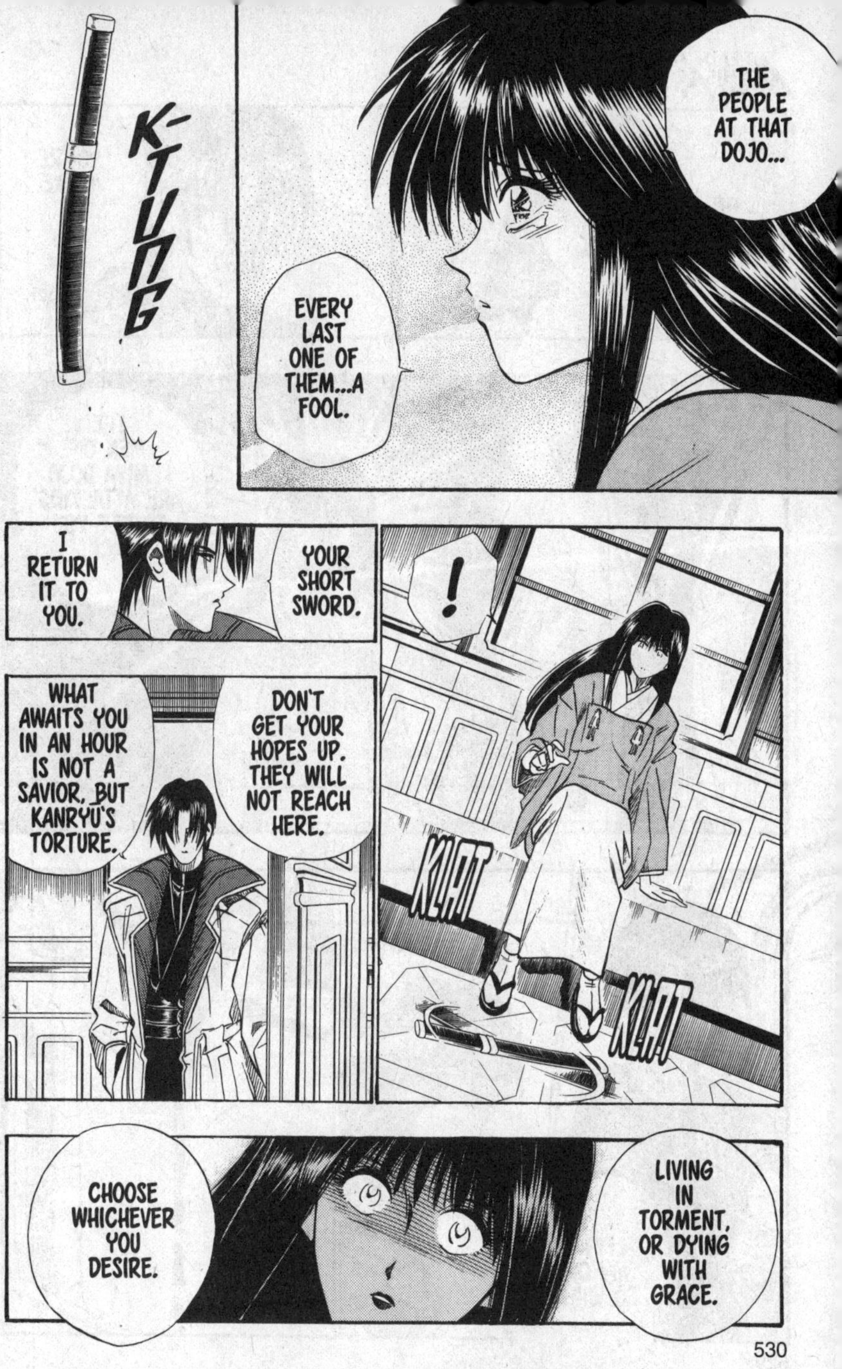
THE PEOPLE AT THAT DOJO...
EVERY LAST ONE OF THEM...A FOOL.
K-TUNG
!
KLAT
KLAT
YOUR SHORT SWORD.
I RETURN IT TO YOU.
DON'T GET YOUR HOPES UP. THEY WILL NOT REACH HERE.
WHAT AWAITS YOU IN AN HOUR IS NOT A SAVIOR, BUT KANRYU'S TORTURE.
LIVING IN TORMENT, OR DYING WITH GRACE.
CHOOSE WHICHEVER YOU DESIRE.

READ THIS WAY

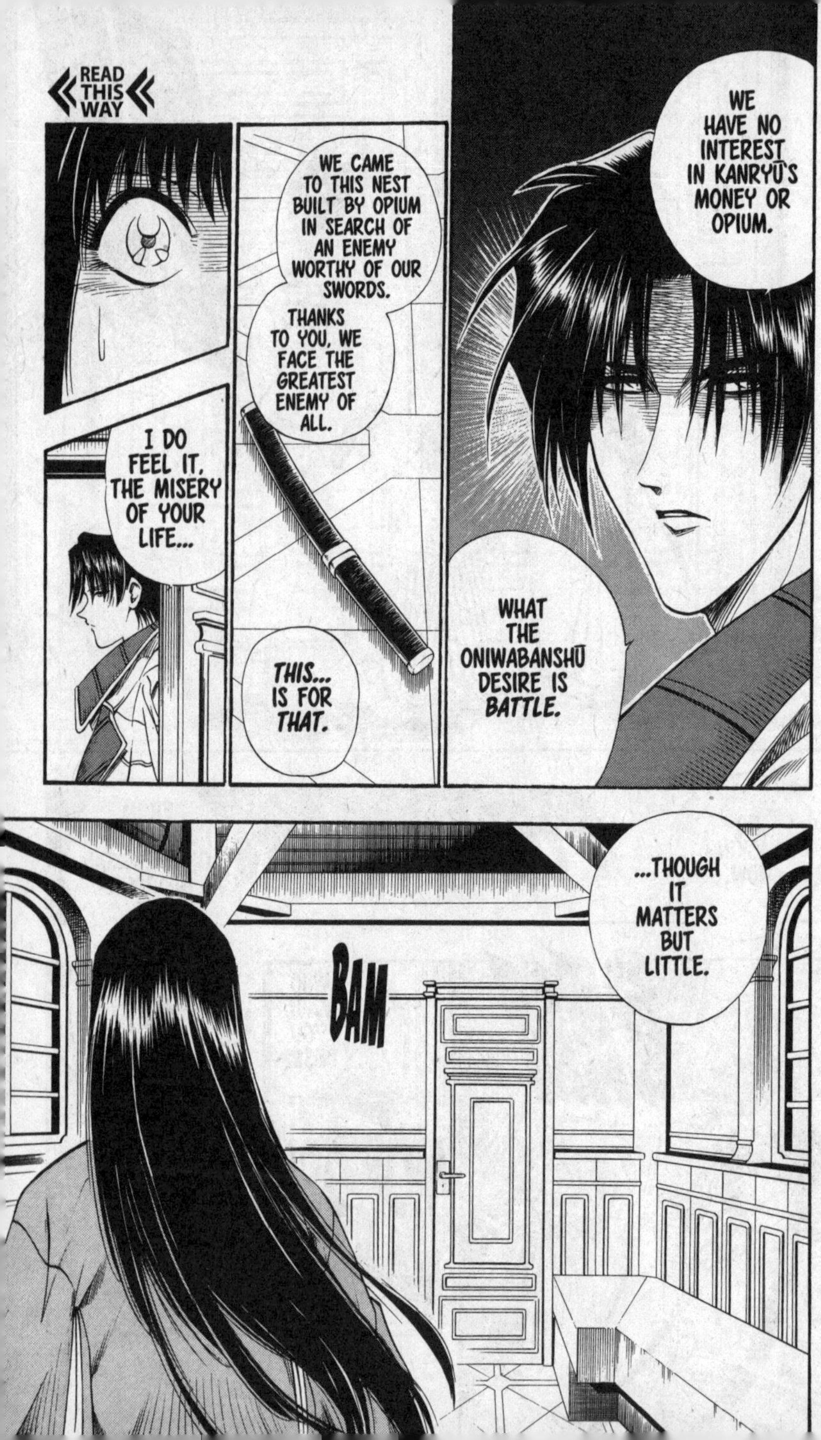
WE HAVE NO INTEREST IN KANRYŪ'S MONEY OR OPIUM.
WHAT THE ONIWABANSHŪ DESIRE IS *BATTLE.*
WE CAME TO THIS NEST BUILT BY OPIUM IN SEARCH OF AN ENEMY WORTHY OF OUR SWORDS.
THANKS TO YOU, WE FACE THE GREATEST ENEMY OF ALL.
THIS... IS FOR *THAT.*
I DO FEEL IT, THE MISERY OF YOUR LIFE...
...THOUGH IT MATTERS BUT LITTLE.
BAM

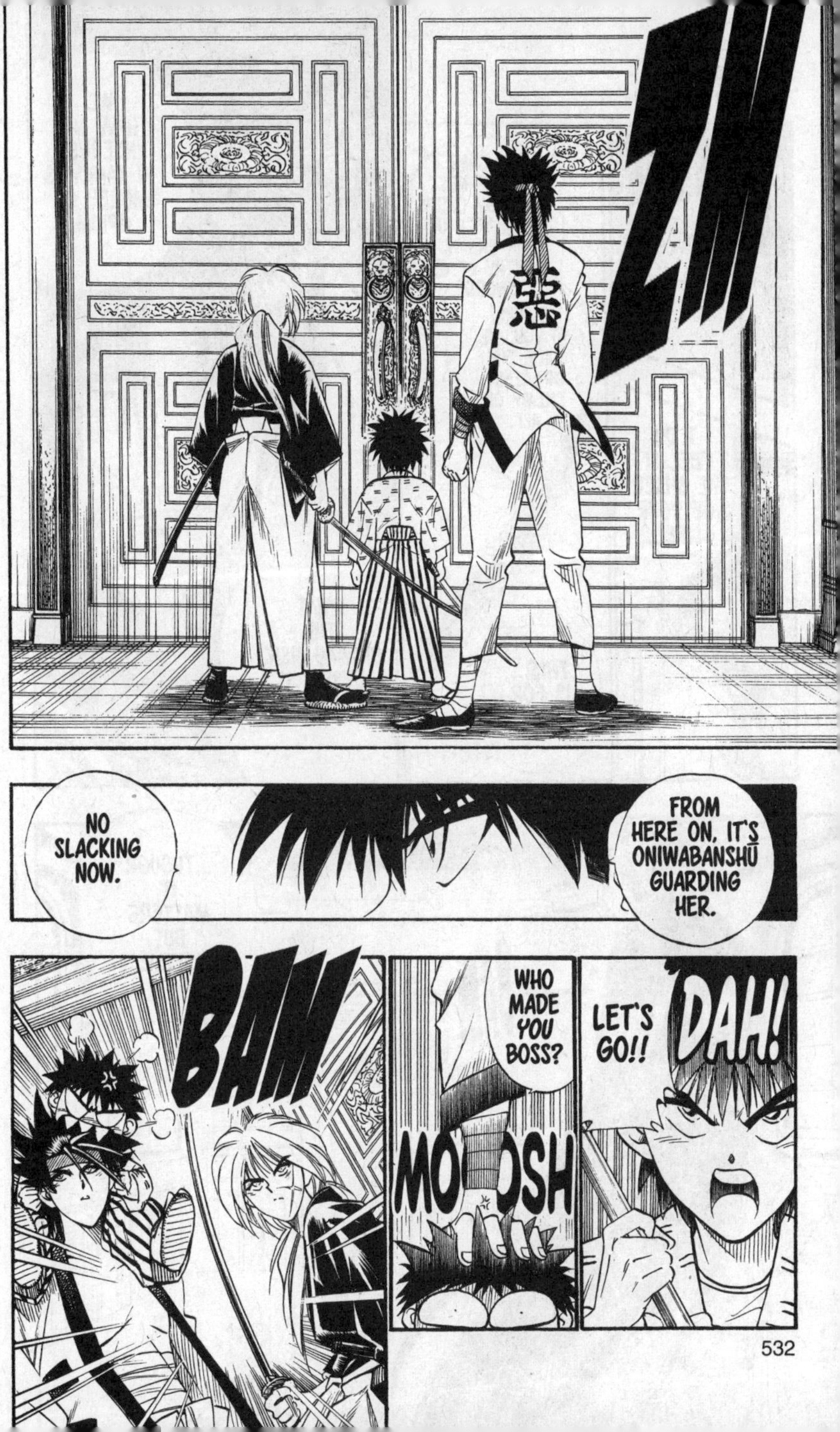
FROM HERE ON, IT'S ONIWABANSHŪ GUARDING HER.
NO SLACKING NOW.
DAH!
LET'S GO!!
WHO MADE YOU BOSS?
BAM

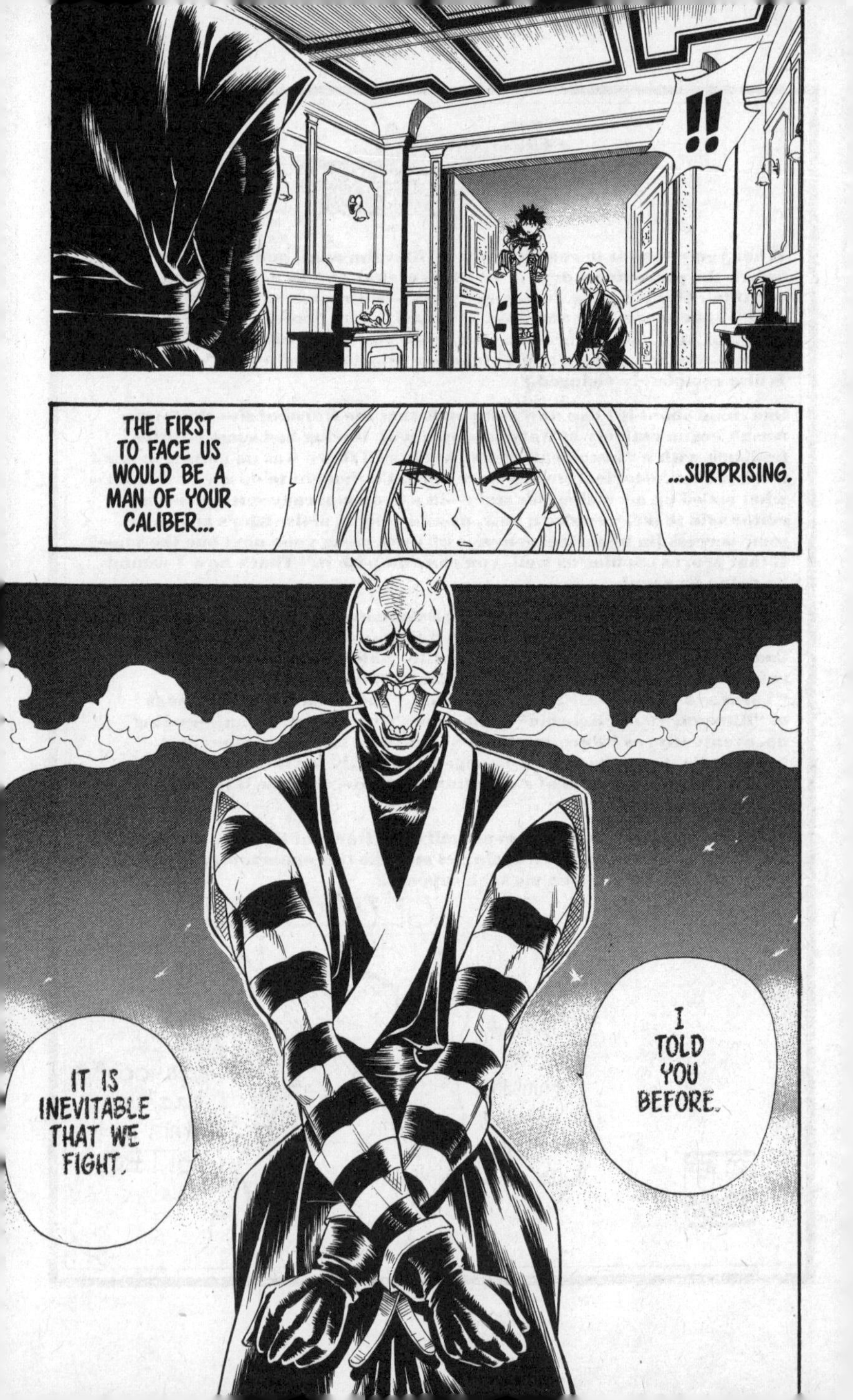
!!
THE FIRST TO FACE US WOULD BE A MAN OF YOUR CALIBER...
...SURPRISING.
I TOLD YOU BEFORE.
IT IS INEVITABLE THAT WE FIGHT.

Rurouni Kenshin

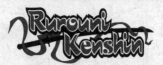

What you're about to read is the very first *Rurouni,* published half a year before the preceding story. If we think of that one as a "side-story," we can think of this one as the series "pilot"—with some of the details being different between then and now. This early story loosely echoes the later "Megumi Arc," as will become clear once you start reading—though, in this version, Megumi, Kaoru and Yahiko are all siblings. (Megumi's personality is also completely changed.)

One thing about it I can now tell you is that the *Rurouni Kenshin* series wasn't begun entirely of Watsuki's own will. Having had some positive feedback with a "historical" debut work, still there was no getting around the fact that historical stories were *hard.* I'd thought to do my next work—what ended up becoming this story—in a contemporary setting, but my editor said to me, "You're a new, up-and-coming artist who's achieved some success [in historical genres]; why not make your next one the same? If that proves popular as well, you can run with it." That's how I wound up doing *Rurouni.*

My goal was to take the time-period (Bakumatsu) from *Moeyo Ken*—Watsuki's bible—and combine it with a *Sugata Sanshirō*-type story. Complicating things further was the title, which went through many revisions. It started as "Nishin (Two-Hearts) Kenshin," went to "Yorozuya (Jack-of-All-Trades) Kenshin," then to several variations of "Rurouni" and "Kenshin"—sometimes with different kanji—ending up, eventually, as "Rurouni, Meiji Swordsman Romantic Story." It took me eight months to do a 45-page story...only for it to fall to the tender editorial mercies of a selection committee. Suffice it to say, the process was *not* easy.

A year and a half to age, and eventually the *Rurouni Kenshin* series we know today was born. Once again, let me take this opportunity to thank all you fans, who've given me such support.

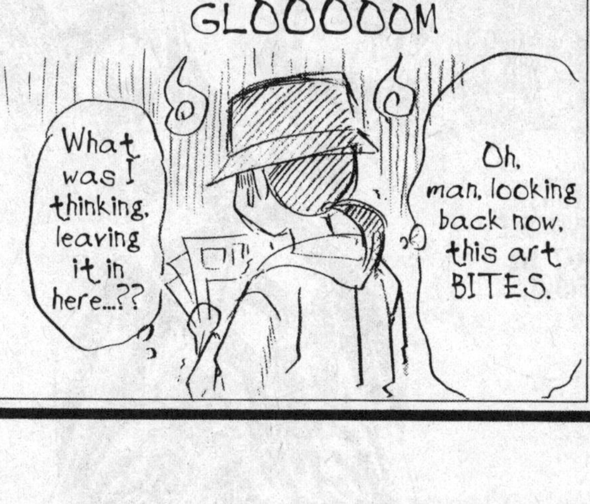
GLOOOOOM
Oh, man, looking back now, this art BITES.
What was I thinking, leaving it in here...??

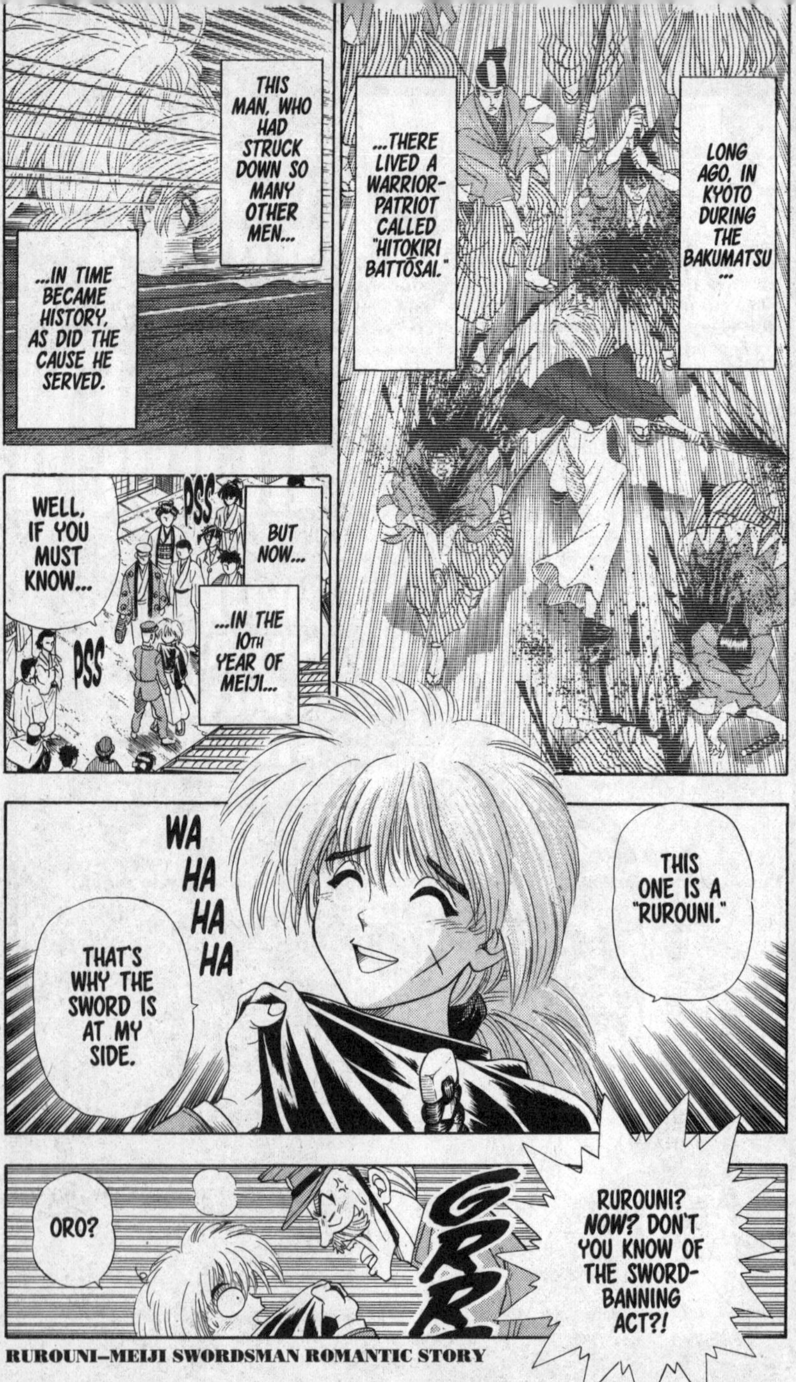
LONG AGO, IN KYOTO DURING THE BAKUMATSU…
…THERE LIVED A WARRIOR-PATRIOT CALLED "HITOKIRI BATTŌSAI."
THIS MAN, WHO HAD STRUCK DOWN SO MANY OTHER MEN…
…IN TIME BECAME HISTORY, AS DID THE CAUSE HE SERVED.
BUT NOW…
…IN THE 10TH YEAR OF MEIJI…
PSS
WELL, IF YOU MUST KNOW…
PSS
THIS ONE IS A "RUROUNI."
WA HA HA HA
THAT'S WHY THE SWORD IS AT MY SIDE.
RUROUNI? NOW? DON'T YOU KNOW OF THE SWORD-BANNING ACT?!
GRR
ORO?

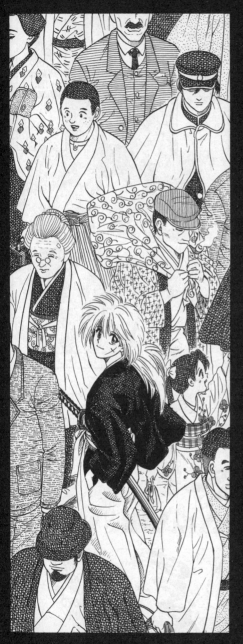

END-OF-VOLUME SPECIAL (2)

RUROUNI

MEIJI SWORDSMAN ROMANTIC STORY

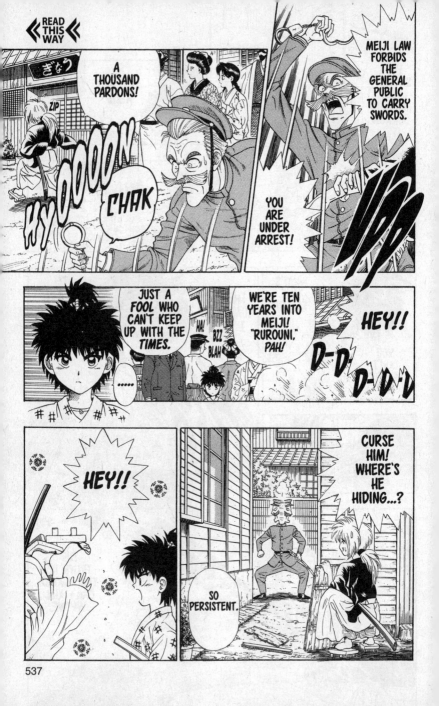

READ THIS WAY

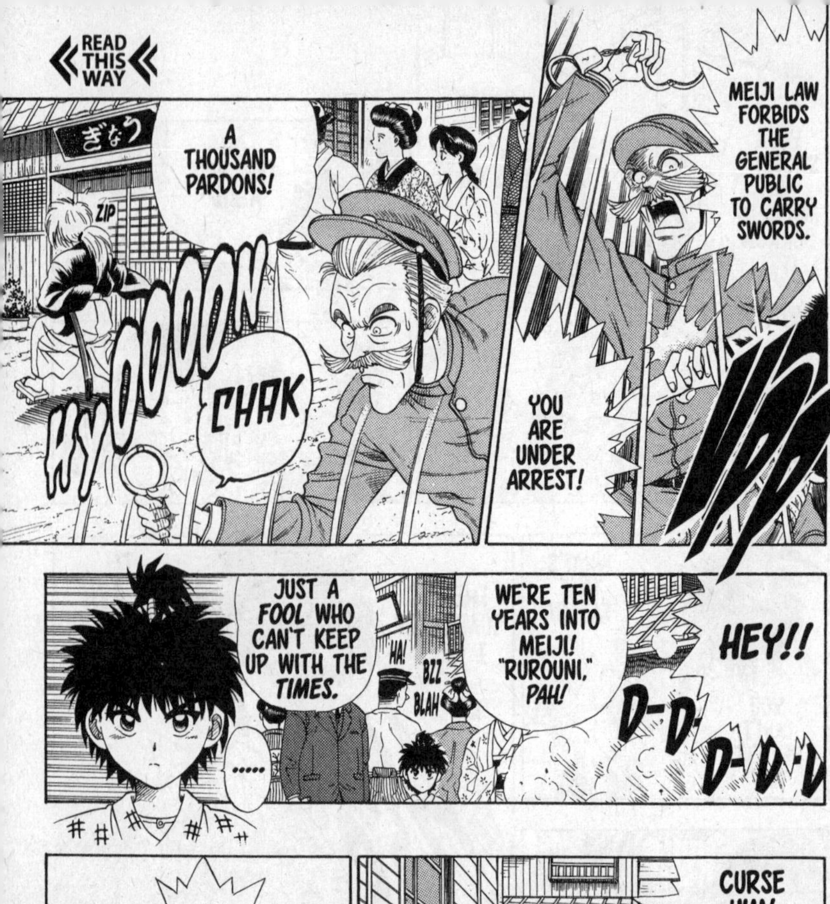
MEIJI LAW FORBIDS THE GENERAL PUBLIC TO CARRY SWORDS.
YOU ARE UNDER ARREST!
A THOUSAND PARDONS!
ZIP
HYOOOON
CHAK
HEY!!
D-D-D-D-D
WE'RE TEN YEARS INTO MEIJI! "RUROUNI," PAH!
BZZ
BLAH
HA!
JUST A FOOL WHO CAN'T KEEP UP WITH THE TIMES.
......
CURSE HIM! WHERE'S HE HIDING...?
SO PERSISTENT.
HEY!!

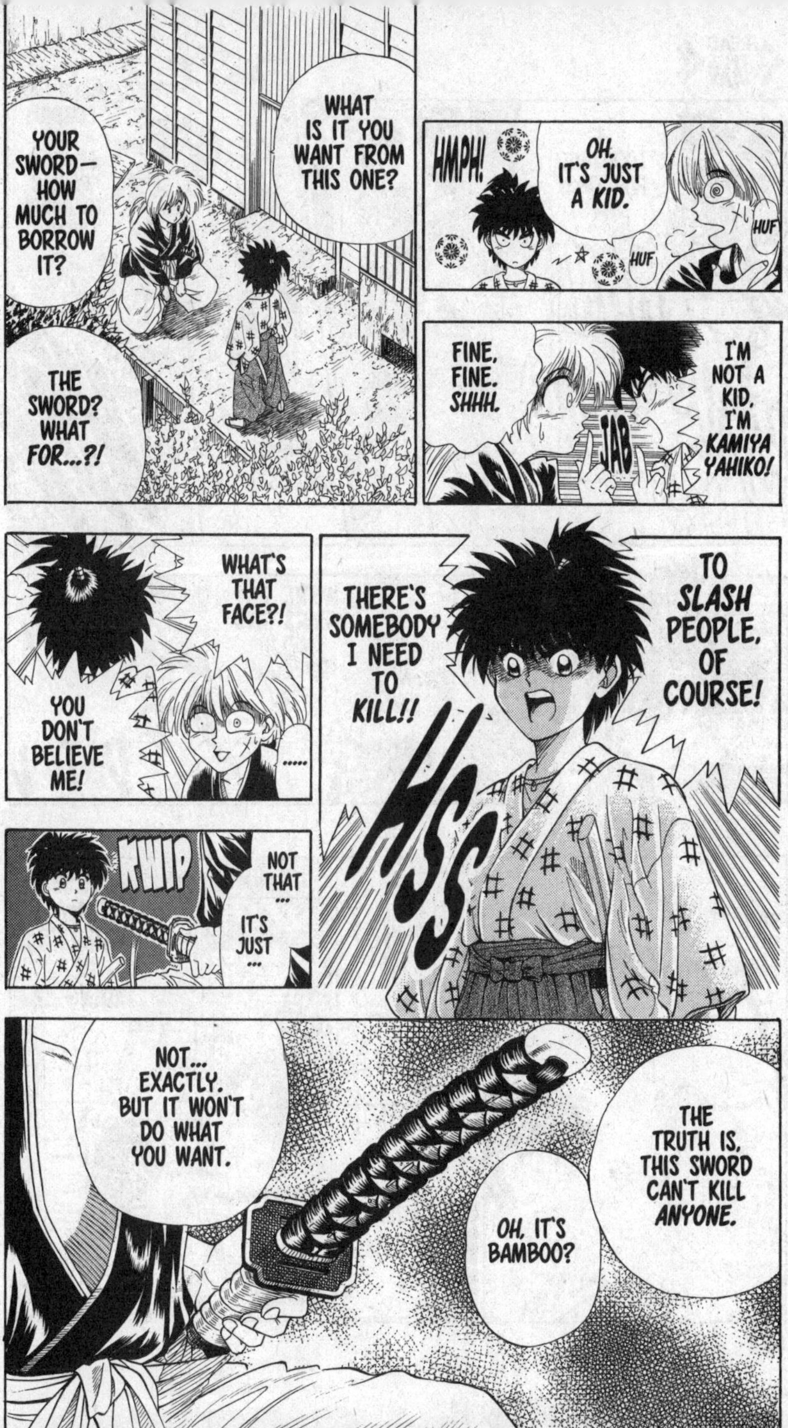
OH, IT'S JUST A KID.
HUF
HUF
HMPH!
I'M NOT A KID, I'M KAMIYA YAHIKO!
JAB
FINE, FINE. SHHH.
WHAT IS IT YOU WANT FROM THIS ONE?
YOUR SWORD— HOW MUCH TO BORROW IT?
THE SWORD? WHAT FOR...?!
TO SLASH PEOPLE, OF COURSE!
THERE'S SOMEBODY I NEED TO KILL!!
HSS
WHAT'S THAT FACE?!
.....
YOU DON'T BELIEVE ME!
NOT THAT... IT'S JUST...
KWIP
THE TRUTH IS, THIS SWORD CAN'T KILL ANYONE.
OH, IT'S BAMBOO?
NOT... EXACTLY. BUT IT WON'T DO WHAT YOU WANT.

READ THIS WAY

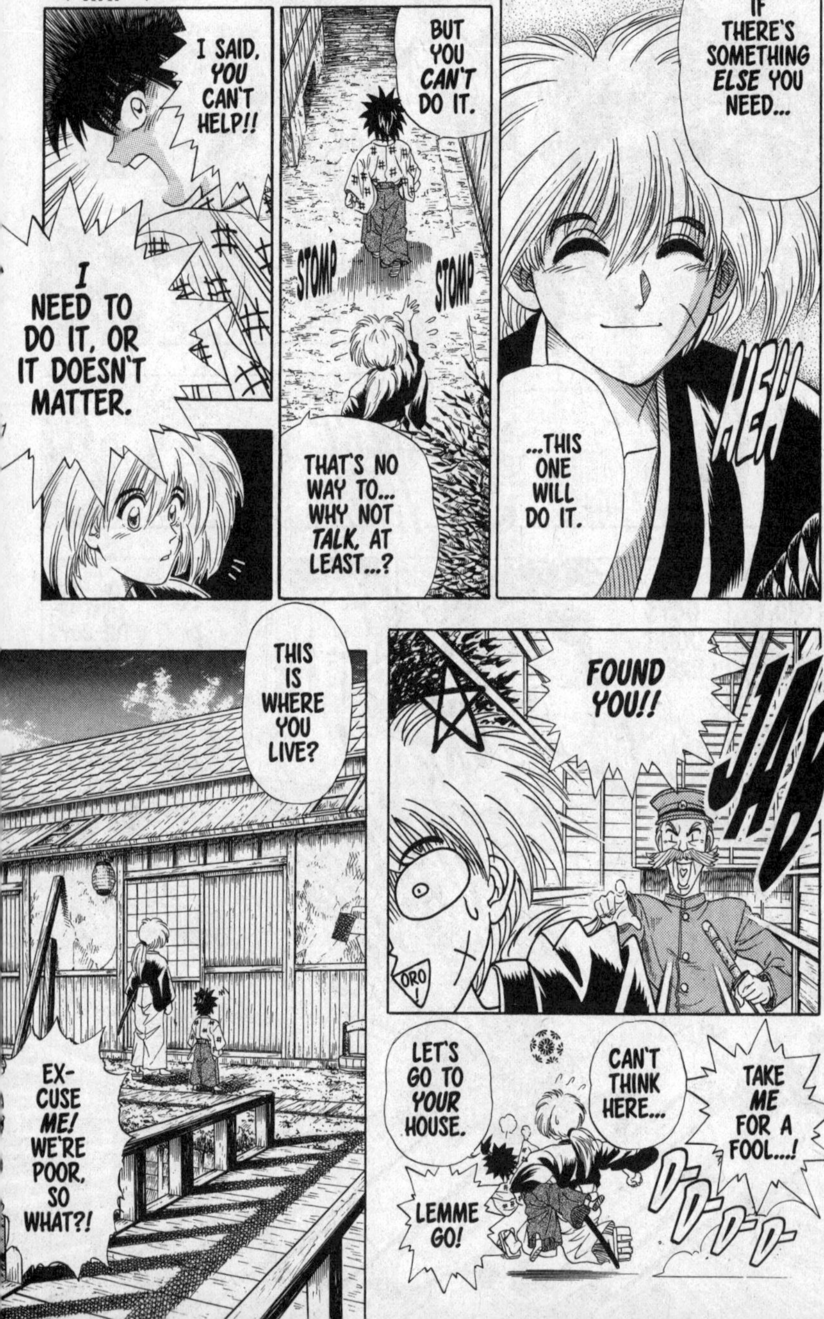
IF THERE'S SOMETHING ELSE YOU NEED...
...THIS ONE WILL DO IT.
HEH
BUT YOU CAN'T DO IT.
STOMP
STOMP
THAT'S NO WAY TO... WHY NOT TALK, AT LEAST...?
I SAID, YOU CAN'T HELP!!
I NEED TO DO IT, OR IT DOESN'T MATTER.
FOUND YOU!!
JAB
ORO!
TAKE ME FOR A FOOL...!
CAN'T THINK HERE...
LET'S GO TO YOUR HOUSE.
LEMME GO!
D-D-D-D
THIS IS WHERE YOU LIVE?
EX-CUSE ME! WE'RE POOR, SO WHAT?!

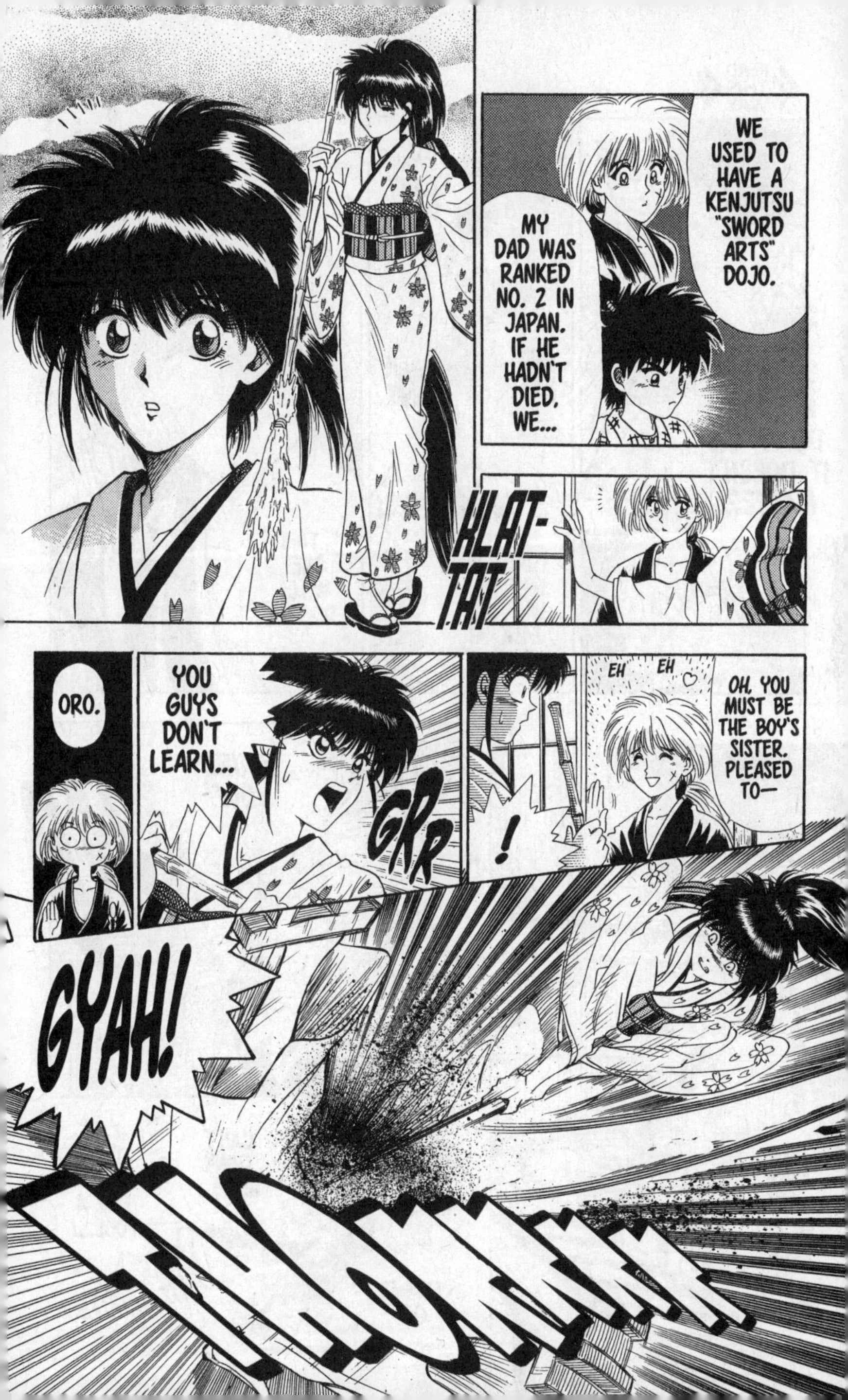
WE USED TO HAVE A KENJUTSU "SWORD ARTS" DOJO.
MY DAD WAS RANKED NO. 2 IN JAPAN. IF HE HADN'T DIED, WE...
KLAT-TAT
EH EH
OH, YOU MUST BE THE BOY'S SISTER. PLEASED TO—
!
YOU GUYS DON'T LEARN...
GRR
ORO.
GYAH!

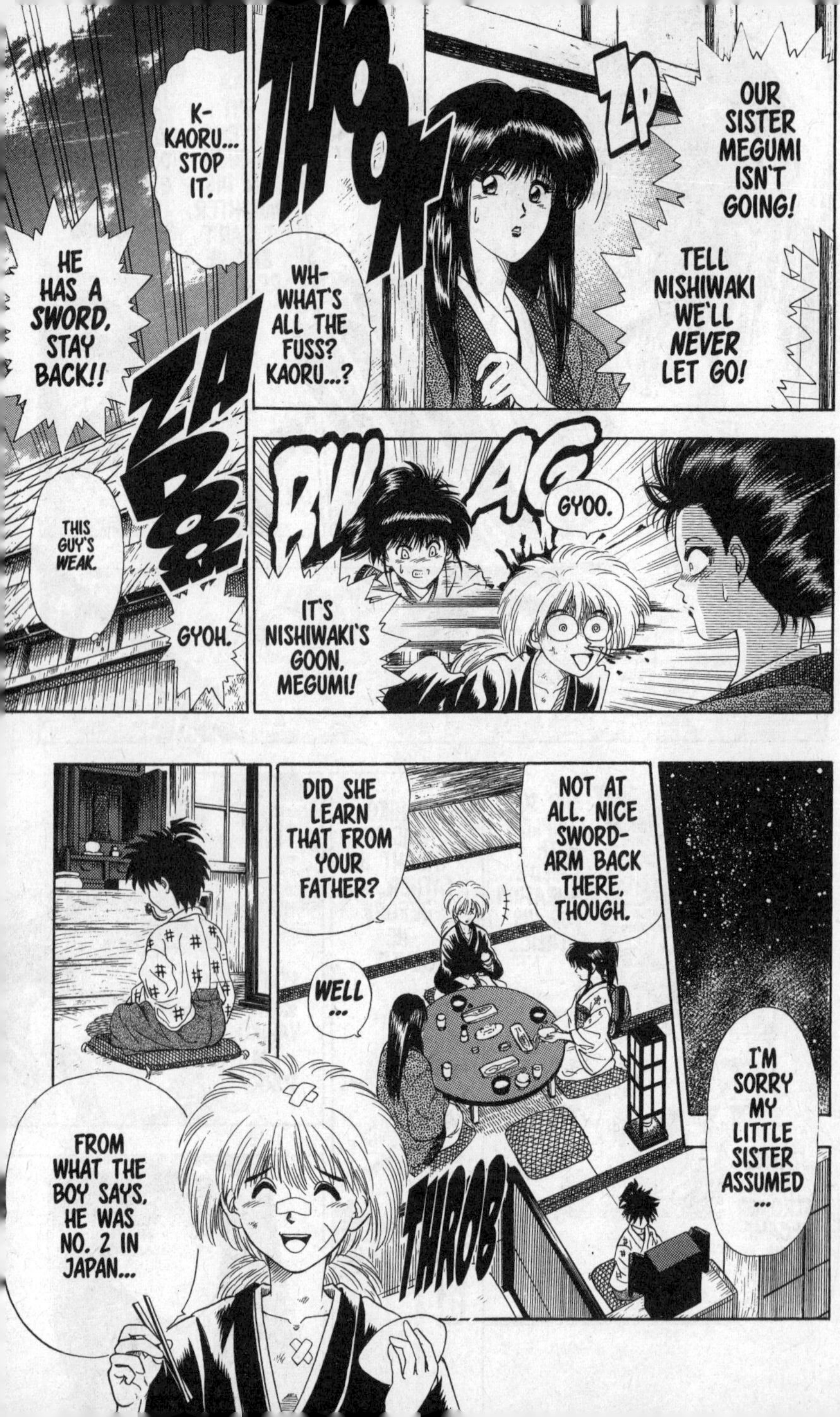
OUR SISTER MEGUMI ISN'T GOING!
TELL NISHIWAKI WE'LL NEVER LET GO!
WH-WHAT'S ALL THE FUSS? KAORU...?
GYOO.
IT'S NISHIWAKI'S GOON, MEGUMI!
K-KAORU... STOP IT.
HE HAS A SWORD. STAY BACK!!
THIS GUY'S WEAK.
GYOH.
I'M SORRY MY LITTLE SISTER ASSUMED...
THROB
NOT AT ALL. NICE SWORD-ARM BACK THERE, THOUGH.
DID SHE LEARN THAT FROM YOUR FATHER?
WELL...
FROM WHAT THE BOY SAYS, HE WAS NO. 2 IN JAPAN...

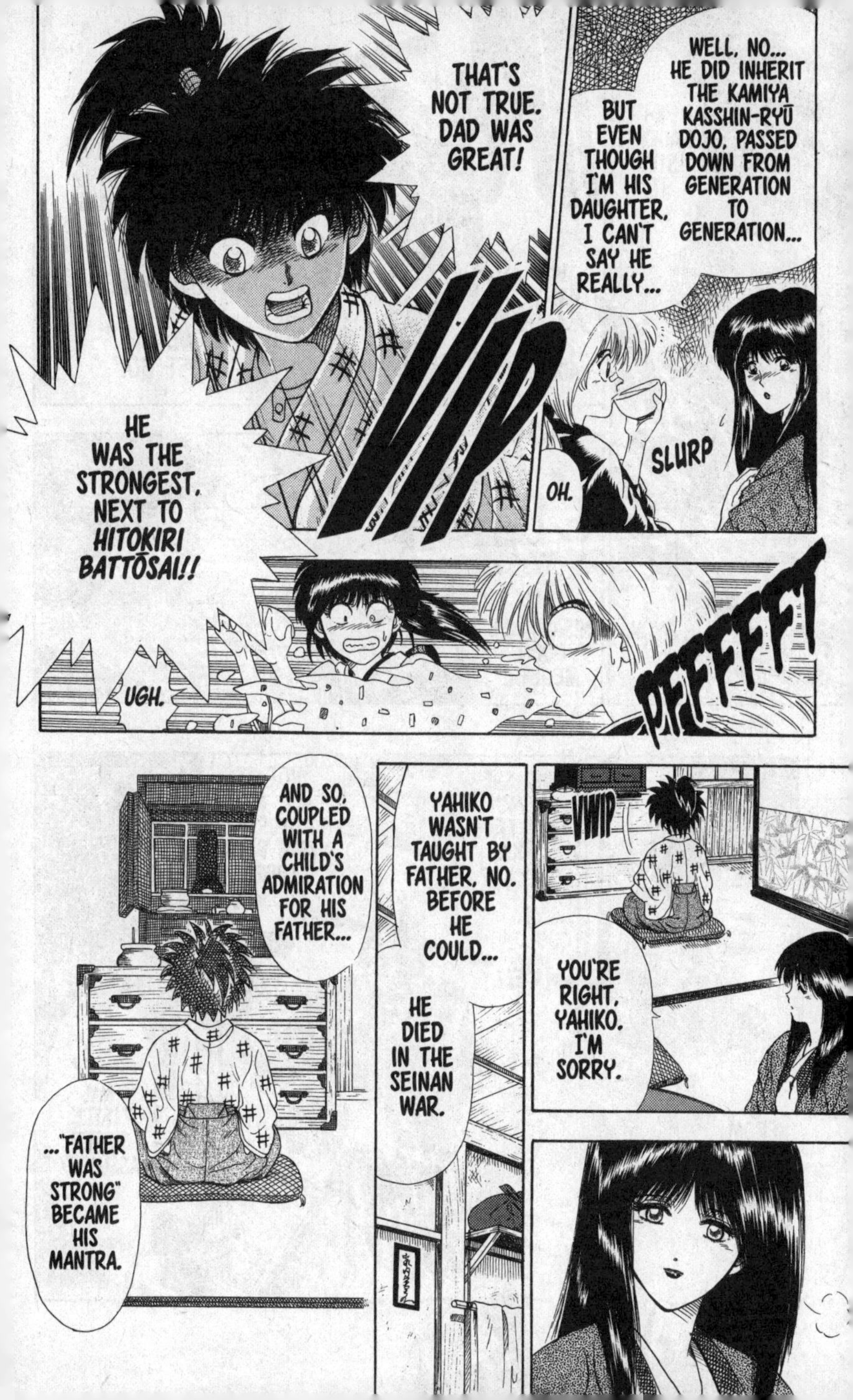
WELL, NO... HE DID INHERIT THE KAMIYA KASSHIN-RYŪ DOJO, PASSED DOWN FROM GENERATION TO GENERATION...
BUT EVEN THOUGH I'M HIS DAUGHTER, I CAN'T SAY HE REALLY...
SLURP
OH.
THAT'S NOT TRUE. DAD WAS GREAT!
VIP
HE WAS THE STRONGEST, NEXT TO HITOKIRI BATTŌSAI!!
PFFFFFT
UGH.
VWIP
YOU'RE RIGHT, YAHIKO. I'M SORRY.
YAHIKO WASN'T TAUGHT BY FATHER, NO. BEFORE HE COULD...
HE DIED IN THE SEINAN WAR.
AND SO, COUPLED WITH A CHILD'S ADMIRATION FOR HIS FATHER...
..."FATHER WAS STRONG" BECAME HIS MANTRA.

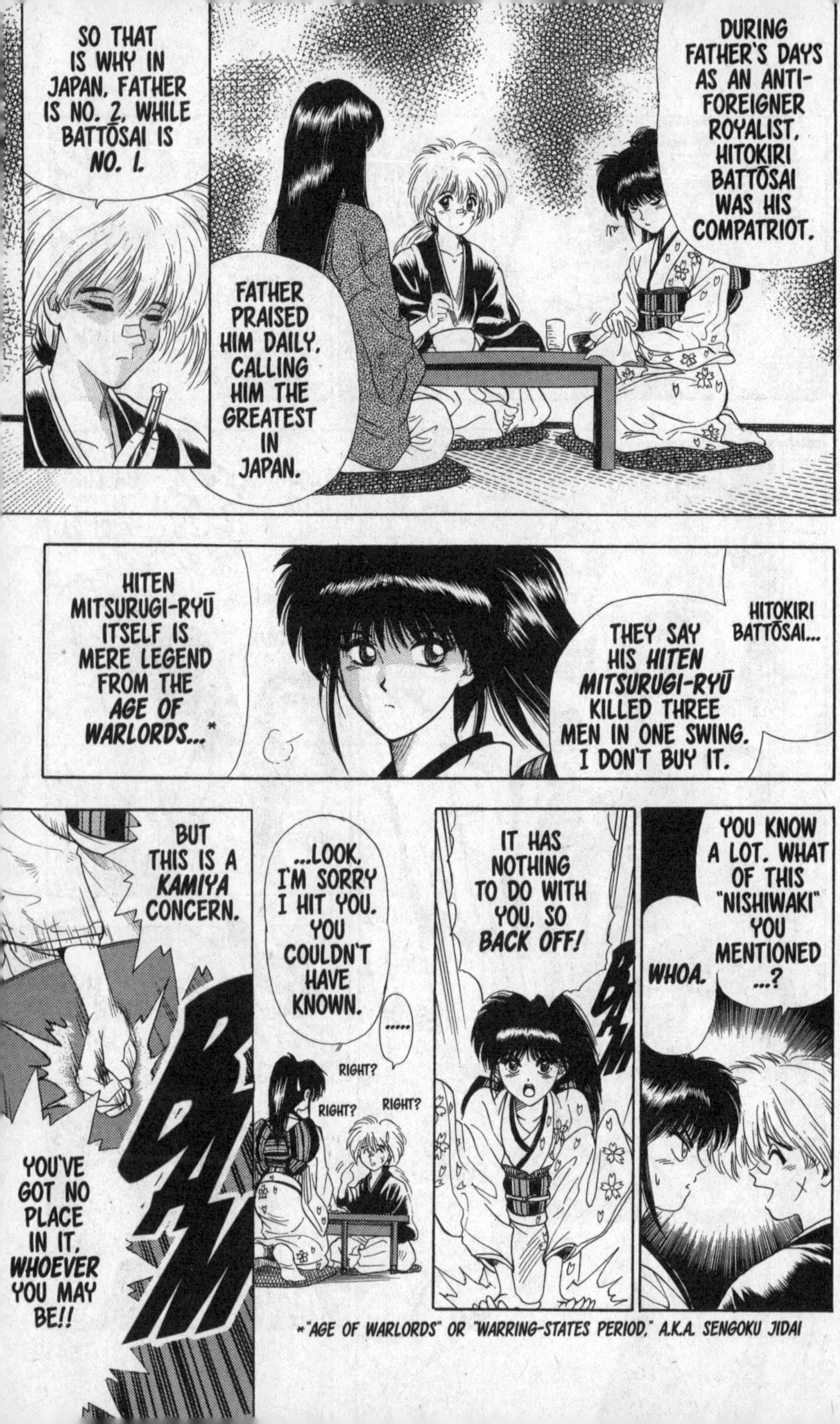
DURING FATHER'S DAYS AS AN ANTI-FOREIGNER ROYALIST, HITOKIRI BATTŌSAI WAS HIS COMPATRIOT.
FATHER PRAISED HIM DAILY, CALLING HIM THE GREATEST IN JAPAN.
SO THAT IS WHY IN JAPAN, FATHER IS NO. 2, WHILE BATTŌSAI IS NO. 1.
HITOKIRI BATTŌSAI...
THEY SAY HIS HITEN MITSURUGI-RYŪ KILLED THREE MEN IN ONE SWING. I DON'T BUY IT.
HITEN MITSURUGI-RYŪ ITSELF IS MERE LEGEND FROM THE AGE OF WARLORDS...*
YOU KNOW A LOT. WHAT OF THIS "NISHIWAKI" YOU MENTIONED ...?
WHOA.
IT HAS NOTHING TO DO WITH YOU, SO BACK OFF!
...LOOK, I'M SORRY I HIT YOU. YOU COULDN'T HAVE KNOWN.
.....
RIGHT?
RIGHT?
RIGHT?
BUT THIS IS A KAMIYA CONCERN.
YOU'VE GOT NO PLACE IN IT, WHOEVER YOU MAY BE!!

*"AGE OF WARLORDS" OR "WARRING-STATES PERIOD," A.K.A. SENGOKU JIDAI

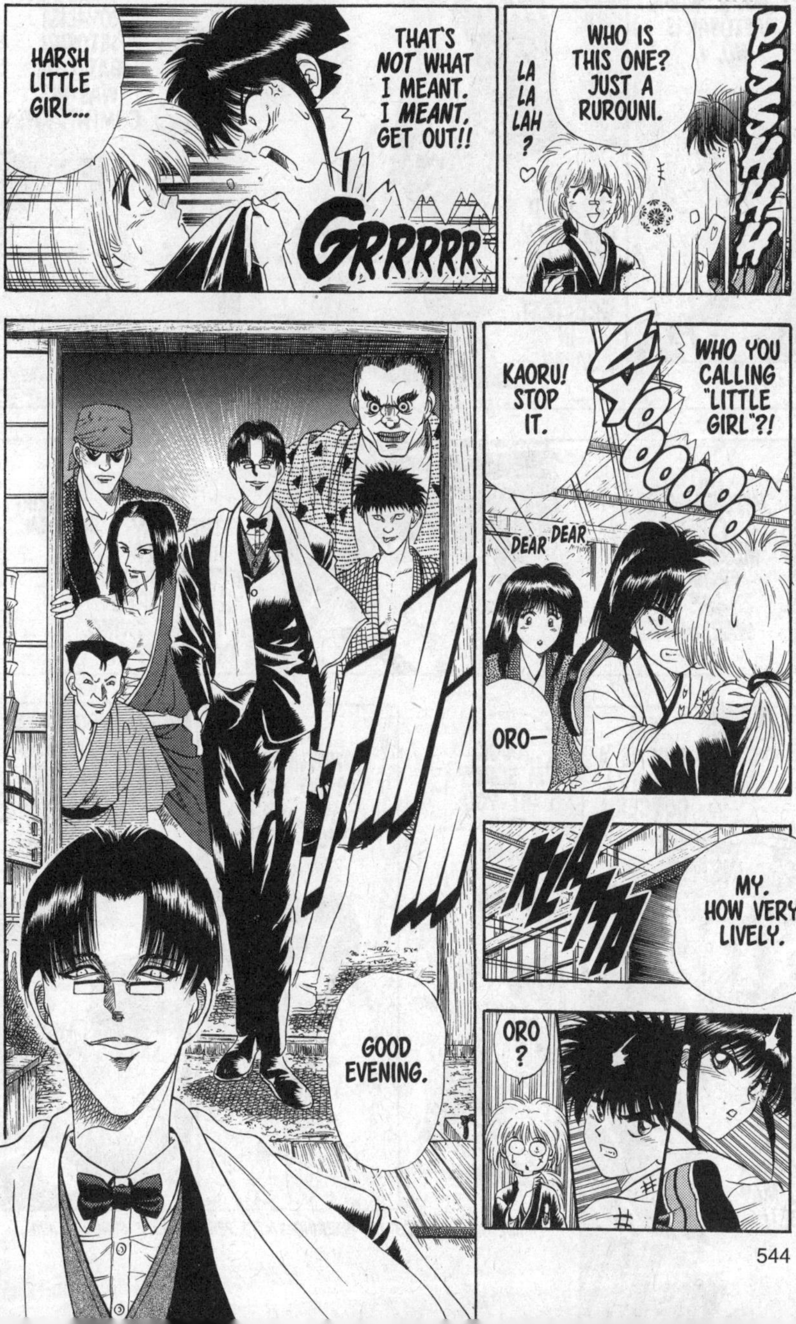
PSSHHH
WHO IS THIS ONE? JUST A RUROUNI.
LA LA LAH ?
THAT'S NOT WHAT I MEANT. I MEANT, GET OUT!!
HARSH LITTLE GIRL...
GRRRRR
WHO YOU CALLING "LITTLE GIRL"?!
GYOOOOOOO
KAORU! STOP IT.
DEAR DEAR
ORO—
MY. HOW VERY LIVELY.
KLAKA
ORO ?
GOOD EVENING.

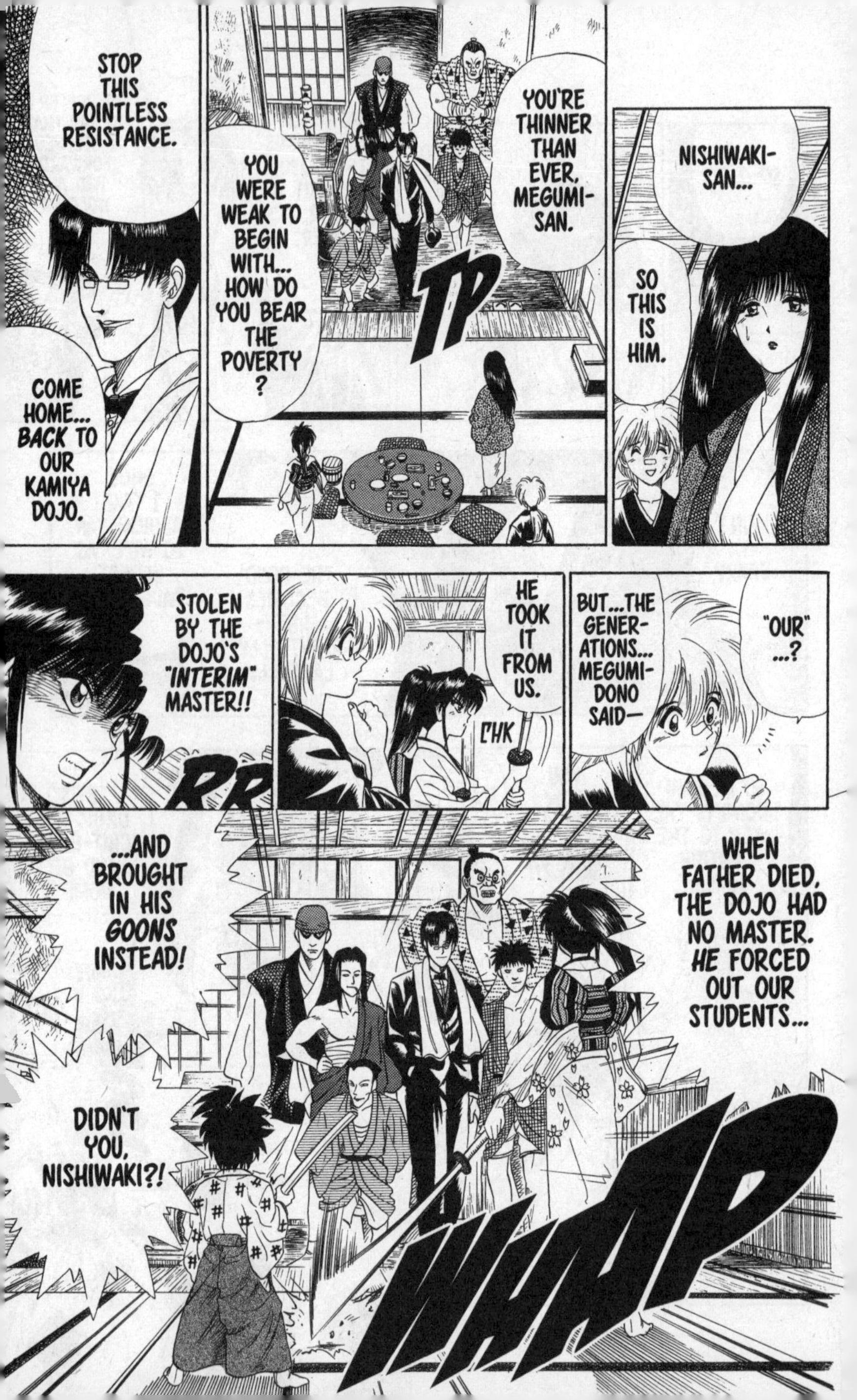
NISHIWAKI-SAN...
SO THIS IS HIM.
YOU'RE THINNER THAN EVER, MEGUMI-SAN.
TP
YOU WERE WEAK TO BEGIN WITH... HOW DO YOU BEAR THE POVERTY?
STOP THIS POINTLESS RESISTANCE.
COME HOME... BACK TO OUR KAMIYA DOJO.
"OUR" ...?
BUT...THE GENERATIONS... MEGUMI-DONO SAID—
HE TOOK IT FROM US.
CHK
STOLEN BY THE DOJO'S "INTERIM" MASTER!!
RR
WHEN FATHER DIED, THE DOJO HAD NO MASTER. HE FORCED OUT OUR STUDENTS...
...AND BROUGHT IN HIS GOONS INSTEAD!
DIDN'T YOU, NISHIWAKI?!
WHAP

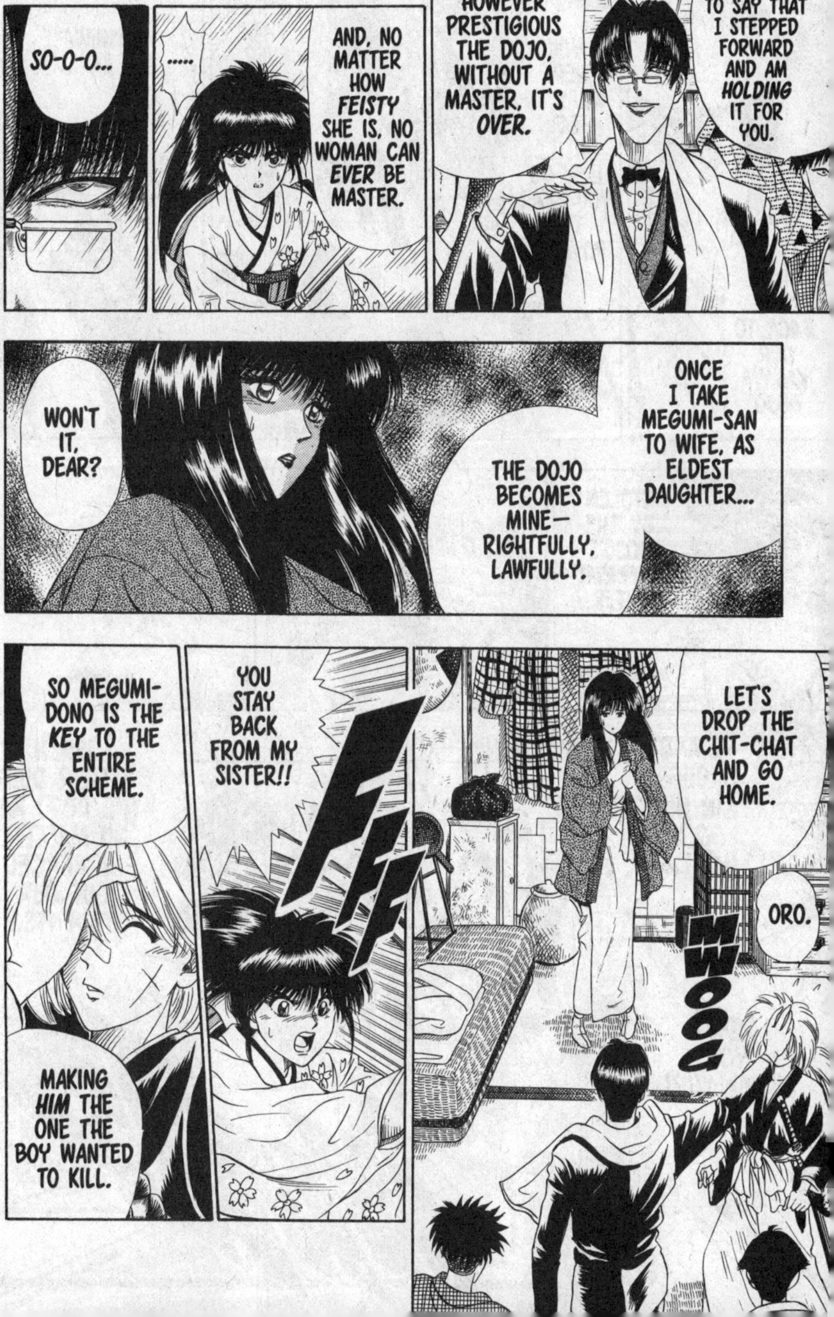
I PREFER TO SAY THAT I STEPPED FORWARD AND AM *HOLDING* IT FOR YOU.
HOWEVER PRESTIGIOUS THE DOJO, WITHOUT A MASTER, IT'S *OVER*.
AND, NO MATTER HOW *FEISTY* SHE IS, NO WOMAN CAN *EVER* BE MASTER.
.....
SO-O-O...
ONCE I TAKE MEGUMI-SAN TO WIFE, AS ELDEST DAUGHTER...
THE DOJO BECOMES MINE— RIGHTFULLY, LAWFULLY.
WON'T IT, DEAR?
LET'S DROP THE CHIT-CHAT AND GO HOME.
MWOOG
ORO.
YOU STAY BACK FROM MY SISTER!!
SO MEGUMI-DONO IS THE *KEY* TO THE ENTIRE SCHEME.
MAKING *HIM* THE ONE THE BOY WANTED TO KILL.

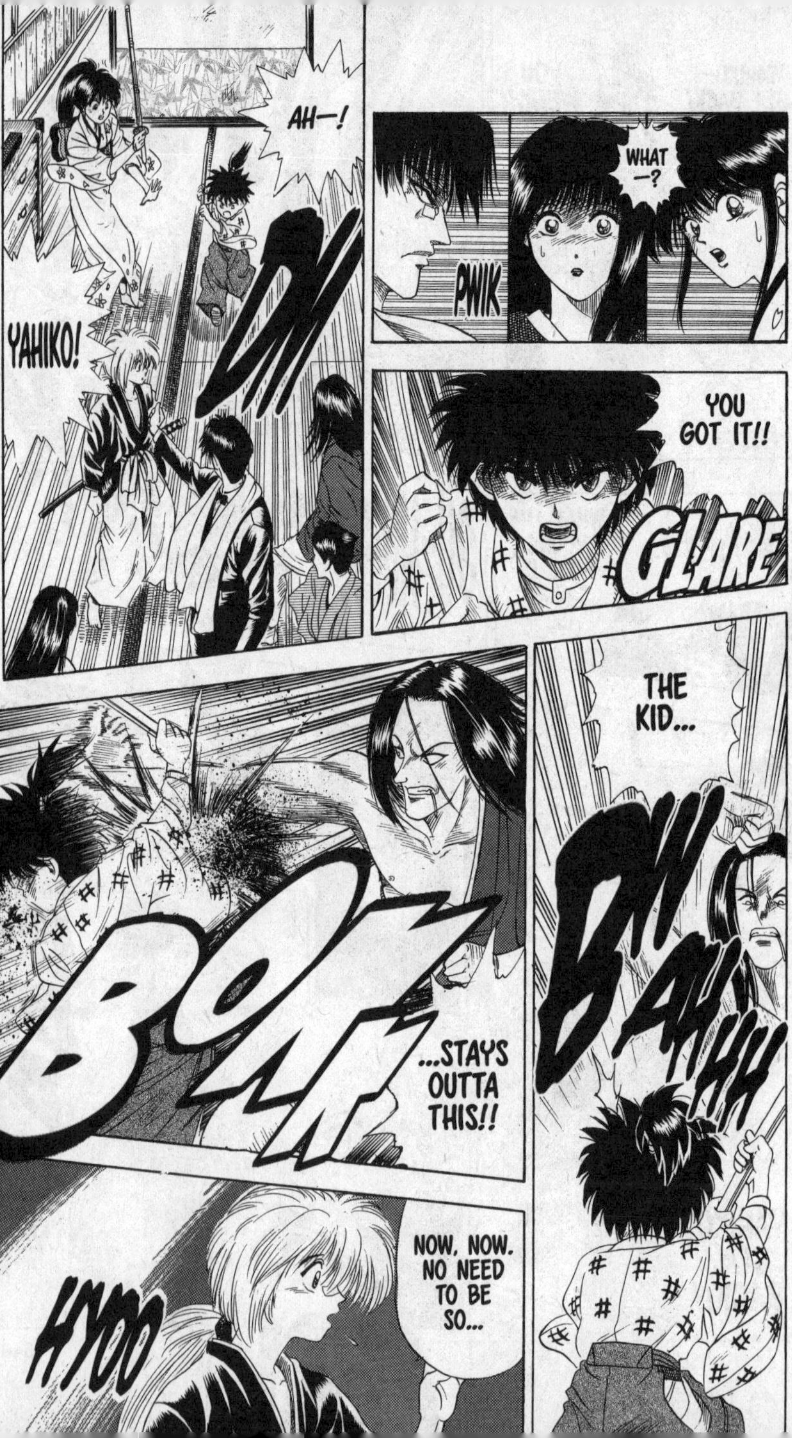
WHAT —?
PWIK
YOU GOT IT!!
GLARE
AH—!
YAHIKO!
THE KID...
...STAYS OUTTA THIS!!
NOW, NOW. NO NEED TO BE SO...
HYOO

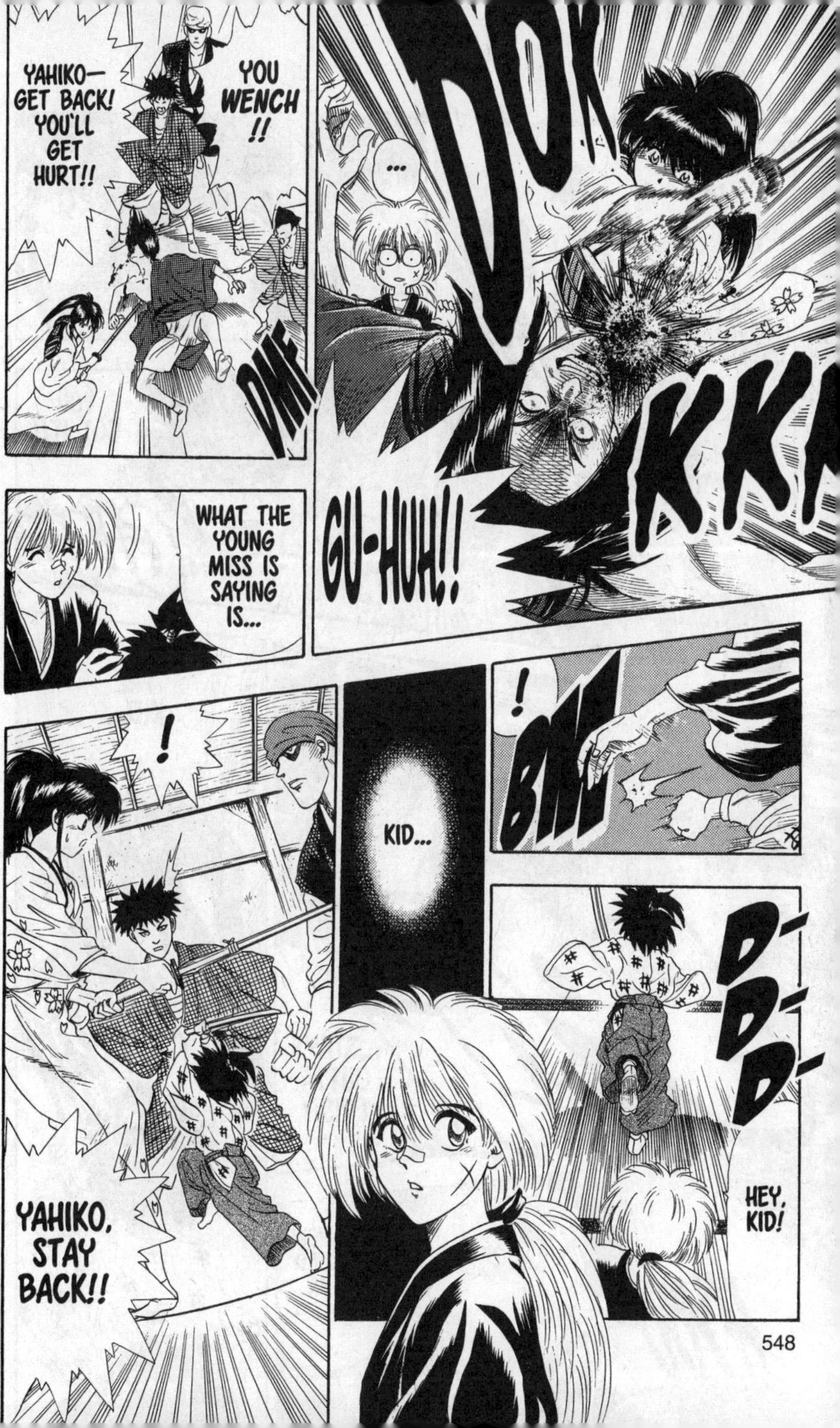
DOK
...
GU-HUH!!
KK
YOU WENCH!!
YAHIKO— GET BACK! YOU'LL GET HURT!!
DMF
WHAT THE YOUNG MISS IS SAYING IS...
!
BAM
D-D-D-
HEY, KID!
KID...
!
YAHIKO, STAY BACK!!

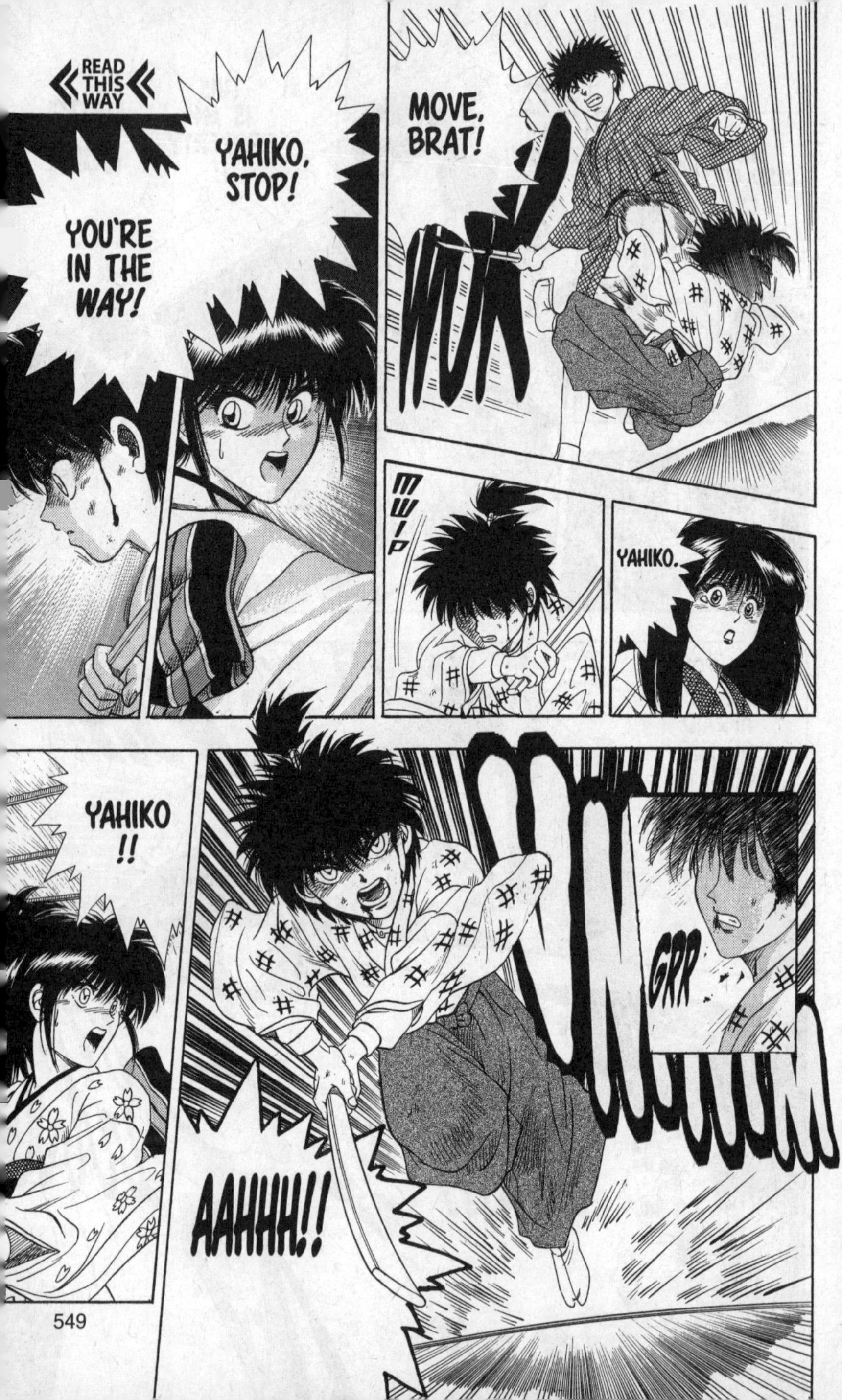
READ THIS WAY
MOVE, BRAT!
YAHIKO.
YAHIKO, STOP!
YOU'RE IN THE WAY!
GRR
AAHHH!!
YAHIKO !!

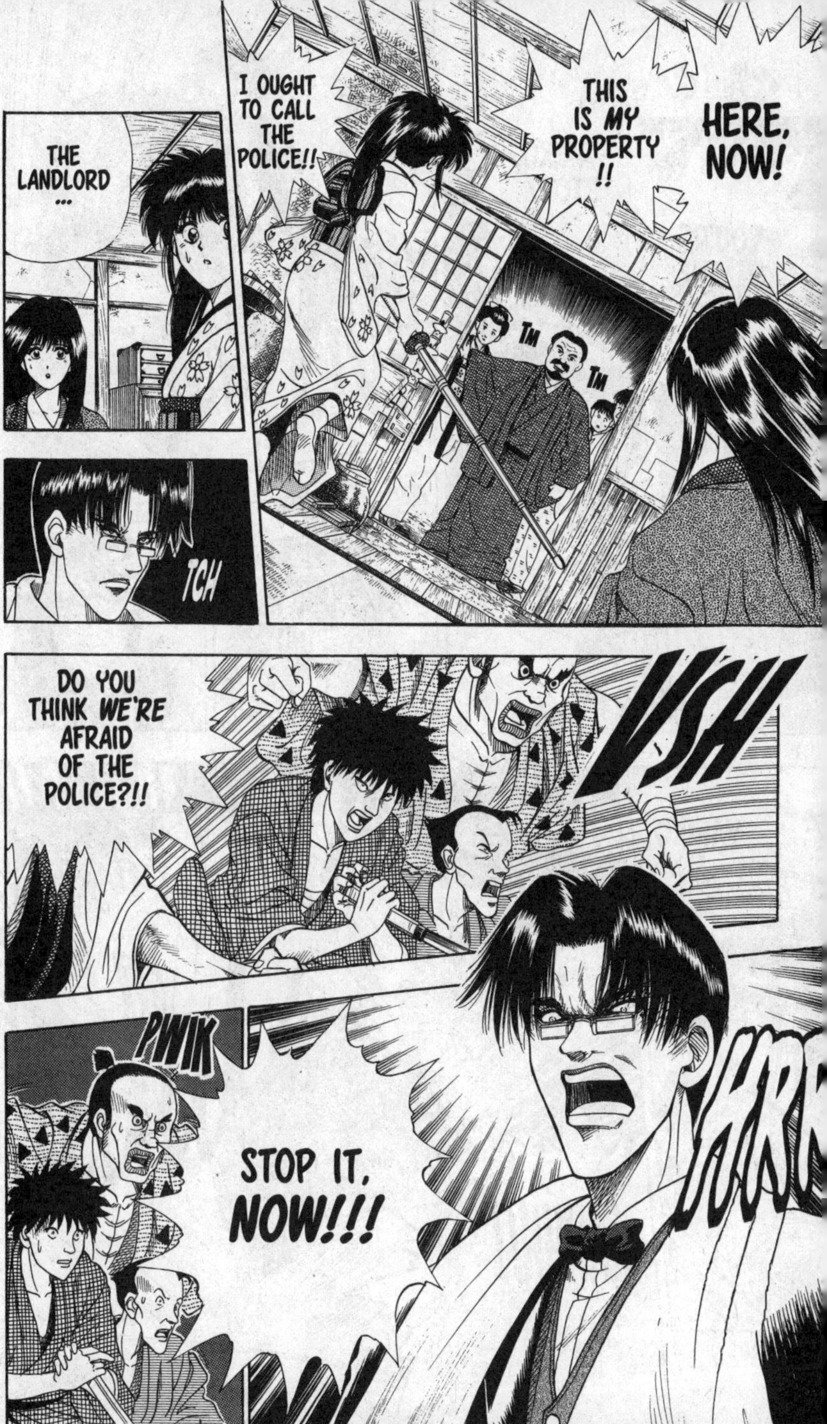
HERE, NOW!
THIS IS MY PROPERTY !!
I OUGHT TO CALL THE POLICE!!
TM
TM
THE LANDLORD ...
TCH
VSH
DO YOU THINK WE'RE AFRAID OF THE POLICE?!!
STOP IT, NOW!!!
PWIK

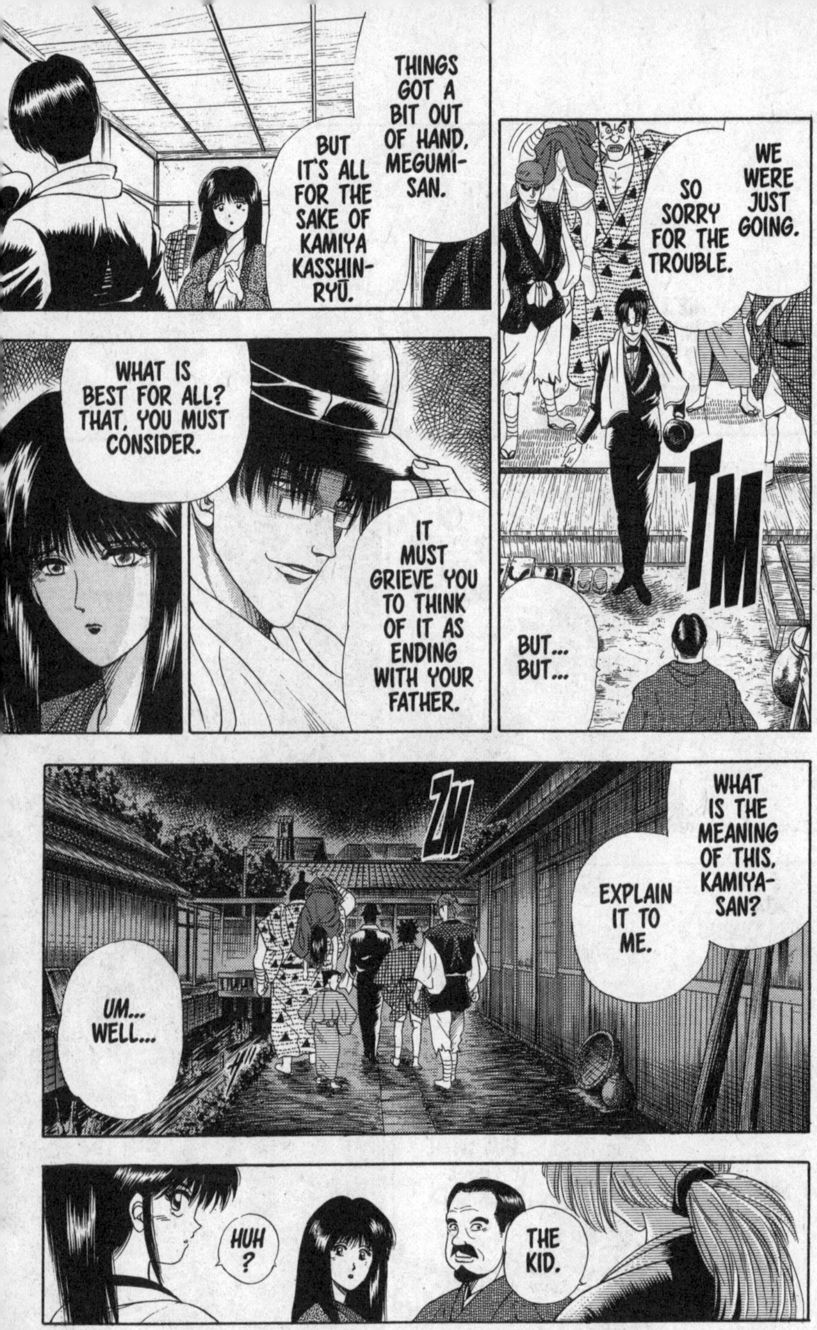
THINGS GOT A BIT OUT OF HAND, MEGUMI-SAN.
BUT IT'S ALL FOR THE SAKE OF KAMIYA KASSHIN-RYŪ.
IT MUST GRIEVE YOU TO THINK OF IT AS ENDING WITH YOUR FATHER.
WHAT IS BEST FOR ALL? THAT, YOU MUST CONSIDER.
WE WERE JUST GOING.
SO SORRY FOR THE TROUBLE.
TM
BUT... BUT...
ZM
WHAT IS THE MEANING OF THIS, KAMIYA-SAN?
EXPLAIN IT TO ME.
UM... WELL...
THE KID.
HUH?

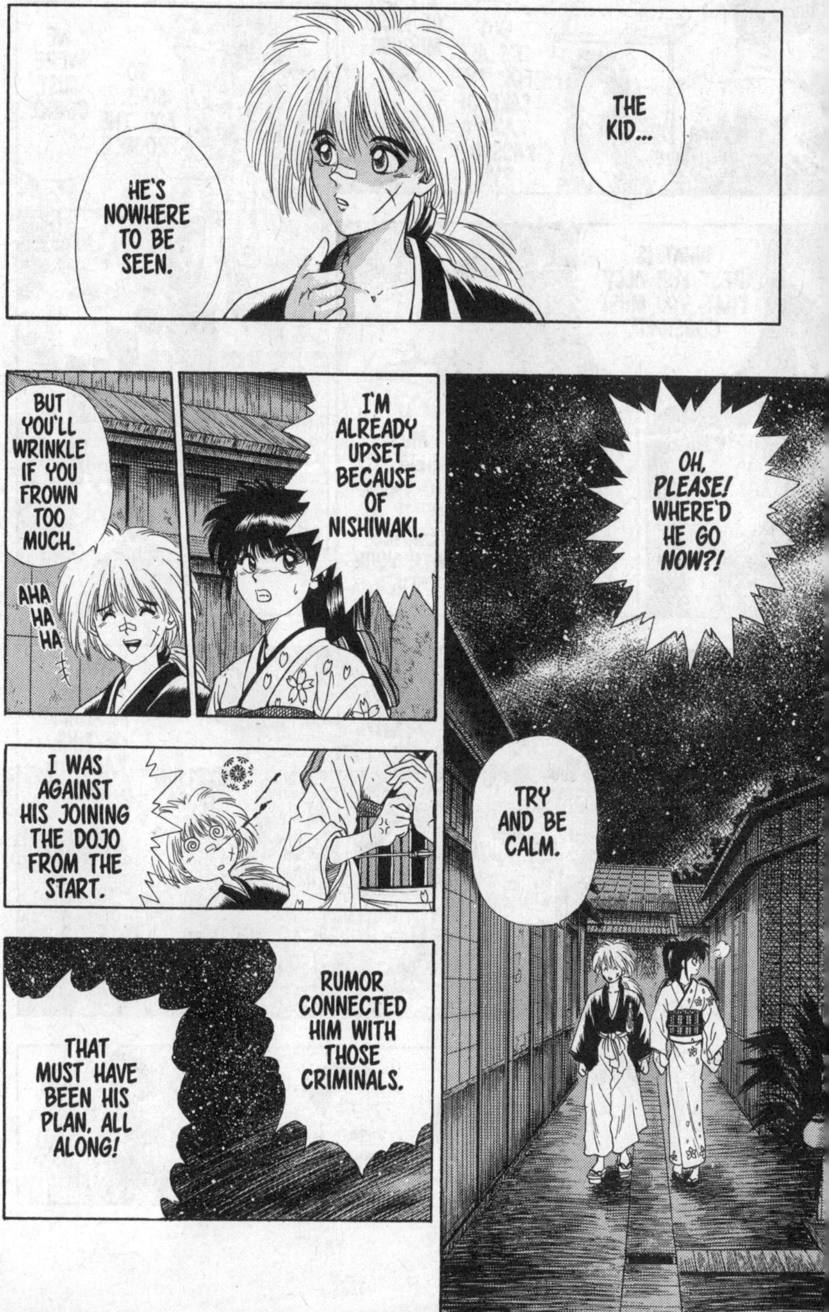
THE KID...
HE'S NOWHERE TO BE SEEN.
OH, PLEASE! WHERE'D HE GO NOW?!
TRY AND BE CALM.
I'M ALREADY UPSET BECAUSE OF NISHIWAKI.
BUT YOU'LL WRINKLE IF YOU FROWN TOO MUCH.
AHA HA HA
I WAS AGAINST HIS JOINING THE DOJO FROM THE START.
RUMOR CONNECTED HIM WITH THOSE CRIMINALS.
THAT MUST HAVE BEEN HIS PLAN, ALL ALONG!

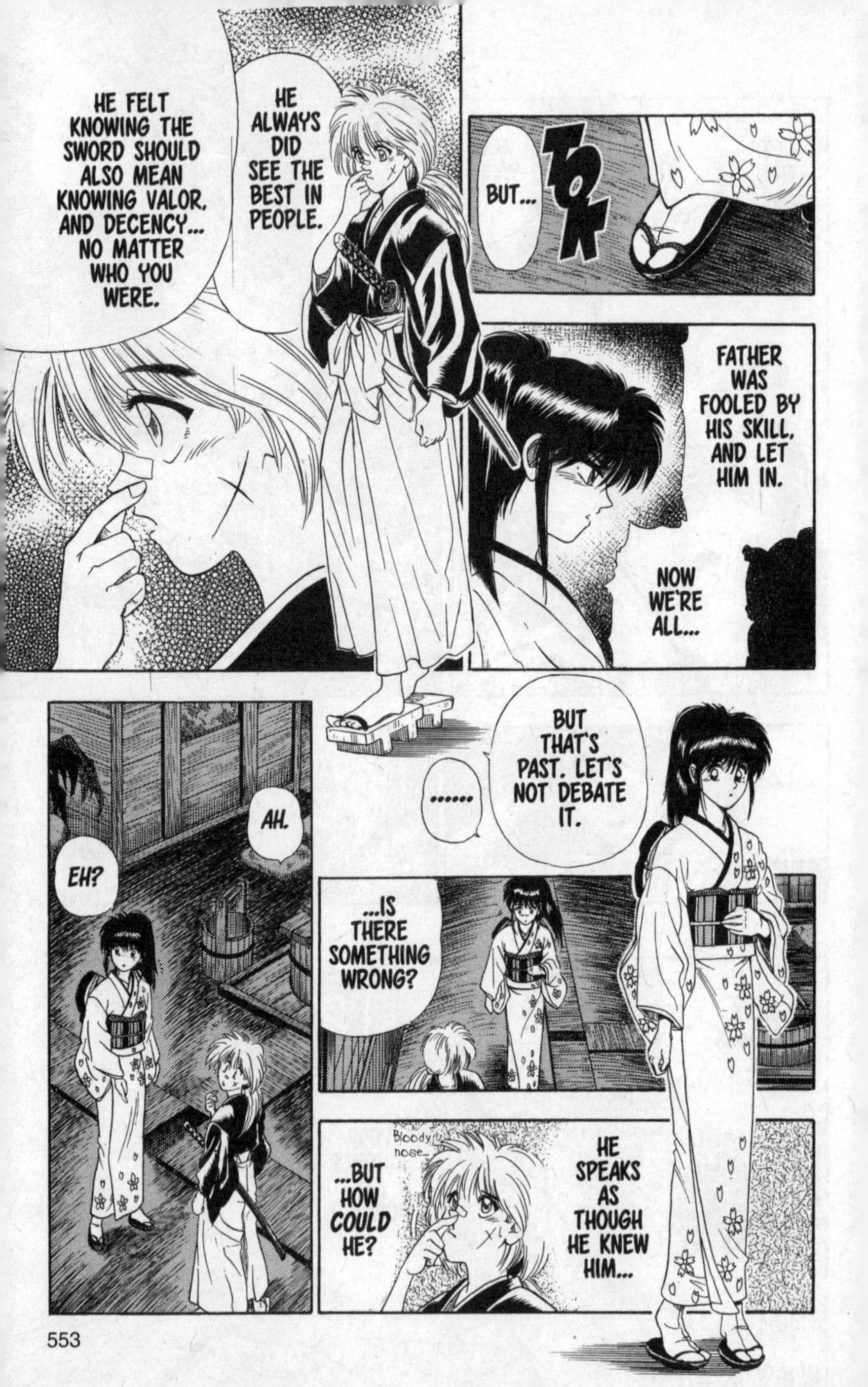
BUT...
TOK
FATHER WAS FOOLED BY HIS SKILL, AND LET HIM IN.
NOW WE'RE ALL...
HE ALWAYS DID SEE THE BEST IN PEOPLE.
HE FELT KNOWING THE SWORD SHOULD ALSO MEAN KNOWING VALOR, AND DECENCY... NO MATTER WHO YOU WERE.
BUT THAT'S PAST. LET'S NOT DEBATE IT.
......
...IS THERE SOMETHING WRONG?
HE SPEAKS AS THOUGH HE KNEW HIM...
Bloody nose...
...BUT HOW COULD HE?
AH.
EH?

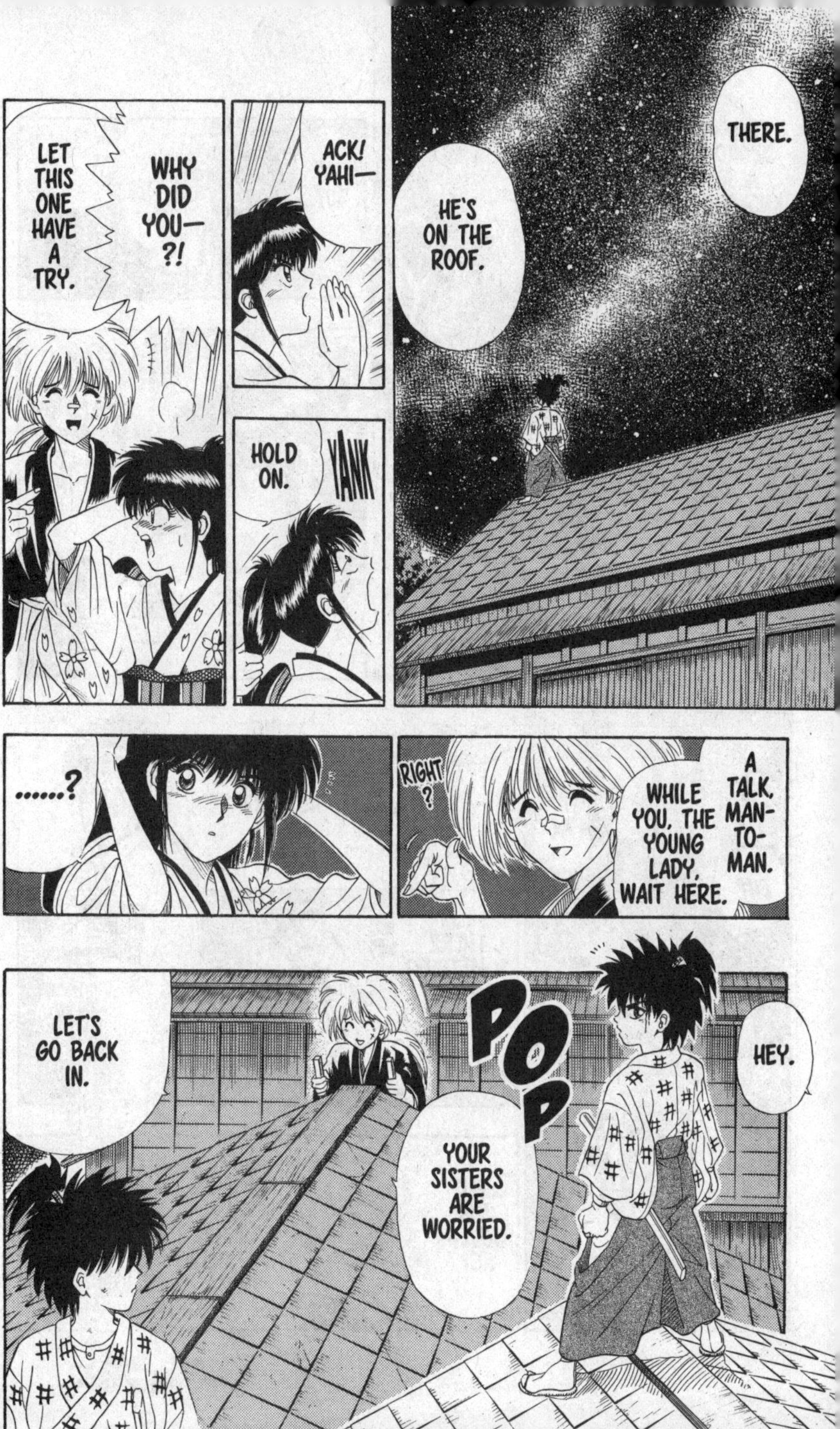
THERE.
HE'S ON THE ROOF.
ACK! YAHI—
HOLD ON.
YANK
WHY DID YOU—?!
LET THIS ONE HAVE A TRY.
A TALK, MAN-TO-MAN.
WHILE YOU, THE YOUNG LADY, WAIT HERE.
RIGHT?
......?
HEY.
POP
YOUR SISTERS ARE WORRIED.
LET'S GO BACK IN.

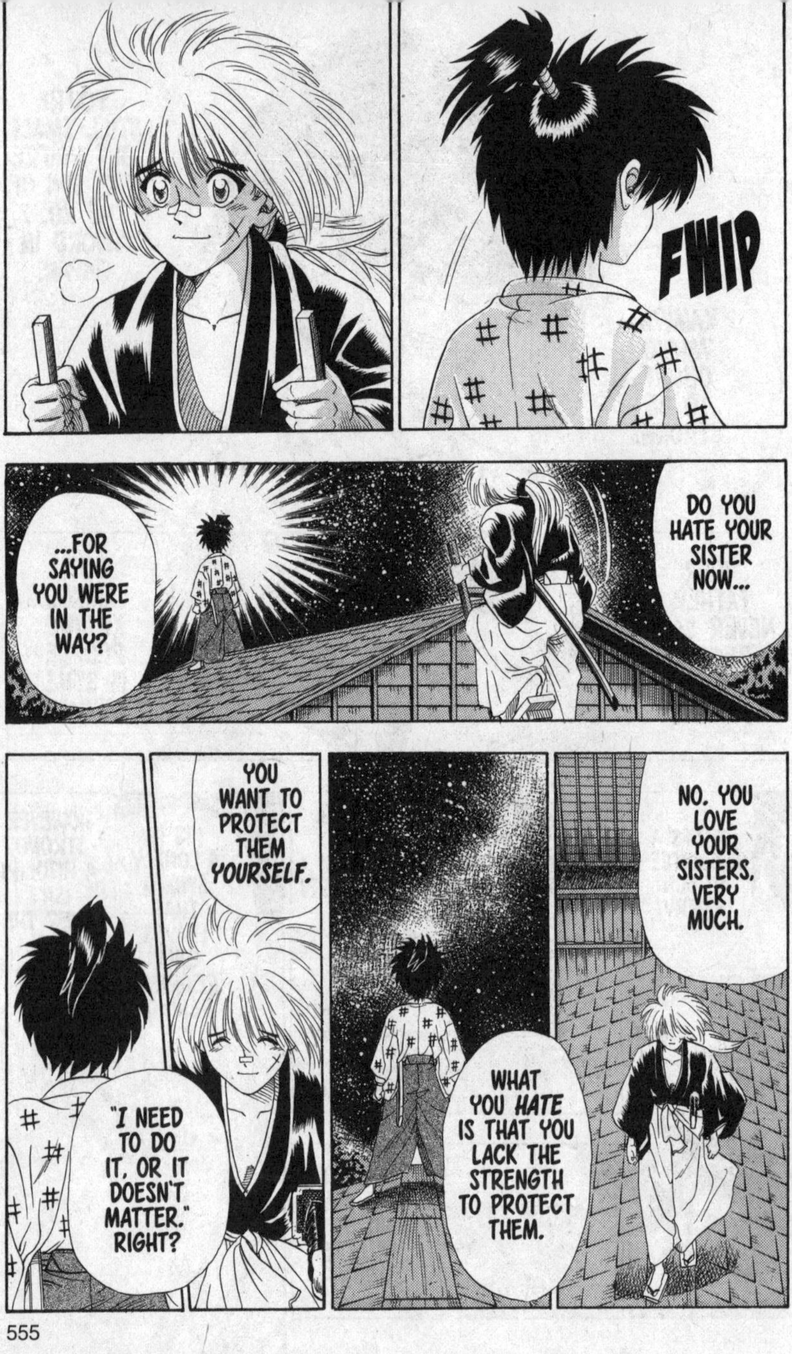
FWIP
DO YOU HATE YOUR SISTER NOW...
...FOR SAYING YOU WERE IN THE WAY?
NO. YOU LOVE YOUR SISTERS, VERY MUCH.
WHAT YOU *HATE* IS THAT YOU LACK THE STRENGTH TO PROTECT THEM.
YOU WANT TO PROTECT THEM *YOURSELF*.
"I NEED TO DO IT, OR IT DOESN'T MATTER." RIGHT?

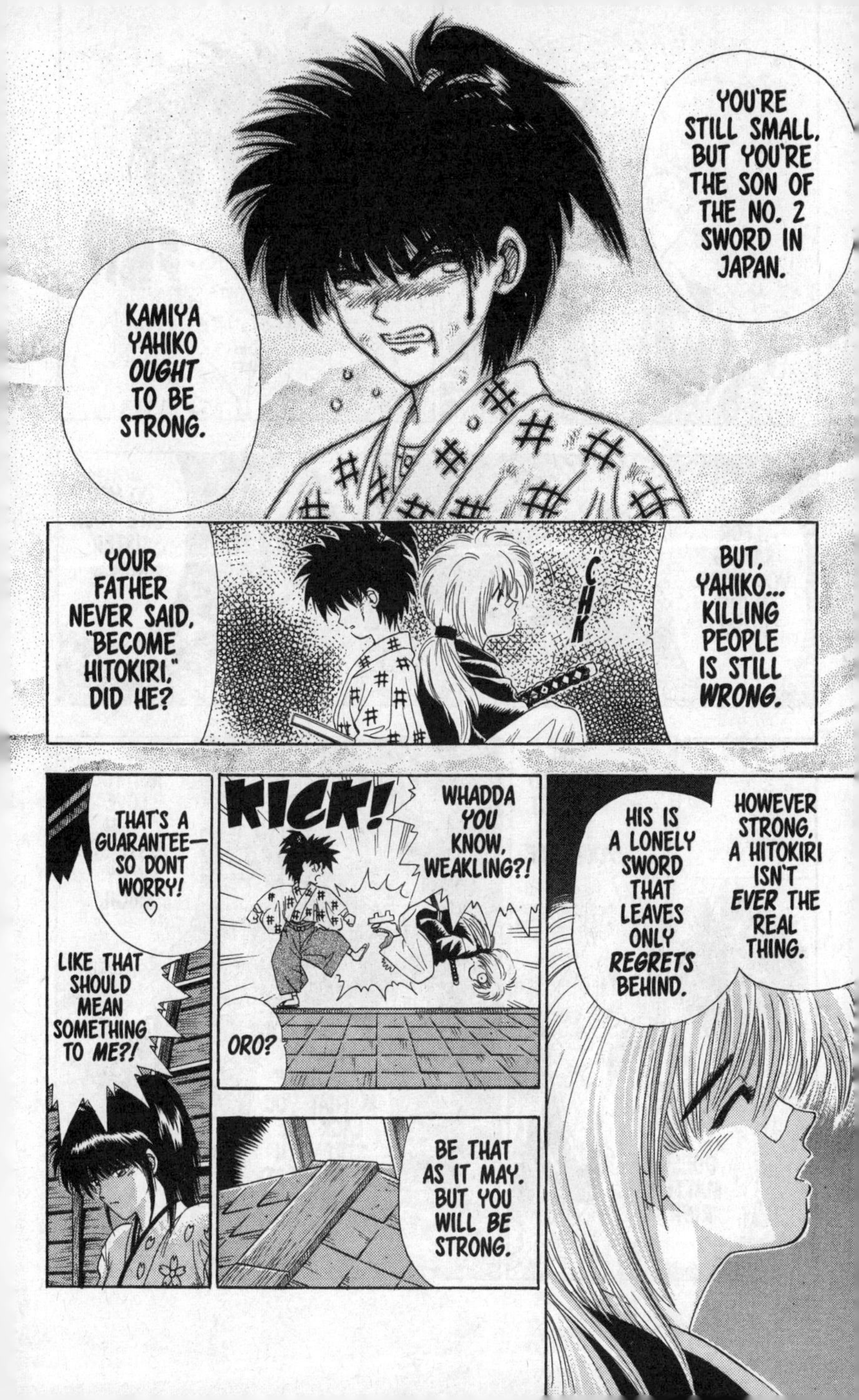
YOU'RE STILL SMALL, BUT YOU'RE THE SON OF THE NO. 2 SWORD IN JAPAN.
KAMIYA YAHIKO OUGHT TO BE STRONG.
BUT, YAHIKO... KILLING PEOPLE IS STILL WRONG.
CHK
YOUR FATHER NEVER SAID, "BECOME HITOKIRI," DID HE?
HOWEVER STRONG, A HITOKIRI ISN'T EVER THE REAL THING.
HIS IS A LONELY SWORD THAT LEAVES ONLY REGRETS BEHIND.
KICK!
WHADDA YOU KNOW, WEAKLING?!
ORO?
BE THAT AS IT MAY. BUT YOU WILL BE STRONG.
THAT'S A GUARANTEE— SO DONT WORRY! ♡
LIKE THAT SHOULD MEAN SOMETHING TO ME?!

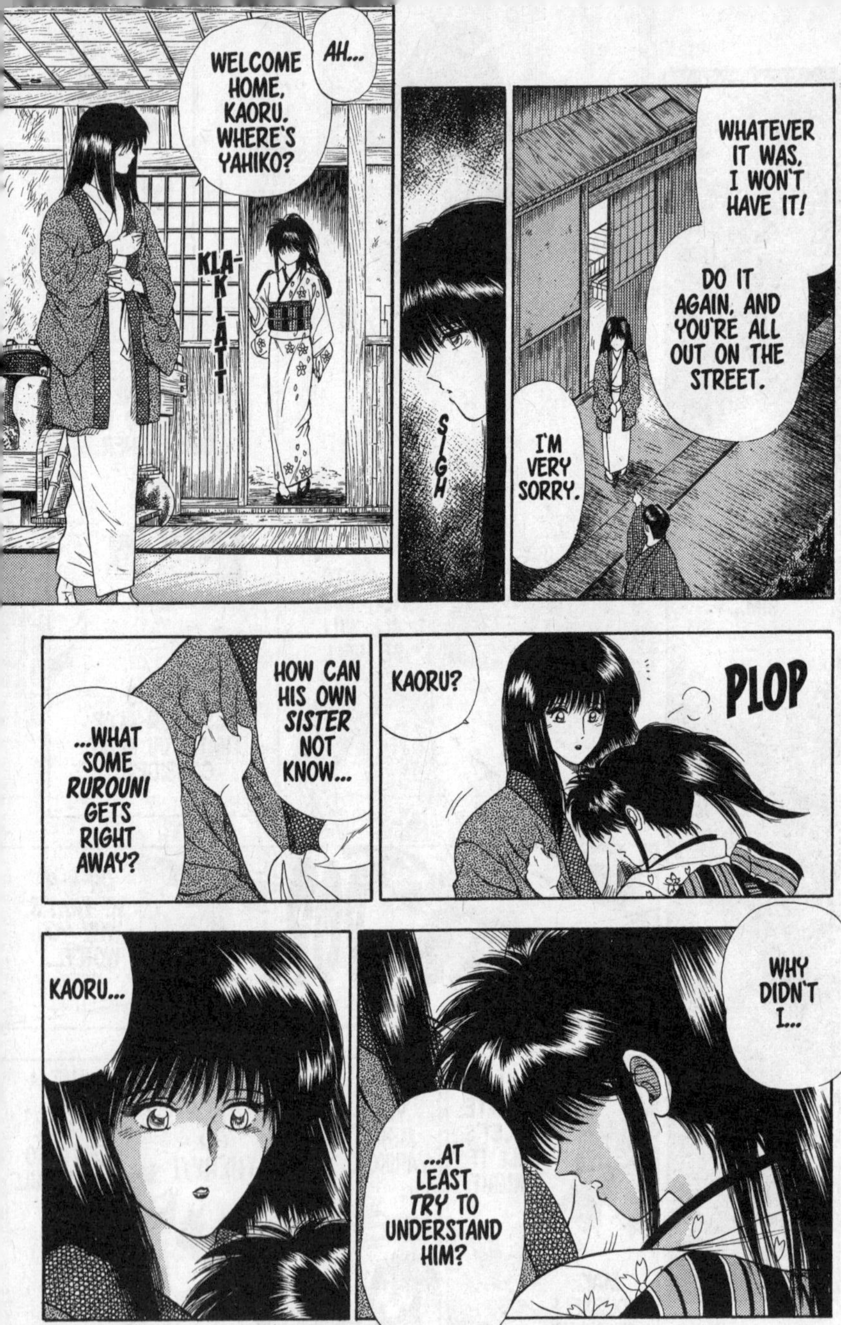
WHATEVER IT WAS, I WON'T HAVE IT!
DO IT AGAIN, AND YOU'RE ALL OUT ON THE STREET.
I'M VERY SORRY.
SIGH
AH...
WELCOME HOME, KAORU. WHERE'S YAHIKO?
KLA-K-KLATT
PLOP
KAORU?
HOW CAN HIS OWN *SISTER* NOT KNOW...
...WHAT SOME *RUROUNI* GETS RIGHT AWAY?
WHY DIDN'T I...
...AT LEAST *TRY* TO UNDERSTAND HIM?
KAORU...

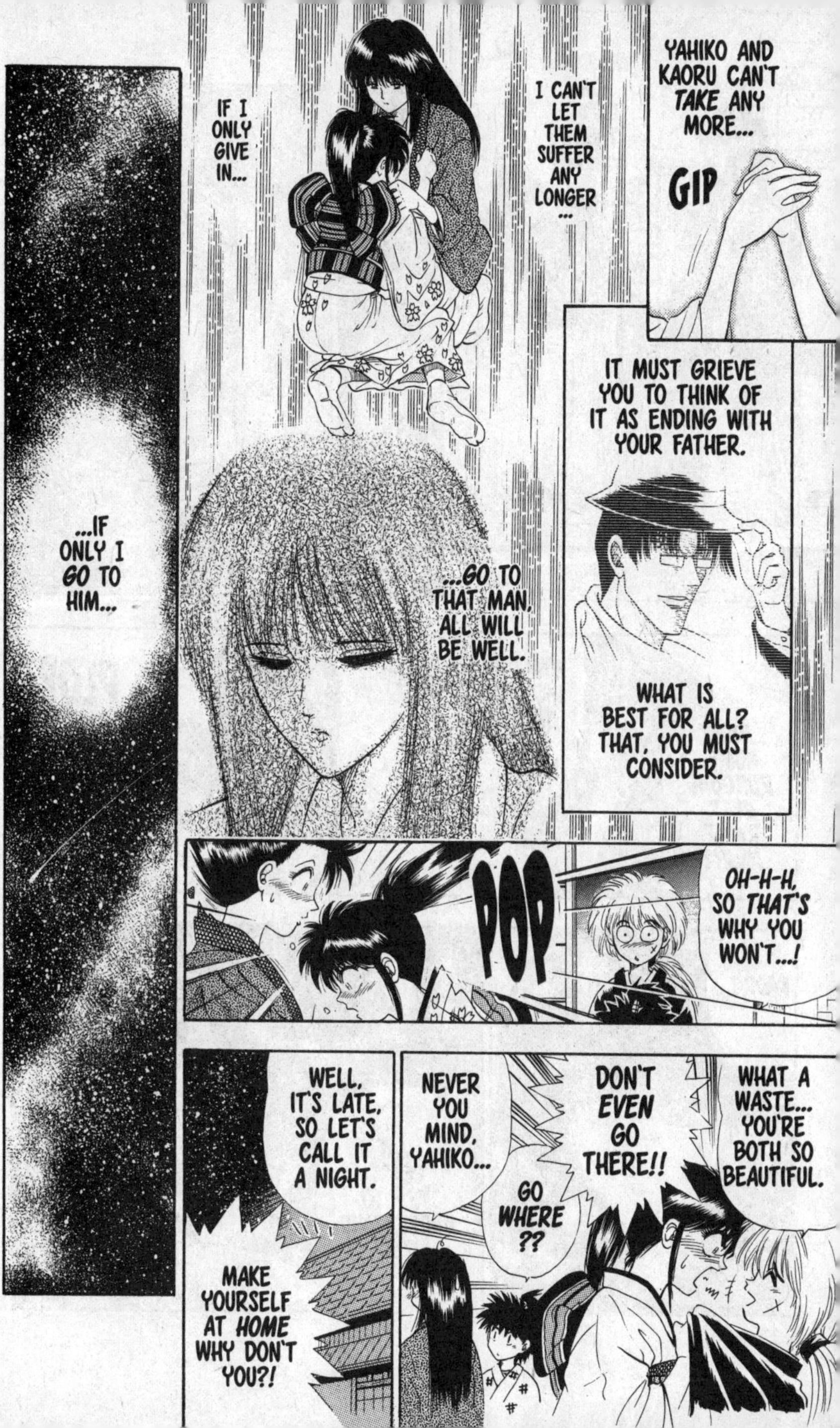
YAHIKO AND KAORU CAN'T TAKE ANY MORE...
GIP
I CAN'T LET THEM SUFFER ANY LONGER...
IF I ONLY GIVE IN...
IT MUST GRIEVE YOU TO THINK OF IT AS ENDING WITH YOUR FATHER.
WHAT IS BEST FOR ALL? THAT, YOU MUST CONSIDER.
...GO TO THAT MAN, ALL WILL BE WELL.
OH-H-H, SO THAT'S WHY YOU WON'T...!
POP
WHAT A WASTE... YOU'RE BOTH SO BEAUTIFUL.
DON'T EVEN GO THERE!!
NEVER YOU MIND, YAHIKO...
GO WHERE ??
WELL, IT'S LATE, SO LET'S CALL IT A NIGHT.
MAKE YOURSELF AT HOME WHY DON'T YOU?!
...IF ONLY I GO TO HIM...

READ THIS WAY

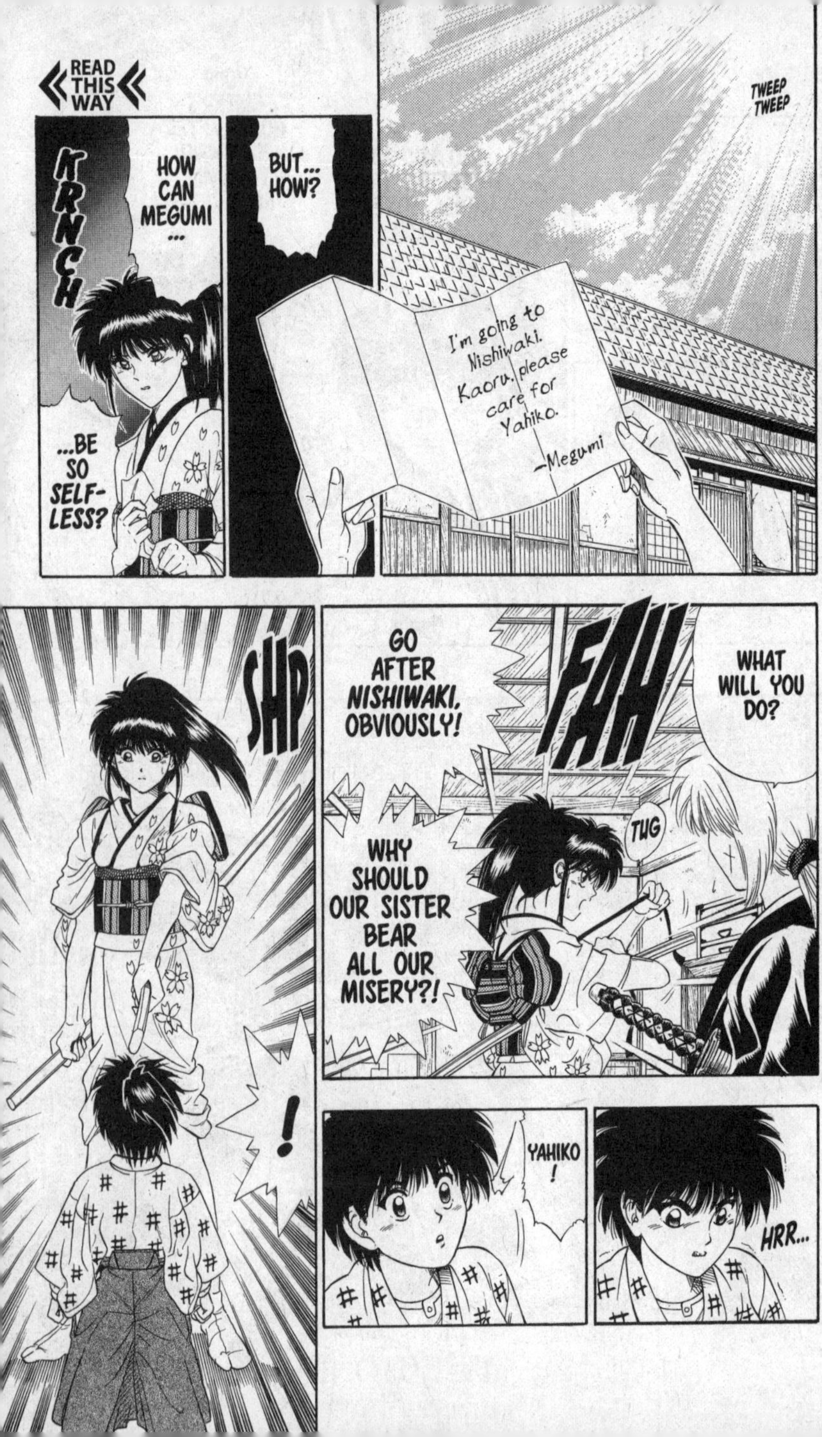

TWEEP TWEEP
I'm going to Nishiwaki. Kaoru, please care for Yahiko.
—Megumi
BUT... HOW?
HOW CAN MEGUMI...
KRNCH
...BE SO SELF-LESS?
WHAT WILL YOU DO?
FAH
GO AFTER NISHIWAKI, OBVIOUSLY!
TUG
WHY SHOULD OUR SISTER BEAR ALL OUR MISERY?!
HRR...
YAHIKO!
SHP
!

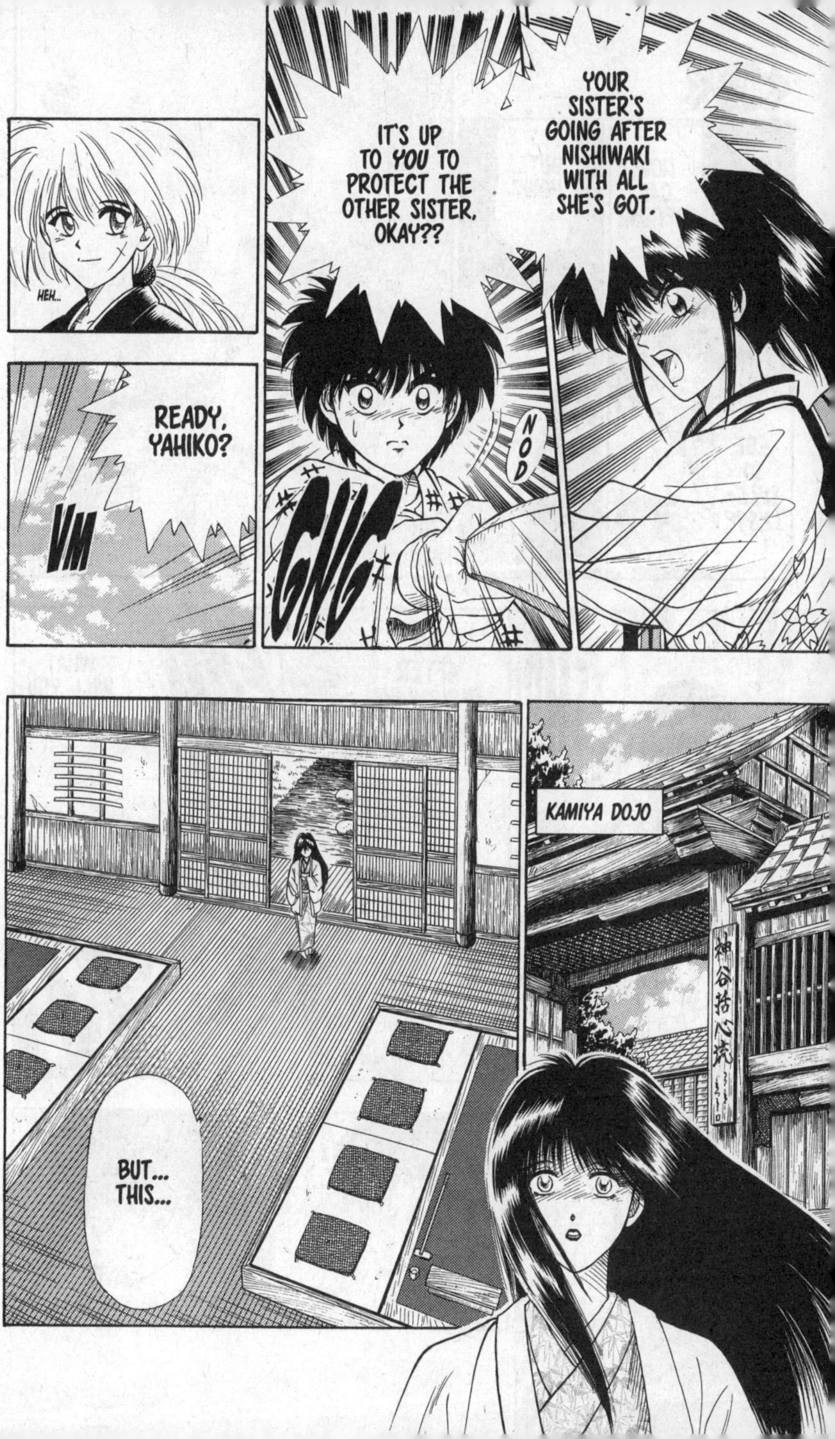
YOUR SISTER'S GOING AFTER NISHIWAKI WITH ALL SHE'S GOT.
IT'S UP TO *YOU* TO PROTECT THE OTHER SISTER, OKAY??
NOD
GNG
HEH...
READY, YAHIKO?
VM
KAMIYA DOJO
神谷活心流
BUT... THIS...

READ THIS WAY

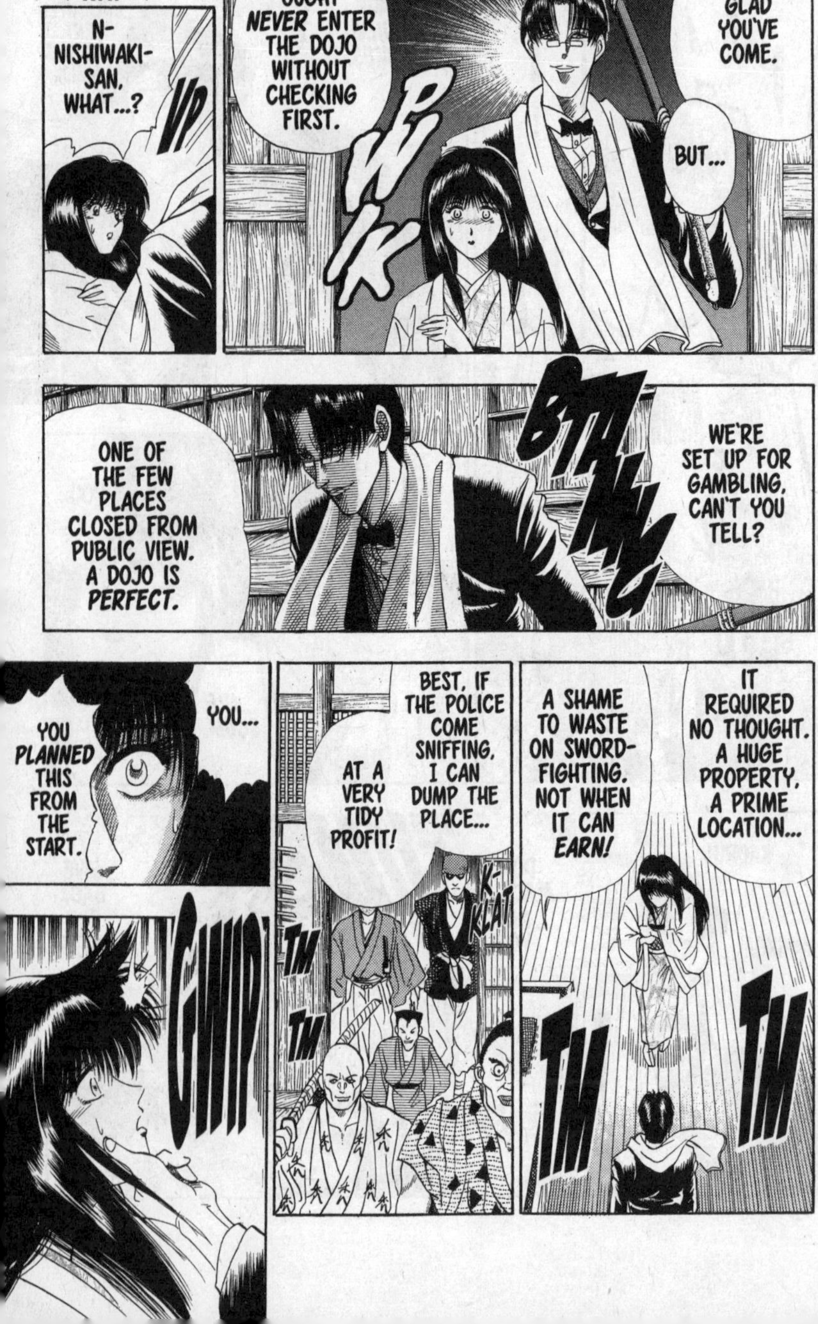
SO GLAD YOU'VE COME.
BUT...
...YOU OUGHT *NEVER* ENTER THE DOJO WITHOUT CHECKING FIRST.
PWIK
N-NISHIWAKI-SAN, WHAT...?
VP
WE'RE SET UP FOR GAMBLING, CAN'T YOU TELL?
ONE OF THE FEW PLACES CLOSED FROM PUBLIC VIEW. A DOJO IS *PERFECT.*
IT REQUIRED NO THOUGHT. A HUGE PROPERTY, A PRIME LOCATION...
A SHAME TO WASTE ON SWORD-FIGHTING. NOT WHEN IT CAN *EARN!*
TM
TM
BEST, IF THE POLICE COME SNIFFING, I CAN DUMP THE PLACE...
AT A VERY TIDY PROFIT!
K-KLAT
TM
TM
YOU...
YOU *PLANNED* THIS FROM THE START.

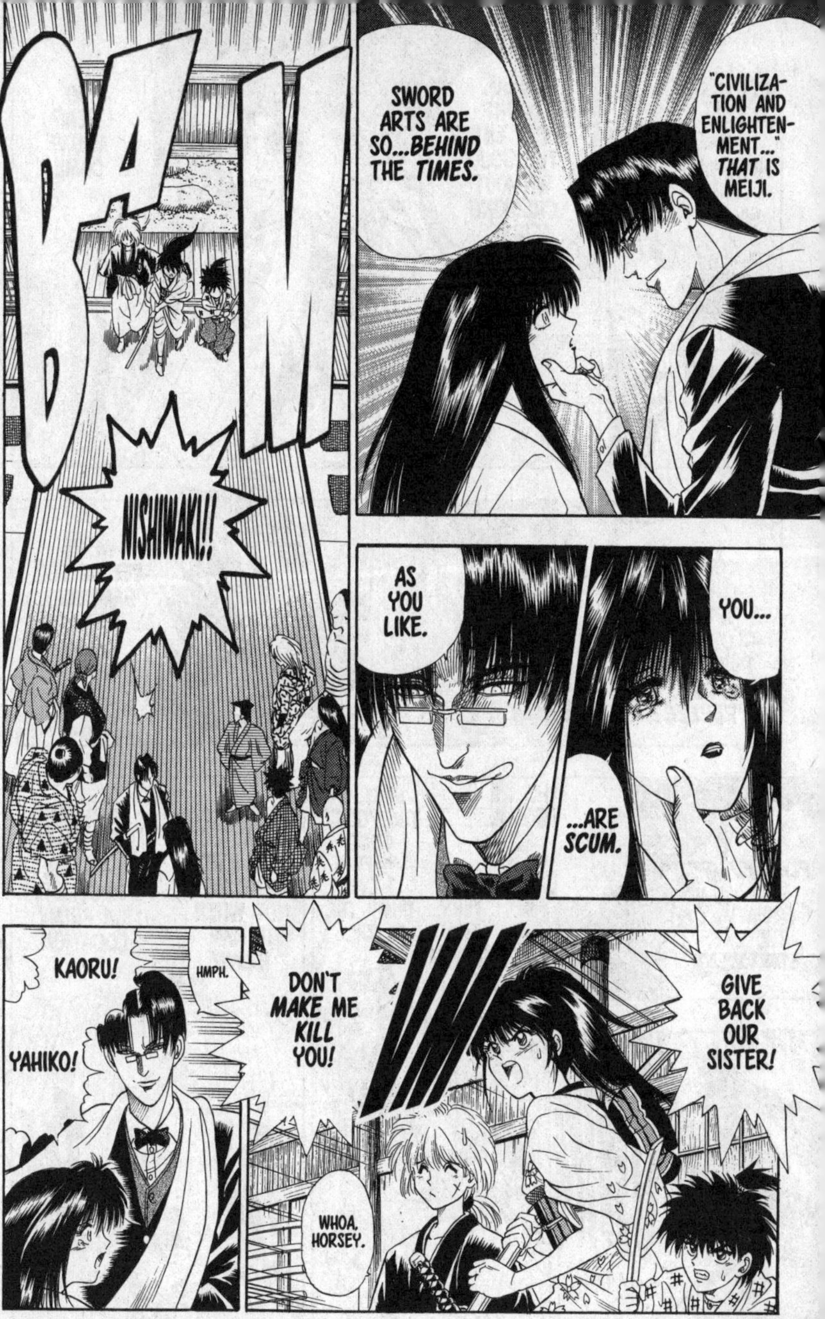
"CIVILIZATION AND ENLIGHTENMENT..." THAT IS MEIJI.
SWORD ARTS ARE SO...BEHIND THE TIMES.
YOU...
...ARE SCUM.
AS YOU LIKE.
BAM!
NISHIWAKI!!
GIVE BACK OUR SISTER!
WHOA. HORSEY.
DON'T MAKE ME KILL YOU!
HMPH.
KAORU!
YAHIKO!

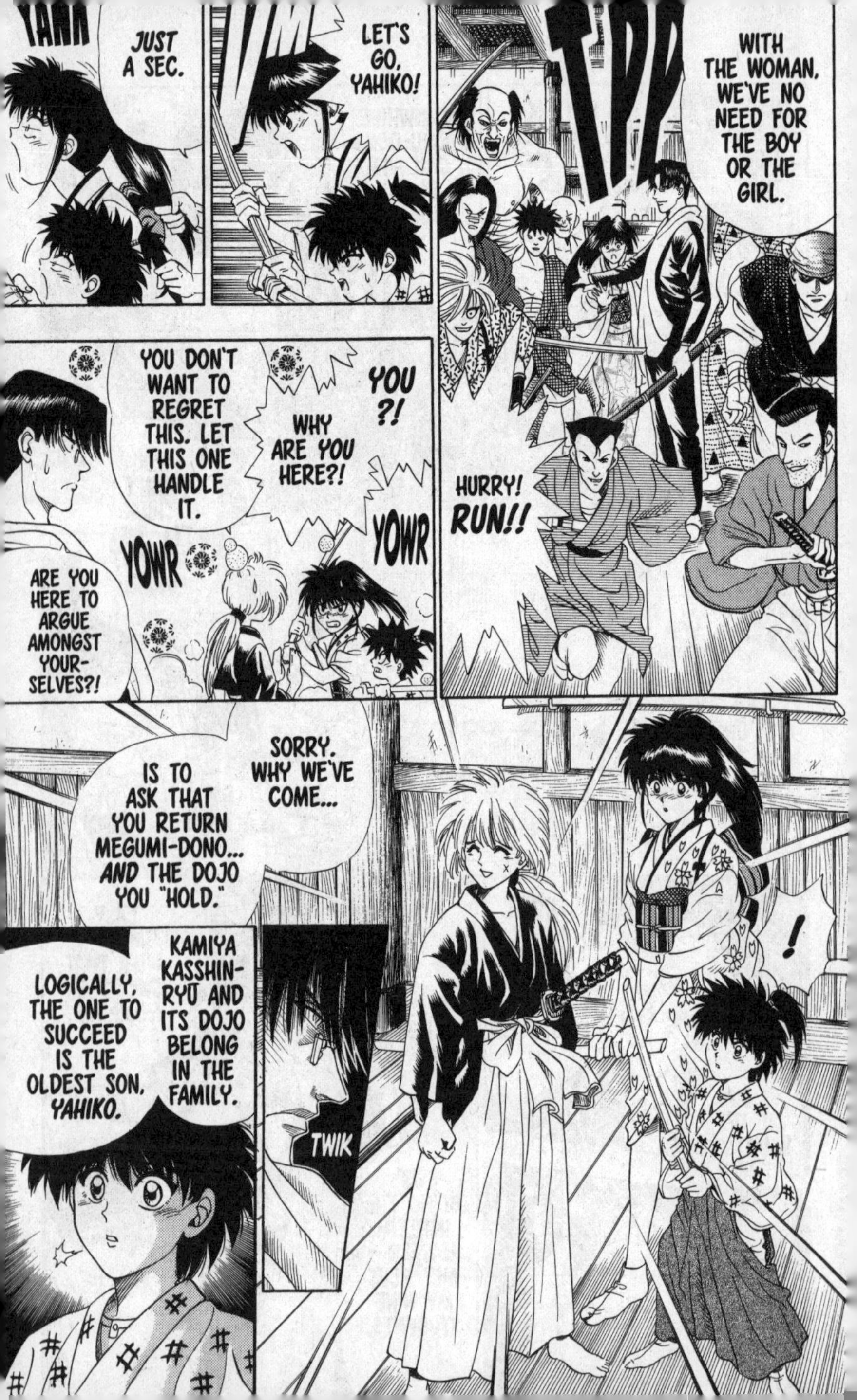

WITH THE WOMAN, WE'VE NO NEED FOR THE BOY OR THE GIRL.
HURRY! RUN!!
LET'S GO, YAHIKO!
JUST A SEC.
YOU?!
WHY ARE YOU HERE?!
YOWR
YOU DON'T WANT TO REGRET THIS. LET THIS ONE HANDLE IT.
YOWR
ARE YOU HERE TO ARGUE AMONGST YOURSELVES?!
SORRY. WHY WE'VE COME...
IS TO ASK THAT YOU RETURN MEGUMI-DONO... AND THE DOJO YOU "HOLD."
!
KAMIYA KASSHIN-RYŪ AND ITS DOJO BELONG IN THE FAMILY.
TWIK
LOGICALLY, THE ONE TO SUCCEED IS THE OLDEST SON, YAHIKO.

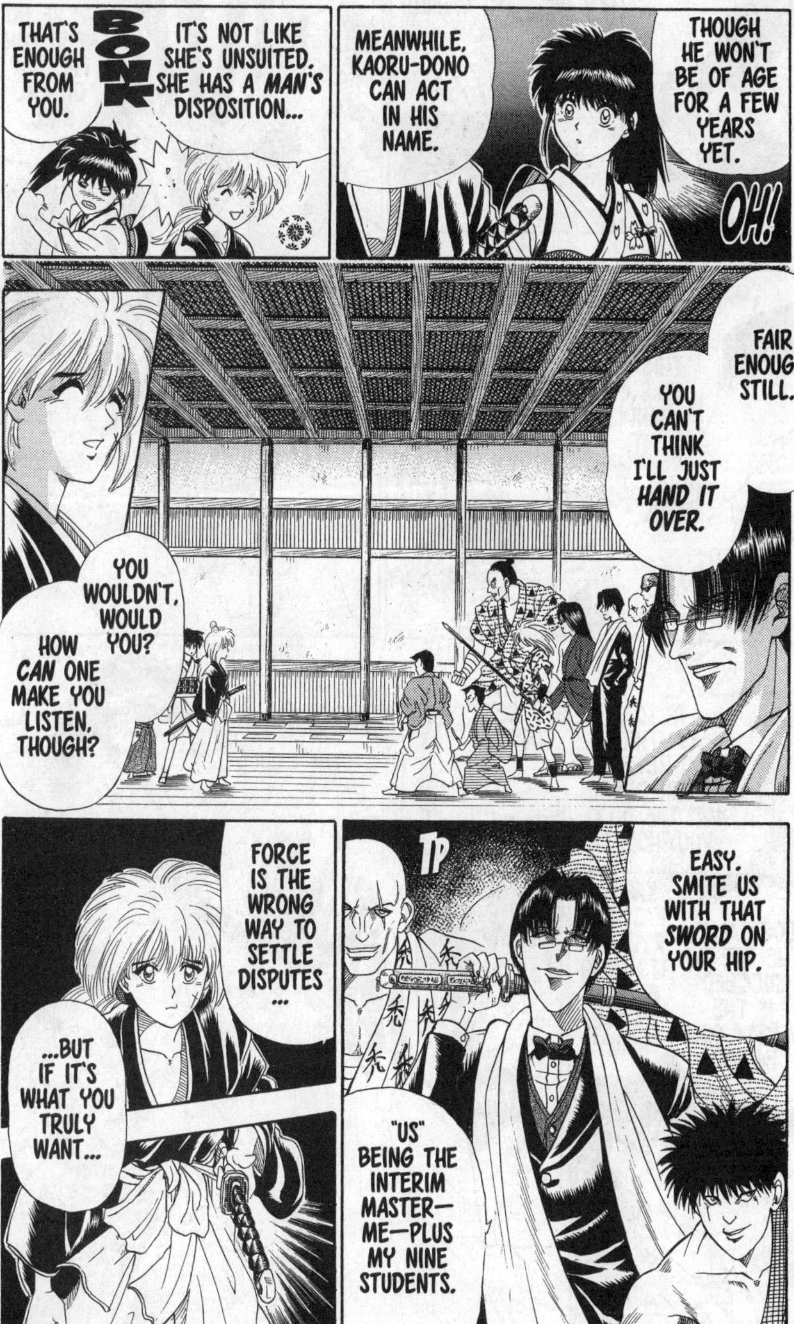
THOUGH HE WON'T BE OF AGE FOR A FEW YEARS YET.
MEANWHILE, KAORU-DONO CAN ACT IN HIS NAME.
OH!
IT'S NOT LIKE SHE'S UNSUITED. SHE HAS A MAN'S DISPOSITION...
BONK
THAT'S ENOUGH FROM YOU.
FAIR ENOUGH. STILL...
YOU CAN'T THINK I'LL JUST HAND IT OVER.
YOU WOULDN'T, WOULD YOU?
HOW CAN ONE MAKE YOU LISTEN, THOUGH?
TP
EASY. SMITE US WITH THAT SWORD ON YOUR HIP.
"US" BEING THE INTERIM MASTER—ME—PLUS MY NINE STUDENTS.
FORCE IS THE WRONG WAY TO SETTLE DISPUTES...
...BUT IF IT'S WHAT YOU TRULY WANT...

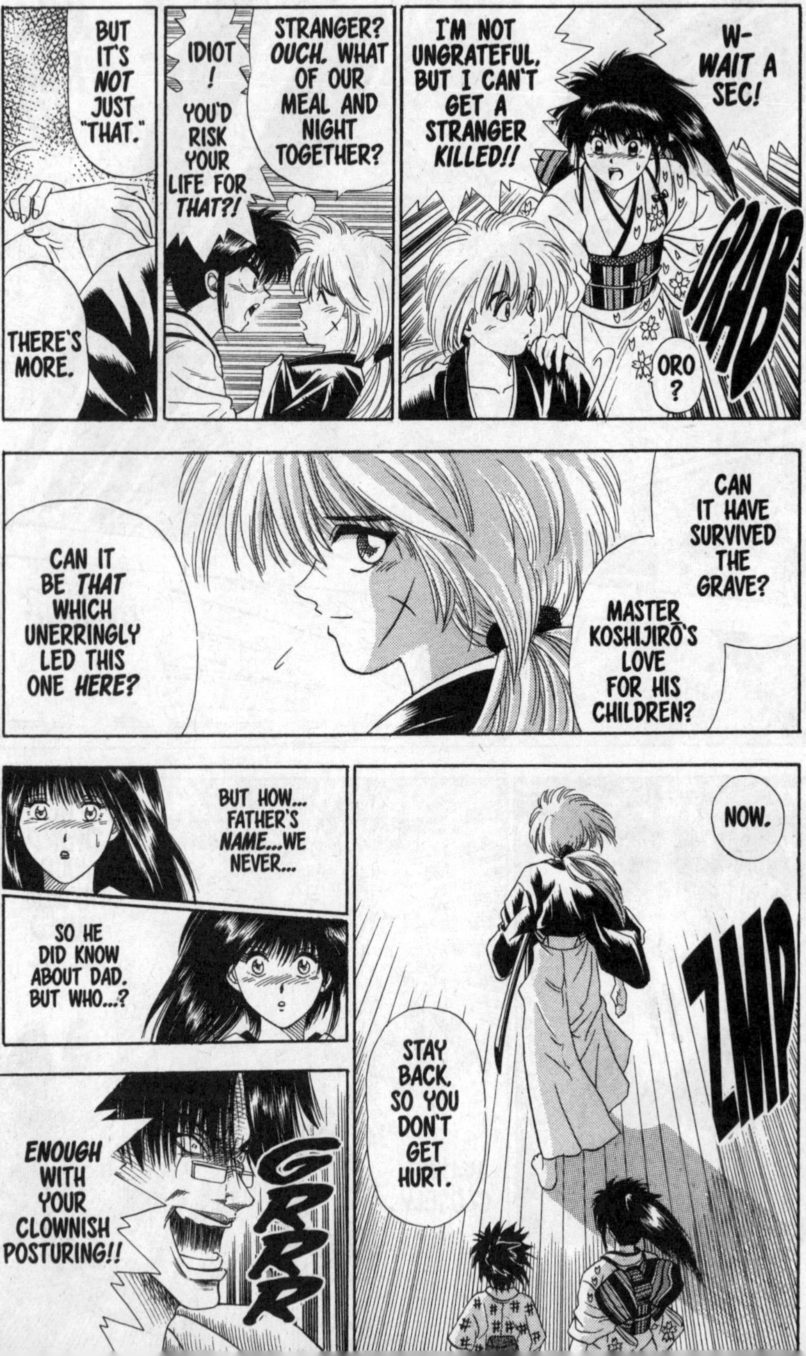
W-WAIT A SEC!
I'M NOT UNGRATEFUL, BUT I CAN'T GET A STRANGER *KILLED!!*
GRAB
ORO?
STRANGER? *OUCH.* WHAT OF OUR MEAL AND NIGHT TOGETHER?
IDIOT! YOU'D RISK YOUR LIFE FOR *THAT?!*
BUT IT'S *NOT* JUST "THAT."
THERE'S MORE.
CAN IT HAVE SURVIVED THE GRAVE?
MASTER KOSHIJIRŌ'S LOVE FOR HIS CHILDREN?
CAN IT BE *THAT* WHICH UNERRINGLY LED THIS ONE *HERE?*
NOW.
ZMP
STAY BACK, SO YOU DON'T GET HURT.
BUT HOW... FATHER'S *NAME*...WE NEVER...
SO HE DID KNOW ABOUT DAD. BUT WHO...?
ENOUGH WITH YOUR CLOWNISH POSTURING!!
GRRR

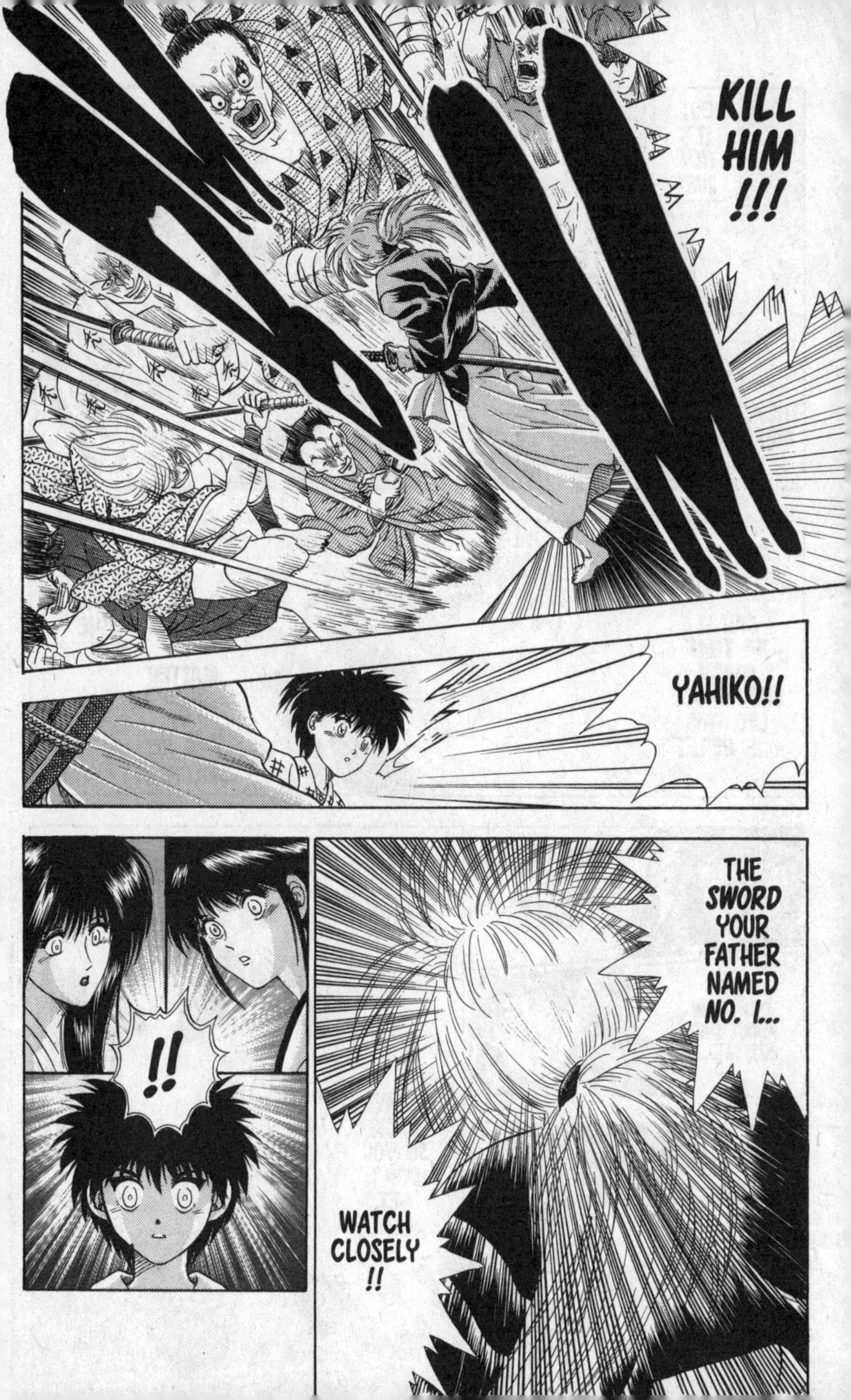
KILL HIM!!!
YAHIKO!!
THE SWORD YOUR FATHER NAMED NO. 1...
WATCH CLOSELY!!
!!

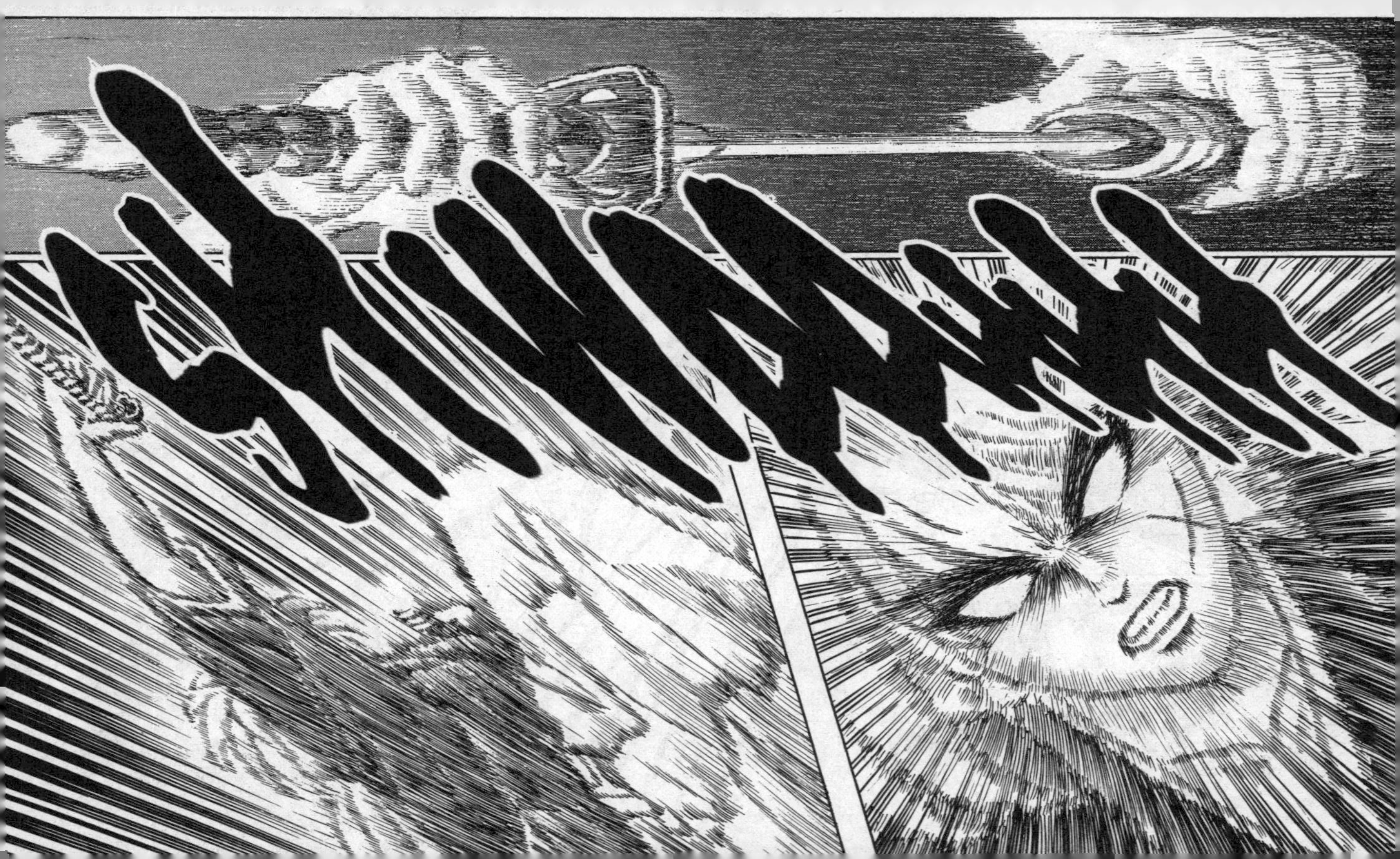

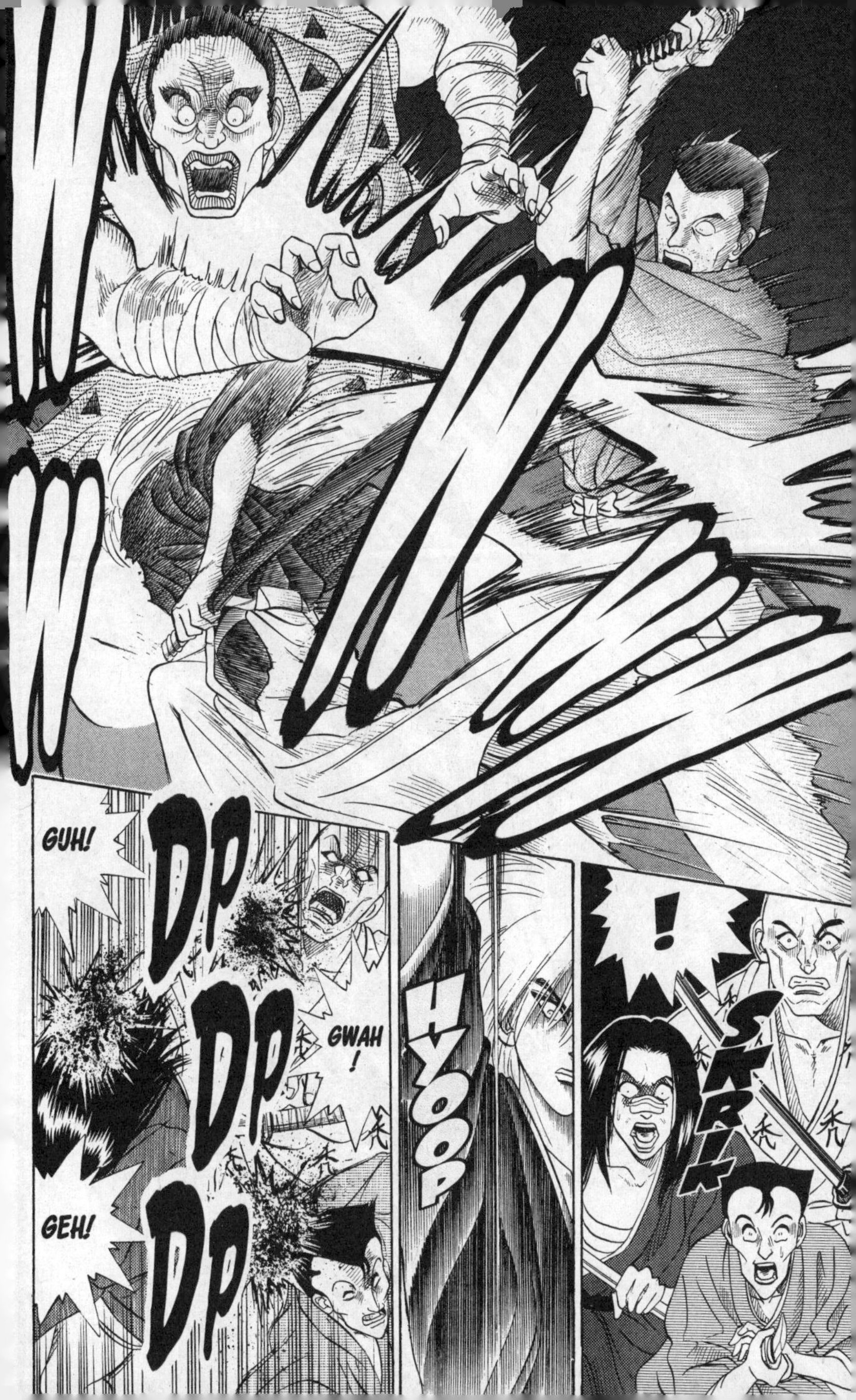
!
SKRIK
HYOOP
GUH!
DP
GWAH!
DP
GEH!
DP

READ THIS WAY

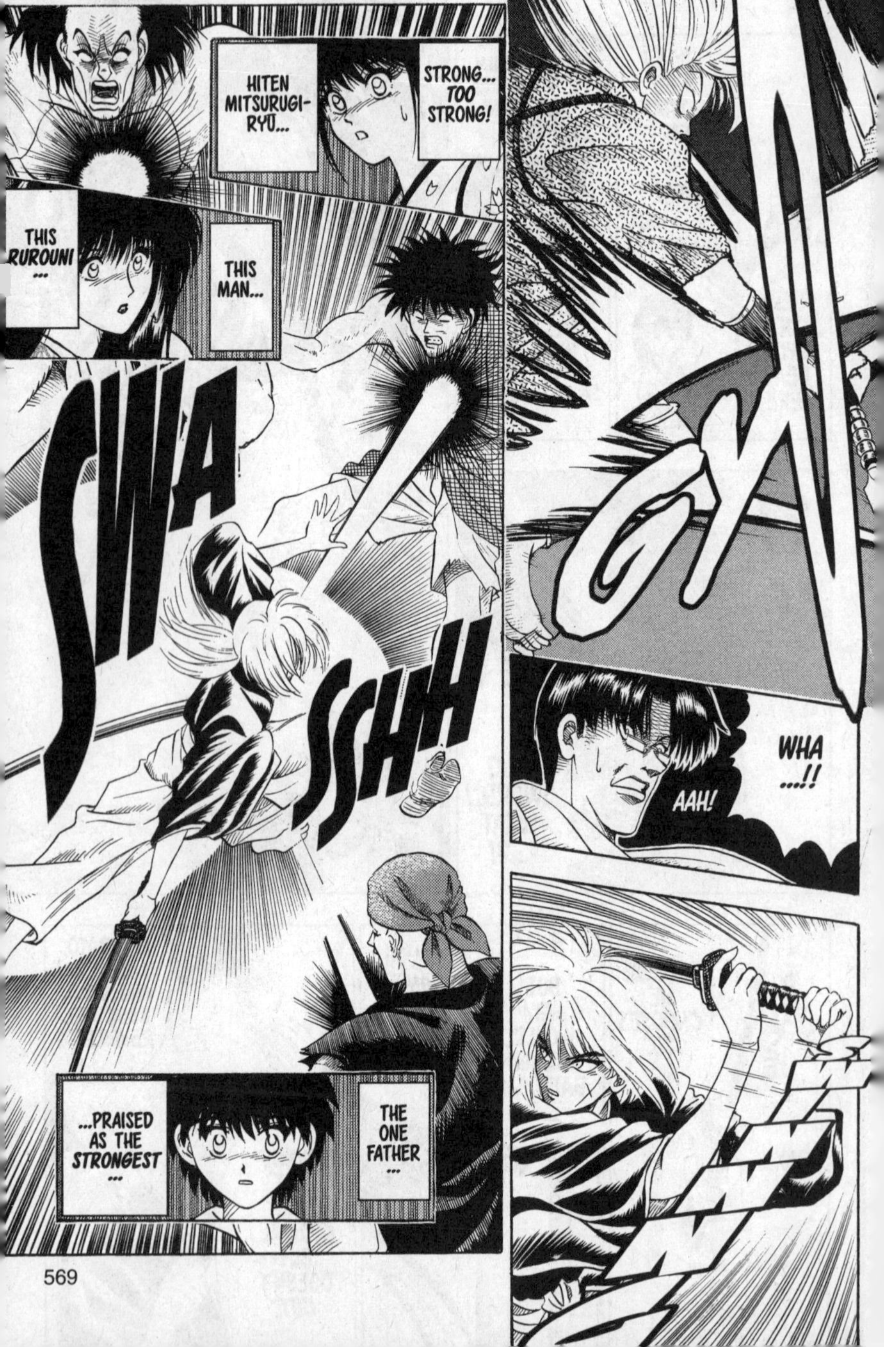
WHA ...!!
AAH!
STRONG... TOO STRONG!
HITEN MITSURUGI-RYŪ...
THIS MAN...
THIS RUROUNI ...
SWASSHH!
THE ONE FATHER ...
...PRAISED AS THE STRONGEST ...

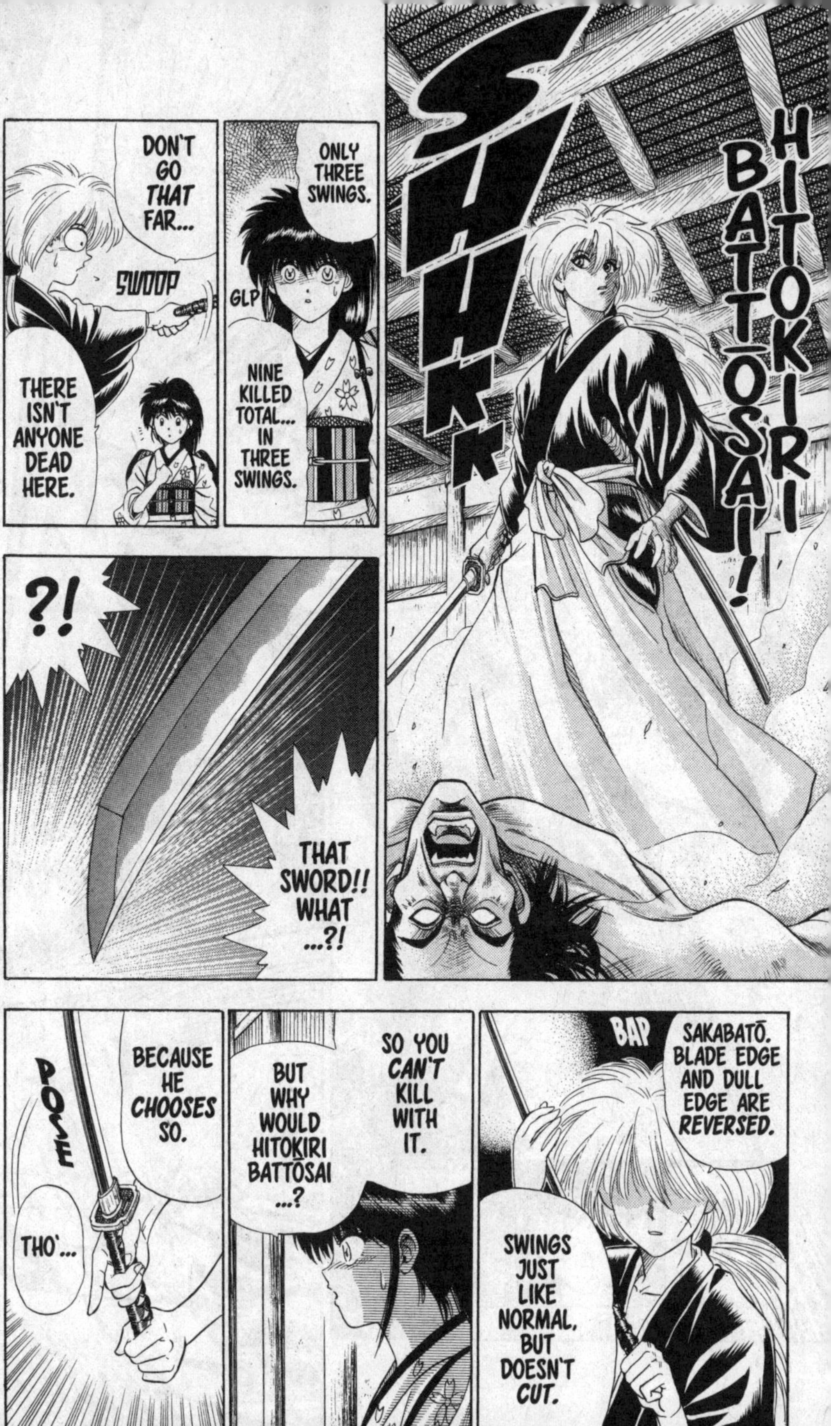
SHHKK
HITOKIRI BATTŌSAI!
ONLY THREE SWINGS.
GLP
NINE KILLED TOTAL... IN THREE SWINGS.
DON'T GO THAT FAR...
SWOOP
THERE ISN'T ANYONE DEAD HERE.
?!
THAT SWORD!! WHAT ...?!
BAP
SAKABATŌ. BLADE EDGE AND DULL EDGE ARE REVERSED.
SWINGS JUST LIKE NORMAL, BUT DOESN'T CUT.
SO YOU CAN'T KILL WITH IT.
BUT WHY WOULD HITOKIRI BATTŌSAI ...?
POSE
BECAUSE HE CHOOSES SO.
THO'...

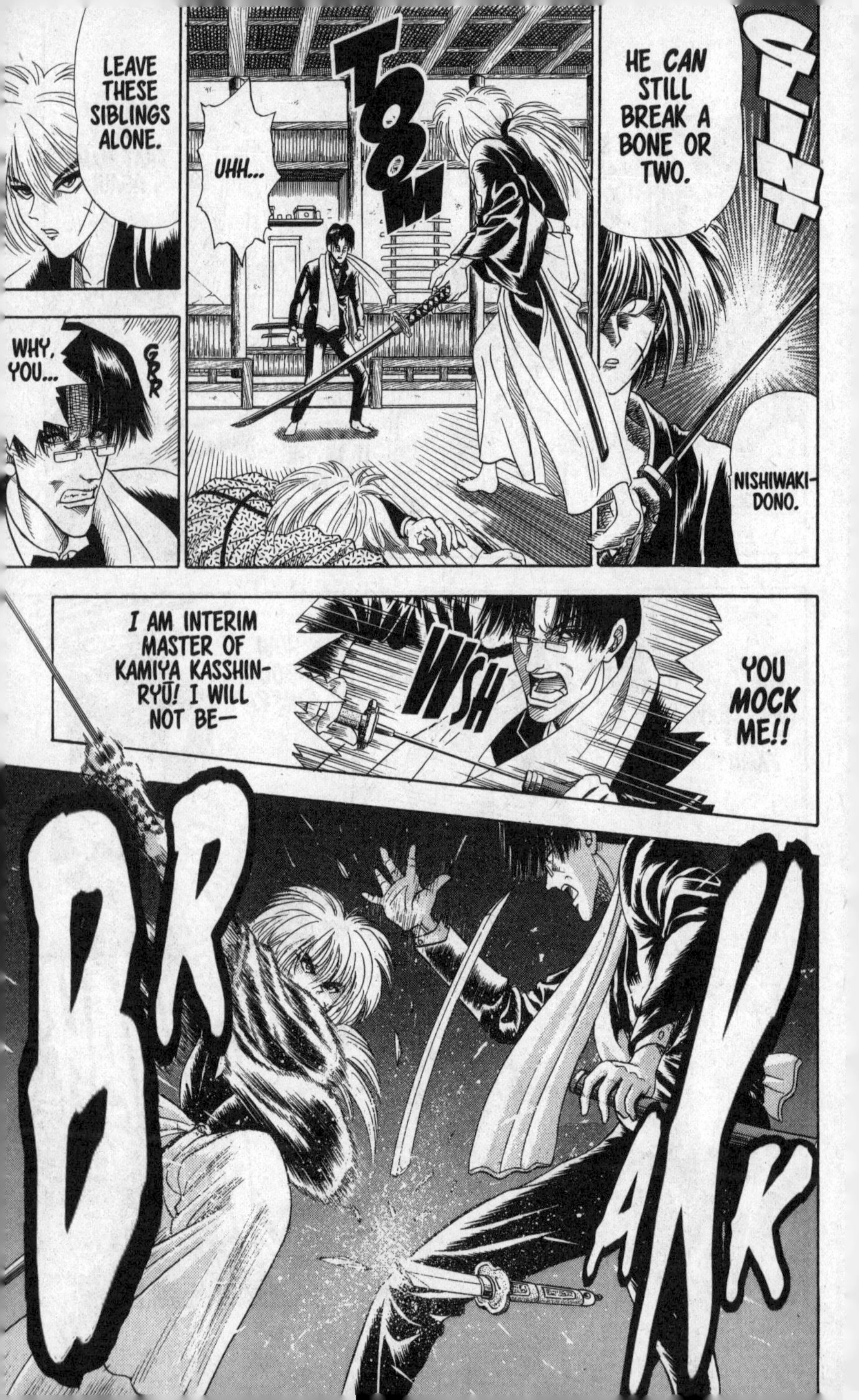
GLINT
HE CAN STILL BREAK A BONE OR TWO.
NISHIWAKI-DONO.
TOOM
UHH...
LEAVE THESE SIBLINGS ALONE.
WHY, YOU...
GRR
YOU MOCK ME!!
WSH
I AM INTERIM MASTER OF KAMIYA KASSHIN-RYŪ! I WILL NOT BE—
BRAK

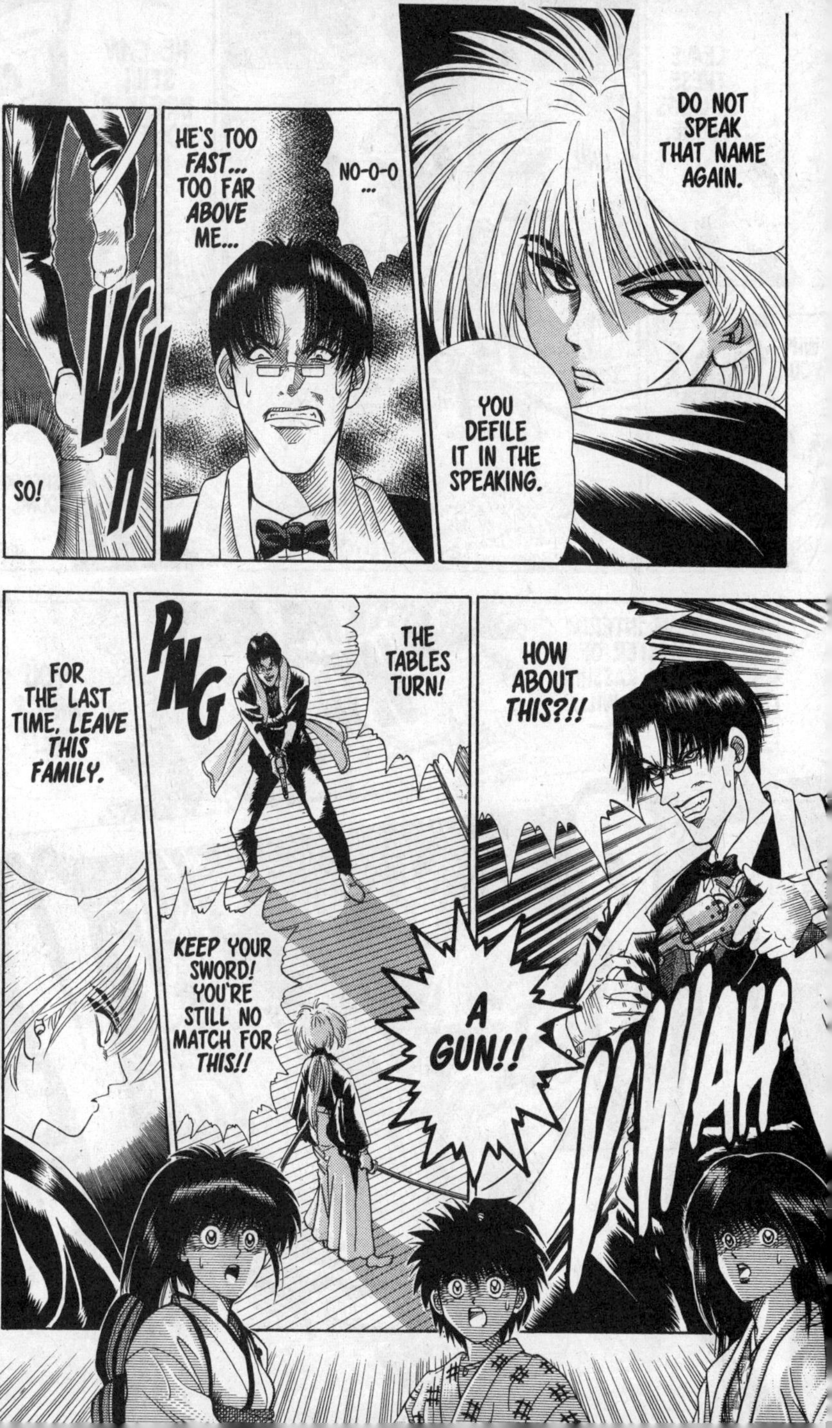
DO NOT SPEAK THAT NAME AGAIN.
YOU DEFILE IT IN THE SPEAKING.
NO-O-O ...
HE'S TOO FAST... TOO FAR ABOVE ME...
VSH
SO!
HOW ABOUT THIS?!!
A GUN!!
WAH!
THE TABLES TURN!
PNG
KEEP YOUR SWORD! YOU'RE STILL NO MATCH FOR THIS!!
FOR THE LAST TIME, LEAVE THIS FAMILY.

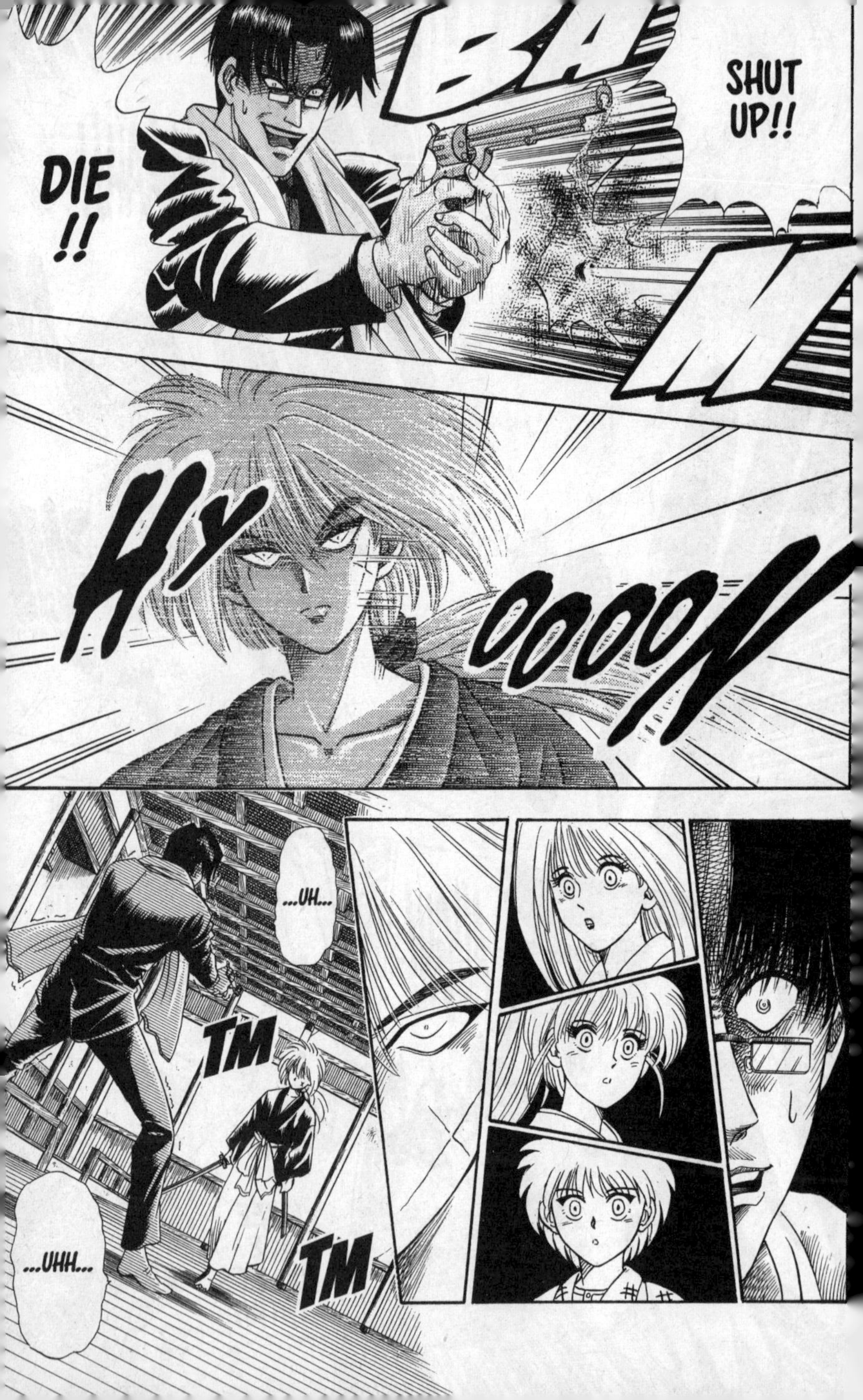
SHUT UP!!
BAM
DIE !!
HyOOOON
...UH...
TM
TM
...UHH...

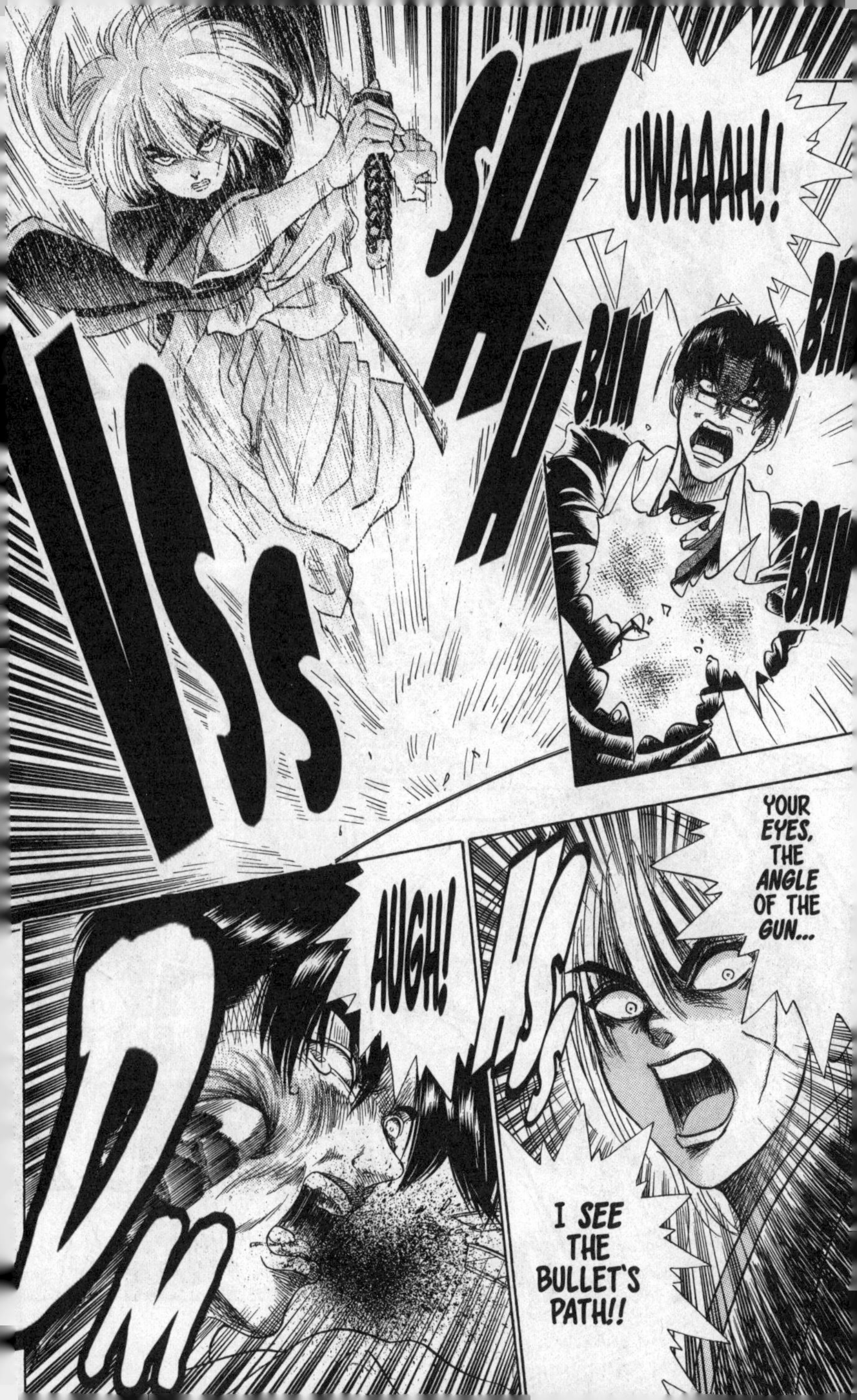
UWAAAH!!
BAM
BAM
BAM
BAM
YOUR EYES, THE ANGLE OF THE GUN...
I SEE THE BULLET'S PATH!!
AUGH!

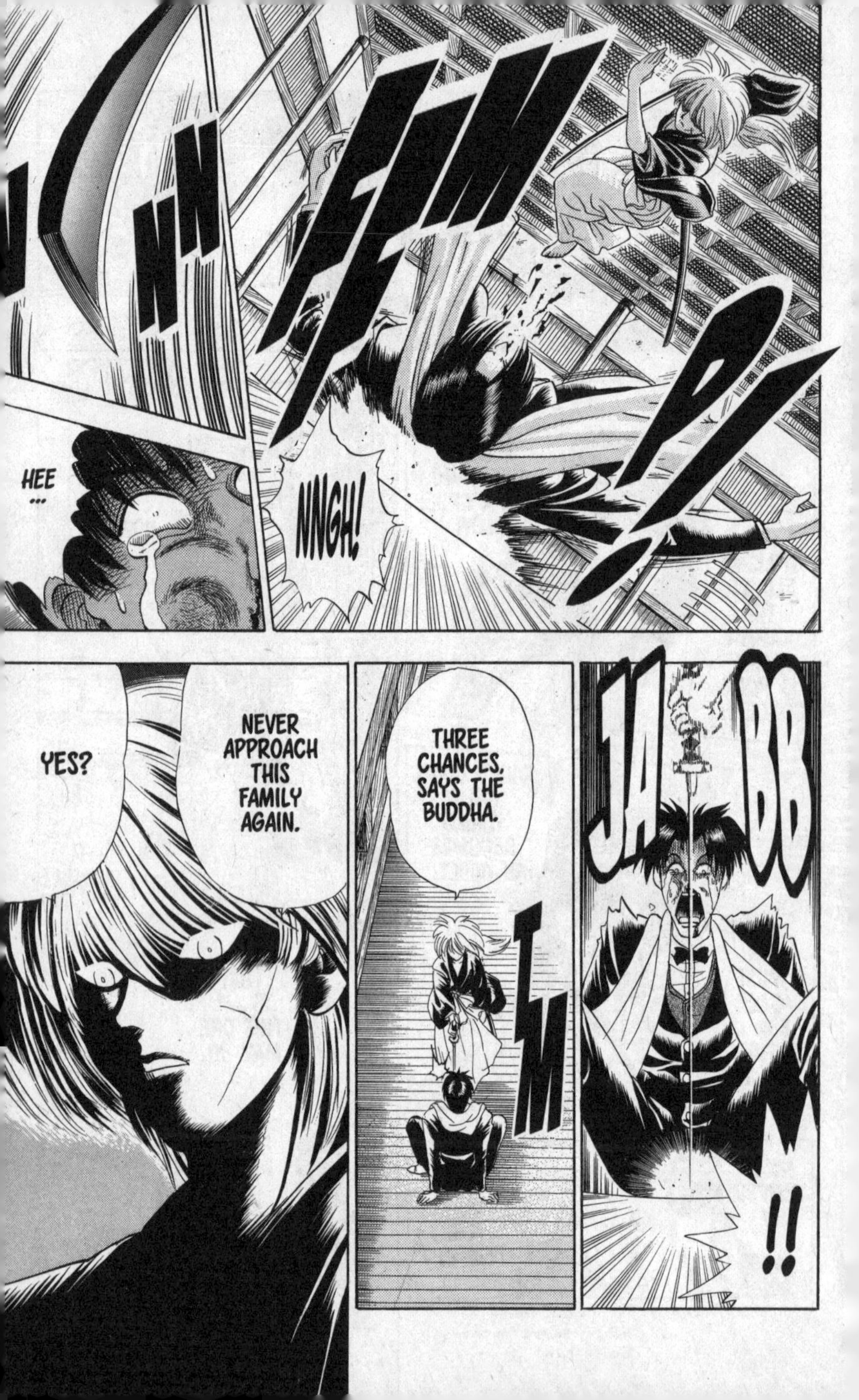
NNGH!
HEE...
JABB
!!
THREE CHANCES, SAYS THE BUDDHA.
NEVER APPROACH THIS FAMILY AGAIN.
YES?

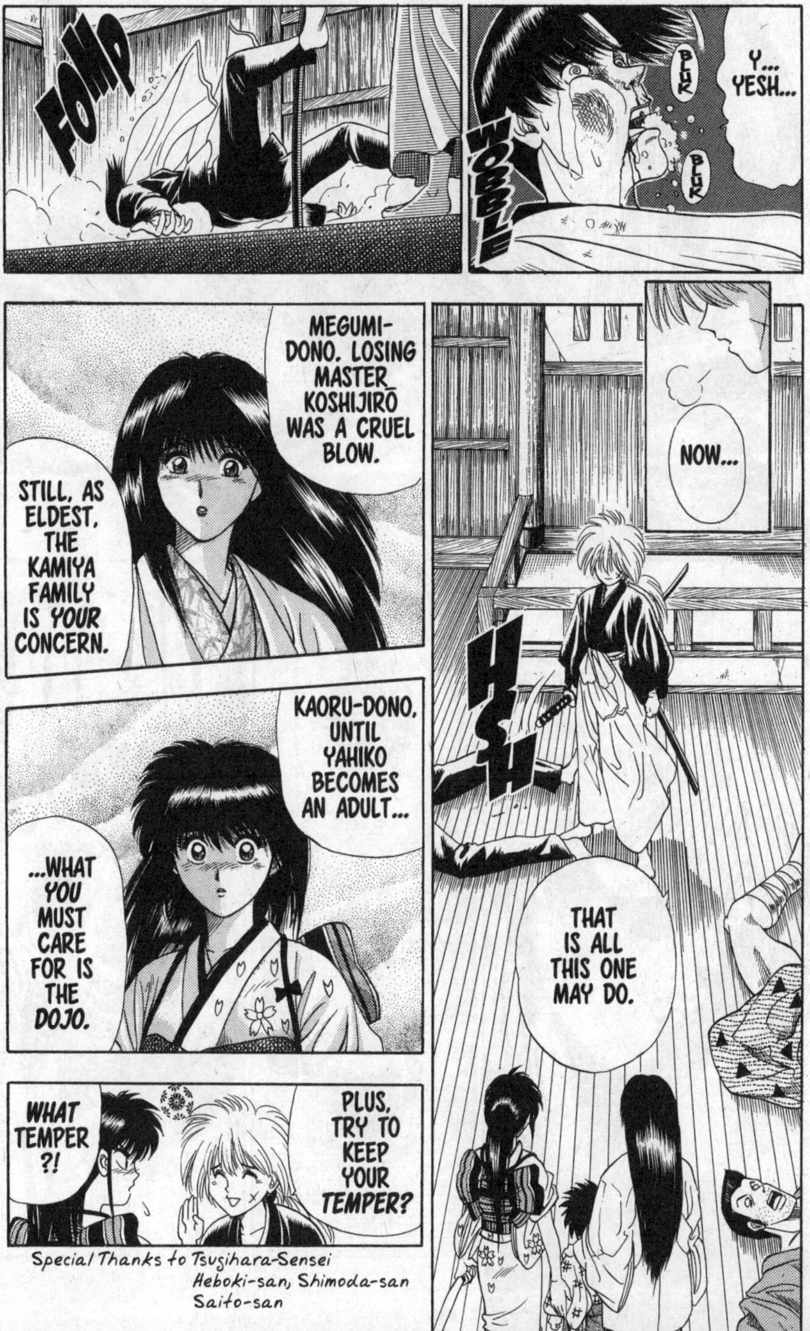

BLUK
Y... YESH...
BLUK
WOBBLE
FOMP
NOW...
HSH
THAT IS ALL THIS ONE MAY DO.
MEGUMI-DONO. LOSING MASTER KOSHIJIRO WAS A CRUEL BLOW.
STILL, AS ELDEST, THE KAMIYA FAMILY IS YOUR CONCERN.
KAORU-DONO, UNTIL YAHIKO BECOMES AN ADULT...
...WHAT YOU MUST CARE FOR IS THE DOJO.
PLUS, TRY TO KEEP YOUR TEMPER?
WHAT TEMPER ?!

Special Thanks to Tsugihara-Sensei
Heboki-san, Shimoda-san
Saito-san

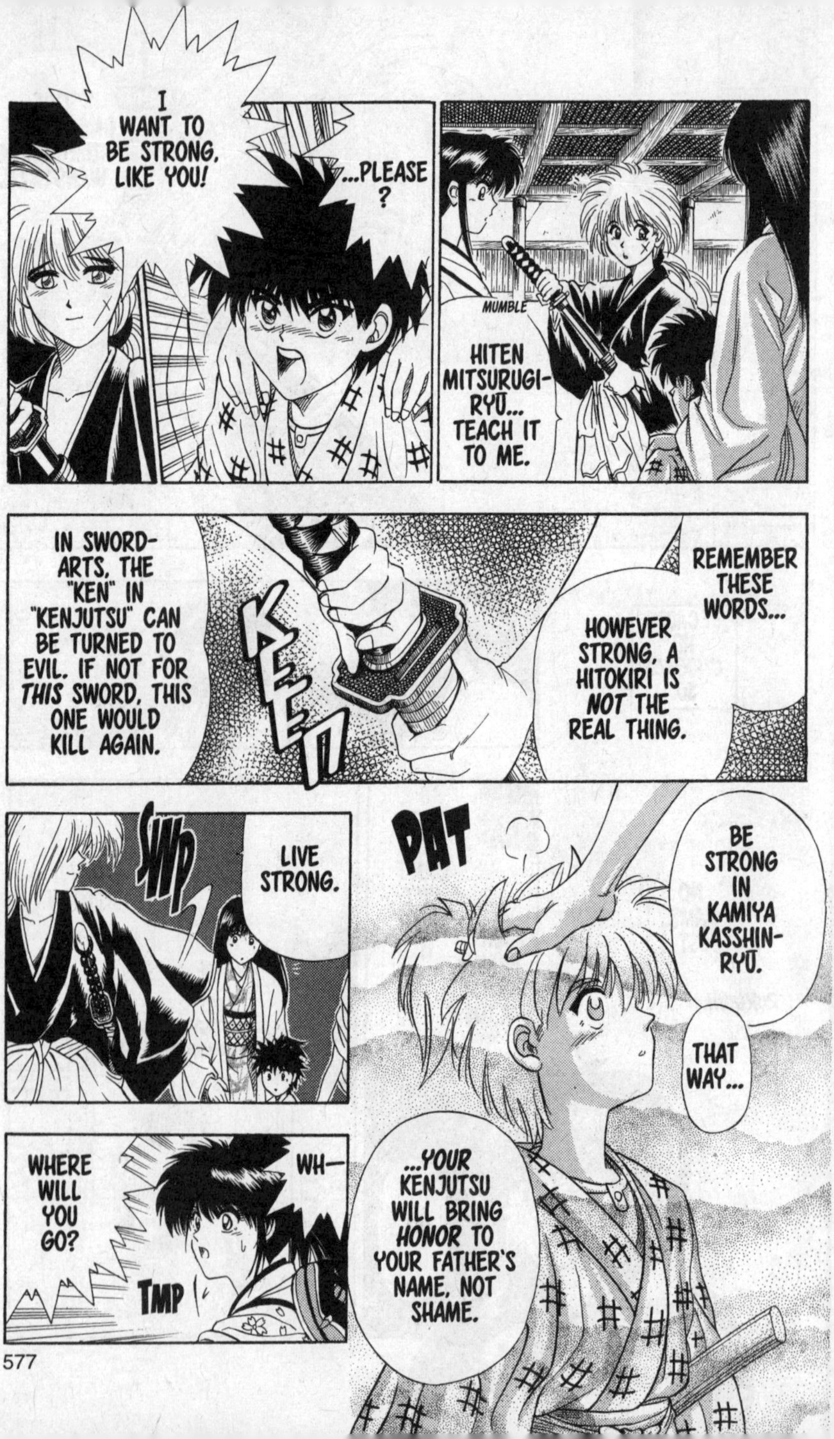
MUMBLE
HITEN MITSURUGI-RYŪ... TEACH IT TO ME.
I WANT TO BE STRONG, LIKE YOU!
...PLEASE ?
REMEMBER THESE WORDS...
HOWEVER STRONG, A HITOKIRI IS *NOT* THE REAL THING.
KEEN
IN SWORD-ARTS, THE "KEN" IN "KENJUTSU" CAN BE TURNED TO EVIL. IF NOT FOR *THIS* SWORD, THIS ONE WOULD KILL AGAIN.
PAT
BE STRONG IN KAMIYA KASSHIN-RYŪ.
THAT WAY...
...*YOUR* KENJUTSU WILL BRING *HONOR* TO YOUR FATHER'S NAME, NOT SHAME.
SWIP
LIVE STRONG.
WH—
WHERE WILL YOU GO?
TMP

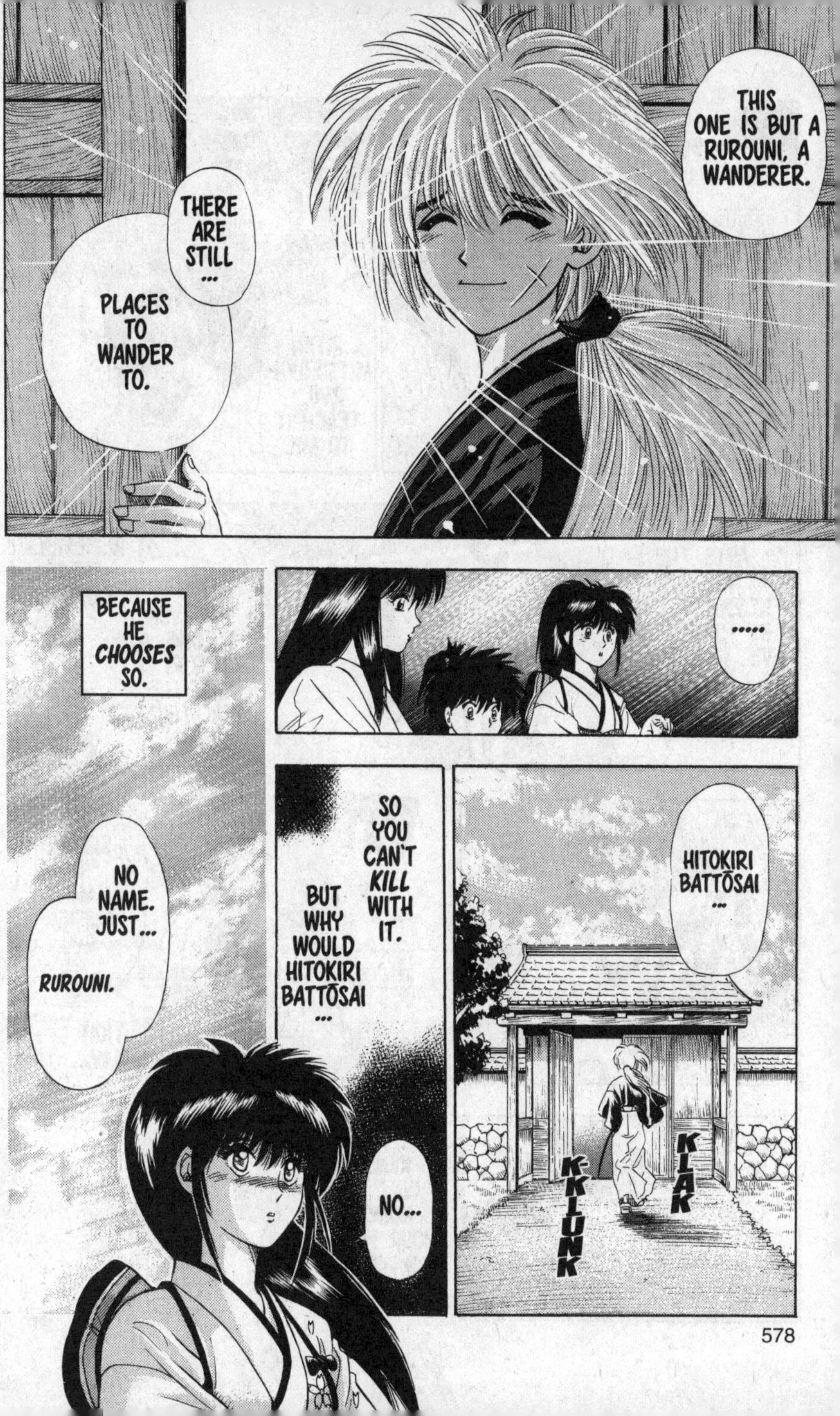
THIS ONE IS BUT A RUROUNI, A WANDERER.
THERE ARE STILL...
PLACES TO WANDER TO.
......
HITOKIRI BATTŌSAI...
KIAK
K-KIUNK
SO YOU CAN'T *KILL* WITH IT.
BUT WHY WOULD HITOKIRI BATTŌSAI...
NO...
BECAUSE HE *CHOOSES* SO.
NO NAME. JUST...
RUROUNI.

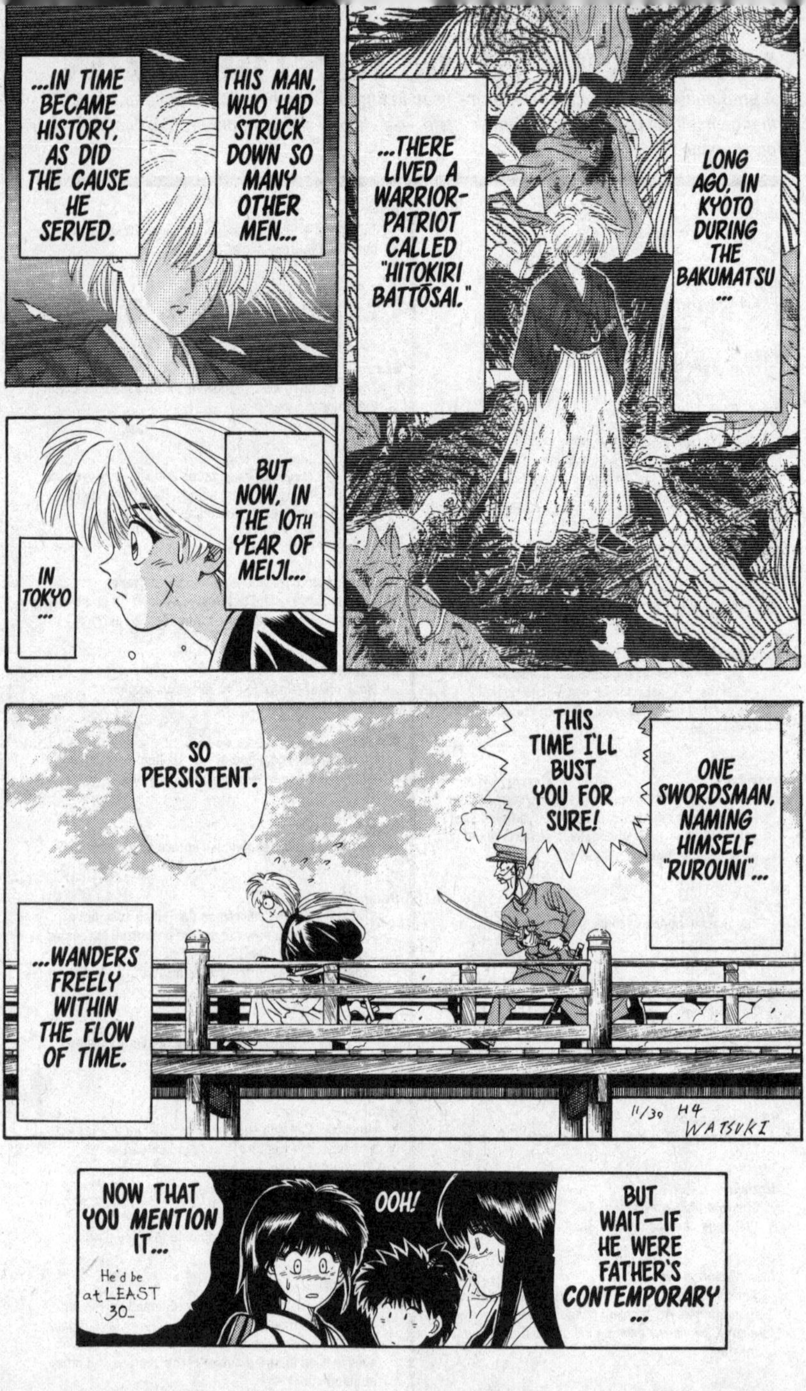
LONG AGO, IN KYOTO DURING THE BAKUMATSU...
...THERE LIVED A WARRIOR-PATRIOT CALLED "HITOKIRI BATTŌSAI."
THIS MAN, WHO HAD STRUCK DOWN SO MANY OTHER MEN...
...IN TIME BECAME HISTORY, AS DID THE CAUSE HE SERVED.
BUT NOW, IN THE 10TH YEAR OF MEIJI...
IN TOKYO...
ONE SWORDSMAN, NAMING HIMSELF "RUROUNI"...
THIS TIME I'LL BUST YOU FOR SURE!
SO PERSISTENT.
...WANDERS FREELY WITHIN THE FLOW OF TIME.
11/30 H4 WATSUKI
BUT WAIT—IF HE WERE FATHER'S CONTEMPORARY...
OOH!
NOW THAT YOU MENTION IT...
He'd be at LEAST 30...

GLOSSARY of the RESTORATION

A brief guide to select Japanese terms used in Rurouni Kenshin. *Both here and in the manga itself, all names are Japanese-style—i.e., last or family name first, with personal or given name following.*

dō
In kendō, a strike to the stomach.

dōgi
Karate uniform, also called a *gi*.

dojo
Martial arts training hall.

-dono
Honorific. More respectful than *-san*; the effect in modern-day Japanese would be along the lines of "Milord So-and-So." As used by Kenshin, it indicates both respect and humility.

Edo
Capital of the Tokugawa shōgunate during the era of shōgun rule (1603-1863), renamed Tokyo ("Eastern Capital") after the Meiji Restoration.

Fudō Myō-ō
In Vajrayana Buddhism, a protector and destroyer of delusions. His fearsome blue visage is typically surrounded by flames, representing the purification of the mind.

genpuku
A ceremony commemorating a young samurai's entrance into adulthood, usually held between the ages of 12 and 18. Traditionally, a samurai could not be married before his genpuku.

geta
Japanese wooden sandals, named after the noise they make.

hachimaki
Originally a charm against evil spirits, these headbands emblazoned with inspiring slogans are still worn today, often by students, as a symbol of determination.

Hijikata Toshizō
Vice-commander of the Shinsengumi.

Hirazuki
The real-life sword technique, associated with the Shinsengumi, upon which Saitō's Gatotsu is based.

Hiten Mitsurugi-ryū
Kenshin's sword technique, used more for defense than offense. An "ancient style that pits one against many," it requires exceptional speed and agility to master.

Aizu
Tokugawa-affiliated domain and site of the fourth battle of the Boshin War.

aku
Kanji character for "evil" worn by Sanosuke.

aku soku zan
"Swift death to evil," a *bushido* motto associated with the Shinsengumi.

Ashura
Often depicted with three faces and six arms, Ashura are low-ranking Buddhist deities. In Japan they're seen as supernatural guardians.

bakufu
Another word for *shōgunate*, bakufu ("tent government") refers to the samurai and other military officials who ruled Japan during the Edo period.

Bakumatsu
Final, chaotic days of the Tokugawa regime.

Bishamon
Often considered a god of war, Bishamon is usually depicted with a halo-like wheel of flames.

bokutō
Wooden kendō weapon also known as a *bokken*.

Boshin War
Civil war of 1868-69 between the failing Tokugawa shōgunate and a new movement organized to restore the Emperor to power. The pro-imperial side won, ushering in a new era of modernization.

Bushido
The "way of the warrior," a code of samurai values dating to the 17th century.

-chan
Honorific. Can be used either as a diminutive (as with a child: "Little Kentarō"), or to indicate affection ("Darling Hanako").

Chōshū
Anti-Tokugawa domain and home to many patriots.

daruma doll
Roly-poly *daruma* figures are traditionally given for good luck to those starting new ventures (a birthday, New Year's, a new business). One of the doll's blank eyes is filled in at the outset of the venture, the other at completion.

Keiō period
    The era just before the Meiji era, spanning from 1865 to 1868.

kenjutsu
    The art of fencing; sword arts; kendō.

Kenshin-gumi
    Literally, "group of Kenshin"—translated (rather playfully) for our purposes as "Team Kenshin."

Kiheitai
    Volunteer militia which, like the Shinsengumi, recruited members based on ability rather than social class. Members ranged from peasant farmers to samurai.

Kinkaku/Ginkaku Temples
    Subject of a famous novel by Yukio Mishima, the Kinkaku-ji or "Temple of the Golden Pavilion" was built as a retirement home for a former shōgun and later converted to a Zen temple. Ginkaku Temple was built by another member of the shōgun's family and incorporates similar designs.

kodachi
    Medium-length sword, shorter than the katana but longer than the *wakizashi*. Its easy maneuverability makes it a strong defensive weapon.

Kōgen Ittō-ryū
    A real historical sword style, *Kōgen Ittō-ryū* is characterized by economy of movement.

-kun
    Honorific. Nowadays it's usually a chummy form of address between male friends. When used in *Rurouni Kenshin*, however, it's more often in the older sense of superior-to-inferior, intended to express a difference in rank as well as affection.

kunoichi
    Female ninja.

"ku-shaped" shuriken
    Shuriken are the "throwing stars" known to lovers of samurai and ninja drama everywhere. "*Ku*-shaped" *shuriken* are shaped like the Japanese character *ku*: basically, a boomerang shape.

Kyoto
    Home of the Emperor from 794 until shortly after the Meiji Restoration, when the imperial court was moved to Edo/Tokyo.

loyalists
    Those who supported the return of the Emperor to power; the Ishin Shishi.

hitokiri
    A skilled sword-wielding assassin, literally "person slasher."

Hitokiri Battōsai
    "Sword-Wielding Manslayer," the name under which Himura Kenshin fought and killed. Swordsmen of the period sometimes adopted "professional" names to keep their birth names private.

Iba Hachirō
    Famed historical swordsman (1843-1869).

Ikeda-ya Incident
    An 1864 plot by a group of samurai to set fire to Kyoto and assassinate or kidnap government officials. The plot was hatched at the Ikeda-ya Inn in Kyoto.

Ishin Shishi
    Famed imperialist patriots who fought to end the reign of the Tokugawa shōgunate and restore the Emperor to his ancient seat of power.

Jigen-ryū
    Aggressive swordsmanship style, literally "revealed reality," which teaches practitioners to kill with a single powerful blow.

Jōdan, Chūdan, Gedan, Hassō, Wakigamae
    The five basic stances of kendō. *Jōdan*: Sword lifted overhead. *Chūdan* (or *seigan*): Cut to the middle. *Gedan*: Low, sweeping block. *Hassō*: Sword held vertically, hands shoulder-level. *Wakigamae*: Horizontal guard position.

kanji
    Japanese system of writing based on Chinese characters.

karakuri
    Intricate mechanized dolls, *karakuri* ("mechanism" or "gimmick") are regarded today as one of Japan's great traditional crafts and a forerunner to modern robotics.

katana
    The standard Japanese longsword, with a curved, single-edge blade normally positioned with the cutting side up. The name is short for *uchigatana*, "striking sword."

Katsu Kaishū
    Founder of the Japanese navy. Called "the greatest man in Japan," Kaishū was born to an impoverished minor samurai family and worked his way up to the head of the Tokugawa shōgunate.

Kawakami Gensai
    This infamous Edo-period assassin, known for being so fast with a sword that he could kill his targets in broad daylight, was the historical inspiration for Himura Kenshin.

rurouni
   Wanderer, vagabond.

Saigō Takamori
   A powerful military and political leader who oversaw the end of the Edo period, Takamori has been called "the last true samurai." Although he supported the restoration of the Emperor, he later led a revolution of disgruntled samurai opposing the rapid modernization of Japan.

sakabatō
   Reversed-edge sword (the dull edge on the side the sharp should be, and vice-versa) carried by Kenshin as a symbol of his resolution never to kill again.

-sama
   Very respectful honorific, used primarily to address a person of much higher rank. But it can also be used romantically: "Ah! Tsukiyama-sama…"

-san
   The basic honorific, equivalent to "Mr." or "Ms." In Japanese, a name should never be spoken without an honorific.

Seinan War
   Failed 1877 uprising of the samurai class against the new Meiji government and the modernization of Japan. Also known as the Satsuma Rebellion.

Seishū, Hanaoka
   Japanese surgeon (1760-1835) whose use of the drug *tsusensan* during a breast cancer operation in 1805 pioneered the use of surgical anesthesia.

Sekihō Army
   A pro-imperial army formed mainly of commoners; the name means "Red Vanguard." After the successful restoration of the Emperor, however, the *Sekihōtai* were scapegoated and blamed for the new regime's failed promises.

sen
   Historical unit of Japanese currency, equal to one hundredth of one yen.

sensei
   Teacher; master. *Sensei* is both the Japanese word for "teacher" and an honorific indicating a position of authority or expertise, including teachers, doctors, lawyers, political leaders, and renowned artists.

shinai
   Wooden practice sword, traditionally constructed of well-seasoned bamboo, first used around 1750.

shingan
   Written with the characters *shin* ("mind," "heart," "soul") and *gan* ("eye," "insight"), *shingan* can be translated as "soul vision" or "mind's eye."

Meiji Restoration
   Period from 1853-1868 during which the Tokugawa shōgunate was destroyed and the Emperor restored as ruler of Japan. Named after Emperor Meiji, whose chosen name was written with the characters for "culture" and "enlightenment."

Mimawarigumi
   A Kyoto police force. Unlike the Shinsengumi, the Mimawarigumi were all upper-class samurai.

Mt. Hiei
   Founded more than 1,200 years ago, the temple atop Mt. Hiei was built to protect Kyoto from evil spirits. Because police were barred from entering the temple grounds, criminals often took sanctuary there.

Obon
   The Buddhist "Day of the Dead," Obon, or Bon, takes place in either July or August, depending on the part of the country. Today it's one of Japan's three major holiday seasons, the others being New Year's in January and "Golden Week" in May.

ohagi
   Autumnal treat made from sweet rice and bean paste. The name comes from *hagi*, or bush clover, which flowers in the fall. A very similar confection called *botamochi*, or tree peony, is eaten in the spring.

okashira
   Leader or boss; literally, "the head."

om
   An ancient meditative symbol in both Buddhism and Hinduism, it is believed to be the sound that was spoken when the universe was created.

onigiri
   These seaweed-wrapped rice balls, usually with fish or vegetable fillings, have long been a portable and convenient staple of the Japanese diet.

Ōnin War
   A fifteenth-century civil war that ushered in the "Warring States Period," an era of near-constant conflict between rival lords.

Oniwabanshū
   Elite group of *onmitsu* ("spies") of the Edo period, now commonly called ninja.

onsen
   Written with the characters for "warmth" and "springs," *onsen*, volcanic hot springs, are an important part of Japanese tradition and remain popular today. The springs are typically the star feature of an inn or other bathing facility that provides visitors with a relaxing experience.

patriots
   Another term for Ishin Shishi, supporters of the Emperor.

Toshimichi Okubo
Samurai and political leader regarded as one of the founders of modern Japan.

wakizashi
A sword similar to the more familiar katana, but shorter, with a blade between 12 and 24 inches.

Wolves of Mibu
Nickname for the Shinsengumi, after the town where they were first stationed.

yakuza
Japanese underworld; "the mob." Like organized criminals in other cultures, they're known for colorful garb (including tattoos, which are traditionally frowned on in Japan) and equally colorful speech.

Yamagata Aritomo
Soldier, statesman and chief founder of the modern Japanese army. A samurai of Chōshū, he studied military science in Europe and returned to Japan in 1870 to head the war ministry.

yatsuhashi
A traditional sweet flavored with sugar and cinnamon. It's one of the best-known *meibutsu*, or regional delicacies, of Kyoto.

zanbatō
A massive, single-edged sword used as an anti-cavalry weapon; the name means "horse-chopping sword."

Zipangu
Japan was once one of the foremost mining countries of the world. Marco Polo heard rumors of *Zipangu*, the "land of gold," while in China, and it was through his writings about the marvelous golden country that Europe was introduced to Japan.

shinobi
Another word for ninja.

Shinsengumi
An elite police force made up of exceptionally skilled swordsmen of all social classes. The Shinsengumi ("newly selected corps") were established by the shōgunate in 1863 to suppress loyalists and restore law and order to the blood-soaked streets of Kyoto.

shizoku
Replaced the term "samurai" in the new era. Made up of ex-samurai and military families, it came to be the gentry class.

shōgi
Strategic board game similar to chess.

shōgun
Feudal military leader of Japan, short for *Sei-i Taishōgun* ("Commander of Expeditionary Force Against Barbarians").

shōgunate
Government ruled by shōguns, with even the Emperor taking orders from the ruling lords.

soba
Buckwheat noodles, about as thick as spaghetti, served either hot or cold.

sukashi
An evasive or defensive move in karate.

suntetsu
Small, handheld blade designed for palming and concealment.

tachi
A long, curved sword usually wielded on horseback.

Toba Fushimi, Battle at
Battle near Kyoto between the forces of the new imperial government and the fallen shōgunate. Ending with an imperial victory, it was the first battle of the Boshin War.

Tokugawa Bakufu
Military feudal government, led by powerful shōguns, that dominated Japan from 1603 to 1867.

Tokugawa Yoshinobu
The 15th and final shōgun of Japan. His peaceful abdication in 1867 marked the end of the Edo period and the beginning of the Meiji era.

tonfa
A two-handed weapon, ideal for defense, often used by police during the Meiji era.

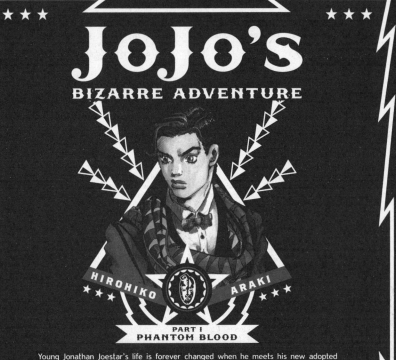
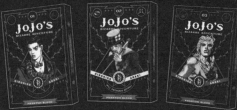

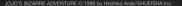

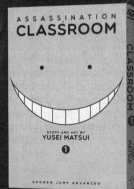

A KILLER COMEDY FROM *WEEKLY SHONEN JUMP*

A S S A S S I N A T I O N
CLASSROOM

STORY AND ART BY
YUSEI MATSUI

Ever caught yourself screaming, "I could just kill that teacher"?
What would it take to justify such antisocial behavior
and weeks of detention? Especially if he's the best
teacher you've ever had? Giving you an "F" on a quiz?
Mispronouncing your name during roll call...*again*? How about
blowing up the moon and threatening to do the same to
Mother Earth—unless you take him out first?! Plus a reward
of a cool 100 million from the Ministry of Defense!

Okay, now that you're committed... How are you going to
pull this off? What does your pathetic class of misfits have
in their arsenal to combat Teach's alien technology, bizarre
powers and...*tentacles*?!

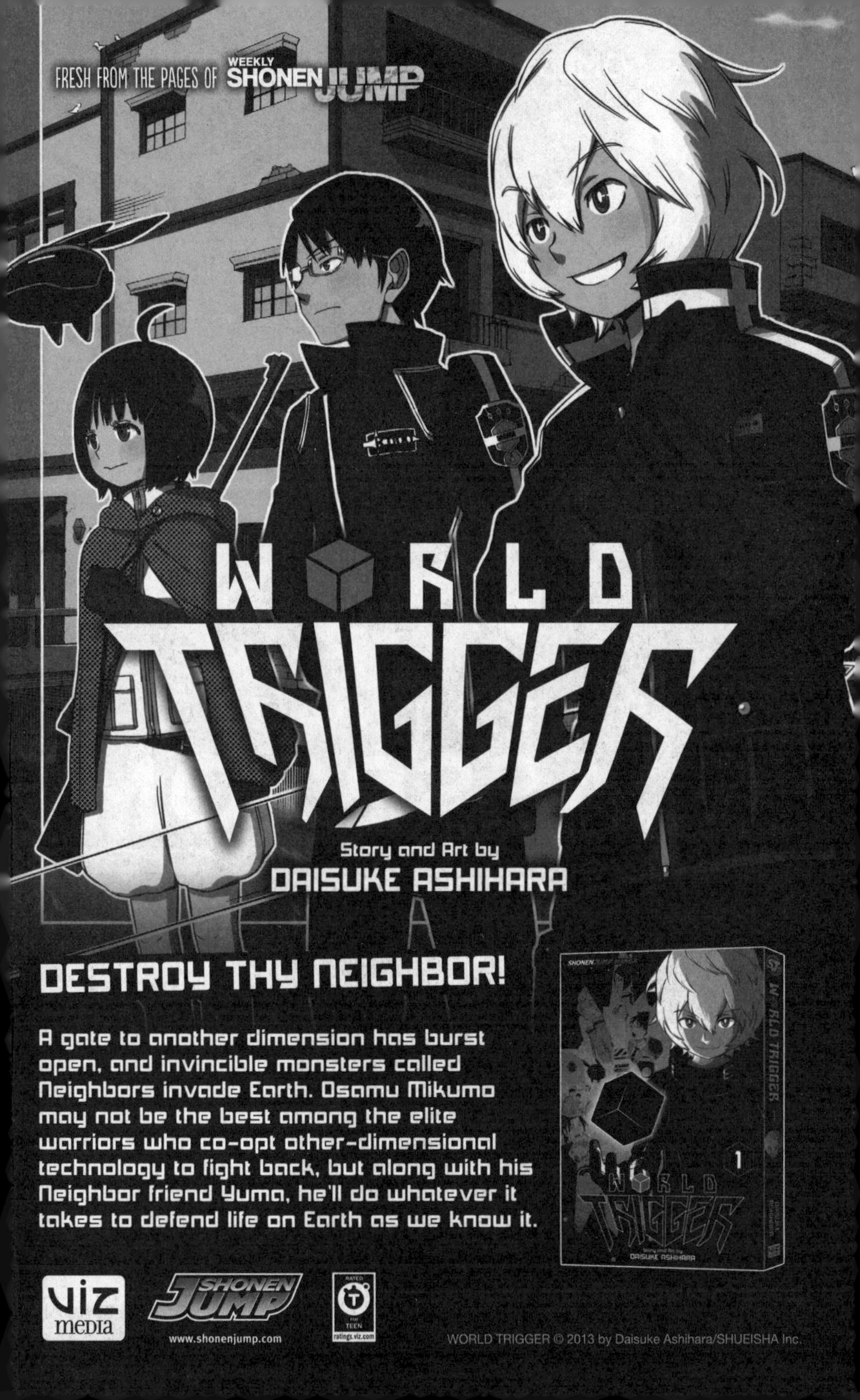
FRESH FROM THE PAGES OF WEEKLY SHONEN JUMP
WORLD TRIGGER
Story and Art by
DAISUKE ASHIHARA
DESTROY THY NEIGHBOR!
A gate to another dimension has burst open, and invincible monsters called Neighbors invade Earth. Osamu Mikumo may not be the best among the elite warriors who co-opt other-dimensional technology to fight back, but along with his Neighbor friend Yuma, he'll do whatever it takes to defend life on Earth as we know it.
SHONEN JUMP MANGA
WORLD TRIGGER
1
Story and Art by
DAISUKE ASHIHARA
viz media
SHONEN JUMP
www.shonenjump.com
RATED T FOR TEEN
ratings.viz.com
WORLD TRIGGER © 2013 by Daisuke Ashihara/SHUEISHA Inc.

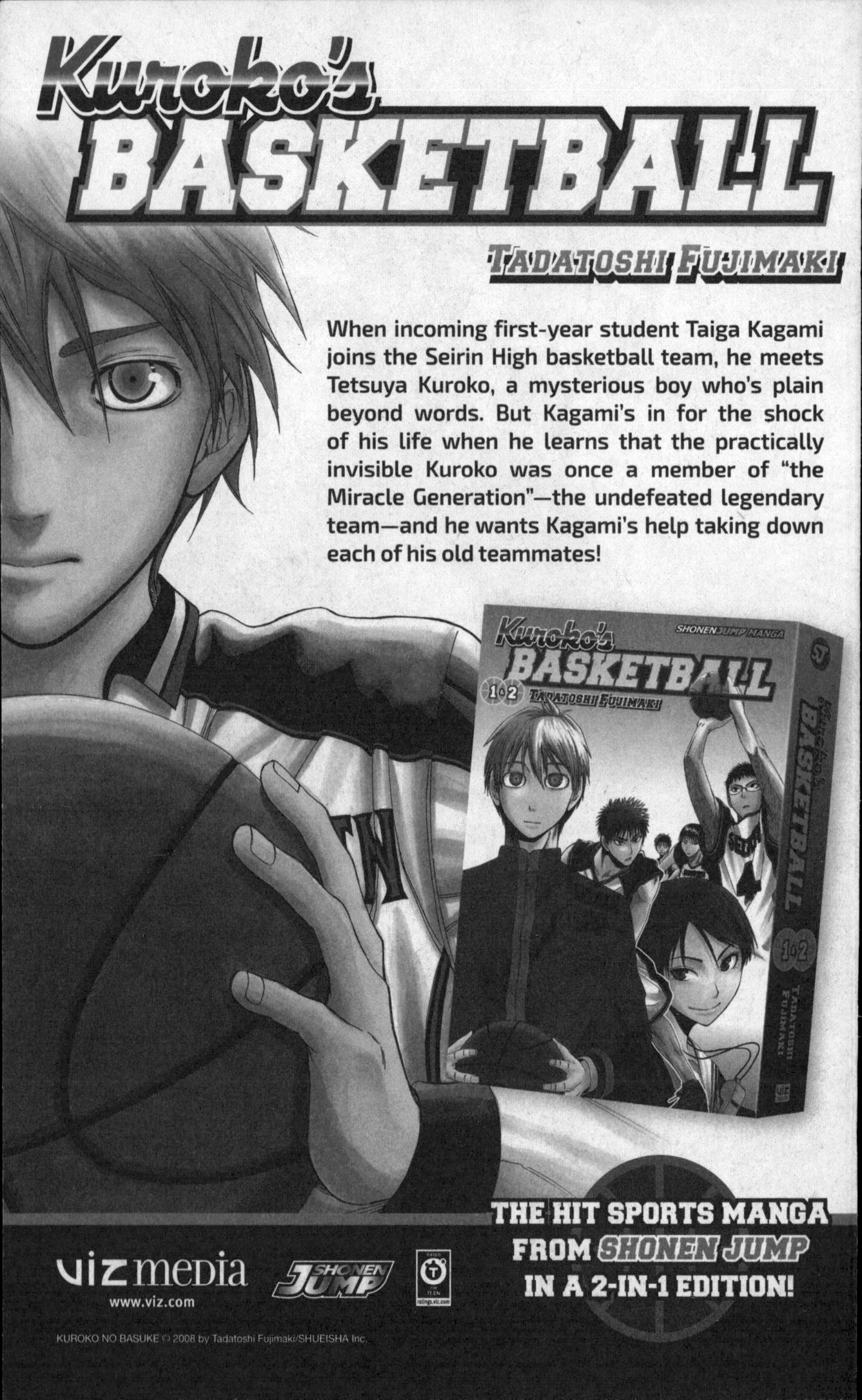

Kuroko's BASKETBALL
TADATOSHI FUJIMAKI
When incoming first-year student Taiga Kagami joins the Seirin High basketball team, he meets Tetsuya Kuroko, a mysterious boy who's plain beyond words. But Kagami's in for the shock of his life when he learns that the practically invisible Kuroko was once a member of "the Miracle Generation"—the undefeated legendary team—and he wants Kagami's help taking down each of his old teammates!
Kuroko's BASKETBALL
SHONEN JUMP MANGA
1•2
TADATOSHI FUJIMAKI
THE HIT SPORTS MANGA FROM SHONEN JUMP IN A 2-IN-1 EDITION!
viz media
www.viz.com
SHONEN JUMP
ratings.viz.com
KUROKO NO BASUKE © 2008 by Tadatoshi Fujimaki/SHUEISHA Inc.

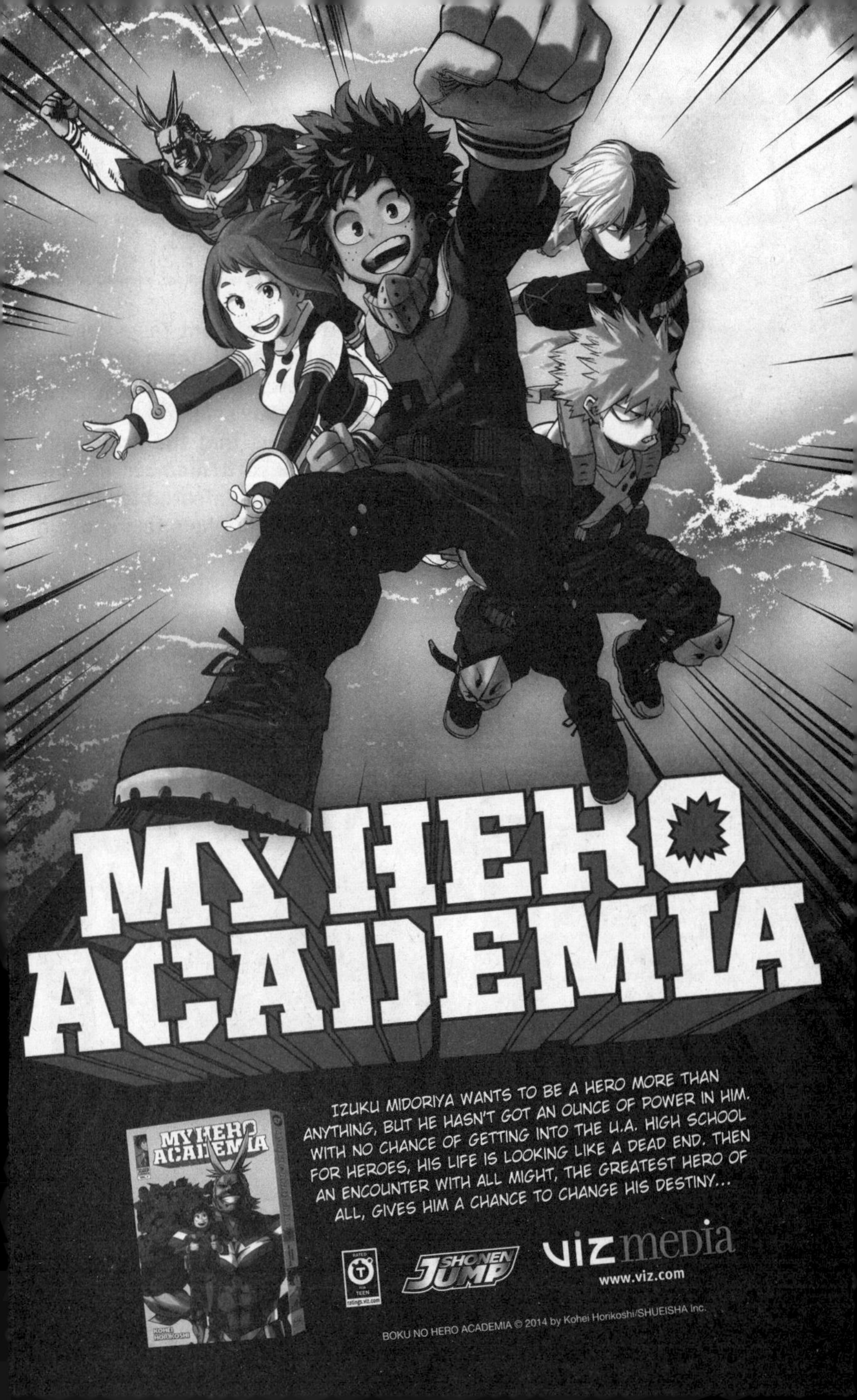
MY HERO ACADEMIA
IZUKU MIDORIYA WANTS TO BE A HERO MORE THAN ANYTHING, BUT HE HASN'T GOT AN OUNCE OF POWER IN HIM. WITH NO CHANCE OF GETTING INTO THE U.A. HIGH SCHOOL FOR HEROES, HIS LIFE IS LOOKING LIKE A DEAD END. THEN AN ENCOUNTER WITH ALL MIGHT, THE GREATEST HERO OF ALL, GIVES HIM A CHANCE TO CHANGE HIS DESTINY...
RATED T TEEN
ratings.viz.com
SHONEN JUMP
viz media
www.viz.com
BOKU NO HERO ACADEMIA © 2014 by Kohei Horikoshi/SHUEISHA Inc.

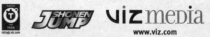

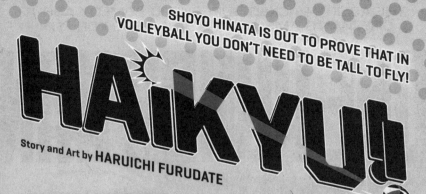
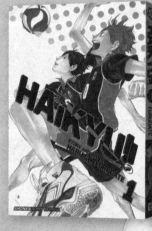
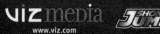

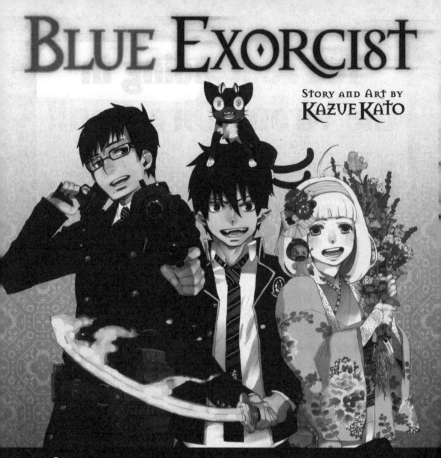
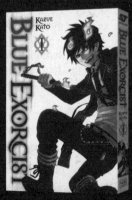

You're Reading the Wrong Direction!!

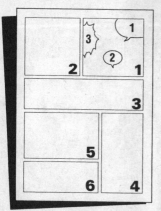

Whoops! Guess what? You're starting at the wrong end of the comic!

…It's true! In keeping with the original Japanese format, **Rurouni Kenshin** is meant to be read from right to left, starting in the upper-right corner.

Unlike English, which is read from left to right, Japanese is read from right to left, meaning that action, sound effects and word-balloon order are completely reversed… something which can make readers unfamiliar with Japanese feel pretty backwards themselves. For this reason, manga or Japanese comics published in the U.S. in English have sometimes been published "flopped"—that is, printed in exact reverse order, as though seen from the other side of a mirror.

By flopping pages, U.S. publishers can avoid confusing readers, but the compromise is not without its downside. For one thing, a character in a flopped manga series who once wore in the original Japanese version a T-shirt emblazoned with "M A Y" (as in "the merry month of") now wears one which reads "Y A M"! Additionally, many manga creators in Japan are themselves unhappy with the process, as some feel the mirror-imaging of their art skews their original intentions.

We are proud to bring you Nobuhiro Watsuki's **Rurouni Kenshin** in the original unflopped format. For now, though, turn to the other side of the book and let the adventure begin…!

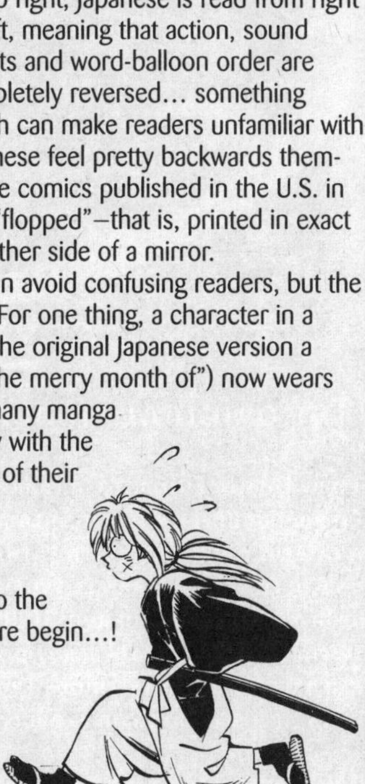

—Editor